CASES AND MATERIALS ON
SEXUALITY, GENDER IDENTITY, AND THE LAW

Sixth Edition

■ ■ ■

Carlos A. Ball
Distinguished Professor of Law & Judge Frederick Lacey Scholar
Rutgers Law School

Jane S. Schacter
William Nelson Cromwell Professor of Law
Stanford Law School

Douglas NeJaime
Professor of Law
UCLA School of Law

William B. Rubenstein
Sidley Austin Professor of Law
Harvard Law School

AMERICAN CASEBOOK SERIES®

WEST ACADEMIC PUBLISHING

The publisher is not engaged in rendering legal or other professional advice, and this publication is not a substitute for the advice of an attorney. If you require legal or other expert advice, you should seek the services of a competent attorney or other professional.

American Casebook Series is a trademark registered in the U.S. Patent and Trademark Office.

ISBN: 978-1-63460-412-3

For Richard. And for our sons, Emmanuel and Sebastian.

C.A.B.

For Juliet, Gabe and Zoe.

J.S.S.

For Shaun. And for my parents, Julie and Michael.

D.N.

PREFACE TO THE SIXTH EDITION

As readers of this casebook undoubtedly know, the legal frameworks surrounding sexual orientation and gender identity are among the most dynamic and rapidly evolving in all of law. Since the last edition of this casebook, there have been significant developments at every level— federal and state; judicial, legislative, and executive; constitutional and statutory. Most importantly, of course, is the U.S. Supreme Court's historic decision on marriage equality. But there have been many other important developments, including the enactment of state laws aimed at preventing the passage of local laws protecting LGBT people from discrimination, the use and adoption of religious freedom laws as mechanisms for limiting the push for LGBT equality, the emergence of bathroom access for transgender individuals as a salient political and legal issue, the interpretation by federal administrative agencies, including the Department of Education and the Equal Employment Opportunity Commission, of federal antidiscrimination laws in ways that provide significant protection to sexual and gender minorities, and the military's lifting of its decades-old policy of excluding individuals on the basis of gender identity.

In light of the range of issues that today attract attention and the directions that both law and research have taken, including most critically the greater engagement of law and politics with questions of gender identity, we have retitled this casebook—*Cases and Materials on Sexuality, Gender Identity, and the Law.*

The intense pace of activity in this context makes it not only impossible for a casebook to stay fully current, but misguided to try. This edition, then, undertakes to be as current as possible as of its publication, but its more fundamental aim remains the one that inspired its creation more than two decades ago: to provide an engaging, interdisciplinary basis for studying the movement for LGBT equality and the law's complex regulation of sexual orientation and gender identity. We hope that the book provides a solid foundation, recognizing that it can and should be supplemented by current developments as they arise.

We are grateful to Harvard Law School, Stanford Law School, Rutgers Law School, and UCLA School of Law for supporting our work on this casebook. We are indebted to colleagues who have consistently provided critical and thoughtful comments and suggestions over multiple editions of this casebook. We owe special thanks to Clifford Rosky at the University of Utah, Steven Homer at the University of New Mexico, and Brad Sears at the Williams Institute at UCLA School of Law. We would also like to thank the many students we have had the privilege of teaching—and learning from—over the years; their contributions are reflected throughout these pages. They include students at nearly a dozen law schools scattered throughout the United States—Harvard, Yale, Stanford, UCLA, Wisconsin, Michigan, Illinois, Rutgers, Penn State, Loyola–Los Angeles, and UC Irvine. For their help with this edition, we especially want to thank UCLA Law students Seth Williams and Morgan Yang.

Acknowledgements

We are indebted to the copyright holders identified below for permission to reprint excerpts from the following copyrighted materials (listed in the order they appear in the book):

How Many People Are Lesbian, Gay, Bisexual, and Transgender?, by Gary J. Gates. Copyright © 2011. Reprinted by permission of Gary J. Gates and the Williams Institute at UCLA School of Law.

Special Report: 3.4% of U.S. Adults Identify as LGBT, by Gary J. Gates and Frank Newport. Copyright © 2012. Reprinted by permission of Gallup, Inc.

Homo Nest Raided, Queen Bees Are Stinging Mad, by Jerry Lisker, from N.Y. Daily News, July 6, 1969. Copyright © Daily News, L.P. Reprinted with permission.

Gay American History, by Jonathan Ned Katz, copyright © 1976 by Jonathan Ned Katz. Reprinted by permission of Jonathan Ned Katz.

Sexuality and Global Forces: Dr. Alfred Kinsey and the Supreme Court of the United States, by Michael Kirby, from 14 Indiana Journal of Global Legal Studies 485 (2007). Copyright © 2007 by the Indiana Journal of Global Legal Studies. Reprinted with permission.

The Social Organization of Sexuality, by Edward O. Laumann, John H. Gagnon, Robert T. Michael, and Stuart Michaels. Copyright © 1994 by Edward O. Laumann, Robert T. Michael, CSG Enterprises, Inc., and Stuart Michaels. Reprinted by permission of The University of Chicago Press and the Author.

The Science of Gaydar, by David France, from New York Magazine (June 17, 2007). Copyright © 2007. Reprinted by permission of David France.

Martha Nussbaum, Essentialism, and Sexuality, by Carlos A. Ball, from 19 Columbia Journal of Gender & the Law 3 (2010). Copyright © 2008 by the Columbia Journal of Gender and the Law. Reprinted by permission of the Columbia Journal of Gender and the Law.

Private Experiences in the Public Domain: Lesbians in Organizations, by Marny Hall. Copyright © 1989, by Marny Hall. Reprinted by permission of Marny Hall.

Allen Grant Richards, Out at Work: A Trans Perspective, Bay Windows, June 27, 2003. Reprinted by permission of author.

Bias in the Workplace: Consistent Evidence of Sexual Orientation and Gender Identity Discrimination 1998–2008, by M.V. Lee Badgett, Brad Sears, Holning Lau, and Deborah Ho, from 84 Chicago-Kent Law Review 559 (2009). Copyright © 2009 by Chicago-Kent Law Review. Reprinted by permission of the Chicago-Kent Law Review.

Covering, by Kenji Yoshino, 111 Yale Law Journal 769 (2002). Copyright © 2002 by the Yale Law Journal. Reprinted by permission of the Yale Law Journal.

Why Gay People Should Seek the Right to Marry, by Thomas Stoddard, from Out/Look: National Lesbian and Gay Quarterly (Fall 1989). Copyright © 1989 by the Out/Look Foundation. Reprinted by permission of Out/Look.

Since When is Marriage a Path to Liberation?, by Paula Ettelbrick, from Out/Look: National Lesbian and Gay Quarterly (Fall 1989). Copyright © 1989 by the Out/Look Foundation. Reprinted by permission of Out/Look.

Brown and Lawrence (and Goodridge), by Michael Klarman. Reprinted from Michigan Law Review, December 2005, vol. 104, no. 3. Copyright © 2005 by the Michigan Law Review Association. Reprinted by permission of the Michigan Law Review and Michael Klarman.

Goodridge in Context, by Mary L. Bonauto, from 40 Harvard Civil Rights-Civil Liberties Law Review 1 (2005). Copyright © 2005 by the President and Fellows of Harvard College and the Harvard Civil Rights–Civil Liberties Law Review.

Gay on Trial, by Gabriel Arana, from *The American Prospect*: December 2009, Volume 20, Issue 10. http.www.prospect.org. *The American Prospect*, 1710 Rhode Island Avenue, NW, Washington, DC 20036. All rights reserved.

Valuing All Families, by Nancy D. Polikoff, from 48 Santa Clara Law Review 741 (2008). Copyright © 2005 by Nancy D. Polikoff. Reprinted by permission of Nancy D. Polikoff and the Santa Clara Law Review.

Marriage Equality and the New Parenthood, by Douglas NeJaime, from 129 Harvard Law Review 1185 (2016). Copyright © 2016 by the Harvard Law Review Association. Reprinted by permission of the

* * *

We have made every effort to obtain permission to reproduce copyrighted material in this volume. If permission has inadvertently been missed or proper acknowledgment has not been made, please contact the authors c/o West Academic Publishing Company.

CARLOS A. BALL
JANE S. SCHACTER
DOUGLAS NEJAIME
WILLIAM B. RUBENSTEIN

October, 2016

SUMMARY OF CONTENTS

TABLE OF CONTENTS

TABLE OF CASES

The principal cases are in bold type.

CASES AND MATERIALS ON
SEXUALITY, GENDER IDENTITY, AND THE LAW

Sixth Edition

CHAPTER 1

BASIC DOCUMENTS

· · ·

I. INTRODUCTION

This Chapter provides foundational materials before the casebook moves into legal doctrine. While the casebook broadly covers the legal regulation of sexuality and gender, the lesbian, gay, bisexual, and transgender (LGBT) population remains the focus population. Accordingly, we begin with that population, including coverage of demographics, history, and political and legal conflict. After this LGBT focus, we move to broader questions regarding the meanings, complexities, and limitations of the very concepts of sexuality and gender. By covering a range of theoretical perspectives, we explore how sexual orientation and gender identity have been constructed as both a legal and cultural matter.

II. THE LGBT POPULATION

HOW MANY PEOPLE ARE LESBIAN, GAY, BISEXUAL, AND TRANSGENDER?*

Gary J. Gates

INTRODUCTION

Increasing numbers of population-based surveys in the United States and across the world include questions designed to measure sexual orientation and gender identity. Understanding the size of the lesbian, gay, bisexual, and transgender (LGBT) population is a critical first step to informing a host of public policy and research topics. * * *

CHALLENGES IN MEASURING THE LGBT COMMUNITY

Estimates of the size of the LGBT community vary for a variety of reasons. These include differences in the definitions of who is included in the LGBT population, differences in survey methods, and a lack of consistent questions asked in a particular survey over time.

In measuring sexual orientation, lesbian, gay, and bisexual individuals may be identified strictly based on their self-identity or it may

---

* Gary Gates, How Many People are Lesbian, Gay, Bisexual, and Transgender?, WILLIAMS INSTITUTE (2011).

be possible to consider same-sex sexual behavior or sexual attraction. Some surveys (not considered in this brief) also assess household relationships and provide a mechanism of identifying those who are in same-sex relationships. Identity, behavior, attraction, and relationships all capture related dimensions of sexual orientation but none of these measures completely addresses the concept.

Defining the transgender population can also be challenging. Definitions of who may be considered part of the transgender community include aspects of both gender identities and varying forms of gender expression or non-conformity. Similar to sexual orientation, one way to measure the transgender community is to simply consider self-identity. Measures of identity could include consideration of terms like transgender, queer, or genderqueer. The latter two identities are used by some to capture aspects of both sexual orientation and gender identity.

Similar to using sexual behaviors and attraction to capture elements of sexual orientation, questions may also be devised that consider gender expression and non-conformity regardless of the terms individuals may use to describe themselves. An example of these types of questions would be consideration of the relationship between the sex that individuals are assigned at birth and the degree to which that assignment conforms with how they express their gender. Like the counterpart of measuring sexual orientation through identity, behavior, and attraction measures, these varying approaches capture related dimensions of who might be classified as transgender but may not individually address all aspects of assessing gender identity and expression.

Another factor that can create variation among estimates of the LGBT community is survey methodology. Survey methods can affect the willingness of respondents to report stigmatizing identities and behaviors. Feelings of confidentiality and anonymity increase the likelihood that respondents will be more accurate in reporting sensitive information. Survey methods that include face-to-face interviews may underestimate the size of the LGBT community while those that include methods that allow respondents to complete questions on a computer or via the internet may increase the likelihood of LGBT respondents identifying themselves. Varied sample sizes of surveys can also increase variation. Population-based surveys with a larger sample can produce more precise estimates.

A final challenge in making population-based estimates of the LGBT community is the lack of questions asked over time on a single large survey. One way of assessing the reliability of estimates is to repeat questions over time using a consistent method and sampling strategy. Adding questions to more large-scale surveys that are repeated over time would substantially improve our ability to make better estimates of the size of the LGBT population.

[Gates then analyzes and compares estimates of the LGBT population from eleven recent United States and international surveys.] * * *

HOW MANY LESBIAN, GAY, BISEXUAL AND TRANSGENDER PEOPLE ARE THERE IN THE UNITED STATES?

Federal data sources designed to provide population estimates in the United States (e.g., the Decennial Census or the American Community Survey) do not include direct questions regarding sexual orientation or gender identity. * * * [N]o single survey offers a definitive estimate for the size of the LGBT community in the United States.

However, combining information from the population-based surveys considered in this brief offers a mechanism to produce credible estimates for the size of the LGBT community. Specifically, estimates for sexual orientation identity will be derived by averaging results from * * * five US surveys. * * *

Separate averages are calculated for lesbian and bisexual women along with gay and bisexual men. An estimate for the transgender population is derived by averaging the findings from * * * Massachusetts and California surveys. * * *

It should be noted that some transgender individuals may identify as lesbian, gay, or bisexual. So it is not possible to make a precise combined LGBT estimate. Instead, Figure 5 presents separate estimates for the number of LGB adults and the number of transgender adults.

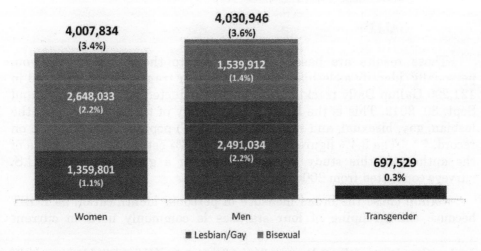

Figure 5. Percent and number of adults who identify as LGBT in the United States.

The analyses suggest that there are more than 8 million adults in the US who are LGB, comprising 3.5% of the adult population. This is split nearly evenly between lesbian/gay and bisexual identified individuals, 1.7% and 1.8%, respectively. There are also nearly 700,000 transgender individuals in the US. Given these findings, it seems reasonable to assert that approximately 9 million Americans identify as LGBT.

Averaging measures of same-sex sexual behavior yields an estimate of nearly 19 million Americans (8.2%) who have engaged in same-sex sexual behavior. The National Survey of Family Growth is the only source of US data on attraction and suggests that 11% or nearly 25.6 million Americans acknowledge at least some same-sex sexual attraction.

SPECIAL REPORT: 3.4% OF U.S. ADULTS IDENTIFY AS LGBT*

Gary J. Gates and Frank Newport

The inaugural results of a new Gallup question—posed to more than 120,000 U.S. adults thus far—shows that 3.4% say "yes" when asked if they identify as lesbian, gay, bisexual, or transgender.

Do you, personally, identify as lesbian, gay, bisexual, or transgender?

	Yes	No	DK/Refused
All Americans	3.4%	92.2%	4.4%

Gallup Daily tracking
June 1-Sept. 30, 2012

GALLUP'

These results are based on responses to the question, "Do you, personally, identify as lesbian, gay, bisexual, or transgender?" included in 121,290 Gallup Daily tracking interviews conducted between June 1 and Sept. 30, 2012. This is the largest single study of the distribution of the lesbian, gay, bisexual, and transgender (LGBT) population in the U.S. on record. * * * The 3.4% figure is similar to a 3.8% estimate made by one of the authors of this study (Gates), averaging a group of smaller U.S. surveys conducted from 2004 to 2008. * * *

Gallup chose the broad measure of personal identification as LGBT because this grouping of four statuses is commonly used in current

---

* Gary J. Gates & Frank Newport, *Special Report: 3.4% of U.S. Adults Identify as LGBT* (2012). Copyright © 2012 Gallup, Inc. All rights reserved. The content is used with permission; however, Gallup retains all rights of republication.

American discourse, and as a result has important cultural and political significance. One obvious limitation of this approach is that it is not possible to separately consider differences among lesbians, gay men, bisexuals, or transgender individuals. A second limitation is that this approach measures broad self-identity, and does not measure sexual or other behavior, either past or present.

The following sections review the percentage identifying as LGBT across specific subgroups of the U.S. population. Overall, the results from this analysis run counter to some media stereotypes that portray the LGBT community as predominantly white, highly educated, and very wealthy.

Nonwhite Individuals More Likely to Identify as LGBT

Nonwhites are more likely than white segments of the U.S. population to identify as LGBT. The survey results show that 4.6% of African-Americans identify as LGBT, along with 4.0% of Hispanics and 4.3% of Asians. The disproportionately higher representation of LGBT status among nonwhite population segments corresponds to the slightly below-average 3.2% of white Americans who identified as LGBT.

Do you, personally, identify as lesbian, gay, bisexual, or transgender?

	Yes	No	DK/Ref
	%	%	%
Non-Hispanic white	3.2	93.9	2.8
Black	4.6	90.1	5.3
Hispanic	4.0	90.2	5.8
Asian	4.3	92.0	3.7

Gallup Daily tracking
June 1-Sept. 30, 2012

GALLUP

Overall, a third of LGBT-identifiers are nonwhite (33%), compared with 27% of non-LGBT individuals.

Women Are More Likely to Identify as LGBT Than Are Men

Although the difference is not large, women are slightly more likely to identify as LGBT than are men (3.6% vs. 3.3%)—a finding that is consistent with other surveys. Put differently, more than 53% of LGBT individuals are women.

Do you, personally, identify as lesbian, gay, bisexual, or transgender?

	Yes	No	DK/Ref
	%	%	%
Men	3.3	92.5	4.2
Women	3.6	91.8	4.6

Gallup Daily tracking
June 1-Sept. 30, 2012

GALLUP'

Younger Americans More Likely to Identify as LGBT

Adults aged 18 to 29 (6.4%) are more than three times as likely as seniors aged 65 and older (1.9%) to identify as LGBT. Among those aged 30 to 64, LGBT identity declines with age—at 3.2% for 30- to 49-year-olds and 2.6% for 50- to 64-year-olds.

Consistent with other recent studies and with the gender gap identified earlier in this report, younger women are more likely to identify as LGBT than are younger men. Among 18- to 29-year-olds, 8.3% of women identify as LGBT, compared with 4.6% of men the same age.

Do you, personally, identify as lesbian, gay, bisexual, or transgender?

	Yes	No	DK/Ref
	%	%	%
18 to 29	6.4	90.1	3.5
30 to 49	3.2	93.6	3.2
50 to 64	2.6	93.1	4.3
65+	1.9	91.5	6.5
18 to 29 Women	8.3	88.0	3.8
18 to 29 Men	4.6	92.1	3.3

Gallup Daily tracking
June 1-Sept. 30, 2012

GALLUP'

It is possible that some of these age differences are due to a greater reluctance on the part of older Americans who may be LGBT to identify as such. In general, younger Americans are more accepting of equal rights and opportunities for gay men and lesbians.

LGBT Americans Tend to Have Lower Levels of Education and Income

Gallup's analysis shows that identification as LGBT is highest among Americans with the lowest levels of education—contrary to what other, more limited, studies have shown. Among those with a high school education or less, 3.5% identify as LGBT, compared with 2.8% of those with a college degree and 3.2% of those with postgraduate education. LGBT identification is highest among those with some college education but not a college degree, at 4.0%.

Do you, personally, identify as lesbian, gay, bisexual, or transgender?

	Yes	No	DK/Ref
	%	%	%
High school or less	3.5	90.3	6.3
Some college	4.0	93.2	2.8
College graduate	2.8	94.7	2.6
Postgraduate education	3.2	94.5	2.3

Gallup Daily tracking
June 1-Sept. 30, 2012

GALLUP

A similar pattern is found across income groups. More than 5% of those with incomes of less than $24,000 a year identify as LGBT, a higher proportion than among those with higher incomes—including 2.8% of those making $60,000 a year or more.

Do you, personally, identify as lesbian, gay, bisexual, or transgender?

	Yes	No	DK/Ref
	%	%	%
Under $24,000	5.1	92.2	2.7
$24,000 to <$60,000	3.6	95.1	1.3
$60,000 to <$90,000	2.8	96.5	0.7
$90,000+	2.8	96.4	0.8

Gallup Daily tracking
June 1-Sept. 30, 2012

GALLUP

Among those who report income, about 16% of LGBT-identified individuals have incomes above $90,000 per year, compared with 21% of the overall adult population. Additionally, 35% of those who identify as LGBT report incomes of less than $24,000 a year, significantly higher than the 24% for the population in general. These findings are consistent with research showing that LGBT people are at a higher risk of poverty. * * *

NOTES

1.   These two reports rely primarily on self-identity to measure and analyze the LGBT population. But as Dr. Gates explains, there are multiple ways to measure sexual orientation and gender identity. We return to these questions later in the chapter.

2.   According to Gallup survey data from 2015, 3.9% of the population identifies as LGBT. *See* Jeffrey M. Jones & Gary J. Gates, *Same-Sex Marriages Up After Supreme Court Ruling*, Gallup (Nov. 5, 2015), http://www.gallup.com/poll/186518/sex-marriages-supreme-court-ruling.aspx. This is slightly higher than the 2012 figure reported above.

3.   In 2016, the Williams Institute released new data on the transgender population, doubling its previous figure and estimating that 1.4 million adults in the U.S. identify as transgender. This is 0.6% of the population. *See* Andrew R. Flores *et al.*, *How Many Adults Identify as Transgender in the United States?*, Williams Institute (June 2016). The larger number is attributable to better data, as well as to the likely increase in self-identification as social stigma decreases.

III. HISTORICAL MATERIALS

Today, we take for granted the existence of an LGBT movement. But widespread mobilization around sexual orientation and gender identity is a relatively recent phenomenon. The materials presented below focus on the emergence of this mobilization and responses to it, over the course of the second half of the twentieth century. They also go back further to paint a picture of the legal, political, medical, and cultural treatment of LGBT people that obstructed, motivated, and shaped LGBT mobilization. Discrimination against lesbians and gay men hindered effective organization around sexual orientation even as it spurred such organization. It is important to note that while gender was entangled with sexuality throughout the period covered by these materials, mobilization around the distinct concept of gender identity emerged more recently.

The origins of the modern LGBT movement are often traced to Stonewall. According to historian Martin Duberman:

> "Stonewall" is *the* emblematic event in modern lesbian and gay history. The site of a series of riots in late June-early July 1969 that resulted from a police raid on a Greenwich Village gay bar, "Stonewall" has become synonymous over the years with gay resistance to oppression. Today, the word resonates with images of insurgency and self-realization and occupies a central place in the iconography of lesbian and gay awareness. The 1969 riots are generally taken to mark the birth of a modern gay and lesbian political movement—that moment in time when gays and lesbians recognized all at once their mistreatment and solidarity. As such, "Stonewall" has become an empowering symbol of global proportions.

MARTIN DUBERMAN, STONEWALL xv (1994).

The fact that Stonewall marked a major turning point should not obscure the history of activism that preceded it. Early organizations like the Mattachine Society and the Daughters of Bilitis, both of which formed on the West Coast in the early 1950s, grew nationally and were active through the 1950s and 1960s. For historical analysis tracing the activities of early groups like these, see JOHN D'EMILIO, SEXUAL POLITICS, SEXUAL COMMUNITIES (1983); LILLIAN FADERMAN, THE GAY REVOLUTION: THE STORY OF THE STRUGGLE (2015); MARCIA M. GALLO, DIFFERENT DAUGHTERS: A HISTORY OF THE DAUGHTERS OF BILITIS AND THE RISE OF THE LESBIAN RIGHTS MOVEMENT (2007); Martin Meeker, *Behind the Mask of Respectability: Reconsidering the Mattachine Society and Male Homophile Practice, 1950s and 1960s*, 10 JOURNAL OF THE HISTORY OF SEXUALITY 78 (2001).

In addition to early political activism, there were social practices that brought gay people together well before Stonewall. According to historian George Chauncey's study of New York:

In the half-century between 1890 and the beginning of the Second World War, a highly visible, remarkably complex, and continually changing gay male world took shape in New York City. That world involved several gay neighborhood enclaves, widely publicized dances and other social events, and a host of commercial establishments where gay men gathered, ranging from saloons, speakeasies, and bars to cheap cafeterias and elegant restaurants. The men who participated in that world forged a distinctive culture with its own language and customs, its own traditions and folk histories, its own heroes and heroines. They organized male beauty contests at Coney Island and drag balls in Harlem; they performed at gay clubs in the Village and at tourist traps in Times Square. Gay writers and performers produced a flurry of gay literature and theater in the 1920's and early 1930's; gay impresarios organized cultural events that sustained and enhanced gay men's communal ties and group identity. Some gay men were involved in long-term monogamous relationships they called marriages; others participated in an extensive sexual underground. . . . The gay male world that flourished before World War II has been almost entirely forgotten in popular memory and overlooked by professional historians; it was not supposed to have existed.

GEORGE CHAUNCEY, GAY NEW YORK: GENDER, URBAN CULTURE, AND THE MAKING OF THE GAY WORLD 1890–1940 1 (1994). For additional historical perspectives on pre-Stonewall lesbian and gay life in the twentieth century, see LILLIAN FADERMAN, ODD GIRLS AND TWILIGHT LOVERS: A HISTORY OF LESBIAN LIFE IN TWENTIETH-CENTURY AMERICA (1991); LILLIAN FADERMAN & STUART TIMMONS, GAY L.A.: A HISTORY OF SEXUAL OUTLAWS, POWER POLITICS, AND LIPSTICK LESBIANS (2006); and DAVID K. JOHNSON, THE LAVENDER SCARE: THE COLD WAR PERSECUTION OF GAYS AND LESBIANS IN THE FEDERAL GOVERNMENT (2004).

In 2010, Professor Chauncey testified as an expert witness in the federal lawsuit challenging California's constitutional ban on marriage for same-sex couples. That case eventually made its way to the U.S. Supreme Court, as discussed in Chapter 5. But because the Supreme Court resolved the case on standing grounds, and thus did not reach the merits, the trial court's decision in *Perry v. Schwarzenegger*, striking down the California ban, became the dispositive ruling. Professor Chauncey's trial testimony covered the history of discrimination against lesbians and gay men in the U.S. and related that history to the emergence of the modern LGBT movement.

In the following passage, Professor Chauncey explains the political and legal struggles that lesbians and gay men faced simply to gather in bars like the Stonewall Inn. Early laws did not simply discriminate against gays and lesbians but rather obstructed their very ability to meet in public. The discrimination, harassment, and stigma that gays and lesbians endured both hindered their effective organization and spurred their eventual political mobilization.

TESTIMONY OF PROFESSOR GEORGE CHAUNCEY*

[I]n 1933, with the repeal of prohibition, first New York state, and then successively many other states, issued regulations that prohibited * * * bars, restaurants, cabarets, or anyplace with a liquor license, from serving drinks to lesbians or gay men, or allowing them to congregate on the premises. * * * [T]his criminalization meant that when people went to a regular bar or restaurant, a normal bar or restaurant, they typically had to be very careful to hide the fact that they were gay, for fear of being excluded.

* * * [T]here were so few places where they could go and be open. But those places, to survive, had to pay bribes to the police, or often to organized criminal syndicates which had relationships with the police, or were even run by organized criminal syndicates. So it meant that gay life was just enmeshed in a web of criminality because of the criminalization of gay and lesbian sociability.

* * * So what the police and the liquor authority agents did, often, was to send plainclothes policemen into the bars, who would strike up conversations with customers, lead them on, and then, at some point, when an invitation was issued to leave the bar and go home, bring out the handcuffs and arrest them.

So that would lead to the arrest of the bar goer. And [that] would also be the best proof possible that homosexuals were at the bar. And so it would then be reported, and that would lead to proceedings to revoke the liquor license.

The other way that was used— * * * [t]he police would actually point to stereotypical gender behavior or cross-gender behavior that was associated with lesbians and gay men, and use that as evidence that a bar was patronized by them.

So, for instance, a police woman might report that she had seen two women dancing together, or women with short hair, or women who were wearing some articles of masculine clothing, or women who seemed

---

*   Testimony of Prof. George Chauncey, Yale University, in Perry v. Schwarzenegger, 704 F. Supp. 2d 921 (N.D. Cal. 2010) (testimony on Jan. 12, 2010).

to * * * swagger around a bar in a way that was more masculine than a woman should walk.

Or, likewise, they would point to men whose clothing was just a little too unconventional, a little too colorful, whose hair was too long, who addressed each other in effeminate ways. * * * [O]ne of the signs the police officer gave that a bar was gay was that he had overheard two men talking about the opera; something that no real man would do in the 1950s.

So there were just a range of ways that sort of unconventional behavior, gender behavior, stereotypically associated with lesbians and gay men was used to identify them.

I think it's actually a kind of striking thing, because it's one of the clearest examples of how the policing of homosexuality has often been used in a very specific legal sense, and then broadly and culturally, to police gender norms so that, actually, people who went into bars, who behaved in unconventional ways, cross-gendered ways, could be suspected of being homosexual.

* * * But, periodically, people did pose a challenge to the idea of this law, that you could actually discriminate against a class of people on the basis of their homosexual status. And in both New York state and in California, in the 1950s, there were rulings by the states' highest court that invalidated that kind of discrimination.

So a famous case in California, the Black Cat Cafe, here in San Francisco, which lost its license, I think, around 1949, filed a suit. It got a state Supreme Court ruling in '51 that said, actually, you couldn't discriminate in this way. And, then, for several years there was relative peace and quiet for bars in San Francisco. And then the San Francisco Police Department started a campaign against homosexuals, '54, '55, sweeps of streets and parks, cracked down on bars. In '55, the state legislature circumvented that [1951] ruling by passing a law that outlawed bars or restaurants that became what it called resorts for sex perverts. And the Alcoholic Beverage Commission, which was just then established, then launched a campaign against such bars and restaurants, which led to many more being closed. Finally, there was another state Supreme Court ruling which said, no, they meant it; you couldn't do this.

And, nonetheless, Mayor George Christopher, here in San Francisco, had had a tough reelection campaign in '59. And his opponent had charged that he had allowed San Francisco to become a mecca for homosexuals. And he was so determined to show that wasn't true, that once he was reelected he launched a two-year-long campaign against gay life in the City. Which led to, by one historian's account, 40 to 60 arrests a week, and about a third of the bars being shut down.

* * * [These bar raids] continued periodically, even in places where they had been ruled unconstitutional. * * * [M]ost famously, of course, in 1969, the police raided the Stonewall Bar, in Greenwich Village, in New York, after in fact the courts had already ruled that it was legitimate to serve lesbians and gay men. In that case, they were going after mob-oriented bars.

[Professor Chauncey then explained how the regulation of gay and lesbian social life was related to the regulation of work, where LGBT people faced widespread and government-sanctioned discrimination.]

[T]he first striking example I'd mention was in the military itself. There had * * * been various regulations affecting homosexual conduct and homosexuals in the military before the second World War, but it was really at the beginning of the second World War that for the first time, facing the necessity of mobilizing literally millions of people very quickly to fight the war, that the military decided to absolutely exclude all homosexuals and to institute screening procedures that would keep homosexuals out.

And so this became a part of the induction process, the screening process for everyone who was volunteered or drafted to serve in the war. Not surprisingly, they didn't ferret out many people, despite this policy. I think it was only five or six thousand. * * *

[A]fter the second World War, the employment of homosexuals in the civilian sectors of employment also became a major issue. And in 1950, Senator Joseph McCarthy announced that he knew the names not only— or had a list of names not only of Communists in the State Department and other agencies, but of sex perverts. This led to a couple of Congressional committees investigating this charge. And one of them, a standing committee, subcommittee which produced a report called, "On the Employment of Homosexuals and Other Sex Perverts in Government in 1950."

And this report * * * was based on investigation of the way the government was dealing with this problem, and took note of the fact that checking Civil Service Commission records, they found that since this had become more of an issue in 1947, two and a half years that they looked at, some 1,700 people had been prohibited from getting civilian jobs because it had been discovered that they were homosexual.

They were concerned that the procedures for identifying homosexuals were inadequate, and for ferreting them out and discharging them. So they recommended a tightening of procedures.

And in 1953, shortly after Dwight Eisenhower became president, one of his first executive orders decreed * * * that homosexuals would be prohibited from civilian as well as military employment in the federal government. And it actually also required private companies, which had contracts with the government, to ferret out and fire their homosexual employees.

* * * [T]hat policy ended for most federal agencies in 1975, when President Carter rescinded that policy. Though, it continued to be in effect for some of the highly-sensitive intelligence agencies, and so forth.

And then it was only in the 1990s that President Clinton both ended the policy bearing on intelligence agencies, and also prohibited discrimination in federal employment.

President Carter said that federal agencies were no longer required to dismiss their homosexual employees or keep homosexuals from their employ. And, then, President Clinton enacted [an] anti-discrimination order that they could not discriminate. So in that intervening period, agencies were not required to discriminate, but they could discriminate. * * *

[Professor Chauncey then discussed the effects of this earlier discrimination on gays and lesbians.]

[I]t meant that gay life really was pushed underground[.] * * * I think some people interpret that to mean that there was very little organized gay life at all. And that's simply not the case. There in fact were meeting places. There were parties in private apartments. People did have a gay social life. But they had to be very, very careful to hide it.

And although this had already been true earlier in the 20th century, most people didn't want to take this risk. It really increased the stakes for people. And so it meant that [there] really became sort of a world within a world. It was very secretive, had its own codes, so that people could talk with one another without alerting outsiders.

Actually, the word "gay" itself is probably the best example of this. Gay liberationists in the 1970s were determined to bring gay people out of the closet. And so * * * they called themselves gay liberationists. But in the 1940s, and '50s, and early '60s, very few straight people realized that gay people, homosexuals, had given "gay" a sort of homosexual meaning. So that a lesbian standing at the office watercooler could say to another woman that she had gone to a gay place the night before, had a gay time, met a gay gal, and really communicate quite a lot to the person she was talking to, without worrying that someone next to her would overhear this and understand what was going on.

But it just meant that there was a level of secrecy required. Of course, this also meant that fewer heterosexuals, or relatively few heterosexuals, thought that they knew gay people.

As the beginning of this section noted, the Stonewall raid provoked a protest that fueled LGBT mobilization. The following contemporaneous account provides further context for understanding the meaning of Stonewall and its reporting by the media.

HOMO NEST RAIDED, QUEEN BEES ARE STINGING MAD*
New York Daily News

She sat there with her legs crossed, the lashes of her mascara-coated eyes beating like the wings of a hummingbird. She was angry. She was so upset she hadn't bothered to shave. A day old stubble was beginning to push through the pancake makeup. She was a he. A queen of Christopher Street.

Last weekend the queens had turned commandos and stood bra strap to bra strap against an invasion of the helmeted Tactical Patrol Force. The elite police squad had shut down one of their private gay clubs, the Stonewall Inn at 57 Christopher St., in the heart of a three-block homosexual community in Greenwich Village. Queen Power reared its bleached blonde head in revolt. New York City experienced its first homosexual riot. "We may have lost the battle, sweets, but the war is far from over," lisped an unofficial lady-in-waiting from the court of the Queens.

"We've had all we can take from the Gestapo," the spokesman, or spokeswoman, continued. "We're putting our foot down once and for all." The foot wore a spiked heel. According to reports, the Stonewall Inn, a two-story structure with a sand painted brick and opaque glass facade, was a mecca for the homosexual element in the village who wanted nothing but a private little place where they could congregate, drink, dance and do whatever little girls do when they get together.

The thick glass shut out the outside world of the street. Inside, the Stonewall bathed in wild, bright psychedelic lights, while the patrons writhed to the sounds of a juke box on a square dance floor surrounded by booths and table. The bar did a good business and the waiters, or waitresses, were always kept busy, as they snaked their way around the dancing customers to the booths and tables. For nearly two years, peace and tranquility reigned supreme for the Alice in Wonderland clientele.

THE RAID LAST FRIDAY

Last Friday the privacy of the Stonewall was invaded by police from the First Division. It was a raid. They had a warrant. After two years, police said they had been informed that liquor was being served on the premises. Since the Stonewall was without a license, the place was being

---

*   Jerry Lisker, *Homo Nest Raided, Queen Bees Are Stinging Mad*, N.Y. DAILY NEWS, July 6, 1969, at 2.

closed. It was the law. All hell broke loose when the police entered the Stonewall. The girls instinctively reached for each other. Others stood frozen, locked in an embrace of fear.

Only a handful of police were on hand for the initial landing in the homosexual beachhead. They ushered the patrons out onto Christopher Street, just off Sheridan Square. A crowd had formed in front of the Stonewall and the customers were greeted with cheers of encouragement from the gallery.

The whole proceeding took on the aura of a homosexual Academy Awards Night. The Queens pranced out to the street blowing kisses and waving to the crowd. A beauty of a specimen named Stella wailed uncontrollably while being led to the sidewalk in front of the Stonewall by a cop. She later confessed that she didn't protest the manhandling by the officer, it was just that her hair was in curlers and she was afraid her new beau might be in the crowd and spot her. She didn't want him to see her this way, she wept.

QUEEN POWER

The crowd began to get out of hand, eye witnesses said. Then, without warning, Queen Power exploded with all the fury of a gay atomic bomb. Queens, princesses and ladies-in-waiting began hurling anything they could get their polished, manicured fingernails on. Bobby pins, compacts, curlers, lipstick tubes and other femme fatale missiles were flying in the direction of the cops. The war was on. The lilies of the valley had become carnivorous jungle plants.

Urged on by cries of "C'mon girls, let[']s go get'em," the defenders of Stonewall launched an attack. The cops called for assistance. To the rescue came the Tactical Patrol Force. Flushed with the excitement of battle, a fellow called Gloria pranced around like Wonder Woman, while several Florence Nightingales administered first aid to the fallen warriors. There were some assorted scratches and bruises, but nothing serious was suffered by the honeys turned Madwoman of Chaillot.

Official reports listed four injured policemen with 13 arrests. The War of the Roses lasted about 2 hours from about midnight to 2 a.m. There was a return bout Wednesday night. Two veterans recently recalled the battle and issued a warning to the cops. "If they close up all the gay joints in this area, there is going to be all out war."

BRUCE AND NAN

Both said they were refugees from Indiana and had come to New York where they could live together happily ever after. They were in their early 20's. They preferred to be called by their married names, Bruce and Nan. "I don't like your paper," Nan lisped matter-of-factly. "It's anti-fag and pro-cop." "I'll bet you didn't see what they did to the Stonewall. Did the pigs tell you that they smashed everything in sight? Did you ask them why they stole money out of the cash register and then smashed it with a sledge hammer? Did you ask them why it took them two years to discover that the Stonewall didn't have a liquor license[?]"

Bruce nodded in agreement and reached over for Nan's trembling hands. "Calm down, doll," he said. "Your face is getting all flushed." Nan wiped her face with a tissue. "This would have to happen right before the wedding. The reception was going to be held at the Stonewall, too," Nan said, tossing her ashen-tinted hair over her shoulder.

"What wedding?," the bystander asked. Nan frowned with a how-could-anybody-be-so-stupid look. "Eric and Jack's wedding, of course. They're finally tieing the knot. I thought they'd never get together."

MEET SHIRLEY

"We'll have to find another place, that's all there is to it," Bruce sighed. "But every time we start a place, the cops break it up sooner or later." "They let us operate just as long as the payoff is regular," Nan said bitterly. "I believe they closed up the Stonewall because there was some trouble with the payoff to the cops. I think that's the real reason. It's a shame. It was such a lovely place. We never bothered anybody. Why couldn't they leave us alone?"

Shirley Evans, a neighbor with two children, agrees that the Stonewall was not a rowdy place and the persons who frequented the club were never troublesome. She lives at 45 Christopher St. "Up until the night of the police raid there was never any trouble there," she said. "The homosexuals minded their own business and never bothered a soul. There were never any fights or hollering, or anything like that. They just wanted to be left alone. I don't know what they did inside, but that's their business. I was never in there myself. It was just awful when the police came. It was like a swarm of hornets attacking a bunch of butterflies."

A reporter visited the now closed Stonewall and it indeed looked like a cyclone had struck the premises. Police said there were over 200 people in the Stonewall when they entered with a warrant. The crowd outside was estimated at 500 to 1,000. According to police, the Stonewall had been under observation for some time. Being a private club, plain clothesmen were refused entrance to the inside when they periodically tried to check the place. "They had the tightest security in the Village," a First Division officer said, "We could never get near the place without a warrant."

POLICE TALK

The men of the First Division were unable to find any humor in the situation, despite the comical overtones of the raid. "They were throwing more than lace hankies," one inspector said. "I was almost decapitated by a slab of thick glass. It was thrown like a discus and just missed my throat by inches." The beer can didn't miss, though, "it hit me right above the temple."

Police also believe the club was operated by Mafia connected owners. The police did confiscate the Stonewall's cash register as proceeds from an illegal operation. The receipts were counted and are on file at the division headquarters. The warrant was served and the establishment closed on the grounds it was an illegal membership club with no license, and no license to serve liquor.

The police are sure of one thing. They haven't heard the last from the Girls of Christopher Street.

NOTE

Stonewall proved to be a major turning point, and it helped to inaugurate a new era of gay advocacy. According to historian John D'Emilio:

> After the second night of disturbances, the anger that had erupted into street fighting was channeled into intense discussion of what many had begun to memorialize as the first gay riot in history. Allen Ginsberg's stature in the 1960s had risen almost to that of guru for many counterculture youth. When he arrived at the Stonewall on Sunday evening, he commented on the change that had already taken place. "You know, the guys there were so beautiful," he told a reporter. "They've lost that wounded look that fags all had ten years ago." The New York Mattachine Society hastily assembled a special riot edition of its newsletter that characterized the events, with camp humor, as "The Hairpin Drop Heard Round the World." It scarcely exaggerated. Before the end of July, women and men in New York had formed the Gay Liberation Front, a self-proclaimed revolutionary organization in the style of the New Left. Word of the Stonewall riot and GLF spread rapidly among the networks of young radicals scattered across the country, and within a year gay liberation groups had sprung into existence on college campuses and in cities around the nation.

John D'Emilio, *A New Beginning: The Birth of Gay Liberation, in* SEXUAL POLITICS: THE MAKING OF A HOMOSEXUAL MINORITY IN THE UNITED STATES, 1940–1970, 231–33 (1983). *See also* PATRICIA CAIN, RAINBOW RIGHTS: THE ROLE OF LAWYERS AND COURTS IN THE LESBIAN AND GAY RIGHTS CIVIL RIGHTS MOVEMENT 91 (2000) (noting that "it is fitting that the event occurred at a gay bar, a place that symbolized the center of the gay community," and that "what the Stonewall riots of June 1969 accomplished was the politicization of the social community"). Notably, other radical LGBT organizations also formed around this time. For example, Stonewall veterans Sylvia Rivera and Marsha P. Johnson formed the Street Transvestite Action Revolutionaries (STAR). FADERMAN, THE GAY REVOLUTION, *supra*, at 200.

Before long, divisions arose within gay liberation groups over whether to devote resources to non-LGBT-focused radical causes and how radical the LGBT-focused efforts themselves should be. In late 1969, less radical and more reform-minded gays and lesbians formed the Gay Activists Alliance (GAA), which, as historian Lillian Faderman describes it, "would be less about promoting gay 'liberation' and more about promoting gay rights." *Id.* at 214.

Eventually, lesbian activists also formed new groups, having been alienated by the gay groups' focus on men and male sexuality and insulted by feminist leader Betty Friedan's concern over "the Lavender Menace" in the National Organization of Women. These activists soon formed Radicalesbians and wrote their manifesto, "The Woman-Identified Woman." *Id.* at 233–34.

It was not only political and legal actors who initiated and perpetuated discrimination against lesbian, gay, and bisexual people— and who in turn inspired LGBT protests. As the following excerpt from 1976 explains, the medical profession also played a significant role in constructing and regulating homosexuality—eventually prompting challenges from LGBT activists.

TREATMENT*
Jonathan Katz

INTRODUCTION

Lesbians and Gay men have long been subjected to a varied, often horrifying list of "cures" at the hands of psychiatric-psychological professionals, treatments usually aimed at asexualization or heterosexual reorientation. This treatment has almost invariably involved a negative value judgment concerning the inherent character of homosexuality. The treatment of Lesbians and Gay men by psychiatrists and psychologists constitutes one of the more lethal forms of homosexual oppression.

Among the treatments are surgical measures: castration, hysterectomy, and vasectomy. In the 1800s, surgical removal of the ovaries and of the clitoris are discussed as a "cure" for various forms of female "erotomania," including, it seems, Lesbianism. Lobotomy was performed as late as 1951. A variety of drug therapies have been employed, including the administration of hormones, LSD, sexual stimulants, and sexual depressants. Hypnosis, used on Gay people in America as early as 1899, was still being used to treat such "deviant behavior" in 1967. Other documented "cures" are shock treatment, both electric and chemical; aversion therapy, employing nausea-inducing

---

*   JONATHAN KATZ, GAY AMERICAN HISTORY: LESBIANS AND GAY MEN IN THE U.S.A. 197–205 (1976).

drugs, electric shock, and/or negative verbal suggestion; and a type of behavior called "sensitization," intended to increase heterosexual arousal, making ingenious use of pornographic photos. Often homosexuals have been the subjects of Freudian psychoanalysis and other varieties of individual and group psychotherapy. Some practitioners (a Catholic one is quoted) have treated homosexuals by urging an effort of the will directed toward the goal of sexual abstinence. Primal therapists, vegetotherapists, and the leaders of each new psychological fad have had their say about treating homosexuals. Even musical analysis has reportedly assisted a doctor in such a "cure." Astrologers, Scientologists, Aesthetic Realists, and other quack philosophers have followed the medical profession's lead with their own suggestions for treatment.

* * *

The treatment of homosexuality by medical practitioners is of relatively recent origin, and is closely tied to the conceptualization of homosexuality as a medical-psychological phenomenon, a "mental illness." This conceptualization is itself a fairly recent invention: European discussion of homosexuality as a medical phenomenon dates to the early 1800s. Before that time, ecclesiastical authorities conceived of homosexuality as essentially a theological-moral phenomenon, a sin. Next, legislative bodies declared it a legal matter, a crime. The historical change in the conception of homosexuality from sin to crime to sickness is intimately associated with the rise to power of a class of petit bourgeois medical professionals, a group of individual medical entrepreneurs, whose stock in trade is their alleged "expert" understanding of homosexuality, a special-interest group whose facade of scientific objectivity covers their own emotional, economic, and career investments in their status as such authorities. At its time of origin, the medical practitioners' concept of homosexuality as a sickness may have been a liberal and humane advance over the conception and punishment of homosexuality as a crime. In 1976, psychiatrists and psychologists are among the major ideologues of homosexual oppression.

Research is now starting to trace the exact historical process by which these medical businessmen (for they are mostly males) acquired the power to define the character of homosexuals—and to trace that political movement by which Gay people are beginning to redefine themselves, struggling for power over that society which affects their lives. Today, Gay liberationists are challenging the long-accepted, medically derived notion that homosexuality is essentially a psychological phenomenon—any more than it is a political, economic, or historical one. They are disputing that view by which the complex human phenomena of homosexual behavior, emotion, lifestyle, culture, and history are reduced to mere psychology. Neither homosexuality nor heterosexuality, they argue, is encompassed by the psychological. Calling for the reconceptualization of homosexuality in broad, humanistic, and social terms, Gay people are today beginning the work of reconceptualizing themselves.

As Katz suggests, in the 1970s, LGBT activists worked to change the medical profession's approach.

When the American Psychiatric Association issued its first official listing of mental disorders (known as the *Diagnostic and Statistical Manual, Mental Disorders (DSM-I)*) in 1952,

> homosexuality and the other sexual deviations were included among the sociopathic personality disturbances. These disorders were characterized by the absence of subjectively experienced distress or anxiety despite the presence of profound pathology. Thus it was possible to include homosexuality in the nosology despite the apparent lack of discomfort or disease on the part of some homosexuals. It was the pattern of behavior that established the pathology. Explicitly acknowledging the centrality of dominant social values in defining such conditions, *DSM-I* asserted that individuals so diagnosed were "ill primarily in terms of society and of conformity with the prevailing cultural milieu."

RONALD BEYER, HOMOSEXUALITY AND AMERICAN PSYCHIATRY: THE POLITICS OF DIAGNOSIS 39 (1981).

The next iteration, *DSM-II*, was published in 1968. It removed homosexuality from the list of sociopathic personality disturbances and instead listed it "with the other sexual deviations—fetishism, pedophilia, transvestitism, exhibitionism, voyeurism, sadism and masochism—among the 'other non-psychotic mental disorders.'" *Id*. At the time, activists made little of the *DSM-II*. But "[t]wo years later the classification of homosexuality in the *Manual* was to become the central focus of the Gay Liberation movement's attack on psychiatry." *Id*. Finally, "in 1973, as the result of three years of challenge on the part of gay activists and their allies within the American Psychiatric Association, homosexuality was [deemed to be no longer a psychiatric disorder]." *Id*. at 40.

NOTES

1. As late as 1967, a majority of the Supreme Court held that a gay Canadian could be deported from the United States under a section of the Immigration and Nationality Act of 1952 that excluded persons "afflicted with psychopathic personality." *Boutilier v. INS*, 387 U.S. 118, 122, 87 S.Ct. 1563, 1566, 18 L.Ed.2d 661 (1967). The dissent objected to the breadth and vagueness of the statutory provision, putting special emphasis on Kinsey's findings about the relative prevalence of homosexual experiences.

Nevertheless, the dissent wrote that "[t]he homosexual is one who, by some freak, is the product of an arrested development. . . ." *Id.* at 127, 87 S.Ct. at 1568 (Douglas, J., dissenting). In 1990, Congress amended the immigration laws to lift the ban on gay applicants. *See* Immigration Act of 1990, Pub. L. No. 101–649, 104 Stat. 4978 (codified as amended in scattered sections of 8 U.S.C.). Ironically, the psychiatric treatment that constituted grounds for deportation in *Boutilier* may now be a reason that bars the United States government from deporting a foreigner; in 1997, the Ninth Circuit held that forced psychiatric treatment in Russia constituted "persecution" enabling a Russian national to claim refugee status in the United States. *Pitcherskaia v. INS*, 118 F.3d 641, 647 (9th Cir. 1997).

2.   Contrast the understandings of homosexuality reflected in the *Boutilier* opinions with the positions taken by the American Psychological Association, the American Psychiatric Association, and associated professional groups in an amicus brief filed in *Lawrence v. Texas*, the landmark 2003 case abolishing anti-sodomy laws, as discussed in Chapter 2. That brief asserted categorically that "the sexual orientation known as homosexuality—which is based on an enduring pattern of sexual or romantic attraction exclusively or primarily to others of one's own sex—is a normal variant of human sexual expression; it is not a mental or psychological disorder; and it is highly resistant to change." Brief of the American Psychological Association et al. as Amici Curiae Supporting Petitioners, *Lawrence v. Texas*, 539 U.S. 558, 123 S.Ct. 2472, 156 L.Ed.2d 508 (2003) (No. 02–102) 2003 WL 152338 (footnote omitted). The brief also went on to address and rebut at some length the idea that sexual orientation can be changed through clinical intervention:

> Some groups and individuals continue to offer interventions—sometimes called "conversion" or "reparative" therapies—that purport to change sexual orientation from homosexual to heterosexual. To date, however, there has been no scientifically adequate research to show that interventions aimed at changing sexual orientation are effective or safe. Moreover, critical examinations of reports of the effectiveness of these therapies have highlighted numerous problems with such claims. . . .

> In addition to the lack of scientific evidence for the effectiveness of efforts to change sexual orientation, there is reason to believe such efforts can be harmful to the psychological well-being of those who attempt them. Clinical observations and self-reports indicate that many individuals who unsuccessfully attempt to change their sexual orientation undergo considerable psychological distress. In fact, the potential psychological risks to some patients undergoing conversion therapies are sufficiently significant that treatment protocols have been developed to assist them in overcoming a wide range of psychological and relational problems. . . .

Accordingly, the mainstream view in the mental health professions is that the most appropriate response of a therapist treating an individual who is troubled about his or her homosexual feelings is to help that person cope with social prejudices against homosexuality and lead a happy and satisfying life as a lesbian or gay man. Reflecting that view, all major national mental health organizations—including *amici* American Psychological Association, American Psychiatric Association, and [National Association of Social Workers], as well as the American Academy of Pediatrics and the American Counseling Association—have adopted policy statements cautioning the profession and the public about treatments that purport to change sexual orientation.

Id. at 4, 13–15 (footnotes omitted). More recently, LGBT advocates have convinced some state lawmakers to prohibit the use of "sexual orientation change efforts" on minors. *See, e.g.,* CAL. BUS. & PROF. CODE § 865 (2013); N.J. STAT. ANN. § 45:1–55 (2013). And these laws have been upheld when challenged by opponents. *See* King v. Governor of the State of New Jersey, 767 F.3d 216 (3d Cir. 2014); Pickup v. Brown, 728 F.3d 1042 (9th Cir. 2013).

In the 1970s, the burgeoning LGBT movement challenged the government's treatment of lesbians and gay men and pushed the medical profession to alter its approach to homosexuality. These advances, though, provoked responses from others opposed to LGBT rights. The nascent "traditional family values" movement opposed the liberalization of norms governing sexuality, gender, and the family. Beginning in the late 1970s, activists successfully countered advances by LGBT advocates.

In his trial testimony in *Perry v. Schwarzenegger*, Professor Chauncey explained some of these developments. As gays and lesbians increasingly came out and sought greater legal protection, local governments began to pass nondiscrimination ordinances. "[B]eginning in the 1970s, about 40 towns and cities enacted antidiscrimination laws. Another 40 did in the 1980s. And this very quickly produced a response." Testimony of Professor George Chauncey, Yale University, in Perry v. Schwarzenegger, 704 F.Supp. 2d 921 (N.D. Cal. 2010) (testimony on Jan. 12, 2010). Anita Bryant's "Save Our Children" campaign began in Dade County, Florida, in 1977 and repealed the local ordinance prohibiting sexual orientation discrimination. Bryant's Florida campaign led to similar efforts across the country. According to Professor Chauncey, "in the 20 years after, there were at least 60 of these campaigns, usually to overturn existing gay rights ordinances, and about three-quarters of which succeeded in doing so." *Id.* We explore ordinances seeking to repeal LGBT rights in Chapter 3 when we consider the successful equal protection challenge to Colorado's Amendment 2 in *Romer v. Evans*.

In the 1980s, the HIV/AIDS epidemic claimed the lives of many gay and bisexual men. In response, the LGBT movement, including many lesbian activists, organized to support research and treatment and to demand greater response from the government. This period saw an expansion of LGBT social services organizations to support gay and bisexual men affected by HIV/AIDS. It also witnessed the rise of protest activity organized around queer politics. The following pamphlet captures some of the activist voices reclaiming the term "queer." Later in the chapter we explore the related queer theoretical move in academic work in the late twentieth century.

QUEERS READ THIS[*]
Anonymous Queers

Being queer is not about a right to privacy; it is about the freedom to be public, to just be who we are. It means everyday fighting oppression; homophobia, racism, misogyny, the bigotry of religious hypocrites and our own self-hatred. (We have been carefully taught to hate ourselves.) And now of course it means fighting a virus as well, and all those homo-haters who are using AIDS to wipe us off the face of the earth.

Being queer means leading a different sort of life. It's not about the mainstream, profit margins, patriotism, patriarchy or being assimilated. It's not about executive directors, privilege and elitism. It's about being on the margins, defining ourselves; it's about gender-fuck and secrets, what's beneath the belt and deep inside the heart; it's about the night. Being queer is "grass roots" because we know that everyone of us, every body, every cunt, every heart and ass and dick is a world of pleasure waiting to be explored. Everyone of us is a world of infinite possibility.

We are an army because we have to be. We are an army because we are so powerful. (We have so much to fight for; we are the most precious of endangered species.) And we are an army of lovers because it is we who know what love is. Desire and lust, too. We invented them. We come out of the closet, face the rejection of society, face firing squads, just to love each other! Every time we fuck, we win.

We must fight for ourselves (no one else is going to do it) and if in that process we bring greater freedom to the world at large then great. (We've given so much to that world: democracy, all the arts, the concepts of love, philosophy and the soul, to name just a few gifts from our ancient Greek Dykes, Fags.) Let's make every space a lesbian and gay space. Every street a part of our sexual geography. A city of yearning and then

---

[*]   ANONYMOUS QUEERS, QUEERS READ THIS; I HATE STRAIGHTS (1990) (pamphlet distributed at New York City's Gay Pride Parade, June 1990).

total satisfaction. A city and a country where we can be safe and free and more. We must look at our lives and see what's best in them, see what is queer and what is straight and let that straight chaff fall away! Remember there is so, so little time. And I want to be a lover of each and every one of you. Next year, we march naked.

* * *

I hate straight people who think they have anything intelligent to say about "outing." I hate straight people who think stories about themselves are "universal" but stories about us are only about homosexuality. I hate straight recording artists who make their careers off of queer people, then attack us, then act hurt when we get angry and then deny having wronged us rather than apologize for it. I hate straight people who say, "I don't see why you feel the need to wear those buttons and t-shirts. I don't go around telling the whole world I'm straight."

I hate that in twelve years of public education I was never taught about queer people. I hate that I grew up thinking I was the only queer in the world, and I hate even more that most queer kids still grow up the same way. I hate that I was tormented by other kids for being a faggot, but more that I was taught to feel ashamed for being the object of their cruelty, taught to feel it was my fault. I hate that the Supreme Court of this country says it's okay to criminalize me because of how I make love. I hate that so many straight people are so concerned about my goddamned sex life. I hate that so many twisted straight people become parents, while I have to fight like hell to be *allowed* to be a father. I hate straights.

* * *

I wear my pink triangle everywhere. I do not lower my voice in public when talking about lesbian love or sex. I always tell people I'm a lesbian. I don't wait to be asked about my "boyfriend." I don't say it's "no one's business."

I don't do this for straight people. Most of them don't know what the pink triangle even means. Most of them couldn't care less that my girlfriend and I are totally in love or having a fight on the street. Most of them don't notice us no matter what we do. I do what I do to reach other lesbians. I do what I do because I don't want lesbians to assume I'm a straight girl. I am out all the time, everywhere, because I WANT TO REACH YOU. Maybe you'll notice me, maybe we'll start talking, maybe we'll exchange numbers, maybe we'll become friends. Maybe we won't say a word but our eyes will meet and I will imagine you naked, sweating, open-mouthed, your back arched as I am fucking you. And we'll be happy to show we aren't the only ones in the world. We'll be happy because we found each other, without saying a word, maybe just for a moment.

But no.

You won't wear a pink triangle on that linen lapel. You won't meet my eyes if I flirt with you on the street. You avoid me on the job because I'm "too" out. You chastise me in bars because I'm "too political." You ignore me in public because I bring "too much" attention to "my" lesbianism. But then you want me to be your lover, you want me to be your friend, you want me to love you, support you, fight for "OUR" right to exist.

* * *

Queer!

Ah, do we really have to use that word? It's trouble. Every gay person has his or her own take on it. For some it means strange and eccentric and kind of mysterious. That's okay, we like that. But some gay girls and boys don't. They think they're more normal than strange. And for others "queer" conjures up those awful memories of adolescent suffering. Queer. It's forcibly bittersweet and quaint at best—weakening and painful at worst. Couldn't we just use "gay" instead. It's a much brighter word. And isn't it synonymous with "happy"? When will you militants grow up and get over the novelty of being different?

WHY QUEER

Well, yes, "gay" is great. It has its place. But when a lot of lesbians and gay men wake up in the morning we feel angry and disgusted, not gay. So we've chosen to call ourselves queer. Using "queer" is a way of reminding us how we are perceived by the rest of the world. It's a way of telling ourselves we don't have to be witty and charming people who keep our lives discreet and marginalized in the straight world. We use queer as gay men loving lesbians and lesbians loving being queer. Queer, unlike GAY, doesn't mean MALE.

And when spoken to other gays and lesbians it's a way of suggesting we close ranks, and forget (temporarily) our individual differences because we face a more insidious common enemy. Yeah, QUEER can be a rough word but it is also a sly and ironic weapon we can steal from the homophobe's hands and use against him.

———————

Having presented a broad overview of the LGBT population, LGBT discrimination, and the movement for LGBT rights, this chapter now turns to more conceptual and theoretical issues. The next section explores the meaning of sexual orientation. Then the last section engages questions of gender, including gender identity and intersexuality.

IV. WHAT IS SEXUAL ORIENTATION?

In this section, we explore the meaning of sexual orientation. The readings below raise the distinction between conduct and status that has been central to the legal regulation of homosexuality. Consider whether it makes sense to separate same-sex sexual behavior from lesbian and gay identity—and what the costs and benefits of such an approach might be. The readings also raise the question of why we define sexual orientation the way that we do—as indicative of the sex of the individuals to whom someone is attracted. Consider what other ways we could understand sexual orientation and what investments we have in our current definition. Finally, the readings introduce the binary around which sexual orientation has been organized—heterosexual and homosexual. This is particularly striking given the percentage of bisexuals in the LGB population, as reported in the readings with which this Chapter opened. Consider why the binary exists and what sexual practices and identities it obscures.

SEXUALITY AND GLOBAL FORCES: DR. ALFRED KINSEY AND THE SUPREME COURT OF THE UNITED STATES*
Michael Kirby

Dr. Alfred Kinsey [began teaching as an assistant professor of biology at Indiana University in Bloomington in 1920.] His research on gall wasps * * * effectively [made him] a world expert on that subject.

Kinsey's obscure but worthy scholarly life might have continued in Bloomington in this way but for one of those shifts of the mind that mark out the greatest of scientists. By the mid-1930s, Kinsey became very interested in great scientists, participating in an undergraduate course, "Life Views of Great Men of Science." Perhaps it was reflecting upon such scientists, and their breakthroughs, that led Kinsey's mind into a new field of biology concerning what he sometimes called "the human animal." He later claimed that published research of Dr. Robert Dickinson, an American leader in sex education, maternal health, and birth control, led him to become interested in sex research in humans. In 1938 he began a marriage course for undergraduates and others at Indiana University. Predictably enough, this attracted opposition from conservative circles, but it was supported by the University Trustees. By the late 1930s, Kinsey was working on a "biometric treatment of data," applying the same meticulous scientific methodologies he had developed in studying gall wasps, so far as that was possible, to the study of human sexual behavior.

* MICHAEL KIRBY, *Sexuality and Global Forces: Dr. Alfred Kinsey and the Supreme Court of the United States*, 14 IND. J. GLOBAL LEGAL STUD. 485, 491–500 (2007).

Books have been written, plays have been staged, and documentaries and films have been screened concerning the way Kinsey began his program of research involving human sexual experience in prisons and elsewhere. One of the early ideas that evolved from his thousands of interviews was that the previous assumption of a strict binary division between "homosexuals" and "heterosexuals" was factually inaccurate. Kinsey was beginning to postulate a rating scale by which individuals could be ranked at different points in relation to their sexual behavior, inclinations, and interests. His was not an enterprise to collect erotic stories for the titillation of particular audiences. It was a case of a "taxonomist working with a taxonomic problem. The methods remain the same; only the material is changed."

Kinsey's questionnaire format was refined during the 1940s. From the beginning, it covered questions on the major sexual outlets of the human subjects: masturbation, sex dreams, petting, and coitus. The last was subdivided into categories based on the identity of the sexual partner. This allowed for sub-classifications including pre-marital, marital, extra-marital, and post-marital coitus as well as intercourse with prostitutes. Kinsey added two almost unexplored areas of sexual activity, namely homosexual relations and sexual contacts with animals. His research was quite unique. No one, with such methodological precision, had ever before attempted such a systematic study of human sexual experience. * * *

[There was] fierce opposition to Kinsey's research from churches, politicians, fellow academics, civic groups, and others. His work on human sexuality survived only because of the strength of his personality, the support of his wife and of his immediate colleagues, and the unwavering insistence of the President of Indiana University, Dr. Herman Wells, that the University existed both for teaching and for the search for truth. * * *

Kinsey's first major report, published in 1948, was titled *Sexual Behavior in the Human Male*. The second report, published in 1953, was *Sexual Behavior in the Human Female*. Each report, but especially the first, burst upon the world as an intellectual bombshell of new ideas. Each report challenged assumptions that were generally accepted throughout the world concerning human sexual experience. Each undermined the strict binary notions of sexual orientation. Each demonstrated widespread human inclination to sexual variety, experimentation, and sexual experience of various kinds throughout life. * * *

The research of Kinsey and his colleagues helped revolutionize thinking about sexual behavior both in the United States and far beyond. The Kinsey approach had eschewed fixed or preordained categories and hypotheses. Instead, it focused on comprehensive fact-gathering from a large but non-random sample of college students, prisoners, and Indianans swept into the giant study at Kinsey's Institute for Sex Research.

The study of male respondents concluded:

Males do not represent two discrete populations, heterosexual and homosexual. The world is not to be divided into sheep and goats. . . . It is a fundamental of taxonomy that nature rarely deals with discrete categories. Only the human mind invents categories and tries to force facts into separated pigeon-holes. The living world is a continuum in each and every one of its aspects. The sooner we learn this concerning human sexual behavior the sooner we shall reach a sound understanding of the realities of sex.

Amongst the most surprising findings recorded in the 1948 Kinsey Report concerned homosexuality. Until that time, American psychologists, Freudian and otherwise, and their counterparts world-wide, had depicted homosexuality as biologically abnormal and psychologically poisonous. The Kinsey findings cast doubt at least on the rarity and abnormality of homosexual orientation.

- 37% of the male population had at least one overt homosexual experience to orgasm between the ages of 16 and 45, while another 13% react erotically to other males without having an experience to orgasm. This means that 50% of the male population had experienced significant homosexual erotic attraction during adulthood.

- 30% of the male population had had at least incidental homosexual experience or reactions (rating one or above on the Kinsey scale) over at least a three-year period between ages 16 and 55.

- 25% of the male population had had more than incidental experience (rating two or above). * * *

- 18% of the male population had had at least as much homosexual as heterosexual experience (rating three or above) over at least a three-year period. * * *

- 10% of the male population had been more or less exclusively homosexual (rating five or six) for at least a three-year period, with 8% being completely homosexual (rating six) for at least that period.

- 4% of the white male population was exclusively homosexual (rating six) for their entire adult lives.

The findings in the 1948 Kinsey Report concerning heterosexual activity were almost as surprising. Contrary to the then accepted mores, Kinsey and his colleagues found that virtually all men masturbated, even after they were married; that many husbands had sexual affairs during their marriage, many of them without guilt (or discovery); and that married couples engaged in a range of sexual activities, including oral and anal sex as well as vaginal sex.

The 1953 study on *Sexual Behavior in the Human Female* reported significant, but much lower, homosexual attraction and activity among women. It found that 28 percent of the women sampled had experienced significant erotic attraction to other women (compared with 50 percent of the male sample), and 13 percent had homosexual experiences to orgasm (compared with 37 percent of the male sample). But Kinsey's great contribution to the study of women's sexuality was to establish beyond reasonable doubt that women are sexually active rather than passive "by nature":

- "Nearly 50% of the sample had engaged in premarital intercourse, a considerable portion with their fiancés in the year or two before marriage." This discovery, unremarkable in today's society, came as a great shock to many in 1953.

- "Among married couples, women tended to be more interested in intercourse later in the marriage, whereas men tended to be most interested early in the marriage."

- "26% of women (in contrast to 50% of the male sample) had engaged in extramarital coitus by the age of forty. Incidence of extramarital inter-course in women was affected by religious background more than any other factor."

- "By age twenty, only 33% of women had masturbated compared with 92% of their male contemporaries."

Kinsey's findings confronted social assumptions that were the foundation of much religious and other moral instruction. They challenged the beliefs about fellow citizens and human beings held by most people and the laws that gave effect to the social postulates about sexual experience. Those laws concerned matters such as the woman's role in marriage and her subordination to the rights of her husband with very limited entitlements to divorce, the woman's access to forms of contraception to control reproduction and to prevent unwanted pregnancies, and the operation of anti-sodomy laws and laws against the so-called unnatural offenses designed to stamp out such "abominable crimes" which one judge in Georgia, in 1904, had declared to be " 'the abominable crime not fit to be named amongst Christians.' " * * *

[B]ig changes in the law and in society have undoubtedly been made in the fifty years since Dr. Kinsey's death [in 1956]. He is not alone responsible for the changes. But his research encouraged other investigations casting doubt on the previously accepted generalizations about homosexuals. One of the foremost followers of Kinsey was Evelyn Hooker, a psychologist who, like Kinsey, was drawn into sex research as a second career. Eventually, this scientific work caused the American Psychological Association to move away from the earlier assumptions and, in 1975, to declare that "[h]omosexuality, per se, implies no impairment in judgment, stability, reliability or general social or vocational capabilities [and mental health professionals should] take the lead in removing the stigma of mental illness that has long been associated with homosexual orientations."

NOTE

While Kinsey's study has been criticized on methodological grounds, it nonetheless constituted a groundbreaking contribution. And his work inspired activists in the mid-twentieth century. In fact, Harry Hay, who founded the Mattachine Society in Los Angeles, was encouraged by Kinsey's 1948 report. *See* FADERMAN, THE GAY REVOLUTION, *supra*, at 54.

THE SOCIAL ORGANIZATION OF SEXUALITY*
Edward O. Laumann et al.

THE MYTH OF 10 PERCENT AND THE KINSEY RESEARCH

* * *

Kinsey's figures are much higher than those found in all the recent population surveys, including ours. There are a number of reasons for this * * * the major difference between Kinsey and recent research is that Kinsey did not use probability sampling. Kinsey's respondents were all purposefully recruited rather than sampled with known probabilities of inclusion. This means both that they were volunteers who may have differed in systematic ways from those who did not participate (e.g., by being more open and comfortable about their sex lives and perhaps more sexually active) and that there is no statistically sound way to generalize from his sample to a population. In fact, Kinsey roamed far and wide in selecting his subjects. He was not averse to using institutional settings, including prisons and reform schools, from which to recruit his subjects. Kinsey also purposely recruited subjects for his research from homosexual friendship and acquaintance networks in big cities. Kinsey combined fantasy, masturbation, and sexual activity with partners in some of his

---

*   EDWARD O. LAUMANN, JOHN H. GAGNON, ROBERT T. MICHAEL & STUART MICHAELS, *Homosexuality, in* THE SOCIAL ORGANIZATION OF SEXUALITY 283, 289–301 (1994).

calculations (e.g., the 50 percent figure). Experiences were collected retrospectively over the whole lifetime and almost as a matter of course were reported to include activity since puberty or since age sixteen. These devices would all tend to bias Kinsey's results toward higher estimates of homosexuality (and other rarer sexual practices) than those that he would have obtained using probability sampling. Almost all the recent sexual behavior research, largely prompted by AIDS and the sexual transmission of disease, has focused on behavior, primarily penetrative sexual practices.

* * *

DIMENSIONS OF HOMOSEXUALITY

To quantify or count something requires unambiguous definition of the phenomenon in question. And we lack this in speaking of homosexuality. When people ask how many gays there are, they assume that everyone knows exactly what is meant. Historians and anthropologists have shown that homosexuality as a category describing same-gender sexual desire and behavior is a relatively recent phenomenon (only about 100 years old) peculiar to the West. But, even within contemporary Western societies, one must ask whether this question refers to same-gender behavior, desire, self-definition, or identification or some combination of these elements. In asking the question, most people treat homosexuality as such a distinctive category that it is as if all these elements must go together. On reflection, it is obvious that this is not true. One can easily think of cases where any one of these elements would be present without the others and that combinations of these attributes, taken two or three at a time, are also possible.

Examples abound. Some people have fantasies or thoughts about sex with someone of their own gender without ever acting on these thoughts or wishes. And the holder of such thoughts may be pleased, excited, or upset and made to feel guilty by them. They may occur as a passing phase, only sporadically, or even as a persisting feature of a person's fantasy life. They may or may not have any effect at all on whether a person thinks of himself or herself as a homosexual in any sense. Clearly, there are people who experience erotic interest in people of both genders and sustain sexual relationships over time with both men and women. Some engage in sex with same-gender partners without any erotic or psychological desire because they have been forced or enticed into doing so. A classic example is sex in prison. Deprived of the opportunity to have sex with opposite-gender partners gives rise to same-gender sex, by volition or as the result of force. Surely this is to be distinguished phenomenally from situations in which people who, given access to both genders, actively seek out and choose to have sex with same-gender partners. Development of self-identification as homosexual or gay is a psychologically and socially complex state, something which, in this society, is achieved only over time, often with considerable personal struggle and self-doubt, not to mention social discomfort. All these motives, attractions, identifications, and behaviors vary over time and circumstances with respect to one another—that is, are dynamically changing features of an individual's sexual expression.

* * *

MEASUREMENT AND PREVALENCE OF SAME-GENDER BEHAVIOR, DESIRE, AND IDENTITY

[Thus,] for the purpose of this analysis, we have divided the questions that relate to homosexual experiences and feelings into three basic dimensions: behavior, desire, and identity. The questions that we asked about behavior always refer to partners or practices in specific time frames. Desire and identity are measured by questions about the respondents' current states of mind. * * *

THE INTERRELATION OF SAME-GENDER SEXUAL BEHAVIOR, DESIRE, AND IDENTITY

How are these three aspects of homosexuality interrelated? To answer this question, we first need to define a simple dichotomous variable denoting the presence or absence of each dimension. We sought relatively broad and inclusive summary measures for this analysis. However, we have excluded people who report their only same-gender sex partners before they turned eighteen. Thus, we have defined *behavior* in terms of a composite measure intended to tap the presence of any same-gender partner after age eighteen. *Desire* combines the *appeal* and *attraction* measures * * * . For this purpose, any respondent who reported either being attracted to people of his or her own gender or finding same-gender sex appealing is considered to have some same-gender desire. Same-gender identity includes people who said that they considered themselves to be either homosexual or bisexual (or an equivalent).

Figure 8.2 displays the overlap among these three conceptually separable dimensions of homosexuality using Venn diagrams. These diagrams make use of overlapping circles to display all the logically possible intersections among different categories. While a Venn diagram distinguishes all possible combinations, it does not attempt to scale the areas in the circles to reflect the relative numbers of respondents in each category because of technical constraints in the geometry of representation. The latter is indicated by the numbers and percentages attached to each area.

The three circles each represent a dimension or component of same-gender sexuality. The totals of 150 women and 143 men, respectively, who report any same-gender behavior, desire, or identity are distributed across all the possible mutually exclusive combinations of the three categories. For example, the area of the circle labeled *desire* that does not overlap with either of the other circles includes only those respondents who reported some same-gender desire but reported neither same-gender partners since eighteen nor self-identification as a homosexual or bisexual. Desire with no corresponding adult behavior or identity is the largest category for both men and women, with about 59 percent of the women and 44 percent of the men in this cell. About 13 percent of the women and 22 percent of the men report a same-gender partner since turning eighteen, but no current desire or identity.

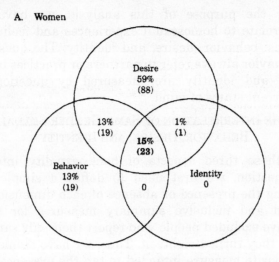

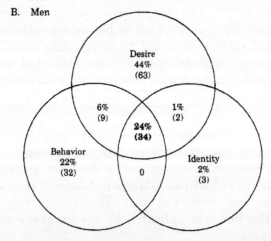

Fig. 8.2 **Interrelation of components of homosexuality. A, For 150 women (8.6 percent of the total 1,749) who report any adult same-gender sexuality. B, For 143 men (10.1 percent of the total 1,410) who report any adult same-gender sexuality.**

No women reported homosexual identity alone. But there were three men who said that they considered themselves homosexual or bisexual even though they did not report desire or partners. This being an unlikely status, it is possible that these men simply misunderstood the categories of self-identification since none of them reported any same-gender experience or interest.

About 15 percent of the women and 24 percent of the men are found in the intersection of all three circles. This is practically all the women (twenty-three out of twenty-four) and the vast majority of the men (thirty-four out of thirty-nine) who identify as homosexual or bisexual. In order to see the relative proportions in each set of categories more clearly, pie charts based on the same data and categories are displayed in figure 8.3.

As it is measured here, sexual identity does not appear to represent an analytically separate dimension because it logically entails the existence of both desire and action. Desire, behavior, and the combination of desire and behavior seem to exist in at least a substantial minority of the cases, but identity independent of the other two is quite rare. It is thus not surprising that no men or women reported behavior and identity without desire. Some sort of homosexual desire seems at the heart of most notions of homosexual identity. To report same-gender partners, *and* to say that one considers oneself to be homosexual or bisexual, *but* to deny any attraction or appeal of homosexuality, seems illogical. On the other hand, the idea of someone reporting desire and identity but no (adult) behavior does not seem so implausible since homosexuality is often thought of as an underlying sexual orientation understood in a psychological sense of fantasy or desire. One can at least imagine people who consider themselves to be homosexual (or bisexual) without necessarily having had any sex partners. In fact, this state appears to be quite rare, with only one woman and two men found in this category.

This analysis demonstrates the high degree of variability in the way that differing elements of homosexuality are distributed in the population. This variability relates to the way that homosexuality is both organized as a set of behaviors and practices and experienced subjectively. It raises quite provocative questions about the definition of *homosexuality.* * * *

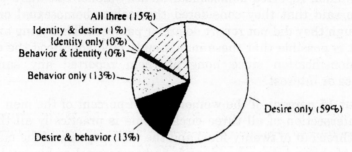

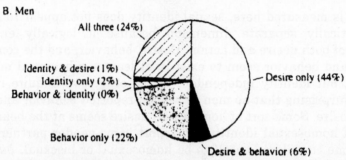

Fig. 8.3   Interrelation of different aspects of same-gender sexuality. A. For 150 women (8.6 percent of the total 1,749) who report any adult same-gender sexuality. B. For 143 men (10.1 percent of the total 1,410) who report any adult same-gender sexuality.

The studies above addressed sexual orientation through the rubrics of desire, behavior, and identity. Others have suggested that sexual orientation may be a fixed characteristic with a genetic or biological basis. While such theories are controversial among LGBT rights supporters, they have had some appeal in law given the attention to "immutability" in equal protection doctrine. This legal question is explored more extensively in Chapter 3. The reading below discusses the ongoing scientific work on the biological basis of sexual orientation, including critiques of that work and potential differences between women and men.

THE SCIENCE OF GAYDAR*
David France

A small constellation of researchers is specifically analyzing the traits and characteristics that, though more pronounced in some than in others, not only make us gay but also make us *appear* gay.

---

*   David France, *The Science of Gaydar*, NEW YORK MAGAZINE (June 17, 2007), *at* http://nymag.com/news/features/33520/.

At first read, their findings seem like a string of unlinked, esoteric observations. Statistically, for instance, gay men and lesbians have about a 50 percent greater chance of being left-handed or ambidextrous than straight men or women. The relative lengths of our fingers offer another hint: The index fingers of most straight men are shorter than their ring fingers, while for most women they are closer in length, or even reversed in ratio. But some researchers have noted that gay men are likely to have finger-length ratios more in line with those of straight women, and a study of self-described "butch" lesbians showed significantly masculinized ratios. The same goes for the way we hear, the way we process spatial reasoning, and even the ring of our voices. One study, involving tape-recordings of gay and straight men, found that 75 percent of gay men *sounded* gay to a general audience. It's unclear what the listeners responded to, whether there is a recognized gay "accent" or vocal quality. And there is no hint as to whether this idiosyncrasy is owed to biology or cultural influences—only that it's unmistakable. * * *

"These are all part and parcel of the idea that being gay is different— that we are different animals to some extent," says Simon LeVay, the British-born neuroscientist who has dedicated himself to studying these issues. " . . . I support the idea that we're a third sex—or a third sex and a fourth sex, gay men and lesbians. Today, there's scientific documentation behind this." * * *

A string of * * * studies, most of them conducted quietly and with small budgets, has offered up a number of other biological indicators. * * * Some of this work has been derided as modern-day phrenology, and obviously possessing one trait or another—a counterclockwise hair whorl here, an elongated ring finger there—doesn't necessarily make a person gay or straight. But researchers point out that these are statistical averages from the community as a whole. And the cumulative findings support the belief now widely held in the scientific community that sexual orientation—perhaps along with the characteristics we typically associate with gayness—is biological. * * *

Because many of these newly identified "gay" traits and characteristics are known to be influenced in utero, researchers think they may be narrowing in on when gayness is set—and identifying its possible triggers. They believe that homosexuality may be the result of some interaction between a pregnant mother and her fetus. Several hypothetical mechanisms have been identified, most pointing to an alteration in the flow of male hormones in the formation of boys and female hormones in the gestation of girls. What causes this? Nobody has any direct evidence one way or another, but a list of suspects includes germs, genes, maternal stress, and even allergy—maybe the mother mounts some immunological response to the fetal hormones. * * *

Some of this research may prove to be significant; some will ultimately get chalked up to coincidence. But the thrust of these developing findings puts activists in a bind and brings gay rights to a major crossroads. * * * If sexual orientation is biological, and we are learning to identify how it happens inside the uterus, doesn't it suggest a future in which gay people can be *prevented*? * * *

That in part is why gay people have not hungered for this breakthrough. Late last year, Martina Navratilova joined activists from PETA to speak out against an experiment that sought to intentionally turn sheep gay (it failed, but another experiment successfully turned ferrets into homosexuals, and the sexual orientations of fruit flies have been switched in laboratories). Some 20,000 angry e-mails clogged the researchers' inboxes, comparing the work to Nazi eugenics and arguing that it held no promise of any kind to gay people. "There are positives, but many negatives" to this kind of research, says Matt Foreman, executive director of the National Gay and Lesbian Task Force. "I will bet my life that if a quote-unquote cure was found, that the religious right would have no problem with genetic or other kind of prenatal manipulations. People who don't think that's a clear and present danger are simply not living in reality."

At the dawn of gay politics a half-century ago, the government treated gay people as a menace to national security, and much of the public, kept from any ordinary depictions of gay life, lived in terror of encountering one of us. * * * The groundwork for change began when Evelyn Hooker, a UCLA psychologist, was approached by a gay former student in the fifties. He had noticed that all research on homosexuals looked at men and women who were imprisoned or institutionalized, thereby advancing the belief that homosexuals were abnormal. He proposed that she study men like him as a counterpoint. Over the next two decades, she did just that, proving that none of the known psychological screens could detect a healthy gay person—that there was no clinical pathology to sexual orientation. Of necessity, research at the time was focused on demonstrating how unremarkable gay men and lesbians are: indistinguishable on all personality inventories, equally good at all jobs, benign as parents, unthreatening as neighbors, and so on. On the strength of Hooker's findings, and a Gandhian effort by activists, the APA [American Psychiatric Association] changed its view on homosexuals 34 years ago.

Thereafter, the field of sexual-orientation research fell dormant until 1991, when Simon LeVay conducted the very first study of homosexual biological uniqueness. He had been a researcher at the Salk Institute in La Jolla, California, when his lover fell ill with AIDS. He took a year off to care for him, but his partner ultimately died. Returning to work, LeVay decided he wanted to concentrate on gay themes. "Just like a lot of gay people who'd been directly affected by the epidemic, I felt a desire to do something more relevant to my identity as a gay man," says LeVay. "Some people have said I was out to try and prove that it wasn't my fault that I was gay. I reject that. In my case, since neuroscience was my work, that just seemed like the way to go."

Ironically, AIDS had also given LeVay opportunity. Before the epidemic, cadavers available for dissecting came with scant personal background besides age and cause of death. But because AIDS was still largely a gay disease, it was possible for the first time to do detailed neuroanatomical studies on the bodies of known gay men. (Being lucky enough to have no proprietary cause of death, lesbians were excluded from the study.)

LeVay decided to make the first detailed comparison of the brain's hypothalamus. * * * It was already known that in (presumably straight) men, a cell cluster in the hypothalamus called INAH3 is more than twice the size of the cluster in (presumably straight) women. * * * LeVay designed a study to see if there were any size differences inside gay brains. His results were startling and unexpected. In gay men, INAH3 is similar in size to straight women's. * * *

At the time, LeVay presented his findings with caution, acknowledging that HIV or AIDS medications might have been responsible for altering brain structure. But more recently, an important study of sheep brains has replicated his findings. * * * A second study in humans also found size differences, though less dramatic, in the hypothalamus cluster identified by LeVay. * * *

If LeVay's research suggested that biology—not environment, vice, or sinfulness—was likely responsible for male homosexuality, the geneticist Dean Hamer, an author and molecular biologist at the National Institutes of Health, hoped to pinpoint the exact biological mechanism responsible. He scanned gene groups in pairs of gay siblings looking for sites where the relatives had inherited the same DNA more frequently than would be expected on the basis of chance. In 1993, he located a region in the human genome, called Xq28, that appeared to be associated with gayness, a finding that has generated some controversy among researchers who have not fully confirmed the results. * * *

Fewer studies have focused specifically on lesbians, perhaps because AIDS didn't provide the same urgent impetus for studying female sexuality. But the research that has been conducted has yielded some interesting, though decidedly cloudy, results. According to some studies, lesbians are more likely to have homosexual relatives than nonlesbians. They also have notably longer bone growth in their arms, legs, and hands, hinting that they had greater androgen exposure during development, according to James Martin, a physiologist with Western University of

Health Sciences in Pomona, California. Another indicator comes in a 2003 study in the journal *Behavioral Neuroscience* that measured something called "prepulse inhibition," which is the part of our startle mechanism that's believed to defy practice or training—something hardwired, in other words. Men tend to blink less than women in such experiments; gay and heterosexual men had similar responses, but lesbians, it turns out, were more like men than not.

In many other studies, though, lesbians have appeared less unique than gay men, leading some people to wonder if their sexual orientation is innate. [Northwestern University psychologist] Michael Bailey—who, as a heterosexual researcher, is a minority in this field—even doubts the existence of female sexual orientation, if by orientation we mean a fundamental drive that defies our conscious choices. He bases this provocative gambit on a sexual-arousal study he and his students conducted. When shown pornographic videos, men have an undeniable response either to gay or straight images but not both, according to sensitive gauges attached to their genitals—it's that binary. Female sexual response is more democratic, opaque, and unpredictable: Arousal itself is harder to track, and there is evidence that it defies easy categorization. "I don't yet understand female partner choices very well, and neither does anyone else," Bailey wrote me in an e-mail. "What I do think it's time to do is admit that female sexuality looks in some ways very different from male sexuality, and that there is no clear analog in women of men's directed sexual-arousal pattern, which I think is their sexual orientation. I am not sure that women don't have a sexual orientation, but it is certainly unclear that they do."

He contends that what they have instead is sexual preference—they might prefer sex with women, but something in their brains can still sizzle at the thought of men. Many feminist scholars agree with this assessment, and consider sexuality more of a fluid than an either-or proposition, but some don't. "I think women do have orientations, but they don't circumscribe the range of desires that women can experience to the same degree as men," says Lisa Diamond, a psychology professor at the University of Utah, who is writing a book on the subject. "For women, there's more wiggle room. You can think of orientation as defining a range of possible responses, and for women, it's much broader." * * *

I suppose the main upside to this kind of work, besides any impact it might have on securing gay rights, is the comfort of self-knowledge. The secrets lurking in the hypothalamus (and the ring finger and the hair whorl) aren't just about who we desire but about a more fundamental organization of our personalities, individually and collectively. Still, some have dismissed all this field-guide work as wrongheaded. Gaydar can no more be proved than a sixth sense, they say. What's being classified as fundamentally gay is nothing more than cultural signals that vary so much from one part of the world to another that they're worthless as clues to anything. * * *

Still, Dr. [Richard] Lippa, [a psychologist at California State University at Fullerton], is publishing a paper in the *Archives of Sexual Behavior* later this year that seems to prove the existence of gay-typical behavior across the globe. * * * "It probably comes as no shock to you that on average men say they're interested in being mechanics, or electrical engineers, or construction workers, whereas on average women are more interested in, say, being an interior decorator or a social worker or an artist," he tells me. "Similarly, the differences between gay men and straight men are pretty large. On average, gay men are interested more in what you would consider female-typical occupations and hobbies than straight men. Same with women. It's not universal. Some gay men like football games and like working on cars and are electrical engineers. But a large majority answer this way."

It could be that his study says more about the limited number of vocations where gay men feel comfortable expressing themselves, and we might be equally drawn to construction sites if we thought we might be accepted there. It could be that the study says as much about the globalization of culture as the biological nature of gayness.

Even Lippa hesitates to say that gay people are *essentially* different from straight. "Essentialism," he explains, "is the enemy of a lot of academics," because it shuts down inquiry into all the possible influences. Perhaps there are a dozen possible routes to homosexuality, any combination of which might produce a number of the traits being catalogued now. It might be that there is no single thing called homosexuality—that there are instead dozens of homosexualities, scores of potential outcomes in terms of personality, and endless potentials for describing them. "For example, do gay men who have older brothers show more or less feminine? Do gay men with counterclockwise hair have more masculine traits? One cause might create a more feminine homosexuality than another."

Of course, biology doesn't determine everything. And some critics of sexual-orientation researchers blame them for minimizing the role of experience in determining our affectional course in life. The feminist biologist Anne Fausto-Sterling has waged a constant battle against their research, which she calls "a big house of cards" that ignores the power of environment in creating personality. Nurture, she argues, can and should be studied as a link to sexual orientation. The baby penguin raised by her two dads is a potential case study—though genetically unrelated to either parent, in the last few mating seasons she has mated with another female.

The rush to declare a biological mandate is motivated by a political agenda, says Fausto-Sterling, the author of *Sexing the Body,* who is married to a woman after a marriage to a man. "For me and for any feminist, I think it's a pretty fragile way to argue for human rights. I want to see the claims for gay rights made on moral, ethical, legal, and constitutional bases that don't rely on a particular scientific view of sexual development."

Especially if that view invites the opponents of gay people to consider dramatic interventions meant to stop the development of homosexual orientation in a fetus. What if prenatal tests were able to show a predisposition to gayness? How long would it be before some pharmaceutical company develops a patch to regulate hormone flow and direct the baby's orientation? Michael Bailey, for one, isn't troubled by the moral implications any more than he would oppose fetal screens for potential birth defects, though he quickly adds his personal belief that homosexuality is "a good" on par with heterosexuality. "There's no reason to ban, or become hysterical about, selecting for heterosexuality," he says. "That's precisely what parenting is about: shaping the children to have traits the parents value."

It's bizarre to think some value systems might lump gayness in with—say—sickle-cell anemia or Down syndrome. As Matt Foreman from the Task Force put it, "It's not playing with the number of toes you have; it's really manipulating your very essence. So many people see gay people only in terms of sexual behavior, as opposed to what sexual orientation is really about, which is how you fit into the world. I don't want to get mushy, but it's about your soul."

Many criticize the scientific search for a genetic or biological basis for sexual orientation because it sidelines more compelling normative and political questions about discrimination and equality. Critics contend that the justification for nondiscrimination should not depend on the immutability of sexual orientation. Critique of the quest for a "gay gene" also emerges from social constructionist accounts of sexual orientation. Scholars argue that sexual orientation as we know it does not exist as a natural, fixed identity but instead emerges as the product of particular political and cultural forces. For an insightful critique of immutability and "gay gene" research, see Janet E. Halley, *Sexual Orientation and the Politics of Biology: A Critique of the Argument from Immutability*, 46 STAN. L. REV. 503 (1994).

The readings below explore the social constructionist understanding of sexual orientation—and homosexuality specifically. This view informs important work in queer theory, which challenges sexual orientation as a coherent identity. *See id.* at 527 (explaining that critiques of "the very impulse to organize around gay and lesbian identity, either because doing so suppresses a sexuality distinct and semi-autonomous from *homo*sexuality, or because it obscures the historical, institutional, and political processes that produce identity[,] . . . are increasingly performed under the rubric 'queer' ").

MARTHA NUSSBAUM, ESSENTIALISM, AND HUMAN SEXUALITY*
Carlos A. Ball

As far as we can tell from the historical record, "erotic and sexual interactions between persons of the same sex are attested in almost all cultures known to us across time and across the globe." Some scholars have looked at this consistency through time and place and concluded that "gay people," that is, individuals who have a distinct identity based on their same-sex erotic preferences, have always existed. These writers, in other words, believe that there are "objective, intrinsic, culture-independent facts about what a person's sexual orientation is."

This so-called essentialist position in matters of sexuality is usually associated with the late historian John Boswell. As he made clear in the title of his 1980 book, *Christianity, Social Tolerance and Homosexuality: Gay People in Western Europe from the Beginning of the Christian Era to the Fourteenth Century,* Boswell believed that "gay people," as a distinct category of individuals, have existed in all Western societies. Although Boswell, like almost everyone else, eschewed the label of "essentialist," he believed that there have always been people whose "erotic inclination toward their own gender [is] a distinguishing characteristic."

Boswell's position * * * was inconsistent with that of Michel Foucault as set forth in his highly influential book *The History of Sexuality, Volume I.* In that book, Foucault famously contended that there is nothing intrinsic or fixed about human sexuality; instead, what we think of as sexuality is a byproduct of the work of systems of knowledge and power as represented, most specifically, by scientific, medical, and psychiatric disciplines. According to Foucault, one of the defining characteristics of the modern era is the extent to which these disciplines have grabbed hold of sexuality by studying, analyzing, and schematizing it through an endless discussion and cataloging of sexual desires, tendencies, and acts. It is from these discursive processes that what had before been viewed simply as the sexual act of sodomy became the basis for a social identity. As Foucault quipped, "[t]he sodomite had been a temporary aberration; the homosexual was now a species." He added that while under

* Carlos A. Ball, *Martha Nussbaum, Essentialism, and Human Sexuality*, 19 COLUM. J. GENDER & L. 3, 6–9 (2010).

ancient civil or canonical codes, sodomy was a category of forbidden acts, . . . [in the] nineteenth-century [the] homosexual became a personage, a past, a case history, and a childhood, in addition to being a type of life, a life form, and a morphology. . . . Nothing that went into his total composition was unaffected by his sexuality.

Foucault's work has served as the foundation for that of many sexuality scholars who have both embraced and elaborated on a socially constructed understanding of sexual identity categories. These writers have in part supported their position linguistically by noting that the word 'homosexual' did not exist before scientific discourses first put it to use in the second half of the nineteenth century. The absence of such a term through most of history strongly suggests to the social constructionists that homosexuality—though not necessarily homosexual sex—is a modern invention. As Robert Padgug puts it, " '[h]omosexual' and 'heterosexual' behavior may be universal; homosexual and heterosexual *identity and consciousness* are modern realities. . . . To 'commit' a homosexual act is one thing; to *be* a homosexual is something entirely different."

In addition, social constructionists point to historical evidence from before the second half of the nineteenth century, which suggests that many societies failed to problematize sexuality along the (for us) familiar homosexual/heterosexual axis. For example, David Halperin * * * points out that the scientific and medical professions in Western countries during the first half of the nineteenth century viewed same-sex sexual acts as a manifestation of "sexual inversion," a categorization of sexual deviance without a clear correlation to what we today consider to constitute homosexuality. * * * Halperin also argues that Aristophanes's famous myth in Plato's *Symposium* shows that the Greeks did not classify or distinguish individuals according to the gender of their sexual partners.

NOTE

In *The History of Sexuality, Volume I*, Michel Foucault described how Western societies in the second half of the nineteenth century—at around the time that "homosexuality" began to be understood as a distinct form of identity—simultaneously silenced and incited sexuality. In the Victorian bourgeoisie home, for example, "silence [was] the rule. The legitimate and procreative couple laid down the law. The couple imposed itself as model, enforced the norm, safeguarded the truth, and reserved the right to speak while retaining the principle of secrecy." MICHEL FOUCAULT, THE HISTORY OF SEXUALITY: AN INTRODUCTION 3 (1978). At the same time, however, well-established institutional discourses regarding sexuality represented "a political, economic, and technical incitement to talk about sex. And not so much in the form of a general theory of sexuality as in the form of analysis, stocktaking, classification, and specification, and of quantitative or causal studies." *Id.* at 23–24. Studies of populations, of birthrates and the appropriate age to marry, of fertility and infertility, of childhood sexuality, of sexual normality and abnormality, of sexual crimes and other infractions against nature, and of debilitating and frustrating sexual desires, all created a discourse on sexuality that was extensive and multifaceted. "What is peculiar to modern societies," Foucault explained, "is not that they consigned sex to a shadow existence, but that they dedicated themselves to speaking of it ad infinitum, while exploiting it as the secret." *Id.* at 35. For essays on Foucault and the theorizing of law, see FOUCAULT AND LAW (Ben Golden & Peter Fitzpatrick eds., 2010).

Foucault's work brings to light how sexuality becomes a set of norms used to privilege particular individuals and groups and punish others. As cultural anthropologist Gayle Rubin argued in a seminal 1984 essay, "discourses on sex, be they religious, psychiatric, popular, or political, delimit a very small portion of human sexual capacity as sanctifiable, safe, healthy, mature, legal, or politically correct." Gayle Rubin, *Thinking Sex: Note for a Radical Theory of the Politics of Sexuality, in* PLEASURE AND DANGER: EXPLORING FEMALE SEXUALITY 267, 282 (Carole Vance ed., 1984). In this "sexual value system," sexuality that is "good" is "heterosexual, marital, monogamous, reproductive, and non-commercial. It should be coupled, relational, within the same generation, and occur at home. It should not involve pornography, fetish objects, sex toys of any sort, or roles other than male and female." *Id.* at 280–81. Sex that is "bad" violates these norms. It "may be homosexual, unmarried, promiscuous, non-procreative, or commercial. It may be masturbatory or take place at orgies, may be casual, may cross generational lines, and may take place in 'public,' or at least in the bushes or the baths. It may involve the use of pornography, fetish objects, sex toys, or unusual roles." *Id.* at 281. Rejecting this hierarchical ordering of sex, Rubin argued instead for "benign sexual variation" and a sexual ethic based on mutuality and consent. *Id.* at 283.

Foucault's work also provided the theoretical foundation for work in queery theory by both legal and non-legal scholars. *See, e.g.,* Ian Halley, *Queer Theory by Men,* 11 DUKE J. GENDER L. & POL'Y 7 (2004) (written by Janet Halley). Professor Janet Halley describes queer theory, which has been notoriously resistant to definition, as having some of the following characteristics: sex affirmative, shame affirmative, irrationalist, affirming practices/performativity/mobility, disaffirming identities/essence/stability, and politically engaged towards the left. *See id.* at 50.

The anti-identitarian position of queer theory leads to a critique of theorizing and organizing around "homosexual identity." As Professor Jed Rubenfeld explains by drawing on Foucault's work:

Homosexuality is first understood as a central, definitive element of a person's identity only from the viewpoint of its "deviancy." Indeed, there is from the outset an imbalance: within its own self-understanding, heterosexuality is merely normality. . . . To the extent that heterosexuality does understand itself as definitive per se, it does so only in the face of and in contradistinction to a homosexuality already classified as abnormal and grotesque.

Jed Rubenfeld, *The Right of Privacy*, 102 HARV. L. REV. 737, 780 (1989).

————————

If sexual orientation is socially constructed, we could imagine alternatives to our contemporary understanding. That is, sexual orientation could connote a different set of practices or identities and could be based on a different set of values. With Foucault and Rubin in mind, consider the reading below, which makes the case for understanding polyamory as a sexual orientation.

POLYAMORY AS A SEXUAL ORIENTATION*
Ann Tweedy

[T]his Article asks whether polyamory—a preference for having multiple romantic relationships simultaneously—should be defined as a type of sexual orientation for purposes of anti-discrimination law. * * *

Today, sexual orientation is almost universally understood to signify whether a person is attracted to members of the same sex, the opposite sex, or both sexes. Thus, of the twenty-one states that had statewide statutes in place as of July 2010 prohibiting discrimination in employment based on sexual orientation, the eighteen states that statutorily defined sexual orientation defined it in terms of heterosexuality, homosexuality, and bisexuality. * * *

The salience of the term in our culture in turn implies that the sex of the objects of each person's attraction says something important about her or him. * * * Although this basic definition of sexual orientation, with its attendant implications, is so common as to be taken for granted as correct, there is nothing intrinsic about either the noun "orientation" or the adjective "sexual" that would tie the term specifically to the sex of those to whom a person is attracted. Instead, as scholars such as Dr. Ruth Hubbard have explained, in the abstract, the limited use of the term employed in common usage appears to be somewhat arbitrary: "the use of the phrase 'sexual orientation' to describe only a person's having sex with members of their own, or the other, sex obscures the fact that many of us have other strong and consistent sexual orientations—toward certain hair colors, body shapes, and racial types." Indeed, as Michel Foucault argued, it appears that our contemporary cultural understanding of the concept of

————————

*   Ann Tweedy, *Polyamory as a Sexual Orientation*, 79 U. CIN. L. REV. 1461, 1462–66, 1474–76, 1479–81, 1514 (2011).

sexual orientation is rooted in the late 1800s, when, as regulation of sexuality increased, those who practiced sodomy began to be imputed with certain essential (and societally undesirable) characteristics[.]

* * * [A] person's sexual orientation may, in actual application, be both broader and narrower than the common use of the term. * * * The facts that the current usage of the term "sexual orientation" is artificially limited and that it poses problems for those whom it is most often invoked to describe, however, do not necessarily lead to the conclusion that, as a matter of anti-discrimination law, the definition should be opened up to include any and all sexual preferences that are either sufficiently strong and consistent or sufficiently settled to technically qualify as a sexual orientation. Rather, it could well be argued that only those sexual preferences that are likely to be the basis for discrimination should be protected by anti-discrimination law.

Polyamory, which is commonly shortened to "poly," "in general describes the practice, state or ability of having more than one sexual [or, for some, romantic] loving relationships at the same time, with the full knowledge and consent of all partners involved." Thus, polyamory, which literally means having more than one lover, is relationship-based and should be distinguished from more casual types of non-monogamy such as swinging. It "is a lifestyle embraced by a minority of individuals who exhibit a wide variety of relationship models and who articulate an ethical vision that . . . encompass[es] five main principles: self-knowledge, radical honesty, consent, self-possession, and privileging love and sex over other emotions and activities such as jealousy." As suggested by these principles, polyamory is not only "a practice," but is also, at least for some of its adherents, "a theory of relationships." * * *

It is estimated that there are more than half a million "openly polyamorous families in the United States * * * with thriving contingents in nearly every major city." * * *

NOTES

1. Why do we define sexual orientation merely in terms of the sex of the individuals to whom someone is attracted? Even if we continue to view sexual orientation as a primary identity category, can we understand it in more expansive and multidimensional terms?

2. As the excerpts above illustrate, queer theoretical work in legal scholarship draws heavily on scholarship from non-legal disciplines. For foundational work, see EVE KOSOFSKY SEDGWICK, EPISTEMOLOGY OF THE CLOSET (1990); LEO BERSANI, HOMOS (1996); JUDITH BUTLER, BODIES THAT MATTER: ON THE DISCURSIVE LIMITS OF SEX (1993); JUDITH BUTLER, GENDER TROUBLE: FEMINISM AND THE SUBVERSION OF IDENTITY (1990); and MICHAEL

WARNER, THE TROUBLE WITH NORMAL: SEX, POLITICS, AND THE ETHICS OF QUEER LIFE (1999).

Even if we limit ourselves to the contemporary usage of sexual orientation, our binary understanding may obscure the lived reality of sexuality. We often discuss sexual orientation within the oppositional framework of heterosexuality and homosexuality. Indeed, we rarely see commentators and the general public explicitly refer to bisexuality, and yet demographic research shows that many people who identify as LGB identify as bisexual. Consider Professor Kenji Yoshino's account of why both heterosexual-identified and homosexual-identified individuals erase bisexuality.

THE EPISTEMIC CONTRACT OF BISEXUAL ERASURE[*]
Kenji Yoshino

Teaching a seminar on Sexual Orientation and the Law, I faced an old inconsistency so frontally that it became difficult to avoid giving it sustained attention. I began the course in what appears to be a common way, by posing basic questions about sexual orientation. I asked why contemporary American society organizes people according to their sexualities; why we do so on the basis of sexual orientation in particular; and why, when classifying by sexual orientation, we insist on doing so with the binary system of heterosexual and homosexual. In discussing the last question, I adduced the view—powerful in modern American culture from at least the publication of the Kinsey studies onward—that sexual orientation arrays itself along a continuum from exclusive heterosexuality to exclusive homosexuality. I noted that this view encouraged us to think of the straight/gay binary as defining the ends of a continuum that could be stretched, accordion-like, to accommodate ever finer gradations of cross-sex and same-sex desire. This meant recognizing a group—often called bisexuals—on the intermediate stretch of the continuum, as well as the possibility of a group—sometimes called asexuals—not represented on the continuum at all. Indeed, I argued that sexual orientation classifications that only used the two "monosexual" terms "heterosexual" and "homosexual" were unstable and naive.

As soon as the introductory unit was over, however, the inconsistency occurred. I found myself and the class falling back into the very "unstable" usages I had worked hard to retire—specifically the usages of the words "heterosexual" and "homosexual" as mutually exclusive, cumulatively exhaustive terms. While we sometimes rallied by using the word "queer" instead of "gay," or by adding the rider "or bisexual" to

---

[*]   Kenji Yoshino, *The Epistemic Contract of Bisexual Erasure*, 52 STAN. L. REV. 353, 356–429 (2000).

"gay," these efforts were token and fitful. In the face of legal discussions and academic commentary that were relentless in reifying the straight/gay binary, it was difficult to hold the bisexual steadily visible, even as a spectral possibility. And while this failure to resist what I had criticized as a distortion was striking in a class that sought to treat the issue of sexual orientation with sophistication, it was simultaneously all too recognizable as an inconsistency that riddles more quotidian discourse. Many who would not deny that bisexuals exist when the subject of bisexuality arises can nonetheless revert to the straight/gay dichotomy when the topic shifts. I myself can speak at length about bisexuals at one moment and then, in the next, field a question such as "Is X straight or gay?" without instinctively feeling as if an important possibility—the bisexual possibility—has been elided.

What is happening here? Why is bisexuality so invisible? If we interpret that invisibility as the product of erasure, why does that erasure occur? Why is bisexuality now becoming sufficiently visible that commentators have begun to theorize its invisibility as the result of erasure? How might contemporary sexual orientation politics and law look different if this trend toward visibility continues?

I.   THE ERASURE OF BISEXUALS

* * * Bisexual invisibility manifests itself in the studied omission of bisexuality in discussions of sexual orientation. * * *

On-line searches for the words "homosexuality" and "bisexuality" in mainstream newspapers, newsmagazines, and academic abstracts reveal a striking discrepancy in the incidence of the two terms. In the period from January 1, 1990 to November 30, 1999, the *Los Angeles Times* had 2790 documents mentioning homosexuality and 121 documents mentioning bisexuality; *USA Today* had 1768 documents mentioning homosexuality and 29 documents mentioning bisexuality; and *The Wall Street Journal* had 396 documents mentioning homosexuality and nine documents mentioning bisexuality. In the same time period, *Time* magazine had 240 documents mentioning homosexuality and fifteen documents mentioning bisexuality; *U.S. News and World Report* had 120 documents mentioning homosexuality and three documents mentioning bisexuality; and *The New Republic* had 144 documents mentioning homosexuality and three documents mentioning bisexuality. While I expected much less of a discrepancy in moving from popular to academic sources, this proved not to be the case. In the same time period, the Social Sciences Abstract Database on Wilson Web had 1122 documents mentioning homosexuality and 87 documents mentioning bisexuality; the General Sciences Abstracts had 221 documents mentioning homosexuality and six documents mentioning bisexuality; the

Humanities Abstracts had 962 documents mentioning homosexuality and 26 documents mentioning bisexuality.

The discrepancy between the relative visibility of homosexuality and bisexuality can be described sociologically as well as statistically. Robin Ochs has argued that bisexuals are invisible not only relative to straights, but also relative to gays. She points out that while we sometimes suspend the general presumption that all individuals are straight, the presumption that replaces it is that all individuals within that context are gay. Thus, "[i]n most families, for example, members are presumed to be heterosexual; conversely, at a women's bar all the women present are presumed lesbians." There are few contexts, however, in which an individual is presumed bisexual. In a similar vein, Marjorie Garber has observed that bisexuals have few recognizable symbols of their identity—the pink and blue "biangle" is one of the few symbols specifically denoting bisexuality and is much less culturally visible than the gay symbols of the pink triangle or the rainbow. Thus, even when the heterosexual presumption that all individuals are straight is suspended, it is replaced by the monosexual presumption that all individuals are straight or gay.

[Yet studies of sexuality suggest that bisexual desire is quite widespread. In Laumann's study,] [s]ubjects were asked to complete the phrase "In general are you sexually attracted to . . . " with one of five responses: "(1) only men; (2) mostly men; (3) both men and women; (4) mostly women; and (5) only women." * * * For men, 0.6 percent (narrow definition) to 3.9 percent (broad definition) were attracted to both men and women, while 2.4 percent (narrow definition) to 3.1 percent (broad definition) reported attraction to men only. For women, 0.8 percent (narrow definition) to 4.1 percent (broad definition) reported attraction to both men and women, while 0.3 percent (narrow definition) to 0.9 percent (broad definition) reported attraction to women only. Taking the narrow and broad definitions as setting the endpoints of a range, the percentages of "bisexuals" are again greater than or comparable to those of "homosexuals." * * *

I conclude that bisexuals are invisible in modern American society and that this invisibility arises from erasure rather than from nonexistence. I now turn to the reasons for this erasure.

II. THE EPISTEMIC CONTRACT OF BISEXUAL ERASURE

* * * My hypothesis is that bisexuals remain invisible because both self-identified straights and self-identified gays have overlapping political interests in bisexual erasure. It is as if self-identified straights and self-identified gays have concluded that whatever their other disagreements, they will agree that bisexuals do not exist. Put another way, the sexual orientation continuum that runs from straight through bisexual to gay is a "loopified" one, in which straights and gays are actually closer to each

other on this issue than either group is to bisexuals. Because of this, self-identified straights and self-identified gays enter into what I will call an epistemic contract of bisexual erasure. * * *

[S]traights and gays have entered into [this] contract * * * because of three different investments: (1) an investment in stabilizing sexual orientation; (2) an investment in retaining the primacy of sex; and (3) an investment in preserving norms of monogamy.

Straights and gays have an investment in stabilizing sexual orientation categories. The shared aspect of this investment is the security that all individuals draw from rigid social orderings. The distinctively straight investment is the retention of heterosexual privilege. And the distinctively gay investment relates to the perception that bisexuality endangers the immutability defense and effective political mobilization.

Both straights and gays may also wish to erase bisexuals because bisexuality has disturbing consequences for the current sex regime. All monosexuals are created through a regime that privileges sex, and they thus have an investment in bisexual erasure that relates to their own constitution. Straights have a specific investment in bisexual erasure because bisexuality disrupts the power heterosexuality has to determine sex performance. And gays have a specific investment because bisexuality interferes with complete sex separatism.

Finally, both straights and gays are disquieted by bisexuals insofar as bisexuals are thought to represent nonmonogamy. Straights and gays have a shared investment in decreasing sexual jealousy. Straights are peculiarly threatened insofar as they believe that bisexual nonmonogamy bridges the gap between the HIV-infected gay population and the uninfected straight population. And gays are distinctively threatened by bisexual nonmonogamy to the extent that they wish to retire the stereotype of gays as nonmonogamous.

These multiple and overlapping investments in bisexual erasure explain the longevity of the epistemic contract. But they are not insurmountable. The very fact that bisexual erasure has been recognized indicates this, for the paradox of status hierarchy is that the oppressed category must have some power to be recognized as such. But this means that even as there are investments in bisexual invisibility, there are simultaneous and countervailing investments in bisexual visibility.

NOTE

Yoshino published his article in 2000. Is bisexuality still subject to erasure? For an updated perspective arguing that bisexuality has become hypervisible, see Elizabeth M. Glazer, *Sexual Reorientation*, 100 GEO. L.J. 997 (2012). On organizing efforts on behalf of bisexuals specifically, see

Benoit Denizet-Lewis, *The Scientific Quest to Prove Bisexuality Exists*, N.Y. TIMES MAG. (Mar. 20, 2014).

V. WHAT IS SEX? WHAT IS GENDER?

Now that we have explored the complexities of defining and understanding sexual orientation, we turn to similar complexities raised by sex and gender. As an initial matter, judges, lawyers, scholars, and commentators frequently use the two terms interchangeably. Nonetheless, sex is often used to connote a biological reality, while gender is often used to connote a set of cultural norms. Scholars, however, have challenged the notion that "sex" is a natural, biological category, rather than itself a social construction. While this issue is addressed more extensively in Chapter 4 in the context of employment discrimination law, in this section we focus on the legal, political, and medical treatment of sex and gender. We do so specifically in the context of transgender and intersex individuals and the challenge to binary notions of sex and gender they present.

Before moving to scholarly accounts, we provide a window into how some judges have approached issues of gender identity. The case below illustrates that, given how thoroughly the gender binary organizes legal and cultural norms, even mundane legal proceedings can give rise to broader questions about the meaning of sex and gender. We see also that in the very quest to determine the litigant's gender within the gender binary, the court's reasoning ends up exposing the incoherence of gender. In addition, we see how in a legal system that polices boundaries of both sex and sexual orientation and punishes deviation from normative identities, the legal treatment of LGB individuals becomes entangled with the legal treatment of transgender individuals.

LITTLETON V. PRANGE

Court of Appeals of Texas, 1999
9 S.W.3d 223

HARDBERGER, C.J.

This case involves the most basic of questions. When is a man a man, and when is a woman a woman? Every schoolchild, even of tender years, is confident he or she can tell the difference, especially if the person is wearing no clothes. These are observations that each of us makes early in life and, in most cases, continue to have more than a passing interest in for the rest of our lives. It is one of the more pleasant mysteries.

The deeper philosophical (and now legal) question is: can a physician change the gender of a person with a scalpel, drugs and counseling, or is a person's gender immutably fixed by our Creator at birth? The answer to that question has definite legal implications that present themselves in this case involving a person named Christie Lee Littleton.

FACTUAL BACKGROUND

A complete stipulation of the facts was made by the parties in this case.

Christie is a transsexual. She was born in San Antonio in 1952, a physically healthy male, and named after her father, Lee Cavazos. At birth, she was named Lee Cavazos, Jr. (Throughout this opinion Christie will be referred to as "She." This is for grammatical simplicity's sake, and out of respect for the litigant, who wishes to be called "Christie," and referred to as "she." It has no legal implications.)

At birth, Christie had the normal male genitalia: penis, scrotum and testicles. Problems with her sexual identity developed early though. Christie testified that she considered herself female from the time she was three or four years old, the contrary physical evidence notwithstanding. Her distressed parents took her to a physician, who prescribed male hormones. These were taken, but were ineffective. Christie sought successfully to be excused from sports and physical education because of her embarrassment over changing clothes in front of the other boys.

By the time she was 17 years old, Christie was searching for a physician who would perform sex reassignment surgery. At 23, she enrolled in a program at the University of Texas Health Science Center that would lead to a sex reassignment operation. For four years Christie underwent psychological and psychiatric treatment by a number of physicians, some of whom testified in this case.

On August 31, 1977, Christie's name was legally changed to Christie Lee Cavazos. Under doctor's orders, Christie also began receiving various treatments and female hormones. Between November of 1979 and February of 1980, Christie underwent three surgical procedures, which culminated in a complete sex reassignment. Christie's penis, scrotum and testicles were surgically removed, and a vagina and labia were constructed. Christie additionally underwent breast construction surgery.

Dr. Donald Greer, a board certified plastic surgeon, served as a member of the gender dysphoria team at UTHSC in San Antonio, Texas during the time in question. Dr. Paul Mohl, a board certified psychiatrist, also served as a member of the same gender dysphoria team. Both participated in the evaluation and treatment of Christie. The gender dysphoria team was a multi-disciplinary team that met regularly to interview and care for transsexual patients. * * *

Dr. Greer and Dr. Mohl would testify that the definition of a transsexual is someone whose physical anatomy does not correspond to their sense of being or their sense of gender, and that medical science has not been able to identify the exact cause of this condition, but it is in medical probability a combination of neuro-biological, genetic and neonatal environmental factors. Dr. Greer and Dr. Mohl would further testify that in arriving at a diagnosis of transsexualism in Christie, the program at UTHSC was guided by the guidelines established by the Johns Hopkins Group and that, based on these guidelines, Christie was diagnosed psychologically and psychiatrically as a genuine male to female transsexual. Dr. Greer and Dr. Mohl also would testify that true male to female transsexuals are, in their opinion, psychologically and psychiatrically female before and after the sex reassignment surgery, and that Christie is a true male to female transsexual.

On or about November 5, 1979, Dr. Greer served as a principal member of the surgical team that performed the sex reassignment surgery on Christie. In Dr. Greer's opinion, the anatomical and genital features of Christie, following that surgery, are such that she has the capacity to function sexually as a female. Both Dr. Greer and Dr. Mohl would testify that, in their opinions, following the successful completion of Christie's participation in UTHSC's gender dysphoria program, Christie is medically a woman.

Christie married a man by the name of Jonathon Mark Littleton in Kentucky in 1989, and she lived with him until his death in 1996. Christie filed a medical malpractice suit under the Texas Wrongful Death and Survival Statute in her capacity as Jonathon's surviving spouse. The sued doctor, appellee here, filed a motion for summary judgment. The motion challenged Christie's status as a proper wrongful death beneficiary, asserting that Christie is a man and cannot be the surviving spouse of another man.

The trial court agreed and granted the summary judgment. The summary judgment notes that the trial court considered the summary judgment evidence, the stipulation, and the argument of counsel. In addition to the stipulation, Christie's affidavit was attached to her response to the motion for summary judgment. In her affidavit, Christie states that Jonathon was fully aware of her background and the fact that she had undergone sex reassignment surgery.

The Legal Issue

Can there be a valid marriage between a man and a person born as a man, but surgically altered to have the physical characteristics of a woman?

Overview of Issue

This is a case of first impression in Texas. The underlying statutory law is simple enough. Texas (and Kentucky, for that matter), like most other states, does not permit marriages between persons of the same sex. In order to have standing to sue under the wrongful death and survival statu[t]es, Christie must be Jonathon's surviving spouse. The defendant's summary judgment burden was to prove she is not the surviving spouse. Referring to the statutory law, though, does not resolve the issue. This court, as did the trial court below, must answer this question: Is Christie a man or a woman? There is no dispute that Christie and Jonathon went through a ceremonial marriage ritual. If Christie is a woman, she may bring this action. If Christie is a man, she may not.

Christie is medically termed a transsexual, a term not often heard on the streets of Texas, nor in its courtrooms. If we look at other states or even other countries to see how they treat marriages of transsexuals, we get little help. Only a handful of other states, or foreign countries, have even considered the case of the transsexual. The opposition to same-sex marriages, on the other hand, is very wide spread. . . . Marriage is tightly defined in the United States: "a legal union between one man and one woman."

Public antipathy toward same-sex marriages notwithstanding, the question remains: is a transsexual still the same sex after a sex-reassignment operation as before the operation? A transsexual, such as Christie, does not consider herself a homosexual because she does not consider herself a man. Her self-identity, from childhood, has been as a woman. Since her various operations, she does not have the outward physical characteristics of a man either. Through the intervention of surgery and drugs, Christie appears to be a woman. In her mind, she has corrected her physical features to line up with her true gender.

"Although transgenderism is often conflated with homosexuality, the characteristic, which defines transgenderism, is not sexual orientation, but sexual identity. Transgenderism describes people who experience a separation between their gender and their biological/anatomical sex." Mary Coombs, *Sexual Dis-Orientation: Transgendered People and Same-Sex Marriage*, 8 UCLA WOMEN'S L.J. 219, 237 (1998).

Nor should a transsexual be confused with a transvestite, who is simply a man who attains some sexual satisfaction from wearing women's clothes. Christie does not consider herself a man wearing women's clothes; she considers herself a woman wearing women's clothes. She has been surgically and chemically altered to be a woman. She has officially changed her name and her birth certificate to reflect her new status. But the question remains whether the law will take note of these changes and treat her as if she had been born a female. To answer this question, we consider the law of those jurisdictions who have previously decided it.

CASE LAW

The English case of *Corbett v. Corbett* appears to be the first case to consider the issue, and is routinely cited in later cases, including those cases from the United States. April Ashley, like Christie Littleton, was born a male, and like Christie, had undergone a sex-reassignment operation. April later married Arthur Corbett. Arthur subsequently asked for a nullification of the marriage based upon the fact that April was a man, and the marriage had never been consummated. April resisted the nullification of her marriage, asserting that the reason the marriage had not been consummated was the fault of her husband, not her. She said she was ready, willing, and able to consummate the marriage.

Arthur testified that he was "mesmerised" by April upon meeting her, and he dated her for three years before their marriage. He said that she "looked like a woman, dressed like a woman and acted like a woman." Arthur and April eventually married, but they were never successful in having sexual relations. Several doctors testified in the case, as they did in the current case.

Based upon the doctors' testimony, the court came up with four criteria for assessing the sexual identity of an individual. These are:

(1) Chromosomal factors;

(2) Gonadal factors (i.e., presence or absence of testes or ovaries);

(3) Genital factors (including internal sex organs); and

(4) Psychological factors.

Chromosomes are the structures on which the genes are carried which, in turn, are the mechanism by which hereditary characteristics are transmitted from parents to off-spring. An individual normally has 23 pairs of chromosomes in his or her body cells; one of each pair being derived from each parent. One pair of chromosomes is known to determine an individual's sex. The English court stated that "[T]he biological sexual constitution of an individual is fixed at birth (at the latest), and cannot be changed, either by the natural development of organs of the opposite sex, or by medical or surgical means. The respondent's operation, therefore, cannot affect her true sex." The court then reasoned that since marriage is essentially a relationship between man and woman, the validity of the marriage depends on whether April is, or is not, a woman. The court held that the criteria for answering this question must be biological and, having so held, found that April, a transsexual, "is not a woman for the purposes of marriage but is a biological male and has been so since birth," and, therefore, the marriage between Arthur and April was void. The court specifically rejected the contention that individuals could "assign" their own sex by their own volition, or by means of an operation. In short, once a man, always a man.

The year after *Corbett* was decided in England, a case involving the validity of a marriage in which one of the partners was transsexual appeared in a United States court. This was the case of *Anonymous v. Anonymous*, 325 N.Y.S.2d 499 (Sup.Ct.1971).

This New York case had a connection with Texas. The marriage ceremony of the transsexual occurred in Belton, while the plaintiff was stationed at Fort Hood. The purpose of the suit was to declare that no marriage could legally have taken place. The court pointed out that this was not an annulment of a marriage because a marriage contract must be between a man and a woman. If the ceremony itself was a nullity, there would be no marriage to annul, but the court would simply declare that no marriage could legally have taken place. The court had no difficulty in doing so, holding: "The law makes no provision for a 'marriage' between persons of the same sex. Marriage is and always has been a contract between a man and a woman."

Factually, the New York case was less complicated than Corbett, and the instant case, because there had been no sexual change operation, and the "wife" still had normal male organs. The plaintiff made this unpleasant discovery on his wedding night. The husband in Anonymous was unaware that he was marrying a transsexual. In both Corbett and the instant case, the husband was fully aware of the true state of affairs, and accepted it. In fact, in the instant case, Christie and her husband were married for seven years, and, according to the testimony, had normal sexual relations. This is a much longer period of time than any of the other reported cases.

The next reported transsexual case came from New Jersey. This is the only United States case to uphold the validity of a transsexual marriage. In *M.T. v. J.T.*, 140 N.J.Super. 77, 355 A.2d 204, 205 (1976), a transsexual wife brought an action for support and maintenance growing out of her marriage. The husband interposed a defense that his wife was male, and that their marriage was void (and therefore he owed nothing). M.T., the wife, testified she was born a male, but she always considered herself a female. M.T. dated men all her life. After M.T. met her husband-to-be, J.T., they decided that M.T. would have an operation so she could "be physically a woman."

In 1971, M.T. had an operation where her male organs were removed and a vagina was constructed. J.T. paid for the operation, and the couple were married the next year. M.T. and J.T. lived as husband and wife and had sexual intercourse. J.T. supported M.T. for over two years; however, in 1974, J.T. left the home, and his support of M.T. ceased. The lawsuit for maintenance and support followed.

The doctor who had performed the sex-reassignment operation testified. He described a transsexual as a person who has "a great discrepancy between the physical genital anatomy and the person's sense of self-identity as a male or as a female." The doctor defined gender identity as "a sense, a total sense of self as being masculine or female; it pervades one's entire concept of one's place in life, of one's place in society and in point of fact the actual facts of the anatomy are really secondary." The doctor said that after the operation his patient had no uterus or cervix, but her vagina had a "good cosmetic appearance" and was "the same as a normal female vagina after a hysterectomy."

The trial court, in ruling for M.T. by finding the marriage valid, stated:

> It is the opinion of the court that if the psychological choice of a person is medically sound, not a mere whim, and irreversible sex reassignment surgery has been performed, society has no right to prohibit the transsexual from leading a normal life. Are we to look upon this person as an exhibit in a circus side show? What harm has said person done to society? The entire area of transsexualism is repugnant to the nature of many persons within our society. However, this should not govern the legal acceptance of a fact.

The appellate court affirmed, holding:

> If such sex reassignment surgery is successful and the postoperative transsexual is, by virtue of medical treatment, thereby possessed of the full capacity to function sexually as male or female, as the case may be, we perceive no legal barrier, cognizable social taboo, or reason grounded in public policy to prevent the persons' identification at least for purposes of marriage to the sex finally indicated.

* * *

DISCUSSION

* * * In our system of government it is for the legislature, should it choose to do so, to determine what guidelines should govern the recognition of marriages involving transsexuals. The need for legislative guidelines is particularly important in this case, where the claim being asserted is statutorily-based. The statute defines who may bring the cause of action: a surviving spouse, and if the legislature intends to recognize transsexuals as surviving spouses, the statute needs to address the guidelines by which such recognition is governed. When or whether the legislature will choose to address this issue is not within the judiciary's control.

It would be intellectually possible for this court to write a protocol for when transsexuals would be recognized as having successfully changed their sex. Littleton has suggested we do so, perhaps using the surgical removal of the male genitalia as the test. As was pointed out by Littleton's counsel, "amputation is a pretty important step." Indeed it is. But this court has no authority to fashion a new law on transsexuals, or anything else. We cannot make law when no law exists: we can only interpret the written word of our sister branch of government, the legislature. Our responsibility in this case is to determine whether, in the absence of legislatively-established guidelines, a jury can be called upon to decide the legality of such marriages. We hold they cannot. In the absence of any guidelines, it would be improper to launch a jury forth on these untested and unknown waters.

There are no significant facts that need to be decided. The parties have supplied them for us. We find the case, at this stage, presents a pure question of law and must be decided by this court.

Based on the facts of this case, and the law and studies of previous cases, we conclude:

(1) Medical science recognizes that there are individuals whose sexual self-identity is in conflict with their biological and anatomical sex. Such people are termed transsexuals.

(2) A transsexual is not a homosexual in the traditional sense of the word, in that transsexuals believe and feel they are members of the opposite sex. Nor is a transsexual a transvestite. Transsexuals do not believe they are dressing in the opposite sex's clothes. They believe they are dressing in their own sex's clothes.

(3) Christie Littleton is a transsexual.

(4) Through surgery and hormones, a transsexual male can be made to look like a woman, including female genitalia and breasts. Transsexual medical treatment, however, does not create the internal sexual organs of a women (except for the vaginal canal). There is no womb, cervix or ovaries in the post-operative transsexual female.

(5) The male chromosomes do not change with either hormonal treatment or sex reassignment surgery. Biologically a post-operative female transsexual is still a male.

(6) The evidence fully supports that Christie Littleton, born male, wants and believes herself to be a woman. She has made every conceivable effort to make herself a female, including a surgery that would make most males pale and perspire to contemplate.

(7) Some physicians would consider Christie a female; other physicians would consider her still a male. Her female anatomy, however, is all man-made. The body that Christie inhabits is a male body in all aspects other than what the physicians have supplied.

We recognize that there are many fine metaphysical arguments lurking about here involving desire and being, the essence of life and the power of mind over physics. But courts are wise not to wander too far into the misty fields of sociological philosophy. Matters of the heart do not always fit neatly within the narrowly defined perimeters of statutes, or even existing social mores. Such matters though are beyond this court's consideration. Our mandate is . . . to interpret the statutes of the state and prior judicial decisions. This mandate is deceptively simplistic in this case: Texas statutes do not allow same-sex marriages, and prior judicial decisions are few.

Christie was created and born a male. Her original birth certificate, an official document of Texas, clearly so states. During the pendency of this suit, Christie amended the original birth certificate to change the sex and name. Under section 191.028 of the Texas Health and Safety Code she was entitled to seek such an amendment if the record was "incomplete or proved by satisfactory evidence to be inaccurate." The trial court that granted the petition to amend the birth certificate necessarily construed the term "inaccurate" to relate to the present, and having been presented with the uncontroverted affidavit of an expert stating that Christie is a female, the trial court deemed this satisfactory to prove an inaccuracy. However, the trial court's role in considering the petition was a ministerial one. It involved no fact-finding or consideration of the deeper public policy concerns presented. No one claims the information contained in Christie's original birth certificate was based on fraud or error. We believe the legislature intended the term "inaccurate" in section 191.028 to mean inaccurate as of the time the certificate was recorded; that is, at the time of birth. At the time of birth, Christie was a male, both anatomically and genetically. The facts contained in the original birth certificate were true and accurate, and the words contained in the amended certificate are not binding on this court.

There are some things we cannot will into being. They just are.

CONCLUSION

We hold, as a matter of law, that Christie Littleton is a male. As a male, Christie cannot be married to another male. Her marriage to Jonathon was invalid, and she cannot bring a cause of action as his surviving spouse.

We affirm the summary judgment granted by the trial court.

ANGELINI, J., concurring.

I concur in the judgment. * * * I note, however, that "real difficulties ... will occur if these three criteria [chromosomal, gonadal and genital tests] are not congruent." *Corbett v. Corbett.* We must recognize the fact that, even when biological factors are considered, there are those individuals whose sex may be ambiguous. *See* Julie A. Greenberg, *Defining Male and Female: Intersexuality and the Collision Between Law and Biology*, 41 ARIZ. L. REV. 265 (1999). Having recognized this fact, I express no opinion as to how the law would view such individuals with regard to marriage. We are, however, not presented with such a case at this time. * * * [I]n the case of Christie Lee Littleton, it appears that all biological and physical factors were congruent and were consistent with those of a typical male at birth. The only pre-operative distinction between Christie Lee Littleton and a typical male was her psychological sense of being a female. Under these facts, I agree that Texas law will not recognize her marriage to a male.

LOPEZ, J., dissenting.

On its surface, the question of whether a person is male or female seems simple enough. Complicated with the issues of surgical alteration, sexual identity, and same-sex marriage, the answer is not so simple. To answer the question, the majority assumes that gender is accurately determined at birth. Consider the basis for such a determination. Traditionally, an attending physician or mid-wife determines a newborn's gender at birth after a visual inspection of the newborn's genitalia. If the child has a penis, scrotum, and testicles, the attendant declares the child to be male. If the child does not have a penis, scrotum, and testicles, the attendant declares the child to be female. This declaration is then memorialized by a certificate of birth, without an examination of the child's chromosomes or an inquiry about how the child feels about its sexual identity. Despite this simplistic approach, the traditional method of determining gender does not always result in an accurate record of gender.

Texas law recognizes that inaccuracies occur in determining, or at least recording, gender. By permitting the amendment of an original birth certificate upon satisfactory evidence, Texas law allows these inaccuracies to be corrected. Indeed, Christie's gender was lawfully corrected by an amended birth certificate months before the trial court ruled on Dr. Prange's motion for summary judgment. Notably, the amended birth certificate reflects the original filing date of April 10, 1952, the original date of birth, and an issuance date of August, 14, 1998. Retention of the original filing date indicates that the amended birth certificate has been substituted for the original birth certificate in the same way an amended pleading is substituted for an original pleading in a civil lawsuit.

Under the rules of civil procedure, a document that has been replaced by an amended document is considered a nullity. Rule 65 provides that the substituted instrument takes the place of the original. Tex. R. Civ. P. 65. Although neither a state statute nor case law address the specific effect of an amended birth certificate, many cases address the effect of an amended pleading. Under this authority, an amended instrument changes the original and is substituted for the original. Although a birth certificate is not a legal pleading, the document is an official state document. Amendment of the state document is certainly analogous to an amended legal pleading. In this case, Christie's amended birth certificate replaced her original birth certificate. In effect, the amended birth certificate nullified the original birth certificate. As a result, summary judgment was issued based on a nullified document. How then can the majority conclude that Christie is a male? If Christie's evidence that she was female was satisfactory enough for the trial court to issue an order to amend her original birth certificate to change both her name and her gender, why is it not satisfactory enough to raise a genuine question of material fact on a motion for summary judgment?

Granted the issues raised by this case are best addressed by the legislature. In the absence of law addressing those issues, however, this court is bound to rely on the standard of review and the evidence presented by the parties. Here, the stipulated evidence alone raises a genuine question about whether Christie is Jonathon's surviving spouse. Every case need not be precedential. In this case, the court is required to determine as a matter of law whether Christie is Jonathon's surviving spouse, not to speculate on the legalities of public policies not yet addressed by our legislature. Under a focused review of this case, a birth certificate reflecting the birth of a male child named Lee Cavazos does not prove that Christie Littleton is not the surviving spouse of Jonathan Littleton. Having failed to prove that Christie was not Jonathon's surviving spouse, Dr. Prange was not entitled to summary judgment. Because Christie's summary judgment evidence raises a genuine question of material fact about whether she is the surviving spouse of Jonathon Littleton, I respectfully dissent.

NOTE

In 2014, the Texas Court of Appeals held that "Texas law recognizes that an individual who has had a 'sex change' is eligible to marry a person of the opposite sex." *In re Estate of Araguz III*, 433 S.W.3d 233, 245 (Tex. App. 2014). In so holding, the court found that "*Littleton* has been legislatively overruled" based on a 2009 family code amendment. *Id.* That amendment provides that "a court order related to an applicant's 'sex change' [is] a form of acceptable proof to establish an applicant's identity and age, and thus, eligibility, to obtain a marriage license." *Id.* at 244 (citing TEX. FAM. CODE. ANN. § 2.005(b)(8)).

Just as sexual orientation has been understood in binary terms (heterosexuality and homosexuality), so too have sex and gender. And just as the sexual orientation binary obscures the fluidity of sexuality and the existence of bisexuality, so too does the sex and gender binary obscure the indeterminacy and fluidity of sex and gender. In the readings below, Professor Dean Spade considers transgender individuals' relationship to the dichotomous and highly stylized understandings of sex and gender central to both medicine and law.

RESISTING MEDICINE, RE/MODELING GENDER[*]
Dean Spade

[S]ex reassignment-related procedures are regulated through a mental health model which promotes regulatory, binary gender expression and denies access to medical procedures to those who fail to perform normative binary gender for their health care providers. * * *

[Professor Spade provides excerpts from writing he did while seeking sex reassignment surgery.]

* * * I was experiencing acutely the gulf between trans community understandings of our bodies, our experiences, and our liberation, and the medical interpretations of our lives. The medical model, ultimately, was what I had to contend with in order to achieve the embodiment I was seeking. I learned quickly that to achieve that embodiment, I needed to perform a desire for gender normativity, to convince the doctors that I suffered from GID and wanted to "be" a "man" in a narrow sense of both words. My quest for body alteration had to be legitimized by a medical reference to, and pretended belief in, a binary gender system that I had been working to dismantle since adolescence. Later, as I contended with my own legal gender status and that of my clients, I would learn that not only medical treatment, but also legal rights and social services for trans people are dependent upon successful navigation of that medical system.

Symptoms of GID [Gender Identity Disorder] in the Diagnostic and Statistical Manual (DSM-IV) describe at length the symptom of childhood participation in stereotypically gender inappropriate behavior. Boys with GID "particularly enjoy playing house, drawing pictures of beautiful girls and princesses, and watching television or videos of their favorite female characters. * * * They avoid rough-and-tumble play and competitive sports and have little interest in cars and trucks." Girls with GID do not want to wear dresses, "prefer boys' clothing and short hair," are

---

    *   Dean Spade, *Resisting Medicine, Re/modeling Gender*, 18 BERKELEY WOMEN'S L.J. 15, 18–29 (2003). © 2003 by Regents of the University of California. Reprinted by permission of the Regents of the University of California.

interested in "contact sports, [and] rough-and-tumble play." Despite the disclaimer in the diagnosis description that this is not to be confused with normal gender non-conformity found in tomboys and sissies, no real line is drawn between "normal" gender non-conformity and gender non-conformity which constitutes GID. The effect is two-fold. First, normative childhood gender is produced by creating and pathologizing a category of deviants: normal kids are simply those who do the opposite of what kids with GID are doing. Non-GID kids can be expected to: play with children of their own sex, play with gender appropriate toys (trucks for boys, dolls for girls), enjoy fictional characters of their own sex (girls, specifically, might have GID if they like Batman or Superman), play gender appropriate characters in games of "house," etc. Secondly, a regulatory mechanism is put into place. Because gender nonconformity is established as a basis for illness, parents now have a "mill of speech," speculation, and diagnosis to feed their children's gender through should it cross the line. As Foucault describes, the invention of a category of deviation, the description of the "ill" behavior that need be resisted or cured, creates not a prohibitive silence about such behavior but an opportunity for increased surveillance and speculation, what he would call "informal-governance."

Another immediate error and danger of the medical model of transsexuality is its separation of gender from cultural forces. The Diagnostic Criteria for Gender Identity Disorder names, as a general category of symptom, "[a] strong and persistent cross-gender identification (not merely a desire for any perceived cultural advantages of being the other sex)." This criterion suggests the possibility of a gender categorization not read through the cultural gender hierarchy. This requires one to imagine a child wanting to be a gender transgressive from the one assigned to hir[1] without having that desire stem from a cultural understanding of gender difference defined by the "advantaging" of certain gender behaviors and identities over others. But gender behavior is learned, and children are not born with some innate sense that girls should wear dresses and boys shouldn't like anything pink. So how can a desire to transgress an assigned gender category be read outside of cultural meaning? Such a standard naturalizes and depoliticizes gender and gender role distress. It creates a fictional transsexual who just knows in hir gut what man is and what woman is, and knows that sie is trapped in the wrong body.

The diagnostic criteria for GID produces a fiction of natural gender in which normal, non-transsexual people grow up with minimal to no gender trouble or exploration, do not crossdress as children, do not play with the wrong-gendered kids, and do not like the wrong kinds of toys or

---

[1]   *Editor's Note*: Spade uses "the gender-neutral pronouns 'sie' (pronounced 'see') and 'hir' (pronounced 'here') to promote the recognition of such pronouns, which resist the need to categorize all subjects neatly into male and female categories."

characters. This story is not believable. Yet, it survives because medicine produces it not through a description of the norm, but through a generalized account of the norm's transgression by gender deviants. By instructing the doctor/parent/teacher to focus on the transgressive behavior, the diagnostic criteria for GID establishes surveillance and regulation effective for keeping both non-transsexuals and transsexuals in adherence to their roles. In order to get authorization for body alteration, the scripted transsexual childhood narrative must be performed, and the GID diagnosis accepted, maintaining an idea of two discrete gender categories that normally contain everyone but occasionally are wrongly assigned, requiring correction to reestablish the norm.

In addition to performing a certain narrative of a gender troubled childhood, the most overt requirement for GID diagnosis is the ability to inhabit and perform the new gender category "successfully." Through my own interactions with medical professionals, accounts of other trans people, and medical scholarship on transsexuality, I have gathered that the favored indication of such "success" seems to be the intelligibility of one's new gender in the eyes of non-trans people. Because the ability to be perceived by non-trans people as a non-trans person is valorized, normative expressions of gender within a singular category are mandated.

* * * What if the propriety of SRS [sex reassignment surgery] was not determined by trans patients' deviations from (non-trans) normative definitions of femininity and masculinity? What if the "success" of transition was not measured by trans people's adherence to (non-trans) normative definitions of femininity and masculinity? I imagine that, like me, some people have a multitude of goals when they seek gender-related body alteration, such as access to different sexual practices, ability to look different in clothing, enhancement of a self-understanding about one's gender that is not entirely reliant on public recognition, public disruption of female and male codes, or any number of other things. Some birth-assigned "men" might want to embody "woman" as butch lesbians in a way that meant they enjoyed occasionally being "sirred" and only sometimes "corrected" the speaker. Some birth-assigned "women" might want to take hormones and become sexy "bearded ladies" who are interpreted a variety of ways but feel great about how they look. When the gatekeepers employ dichotomous gender standards, they foreclose such norm-resistant possibilities.

Many of the trans people I have talked to do not imagine themselves entering a realm of "real manness" or "real womanness," even if they pass as non-trans all the time. Rather, they recognize the absence of meaning in such terms. They regard their transformations as freeing them to express more of themselves, and enabling more comfortable and exciting self understandings and images. While some do rely on passing as non-trans women or men in various aspects of their lives, and some embrace non-trans male or female identity, I think that all are disserved by the requirement that trans people exhibit hyper-masculine or hyper-feminine characteristics to get through medical gatekeeping.

For most of us, negotiating medical standards—whether we are seeking to change our bodies or identity documents, or seeking to enforce our rights—is fraught with difficulty. The medical approach to our gender identities forces us to rigidly conform ourselves to medical providers' opinions about what "real masculinity" and "real femininity" mean, and to produce narratives of struggle around those identities that mirror the diagnostic criteria of GID. For those of us seeking to disrupt the very definitions and categories upon which the medical model of transsexuality relies, the gender-regulating processes of this medical treatment can be dehumanizing, traumatic, or impossible to complete.

NOTE

The latest version of the American Psychiatric Association's *Diagnostic and Statistical Manual, DSM-5*, addresses some of the critiques of "gender identity disorder" in *DSM-IV*. *DSM-5* replaces the diagnostic term "gender identity disorder" with "gender dysphoria," attempting to shift the focus from "identity per se" to "distress that may accompany the incongruence between one's experienced or expressed gender and one's assigned gender." AMERICAN PSYCHOLOGICAL ASSOCIATION, DIAGNOSTIC AND STATISTICAL MANUAL 451 (5th ed. 2013). *DSM-5* also includes a separate diagnosis for children with criteria that attempt to ratchet up the required showing. In addition to a "strong desire to be of the other gender or an insistence that one is the other gender (or some alternative gender different from one's assigned gender)," the child must show at least five of the following:

- In boys (assigned gender), a strong preference for cross-dressing or simulating female attire; or in girls (assigned gender), a strong preference for wearing only typical masculine clothing and a strong resistance to the wearing of typical feminine clothing.

- A strong preference for cross-gender roles in make-believe or fantasy play.

- A strong preference for the toys, games, or activities stereotypically used or engaged in by the other gender.

- A strong preference for playmates of the other gender.

- In boys (assigned gender), a strong rejection of typically masculine toys, games, and activities and a strong avoidance of rough-and-tumble play; or in girls (assigned gender), a strong rejection of typically feminine toys, games, and activities.

- A strong dislike of one's sexual anatomy.

- A strong desire for the primary and/or secondary sex characteristics that match one's experienced gender.

Id. at 451–52.

A member of the subgroup that formulated the criteria explained, "It's really a narrowing of the criteria because you have to want the diagnosis. It takes psychiatrists out of the business of labeling children or others simply because they show gender-atypical behavior." Mark Moran, *New Gender Dysphoria Criteria Replace GID*, PSYCHIATRIC NEWS, Apr. 5, 2013, at 9 (quoting Dr. Jack Drescher). Do you agree? Does Professor Spade's critique of *DSM-IV* apply with equal force to the diagnostic criteria for children in *DSM-5*?

While the previous reading focused on the medical profession's treatment of gender identity within a system organized around male and female and masculine and feminine, in the excerpt below Professor Spade explores the relationship between, on one hand, the medicalization of transgender identity and, on the other hand, a legal regime and administrative state shaped by the gender binary.

DOCUMENTING GENDER[*]
Dean Spade

Over the past forty years, increasing numbers of identity document issuing agencies, such as departments of health, DMVs [Departments of Motor Vehicles], and the SSA [Social Security Administration], have created policies or practices allowing individuals to change the gender marker on their documents and records from "M" to "F" (male to female) or "F" to "M" (female to male). These policies emerged from a growing awareness of the existence of a population of people, currently labeled "transgender," who live their lives identifying as and expressing a different gender than the one assigned to them at birth. Recognizing the social and economic difficulties faced by those whose lived expression of gender does not match their identity documentation, state and federal agencies have over time created a variety of policies aimed at allowing gender marker change on documents commonly used to verify identity.

Many people are under the impression that everyone has a clear "legal gender" on record with the government, and that changing "legal gender" involves presenting some kind of evidence to a specific agency or institution in order to make a decisive and clear change to the new category. Because of the long history linking transgender identity with

---

[*]   Dean Spade, *Documenting Gender*, 59 HASTINGS L.J. 731, 733–38 (2008).

medical authority and popular cultural beliefs that changing gender involves surgical procedures, some may assume that achieving gender reclassification requires presenting medical evidence to an appropriate administrative or judicial decisionmaker. As it turns out, the reality of the rules that govern gender reclassification in the United States is far more complex.

The rules of gender reclassification * * * differ across jurisdictions and "expert" agencies responsible for creating and enforcing these policies, producing bureaucratic confusion and serious consequences for those directly regulated. [Professor Spade then explains that a variety of policies exist, ranging from those that completely refuse reclassification to those that use medical authority to determine whether reclassification is allowed to those that reclassify based on self-identification.] * * *

Two examples where gender can never be changed from birth-assigned gender are Tennessee's birth certificate policy and prison placement policies across the United States. Tennessee has a statute explicitly forbidding the changing of gender markers on birth certificates, so that transgender people born in that state can never obtain a certificate indicating a gender other than that assigned at birth. Similarly, placement policies in prisons across the United States generally use a "never" rule. Transgender women are placed in men's prisons and transgender men are placed in women's prisons. Of the nine jurisdictions that have written policies regarding treatment of transgender prisoners, none allow placement of transgender prisoners according to current gender identity.

In contrast to those policies, a large subset of gender reclassification policies require medical intervention for reclassification. The type of medical intervention, however, differs significantly from policy to policy. Three different birth certificate policies can be used as examples to show a range of requirements. California's birth certificate gender change policy requires the applicant show that he or she has undergone any of a variety of gender confirmation surgeries, which could include chest surgery (breast enhancement for transwomen or mastectomy and reconstruction for trans men), tracheal shave ("Adam's Apple" reduction), penectomy (removal of the penis), orchiectomy (removal of the testicles), vaginoplasty (creation of a vagina), phalloplasty (creation of a penis), hysterectomy (removal of internal pelvic organs), or any one of a range of other gender-related surgeries. New York City and New York State, however, each require genital surgery, and, interestingly, have differing requirements. People born in New York City are required to provide evidence that they have undergone phalloplasty or vaginoplasty, while people born in New York State must provide evidence that they have undergone penectomy or hysterectomy and mastectomy. The fact that two jurisdictions issuing birth certificates in the same state have come up with entirely different requirements for recognition of gender change, alone, attests to the inconsistency in this area. The Massachusetts DMV gender reclassification policy requires that an applicant prove that he or she has undergone some kind of surgery, which is not specified, as well as provide a birth certificate that indicates the new gender. Further, * * * gender reclassification policies often include requirements of recognition by other agencies or institutions.

The SSA's policy requires genital surgery but is non-specific as to which surgeries will be accepted. Some DMV gender reclassification policies, such as those of Colorado, New York, and the District of Columbia do not require evidence of surgery, but still require medical documentation in the form of a doctor's letter attesting that the person is transgender and is living in the new gender.

Still other policies require no medical evidence at all. The homeless shelter placement policies of Boston, San Francisco, and New York City are examples of policies that allow individuals to be recognized according to their current gender identity based solely on self-identity. These policies require that homeless transgender people be placed in the shelter associated with their gender identity without being required to provide any medical documentation or ID as verification of that identity.

* * * Because multiple policies with conflicting criteria for gender reclassification operate within single jurisdictions and upon individuals, the conflicts cause a number of problems. For one, similarly situated people are often treated differently under these policies, because of the ways the differing criteria for gender reclassification interrelate. One brief example will illustrate. Two transgender men living in Massachusetts, one born in California and the other in New York City, seek to obtain drivers' licenses indicating their male gender. Both have undergone mastectomy and no other surgical procedures. The California-born man will be able to obtain the reclassification he seeks, because California will amend his birth certificate and Massachusetts will accept this, and evidence of his surgery, as sufficient to change the document. The New York City-born man will be unable to obtain a corrected document, because he will not be able to provide an amended birth certificate. This man will have to carry an ID with a gender marker that does not match his identity, possibly leading to difficulty and exposure to discrimination in every context in which he might have to present ID, such as police interactions, employment, and travel.

Additionally, as new initiatives from the Department of Homeland Security, primarily focused on the enforcement of immigration laws, have increasingly led to comparisons of records between agencies with differing gender reclassification policies, the conflicts between these policies ha[ve] created a new range of problems. For example, in New York, Maryland,

and other states, DMV records were compared with Social Security records in order to find mismatching information that might indicate the misuse of a Social Security Number (SSN) to falsely obtain a DMV ID. People whose identities came up with "no match" information were sent letters warning that their licenses would be revoked, and hundreds of thousands of people lost their licenses. Many transgender people came up as "no matches" because the gender designation on their DMV records did not match that on their SSA records, especially in states where DMV gender reclassification requirements did not require genital surgery, which is required for such reclassification by the SSA. Similar record comparisons have been used to find people misusing SSNs to obtain employment, and employers across the United States have received "no match" letters indicating that their employees have a different gender marker on their SSA records than on their employee records. For transgender employees, this has led to being outed as transgender to their employers.

Professor Spade critiques dichotomous notions of sex and gender from the perspective of transgender individuals. In the following excerpt, Professor Julie Greenberg's analysis of intersexuality further problematizes the sex and gender binary. Given the relationship between transgender individuals and the medical profession that Spade exposes, consider the role that medical regulation plays in the context of intersexuality—and ask yourself what role it *should* play.

DEFINING MALE AND FEMALE: INTERSEXUALITY AND THE COLLISION BETWEEN LAW AND BIOLOGY*
Julie A. Greenberg

"He was a boy, became a girl, and then a boy again." This provocative headline sounds like it should have appeared in a supermarket tabloid. This headline actually appeared in the Los Angeles Times and cited a critical study that had just been reported in the Archives of Pediatric & Adolescent Medicine.

For many decades, the medical and psychological communities have attempted to resolve the issue of how one's sex (whether an individual is a male or female) should be determined for medical purposes. Until recently, however, legal authorities generally have been blind to the need to define the terms "male" and "female" for legal purposes. The law typically has operated under the assumption that the terms "male" and

---

    *   Julie A. Greenberg, *Defining Male and Female: Intersexuality and the Collision Between Law and Biology*, 41 ARIZ. L. REV. 265, 266–79 (1999).

"female" are fixed and unambiguous despite medical literature demonstrating that these assumptions are not true.

Although the law generally presumes these terms are unambiguous, courts and administrative agencies have been forced to determine an individual's legal sex under some limited circumstances. These cases typically have involved transsexuals—individuals whose biological sex does not conform with their self-identified sex.

The law has largely ignored other medical conditions in which an individual's sex may be ambiguous. Recent medical literature indicates that approximately one to four percent of the world's population may be intersexed and have either ambiguous or noncongruent sex features. Thus, the manner in which the law defines "male," "female," and "sex" will have a profound impact on at least 2.7 million persons in the United States. If, as some experts believe, the number of intersexed people is four percent, approximately ten million people in the United States will be affected.

* * * [S]ome individuals with an XY chromosomal pattern (male genotype) and testes (male gonads) have a female phenotype (external appearance) and female genitalia. In all senses, these XY women look, feel, and are viewed by society as female. Many of these women are unaware that they carry a Y chromosome and are unaware of their undescended testes. The issue that must be resolved is whether the law will view them as female, based upon their sexual identity and external appearance, or will instead rely on seemingly objective criteria, such as a chromosomal or gonadal analysis, to define them as male. If the law defines sex based on a chromosomal or gonadal analysis, these women would be prohibited from marrying males. Ironically, these same women would be permitted to marry females—a result directly contrary to the legislative intent to prohibit gay and lesbian marriages.

Regardless of the legal, moral, and societal implications of prohibiting same-sex marriages, [the federal Defense of Marriage Act] highlights the difficulty of using objective laboratory tests to effectuate its prohibitions. A variety of factors could contribute to the determination of whether an individual should be considered male or female for legal purposes. These factors include: chromosomal sex, gonadal sex, external morphologic sex, internal morphologic sex, hormonal patterns, phenotype, assigned sex, and sexual identity. In most individuals, these factors are all congruent. For millions of individuals, however, these factors are incongruent or ambiguous. For these individuals, DOMA and its state equivalents must establish which factor(s) will control.

The manner in which legal institutions define the terms "sex," "male," and "female" will also have a significant impact on a variety of areas other than marriage. How the terms "sex," "male," and "female" are defined will also affect the ability to control one's sex designation on official documents such as birth certificates, driver's licenses, and passports, as well as the ability to claim sex discrimination under employment discrimination statutes. * * *

II. A BINARY SEX AND GENDER PARADIGM

A variety of federal and state statutes and regulations differentiate between individuals based upon their sex and gender, or their status as males and females or men and women. Given the prevalence of such regulations, one might assume that these terms have clear legal meanings. In reality, the law defines these terms inconsistently or frequently fails to define them at all. The definition of these terms is critical, however, to the proper enforcement of legislation that seeks to regulate behavior based upon one's status as a male or female. Legal scholars and scholars in other disciplines, such as medicine, sociology, psychology, and gender studies, are investigating and redefining the meanings of these terms.

A. Sex

Sex is commonly used to denote one's status as a man or woman based upon biological factors. Although sex is a reflection of one's biology, as opposed to gender, which is generally considered to be socially constructed, the biological aspect of one's body that determines one's sex has not been legally or medically resolved.

An individual's sex is established for legal purposes on a person's birth certificate. The sex designation on the birth certificate is determined by the birth attendant. If external genitalia appear unambiguous, the external genitalia typically determine the sex designated on the birth certificate.

If the genitalia appear ambiguous, sex is assigned in part based on sex-role stereotypes. The presence of an "adequate" penis in an XY infant leads to the label male, while the absence of an adequate penis leads to the label female. A genetic male with an "inadequate" penis (one that is incapable of penetrating a female's vagina) is "turned into" a female even if it means destroying his reproductive capacity. A genetic female who may be capable of reproducing, however, is generally assigned the female sex to preserve her reproductive capability regardless of the appearance of her external genitalia. If her "phallus" is considered to be "too large" to meet the guidelines for a typical clitoris, it is surgically reduced even if it means that her capacity for satisfactory sex may be reduced or destroyed. In other words, men are defined based upon their ability to penetrate females and females are defined based upon their ability to procreate. Sex, therefore, can be viewed as a social construct rather than a biological fact.

In the presence of ambiguous genitalia, medical professionals generally suggest that surgery be performed to "fix" the genitalia so that they appear clearly male or female. Because one's birth certificate will often be used to obtain other legal documents, an individual's legal sex is generally fixed based upon the appearance of the person's external genitalia at birth.

Although the appearance of the external genitalia generally establishes an individual's sex at birth, other criteria may be used later to determine an individual's sex for other purposes. For instance, before 1968, athletic organizations examined a female athlete's external genitalia to determine her right to participate as a female in athletic competitions. In recent years, however, some athletic organizations, including the International Olympic Organizing Committee, have been using a chromosomal test instead. Individuals with XY chromosomes are defined as males and individuals with XX chromosomes are defined as females.

The absurdity of using a test that defines an individual as a woman based on the presence of two X chromosomes is best illustrated by the story of Maria Patino, a Spanish hurdler. Ms. Patino planned to compete in the World University Games in 1985. She knew that she would be subjected to a sex verification test, but she had no reason to believe that the test would indicate that she was anything other than a female. Although Ms. Patino was not aware of it, she had Androgen Insensitivity Syndrome ("AIS"). Therefore, she had the chromosomal make-up of a male (XY) even though her external morphologic sex, phenotype, and self-identification were clearly female.

Ms. Patino failed the sex chromatin test and was banned from the 1985 competition. She was later barred from further competition by the Spanish national team. The irony of using the sex chromatin test to deter unfair competition is that Ms. Patino's condition may have put her at a competitive disadvantage compared to the typical XX female athlete.

Therefore, although sex is typically defined according to biological factors, the biological factor(s) that control sex determination may vary depending upon the purpose for which sex is being defined. At birth, the appearance of the external genitalia typically determine the sex assigned while the right to participate in some athletic competitions as a female may be controlled by the chromosomal structure.

B. Gender

Gender is generally used to refer to the cultural or attitudinal qualities that are characteristic of a particular sex. Gender, as used in this sense, is socially constructed. Individuals with characteristics that are typically associated with men have a masculine gender while individuals with characteristics that are typically associated with women have a feminine gender. Most legislation utilizes the word "sex," yet courts, legislators, and administrative agencies often substitute the word "gender" for "sex" when they interpret these statutes. Despite the different meanings of the terms "sex" and "gender," they are often used interchangeably.

C. Binary Assumptions

Implicit in legislation utilizing the terms "sex" and "gender" are the assumptions that only two biological sexes exist and that all people fit neatly into either the category male or female. In other words, despite medical and anthropological studies to the contrary, the law presumes a binary sex and gender model. The law ignores the millions of people who are intersexed.

A binary sex paradigm does not reflect reality. Instead, sex and gender range across a spectrum. Male and female occupy the two ends of the poles, and a number of intersexed conditions exist between the two poles. Millions of individuals are intersexed and have some sexual characteristics that are typically associated with males and some sexual characteristics that are typically associated with females.

Although the American legal system blindly clings to a binary sex and gender paradigm, anthropologists who have studied other societies have found cultures that reject binary sex and gender systems. These societies formally recognize that more than two sexes and/or two genders exist.

* * * [R]ules governing intersexuals have existed throughout history in a variety of cultures and religions. Although the United States, other modern societies, and some religions utilize a binary sex paradigm in which intersexuals are classified as either male or female for legal purposes, other societies have recognized a multi-sexual and multi-gender model.

The currently accepted binary model that determines an individual's sex based primarily on the appearance of his/her external genitalia at birth is an inadequate system. * * *

III. INTERSEXED MEDICAL CONDITIONS

Medical experts recognize that many factors contribute to the determination of an individual's sex. According to medical professionals, the typical criteria of sex include:

1. Genetic or chromosomal sex—XY or XX;

2. Gonadal sex (reproductive sex glands)—testes or ovaries;

3. Internal morphologic sex (determined after three months gestation)—seminal vesicles/prostrate or vagina/uterus/fallopian tubes;

4. External morphologic sex (genitalia)—penis/scrotum or clitoris/labia;

5. Hormonal sex—androgens or estrogens;

6. Phenotypic sex (secondary sexual features)—facial and chest hair or breasts;

7. Assigned sex and gender of rearing; and

8. Sexual identity.

For most people, these factors are all congruent, and one's status as a man or woman is uncontroversial. For intersexuals, some of these factors may be incongruent, or an ambiguity within a factor may exist.

The assumption is that there are two separate roads, one leading from XY chromosomes at conception to manhood, the other from XX chromosomes at conception to womanhood. The fact is that there are not two roads, but one road with a number of forks that turn in the male or female direction. Most of us turn in the same direction at each fork.

The bodies of the millions of intersexed people have taken a combination of male and female forks and have followed the road less traveled. These individuals have noncongruent sexual attributes. For these individuals, the law must determine which of the eight sexual factors will determine their sex and whether any one factor should be dispositive for all legal purposes.

NOTES

1. In the U.S., advocacy on behalf of the intersex population has not been directly attached to LGBT organizing. Nonetheless, organizations, such as interACT advocate for intersex youth and seek to protect rights to bodily self-determination.

2. For additional readings on intersexuality, including its legal regulation, see JULIE A. GREENBERG, INTERSEXUALITY AND THE LAW: WHY SEX MATTERS (2012); INTERSEX AND AFTER (Iain Morland ed. 2009); ETHICS AND INTERSEX (Sharon Sytsma ed. 2006).

CHAPTER 2

SEXUALITY & LIBERTY

• • •

The criminal law has been a primary means for society's regulation of sex and sexuality. Various forms of sexual conduct and relationships have been historically proscribed and some remain illegal today. These include prostitution (sex for money), fornication (sex between unmarried persons), adultery (sex between married persons and others who are not their spouses), bestiality (sex with an animal), incest (sex between persons closely related to one another), rape and molestation (sex without consent or with a person, such as a minor, who lacks the legal capacity to consent), and sodomy (defined in various ways, as discussed below). Society has also regulated sex and sexuality through restrictions on the use of contraception and abortion.

The Chapter's first Section explores how the Supreme Court has dealt with regulations that restrict contraception and abortion. These rulings constituted the Court's first forays into the application of substantive due process principles (as well as other constitutional principles) to matters related to sex and sexuality. The rulings also contain some of the most important constitutional foundations for the Court's later treatment of sodomy laws and same-sex marriage bans.

The chapter's second Section investigates the scope of the right to sexual intimacy. It begins by addressing the legal regulation of sodomy, including its justification and constitutionality. In doing so, the Section pays considerable attention to the Supreme Court's ruling in *Lawrence v. Texas*.[1] The Section then discusses additional forms of government regulation of sex and sexuality, including bans on polygamy, the use of sex toys, incest, public sex, and sexual sadomasochism (S/M).

I. CONTRACEPTION AND ABORTION

The constitutional right to privacy and autonomy in matters related to sex, sexual intimacy, and reproductive freedom was first articulated by Justice John Harlan in his 1961 dissent in *Poe v. Ullman*.[2] At issue in *Poe* was the constitutionality of a Connecticut statute that criminalized the use of contraceptives. The Court refused to reach the merits of the case on

Poe
Harlan
dissent

---

[1]   539 U.S. 558, 123 S.Ct. 2472, 156 L.Ed.2d 508 (2003).

[2]   367 U.S. 497, 81 S.Ct. 1752, 6 L.Ed.2d 989 (1961).

the ground that, since it was unlikely that the statute would be enforced against the plaintiffs, which including a married couple, the lawsuit did not raise a justiciable controversy. Justice Harlan, after disagreeing with the Court on the justiciability issue, proceeded to address the merits of the plaintiffs' constitutional claim, one grounded in substantive due process.

In concluding that the statute was unconstitutional, Harlan emphasized two points. The first was the degree of governmental intrusion into the intimate decisions of couples—including married ones—that was required in order to successfully investigate and prosecute the crime. The enforcement of the contraception statute, Harlan noted, "is an intolerable and unjustifiable invasion of privacy in the conduct of the most intimate concerns of an individual's personal life."[3]

Harlan's second concern was that the statute intruded into the home, a site protected not only by the Fourth Amendment right against unreasonable searches and seizures, but also, he believed, by the Fourteenth Amendment's Liberty Clause. As Harlan put it, "the enactment involves what, by common understanding throughout the English-speaking world, must be granted to be a most fundamental aspect of 'liberty,' the privacy of the home in its most basic sense, and it is this which requires that the statute be subjected to 'strict scrutiny.' "[4]

At the same time, Harlan made clear that the constitutional right in question did not prevent the government from criminalizing adultery, fornication, and same-sex sexual conduct, "however privately practiced."[5] As he explained, "*not to discriminate* between what is involved in this case and . . . the traditional offenses against good morals or crimes which . . . may . . . happen to have been committed or concealed in the home, would entirely misconceive the argument that is being made."[6] Harlan added that "[a]dultery, homosexuality and the like are sexual intimacies which the State forbids altogether, but the intimacy of husband and wife is necessarily an essential and accepted feature of the institution of marriage, an institution which the State not only must allow, but which always and in every age it has fostered and protected."[7]

Four years later, the Supreme Court returned to the question of the constitutionality of Connecticut's contraception ban. This time, a majority of the Court agreed that the statute was unconstitutional.

---

3   *Poe*, 367 U.S. at 539 (Harlan, J., dissenting).
4   *Id.* at 548 (citation omitted).
5   *Id.* at 553.
6   *Id.* (emphasis added).
7   *Id.*

GRISWOLD V. CONNECTICUT

Supreme Court of the United States, 1965
381 U.S. 479, 85 S.Ct. 1678, 14 L.Ed.2d 510

MR. JUSTICE DOUGLAS delivered the opinion of the Court.

Appellant Griswold is Executive Director of the Planned Parenthood League of Connecticut. Appellant Buxton is a licensed physician and a professor at the Yale Medical School who served as Medical Director for the League at its Center in New Haven—a center open and operating from November 1 to November 10, 1961, when appellants were arrested.

They gave information, instruction, and medical advice to *married persons* as to the means of preventing conception. They examined the wife and prescribed the best contraceptive device or material for her use. Fees were usually charged, although some couples were serviced free.

The statutes whose constitutionality is involved in this appeal are §§ 53–32 and 54–196 of the General Statutes of Connecticut (1958 rev.). The former provides:

> Any person who uses any drug, medicinal article or instrument for the purpose of preventing conception shall be fined not less than fifty dollars or imprisoned not less than sixty days nor more than one year or be both fined and imprisoned.

Section 54–196 provides:

> Any person who assists, abets, counsels, causes, hires or commands another to commit any offense may be prosecuted and punished as if he were the principal offender.

The appellants were found guilty as accessories and fined $100 each, against the claim that the accessory statute as so applied violated the Fourteenth Amendment. The Appellate Division of the Circuit Court affirmed. The Supreme Court of Errors affirmed that judgment. We noted probable jurisdiction.

We think that appellants have standing to raise the constitutional rights of the married people with whom they had a professional relationship. * * * The rights of husband and wife, pressed here, are likely to be diluted or adversely affected unless those rights are considered in a suit involving those who have this kind of confidential relation to them.

Coming to the merits, we are met with a wide range of questions that implicate the Due Process Clause of the Fourteenth Amendment. Overtones of some arguments suggest that Lochner v. State of New York, 198 U.S. 45, 25 S.Ct. 539, 49 L.Ed. 937, should be our guide. But we decline that invitation. * * * We do not sit as a super-legislature to determine the wisdom, need, and propriety of laws that touch economic problems, business affairs, or social conditions. This law, however, operates directly on an intimate relation of husband and wife and their physician's role in one aspect of that relation.

The association of people is not mentioned in the Constitution nor in the Bill of Rights. The right to educate a child in a school of the parents' choice—whether public or private or parochial—is also not mentioned. Nor is the right to study any particular subject or any foreign language. Yet the First Amendment has been construed to include certain of those rights.

* * * [S]pecific guarantees in the Bill of Rights have penumbras, formed by emanations from those guarantees that help give them life and substance. *See* Poe v. Ullman, 367 U.S. 497, 516–522, 81 S.Ct. 1752, 6 L.Ed.2d 989 (dissenting opinion). Various guarantees create zones of privacy. The right of association contained in the penumbra of the First Amendment is one, as we have seen. The Third Amendment in its prohibition against the quartering of soldiers 'in any house' in time of peace without the consent of the owner is another facet of that privacy. The Fourth Amendment explicitly affirms the "right of the people to be secure in their persons, houses, papers, and effects, against unreasonable searches and seizures." The Fifth Amendment in its Self-Incrimination Clause enables the citizen to create a zone of privacy which government may not force him to surrender to his detriment. The Ninth Amendment provides: "The enumeration in the Constitution, of certain rights, shall not be construed to deny or disparage others retained by the people."

The Fourth and Fifth Amendments were described in Boyd v. United States, 116 U.S. 616, 630, 6 S.Ct. 524, 532, 29 L.Ed. 746, as protection against all governmental invasions "of the sanctity of a man's home and the privacies of life." We recently referred in Mapp v. Ohio, 367 U.S. 643, 656, 81 S.Ct. 1684, 1692, 6 L.Ed.2d 1081, to the Fourth Amendment as creating a "right to privacy, no less important than any other right carefully and particularly reserved to the people." * * *

The present case, then, concerns a relationship lying within the zone of privacy created by several fundamental constitutional guarantees. And it concerns a law which, in forbidding the use of contraceptives rather than regulating their manufacture or sale, seeks to achieve its goals by means having a maximum destructive impact upon that relationship. Such a law cannot stand in light of the familiar principle, so often applied by this Court, that a "governmental purpose to control or prevent activities constitutionally subject to state regulation may not be achieved by means which sweep unnecessarily broadly and thereby invade the area of protected freedoms." Would we allow the police to search the sacred precincts of marital bedrooms for telltale signs of the use of contraceptives? The very idea is repulsive to the notions of privacy surrounding the marriage relationship.

We deal with a right of privacy older than the Bill of Rights—older than our political parties, older than our school system. Marriage is a coming together for better or for worse, hopefully enduring, and intimate to the degree of being sacred. It is an association that promotes a way of life, not causes; a harmony in living, not political faiths; a bilateral loyalty, not commercial or social projects. Yet it is an association for as noble a purpose as any involved in our prior decisions.

Reversed.

MR. JUSTICE GOLDBERG, whom THE CHIEF JUSTICE and MR. JUSTICE BRENNAN join, concurring.

I agree with the Court that Connecticut's birth-control law unconstitutionally intrudes upon the right of marital privacy, and I join in its opinion and judgment. Although I have not accepted the view that "due process" as used in the Fourteenth Amendment includes all of the first eight Amendments, I do agree that the concept of liberty protects those personal rights that are fundamental, and is not confined to the specific terms of the Bill of Rights. My conclusion that the concept of liberty is not so restricted and that it embraces the right of marital privacy though that right is not mentioned explicitly in the Constitution is supported both by numerous decisions of this Court, referred to in the Court's opinion, and by the language and history of the Ninth Amendment. In reaching the conclusion that the right of marital privacy is protected, as being within the protected penumbra of specific guarantees of the Bill of Rights, the Court refers to the Ninth Amendment. I add these words to emphasize the relevance of that Amendment to the Court's holding. * * *

This Court, in a series of decisions, has held that the Fourteenth Amendment absorbs and applies to the States those specifics of the first eight amendments which express fundamental personal rights. The language and history of the Ninth Amendment reveal that the Framers of the Constitution believed that there are additional fundamental rights, protected from governmental infringement, which exist alongside those fundamental rights specifically mentioned in the first eight constitutional amendments.

The Ninth Amendment reads, "The enumeration in the Constitution, of certain rights, shall not be construed to deny or disparage others retained by the people." * * *

I [do not] mean to state that the Ninth Amendment constitutes an independent source of rights protected from infringement by either the States or the Federal Government. Rather, the Ninth Amendment shows a belief of the Constitution's authors that fundamental rights exist that are not expressly enumerated in the first eight amendments and an intent that the list of rights included there not be deemed exhaustive. * * * The Ninth Amendment simply shows the intent of the Constitution's authors that other fundamental personal rights should not be denied such protection or disparaged in any other way simply because they are not specifically listed in the first eight constitutional amendments. I do not see how this broadens the authority of the Court; rather it serves to support what this Court has been doing in protecting fundamental rights. * * *

In determining which rights are fundamental, judges are not left at large to decide cases in light of their personal and private notions. Rather, they must look to the "traditions and (collective) conscience of our people' to determine whether a principle is so rooted (there) . . . as to be ranked as fundamental." The inquiry is whether a right involved "is of such a character that it cannot be denied without violating those fundamental principles of liberty and justice which lie at the base of all our civil and political institutions. . . ."

* * * Of this whole "private realm of family life" it is difficult to imagine what is more private or more intimate than a husband and wife's marital relations. The entire fabric of the Constitution and the purposes that clearly underlie its specific guarantees demonstrate that the rights to marital privacy and to marry and raise a family are of similar order and magnitude as the fundamental rights specifically protected.

Although the Constitution does not speak in so many words of the right of privacy in marriage, I cannot believe that it offers these fundamental rights no protection. The fact that no particular provision of the Constitution explicitly forbids the State from disrupting the traditional relation of the family—a relation as old and as fundamental as our entire civilization—surely does not show that the Government was meant to have the power to do so. Rather, as the Ninth Amendment expressly recognizes, there are fundamental personal rights such as this one, which are protected from abridgment by the Government though not specifically mentioned in the Constitution. * * *

MR. JUSTICE HARLAN, concurring in the judgment.

I fully agree with the judgment of reversal, but find myself unable to join the Court's opinion. * * * In my view, the proper constitutional inquiry in this case is whether this Connecticut statute infringes the Due Process Clause of the Fourteenth Amendment because the enactment violates basic values "implicit in the concept of ordered liberty," Palko v. State of Connecticut, 302 U.S. 319, 325, 58 S.Ct. 149, 152, 82 L.Ed. 288. For reasons stated at length in my dissenting opinion in *Poe v. Ullman*, supra, I believe that it does. While the relevant inquiry may be aided by resort to one or more of the provisions of the Bill of Rights, it is not dependent on them or any of their radiations. The Due Process Clause of the Fourteenth Amendment stands, in my opinion, on its own bottom. * * *

[A concurring opinion by JUSTICE WHITE is omitted.]

MR. JUSTICE BLACK, with whom MR. JUSTICE STEWART joins, dissenting.

I agree with my Brother STEWART's dissenting opinion. And like him I do not to any extent whatever base my view that this Connecticut law is constitutional on a belief that the law is wise or that its policy is a good one. In order that there may be no room at all to doubt why I vote as I do, I feel constrained to add that the law is every bit as offensive to me as it is my Brethren of the majority and my Brothers HARLAN, WHITE and GOLDBERG who, reciting reasons why it is offensive to them, hold it unconstitutional. There is no single one of the graphic and eloquent strictures and criticisms fired at the policy of this Connecticut law either by the Court's opinion or by those of my concurring Brethren to which I cannot subscribe—except their conclusion that the evil qualities they see in the law make it unconstitutional. * * *

The Court talks about a constitutional 'right of privacy' as though there is some constitutional provision or provisions forbidding any law ever to be passed which might abridge the 'privacy' of individuals. But there is not. * * * So far as I am concerned, Connecticut's law as applied here is not forbidden by any provision of the Federal Constitution as that Constitution was written, and I would therefore affirm.

MR. JUSTICE STEWART, whom MR. JUSTICE BLACK joins, dissenting.

Since 1879 Connecticut has had on its books a law which forbids the use of contraceptives by anyone. I think this is an uncommonly silly law. As a practical matter, the law is obviously unenforceable, except in the oblique context of the present case. As a philosophical matter, I believe the use of contraceptives in the relationship of marriage should be left to personal and private choice, based upon each individual's moral, ethical, and religious beliefs. As a matter of social policy, I think professional counsel about methods of birth control should be available to all, so that each individual's choice can be meaningfully made. But we are not asked in this case to say whether we think this law is unwise, or even asinine. We are asked to hold that it violates the United States Constitution. And that I cannot do. * * *

It is the essence of judicial duty to subordinate our own personal views, our own ideas of what legislation is wise and what is not. If, as I should surely hope, the law before us does not reflect the standards of the people of Connecticut, the people of Connecticut can freely exercise their true Ninth and Tenth Amendment rights to persuade their elected representatives to repeal it. That is the constitutional way to take this law off the books.

EISENSTADT V. BAIRD
Supreme Court of the United States, 1972
405 U.S. 438, 92 S.Ct. 1029, 31 L.Ed.2d 349

MR. JUSTICE BRENNAN delivered the opinion of the Court.

Appellee William Baird was convicted at a bench trial in the Massachusetts Superior Court under Massachusetts General Laws Ann., c. 272, § 21, first, for exhibiting contraceptive articles in the course of delivering a lecture on contraception to a group of students at Boston University and, second, for giving a young woman a package of Emko vaginal foam at the close of his address. The Massachusetts Supreme Judicial Court unanimously set aside the conviction for exhibiting contraceptives on the ground that it violated Baird's First Amendment rights, but by a four-to-three vote sustained the conviction for giving away the foam. * * *

Massachusetts General Laws Ann., c. 272, § 21, under which Baird was convicted, provides a maximum five-year term of imprisonment for "whoever . . . gives away . . . any drug, medicine, instrument or article whatever for the prevention of conception," except as authorized in § 21A. Under § 21A, "[a] registered physician may administer to or prescribe for any married person drugs or articles intended for the prevention of pregnancy or conception. [And a] registered pharmacist actually engaged in the business of pharmacy may furnish such drugs or articles to any married person presenting a prescription from a registered physician." As interpreted by the State Supreme Judicial Court, these provisions make it a felony for anyone, other than a registered physician or pharmacist acting in accordance with the terms of § 21A, to dispense any article with the intention that it be used for the prevention of conception. The statutory scheme distinguishes among three distinct classes of distributees—first, married persons may obtain contraceptives to prevent pregnancy, but only from doctors or druggists on prescription; second, single persons may not obtain contraceptives from anyone to prevent pregnancy; and, third, married or single persons may obtain contraceptives from anyone to prevent, not pregnancy, but the spread of disease.

The legislative purposes that the statute is meant to serve are not altogether clear. In *Commonwealth v. Baird*, the Supreme Judicial Court noted only the State's interest in protecting the health of its citizens: "[T]he prohibition in § 21," the court declared, "is directly related to" the State's goal of "preventing the distribution of articles designed to prevent conception which may have undesirable, if not dangerous, physical consequences." In a subsequent decision, the court, however, found "a second and more compelling ground for upholding the statute"—namely, to protect morals through "regulating the private sexual lives of single persons." The Court of Appeals, for reasons that will appear, did not consider the promotion of health or the protection of morals through the deterrence of fornication to be the legislative aim. Instead, the court concluded that the statutory goal was to limit contraception in and of itself—a purpose that the court held conflicted "with fundamental human rights" under *Griswold v. Connecticut*, 381 U.S. 479, 85 S.Ct. 1678, 14 L.Ed.2d 510 (1965), where this Court struck down Connecticut's prohibition against the use of contraceptives as an unconstitutional infringement of the right of marital privacy.

We agree that the goals of deterring premarital sex and regulating the distribution of potentially harmful articles cannot reasonably be regarded as legislative aims of §§ 21 and 21A. And we hold that the statute, viewed as a prohibition on contraception per se, violates the rights of single persons under the Equal Protection Clause of the Fourteenth Amendment.

[The Court first concluded that Baird had standing "to assert the rights of unmarried persons" because, inter alia, "[e]nforcement of the Massachusetts statute will materially impair the ability of single persons to obtain contraceptives. In fact, the case for according standing to assert third-party rights is stronger in this regard here than in *Griswold* because unmarried persons denied access to contraceptives in Massachusetts, unlike the users of contraceptives in Connecticut, are not themselves subject to prosecution and, to that extent, are denied a forum in which to assert their own rights. The Massachusetts statute, unlike the Connecticut law considered in *Griswold*, prohibits, not use, but distribution."]

The question for our determination in this case is whether there is some ground of difference that rationally explains the different treatment accorded married and unmarried persons under Massachusetts General Laws Ann., c. 272, §§ 21 and 21A. For the reasons that follow, we conclude that no such ground exists. * * *

It would be plainly unreasonable to assume that Massachusetts has prescribed pregnancy and the birth of an unwanted child as punishment for fornication, which is a misdemeanor under Massachusetts General Laws Ann., c. 272, § 18. Aside from the scheme of values that assumption would attribute to the State, it is abundantly clear that the effect of the ban on distribution of contraceptives to unmarried persons has at best a marginal relation to the proffered objective. What Mr. Justice Goldberg said in *Griswold v. Connecticut* concerning the effect of Connecticut's prohibition on the use of contraceptives in discouraging extramarital sexual relations, is equally applicable here. "The rationality of this justification is dubious, particularly in light of the admitted widespread availability to all persons in the State of Connecticut, unmarried as well as married, of birth-control devices for the prevention of disease, as distinguished from the prevention of conception." Like Connecticut's laws, §§ 21 and 21A do not at all regulate the distribution of contraceptives when they are to be used to prevent, not pregnancy, but the spread of disease. Nor, in making contraceptives available to married persons without regard to their intended use, does Massachusetts attempt to deter married persons from engaging in illicit sexual relations with unmarried persons. Even on the assumption that the fear of pregnancy operates as a deterrent to fornication, the Massachusetts statute is thus so riddled with exceptions that deterrence of premarital sex cannot reasonably be regarded as its aim. * * *

The Supreme Judicial Court * * * held that the purpose of the amendment was to serve the health needs of the community by regulating the distribution of potentially harmful articles. * * * [But] we must agree with the Court of Appeals[:] * * * "If the prohibition (on distribution to unmarried persons) * * * is to be taken to mean that the same physician who can prescribe for married patients does not have sufficient skill to protect the health of patients who lack a marriage certificate, or who may be currently divorced, it is illogical to the point of irrationality." Furthermore, we must join the Court of Appeals in noting that not all contraceptives are potentially dangerous. As a result, if the Massachusetts statute were a health measure, it would not only invidiously discriminate against the unmarried, but also be overbroad with respect to the married, a fact that the Supreme Judicial Court itself seems to have conceded in *Sturgis v. Attorney General*, 260 N.E.2d at 690, where it noted that "it may well be that certain contraceptive medication and devices constitute no hazard to health, in which event it could be argued that the statute swept too broadly in its prohibition." "In this posture," as the Court of Appeals concluded, "it is impossible to think of the statute as intended as a health measure for the unmarried, and it is almost as difficult to think of it as so intended even as to the married." * * *

[Furthermore,] whatever the rights of the individual to access to contraceptives may be, the rights must be the same for the unmarried and the married alike. If under *Griswold* the distribution of contraceptives to married persons cannot be prohibited, a ban on distribution to unmarried persons would be equally impermissible. It is true that in *Griswold* the right of privacy in question inhered in the marital relationship. Yet the marital couple is not an independent entity with a mind and heart of its own, but an association of two individuals each with a separate intellectual and emotional makeup. If the right of privacy means anything, it is the right of the individual, married or single, to be free from unwarranted governmental intrusion into matters so fundamentally affecting a person as the decision whether to bear or beget a child. *See* Stanley v. Georgia, 394 U.S. 557, 89 S.Ct. 1243, 22 L.Ed.2d 542 (1969). *See also* Skinner v. Oklahoma ex rel. Williamson, 316 U.S. 535, 62 S.Ct. 1110, 86 L.Ed. 1655 (1942); Jacobson v. Massachusetts, 197 U.S. 11, 29, 25 S.Ct. 358, 362, 49 L.Ed. 643 (1905).

On the other hand, if *Griswold* is no bar to a prohibition on the distribution of contraceptives, the State could not, consistently with the Equal Protection Clause, outlaw distribution to unmarried but not to married persons. In each case the evil, as perceived by the State, would be identical, and the underinclusion would be invidious. Mr. Justice Jackson, concurring in Railway Express Agency v. New York, 336 U.S. 106, 112–113, 69 S.Ct. 463, 466, 93 L.Ed. 533 (1949), made the point:

> The framers of the Constitution knew, and we should not forget today, that there is no more effective practical guaranty against arbitrary and unreasonable government than to require that the principles of law which officials would impose upon a minority must be imposed generally. Conversely, nothing opens the door to arbitrary action so effectively as to allow those officials to pick and choose only a few to whom they will apply legislation and thus to escape the political retribution that might be visited upon them if larger numbers were affected. Courts can take no better measure to assure that laws will be just than to require that laws be equal in operation.

Although Mr. Justice Jackson's comments had reference to administrative regulations, the principle he affirmed has equal application to the legislation here. We hold that by providing dissimilar treatment for married and unmarried persons who are similarly situated, Massachusetts General Laws Ann., c. 272, §§ 21 and 21A, violate the Equal Protection Clause. The judgment of the Court of Appeals is affirmed.

[Concurring opinions by JUSTICES DOUGLAS and WHITE are omitted.]

MR. CHIEF JUSTICE BURGER, dissenting.

* * * The choice of a means of birth control, although a highly personal matter, is also a health matter in a very real sense, and I see nothing arbitrary in a requirement of medical supervision. It is generally acknowledged that contraceptives vary in degree of effectiveness and potential harmfulness. There may be compelling health reasons for certain women to choose the most effective means of birth control available, no matter how harmless the less effective alternatives. Others might be advised not to use a highly effective means of contraception because of their peculiar susceptibility to an adverse side effect. Moreover, there may be information known to the medical profession that a particular brand of contraceptive is to be preferred or avoided, or that it has not been adequately tested. * * *

I see nothing in the Fourteenth Amendment or any other part of the Constitution that even vaguely suggests that these medicinal forms of contraceptives must be available in the open market. I do not challenge *Griswold v. Connecticut*, despite its tenuous moorings to the text of the Constitution, but I cannot view it as controlling authority for this case. The Court was there confronted with a statute flatly prohibiting the use of contraceptives, not one regulating their distribution. I simply cannot believe that the limitation on the class of lawful distributors has significantly impaired the right to use contraceptives in Massachusetts. By relying [on] *Griswold* in the present context, the Court has passed beyond the penumbras of the specific guarantees into the uncircumscribed area of personal predilections.

NOTES

1.   Which of the different constitutional bases mentioned in the Court's ruling in *Griswold* and in the concurring opinions for striking down the Connecticut contraceptive statute is most persuasive? Is the issue fundamentally one of liberty, privacy, or association (or a combination of all three)? Are the Court's (in)famous references to constitutional "penumbras" helpful or do they undermine the ruling's legitimacy?

2.   Was the *Griswold* Court justified in placing so much importance on the impact of the contraception ban on married couples? Why should marital relationships be constitutionally privileged? Should married couples have greater rights to liberty and privacy in matters related to sex and sexuality than unmarried ones?

3.   Although *Eisenstadt* is not, strictly speaking, a substantive due process case given that the Court relied on the Equal Protection Clause to strike down the contraceptive statute at issue, considerations of privacy and autonomy nonetheless play an important role in the Court's reasoning. Indeed, *Eisenstadt* is generally understood today to be part of the Court's substantive due process line of cases. Is it clear that once the government is prohibited from interfering with the intimacy choices of married couples, it also cannot do the same with regards to unmarried couples? And what about sexual actors who are not in ongoing relationships?

4.   What role does the *capacity* to procreate play in *Griswold* and *Eisenstadt*? Do the opinions provide grounds for constitutionally protecting the sexual intimacy choices of different-sex couples who cannot procreate? Of same-sex couples?

ROE V. WADE

Supreme Court of the United States, 1973
410 U.S. 113, 93 S.Ct. 705, 35 L.Ed.2d 147

MR. JUSTICE BLACKMUN delivered the opinion of the Court.

This [appeal presents] constitutional challenges to state criminal abortion legislation. The Texas statutes under attack here [which make procuring an abortion a crime except "by medical advice for the purpose of saving the life of the mother"] are typical of those that have been in effect in many States for approximately a century.

* * * [T]he restrictive criminal abortion laws in effect in a majority of States today are of relatively recent vintage. * * * [T]hey derive from statutory changes effected, for the most part, in the latter half of the 19th century.

* * * [A]bortion was practiced in Greek times as well as in the Roman Era. * * * If abortion was prosecuted in some places, it seems to have been based on a concept of a violation of the father's right to his offspring. Ancient religion did not bar abortion.

* * * [A]t common law, abortion performed before "quickening"—the first recognizable movement of the fetus in utero, appearing usually from the 16th to the 18th week of pregnancy—was not an indictable offense. [The opinion then concludes that it was not until the mid-to-late 1800s that the "quickening" distinction was abandoned and the degree of the offense and punishments for offense increased.]

* * * It is thus apparent that at common law, at the time of the adoption of our Constitution, and throughout the major portion of the 19th century, abortion was viewed with less disfavor than under most American statutes currently in effect. Phrasing it another way, a woman enjoyed a substantially broader right to terminate a pregnancy than she does in most States today. At least with respect to the early stage of pregnancy, and very possibly without such a limitation, the opportunity to make this choice was present in this country well into the 19th century. * * *

Three reasons have been advanced to explain historically the enactment of criminal abortion laws in the 19th century and to justify their continued existence.

It has been argued occasionally that these laws were the product of a Victorian social concern to discourage illicit sexual conduct. Texas, however, does not advance this justification in the present case, and it appears that no court or commentator has taken the argument seriously. * * *

A second reason is concerned with abortion as a medical procedure. When most criminal abortion laws were first enacted, the procedure was a hazardous one for the woman. This was particularly true prior to the development of antisepsis. Antiseptic techniques, of course, were based on discoveries by Lister, Pasteur, and others first announced in 1867, but were not generally accepted and employed until about the turn of the century. Abortion mortality was high. Even after 1900, and perhaps until as late as the development of antibiotics in the 1940's, standard modern techniques such as dilation and curettage were not nearly so safe as they are today. Thus, it has been argued that a State's real concern in enacting a criminal abortion law was to protect the pregnant woman, that is, to restrain her from submitting to a procedure that placed her life in serious jeopardy.

Modern medical techniques have altered this situation. * * * Mortality rates for women undergoing early abortions, where the procedure is legal, appear to be as low as or lower than the rates for normal childbirth. * * * Of course, important state interests in the areas of health and medical standards do remain. The State has a legitimate interest in seeing to it that abortion, like any other medical procedure, is performed under circumstances that insure maximum safety for the patient. * * * Thus, the State retains a definite interest in protecting the woman's own health and safety when an abortion is proposed at a late stage of pregnancy.

The third reason is the State's interest—some phrase it in terms of duty—in protecting prenatal life. Some of the argument for this justification rests on the theory that a new human life is present from the moment of conception. * * * In assessing the State's interest, recognition may be given to the less rigid claim that as long as at least *potential* life is involved, the State may assert interests beyond the protection of the pregnant woman alone. * * *

The Constitution does not explicitly mention any right of privacy. In a line of decisions, however, going back perhaps as far as Union Pacific R. Co. v. Botsford, 141 U.S. 250, 251, 11 S.Ct. 1000, 1001, 35 L.Ed. 734 (1891), the Court has recognized that a right of personal privacy, or a guarantee of certain areas or zones of privacy, does exist under the Constitution. In varying contexts, the Court or individual Justices have, indeed, found at least the roots of that right in the First Amendment, Stanley v. Georgia, 394 U.S. 557, 564, 89 S.Ct. 1243, 1247, 22 L.Ed.2d 542 (1969); in the Fourth and Fifth Amendments, Terry v. Ohio, 392 U.S. 1, 8–9, 88 S.Ct. 1868, 1872–1873, 20 L.Ed.2d 889 (1968), Katz v. United States, 389 U.S. 347, 350, 88 S.Ct. 507, 510, 19 L.Ed.2d 576 (1967); Boyd v. United States, 116 U.S. 616, 6 S.Ct. 524, 29 L.Ed. 746 (1886), see Olmstead v. United States, 277 U.S. 438, 478, 48 S.Ct. 564, 572, 72 L.Ed. 944 (1928) (Brandeis, J., dissenting); in the penumbras of the Bill of

Rights, Griswold v. Connecticut, 381 U.S., at 484–485, 85 S.Ct., at 1681–1682; in the Ninth Amendment, id., at 486, 85 S.Ct. at 1682 (Goldberg, J., concurring); or in the concept of liberty guaranteed by the first section of the Fourteenth Amendment, see Meyer v. Nebraska, 262 U.S. 390, 399, 43 S.Ct. 625, 626, 67 L.Ed. 1042 (1923). These decisions make it clear that only personal rights that can be deemed "fundamental" or "implicit in the concept of ordered liberty," Palko v. Connecticut, 302 U.S. 319, 325, 58 S.Ct. 149, 152, 82 L.Ed. 288 (1937), are included in this guarantee of personal privacy. They also make it clear that the right has some extension to activities relating to marriage, Loving v. Virginia, 388 U.S. 1, 12, 87 S.Ct. 1817, 1823, 18 L.Ed.2d 1010 (1967); procreation, Skinner v. Oklahoma, 316 U.S. 535, 541–542, 62 S.Ct. 1110, 1113–1114, 86 L.Ed. 1655 (1942); contraception, Eisenstadt v. Baird, 405 U.S., at 453–454, 92 S.Ct., at 1038–1039; id., at 460, 463–465, 92 S.Ct. at 1042, 1043–1044 (White, J., concurring in result); family relationships, Prince v. Massachusetts, 321 U.S. 158, 166, 64 S.Ct. 438, 442, 88 L.Ed. 645 (1944); and child rearing and education, Pierce v. Society of Sisters, 268 U.S. 510, 535, 45 S.Ct. 571, 573, 69 L.Ed. 1070 (1925), Meyer v. Nebraska, supra.

privacy

This right of privacy, whether it be founded in the Fourteenth Amendment's concept of personal liberty and restrictions upon state action, as we feel it is, or, as the District Court determined, in the Ninth Amendment's reservation of rights to the people, is broad enough to encompass a woman's decision whether or not to terminate her pregnancy. The detriment that the State would impose upon the pregnant woman by denying this choice altogether is apparent. Specific and direct harm medically diagnosable even in early pregnancy may be involved. Maternity, or additional offspring, may force upon the woman a distressful life and future. Psychological harm may be imminent. Mental and physical health may be taxed by child care. There is also the distress, for all concerned, associated with the unwanted child, and there is the problem of bringing a child into a family already unable, psychologically and otherwise, to care for it. In other cases, as in this one, the additional difficulties and continuing stigma of unwed motherhood may be involved. All these are factors the woman and her responsible physician necessarily will consider in consultation.

broad

harm

On the basis of elements such as these, appellant and some amici argue that the woman's right is absolute and that she is entitled to terminate her pregnancy at whatever time, in whatever way, and for whatever reason she alone chooses. With this we do not agree. * * * The Court's decisions recognizing a right of privacy also acknowledge that some state regulation in areas protected by that right is appropriate. As noted above, a State may properly assert important interests in safeguarding health, in maintaining medical standards, and in protecting potential life. * * *

limitation

[But], we [also] do not agree that, by adopting one theory of life, Texas may override the rights of the pregnant woman that are at stake. We repeat, however, that the State does have an important and legitimate interest in preserving and protecting the health of the pregnant woman, whether she be a resident of the State or a non-resident, who seeks medical consultation and treatment there, and that it has still another important and legitimate interest in protecting the potentiality of human life. These interests are separate and distinct. Each grows in substantiality as the woman approaches term and, at a point during pregnancy, each becomes "compelling."

With respect to the State's important and legitimate interest in the health of the mother, the "compelling" point, in the light of present medical knowledge, is at approximately the end of the first trimester. This is so because of the now-established medical fact * * * that until the end of the first trimester mortality in abortion may be less than mortality in normal childbirth. It follows that, from and after this point, a State may regulate the abortion procedure to the extent that the regulation reasonably relates to the preservation and protection of maternal health. Examples of permissible state regulation in this area are requirements as to the qualifications of the person who is to perform the abortion; as to the licensure of that person; as to the facility in which the procedure is to be performed, that is, whether it must be a hospital or may be a clinic or some other place of less-than-hospital status; as to the licensing of the facility; and the like.

This means, on the other hand, that, for the period of pregnancy prior to this "compelling" point, the attending physician, in consultation with his patient, is free to determine, without regulation by the State, that, in his medical judgment, the patient's pregnancy should be terminated. If that decision is reached, the judgment may be effectuated by an abortion free of interference by the State.

With respect to the State's important and legitimate interest in potential life, the "compelling" point is at viability. This is so because the fetus then presumably has the capability of meaningful life outside the mother's womb. State regulation protective of fetal life after viability thus has both logical and biological justifications. If the State is interested in protecting fetal life after viability, it may go so far as to proscribe abortion during that period, except when it is necessary to preserve the life or health of the mother.

[The concurring opinions of Justices Stewart and Douglas and Chief Justice Burger, as well as the dissenting opinions of Justices White and Rehnquist, are omitted.]

PLANNED PARENTHOOD OF SOUTHEASTERN PENNSYLVANIA V. CASEY

Supreme Court of the United States, 1992
505 U.S. 833, 112 S.Ct. 2791, 120 L.Ed.2d 674

JUSTICE O'CONNOR, JUSTICE KENNEDY, and JUSTICE SOUTER announced the judgment of the Court.

I

Liberty finds no refuge in a jurisprudence of doubt. Yet 19 years after our holding that the Constitution protects a woman's right to terminate her pregnancy in its early stages, *Roe v. Wade,* 410 U.S. 113, 93 S.Ct. 705, 35 L.Ed.2d 147 (1973), that definition of liberty is still questioned. Joining the respondents as *amicus curiae,* the United States, as it has done in five other cases in the last decade, again asks us to overrule *Roe.* * * *

After considering the fundamental constitutional questions resolved by *Roe,* principles of institutional integrity, and the rule of *stare decisis,* we are led to conclude this: the essential holding of *Roe v. Wade* should be retained and once again reaffirmed. * * *

II

Constitutional protection of the woman's decision to terminate her pregnancy derives from the Due Process Clause of the Fourteenth Amendment. It declares that no State shall "deprive any person of life, liberty, or property, without due process of law." The controlling word in the cases before us is "liberty." Although a literal reading of the Clause might suggest that it governs only the procedures by which a State may deprive persons of liberty, for at least 105 years, the Clause has been understood to contain a substantive component as well, one "barring certain government actions regardless of the fairness of the procedures used to implement them." * * *

Men and women of good conscience can disagree, and we suppose some always shall disagree, about the profound moral and spiritual implications of terminating a pregnancy, even in its earliest stage. * * * Our obligation is to define the liberty of all, not to mandate our own moral code. The underlying constitutional issue is whether the State can resolve these philosophic questions in such a definitive way that a woman lacks all choice in the matter, except perhaps in those rare circumstances in which the pregnancy is itself a danger to her own life or health, or is the result of rape or incest.

It is conventional constitutional doctrine that where reasonable people disagree the government can adopt one position or the other. That theorem, however, assumes a state of affairs in which the choice does not intrude upon a protected liberty. * * *

III

A

* * * [W]hen this Court reexamines a prior holding, its judgment is customarily informed by a series of prudential and pragmatic considerations designed to test the consistency of overruling a prior decision with the ideal of the rule of law, and to gauge the respective costs of reaffirming and overruling a prior case. * * *

So in this case we may enquire whether *Roe*'s central rule has been found unworkable; whether the rule's limitation on state power could be removed without serious inequity to those who have relied upon it or significant damage to the stability of the society governed by it; whether the law's growth in the intervening years has left *Roe*'s central rule a doctrinal anachronism discounted by society; and whether *Roe*'s premises of fact have so far changed in the ensuing two decades as to render its central holding somehow irrelevant or unjustifiable in dealing with the issue it addressed.

1

Although *Roe* has engendered opposition, it has in no sense proven "unworkable," representing as it does a simple limitation beyond which a state law is unenforceable. While *Roe* has, of course, required judicial assessment of state laws affecting the exercise of the choice guaranteed against government infringement, and although the need for such review will remain as a consequence of today's decision, the required determinations fall within judicial competence.

2

The inquiry into reliance counts the cost of a rule's repudiation as it would fall on those who have relied reasonably on the rule's continued application.

* * * Abortion is customarily chosen as an unplanned response to the consequence of unplanned activity or to the failure of conventional birth control, and except on the assumption that no intercourse would have occurred but for *Roe*'s holding, such behavior may appear to justify no reliance claim. Even if reliance could be claimed on that unrealistic assumption, the argument might run, any reliance interest would be *de minimis*. This argument would be premised on the hypothesis that reproductive planning could take virtually immediate account of any sudden restoration of state authority to ban abortions.

To eliminate the issue of reliance that easily, however, one would need to limit cognizable reliance to specific instances of sexual activity. But to do this would be simply to refuse to face the fact that for two decades of economic and social developments, people have organized intimate relationships and made choices that define their views of themselves and their places in society, in reliance on the availability of abortion in the event that contraception should fail. The ability of women to participate equally in the economic and social life of the Nation has been facilitated by their ability to control their reproductive lives. The Constitution serves human values, and while the effect of reliance on *Roe* cannot be exactly measured, neither can the certain cost of overruling *Roe* for people who have ordered their thinking and living around that case be dismissed.

3

No evolution of legal principle has left *Roe*'s doctrinal footings weaker than they were in 1973. No development of constitutional law since the case was decided has implicitly or explicitly left *Roe* behind as a mere survivor of obsolete constitutional thinking.

It will be recognized, of course, that *Roe* stands at an intersection of two lines of decisions, but in whichever doctrinal category one reads the case, the result for present purposes will be the same. The *Roe* Court itself placed its holding in the succession of cases most prominently exemplified by *Griswold v. Connecticut*, 381 U.S. 479, 85 S.Ct. 1678, 14 L.Ed.2d 510 (1965). When it is so seen, *Roe* is clearly in no jeopardy, since subsequent constitutional developments have neither disturbed, nor do they threaten to diminish, the scope of recognized protection accorded to the liberty relating to intimate relationships, the family, and decisions about whether or not to beget or bear a child.

Roe, however, may be seen not only as an exemplar of *Griswold* liberty but as a rule (whether or not mistaken) of personal autonomy and bodily integrity, with doctrinal affinity to cases recognizing limits on governmental power to mandate medical treatment or to bar its rejection. If so, our cases since *Roe* accord with *Roe*'s view that a State's interest in the protection of life falls short of justifying any plenary override of individual liberty claims. * * *

4

We have seen how time has overtaken some of *Roe*'s factual assumptions: advances in maternal health care allow for abortions safe to the mother later in pregnancy than was true in 1973, and advances in neonatal care have advanced viability to a point somewhat earlier. But these facts go only to the scheme of time limits on the realization of competing interests, and the divergences from the factual premises of 1973 have no bearing on the validity of *Roe*'s central holding, that viability marks the earliest point at which the State's interest in fetal life is constitutionally adequate to justify a legislative ban on nontherapeutic abortions. The soundness or unsoundness of that constitutional judgment in no sense turns on whether viability occurs at approximately 28 weeks, as was usual at the time of *Roe,* at 23 to 24 weeks, as it sometimes does today, or at some moment even slightly earlier in pregnancy, as it may if fetal respiratory capacity can somehow be enhanced in the future. Whenever it may occur, the attainment of viability may continue to serve as the critical fact, just as it has done since *Roe* was decided; which is to say that no change in *Roe*'s factual underpinning has left its central holding obsolete, and none supports an argument for overruling it. * * *

From what we have said so far it follows that it is a constitutional liberty of the woman to have some freedom to terminate her pregnancy. We conclude that the basic decision in *Roe* was based on a constitutional analysis which we cannot now repudiate. The woman's liberty is not so unlimited, however, that from the outset the State cannot show its concern for the life of the unborn, and at a later point in fetal development the State's interest in life has sufficient force so that the right of the woman to terminate the pregnancy can be restricted.

That brings us, of course, to the point where much criticism has been directed at *Roe,* a criticism that always inheres when the Court draws a specific rule from what in the Constitution is but a general standard. We conclude, however, that the urgent claims of the woman to retain the ultimate control over her destiny and her body, claims implicit in the meaning of liberty, require us to perform that function. Liberty must not be extinguished for want of a line that is clear. And it falls to us to give some real substance to the woman's liberty to determine whether to carry her pregnancy to full term.

We conclude the line should be drawn at viability, so that before that time the woman has a right to choose to terminate her pregnancy. We adhere to this principle for two reasons. First, as we have said, is the doctrine of *stare decisis.* * * * The second reason is that the concept of viability, as we noted in *Roe,* is the time at which there is a realistic possibility of maintaining and nourishing a life outside the womb, so that the independent existence of the second life can in reason and all fairness be the object of state protection that now overrides the rights of the woman. Consistent with other constitutional norms, legislatures may draw lines which appear arbitrary without the necessity of offering a justification. But courts may not. We must justify the lines we draw. And there is no line other than viability which is more workable. To be sure, as we have said, there may be some medical developments that affect the precise point of viability, but this is an imprecision within tolerable limits given that the medical community and all those who must apply its discoveries will continue to explore the matter. The viability line also has, as a practical matter, an element of fairness. In some broad sense it might be said that a woman who fails to act before viability has consented to the State's intervention on behalf of the developing child.

The woman's right to terminate her pregnancy before viability is the most central principle of *Roe v. Wade.* It is a rule of law and a component of liberty we cannot renounce. * * *

Yet it must be remembered that *Roe v. Wade* speaks with clarity in establishing not only the woman's liberty but also the State's "important and legitimate interest in potential life." That portion of the decision in *Roe* has been given too little acknowledgment and implementation by the Court in its subsequent cases. Those cases decided that any regulation touching upon the abortion decision must survive strict scrutiny, to be sustained only if drawn in narrow terms to further a compelling state interest. Not all of the cases decided under that formulation can be reconciled with the holding in *Roe* itself that the State has legitimate interests in the health of the woman and in protecting the potential life within her. In resolving this tension, we choose to rely upon *Roe,* as against the later cases.

Roe established a trimester framework to govern abortion regulations. Under this elaborate but rigid construct, almost no regulation at all is permitted during the first trimester of pregnancy; regulations designed to protect the woman's health, but not to further the State's interest in potential life, are permitted during the second trimester; and during the third trimester, when the fetus is viable, prohibitions are permitted provided the life or health of the mother is not at stake. Most of our cases since *Roe* have involved the application of rules derived from the trimester framework.

The trimester framework no doubt was erected to ensure that the woman's right to choose not become so subordinate to the State's interest in promoting fetal life that her choice exists in theory but not in fact. We do not agree, however, that the trimester approach is necessary to accomplish this objective. A framework of this rigidity was unnecessary and in its later interpretation sometimes contradicted the State's permissible exercise of its powers.

Though the woman has a right to choose to terminate or continue her pregnancy before viability, it does not at all follow that the State is prohibited from taking steps to ensure that this choice is thoughtful and informed. Even in the earliest stages of pregnancy, the State may enact rules and regulations designed to encourage her to know that there are philosophic and social arguments of great weight that can be brought to bear in favor of continuing the pregnancy to full term and that there are procedures and institutions to allow adoption of unwanted children as well as a certain degree of state assistance if the mother chooses to raise the child herself. "[T]he Constitution does not forbid a State or city, pursuant to democratic processes, from expressing a preference for normal childbirth." It follows that States are free to enact laws to provide a reasonable framework for a woman to make a decision that has such profound and lasting meaning. This, too, we find consistent with *Roe's* central premises, and indeed the inevitable consequence of our holding that the State has an interest in protecting the life of the unborn.

We reject the trimester framework, which we do not consider to be part of the essential holding of *Roe.* * * *

As our jurisprudence relating to all liberties save perhaps abortion has recognized, not every law which makes a right more difficult to exercise is, *ipso facto,* an infringement of that right. An example clarifies the point. We have held that not every ballot access limitation amounts to an infringement of the right to vote. Rather, the States are granted substantial flexibility in establishing the framework within which voters choose the candidates for whom they wish to vote.

The abortion right is similar. Numerous forms of state regulation might have the incidental effect of increasing the cost or decreasing the availability of medical care, whether for abortion or any other medical procedure. The fact that a law which serves a valid purpose, one not designed to strike at the right itself, has the incidental effect of making it more difficult or more expensive to procure an abortion cannot be enough to invalidate it. Only where state regulation imposes an undue burden on a woman's ability to make this decision does the power of the State reach into the heart of the liberty protected by the Due Process Clause. * * *

[I]t is an overstatement to describe it as a right to decide whether to have an abortion "without interference from the State." *Planned Parenthood of Central Mo. v. Danforth,* 428 U.S. 52, 61, 96 S.Ct. 2831, 2837, 49 L.Ed.2d 788 (1976). All abortion regulations interfere to some degree with a woman's ability to decide whether to terminate her pregnancy. It is, as a consequence, not surprising that despite the protestations contained in the original *Roe* opinion to the effect that the Court was not recognizing an absolute right, the Court's experience applying the trimester framework has led to the striking down of some abortion regulations which in no real sense deprived women of the ultimate decision. Those decisions went too far because the right recognized by *Roe* is a right "to be free from unwarranted governmental intrusion into matters so fundamentally affecting a person as the decision whether to bear or beget a child." *Eisenstadt v. Baird,* 405 U.S., at 453, 92 S.Ct., at 1038. Not all governmental intrusion is of necessity unwarranted; and that brings us to the other basic flaw in the trimester framework: even in *Roe's* terms, in practice it undervalues the State's interest in the potential life within the woman.

Roe v. Wade was express in its recognition of the State's "important and legitimate interest[s] in preserving and protecting the health of the pregnant woman [and] in protecting the potentiality of human life." The trimester framework, however, does not fulfill *Roe*'s own promise that the State has an interest in protecting fetal life or potential life. *Roe* began the contradiction by using the trimester framework to forbid any regulation of abortion designed to advance that interest before viability. Before viability, *Roe* and subsequent cases treat all governmental attempts to influence a woman's decision on behalf of the potential life within her as unwarranted. This treatment is, in our judgment, incompatible with the recognition that there is a substantial state interest in potential life throughout pregnancy.

The very notion that the State has a substantial interest in potential life leads to the conclusion that not all regulations must be deemed unwarranted. Not all burdens on the right to decide whether to terminate a pregnancy will be undue. In our view, the undue burden standard is the appropriate means of reconciling the State's interest with the woman's constitutionally protected liberty.

A finding of an undue burden is a shorthand for the conclusion that a state regulation has the purpose or effect of placing a substantial obstacle in the path of a woman seeking an abortion of a nonviable fetus. A statute with this purpose is invalid because the means chosen by the State to further the interest in potential life must be calculated to inform the woman's free choice, not hinder it. And a statute which, while furthering the interest in potential life or some other valid state interest, has the effect of placing a substantial obstacle in the path of a woman's choice cannot be considered a permissible means of serving its legitimate ends. * * *

[Pennsylvania required a woman seeking an abortion to wait 24 hours (unless it was a medical emergency), so she would consider information required to be transmitted by the physician. Pennsylvania also required minors to obtain a parent's consent, but included a judicial bypass mechanism. And Pennsylvania required married women to notify their spouse before seeking an abortion. The Joint Opinion struck down only the spousal notification provision, based on its finding that that provision placed an "undue burden" on the abortion right.] * * *

Our Constitution is a covenant running from the first generation of Americans to us and then to future generations. It is a coherent succession. Each generation must learn anew that the Constitution's written terms embody ideas and aspirations that must survive more ages than one. We accept our responsibility not to retreat from interpreting the full meaning of the covenant in light of all of our precedents. We invoke it once again to define the freedom guaranteed by the Constitution's own promise, the promise of liberty. * * *

[The opinions of Justices Blackmun and Stevens are omitted. They concurred in the refusal to overrule *Roe* and the invalidation of the spousal notice requirement, but dissented as to the constitutionality of the other provisions.]

CHIEF JUSTICE REHNQUIST, with whom JUSTICE WHITE, JUSTICE SCALIA, and JUSTICE THOMAS join, concurring in the judgment in part and dissenting in part.

The joint opinion, following its newly minted variation on *stare decisis,* retains the outer shell of *Roe v. Wade,* but beats a wholesale retreat from the substance of that case. We believe that *Roe* was wrongly decided, and that it can and should be overruled consistently with our traditional approach to *stare decisis* in constitutional cases. We would * * * uphold the challenged provisions of the Pennsylvania statute in their entirety.

I

* * * In *Roe v. Wade,* the Court recognized a "guarantee of personal privacy" which "is broad enough to encompass a woman's decision whether or not to terminate her pregnancy." We are now of the view that, in terming this right fundamental, the Court in *Roe* read the earlier opinions upon which it based its decision much too broadly. Unlike marriage, procreation, and contraception, abortion "involves the purposeful termination of a potential life." *Harris v. McRae,* 448 U.S. 297, 325, 100 S.Ct. 2671, 2692, 65 L.Ed.2d 784 (1980). The abortion decision must therefore "be recognized as *sui generis,* different in kind from the others that the Court has protected under the rubric of personal or family privacy and autonomy." *Thornburgh v. American College of Obstetricians and Gynecologists,* 476 U.S., at 792, 106 S.Ct., at 2195 (WHITE, J., dissenting). One cannot ignore the fact that a woman is not isolated in her pregnancy, and that the decision to abort necessarily involves the destruction of a fetus.

Nor do the historical traditions of the American people support the view that the right to terminate one's pregnancy is "fundamental." The common law which we inherited from England made abortion after "quickening" an offense. At the time of the adoption of the Fourteenth Amendment, statutory prohibitions or restrictions on abortion were commonplace; in 1868, at least 28 of the then-37 States and 8 Territories had statutes banning or limiting abortion. By the turn of the century virtually every State had a law prohibiting or restricting abortion on its books. By the middle of the present century, a liberalization trend had set in. But 21 of the restrictive abortion laws in effect in 1868 were still in effect in 1973 when *Roe* was decided, and an overwhelming majority of the States prohibited abortion unless necessary to preserve the life or health of the mother. On this record, it can scarcely be said that any deeply rooted tradition of relatively unrestricted abortion in our history supported the classification of the right to abortion as "fundamental" under the Due Process Clause of the Fourteenth Amendment.

We think, therefore, both in view of this history and of our decided cases dealing with substantive liberty under the Due Process Clause, that the Court was mistaken in *Roe* when it classified a woman's decision to terminate her pregnancy as a "fundamental right" that could be abridged only in a manner which withstood "strict scrutiny." * * *

We believe that the sort of constitutionally imposed abortion code of the type illustrated by our decisions following *Roe* is inconsistent "with the notion of a Constitution cast in general terms, as ours is, and usually speaking in general principles, as ours does." The Court in *Roe* reached too far when it analogized the right to abort a fetus to the rights involved in *Pierce, Meyer, Loving,* and *Griswold,* and thereby deemed the right to abortion fundamental. * * *

II

* * * The joint opinion discusses several *stare decisis* factors which, it asserts, point toward retaining a portion of *Roe.* Two of these factors are that the main "factual underpinning" of *Roe* has remained the same, and that its doctrinal foundation is no weaker now than it was in 1973. Of course, what might be called the basic facts which gave rise to *Roe* have remained the same—women become pregnant, there is a point somewhere, depending on medical technology, where a fetus becomes viable, and women give birth to children. But this is only to say that the same facts which gave rise to *Roe* will continue to give rise to similar cases. It is not a reason, in and of itself, why those cases must be decided in the same incorrect manner as was the first case to deal with the question. And surely there is no requirement, in considering whether to depart from *stare decisis* in a constitutional case, that a decision be more wrong now than it was at the time it was rendered. If that were true, the most outlandish constitutional decision could survive forever, based simply on the fact that it was no more outlandish later than it was when originally rendered. * * *

The joint opinion thus turns to what can only be described as an unconventional—and unconvincing—notion of reliance, a view based on the surmise that the availability of abortion since *Roe* has led to "two decades of economic and social developments" that would be undercut if the error of *Roe* were recognized. The joint opinion's assertion of this fact is undeveloped and totally conclusory. In fact, one cannot be sure to what economic and social developments the opinion is referring. Surely it is dubious to suggest that women have reached their "places in society" in reliance upon *Roe,* rather than as a result of their determination to obtain higher education and compete with men in the job market, and of society's increasing recognition of their ability to fill positions that were previously thought to be reserved only for men. * * *

[The dissenting opinion of JUSTICE SCALIA is omitted.]

NOTES

1.   The question of abortion, and its regulation by the state, raises many difficult constitutional, moral, and policy questions. For purposes of exploring the subject matter of this casebook, you may want to focus on the following ones. First, was the Court correct in *Roe* and *Casey* that a woman's right to terminate a pregnancy before viability is, in effect, an exemplar of the rights to liberty and privacy recognized in *Griswold*? How are contraceptive and abortion regulations similar? How are they different? If the government is constitutionally precluded from denying access to contraceptives, does it also lack the constitutional authority to ban abortions?

2.   Second, what do *Roe* and *Casey* mean for questions of sexual freedom and liberty? Is the reasoning in the two cases limited to issues of procreation and whether to carry a fetus to term or does the reasoning extend to questions regarding the authority of the state to regulate sex and sexuality more broadly?

3.   Third, abortion regulations clearly impact women more directly than men. Should the Court in *Roe* and *Casey* have grappled with the equality implications of abortion regulations? As perhaps suggested by the Court's reasoning in *Eisenstadt*, does the Equal Protection Clause provide a viable constitutional basis for limiting the authority of the state to burden the choices of particular classes of individuals in matters related to sex and procreation? Do restrictions on abortion rely on gender-based judgments about women's roles? That is, might a prohibition on abortion reflect judgments about the "natural" relationship between pregnancy and motherhood? For an insightful analysis of the history of abortion regulation and its relationship to role stereotypes, see Reva B. Siegel, *Reasoning from the Body: An Historical Perspective on Abortion Regulation and Questions of Equal Protection*, 44 STAN. L. REV. 261 (1992).

4.   Finally, how persuasive are the *stare decisis* arguments contained in the joint opinion and in Chief Justice Rehnquist's dissenting opinion in *Casey*? It is fair to say that the two most controversial substantive due process decisions of the last fifty years are *Roe* and *Bowers v. Hardwick*, 478 U.S. 186, 106 S.Ct. 2841, 92 L.Ed.2d 140 (1986), in which the Court refused to extend liberty and privacy protections to same-sex sexual conduct. (We will explore *Bowers* shortly.) You should keep questions regarding *stare decisis* in mind later in this chapter when assessing the Court's willingness in *Lawrence v. Texas*, 539 U.S. 558, 123 S.Ct. 2472, 156 L.Ed.2d 508 (2003), decided a little more than a decade after *Casey*, to overrule *Bowers*. As you will see, Justice Scalia, in his *Lawrence* dissent, contends that the Court got it precisely wrong: *Stare decisis* principles required the overturning of *Roe*

and the upholding of *Bowers*. *See Lawrence*, 539 U.S. at 587–88 (Scalia, J., dissenting). Do you agree?

5.   In *Gonzalez v. Carhart*, 550 U.S. 124, 127 S.Ct. 1610, 167 L.E.2d 480 (2007), the Supreme Court upheld the constitutionality of a federal statute, known as the Partial-Birth Abortion Ban Act of 2003, which prohibited a particular kind of abortion procedure known as "intact dilation and evacuation." The Court, in a 5 to 4 ruling, rejected the argument that the statute constituted an undue burden on a woman's right to choose because it was overbroad and lacked an exception in cases when the procedure was required to protect a pregnant woman's health. On the latter point, the Court concluded that there were conflicting medical views on whether the procedure in question was, in some instances, the safest way of conducting an abortion while protecting women's health. As a result, the Court deemed it appropriate to defer to Congress's view that the procedure is never medically necessary. *Id.* at 163.

6.   In 2013, Texas enacted a law that *inter alia* required abortion practitioners to hold admitting privileges at nearby hospitals and abortion clinics to meet the standards, including those related to facilities, equipment, and staffing, of ambulatory surgical centers. *See* Tex. Health & Safety Code §§ 171.044, 171.063(a), 171.0031(a), 245.010(a). In 2016, the Supreme Court, in a 5–3 ruling, struck down the law's two requirements. *Whole Woman's Health v. Hellerstedt*, ___ U.S. ___, 136 S.Ct. 2292, 195 L.Ed.2d 665 (2016). The Court explained that "neither of these provisions confers medical benefits sufficient to justify the burdens upon access that each imposes. Each places a substantial obstacle in the path of women seeking a previability abortion, each constitutes an undue burden on abortion access, and each violates the Federal Constitution." *Id.* at 2300 (citing to *Casey*). The Court reasoned that *Casey* "requires that courts consider the burdens a law imposes on abortion access together with the benefits those laws confer." *Id.* at 2309. In striking down the requirements, the majority relied heavily on the district court's factual findings. Those findings "demonstrate[d] that, before the act's passage, abortion in Texas was extremely safe with particularly low rates of serious complications and virtually no deaths occurring on account of the procedure." *Id.* at 2302 (quoting *Whole Women's Health v. Lakey*, 46 F.Supp.3d 673, 684 (W.D. Tex. 2014)). The Court added that "the record contains sufficient evidence that the admitting-privileges requirement led to the closure of half of Texas' clinics, or thereabouts. Those closures meant fewer doctors, longer waiting times, and increased crowding." *Id.* at 2312. In addition, the Court noted the parties' stipulation that the surgical-center requirement "would further reduce the number of abortion facilities available to seven or eight facilities" from a total of about 40. Furthermore, the majority pointed out that "[n]ationwide, childbirth is 14 times more likely than abortion to result in death, but Texas law allows a midwife to oversee childbirth in the patient's own home. Colonoscopy, a procedure that typically takes place outside a hospital (or surgical center) setting, has a mortality rate 10 times higher than an abortion. * * * These facts indicate that the surgical-

center provision imposes a requirement that simply is not based on differences between abortion and other surgical procedures that are reasonably related to preserving women's health, the asserted purpose of the Act in which it is found." *Id.* at 2315 (internal citations omitted).

II. THE RIGHT TO SEXUAL INTIMACY

A. SODOMY

1. History and Background

AMICI CURIAE BRIEF OF PROFESSORS OF HISTORY*

Lawrence v. Texas

Prohibitions against sodomy are rooted in the teachings of Western Christianity, but those teachings have always been strikingly inconsistent in their definition of the acts encompassed by the term. When the term "sodomy" was first emphasized by medieval Christian theologians in the eleventh century, they applied it inconsistently to a diverse group of non-procreative sexual practices. In subsequent Latin theology, canon law, and confessional practice, the term was notoriously confused with "unnatural acts," which had a very different origin and ranged even more widely (to include, for example, procreative sexual acts in the wrong position or with contraceptive intent). "Unnatural acts" is the older category, because it comes directly from Paul in Romans 1, but Paul does not associate such acts with (or even mention) the story of Sodom (Genesis 19) and appears not to have considered that story to be concerned with same-sex activity.

Later Christian authors did combine Romans 1 with Genesis 19, but they could not agree on what sexual practices were meant by either "unnatural acts" or "sodomy." For example, in Peter Damian, who around 1050 championed the term "sodomy" as an analogy to "blasphemy," the "sins of the Sodomites" include solitary masturbation. In Thomas Aquinas, about two centuries later, "unnatural acts" cover every genital contact intended to produce orgasm except penile-vaginal intercourse in an approved position. Many later Christian writers denied that women could commit sodomy at all; others believed that the defining characteristic of unnatural or sodomitic sex was that it could not result in procreation, regardless of the genders involved. In none of these authors does the term "sodomy" refer systematically and exclusively to same-sex

---

*   Brief of Professors of History George Chauncey, Nancy F. Cott, John D'Emilio, Estelle B. Freedman, Thomas C. Holt, John Howard, Lynn Hunt, Mark D. Jordan, Elizabeth Lapovsky Kennedy, and Linda P. Kerber as Amici Curiae Supporting Petitioners, *Lawrence v. Texas*, 539 U.S. 558, 123 S. Ct. 2472, 156 L.Ed.2d 508 (2003).

conduct. Certainly it was not used consistently through the centuries to condemn that conduct. * * *

The English Reformation Parliament of 1533 turned the religious injunction against sodomy into the secular crime of buggery when it made "the detestable and abominable vice of buggery committed with mankind or beast" punishable by death. The English courts interpreted this to apply to sexual intercourse between a human and animal and anal intercourse between a man and woman as well as anal intercourse between two men.

Colonial American statutes variously drew on the religious and secular traditions and shared their imprecision in the definition of the offense. Variously defining the crime as (the religious) sodomy or (the secular) buggery, they generally proscribed anal sex between men and men, men and women, and humans and animals, but their details and their rationale varied, and the New England colonies penalized a wider range of "carnall knowledge," including (but by no means limited to) "men lying with men." Puritan leaders in the New England colonies were especially vigorous in their denunciation of sodomitical sins as contrary to God's will, but their condemnation was also motivated by the pressing need to increase the population and to secure the stability of the family. Thus John Winthrop mused that the main offense of one man hanged in New Haven in 1646 for having engaged in masturbation with numerous youths—not, in other words, for "sodomy" as it is usually understood today—was his "frustratinge of the Ordinance of marriage & the hindringe the generation of mankinde."

Another indication that the sodomy statutes were not the equivalent of a statute against "homosexual conduct" is that with one brief exception they applied exclusively to acts performed by men, whether with women, girls, men, boys, or animals, and not to acts committed by two women. Only the New Haven colony penalized "women lying with women," and this for only ten years. For the entire colonial period we have reports of only two cases involving two women engaged in acts with one another. * * *

Statutes enacted in the early decades after independence followed the English authorities, but by the mid-nineteenth century most statutes defined the offense as a crime against nature rather than as a crime against God. Such statutes were still not the equivalent of a statute proscribing "homosexual conduct." In 1868, no statute criminalized oral sex, whether between two men, two women, or a man and woman. * * *

* * * [T]hroughout American history, the authorities have rarely enforced statutes prohibiting sodomy, however defined. Even in periods when enforcement increased, it was rare for people to be prosecuted for consensual sexual relations conducted in private, even when the parties

were of the same sex. Indeed, records of only about twenty prosecutions and four or five executions have surfaced for the entire colonial period. Even in the New England colonies, whose leaders denounced "sodomy" with far greater regularity and severity than did other colonial leaders and where the offense carried severe sanctions, it was rarely prosecuted. The trial of Nicholas Sension, a married man living in Westhersfield, Connecticut, in 1677, revealed that he had been widely known for soliciting sexual contacts with the town's men and youth for almost forty years but remained widely liked. Likewise, a Baptist minister in New London, Connecticut, was temporarily suspended from the pulpit in 1757 because of his repeatedly soliciting sex with men, but the congregation voted to restore him to the ministry after he publicly repented. They understood his sexual transgressions to be a form of sinful behavior in which anyone could engage and from which anyone could repent, not as a sin worthy of death or the condition of a particular class of people.

The relative indifference of the public and the authorities to the crime of sodomy continued in the first century of independence. For instance, only twenty-two men were indicted for sodomy in New York City in the nearly eight decades from 1796 to 1873. The number of sodomy prosecutions increased sharply in the last two decades of the nineteenth century and in the twentieth century. This was made possible by the decision of many States to criminalize oral intercourse for the first time. But it resulted in large measure from the pressure applied on district attorneys by privately organized and usually religiously inspired anti-vice societies, whose leaders feared that the growing size and complexity of cities had loosened the constraints on sexual conduct and increased the vulnerability of youth and the disadvantaged. The increase in sodomy prosecutions was only one aspect of a general escalation in the policing of sexual activity, which also included stepped-up campaigns against prostitution, venereal disease, and contraception use. Although in this context a growing number of sodomy prosecutions involved adult males who had engaged in consensual relations, most such relations had taken place in semi-public spaces rather than in the privacy of the home, and the great majority of cases continued to involve coercion and/or minor boys or girls. * * *

Over the generations, sodomy legislation proscribed a diverse and inconsistent set of sexual acts engaged in by various combinations of partners. Above all, it regulated conduct in which anyone (or, at certain times and in certain places, any male person) could engage. Only in the late nineteenth century did the idea of the homosexual as a distinct category of person emerge, and only in the twentieth century did the state begin to classify and penalize citizens on the basis of their identity or status as homosexuals. The States began to enact discriminatory measures in the 1920s and 1930s, but such measures and other forms of anti-gay harassment reached a peak in the twenty years following the Second World War, when government agencies systematically discriminated against homosexuals.

The unprecedented decision of Texas and several other states, primarily in the 1970s, to enact sodomy laws singling out "homosexual sodomy" for penalty, is best understood historically in the context of these discriminatory measures. The new sodomy laws essentially recast the historic purpose of such laws, which had been to regulate conduct generally, by adding them to the array of discriminatory measures directed specifically against homosexuals. Such discriminatory measures against homosexuals, although popularly imagined to be longstanding, are in fact not ancient but a unique and relatively short-lived product of the twentieth century.

It was only in the late nineteenth century that the very concept of the homosexual as a distinct category of person developed. The word "homosexual" appeared for the first time in a German pamphlet in 1868, and was introduced to the American lexicon only in 1892. As Michel Foucault has famously described this evolution, "the sodomite had been a temporary aberration; the homosexual was now a species." 1 Michel Foucault, The History of Sexuality 43 (Robert Hurley trans. 1978).

As of 1961, all 50 states in the United States had some sort of sodomy law on their books. During the following four decades, many jurisdictions repealed their sodomy laws, particularly as state legislatures adopted the Model Penal Code. Drafted in the 1950s by the American Law Institute (ALI)—an influential body of lawyers and law professors—the Model Penal Code was meant to update and unify American criminal law. A critical development in the Code was the de-criminalization of sexual behavior, including same-sex sexual conduct, between consenting adults in private. The drafters of the Model Penal Code were influenced by a 1957 report to the British Parliament by England's Committee on Homosexual Offenses and Prostitution (the Wolfenden Report) that recommended that consensual same-sex sexual conduct be de-criminalized. The report stated that "[u]nless a deliberate attempt is to be made by society, acting through the agency of the law, to equate the sphere of crime with that of sin, there must remain a realm of private morality and immorality which is, in brief and crude terms, not the law's business. To say this is not to condone or encourage private immorality."[8]

Legislative repeal was the route by which most states rid themselves of sodomy statutes. By the time the U.S. Supreme Court decided

---

[8]   DEPARTMENTAL COMMITTEE ON HOMOSEXUAL OFFENSES AND PROSTITUTION, REPORT TO THE SECRETARY OF STATE FOR THE HOME DEPARTMENT ("THE WOLFENDEN REPORT") 24, ¶ 61 (1957).

Lawrence v. Texas in 2003, 28 state legislatures (AK, AZ, CA, CO, CT, DE, FL, HA, IL, IN, IA, ME, NB, ND, NH, NJ, NM, NV, NY, OH, OR, RI, SD, VT, WA, WI, WV, and WY) had repealed their sodomy laws. (By the time *Lawrence* was decided, courts in nine additional states had questioned the constitutionality of sodomy statutes: AR, GA, KY, MA, MD, MI, MT, PA, and TN.) The first legislative repeal was Illinois's in 1961; no state followed for a decade until Connecticut did so in 1971. Twenty of the legislative repeals took place during the 1970s. The number of repeals fell considerably after that, with only two in the 1980s (Alaska and Wisconsin) and three in the 1990s (Nevada, Rhode Island, and the District of Columbia). The last two legislative repeals before *Lawrence* occurred in 2001 (Arizona and New York).

While many states were repealing their sodomy statutes, a handful of others amended their laws so as to criminalize same-sex sodomy only. This process of "specification" occurred in eight states: Kansas (1969); Montana and Texas (1973); Kentucky (1974); Arkansas, Missouri and Nevada (1977); and Tennessee (1989). Nan Hunter has noted that

> [t]he specification trend coincided with the emergence of the contemporary versions of both the lesbian and gay rights movement and a renewed movement for religious fundamentalism in American politics. In 1973, * * * two critical events occurred: The American Psychiatric Association removed homosexuality from its list of mental diseases and the United States Civil Service Commission forbade personnel supervisors from finding a person unsuitable for a federal government job based solely on homosexuality. By 1985, anti-discrimination laws had been adopted by the District of Columbia, San Francisco, Los Angeles, Minneapolis, Philadelphia and several smaller cities. Anti-equality forces mobilized during the 1970s also, securing repeal of a civil rights law in Dade County, Florida, and conducting two electoral campaigns to enact laws mandating the firing of state schools systems employees who advocated homosexuality—one unsuccessfully (California) and the other successfully (Oklahoma). For states revising their criminal codes, the specification of homosexual acts as a crime marked both the greater visibility of homosexuality in a positive sense and the tremendous social anxiety which that visibly generated.

Nan D. Hunter, *Life After* Hardwick, 27 HARV. C.R.-C.L. L. REV. 531, 539–40 (1992).

2. Constitutional Litigation

The first constitutional challenges to sodomy statutes were grounded on the idea that they violated due process because they were unduly vague, thus giving citizens insufficient notice as to what conduct would result in criminal liability. Most of those challenges were unsuccessful.

For example, the U.S. Supreme Court in 1973 concluded that Florida's "abominable and detestable crime against nature statute" was not unconstitutionally vague.[9] The Court reached the same conclusion two years later when assessing Tennessee's crime against nature statute.[10]

Those interested in challenging sodomy statutes next turned to the due process right to privacy. The first privacy-based challenge to a sodomy statute to reach the U.S. Supreme Court was *Doe v. Commonwealth's Attorney*.[11] The lower court in *Doe* determined that the Supreme Court's privacy cases only "condemn[ ] State legislation that trespasses upon the privacy of the incidents of marriage, upon the sanctity of the home, or upon the nurture of family life."[12] The court concluded that there is "no authoritative judicial bar to the proscription of homosexuality * * * since it is obviously no part of marriage, home or family life * * * ."[13] The *Doe* case was appealed to the Supreme Court, which summarily affirmed, over a dissent by Justices William Brennan, Thurgood Marshall, and John Paul Stevens.[14]

Notwithstanding *Doe*, a federal district court in Texas struck down that state's sodomy law as violating the federal Constitution in 1982.[15] Relying on *Doe v. Commonwealth's Attorney*, the U.S. Court of Appeals for the Fifth Circuit reversed.[16]

Although pre-*Bowers* challenges to sodomy statutes were unsuccessful in the federal courts, progress was made in some state courts. In 1980, the highest courts in New York and Pennsylvania struck down their state's sodomy laws on both federal and state constitutional grounds.[17] Two years later, an Atlanta police officer entered the apartment of a man by the name of Michael Hardwick while Hardwick was engaged in oral sex with another man. The officer then arrested both men for committing sodomy.

---

[9]   *See Wainwright v. Stone*, 414 U.S. 21, 22–23, 94 S.Ct. 190, 192–93, 38 L.Ed.2d 179, 181–82 (1973) (per curiam).

[10]   *See Rose v. Locke*, 423 U.S. 48, 96 S.Ct. 243, 46 L.Ed.2d 185 (1975) (per curiam).

[11]   403 F.Supp. 1199 (D. Va. 1975), *aff'd*, 425 U.S. 901, 96 S.Ct. 1489, 47 L.Ed.2d 751 (1976).

[12]   403 F.Supp. at 1200.

[13]   *Id.* at 1202.

[14]   *See Doe v. Commonwealth's Attorney*, 425 U.S. 901, 96 S.Ct. 1489, 47 L.Ed.2d 751 (1976).

[15]   *Baker v. Wade*, 553 F.Supp. 1121 (D. Tex. 1982), *rev'd*, 769 F.2d 289, 292 (5th Cir. 1985) (en banc).

[16]   *Baker v. Wade*, 769 F.2d 289, 292 (5th Cir. 1985) (en banc).

[17]   *New York v. Onofre*, 415 N.E.2d 936, 51 N.Y.2d 476, 434 N.Y.S.2d 947 (1980); *Commonwealth v. Bonadio*, 415 A.2d 47, 490 Pa. 91 (1980).

BOWERS V. HARDWICK

Supreme Court of the United States, 1986
478 U.S. 186, 106 S.Ct. 2841, 92 L.Ed.2d 140

JUSTICE WHITE.

In August 1982, respondent Hardwick (hereafter respondent) was charged with violating the Georgia statute criminalizing sodomy[1] by committing that act with another adult male in the bedroom of respondent's home. After a preliminary hearing, the District Attorney decided not to present the matter to the grand jury unless further evidence developed. * * *

Respondent then brought suit in the Federal District Court, challenging the constitutionality of the statute insofar as it criminalized consensual sodomy.[2] * * * The District Court granted the defendants' motion to dismiss for failure to state a claim, relying on *Doe v. Commonwealth's Attorney for the City of Richmond*, 403 F.Supp. 1199 (E.D.Va.1975), which this Court summarily affirmed, 425 U.S. 901 (1976).

A divided panel of the Court of Appeals for the Eleventh Circuit reversed. 760 F.2d 1202 (1985). * * *

This case does not require a judgment on whether laws against sodomy between consenting adults in general, or between homosexuals in particular, are wise or desirable. It raises no question about the right or propriety of state legislative decisions to repeal their laws that criminalize homosexual sodomy, or of state-court decisions invalidating those laws on state constitutional grounds. The issue presented is whether the Federal Constitution confers a fundamental right upon homosexuals to engage in sodomy and hence invalidates the laws of the many States that still make such conduct illegal and have done so for a very long time. The case also calls for some judgment about the limits of the Court's role in carrying out its constitutional mandate.

---

[1]   Georgia Code Ann., § 16–6–2 (1984) provides, in pertinent part, as follows:

"(a) A person commits the offense of sodomy when he performs or submits to any sexual act involving the sex organs of one person and the mouth or anus of another. * * *

"(b) A person convicted of the offense of sodomy shall be punished by imprisonment for not less than one nor more than 20 years. * * * "

[2]   John and Mary Doe were also plaintiffs in the action. They alleged that they wished to engage in sexual activity proscribed by § 16–6–2 in the privacy of their home, and that they had been "chilled and deterred" from engaging in such activity by both the existence of the statute and Hardwick's arrest. The District Court held, however, that because they had neither sustained, nor were in immediate danger of sustaining, any direct injury from the enforcement of the statute, they did not have proper standing to maintain the action. The Court of Appeals affirmed the District Court's judgment dismissing the Does' claim for lack of standing, 760 F.2d 1202, 1206–1207 (11th Cir. 1985), and the Does do not challenge that holding in this Court.

The only claim properly before the Court, therefore, is Hardwick's challenge to the Georgia statute as applied to consensual homosexual sodomy. We express no opinion on the constitutionality of the Georgia statute as applied to other acts of sodomy.

We first register our disagreement with the Court of Appeals and with respondent that the Court's prior cases have construed the Constitution to confer a right of privacy that extends to homosexual sodomy and for all intents and purposes have decided this case. The reach of this line of cases was sketched in *Carey v. Population Services International*, 431 U.S. 678, 685 (1977). *Pierce v. Society of Sisters*, 268 U.S. 510 (1925), and *Meyer v. Nebraska*, 262 U.S. 390 (1923), were described as dealing with child rearing and education; *Prince v. Massachusetts*, 321 U.S. 158 (1944), with family relationships; *Skinner v. Oklahoma ex rel. Williamson*, 316 U.S. 535 (1942), with procreation; *Loving v. Virginia*, 388 U.S. 1 (1967), with marriage; *Griswold v. Connecticut, supra*, and *Eisenstadt v. Baird, supra*, with contraception; and *Roe v. Wade*, 410 U.S. 113 (1973), with abortion. The latter three cases were interpreted as construing the due process clause of the Fourteenth Amendment to confer a fundamental individual right to decide whether or not to beget or bear a child. *Carey v. Population Services International, supra*, at 688–689.

Accepting the decisions in these cases and the above description of them, we think it evident that none of the rights announced in those cases bears any resemblance to the claimed constitutional right of homosexuals to engage in acts of sodomy that is asserted in this case. No connection between family, marriage, or procreation on the one hand and homosexual activity on the other has been demonstrated, either by the Court of Appeals or by respondent. Moreover, any claim that these cases nevertheless stand for the proposition that any kind of private sexual conduct between consenting adults is constitutionally insulated from state proscription is unsupportable. Indeed, the Court's opinion in *Carey* twice asserted that the privacy right, which the *Griswold* line of cases found to be one of the protections provided by the due process clause, did not reach so far.

Precedent aside, however, respondent would have us announce, as the Court of Appeals did, a fundamental right to engage in homosexual sodomy. This we are quite unwilling to do. It is true that despite the language of the due process clauses of the Fifth and Fourteenth Amendments, which appears to focus only on the processes by which life, liberty, or property is taken, the cases are legion in which those clauses have been interpreted to have substantive content, subsuming rights that to a great extent are immune from federal or state regulation or proscription. Among such cases are those recognizing rights that have little or no textual support in the constitutional language. *Meyer, Prince*, and *Pierce* fall in this category, as do the privacy cases from *Griswold* to *Carey*.

Striving to assure itself and the public that announcing rights not readily identifiable in the Constitution's text involves much more than the imposition of the Justices' own choice of values on the States and the Federal Government, the Court has sought to identify the nature of the rights qualifying for heightened judicial protection. In *Palko v. Connecticut*, 302 U.S. 319, 325, 326 (1937), it was said that this category includes those fundamental liberties that are "implicit in the concept of ordered liberty," such that "neither liberty nor justice would exist if [they] were sacrificed." A different description of fundamental liberties appeared in *Moore v. East Cleveland*, 431 U.S. 494, 503 (1977) (opinion of Powell, J.), where they are characterized as those liberties that are "deeply rooted in this Nation's history and tradition." *Id.*, at 503 (Powell, J.).

It is obvious to us that neither of these formulations would extend a fundamental right to homosexuals to engage in acts of consensual sodomy. Proscriptions against that conduct have ancient roots. *See generally*, Survey on the Constitutional Right to Privacy in the Context of Homosexual Activity, 40 U. Miami L. Rev. 521, 525 (1986). Sodomy was a criminal offense at common law and was forbidden by the laws of the original thirteen states when they ratified the Bill of Rights. In 1868, when the Fourteenth Amendment was ratified, all but 5 of the 37 States in the Union had criminal sodomy laws. In fact, until 1961, all 50 States outlawed sodomy, and today, 24 states and the District of Columbia continue to provide criminal penalties for sodomy performed in private and between consenting adults. *See* Survey, U. Miami L. Rev., *supra*, at 524, n. 9. Against this background, to claim that a right to engage in such conduct is "deeply rooted in this nation's history and tradition" or "implicit in the concept of ordered liberty" is, at best, facetious.

Nor are we inclined to take a more expansive view of our authority to discover new fundamental rights imbedded in the due process clause. The Court is most vulnerable and comes nearest to illegitimacy when it deals with judge-made constitutional law having little or no cognizable roots in the language or design of the Constitution. That this is so was painfully demonstrated by the face-off between the Executive and the Court in the 1930s, which resulted in the repudiation of much of the substantive gloss that the Court had placed on the Due Process Clauses of the Fifth and Fourteenth Amendments. There should be, therefore, great resistance to expand the substantive reach of those Clauses, particularly if it requires redefining the category of rights deemed to be fundamental. Otherwise, the Judiciary necessarily takes to itself further authority to govern the country without express constitutional authority. The claimed right pressed on us today falls far short of overcoming this resistance.

Respondent, however, asserts that the result should be different where the homosexual conduct occurs in the privacy of the home. He relies on *Stanley v. Georgia*, 394 U.S. 557 (1969), where the Court held that the First Amendment prevents conviction for possessing and reading obscene material in the privacy of one's home: "If the First Amendment means anything, it means that a State has no business telling a man, sitting alone in his house, what books he may read or what films he may watch." *Id.*, at 565.

Stanley did protect conduct that would not have been protected outside the home, and it partially prevented the enforcement of state obscenity laws; but the decision was firmly grounded in the First Amendment. The right pressed upon us here has no similar support in the text of the Constitution, and it does not qualify for recognition under the prevailing principles for construing the Fourteenth Amendment. Its limits are also difficult to discern. Plainly enough, otherwise illegal conduct is not always immunized whenever it occurs in the home. Victimless crimes, such as the possession and use of illegal drugs, do not escape the law where they are committed at home. *Stanley* itself recognized that its holding offered no protection for the possession in the home of drugs, firearms, or stolen goods. *Id.*, at 568, n. 11. And if respondent's submission is limited to the voluntary sexual conduct between consenting adults, it would be difficult, except by fiat, to limit the claimed right to homosexual conduct while leaving exposed to prosecution adultery, incest, and other sexual crimes even though they are committed in the home. We are unwilling to start down that road.

Even if the conduct at issue here is not a fundamental right, respondent asserts that there must be a rational basis for the law and that there is none in this case other than the presumed belief of a majority of the electorate in Georgia that homosexual sodomy is immoral and unacceptable. This is said to be an inadequate rationale to support the law. The law, however, is constantly based on notions of morality, and if all laws representing essentially moral choices are to be invalidated under the Due Process Clause, the courts will be very busy indeed. Even respondent makes no such claim, but insists that majority sentiments about the morality of homosexuality should be declared inadequate. We do not agree, and are unpersuaded that the sodomy laws of some 25 States should be invalidated on this basis.

Accordingly, the judgment of the Court of Appeals is *Reversed*.

CHIEF JUSTICE BURGER, concurring.

I join the Court's opinion, but I write separately to underscore my view that in constitutional terms there is no such thing as a fundamental right to commit homosexual sodomy.

As the Court notes, the proscriptions against sodomy have very "ancient roots." Decisions of individuals relating to homosexual conduct have been subject to state intervention throughout the history of Western civilization. Condemnation of those practices is firmly rooted in Judeao-Christian moral and ethical standards. Homosexual sodomy was a capital crime under Roman law. *See* Code Theod. 9.7.6; Code Just. 9.9.31. *See* *also* D. Bailey, Homosexuality and the Western Christian Tradition, 70–81 (1975). During the English Reformation when powers of the ecclesiastical courts were transferred to the King's Courts, the first English statute criminalizing sodomy was passed. 25 Hen. VIII, ch. 6. Blackstone described "the infamous *crime against nature*" as an offense of "deeper malignity" than rape, a heinous act "the very mention of which is a disgrace to human nature," and "a crime not fit to be named." 4 W. Blackstone, Commentaries *215. The common law of England, including its prohibition of sodomy, became the received law of Georgia and the other Colonies. In 1816 the Georgia Legislature passed the statute at issue here, and that statute has been continuously in force in one form or another since that time. To hold that the act of homosexual sodomy is somehow protected as a fundamental right would be to cast aside millennia of moral teaching.

This is essentially not a question of personal "preferences" but rather of the legislative authority of the State. I find nothing in the Constitution depriving a State of the power to enact the statute challenged here.

JUSTICE POWELL, concurring.

I join the opinion of the Court. I agree with the Court that there is no fundamental right—*i.e.*, no substantive right under the due process clause—such as that claimed by respondent Hardwick, and found to exist by the Court of Appeals. This is not to suggest, however, that respondent may not be protected by the Eighth Amendment of the Constitution. The Georgia statute at issue in this case, Ga. Code Ann., § 16–6–2 (1984), authorizes a court to imprison a person for up to 20 years for a single private, consensual act of sodomy. In my view, a prison sentence for such conduct—certainly a sentence of long duration—would create a serious Eighth Amendment issue. Under the Georgia statute a single act of sodomy, even in the private setting of a home, is a felony comparable in terms of the possible sentence imposed to serious felonies such as aggravated battery, § 16–5–24, first-degree arson, § 16–7–60, and robbery, § 16–8–40.

In this case, however, respondent has not been tried, much less convicted and sentenced. Moreover, respondent has not raised the Eighth Amendment issue below. For these reasons this constitutional argument is not before us.

JUSTICE BLACKMUN, with whom JUSTICE BRENNAN, JUSTICE MARSHALL, and JUSTICE STEVENS join, dissenting.

This case is no more about "a fundamental right to engage in homosexual sodomy," as the Court purports to declare, than *Stanley v. Georgia*, 394 U.S. 557 (1969), was about a fundamental right to watch obscene movies, or *Katz v. United States*, 389 U.S. 347 (1967), was about a fundamental right to place interstate bets from a telephone booth.

Rather, this case is about "the most comprehensive of rights and the right most valued by civilized men," namely, "the right to be let alone." *Olmstead v. United States*, 277 U.S. 438, 478 (1928) (Brandeis, J., dissenting).

The statute at issue, Ga. Code Ann. § 16–6–2 (1984), denies individuals the right to decide for themselves whether to engage in particular forms of private, consensual sexual activity. The Court concludes that § 16–6–2 is valid essentially because "the laws of * * * many States * * * still make such conduct illegal and have done so for a very long time." But the fact that the moral judgments expressed by statutes like § 16–6–2 may be " 'natural and familiar * * * ought not to conclude our judgment upon the question whether statutes embodying them conflict with the Constitution of the United States.' " *Roe v. Wade*, 410 U.S. 113, 117 (1973), quoting *Lochner v. New York*, 198 U.S. 45, 76 (1905) (Holmes, J., dissenting). Like Justice Holmes, I believe that "[it] is revolting to have no better reason for a rule of law than that so it was laid down in the time of Henry IV. It is still more revolting if the grounds upon which it was laid down have vanished long since, and the rule simply persists from blind imitation of the past." Holmes, "The Path of the Law," 10 Harv. L. Rev. 457, 469 (1897). I believe we must analyze respondent Hardwick's claim in the light of the values that underlie the constitutional right to privacy. If that right means anything, it means that, before Georgia can prosecute its citizens for making choices about the most intimate aspects of their lives, it must do more than assert that the choice they have made is an " 'abominable crime not fit to be named among Christians.' " *Herring v. State*, 46 S.E. 876, 882 (Ga. 1904). * * *

Only the most willful blindness could obscure the fact that sexual intimacy is "a sensitive, key relationship of human existence, central to family life, community welfare, and the development of human personality," *Paris Adult Theatre I v. Slaton*, 413 U.S. 49, 63 (1973); *see also Carey v. Population Services International*, 431 U.S. 678, 685 (1977). The fact that individuals define themselves in a significant way through their intimate sexual relationships with others suggests, in a nation as diverse as ours, that there may be many "right" ways of conducting those relationships, and that much of the richness of a relationship will come from the freedom an individual has to *choose* the form and nature of these intensely personal bonds. * * *

The behavior for which Hardwick faces prosecution occurred in his own home, a place to which the Fourth Amendment attaches special significance. The Court's treatment of this aspect of the case is symptomatic of its overall refusal to consider the broad principles that have informed our treatment of privacy in specific cases. Just as the right to privacy is more than the mere aggregation of a number of entitlements to engage in specific behavior, so too, protecting the physical integrity of the home is more than merely a means of protecting specific activities that often take place there. Even when our understanding of the contours of the right to privacy depends on "reference to a 'place,' " *Katz v. United States*, 389 U.S., at 361 (Harlan, J., concurring), "the essence of a Fourth Amendment violation is 'not the breaking of [a person's] doors, and the rummaging of his drawers,' but rather is 'the invasion of his indefeasible right of personal security, personal liberty and private property.' " *California v. Ciraolo*, 476 U.S. 207, 226 (1986) (Powell, J., dissenting), quoting *Boyd v. United States*, 116 U.S. 616, 630 (1886).

JUSTICE STEVENS, with whom JUSTICE BRENNAN and JUSTICE MARSHALL join, dissenting.

Our prior cases make two propositions abundantly clear. First, the fact that the governing majority in a State has traditionally viewed a particular practice as immoral is not a sufficient reason for upholding a law prohibiting the practice; neither history nor tradition could save a law prohibiting miscegenation from constitutional attack. Second, individual decisions by married persons, concerning the intimacies of their physical relationship, even when not intended to produce offspring, are a form of "liberty" protected by the due process clause of the Fourteenth Amendment. *Griswold v. Connecticut*, 381 U.S. 479 (1965). Moreover, this protection extends to intimate choices by unmarried as well as married persons. *Carey v. Population Services International*, 431 U.S. 678 (1977); *Eisenstadt v. Baird*, 405 U.S. 438 (1972). * * *

If the Georgia statute cannot be enforced as it is written—if the conduct it seeks to prohibit is a protected form of liberty for the vast majority of Georgia's citizens—the State must assume the burden of justifying a selective application of its law. Either the persons to whom Georgia seeks to apply its statute do not have the same interest in "liberty" that others have, or there must be a reason why the State may be permitted to apply a generally applicable law to certain persons that it does not apply to others.

The first possibility is plainly unacceptable. Although the meaning of the principle that "all men are created equal" is not always clear, it surely must mean that every free citizen has the same interest in "liberty" that the members of the majority share. From the standpoint of the individual, the homosexual and the heterosexual have the same interest in deciding how he will live his own life, and, more narrowly, how he will conduct himself in his personal and voluntary associations with his companions. State intrusion into the private conduct of either is equally burdensome.

The second possibility is similarly unacceptable. A policy of selective application must be supported by a neutral and legitimate interest— something more substantial than a habitual dislike for, or ignorance about, the disfavored group. Neither the State nor the Court has identified any such interest in this case. The Court has posited as a justification for the Georgia statute "the presumed belief of a majority of the electorate in Georgia that homosexual sodomy is immoral and unacceptable." But the Georgia electorate has expressed no such belief— instead, its representatives enacted a law that presumably reflects the belief that *all sodomy* is immoral and unacceptable. Unless the Court is prepared to conclude that such a law is constitutional, it may not rely on the work product of the Georgia legislature to support its holding. For the Georgia statute does not single out homosexuals as a separate class meriting special disfavored treatment.

Nor, indeed, does the Georgia prosecutor even believe that all homosexuals who violate this statute should be punished. This conclusion is evident from the fact that the respondent in this very case has formally acknowledged in his complaint and in court that he has engaged, and intends to continue to engage, in the prohibited conduct, yet the State has elected not to process criminal charges against him. As Justice Powell points out, moreover, Georgia's prohibition on private, consensual sodomy has not been enforced for decades. The record of nonenforcement, in this case and in the last several decades, belies the Attorney General's representations about the importance of the State's selective application of its generally applicable law.

Both the Georgia statute and the Georgia prosecutor thus completely fail to provide the Court with any support for the conclusion that homosexual sodomy, *simpliciter*, is considered unacceptable conduct in that State, and that the burden of justifying a selective application of the generally applicable law has been met.

NOTES

1. After *Bowers*, states remained free, as a matter of federal constitutional law, to criminalize same-sex sexual activity. The reality, however, was that by the time *Bowers* was decided, law enforcement officials were rarely bringing sodomy prosecutions in cases involving consensual sexual conduct in private. *Bowers*, therefore, had a greater practical impact on civil cases than it did on criminal cases. The fact that states could, if they so chose, impose criminal liability for consensual same-sex sexual conduct was used to justify the continued discrimination against lesbians, gay men, and bisexuals in matters as diverse as those affecting public employment, family law, and immigration. *See generally* Diana Hassel, *The Use of Criminal Sodomy Laws in Civil Litigation*, 79 TEX. L. REV. 813 (2001); Christopher R. Leslie, *Creating Criminals: The Injuries Inflicted by "Unenforced" Sodomy Laws*, 35 HARV. C.R.-C.L. L. REV. 103 (2000).

2. Even though *Bowers* was a due process case, the ruling had important repercussions on questions of equal protection as several courts used the opinion to justify denying suspect class status to lesbians and gay

men. If the state could criminalize the conduct that defines the class, the argument went, then the class should not receive heightened scrutiny under the Equal Protection Clause. *See, e.g., High Tech Gays v. Defense Indus. Sec. Clearance Office*, 895 F.2d 563, 571 (9th Cir. 1990) (noting that "if there is no fundamental right to engage in homosexual sodomy * * *, it would be incongruous to expand the reach of equal protection to find a fundamental right of homosexual conduct under the equal protection component of the Due Process Clause of the Fifth Amendment"); *Woodward v. United States*, 871 F.2d 1068, 1076 (Fed. Cir. 1989) (arguing that "[a]fter *Hardwick* it cannot logically be asserted that discrimination against homosexuals is constitutionally infirm"). The issue of sexual orientation and suspect classification is explored further below, in Chapter 3, Section II.B.

3.   Once the question of the federal constitutionality of sodomy statutes was answered by the U.S. Supreme Court in *Bowers*, parties interested in challenging the statutes turned their attention more specifically to state courts, where, as already noted, there were some pre-*Bowers* litigation successes. *E.g., New York v. Onofre*, 415 N.E.2d 936, 51 N.Y.2d 476, 434 N.Y.S.2d 947 (1980); *Commonwealth v. Bonadio*, 415 A.2d 47, 490 Pa. 91 (1980). This shift was consistent with a growing body of commentary embracing the use of state constitutions to try to expand civil rights and liberties protections. *See generally* William J. Brennan, Jr., *State Constitutions and the Protection of Individual Rights*, 90 HARV. L. REV. 489 (1977). Six years after *Bowers*, the Kentucky Supreme Court became the first highest court of a state to strike down a sodomy statute on state constitutional grounds. *See Commonwealth v. Wasson*, 842 S.W.2d 487 (Ky. 1992) (violation of privacy and equal protection). Other state supreme courts followed with similar rulings, *see Gryczan v. State*, 942 P.2d 112, 283 Mont. 433 (1997); *Jegley v. Picado*, 80 S.W.3d 332, 349 Ark. 600 (2002), including the Georgia Supreme Court in a case involving the same statute at issue in *Bowers. Powell v. State*, 510 S.E.2d 18, 270 Ga. 327 (1998). *Contra State v. Smith*, 766 So.2d 501 (La. 2000) (upholding constitutionality of "crime against nature" statute).

——————

After *Bowers*, the next important substantive due process opinion issued by the U.S. Supreme Court was *Planned Parenthood of Southeastern Pennsylvania v. Casey*.[18] *See supra* Section I. Five years later, the Court returned to the question of substantive due process in *Washington v. Glucksberg*.[19] The Court in *Glucksberg* held that Washington's prohibition of physician-assisted suicide did not violate the Fourteenth Amendment's Liberty Clause. The Court stated that

[o]ur established method of substantive-due-process analysis has two primary features: First, we have regularly observed that the

——————

[18]   505 U.S. 833, 112 S. Ct. 2791, 120 L. Ed. 2d 674 (1992).
[19]   521 U.S. 702, 117 S. Ct. 2258, 138 L. Ed. 2d 772 (1997).

Due Process Clause specially protects those fundamental rights and liberties which are, objectively, "deeply rooted in this Nation's history and tradition," and "implicit in the concept of ordered liberty," such that "neither liberty nor justice would exist if they were sacrificed." Second, we have required in substantive-due-process cases a "careful description" of the asserted fundamental liberty interest. Our Nation's history, legal traditions, and practices thus provide the crucial "guideposts for responsible decisionmaking" that direct and restrain our exposition of the Due Process Clause. * * *

In our view * * * the development of this Court's substantive-due-process jurisprudence * * * has been a process whereby the outlines of the "liberty" specially protected by the Fourteenth Amendment—never fully clarified, to be sure, and perhaps not capable of being fully clarified—have at least been carefully refined by concrete examples involving fundamental rights found to be deeply rooted in our legal tradition. This approach tends to rein in the subjective elements that are necessarily present in due-process judicial review. In addition, by establishing a threshold requirement—that a challenged state action implicate a fundamental right—before requiring more than a reasonable relation to a legitimate state interest to justify the action, it avoids the need for complex balancing of competing interests in every case.[20]

In reviewing the historical record in *Glucksberg*, the Court noted that "we are confronted with a consistent and almost universal tradition that has long rejected the asserted right, and continues explicitly to reject it today, even for terminally ill, mentally competent adults. To hold for respondents, we would have to reverse centuries of legal doctrine and practice, and strike down the considered policy choice of almost every State."[21]

THE UNKNOWN PAST OF *LAWRENCE V. TEXAS*[*]

Dale Carpenter

Below I offer a brief history of the Texas sodomy law, in its various statutory iterations. I do so for two reasons. First, though the law never distinguished between acts committed in broad daylight and acts

----

[20]   *Id.* at 720–22, 117 S. Ct. at 2268, 138 L. Ed. 2d at 787–89.

[21]   *Id.* at 723, 117 S. Ct. at 2269, 138 L. Ed. 2d at 793.

[*]   Dale Carpenter, *The Unknown Past of* Lawrence v. Texas 102 MICH.L.REV. 1464, 1468–74 (2004).

committed in the home, it was almost never enforced against the latter. That is, it was almost never enforced against the most prevalent instances of sodomy. Thus, the law's concern was not with preventing sodomy. The law was intended to send a symbolic message of disdain about the people thought to commonly engage in sodomy.

Second, the history of the law's development establishes an important point: the Texas law, like other sodomy laws around the country, initially applied to certain acts, regardless of the sex of the people involved in the act. It was only through a process of specification that it came to be aimed at certain people engaged in certain acts. The Texas law, like many such laws, instantiates a particular cultural view of homosexuals as hyper-sexualized and dangerous in some way. * * *

1. THE 1860 STATUTE

The criminal code of the Republic of Texas, in force from 1836 to 1845 while Texas was an independent nation, contained no prohibition on sodomy, although common-law crimes were recognized. In its first fifteen years as a state, Texas had no statutory sodomy law.

The state adopted its first sodomy law in 1860, using the common-law definition for the crime. It provided: "If any person shall commit with mankind or beast the abominable and detestable crime against nature * * * he shall be punished by confinement in the penitentiary for not less than five nor more than fifteen years." Commentators and courts of the era understood this language to prohibit anal sex between a man and a woman or between two men. It did not prohibit oral sex, and it did not prohibit any sex between women. The category "homosexual conduct" would have been literally incomprehensible to Texas legislators of the era since there was no word for "homosexual" at the time. * * *

2. THE 1943 STATUTE

In 1943, the Texas legislature revised the state sodomy law a second time. The new version, which passed by votes of 127–0 and 24–0 in the state house and senate, respectively, made oral sex a crime for the first time in Texas:

Whoever has carnal copulation with a beast, or in an opening of the body, except sexual parts, with another human being, or whoever shall use his mouth on the sexual parts of another human being for the purpose of having carnal copulation, or who shall voluntarily permit the use of his own sexual parts in a lewd or lascivious manner by any minor, shall be guilty of sodomy, and upon conviction thereof shall be deemed guilty of a felony, and shall be confined in the penitentiary not less than two (2) nor more than fifteen (15) years.

The 1943 revision is bizarre in more ways than one. It suggests that while oral sex for the purpose of "carnal copulation" is illegal, oral sex for some other purpose is just fine. It also suggests that while sexual intercourse with an animal is illegal, oral sex performed on an animal is not a problem since it is only oral sex performed on "another human being" that is criminal. Still, the law on its face applied equally to heterosexual and homosexual sex.

3.   THE 1973 STATUTE

In 1973, during a comprehensive criminal code revision, the Texas legislature changed the sodomy law a third time. Now for the first time calling the law "Homosexual Conduct," the legislature banned oral and anal sex only between persons of the same sex. It first defined "deviate sexual intercourse" as "any contact between any part of the genitals of one person and the mouth or anus of another person." Next, it made deviate sexual intercourse a crime only if performed "with another individual of the same sex." The 1973 revision made homosexual conduct a Class C misdemeanor punishable only by a fine of up to $200. It made lesbian sex criminal for the first time.

Also in 1973, the Texas legislature generally liberalized its sex laws, decriminalizing adultery, fornication, seduction, and even bestiality. And while opposite-sex couples were now free to engage in "deviate sexual intercourse," same-sex couples were not.

Thus, the 1973 Texas Homosexual Conduct law represented an expansion of the types of acts historically prohibited. Both anal and oral sex were now covered, though only anal sex was covered before 1943. At the same time, it also represented a narrowing of the class of people historically covered. Same-sex, but not opposite-sex, couples were now covered. * * *

Enforcement of the Texas Sodomy Law

In the entire 143-year history of the Texas sodomy law, * * * there are no publicly reported court decisions involving the enforcement of the law against consensual sex between adult persons in a private space. In some reported decisions, the facts given by the court are too sketchy to determine whether the prosecution was for private, adult, consensual activity. Especially in early cases, the decisions are very short, often no more than a paragraph or two in length. Courts have often seemed too bashful even to present the facts. In a typical example, affirming a sodomy conviction after a guilty plea, one Kentucky court said simply, "It is not necessary to set out the revolting facts." *Medrano v. State*, 205 S.W. 2d 588, 588 (Ky. 1947)

All of the reported Texas cases detailing the circumstances of an arrest for sodomy involve some element that makes them distinct from

Lawrence. Many involve charges of sodomy violations in a public or quasi-public place, such as a jail. Some cases involve some element of force or coercion. Others involve sex with minors. Indeed, in litigation challenging the state sodomy law, the state has contended that it has only enforced the law in cases where force was used, cases involving minors, and cases involving public sex. This alone makes the arrest and prosecution of Lawrence and Garner, whose case involved none of these factors, anomalous.

However, the absence of reported decisions does not mean that the Texas sodomy law was never enforced against private activity. Instead, perhaps because of the shame long associated with homosexuality and homosexual acts, defendants arrested and charged with violating the law routinely pleaded guilty to the offense, paid whatever fine was imposed, and hushed up about their convictions. As a result, almost all of the uses and misuses by police of the Texas sodomy law (and of sodomy laws in other states) against private acts will never be known. They are lost to history because of shame and fear.

LAWRENCE V. TEXAS

Supreme Court of the United States, 2003
539 U.S. 558, 123 S.Ct. 2472, 156 L.Ed.2d 508

JUSTICE KENNEDY delivered the opinion of the Court.

Liberty protects the person from unwarranted government intrusions into a dwelling or other private places. In our tradition the State is not omnipresent in the home. And there are other spheres of our lives and existence, outside the home, where the State should not be a dominant presence. Freedom extends beyond spatial bounds. Liberty presumes an autonomy of self that includes freedom of thought, belief, expression, and certain intimate conduct. The instant case involves liberty of the person both in its spatial and in its more transcendent dimensions.

The question before the Court is the validity of a Texas statute making it a crime for two persons of the same sex to engage in certain intimate sexual conduct.

In Houston, Texas, officers of the Harris County Police Department were dispatched to a private residence in response to a reported weapons disturbance. They entered an apartment where one of the petitioners, John Geddes Lawrence, resided. The right of the police to enter does not seem to have been questioned. The officers observed Lawrence and another man, Tyron Garner, engaging in a sexual act. The two petitioners were arrested, held in custody overnight, and charged and convicted before a Justice of the Peace.

The complaints described their crime as "deviate sexual intercourse, namely anal sex, with a member of the same sex (man)." App. to Pet. for Cert. 127a, 139a. The applicable state law is Tex. Penal Code Ann. § 21.06(a) (2003). It provides: "A person commits an offense if he engages in deviate sexual intercourse with another individual of the same sex." The statute defines "[d]eviate sexual intercourse" as follows:

statute

"(A) any contact between any part of the genitals of one person and the mouth or anus of another person; or

"(B) the penetration of the genitals or the anus of another person with an object." § 21.01(1). * * *

The petitioners were adults at the time of the alleged offense. Their conduct was in private and consensual.

Private + consensual

We conclude the case should be resolved by determining whether the petitioners were free as adults to engage in the private conduct in the exercise of their liberty under the Due Process Clause of the Fourteenth Amendment to the Constitution. For this inquiry we deem it necessary to reconsider the Court's holding in *Bowers*.

Δ reconsider Bowers

There are broad statements of the substantive reach of liberty under the Due Process Clause in earlier cases * * * but the most pertinent beginning point is our decision in *Griswold v. Connecticut*, 381 U.S. 479 (1965). * * *

Griswold

In *Griswold* the Court invalidated a state law prohibiting the use of drugs or devices of contraception and counseling or aiding and abetting the use of contraceptives. The Court described the protected interest as a right to privacy and placed emphasis on the marriage relation and the protected space of the marital bedroom. *Id.*, at 485.

Privacy

After *Griswold* it was established that the right to make certain decisions regarding sexual conduct extends beyond the marital relationship. In *Eisenstadt v. Baird*, 405 U.S. 438 (1972), the Court invalidated a law prohibiting the distribution of contraceptives to unmarried persons. The case was decided under the Equal Protection Clause, *id.*, at 454 * * * ; but with respect to unmarried persons, the Court went on to state the fundamental proposition that the law impaired the exercise of their personal rights, *ibid.* It quoted from the statement of the Court of Appeals finding the law to be in conflict with fundamental human rights, and it followed with this statement of its own: "It is true that in *Griswold* the right of privacy in question inhered in the marital relationship. * * * If the right of privacy means anything, it is the right of the *individual*, married or single, to be free from unwarranted governmental intrusion into matters so fundamentally affecting a person as the decision whether to bear or beget a child." *Id.* at 453.

Eisenstadt

EP

Δπ

The opinions in *Griswold* and *Eisenstadt* were part of the background for the decision in *Roe v. Wade*, 410 U.S. 113 (1973). * * * *Roe* recognized the right of a woman to make certain fundamental decisions affecting her destiny and confirmed once more that the protection of liberty under the Due Process Clause has a substantive dimension of fundamental significance in defining the rights of the person.

In *Carey v. Population Services Int'l*, 431 U.S. 678 (1977), the Court confronted a New York law forbidding sale or distribution of contraceptive devices to persons under 16 years of age. Although there was no single opinion for the Court, the law was invalidated. Both *Eisenstadt* and *Carey*, as well as the holding and rationale in *Roe*, confirmed that the reasoning of *Griswold* could not be confined to the protection of rights of married adults. This was the state of the law with respect to some of the most relevant cases when the Court considered *Bowers v. Hardwick*. * * *

The Court began its substantive discussion in *Bowers* as follows: "The issue presented is whether the Federal Constitution confers a fundamental right upon homosexuals to engage in sodomy and hence invalidates the laws of the many States that still make such conduct illegal and have done so for a very long time." That statement, we now conclude, discloses the Court's own failure to appreciate the extent of the liberty at stake. To say that the issue in *Bowers* was simply the right to engage in certain sexual conduct demeans the claim the individual put forward, just as it would demean a married couple were it to be said marriage is simply about the right to have sexual intercourse. The laws involved in *Bowers* and here are, to be sure, statutes that purport to do no more than prohibit a particular sexual act. Their penalties and purposes, though, have more far-reaching consequences, touching upon the most private human conduct, sexual behavior, and in the most private of places, the home. The statutes do seek to control a personal relationship that, whether or not entitled to formal recognition in the law, is within the liberty of persons to choose without being punished as criminals.

This, as a general rule, should counsel against attempts by the State, or a court, to define the meaning of the relationship or to set its boundaries absent injury to a person or abuse of an institution the law protects. It suffices for us to acknowledge that adults may choose to enter upon this relationship in the confines of their homes and their own private lives and still retain their dignity as free persons. When sexuality finds overt expression in intimate conduct with another person, the conduct can be but one element in a personal bond that is more enduring. The liberty protected by the Constitution allows homosexual persons the right to make this choice.

Having misapprehended the claim of liberty there presented to it, and thus stating the claim to be whether there is a fundamental right to engage in consensual sodomy, the *Bowers* Court said: "Proscriptions against that conduct have ancient roots." * * * [T]he following considerations counsel against adopting the definitive conclusions upon which *Bowers* placed such reliance.

At the outset it should be noted that there is no longstanding history in this country of laws directed at homosexual conduct as a distinct matter. Beginning in colonial times there were prohibitions of sodomy derived from the English criminal laws passed in the first instance by the Reformation Parliament of 1533. The English prohibition was understood to include relations between men and women as well as relations between men and men. Nineteenth-century commentators similarly read American sodomy, buggery, and crime-against-nature statutes as criminalizing certain relations between men and women and between men and men. The absence of legal prohibitions focusing on homosexual conduct may be explained in part by noting that according to some scholars the concept of the homosexual as a distinct category of person did not emerge until the late 19th century. Thus early American sodomy laws were not directed at homosexuals as such but instead sought to prohibit nonprocreative sexual activity more generally. This does not suggest approval of homosexual conduct. It does tend to show that this particular form of conduct was not thought of as a separate category from like conduct between heterosexual persons.

Laws prohibiting sodomy do not seem to have been enforced against consenting adults acting in private. A substantial number of sodomy prosecutions and convictions for which there are surviving records were for predatory acts against those who could not or did not consent, as in the case of a minor or the victim of an assault. As to these, one purpose for the prohibitions was to ensure there would be no lack of coverage if a predator committed a sexual assault that did not constitute rape as defined by the criminal law. Thus the model sodomy indictments presented in a 19th-century treatise addressed the predatory acts of an adult man against a minor girl or minor boy. Instead of targeting relations between consenting adults in private, 19th-century sodomy prosecutions typically involved relations between men and minor girls or minor boys, relations between adults involving force, relations between adults implicating disparity in status, or relations between men and animals.

To the extent that there were any prosecutions for the acts in question, 19th-century evidence rules imposed a burden that would make a conviction more difficult to obtain even taking into account the problems always inherent in prosecuting consensual acts committed in private. Under then-prevailing standards, a man could not be convicted of sodomy based upon testimony of a consenting partner, because the partner was considered an accomplice. A partner's testimony, however, was admissible if he or she had not consented to the act or was a minor, and therefore incapable of consent. The rule may explain in part the infrequency of these prosecutions. In all events that infrequency makes it difficult to say that society approved of a rigorous and systematic punishment of the consensual acts committed in private and by adults. The longstanding criminal prohibition of homosexual sodomy upon which the *Bowers* decision placed such reliance is as consistent with a general condemnation of nonprocreative sex as it is with an established tradition of prosecuting acts because of their homosexual character.

The policy of punishing consenting adults for private acts was not much discussed in the early legal literature. We can infer that one reason for this was the very private nature of the conduct. Despite the absence of prosecutions, there may have been periods in which there was public criticism of homosexuals as such and an insistence that the criminal laws be enforced to discourage their practices. But far from possessing "ancient roots," American laws targeting same-sex couples did not develop until the last third of the 20th century. The reported decisions concerning the prosecution of consensual, homosexual sodomy between adults for the years 1880–1995 are not always clear in the details, but a significant number involved conduct in a public place.

It was not until the 1970's that any State singled out same-sex relations for criminal prosecution, and only nine States have done so. Post-*Bowers* even some of these States did not adhere to the policy of suppressing homosexual conduct. Over the course of the last decades, States with same-sex prohibitions have moved toward abolishing them.

In summary, the historical grounds relied upon in *Bowers* are more complex than the majority opinion and the concurring opinion by Chief Justice Burger indicate. Their historical premises are not without doubt and, at the very least, are overstated.

It must be acknowledged, of course, that the Court in *Bowers* was making the broader point that for centuries there have been powerful voices to condemn homosexual conduct as immoral. The condemnation has been shaped by religious beliefs, conceptions of right and acceptable behavior, and respect for the traditional family. For many persons these are not trivial concerns but profound and deep convictions accepted as ethical and moral principles to which they aspire and which thus determine the course of their lives. These considerations do not answer the question before us, however. The issue is whether the majority may use the power of the State to enforce these views on the whole society through operation of the criminal law. "Our obligation is to define the liberty of all, not to mandate our own moral code." *Planned Parenthood of Southeastern Pa. v. Casey*, 505 U.S. 833 (1992).

* * * In all events we think that our laws and traditions in the past half century are of most relevance here. These references show an emerging awareness that liberty gives substantial protection to adult persons in deciding how to conduct their private lives in matters pertaining to sex. "[H]istory and tradition are the starting point but not in all cases the ending point of the substantive due process inquiry." *County of Sacramento v. Lewis*, 523 U.S. 833, 857 (1998) (Kennedy, J., concurring).

liberty/ privacy

This emerging recognition should have been apparent when *Bowers* was decided. In 1955 the American Law Institute promulgated the Model Penal Code and made clear that it did not recommend or provide for "criminal penalties for consensual sexual relations conducted in private." * * * In 1961 Illinois changed its laws to conform to the Model Penal Code. Other States soon followed. [By the time of the Court's decision in *Bowers*, only] 24 States and the District of Columbia had sodomy laws. Justice Powell pointed out that these prohibitions often were being ignored, however. Georgia, for instance, had not sought to enforce its law for decades. ([Justice Powell stated that:] "The history of nonenforcement suggests the moribund character today of laws criminalizing this type of private, consensual conduct.")

MPC

[Moreover, a] committee advising the British Parliament recommended in 1957 repeal of laws punishing homosexual conduct. *The Wolfenden Report: Report of the Committee on Homosexual Offenses and Prostitution* (1963). Parliament enacted the substance of those recommendations 10 years later.

Of even more importance, almost five years before *Bowers* was decided the European Court of Human Rights considered a case with parallels to *Bowers* and to today's case. An adult male resident in Northern Ireland alleged he was a practicing homosexual who desired to engage in consensual homosexual conduct. The laws of Northern Ireland forbade him that right. He alleged that he had been questioned, his home had been searched, and he feared criminal prosecution. The court held that the laws proscribing the conduct were invalid under the European Convention on Human Rights. *Dudgeon v. United Kingdom*, 45 Eur. Ct. H.R. (1981) & ¶ 52. Authoritative in all countries that are members of the Council of Europe (21 nations then, 45 nations now), the decision is at odds with the premise in *Bowers* that the claim put forward was insubstantial in our Western civilization.

Dudgeon

In our own constitutional system the deficiencies in *Bowers* became even more apparent in the years following its announcement. The 25 States with laws prohibiting the relevant conduct referenced in the *Bowers* decision are reduced now to 13, of which 4 enforce their laws only against homosexual conduct. In those States where sodomy is still

fewer states w/ these laws

[margin note: nonenforcement]

proscribed, whether for same-sex or heterosexual conduct, there is a pattern of nonenforcement with respect to consenting adults acting in private. The State of Texas admitted in 1994 that as of that date it had not prosecuted anyone under those circumstances. *State v. Morales*, 869 S.W.2d 941, 943.

Two principal cases decided after *Bowers* cast its holding into even more doubt. In *Planned Parenthood of Southeastern Pa. v. Casey*, 505 U.S. 833 (1992), the Court reaffirmed the substantive force of the liberty protected by the Due Process Clause. The *Casey* decision again confirmed that our laws and tradition afford constitutional protection to personal decisions relating to marriage, procreation, contraception, family relationships, child rearing, and education. In explaining the respect the Constitution demands for the autonomy of the person in making these choices, we stated as follows:

[margin note: PP v. Casey]

> These matters, involving the most intimate and personal choices a person may make in a lifetime, choices central to personal dignity and autonomy, are central to the liberty protected by the Fourteenth Amendment. At the heart of liberty is the right to define one's own concept of existence, of meaning, of the universe, and of the mystery of human life. Beliefs about these matters could not define the attributes of personhood were they formed under compulsion of the State.

Persons in a homosexual relationship may seek autonomy for these purposes, just as heterosexual persons do. The decision in *Bowers* would deny them this right.

[margin note: seems like an equality argument]

The second post-*Bowers* case of principal relevance is *Romer v. Evans*, 517 U.S. 620 (1996). There the Court struck down class-based legislation directed at homosexuals as a violation of the Equal Protection Clause. * * *

[margin note: Romer] *[margin note: EP]*

As an alternative argument in this case, counsel for the petitioners and some *amici* contend that *Romer* provides the basis for declaring the Texas statute invalid under the Equal Protection Clause. That is a tenable argument, but we conclude the instant case requires us to address whether *Bowers* itself has continuing validity. Were we to hold the statute invalid under the Equal Protection Clause some might question whether a prohibition would be valid if drawn differently, say, to prohibit the conduct both between same-sex and different-sex participants.

Equality of treatment and the due process right to demand respect for conduct protected by the substantive guarantee of liberty are linked in important respects, and a decision on the latter point advances both interests. If protected conduct is made criminal and the law which does so remains unexamined for its substantive validity, its stigma might remain even if it were not enforceable as drawn for equal protection reasons. When homosexual conduct is made criminal by the law of the State, that declaration in and of itself is an invitation to subject homosexual persons to discrimination both in the public and in the private spheres. The central holding of *Bowers* has been brought in question by this case, and it should be addressed. Its continuance as precedent demeans the lives of homosexual persons.

The stigma this criminal statute imposes, moreover, is not trivial. The offense, to be sure, is but a class C misdemeanor, a minor offense in the Texas legal system. Still, it remains a criminal offense with all that imports for the dignity of the persons charged. The petitioners will bear on their record the history of their criminal convictions. * * * We are advised that if Texas convicted an adult for private, consensual homosexual conduct under the statute here in question the convicted person would come within the registration laws of a least four States were he or she to be subject to their jurisdiction. This underscores the consequential nature of the punishment and the state-sponsored condemnation attendant to the criminal prohibition. Furthermore, the Texas criminal conviction carries with it the other collateral consequences always following a conviction, such as notations on job application forms, to mention but one example.

The foundations of *Bowers* have sustained serious erosion from our recent decisions in *Casey* and *Romer*. When our precedent has been thus weakened, criticism from other sources is of greater significance. In the United States criticism of *Bowers* has been substantial and continuing, disapproving of its reasoning in all respects, not just as to its historical assumptions. *See, e.g.,* C. Fried, *Order and Law: Arguing the Reagan Revolution—A Firsthand Account* 81–84 (1991); R. Posner, *Sex and Reason* 341–350 (1992). The courts of five different States have declined to follow it in interpreting provisions in their own state constitutions parallel to the Due Process Clause of the Fourteenth Amendment.

To the extent *Bowers* relied on values we share with a wider civilization, it should be noted that the reasoning and holding in *Bowers* have been rejected elsewhere. The European Court of Human Rights has followed not *Bowers* but its own decision in *Dudgeon v. United Kingdom*. Other nations, too, have taken action consistent with an affirmation of the protected right of homosexual adults to engage in intimate, consensual conduct. The right the petitioners seek in this case has been accepted as an integral part of human freedom in many other countries. There has been no showing that in this country the governmental interest in circumscribing personal choice is somehow more legitimate or urgent.

The doctrine of *stare decisis* is essential to the respect accorded to the judgments of the Court and to the stability of the law. It is not, however,

overruling

reliance - not here

an inexorable command. In *Casey* we noted that when a Court is asked to overrule a precedent recognizing a constitutional liberty interest, individual or societal reliance on the existence of that liberty cautions with particular strength against reversing course. The holding in *Bowers*, however, has not induced detrimental reliance comparable to some instances where recognized individual rights are involved. Indeed, there has been no individual or societal reliance on *Bowers* of the sort that could counsel against overturning its holding once there are compelling reasons to do so. *Bowers* itself causes uncertainty, for the precedents before and after its issuance contradict its central holding.

The rationale of *Bowers* does not withstand careful analysis. In his dissenting opinion in *Bowers*, Justice Stevens came to these conclusions:

immorality not suff.

> Our prior cases make two propositions abundantly clear. First, the fact that the governing majority in a State has traditionally viewed a particular practice as immoral is not a sufficient reason for upholding a law prohibiting the practice; neither history nor tradition could save a law prohibiting miscegenation from constitutional attack. Second, individual decisions by married persons, concerning the intimacies of their physical relationship, even when not intended to produce offspring, are a form of 'liberty' protected by the Due Process Clause of the Fourteenth Amendment. Moreover, this protection extends to intimate choices by unmarried as well as married persons.

privacy

Justice Stevens' analysis, in our view, should have been controlling in *Bowers* and should control here.

Bowers was not correct when it was decided, and it is not correct today. It ought not to remain binding precedent. *Bowers v. Hardwick* should be and now is overruled.

The present case does not involve minors. It does not involve persons who might be injured or coerced or who are situated in relationships where consent might not easily be refused. It does not involve public conduct or prostitution. It does not involve whether the government must give formal recognition to any relationship that homosexual persons seek to enter. The case does involve two adults who, with full and mutual consent from each other, engaged in sexual practices common to a homosexual lifestyle. The petitioners are entitled to respect for their private lives. The State cannot demean their existence or control their destiny by making their private sexual conduct a crime. Their right to liberty under the Due Process Clause gives them the full right to engage in their conduct without intervention of the government. "It is a promise of the Constitution that there is a realm of personal liberty which the government may not enter." *Casey*, 505 U.S. at 47. The Texas statute

liberty DP

furthers no legitimate state interest which can justify its intrusion into the personal and private life of the individual.

Had those who drew and ratified the Due Process Clauses of the Fifth Amendment or the Fourteenth Amendment known the components of liberty in its manifold possibilities, they might have been more specific. They did not presume to have this insight. They knew times can blind us to certain truths and later generations can see that laws once thought necessary and proper in fact serve only to oppress. As the Constitution endures, persons in every generation can invoke its principles in their own search for greater freedom.

JUSTICE O'CONNOR, concurring in the judgment.

The Court today overrules *Bowers.* I joined *Bowers,* and do not join the Court in overruling it. Nevertheless, I agree with the Court that Texas' statute banning same-sex sodomy is unconstitutional. Rather than relying on the substantive component of the Fourteenth Amendment's Due Process Clause, I base my conclusion on the Fourteenth Amendment's Equal Protection Clause. * * *

The statute at issue here makes sodomy a crime only if a person "engages in deviate sexual intercourse with another individual of the same sex." Sodomy between opposite-sex partners, however, is not a crime in Texas. That is, Texas treats the same conduct differently based solely on the participants. Those harmed by this law are people who have a same-sex sexual orientation and thus are more likely to engage in behavior prohibited by § 21.06.

The Texas statute makes homosexuals unequal in the eyes of the law by making particular conduct—and only that conduct—subject to criminal sanction. It appears that prosecutions under Texas' sodomy law are rare. This case shows, however, that prosecutions under § 21.06 *do* occur. And while the penalty imposed on petitioners in this case was relatively minor, the consequences of conviction are not. As the Court notes, petitioners' convictions, if upheld, would disqualify them from or restrict their ability to engage in a variety of professions, including medicine, athletic training, and interior design. Indeed, were petitioners to move to one of four States, their convictions would require them to register as sex offenders to local law enforcement.

And the effect of Texas' sodomy law is not just limited to the threat of prosecution or consequence of conviction. Texas' sodomy law brands all homosexuals as criminals, thereby making it more difficult for homosexuals to be treated in the same manner as everyone else. Indeed, Texas itself has previously acknowledged the collateral effects of the law, stipulating in a prior challenge to this action that the law "legally sanctions discrimination against [homosexuals] in a variety of ways unrelated to the criminal law," including in the areas of "employment, family issues, and housing." *State v. Morales*, 826 S.W.2d 201, 203 (Tex. App. 1992).

Texas attempts to justify its law, and the effects of the law, by arguing that the statute satisfies rational basis review because it furthers the legitimate governmental interest of the promotion of morality. In *Bowers*, we held that a state law criminalizing sodomy as applied to homosexual couples did not violate substantive due process. We rejected the argument that no rational basis existed to justify the law, pointing to the government's interest in promoting morality. The only question in front of the Court in *Bowers* was whether the substantive component of the Due Process Clause protected a right to engage in homosexual sodomy. *Bowers* did not hold that moral disapproval of a group is a rational basis under the Equal Protection Clause to criminalize homosexual sodomy when heterosexual sodomy is not punished.

This case raises a different issue than *Bowers*: whether, under the Equal Protection Clause, moral disapproval is a legitimate state interest to justify by itself a statute that bans homosexual sodomy, but not heterosexual sodomy. It is not. Moral disapproval of this group, like a bare desire to harm the group, is an interest that is insufficient to satisfy rational basis review under the Equal Protection Clause. *See, e.g.*, *Department of Agriculture v. Moreno*, 413 U.S. 528, 534 (1973); *Romer v. Evans*, 517 U.S. 620, 634–35 (1996). Indeed, we have never held that moral disapproval, without any other asserted state interest, is a sufficient rationale under the Equal Protection Clause to justify a law that discriminates among groups of persons.

Moral disapproval of a group cannot be a legitimate governmental interest under the Equal Protection Clause because legal classifications must not be "drawn for the purpose of disadvantaging the group burdened by the law." *Id*. at 633. Texas' invocation of moral disapproval as a legitimate state interest proves nothing more than Texas' desire to criminalize homosexual sodomy. But the Equal Protection Clause prevents a State from creating "a classification of persons undertaken for its own sake." *Id*. at 635. And because Texas so rarely enforces its sodomy law as applied to private, consensual acts, the law serves more as a statement of dislike and disapproval against homosexuals than as a tool to stop criminal behavior. The Texas sodomy law "raises the inevitable inference that the disadvantage imposed is born of animosity toward the class of persons affected." *Id*. at 634.

Texas argues, however, that the sodomy law does not discriminate against homosexual persons. Instead, the State maintains that the law discriminates only against homosexual conduct. While it is true that the law applies only to conduct, the conduct targeted by this law is conduct that is closely correlated with being homosexual. Under such circumstances, Texas' sodomy law is targeted at more than conduct. It is instead directed toward gay persons as a class. After all, there can hardly be more palpable discrimination against a class than making the conduct that defines the class criminal. *Id.* at 641 (Scalia, J. dissenting).

Indeed, Texas law confirms that the sodomy statute is directed toward homosexuals as a class. In Texas, calling a person a homosexual is slander *per se* because the word "homosexual" "imputes the commission of a crime." *Plumley v. Landmark Chevrolet, Inc.*, 122 F.3d 308, 310 (5th Cir. 1997) (applying Texas law). The State has admitted that because of the sodomy law, *being* homosexual carries the presumption of being a criminal. *See State v. Morales*, 826 S.W.2d, at 202–203 ("The statute brands lesbians and gay men as criminals and thereby legally sanctions discrimination against them in a variety of ways unrelated to the criminal law."). Texas' sodomy law therefore results in discrimination against homosexuals as a class in an array of areas outside the criminal law. In *Romer v. Evans*, we refused to sanction a law that singled out homosexuals "for disfavored legal status." The same is true here. The Equal Protection Clause " 'neither knows nor tolerates classes among citizens.' " *Id.*, at 623 (quoting *Plessy v. Ferguson*, 163 U.S. 537, 559 (1896) (Harlan, J. dissenting)).

A State can of course assign certain consequences to a violation of its criminal law. But the State cannot single out one identifiable class of citizens for punishment that does not apply to everyone else, with moral disapproval as the only asserted state interest for the law. The Texas sodomy statute subjects homosexuals to "a lifelong penalty and stigma. A legislative classification that threatens the creation of an underclass * * * cannot be reconciled with" the Equal Protection Clause. *Plyler v. Doe*, 457 U.S. 202, 239 (1982) (Powell, J., concurring).

Whether a sodomy law that is neutral both in effect and application would violate the substantive component of the Due Process Clause is an issue that need not be decided today. I am confident, however, that so long as the Equal Protection Clause requires a sodomy law to apply equally to the private consensual conduct of homosexuals and heterosexuals alike, such a law would not long stand in our democratic society. In the words of Justice Jackson:

> The framers of the Constitution knew, and we should not forget today, that there is no more effective practical guaranty against arbitrary and unreasonable government than to require that the principles of law which officials would impose upon a minority be imposed generally. Conversely, nothing opens the door to arbitrary action so effectively as to allow those officials to pick and choose only a few to whom they will apply legislation and thus to escape the political retribution that might be visited

upon them if larger numbers were affected. *Railway Express Agency, Inc. v. New York,* 336 U.S. 106, 112–113 (1949) (concurring opinion).

That this law as applied to private, consensual conduct is unconstitutional under the Equal Protection Clause does not mean that other laws distinguishing between heterosexuals and homosexuals would similarly fail under rational basis review. Texas cannot assert any legitimate state interest here, such as national security or preserving the traditional institution of marriage. Unlike the moral disapproval of same-sex relations—the asserted state interest in this case—other reasons exist to promote the institution of marriage beyond mere moral disapproval of an excluded group.

A law branding one class of persons as criminal solely based on the State's moral disapproval of that class and the conduct associated with that class runs contrary to the values of the Constitution and the Equal Protection Clause, under any standard of review. I therefore concur in the Court's judgment that Texas' sodomy law banning "deviate sexual intercourse" between consenting adults of the same sex, but not between consenting adults of different sexes, is unconstitutional.

JUSTICE SCALIA, with whom the CHIEF JUSTICE and JUSTICE THOMAS join, dissenting.

I begin with the Court's surprising readiness to reconsider a decision rendered a mere 17 years ago in *Bowers v. Hardwick.* * * *

Today's approach to *stare decisis* invites us to overrule an erroneously decided precedent (including an "intensely divisive" decision) if: (1) its foundations have been "eroded" by subsequent decisions; (2) it has been subject to "substantial and continuing" criticism; and (3) it has not induced "individual or societal reliance" that counsels against overturning. The problem is that *Roe* itself—which today's majority surely has no disposition to overrule—satisfies these conditions to at least the same degree as *Bowers.* * * *

"[T]here has been," the Court says, "no individual or societal reliance on *Bowers* of the sort that could counsel against overturning its holding. . . ." It seems to me that the "societal reliance" on the principles confirmed in *Bowers* and discarded today has been overwhelming. Countless judicial decisions and legislative enactments have relied on the ancient proposition that a governing majority's belief that certain sexual behavior is "immoral and unacceptable" constitutes a rational basis for regulation. We ourselves relied extensively on *Bowers* when we concluded, in *Barnes v. Glen Theatre, Inc.,* 501 U.S. 560, 569 (1991), that Indiana's public indecency statute furthered "a substantial government interest in protecting order and morality." State laws against bigamy, same-sex marriage, adult incest, prostitution, masturbation, adultery, fornication, bestiality, and obscenity are likewise sustainable only in light of *Bowers'* validation of laws based on moral choices. Every single one of these laws is called into question by today's decision; the Court makes no effort to cabin the scope of its decision to exclude them from its holding. The impossibility of distinguishing homosexuality from other traditional "morals" offenses is precisely why *Bowers* rejected the rational-basis challenge. * * *

What a massive disruption of the current social order, therefore, the overruling of *Bowers* entails. Not so the overruling of *Roe*, which would simply have restored the regime that existed for centuries before 1973, in which the permissibility of, and restrictions upon, abortion were determined legislatively State-by-State. *Casey*, however, chose to base its *stare decisis* determination on a different "sort" of reliance. "People," it said, "have organized intimate relationships and made choices that define their views of themselves and their places in society, in reliance on the availability of abortion in the event that contraception should fail." 505 U.S., at 856 This falsely assumes that the consequence of overruling *Roe* would have been to make abortion unlawful. It would not; it would merely have *permitted* the States to do so. Many States would unquestionably have declined to prohibit abortion, and others would not have prohibited it within six months (after which the most significant reliance interests would have expired). Even for persons in States other than these, the choice would not have been between abortion and childbirth, but between abortion nearby and abortion in a neighboring State.

To tell the truth, it does not surprise me, and should surprise no one, that the Court has chosen today to revise the standards of *stare decisis* set forth in *Casey*. It has thereby exposed *Casey's* extraordinary deference to precedent for the result-oriented expedient that it is.

Having decided that it need not adhere to *stare decisis*, the Court still must establish that *Bowers* was wrongly decided and that the Texas statute, as applied to petitioners, is unconstitutional. Texas Penal Code Ann. § 21.06(a) (2003) undoubtedly imposes constraints on liberty. So do laws prohibiting prostitution, recreational use of heroin, and, for that matter, working more than 60 hours per week in a bakery. But there is no right to "liberty" under the Due Process Clause, though today's opinion repeatedly makes that claim. The Fourteenth Amendment *expressly allows* States to deprive their citizens of "liberty," *so long as "due process of law" is provided.* Our opinions applying the doctrine known as "substantive due process" hold that the Due Process Clause prohibits States from infringing *fundamental* liberty interests, unless the infringement is narrowly tailored to serve a compelling state interest. We have held repeatedly, in cases the Court today does not overrule, that *only* fundamental rights qualify for this so-called "heightened scrutiny" protection—that is, rights which are "deeply rooted in this Nation's history and tradition." All other liberty interests may be abridged or abrogated pursuant to a validly enacted state law if that law is rationally related to a legitimate state interest.

Bowers held, first, that criminal prohibitions of homosexual sodomy are not subject to heightened scrutiny because they do not implicate a "fundamental right" under the Due Process Clause. Noting that "[p]roscriptions against that conduct have ancient roots," that "[s]odomy was a criminal offense at common law and was forbidden by the laws of the original 13 States when they ratified the Bill of Rights," and that many States had retained their bans on sodomy, *Bowers* concluded that a right to engage in homosexual sodomy was not "deeply rooted in this Nation's history and tradition."

The Court today does not overrule this holding. Not once does it describe homosexual sodomy as a "fundamental right" or a "fundamental liberty interest," nor does it subject the Texas statute to strict scrutiny. Instead, having failed to establish that the right to homosexual sodomy is "deeply rooted in this Nation's history and tradition," the Court concludes that the application of Texas's statute to petitioners' conduct fails the rational-basis test, and overrules *Bowers*' holding to the contrary. * * *

After discussing the history of antisodomy laws, the Court proclaims that, "it should be noted that there is no longstanding history in this country of laws directed at homosexual conduct as a distinct matter." This observation in no way casts into doubt the "definitive [historical] conclusion," on which *Bowers* relied: that our Nation has a longstanding history of laws prohibiting *sodomy in general*—regardless of whether it was performed by same-sex or opposite-sex couples. * * *

It is (as *Bowers* recognized) entirely irrelevant whether the laws in our long national tradition criminalizing homosexual sodomy were "directed at homosexual conduct as a distinct matter." Whether homosexual sodomy was prohibited by a law targeted at same-sex sexual relations or by a more general law prohibiting both homosexual and heterosexual sodomy, the only relevant point is that it *was* criminalized— which suffices to establish that homosexual sodomy is not a right "deeply rooted in our Nation's history and tradition." The Court today agrees that homosexual sodomy was criminalized and thus does not dispute the facts on which *Bowers actually* relied.

Next the Court makes the claim, again unsupported by any citations, that "[l]aws prohibiting sodomy do not seem to have been enforced against consenting adults acting in private." The key qualifier here is "acting in private"—since the Court admits that sodomy laws *were* enforced against consenting adults (although the Court contends that prosecutions were "infrequent"). I do not know what "acting in private" means; surely consensual sodomy, like heterosexual intercourse, is rarely performed on stage. If all the Court means by "acting in private" is "on private premises, with the doors closed and windows covered," it is entirely unsurprising that evidence of enforcement would be hard to come by. (Imagine the circumstances that would enable a search warrant to be obtained for a residence on the ground that there was probable cause to believe that consensual sodomy was then and there occurring.) Surely that lack of evidence would not sustain the proposition that consensual sodomy on private premises with the doors closed and windows covered was regarded as a "fundamental right," even though all other consensual sodomy was criminalized. There are 203 prosecutions for consensual, adult homosexual sodomy reported in the West Reporting system and official state reporters from the years 1880–1995. *See* W. Eskridge, *Gaylaw: Challenging the Apartheid of the Closet* 375 (1999) (hereinafter *Gaylaw*). There are also records of 20 sodomy prosecutions and 4 executions during the colonial period. J. Katz, *Gay/Lesbian Almanac* 29, 58, 663 (1983). *Bowers'* conclusion that homosexual sodomy is not a fundamental right "deeply rooted in this Nation's history and tradition" is utterly unassailable.

Realizing that fact, the Court instead says: "[W]e think that our laws and traditions in the past half century are of most relevance here. These references show *an emerging awareness* that liberty gives substantial protection to adult persons in deciding how to conduct their private lives *in matters pertaining to sex*." Apart from the fact that such an "emerging awareness" does not establish a "fundamental right," the statement is factually false. States continue to prosecute all sorts of crimes by adults "in matters pertaining to sex": prostitution, adult incest, adultery, obscenity, and child pornography. Sodomy laws, too, have been enforced "in the past half century," in which there have been 134 reported cases involving prosecutions for consensual, adult, homosexual sodomy. *Gaylaw* at 375. In relying, for evidence of an "emerging recognition," upon the American Law Institute's 1955 recommendation not to criminalize "'consensual sexual relations conducted in private,'" the Court ignores the fact that this recommendation was "a point of resistance in most of the states that considered adopting the Model Penal Code." *Gaylaw* at 159.

In any event, an "emerging awareness" is by definition not "deeply rooted in this Nation's history and tradition[s]," as we have said "fundamental right" status requires. Constitutional entitlements do not spring into existence because some States choose to lessen or eliminate criminal sanctions on certain behavior. Much less do they spring into existence, as the Court seems to believe, because *foreign nations* decriminalize conduct. The *Bowers* majority opinion *never* relied on "values we share with a wider civilization," but rather rejected the claimed right to sodomy on the ground that such a right was not "deeply rooted in *this Nation's* history and tradition." *Bowers'* rational-basis holding is likewise devoid of any reliance on the views of a "wider civilization." The Court's discussion of these foreign views (ignoring, of course, the many countries that have retained criminal prohibitions on sodomy) is therefore meaningless dicta. Dangerous dicta, however, since "this Court * * * should not impose foreign moods, fads, or fashions on Americans." *Foster v. Florida*, 537 U.S. 990 (2002) (Thomas, J., concurring in denial of certiorari).

I turn now to the ground on which the Court squarely rests its holding: the contention that there is no rational basis for the law here under attack. This proposition is so out of accord with our jurisprudence—indeed, with the jurisprudence of *any* society we know—that it requires little discussion.

The Texas statute undeniably seeks to further the belief of its citizens that certain forms of sexual behavior are "immoral and unacceptable"—the same interest furthered by criminal laws against fornication, bigamy, adultery, adult incest, bestiality, and obscenity. *Bowers* held that this *was* a legitimate state interest. The Court today reaches the opposite conclusion. * * * This effectively decrees the end of all morals legislation. If, as the Court asserts, the promotion of majoritarian sexual morality is not even a *legitimate* state interest, none of the above-mentioned laws can survive rational-basis review.

Finally, I turn to petitioners' equal-protection challenge, which no Member of the Court save Justice O'Connor embraces. * * *

No purpose to discriminate against men or women as a class can be gleaned from the Texas law, so rational-basis review applies. That review is readily satisfied here by the same rational basis that satisfied it in *Bowers*—society's belief that certain forms of sexual behavior are "immoral and unacceptable." This is the same justification that supports many other laws regulating sexual behavior that make a distinction based upon the identity of the partner—for example, laws against adultery, fornication, and adult incest, and laws refusing to recognize homosexual marriage. * * *

Even if the Texas law *does* deny equal protection to "homosexuals as a class," that denial *still* does not need to be justified by anything more than a rational basis, which our cases show is satisfied by the enforcement of traditional notions of sexual morality.

* * * [Justice O'Connor's] reasoning leaves on pretty shaky grounds state laws limiting marriage to opposite-sex couples. Justice O'Connor seeks to preserve them by the conclusory statement that "preserving the traditional institution of marriage" is a legitimate state interest. But "preserving the traditional institution of marriage" is just a kinder way of describing the State's *moral disapproval* of same-sex couples. Texas's

interest in § 21.06 could be recast in similarly euphemistic terms: "preserving the traditional sexual mores of our society." In the jurisprudence Justice O'Connor has seemingly created, judges can validate laws by characterizing them as "preserving the traditions of society" (good); or invalidate them by characterizing them as "expressing moral disapproval" (bad).

Today's opinion is the product of a Court, which is the product of a law-profession culture, that has largely signed on to the so-called homosexual agenda, by which I mean the agenda promoted by some homosexual activists directed at eliminating the moral opprobrium that has traditionally attached to homosexual conduct. I noted in an earlier opinion the fact that the American Association of Law Schools (to which any reputable law school *must* seek to belong) excludes from membership any school that refuses to ban from its job-interview facilities a law firm (no matter how small) that does not wish to hire as a prospective partner a person who openly engages in homosexual conduct. *See Romer, supra,* at 653, 116 S. Ct. 1620.

One of the most revealing statements in today's opinion is the Court's grim warning that the criminalization of homosexual conduct is "an invitation to subject homosexual persons to discrimination both in the public and in the private spheres." It is clear from this that the Court has taken sides in the culture war, departing from its role of assuring, as neutral observer, that the democratic rules of engagement are observed. Many Americans do not want persons who openly engage in homosexual conduct as partners in their business, as scoutmasters for their children, as teachers in their children's schools, or as boarders in their home. They view this as protecting themselves and their families from a lifestyle that they believe to be immoral and destructive. The Court views it as "discrimination" which it is the function of our judgments to deter. So imbued is the Court with the law profession's anti-anti-homosexual culture, that it is seemingly unaware that the attitudes of that culture are not obviously "mainstream"; that in most States what the Court calls "discrimination" against those who engage in homosexual acts is perfectly legal; that proposals to ban such "discrimination" under Title VII have repeatedly been rejected by Congress, see Employment Non-Discrimination Act of 1994, S. 2238, 103d Cong., 2d Sess. (1994); Civil Rights Amendments, H.R. 5452, 94th Cong., 1st Sess. (1975); that in some cases such "discrimination" is *mandated* by federal statute, see 10 U.S.C. § 654(b)(1) (mandating discharge from the Armed Forces of any service member who engages in or intends to engage in homosexual acts); and that in some cases such "discrimination" is a constitutional right, *see Boy Scouts of America v. Dale,* 530 U.S. 640, 120 S. Ct. 2446, 147 L. Ed. 2d 554 (2000).

Let me be clear that I have nothing against homosexuals, or any other group, promoting their agenda through normal democratic means. Social perceptions of sexual and other morality change over time, and every group has the right to persuade its fellow citizens that its view of such matters is the best. That homosexuals have achieved some success in that enterprise is attested to by the fact that Texas is one of the few remaining States that criminalize private, consensual homosexual acts. But persuading one's fellow citizens is one thing, and imposing one's views in absence of democratic majority will is something else. I would no more *require* a State to criminalize homosexual acts—or, for that matter, display *any* moral disapprobation of them—than I would *forbid* it to do so. What Texas has chosen to do is well within the range of traditional democratic action, and its hand should not be stayed through the invention of a brand-new "constitutional right" by a Court that is impatient of democratic change. It is indeed true that "later generations can see that laws once thought necessary and proper in fact serve only to oppress;" and when that happens, later generations can repeal those laws. But it is the premise of our system that those judgments are to be made by the people, and not imposed by a governing caste that knows best. * * *

At the end of its opinion—after having laid waste the foundations of our rational-basis jurisprudence—the Court says that the present case "does not involve whether the government must give formal recognition to any relationship that homosexual persons seek to enter." Do not believe it. * * * Today's opinion dismantles the structure of constitutional law that has permitted a distinction to be made between heterosexual and homosexual unions, insofar as formal recognition in marriage is concerned. If moral disapprobation of homosexual conduct is "no legitimate state interest" for purposes of proscribing that conduct, and if, as the Court coos (casting aside all pretense of neutrality), "[w]hen sexuality finds overt expression in intimate conduct with another person, the conduct can be but one element in a personal bond that is more enduring," what justification could there possibly be for denying the benefits of marriage to homosexual couples exercising "[t]he liberty protected by the Constitution"? Surely not the encouragement of procreation, since the sterile and the elderly are allowed to marry. This case "does not involve" the issue of homosexual marriage only if one entertains the belief that principle and logic have nothing to do with the decisions of this Court. Many will hope that, as the Court comfortably assures us, this is so.

The matters appropriate for this Court's resolution are only three: Texas's prohibition of sodomy neither infringes a "fundamental right" (which the Court does not dispute), nor is unsupported by a rational relation to what the Constitution considers a legitimate state interest, nor denies the equal protection of the laws. I dissent.

JUSTICE THOMAS, dissenting.

I join Justice Scalia's dissenting opinion. I write separately to note that the law before the Court today "is * * * uncommonly silly." *Griswold*, 381 U.S. at 527 (Stewart, J., dissenting). If I were a member of the Texas Legislature, I would vote to repeal it. Punishing someone for expressing his sexual preference through noncommercial consensual conduct with another adult does not appear to be a worthy way to expend valuable law enforcement resources.

Notwithstanding this, I recognize that as a member of this Court I am not empowered to help petitioners and others similarly situated. My duty, rather, is to "decide cases 'agreeably to the Constitution and laws of the United States.' " *Id.* at 530. And, just like Justice Stewart, I "can find [neither in the Bill of Rights nor any other part of the Constitution a] general right of privacy," or as the Court terms it today, the "liberty of the person both in its spatial and more transcendent dimensions."

———————

Professor Dale Carpenter has sought to determine exactly what happened on the night that Lawrence and Garner were arrested. The former was a fifty-five year old white man who worked as a laboratory technician at a Houston hospital. Garner was a thirty-one year old black man who had worked as a cook and a waiter.[22] The two men were introduced by Robert Eubanks, a former roommate of Lawrence who had previously dated Garner. "After Eubanks introduced them in the mid-1990s, Lawrence and Garner never became much more than acquaintances."[23]

On the evening of the arrest, the three men spent several hours in Lawrence's apartment. At some point, Eubanks became upset with the other two men and left the apartment to call the police to report falsely that there was a man with a gun in Lawrence's apartment.

The following version of what happened next is based largely on Professor Carpenter's interviews with the arresting officers:

> Eubanks waited for the deputies at the bottom of the stairs leading to Lawrence's apartment. He didn't have to wait long. Deputy Joseph Quinn was on patrol nearby and arrived within minutes of the call. Quinn was the first deputy on the scene, followed shortly thereafter by deputies William D. Lilly, Donald

———————

[22]   DALE CARPENTER, FLAGRANT CONDUCT: THE STORY OF *LAWRENCE V. TEXAS*: HOW A BEDROOM ARREST DECRIMINALIZED GAY AMERICANS 43–44 (2012).

[23]   *Id.* at 45.

Tipps, and Kenneth Landry. According to standard procedure, Quinn took the lead on the scene because he was the first deputy to arrive. The deputies, weapons drawn, began looking for the man who had called in the report and for the apartment containing the armed suspect. Eubanks saw the deputies and motioned toward them, saying, "Over here! Over here!" The deputies could tell that Eubanks was upset because he was visibly shaking and crying. Quinn asked, "Where is the man with the gun?" Eubanks pointed up the stairs toward Lawrence's apartment, saying, "He is in that apartment up there and he has a gun."

Quinn, Lilly, Tipps and Landry headed up the stairwell in what is known as a "tactical stack," one deputy right behind the other, with Quinn at the front of the stack. When they reached the apartment Quinn saw that the door was mostly closed, but not pulled completely shut. It was resting against the door jam, slightly ajar, as Eubanks had left it. Quinn could not see into the apartment. He turned the door knob and determined it was unlocked. Quinn knocked on the door, which pushed it open slightly and allowed him to get a peek inside. The light was on but no sound could be heard. Seeing no armed suspect or other person, Quinn pushed the door wide open into a standard living room. Still no one could be seen inside. Announcing "Sheriff's Department! Sheriff's Department!" in a loud voice, Quinn and the deputies quickly entered the apartment. * * *

Guns still drawn, Quinn and Lilly moved toward Lawrence's bedroom. Lilly took the lead in approaching the bedroom, with Quinn right behind him. With the aid of the lights from other rooms Lilly made out the moving shapes of two nude men in the bedroom. Startled at the sight, he jumped back. Quinn, who had not yet seen the naked men, guessed that Lilly must have seen the reported gunman. In a crouched position, Quinn came around low on Lilly's right side with his gun pointed ahead. The deputies entered the room, with their fingers on the triggers of their guns, ready to fire. Lilly turned the bedroom light on and the two deputies saw Lawrence and Garner standing there in the nude, shocked looks on their faces. Quinn shouted at the men, "Let me see your hands!" Lawrence and Garner complied, raising their hands.

Hearing this, Tipps and Landry immediately came to see what was happening. The deputies ordered the men to put on their underwear, handcuffed them, and led them into the living room where they sat the * * * men down to figure out what was going on. Lawrence, genuinely upset and bewildered at the deputies' intrusion into his home, asked, "What the fuck are y'all doing here? You don't have any right to be here." Quinn replied that they had every right to enter the apartment under the circumstances.

A deputy fetched Eubanks and brought him up to the apartment. The deputies quickly determined Eubanks had lied about an armed black man because he was jealous of the attention Lawrence and Garner were paying to each other. At one point Eubanks became so angry he stood up, shouted at Garner, and had to be forced to sit back down. When the deputies learned the report had been false, their frustration and anger grew. From their perspective, the prank could easily have resulted in a fatal shooting.

"Do you realize that not once but twice we called out?" Quinn told the men. "You were close to being shot." Lawrence remained angry, calling the deputies "gestapo" and "storm troopers" and "jack-booted thugs."

As the deputies looked around the apartment, they found stacks of gay pornography and explicit images hanging as art on the walls. "The apartment was loaded with pornography," says Quinn. "Everywhere you looked there was some kind." In particular, the deputies noticed "two pencil sketchings of James Dean, naked with an extremely oversized penis on him." The sketches "were hung up like regular pictures," says Quinn. Quinn and Tipps laughed about the Dean etchings, joking, "This is the kind of thing I would have in my house!"

Tipps asked Quinn, "Did you see anyone with a gun?" Quinn, angry about the false report, shocked at seeing two nude men in a bedroom together, offended by the gay pornographic images in the apartment, and frustrated with Lawrence for being uncooperative and name-calling the deputies, glanced at Lilly and made a split-second decision to charge them with homosexual conduct, which Quinn knew was a crime in Texas. "No," he replied. "But you ain't gonna believe this. Those guys were having sex." "Really?" asked Tipps, incredulous. "Yep," responded Quinn, "we caught 'em in the act." Quinn figured he would teach Lawrence and Garner a lesson not to disrespect law enforcement authorities. He also had nothing to lose in citing them. They were obviously not rich or important men. They would probably just pay their fines and move on. Lilly remained quiet, figuring this was Quinn's show, that he (Lilly) would not be filing the charges, and that Lawrence and Garner had probably been having sex at some point anyway. With the men caught naked and now sitting there in their underwear, Tipps and Landry had no reason to doubt Quinn's word.

Lawrence accused the deputies of "harassing" them because they were gay. Quinn responded: "I don't know you. And I don't know your sexual orientation. So how can I be harassing you because you're homosexual other than that I caught you in the act?" Lawrence and Garner understood that they were being charged with "homosexual conduct" which, for all they knew, included any gay sexual activity.

By now, several other deputies had arrived, including Sgt. Kenneth O. Adams. Quinn discussed with Adams what to do about Lawrence and Garner. Because Homosexual Conduct was a Class C misdemeanor (like a traffic ticket), punishable in Texas by fine but not prison, Quinn knew that the deputies had the option to issue no citation, or to issue a citation without actually taking the men to jail. But Quinn recommended that the men not only be charged with violating the Homosexual Conduct law but also be taken to prison. "I think the totality of the circumstances where I think there's a guy with a gun and I almost have to shoot, that it warranted me giving them a citation" and taking them to jail, Quinn says. "It was a lovers' triangle that could have got somebody hurt. I could have killed these guys over having sex. They were stupid enough to let it go that far."

Adams agreed with Quinn and it was decided to call the assistant D.A. on duty (in Harris County, Texas, there is a D.A. available twenty-four-hours a day, offering legal counsel to the deputies in the field) to get approval for the citation and arrest. The D.A. on duty was Ira Jones. Quinn told Jones that he had seen Lawrence and Garner having anal sex and then asked Jones if it mattered, under the Homosexual Conduct law, whether the conduct occurred in a home or in a public place. Jones looked at the statute and confirmed it did not matter where the offense occurred.

Eubanks was charged with filing a false report, a more serious Class B misdemeanor. He later served more than two weeks in prison for it. * * *

Enraged by the deputies' intrusion into his home, their behavior, and the charge, Lawrence engaged in his own form of civil disobedience. He refused to put on more than his underwear for his trip to jail. He demanded to see a lawyer. He also refused to walk out of his home and was physically carried by the deputies down the stairs, in his underwear, to a patrol car.

Lawrence's legs dragged on the ground as the deputies carried him down the stairs, resulting in minor cuts and bruises. Quinn says that Lawrence could have been cited for resisting transport while under arrest. But Quinn did not cite him because Lawrence "was doing all this to entice me to do something that could show I hated homosexuals."

As the deputies prepared to leave the scene, Quinn advised them to wash their hands. "You have to wonder," says Quinn, " 'What have we touched? Have we come into contact with any fluids?' " Quinn recalls that, "I made sure I doused myself with sanitizer" that he kept handy in his patrol car.

Lawrence, Garner, and Eubanks were led away to the station in separate patrol cars. Eubanks rode with Quinn. Once they arrived at the station, Lawrence continued to be angry and uncooperative throughout the standard intake procedures. By contrast, Garner was quiet and cooperative. Garner had had enough prior experience with the police to know better than to provoke them. Lawrence and Garner were given orange prisoners' jump-suits and spent the night in jail.

The next evening, September 18, Lawrence and Garner appeared before a hearing officer and pleaded "Not guilty." Lawrence requested a trial by jury; Garner, a trial by judge. They were released on personal recognizance, with bond set at $200, the maximum fine allowed for violating the state sodomy law.[24]

Professor Carpenter reports that, for many years, Lawrence and Garner's attorneys advised them not to talk about whether they actually had been having sex when the police stormed into the apartment. Carpenter notes, however, that there were reasons to believe that Lawrence and Garner may not have had sex on that evening. Although the lawyers claimed that they wanted to protect the men's privacy, Carpenter suggests that the attorneys instead may have wanted to prevent "the disclosure of information—the likelihood that sex had not occurred—that they believed would be unhelpful to the case and larger cause."[25]

In any event, the attorneys eventually relented when Lawrence, several years after the Supreme Court's ruling, insisted that he wanted to set the record straight so that "the police were not allowed to get away

---

[24]   Dale Carpenter, The Unknown Past of *Lawrence v. Texas*, 102 MICH. L. REV. 1464, 1508–13 (2004).

[25]   DALE CARPENTER, FLAGRANT CONDUCT: THE STORY OF *LAWRENCE V. TEXAS*: HOW A BEDROOM ARREST DECRIMINALIZED GAY AMERICANS 70 (2012).

with their tall tale of seeing uncontrollable gay sex."[26] In 2011, Lawrence told Professor Carpenter that Garner and he were watching the late-evening news on television in his living room when the police burst in demanding to know the gun's whereabouts. " 'There was no sex,' insisted Lawrence. * * * In fact, he said, Garner and he were not physically touching one another, and were seated as much as fifteen feet apart."[27] Although Lawrence acknowledged that he sometimes flirted with Garner, the two "had never before or since had sex. The police invented the story, he declared. 'They told bald-faced lies.' "[28]

NOTES

1. *Rational Basis vs. Heightened Scrutiny.* One of the intriguing, and perhaps frustrating, aspects of *Lawrence* is that much of the Court's lofty language about liberty, when coupled with its use of precedents (such as *Griswold* and *Roe*), makes the opinion sound like a fundamental rights case. The Court, however, did not explicitly apply heightened scrutiny. Instead, in assessing the state's interest in enacting the sodomy statute, it used terms traditionally associated with the rational basis test. *See Lawrence*, 539 U.S. at 578, 123 S.Ct. at 2484 ("The Texas statute furthers no legitimate state interest. . . ."). It may be that the Court believed that the state's interest in support of the law was so weak that it could not withstand constitutional scrutiny even under the most deferential form of judicial review, making it unnecessary for it to hold explicitly that a fundamental right was at issue in the case. Or, alternatively, it may be that the Court was unwilling to state explicitly what it seemed to believe implicitly given the rhetoric of the opinion, namely, that it would be skeptical of *any* purported justification for a law that so significantly compromised the liberty of individuals and the dignity of their relationships. Either way, Justice Scalia in his dissent was quick to deem *Lawrence* a non-fundamental rights case. *See id.* at 594, 123 S. Ct. at 2492 (Scalia, J., dissenting).

The lower courts have disagreed on the question of whether *Lawrence* calls for heightened scrutiny when assessing the constitutionality of government regulations relating to matters of sex and sexuality. Compare *Lofton v. Secretary of the Department of Children & Family Services*, 358 F.3d 804, 816 (11th Cir. 2004), *cert. denied*, 543 U.S. 1081, 125 S.Ct. 869, 160 L.Ed.2d 825 (2005) ("We are particularly hesitant to infer a new fundamental liberty interest from an opinion whose language and reasoning are inconsistent with standard fundamental-rights analysis.") *with Witt v. Department of the Air Force*, 527 F.3d 806, 816 (9th Cir. 2008) ("We cannot reconcile what the Supreme Court did in *Lawrence* with the minimal protections afforded by traditional rational basis review."). We will explore

---

[26]   *Id.*

[27]   *Id.* at 71.

[28]   *Id.*

the question of the level of scrutiny required by *Lawrence* throughout the remainder of this chapter.

2.   *Liberty vs. Privacy.* Although the *Lawrence* Court on a few occasions noted the "private" nature of the conduct in question, it relied very little on a right to privacy as such in its interpretation of the Fourteenth Amendment. In this way, *Lawrence* is a departure from the Court's opinions in *Griswold*, *Eisenstadt*, and *Roe* (as well as from Justice Blackmun's dissent in *Bowers*), all of which relied heavily on a right to privacy in their reasoning. Rather than emphasizing "privacy," the *Lawrence* Court elaborated on the meaning of "liberty," perhaps giving the opinion greater constitutional legitimacy since that is the word used in the Fourteenth Amendment. It remains to be seen whether *Lawrence* represents the beginning of a shift away from the right to privacy in the Court's substantive due process jurisprudence, or, alternatively, whether the Court in future cases goes back to using privacy as the normative foundation for that jurisprudence.

3.   *Due Process vs. Equal Protection.* Justice Kennedy reasoned that it was preferable to decide *Lawrence* on due process grounds because such a decision would address the very authority of the state to enact sodomy laws. To decide the case on equal protection grounds, Justice Kennedy noted, might simply lead the state to enact a broader sodomy law. *See Lawrence*, 539 U.S. at 574–75, 123 S.Ct. at 2481–81. Nonetheless, Justice Kennedy noted that equal treatment and due process are "linked in important respects, and a decision on the latter point advances both interests." *Id.* at 575, 123 S. Ct. at 2482. He then proceeded to elaborate at some length on the equality implications of sodomy laws by detailing how they were used to justify both private and public discrimination against lesbians and gay men. *See id.*

Justice O'Connor, who did not wish to overrule *Bowers*, concluded in her concurring opinion that the sodomy law represented a form of impermissible moral disapproval of lesbians and gay men as a group, and as such, violated the Equal Protection Clause. *See id.* at 582–83, 123 S. Ct. at 2486–87 (O'Connor, J., concurring). Her willingness to leave *Bowers* in place leads to the question of why moral disapproval may be a sufficient justification for a law to pass constitutional muster under the Due Process Clause but not under the Equal Protection Clause.

4.   *Sodomy   vs.   Same-Sex   Marriage   Part   I.* Justice Kennedy distinguished between sodomy laws and bans on same-sex marriage when he noted that the case did "not involve [the question of] whether the government must give formal recognition to any relationships that homosexual persons seek to enter." *Lawrence*, 539 U.S. at 578, 123 S.Ct. at 2484. Justice O'Connor went further by suggesting that while sodomy laws are unconstitutional, same-sex marriage bans are not because "unlike the moral disapproval of same-sex relations—the asserted state interest in this case—other reasons exist to promote the institution of marriage beyond mere moral disapproval of an excluded group." *Id.* at 585, 123 S. Ct. at 2488 (O'Connor, J., concurring). Justice Scalia, on the other hand, concluded that once sodomy statutes fall, so

must the marriage bans. *See id.* at 604–05, 123 S. Ct. at 2498 (Scalia, J., dissenting).

Five months after *Lawrence*, the Massachusetts Supreme Judicial Court struck down that state's same-sex marriage ban in *Goodridge v. Department of Public Health*, 798 N.E.2d 941, 440 Mass. 309 (2003) (discussed below, Chapter 5, Section III). While the *Goodridge* court based its holding on state rather than federal constitutional grounds, it seems to have been influenced by *Lawrence*. The Massachusetts court, for example, noted that the *Lawrence* "Court affirmed that the core concept of common human dignity protected by the Fourteenth Amendment to the United States Constitution precludes government intrusion into the deeply personal realms of consensual adult expressions of intimacy and one's choice of an intimate partner. The Court also reaffirmed the central role that decisions whether to marry or have children bear in shaping one's identity." *Id.* at 948, 440 Mass. at 313.

Other courts, however, concluded that there was no connection between the State's constitutional inability to criminalize same-sex sexual conduct and its ability to prohibit same-sex marriage. This is what the New York Court of Appeals held in *Hernandez v. Robles*, 855 N.E.2d 1, 7 N.Y.3d 338, 821 N.Y.S.2d 770 (2006). The *Hernandez* court explained that the "[p]laintiffs here do not, as the petitioners in *Lawrence* did, seek protection against state intrusion on intimate, private activity. They seek from the courts access to a state-conferred benefit that the Legislature has rationally limited to opposite-sex couples. We conclude that, by defining marriage as it has, the New York Legislature has not restricted the exercise of a fundamental right." 855 N.E.2d at 10, 7 N.Y.3d at 363, 821 N.Y.S.2d at 779. *See also Standhardt v. Superior Court*, 77 P.3d 451, 457, 206 Ariz. 276, 282 (2003) ("[w]e view [*Lawrence*] as acknowledging a homosexual person's right to define his or her own existence, and achieve the type of individual fulfillment that is a hallmark of a free society, by entering into a homosexual relationship. We do not view [*Lawrence*] as stating that such a right includes the choice to enter a state-sanctioned, same-sex marriage.").

5.   *Sodomy vs. Same-Sex Marriage Part II*. Although Justice Kennedy in *Lawrence* claimed that the case had nothing to do with marriage, he twice turned to its reasoning, a decade later, in writing the majority opinion striking down part of the federal Defense of Marriage Act. *See United States v. Windsor*, ___ U.S. ___, 133 S.Ct. 2675, 186 L.Ed.2d 808 (2013). First, Kennedy noted that "the States' interest in defining and regulating the marital relation . . . stems from the understanding that marriage is more than a routine classification for purposes of certain statutory benefits. Private, consensual sexual intimacy between two adult persons of the same sex may not be punished by the State, and it can form 'but one element in a personal bond that is more enduring.' "*Id.* at 2692 (citing *Lawrence*, 539 U.S. at 567). By recognizing same-sex relationships as marital, Kennedy explained, some states had chosen to "give further protection and dignity to that bond." *Id.*

Second, Kennedy turned to *Lawrence* to explain how the Defense of Marriage Act demeaned the marital relationships of same-sex couples: "DOMA undermines both the public and private significance of state-sanctioned same-sex marriages; for it tells those couples, and all the world, that their otherwise valid marriages are unworthy of federal recognition. This places same-sex couples in an unstable position of being in a second-tier marriage. The differentiation demeans the couple, whose moral and sexual choices the Constitution protects, see *Lawrence,* 539 U.S. 558, 123 S.Ct. 2472, and whose relationship the State has sought to dignify." *Windsor,* 133 S.Ct. at 2694. For a detailed exploration of *Windsor,* see *infra* Chapter 5, Section IV.

6. *Sodomy vs. Same-Sex Marriage Part III.* Two years after *Windsor,* Justice Kennedy also turned to *Lawrence* to explain why states were, in fact, constitutionally *required* to allow same-sex couples to marry. In writing for the Court in *Obergefell v. Hodges,* ___ U.S. ___, 135 S.Ct. 2584, 192 L.Ed.2d 609 (2015), Kennedy relied on *Lawrence* to defend four propositions. First, that "[l]ike choices concerning contraception, family relationships, procreation, and childrearing, all of which are protected by the Constitution, decisions concerning marriage are among the most intimate that an individual can make." *Id.* at 2599. Second, that "same-sex couples have the same right as opposite-sex couples to enjoy intimate association." *Id.* at 2600. Third, that the liberty protected by the Constitution goes beyond the right to "engage in intimate association without criminal liability. . . . Outlaw to outcast may be a step forward, but it does not achieve the full promise of liberty." *Id.* Finally, that the fact that same-sex couples were traditionally denied the right to marry did not preclude a finding that they, too, were entitled to benefit from the fundamental right to marry. As Kennedy explained, "if rights were defined by who exercised them in the past, then received practices could serve as their own continued justification and new groups could not invoke rights once denied." *Id.* at 2602. Does Kennedy's heavy reliance on *Lawrence* in *Obergefell* suggest that Justice Scalia was correct when he complained that the majority in *Lawrence* was not being entirely forthright when it claimed that the sodomy ruling had nothing to do with the question of which intimate relationships the state should recognize as marital? *See Lawrence,* 539 U.S. at 605 ("This case 'does not involve' the issue of homosexual marriage only if one entertains the belief that principle and logic have nothing to do with the decisions of this Court.") (Scalia, J., dissenting). For a detailed exploration of *Obergefell,* see *infra* Chapter 5, Section IV.

7. *Sex vs. No Sex.* What if Lawrence and Garner did not have sex, as Carpenter's account suggests, on the night of their arrest? Should that change our understanding of the decision? On the one hand, it would seem odd if the two men, on the night of their arrest, had not engaged in the sexual conduct that the Court concluded was constitutionally protected. On the other hand, notice that the decision recognized a constitutional right to engage in sexual conduct, but did not speak in direct terms about any specific

sexual activity. Instead, it spoke euphemistically about sex, referring, for example, to an enduring "bond" and to "intimate conduct." In addition, the opinion focused more on the respect and dignity the two men deserved than on the importance of the sexual activity itself. What does this then mean for Carpenter's revelation, if true, for the legacy of *Lawrence*?

8. *How Would You Vote and Rule?* Consider the activities listed in the first column and then decide whether you would, first, as a legislator vote to criminalize the activity; and, second, as a judge find that *Lawrence* prohibits a state from criminalizing the activity.

	If you were a legislator, would you vote in favor of a law that would criminalize this conduct?	If you were a judge, would *Lawrence* allow you to strike down a law that criminalizes this conduct?
S & M sexual relations in private whereby a 35 year old woman lightly whips a 33 year old man		
S & M sexual relations in private whereby a 35 year old woman badly beats a 33 year old man		
Consensual sexual relations in private between a 35 year old woman and her 33 year old brother		
Consensual sexual relations in private between a 35 year old woman and her 55 year old father		
Consensual sexual relations in private between a 35 year old woman and a 16 year old boy or girl		
A marriage of one man and three women		
A marriage of eight men to one another		
Sexual relations between an unmarried woman and an unmarried man (fornication)		

Sexual relations between a married woman and a man to whom she is not married (adultery)		
Sexual relations between a 35 year old woman and another woman she pays to have sex with her (prostitution)		

3. Post-*Lawrence* Scholarship

The Supreme Court's opinion in *Lawrence* has produced an extensive body of academic commentary. We provide excerpts from three of those articles below. In the first excerpt, Professor Katherine Franke criticizes *Lawrence* for "domesticating" sexual liberty, that is, for valuing sexual intimacy as an expression of liberty only when it takes place from within ongoing relationships. The second excerpt, by Professors Nelson Lund and John McGinnis, is a frontal attack on what they call the "ad hoc" due process approach of the *Lawrence* opinion. Finally, Professor Laurence Tribe, in the final excerpt, praises the Court for grounding its due process analysis in considerations of equal dignity, and for moving away from a focus on distinct activities (such as particular sexual acts) and toward a more holistic and comprehensive understanding of liberty.

THE DOMESTICATED LIBERTY OF *LAWRENCE V. TEXAS**
Katherine M. Franke

In this commentary I provide a critical reading of both the *Lawrence* opinion and the gay community's response to it. I argue that in *Lawrence* the Court relies on a narrow version of liberty that is both geographized and domesticated—not a robust conception of sexual freedom or liberty, as is commonly assumed. In this way, *Lawrence* both echoes and reinforces a pull toward domesticity in current gay and lesbian organizing. * * *

Justice Kennedy in *Lawrence* takes it as given that the sex between John Lawrence and Tyron Garner took place within the context of a relationship. With respect to the right to make decisions about intimate affiliations in private settings, Justice Kennedy notes that "[p]ersons in a homosexual relationship may seek autonomy for these purposes, just as heterosexual persons do," and that the statutes at issue in *Lawrence* and in *Bowers* "seek to control a personal relationship that, whether or not entitled to formal recognition in the law, is within the liberty of persons to choose without being punished as criminals." Note that the analogy here

*   Katherine M. Franke, *The Domesticated Liberty of* Lawrence v. Texas, 104 COLUM. L. REV. 1399, 1400, 1407–16 (2004).

is between persons in a homosexual *relationship* and heterosexual persons. Thus, the issue in *Lawrence*, as well as in *Bowers*, was not the right to engage in certain sexual conduct—that, says Kennedy, would be demeaning to John Lawrence and Tyron Garner. *They* would be disgraced just as a *married couple* would be if the claim were made that "marriage is simply about the right to have sexual intercourse." Kennedy writes that "[sexual conduct] can be but one element in a personal bond that is more enduring." More enduring than what? Than sex?

In two paragraphs, Justice Kennedy does a thorough job of domesticating John Lawrence and Tyron Garner—Lawrence an older white man, Garner a younger black man, who for all we know from the opinion, might have just been tricking with each other. Did they even know each other's name at the point police entered Lawrence's apartment? Did they plan on seeing each other again? None of these facts is in the record, none of the briefing in the case indicated that they were in a relationship. Nevertheless, the Court took it as given that Lawrence and Garner were in a relationship, and the fact of that relationship does important normative work in the opinion. Remember, sex is but one element in a personal bond that is more enduring.

Just as the Court's earlier *Bowers* decision and the military's "don't ask, don't tell" policy overdetermined gay men and lesbians in sexual terms, we now celebrate a victory that at its heart underdetermines, if not writes out entirely, their sexuality. Previously, when courts considered the legal status of gay men, they approached the specter of homosexual sex with a horror ordinarily reserved for incest cases. Now gay men are portrayed as domesticated creatures, settling down into marital-like relationships in which they can both cultivate and nurture desires for exclusivity, fidelity, and longevity in place of other more explicitly erotic desires. "The instant case involves liberty of the person both in its spatial and more transcendent dimensions," writes Justice Kennedy. We come to learn later in the opinion that by "spatial" he means private, and by "transcendent" he means to refer to relationship-based intimacy. The price of the victory in *Lawrence* has been to trade sexuality for domesticity—a high price indeed, and a difficult spot from which to build a politics of sexuality. * * *

[D]ecriminalization merely disables a form of public regulation of private adult activity. Indeed, it neither sanctions nor suggests any alternative form of legitimization. So too, it does not render viable any particular kind of sexual politics or political legibility. Without more, *Lawrence*-like decriminalization merely signals a public tolerance of the behavior, so long as it takes place in private and between two consenting adults in a relationship. * * *

There is no denying that rights in general, and liberty in particular, are something we cannot not want. * * * But rights, particularly in the form articulated in *Lawrence*, cannot exhaust our political projects. *Lawrence* recognizes, in a manner far more robust than *Romer v. Evans*, that homosexuals are rights-bearing subjects. But the political agenda leveraged by that recognition does not exceed honor of the domesticated private. The most likely project to be launched from this conception of subjectivity is, of course, marriage. And, of course, that's exactly what *Lawrence* has unleashed. Less than six months after the Supreme Court issued the *Lawrence* decision, the Massachusetts Supreme Judicial Court found that Massachusetts's refusal to license same-sex marriage was unconstitutional, and in so finding it relied very heavily upon *Lawrence*. For a short period thereafter, gay and lesbian couples overwhelmed public officials in a handful of cities demanding marriage licenses. The relevant officials in San Francisco, New Paltz, and a couple of other jurisdictions accommodated those demands and married thousands of gay and lesbian couples. As such, the subjects of gay and lesbian political organizing at this moment have become same-sex *couples*, not persons who seek nonnormative kinship formations or individuals who engage in nonnormative sex.

But it is wrong to understand the fight for gay marriage as a fight for sexual freedom or, for that matter, relationship-based freedom. Marriage is not a freedom. Rather, it is a *power* understood in Hohfeldian terms, and as a *power* it is the less interesting *pouvoir*, not *puissance*. The states have created a civil status called marriage, just as the states have created voting criteria and rights to inheritance. One either is or is not the kind of person to whom the state has given the power to enter into a civil marriage, to exercise the vote, or to inherit property. One has the power, not the freedom, to marry, to vote, and to inherit property. * * * The state creates rules and conventions that govern these sorts of powers, and the denial of the ability to participate does not trammel upon a fundamental freedom, understood in traditional liberal terms. To the extent that same-sex couples are denied the ability to marry, that denial best surfaces in law as a problem of equality, of indefensible differential treatment, but not as a matter of freedom. * * *

I fear that *Lawrence* and the gay rights organizing that has taken place in and around it have created a path dependency that privileges privatized and domesticated rights and legal liabilities, while rendering less viable projects that advance nonnormative notions of kinship, intimacy, and sexuality. * * *

Lawrence is a slam-dunk victory for a politics that is exclusively devoted to creating safe zones for homo- and hetero-sex/intimacy, while at the same time rendering all other zones more dangerous for nonnormative sex. It can be used to float political projects that render

certain normative heterosexual couples as its primary reference points
and ethical paradigms. *Lawrence* and the ethics from which it evolved do
little to open up new forms of public and private sexual intelligibility that
are not always already domestinormative. The landscape post-*Lawrence*
is not one that makes formal legal distinctions between heterosexual and
homosexual practices, but rather one that likely renders different legal
treatment to those who express their sexuality in domesticated ways and
those who don't—regardless of orientation. The world post-*Lawrence*
remains invested in forms of social membership and, indeed, citizenship
that are structurally identified with domesticated heterosexual marriage
and intimacy. *Lawrence* offers us no tools to investigate "kinds of
intimacy [and sex] that bear no necessary relation to domestic space, to
kinship, to the couple form, to property, or to the nation."[84] In this regard,
the opinion's implications are at once modest and quite broad in scope.
The legal program that is most easily suggested by *Lawrence* is one
undertaken by adult gay couples who seek recognition for their
relationships and whose sexuality is not merely backgrounded, but
closeted behind the closed doors of the bedroom. This is a project devoted
to celebrating our *relationships*; it is not a project of sexual rights or the
politics of sexuality. Indeed, against this framing of the "gay agenda," the
heterosexual reproductive rights cases start looking pretty darn radical.
In this sense, overreliance on *Lawrence* risks domesticating rights, sex,
and politics, and charting us down a path of domestinormative sexual
citizenship. The political subjects it predetermines are husbands and
wives, and the legal projects it maps out do not extend beyond gay
marriage. * * *

Lawrence announces that the criminalization of same-sex sodomy is
unconstitutional because it interferes with gay people's right to enter into
serious domestic relationships, but that should not be taken to define the
political dimension of sexuality or sexual citizenship. Sex gets figured, if
at all, in *Lawrence* as instrumental to the formation of intimate
relationships—it seems not to have a social or legal status in its own
right. As a result, sexual rights qua sexual are exiled from the legal
struggle on behalf of gay men and lesbians.

LAWRENCE V. TEXAS AND JUDICIAL HUBRIS*

Nelson Lund & John O. McGinnis

Lawrence is a paragon of the most anticonstitutional branch of
constitutional law: substantive due process. The decision also reflects a
breakdown of the Court's most recent attempt to put doctrinal restraints

---

84   Lauren Berlant & Michael Warner, *Sex in Public*, 24 CRITICAL INQUIRY 547, 558
(1998).

*   Nelson Lund & John O. McGinnis, Lawrence v. Texas *and Judicial Hubris*, 102 MICH.
L. REV. 1555, 1557, 1578–80, 1584–85, 1606–07 (2004).

on that intoxicating doctrine. It is a commonplace observation—often repeated by members of the Court itself—that substantive due process makes judges into unelected and unremovable superlegislators. History has recorded several efforts to tame the doctrine in ways designed to give it a more law-like nature, and thereby to protect the properly judicial function of the Court from its all-too-human members. In *Lawrence*, the latest effort fell apart.

The *Lawrence* opinion is a tissue of sophistries embroidered with a bit of sophomoric philosophizing. It is a serious matter when the Supreme Court descends to the level of analysis displayed in this opinion, especially in a high-visibility case that all but promises future adventurism unconstrained by anything but the will of the judicial majority. This performance deserves to be condemned rather than celebrated, even by those—like us—who have no sympathy for the statute that the Court struck down. Nor does *Lawrence*, which displays a dismissive contempt for both the Constitution and the work of prior Courts, deserve to be preserved by the doctrine of stare decisis. * * *

As an initial matter, *Lawrence* does not bother even to say what standard of review it is purporting to apply. Since *Carolene Products*, the most important threshold question in substantive due process cases has been whether they involve a fundamental right. If such a right is found, the Court demands a strong justification for infringing it, and gives little or no deference to legislative judgments; if no fundamental right has been infringed, rational basis review applies, and the legislature will receive almost unquestioning deference. *Lawrence* refuses to make express use of these categories, leaving its standard of review indeterminate.

Even more significantly, the Court neither analyzes the interests of the government, as heightened scrutiny would require, nor makes any effort to imagine what legitimate purpose the statute might serve, as rational basis review would require. Nor, as we shall see, does the Court supply any alternative rational analysis, legal or otherwise. Inflated and empty pronouncements about more transcendent dimensions and defining one's own concept of meaning do not constitute rational analysis. And without such analysis, we have not been told more than what the Court wants and that it has the power to do what it wants. * * *

* * * [T]he Court could have tried to articulate a logically coherent argument based on existing case law, for *Bowers* is difficult or impossible to reconcile with the *Griswold-Roe* line of cases. But that is not the basis on which *Lawrence* overrules *Bowers*. The Court comes closest to making a legal argument when it contends that the deeply rooted tradition of proscribing sodomy, on which *Bowers* had relied, did not support the holding in that case because sodomy laws traditionally applied to heterosexual conduct as well as homosexual conduct: "[T]here is no

longstanding history in this country of laws directed at homosexual conduct *as a distinct matter."* By the *Lawrence* Court's logic, the traditional proscription against prostitution must be quite compatible with a fundamental right to engage in homosexual prostitution, or heterosexual prostitution for that matter, since the law has generally not singled out either of them "as a distinct matter." That is absurd.

Let us assume, furthermore, that *Lawrence* is right to claim that *Bowers* overstated what the Court calls its "historical premises" about anti-sodomy laws. Even if this were true, it would be no more than a red herring. The *Lawrence* Court's perfectly plausible claim that the states have not aggressively and consistently punished homosexual conduct does not advance one whit the argument that a *right* to homosexual sex specifically, or nonprocreative sex in general, is deeply rooted in the Nation's history and tradition. The absence of consistent condemnation does not imply the existence of consistent protection. If it did, there would be deeply rooted traditional rights to incest, prostitution, bestiality, cocaine, gambling, child labor, animal cruelty, and thousands of other practices that have been tolerated at some times but not others. * * *

Nowhere in the *Lawrence* opinion does the Court so much as entertain the possibility that state legislatures could have any valid reason for proscribing sodomy in general or homosexual sodomy in particular. Furthermore, the Court comes very close to implying that one obvious basis for such proscriptions—a desire to discourage behavior considered immoral by the majority—is inherently illegitimate. Even if we leave aside other possible rationales for the statute, such as public health and promoting the institution of marriage, how is the desire to discourage putatively immoral behavior really different in any way marked out by the Constitution from the paternalistic desire to discourage other forms of putatively dangerous or self-destructive behavior? When the government outlaws conduct that it regards as risky or unhealthy—such as the recreational use of drugs, or working long hours in a bakery, or driving a motorcycle without a helmet—it is making a *moral* decision that assigns a higher value to health and physical safety than to the spiritual insights that some people have said they get from LSD, or the moral satisfaction that some people get from following a strict work ethic, or the mystical exhilaration of flirting with danger on the open road. Unless the Court were to distinguish without any constitutional justification between the different moral judgments reflected in different forms of paternalistic legislation, it is hard to see how any regulatory statute could survive unless it is demonstrably necessary to prevent immediate injuries to people other than those who want to engage in the conduct.

We certainly do not believe that the *Lawrence* Court consciously decided to embrace any such radically libertarian interpretation of the

Due Process Clauses. Nor do we assume that the apparent sympathy for the more limited Playboy Philosophy actually reflects a conscious adoption of Hugh Hefner's views by all the Justices who joined the majority opinion. In fact, we think that the most salient characteristic of *Lawrence* is the impossibility of determining what it means, other than that five Justices have decided to forbid laws proscribing sodomy. Whatever new rights the Court may find or refuse to find among "the components of liberty in its manifold possibilities," *Lawrence* will stand primarily for the proposition that due process jurisprudence has transcended the bounds of rational discourse. * * *

[T]he ad hoc due process approach that has culminated in *Lawrence* is the more likely alternative to genuine common law reasoning. Judicial behavior becomes indistinguishable from naked political judgments: judges reach their decisions by deciding what they think is just and socially beneficial, what will please the elites who shape their reputations, and what they guess the nation will tolerate.

This openly discretionary mode of judging has long term costs—costs that the Justices can impose on future generations with relative impunity. If constitutional debates about contentious issues of the day become simply politics by other means, the Constitution will have failed in one of its primary purposes—to create a framework by which disputes are authoritatively and predictably settled without simply replicating the strong moral and political disagreements that lead to the need for such rules in the first place. When the Court refuses to resolve such disputes by resorting to settled legal rules, and instead injects its members' personal ideological preferences, it sharply reduces the value of this settlement function. Other politicians, moreover, and occasionally even the people themselves, will come to recognize that the Court is engaging in ordinary politics while exempting itself from the mechanisms of political accountability. Once this extraordinary leverage is widely recognized, it is likely that Justices will be nominated and confirmed on increasingly narrow ideological grounds, which eventually may threaten a general dissolution of the Court's constitutional function.

The Court's increasingly casual imposition of elite—and even foreign—views about the appropriate content of constitutional rights may also have the cost of alienating the people from their Constitution. If the Supreme Court doesn't take the Constitution seriously, why should anybody else? And if the Constitution is not actually our unifying law, why should the people treat the constitutional order with more than benign neglect? One important feature of the American tradition is the bond of affection that citizens have for their founding document, in some measure because it is theirs. Imposing elitist views in general, and citing international or foreign judicial decisions as justification for doing so, exacerbates this danger. Flaunting a cosmopolitan sensibility may be quite chic, but this high style comes with a price. The emphatically American nature of our Constitution has been a source of affection and pride that have contributed to our social stability.

LAWRENCE V. TEXAS: THE "FUNDAMENTAL RIGHT" THAT DARE NOT SPEAK ITS NAME[*]

Laurence H. Tribe

There is a certain conventional understanding, largely unexamined and too often uncritically accepted, of what it means for the state to deprive someone of "liberty" without "due process of law" in the substantive sense of that phrase. According to this understanding, courts more or less passively identify a set of personal activities in which individuals may engage free of government regulation. This list derives from American constitutional text and tradition, fixed, if not at the nation's founding, then, at the very latest, at the time of the post-Civil War constitutional upheaval that left its textual mark principally in the Fourteenth Amendment. To name the activities on that list is to know what substantive areas are marked off as presumptively beyond the reach of governmental power, both state and federal. And, according to that understanding, if one is to broaden the vistas of freedom beyond the list, one must turn from the properly conservative and suitably backward-looking domain of substantive due process to the domain of a norm focused more on the present and the future—the more aspirational domain of equal protection. Indeed, proponents of this theory emphasize, it is in the name of equal protection that judges since the late nineteenth century have taken the crucially progressive steps toward first racial and then gender equality, steps that broke sharply with history and tradition precisely because the Equal Protection Clause was understood from the beginning to call for the rejection of certain received ways of doing things.

But this sketch tells at best a half-truth. Trying to make sense of the conclusions judges have reached by attending carefully to the rulings they have actually rendered in the name of substantive due process reveals a very different narrative. It is a narrative in which due process and equal protection, far from having separate missions and entailing different inquiries, are profoundly interlocked in a legal double helix. It is a single, unfolding tale of equal liberty and increasingly universal dignity. This tale centers on a quest for genuine self-government of groups small and large, from the most intimate to the most impersonal. It reflects the fact that within any group, the project of self-government is necessarily a process that extends over time (and, at times, even across generations) as the group's experiences, and typically its membership, evolve. * * *

---

[*]   Laurence H. Tribe, Lawrence v. Texas: *The "Fundamental Right" That Dare Not Speak Its Name,* 117 HARV. L. REV. 1893, 1897–99, 1902–06, 1934–37 (2004).

Lawrence, more than any other decision in the Supreme Court's history, both presupposed and advanced an explicitly equality-based and relationally situated theory of substantive liberty. The "liberty" of which the Court spoke was as much about equal dignity and respect as it was about freedom of action—more so, in fact. And the Court left no doubt that it was protecting the equal liberty and dignity not of atomistic individuals torn from their social contexts, but of people as they relate to, and interact with, one another. Although this concept of liberty far transcends the enumerated "specifics" of the Bill of Rights, *Lawrence*, when viewed through the lens of the Constitution as a framework for individual and group self-government, has much to teach about what those "specific" provisions represent and protect and about how they operate. To be sure, the broad and bold strokes with which the Court painted in *Lawrence* left a good bit of this picture to the reader's imagination, but this mode of exposition hardly seems inapt for a decision laying down a landmark that opens vistas rather than enclosing them.

In particular, the Court gave short shrift to the notion that it was under some obligation to confine its implementation of substantive due process to the largely mechanical exercise of isolating "fundamental rights" as though they were a historically given set of data points on a two-dimensional grid, with one dimension representing time and the other representing a carefully defined and circumscribed sequence of protected primary activities (speaking, praying, raising children, using contraceptives in the privacy of the marital bedroom, and the like). By implicitly rejecting the notion that its task was simply to name the specific activities textually or historically treated as protected, the Court lifted the discussion to a different and potentially more instructive plane. It treated the substantive due process precedents invoked by one side or the other not as a record of the inclusion of various activities in—and the exclusion of other activities from—a fixed list defined by tradition, but as reflections of a deeper pattern involving the allocation of decisionmaking roles, not always fully understood at the time each precedent was added to the array. The Court, it seems, understood that the unfolding logic of this pattern is constructed as much as it is discovered. Constructing that logic is in some ways akin to deriving a regression line from a scatter diagram, keeping in mind, of course, that the choice of one method of extrapolation over another is, at least in part, a subjective one. As if to demonstrate the inevitable dependence of the diagram upon the diagrammer, the *Lawrence* Court, beyond overruling *Bowers v. Hardwick*, took the *Bowers* Court to task for the very way it had formulated the question posed for decision. In doing so, *Lawrence* significantly altered the historical trajectory of substantive due process and thus of liberty. * * *

The *Lawrence* Court's blend of equal protection and substantive due process themes was neither unprecedented nor accidental: "Equality of treatment and the due process *right to demand respect* for conduct protected by the substantive guarantee of liberty are linked in important respects," Justice Kennedy wrote for the Court, "and a decision on the latter point advances both interests." How might we unpack this rather cryptic statement to view more vividly what was driving the majority in *Lawrence*? It seems to me that two crucial and interrelated concepts are bound up in Justice Kennedy's thesis:

First. The vice of the Texas prohibition of same-sex sodomy was not principally, as some have argued, the cruelty of punishing some people for the only mode of sexual gratification available to them. Nor was it principally the lack of "fair notice" and the danger of "arbitrary and unpredictable enforcement" in dealing with a law that either had become moribund or never was seriously enforced and that, in either case, was "able to persist only because it [was] enforced so rarely." Rather, the prohibition's principal vice was its stigmatization of intimate personal relationships between people of the same sex: the Court concluded that these relationships deserve to be protected in the same way that nonprocreative intimate relationships between opposite-sex adult couples—whether marital or nonmarital, lifelong or ephemeral—are protected. Focusing on the centrality of the relationship in which intimate conduct occurs rather than on the nature of the intimate conduct itself, the Court emphasized its view that "[t]o say that the issue in *Bowers* was simply the right to engage in certain sexual conduct demeans the claim the individual put forward, just as it would demean a married couple were it to be said marriage is simply about the right to have sexual intercourse." Justice Scalia, dissenting, evidently thought he had scored a major point by parsing the majority opinion and concluding, triumphantly: "Not once does it describe homosexual sodomy as a 'fundamental right' or a 'fundamental liberty interest.'" Of course not! How can one put it more clearly? Try this: "It's not the sodomy. It's the relationship!"

And what kind of relationship was it? Apparently, it was quite fleeting, lasting only one night and lacking any semblance of permanence or exclusivity. The Court nonetheless spoke in relational terms: "when sexuality finds overt expression in intimate conduct with another person," Justice Kennedy wrote, "the conduct can be but one element in a personal bond that is more enduring." The Court clearly proceeded from a strong constitutional presumption against allowing government, including its judicial branch, "to define the meaning of [any given personal] relationship or to set its boundaries absent injury to a person or abuse of an institution the law protects." And in unflinchingly applying that presumption despite the seemingly casual character of the encounter involved, the Court evidently recognized an obligation to extend constitutional protection to some brief interactions that might not ripen into meaningful connections over time—even to some that might be chosen precisely for their fleeting and superficial character and their lack of emotional involvement. Had the Court done otherwise, it would have ceded to the state the power to determine what count as meaningful relationships and to decide when and how individuals might enter into such relationships. Doing so would have drained those relationships of their unique significance as expressions of self-government.

Second. The stigmatization of same-sex relationships is concretized and aggravated by the law's denunciation as criminal of virtually the only ways of consummating sexual intimacy possible in such relationships. For although "sodomy" is by no means a "gays only" act, the term has come to carry a strong cultural association with gay male, and to a much lesser extent lesbian, sexual activities—an association that the *Bowers* Court's conflation of sodomy with gay sex both underscored and helped to perpetuate. Many heterosexuals, even those who regularly engage in one or another form of opposite-sex sodomy, no doubt associate "sodomy" with acts that strike them as perverse and alien. Even worse, in their eyes such acts might uncomfortably resemble their own intimacies, simultaneously caricaturing or demeaning these intimacies and inspiring fear of suppressed homosexual proclivities and desires. It follows that even if the Texas law, like the Georgia law at issue in *Bowers*, had been applied to opposite-sex as well as same-sex sodomy and had been enforced equally against both (or not enforced at all), it would still have been "anti-gay" in terms of both its practical impact and its cultural significance. * * *

The *Lawrence* Court's explicit recognition of the "due process right to demand respect for conduct protected by the substantive guarantee of liberty" and of the way in which that right is linked to "[e]quality of treatment" was an obviously important doctrinal innovation. But the Court developed its substantive due process jurisprudence in a way that connected *Lawrence* with the long line of decisions that described the protected liberties at higher levels of generality than any "protected activities" catalog could plausibly accommodate, and typically did so in temporally extended, relationship-focused terms rather than in strictly solitary, atomistic terms. Thus *Meyer* and *Pierce*, the two sturdiest pillars of the substantive due process temple—both survivors of the largely discredited Lochner era—described what they were protecting from the standardizing hand of the state in language that spoke of the family as a center of value-formation and value-transmission that was not to be commandeered by state power. Their language bespoke the authority of parents to make basic choices directing the upbringing of their children. Those judicial decisions did not describe what they were protecting merely as the personal activities of sending one's child to a religious school (*Pierce v. Society of Sisters*) or * * * of hiring a teacher to educate one's child in the German language (*Meyer*).

In much the same way, *Lawrence* makes clear, if only by conspicuous omission, that any such exercise in enumeration is a fool's errand that misconceives the structure of liberty and of the constitutional doctrines that provide its contents. Indeed, *Lawrence* is likely to endure in large part because it highlights the futility of describing liberty in so one-dimensional a manner. The Court left no doubt about *its* understanding of the fundamental claim to "liberty" being advanced in *Lawrence* and in *Bowers* alike: at stake in both cases were claims that a state may not undertake to "control a personal relationship" in the way that Georgia had in *Bowers* and Texas had in *Lawrence*.

Lawrence's focus on the role of self-regulating relationships in American liberty suggests that the "Trivial Pursuit" version of the due process "name that liberty" game arguably validated by *Glucksberg* has finally given way to a focus on the underlying pattern of self-government (rather than of state micromanagement) defined by the rights enumerated or implicit in the Constitution or recognized by the landmark decisions construing it. It's always possible to persuade oneself that data points lying along a great arc are in fact just so many isolated points—to see the dots but not the path that passes through them. *Bowers* might not seem aberrant to someone of that sort—someone who collects and categorizes the continuous stream of rulings about human freedom as though cataloging so many discrete data points rather than searching for and constructing a regression line that satisfyingly explains the relationship of the points to one another and to liberty as a whole. Count them, if you will: one data point for the right to become a parent (*Skinner*); several more points marking the rights of parents to direct the upbringing of their children (*Meyer, Pierce, Troxel*); a pair of points for the right to keep one's children safe from the distractions and temptations of a too-diverse world, coupled with a right either to inculcate one's religion (*Yoder*) or to transmit one's views of morality (*Boy Scouts*); yet another point for the rights of married couples to have sexual intercourse without risking pregnancy and parenthood (*Griswold*); another pair for the rights of individuals (married or unmarried) not to risk unwanted pregnancy or sexually transmitted disease as penalties inflicted (without trial!) for breaking the state's codes of sexual conduct (*Eisenstadt, Carey*); two points more to mark the rights of pregnant women to end their pregnancies (*Roe, Casey*) or, if they wish, to continue their pregnancies to term (*Casey*); and three last points celebrating the rights of straight couples to marry without restrictions based on race (*Loving*), poverty (*Zablocki*), or imprisonment (*Turner*). So many points, so many disconnected dots!

Lawrence eschewed such isolated point-plotting. The whole of substantive due process, *Lawrence* teaches us, is larger than, and conceptually different from, the sum of its parts. *Lawrence* contrasts with Justice Harlan's justly celebrated "rational continuum" that purported to connect the Bill of Rights with a discourse defined by our society's specific historical experience and that led Justice Harlan, dissenting in *Poe v. Ullman*, to put intimate marital relations on a pedestal and to relegate fornication and homosexuality to a disconnected netherworld. Justice Kennedy's opinion for the Court in *Lawrence* instead suggests the globally unifying theme of shielding from state control *value-forming* and *value-transmitting* relationships, procreative and nonprocreative alike, drawing from *Griswold* a right to decouple sex from conception in an intimate marital relationship and from *Eisenstadt* a right to an intimate sexual relationship distinct from marriage. *Lawrence* also suggests this theme when it looks beyond the American historical experience for insight both contemporary and cross-cultural into the range of relationships through which individuals might seek to transcend the boundaries of the self.

NOTE

For a sampling of additional scholarly commentary on *Lawrence*, see Carlos A. Ball, *The Positive in the Fundamental Right to Marry: Same-Sex Marriage and the Aftermath of* Lawrence v. Texas, 88 MINN. L. REV. 1184 (2004); Thomas P. Crocker, *From Privacy to Liberty: The Fourth Amendment After* Lawrence, 57 UCLA L. Rev. 1 (2009); Mary Anne Case, *Of "This" and "That" in* Lawrence v. Texas, 2003 SUP. CT. REV. 75; William N. Eskridge, Jr., Lawrence's *Jurisprudence of Tolerance: Judicial Review to Lower the Stakes of Identity Politics*, 88 MINN. L. REV. 1021 (2004); Chai R. Feldblum, *The Right to Define One's Own Concept of Existence: What* Lawrence *Can Mean for Intersex and Transgender People*, 7 GEO. J. GENDER & L. 115 (2006); Suzanne B. Goldberg, *Morals-Based Justifications for Lawmaking: Before and After* Lawrence v. Texas, 88 MINN. L. REV. 1233 (2004); Nan D. Hunter, *Living with* Lawrence, 88 MINN. L. REV. 1103 (2004); Pamela S. Karlan, *Loving* Lawrence, 102 MICH. L. REV. 1447 (2004); Sonya Katyal, *Sexuality and Sovereignty: The Global Limits and Possibilities of* Lawrence, 14 WM. & MARY BILL RTS. J. 1429 (2006); Miranda Oshige McGowan, *From Outlaws to Ingroup:* Romer, Lawrence *and the Inevitable Normativity of Group Recognition*, 88 MINN. L. REV. 1312 (2004); Jane S. Schacter, Lawrence v. Texas *and the Fourteenth Amendment's Democratic Aspirations*, 13 TEMP. POL. & CIV. RTS. L. REV. 733 (2004); Cass R. Sunstein, *What Did* Lawrence *Hold? Of Autonomy, Desuetude, Sexuality, and Marriage*, 2003 SUP. CT. REV. 276; Francisco Valdes, *Anomalies, Warts and All: Four Score of Liberty, Privacy and Equality*, 65 OHIO ST. L.J. 1341 (2004).

B. POLYGAMY

STATE V. HOLM

Utah Supreme Court, 2006
137 P.3d 726

DURRANT, JUSTICE:

In this case, we are asked to determine whether Rodney Hans Holm was appropriately convicted for bigamy and unlawful sexual conduct with a minor. Specifically, we are asked to determine whether Holm's behavior violated Utah's bigamy statute and whether that statute is constitutional. * * * We conclude that Holm's behavior falls squarely within the realm of behavior criminalized by our State's bigamy statute and that the protections enshrined in the federal constitution, as well as our state constitution, guaranteeing the free exercise of religion and conscience, due process, and freedom of association do not shield Holm's polygamous practices from state prosecution. * * * Accordingly, we affirm the defendant's conviction under Utah Code section 76–7–101 for bigamy and under Utah Code section 76–5–401.2 for unlawful sexual conduct with a minor.

Holm was legally married to Suzie Stubbs in 1986. Subsequent to this marriage, Holm, a member of the Fundamentalist Church of Jesus Christ of Latter-day Saints (the "FLDS Church"),[1] participated in a religious marriage ceremony with Wendy Holm. Then, when Rodney Holm was thirty-two, he participated in another religious marriage ceremony with then-sixteen-year-old Ruth Stubbs, Suzie Stubbs's sister. After the ceremony, Ruth moved into Holm's house, where her sister Suzie Stubbs, Wendy Holm, and their children also resided. By the time Ruth turned eighteen, she had conceived two children with Holm, the second of which was born approximately three months after her eighteenth birthday.

Holm was subsequently arrested in Utah and charged with three counts of unlawful sexual conduct with a sixteen- or seventeen-year-old, in violation of Utah Code section 76–5–401.2 (2003), and one count of bigamy, in violation of Utah Code section 76–7–101 (2003)[3]—all third degree felonies. * * *

---

[1] The FLDS Church is one of a number of small religious communities in Utah that continue to interpret the early doctrine of the Church of Jesus Christ of Latter-day Saints (the "LDS Church" or "Mormon Church") as supporting the practice of "plural marriage," or polygamy. Though often referred to as "fundamentalist Mormons," these groups have no connection to the LDS Church, which renounced the practice of polygamy in 1890.

[3] Utah Code section 76–7–101 provides, in pertinent part, as follows: "A person is guilty of bigamy when, knowing he has a husband or wife or knowing the other person has a husband or wife, the person purports to marry another person or cohabits with another person."

* * * Stubbs * * * testified that she had moved in with Holm; that Holm had provided, at least in part, for Stubbs and their children; and that she and Holm had "regularly" engaged in sexual intercourse at the house in Hildale, Utah. Evidence was also introduced at trial that Holm and Stubbs "regarded each other as husband and wife." * * *

The jury returned a guilty verdict on each of the charges, indicating on a special verdict form that Holm was guilty of bigamy both because he "purported to marry Ruth Stubbs" and because he had "cohabited with Ruth Stubbs." The trial court sentenced Holm to up to five years in state prison on each conviction, to be served concurrently, and imposed a $3,000 fine. Both the prison time and the fine were suspended in exchange for three years on probation, one year in the county jail with work release, and two hundred hours of community service.

[The court rejected Holm's argument that the bigamy statute did not apply to him because he had entered into only one legal marriage, explaining that "the bigamy statute is not confined to legal marriage and is, in fact, broad enough to cover the type of religious solemnization engaged in by Holm and Stubbs."]

Holm [also] argues that the State of Utah is foreclosed from criminalizing polygamous behavior because the freedom to engage in such behavior is a fundamental liberty interest that can be infringed only for compelling reasons and that the State has failed to identify a sufficiently compelling justification for its criminalization of polygamy. * * * In arguing that his behavior is constitutionally protected as a fundamental liberty interest, Holm relies primarily on the United States Supreme Court's decision in *Lawrence v. Texas,* 539 U.S. 558, 123 S.Ct. 2472, 156 L.Ed.2d 508 (2003). * * *

Despite its use of seemingly sweeping language, the holding in *Lawrence* is actually quite narrow. Specifically, the Court takes pains to limit the opinion's reach to decriminalizing private and intimate acts engaged in by consenting adult gays and lesbians. In fact, the Court went out of its way to exclude from protection conduct that causes "injury to a person or abuse of an institution the law protects." *Id.* at 567, 123 S.Ct. 2472. Further, after announcing its holding, the Court noted the following: "The present case does not involve minors. It does not involve persons who might be injured or coerced or who are situated in relationships where consent might not easily be refused. It does not involve public conduct. * * * " *Id.* at 578, 123 S.Ct. 2472.

In marked contrast to the situation presented to the Court in *Lawrence,* this case implicates the public institution of marriage, an institution the law protects, and also involves a minor. In other words, this case presents the exact conduct identified by the Supreme Court in *Lawrence* as outside the scope of its holding.

* * * [T]he behavior at issue in this case is not confined to personal decisions made about sexual activity, but rather raises important questions about the State's ability to regulate marital relationships and prevent the formation and propagation of marital forms that the citizens of the State deem harmful. Sexual intercourse * * * is the most intimate behavior in which the citizenry engages. [*Lawrence*] spoke to this discreet, personal activity. Marriage, on the other hand, includes both public and private conduct. Within the privacy of the home, marriage means essentially whatever the married individuals wish it to mean. Nonetheless, marriage extends beyond the confines of the home to our society.

The very "concept of marriage possesses undisputed social value." Utah's own constitution enshrines a commitment to prevent polygamous behavior. That commitment has undergirded this State's establishment of "a vast and convoluted network of . . . laws . . . based exclusively upon the practice of monogamy as opposed to plural marriage." *Potter v. Murray City,* 760 F.2d 1065, 1070 (10th Cir. 1985). Our State's commitment to monogamous unions is a recognition that decisions made by individuals as to how to structure even the most personal of relationships are capable of dramatically affecting public life.

The dissent states quite categorically that the State of Utah has no interest in the commencement of an intimate personal relationship so long as the participants do not present their relationship as being state-sanctioned. On the contrary, the formation of relationships that are marital in nature is of great interest to this State, no matter what the participants in or the observers of that relationship venture to name the union. We agree with the dissent's statement that any two people may make private pledges to each other and that these relationships do not receive legal recognition unless a legal adjudication of marriage is sought. That does not, however, prevent the legislature from having a substantial interest in criminalizing such behavior when there is an existing marriage.

As the dissent recognizes, a marriage license significantly alters the bond between two people because the State becomes a third party to the marital contract. It is precisely that third-party contractual relationship that gives the State a substantial interest in prohibiting unlicensed marriages when there is an existing marriage. Without this contractual relationship, the State would be unable to enforce important marital rights and obligations. In situations where there is no existing marriage, the Legislature has developed a mechanism for legally determining that a marriage did in fact exist, even where the couple did not seek legal recognition of that marriage, so that the State may enforce marital obligations such as spousal support or prevent welfare abuse. *See* Utah

Code Ann. § 30–1–4.5 (Supp.2005).[12] There is no such mechanism for protecting the State's interest in situations where there is an existing marriage because, under any interpretation of the bigamy statute, a party cannot seek a legal adjudication of a second marriage. Thus, the State has a substantial interest in criminalizing such an unlicensed second marriage.

Moreover, marital relationships serve as the building blocks of our society. The State must be able to assert some level of control over those relationships to ensure the smooth operation of laws and further the proliferation of social unions our society deems beneficial while discouraging those deemed harmful. The people of this State have declared monogamy a beneficial marital form and have also declared polygamous relationships harmful. As the Tenth Circuit stated in *Potter*, Utah "is justified, by a compelling interest, in upholding and enforcing its ban on plural marriage to protect the monogamous marriage relationship." 760 F.2d at 1070; *see also Green*, 2004 UT 76, ¶ 72, 99 P.3d 820 (Durrant, J., concurring) ("[Utah] has a compelling interest in prohibiting conduct, such as the practice of polygamy, which threatens [monogamous marriage].").

Further, this case features another critical distinction from *Lawrence*; namely, the involvement of a minor. Stubbs was sixteen years old at the time of her betrothal, and evidence adduced at trial indicated that she and Holm regularly engaged in sexual activity. Further, it is not unreasonable to conclude that this case involves behavior that warrants inquiry into the possible existence of injury and the validity of consent.

Given the above, we conclude that *Lawrence* does not prevent our Legislature from prohibiting polygamous behavior. The distinction between private, intimate sexual conduct between consenting adults and the public nature of polygamists' attempts to extralegally redefine the acceptable parameters of a fundamental social institution like marriage is plain. The contrast between the present case and *Lawrence* is even more dramatic when the minority status of Stubbs is considered. Given the critical differences between the two cases, and the fact that the United States Supreme Court has not extended its jurisprudence to such a

---

[12]   *See, e.g., Clark v. Clark*, 2001 UT 44, 27 P.3d 538 (seeking legal adjudication of marriage and a divorce to receive division of the marital assets); *Whyte v. Blair*, 885 P.2d 791 (Utah 1994) (seeking legal adjudication of marriage to receive automobile insurance benefits); *Kelley v. Kelley*, 2003 UT App 317, 79 P.3d 428 (extending alimony rights to include time of unsolemnized marriage); *Walters v. Walters*, 812 P.2d 64 (Utah Ct.App.1991) (seeking legal adjudication of marriage to receive property distribution and portion of retirement benefits); Floor Debate, 47th Leg., Gen. Sess. (Utah Feb. 17, 1987) (Senate recording tape no. 75) (statement of Sen. Stephen Rees) (stating that the purpose of the unsolemnized marriage statute is to "close some loopholes in welfare abuse"); *id.* (statement of Norman Angus, Director of State Social Services Administration) ("[A] woman with children . . . may . . . be living with an individual who could and in all probability does provide a substantial amount of support to that household and still we cannot consider any of the income or the resources of that individual available and therefore the woman can in fact qualify for a full public assistance grant. . . .").

degree as to protect the formation of polygamous marital arrangements, we conclude that the criminalization of the behavior engaged in by Holm does not run afoul of the personal liberty interests protected by the Fourteenth Amendment. Having so concluded, we now address Holm's contention that our State's bigamy statute violates equal protection guarantees.

[The court also rejected the defendant's contention that "his conviction for bigamy is unconstitutional because the bigamy statute unfairly discriminates against individuals who are religiously compelled to practice polygamy." In addition, the court rejected his contention that the statute violated his right of association and was unconstitutionally vague. Finally, the court upheld the conviction for unlawful sexual conduct with a minor.]

[A concurring opinion by JUSTICE NEHRING is omitted]

DURHAM, CHIEF JUSTICE, concurring in part and dissenting in part:

I join the majority in upholding Holm's conviction for unlawful sexual conduct with a minor. As to the remainder of its analysis, I respectfully dissent. As interpreted by the majority, Utah Code section 76–7–101 defines "marriage" as acts undertaken for religious purposes that do not meet any other legal standard for marriage—acts that are unlicensed, unsolemnized by any civil authority, acts that are indeed entirely outside the civil law, and unrecognized as marriage for any other purpose by the state—and criminalizes those acts as "bigamy." I believe that in doing so the statute oversteps lines protecting the free exercise of religion and the privacy of intimate, personal relationships between consenting adults. The majority upholds Holm's criminal bigamy conviction based solely on his participation in a private religious ceremony because the form of that ceremony—though not its intent—resembled what we think of as a wedding, a ritual that serves to solemnize lawful marriages and in which the parties formally undertake the legal rights, obligations, and duties that belong to that state-approved institution. In resting its conclusion on that basis, the majority, in my view, ignores the legislature's intent that the concept of marriage in Utah law be confined to a legally recognized union. I also believe that the majority's reasoning fails to distinguish between conduct that has public import of a sort that the state may legitimately regulate and conduct of the most private nature.

* * * Because I conclude that Holm's bigamy conviction violates the Utah Constitution's religious freedom guarantees, my dissenting vote is not based on the majority's analysis of Holm's federal constitutional claims. I do, however, wish to register my disagreement with the majority's treatment of Holm's claim that his conviction violates his Fourteenth Amendment right under the Due Process Clause to individual liberty, as recognized by the United States Supreme Court in *Lawrence v.*

Texas, 539 U.S. 558, 123 S.Ct. 2472, 156 L.Ed.2d 508 (2003). As the majority acknowledges, the Court in *Lawrence* stated the principle that "absent injury to a person or abuse of an institution the law protects," adults are free to choose the nature of their relationships "in the confines of their homes and their own private lives." *Id.* at 567, 123 S.Ct. 2472. The majority concludes that the private consensual behavior of two individuals who did not claim legal recognition of their relationship somehow constitutes an abuse of the institution of marriage, thus rendering *Lawrence* inapplicable. On that basis, the majority summarily rejects Holm's due process claim as beyond the scope of *Lawrence*'s holding.[34] I disagree with this analysis.

* * * I do not believe that the conduct at issue threatens the institution of marriage, and I therefore cannot agree that it constitutes an "abuse" of that institution. The majority fails to offer a persuasive justification for its view to the contrary. It asserts that "the behavior at issue in this case" implicates "the state's ability to regulate marital relationships." According to the majority, this regulation includes the state's ability to impose a legal marriage on an individual against his or her will in order to enforce spousal support obligations or prevent welfare abuse. In regard to spousal support, I am unpersuaded that the potential interests of consenting adults who voluntarily enter legally unrecognized relationships despite the financial risks they might face in the future justify the imposition of criminal penalties on the parties to those relationships. Under the majority's rationale, the state would be justified in imposing criminal penalties on unmarried persons who enter same-sex relationships simply because the state, under the applicable constitutional and statutory provisions, is unable to hold them legally married. In regard to welfare abuse, I find it difficult to understand how those in polygamous relationships that are ineligible to receive legal sanction are committing welfare abuse when they seek benefits available to unmarried persons.

The majority also offers the view that "[t]he state must be able to . . . further the proliferation of social unions our society deems beneficial while discouraging those deemed harmful." The Supreme Court in *Lawrence,* however, rejected the very notion that a state can criminalize behavior merely because the majority of its citizens prefers a different form of personal relationship. Striking down Texas's criminal sodomy statute as unconstitutional, the Court in *Lawrence* recognized that the Fourteenth Amendment's individual liberty guarantee "gives substantial protection to adult persons in deciding how to conduct their private lives

---

[34] The majority could have limited its rejection of Holm's liberty claim to the fact that Holm's behavior involved a minor. That fact alone, in my view, justifies the conclusion that Holm's bigamy conviction does not violate his right to individual liberty under the Due Process Clause of the Fourteenth Amendment to the United States Constitution.

in matters pertaining to sex." 539 U.S. at 572, 123 S.Ct. 2472. As described in *Lawrence,* this protection encompasses not merely the consensual act of sex itself but the "autonomy of the person" in making choices "relating to . . . family relationships." *Id.* at 574, 123 S.Ct. 2472. The sodomy statute was thus held unconstitutional because it sought "to control a personal relationship that, whether or not entitled to formal recognition in the law, is within the liberty of persons to choose without being punished as criminals." *Id.* at 567, 123 S.Ct. 2472.

I agree with the majority that marriage, when understood as a legal union, qualifies as "an institution the law protects." However, the Court's statement in *Lawrence* that a state may interfere when such an institution is "abuse[d]," together with its holding that the sodomy statute was unconstitutional, leads me to infer that, in the Court's view, sexual acts between consenting adults and the private personal relationships within which these acts occur, do not "abuse" the institution of marriage simply because they take place outside its confines. *See id.* at 585, 123 S.Ct. 2472 (O'Connor, J., concurring in the judgment) (indicating that Texas's criminal sodomy law did not implicate the state's interest in "preserving the traditional institution of marriage" but expressed "mere moral disapproval of an excluded group"). In the wake of *Lawrence,* the Virginia Supreme Court has come to the same conclusion, striking down its state law criminalizing fornication. *Martin v. Ziherl,* 269 Va. 35, 607 S.E.2d 367, 371 (2005). In my opinion, these holdings correctly recognize that individuals in today's society may make varied choices regarding the organization of their family and personal relationships without fearing criminal punishment.

The majority does not adequately explain how the institution of marriage is abused or state support for monogamy threatened simply by an individual's choice to participate in a religious ritual with more than one person outside the confines of legal marriage. Rather than offering such an explanation, the majority merely proclaims that "the public nature of polygamists' attempts to extralegally redefine the acceptable parameters of a fundamental social institution like marriage is plain." It is far from plain to me.

I am concerned that the majority's reasoning may give the impression that the state is free to criminalize any and all forms of personal relationships that occur outside the legal union of marriage. While under *Lawrence* laws criminalizing isolated acts of sodomy are void, the majority seems to suggest that the relationships within which these acts occur may still receive criminal sanction. Following such logic, nonmarital cohabitation might also be considered to fall outside the scope of federal constitutional protection. Indeed, the act of living alone and unmarried could as easily be viewed as threatening social norms.

In my view, any such conclusions are foreclosed under *Lawrence.* Essentially, the Court's decision in *Lawrence* simply reformulates the longstanding principle that, in order to "secure individual liberty, ... certain kinds of highly personal relationships" must be given "a substantial measure of sanctuary from unjustified interference by the State." *Roberts v. U.S. Jaycees,* 468 U.S. 609, 618, 104 S.Ct. 3244, 82 L.Ed.2d 462 (1984); *see also Laurence H. Tribe, Lawrence v. Texas: The "Fundamental Right" That Dare Not Speak Its Name,* 117 Harv. L.Rev. 1893, 1922 (2004) ("[T]he claim *Lawrence* accepted . . . is that intimate relations may not be micromanaged or overtaken by the state."). Whether referred to as a right of "intimate" or "intrinsic" association, as in *Roberts,* 468 U.S. at 618, 104 S.Ct. 3244, a right to "privacy," as in *Griswold v. Connecticut,* 381 U.S. 479, 485, 85 S.Ct. 1678, 14 L.Ed.2d 510 (1965), and *Eisenstadt v. Baird,* 405 U.S. 438, 453, 92 S.Ct. 1029, 31 L.Ed.2d 349 (1972), a right to make "choices concerning family living arrangements," as in *Moore v. City of East Cleveland,* 431 U.S. 494, 499, 97 S.Ct. 1932, 52 L.Ed.2d 531 (1977) (plurality), or a right to choose the nature of one's personal relationships, as in *Lawrence,* 539 U.S. at 574, 123 S.Ct. 2472, this individual liberty guarantee essentially draws a line around an individual's home and family and prevents governmental interference with what happens inside, as long as it does not involve injury or coercion or some other form of harm to individuals or to society.

————————

In the ruling that follows, a federal district court struck down the section of Utah's bigamy statute that prohibits married individuals from cohabiting with others who are not their spouses. The U.S. Court of Appeals for the Tenth Circuit eventually vacated the lower court's ruling on jurisdictional grounds—the appellate court concluded the case was moot because the county attorney had stated that he would not prosecute individuals under the statute unless they had committed another crime (such as domestic violence or child abuse)—without reaching the merits.[29] Although the district court's ruling is no longer good law, we include an excerpt from it because it provides an extensive discussion of historical and constitutional issues associated with the regulation of polygamous relationships.

———————————————————

[29]   Brown v. Buhman, 822 F.3d 1151 (10th Cir.2016).

BROWN V. BUHMAN

Federal Court for the District of Utah, 2013
947 F. Supp.2d 1170, *vacated by* 822 F.3d 1151 (10th Cir.)

WADDOUPS, J.

Before the court are the parties' cross motions for summary judgment relating to Plaintiffs' facial and as-applied constitutional challenges to Utah's bigamy statute, Utah Code Ann. § 76–7–101 (2013). * * * Plaintiffs named Utah Governor Gary R. Herbert, Utah Attorney General Mark Shurtleff, and Utah County Attorney Jeffrey R. Buhman in a lawsuit challenging the Statute as unconstitutional filed on July 13, 2011. * * *

FACTUAL BACKGROUND

[T]he court * * * finds the following undisputed material facts * * * to be relevant to its resolution of the pending motions:

1. The Statute covers not only polygamy but "cohabitation"—a term that encompasses a broad category of private relations in which a married person "purports to marry another person or cohabits with another person."

2. The practice of married individuals cohabiting with other people can include adulterous relations.

3. The Browns are members of a religious group that believes polygamy is a core religious practice.

4. The Brown family does not have multiple marriage licenses.

5. There is only one recorded marriage license in the Brown family—that of Kody and Meri Brown.

6. Prosecutions under the Statute have been rare and published cases in the last three decades only involve religious polygynists.

7. Utah government officials are aware of thousands of polygamist families in the state and regularly interact with such families as part of the "Safety Net" program and other governmental programs.

8. "The Sister Wives" is a reality show that explores the daily issues and realities of a plural family.

9. The content of "The Sister Wives" program includes the defense of plural families and discussion of the Browns' religious beliefs in polygamy.

10. Utah government officials were aware that the Brown family was a plural or polygamist family for years before the first episode of "The Sister Wives" aired on TLC Network.

11. The investigation of the Browns occurred only [after] the first episode of "The Sister Wives" aired.

12. State officials have acknowledged that "The Sister Wives" program triggered their investigation.

13. State officials publicly denounced the Browns as committing crimes every night on television.

14. One official connected to the investigation publicly stated the program made prosecution "easier."

15. The prosecutors stated that the Brown family moving to Nevada would not prevent them from prosecuting the family.

16. The Defendant admitted, through counsel in the December 16, 2011 hearing, that prosecutors gave interviews discussing the Brown family, their alleged crime of polygamy, and the public investigation.

17. The Defendant has found no evidence of any crime by the Browns though he maintains future prosecutors can charge them as a matter of discretion and policy. Shortly before [Plaintiffs filed their Motion for Summary Judgment], the Defendant filed a Motion to Dismiss for Mootness and confirmed that the long investigation of the Brown[s] has been closed shortly before the planned summary judgment motions. He seeks to avoid review of the Statute based on the assurance that, while he cannot guarantee that they will not be prosecuted by others for polygamy in the future, he will not prosecute them unless he finds that they have also committed a collateral crime.

18. The Defendant has said that there is no guarantee that the Browns will not be prosecuted in the future for polygamy.

19. There has been no allegation of child or spousal abuse by members of the Brown family.

20. No member of the Brown family has ever been charged with a crime.

In addition to the preceding undisputed material facts quoted from Plaintiffs' Motion, the court finds the following additional undisputable material facts relevant to the disposition of the current motions:

21. Defendant swore under penalty of perjury that "[a]s Utah County Attorney, I have now adopted a formal office policy not to prosecute the practice of bigamy unless the bigamy occurs in the conjunction with another crime or a person under the age of 18 was a party to the bigamous marriage or relationship."

22. Counsel for Defendant represented at oral argument on January 17, 2013 that the Statute is not intended to capture mere adultery or adulterous cohabitation, but that it is illegal under the Statute to participate in a wedding ceremony between a legally married individual and a person with whom he or she is cohabiting and/or to call that person a wife.

HISTORICAL BACKGROUND

This decision is fraught with both religious and historical significance for the State of Utah because it deals with the question of polygamy, an issue that played a central role in the State's development and that of its dominant religion, The Church of Jesus Christ of Latter-day Saints (the "LDS Church" or "Mormon Church"). The Brown Plaintiffs are not members of the LDS Church, but do adhere to the beliefs of a fundamentalist church that shares its historical roots with Mormonism.

The proper outcome of this issue has weighed heavily on the court for many months as it has examined, analyzed, and re-analyzed the numerous legal, practical, moral, and ethical considerations and implications of today's ruling. It would be an easy enough matter for the court to do as the Defendant urges and find against the Plaintiffs on the question of religious cohabitation under the Statute, defaulting simply to *Reynolds v. United States,* 98 U.S. 145, 25 L.Ed. 244 (1879), without seriously addressing the much developed constitutional jurisprudence that now protects individuals from the criminal consequences intended by legislatures to apply to certain personal choices, though such legislatures may sincerely believe that such criminal sanctions are in the best interest of society. The court has concluded that this would not be the legally or morally responsible approach in this case given the current contours of the constitutional protections at issue.

The court notes that 133 years after *Reynolds,* non-Mormon counsel for Plaintiffs have vigorously advanced arguments in favor of the right of religious polygamists to practice polygamy (through private "spiritual" marriages not licensed or otherwise sanctioned by the state, a relationship to which the court will refer as "religious cohabitation") that would have perhaps delighted Mormon Apostles and polygamy apologists throughout the period from 1852 to approximately 1904. To state the obvious, the intervening years have witnessed a significant strengthening of numerous provisions of the Bill of Rights, and a practical and morally defensible identification of "penumbral" rights "of privacy and repose" emanating from those key provisions of the Bill of Rights, as the Supreme Court has over decades assumed a general posture that is less inclined to allow majoritarian coercion of unpopular or disliked minority groups, especially when blatant racism (as expressed through Orientalism/imperialism), religious prejudice, or some other constitutionally suspect motivation, can be discovered behind such legislation. * * *

[I]t is perhaps a bitter irony of the history at issue here that it is possible to view the LDS Church as playing the role of both victim and violator in the saga of religious polygamy in Utah (and America). When the federal government targeted Mormon polygamy for elimination during the half century from the passage of the Morrill Anti-Bigamy Act of 1862 through the Congressional inquiry into the seating of Utah Senator Reed Smoot from 1904 to 1907, the "good order and morals of society" served as an acceptable basis for a legislature, it was believed, to identify "fundamental values" through a religious or other perceived ethical or moral consensus, enact criminal laws to force compliance with these values, and enforce those laws against a targeted group. In fact, with the exception of targeting a specific group, this has remained true in various forms (depending on the particular right and constitutional provision at issue) until the Supreme Court's decision in *Lawrence v. Texas,* 539 U.S. 558, 123 S.Ct. 2472, 156 L.Ed.2d 508 (2003) created ambiguity about the status of such "morals legislation." But the LDS Church was a victim of such majoritarian consensus concerning its practice of polygamy as a foundational and identifying tenet of religious faith. *See Reynolds,* 98 U.S. at 166–67 (noting that Congress was "deprived of all legislative power over mere opinion, but was left free to reach actions which were in violation of social duties or subversive of good order"). Although the court doubts that *Lawrence* actually must be interpreted to signal the end of the era in which the "good order and morals of society" are a rational basis for majoritarian legislation, there is no question this was the prevailing view in the 1870s. And, in fact, the decades-long "war" by the United States against the LDS Church— beginning with the Republican Party's 1856 platform of abolishing American chattel slavery and Mormon polygamy as the "twin relics of barbarism" and culminating, depending on how one views the historical episode, with either the Enabling Act in 1894 requiring that Utah ensure that "polygamist or plural marriages are forever prohibited" in Utah as a condition for joining the Union as a State, or the seating of Utah Senator Reed Smoot in 1907—was based on a majoritarian consensus that Mormons were indeed "subversive of good order" in their practice of polygamy.

But what exactly was the "social harm" identified by the *Reynolds* Court in the Mormon practice of polygamy that made the practice "subversive of good order"? "Polygamy has always been odious among the northern and western nations of Europe, and, until the establishment of the Mormon Church, was almost exclusively a feature of the life of Asiatic and of African people." *Reynolds,* 98 U.S. at 164. Though Professor [Edward] Said did not cite *Reynolds* in his text on Orientalism, this expression of the social harm identified in the Mormon practice of polygamy aptly exemplifies the concept. A decade later, the Supreme Court clarified the social harm further, explaining that Mormons were degrading the morals of the country through their religious practices, such as polygamy, which, the Supreme Court declared, constituted "a return to barbarism" and were "contrary to the spirit of Christianity." *Late Corp. of The Church of Jesus Christ of Latter-Day Saints v. United States,* 136 U.S. 1, 49, 10 S.Ct. 792, 34 L.Ed. 478 (1890). * * *

In other words, the social harm was introducing a practice perceived to be characteristic of non-European people—or non-white races—into white American society. "The organization of a community for the spread and practice of polygamy is, in a measure, a return to barbarism. It is contrary to the spirit of Christianity and of the civilization which Christianity has produced in the Western world." *Late Corp.,* 136 U.S. at 49, 10 S.Ct. 792. This observation in *Late Corp.*—unthinkable as part of the legal analysis in a modern Supreme Court decision given the significant (and appropriate) development in the interpretation of the protections afforded to religious minorities under both the Establishment Clause and the Free Exercise Clause in the latter half of the twentieth century, and racial minorities under the Due Process and Equal Protection Clauses of the Fourteenth Amendment, as also recognized in the latter half of the twentieth century—was only a reiteration of the definitive position already taken by the Supreme Court more than a decade earlier in *Reynolds.* Such an assessment arising from derisive societal views about race and ethnic origin prevalent in the United States at that time has no place in discourse about religious freedom, due process, equal protection or any other constitutional guarantee or right in the genuinely and intentionally racially and religiously pluralistic society that has been strengthened by the Supreme Court's twentieth-century rights jurisprudence. * * *

[The court concluded that while *Reynolds* allowed the state to ban] actual polygamy (multiple purportedly legal unions), the cohabitation prong of the Statute is not operationally neutral or of general applicability because of its targeted effect on specifically religious cohabitation. It is therefore subject to strict scrutiny under the Free Exercise Clause and fails under that standard. * * * Alternatively, following *Lawrence* and based on the arguments presented by Defendant in both his filings and at oral argument, the State of Utah has no rational basis under the Due Process Clause on which to prohibit the type of religious cohabitation at issue here; thus, the cohabitation prong of the Statute is facially unconstitutional, though the broader Statute survives in prohibiting bigamy. * * *

I.   COHABITATION IN THE 1973 STATUTE

A.   THE UTAH SUPREME COURT'S INTERPRETATION OF "MARRY" IN THE STATUTE

Plaintiffs challenge the constitutionality of the Statute on multiple grounds, arguing both that the Statute is facially unconstitutional and unconstitutional as applied to the Plaintiffs. The Statute provides that "[a] person is guilty of bigamy when, knowing he has a husband or wife or knowing the other person has a husband or wife, the person purports to marry another person or cohabits with another person." Utah Code Ann. § 76–7–101(1) (2013). It is axiomatic that state courts are the final arbiters of state law. The court is therefore bound by the Utah Supreme Court's interpretation of the Statute.

In *Holm,* the Utah Supreme Court affirmed the defendant's conviction for unlawful sexual conduct with a minor under section 76–5–401.2 of the Utah Code as well as bigamy under the Statute, but did not find occasion to construe the phrase "or cohabits with another person" because it rested its holding as to the bigamy conviction on its interpretation of the term "marry" and the phrase "purports to marry." * * * [The court in *Holm*] held that "the term 'marry,' as used in the bigamy statute, includes both legally recognized marriages and those that are not state-sanctioned."

As Plaintiffs correctly note, the Utah Supreme Court's interpretation of "marry" in the Statute in *Holm* means that the Statute "criminalizes not only privately 'marrying' someone after having legally married, but also merely cohabiting with a second adult partner after having married a first partner." This, argue Plaintiffs, is unconstitutional under numerous independent constitutional provisions, as discussed below.

B.   STRICT OR HEIGHTENED SCRUTINY

Though the court is bound by the Utah Supreme Court's interpretation of the Statute in *Holm* (with the particular relevance of its broad construction of the word "marry"), it is not bound by that Court's denial of Holm's federal constitutional claims. At oral argument, Plaintiffs suggested that "the narrowest ground upon which this court can find for the plaintiff is under the Due Process Clause." The court will therefore first examine the constitutionality of the Statute, as interpreted by the Utah Supreme Court in *Holm,* under the Due Process Clause of the Fourteenth Amendment.

Heightened Scrutiny Under the
Glucksberg Framework

* * *

a. Polygamy. * * * [T]he court finds that there is no "fundamental right" to polygamy under *Glucksberg*. To phrase it with a "careful description" of the asserted right, no "fundamental right" exists to have official State recognition or legitimation of individuals' "purported" polygamous marriages—relationships entered into knowing that one of the parties to such a plural marriage is already legally married in the eyes of the State. * * *

b. Religious Cohabitation. The relationship at issue in this lawsuit, which the court has termed "religious cohabitation," has been aptly described by then Chief Justice Durham of the Utah Supreme Court. Religious cohabitation occurs when "[t]hose who choose to live together without getting married enter into a personal relationship that resembles a marriage in its intimacy but claims no legal sanction." *Holm*, 2006 UT at ¶ 172, 137 P.3d at 773 (Durham, C.J., dissenting). * * * [T]his religious cohabitation also fails to qualify as a fundamental right or fundamental liberty interest triggering heightened scrutiny under the *Glucksberg* substantive due process analysis.

Plaintiffs provide the "careful description" of the asserted fundamental right—the required first step of the analysis in the Tenth Circuit, *see Seegmiller* [*v. LaVerkin City*], 528 F.3d [762, 769 (10th Cir. 2008)][30]—as follows: "a fundamental liberty interest in choosing to cohabit and maintain romantic and spiritual relationships, even if those relationships are termed 'plural marriage'." Plaintiffs truncate the *Glucksberg* analysis by reference to *Lawrence*, which they argue establishes "a fundamental liberty interest in intimate sexual conduct," thus prohibiting the state "from imposing criminal sanctions for intimate sexual conduct in the home. * * * *Lawrence* was the latest iteration in a long series of constitutional decisions amplifying a core principle: the Due Process Clause circumscribes and in some cases virtually forbids state intervention in private relationships and conduct."

Plaintiffs' arguments about the meaning and implications of *Lawrence* for the State's ability to criminalize their private conduct of religious cohabitation are very persuasive. But *Lawrence* provides less specific guidance than would be desirable, primarily because the

---

[30]   *Editor's Note*: The plaintiff in *Seegmiller*, a police officer, was reprimanded by her department after she had consensual private sex with another officer while attending a conference paid by her employer. In assessing her substantive due process claim, the court refused to apply heightened scrutiny, concluding that *Lawrence* did not require it to do so. The court then upheld the constitutionality of the employer's reprimand based on the department's interests in avoiding appearances of impropriety by officers and in "further[ing] internal discipline." *Seegmiller*, 528 F.3d at 772.

enigmatic decision eschews a formal, technical analysis of the level of detail modeled in the *Glucksberg* framework for analyzing claims to substantive due process protecting carefully described fundamental rights. Unfortunately, the decision also never explicitly identifies the standard of review applied and, though providing a substantive due process discussion that could fairly easily support an interpretation that heightened scrutiny was indeed applied, the Court used some terminology arguably characteristic of rational basis review in ruling Texas' anti-sodomy statute unconstitutional. *See Lawrence,* 539 U.S. at 586, 123 S.Ct. 2472 (SCALIA, J., dissenting) (arguing that the majority applied "an unheard of form of rational basis review" to strike down Texas' anti-sodomy law). *But see* Laurence H. Tribe, Lawrence v. Texas: *The "Fundamental Right" That Dare Not Speak Its Name,* 117 HARV. L. REV.. 1893, 1917 (2004) (arguing that "the strictness of the Court's standard in *Lawrence,* however articulated, could hardly have been more obvious" and to assume that rational basis review was applied "requires overlooking passage after passage in which the Court's opinion indeed invoked the talismanic verbal formula of substantive due process but did so by putting the key words in one unusual sequence or another"). * * *

Despite the moral and philosophical appeal of *Lawrence*'s discussion about the Fourteenth Amendment's commitment to a concept of liberty that "protects the person from unwarranted government intrusions into a dwelling or other private places" because it "presumes an autonomy of self that includes . . . certain intimate conduct," *Lawrence,* 539 U.S. at 562, 123 S.Ct. 2472, and therefore "gives substantial protection to adult persons in deciding how to conduct their lives in matters pertaining to sex," *id.* at 571, 123 S.Ct. 2472, and the resulting inherent persuasiveness of Plaintiffs' arguments that this broadly outlined substantive due process liberty interest applies to the religious cohabitation at issue here, the court is bound by the Tenth Circuit's interpretation of *Lawrence* in *Seegmiller*. It therefore need look no further than *Seegmiller* to find that such religious cohabitation does not qualify for heightened scrutiny under the substantive due process analysis in the Tenth Circuit. * * *

Although *Seegmiller* is factually distinguishable and therefore not directly controlling, the court cannot ignore the Tenth Circuit's specific substantive due process analysis of the asserted "fundamental liberty interest in sexual privacy." In particular, the Tenth Circuit went out of its way to interpret *Lawrence* in this context. [T]he Tenth Circuit in *Seegmiller* observed that "[a] broadly-defined 'right to sexual activity' will clearly not suffice. The Supreme Court has never identified such a right at that level of generality."

In support of this conclusion, the *Seegmiller* Court noted * * * that *Lawrence* "counsels against finding a broad-based fundamental right to engage in private sexual conduct." The Tenth Circuit observed that "nowhere in *Lawrence* does the [Supreme] Court describe the right at issue [the right to engage in private, consensual homosexual sodomy] as a fundamental right or a fundamental liberty interest. . . . It instead applied rational basis review to the law and found it lacking." * * * The court views the Tenth Circuit's analysis and interpretation of *Lawrence* as binding for this case and, accordingly, finds that it precludes the application of heightened scrutiny to Plaintiffs' substantive due process claim as well, supported as it is by the contention that *Lawrence* establishes "a fundamental liberty interest in intimate sexual conduct." The cohabitation prong of the Statute, however, cannot withstand rational basis review under the substantive due process analysis. * * *

C. RATIONAL BASIS REVIEW UNDER THE DUE PROCESS CLAUSE

* * * Though the court has followed the Tenth Circuit's lead in *Seegmiller* as to the application of *Lawrence* to the fundamental rights question, *Lawrence* becomes controlling for the rational basis review analysis. Following the Eleventh Circuit in *Williams IV*, the Tenth Circuit held in *Seegmiller* that *Lawrence* applied rational basis review in striking down Texas' homosexual sodomy statute. *Seegmiller,* 528 F.3d at 771. In doing so, the *Seegmiller* Court also stated that "no one disputes a right to be free from government interference in matters of consensual sexual privacy." *Id.* at 769.

Consensual sexual privacy is the touchstone of the rational basis review analysis in this case, as in *Lawrence*. The court believes that Plaintiffs are correct in their argument that, in prohibiting cohabitation under the Statute, "it is, of course, the state that has equated private sexual conduct with marriage." That is, in the case of people who have not even claimed to be legally married—are not making any claim to legal recognition of their unions or the network of laws surrounding the institution of marriage—"[i]t is the state that is treating the relationship as a form of marriage and prosecuting on that basis." As such, this, in effect, criminalizes "the private consensual relations of adults." * * * Once again, the court looks to Chief Justice Durham's astute and commanding analysis in recognizing the concern that the *Holm* majority's approach "may give the impression that the state is free to criminalize any and all forms of personal relationships that occur outside the legal union of marriage." *Holm,* 2006 UT at ¶ 185, 137 P.3d at 778 (Durham, C.J., dissenting).

* * * Adultery, including adulterous cohabitation, is not prosecuted. [In 2006 Chief Justice Durham reported not being able to find any [adultery] prosecutions * * * and noted that it appeared that "[t]he most recent adultery prosecution to have reached [the Utah Supreme Court] appears to have been in 1928 under a previous criminal provision." Id. at

¶ 169 n. 22, 137 P.3d at 772 (Durham, C.J., dissenting).] Religious cohabitation, however, is subject to prosecution at the limitless discretion of local and State prosecutors, despite a general policy *not* to prosecute religiously motivated polygamy. The court finds no rational basis to distinguish between the two, not least with regard to the State interest in protecting the institution of marriage. * * *

This court shares serious concerns about the potential for injury and harm in closed religious polygamist communities, but notes that each such crime can and should be prosecuted on its own independent basis under the Utah statutes specifically designated for those purposes, including "criminal laws punishing incest, rape, unlawful sexual conduct with a minor, and domestic and child abuse." *Holm,* 2006 UT at ¶ 176, 137 P.3d at 775 (Durham, C.J., dissenting). Defendant referred to various reports documenting such abuses in Utah's religious polygamist communities. "But based on stories like these, Utah has made a legislative policy determination that the practice of polygamy is harmful to society and therefore should be prohibited." (Def.'s Reply 11 [Dkt. No. 73].) This cannot be a rational basis for the cohabitation prong of the Statute, however, because the State has specifically formulated a general policy not to prosecute religiously motivated polygamy, though when it has proceeded anyway, it has invariably been against religiously cohabiting individuals, usually in cases in which the defendant has been convicted of the "collateral crime" at issue anyway. Again, the court finds that there can be no rational basis for this approach, particularly under *Lawrence* and its focus on the deeper liberty interests at issue in the home and personal relationships. * * *

II. "PURPORTS TO MARRY" IN THE 1973 STATUTE

The court has found the phrase "or cohabits with another person" to be unconstitutional under various constitutional provisions and has ordered it to be stricken. With the cohabitation prong thus stricken, the Statute now reads as follows: "A person is guilty of bigamy when, knowing he has a husband or wife or knowing the other person has a husband or wife, the person purports to marry another person." Utah Code Ann. § 76–7–101(1) (2013). As noted above, the court must interpret the Statute in conformity with the broad construction of the Utah Supreme Court's most recent consideration of the Statute in *Holm.*

* * * Under [the state court's] broad interpretation of the term "marry," the phrase "purports to marry another person" raises the same constitutional concerns addressed in relation to the cohabitation prong above. But the court cannot resolve this difficulty by similarly striking the "purports to marry" prong because without it, the Statute becomes both legally and syntactically meaningless. And yet, it is not the role of federal courts in the constitutional framework of checks and balances to

"rewrite a state law to conform it to constitutional requirements." The court must therefore apply the "canon of constitutional avoidance," under which "[t]he elementary rule is that every reasonable construction must be resorted to, in order to save a statute from unconstitutionality." "Courts employ two mechanisms to preserve unconstitutional statutes from wholesale invalidation. First, if a statute is readily susceptible to a narrowing construction that will remedy the constitutional infirmity, the statute will be upheld. If the language is not readily susceptible to a narrowing construction, but the unconstitutional language is severable from the remainder of the statute, that which is constitutional may stand while that which is unconstitutional will be rejected."

As discussed in Part II above, the unsalvageable cohabitation prong has been stricken as unconstitutional. But as to the remainder of the Statute, "[i]t is well-settled that a federal court must uphold a statute if it is 'readily susceptible' to a narrowing construction that would make it constitutional." To be "readily susceptible" to a "narrowing construction that would make it constitutional," such narrowing or alternative construction must be "reasonable and readily apparent."

The Statute can be saved after striking the cohabitation prong by adopting Chief Justice Durham's interpretation of the "purports to marry" phrase (and the term "marry") from her dissent in *Holm* as the "reasonable and readily apparent" narrowing construction. [Stated succinctly, the one and only factor that is officially indicative of marriage is the marriage license which must be present before any kind of solemnization ritual has legal effect creating a marriage, and fraudulently obtaining more than one license constitutes bigamy.]

NOTES

1. Notice that the question of whether the government should recognize certain unions as marital is distinct from the question of whether it should criminalize the entering into those unions. For example, while no state, until relatively recently, recognized same-sex marriages, the entering into "unofficial" same-sex marriages was not by itself a crime (though, of course, consensual sodomy remained illegal in some jurisdictions before *Lawrence*). Why has our society *criminalized* the entering into a second marriage by an already married person? Why is the refusal to recognize legally a married person's additional marriages not enough to advance whatever interests the state may have in discouraging plural marriages?

2. In 2011, the Supreme Court of British Columbia upheld the constitutionality of Canada's criminalization of polygamy. *Reference re: Section 293 of the Criminal Code of Canada,* 2011 BCSC 1588. Although the court believed that the statute "offends the freedom of religion" protected by the Canadian Charter of Rights and Freedoms, it concluded the

criminalization was justified because of the harms engendered by polygamy. According to the court,

> Women in polygamous relationships are at an elevated risk of physical and psychological harm. They face higher rates of domestic violence and abuse, including sexual abuse. * * * They tend to have less autonomy, and report higher rates of marital dissatisfaction and lower levels of self-esteem. They also fare worse economically, as resources may be inequitably divided or simply insufficient.

> Children in polygamous families face higher infant mortality, even controlling for economic status and other relevant variables. They tend to suffer more emotional, behavioural and physical problems, as well as lower educational achievement than children in monogamous families. These outcomes are likely the result of higher levels of conflict, emotional stress and tension in polygamous families. * * *

> Early marriage for girls is common, frequently to significantly older men. The resultant early sexual activity, pregnancies and childbirth have negative health implications for girls, and also significantly limit their socio-economic development. Shortened inter-birth intervals pose a heightened risk of various problems for both mother and child.

> The sex ratio imbalance inherent in polygamy means that young men are forced out of polygamous communities to sustain the ability of senior men to accumulate more wives. These young men and boys often receive limited education as a result and must navigate their way outside their communities with few life skills and social support.

> Another significant harm to children is their exposure to, and potential internalization of, harmful gender stereotypes.

> Polygamy has negative impacts on society flowing from the high fertility rates, large family size and poverty associated with the practice. It generates a class of largely poor, unmarried men who are statistically predisposed to violence and other anti-social behaviour. Polygamy also institutionalizes gender inequality. Patriarchal hierarchy and authoritarian control are common features of polygamous communities. Individuals in polygynous societies tend to have fewer civil liberties than their counterparts in societies which prohibit the practice.

> Polygamy's harm to society includes the critical fact that a great many of its individual harms are not specific to any particular religious, cultural or regional context. They can be generalized and expected to occur wherever polygamy exists.

Id. What do you think of the Canadian court's claims regarding the question of harms? Do you find them persuasive? Notice the role that gender plays in the court's analysis. Does the promotion of gender equality constitute a valid basis for criminalizing polygamy? Given the fact that the practice of polygamy in the United States, as in Canada, has almost always involved one man and more than one woman, is it appropriate for the government to "protect" women from polygamous marriages?

3. For the *Brown* court, there was a constitutionally relevant difference between what it called "actual polygamy" (the entering into more than one legal union) and cohabitation involving one man, his legal wife, and several other women. Are the state's interests in preventing polygamous marriages also present in the type of cohabitation at issue in *Brown*? Should individuals have a greater right to cohabit with whom they want (even if it is with more than one person) than to marry the individual(s) of their choice? Does the state have a greater interest in setting criteria for marriage because it is one of "its" institutions while cohabitation is not a state institution at all?

4. For an autonomy-based argument in favor of recognizing polygamous marriages, see Joseph J. Fischel, *A More Promiscuous Politics: LGBT Rights without the LGBT Rights, in* AFTER MARRIAGE EQUALITY: THE FUTURE OF LGBT RIGHTS 181 (Carlos A. Ball, ed. 2016). For an extended discussion of why the law should allow polygamous marriages, see RONALD C. DEN OTTER, IN DEFENSE OF PLURAL MARRIAGE (2015). For the contrary view, see STEPHEN MACEDO, JUST MARRIED: SAME-SEX COUPLES, MONOGAMY & THE FUTURE OF MARRIAGE (2016). Macedo distinguishes polygamy from same-sex marriage by arguing that "same-sex sexual orientation appears to be quite universal and is found in societies that are extremely repressive. On the other hand, people's felt desire for polygamous marriages appears to be highly variable and dependent on prevalent institutions and culture." *Id.* at 163. Macedo also contends that jealousy and conflict are more likely to arise in polygamous families: "As compared with the families of intact monogamous couples, polygamous households are characterized by greater complexity in the relations and 'genetic' relatedness of adults and children. It hardly seems surprising that the opportunities for jealousy, rivalry, factionalism, and conflict would be greatly multiplied in households in which several wives and many half-brothers and sisters cohabit." *Id.* at 168. In addition, Macedo contends that "[e]vidence suggests that if we grant people in general permission to marry multiple spouses, the opportunity will be taken up unevenly and will tend to be to the advantage of higher-status, more powerful, and wealthier males." *Id.* at 164.

C. SEX TOYS

WILLIAMS V. ATTORNEY GENERAL OF ALABAMA

U.S. Court of Appeals, Eleventh Circuit, 2004
378 F.3d 1232

BIRCH, CIRCUIT JUDGE.

In this case, the American Civil Liberties Union ("ACLU") invites us to add a new right to the current catalogue of fundamental rights under the Constitution: a right to sexual privacy. It further asks us to declare Alabama's statute prohibiting the sale of "sex toys" to be an impermissible burden on this right. Alabama responds that the statute exercises a time-honored use of state police power—restricting the sale of sex. We are compelled to agree with Alabama and must decline the ACLU's invitation.

I. BACKGROUND

Alabama's Anti-Obscenity Enforcement Act prohibits, among other things, the commercial distribution of "any device designed or marketed as useful primarily for the stimulation of human genital organs for any thing of pecuniary value." Ala. Code § 13A–12–200.2 (Supp.2003).

The Alabama statute proscribes a relatively narrow bandwidth of activity. It prohibits only the sale—but not the use, possession, or gratuitous distribution—of sexual devices (in fact, the users involved in this litigation acknowledge that they already possess multiple sex toys). The law does not affect the distribution of a number of other sexual products such as ribbed condoms or virility drugs. Nor does it prohibit Alabama residents from purchasing sexual devices out of state and bringing them back into Alabama. Moreover, the statute permits the sale of ordinary vibrators and body massagers that, although useful as sexual aids, are not "designed or marketed * * * primarily" for that particular purpose. *Id.* Finally, the statute exempts sales of sexual devices "for a bona fide medical, scientific, educational, legislative, judicial, or law enforcement purpose." *Id.* § 13A–12–200.4.

This case, which is now before us on appeal for the second time, involves a challenge to the constitutionality of the Alabama statute. The ACLU, on behalf of various individual users and vendors of sexual devices, initially filed suit seeking to enjoin the statute on 29 July 1998, a month after the statute took effect. The ACLU argued that the statute burdens and violates sexual-device users' right to privacy and personal autonomy under the Fourteenth Amendment to the United States Constitution.

Following a bench trial, the district court concluded that there was no currently recognized fundamental right to use sexual devices and declined the ACLU's invitation to create such a right. *Williams v. Pryor*, 41 F. Supp. 2d. 1257, 1282–84 (N.D. Ala. 1999) (*Williams I*). The district court then proceeded to scrutinize the statute under rational basis review. *Id.* at 1284. Concluding that the statute lacked any rational basis, the district court permanently enjoined its enforcement. *Id.* at 1293.

On appeal, we reversed in part and affirmed in part. *Williams v. Pryor*, 240 F.3d 944 (11th Cir. 2001) (*Williams II*). We reversed the district court's conclusion that the statute lacked a rational basis and held that the promotion and preservation of public morality provided a rational basis. *Id.* at 952. However, we affirmed the district court's rejection of the ACLU's *facial* fundamental-rights challenge to the statute. *Id.* at 955. We then remanded the action to the district court for further consideration of the *as-applied* fundamental-rights challenge. *Id.* at 955.

On remand, the district court again struck down the statute. *Williams v. Pryor*, 220 F. Supp. 2d 1257 (N.D. Ala. 2002) (*Williams III*). On cross motions for summary judgment, the district court held that the statute unconstitutionally burdened the right to use sexual devices within private adult, consensual sexual relationships. *Id.* After a lengthy discussion of the history of sex in America, the district court announced a fundamental right to "sexual privacy," which, although unrecognized under any existing Supreme Court precedent, the district court found to be deeply rooted in the history and traditions of our nation. *Id.* at 1296. The district court further found that this right "encompass[es] the right to use sexual devices like the vibrators, dildos, anal beads, and artificial vaginas" marketed by the vendors involved in this case. *Id.* The district court accordingly applied strict scrutiny to the statute. *Id.* Finding that the statute failed strict scrutiny, the district court granted summary judgment to the ACLU and once again enjoined the statute's enforcement. *Id.* at 1307.

Alabama now appeals that decision. The only question on this appeal is whether the statute, as applied to the involved users and vendors, violates any fundamental right protected under the Constitution. The proper analysis for evaluating this question turns on whether the right asserted by the ACLU falls within the parameters of any presently recognized fundamental right or whether it instead requires us to recognize a hitherto unarticulated fundamental right.

II. DISCUSSION

A. Asserted Right

* * * The ACLU invokes "privacy" and "personal autonomy" as if such phrases were constitutional talismans. In the abstract, however, there is no fundamental right to either. *See, e.g., Glucksberg*, 521 U.S. at 725 (fundamental rights are "not simply deduced from abstract concepts of personal autonomy"). Undoubtedly, many fundamental rights currently recognized under Supreme Court precedent touch on matters of personal autonomy and privacy. However, "[t]hat many of the rights and liberties protected by the Due Process Clause sound in personal autonomy does not warrant the sweeping conclusion that any and all important, intimate, and personal decisions are so protected." *Id.* at 727. Such rights have been denominated "fundamental" not simply because they implicate deeply personal and private considerations, but because they have been identified as "deeply rooted in this Nation's history and tradition and implicit in the concept of ordered liberty, such that neither liberty nor justice would exist if they were sacrificed." *Id.* at 720–21.

Nor, contrary to the ACLU's assertion, have the Supreme Court's substantive-due-process precedents recognized a free-standing "right to sexual privacy." The Court has been presented with repeated opportunities to identify a fundamental right to sexual privacy—and has invariably declined. * * *

The Supreme Court's most recent opportunity to recognize a fundamental right to sexual privacy came in *Lawrence v. Texas*, where petitioners and *amici* expressly invited the court to do so. That the *Lawrence* Court had declined the invitation was this court's conclusion in our recent decision in *Lofton v. Sec. of Dept. of Children & Family Servs.*, 358 F.3d 804, 815–16 (11th Cir. 2004). In *Lofton*, we addressed in some detail the "question of whether *Lawrence* identified a new fundamental right to private sexual intimacy." *Id.* at 815. We concluded that, although *Lawrence* clearly established the unconstitutionality of criminal prohibitions on consensual adult sodomy, "it is a strained and ultimately incorrect reading of *Lawrence* to interpret it to announce a new fundamental right"—whether to homosexual sodomy specifically or, more broadly, to all forms of sexual intimacy. We noted in particular that the *Lawrence* opinion did not employ fundamental-rights analysis and that it ultimately applied rational-basis review, rather than strict scrutiny, to the challenged statute.

The dissent seizes on scattered *dicta* from *Lawrence* to argue that *Lawrence* recognized a *substantive* due process right of consenting adults to engage in private intimate sexual conduct, such that all infringements of this right must be subjected to strict scrutiny. As we noted in *Lofton*, we are not prepared to infer a new fundamental right from an opinion that never employed the usual *Glucksberg* analysis for identifying such rights. Nor are we prepared to assume that *Glucksberg*—a precedent that *Lawrence* never once mentions—is overruled by implication.

The dissent in turn argues that the right recognized in *Lawrence* was a longstanding right that preexisted *Lawrence*, thus obviating the need for any *Glucksberg*-type fundamental rights analysis. But the dissent never identifies the source, textual or precedential, of such a preexisting right to sexual privacy. It does cite *Griswold, Eisenstadt, Roe,* and *Carey.* However, although these precedents recognize various substantive rights *closely related* to sexual intimacy, none of them recognize the overarching right to sexual privacy asserted here. *Griswold* (marital privacy and contraceptives); *Eisenstadt* (equal protection extension of *Griswold*); *Roe* (abortion); *Carey* (contraceptives). * * * [I]n the most recent of these decisions, *Carey,* the Court specifically observed that it had not answered the question of whether there is a constitutional right to private sexual conduct. Moreover, nearly two decades later, the *Glucksberg* Court, listing the current catalog of fundamental rights, did not include such a right.

In short, we decline to extrapolate from *Lawrence* and its *dicta* a right to sexual privacy triggering strict scrutiny. To do so would be to impose a fundamental-rights interpretation on a decision that rested on rational-basis grounds, that never engaged in *Glucksberg* analysis, and that never invoked strict scrutiny. Moreover, it would be answering questions that the *Lawrence* Court appears to have left for another day. Of course, the Court may in due course expand *Lawrence's* precedent in the direction anticipated by the dissent. But for us preemptively to take that step would exceed our mandate as a lower court.

B. *Glucksberg Analysis*

1. *Careful Description*

* * * In searching for, and ultimately finding, [a] right to sexual privacy, the district court did little to define its scope and bounds. As formulated by the district court, the right potentially encompasses a great universe of sexual activities, including many that historically have been, and continue to be, prohibited. At oral arguments, the ACLU contended that "no responsible counsel" would challenge prohibitions such as those against pederasty and adult incest under a "right to sexual privacy" theory. However, mere faith in the responsibility of the bar scarcely provides a legally cognizable, or constitutionally significant, limiting principle in applying the right in future cases.

The sole limitation provided by the district court's ruling was that the right would extend only to *consenting adults.* The consenting-adult formula, of course, is a corollary to John Stuart Mill's celebrated "harm principle," which would allow the state to proscribe only conduct that causes identifiable harm to another. *See generally* John Stuart Mill, *On Liberty* (Elizabeth Rapaport ed., Hackett Pub. Co. 1978) (1859). Regardless of its force as a policy argument, however, it does not translate *ipse dixit* into a constitutionally cognizable standard.

If we were to accept the invitation to recognize a right to sexual intimacy, this right would theoretically encompass such activities as prostitution, obscenity, and adult incest—even if we were to limit the right to consenting adults. This in turn would require us to subject all infringements on such activities to strict scrutiny. In short, by framing our inquiry so broadly as to look for a general right to sexual intimacy, we would be answering many questions not before us on the present facts.

Indeed, the requirement of a "careful description" is designed to prevent the reviewing court from venturing into vaster constitutional vistas than are called for by the facts of the case at hand. * * *

[T]he scope of the liberty interest at stake here must be defined in reference to the scope of the Alabama statute. We begin by observing that the broad rights to "privacy" and "sexual privacy" invoked by the ACLU are not at issue. The statute invades the privacy of Alabama residents in their bedrooms no more than does any statute restricting the availability of commercial products for use in private quarters as sexual enhancements.[12] Instead, the challenged Alabama statute bans the commercial distribution of sexual devices. At a minimum, therefore, the putative right at issue is the right to sell and purchase sexual devices.

It is more than that, however. For purposes of constitutional analysis, restrictions on the ability to purchase an item are tantamount to restrictions on the use of that item. Thus it was that the *Glucksberg* Court analyzed a ban on *providing* suicide assistance as a burden on the right to *receive* suicide assistance. Similarly, prohibitions on the *sale* of contraceptives have been analyzed as burdens on the *use* of contraceptives. Because a prohibition on the distribution of sexual devices would burden an individual's ability to use the devices, our analysis must be framed not simply in terms of whether the Constitution protects a right to *sell* and *buy* sexual devices, but whether it protects a right to *use* such devices.

2. *"History and Tradition" and "Implicit in the Concept of Ordered Liberty"*

With this "careful description" in mind, we turn now to the second prong of the fundamental-rights inquiry. The crucial inquiry under this prong is whether the right to use sexual devices when engaging in lawful, private sexual activity is (1) "objectively, deeply rooted in this Nation's history and tradition" and (2) "implicit in the concept of ordered liberty, such that neither liberty nor justice would exist if [it] were sacrificed." *Glucksberg*, 521 U.S. at 721.

---

[12]   The mere fact that a product is used within the privacy of the bedroom, or that it enhances intimate conduct, does not in itself bring the use of that article within the right to privacy. If it were otherwise, individuals whose sexual gratification requires other types of material or instrumentalities—perhaps hallucinogenic substances, depictions of child pornography or bestiality, or the services of a willing prostitute—likewise would have a colorable argument that prohibitions on such activities and materials interfere with their privacy in the bedchamber. Under this theory, all such sexual-enhancement paraphernalia (as long as it was used only in consensual encounters between adults) would also be encompassed within the right to privacy—and any burden thereon subject to strict scrutiny.

a.   The Scope of the District Court's History and Tradition Analysis

The district court began its *Glucksberg*-mandated history and tradition inquiry by defining its task as one of determining whether to "recognize a fundamental right to sexual privacy." *Williams III*, 220 F.Supp.2d at 1277. After an extensive survey of the history of sex in American culture and law—replete with cites to the Kinsey studies and Michel Foucault—the district court concluded that "there exists a constitutionally inherent right to sexual privacy that firmly encompasses state non-interference with private, adult, consensual sexual relationships." *Id.* at 1296. As examined above, the Supreme Court's own reticence in this area, and its admonition to carefully define the right at stake, convince us that the district court erred in undertaking to find a generalized "right to sexual privacy." Given this over-broad starting point, the district court's subsequent inquiry, predictably, was likewise broader than called for by the facts of the case. The inquiry should have been focused not broadly on the vast topic of sex in American cultural and legal history, but narrowly and more precisely on the treatment of *sexual devices* within that history and tradition.

b.   The District Court's Focus on "Contemporary Practice"

In reaching its holding, the district court relied heavily on "contemporary practice," emphasizing the "contemporary trend of legislative and societal liberalization of attitudes toward consensual, adult sexual activity." *Id.* at 1294. * * *

Our first concern is the legal significance, or the lack thereof, of much of the district court's source material for this contemporary practice. In addition to invoking a cluster of Supreme Court precedents touching on matters of procreation and familial integrity, the district court looked to social science data respecting premarital intercourse, marriage and divorce rates, and the like. It further noted the revolutionary impact of the Kinsey studies, the "imagery and implements of adult sexual relationships [that] pervade modern American society," the availability of "pornography of the grossest sort," and the "widespread marketing of Viagra." *Id.* at 1294. While such evidence undoubtedly confirms the district court's discovery of "the specter of a twentieth century sexual liberalism," *id.* at 1291, its relevance under *Glucksberg* is scant. * * *

c.   The District Court's Faulty Equation of Historical Non-Interference with Historical Protection

The district court's central holding—its discovery of a constitutional "right to use sexual devices like * * * vibrators, dildos, anal beads, and artificial vaginas"—was not based on any evidence of a history and tradition of *affirmative protection* of this right. *Williams III*, 220 F.Supp.2d at 1296. The district court's lengthy opinion cites no reference to such a right in the usual repositories of our freedoms, such as federal and state constitutional provisions, constitutional doctrines, statutory provisions, common-law doctrines, and the like. Instead, the critical evidence for the district court was the relative scarcity of statutes explicitly banning sexual devices and the rarity of reported cases of sexual-devices prosecutions—along with various factual assertions from declarations by the ACLU's experts. From this, the district court inferred "that history and contemporary practice demonstrate a conscious avoidance of regulation of [sexual] devices by the states." *Id.* at 1296.

This negative inference essentially inverted *Glucksberg's* history and tradition inquiry. *Glucksberg*, 521 U.S. at 721. The district court—rather than requiring a showing that the right to use sexual devices is "deeply rooted in this Nation's history and tradition," *id.*—looked for a showing that *proscriptions* against sexual devices are deeply rooted in history and tradition. Under this approach, the freedom to smoke, to pollute, to engage in private discrimination, to commit marital rape—at one time or another—all could have been elevated to fundamental-rights status. Moreover, it would create the perverse incentive for legislatures to regulate every area within their plenary power for fear that their restraint in any area might give rise to a right of constitutional proportions. * * *

[N]othing in *Glucksberg* indicates that an absence of historical *prohibition* is tantamount, for purposes of fundamental-rights analysis, to an historical record of *protection* under the law. * * * Not only does the record before us fail to evidence such a deeply rooted right, but it suggests that, to the extent that sex toys historically have attracted the attention of the law, it has been in the context of proscription, not protection.

The chief example of this proscription is the "Comstock Laws," federal and state legislation adopted in the late 1800s. The federal Comstock Act of 1873 was a criminal statute directed at "the suppression of Trade in and Circulation of obscene Literature and Articles of immoral Use." *See Bolger v. Youngs Drug Prods. Corp.*, 463 U.S. 60, 70 (1983). The Act prohibited importation of and use of the mails for transporting, among other things, "every article or thing intended or adapted for any indecent or immoral use." *United States v. Chase*, 135 U.S. 255, 257, 10 S. Ct. 756, 756, 34 L. Ed. 117 (1890). Various states also enacted similar statutes prohibiting the sale of such articles. * * *

[T]he negative inference drawn by the district court—that the scarcity of explicit reference to sexual devices in statutory schemes and reported cases reflects a "deliberate non-interference," *id.* at 1286—is too speculative a basis for constitutionalizing a hitherto unrecognized right. This is especially true given the lack of any indicia of affirmative protection under the law. In short, there is no competent evidence in the record before us indicating that the lack of explicit and aggressive proscription of sex toys was, as the district court surmised, "conscious avoidance of regulation of these devices by the states." *Id.* at 1296. * * *

We REVERSE the district court's grant of the ACLU's motion for summary judgment and REMAND to the district court for further proceedings consistent with this opinion.

BARKETT, CIRCUIT JUDGE, dissenting.

The majority's decision rests on the erroneous foundation that there is no substantive due process right to adult consensual sexual intimacy in the home and erroneously assumes that the promotion of public morality provides a rational basis to criminally burden such private intimate activity. These premises directly conflict with the Supreme Court's holding in *Lawrence v. Texas*, 539 U.S. 558 (2003).

This case is not, as the majority's demeaning and dismissive analysis suggests, about sex or about sexual devices. It is about the tradition of American citizens from the inception of our democracy to value the constitutionally protected right to be left alone in the privacy of their bedrooms and personal relationships. As Justice Brandeis stated in the now famous words of his dissent in *Olmstead v. United States*, 277 U.S. 438 (1928), when "[t]he makers of our Constitution undertook to secure conditions favorable to the pursuit of happiness * * * [t]hey conferred, as against the government, the right to be let alone—the most comprehensive of rights and the right most valued by civilized men." [*Id.*] at 478.

The majority claims that *Lawrence*, like *Bowers v. Hardwick*, 478 U.S. 186, 106 S. Ct. 2841, 92 L. Ed. 2d 140 (1986), failed to recognize the substantive due process right of consenting adults to engage in private sexual conduct. Conceding that *Lawrence* must have done *something*, the majority acknowledges that *Lawrence* "established the unconstitutionality of criminal prohibitions on consensual adult sodomy." The majority refuses, however, to acknowledge *why* the Court in *Lawrence* held that criminal prohibitions on consensual sodomy are unconstitutional. This failure underlies the majority's flawed conclusion in this case.

* * * *Lawrence* held that a state may not criminalize sodomy because of the existence of the very right to private sexual intimacy that the majority refuses to acknowledge. *Lawrence* reiterated that its prior fundamental rights cases protected individual choices "concerning the intimacies of [a] physical relationship." *Lawrence*, 123 S. Ct. at 2483. Because of this precedent, the *Lawrence* Court overruled *Bowers*, concluding that *Bowers* had "misapprehended the claim of liberty there presented" as involving a particular sexual act rather than the broader right of adult sexual privacy. *Id.* at 2478. Instead of heeding the Supreme Court's instruction regarding *Bowers*' error, the majority *repeats* it,

ignoring *Lawrence*'s teachings about how to correctly frame a liberty interest affecting sexual privacy.

Compounding this error, the majority also ignores *Lawrence*'s holding that although history and tradition may be used as a "starting point," they are not the "ending point" of a substantive due process inquiry. *Id.* at 2480. In cases solely involving adult consensual sexual privacy, the Court has never required that there be a long-standing history of *affirmative* legal protection of *specific conduct* before a right can be recognized under the Due Process Clause. To the contrary, because of the fundamental nature of this liberty interest, this right has been protected by the Court despite historical, legislative *restrictions* on private sexual conduct. Applying the analytical framework of *Lawrence* compels the conclusion that the Due Process Clause protects a right to sexual privacy that encompasses the use of sexual devices.

Finally, even under the majority's own constrained and erroneous interpretation of *Lawrence*, we are, at a bare minimum, obliged to revisit this Court's previous conclusion in *Williams v. Pryor*, 240 F.3d 944 (11th Cir. 2001) ("*Williams II*"), that Alabama's law survives the most basic level of review, that of rational basis. *See* 240 F.3d at 949. That decision explicitly depended upon the finding in *Bowers* that the promotion of public morality provided a rational basis to restrict private sexual activity. While the majority recognizes that *Bowers* has been overruled, it inexplicably fails to offer any explanation whatsoever for why public morality provides a rational basis to criminalize the private sexual activity in this case, when it was clearly not found to be a legitimate state interest in *Lawrence*.

NOTES

1.   The following question can be asked after a ruling like *Williams*: Why is consensual sexual conduct involving body parts (a penis and an anus, for example) constitutionally protected, while consensual sexual conduct involving a device and a body part (a vibrator and a vagina, for example) is not?

2.   The *Williams* court remanded the case for a determination of whether the Alabama statute survived rational basis review. A federal district court subsequently held that it did, see *Williams v. King*, 420 F.Supp.2d 1224 (N.D.Ala. 2006) (*Williams V*), and the Eleventh Circuit affirmed. *See Williams v. Morgan*, 478 F.3d 1316 (11th Cir. 2007) (*Williams VI*). In affirming, the appellate court explained that "while the statute at issue in *Lawrence* criminalized *private* sexual conduct, the statute at issue in this case forbids *public, commercial* activity. To the extent *Lawrence* rejects public morality as a legitimate government interest, it invalidates only those laws that target conduct that is *both* private *and* non-commercial. Unlike *Lawrence,* the activity regulated here is *neither* private *nor* non-commercial.

This statute targets *commerce* in sexual devices, an inherently public activity, whether it occurs on a street corner, in a shopping mall, or in a living room." *Id.* at 1322. (Is this reasoning inconsistent with the same court's statement in the main case that "for purposes of constitutional analysis, restrictions on the ability to purchase an item are tantamount to restrictions on the use of that item?" *Williams v. Attorney General of Alabama*, 378 F.3d 1232, 1242 (11th Cir. 2004).) The *Williams VI* court then went on to make clear that it did "not read *Lawrence* [or] the overruling of *Bowers* * * * to have rendered public morality altogether illegitimate as a rational basis. The principle that '[t]he law * * * is constantly based on notions of morality,' *Bowers*, 478 U.S. at 196, 106 S.Ct. at 2846, was not announced for the first time in *Bowers* and remains in force today." *Williams*, 478 F.3d at 1323.

3.   The U.S. Court of Appeals for the Fifth Circuit disagreed with *Williams* when it held that *Lawrence* required it to strike down Texas's statute prohibiting the sale of sexual devices. *See Reliable Consultants, Inc. v. Earle*, 517 F.3d 738, 745–46 (5th Cir. 2008). The court explained: "Because of *Lawrence*, the issue before us is whether the Texas statute impermissibly burdens the individual's substantive due process right to engage in private intimate conduct of his or her choosing." *Id.* at 744. In finding an impermissible burden, the court did not read *Lawrence* as a fundamental rights case: "*Lawrence* did not categorize the right to sexual privacy as a fundamental right, and we do not purport to do so here. Instead, we simply follow the precise instructions from *Lawrence* and hold that the statute violates the right to sexual privacy, however it is otherwise described." *Id.* at 745 n.32.

The court rejected the government's effort to justify the statute on moral grounds, explaining that "if in *Lawrence* public morality was an insufficient justification for a law that restricted 'adult consensual intimacy in the home,' then public morality also cannot serve as a rational basis for Texas's statute, which also regulates private sexual intimacy." *Id.* at 745 (quoting *Lawrence*, 539 U.S. at 564, 123 S.Ct. at 2476) (footnote omitted).

The *Reliable Consultants* court also rejected a second rationale proffered by the state: that the statute was needed to protect the sensibilities of "unwilling adults from exposure to sexual devices and their advertisement." *Reliable Consultants*, 517 F.3d at 746. In rejecting this government interest, the court noted that it "bears no rational relation to the restriction on sales of sexual devices because an adult cannot buy a sexual device without making the affirmative decision to visit a store and make the purchase." *Id.*

Finally, the court rejected the argument that striking down the statute essentially provides constitutional protection to the "commercial sale of sex." *Id.* at 746. Instead, the court explained that "[t]he sale of a device that an individual may choose to use during intimate conduct with a partner in the home is not the 'sale of sex' (prostitution)." *Id.*

4.   After the almost decade-long *Williams* litigation finally came to an end in 2007, the Alabama Supreme Court added its two cents by upholding

the validity of the sexual device statute under both the federal and state constitutions. *See 1568 Montgomery Hwy. Inc. v. City of Hoover*, 45 So.3d 319 (Ala.Sup.Ct. 2010). Prior to *Lawrence*, three state supreme courts had struck down their respective statutes prohibiting the sale, distribution, and promotion of obscene devices. *See Colorado v. Seven Thirty-Five East Colfax, Inc.*, 697 P.2d 348 (Colo. 1985); *Kansas v. Hughes*, 792 P.2d 1023, 246 Kan. 607 (1990); *Louisiana v. Brenan*, 772 So.2d 64 (La. 2000). The U.S. Court of Appeals for the Eleventh Circuit, the same court that upheld Alabama's law in *Williams*, had struck down Georgia's statute, which not only prohibited the sale of sexual devices, but also their advertisement. The court concluded that the latter restriction was a violation of the First Amendment. *See This That and the Other Gift and Tobacco, Inc. v. Cobb County*, 285 F.3d 1319, 1323 (11th Cir. 2002). There remain, in addition to Alabama, only two states with such laws: Mississippi, see MISS. CODE. ANN. § 97–29–105 (2010) and Virginia, see VA. CODE. ANN. § 18.2373 (2010). The Mississippi statute was upheld by the state supreme court in *PHE, Inc. v. State*, 877 So.2d 1244 (Miss. 2004).

D. INCEST

LOWE V. SWANSON

U.S. Court of Appeals, Sixth Circuit, 2011
663 F.3d 258

GRIFFIN, CIRCUIT JUDGE.

Petitioner Paul Lowe appeals the district court's denial of his petition for a writ of habeas corpus, arguing that the Ohio Supreme Court unreasonably applied federal law as clearly established by the Supreme Court in *Lawrence v. Texas*, 539 U.S. 558, 123 S.Ct. 2472, 156 L.Ed.2d 508 (2003), when it upheld his incest conviction for engaging in sexual conduct with his stepdaughter. We disagree and therefore affirm.

Lowe was charged with one count of sexual battery for engaging in sexual conduct by means of sexual intercourse with his 22-year-old stepdaughter, in violation of Ohio Rev.Code § 2907.03(A)(5), which makes it a crime to "engage in sexual conduct with another, not the spouse of the offender, when . . . [t]he offender is the other person's natural or adoptive parent, or a stepparent, or guardian, custodian, or person in loco parentis of the other person." Lowe moved to dismiss the charge in the trial court, arguing that the facts alleged in the indictment did not constitute an offense under Ohio Rev.Code § 2907.03(A)(5) because there was a "clear legislative intent to have the law apply to children, not adults." Lowe also argued that the statute was unconstitutional as applied to him because the government had no legitimate interest in regulating sexual activity between consenting adults. *See State v. Lowe*, 112 Ohio St.3d 507, 861 N.E.2d 512, 514 (2007). The court disagreed and overruled his motion.

Thereafter, Lowe pled no contest to the charge and was sentenced to 120 days of incarceration and three years of community control and was classified as a sex offender.

The Ohio Court of Appeals upheld Lowe's conviction on direct review. It concluded that Ohio Rev.Code § 2907.03(A)(5) prohibits sexual conduct between a stepparent and stepchild regardless of the stepchild's age and found that Lowe "d[id] not have a constitutionally protected right to engage in sex with his stepdaughter." On discretionary review, the Ohio Supreme Court also affirmed. *Lowe*, 861 N.E.2d at 518. It determined that "*Lawrence* did not announce a 'fundamental' right to all consensual adult sexual activity, let alone consensual sex with one's adult children or stepchildren" and that "the statute in *Lawrence* was subjected to a rational-basis rather than a strict-scrutiny test. . . ." *Id.* at 517. Accordingly, the court held that Lowe's conviction was constitutional because "as applied in this case, R.C. 2907.03(A)(5) bears a rational relationship to the legitimate state interest in protecting the family . . . from the destructive influence of sexual relationships between parents or stepparents and their children or stepchildren." *Id.* at 518.

Lowe then filed a 28 U.S.C. § 2254 petition for habeas relief with the federal district court, arguing that the Ohio Supreme Court unreasonably applied federal law as clearly established by the Supreme Court in *Lawrence*. The magistrate judge issued a report and recommendation to deny Lowe's petition, concluding that the Ohio Supreme Court's decision was not unreasonable because, as evidenced by a split among the federal circuits, *Lawrence* was not clear as to the nature of the right it considered or the standard of review it applied to the Texas statute. *See Lowe v. Swanson*, 639 F.Supp.2d 857, 859 (N.D. Ohio 2009). The district court adopted the magistrate judge's report and recommendation and denied the petition. We subsequently granted Lowe's request for a certificate of appealability, explaining that "the conflicting authority by our sister circuits establishes that the issues presented by this habeas petition are substantial and warrant further review."

* * * Lowe argues that he is entitled to habeas relief because the Ohio Supreme Court "unreasonably applied the federal law announced in *Lawrence*." According to Lowe, the Ohio Supreme Court "made the same mistake as the *Bowers* Court by framing the issue as 'whether [Mr.] Lowe is guaranteed a fundamental right to engage in sexual intercourse with his consenting adult stepdaughter,'" rather than framing the issue more broadly as "the recognition of the right, as between consenting adults, to engage in private sexual conduct." *See Lowe*, 861 N.E.2d at 516; *see also Lawrence*, 539 U.S. at 578, 123 S.Ct. 2472 (quoting *Bowers v. Hardwick*, 478 U.S. 186, 216, 106 S.Ct. 2841, 92 L.Ed.2d 140 (1986) (Stevens, J., dissenting) (opining that "individual decisions by married [or unmarried] persons, concerning the intimacies of their physical relationship . . . are a

form of 'liberty' protected by the Due Process Clause of the Fourteenth Amendment ... "). Lowe also contends that this broad right is a fundamental one requiring strict scrutiny because of the *Lawrence* Court's citations to fundamental rights cases and its references to "the right to make certain decisions regarding sexual conduct," a person's interest in making "certain fundamental decisions affecting her destiny," and the "emerging awareness that liberty gives substantial protection to adult persons in deciding how to conduct their private lives in matters pertaining to sex." *See Lawrence,* 539 U.S. at 565, 572, 123 S.Ct. 2472.

Lowe's arguments have some support. In *Cook v. Gates,* 528 F.3d 42 (1st Cir.2008), the First Circuit, considering a challenge by members of the United States Armed Forces who claimed that the "Don't Ask, Don't Tell" statute, 10 U.S.C. § 654 (2007), violated their substantive due process rights, found that *Lawrence* announced a broad Fourteenth Amendment right to sexual privacy. The court noted that "[t]he *Lawrence* Court characterized the constitutional question as whether petitioners' criminal convictions for adult consensual sexual intimacy in the home violate their vital interests in liberty and privacy protected by the Due Process Clause"; and it further explained that "[t]aking into account the precedent relied on by *Lawrence,* the tenor of its language, its special reliance on Justice Stevens' *Bowers* dissent, and its rejection of morality as an adequate basis for the law in question, we are convinced that *Lawrence* recognized that adults maintain a protected liberty interest to engage in certain 'consensual sexual intimacy in the home.'" *Id.* at 49, 53. The Fifth Circuit came to a similar conclusion in *Reliable Consultants, Inc. v. Earle,* 517 F.3d 738 (5th Cir.2008), asserting that "[t]he right the Court recognized [in *Lawrence*] was not simply a right to engage in the sexual act itself, but instead a right to be free from governmental intrusion regarding 'the most private human contact, sexual behavior.'" *Id.* at 744.

Also, were *Lawrence* applicable, there is authority for Lowe's position that a heightened standard, greater than a rational basis, may govern. Again, Lowe relies on *Cook,* where the First Circuit held that *Lawrence* "applies a standard of review that lies between strict scrutiny and rational basis" because it "balanced the strength of the state's asserted interest in prohibiting immoral conduct against the degree of intrusion into the petitioners' private sexual life caused by the statute in order to determine whether the law was unconstitutionally applied." *Cook,* 528 F.3d at 56. In *Witt v. Dep't of the Air Force,* 527 F.3d 806 (9th Cir.2008), the Ninth Circuit also considered the "Don't Ask, Don't Tell" policy post-*Lawrence* and concluded that the *Lawrence* Court must have applied something more stringent than rational basis review. It noted that the Supreme Court rejected *Bowers* not because the *Bowers* Court wrongly held that the statute at issue satisfied rational basis review, but because of "the Court's own failure to appreciate the extent of the liberty at stake," *id.* at 813 (quoting *Lawrence,* 539 U.S. at 567, 123 S.Ct. 2472); that "the cases on which the Supreme Court explicitly based its decision in *Lawrence* are based on heightened scrutiny"; and that "[w]ere the Court applying rational basis review, it would not [have] identif[ied] a legitimate state interest to 'justify' the particular intrusion of liberty at issue," *id.* at 817.

Other circuit courts, however, have concluded just the opposite. In *Seegmiller v. LaVerkin City,* 528 F.3d 762 (10th Cir.2008), the Tenth Circuit considered a plaintiff's claim that her employer, LaVerkin City, Utah, and its agents, "violated her fundamental liberty interest to 'engage in a private act of consensual sex.'" *Id.* at 770. The court noted that "[b]roadly speaking, no one disputes a right to be free from government interference in matters of consensual sexual privacy. But as the case law teaches us, a plaintiff asserting a substantive due process right must both (1) carefully describe the right and its scope; and (2) show how the right as described fits within the Constitution's notions of ordered liberty." *Id.* at 769 (citing *Washington v. Glucksberg,* 521 U.S. 702, 721, 117 S.Ct. 2258, 138 L.Ed.2d 772 (1997)). Applying that standard, the court concluded that *Lawrence* did not announce a fundamental right, noting that "nowhere in *Lawrence* does the Court describe the right at issue in that case as a fundamental right or a fundamental liberty interest. It instead applied rational basis review to the law and found it lacking." *Id.* at 771.

The Court of Appeals for the Eleventh Circuit has similarly construed *Lawrence.* In *Lofton v. Sec'y of Dep't of Children & Family Servs.,* 358 F.3d 804 (11th Cir.2004), *cert. denied,* 543 U.S. 1081, 125 S.Ct. 869, 160 L.Ed.2d 825 (2005), it held that "it is a strained and ultimately incorrect reading of *Lawrence* to interpret it to announce a new fundamental right" when the *Lawrence* opinion "contains virtually no inquiry into the question of whether the petitioners' asserted right is one of those fundamental rights and liberties which are, objectively, deeply rooted in this Nation's history and tradition and implicit in the concept of ordered liberty . . . "; "never provides the careful description of the asserted fundamental liberty interest that is to accompany fundamental-rights analysis"; and "[m]ost significant[ly] . . . never applied strict scrutiny, the proper standard when fundamental rights are implicated, but instead invalidated the Texas statute on rational basis grounds. . . ." *Id.* at 816–17; *see also Williams v. Att'y Gen. of Ala.,* 378 F.3d 1232, 1237 (11th Cir.2004) ("As we noted in *Lofton,* we are not prepared to infer a new fundamental right from an opinion that never employed the usual *Glucksberg* analysis for identifying such rights. Nor are we prepared to assume that *Glucksberg*—a precedent that *Lawrence* never once mentions—is overruled by implication.").

In the present case, as the magistrate judge and district court correctly concluded, this split of authority provides strong support * * * to affirm the decision of the Ohio Supreme Court. In light of the disagreement among the circuits and the well-reasoned authority in favor of respondent, we hold that the Ohio Supreme Court did not unreasonably apply clearly established federal law in reviewing Ohio Rev.Code § 2907.03(A)(5) for a rational basis. *See Wright v. Van Patten,* 552 U.S. 120, 126, 128 S.Ct. 743, 169 L.Ed.2d 583 (2008) (explaining that "[b]ecause our cases give no clear answer to the question presented, let alone one in [the defendant's] favor, it cannot be said that the state court unreasonably applied clearly established Federal law").

Furthermore, assuming that *Lawrence* clearly established a fundamental right and/or a higher standard of review, we hold that neither the right nor standard is implicated in the present case. In this regard, we agree with the Seventh Circuit's decision in *Muth v. Frank,* 412 F.3d 808 (7th Cir.), *cert. denied,* 546 U.S. 988, 126 S.Ct. 575, 163 L.Ed.2d 480 (2005). There, the defendant was convicted of incest in a Wisconsin state court and argued that "Wisconsin's incest statute is unconstitutional insofar as it seeks to criminalize a sexual relationship between two consenting adults." *Id.* at 810. The defendant filed a petition for habeas corpus relief that the federal district court denied. On appeal, the Seventh Circuit affirmed, concluding that "[g]iven ... the specific focus in *Lawrence* on homosexual sodomy, the absence from the Court's opinion of its own 'established method' for resolving a claim that a particular practice implicates a fundamental liberty interest, and the absence of strict scrutiny review," there was no clearly established federal law "that supports [the defendant's] claim that he has a fundamental right to engage in incest free from government proscription." *Id.* at 818.

A similar conclusion applies here. As the Seventh Circuit held, *Lawrence* did not address or clearly establish federal law regarding state incest statutes. Indeed, the *Lawrence* Court expressly distinguished statutes like Ohio Rev.Code § 2907.03(A)(5) when it emphasized that "[t]he present case does not involve * * * persons who might be injured or coerced or who are situated in relationships where consent might not easily be refused." *Lawrence,* 539 U.S. at 578, 123 S.Ct. 2472. Unlike sexual relationships between unrelated same-sex adults, the stepparent-stepchild relationship is the kind of relationship in which a person might be injured or coerced or where consent might not easily be refused, regardless of age, because of the inherent influence of the stepparent over the stepchild.

Moreover, the State of Ohio's interest in criminalizing incest is far greater and much different than the interest of the State of Texas in prosecuting homosexual sodomy. Ohio's paramount concern is protecting the family from the destructive influence of intra-family, extra-marital sexual contact. This is an important state interest that the *Lawrence* Court did not invalidate. For these reasons, we hold that the Ohio Supreme Court's decision was not contrary to and did not involve an unreasonable application of clearly established federal law.

Lowe's remaining arguments are meritless. His claim that the Ohio law is contrary to *Lawrence* because it is morality-based fails for two reasons. First, the state has a legitimate and important interest in protecting families. *See Michael H. v. Gerald D.*, 491 U.S. 110, 123–24, 109 S.Ct. 2333, 105 L.Ed.2d 91 (1989) ("Our decisions establish that the Constitution protects the sanctity of the family precisely because the institution of the family is deeply rooted in this Nation's history and tradition."); *see, e.g., Camp v. State,* 288 Ark. 269, 704 S.W.2d 617, 619 (1986) ("[S]ociety is as concerned with the integrity of the family, including step and adoptive relationships as well as those of blood relationships, and sexual activity is equally disruptive, whatever the makeup of the family."). Second, the *Lawrence* Court did not categorically invalidate criminal laws that are based in part on morality. *Cf. Williams v. Morgan,* 478 F.3d 1316, 1323 (11th Cir. 2007) (concluding that "public morality survives as a rational basis for legislation even after *Lawrence*"). Finally, Lowe's assertion that Ohio's "generalized interest in protecting the family unit" cannot support the statute as applied in this case because "there is no evidence in the record that beyond [his] technical status as stepfather an actual family unit even existed" is also without merit. Ohio has an interest in protecting *all* families against destructive sexual contacts irrespective of the particular factual family dynamic. * * *

For these reasons, we affirm the judgment of the district court.

THE PSYCHODYNAMICS OF SEXUAL CHOICE[*]

Anne C. Dailey

Sigmund Freud considered the incest taboo to be a universal feature of civilized societies. Anthropologists confirm the widespread existence of the moral sanction against adult incest. A few countries today do not criminalize sexual relations between consenting adult family members, but social disapproval of adult incestuous relations is almost universal. In the United States, criminal laws against adult incest remain firmly entrenched in 47 states, with some states allowing life imprisonment as the penalty for the crime.[30] No state allows marriage between immediate family members. The issue of adult incest is not merely hypothetical. In

---

[*]   Anne C. Dailey, *The Psychodynamics of Sexual Choice,* 57 ARIZ. L. REV. 343, 350–53 (2015).

[30]   In the United States, Connecticut, Rhode Island, and New Jersey have decriminalized adult incest.

2010, a professor at Columbia University was charged with felony incest for sleeping with his 24-year-old daughter over a three-year period. In 1997, Katherine Harrison published her memoir detailing her several-year adult sexual relationship with her father. Persons convicted of adult incest can be fined, sentenced to prison, denied parental rights, and classified as sex offenders.

Since Sophocles, adult incest has captured the literary imagination. The Marquis de Sade covered the topic in several of his works. Among the many modern authors taken with the subject, F. Scott Fitzgerald, Lawrence Durrell, Gabriel Garcia Marquez, Vladimir Nabokov, John Irving, and Jeffrey Eugenides, explore incestuous relationships in their books. Incest also plays a regular part in American films. The relatively frequent presence of the topic in literature and film reflects a cultural fascination with the transgression of this elemental boundary. Is it repulsion, temptation, or both that stands behind the incest taboo? We assume the incest taboo expresses universal disgust for the practice, but perhaps, as Freud believed, the prohibition has a hold on our imagination precisely because it is needed to contain powerful and transgressive unconscious desires. History shows us that the crossing of sexual boundaries with a more powerful figure proves a seductive fantasy. Removing the barrier to adult incest might in fact reduce its transgressive allure.

Given the modern ideal of sexual autonomy, the ban on adult incest requires justification. No one objects to the incest taboo when it comes to sexual relations with children, for obvious reasons. Children are vulnerable, sexually immature, and dependent on their parental caregivers. Sexual conduct at too early an age can result in severe and long-lasting trauma. But few people regard the incest taboo as objectionable when it comes to *adult* incest, either. We may think the reasons for the adult incest prohibition are obvious, but close examination reveals surprising weaknesses in the traditional justifications for the rule.

The topic of adult incest provokes near universal disgust. Most people view the act as morally repugnant and unnatural, a perversion rising to the level of bestiality and cannibalism. Yet the principle of sexual autonomy protects individuals from the moral condemnation of society, as we learned from the Supreme Court's decision in *Lawrence* on homosexual sodomy. Many sex acts might be viewed as perversions, but we allow them precisely because we believe individuals have the right to control their intimate lives so long as they do not harm anyone else. In the aftermath of *Lawrence*, moral distaste cannot justify laws regulating private, consensual sexual activity—something more must be at stake.

Defenders argue that incest laws are justified as health measures because they protect against offspring with genetic abnormalities. Yet the scientific support for this proposition remains inconclusive. Even if we accept the point as true, the argument has serious weaknesses. Many people desiring incestuous relations are not biologically able to reproduce, either because of age or reproductive disability, but they are nevertheless included within the scope of these statutes. Homosexual couples fall within the prohibition, as do step-relatives and adoptive relatives in many states. Most problematic, the genetic abnormalities argument goes to the issue of procreation, not sex. Although many people in nonincestuous relationships have an even greater likelihood of having children with hereditary defects, we allow them to engage in sexual relations unrestrained. Equal treatment would require prohibiting all of these relationships as well. Yet banning all sexual relations posing heightened risks for genetic abnormalities or disease in offspring would obviously be an intolerable invasion of individual rights. The idea recalls Justice Holmes' infamous opinion in *Buck v. Bell*, in which he upheld the forced sterilization of a mentally disabled woman with the remark: "Three generations of imbeciles are enough." The Supreme Court has long since abandoned support for eugenics, suggesting that individuals have a fundamental right to procreate, whatever the genetic consequences.

Some might argue that allowing adult incest would make policing the incest taboo during childhood just that much harder. It is true that the possibility of sexual relations in the future might lead some adults to "jump the gun," particularly with older adolescents. But this argument could apply just as easily to all relationships, not just incestuous ones. The possibility of future sexual relations might lead any adult so inclined to pursue sexual relations with adolescents regardless of family ties. One might argue that adults in the family have greater access to children, and so the opportunity for developing—and the temptation to develop—sexual relations prematurely is greater. This may be true, but we already have laws in place to address this problem, including statutory rape laws, child sexual assault laws, child abuse laws, and child endangerment laws. Statutory rape is a strict liability crime that does not require the prosecution to prove lack of consent, so it is especially effective at deterring adult sex with minors. It is unclear why a special statute banning all adult incest is needed to restrain individuals who exploit children.

A last justification for the prohibition on adult incest seems more promising, at least initially. Some argue that the possibility of adult incest will encourage adults to regard children as future sexual mates. Parents in the home might be tempted to groom their children to be their adult sexual partners. But again, child welfare laws are already in place that criminalize conduct occurring while the child is a minor. If the argument centers on adult fantasies about future sexual relations, then this argument must identify how fantasy about the future translates into present harm when it does not result in actual sexual conduct. We should want to know more about "grooming" before imposing an absolute lifetime ban on adult incestuous relationships. Moreover, it is unclear why this argument applies only to family relationships, and not to adult-child relationships outside the family. Adults may consider any child a potential future mate. Indeed it may be more likely that unrelated adults would have such thoughts and fantasies, but we do not respond by banning the eventual adult relationships. Coaches, teachers, neighbors, and camp counselors all have close contact with children, but they are not prohibited from entering into relationships once the children reach the age of majority. A defense of incest laws that turns on the harm of sexualizing children must explain why the harm to children is greater in families than in other contexts. The fact that sexual abuse of children may happen most frequently in the family context does not necessarily justify the lifetime ban on adults.

The adult-incest prohibition thus comes across, upon reflection, as an overly broad, morally discriminatory, and unnecessary intrusion on the right of sexual autonomy. We believe that incest between a parent and an adult child is wrong, but we have no justification beyond moral condemnation of a parent who would pursue a sexual relationship with an adult child.

[Professor Dailey goes on to argue that adult incest prohibitions are best justified on the ground that an adult child's capacity to consent to a sexual relationship with a parent "is likely to be deeply compromised" because the strong emotional reactions that can surface with any sexual encounter may "trigger in the adult child a psychological 'regression' to more elementary, child-like modes of thinking rooted in the early parent-child relationship. This kind of cognitive regression—where the individual experiences an unconscious breakdown in adult reflective thinking—renders the adult child more psychically vulnerable. Present and past collapse as the adult child loses the capacity for mature deliberative thought brought about by a sexual relationship with a psychologically more powerful figure."]

NOTES

1.   Incest regulations fall into two broad categories. First, there are laws that prohibit marriages between individuals who are thought to be too closely related to marry. Second, there are laws, such as the one at issue in *Lowe*, which criminalize sexual conduct among family members. Are the justifications for the two sets of laws the same? Should the state have greater discretion to prohibit, for example, two first cousins from marrying than to prohibit them from engaging in sexual acts? (About half the states today do

not allow first cousins to marry.) If two individuals are constitutionally entitled to decide whether they should have sex with each other, does that mean that they should also be constitutionally entitled to marry?

2.   What is the proper role of consent by adults in questions related to incest? What justifies vitiating the consent, for example, of adult stepchildren to have sexual relations with their stepparents or of adult siblings to have sex with each other? Is the problem that consent in intra-family contexts cannot be meaningful (analogous perhaps to the ways in which a minor lacks the capacity to consent to have sex with an adult)? Or is the problem that even if consent to sex can be meaningful in at least some intra-family circumstances, there are other social interests that outweigh considerations of consent and personal liberty?

3.   Consider the following argument by political scientist Stephen Macedo:

> The distinctive forms of love and trust that characterize healthy family relations * * * depend on the exclusion of sexual relations. For siblings or parents and children to consider each other as eligible sexual partners *prospectively* is inherently corrupting of norms that sustain healthy and valuable family relations, and these are vital to human well-being. If we were to announce permission for adult siblings, or parents and their adult children, past a certain age to have sexual relations, this would reshape the way that siblings and parents and children regard one another generally, including from the time children are very young. I see no way for the consequences to be limited to those truly voluntarily agreeing in the later stages of life. * * * Once the idea becomes socially acceptable, it becomes a prospective possibility, available to all, shaping * * * the imaginations of the young and older family members. It becomes thinkable for parents to consider raising their children to be prospective sexual partners, but of course, only at the proper age. How could we trust, if ever this happened, that the parent had not manipulated and subverted the education for independence and equal freedom that every child is owed (like Humbert Humbert's rearing of Lolita)?

MACEDO, *supra*, at 195.

4.   The courts have consistently rejected the claim that *Lawrence* requires the striking down of incest bans. In addition to the court's ruling in *Lowe*, see, e.g., *Muth v. Frank*, 412 F.3d 808 (7th Cir. 2005); *People v. McEvoy*, 215 Cal.App.4th 431, 154 Cal.Rpt.3d 914 (2013); *People v. Scott*, 157 Cal.App.4th 189, 68 Cal.Rptr.3d 592 (2007); *Prather v. Kentucky*, 2014 WL 2536866 (Ky.Ct.App.); *State v. Freeman*, 801 N.E.2d 906, 155 Ohio App.3d 492 (2003).

E. PUBLIC SEX

The defendants in *Lawrence* were arrested for allegedly engaging in consensual sex in the home. What if they had been arrested for engaging in sex in a less private place, such as a sex club, public bathroom or park? Would the liberty interest recognized in *Lawrence* to engage in consensual sexual conduct apply then? The following materials address that question.

SINGSON V. COMMONWEALTH

Court of Appeals of Virginia, 2005
621 S.E.2d 682, 46 Va.App. 724

ROBERT J. HUMPHREYS, JUDGE.

Appellant Joel Dulay Singson ("Singson") appeals his conviction, following a conditional guilty plea, for solicitation to commit oral sodomy, in violation of Code §§ 18.2–29 (criminal solicitation) and 18.2–361 (crimes against nature). Based on the holding of the United States Supreme Court in *Lawrence v. Texas*, 539 U.S. 558 (2003), Singson contends that Code § 18.2–361 is facially unconstitutional because it prohibits private acts of consensual sodomy, in violation of the Due Process Clause of the Fourteenth Amendment. Thus, Singson argues that he cannot be convicted for attempting, through solicitation, to violate that statute. * * *

The relevant facts are not in dispute. At approximately 4:00 p.m. on March 20, 2003, Singson walked into a men's restroom located in a department store. The restroom is freely accessible to members of the public, including children. Once in the restroom, Singson entered the handicapped bathroom stall and remained in that stall for approximately thirty minutes. Singson then left the handicap bathroom stall and approached a stall occupied by an undercover police officer. Singson "stopped in front of the stall, leaned forward," and "peered into [the] stall through the crack in the stall door." The undercover police officer, who was in "a state of undress," asked Singson "What's up?" and "What are you looking for?" Singson replied, "Cock." The officer then asked "What do you want to do," and Singson replied, "I want to suck cock." The undercover officer asked if Singson wanted to suck his penis, and Singson responded, "Yes." When the officer asked, "Do you want to do it in here," Singson nodded towards the handicap stall. The officer then asked if Singson wanted to suck his penis in the handicap stall, and Singson responded, "Yes."

A grand jury indicted Singson for "command[ing], entreat[ing] or otherwise attempt[ing] to persuade another to commit a felony other than murder," specifically, "Crimes Against Nature," in violation of Code §§ 18.2–29 and 18.2–361. Singson moved to dismiss the indictment, arguing that Code § 18.2–361 "is overbroad and vague, [and] violates the defendant's rights to Due Process under the United States Constitution as outlined in the recent U.S. Supreme Court opinion in [*Lawrence v. Texas*, 539 U.S. 558]."

The trial court overruled the motion to dismiss, reasoning that *Lawrence* did not apply because "the restrooms within [s]tores open to the public are not within the zone of privacy as contemplated by the United States Supreme Court." The court further noted that it could not "imagine too much more [of a] public place than a restroom in a shopping mall." Singson entered a conditional guilty plea, and the trial court, noting Singson's extensive criminal history of prior, similar behavior, imposed a sentence of three years in prison. The court suspended two and one-half years of Singson's sentence, resulting in a total active sentence of six months. * * *

Citing the United States Supreme Court's decision in *Lawrence v. Texas*, Singson * * * contends that Code § 18.2–361 is facially unconstitutional because it encompasses private acts of consensual sodomy, thus offending the Due Process Clause of the Fourteenth Amendment. However, because Singson's conduct occurred in a public place—not a private location—we hold that he lacks standing to challenge the constitutionality of Code § 18.2–361 on this ground. Accordingly, we do not reach the issue of whether, applying *Lawrence*, Code § 18.2–361 is facially unconstitutional under the Fourteenth Amendment because it encompasses private—as well as public—acts of consensual sodomy. And, because application of Code § 18.2–361 under the circumstances of this case neither implicates nor violates Singson's constitutional right to due process of law, we conclude that this assignment of error has no merit. * * *

[A] litigant "has standing to challenge the constitutionality of a statute only insofar as it has an adverse impact on his own rights." *County Court of Ulster County v. Allen*, 442 U.S. 140, 154–55 (1979). Thus, "[a]s a general rule, if there is no constitutional defect in the application of the statute to the litigant, he does not have standing to argue that it would be unconstitutional if applied to third parties in hypothetical situations." *Id.* at 155. * * *

Accordingly * * * we hold that Singson lacks standing to mount a facial challenge to Code § 18.2–361. Rather, this Court is constrained to deciding whether Code § 18.2–361 is constitutional as applied to the circumstances of this case. And, for the reasons that follow, we hold that application of Code § 18.2–361 to Singson's proposed conduct does not offend the Due Process Clause of the Fourteenth Amendment. * * *

[I]n *Lawrence*, the Supreme Court explicitly noted that the case being decided on appeal did not "involve public conduct or prostitution." *Id.* The

Court, therefore, only addressed the constitutionality of criminalizing "adult consensual sexual intimacy in the home," *id.* at 564, leaving undisturbed the states' authority to prohibit sexual conduct that occurs in a public—rather than private—arena. *See, e.g., State v. Thomas*, 891 So.2d 1233, 1236, 1238 (La.2005) (declining to use *Lawrence* to strike down a law criminalizing solicitation of a crime against nature, noting that "the majority opinion in *Lawrence* specifically states the court's decision does not disturb state statutes prohibiting public sexual conduct or prostitution"); *State v. Pope*, 608 S.E.2d 114, 116 (reversing dismissal of indictment based upon the defendant's "encounter with undercover police officers in which she indicated she would perform oral sex in exchange for money," reasoning that, "[a]s the *Lawrence* Court expressly excluded prostitution and public conduct from its holding, the State of North Carolina may properly criminalize the solicitation of a sexual act it deems a crime against nature"), *review denied*, 612 S.E.2d 636 (N.C.2005).

Singson argues, however, that, in *Lawrence*, the Supreme Court effectively declared all sodomy statutes facially unconstitutional. Singson points to the Court's statement that "*Bowers* was not correct when it was decided, and it is not correct today," 539 U.S. at 578, 123 S. Ct. at 2484, as evidencing the Supreme Court's belief that no statute encompassing private acts of sodomy can survive scrutiny under the Due Process Clause. We disagree.

In *Bowers*, the appellant was prosecuted for engaging in homosexual acts of sodomy in the privacy of his own home. *See* 478 U.S. at 187–88. After the indictment was dismissed, the appellant brought a suit in federal district court seeking, in essence, a declaratory judgment that the Georgia statute was unconstitutional "as applied to consensual homosexual sodomy." *Id.* at 188 n. 2. The *Bowers* majority carefully stated that its decision "express[ed] no opinion on the constitutionality of the Georgia statute as applied to other acts of sodomy," *id.*, later noting that the issue being resolved in the appeal involved the continuing imposition of "criminal penalties for sodomy performed in private and between consenting adults," *id.* at 194. Similarly, the principal dissent in *Bowers* noted that the issue being decided concerned "the right of an individual to conduct intimate relationships in the intimacy of his or her own home." *Id.* at 208 (Blackmun, J., dissenting). Thus, despite Singson's argument to the contrary, *Bowers* did not involve a facial challenge to the Georgia sodomy statute. At best, then, the *dicta* in *Lawrence* indicates that the as-applied challenge in *Bowers* should have been upheld, and the statement does not—as Singson contends—announce a *per se* rule that all sodomy statutes are facially unconstitutional.

Singson also argues, however, that the decision of the Virginia Supreme Court in *Martin v. Ziherl*, 607 S.E.2d 367 (2005), effectively declared Code § 18.2–361 facially unconstitutional. In *Martin*, the Virginia Supreme Court held that Code § 18.2–344, which prohibits unmarried individuals from "voluntarily [ ] hav[ing] sexual intercourse with any other person," was unconstitutional in light of the decision in *Lawrence*. However, the Virginia Supreme Court carefully noted that its decision "does not involve minors, non-consensual activity, prostitution, *or public activity*." 607 S.E.2d at 371 (emphasis added). Rather, the Court explicitly restricted its holding to "private, consensual conduct between adults and the respective statutes' impact on such conduct," further noting that its decision "does not affect the Commonwealth's police power regarding regulation of public fornication, prostitution, or other such crimes." *Id.*

Thus, to the extent that Code § 18.2–361 prohibits individuals from engaging in *public* acts of sodomy, the statute survives constitutional scrutiny under the Due Process Clause. And, because Singson's proposed conduct occurred in a public location, application of Code § 18.2–361 under the circumstances of this case does not implicate Singson's constitutionally-protected right to engage in private, consensual acts of sodomy.

Our decision in *DePriest*, 537 S.E.2d 1, is instructive on this point. In *DePriest*, we affirmed the appellants' convictions for solicitation to commit oral sodomy, holding that application of Code § 18.2–361 under the circumstances of that case did not "infringe [ ] [the appellants'] right to privacy" because "the appellants' conduct was not private." [*Id.*] at 5. The appellants in *DePriest* approached "strangers in public parks" and "proposed to commit sodomy in the public parks." *Id.* at 763, 537 S.E.2d at 5. We held that "[t]he appellants' acts and their proposed conduct were clothed with no circumstance giving rise to a supportable claim of privacy," reasoning that, "[w]hatever may be the constitutional privacy rights of one who engages in sodomy in private, those rights do not attach to one who does the same thing in public." *Id.*

Similarly, here, * * * Singson approached a stranger in a public restroom in a public department store during business hours, and he proposed to commit sodomy in that restroom. Because Singson's proposed conduct involved a public rather than private location, application of Code § 18.2–361 under the circumstances of this case does not implicate the narrow liberty interest recognized in *Lawrence*. * * * *Affirmed.*

PRIVACY, PROPERTY, AND PUBLIC SEX*

Carlos A. Ball

For the gay rights movement, *Lawrence* represented the culmination of a twenty year effort to convince the courts to include gay sexual intimacy within the scope of constitutional protection afforded to other sexual conduct that takes place in the home. Many queer theorists, however, are troubled by this effort to "domesticate" sexual liberty. From th[eir] perspective, the home, as a sexual site, can serve as an extension of the closet, a place where sex is permitted (or tolerated) precisely because it is hidden from view. The notion that the only gay sex that is permissible is that which takes place in the privacy of the bedroom reinforces the idea that such sex is shameful and debasing. When lesbians and gay men limit their sexuality to sex with their partners in the privacy of their homes, the argument goes, they replicate the traditional sexual practices and mores of heterosexuals. The bedroom, then, acts as a sanitizing site through which gay sex is cleansed and made more acceptable (i.e., made more like heterosexual sex). In contrast, when gay sex takes place outside of the privacy of the home, its publicness transforms it into *queer* sex. It becomes, in other words, a form of transgressive sex that challenges heteronormative values and practices.

Part of the transgressiveness of public (or non-domesticated) sex lies in the fact that it is usually both anonymous and lacking in emotional commitment. Some queer theorists are critical of the efforts by the gay rights movement to "mainstream" gay sexuality by, for example, seeking admission into the institution of marriage. From this queer theory perspective, the struggle to gain marital recognition of same-sex relationships is a misguided effort to normalize gay sexuality by creating the illusion that all gay people want the same thing, in terms of sexual intimacy, that ostensibly most straight people seek, that is, a life-long commitment with one sexual partner. The anonymity and lack of emotional commitment that usually accompany public sex, then, become for some an appealingly transgressive alternative to the assimilationist and conservative goal of encouraging individuals, regardless of sexual orientation, to marry.

Queer theorists value public sex not only because of its transgressiveness, but also because of its accessibility. Not everyone has a bedroom to call her own, and [young] gay people in particular may have a hard time finding spaces in their family homes where they can have sex. In contrast to bedrooms, public sex sites are generally accessible by anyone who is interested in the type of sex that takes place therein.

* Carlos A. Ball, *Privacy, Property, and Public Sex*, 18 COLUM. J. GENDER & L. 1, 6–10, 13–14, 42–45, 21–22, 48–51 (2008).

The accessibility of public sex, in turn, plays an important role in transmitting knowledge about gay sexuality. Michael Warner notes that gay people have a limited opportunity to learn about gay sex, and that the ability to observe others engaging in that sex, whether in person or through pornographic materials, helps to educate gay people sexually. Warner points out that "[s]exual knowledges can be made cumulative," so that when queers see others like themselves having sex, they come to realize "that each touch, gesture, or sensation condenses lessons learned not only through one's own experience, but through the experience of others."[34] * * *

A truly radical understanding of sexual liberty * * * could seek to defend the rights of individuals to have sex anywhere, at any time, and in front of anybody. There are, however, at least three reasons why not even the most radical proponents of public sex defend such an expansive understanding of sexual liberty. The first is that those who do not want to observe the sex in question—individuals whom we can refer to as "unwilling gazers"—have a legitimate interest in not having sex thrust upon them. The second reason is that while a *willing* gaze by consenting observers may enhance the pleasurable experience arising from sex for some sexual actors, an *unwilling* gaze by hostile observers is likely to have the opposite effect by creating tension and discomfort, thus inhibiting or constraining the sexual actors. Finally, unwilling gazes can lead to the harassment of sexual actors by hostile gazers or by law enforcement officials. * * *

[It turns out that] privacy is an exceedingly important consideration for those who choose to engage in public sex. In fact, the likelihood of privacy serves as the crucial factor that helps to distinguish the vast number of public places that are not used as public sex sites from the limited number that are. The important point is this: *without privacy, a public place cannot function as a public sex site.* * * *

[I]t is possible to create zones of privacy in public places [where individuals engage in sex]. An expectation of privacy at these sites may be reasonable if the sexual actors have taken the necessary steps to shield their conduct from unwilling gazers. It would seem, for example, that individuals have a reasonable expectation of privacy when they have sex at a commercial [sex] establishment behind the closed doors of a cubicle or booth. The doors serve as physical barriers that, when coupled with a prevailing norm that other patrons will not enter unless invited, make it unlikely that the sex will be observed by unwilling gazers.

Admittedly, not all of the sexual conduct that occurs in commercial sex establishments takes place behind closed doors. Nonetheless, some

---

[34] MICHAEL WARNER, THE TROUBLE WITH NORMAL: SEX POLITICS AND THE ETHICS OF QUEER LIFE 178 (2000).

commercial sex establishments are configured in ways that make it unlikely that sex which takes place outside of booths and cubicles will be observed by unwilling gazers. The use of the backroom in [a] gay adult bookstore [in Washington, D.C.,] is an example of such a configuration. In order to enter that backroom, patrons have to pay a fee, and then go through a set of curtains to enter a dimly lit area. "The important characteristics [of this backroom] are several: the site is marked, explicitly, for erotic activity, and persons who enter the site may freely assume that they share similar erotic interests with persons already on-site."[154] It is reasonable to assume, therefore, that individuals who enter that particular backroom have consented to observe, and to be observed engaging in, sexual conduct.

It is also, however, reasonable to assume that the likelihood that sex will be observed by unwilling gazers increases, and the extent of the reasonableness of the privacy expectations of the sexual actors therefore decreases, when shifting from private commercial sites to open access areas [such as parks and public bathrooms]. Nonetheless, the sociological literature on public sex shows that it is possible, at least under some circumstances, for sexual actors to use open access spaces in ways that go undetected by potential unwilling gazers.

A * * * study by John Hollister of a highway rest stop that functions as a sexual site [shows] how sexual actors go about privatizing open access areas.[79] Hollister explains, for example, that where individuals park their automobiles (far from or near the restroom facility) and where they stroll after they park (away from or toward the facility) communicate sexual intentions, *but only to the initiated.* As Hollister puts it, "[c]ommunication takes place in relation to the space, and the likely possibilities for the use of that space. Participants reach conclusions as to a man's sexual availability based on how he approaches and occupies the space, and they [in turn] use the space in ways that the other man might recognize." He adds that "[t]he communication is rarely so obvious or direct as to expose the situation to someone who is there by accident, or who may respond violently."

* * * Hollister [found] that the private/sexual and public/nonsexual uses of the highway rest stop coexist with little interference from each other: "Rest area cruisers take great care in camouflaging themselves. The few who don't are as effective in inducing [other cruisers] to leave as

---

154   William L. Leap, *Sex in "Private" Places: Gender, Erotics, and Detachment in Two Urban Locales, in* PUBLIC SEX/GAY SPACE (William L. Leap ed., 1999), at 115, 127. When Leap interviewed the patrons of this particular establishment, they repeatedly "use[d] the term 'private' * * * to identify and describe [the backroom]." *Id.* at 129.

79   *See* John Hollister, *A Highway Rest Area as a Socially Reproducible Site, in* PUBLIC SEX/GAY SPACE (William L. Leap ed., 1999), at 55, 58.

a policeman * * * [T]he sites I observed were concealed from nonparticipants." * * *

It may be argued that the possibility that sex in open access areas may be observed by a third party renders unreasonable the sexual actors' expectations of privacy. What should ultimately matter in establishing the scope of the right to sexual liberty, however, should not be whether the sex is observed but whether such observation is consensual. The state's interest in regulating sexual conduct is implicated only once it is likely that the sex will be observed by unwilling gazers. There is no harm that justifies the interference with sexual liberty when there is consent on the part of both the observers and the sexual actors. As Richard Mohr argues, "[w]e need to abandon the idea that in order for sex to be considered private, it must be hidden away behind four walls. It is not geography or mere physical enclosure that makes sex private. * * * If the participants are all consenting to be there with each other for the possibility of sex polymorphic, then they fulfill the criterion of the private in the realm of the sexual." * * *

There can be, of course, no guarantee that sex in open access areas, such as public bathrooms and highway rest stops, will remain undetected. It is always possible that, despite significant precautions taken by sexual actors, unsuspecting individuals may nonetheless stumble across sexual conduct that they will find offensive. The question, however, should not be whether it is possible that an unwilling gazer will observe the sex. It is, after all, possible that an unwilling gazer (such as an unexpected visitor) will stumble across sexual conduct that takes place in the home. The question instead should be whether it is *likely* that a nonconsenting third party will observe the sex. The public sex literature suggests that such an outcome is unlikely in at least some open access sites under some circumstances. * * *

We should, therefore, resist the urge to jump to the conclusion that sex in open access areas should always be constitutionally unprotectable. This is particularly true in cases in which law enforcement officials have to engage in intrusive or deceptive practices to observe the sexual conduct in question. Public sex advocates argue that much of the sex that takes place in open access areas would go undetected *but for* the aggressive investigative tools used by government officials. Pat Califia, for example, notes that "[i]f people are going to see what is going on in these places, they must intrude. They must actively look for things that will offend them either by penetrating physical barriers, by setting up covert surveillance, or by posing as potential participants."[165] The greater the efforts that must be engaged in by law enforcement officials and others to observe public sex, the more likely it is that the sexual actors in question

---

[165]   PAT CALIFIA, PUBLIC SEX: THE CULTURE OF RADICAL SEX 76 (1994).

are taking the necessary steps to exclude unwilling gazers and other potential intruders.

UNITED STATES V. LANNING

U.S. Court of Appeals for the Fourth Circuit, 2013
723 F.3d 476

WYNN, CIRCUIT JUDGE.

In the context of a sting operation specifically targeting gay men, an undercover ranger approached Defendant, initiated a sexually suggestive conversation with him, and then expressly agreed to have sex with him. In response, Defendant backed up to the ranger and "[v]ery briefly" touched the ranger's fully-clothed crotch. That conduct gave rise to Defendant's conviction for disorderly conduct under 36 C.F.R. § 2.34, which prohibits conduct that is "obscene," "physically threatening or menacing," or "likely to inflict injury or incite an immediate breach of the peace." 36 C.F.R. § 2.34(a)(2).

Upon review, we hold that the term "obscene" is unconstitutionally vague as applied to Defendant. We further hold that no rational trier of fact could find beyond a reasonable doubt that Defendant's brief touch of the ranger's crotch, done in response to the ranger's deliberate attempt to convince Defendant that he would have sex with him, was "physically threatening or menacing" or "likely to inflict injury or incite an immediate breach of the peace." Accordingly, we reverse and remand for a judgment of acquittal.

After receiving complaints about male-on-male sexual activity around the Sleepy Gap Overlook of the Blue Ridge Parkway in Buncombe County, North Carolina, the National Park Service and the United States Forest Service conducted a joint operation "designed to enable officers to identify and arrest men who were using the area for sexual solicitation and activity with other men." Appellee's Br. at 3. Joseph Darling, a thirty-three-year-old, two-hundred-pound park ranger, participated in the sting operation as an undercover officer. In November 2009, in the course of the sting operation, Darling saw Defendant, a sixty-two-year-old male retiree, on a nearby trail. As Darling walked past Defendant, Defendant grabbed his own groin and kept walking. Darling said hello and also kept walking.

Five or ten minutes later, after walking around in the woods and talking to a few other people, Darling went looking for Defendant and found him standing by himself on an unofficial trail. Darling engaged Defendant in a casual conversation about the weather for several minutes. Darling then commented that Asheville was "an open community," accepting of a homosexual lifestyle. Defendant responded that he "wanted to be F'ed." Darling replied "okay or yes, or something to that affirmative[,]" and "gave [Defendant] every reason to believe that

[Darling] was good to go." At that point, Defendant—who was facing Darling and standing approximately three to five feet away from him—turned around, took one or two steps backward towards Darling, and, with his left hand, reached back and "[v]ery briefly" touched Darling's fully-clothed crotch. Darling described the touch as "a fairly firm grasp" that lasted "[v]ery briefly[,] [u]ntil I could get the words out: 'Police officer, you're under arrest.'"

Defendant was charged with disorderly conduct in violation of 36 C.F.R. § 2.34(a)(2). Before trial, Defendant unsuccessfully moved to dismiss the case. At trial, Darling was the only witness. And at the close of the government's evidence, Defendant moved for judgment of acquittal. This, too, the magistrate judge denied. The magistrate judge then found Defendant guilty of disorderly conduct, giving no specific reasons for his decision and noting only that he was "convinced beyond a reasonable doubt" that Defendant had violated the statute. The magistrate judge sentenced Defendant to 15 days' imprisonment, a $1000 fine, and a two-year ban on visiting government forests and parks.

Defendant appealed to the district court. The district court affirmed Defendant's conviction, [but] vacated and remanded Defendant's sentence because the magistrate judge lacked the authority to ban Defendant from government parks. The magistrate judge resentenced Defendant to 15 days' imprisonment and a $500 fine, and the district court affirmed. Defendant then appealed to this Court.

Section 2.34 is an enactment of the Secretary of the Interior, who is authorized to promulgate regulations "necessary or proper for the use and management" of parks under the jurisdiction of the National Park Service, including the Blue Ridge Parkway. * * * Section 2.34(a)(2) [states as follows:]

> A person commits disorderly conduct when, with intent to cause public alarm, nuisance, jeopardy or violence, or knowingly or recklessly creating a risk thereof, such person * * * [u]ses language, an utterance, or gesture, or engages in a display or act that is obscene, physically threatening or menacing, or done in a manner that is likely to inflict injury or incite an immediate breach of the peace.

36 C.F.R. § 2.34(a)(2). * * * Defendant argues that the government failed to prove the second element of disorderly conduct under Section 2.34(a)(2). We therefore must analyze each prong of that element—that is, whether the conduct at issue was "obscene," "physically threatening or menacing," or "likely to inflict injury or incite an immediate breach of the peace"—to determine whether the government met its burden. * * *

* * * [T]he provision's legislative history reveals that the rule's promulgator believed "[t]he harms that the regulation seeks to avoid [to

be] *commonly understood.*" 48 Fed.Reg. 30252, 30270 (June 30, 1983) (emphasis added). Similarly, in *United States v. Coutchavlis,* the Ninth Circuit declared that "the regulation contained only 'common words,' easily understandable by 'people of ordinary intelligence.' The words of § 2.34 are not so obscure that they require any special skill to interpret." 260 F.3d 1149, 1155 (9th Cir.2001).

We regularly turn to the dictionary for the "ordinary, contemporary, common meaning" of words undefined by statute, as is the case with "obscene" here. *The American Heritage Dictionary* defines "obscene" as "[o]ffensive to accepted standards of decency" and "[m]orally repulsive[.]" *Id.* at 1216 (5th ed.2011). *The Oxford English Dictionary* defines "obscene" as "[o]ffensively or grossly indecent, lewd[.]" *Oxford English Dictionary Online,* http://www.oed.com/view/Entry/129823?redirected From=obscene (last visited April 10, 2013).

The government argues that "the standard dictionary definition" of obscene "appl[ies] in determining whether a defendant is guilty of 'disorderly conduct'" and, when doing so here, "the evidence amply supports the magistrate judge's finding that Defendant's conduct was obscene." Defendant counters that if a dictionary definition of obscene applies, then Section 2.34(a)(2) is "unconstitutionally vague as applied." Under the circumstances of this case, we must agree with Defendant.

It is axiomatic that a law fails to meet the dictates of the Due Process Clause "if it is so vague and standardless that it leaves the public uncertain as to the conduct it prohibits. * * *" *City of Chicago v. Morales,* 527 U.S. 41, 56, 119 S.Ct. 1849, 144 L.Ed.2d 67 (1999). "A statute can be impermissibly vague for either of two independent reasons. First, if it fails to provide people of ordinary intelligence a reasonable opportunity to understand what conduct it prohibits. Second, if it authorizes or even encourages arbitrary and discriminatory enforcement." *Hill v. Colorado,* 530 U.S. 703, 732, 120 S.Ct. 2480, 147 L.Ed.2d 597 (2000). As the Supreme Court has noted, "perhaps the most meaningful aspect of the vagueness doctrine is not actual notice, but the other principal element of the doctrine—the requirement that a legislature establish minimal guidelines to govern law enforcement." *Smith v. Goguen,* 415 U.S. 566, 574, 94 S.Ct. 1242, 39 L.Ed.2d 605 (1974).

Turning first to the notice issue, we agree with Defendant that Section 2.34(a)(2) would not have provided him, or anyone of ordinary intelligence, fair warning that the complained-of conduct was obscene. The evidence, even when viewed in the light most favorable to the government, shows that: Defendant grabbed his own clothed groin once while walking; after being engaged in a flirtatious conversation by an undercover ranger who noted that "Asheville [was] an open community;" Defendant told the undercover ranger that "he wanted to be F'ed[,]"; and, after the ranger accepted Defendant's sexual proposition, Defendant quickly walked backwards toward the ranger and grabbed the ranger's clothed crotch "fairly firm[ly] * * * [v]ery briefly[,] [u]ntil [the ranger] could get the words out: 'Police officer, you're under arrest.' " Under these circumstances, we cannot conclude that anyone "of ordinary intelligence," would understand that such conduct is "[m]orally repulsive," or "[o]ffensively or grossly indecent, lewd[,]" so as to be "obscene" and thus proscribed by Section 2.34(a)(2).[3]

Further, the facts of this case illustrate the real risk that the provision may be "arbitrar[ily] and discriminator[ily] enforce[d]." *Hill*, 530 U.S. at 732, 120 S.Ct. 2480. The sting operation that resulted in Defendant's arrest was aimed not generally at sexual activity in the Blue Ridge Parkway; rather, it specifically targeted gay men. Perhaps not surprisingly, then, the all-male undercover rangers arrested only men on the basis of disorderly homosexual conduct.

The impetus for the sting operation: citizen complaints. Darling testified that "the public was concerned" about "male on male [sexual] activity in that area that was targeted."[4] Darling testified that every single one of the citizen complaints had been about homosexuals.

It may be that gay men engage more frequently in sexual activity in the Blue Ridge Parkway and therefore generate more citizen complaints. Yet it is also entirely plausible that the public in and around the Blue Ridge Parkway subjectively finds homosexual conduct, even relatively innocuous conduct such as that at issue here, particularly "morally repulsive" and "grossly indecent," and therefore complains. If the public is, by contrast, not similarly troubled by a woman propositioning her boyfriend for sex and then briefly touching his clothed crotch, there would exist no citizen complaint and no related sting, even for otherwise identical heterosexual conduct. Simply enforcing the disorderly conduct

---

[3]   Perhaps recognizing its weak hand, the government suggests that "the magistrate judge could reasonably *infer* from Defendant's conduct that he, in fact, *intended* to have sexual intercourse in the very location in which he backed into Ranger Darling and grabbed Ranger Darling's [clothed] genitals." Yet Defendant's conviction was for disorderly *conduct*—not disorderly thoughts or desires. And it is undisputed that Defendant's actual conduct never went further than his backing up to Darling and very briefly grabbing Darling's clothed crotch. Moreover, even Darling agreed that, "for all [he] knew, [Defendant] could have very well intended for [the intercourse] to happen at [Defendant's] house." And such private sexual conduct would, of course, have been perfectly legal. As the Supreme Court pronounced a decade ago, "[l]iberty presumes an autonomy of self that includes freedom of thought, belief, expression, and certain intimate conduct" and "allows homosexual persons the right to" engage in consensual intimate conduct in the privacy of their homes. *Lawrence v. Texas*, 539 U.S. 558, 567, 123 S.Ct. 2472, 156 L.Ed.2d 508 (2003).

[4]   One wonders why a sting operation was implemented in the first place. If instead the rangers had, for example, hidden themselves, monitored the area, and arrested individuals who engaged in public sexual conduct, many of the questionable aspects of this case, from the discriminatory targeting to the alleged inchoate conduct the government attempts to inject into this matter would almost surely fall away.

regulation on the basis of citizen complaints therefore presents a real threat of anti-gay discrimination.

To be sure, in concluding that Section 2.34(a)(2)'s "obscene" is unconstitutionally vague as applied to Defendant, we do not mean to suggest that the statute is impermissibly vague per se. As the Supreme Court has recognized, "there are statutes that by their terms or as authoritatively construed apply without question to certain activities, but whose application to other behavior is uncertain." *Smith*, 415 U.S. at 577–78, 94 S.Ct. 1242.

Section 2.34(a)(2) may be just such a law. For example, we have no doubt that the court [in *United States v. Mather*, 902 F.Supp. 560 (E.D.Pa.1995)] correctly held that the conduct at issue there—i.e., two individuals with their pants down, masturbating in front of one another and engaging in fellatio in a national park—was obscene and disorderly under Section 2.34(a)(2). Unquestionably, it was; and were that conduct before us, this would surely be a radically different opinion.

The conduct at issue here, however, is of a qualitatively different, significantly more benign nature. We do not believe that a reasonable defendant would know that by engaging in such conduct under the circumstances of this case, he would be subjecting himself to criminal liability. That, coupled with our serious concern regarding discriminatory enforcement, leads us to conclude that Section 2.34(a)(2) is unconstitutionally vague as applied and that the "obscene" prong of the regulation therefore cannot serve as a basis for Defendant's conviction.

We also acknowledge the dissenting opinion's assertion that we fail to "accord[ ] the level of deference to the magistrate judge's findings of fact required by our standard of review." But that assertion misses the mark as to the regulation's obscenity prong, because even where a rational trier of fact could find facts sufficient to support a conviction, a statute can still be unconstitutional because it "authorizes or even encourages arbitrary and discriminatory enforcement." *Hill*, 530 U.S. at 732, 120 S.Ct. 2480. Indeed, the sufficiency of the evidence seems irrelevant to such a constitutional analysis.

Turning to the next prong of the regulation's second element, we analyze whether Defendant's conduct was "physically threatening or menacing." 36 C.F.R. § 2.34(a)(2).

Even the government concedes that an objective reasonable person standard applies to this inquiry. Stated differently, a fact finder must focus not on whether a particular victim subjectively felt physically threatened or menaced, but instead must ask whether a reasonable person objectively would have felt so under the circumstances of the case. * * *

* * * [A]lthough Darling testified that Defendant's touch was "firm," the government presented no evidence that Darling experienced any pain or suffered any injury as a consequence. * * * [It is true that] Darling testified that he felt "shocked" and "caught * * * off guard" by Defendant's touch. But the disorderly conduct regulation requires "physically threatening or menacing" conduct, not merely surprising conduct. 36 C.F.R. § 2.34(a)(2). And even if surprise were sufficient to trigger the regulation (it is not), and even if Darling's subjective reaction were relevant to our inquiry (it is not), it defies logic that Darling was shocked by Defendant's touch when it was, in fact, precisely what Darling had been "string[ing Defendant] along" to do—"to cross a certain line."

Facts matter. Had Defendant and Darling engaged in flirtatious conversation that did not involve an agreement to have sex, a reasonable person might well have felt physically threatened or menaced by Defendant's "[v]ery briefly" touching Darling's clothed crotch. Likewise, had Defendant pinned Darling down and attempted to remove Darling's clothing, a reasonable person, even one who had consented to sex, might well have felt physically threatened or menaced by that conduct. But given the totality of the circumstances actually before us, even when viewing the evidence in the light most favorable to the government, no rational fact finder could conclude that a reasonable person would feel physically threatened or menaced by Defendant's conduct. * * *

[Finally], we point to a recent Sixth Circuit decision, *Alman v. Reed,* which we find insightful, even if distinguishable.703 F.3d 887 (6th Cir.2013). In *Alman,* law enforcement arrested a gay man during an undercover sting at a Michigan park. The *Alman* sting, too, resulted from complaints of sexual activity in the park. There as here, an undercover officer approached Alman and initiated conversation. While the two men engaged in apparently flirtatious conversation, unlike in this case, the undercover officer never expressly agreed to engage in anal intercourse, or anything else for that matter. Nevertheless, "Alman leaned forward and reached out and touched the zipper area on the front of [the undercover officer's] crotch." *Id.* at 893. The undercover officer backed away and soon thereafter "pulled out his badge and told Alman that he was under arrest." *Id.* Alman was charged with being a disorderly person, battery, soliciting and accosting, and criminal sexual conduct in the fourth degree. Ultimately, all of the charges were dismissed.

Alman (along with his partner and a gay rights organization) brought a Section 1983 suit alleging that law enforcement violated his constitutional rights. The district court dismissed the case, but the Sixth Circuit resuscitated it, expressly holding that law enforcement, as a matter of law, lacked probable cause as to each offense with which Alman had been charged. The Sixth Circuit held that "there is nothing in the record describing circumstances that would be sufficient to create a reasonable fear of dangerous consequences." *Id.* at 897. The Court expressly refused to make "assumptions about Alman's intentions that the record does not substantiate" and noted that "a reasonable officer would have needed more evidence of Alman's intentions before concluding that he was inviting [the undercover officer] to do a public lewd act." *Id.* at 899. Under the circumstances, the Sixth Circuit concluded that "no reasonable officer" would have thought that Alman committed, or was about to commit, any of the crimes with which he was charged. * * *

REVERSED AND REMANDED

DUNCAN, CIRCUIT JUDGE, dissenting:

I respect the thoughtfulness of the majority opinion and share its distaste for Officer Darling's conduct. I also appreciate the narrowness of its focus and its careful tethering to the specific facts before us. However, the concern that prompts my brief dissent is that I am unable to agree that the majority opinion accords the level of deference to the magistrate judge's findings of fact required by our standard of review. I believe that a rational trier of fact could have found a physical touching such as this implying an immediate intent to engage in sexual activity in public both obscene and physically threatening or menacing within the meaning of 36 C.F.R. § 2.34(a)(2).

NOTES

1.   Notice that although the court in *Lanning* struck down the disorderly conduct regulation on the due process ground that it was impermissibly vague as applied, it was also troubled by the unequal enforcement of the regulation against gay men. Indeed, law enforcement agencies have historically targeted gay men in enforcing disorderly conduct, solicitation, and public lewdness laws. *See* Christopher R. Leslie, *Standing in the Way of Equality: How States use Standing Doctrine to Insulate Sodomy Laws from Constitutional Attack*, 2001 WIS. L. REV. 29, 84 (noting that "[m]any police departments employ undercover operations designed to entrap gay men into offering or requesting oral sex."). *See also* Amber Arellano et al., *Group Says Detroit Cops Target Gays*, DETROIT FREE PRESS, July 6, 2001, at 1B; Matt Lait, *LAPD Officers Target Gays, Police Commission is Told*, L.A. TIMES, May 6, 1998, at B3. The actions of the Detroit police led the city council to approve an award of $170,000 to settle litigation challenging a pattern of entrapment in the enforcement of public lewdness laws against gay men at a local park. *See* Darren Nichols, *Detroit Settles Lawsuit Over Police Sting on Gays*, DETROIT NEWS, May 16, 2002, at D2. *See also Martinez v. Port Authority of New York & New Jersey*, 2005 WL 2143333 (S.D.N.Y 2005), *aff'd*, 445 F.3d 158 (2nd Cir. 2006) (defendants ordered to pay $464,000 to compensate plaintiff for police policy of arresting men perceived to be gay for public lewdness at a subway station without probable cause).

2. A few years after *Singer*, the U.S. Court of Appeals for the Fourth Circuit held that Virginia's sodomy statute was *facially* unconstitutional. *See MacDonald v. Moose*, 710 F.3d 154, 166 (4th Cir. 2013), *cert. denied*, 134 S.Ct. 200 (2013). A short time later, the Virginia legislature amended it "crime against nature" provision so that it covered bestiality only and not consensual sex between adults. *See* Virginia Senate Bill 14 (2014).

3. Although in most instances, the challenges to the enforcement of solicitation and public lewdness statutes relate to laws that are neutral on their face, some laws explicitly targeted lesbians and gay men. Ohio, for example, until 2003 proscribed the crime of "importuning," defined as the "solicit[ation] [of] a person of the same sex to engage in sexual activity with the offender, when the offender knows such solicitation is offensive to the other person." OHIO REV. CODE ANN. § 2907.07B (2007). The Ohio Supreme Court in 1979 upheld the constitutionality of the importuning statute, concluding that same-sex solicitation is "often grossly offensive and emotionally disturbing." *State v. Phipps*, 389 N.E.2d 1128, 1134, 58 Ohio St.2d 271, 279 (1979). The same court struck down the statute in 2002, concluding that it was a content-based restriction on speech, which by extension violated state and federal equal protection guarantees. *See State v. Thompson*, 767 N.E.2d 251, 95 Ohio St.3d 264 (2002). The Ohio legislature repealed the law the following year.

4. In 1998, the Phoenix city council enacted an ordinance that prohibited "the operation of a business for purposes of providing the opportunity to engage in * * * or view * * * live sex acts." PHOENIX, AZ., CITY CODE ch. 23, art. IV, § 23–54 (1998). Fleck and Associates operated a health club in the city, and as part of their operations, they rented rooms inside the facility to men for the purpose of engaging in sexual activity. The club brought a lawsuit against the city seeking an injunction against the enforcement of the ordinance arguing inter alia that it violated their patrons' constitutional rights after *Lawrence*. The court refused to issue the injunction, concluding that "*Lawrence* does not suggest that sexual activities in a place of public accommodation are Constitutionally protected. Because [the plaintiff's] club is not private, the sexual activities that take place there likewise are not private." *Fleck & Assocs., Inc. v. Phoenix*, 356 F.Supp.2d 1034, 1041 (D.Ariz.2005), *rev'd on other grounds*, 471 F.3d 1100 (9th Cir. 2006). *See also 832 Corp., Inc. v. Gloucester*, 404 F.Supp.2d 614, 623 (D.N.J. 2005) (contrary to argument raised by owners of a nightclub where consensual sex took place, "*Lawrence* did not recognize a broad right to engage in sexual conduct outside of private settings."); *Commonwealth v. Can-Port Amusement Corp.*, 2005 WL 2009672 (Mass.Super.Ct.2005) (holding that *Lawrence* did not protect same-sex sexual conduct that took place in adult movie theater).

F. SADOMASOCHISM (S/M)

THE PSYCHODYNAMICS OF SEXUAL CHOICE*

Anne C. Dailey

Sexual masochists, as they are sometimes called, seek, and perhaps need, physical suffering and degradation in order to achieve sexual pleasure or gratification. In contrast to adult incest * * *, sadomasochistic sexual relations on the surface look nonconsensual. The submissive partner may be bound, chained, or gagged. He may be whipped, genitally pierced, bitten, smothered, injected with liquid, or covered in hot wax. Most people might find it difficult to imagine that anyone would consent to such acts, but a minority of people engage in these intimate enactments of sexual submission.

Most states prohibit sadomasochistic practices that cause or have a risk of causing serious physical injury. The dominant partner can be prosecuted for physical assault, generally defined as intentionally causing serious bodily injury to another person. Consent is not a defense to the charge of assault because, "as a matter of public policy, a person cannot avoid criminal responsibility for an assault that causes injury or carries a risk of serious harm, even if the victim asked for or consented to the act."[138] Although consensual sadomasochism does not usually result in serious injury, courts in practice "exaggerate or mischaracterize [sadomasochistic] activities in order to force the resulting injuries into the category of 'serious bodily injury.' "[139] Moreover, even where sexual harm is threatened, the "no consent" policy as applied to sadomasochism is not entirely consistent with the treatment of certain athletic activities such as boxing, mixed marital arts, and football. Finally, we allow consent as a defense to rape because we understand that consent is what distinguishes pleasurable sexual activity from violation. Why then do we rule out consent as a defense to sadomasochistic sex? Given the fundamental right of sexual autonomy, what justifies the prohibition on consensual sadomasochistic relations?

We already know that the prohibition on sadomasochistic sex cannot be based solely on our revulsion at the practice, for *Lawrence* eliminates moral condemnation as a basis for denying individuals the right to sexual autonomy. But more plausible justifications for the absolute ban should be considered. For example, we might prohibit sadomasochistic sex because we do not consider the submissive partner in these encounters to be a fully willing participant. Given the intensity of the degradation and

---

* Anne C. Dailey, *The Psychodynamics of Sexual Choice*, 57 ARIZ. L. REV. 343, 372–80 (2015).

138 State v. Van, 688 N.W.2d 600, 614 (Neb. 2004) (quoting People v. Jovanovic, 263 A.2d 182, 198 n.5 (N.Y. 1999)).

139 *See* Margo Kaplan, *Sex-Positive Law*, 89 N.Y.U. L. REV. 89, 122 (2014).

pain, we assume that no rational person would consent. The submissive partner might appear to be willing, but we think that at some level he is driven by a pathological need for punishment. The facts of some cases suggest as much. In *State v. Van*, for example, the submissive partner testified that he felt himself to be a "fundamentally * * * bad person," that he was looking for a "very physically and mentally abusive punishment relationship," and that "he expected to be tortured, humiliated, and to eventually die as a result of his relationship with [his master.]"[145] Cases such as *Van* support a common inference that the submissive partner must be psychologically ill because no rational person would willingly submit to such pain and degradation, and even risk of death. Thus, we deny the submissive partner the right to choose because we believe it is no choice at all. We position the submissive partner in the same way as the adult incestuous partner. Indeed, the masochist looks to be acting out exactly the kind of surrender to a more powerful other that we deemed indicative of the absence of choice with * * * adult incest * * * .

Yet upon closer examination, the "no rational person would consent" argument does not hold up. The law routinely accepts the idea that rational people consent to pain and injury. Football players, boxers, hockey players, and mixed martial-arts fighters all lawfully consent to risk of serious injury; skydivers and mountain climbers regularly risk death as well. The public generally admires players and athletes who risk serious injury or death for the mastery of the sport. We see these players and athletes as demonstrating exceptional courage and a sense of adventure, living life at a heightened level of energy, excitement, and skill. Moreover, all of us are implicated in the enjoyment of these games as spectators. As Robert Cover observed, "almost all people are fascinated and attracted by violence, even though they are at the same time repelled by it." We might want to argue that the pain and injury are just secondary to our real interest: the athleticism or skill. But the fact is that gratuitous pain and risk of injury are exactly what draw many people to these spectator sports.

The "no rational person would consent" argument has deeper problems as well. While not talked about in polite company, many people are specifically drawn to violence in sex. The idea that no rational person would willingly submit to sexual pain constructs a false barrier between "normal" sex and "perverse" sadomasochistic sex. We shut our eyes to the truth when we deny the physical aggression present in many, more ordinary, sexual encounters. Whatever their normative status and cultural derivations, fantasies of violent sex are not uncommon. Culturally, sadomasochistic sex has come out of the closet. Novels depicting sadomasochistic sex are bestsellers; sadomasochistic films are box office successes; artists depicting sadomasochistic activities enjoy

---

[145]   *Van*, 688 N.W.2d at 609.

widespread acclaim. Of course, sadomasochistic practices often cross the line into a realm of pain and degradation beyond what most people would ever imagine or desire. But sadomasochism lies along a continuum of consensual sexual aggression, running from conventional sex play at one end to severe pain and degradation at the other. Without overly romanticizing physical degradation and domination, the point here is that taking pleasure in rough play, bondage, or pain—whether mild or severe, real or fantasied—is not in itself an indication of impaired choice. We cannot use the presence of violence alone to infer the absence of consent.

Nevertheless, the absence of consent in sadomasochistic sex might be measured by considering the degree of aggression. Fantasy or rough play in conventional sex hardly compares to genital piercing and hot wax. But we have already identified the popular participation in extreme sports as an obvious example of a fully consensual activity posing an equally, if not sometimes higher, risk of injury or death. We might try to distinguish sadomasochism by focusing on the submissive partner's pleasure in the extreme pain, but it could actually be the case that many athletes, for example long-distance runners or bikers, similarly take pleasure in pushing their bodies beyond comfortable bounds. Finally, we might try to distinguish sadomasochistic sex on the ground that extreme sports bring social honor, fortune, and a sense of accomplishment, whereas sadomasochistic sex elicits social degradation and shame. But the right of sexual autonomy prevents us from imposing moral judgment through law on adult, consensual sexual practices. Moreover, shame and disgrace arising from sexual practices is hardly confined to sadomasochism. History has shown us that powerful people are often brought to ruin because of far less exotic sex practices. Top political leaders' careers have ended in disgrace after adulterous sexual liaisons have come to light. Socially condemned sexual behavior is hardly a road that the sexual masochist travels alone.

But the real problem with the argument that submissive partners do not consent is that it simply does not fit the facts. It turns out that submissive partners *do* consent, deliberately and carefully. In fact, sadomasochistic partners are exemplary in their commitment to consensual practices. Setting clear limits defines the community's culture. The partners may work out the terms of the sexual encounter together and in writing, injecting an element of reasoned deliberation into the process. Safe words are identified, which, when spoken, will put a stop to the activity. Furthermore, partners are careful not to engage in activities that pose a risk of serious, permanent injury. As author Pat Califia explains:

> Sadomasochism is not a form of sexual assault. It is a consensual activity that involves polarized roles and intense sensations. An S/M scene is always preceded by a negotiation in

which the top and bottom decide whether or not they will play, what activities are likely to occur, what activities will not occur, and about how long the scene will last. The bottom is usually given a "safe word" or "code action" she can use to stop the scene.[162]

These negotiated parameters and safe words demarcate the continuing consensual nature of the sexual activity. A masochistic contract, as it is sometimes called, reflects the submissive partner's control over the terms of the sexual encounter. As psychoanalyst Theodor Reik argued, to the extent coercion operates at the psychological level, it may in fact be the masochist who overtakes the will of his partner. Optimally, the exchange of pleasure rather than malignant domination defines the experience. Upending our expectations, therefore, sadomasochistic sex actually provides a template for the role of reasoned deliberation in safeguarding consensual sexual activity.

The sadomasochistic encounter highlights the importance of treating "no" as performative rather than communicative, an utterance signaling the end of consent and triggering legal responsibility for the immediate cessation of sex. Yet is the choice to engage in masochistic sex compromised by a relationship that so obviously engages the dynamics of domination and submission? While sadomasochistic sex enacts a scene of sexual domination and submission, the actual psychodynamics of the relationship are not structured around forced compliance. Sadomasochism is understood to be theater. As Califia emphasizes, "[t]he key word to understand S/M is *fantasy*." When the parameters of the encounter are expressly consented to, the sadomasochistic scene of domination and submission remains staged. The scenes are typically scripted. Indeed, the "victim" often designs the scene and maintains control over how it will unfold. Safe words are performative rather than communicative, triggering an immediate cessation to the activity. Domination retains its fantasized character up to the point where safe words are ignored and the scene goes beyond the agreed-upon terms.

* * * [D]espite the fact that sexual masochism may be motivated by unconscious needs and desires, we may not be justified in imposing paternalistic limits on the behavior. With masochism, we are not dealing with the kind of totalizing psychological submission to authority and loss of reality testing that we have seen characterize adult incest * * * . Unlike adult incest * * *, there is nothing inherent in the sadomasochistic relationship that distinguishes it from the kinds of vulnerabilities and exploitation we find in many non-sadomasochistic relationships. Certainly, masochists are not any more likely to be psychologically ill than anyone else. The Diagnostic and Statistical Manual of Mental

---

[162]   Pat Califia, *Feminism and Sadomasochism, in* PUBLIC SEX: THE CULTURE OF RADICAL 165, 168 (1994).

Disorders now requires personal distress about the sexual masochism or harm to others in order for a diagnosis to be given, reflecting the current belief that people with "atypical sexual interests do not have a mental disorder." As one commentator puts it: "At the core of the [S/M] community are mostly sensible, rational, respectable, otherwise quite ordinary people." The fact that sadomasochistic partners negotiate the terms of their sexual scene in advance only makes it more likely that the individual chooses, rather than blindly submits to, physical subjugation. While recognizing the extent to which choice is determined by unconscious factors, psychoanalysis nevertheless does not rule out human agency in the sadomasochistic encounter. For while it appears that sadomasochistic sex can be infused with unconscious super-ego fantasies of guilt and punishment, it is nevertheless explicitly and consciously bounded by and within reason.

Of course there are limits to the sexual activities to which an individual may consent. No civilized society need tolerate sexual practices that involve death, mutilation, or other severe long-term bodily injury in the name of sexual pleasure. But we must be clear about the justification for prohibiting this behavior. It is not because sexual autonomy is lacking. Rather, the ban on extreme forms of self-injury reflects a social norm that irrevocable bodily injury outweighs the individual's right to sexual freedom. We see this balancing of values in other contexts involving self-injury. Prohibitions on suicide reflect limits on self-injury deriving from the competing value of human life. In the case of suicide, countervailing normative commitments lead us to conclude that the social harm outweighs the individual's fundamental right to choose. But in the context of sadomasochistic sex, no countervailing social values against non-life-threatening injury clearly outweigh the fundamental right of sexual autonomy. If legal limits are to be set, then balancing the right to sexual autonomy against perceived social harms must take place.

In this regard, some feminists have raised legitimate concerns that sadomasochism risks sexualizing violence in ways that promote unconsented-to violence and rape among intimate partners. In fact, many of the published cases on sadomasochism do appear to involve nonconsensual sexual activity. In *Twyman v. Twyman*, for example, Sheila Twyman brought suit for intentional infliction of emotional distress against her husband for coercing her into bondage activities despite his knowing that she had been raped at knifepoint before their marriage.[182] The absence of a consent defense in sadomasochism prosecutions provides the state with an easy way to prosecute dominant partners who violate the agreed upon terms. But the same could also be said about rape statutes generally; it would certainly be easier for prosecutors if consent were not a defense to rape, but we do not take that

---

[182]   855 S.W.2d 619, 620 n.1 (Tex. 1993).

fact to be a reason to do away with the consent defense to rape charges. Some feminists argue, in fact, that because sadomasochistic sex highlights power dynamics in a self-conscious way, it allows for social critique and transformation of prevailing gender and sexual norms.

Given concerns about sexual autonomy, sadomasochistic sex should lead to criminal liability only when clearly negotiated consent was lacking or exceeded, or the injuries are truly severe or life threatening. However, because of the heightened risk of injury, we might impose a higher standard of care for establishing that the submissive partner consented to the specific activity. We might require that consent be in writing. We might insist that safe words be identified. We might be vigilant in prohibiting sexual imprisonment of any kind because it runs the risk of "traumatic bonding," a type of dependency relationship experienced by individuals physically controlled by another over a period of time. But an absolute ban on sadomasochistic sex would appear to run afoul of the fundamental right to sexual autonomy. In the absence of serious mental impairment, no compelling basis exists to deny individuals the right to engage in sadomasochistic sex.

ROE V. RECTOR AND VISITORS OF GEORGE MASON UNIVERSITY

Federal District Court for the Eastern District of Virginia, 2016
149 F. Supp.3d 602

T.S. ELLIS, III, DISTRICT JUDGE.

Plaintiff in this Fourteenth Amendment due process and free speech case is a former George Mason University ("GMU") student who was expelled in December 2014 following an administrative process that found him responsible for violating two of GMU's student conduct regulations, one pertaining to sexual misconduct and one pertaining to threats. In response to this expulsion, plaintiff filed the instant action in February 2015 against GMU and three of its officials in their individual and official capacities, alleging violations of various state and federal constitutional rights, state common law duties, and federal law. By Order and Memorandum Opinion dated September 16, 2015, defendants' motion to dismiss plaintiff's Second Amended Complaint was granted in part and denied in part. As a result of this Order, plaintiff's remaining claims are for (i) deprivation of a constitutionally protected liberty interest without due process of law and (ii) violation of plaintiff s right to free speech. * * *.

The facts giving rise to the instant suit began in August 2012, when plaintiff matriculated as a freshman at GMU. Shortly thereafter, plaintiff began a romantic relationship with a woman—referred to pseudonymously as Jane Roe—who was a student at a different university. This relationship included certain sexual practices known collectively as "BDSM," which is an acronym for the practices it entails, namely bondage, discipline, dominance, submission, sadism, and masochism. Thus, a BDSM relationship might involve as part of the sexual activity such actions as biting, choking, spanking, or the use of restraints. In order to protect Roe, who was the submissive party in the relationship, plaintiff and Roe agreed on a safe word—"red"—that Roe could use to indicate when she wanted sexual activity to cease. According to plaintiff, the ground rules for his BDSM relationship with Roe included that plaintiff should not stop sexual activity unless and until Roe used the safe word. Thus, under the rules of the relationship statements such as "stop" or physical resistance to sexual conduct were not a withdrawal of consent; only the safe word "red" would signal a withdrawal of consent. * * *

[The] plaintiff and Roe * * * engaged in certain of their BDSM activities in plaintiff's dormitory room. One such occasion was October 27, 2013. On that night, Roe went to plaintiff's dormitory room and sexual activity ensued. During this sexual encounter, Roe at one point pushed plaintiff away, but plaintiff continued the sexual activity. At another point, plaintiff asked Roe whether she wished to continue sexual activity, to which Roe responded "I don't know." Plaintiff continued with the sexual activity despite the equivocation, given that Roe did not use the agreed safe word "red."

A few months after the October 27, 2013 incident, plaintiff and Roe ended their relationship. In the following months, plaintiff occasionally attempted to communicate with Roe, often to no avail. One such attempt was a March 2014 text message in which plaintiff told Roe that if she did not respond, then plaintiff would shoot himself. In April 2014, Roe reported incidents of harassment by plaintiff and allegations of the abusive nature of their prior relationship to her university. * * *

Roe also began working with the GMU police. Specifically, in July 2014, Roe cooperated with the GMU police to record a telephone conversation between herself and plaintiff. Over the course of that conversation, Roe asked plaintiff "why [he] never stopped when [she] used the safe word," to which plaintiff replied that he "felt like [she] could handle it." This recording was eventually used as evidence in a July 2014 hearing before the Fairfax County General District Court in which Roe successfully sought a protective order against plaintiff.

Ultimately, Roe decided to press student disciplinary charges against plaintiff through GMU. * * * [A few days later, the university informed plaintiff that he] (i) was the subject of "an alleged violation to [GMU's] sexual misconduct policy" and (ii) that plaintiff was charged with four violations of the Code of Conduct:

(1) Infliction of physical harm to any person(s), including self (Code 2013.7. A);

(2) Deliberate touching or penetration of another person without consent (Code 2013.8.A);

(3) Conduct of a sexual nature (Code 2013.8.C); and

(4) Communication that may cause injury, distress, or emotional or physical discomfort (Code 2013.9.B).

Under GMU policy, allegations of sexual misconduct are adjudicated by a three-member panel of the Sexual Misconduct Board, which consists of GMU faculty members and staff. On September 5, 2014, a panel convened a hearing on the allegations against plaintiff. This hearing lasted ten hours, and both plaintiff and Roe had the opportunity to testify subject to cross-examination, to call witnesses, and to submit evidence. In the course of the hearing, Roe testified as to her allegations about the events of October 27, 2013. Plaintiff, in turn, testified about the BDSM nature of his relationship with Roe, including the rule pertaining to the safe word. In at least one instance, the panel explored the nature of the BDSM relationship by inquiring about events beyond October 27, 2013. Specifically, at one point a panelist asked plaintiff if there were "instances outside of October 27th where the word 'red' was used and [plaintiff] did not stop." Plaintiff responded that in "very rare" and "unusual circumstances," he would be "set in the routine of things" and Roe would need to say "red" again, at which point plaintiff "would stop immediately." But as plaintiff explained, upon hearing the safe word he "would not just blatantly ignore and then continue" with intercourse. On September 12, 2014, the panel issued a decision finding plaintiff not responsible as to each of the four charges against him concerning plaintiff's "involvement in an incident that occurred on or around October 27, 2013."

[Roe successfully appealed the panel's decision to the Assistant Dean of Students, who overturned the panel's decision and concluded that the plaintiff had "violat[ed] Code 2013.8.A (deliberate touching or penetration of another person without consent) and Code 2013.9.B (communication that may cause injury, distress, or emotional or physical discomfort). The plaintiff then unsuccessfully appealed that decision to the Dean of Students.

The court concluded that university officials violated the plaintiff's procedural due process rights, in part because officials failed to provide him with adequate notice and because they engaged in off the record and *ex parte* meetings with Roe while they considered his appeals. The court also concluded that officials violated the plaintiff's rights to free speech when they penalized him for the March 2014 text that he sent to Roe. The content of that text, the court concluded, constituted neither fighting words nor a true threat under the Free Speech Clause. As a result, the court concluded that the university was required to reinstate the plaintiff. The court then turned to the substantive due process issue.]

When plaintiff initiated this lawsuit, he asserted a claim for a violation of his substantive due process rights, alleging that [the Assistant Dean of Students] 'disregarded' the BDSM context of the relationship and how it 'affected matters like consent and related issues' and treated a BDSM relationship as '*per se* sexual misconduct.' " *Doe*, ___ F.Supp.3d ___, 2015 WL 5553855, at *10. This, plaintiff argued, constituted a violation of plaintiff's right to sexual liberty as protected under *Lawrence v. Texas*, 539 U.S. 558, 578, 123 S.Ct. 2472, 156 L.Ed.2d 508 (2003), which held that a state could not criminalize intimate sexual conduct between consenting adults. * * *

The Supreme Court's cases recognizing judicially-enforceable fundamental liberty interests disclose two equal but distinct lines of precedent with respect to the appropriate methodology to be used when considering whether a liberty is fundamental and therefore protected as judicially enforceable under the Fourteenth Amendment. One approach is a common law methodology articulated by Justice Harlan in dissent in *Poe v. Ullman*, 367 U.S. 497, 543, 81 S.Ct. 1752, 6 L.Ed.2d 989 (1961), and later embraced in cases such as *Planned Parenthood of Southeastern Pa. v. Casey*, 505 U.S. 833, 848–49, 112 S.Ct. 2791, 120 L.Ed.2d 674 (1992), and *Obergefell*, 135 S.Ct. at 2598–99. This methodology balances private interests against social needs by reference to, but not bound by, historical practice. In contrast, a more restrictive and historical-focused approach was articulated in *Washington v. Glucksberg*, 521 U.S. 702, 721, 117 S.Ct. 2258, 138 L.Ed.2d 772 (1997), in which the Supreme Court held that a judicially enforceable implied fundamental liberty interest must be (i) deeply rooted in the nation's history and traditions and (ii) implicit in the concept of ordered liberty.

Under the *Glucksberg* mode of analysis, plaintiff's asserted fundamental liberty interest in engaging in BDSM sexual activity is clearly not protected as judicially enforceable under the Fourteenth Amendment. Defined with specificity and cast as a negative liberty, as *Glucksberg* counsels, plaintiff's asserted liberty is a freedom from state regulation of consensual BDSM sexual activity. There is no basis to conclude that tying up a willing submissive sex partner and subjecting him or her to whipping, choking, or other forms of domination is deeply rooted in the nation's history and traditions or implicit in the concept of ordered liberty.

Perhaps in recognition of the futility of his argument under *Glucksberg*, plaintiff bases his fundamental liberty interest argument on *Lawrence*, a case in the Justice Harlan common law tradition. In order to understand fully the methodology employed under this line of cases, analysis properly begins by considering the most recent of the Supreme Court's decisions in this line, namely *Obergefell*. Importantly, *Obergefell* explicitly establishes that the Due Process and Equal Protection Clauses are "interlocking" and each "leads to a stronger understanding of the other." *See* 135 S.Ct. at 2603–04. In other words, *Obergefell* highlights that the decision to recognize an implied fundamental liberty interest as judicially enforceable turns, in part, on whether the liberty interest at issue has historically been denied on the basis of impermissible animus or, alternatively, on a legitimate basis aimed at protecting a vulnerable group. *See, e.g., id.* at 2596. *Lawrence* is not to the contrary. There, the Supreme Court reasoned that a statute criminalizing homosexual sodomy violated a judicially enforceable implied fundamental liberty interest in sexual intimacy because of the history of animus towards homosexuals. *See Lawrence*, 539 U.S. at 571, 123 S.Ct. 2472 (noting that "powerful voices * * * condemn homosexual conduct as immoral" but that this does not permit "the majority [to] use the power of the State to enforce these views on the whole society through the operation of the criminal law"). Indeed, the Supreme Court has since noted that *Lawrence* "acknowledged, and sought to remedy, the continuing inequality that resulted from laws making intimacy in the lives of gays and lesbians a crime against the State" and "therefore drew upon principles of liberty and equality to define and protect the rights of gays and lesbians." *Obergefell*, 135 S.Ct. at 2604.

Under the *Lawrence* methodology, history and tradition continue to inform the analysis. *See id.* at 2598 ("History and tradition guide and discipline [the implied fundamental liberty interests] inquiry but do not set its outer boundaries."). Yet, courts must consider not only the history and tradition of freedom to engage in certain conduct, but also any history and tradition of impermissible animus that motivates the legislative restriction on the freedom in order to weigh with appropriate rigor whether the government's interest in limiting some liberty is a justifiable use of state power or an arbitrary abuse of that power. In this respect, the conclusion reached here under the *Glucksberg* line of reasoning that there is no deeply rooted history or tradition of BDSM sexual activity remains relevant and important to the analysis. Also relevant and important to the analysis is the *absence* of a history of impermissible animus as the basis for the restriction at issue here. Sexual activity that involves binding and gagging or the use of physical force such as spanking or choking poses certain inherent risks to personal safety not present in more traditional types of sexual activity. Thus, as in * * * *Glucksberg*, a legislative restriction on BDSM activity is justifiable by reference to the state's interest in the protection of vulnerable persons, *i.e.* sexual partners placed in situations with an elevated risk of physical harm. Accordingly, consistent with the logic of *Lawrence*, plaintiff has no constitutionally protected and judicially enforceable fundamental liberty interest under the Due Process Clause of the Fourteenth Amendment to engage in BDSM sexual activity.

NOTES

1.   More than two decades before *Lawrence*, the Massachusetts Supreme Judicial Court rejected the claim that a constitutional right to privacy prevents a conviction for assault and battery arising from sexual S/M. As the court explained,

> [t]he fact that violence may be related to sexual activity (or may even be sexual activity to the person inflicting pain on another . . .) does not prevent the State from protecting its citizens against physical harm. The invalidity of the victim's consent to a battery by means of a dangerous weapon would be the same, however, whether or not the battery was related to sexual activity. The general rule is: "It is settled that to commit a battery upon a person with such violence that bodily harm is likely to result is unlawful, and consent thereto is immaterial." Regardless of whether sexual activity was involved in the incident in question, [the victim's] consent to assault and battery upon him by [the defendant] by means of a dangerous weapon cannot absolve [the latter] of the crime charged.

Commonwealth v. Appleby, 380 Mass. 296, 311 402 N.E.2d 1051, 1061 (1980).

2.   Does the notion of a constitutional right to engage in S/M sex go too far? Should the government not be able to draw the line once there is a plausible risk of physical injury to sexual partners? Or is Professor Dailey correct that the right to sexual autonomy must include the right to consent to physical harm resulting from sexual contact and the exploring of sexual fantasies as long as the potential injuries are not severe or life threatening?

3.   Why did the court in *Doe* reject the claim that the plaintiff had a constitutional right to engage in S/M sex? Did the Court appropriately apply *Lawrence*? What role, if any, did questions of consent to S/M sexual conduct play in the court's analysis?

4.   Notice that Roe seemed to operate under the understanding that when she said the "safe word (red)," the plaintiff would stop all sexual activity and physical contact. Yet, the plaintiff claimed that, on a few occasions, Roe did not want him to stop altogether even after she used the word "red." Do the facts in *Doe* complicate the claim that S/M sexual partners can reach clear understandings regarding the type of physical contact that the "submissive" partner agrees may be engaged in by the "dominant" partner?

CHAPTER 3

SEXUALITY, GENDER, & EQUALITY

▪ ▪ ▪

I. INTRODUCTION

The equal protection clause is designed to police group-based discrimination by the government. If a group is excluded from a government program or government employment—for instance, if schools will not hire black teachers because of their race—the equal protection clause is implicated. The U.S. Supreme Court has, over the last several decades, developed an elaborate jurisprudential scheme for adjudicating equal protection claims. According to the type of discrimination being considered, the Court's doctrine states that three levels of review will be used in equal protection cases: strict, intermediate, and what is called "rational basis" review.

Under this doctrine, some classifications made by the government—classifications based on race or national origin, for example—are "suspect" and require "strict" judicial scrutiny to ensure that they are not illegitimate attempts to discriminate on these bases. In these cases, the judge's task is to ensure that the government's classification is supported by a "compelling governmental interest" and is narrowly tailored to serve that purpose. It is usually very difficult for the government to justify a classification under this strict standard.

At the opposite end of the spectrum are governmental distinctions that are considered ordinary, like those routinely made in the realm of economic regulation. The government must justify these types of distinctions by showing only that the classification challenged is "rationally related to a legitimate state interest." This is a standard that the government can almost always meet, although there are significant exceptions to that truism that will be explored below.

A third, intermediate category, has also developed, in which classifications, such as those based on sex, are sometimes thought to be based on legitimate differences between the sexes, but are other times found to be discriminatory. Thus, courts are instructed to employ a medium level of scrutiny to ensure that such classifications "serve important governmental objectives and [are] substantially related to achievement of those objectives."

This schema has been severely criticized, both by some members of the Court itself,[1] and by academic commentators.[2] One of the primary criticisms of this method of jurisprudence is that the level of scrutiny a court employs frequently—though not invariably—determines whether a plaintiff prevails.[3] Thus, much of the fight in equal protection cases has traditionally concerned the level of scrutiny applicable to the case. The Supreme Court has articulated a series of principles that determine whether a classification should trigger heightened judicial scrutiny. These include whether there has been a history of discrimination against the group at issue, whether the discrimination is unrelated to the individual group members' abilities, and whether the members of the group are so poorly represented in the political processes that those processes could not be expected to correct the harm at issue.[4] Some courts have also said that the trait that defines the class must be "immutable" for the group to be deserving of heightened judicial scrutiny.[5]

A second criticism focuses on the inconsistency in the doctrine and notes the ways that the tiers of scrutiny have been breaking down in recent years. Indeed, as the material in this Chapter will show, cases in the sexual orientation area illustrate this breakdown particularly well. There have been significant victories for LGBT equality in cases where the Court—puzzlingly—either purports to use the "rational basis" standard that typically guarantees a victory for the government or simply fails to identify the standard of review.

This Chapter will focus on the rubrics used by courts to evaluate constitutional claims of discrimination based on sex, sexual orientation and gender identity. The first Section lays out the constitutional framework for sex discrimination claims, including the early debate about whether sex should—like race—be a suspect classification, and presents some of the cases settling on intermediate scrutiny as the relevant standard. We next ask whether discrimination based on sexual orientation or gender identity ought to be seen as a form of sex discrimination. We then turn to the standard the Court should use for constitutional claims of sexual orientation discrimination and gender identity discrimination, respectively, if these claims are *not* seen as a

---

[1] *See, e.g., Adarand Constructors, Inc. v. Pena,* 515 U.S. 200, 247, 115 S.Ct. 2097, 2122, 132 L.Ed.2d 158, 195 (1995) (Stevens, J., dissenting); *San Antonio Indep. Sch. Dist. v. Rodriguez,* 411 U.S. 1, 98–99, 93 S.Ct. 1278, 1330, 36 L.Ed.2d 16, 81–82 (1973) (Marshall, J., dissenting).

[2] *See, e.g.,* Suzanne B. Goldberg, *Equality Without Tiers,* 77 S. CAL. L. REV. 481, 508–18 (2004); Gerald Gunther, *The Supreme Court 1971 Term—Foreword: In Search of Evolving Doctrine on a Changing Court: A Model for a Newer Equal Protection,* 86 HARV. L. REV. 1, 17–18 (1972).

[3] Gunther, 86 HARV. L. REV. at 8.

[4] *Frontiero v. Richardson,* 411 U.S. 677, 684–87, 93 S.Ct. 1764, 1769–71, 36 L.Ed.2d 583, 590–92 (1973).

[5] *See id.* at 686, 93 S. Ct. at 1770.

form of sex discrimination. We close with a look at the Supreme Court's approach to equal protection and sexual orientation.

II. THE LEVEL OF SCRUTINY DEBATE

A. THE CONSTITUTION AND SEX DISCRIMINATION

The constitutional law of sex discrimination under the equal protection clause began to evolve in earnest in the early 1970s. That body of law has set the conceptual stage in various ways for the unfolding constitutional law of sexual orientation discrimination. Consider the following leading constitutional cases on sex discrimination. Bear in mind some key questions as you read: What ideas of sex and gender underpin the Court's approach? What standard of review does the Court arrive at for sex-based classifications? What is the relevance of the Court's arguments regarding sex-based claims for the question of what standard of review should be applied to sexual orientation- and gender identity-based claims?

FRONTIERO V. RICHARDSON
Supreme Court of the United States, 1973
411 U.S. 677, 93 S.Ct. 1764, 36 L.Ed.2d 583

JUSTICE BRENNAN announced the judgment of the Court and an opinion in which JUSTICE DOUGLAS, JUSTICE WHITE, and JUSTICE MARSHALL join.

The question before us concerns the right of a female member of the uniformed services to claim her spouse as a "dependent" for the purposes of obtaining increased quarters allowances and medical and dental benefits under 37 U.S.C. 401, 403, and 10 U.S.C. 1072, 1076, on an equal footing with male members. Under these statutes, a serviceman may claim his wife as a "dependent" without regard to whether she is in fact dependent upon him for any part of her support. 37 U.S.C. 401(1); 10 U.S.C. 1072(2)(A). A servicewoman, on the other hand, may not claim her husband as a "dependent" under these programs unless he is in fact dependent upon her for over one-half of his support. 37 U.S.C. 401; 10 U.S.C. 1072(2)(c). Thus, the question for decision is whether this difference in treatment constitutes an unconstitutional discrimination against servicewomen in violation of the Due Process Clause of the Fifth Amendment. * * *

Appellant Sharron Frontiero, a lieutenant in the United States Air Force, sought increased quarters allowances, and housing and medical benefits for her husband, appellant Joseph Frontiero, on the ground that he was her "dependent." Although such benefits would automatically have been granted with respect to the wife of a male member of the uniformed services, appellant's application was denied because she failed to demonstrate that her husband was dependent on her for more than one-half of his support. * * *

Although the legislative history of these statutes sheds virtually no light on the purposes underlying the differential treatment accorded male and female members, a majority of the three-judge District Court surmised that Congress might reasonably have concluded that, since the husband in our society is generally the "breadwinner" in the family—and the wife typically the "dependent" partner—"it would be more economical to require married female members claiming husbands to prove actual dependency than to extend the presumption of dependency to such members." 341 F. Supp., at 207. Indeed, given the fact that approximately 99% of all members of the uniformed services are male, the District Court speculated that such differential treatment might conceivably lead to a "considerable saving of administrative expense and manpower." *Ibid.*

At the outset, appellants contend that classifications based upon sex, like classifications based upon race, alienage, and national origin, are inherently suspect and must therefore be subjected to close judicial scrutiny. We agree and, indeed, find at least implicit support for such an approach in our unanimous decision only last Term in *Reed v. Reed.* * * *

There can be no doubt that our Nation has had a long and unfortunate history of sex discrimination. Traditionally, such discrimination was rationalized by an attitude of "romantic paternalism" which, in practical effect, put women, not on a pedestal, but in a cage. Indeed, this paternalistic attitude became so firmly rooted in our national consciousness that, 100 years ago, a distinguished Member of this Court was able to proclaim:

> "Man is, or should be, woman's protector and defender. The natural and proper timidity and delicacy which belongs to the female sex evidently unfits it for many of the occupations of civil life. The constitution of the family organization, which is founded in the divine ordinance, as well as in the nature of things, indicates the domestic sphere as that which properly belongs to the domain and functions of womanhood. The harmony, not to say identity, of interests and views which belong, or should belong, to the family institution is repugnant to the idea of a woman adopting a distinct and independent career from that of her husband. . . . The paramount destiny and mission of woman are to fulfil the noble and benign offices of wife and mother. This is the law of the Creator." *Bradwell v. State.*

As a result of notions such as these, our statute books gradually became laden with gross, stereotyped distinctions between the sexes and, indeed, throughout much of the 19th century the position of women in our society was, in many respects, comparable to that of blacks under the pre-

Civil War slave codes. Neither slaves nor women could hold office, serve on juries, or bring suit in their own names, and married women traditionally were denied the legal capacity to hold or convey property or to serve as legal guardians of their own children. * * *

And although blacks were guaranteed the right to vote in 1870, women were denied even that right—which is itself "preservative of other basic civil and political rights"—until adoption of the Nineteenth Amendment half a century later.

It is true, of course, that the position of women in America has improved markedly in recent decades. Nevertheless, it can hardly be doubted that, in part because of the high visibility of the sex characteristic, women still face pervasive, although at times more subtle, discrimination in our educational institutions, in the job market and, perhaps most conspicuously, in the political arena. * * *

Moreover, since sex, like race and national origin, is an immutable characteristic determined solely by the accident of birth, the imposition of special disabilities upon the members of a particular sex because of their sex would seem to violate "the basic concept of our system that legal burdens should bear some relationship to individual responsibility. . . ." And what differentiates sex from such nonsuspect statuses as intelligence or physical disability, and aligns it with the recognized suspect criteria, is that the sex characteristic frequently bears no relation to ability to perform or contribute to society. As a result, statutory distinctions between the sexes often have the effect of invidiously relegating the entire class of females to inferior legal status without regard to the actual capabilities of its individual members.

We might also note that, over the past decade, Congress has itself manifested an increasing sensitivity to sex-based classifications. In Tit. VII of the Civil Rights Act of 1964, for example, Congress expressly declared that no employer, labor union, or other organization subject to the provisions of the Act shall discriminate against any individual on the basis of "race, color, religion, sex, or national origin." Similarly, the Equal Pay Act of 1963 provides that no employer covered by the Act "shall discriminate . . . between employees on the basis of sex." And § 1 of the Equal Rights Amendment, passed by Congress on March 22, 1972, and submitted to the legislatures of the States for ratification, declares that "[e]quality of rights under the law shall not be denied or abridged by the United States or by any State on account of sex." Thus, Congress itself has concluded that classifications based upon sex are inherently invidious, and this conclusion of a coequal branch of Government is not without significance to the question presently under consideration.

With these considerations in mind, we can only conclude that classifications based upon sex, like classifications based upon race, alienage, or national origin, are inherently suspect, and must therefore be subjected to strict judicial scrutiny. Applying the analysis mandated by that stricter standard of review, it is clear that the statutory scheme now before us is constitutionally invalid. * * *

Moreover, the Government concedes that the differential treatment accorded men and women under these statutes serves no purpose other than mere "administrative convenience." In essence, the Government maintains that, as an empirical matter, wives in our society frequently are dependent upon their husbands, while husbands rarely are dependent upon their wives. Thus, the Government argues that Congress might reasonably have concluded that it would be both cheaper and easier simply conclusively to presume that wives of male members are financially dependent upon their husbands, while burdening female members with the task of establishing dependency in fact. * * *

[O]ur prior decisions make clear that, although efficacious administration of governmental programs is not without some importance, "the Constitution recognizes higher values than speed and efficiency." *Stanley v. Illinois*, 405 U.S. 645, 656, 92 S.Ct. 1208, 1215, 31 L.Ed.2d 551 (1972). And when we enter the realm of "strict judicial scrutiny," there can be no doubt that "administrative convenience" is not a shibboleth, the mere recitation of which dictates constitutionality. On the contrary, any statutory scheme which draws a sharp line between the sexes, solely for the purpose of achieving administrative convenience, necessarily commands "dissimilar treatment for men and women who are . . . similarly situated," and therefore involves the "very kind of arbitrary legislative choice forbidden by the [Constitution]. . . ." *Reed v. Reed*, 404 U.S., at 77, 76, 92 S.Ct., at 254. We therefore conclude that, by according differential treatment to male and female members of the uniformed services for the sole purpose of achieving administrative convenience, the challenged statutes violate the Due Process Clause of the Fifth Amendment insofar as they require a female member to prove the dependency of her husband.

Reversed.

NOTE

Justice Brennan's argument to apply strict scrutiny to sex-based classifications failed to command a majority on the Supreme Court; only four justices took that view. A few years later, the Court decided *Craig v. Boren*, 429 U.S. 190, 97 S.Ct. 451, 50 L.Ed.2d 397 (1976), a case challenging the constitutionality of prohibiting the sale of "nonintoxicating" beer to males under the age of 21 and to females under the age of 18. The Court struck down the law, rejected the statistical evidence purporting to justify the stricter rule for males, and articulated a standard of review that has come to be known as intermediate scrutiny. The majority opinion said:

To withstand constitutional challenge, previous cases establish that classifications by gender must serve important governmental objectives and must be substantially related to achievement of those objectives. Thus, in *Reed*, the objectives of "reducing the workload on probate courts," 404 U.S. at 76, and "avoiding intrafamily controversy," *id.*, at 77, were deemed of insufficient importance to sustain use of an overt gender criterion in the appointment of administrators of intestate decedents' estates. Decisions following *Reed* similarly have rejected administrative ease and convenience as sufficiently important objectives to justify gender-based classifications. *See, e. g., Stanley v. Illinois*; *Frontiero v. Richardson*; *cf. Schlesinger v. Ballard.* * * *

Reed v. Reed has also provided the underpinning for decisions that have invalidated statutes employing gender as an inaccurate proxy for other, more germane bases of classification. Hence, "archaic and overbroad" generalizations, *Schlesinger v. Ballard*, concerning the financial position of servicewomen, *Frontiero v. Richardson*, and working women, *Weinberger v. Wiesenfeld*, could not justify use of a gender line in determining eligibility for certain governmental entitlements. Similarly, increasingly outdated misconceptions concerning the role of females in the home rather than in the "marketplace and world of ideas" were rejected as loose-fitting characterizations incapable of supporting state statutory schemes that were premised upon their accuracy. *Stanton v. Stanton*; *Taylor v. Louisiana*. In light of the weak congruence between gender and the characteristic or trait that gender purported to represent, it was necessary that the legislatures choose either to realign their substantive laws in a gender-neutral fashion, or to adopt procedures for identifying those instances where the sex-centered generalization actually comported with fact.

Craig, 429 U.S. at 197–99, 97 S.Ct. 451, 457–58, 50 L.Ed.2d at 407–08.

The next case is a leading decision on the constitutional law of sex discrimination.

UNITED STATES V. VIRGINIA

Supreme Court of the United States, 1996
518 U.S. 515, 116 S.Ct. 2264, 135 L.Ed.2d 735

JUSTICE GINSBURG delivered the opinion of the Court.

Virginia's public institutions of higher learning include an incomparable military college, Virginia Military Institute (VMI). The United States maintains that the Constitution's equal protection guarantee precludes Virginia from reserving exclusively to men the unique educational opportunities VMI affords. We agree.

Founded in 1839, VMI is today the sole single-sex school among Virginia's 15 public institutions of higher learning. VMI's distinctive mission is to produce "citizen-soldiers," men prepared for leadership in civilian life and in military service. VMI pursues this mission through pervasive training of a kind not available anywhere else in Virginia. Assigning prime place to character development, VMI uses an "adversative method" modeled on English public schools and once characteristic of military instruction. VMI constantly endeavors to instill physical and mental discipline in its cadets and impart to them a strong moral code. The school's graduates leave VMI with heightened comprehension of their capacity to deal with duress and stress, and a large sense of accomplishment for completing the hazardous course. * * *

Neither the goal of producing citizen-soldiers nor VMI's implementing methodology is inherently unsuitable to women. And the school's impressive record in producing leaders has made admission desirable to some women. Nevertheless, Virginia has elected to preserve exclusively for men the advantages and opportunities a VMI education affords. * * *

VMI today enrolls about 1,300 men as cadets. Its academic offerings in the liberal arts, sciences, and engineering are also available at other public colleges and universities in Virginia. But VMI's mission is special. It is the mission of the school

> " 'to produce educated and honorable men, prepared for the varied work of civil life, imbued with love of learning, confident in the functions and attitudes of leadership, possessing a high sense of public service, advocates of the American democracy and free enterprise system, and ready as citizen-soldiers to defend their country in *522 time of national peril.' " 766 F. Supp. 1407, 1425 (W.D.Va.1991) (quoting Mission Study Committee of the VMI Board of Visitors, Report, May 16, 1986). * * *

VMI attracts some applicants because of its reputation as an extraordinarily challenging military school, and "because its alumni are exceptionally close to the school." 766 F.Supp., at 1421. * * *

The District Court ruled in favor of VMI * * * The District Court reasoned that education in "a single-gender environment, be it male or female," yields substantial benefits. 766 F.Supp., at 1415. VMI's school for men brought diversity to an otherwise coeducational Virginia system, and that diversity was "enhanced by VMI's unique method of instruction." *Ibid.* If single-gender education for males ranks as an important governmental objective, it becomes obvious, the District Court concluded, that the only means of achieving the objective "is to exclude women from the all-male institution—VMI." *Ibid.*

"Women are [indeed] denied a unique educational opportunity that is available only at VMI," the District Court acknowledged. Id., at 1432. But "[VMI's] single-sex status would be lost, and some aspects of the [school's] distinctive method would be altered," if women were admitted, id., at 1413: "Allowance for personal privacy would have to be made," id., at 1412; "[p]hysical education requirements would have to be altered, at least for the women," id., at 1413; the adversative environment could not survive unmodified, id., at 1412–1413. Thus, "sufficient constitutional justification" had been shown, the District Court held, "for continuing [VMI's] single-sex policy." Id., at 1413. * * *

The Court of Appeals for the Fourth Circuit disagreed and vacated the District Court's judgment. * * * Remanding the case ... the court suggested these options for the Commonwealth: Admit women to VMI; establish parallel institutions or programs; or abandon state support, leaving VMI free to pursue its policies as a private institution. 976 F.2d 890, 900 (1992). * * *

In response to the Fourth Circuit's ruling, Virginia proposed a parallel program for women: Virginia Women's Institute for Leadership (VWIL). The 4-year, state-sponsored undergraduate program would be located at Mary Baldwin College, a private liberal arts school for women, and would be open, initially, to about 25 to 30 students. Although VWIL would share VMI's mission—to produce "citizen-soldiers"—the VWIL program would differ, as does Mary Baldwin College, from VMI in academic offerings, methods of education, and financial resources. *See* 852 F.Supp. 471, 476–477 (W.D. Va.1994). * * *

[T]his suit present two ultimate issues. First, does Virginia's exclusion of women from the educational opportunities provided by VMI—extraordinary opportunities for military training and civilian leadership development—deny to women "capable of all of the individual activities required of VMI cadets," 766 F.Supp., at 1412, the equal protection of the laws guaranteed by the Fourteenth Amendment? Second, if VMI's "unique" situation, id., at 1413—as Virginia's sole single-sex public institution of higher education—offends the Constitution's equal protection principle, what is the remedial requirement?

We note, once again, the core instruction of this Court's pathmarking decisions in *J.E.B. v. Alabama ex rel. T.B.*, and *Mississippi Univ. for Women*: Parties who seek to defend gender-based government action must demonstrate an "exceedingly persuasive justification" for that action. Today's skeptical scrutiny of official action denying rights or opportunities based on sex responds to volumes of history. As a plurality of this Court acknowledged a generation ago, "our Nation has had a long and unfortunate history of sex discrimination." *Frontiero v. Richardson.* Through a century plus three decades and more of that history, women did not count among voters composing "We the People"; not until 1920 did women gain a constitutional right to the franchise. *Id.*, at 685. And for a half century thereafter, it remained the prevailing doctrine that government, both federal and state, could withhold from women opportunities accorded men so long as any "basis in reason" could be conceived for the discrimination. *See, e.g., Goesaert v. Cleary* (rejecting challenge by female tavern owner and her daughter to Michigan law denying bartender licenses to females—except for wives and daughters of male tavern owners; Court would not "give ear" to the contention that "an unchivalrous desire of male bartenders to . . . monopolize the calling" prompted the legislation).

In 1971, for the first time in our Nation's history, this Court ruled in favor of a woman who complained that her State had denied her the equal protection of its laws. *Reed v. Reed* (holding unconstitutional Idaho Code prescription that, among " 'several persons claiming and equally entitled to administer [a decedent's estate], males must be preferred to females' "). Since *Reed*, the Court has repeatedly recognized that neither federal nor state government acts compatibly with the equal protection principle when a law or official policy denies to women, simply because they are women, full citizenship stature—equal opportunity to aspire, achieve, participate in and contribute to society based on their individual talents and capacities. * * *

Without equating gender classifications, for all purposes, to classifications based on race or national origin, the Court, in post-*Reed* decisions, has carefully inspected official action that closes a door or denies opportunity to women (or to men). *See J.E.B.* (Kennedy, J., concurring in judgment) (case law evolving since 1971 "reveal[s] a strong presumption that gender classifications are invalid"). To summarize the Court's current directions for cases of official classification based on gender: Focusing on the differential treatment or denial of opportunity for which relief is sought, the reviewing court must determine whether the proffered justification is "exceedingly persuasive." The burden of justification is demanding and it rests entirely on the State. *See Mississippi Univ. for Women.* The State must show "at least that the [challenged] classification serves 'important governmental objectives and that the discriminatory means employed' are 'substantially related to the achievement of those objectives.' " * * *

The justification must be genuine, not hypothesized or invented post hoc in response to litigation. And it must not rely on overbroad generalizations about the different talents, capacities, or preferences of males and females. * * *

The heightened review standard our precedent establishes does not make sex a proscribed classification. Supposed "inherent differences" are no longer accepted as a ground for race or national origin classifications. *See Loving v. Virginia.* Physical differences between men and women, however, are enduring: "[T]he two sexes are not fungible; a community made up exclusively of one [sex] is different from a community composed of both." * * *

"Inherent differences" between men and women, we have come to appreciate, remain cause for celebration, but not for denigration of the members of either sex or for artificial constraints on an individual's opportunity. Sex classifications may be used to compensate women "for particular economic disabilities [they have] suffered," *Califano v. Webster,* to "promot[e] equal employment opportunity," *see California Federal Sav. & Loan Assn. v. Guerra,* to advance full development of the talent and capacities of our Nation's people. But such classifications may not be used, as they once were, *see Goesaert,* to create or perpetuate the legal, social, and economic inferiority of women.

Measuring the record in this case against the review standard just described, we conclude that Virginia has shown no "exceedingly persuasive justification" for excluding all women from the citizen-soldier training afforded by VMI. We therefore affirm the Fourth Circuit's initial judgment, which held that Virginia had violated the Fourteenth Amendment's Equal Protection Clause. Because the remedy proffered by Virginia—the Mary Baldwin VWIL program—does not cure the constitutional violation, i.e., it does not provide equal opportunity, we reverse the Fourth Circuit's final judgment in this case.

NOTES

1.   How would you state the standard of review that the Court uses for sex-based classifications? Is there a difference between the principles articulated in *Craig* and those offered in the *Virginia* case?

2.   Recall the materials in Chapter 1 on the complexity of defining sex and gender. How might the evolving constitutional law of sex discrimination and sex-based classifications be consistent or be in tension with the ideas stressed in those accounts? Note that the terms "sex" and "gender" are sometimes used interchangeably in the cases. Should the terms, properly understood, be given different meanings? Consider Professor Katherine Franke's perspective:

> Contemporary sex discrimination jurisprudence accepts as one of its foundational premises the notion that sex and gender are two distinct aspects of human identity. That is, it assumes that the identities male and female are different from the characteristics masculine and feminine. Sex is regarded as a product of nature, while gender is understood as a function of culture. This disaggregation of sex from gender represents a central mistake of equality jurisprudence.

Antidiscrimination law is founded upon the idea that sex, conceived as biological difference, is prior to, less normative than, and more real than gender. Yet in every way that matters, sex bears an epiphenomenal relationship to gender; that is, under close examination, almost every claim with regard to sexual identity or sex discrimination can be shown to be grounded in normative gender rules and roles. Herein lies the mistake. In the name of avoiding "the grossest discrimination," that is, "treating things that are different as though they were exactly alike," sexual equality jurisprudence has uncritically accepted the validity of biological sexual differences. By accepting these biological differences, equality jurisprudence reifies as foundational *fact* that which is really an *effect* of normative gender ideology. This jurisprudential error not only produces obvious absurdities at the margin of gendered identity, but it also explains why sex discrimination laws have been relatively ineffective in dismantling profound sex segregation in the wage-labor market, in shattering "glass ceilings" that obstruct women's entrance into the upper echelons of corporate management, and in increasing women's wages, which remain a fraction of those paid men. The targets of antidiscrimination law, therefore, should not be limited to the "gross, stereotyped distinctions between the sexes" but should also include the social processes that construct and make coherent the categories male and female. In many cases, biology operates as the excuse or cover for social practices that hierarchize individual members of the social category "man" over individual members of the social category "woman." In the end, biology or anatomy serve as metaphors for a kind of inferiority that characterizes society's view of women.

The authority to define particular categories or types of people and to decide to which category a particular person belongs is a profoundly powerful social function. While the state has always performed this role, its actions have rarely been subject to equal protection scrutiny. Given the epiphenomenal relationship between identity and equality, the Fourteenth Amendment and Title VII should apply with equal force to acts of classification as well as to disparate treatment of classes. Rather than accepting sexual differences as the starting point of equality discourse, sex discrimination jurisprudence should consider the role that the ideology of sexual differences plays in perpetuating and ensuring sexual hierarchy.

A reconceptualization of the two most fundamental elements of sexual equality jurisprudence is necessary to correct this foundational error. First, sexual identity—that is, what it means to be a woman and what it means to be a man—must be understood not in deterministic, biological terms, but according to a set of behavioral, performative norms that at once enable and constrain a degree of human agency and create the background conditions for a person to assert, *I am a woman.* To say that someone is a woman demands a complex description of the history and experience of persons so labeled. This conception of sexual identity ultimately provides the basis for a fundamental right to determine gendered identity independent of biological sex.

Second, what it means to be discriminated against *because of one's sex* must be reconceived beyond biological sex as well. To the extent that the wrong of sex discrimination is limited to conduct or treatment which would not have occurred *but for* the plaintiff's biological sex, antidiscrimination law strives for too little. Notwithstanding an occasional gesture to the contrary, courts have not interpreted the wrong of sex discrimination to reach rules and policies that reinforce masculinity as the authentic and natural exercise of male agency and femininity as the authentic and natural exercise of female agency. . . .

Katherine M. Franke, *The Central Mistake of Sex Discrimination Law: The Disaggregation of Sex from Gender*, 144 U. PA. L. REV. 1, 1–4 (1995). For other perspectives on this question and its relationship to sexual orientation and gender identity, see Melina Constantine Bell, *Gender Essentialism and American Law: Why and How to Sever the Connection*, 23 DUKE J. GENDER & POL'Y 163 (2016); Mary Anne C. Case, *Disaggregating Gender from Sex and Sexual Orientation: The Effeminate Man in the Law and Feminist Jurisprudence*, 105 YALE L.J. 1 (1995); Stevie V. Tran and Elizabeth M. Glazer, *Transgenderless*, 35 HARV. J. L. & GENDER 299 (2012); Francisco Valdes, *Queers, Sissies, Dykes and Tomboys: Deconstructing the Conflation of "Sex," "Gender," and "Sexual Orientation" in Euro-American Law and Society*, 83 CALIF. L. REV. 3 (1995).

B. SEXUAL ORIENTATION DISCRIMINATION AS A FORM OF SEX DISCRIMINATION

There would be no need to determine the standard of review to apply to claims of sexual orientation discrimination if such discrimination were itself seen as a form of sex discrimination. In that case, intermediate scrutiny would presumably apply. This argument has featured prominently in recent litigation and scholarship.

1. Variations on a Theme

a. *The Formal Argument*

Baehr v. Lewin was an early and influential case concerning the rights of same-sex couples to marry. Indeed, it may fairly be said to have inaugurated the current debate about marriage by putting the possibility of same-sex marriage on the national screen for the first time. The case is addressed further in Chapter 5, but for present purposes, focus on the argument made by the court that denial of marriage rights to same-sex partners can be seen as a form of sex discrimination. Then, read the majority and dissenting opinions in the *Hernandez v. Robles* marriage decision that follows *Baehr* and consider how the justices on New York's highest court debated the issue.

BAEHR V. LEWIN

Supreme Court of Hawaii, 1993
852 P.2d 44, 74 Haw. 645

LEVINSON, JUDGE, in which MOON, CHIEF JUDGE, joins.

The equal protection clauses of the United States and Hawaii Constitutions are not mirror images of one another. The fourteenth amendment to the United States Constitution somewhat concisely provides, in relevant part, that a state may not "deny to any person within its jurisdiction the equal protection of the laws." Hawaii's counterpart is more elaborate. Article I, section 5 of the Hawaii Constitution provides in relevant part that "[n]o person shall ... be denied the equal protection of the laws, *nor be denied the enjoyment of the person's civil rights or be discriminated against in the exercise thereof because of race, religion, sex, or ancestry.*" (Emphasis added.) Thus, by its plain language, the Hawaii Constitution prohibits state-sanctioned discrimination against any person in the exercise of his or her civil rights on the basis of sex.

"The freedom to marry has long been recognized as one of the vital personal rights essential to the orderly pursuit of happiness by free [people]." *Loving*, 388 U.S. at 12. So "fundamental" does the United States Supreme Court consider the institution of marriage that it has deemed marriage to be "one of the 'basic civil rights of [men and women].'" *Id.* (quoting *Skinner*, 316 U.S. at 541).

* * * This court has held, in another context, that such "privilege[s] of citizenship ... cannot be taken away [on] any of the prohibited bases of race, religion, sex or ancestry" enumerated in article I, section 5 of the Hawaii Constitution and that to do so violates the right to equal protection of the laws as guaranteed by that constitutional provision. * * *

Rudimentary principles of statutory construction render manifest the fact that, by its plain language, HRS § 572–1 restricts the marital relation to a male and a female. . . . Accordingly, on its face and (as Lewin admits) as applied, HRS § 572–1 denies same-sex couples access to the marital status and its concomitant rights and benefits. It is the state's regulation of access to the status of married persons, on the basis of the applicants' sex, that gives rise to the question whether the applicant couples have been denied the equal protection of the laws in violation of article I, section 5 of the Hawaii Constitution. * * *

As we have indicated, HRS § 572–1, on its face and as applied, regulates access to the marital status and its concomitant rights and benefits on the basis of the applicants' sex. As such, HRS § 572–1 establishes a sex-based classification. * * *

Our decision in *Holdman* [*v. Olim*, an earlier case brought under the Hawaii constitution] is key to the present case in several respects. First, we clearly and unequivocally established, for purposes of equal protection analysis under the Hawaii Constitution, that sex-based classifications are subject, as a per se matter, to some form of "heightened" scrutiny, be it "strict" or "intermediate," rather than mere "rational basis" analysis. Second, we assumed, arguendo, that such sex-based classifications were subject to "strict scrutiny." Third, we reaffirmed the longstanding principle that this court is free to accord greater protections to Hawaii's citizens under the state constitution than are recognized under the United States Constitution. And fourth, we looked to the then current case law of the United States Supreme Court for guidance.

Of the decisions of the United States Supreme Court cited in *Holdman, Frontiero v. Richardson* was by far the most significant. * * *

Particularly noteworthy in *Frontiero*, however, was the concurring opinion of Justice Powell, joined by the Chief Justice and Justice Blackmun (the Powell group). The Powell group agreed that "the challenged statutes constitute[d] an unconstitutional discrimination against servicewomen," but deemed it "unnecessary for the Court in this case to characterize sex as a suspect classification, with all of the far-reaching implications of such a holding." Central to the Powell group's thinking was the following explanation:

> There is another . . . reason for deferring a general categorizing of sex classifications as invoking the strictest test of judicial scrutiny. The Equal Rights Amendment, which if adopted will resolve the substance of this precise question, has been approved by Congress and submitted for ratification by the States. If this Amendment is duly adopted, it will represent the will of the people accomplished in the manner prescribed by the Constitution. By acting prematurely and unnecessarily, . . . the Court has assumed a decisional responsibility at the very time when state legislatures, functioning within the traditional democratic process, are debating the proposed Amendment. It seems . . . that this reaching out to preempt by judicial action a major political decision which is currently in process of resolution does not reflect appropriate respect for duly prescribed legislative processes.

411 U.S. at 727 (emphasis added).

The Powell group's concurring opinion therefore permits but one inference: had the Equal Rights Amendment been incorporated into the United States Constitution, at least seven members (and probably eight) of the *Frontiero* Court would have subjected statutory sex-based classifications to "strict" judicial scrutiny.

In light of the interrelationship between the reasoning of the Brennan plurality and the Powell group in *Frontiero*, on the one hand, and the presence of article I, section 3—the Equal Rights Amendment—in the Hawaii Constitution, on the other, it is time to resolve once and for all the question left dangling in *Holdman*. Accordingly, we hold that sex is a "suspect category" for purposes of equal protection analysis under article I, section 5 of the Hawaii Constitution[33] and that HRS § 572–1 is subject to the "strict scrutiny" test. It therefore follows, and we so hold, that (1) HRS § 572–1 is presumed to be unconstitutional (2) unless Lewin, as an agent of the State of Hawaii, can show that (a) the statute's sex-based classification is justified by compelling state interests and (b) the statute is narrowly drawn to avoid unnecessary abridgements of the applicant couples' constitutional rights. * * *

Because, for the reasons stated in this opinion, the circuit court erroneously granted Lewin's motion for judgment on the pleadings and dismissed the plaintiffs' complaint, we vacate the circuit court's order and judgment and remand this matter for further proceedings consistent with this opinion. On remand, in accordance with the "strict scrutiny" standard, the burden will rest on Lewin to overcome the presumption that HRS § 572–1 is unconstitutional by demonstrating that it furthers compelling state interests and is narrowly drawn to avoid unnecessary abridgements of constitutional rights.

HERNANDEZ V. ROBLES

Court of Appeals of New York, 2006
855 N.E.2d 1, 7 N.Y.3d 338, 821 N.Y.S.2d 770

SMITH, JUDGE.

Plaintiffs claim that the distinction made by the Domestic Relations Law between opposite-sex and same-sex couples deprives them of the equal protection of the laws. [The Court notes that plaintiffs argued that the denial of marriage rights to same-sex couples constituted sex discrimination, and rejects this claim.] * * *

By limiting marriage to opposite-sex couples, New York is not engaging in sex discrimination. The limitation does not put men and women in different classes, and give one class a benefit not given to the

---

[33] Our holding in this regard is *not*, as the dissent suggests, "[t]hat Appellants are a 'suspect class.'"

other. Women and men are treated alike—they are permitted to marry people of the opposite sex, but not people of their own sex. This is not the kind of sham equality that the Supreme Court confronted in *Loving*; the statute there, prohibiting black and white people from marrying each other, was in substance anti-black legislation. Plaintiffs do not argue here that the legislation they challenge is designed to subordinate either men to women or women to men as a class.

KAYE, CHIEF JUDGE, dissenting.

The exclusion of same-sex couples from civil marriage also discriminates on the basis of sex, which provides a further basis for requiring heightened scrutiny. * * *

Under the Domestic Relations Law, a woman who seeks to marry another woman is prevented from doing so on account of her sex—that is, because she is not a man. If she were, she would be given a marriage license to marry that woman. That the statutory scheme applies equally to both sexes does not alter the conclusion that the classification here is based on sex. The "equal application" approach to equal protection analysis was expressly rejected by the Supreme Court in *Loving*: "We reject the notion that the mere 'equal application' of a statute containing [discriminatory] classifications is enough to remove the classifications from the [constitutional] proscription of all invidious . . . discriminations" (388 U.S. at 8). Instead, the *Loving* Court held that "there can be no question but that Virginia's miscegenation statutes rest solely upon distinctions drawn according to race [where the] statutes proscribe generally accepted conduct if engaged in by members of different races."

b. The Argument from Gender Roles

A different approach to conceptualizing sexual orientation discrimination as sex discrimination has been advanced by various scholars. Consider the argument set out in an influential early article by Professor Sylvia Law, and think about how it is different from the argument presented above.

HOMOSEXUALITY AND THE SOCIAL MEANING OF GENDER[*]
Sylvia A. Law

[H]omosexuality is censured because it violates the prescriptions of gender role expectations. A panoply of legal rules and cultural institutions reinforce the assumption that heterosexual intimacy is the only natural and legitimate form of sexual expression. The presumption and prescription that erotic interests are exclusively directed to the

---

[*]   Sylvia A. Law, *Homosexuality and the Social Meaning of Gender*, 1988 WIS. L. REV. 187, 196–202 (1998).

opposite sex define an important aspect of masculinity and femininity. Real men are and should be sexually attracted to women, and real women invite and enjoy that attraction. Though complex rules govern the ways in which heterosexual attraction may appropriately be expressed, the allure of the opposite sex is pervasively assumed. Conversely, the culture and law presume and prescribe an absence of sexual attraction between people of the same sex.

But sexual intimacies are only one piece of the presumption and prescription of heterosexuality. In our culture, the adult heterosexual couple forms the nucleus of networks of social and kinship relations, which are socially supported and privileged. The pleasure most people feel when a single friend forms a close relationship with a congenial person of the opposite sex is not based simply, or even primarily, on an appreciation of erotic or procreative possibilities. Rather, it reflects a broad understanding that life as half of a heterosexual couple is generally easier, and more pleasant and satisfying, in part because dominant prevailing structures of social and family life make it so.

Homosexual relationships challenge dichotomous concepts of gender. These relationships challenge the notion that social traits, such as dominance and nurturance, are naturally linked to one sex or the other. Moreover, those involved in homosexual relations implicitly reject the social institutions of family, economic and political life that are premised on gender inequality and differentiation. * * *

In the nineteenth century, industrialization and urbanization profoundly altered American family circumstances and values. Economically, families were no longer integrated units of production. Rather, men sold their labor in exchange for a wage, and women were assigned and assumed responsibility for maintaining the home as locus of consumption, reproduction and refuge. In many ways, women's situation improved: birth rates declined, women acquired wider educational opportunities and minimal legal rights, and a feminist movement gave voice to their interests. Urban families were less integrated with the community. Individuals, particularly men and people of means, could exercise greater choice over their family arrangements; some chose to avoid the expectations of patriarchal family life.

These profound changes in the economic and social function of the family and its relation to a larger community generated great anxiety and produced strong reaction from many sources. For the first time, the American family developed a self-conscious "image." Central to this new image was a perception of a sharp separation between public and private, male and female. The sense of individual identity, of oneness with others, and of purpose to life that were once associated with patriarchal family and religion were now more closely tied to gender.

Many social forces worked to reinforce this new gender-dichotomous concept of family. Conventional morality praised the purity of women and of the home. Late nineteenth century social purity movements promoted temperance and suppression of sexually explicit materials, including contraceptive information. In England, the historic concept of "sodomy" was broadened to encompass all forms of non-procreative sex, including advocacy of birth control. Feminists promoted "voluntary motherhood," a concept which glorified the maternal role, urged male self-restraint, and sought to empower women within the family. With the development of opportunities for independent living in the nineteenth century, homosexual identity first became possible.

Only when individuals began to make their living through wage labor instead of as parts of an interdependent family unit, was it possible for homosexual desire to coalesce into a personal identity—an identity based on the ability to remain outside the heterosexual family and to construct a personal life based on attraction to one's own sex.

Simultaneous with the emergence of the possibility of homosexual identity, nineteenth century social condemnation of homosexuality intensified and sought to reinforce sharp differences in the meaning of gender. As the material and social functions of the family became less clear, and family size decreased, the attractiveness of the ideological and emotional ideal of the family intensified. Many trends made homosexual liaisons more threatening: as the economic basis of family cohesion attenuated, emotional expectations increased; with smaller families, each child bore greater responsibility for carrying on the family line; women's claims for emancipation and participation in wage labor challenged traditional division of functions.

Nineteenth century grounds for ostracism of homosexuals differed for men and women. Lesbians were censured by silence; sexual acts between two women were unimaginable. Men, by contrast, were judged guilty of effeminacy. For both men and women, homosexual behavior came to be seen as a manifestation of "inversion." Effeminate men or masculine women violated the prescriptions of gender. The men particularly served as popular symbols of perversion and moral contagion.

NOTES

1.   Professor Law emphasizes the role that prescriptive gender roles play in the regulation of sexual orientation. Her approach has affinities with ideas about sex stereotyping and employment embraced by the U.S. Supreme Court in *Price Waterhouse v. Hopkins*, 490 U.S. 228, 109 S.Ct. 1775, 104 L.Ed.2d 268 (1989), a leading case on statutory sex discrimination claims under Title VII (*see* Chapter 4, Section II.B.)

2.   When the Supreme Court ruled in favor of marriage equality in *Obergefell v. Hodges*, ___ U.S. ___, 135 S.Ct. 2584, 192 L.Ed.2d 609 (2015), it did not embrace, or even discuss, the issue of sex discrimination. Chief Justice Roberts, however, had raised the issue at oral argument in the case. Noting that "if Sue loves Joe and Tom loves Joe, Sue can marry him and Tom can't," he asked counsel for the states why it wasn't a case about sex discrimination. *Obergefell v. Hodges*, Transcript of Oral Argument, https://www.supremecourt.gov/oral_arguments/argument_transcripts/14-556q1_l5gm.pdf at 62. For perspectives on the Supreme Court declining to embrace the sex discrimination argument in this context, see Mary Anne Case, *Missing Sex Talk in the Supreme Court's Same-Sex Marriage Cases*, 84 U.M.K.C. L. Rev. 675 (2016); Suzanne B. Goldberg, *Risky Arguments in Social-Justice Litigation: The Case of Sex Discrimination and Marriage Equality*, 114 Colum. L. Rev. 2087 (2014).

2.   Debating the Sex Discrimination Argument

EVALUATING THE SEX DISCRIMINATION ARGUMENT FOR LESBIAN AND GAY RIGHTS[*]

Edward Stein

In order to elucidate the problems with the sex discrimination argument, consider a hypothetical argument that could be made against antimiscegenation laws. Various scholars have noted that there were sex hierarchies implicit in antimiscegenation statutes—a significant purpose of such laws was to protect white women from black men. Sex classifications clearly played a role in the development and articulation of antimiscegenation laws. In light of this fact, one could make a sex discrimination argument against antimiscegenation laws, pointing out that women were disadvantaged by antimiscegenation laws and that such laws were justified by sexism. * * *

Overturning antimiscegenation laws because they discriminate on the basis of sex would mischaracterize the core of the problem with such laws.

To put a finer point on my claim, there are three related problems with the sex discrimination argument against antimiscegenation laws in particular and against racially discriminatory laws in general. First, this argument misidentifies the class disadvantaged by antimiscegenation laws. Nonwhites, more than women, are disadvantaged by such a law. Call this the *sociological* mistake of the sex discrimination argument against antimiscegenation laws. The sex discrimination argument against antimiscegenation laws overemphasizes the ways these laws

---

[*]   Edward Stein, *Evaluating the Sex Discrimination Argument for Lesbian and Gay Rights*, 49 UCLA L. REV. 471, 496–504, 509–15 (2001).

disadvantage women as compared to the ways they disadvantage people of color. * * *

Second, the sex discrimination argument against antimiscegenation laws misidentifies the belief system that justifies antimiscegenation laws. Even granting that racism and sexism complement each other in providing the justification for antimiscegenation laws, racism, not sexism, is the belief system that primarily underlies these laws. Call this the *theoretical* mistake of the sex discrimination argument against antimiscegenation laws. * * *

Third, a court that overturned an antimiscegenation law on the grounds that the law discriminated on the basis of sex would, in so doing, fail to take a stand on the central moral issue underlying the legal questions about antimiscegenation laws, namely that racial discrimination is morally wrong. If the *Loving* Court, in overturning Virginia's antimiscegenation law, had focused on the sexist rather than the racist assumptions that justified the law, it would have made a moral mistake, not just a theoretical one. Call this the *moral* mistake of the sex discrimination argument against antimiscegenation laws. The three mistakes of the sex discrimination argument against antimiscegenation laws—the sociological, the theoretical, and the moral—are interconnected. The theoretical mistake builds on the sociological mistake: If women are in fact greatly disadvantaged by antimiscegenation laws, then it would make sense to say that sexism plays a role in the justification of such laws. The moral mistake builds on the other two: It is tempting to see the moral issue of antimiscegenation laws in terms of mistaken and unjust views of women because of the sociological and theoretical claims linking racism and sexism.

The three problems with the sex discrimination argument against antimiscegenation laws parallel problems with the sex discrimination argument as applied to laws that discriminate against lesbians, gay men, and bisexuals. I turn now to these parallel problems with the sex discrimination argument for lesbian and gay rights. * * *

Various scholars have argued for the need to analyze sexual orientation and sex separately. For example, Cheshire Calhoun, in her article *Separating Lesbian Theory from Feminist Theory*, says that:

> patriarchy and heterosexual dominance are two, in principle, separable systems. Even where they work together, it is possible conceptually to pull the patriarchal aspect of male-female relationships apart from their heterosexual dimensions. . . . Even if empirically and historically heterosexual dominance and patriarchy are completely intertwined, it does not follow from this fact that the collapse [or weakening] of patriarchy will bring about the collapse [or weakening] of heterosexual dominance.

While an advocate of the sex discrimination argument might admit that sexual-orientation inequality and homophobia could continue to exist even if there were sex equality and no sexism, I want to make a stronger claim. Building on the work of Calhoun and of others, I claim that there are actual and significant differences between sexism and homophobia in contemporary American and other western societies. Simply put, sexism and homophobia are coming apart. Consider, for example, the dramatic changes in family law in the past century. Whereas women were once viewed as the property of their husbands and had few rights as wives, today the legal status of women and men in the context of the family are basically equal. In contrast, with the notable exception of the creation of civil unions in Vermont, the legal recognition for lesbian and gay relationships and families lags dramatically behind those of heterosexuals. This one example illustrates how homophobia, though it has gradually become disentangled from sexism, remains entrenched in our society. * * *

It mischaracterizes the nature of laws that discriminate against lesbians and gay men to see them as primarily harming women (or even as harming women as much as they harm gay men, lesbians, and bisexuals). Further, it mischaracterizes laws that discriminate on the basis of sexual orientation to see them as primarily justified by sexism rather than by homophobia. * * *

[T]o simply deploy the sex discrimination argument against sodomy laws would, for example, ignore the central role that conceptions of sexual desire play in such laws. Making the sex discrimination argument also overlooks the distinctive role that "the closet," and the associated invisibility of lesbians, gay men, and bisexuals, play in the justification and maintenance of sodomy laws and of sexual orientation discrimination generally. Various theorists have shown how the element of secrecy, sometimes in the form of an "open secret," is a central aspect of the experience of lesbians, gay men, and bisexuals. The centrality of the closet can be seen in such legal policies as the military's "don't ask, don't tell" policy and the varied policies of public school districts towards teachers who are open about their homosexuality or bisexuality. * * *

I agree that some laws that disadvantage one group may also disadvantage another and that more than one belief system may undergird some laws. Sometimes, however, one group may be more disadvantaged than another and one belief system may play a much more central role than another. * * *

A parallel point can be made concerning the sex discrimination argument for lesbian and gay rights: Women, compared to men, may be more disadvantaged by laws that discriminate on the basis of sexual orientation, but lesbians, gay men, and bisexuals are more significantly disadvantaged by such laws than are women in general. Similarly, while sexism plays a role in maintaining laws relating to sexual orientation, homophobia plays a much more central role. * * *

In an essay written before *Loving* but after *Brown v. Board of Education*, Herbert Wechsler argued that the questions posed by state-enforced segregation (in both education and marriage) do not primarily concern discrimination or equal protection but rather primarily concern freedom of association. He argued that the prohibition of miscegenation affected both whites and nonwhites; the prohibition, properly understood, did not discriminate against blacks and did not violate the Equal Protection Clause but rather restricted the freedom of association of everyone, regardless of race.

Charles Black, in response, said that as a member of this society, he has no doubt why segregation laws exist. He argued that Wechsler ignored the obvious ways in which segregation (in marriage, education, and other contexts) clearly offends equality. It was ridiculous to claim that such laws were unconstitutional because they restrict the right to free association:

> [I]f a whole race of people finds itself confined within a system which is set up and continued for the very purpose of keeping it in an inferior station, and if the question is then solemnly propounded whether such a race is being treated "equally," I think we ought to exercise one of the sovereign prerogatives of philosophers—that of laughter.

Black convincingly—and presciently (in light of the Court's decision in *Loving*)—argued that segregation was designed to keep African Americans "in their place" and to sustain white supremacy.

The moral objection to the sex discrimination argument is similar to Black's objection to Wechsler's argument against segregation: Laws that discriminate against lesbians, gay men, and bisexuals should be overturned on the grounds that they make invidious distinctions on the basis of sexual orientation, not on other grounds. Overturning laws that discriminate on the basis of sexual orientation because they discriminate on the basis of sex (or gender) mischaracterizes the core wrong of these laws. . . . By failing to address arguments about the morality of same-sex sexual acts and the moral character of lesbians, gay men, and bisexuals, the sex discrimination argument "closets," rather than confronts, homophobia. * * *

In virtue of the fact that sex and sexual orientation are conceptually and culturally distinct, not all laws that discriminate on the basis of sexual orientation in fact make use of sex classifications. In his book, *Gaylaw*, William Eskridge distinguishes among three different types of laws that discriminate on the basis of sexual orientation: (1) laws that explicitly discriminate on the basis of sexual orientation (*type-1 laws*; an example would be the military's policy concerning homosexuality); (2) laws that discriminate on the basis of sex but that have their primary effect on gay people (*type-2 laws*; an example would be marriage laws that prohibit same-sex couples from marrying); and (3) other laws that do not facially discriminate against either sex or sexual orientation but that have discriminatory effects on lesbians and gay men (*type-3 laws*).

As an example of a type-1 law, consider the military's policy concerning homosexuality. This law and the regulations that implement it, often referred to collectively as the "don't ask, don't tell" policy, do not facially discriminate on the basis of sex or even mention sex classifications. Under this policy, one of the several ways that lesbians, gay men, and bisexuals can be discharged is if they engage in sexual activities with people of the same-sex. This policy does not, however, discharge *heterosexuals* who engage in same-sex sexual acts (as some heterosexuals do). Specifically, the law provides for an exemption from discharge of a member of the armed forces who "engages in a homosexual act . . . [if] such conduct is a departure from the member's usual and customary behavior; such conduct . . . is unlikely to recur; . . . and the member does not have a propensity or intent to engage in homosexual acts." In other words, heterosexuals who occasionally engage in same-sex sexual acts might not be discharged for engaging in such acts, even if such acts are discovered. Only lesbians, gay men, and bisexuals will be discharged for engaging in same-sex sexual acts, because, by virtue of their sexual orientations, only they have the propensity to engage in such acts. In light of this exemption, the military policy is a type-1 law: It does not discriminate on the basis of sex, but it discriminates on the basis of sexual orientation—it discharges lesbians, gay men, and bisexuals for engaging in a behavior for which heterosexuals are not discharged.

Although the sex discrimination argument could be applied to type-1 laws as well as to type-3 laws, the sex discrimination argument has its greatest potential applied to type-2 laws, that is, laws that discriminate on the basis of sex. The sex discrimination argument will be much harder for judges to accept when it is applied to type-1 laws or to type-3 laws, that is, laws that discriminate on the basis of sexual orientation that do *not* make use of sex classifications. This is a significant practical limitation of the sex discrimination argument. * * *

Legislatures that wish to restrict lesbian and gay rights will try to immunize themselves against the sex discrimination argument by not using sex classifications in laws relating to sexual orientation and by explicitly stating that such laws do not discriminate against sex. * * *

[Another] practical problem for the sex discrimination argument for lesbian and gay rights is that any practical successes for the sex discrimination argument could lead to a weakening of protections against sex discrimination. This is because a strong backlash typically occurs when lesbians, gay men, and bisexuals make legal and political advances. In fact, some have argued that the link to lesbian and gay rights, especially to same-sex marriage, had a deleterious effect on the Equal Rights Amendment. A backlash to any success of the sex discrimination argument could undermine both women's rights and lesbian and gay rights. In effect, this is what happened in Hawaii. The 1999 decision of the state's supreme court construed the 1998 constitutional amendment as taking Hawaii's marriage law "out of the ambit of the equal protection clause of the Hawaii constitution," thereby weakening sex discrimination jurisprudence in Hawaii. * * *

[M]y view is that the sex discrimination argument, given its practical and theoretical pitfalls, if presented at all, should be used with caution. Making this argument in conjunction with other sorts of arguments for lesbian and gay rights might mitigate some of the practical problems with the sex discrimination argument, but some serious worries would remain. A law that discriminates on the basis of sexual orientation that is overturned in the face of the sex discrimination argument could reappear in a slightly different form, recast so that it does not make use of sex classifications. Further, when a law that discriminates on the basis of sexual orientation is overturned in the face of the sex discrimination argument, the central moral debates about homosexuality are bracketed. Perhaps Herbert Wechsler's argument that appealed to the freedom of association could have worked to persuade judges who would have otherwise upheld racial segregation, but such an argument would have lacked the moral force of the Supreme Court's opinion in *Loving*. When the basic human rights of a despised minority are at issue, the judiciary needs to speak in a strong moral voice.

DEFENDING THE SEX DISCRIMINATION ARGUMENT FOR LESBIAN AND GAY RIGHTS: A REPLY TO EDWARD STEIN*

Andrew Koppelman

So many things are wrong with laws that discriminate against gay people that it is hard to know where to begin. They intrude on citizens' privacy. They enforce indefensible beliefs about sexual morality. They give the state's imprimatur to a theology, and a dubious one at that. They interfere with matters in which the law has no competence and that are none of the state's business. They oppress a long-suffering minority. Their enforcement typically involves cruelty and hypocrisy.

* Andrew Koppelman, *Defending the Sex Discrimination Argument for Lesbian and Gay Rights: A Reply to Edward Stein*, 49 UCLA L. REV. 519, 519–34 (2001).

They also discriminate on the basis of sex, and they depend on and reinforce the subordination of women.

Each of the preceding seven sentences is an inadequate portrait of antigay oppression to the extent that it fails to mention the wrongs cited by the others. This is one of the limitations of language. Edward Stein's critique of the sex discrimination argument for gay rights is concerned about what the argument leaves out. I do not want to leave them out, either. But that is not a reason to neglect the wrongs specifically revealed by the sex discrimination argument. * * *

The formal argument that discrimination against gays is a kind of sex discrimination is stated briefly and accurately by Stein:

> If a person's sexual orientation is a dispositional property that concerns the sex of people to whom he or she is attracted, then, to determine a person's sexual orientation, one needs to know the person's sex and the sex of the people to whom he or she is primarily sexually attracted. For example, if A is sexually attracted exclusively to men, then A is a heterosexual only if A is a woman, and A is a homosexual only if A is a man.

This argument is formally incomplete, Stein thinks, because a law that discriminates against gays may just as easily be understood as treating both sexes equally by forbidding both to engage in sexual conduct with persons of the same sex. "Deciding whether a statute that discriminates on the basis of sexual orientation discriminates on the basis of sex seems, in light of this problem, like deciding whether a glass is half empty or half full."

Stein acknowledges that the miscegenation cases presented a similar problem, and that the U.S. Supreme Court ultimately rejected the idea that both races were treated identically by laws against interracial marriage. But, he claims, in those cases there was "a fit between the class disadvantaged by the law and the suspect classification the law employs." And he proceeds to raise questions about the sociological connection between antigay animus and sexism.

This, however, leaves legal doctrine behind, because it misstates what the Court did in the miscegenation cases. Stein is correct that *Loving v. Virginia* noted a connection between the miscegenation prohibition and racism. But *Loving* was preceded by *McLaughlin v. Florida*, in which the Court unanimously invalidated a criminal statute prohibiting an unmarried interracial couple from habitually living in and occupying the same room at night. "It is readily apparent," the Court held, that the statute "treats the interracial couple made up of a white person and a Negro differently than it does any other couple." Racial classifications, it concluded, can only be sustained by a compelling state interest. Because the State had failed to establish that the statute served "some overriding statutory purpose requiring the proscription of the specified conduct when engaged in by a white person and a Negro, but not otherwise," the statute necessarily fell as "an invidious discrimination forbidden by the Equal Protection Clause."

McLaughlin, not *Loving*, was the groundbreaking case that laid the equal application argument to rest, and *McLaughlin*, not *Loving*, is the crucial precedent on which the sex discrimination argument relies. It should not even be necessary to cite it as a precedent, because it stated the obvious. If prohibited conduct is defined by reference to the actor's own race or sex, the prohibition is not neutral with reference to that characteristic. Indeed, in the states that specifically prohibit homosexual sex, the defendant's own sex would appear to be one of the essential elements of the crime that the prosecution must prove.

McLaughlin did not rely on any claims whatsoever about the motive for the law or about the class that was harmed by the law. It simply noted that there was a racial classification and applied heightened scrutiny. The sex discrimination argument for protecting gays from discrimination requires nothing more. * * *

Stein correctly observes that sex discrimination doctrine permits discrimination in cases in which the discrimination reflects real differences between men and women. Courts have relied on that doctrine to reject the sex discrimination argument. But does current doctrine permit this result? There are a few cases, which Stein notes, that do permit reliance on those differences. The laws upheld in those decisions, however, reflected accurate empirical rather than normative generalizations. More importantly, the generalizations they reflected were exceptionless. If it were otherwise—if a sex-based classification could be justified by what is usually the case, or what is true about most members of either sex—then the constitutional doctrine would be eviscerated, because even the most invidiously sexist laws have been justifiable in terms of some argument of this sort.

What "real differences" could courts cite? Stein notes that some states have tried to defend some kinds of discrimination by arguing:

> that marriage is related to childrearing (and that . . . lesbians and gay men are bad parents compared to heterosexuals), that lesbians and gay men are less able to sustain the sort of long-term commitments the state wants to encourage in its citizens, and that the incidence of sodomy can be reduced by preventing homosexuals from marrying.

All of these claims involve the kind of stereotyping that the Court has consistently rejected in the sex discrimination cases. Some, such as the claim about parenting, are not even statistically accurate. More importantly, none of them are true of all gay couples. Such generalizations have been relied on by courts denying gays' sex discrimination claims. But such generalizations have also been relied on to justify *all* forms of sex discrimination. * * *

Drawing on a taxonomy developed by William Eskridge, Jr., Stein observes that the sex discrimination argument does not reach all antigay laws. Specifically, he claims that sex classifications are found neither in laws that explicitly discriminate on the basis of sexual orientation (what he calls "type-1 laws"), nor in laws that do not facially discriminate but have discriminatory effects on gays ("type-3 laws").

With respect to type-3 laws, Stein is undoubtedly correct. This objection is not confined to the sex discrimination argument, however. It also deflates the argument that homosexuality is a suspect classification like race and the argument that sexual orientation discrimination is like religious discrimination. Disparate impact based on race or religion is not now recognized as a basis for a constitutional claim. In this regard, the sex discrimination argument fares no worse than its rivals.

The sex discrimination argument does, however, reach type-1 laws. Any law that discriminates against gays as such must be predicated on some procedure for determining who is gay. Stein acknowledges that "to determine a person's sexual orientation, one needs to know the person's sex and the sex of the people to whom he or she is primarily sexually attracted." He thinks that the sex discrimination argument would not reach a law that prohibited gay people from marrying anyone of either sex. In order to enforce this law, though, the registrar of marriages would need to know what A's sex is in order to decide whether A's attraction to B marks A as a gay person. Imagine a law that discriminated against "miscegenosexuals" and denied them the right to marry or other benefits. Does Stein really think that such a law is not racially discriminatory, or that it would not be immediately recognized as such? * * *

The big problem with his sociological objection is that it implies that *Loving* was wrong to talk about white supremacy. The same objection could have been raised in that case: Miscegenation laws primarily harmed, not blacks as such, but interracial heterosexual couples (a group that, by definition, included equal numbers of blacks and whites). While the harm to blacks was recognized even by the most obtuse judges as a "stigma, of the deepest degradation . . . fixed upon the whole [black] race," it would be callous not to notice that the persons who were *most* severely harmed by those laws were the ones whose marriages were voided and who were, in many cases, sent to prison. If the harm to blacks counts against the miscegenation laws, then for the same reasons, the harm to women should count against antigay laws. * * *

What Stein calls the "theoretical" objection (it appears just as sociological as its predecessor) is that "while sexism plays a role in the justification of laws that discriminate against lesbians, gay men, and bisexuals, homophobia plays a more central role." I do not know how to evaluate that comparative claim, which pertains to complex social and psychological processes that are largely mysterious (and that take very different forms in the psyches of different people). * * *

At one point Stein makes the stronger claim that in contemporary America, "sexism and homophobia are coming apart." I would have to see better evidence than that which Stein cites before I believed this. The most thorough documentation of the linkage is the work of Francisco Valdes, which illustrates the ways in which literature, the discourse of scholarly psychologists, politics, public opinion, popular culture, and judicial decisionmaking have conflated sex, gender, and sexual orientation throughout the last century. Valdes concludes that "sex, gender, and sexual orientation *never* have been constructed independently of each other in our society." If someone wanted to refute him, they could begin by citing instances of discourse in which sexual orientation is constructed without reference to gender norms. However, this would not be an easy task. I cannot imagine where they would begin. The mere fact that women's status has improved, which is all that Stein cites, hardly suffices. The status of gays has improved at the same time, and those who have struggled against heterosexism and sexism are acutely conscious of the link. * * *

Finally, Stein objects that the sex discrimination argument "mischaracterizes the core wrong" of antigay laws. "By failing to address arguments about the morality of same-sex sexual acts and the moral character of lesbians, gay men, and bisexuals, the sex discrimination argument 'closets,' rather than confronts, homophobia."

This is a powerful claim. Stein is only the latest of many writers who have worried that the sex discrimination argument marginalizes gays' moral claims. Jack Balkin writes that the sex discrimination argument implies "that discrimination against homosexuals is merely a 'side effect' of discrimination against women, and therefore somehow less important." John Gardner thinks that "those committed to the moral wrongfulness of sexuality discrimination should not be at all happy to find this wrongfulness appended to the moral margins of somebody else's grievance, namely the grievance of those who are victims of sex discrimination." William Eskridge writes that the sex discrimination argument has "a transvestite quality," because "it dresses a gay rights issue up in gender rights garb." Danielle Kie Hart argues that the sex discrimination argument "makes the lives of homosexuals invisible; it sends a clear message to society that it is not acceptable to discuss homosexuality in a public forum; and it reflects and may perpetuate negative attitudes about lesbians and gay men."

All these concerns are valid. One can make the same point about the interracial couple prosecuted in *Loving*: the racist system primarily harmed blacks, but the white husband's interests were hardly unimportant. Balkin's rephrasing of the point is helpful: "gender categories are general forms of social subordination that subordinate the feminine and all things associated with the feminine. Thus, this system subordinates not only women, but homosexuals, bisexuals, and effeminate men."

The problem here is the problem with any legal claim. Law always picks and chooses among facts in the world, deeming some relevant and ignoring others. It thus flattens the richness of human life. Law is not literature. Its capacity "to speak in a strong moral voice" is inevitably limited. When we evaluate a human life, we do not just ask whether the person followed the rules. Othello and Iago both killed their wives; the law would make no distinction between them, even though any reader of Shakespeare's play knows that the two men lived in different moral universes. Facts are messy. Legal categories make them clean, usually by stripping off the living flesh. There is a danger, which should always be resisted, that stories deemed irrelevant for legal purposes will be deemed irrelevant *simpliciter*.

The sex discrimination argument relies on settled law that was established for the benefit of women, not of gays. It can be relied on because it is settled, but it is settled only because it was devised without thinking about (to some extent, by deliberately ignoring) the claims of gays. Accepting and relying on the sex discrimination argument thus means accepting and relying on a view of the world in which gays are at best marginal.

On the other hand, the marginalization of gays is precisely why the argument has the comparative advantages that it does. Each of the other principal arguments for gay equality—the privacy and suspect classification arguments—depend on an innovative extension of existing law to cover gays. The sex discrimination argument does not. On the contrary, it is its opponents who must ask for legal innovation, by carving out an exception to a settled rule.

NOTE

Who do you think has the better of this exchange? What light is shed on the questions debated by Professors Stein and Koppelman by the argument offered by Professor Law earlier in this Chapter?

C. GENDER IDENTITY DISCRIMINATION AS A FORM OF SEX DISCRIMINATION

A related, but distinct, issue is the extent to which unconstitutional discrimination based on gender identity has been, and should be, seen as a form of sex discrimination. As you will see in Chapter 4, most of the law regarding employment discrimination based on gender identity has developed under statutory frameworks, and the trend in that context has been toward recognizing gender identity discrimination as a form of sex discrimination. But the conceptual frameworks utilized in the statutory context are not always carried over to the constitutional domain. The next case is important because it utilizes the equal protection clause and thus can offer a blueprint for constitutional claims against state actors in employment, as well as other realms.

GLENN V. BRUMBY

United States Court of Appeals, Eleventh Circuit, 2011
663 F.3d 1312

BARKETT, CIRCUIT JUDGE.

* * * Vandiver Elizabeth Glenn was born a biological male. Since puberty, Glenn has felt that she is a woman, and in 2005, she was diagnosed with GID, a diagnosis listed in the American Psychiatric Association's Diagnostic and Statistical Manual of Mental Disorders.

Starting in 2005, Glenn began to take steps to transition from male to female under the supervision of health care providers. This process included living as a woman outside of the workplace, which is a prerequisite to sex reassignment surgery. In October 2005, then known as Glenn Morrison and presenting as a man, Glenn was hired as an editor by the Georgia General Assembly's OLC. Sewell Brumby is the head of the OLC and is responsible for OLC personnel decisions, including the decision to fire Glenn.

In 2006, Glenn informed her direct supervisor, Beth Yinger, that she was a transsexual and was in the process of becoming a woman. On Halloween in 2006, when OLC employees were permitted to come to work wearing costumes, Glenn came to work presenting as a woman. When Brumby saw her, he told her that her appearance was not appropriate and asked her to leave the office. Brumby deemed her appearance inappropriate "[b]ecause he was a man dressed as a woman and made up as a woman." Brumby stated that "it's unsettling to think of someone dressed in women's clothing with male sexual organs inside that clothing," and that a male in women's clothing is "unnatural." Following this incident, Brumby met with Yinger to discuss Glenn's appearance on Halloween of 2006 and was informed by Yinger that Glenn intended to undergo a gender transition.

In the fall of 2007, Glenn informed Yinger that she was ready to proceed with gender transition and would begin coming to work as a woman and was also changing her legal name. Yinger notified Brumby, who subsequently terminated Glenn because "Glenn's intended gender transition was inappropriate, that it would be disruptive, that some people would view it as a moral issue, and that it would make Glenn's coworkers uncomfortable."

Glenn sued, alleging two claims of discrimination under the Equal Protection Clause. First, Glenn alleged that Brumby "discriminat[ed] against her because of her sex, including her female gender identity and her failure to conform to the sex stereotypes associated with the sex Defendant[ ] perceived her to be." [Glenn also alleged that Brumby discriminated against her because of a medical condition]. * * *

The Equal Protection Clause requires the State to treat all persons similarly situated alike or, conversely, to avoid all classifications that are "arbitrary or irrational" and those that reflect "a bare . . . desire to harm a politically unpopular group." States are presumed to act lawfully, and therefore state action is generally upheld if it is rationally related to a legitimate governmental purpose. However, more than a rational basis is required in certain circumstances. * * * In *United States v. Virginia*, the Supreme Court reaffirmed its prior holdings that sex-based discrimination is subject to intermediate scrutiny under the Equal Protection Clause. This standard requires the government to show that its "gender classification . . . is substantially related to a sufficiently important government interest." Moreover, this test requires a "genuine" justification, not one that is "hypothesized or invented *post hoc* in response to litigation." In *Virginia*, the state's policy of excluding women from the Virginia Military Institute failed this test because the state could not rely on generalizations about different aptitudes of males and females to support the exclusion of women. * * *

The question here is whether discriminating against someone on the basis of his or her gender non-conformity constitutes sex-based discrimination under the Equal Protection Clause. For the reasons discussed below, we hold that it does.

In *Price Waterhouse v. Hopkins*, the Supreme Court held that discrimination on the basis of gender stereotype is sex-based discrimination. In that case, the Court considered allegations that a senior manager at Price Waterhouse was denied partnership in the firm because she was considered "macho," and "overcompensated for being a woman." * * *

A person is defined as transgender precisely because of the perception that his or her behavior transgresses gender stereotypes. "[T]he very acts that define transgender people as transgender are those that contradict stereotypes of gender-appropriate appearance and behavior." Ilona M. Turner, *Sex Stereotyping Per Se: Transgender Employees and Title VII*, 95 Cal. L. Rev. 561, 563 (2007); *see also* Taylor Flynn, *Transforming the Debate: Why We Need to Include Transgender Rights in the Struggles for Sex and Sexual Orientation Equality*, 101 Colum. L. Rev. 392, 392 (2001) (defining transgender persons as those whose "appearance, behavior, or other personal characteristics differ from traditional gender norms"). There is thus a congruence between discriminating against transgender and transsexual individuals and discrimination on the basis of gender-based behavioral norms. Accordingly, discrimination against a transgender individual because of her gender-nonconformity is sex discrimination, whether it's described as being on the basis of sex or gender. * * *

All persons, whether transgender or not, are protected from discrimination on the basis of gender stereotype. For example, courts have held that plaintiffs cannot be discriminated against for wearing jewelry that was considered too effeminate, carrying a serving tray too gracefully, or taking too active a role in child-rearing. An individual cannot be punished because of his or her perceived gender-nonconformity. Because these protections are afforded to everyone, they cannot be denied to a transgender individual. The nature of the discrimination is the same; it may differ in degree but not in kind, and discrimination on this basis is a form of sex-based discrimination that is subject to heightened scrutiny under the Equal Protection Clause. Ever since the Supreme Court began to apply heightened scrutiny to sex-based classifications, its consistent purpose has been to eliminate discrimination on the basis of gender stereotypes.

* * * Accordingly, governmental acts based upon gender stereotypes—which presume that men and women's appearance and behavior will be determined by their sex—must be subjected to heightened scrutiny because they embody "the very stereotype the law condemns." *J.E.B. v. Alabama* (declaring unconstitutional a government attorney's use of peremptory juror strikes based on the presumption that potential jurors' views would correspond to their sexes). * * *

* * * In this case, Brumby testified at his deposition that he fired Glenn because he considered it "inappropriate" for her to appear at work dressed as a woman and that he found it "unsettling" and "unnatural" that Glenn would appear wearing women's clothing. Brumby testified that his decision to dismiss Glenn was based on his perception of Glenn as "a man dressed as a woman and made up as a woman," and Brumby admitted that his decision to fire Glenn was based on "the sheer fact of the transition." Brumby's testimony provides ample direct evidence to support the district court's conclusion that Brumby acted on the basis of Glenn's gender non-conformity.

[The remainder of the opinion is excerpted in Chapter 4, Section III.A.]

NOTES

1.   Compared to sexual orientation claims, are claims of discrimination based on gender identity more easily seen as a form of sex discrimination? Note one possible puzzle. Sex is conventionally seen as an "immutable characteristic," as Justice Brennan wrote in in his opinion in *Frontiero*. Is the idea of gender reassignment inconsistent with that idea of immutability? Is the rejection of the gender binary that some transgender activists champion likewise at odds with this concept of immutability?

2.   To what extent would Professor Stein's critiques of the sex discrimination argument for sexual orientation apply to gender identity as well? Do you think anything important is lost in framing gender identity claims in these terms, as opposed to arguing that gender identity discrimination is its own distinctive phenomenon and should be constitutionally analyzed as such? (*See* Section II.E., below for more on seeing gender identity discrimination as an independent basis for heightened scrutiny).

3.   For more on transgender rights and sex discrimination, see Taylor Flynn, *Transforming the Debate: Why We Need to Include Transgender Rights in the Struggles for Sex and Sexual Orientation Equality*, 101 Colum. L. Rev. 392 (2001); Franklin H. Romeo, *Beyond a Medical Model: Advocating for a New Conception of Gender Identity in the Law*, 36 Colum. Hum. Rts. L. Rev. 713 (2005); Stevie V. Tran & Elizabeth M. Glazer, *Transgenderless*, 35 Harv. J.L. & Gender 399 (2012); Dylan Vade, *Expanding Gender and Expanding the Law: Toward a Social and Legal Conceptualization of Gender That Is More Inclusive of Transgender People*, 11 Mich. J. Gender & L. 253 (2005). While many transgender rights cases are litigated under a theory of sex discrimination, advocates have used a variety of other legal strategies, including disability law, the First Amendment and substantive due process. For articles advocating transgender rights through such alternative means, see Jeffrey Kosbie, *(No) State Interests in Regulating Gender: How Suppression of Gender Nonconformity Violates Freedom of Speech*, 19 Wm. & Mary J. Women & L. 187 (2013); S. Elizabeth Malloy, *What Best to Protect Transsexuals from Discrimination: Using Current Legislation or Adopting a New Judicial Framework*, 32 Women's Rts. L. Rep. 283 (2011); Daniella A. Schmidt, *Bathroom Bias: Making the Case for Trans Rights Under Disability Law*, 20 Mich. J. Gender & L. 155 (2013)

4.   Although the question of bathroom usage has been a significant part of the struggle for transgender equality for many years, the issue came dramatically to the fore in 2016, when the state of North Carolina passed House Bill 2. In relevant part, this controversial law requires that, in schools and public buildings, people use the bathroom that corresponds to their "biological sex," which the law defines as "[t]he physical condition of being

male or female, which is stated on a persons's birth certificate." After the bill passed, several lawsuits were filed to challenge it, including one brought by LGBT individuals. *Carcaño v. McCrory*, U.S. District Court for the Middle District of North Carolina, No. 1:16cv2346 (March 28, 2016). These plaintiffs claimed that the law violates the equal protection clause. How would you frame an equal protection claim against this law? What facts about the law would you want to know to predict how a court might rule? How is the issue of bathroom access like and unlike the employment issue posed in *Brumby*? For analyses of equal protection in the context of gender identity and bathrooms, see Diana Elkind, Comment, *The Constitutional Implications of Bathroom Access Based on Gender Identity: An Examination of Recent Developments Paving the Way for the Next Frontier of Equal Protection*, 9 U. Pa. J. Const. L. 895, 901 (2007); Chinyere Ezie, *Deconstructing the Body: Transgender and Intersex Identities and Sex Discrimination—The Need for Strict Scrutiny*, 20 Colum. J. Gender & L. 141 (2011); Jennifer Levi and Daniel Redman, *The Cross-Dressing Case for Bathroom Equality*, 34 Seattle U. L. Rev. 133 (2010); cf. Kelly Levy, *Equal, But Still Separate?: The Constitutional Debate of Sex-Segregated Public Restrooms in the Twenty-First Century*, 32 Women's Rts. L. Rep. 248 (2011) (questioning the constitutionality of sex segregation in bathrooms).

For more on employment disputes relating to gender identity and bathrooms, see Chapter 4, Section II.B.3.

D. HEIGHTENED SCRUTINY FOR SEXUAL ORIENTATION?

Setting aside the sex discrimination question, what level of scrutiny should be applied to constitutional claims of sexual orientation-based discrimination framed as such? Are LGB persons a suspect or quasi-suspect class? For many years, advocates have made the case for heightened scrutiny. As we explore later in this chapter, the Supreme Court has shown little interest in formally assigning sexual orientation-based discrimination a heightened level of scrutiny and has never even explicitly taken up the question. Several lower courts, however, have engaged this inquiry, most often in the context of marriage equality cases. (The same-sex marriage debate is explored in detail in Chapter 5). In the cases that follow, which predated the Supreme Court's ruling in favor of marriage equality in *Obergefell v. Hodges*, ___ U.S. ___, 135 S.Ct. 2584, 192 L.Ed.2d 609 (2015), you will see how the Connecticut and Washington state supreme courts reached different conclusions. In each of the cases below, same-sex couples, asserted that a state law preventing them from marrying violated rights protected by a state constitution. In each, the court was called upon to decide what level of scrutiny to apply. Note that, while the courts analyzed these claims under the provisions of a state constitution, they nevertheless chose to ground their approaches in federal equal protection precedents. As you read the cases, consider what factors seem to be the most important to these justices, and which court's approach better conceptualizes and applies these factors. Are the courts applying the same test, with different interpretations of the facts, or are they applying different tests?

KERRIGAN v. COMMISSIONER OF PUBLIC HEALTH

Connecticut Supreme Court, 2008
289 Conn. 135, 957 A.2d 407

PALMER, JUDGE.

IV

QUASI-SUSPECT CLASSIFICATIONS UNDER THE STATE CONSTITUTION

Although this court has indicated that a group may be entitled to heightened protection under the state constitution because of its status as a quasi-suspect class, we previously have not articulated the specific criteria to be considered in determining whether recognition as a quasi-suspect class is warranted. The United States Supreme Court, however, consistently has identified two factors that must be met, for purposes of the federal constitution, if a group is to be accorded such status. These two required factors are: (1) the group has suffered a history of invidious discrimination; * * * and (2) the characteristics that distinguish the group's members bear "no relation to [their] ability to perform or contribute to society." * * * The United States Supreme Court also has cited two other considerations that, in a given case, may be relevant in determining whether statutory provisions pertaining to a particular group are subject to heightened scrutiny. These two additional considerations are: (1) the characteristic that defines the members of the class as a discrete group is immutable or otherwise not within their control; * * * and (2) the group is "a minority or politically powerless." (Internal quotation marks omitted.) * * *

Because of the evident correlation between the indicia of suspectness identified by the United States Supreme Court and the issue of whether a class that has been singled out by the state for unequal treatment is entitled to heightened protection under the federal constitution, we conclude that those factors also are pertinent to the determination of whether a group comprises a quasi-suspect class for purposes of the state constitution. * * * It is evident, moreover, that immutability and minority status or political powerlessness are subsidiary to the first two primary factors because, as we explain more fully hereinafter, the United States Supreme Court has granted suspect class status to a group whose distinguishing characteristic is not immutable; see *Nyquist v. Mauclet*, (rejecting immutability requirement in treating group of resident aliens as suspect class despite their ability to opt out of class voluntarily); and has accorded quasi-suspect status to a group that had not been a minority or truly politically powerless. *See Frontiero v. Richardson*, supra, (plurality opinion) (according women heightened protection despite court's acknowledgment that women "do not constitute a small and powerless minority"). * * *

Finally, we note that courts generally have applied the same criteria to determine whether a classification is suspect, quasi-suspect or neither. * * * Just as there is no uniformly applied formula for determining whether a group is entitled to heightened protection under the constitution, there also is no clear test for determining whether a group that deserves such protection is entitled to designation as a suspect class or as a quasi-suspect class. * * * With these principles in mind, we consider the plaintiffs' contention that they are entitled to recognition as a quasi-suspect class.

V

STATUS OF GAY PERSONS AS A QUASI-SUSPECT CLASS

For the reasons that follow, we agree with the plaintiffs' claim that sexual orientation meets all of the requirements of a quasi-suspect classification. Gay persons have been subjected to and stigmatized by a long history of purposeful and invidious discrimination that continues to manifest itself in society. The characteristic that defines the members of this group—attraction to persons of the same sex—bears no logical relationship to their ability to perform in society, either in familial relations or otherwise as productive citizens. Because sexual orientation is such an essential component of personhood, even if there is some possibility that a person's sexual preference can be altered, it would be wholly unacceptable for the state to require anyone to do so. Gay persons also represent a distinct minority of the population. It is true, of course, that gay persons recently have made significant advances in obtaining equal treatment under the law. Nonetheless, we conclude that, as a minority group that continues to suffer the enduring effects of centuries of legally sanctioned discrimination, laws singling them out for disparate treatment are subject to heightened judicial scrutiny to ensure that those laws are not the product of such historical prejudice and stereotyping.

A

History of Discrimination

The defendants do not dispute that gay persons historically have been, and continue to be, the target of purposeful and pernicious discrimination due solely to their sexual orientation. * * * As the United States Supreme Court has recognized, "[p]roscriptions against [homosexual sodomy] have ancient roots." *Bowers v. Hardwick*, 478 U.S. 186, 192 (1986), overruled on other grounds by *Lawrence v. Texas*, 539

U.S. 558 (2003); see also *High Tech Gays v. Defense Industrial Security Clearance Office*, 909 F.2d 375, 382 (9th Cir. 1990) (Canby, J., dissenting) ("mainstream society has mistreated [homosexuals] for centuries"); *Baker v. Wade*, 769 F.2d 289, 292 (5th Cir. 1985) ("the strong objection to homosexual conduct . . . has prevailed in Western culture for the past seven centuries"), cert. denied, 478 U.S. 1022 (1986). . . .

There is no question, therefore, that gay persons historically have been, and continue to be, the target of purposeful and pernicious discrimination due solely to their sexual orientation. We therefore turn to the second required factor, namely, whether the sexual orientation of gay persons has any bearing on their ability to participate in society.

B

Whether Sexual Orientation Is Related to a Person's Ability to Participate in or Contribute to Society

The defendants also concede that sexual orientation bears no relation to a person's ability to participate in or contribute to society, a fact that many courts have acknowledged, as well. See, e.g., *Watkins v. United States Army*, 875 F.2d 699, 725 (9th Cir. 1989) (Norris, J., concurring in the judgment) ("[s]exual orientation plainly has no relevance to a person's ability to perform or contribute to society" [internal quotation marks omitted]), cert. denied, 498 U.S. 957, 111 S. Ct. 384, 112 L. Ed. 2d 395 (1990). In this critical respect, gay persons stand in stark contrast to other groups that have been denied suspect or quasi-suspect class recognition, despite a history of discrimination, because the distinguishing characteristics of those groups adversely affect their ability or capacity to perform certain functions or to discharge certain responsibilities in society. See, e.g., *Cleburne v. Cleburne Living Center, Inc.*, supra, 473 U.S. 442 (for purposes of federal constitution, mental retardation is not quasi-suspect classification because, inter alia, "it is undeniable . . . that those who are mentally retarded have a reduced ability to cope with and function in the everyday world"); *Massachusetts Board of Retirement v. Murgia*, supra, 427 U.S. 315 (age is not suspect classification because, inter alia, "physical ability generally declines with age"). . . .

C

Immutability of the Group's Distinguishing Characteristic

A third factor that courts have considered in determining whether the members of a class are entitled to heightened protection for equal protection purposes is whether the attribute or characteristic that distinguishes them is immutable or otherwise beyond their control. See, e.g., *Bowen v. Gilliard*, supra, 483 U.S. 602. Of course, the characteristic that distinguishes gay persons from others and qualifies them for recognition as a distinct and discrete group is the characteristic that historically has resulted in their social and legal ostracism, namely, their attraction to persons of the same sex. * * *

A number of courts that have considered this factor have rejected the claim that sexual orientation is an immutable characteristic. Other courts, however, as well as many, if not most, scholarly commentators, have reached a contrary conclusion. Although we do not doubt that sexual orientation—heterosexual or homosexual—is highly resistant to change, it is not necessary for us to decide whether sexual orientation is immutable in the same way and to the same extent that race, national origin and gender are immutable, because, even if it is not, the plaintiffs nonetheless have established that they fully satisfy this consideration. * * *

In view of the central role that sexual orientation plays in a person's fundamental right to self-determination, we fully agree with the plaintiffs that their sexual orientation represents the kind of distinguishing characteristic that defines them as a discrete group for purposes of determining whether that group should be afforded heightened protection under the equal protection provisions of the state constitution. This prong of the suspectness inquiry surely is satisfied when, as in the present case, the identifying trait is "so central to a person's identity that it would be abhorrent for government to penalize a person for refusing to change [it]. . . ." *Watkins v. United States Army*, supra, 875 F.2d 726 (Norris, J., concurring in the judgment); * * * In other words, gay persons, because they are characterized by a "central, defining [trait] of personhood, which may be altered [if at all] only at the expense of significant damage to the individual's sense of self" * * *

D

Whether the Group Is a Minority or Lacking in Political Power

* * *

1

We commence our analysis by noting that, in previous cases involving groups seeking heightened protection under the federal equal protection clause, the United States Supreme Court described this factor without reference to the minority status of the subject group, focusing instead on the group's lack of political power. See, e.g., *Massachusetts Board of Retirement v. Murgia*, supra, 427 U.S. 313 (explaining that "a suspect class is one saddled with such disabilities, or subjected to such a history of purposeful unequal treatment, or relegated to such a position of political powerlessness as to command extraordinary protection from the majoritarian political process" [internal quotation marks omitted]); *San Antonio Independent School District v. Rodriguez*, supra, 411 U.S. 28

(same). In its most recent formulation of the test for determining whether a group is entitled to suspect or quasi-suspect classification, however, the Court has indicated that this factor is satisfied upon a showing either that the group is a minority or that it lacks political power. *Bowen v. Gilliard,* supra, 483 U.S. 602; *Lyng v. Castillo,* supra, 477 U.S. 638. Indeed, in characterizing this factor in disjunctive terms, the Court cited to *Murgia; Bowen v. Gilliard,* supra, 602–603; *Lyng v. Castillo,* supra, 638; thereby also indicating that, for purposes of this aspect of the inquiry, the test always has involved a determination of whether the group is a "discrete and insular" minority; *United States v. Carolene Products Co.,* 304 U.S. 144, 152–53 n.4, 58 S. Ct. 778, 82 L. Ed. 1234 (1938); or, if not a true minority; see, e.g., *Frontiero v. Richardson,* supra, 411 U.S. 686 n.17, 688 (plurality opinion) (women accorded protected status although not minority); the group nonetheless is lacking in political power. This disjunctive test properly recognizes that a group may warrant heightened protection even though it does not fit the archetype of a discrete and insular minority. The test also properly recognizes that legislation singling out a true minority that meets the first three prongs of the suspectness inquiry must be viewed with skepticism because, under such circumstances, there exists an undue risk that legislation involving the historically disfavored group has been motivated by improper considerations borne of prejudice or animosity.

When this approach is applied to the present case, there is no doubt that gay persons clearly comprise a distinct minority of the population. Consequently, they clearly satisfy the first part of the disjunctive test and, thus, may be deemed to satisfy this prong of the suspectness inquiry on that basis alone.

2

* * * In support of their claim, the defendants rely primarily on this state's enactment of the gay rights and civil union laws, which, of course, were designed to provide equal rights for gay persons, and which undoubtedly reflect a measure of political power. The defendants also rely on the fact that several state legislators in Connecticut are openly gay. From the defendants' standpoint, these significant advances undermine the plaintiffs' claim that gay persons are so lacking in political power that they are entitled to heightened judicial protection. * * *

In this state, no openly gay person ever has been elected to *statewide* office, and only five of the 187 members of the state legislature are openly gay or lesbian. No openly gay man or lesbian ever has been appointed to the state Supreme Court or Appellate Court, and we are aware of only one openly gay or lesbian judge of the Superior Court. By contrast, this state's current governor, comptroller and secretary of the state are women, as are the current chief justice and two associate justices of the state Supreme Court, and other women now hold and previously have held statewide office and positions in the United States House of Representatives. By any standard, therefore, gay persons "remain a political underclass in our [state and] nation." *Andersen v. King County*, supra, 158 Wash.2d at 105, 138 P.3d 963 (Bridge, J., concurring in dissent).

advances in rights

In recent years, our legislature has taken substantial steps to address discrimination against gay persons. These efforts are most notably reflected in this state's gay rights law; see General Statutes §§ 46a–81a through 46a–81r; which broadly prohibits discrimination against a person because of his or her "preference for heterosexuality, homosexuality or bisexuality, having a history of such preference or being identified with such preference. . . ." General Statutes § 46a–81a. This public policy extends to a wide range of activities, including membership in licensed professional associations; see General Statutes § 46a–81b; employment; see General Statutes § 46a–81c; public accommodations; see General Statutes § 46a–81d; housing; see General Statutes § 46a–81e; credit practices; see General Statutes § 46a–81f; employment in state agencies; see General Statutes §§ 46a–81h and 46a–81j; the granting of state licenses; see General Statutes § 46a–81k; educational and vocational programs of state agencies; see General Statutes § 46a–81m; and the allocation of state benefits. *See* General Statutes § 46a–81n. Other statutes also seek to prohibit discrimination against same sex couples and gay persons. *See* General Statutes § 45a–724 et seq. (permitting same sex couples to adopt children); General Statutes §§ 53a–181j, 53a–181k and 53a–181 *l* (recognizing crimes of intimidation based on bigotry or bias for conduct directed at another on account of that person's actual or perceived sexual orientation). These antidiscrimination provisions, along with the civil union law, reflect the fact that gay persons are able to exert some degree of political influence in the state.

Notwithstanding these provisions, however, the legislature expressly has stated that the gay rights law shall *not* be "deemed or construed (1) to mean the state of Connecticut condones homosexuality or bisexuality or any equivalent lifestyle, (2) to authorize the promotion of homosexuality or bisexuality in educational institutions or require the teaching in educational institutions of homosexuality or bisexuality as an acceptable lifestyle, (3) to authorize or permit the use of numerical goals or quotas, or other types of affirmative action programs, with respect to homosexuality or bisexuality in the administration or enforcement of the [state's antidiscrimination laws], (4) to authorize the recognition of or the right of marriage between persons of the same sex, or (5) to establish sexual orientation as a specific and separate cultural classification in society." General Statutes § 46a–81r. By singling out same sex relationships in this manner—there is, of course, no such statutory disclaimer for opposite sex relationships—the legislature effectively has proclaimed, as a matter of state policy, that same sex relationships are disfavored. That policy, which is unprecedented among the various antidiscrimination measures enacted in this state, represents a kind of state-sponsored disapproval of same sex relationships and, consequently, serves to undermine the legitimacy of homosexual relationships, to perpetuate feelings of personal inferiority and inadequacy among gay persons, and to diminish the effect of the laws barring discrimination against gay persons. Indeed, the purposeful description of homosexuality as a "lifestyle" not condoned by the state stigmatizes gay persons and equates their identity with conduct that is disfavored by the state. Furthermore, although the legislature eventually enacted the gay rights law, its enactment was preceded by nearly a decade of numerous, failed attempts at passage. In addition, the bill that did become law provides more limited protection than the proposals that had preceded it, all of which would have added sexual orientation to the existing nondiscrimination laws and would have treated the classification in the same manner as other protected classes. Finally, as we have explained, the legislation that ultimately emerged from this process passed only after a compromise was reached that resulted in, inter alia, an unprecedented proviso expressing the position of the legislature that it does not condone homosexuality. Thus, to the extent that those civil rights laws, as well as the civil union law, reflect the fact that gay persons wield a measure of political power, the public policy articulated in § 46a–81r is clear evidence of the limits of that political influence. * * *

4

In sum, the relatively modest political influence that gay persons possess is insufficient to rectify the invidious discrimination to which they have been subjected for so long. Like the political gains that women had made prior to their recognition as a quasi-suspect class, the political advances that gay persons have attained afford them inadequate protection, standing alone, in view of the deep-seated and pernicious nature of the prejudice and antipathy that they continue to face. Today, moreover, women have far greater political power than gay persons, yet they continue to be accorded status as a quasi-suspect class. See Breen v. Carlsbad Municipal Schools, supra, 138 N.M. 338 (explaining that intermediate scrutiny is appropriate with respect to discrimination based on sex "even though the darkest period of discrimination may have passed for [the] historically maligned group" and that "[such] scrutiny should still be applied to protect against more subtle forms of unconstitutional discrimination created by unconscious or disguised prejudice"). We conclude, therefore, that, to the extent that gay persons possess some political power, it does not disqualify them from recognition as a quasi-suspect class under the state constitution in view of the pervasive and invidious discrimination to which they historically have been subjected due to an innate personal characteristic that has absolutely no bearing on their ability to perform in or contribute to society.

ANDERSEN V. KING COUNTY

Supreme Court of Washington, 2006
158 Wash.2d 1, 138 P.3d 963

MADSEN, JUDGE.

To qualify as a suspect class for purposes of an equal protection analysis, the class must have suffered a history of discrimination, have as the characteristic defining the class an obvious, immutable trait that frequently bears no relation to ability to perform or contribute to society, and show that it is a minority or politically powerless class. *Hanson,* 83 Wash.2d at 199, 517 P.2d 599; *City of Cleburne v. Cleburne Living Ctr., Inc.,* 473 U.S. 432, 440–41, 105 S.Ct. 3249, 87 L.Ed.2d 313 (1985); *High Tech Gays v. Def. Indus. Sec. Clearance Office,* 895 F.2d 563 (9th Cir.1990). Race, alienage, and national origin are examples of suspect classifications. *City of Cleburne,* 473 U.S. at 440, 105 S.Ct. 3249. Suspect classifications require heightened scrutiny because the defining characteristic of the class is "so seldom relevant to the achievement of any legitimate state interest that laws grounded in such considerations are deemed to reflect prejudice and antipathy—a view that those in the burdened class are not as worthy or deserving as others." *Id.* There is no dispute that gay and lesbian persons have been discriminated against in the past.

The parties dispute whether homosexuality is immutable. The State relies on the decision in *High Tech Gays* that homosexuality is behavioral, and thus not immutable. The plaintiffs counter that the Ninth Circuit has since "corrected" *High Tech Gays* and held that gay and lesbian persons constitute a suspect class. They rely on *Hernandez-Montiel v. Immigration & Naturalization Serv.,* 225 F.3d 1084 (9th Cir. 2000), *overruled in part on other grounds by Thomas v. Gonzales,* 409 F.3d 1177 (9th Cir. 2005), where the court determined that asylum should be granted to an immigration applicant, reasoning among other things that as a gay man with a female sexual identity the applicant had a well-grounded fear of persecution as a member of a particular social group. The court concluded the applicant was a member of a particular social group because "[s]exual orientation and sexual identity are immutable; they are so fundamental to one's identity that a person should not be required to abandon them." *Id.* at 1093. This conclusion was drawn from other immigration cases and secondary authority.

Notwithstanding *Hernandez-Montiel,* the Ninth Circuit has since referenced *High Tech Gays* for its holding that gay and lesbian persons do not constitute a suspect class. *Flores v. Morgan Hill Unified Sch. Dist.*, 324 F.3d 1130, 1137 (9th Cir. 2003) (citing *High Tech Gays*).

The plaintiffs do not cite other authority or any secondary authority or studies in support of the conclusion that homosexuality is an immutable characteristic. They focus instead on the lack of any relation between homosexuality and ability to perform or contribute to society. But plaintiffs must make a showing of immutability, and they have not done so in this case.

Finally, with regard to the ability to obtain redress through the legislative process (the political powerless prong), several state statutes and municipal codes provide protection against discrimination based on sexual orientation and also provide economic benefit for same sex couples. Recently, the legislature amended the Washington State Law Against Discrimination to prohibit discrimination on the basis of sexual orientation. Engrossed Substitute H.B. 2661, 59th Leg., Reg. Sess. (Wash.2006). In addition, the Intervenors point to evidence that a number of openly gay candidates were elected to national, state, and local offices in 2004.

The enactment of provisions providing increased protections to gay and lesbian individuals in Washington shows that as a class gay and lesbian persons are not powerless but, instead, exercise increasing political power. Indeed, the recent passage of the amendments to chapter 49.60 RCW is particularly significant given that, as the plaintiffs point out, the legislature had previously declined on numerous occasions to add sexual orientation to the laws against discrimination. We conclude that plaintiffs have not established that they satisfy the third prong of the suspect classification test.

Our conclusion here, that plaintiffs have not established that they are members of a suspect class, accords with the decisions of the overwhelming majority of courts, which find that gay and lesbian persons do not constitute a suspect class. *See Lofton v. Sec'y of the Dep't of Children & Family Servs.*, 358 F.3d 804, 818 & n.4 (11th Cir. 2004), *cert. denied,* 543 U.S. 1081 (2005) (concluding that gay and lesbian persons are not a suspect class and citing cases from the Fourth, Fifth, Sixth, Seventh, Ninth, and Tenth Circuits that have reached the same conclusion). The Second and Eighth Circuits have reached the same conclusion. *Able v. United States*, 155 F.3d 628, 632 (2d Cir. 1998); *Richenberg v. Perry*, 97 F.3d 256, 260 (8th Cir. 1996). The Court of Appeals held in *Singer*, 11 Wn. App. 247, that gay and lesbian persons do not constitute a suspect class. And even two state courts deciding that same-sex couples have a right to a civil union or marriage did not find a suspect class. *Baker v. State*, 170 Vt. 194, 744 A.2d 864 (1999) (under the state constitution's common benefits clause, plaintiffs seeking same-sex marriage are entitled to benefits and obligations like those accompanying marriage); *Goodridge v. Dep't of Pub. Health*, 440 Mass. 309, 798 N.E.2d 941 (2003) (denial of civil marriage to same-sex [*22] couples violates state equal protection principles). And, while the plaintiffs cite cases they say hold that gay and lesbian persons constitute a suspect class, most do not support the proposition or are otherwise distinguishable. * * *

The plaintiffs also suggest that *Miguel v. Guess,* 112 Wash.App. 536, 51 P.3d 89 (2002), *Romer,* 517 U.S. 620, 116 S.Ct. 1620, 134 L.Ed.2d 855, and *Lawrence v. Texas,* 539 U.S. 558, 123 S.Ct. 2472, 156 L.Ed.2d 508 (2003) indicate a trend toward heightened scrutiny where gay and lesbian persons are concerned. *Miguel* and *Romer* are based on another constitutional principle, however. In *Romer,* the Court invalidated on equal protection grounds Colorado's constitutional Amendment 2, which prohibited all legislative, executive, or judicial action designed to protect gay and lesbian persons from discrimination. The Court noted that "if a law neither burdens a fundamental right nor targets a suspect class, we will uphold the legislative classification so long as it bears a rational relation to some legitimate end." *Romer,* 517 U.S. at 631, 116 S.Ct. 1620. The Court said that Amendment 2 "fails, indeed defies" this inquiry. *Id.* at 632, 116 S.Ct. 1620. The court noted that central to equal protection is the principle that "government and each of its parts remain open . . . to all who seek its assistance," and "[a] law declaring that in general it shall be more difficult for one group of citizens than for all others to seek aid from the government is itself a denial of equal protection in the most literal sense." *Id.* at 633, 116 S.Ct. 1620. The Court found that there was no legitimate government purpose of Amendment 2 and held the amendment did not satisfy rational relation review.

Similarly, in *Miguel,* where the plaintiff claimed her civil rights were violated as a result of discrimination based on being a lesbian, the court found that a discriminatory classification based on prejudice or bias is not rationally related to a legitimate governmental purpose as a matter of law. *See also Cleburne Living Ctr.,* 473 U.S. at 448, 105 S.Ct. 3249 (noting that while private biases may be outside the reach the law, the law cannot give them effect). Both *Miguel* and *Romer* rest on the principle that equal protection is denied where the law's purpose is discrimination and it has no legitimate government purpose. Neither case supports the proposition that gay and lesbian persons constitute a suspect class. Indeed, as plaintiffs recognize, neither case addressed suspect classifications; the court in *Miguel* expressly declined to decide whether gay and lesbian persons constitute a suspect class. *Miguel,* 112 Wash.App. at 552 n. 3, 51 P.3d 89.

In *Lawrence,* the Court held that Texas's sodomy law violated equal protection under a rational basis analysis, thus overruling its decision in *Bowers v. Hardwick,* 478 U.S. 186, 106 S.Ct. 2841, 92 L.Ed.2d 140 (1986).

Lawrence is widely viewed as reflecting changing societal attitudes toward gay and lesbian persons. The Court emphasized "an emerging awareness that liberty gives substantial protection to adult persons in deciding how to conduct their private lives in matters pertaining to sex." *Lawrence,* 539 U.S. at 572, 123 S.Ct. 2472. However, the Court did not address suspect classification and invalidated the challenged law on the basis that it did not satisfy rational basis review, a standard that would not apply if the court had found an inherently suspect class.

In light of the lack of a sufficient showing of immutability and the overwhelming authority finding that gay and lesbian persons are not a suspect class for purposes of the equal protection clause, we decline to conclude that gay and lesbian persons constitute an inherently suspect class for purposes of article I, section 12.

NOTES

1.   Note the difference in how the Connecticut and Washington courts treat the issue of immutability. Which court has the better approach? What role—if any—do you think immutability should play in determining a level of scrutiny?

2.   How does the practice of gay "conversion therapy" bear on the immutability of sexual orientation? Such therapy involves controversial treatment designed to change a person's sexual orientation to heterosexual. As this edition of the Casebook goes to press, California, New Jersey, Illinois, Oregon, Vermont and the District of Columbia have legislatively banned this treatment for young persons, and bills to do the same have been introduced in other states. Michael K. Lavers, *Vermont Governor Signs Conversion Therapy Ban,* WASH. BLADE, May 25, 2016 (http://www.washingtonblade.com/ 2016/05/25/vermont-governor-signs-conversion-therapy-ban/). The California ban on conversion therapy was challenged as a violation of the First Amendment. The Ninth Circuit upheld the law in *Pickup v. Brown,* 728 F.3d 1042 (9th Cir. 2013), amended and superseded by *Pickup v. Brown,* 740 F.3d 1208 (9th Cir. 2014), *cert. denied,* 134 S.Ct. 2871 (2014); see also *King v. Christie,* 767 F.3d 216 (3rd Circ. 2014), *cert. denied,* 135 S.Ct. 2048 (2015) (upholding similar New Jersey law). Opponents of the therapy argue that it does not work and harms those subject to it. Is the treatment's efficacy relevant to the immutability question?

3.   For constitutional analysis, does it matter whether a characteristic is literally immutable versus difficult to change? Should the law require individuals to change a personal characteristic to avoid discrimination? Does it matter whether the trait in question is deemed especially central to personal identity? For a critique of immutability that charts a transition from the "old" version (which embodies "protection from chance") to a "new" one (which embodies "protection of choice"), see Jessica A. Clarke, *Against Immutability,* 125 YALE L.J. 2 (2015).

what about religion?

4.   Note the contrasting discussions of lesbian and gay political power in the Connecticut and Washington opinions. In view of legislative gains made on issues such as repealing sodomy laws and enacting anti-discrimination laws based on sexual orientation, can it be persuasively said that LGB persons are politically powerless? Does it depend on how "political power" is defined for purposes of heightened scrutiny review? Two political scientists debated this point at great length in their expert testimony in the federal lawsuit challenging the constitutionality of California's Proposition 8. *See Perry v. Schwarzenegger*, 704 F. Supp. 2d 921, 937, 943–44, 950–52 (N.D. Cal. 2010). For more on the issue of political power, see Darren Lenard Hutchinson, *'Not Without Political Power': Gays and Lesbians, Equal Protection and the Suspect Class Doctrine*, 65 ALA. L. REV. 975 (2014); Jane S. Schacter, *Ely at the Altar: Political Process Theory Through the Lens of the Marriage Debate*, 109 MICH. L. REV. 1363 (2011); Nicholas Stephanopolous, *Political Powerlessness*, 90 N.Y.U. L. REV. 1527 (2015).

5.   At the time that the Connecticut and Washington courts wrote, judicial action on marriage equality was crucially important because no state legislature had yet enacted marriage equality into law. In later years, however, it became more common for legislatures to support marriage equality. What significance should those changed institutional dynamics have in assessing the political power of the LGB community?

6.   In February 2011, then-Attorney general Eric Holder informed the Speaker of the House of Representatives that the Department of Justice would no longer defend the Defense of Marriage Act. As part of his letter (which appears in Chapter 5, Section III.E.2.), Holder made the case that sexual orientation-based distinctions should trigger heightened scrutiny. In 2012, following the Holder letter, the Second Circuit upheld a district court ruling invalidating DOMA. Unlike the district court in that case, however, the Second Circuit employed intermediate scrutiny. *Windsor v. United States*, 699 F.3d 169 (2d Cir. 2012). The opinion acknowledged that "homosexuals" had "clearly" achieved some political successes but said the key question is whether the group has "the strength to politically protect [itself] from wrongful discrimination." 699 F.3d at 184. When the decision was affirmed by the Supreme Court, Justice Kennedy's majority opinion seemed to apply rational basis in striking down DOMA and made no comment about the appropriateness of heightening scrutiny. *United States v. Windsor*, ___ U.S. ___, 133 S.Ct. 2675, 186 L.Ed.2d 808 (2013). That decision is covered at length in Chapter 5. Nevertheless, the approach taken by the Second Circuit reflected the first time a federal court of appeals embraced intermediate scrutiny for sexual orientation-based equal protection claims. In a case involving jury discrimination, the Ninth Circuit followed suit in 2014. *SmithKline Beecham v. Abbott Labs*, 740 F.3d 471 (9th Cir. 2014).

E. HEIGHTENED SCRUTINY FOR GENDER IDENTITY?

If constitutional claims of gender identity discrimination are not conceptualized in terms of sex discrimination, should they trigger heightened scrutiny on an independent basis? Very few courts have analyzed this question. Compare the two decisions below, and then consider a recent scholarly perspective on the issue.

RAMONA HOLLOWAY V. ARTHUR ANDERSEN & CO.

United States Court of Appeals for the Ninth Circuit (1977)
566 F.2d 659

[Ramona Holloway, a transgender woman, was fired from her position at an accounting firm and alleged that her gender transition was the cause. She argued that she was protected by the provisions of Title VII that ban discrimination based on gender. She also argued that, if transgender persons (typically called "transsexuals at the time of the decision) were excluded from protection under Title VII, that exclusion would give rise to an equal protection claim. In the course of addressing that equal protection claim, the Ninth Circuit addressed the standard of review].

[If] appellant has properly raised an equal protection argument, we find no merit to it. Normally, any rational classification or discrimination is presumed valid. That is, a statute is constitutional if the classification or discrimination it contains has some rational relationship to a legitimate government interest, unless the statute is based upon an inherently suspect classification, in which case the statute requires close judicial scrutiny.

This court cannot conclude that transsexuals are a suspect class. Examining the traditional indicia of suspect classification, we find that transsexuals are not necessarily a "discrete and insular minority," nor has it been established that transsexuality is an "immutable characteristic determined solely by the accident of birth" like race or national origin. Furthermore, the complexities involved merely in defining the term "transsexual" would prohibit a determination of suspect classification for transsexuals. Thus, the rational relationship test is the standard to apply. In applying this standard to this statute, it can be said without question that the prohibition of employment discrimination between males and females and on the basis of race, religion or national origin is rationally related to a legitimate governmental interest. * * *

ADKINS V. NEW YORK

United States District Court, S.D. New York, 2015
143 F.Supp.3d 134

[Plaintiff Justin Adkins, a transgender man, was arrested in 2011 in an Occupy Wall Street protest. Alleging mistreatment by the police, he sued. Among other claims, Adkins asserted an equal protection claim. In sustaining portions of that claim against a motion to dismiss, the district court addressed the standard of review.]

[P]laintiff has adequately alleged that he was treated differently than others similarly situated as a result of intentional or purposeful discrimination. Plaintiff claims he was originally held with other male detainees in a general cell. But plaintiff, allegedly the only transgender detainee, was removed and held by himself in more deleterious conditions—handcuffed to a wall without food. Plaintiff alleges that this disparate treatment was purposeful because it was pursuant to the NYPD's custom of subjecting transgender detainees to special conditions, *viz.*, handcuffing them to railings. He also alleges discriminatory intent on the basis of individual police officers' responses to learning of his transgender status, which included gawking, giggling, and inquiring about his genitalia. These allegations render plaintiff's claims of intentional discrimination plausible. * * *

The Court concludes that transgender people are [a "quasi-suspect" class]. * * *

First, transgender people have suffered a history of persecution and discrimination. As the Second Circuit put it with respect to gay people, this is "not much in debate." Moreover, this history of persecution and discrimination is not yet history. Plaintiff cites data indicating that transgender people report high rates of discrimination in education, employment, housing, and access to healthcare.

Second, transgender status bears no relation to ability to contribute to society. Some transgender people experience debilitating dysphoria while living as the gender they were assigned at birth, but this is the product of a long history of persecution forcing transgender people to live as those who they are not. The Court is not aware of any data or argument suggesting that a transgender person, simply by virtue of transgender status, is any less productive than any other member of society.

Third, transgender status is a sufficiently discernible characteristic to define a discrete minority class. The test is "whether there are 'obvious, immutable, or distinguishing characteristics that define ... a discrete group.' " * * * Specifically, "[w]hat seems to matter is whether the characteristic of the class calls down discrimination when it is manifest." * * * [M]any forms of identification required for asserting legal rights, such as birth certificates, indicate the bearer's gender. A mismatch between the gender indicated on the document and the gender of the holder calls down discrimination, among other problems. Document troubles aside, transgender people often face backlash in everyday life when their status is discovered. For instance, plaintiff alleges that, upon learning that he was transgender, police officers gawked and giggled at him and asked him what he had "down there."

Fourth, transgender people are a politically powerless minority. "The question is whether they have the strength to politically protect themselves from wrongful discrimination." Particularly in comparison to gay people at the time of *Windsor,* transgender people lack the political strength to protect themselves. * * * [L]ike gay people, it is difficult to assess the degree of underrepresentation of transgender people in positions of authority without knowing their number relative to the cisgender population. However, in at least one way this underrepresentation inquiry is easier with respect to transgender people: for, although there are and were gay members of the United States Congress (since *Windsor,* in both houses), as well as gay federal judges, there is no indication that there have ever been any transgender members of the United States Congress or the federal judiciary. * * *

politically powerless

A BARE DESIRE TO HARM: TRANSGENDER PEOPLE AND THE EQUAL PROTECTION CLAUSE*

Kevin M. Barry, Brian Farrell, Jennifer L. Levi and Neelima Vanguri

[The point of departure for the authors' analysis is the exclusion of persons with "transvestism," "gender identity disorders not resulting from physical impairments," and "transsexualism" from the protections of the Americans with Disabilities Act. The article addresses whether that exclusion violates the equal protection clause and makes an argument for heightened scrutiny]

a. Transgender Individuals Have Suffered a History of Discrimination

* * * Transgender people are disproportionately at risk for discrimination in almost all aspects of life, including employment, housing, education, public accommodations, and access to government services. Experiences of employment discrimination, in particular, are nearly universal for transgender individuals. According to The National Transgender Discrimination Survey Report ("National Survey"), the most extensive survey of transgender discrimination ever taken, 97% of nearly 6500 respondents experienced harassment or mistreatment on the job or took actions like hiding their gender transition to avoid such treatment, and 47% of respondents lost their jobs, were denied a promotion, or were denied a job as result of being transgender. In fact, survey respondents experienced unemployment at twice the rate of the general population, with rates up to four times higher for transgender people of color.

* Kevin M. Barry, Brian Farrell, Jennifer L. Levi, & Neelima Vanguri, *A Bare Desire to Harm: Transgender People and the Equal Protection Clause*, 57 B.C. L. REV. 507, 551-565 (2016).

These barriers to employment contribute to tremendous economic insecurity; respondents were four times more likely than the general population to have a household income of less than $10,000 per year, and 16% of respondents were compelled to work in the underground economy, such as sex work or selling drugs. A report by the Williams Institute at UCLA School of Law, which summarized six studies of transgender employment discrimination conducted between 1996 and 2006, similarly revealed that as high as 60% of transgender respondents reported being unemployed and as high as 64% earned incomes less than $25,000 per year.

Given these employment barriers, it is not surprising that transgender individuals also face significant housing instability. According to the National Survey, 19% of respondents had been homeless at some point in their lives (2.5 times the rate of the national population) and almost 2% of respondents were currently homeless (nearly twice the percentage of the national population). For those who had attempted to access homeless shelters, 29% were turned away altogether because they were transgender, 42% were forced to stay in facilities designated for the wrong gender, and 55% experienced harassment, including physical and sexual assault.

Education is another area in which transgender people experience significant discrimination. Transgender individuals in grades K–12 frequently experience harassment (78%), physical assault (35%), and sexual assault (12%) by students as well as by teachers and staff. In fact, 15% of respondents in K–12 and higher education left school altogether because of such harassment. Nineteen percent of respondents in higher education were denied access to gender-appropriate housing.

In places of public accommodation, transgender individuals frequently experience discrimination—from outright denial of services (44%) to verbal harassment (53%) and physical assault (8%). For example, in doctor's offices, hospitals, emergency rooms, and mental health clinics, 28% of respondents experienced harassment and 19% were denied services altogether. In retail stores, discrimination was even worse, with 37% of respondents reporting harassment and 32% reporting denial of services. Twenty-two percent of respondents reported verbal harassment and 4% were physically attacked on buses, trains, and taxis.

Because transgender individuals are more likely to be the victims of violent crime, to be on the street due to homelessness, or to work in the underground economy, they are also more likely to interact with police. These interactions often involve discrimination. For example, 22% of respondents reported harassment by police, including being profiled as sex workers and arrested (a practice known colloquially as "Walking While Transgender"), and 20% reported being denied services by the police. Six percent of respondents reported being physically assaulted by police, and 2% reported being sexually assaulted by police; for transgender people of color, these numbers more than double to 15% and 7%, respectively. Not surprisingly, this discrimination has a chilling effect, with 46% of respondents reporting being uncomfortable seeking police assistance. Incarcerated transgender individuals also experience discrimination in the form of harassment by correctional officers (37%) and other inmates (35%), physical and sexual assault (16% and 15%, respectively), and even the denial of routine health care (12%).

Discrimination jeopardizes not only transgender rights, but also transgender health and, quite literally, transgender lives. As the APA has concluded, "discrimination and lack of equal civil rights is damaging to the mental health of transgender and gender variant individuals." The DSM agrees that for transgender people, "high levels of stigmatization, discrimination, and victimization" can "lead[ ] to negative self-concept, increased rates of mental disorder comorbidity, school dropout, and economic marginalization, including unemployment, with attendant social and mental health risks, especially in individuals from resource-poor family backgrounds." Indeed, such discrimination can also lead to death. According to the National Survey, 41% of respondents reported attempting suicide compared to just 1.6% of the general population. These numbers are consistent with those of another study reported by the APA, which found that "gender-based discrimination and victimization were found to be independently associated with attempted suicide in a population of transgender individuals, 32% of whom had histories of trying to kill themselves." These statistics reveal perhaps the most troubling truth about discrimination's toll on the lives of transgender people: many contemplate death over living in a society that persistently discriminates against them.

The animus leveled at transgender individuals often extends beyond discrimination, culminating in horrific hate crimes. In 2014, the National Council of Anti-Violence Programs reported the hate-motivated murder of eighteen members of the LGBT community in the prior year. Thirteen of those murdered were transgender individuals, all but one of whom was a transgender woman of color. These numbers continue a three-year trend in which transgender women—and transgender people of color, in particular—experienced a greater risk of homicide than others in the LGBT community. Due to the compelling need for protections for transgender people against hate violence, Congress passed and President Obama signed into law the Matthew Shepard and James Byrd, Jr., Hate Crimes Prevention Act of 2009, which extended federal protections against crimes based on gender, disability, gender identity or sexual orientation. In passing this law, the House of Representatives Judiciary Committee emphasized the "particularly violent" nature of hate crimes against transgender people and the "extreme bias against gender nonconformity." * * *

This historical discrimination against transgender people is perhaps best epitomized by Congress's explicit exclusion of transgender people from four federal civil rights laws over the past thirty years. In 1988, Congress excluded "transvestites" from the Fair Housing Act. In 1990, Congress excluded GID, transsexualism, and transvestism from the ADA. The following year, Congress added an identical exclusion to the Rehabilitation Act of 1973, thereby stripping transgender people of civil rights protections they had enjoyed for nearly twenty years. And in 2008, Congress passed the ADA Amendments Act ("ADAAA"), which maintained the transgender exclusions while expanding the definition of disability under the ADA and Rehabilitation Act for all other impairments. By explicitly excluding transgender people from these civil rights protections, Congress expressly sanctioned blatant discrimination against transgender people, codifying their unequal status in law. * * *

b. *Transgender Individuals Have the Ability to Participate in and Contribute to Society*

* * * The incongruence between a transgender person's gender identity and assigned sex, like sexual orientation, race, national origin, and alienage, "bears no relation to ability to perform or contribute to society." * * *

Importantly, "transgender" and "impairment" are not synonymous. Although some transgender people experience Gender Dysphoria— distress and discomfort with their assigned sex which, if left untreated, may limit their ability to work or engage in other life functions—many do not. Indeed, many transgender people are completely comfortable living just the way they are. Stated another way, while everyone who experiences Gender Dysphoria is necessarily transgender, not everyone who is transgender necessarily experiences Gender Dysphoria. The mere fact that some members of a suspect class may sometimes experience impairment does not diminish their status as a suspect class and the requisite scrutiny accorded such classifications. Accordingly, transgender individuals are perfectly able to participate in and contribute to society. * * *

c. *Transgender Individuals Exhibit Immutable Distinguishing Characteristics*

* * * Transgender status is neither chosen nor changeable; it is immutable. According to the APA, children typically begin "expressing gendered behaviors and interests" between ages two and four years. The formation of one's gender identity begins even earlier, likely within the first two years and perhaps even before birth. This, of course, well precedes a child's ability to choose. Indeed, it strains logic to say that a

person chooses to become part of the transgender class—membership in which quadruples one's risk of suicide and exposes the person to almost certain discrimination in nearly every aspect of life.

In addition to lack of choice, over fifty years of medical research has confirmed that transgender status, like sexual orientation, is not "correctable." In the past, some practitioners tried to "cure" transgender people through aversion therapies and other techniques intended to alter crossgender identification. Those efforts were not only unsuccessful, but caused severe psychological damage. In "The Transsexual Phenomenon," Dr. Benjamin declared attempts to cure a "useless undertaking." Today, efforts to alter a person's core gender identity are viewed as futile and unethical. Accordingly, the treatment paradigm has shifted from attempting to "cure" the transgender person "to facilitating acceptance and management of a gender role transition." As courts have repeatedly found with respect to sexual orientation, gender identity is such a "central, defining [trait] of personhood" that it "may be altered [if at all] only at the expense of significant damage to the individual's sense of self." * * *

Importantly, transgender people who undergo transition from one gender to another do not "abandon" their transgender status. Although transition aligns one's gender identity with one's outward expression of gender, it does not eliminate the incongruence between one's gender identity and assigned sex at birth. For example, a post-operative male-to-female transgender person has a gender identity (female) that does not align with her assigned sex at birth (male). A person who transitions is still a transgender person.

One might argue that transgender status is not immutable because it is not always obvious; some transgender people "pass" as the other gender, whereas others do not outwardly express their gender identity out of fear of prejudice or worse. This argument seems wrong in both law and fact. Under Supreme Court case law, visibility is not a prerequisite for finding that a distinguishing characteristic is immutable. * * *

d. *Transgender Individuals Are a Minority and Lack Political Power*

* * * [Transgender people] are clearly a minority; researchers estimate that transgender individuals make up approximately 0.3% of the adult population. Transgender people are also politically powerless, for two reasons. First, they are woefully underrepresented in government and in other positions of power. No acknowledged transgender person has ever been elected to the U.S. Congress, served as President, or served on the federal judiciary or the Supreme Court. This underrepresentation pervades all levels of local, state, and federal government. * * *

Second, in addition to their exclusion from positions of power, transgender people are severely limited in their ability to attract the attention of lawmakers. The hostility transgender people experience undermines transgender advocacy, "suppress[ing] some degree of political activity by inhibiting the kind of open association that advances political agendas." This lack of political power is epitomized by the exclusion of transgender people from four federal civil rights laws—the Fair Housing Act, Rehabilitation Act, ADA, and the ADAAA—for no reason other than moral animus.

Transgender people's limited ability to attract the attention of lawmakers is also underscored by their lack of political power relative to lesbian, gay, and bisexual people. In 2011, for example, the U.S. Department of Defense repealed its "Don't Ask Don't Tell" policy for LGB people, but not for transgender people. The armed forces can still refuse transgender applicants for admission, and the estimated 15,500 transgender service members in the U.S. military can still be discharged for being transgender. Additionally, in 2007, the "last-minute jitters [of] some Democrats" over the Employment-Non Discrimination Act's ("ENDA") trans-inclusive language prompted members of Congress to introduce a "compromise" bill that stripped out "gender identity," fracturing the coalition of transgender and gay rights organizations in the process. Although the LGBT community now stands united behind a trans-inclusive ENDA, the compromise bill's support in Congress, and among some LGB advocacy groups, demonstrates transgender people's weak political position relative to the lesbian, gay, and bisexual community. * * *

NOTES

1. The District Court's decision in *Adkins* broke new ground with its argument that transgender people are a quasi-suspect class. Most courts confronted with the question have either followed the older *Holloway* decision or simply rejected the claim summarily. For a collection of decisions pre-dating *Adkins*, see Julia C. Maddera, Note, *Batson in Transition: Prohibiting Peremptoy Challenges on the Basis of Gender Identity of Expression*, 116 Colum. L. Rev. 195, 213–217 (2016).

2. In arguing that transgender people lack political power, Barry, et al note that when the Don't Ask, Don't Tell policy was repealed, the military retained its authority to exclude based on gender identity. The judge in *Adkins* alluded to this point as well in a portion of the opinion not excerpted above. After both were published, the federal government lifted the ban on transgender military service. [This issue is addressed in Chapter 4, Section III.B.3.] Does the lifting of that ban weaken the case for political powerlessness?

3.   Barry, et al note that the transgender label groups together people who are not alike in all respects. They point out that while some transgender people experience intense "distress and discomfort with their assigned sex," others do not and "are completely comfortable living just the way they are." How does this plurality of experiences bear on heightened scrutiny? Does the case for heightening scrutiny apply with equal force to those who disclaim gender dysphoria? To those who challenge the gender binary? Who identify themselves as gender fluid?

4.   Recall the material in the final section of chapter 1 about intersexuality. Do the arguments for heightened scrutiny in *Adkins* and Barry, et al also apply to persons born with ambiguous genitalia? In thinking about this question, is it relevant that the social movements supporting intersex and transgender have had different points of emphasis? In the words of gender theorist Judith Butler, "intersex and transsex sometimes seem to be movements at odds with each other, the first opposing unwanted surgery, the second sometimes calling for elective surgery." JUDITH BUTLER, UNDOING GENDER 6 (2004). For an analysis of these differences, see Noa Ben-Asher, *The Necessity of Sex Change: A Struggle for Intersex and Transsexual Liberties*, 29 HARV. J. L.& GENDER 51 (2006).

F.   SCHOLARLY PERSPECTIVES ON THE HEIGHTENED SCRUTINY DEBATE

A significant body of scholarship has developed around the approaches courts have used to assess the need for heightened scrutiny. In an influential book, John Hart Ely built on the famous footnote 4 in the U.S. Supreme Court's decision in *United States v. Carolene Prods. Co.*, 304 U.S. 144, 152 n.4, 58 S.Ct. 778 n.4, 82 L.Ed. 1234 n.4 (1938), which suggested that "prejudice against discrete and insular minorities may be a special condition ... curtail[ing] the operation of those political processes ordinarily to be relied upon to protect minorities, and [so] may call for a correspondingly more searching judicial inquiry." In Ely's view, judicial review should compensate for malfunctions in the democratic process, which occur when "representatives beholden to an effective majority are systematically disadvantaging some minority out of simple hostility or a prejudiced refusal to recognize commonalities of interest, and thereby denying that minority the protection afforded other groups by a representative system." John Hart Ely, Democracy and Distrust: A Theory of Judicial Review 103 (1980). Ely argued that "a combination of the factors of [anti-gay] prejudice and hideability" warranted heightened scrutiny because they impaired the ability of gay persons to advocate effectively in the political process. Id. at 163.

The first two readings that follow challenge aspects of the approach suggested by Ely and footnote 4. The third reading considers the relevance of immutability.

BEYOND CAROLENE PRODUCTS[*]

Bruce A. Ackerman

IV. *Discrete* and Insular Minorities?

[I]t is not obvious whether most constitutional lawyers endow the word "discrete" with independent significance in their understanding of the *Carolene* doctrine. Nonetheless, we can conceive the term in a way that adds something important to the overall formula. I propose to define a minority as "discrete" when its members are marked out in ways that make it relatively easy for others to identify them. For instance, there is nothing a black woman may plausibly do to hide the fact that she is black or female. Like it or not, she will have to deal with the social expectations and stereotypes generated by her evident group characteristics. In contrast, other minorities are socially defined in ways that give individual members the chance to avoid easy identification. A homosexual, for example, can keep her sexual preference a very private affair and thereby avoid much of the public opprobrium attached to her minority status. It is for this reason that I shall call homosexuals, and groups like them, "anonymous" minorities and contrast them with "discrete" minorities of the kind paradigmatically exemplified by blacks.

[margin note: of identifiable]

[margin note: of anonymous]

This way of defining terms allows us to complement our analysis of insularity in a natural way. While the insularity-diffuseness continuum measures the intensity and breadth of intra-group interaction, the discreteness-anonymity continuum measures the ease with which people outside a group can identify group members. It should be plain that these two continua are not invariably associated with one another. Blacks, for example, are both discrete and insular, whereas women are discrete yet diffuse; homosexuals are anonymous but may be somewhat insular,[28] whereas the poor are both relatively anonymous and diffuse. Because there is no necessary correlation between discreteness and insularity, I shall treat discreteness as a distinct subject for analysis and consider how a group's place on the discreteness-anonymity continuum can be expected to add to, or detract from, its probable political influence.

Carolene takes a straightforward position on this question. In its view, discreteness is a political liability. Once again, however, the only thing that is obvious is that this is not obvious. The main reason why has been elegantly developed in Albert Hirschman's modern classic, *Exit,*

---

[*]   Bruce A. Ackerman, *Beyond* Carolene Products, 98 HARV. L. REV. 713, 728–31 (1985).

[28]   At this point the distinction between intensity and breadth may be helpful in refining the text's qualifying "somewhat." Although homosexuals do not characteristically share a broad range of social settings in which they interact as homosexuals, a few social contexts do serve as loci for an intense reaffirmation of homosexual identities—most notably, the network of homosexual bars and restaurants found in major American cities. Predictably, this network provided an important organizational focus for the recent political movement on behalf of homosexual rights. *See* J. D'EMILIO, SEXUAL POLITICS, SEXUAL COMMUNITIES 129–250 (1983).

Voice and Loyalty (1970). The book's title refers to three nonviolent ways of responding to an unsatisfactory situation: if you dislike something, you may try to avoid it (exit), you may complain about it (voice), or you may grin-and-hope-for-improvement (loyalty). Although these three responses may be related to one another in a number of ways, the relationship between two of them—exit and voice—is of special relevance here. People do not respond to a bad situation by engaging in a random pattern of avoidance and protest. Instead, according to Hirschman, an inverse relationship obtains: the more exit, the less voice, and vice versa. The reason for this is straightforward: the easier it is to avoid a bad situation, the less it will seem worthwhile to complain, and vice versa.

This inverse relationship holds significant implications for the relative political strength of minorities at different points on the discreteness-anonymity scale. If you are a black in America today, you know there is no way you can avoid the impact of the larger public's views about the significance of blackness. Because exit is not possible, there is only one way to do something about disadvantageous racial stereotypes: complain about them. Among efficacious forms of complaint, the possibility of organized political action will surely rank high.

This is not to say, of course, that individual blacks, or members of other discrete minorities, will necessarily lend their support to interest-group activity. They may, instead, succumb to the temptations of free-riding and thus deprive the group of vital political resources. But even if discreteness is no cure-all for selfishness, it does free a minority from the organizational problem confronting an anonymous group of comparable size. To see my point, compare the problem faced by black political organizers with the one confronting organizers of the homosexual community. As a member of an anonymous group, each homosexual can seek to minimize the personal harm due to prejudice by keeping his or her sexual preference a tightly held secret. Although this is hardly a fully satisfactory response, secrecy does enable homosexuals to "exit" from prejudice in a way that blacks cannot. This means that a homosexual group must confront an organizational problem that does not arise for its black counterpart: somehow the group must induce each anonymous homosexual to reveal his or her sexual preference to the larger public and to bear the private costs this public declaration may involve.

Although some, perhaps many, homosexuals may be willing to pay this price, the fact that each must individually choose to pay it means that this anonymous group is less likely to be politically efficacious than is an otherwise comparable but discrete minority. For, by definition, discrete groups do not have to convince their constituents to "come out of the closet" before they can engage in effective political activity. So it would seem that *Carolene Products* is wrong again: a court concerned with pluralist bargaining power should be more, not less, attentive to the claims of anonymous minorities than to those of discrete ones.

ELY AT THE ALTER: POLITICAL PROCESS THEORY THROUGH THE LENS OF THE MARRIAGE DEBATE*

Jane S. Schacter

In the absence of clearer substantive commitments about what makes a political process fair and how much/what kind of political power a group "should" have, [process] theory offers little to resolve questions of application like those raised in the marriage debate. * * * Process theory essentially asks whether LGBT people—or other disadvantaged groups— have "sufficient" power to be left to their own political devices, rather than receiving solicitous treatment from a court. Answering this question depends not only on how political power is defined, but on how sufficiency is understood. Therein lies the baseline question. To assess meaningfully whether historical prejudice undermines a group's power, we, presumably, need to know something about what the group's political power would look like in a properly functioning political process. * * *

[I]dentifying the relevant baseline begins to get both enigmatic and interesting when we recognize that there is no particular reason to believe that LGBT people would be politically organized and active as LGBT people in the way that has become familiar *but for* the phenomena that called into being the organization of their social movement. The animating goal that gave rise to the gay rights movement was, precisely, to dislodge longstanding structures of discrimination. . . . The dilemma is this: if the need to politically organize is itself generated by long-term historical subordination, it is difficult to conjure the untainted baseline political process against which to measure the current process, because there are good grounds to wonder whether LGBT people would be legislatively active as LGBT people in the absence of that subordination. * * *

A second set of problems with process theory that the marriage debate reveals—and a second way in which process theory is thin— relates to its institutional assumptions. There is a distinctly caricatured quality to the roles that process theory assigns to courts and to legislatures.

Process theory is built on the assumption that, while legislatures will predictably fall prey to—and remain mired in—forms of prejudice that will skew and distort their approach to public policy, courts can and will overcome such prejudice in adjudication. * * *

---

* Jane S. Schacter, *Ely at the Altar: Political Process Theory Through the Lens of the Marriage Debate*, 109 MICH. L. REV. 1363, 1390, 1392–93, 1397–99 (2011).

[A] core empirical problem with this view is that, while the vision of courts as consistent countermajoritarian forces has deep and enduring normative appeal, it is not empirically well supported. . . . [C]ourts, across the long march of history, are not often all that far out of step with popular opinion or out front on controversial social issues. * * *

Indeed, in every state whose supreme court issued a judicial decision favorable to same-sex couples, the political process had taken significant strides toward recognizing gay civil rights by the time the court ruled. * * * [C]ontrary to the assumption of process theory, it is strikingly implausible to think that judges in [the states most hostile to LGBT rights] can or will stand apart from prevailing public opinion and take action to compensate for anti-gay bias decades before the political process shows movement on marriage or other issues of concern to LGBT citizens of the state. Such a prospect, indeed, depends in the first instance on the improbable notion that courts in these states would *characterize* as anti-gay bias the resistance of legislators and citizens to gay equality claims. * * *

THE CONSTITUTION OF STATUS*
J.M. Balkin

Analyzing discrimination in terms of status groups also helps us understand our objections to discrimination more clearly in situations where courts hold that the Constitution already proscribes it. Discrimination against blacks, for example, is not unjust simply because race is an immutable characteristic. Focusing on immutability per se confuses biological with sociological considerations. It confuses the physical existence of the trait with what the trait means in a social system. Racial discrimination is wrong because of the historical creation of a status hierarchy organized around the meaning of skin color. The question to ask is not whether a trait is immutable, but whether there has been a history of using the trait to create a system of social meanings, or define a social hierarchy, that helps dominate and oppress people. Any conclusions about the importance of immutability already presuppose a view about background social structure.

Indeed, a focus on immutability makes sense only as long as we recognize its relationship to social structure. Social hierarchies often assign differential social meanings to immutable traits because they make exit from low status more difficult. But not all immutable characteristics are or have been the basis for unjust social hierarchies, and not all unjust social hierarchies are founded on immutable characteristics.

---

* J.M. Balkin, *The Constitution of Status*, 106 YALE L.J. 2313, 2365–67 (1997).

Religion is not an immutable trait—many religions are always looking for new converts—but status-based discrimination against religious groups is surely also unjust. Defenders of the immutability criterion can point to the Religion Clauses as an independent justification for protection of religious minorities; but this puts the cart before the horse. The Religion Clauses exist in part because the Framers recognized that religious intolerance was an evil long before they recognized that racial intolerance was.

The importance of immutability as a criterion of judgment is also sometimes defended on the grounds that immutable characteristics—for example, race—are morally irrelevant. But this argument, too, really depends on a view about the justness of a particular status hierarchy. When status distinctions are internalized in a culture, status hierarchies *make* traits morally relevant. They become signs of positive and negative associations. They become permissible proxies for inferences about character, honesty, ability, and judgment. Such traits are morally irrelevant only to persons not in the grip of that particular hierarchy. In the aristocracy of pre-Revolutionary America, for example, high birth was viewed as correlating with many other positive attributes—honesty, sagacity, learning, and good manners—and society was organized to make these positive associations a self-fulfilling prophecy. Generations of whites thought blacks naturally inferior; succeeding generations who learned not to make biological arguments have nevertheless continued to regard blacks as culturally inferior—as displaying negative qualities of sloth, violence, and licentiousness. A characteristic becomes "morally irrelevant" precisely when we understand the status hierarchy it is based on to be unjust. Only then do we become embarrassed to use the trait as a signifier of, or a proxy for, positive or negative associations. Our objection to the moral relevance of the characteristic is really our objection to the system of social meanings and the hierarchy of social status that uses this trait as a criterion for judgment. The real issue is whether society has created an unjust status hierarchy organized around a particular trait or set of traits, whether those traits are immutable, or—like religion— voluntarily chosen or instilled through socialization.

G. THE SUPREME COURT AND SEXUAL ORIENTATION EQUALITY

For all the attention traditionally paid to heightened scrutiny in the realm of equal protection, the Supreme Court's major decisions on sexual orientation equality have been surprisingly silent, even cryptic, on the question of standard of review. Indeed, in many ways the evolution of the Court's caselaw on equality in this area might signal that the scrutiny question is no longer as central to the Court as it once seemed to be.

The Court's first foray into sexual orientation-based discrimination and equal protection came with its 1996 decision in *Romer v. Evans*. More recently, the Court considered equal protection as part of its landmark marriage equality decisions in *Windsor* and *Obergefell*. In this section, we trace the evolution of this jurisprudence. As you review the cases, consider what legal principles and ideas thread through them.

In *Romer*, the Supreme Court struck down a voter initiative hostile to gay civil rights statutes that added sexual orientation to statutory anti-discrimination laws. Initiatives like this one date to the 1970s, but, in the early 1990s, the opponents of gay equality initiated a new round of measures designed to counter advances made by lesbians, gay men, and bisexuals. Initiatives were proposed to ban protections against anti-gay discrimination in two California cities (Riverside and Concord), but both were declared unconstitutional and barred from being placed on the ballot.[6] In 1992, statewide initiatives were promulgated by opponents of sexual orientation laws in Oregon and Colorado. The Oregon measure was defeated at the polls, but the Colorado initiative, known as Amendment 2, was enacted by the voters by a 53.4%–46.6% margin. Amendment 2 repealed existing protections against discrimination based on sexual orientation—including ordinances in the cities of Aspen, Boulder, and Denver; a statewide Executive Order prohibiting discrimination in state employment; and an insurance code provision prohibiting health insurers from determining insurability and premiums based on an applicant's sexual orientation.[7] Amendment 2 also barred state and local governmental units from enacting such protections in the future.

The constitutionality of Amendment 2 was immediately challenged in the Colorado state courts and, due to the issuance of an injunction pending the outcome of the case, Amendment 2 never went into effect. In two decisions, the Colorado Supreme Court found Amendment 2 unconstitutional. In *Evans I*, the court held that the Amendment had the effect of burdening the plaintiffs' fundamental right "to participate equally in the political process" and thus that it could be sustained only if the state could show at trial that it was necessary to serve a compelling governmental interest and that it did so in the least restrictive manner possible. *Evans v. Romer*, 854 P.2d at 1276 (Colo. 1993), *cert. denied*, 510 U.S. 959, 114 S.Ct. 419, 126 L.Ed.2d 365 (1993). The Colorado high court based its decision in *Evans I* on a series of cases involving similar referenda that arose in the race context, *e.g.*, *Hunter v. Erickson*, 393 U.S. 385, 89 S.Ct. 557, 21 L.Ed.2d 616 (1969). The state argued unsuccessfully that the application of heightened scrutiny in these earlier cases was

---

[6]   *See Citizens for Responsible Behavior v. Superior Court*, 2 Cal.Rptr.2d 648, 661, 1 Cal.App. 4th 1013, 1036 (1991); *Jester v. City of Concord*, No. C91–05455 (Cal. Super. Ct. 1992).

[7]   *See Evans v. Romer*, 854 P.2d 1270, 1284–85 & n.26 (Colo. 1993).

solely a function of the classifications therein being racial, not a result of the presence of a fundamental right. Following a lengthy trial, the lower court rejected all of the reasons the state put forward as compelling state interests; its decision was affirmed by the Colorado Supreme Court in *Evans II, Evans v. Romer*, 882 P.2d 1335, 1350 (Colo. 1994), *cert. granted*, 513 U.S. 1146, 115 S. Ct. 1092, 130 L. Ed. 2d 1061 (1995).

In 1996, the U.S. Supreme Court affirmed the Colorado Supreme Court's conclusion that Amendment 2 violated the federal constitution, but it reached that conclusion through a different route.

ROMER V. EVANS

Supreme Court of the United States, 1996
517 U.S. 620, 116 S.Ct. 1620, 134 L.Ed.2d 855

JUSTICE KENNEDY delivered the opinion of the Court.

One century ago, the first Justice Harlan admonished this Court that the Constitution "neither knows nor tolerates classes among citizens." *Plessy v. Ferguson*, 163 U.S. 537, 559 (1896) (dissenting opinion). Unheeded then, those words now are understood to state a commitment to the law's neutrality where the rights of persons are at stake. The Equal Protection Clause enforces this principle and today requires us to hold invalid a provision of Colorado's Constitution.

I

The enactment challenged in this case is an amendment to the Constitution of the State of Colorado, adopted in a 1992 statewide referendum. The parties and the state courts refer to it as "Amendment 2," its designation when submitted to the voters. The impetus for the amendment and the contentious campaign that preceded its adoption came in large part from ordinances that had been passed in various Colorado municipalities. For example, the cities of Aspen and Boulder and the City and County of Denver each had enacted ordinances which banned discrimination in many transactions and activities, including housing, employment, education, public accommodations, and health and welfare services. What gave rise to the statewide controversy was the protection the ordinances afforded to persons discriminated against by reason of their sexual orientation. *See* Boulder Rev. Code § 12–1–1 (defining "sexual orientation" as "the choice of sexual partners, i.e., bisexual, homosexual or heterosexual"); Denver Rev. Municipal Code, Art. IV § 28–92 (defining "sexual orientation" as "the status of an individual as to his or her heterosexuality, homosexuality or bisexuality"). Amendment 2 repeals these ordinances to the extent they prohibit discrimination on the basis of "homosexual, lesbian or bisexual orientation, conduct, practices or relationships."

Yet Amendment 2, in explicit terms, does more than repeal or rescind these provisions. It prohibits all legislative, executive or judicial action at any level of state or local government designed to protect the named class, a class we shall refer to as homosexual persons or gays and lesbians. The amendment reads:

> "No Protected Status Based on Homosexual, Lesbian, or Bisexual Orientation. Neither the State of Colorado, through any of its branches or departments, nor any of its agencies, political subdivisions, municipalities or school districts, shall enact, adopt or enforce any statute, regulation, ordinance or policy whereby homosexual, lesbian or bisexual orientation, conduct, practices or relationships shall constitute or otherwise be the basis of or entitle any person or class of persons to have or claim any minority status, quota preferences, protected status or claim of discrimination. This Section of the Constitution shall be in all respects self-executing."

Soon after Amendment 2 was adopted, this litigation to declare its invalidity and enjoin its enforcement was commenced in the District Court for the City and County of Denver. Among the plaintiffs (respondents here) were homosexual persons, some of them government employees. They alleged that enforcement of Amendment 2 would subject them to immediate and substantial risk of discrimination on the basis of their sexual orientation. Other plaintiffs (also respondents here) included the three municipalities whose ordinances we have cited and certain other governmental entities which had acted earlier to protect homosexuals from discrimination but would be prevented by Amendment 2 from continuing to do so. Although Governor Romer had been on record opposing the adoption of Amendment 2, he was named in his official capacity as a defendant, together with the Colorado Attorney General and the State of Colorado.

The trial court granted a preliminary injunction to stay enforcement of Amendment 2, and an appeal was taken to the Supreme Court of Colorado. Sustaining the interim injunction and remanding the case for further proceedings, the State Supreme Court held that Amendment 2 was subject to strict scrutiny under the Fourteenth Amendment because it infringed the fundamental right of gays and lesbians to participate in the political process. *Evans v. Romer*, 854 P.2d 1270 (Colo. 1993) (*Evans I*). To reach this conclusion, the state court relied on our voting rights cases, *e.g.*, *Reynolds v. Sims*, 377 U.S. 533 (1964); *Carrington v. Rash*, 380 U.S. 89 (1965); *Harper v. Virginia Bd. of Elections*, 383 U.S. 663 (1966); *Williams v. Rhodes*, 393 U.S. 23 (1968), and on our precedents involving discriminatory restructuring of governmental decisionmaking, *see e.g.*, *Hunter v. Erickson*, 393 U.S. 385 (1969); *Reitman v. Mulkey*, 387 U.S. 369 (1967); *Washington v. Seattle School Dist. No. 1*, 458 U.S. 457 (1982);

Gordon v. Lance, 403 U.S. 1 (1971). On remand, the State advanced various arguments in an effort to show that Amendment 2 was narrowly tailored to serve compelling interests, but the trial court found none sufficient. It enjoined enforcement of Amendment 2, and the Supreme Court of Colorado, in a second opinion, affirmed the ruling. *Evans v. Romer*, 882 P.2d 1335 (Colo. 1994) (*Evans II*). We granted certiorari and now affirm the judgment, but on a rationale different from that adopted by the State Supreme Court.

Failed SS

II

The State's principal argument in defense of Amendment 2 is that it puts gays and lesbians in the same position as all other persons. So, the State says, the measure does no more than deny homosexuals special rights. This reading of the amendment's language is implausible. We rely not upon our own interpretation of the amendment but upon the authoritative construction of Colorado's Supreme Court. The state court, deeming it unnecessary to determine the full extent of the amendment's reach, found it invalid even on a modest reading of its implications. The critical discussion of the amendment, set out in *Evans I*, is as follows:

A State's argument ↓ don't want to give LGBTQ MORE right than anyone else

> The immediate objective of Amendment 2 is, at a minimum, to repeal existing statutes, regulations, ordinances, and policies of state and local entities that barred discrimination based on sexual orientation. *See* Aspen, Colo., Mun. Code § 13–98 (1977) (prohibiting discrimination in employment, housing and public accommodations on the basis of sexual orientation); Boulder, Colo., Rev. Code §§ 12–1–2 to –4 (1987) (same); Denver, Colo., Rev. Mun. Code art. IV, §§ 28–91 to –116 (1991) (same); Executive Order No. D0035 (December 10, 1990) (prohibiting employment discrimination for "all state employees, classified and exempt" on the basis of sexual orientation); Colorado Insurance Code, § 10–3–1104, 4A C.R.S. (1992 Supp.) (forbidding health insurance providers from determining insurability and premiums based on an applicant's, a beneficiary's, or an insured's sexual orientation); and various provisions prohibiting discrimination based on sexual orientation at state colleges.[26] "The 'ultimate effect' of Amendment 2 is to prohibit any governmental entity from adopting similar, or more protective statutes, regulations, ordinances, or policies in the future unless the state constitution is first amended to permit such measures." 854 P.2d, at 1284–1285, and n. 26.

---

[26] Metropolitan State College of Denver prohibits college sponsored social clubs from discriminating in membership on the basis of sexual orientation and Colorado State University has an antidiscrimination policy which encompasses sexual orientation.

Sweeping and comprehensive is the change in legal status effected by this law. So much is evident from the ordinances that the Colorado Supreme Court declared would be void by operation of Amendment 2. Homosexuals, by state decree, are put in a solitary class with respect to transactions and relations in both the private and governmental spheres. The amendment withdraws from homosexuals, but no others, specific legal protection from the injuries caused by discrimination, and it forbids reinstatement of these laws and policies.

The change that Amendment 2 works in the legal status of gays and lesbians in the private sphere is far-reaching, both on its own terms and when considered in light of the structure and operation of modern anti-discrimination laws. That structure is well illustrated by contemporary statutes and ordinances prohibiting discrimination by providers of public accommodations. "At common law, innkeepers, smiths, and others who 'made profession of a public employment,' were prohibited from refusing, without good reason, to serve a customer." *Hurley v. Irish-American Gay, Lesbian & Bisexual Group of Boston, Inc.*, 515 U.S. 557, 571 (1995). The duty was a general one and did not specify protection for particular groups. The common law rules, however, proved insufficient in many instances, and it was settled early that the Fourteenth Amendment did not give Congress a general power to prohibit discrimination in public accommodations, *Civil Rights Cases*, 109 U.S. 3, 25 (1883). In consequence, most States have chosen to counter discrimination by enacting detailed statutory schemes.

Colorado's state and municipal laws typify this emerging tradition of statutory protection and follow a consistent pattern. The laws first enumerate the persons or entities subject to a duty not to discriminate. The list goes well beyond the entities covered by the common law. The Boulder ordinance, for example, has a comprehensive definition of entities deemed places of "public accommodation." They include "any place of business engaged in any sales to the general public and any place that offers services, facilities, privileges, or advantages to the general public or that receives financial support through solicitation of the general public or through governmental subsidy of any kind." Boulder Rev. Code § 12–1–1(j) (1987). The Denver ordinance is of similar breadth, applying, for example, to hotels, restaurants, hospitals, dental clinics, theaters, banks, common carriers, travel and insurance agencies, and "shops and stores dealing with goods or services of any kind," Denver Rev. Municipal Code, Art. IV, § 28–92.

These statutes and ordinances also depart from the common law by enumerating the groups or persons within their ambit of protection. Enumeration is the essential device used to make the duty not to discriminate concrete and to provide guidance for those who must comply. In following this approach, Colorado's state and local governments have not limited anti-discrimination laws to groups that have so far been given the protection of heightened equal protection scrutiny under our cases. *See, e.g., J.E.B. v. Alabama ex rel. T.B.,* 511 U.S. 127 (1994) (sex); *Lalli v. Lalli,* 439 U.S. 259, 265 (1978) (illegitimacy); *McLaughlin v. Florida,* 379 U.S. 184, 191–192 (1964) (race); *Oyama v. California,* 332 U.S. 633 (1948) (ancestry). Rather, they set forth an extensive catalogue of traits which cannot be the basis for discrimination, including age, military status, marital status, pregnancy, parenthood, custody of a minor child, political affiliation, physical or mental disability of an individual or of his or her associates and, in recent times, sexual orientation.

enumerated groups

Amendment 2 bars homosexuals from securing protection against the injuries that these public accommodations laws address. That in itself is a severe consequence, but there is more. Amendment 2, in addition, nullifies specific legal protections for this targeted class in all transactions in housing, sale of real estate, insurance, health and welfare services, private education, and employment. *See, e.g.,* Aspen Municipal Code §§ 13–98(b), (c) (1977); Boulder Rev. Code §§ 12–1–2, 12–1–3 (1987); Denver Rev. Municipal Code, Art. IV §§ 28–93 to 28–95, § 28–97 (1991).

consequences

Not confined to the private sphere, Amendment 2 also operates to repeal and forbid all laws or policies providing specific protection for gays or lesbians from discrimination by every level of Colorado government. The State Supreme Court cited two examples of protections in the governmental sphere that are now rescinded and may not be reintroduced. The first is Colorado Executive Order D0035 (1990), which forbids employment discrimination against " 'all state employees, classified and exempt' on the basis of sexual orientation." 854 P.2d, at 1284. Also repealed, and now forbidden, are "various provisions prohibiting discrimination based on sexual orientation at state colleges." *Id.,* at 1284, 1285. The repeal of these measures and the prohibition against their future reenactment demonstrates that Amendment 2 has the same force and effect in Colorado's governmental sector as it does elsewhere and that it applies to policies as well as ordinary legislation.

repeals/ forbids

Amendment 2's reach may not be limited to specific laws passed for the benefit of gays and lesbians. It is a fair, if not necessary, inference from the broad language of the amendment that it deprives gays and lesbians even of the protection of general laws and policies that prohibit arbitrary discrimination in governmental and private settings. *See, e.g.,* Colo. Rev. Stat. § 24–4–106(7) (1988) (agency action subject to judicial review under arbitrary and capricious standard); § 18–8–405 (making it a criminal offense for a public servant knowingly, arbitrarily or capriciously to refrain from performing a duty imposed on him by law); § 10–3–1104(1)(f) (prohibiting "unfair discrimination" in insurance); 4 Colo. Code of Regulations 801–1, Policy 11–1 (1983) (prohibiting discrimination in state employment on grounds of specified traits or "other non-merit factor"). At some point in the systematic administration of these laws, an official must determine whether homosexuality is an arbitrary and thus forbidden basis for decision. Yet a decision to that effect would itself amount to a policy prohibiting discrimination on the basis of homosexuality, and so would appear to be no more valid under Amendment 2 than the specific prohibitions against discrimination the state court held invalid.

If this consequence follows from Amendment 2, as its broad language suggests, it would compound the constitutional difficulties the law creates. The state court did not decide whether the amendment has this effect, however, and neither need we. In the course of rejecting the argument that Amendment 2 is intended to conserve resources to fight discrimination against suspect classes, the Colorado Supreme Court made the limited observation that the amendment is not intended to affect many anti-discrimination laws protecting non-suspect classes, *Romer II*, 882 P.2d at 1346, n. 9. In our view that does not resolve the issue. In any event, even if, as we doubt, homosexuals could find some safe harbor in laws of general application, we cannot accept the view that Amendment 2's prohibition on specific legal protections does no more than deprive homosexuals of special rights. To the contrary, the amendment imposes a special disability upon those persons alone. Homosexuals are forbidden the safeguards that others enjoy or may seek without constraint. They can obtain specific protection against discrimination only by enlisting the citizenry of Colorado to amend the state constitution or perhaps, on the State's view, by trying to pass helpful laws of general applicability. This is so no matter how local or discrete the harm, no matter how public and widespread the injury. We find nothing special in the protections Amendment 2 withholds. These are protections taken for granted by most people either because they already have them or do not need them; these are protections against exclusion from an almost limitless number of transactions and endeavors that constitute ordinary civic life in a free society.

III

The Fourteenth Amendment's promise that no person shall be denied the equal protection of the laws must co-exist with the practical necessity that most legislation classifies for one purpose or another, with resulting disadvantage to various groups or persons. *Personnel Administrator of Mass. v. Feeney*, 442 U.S. 256, 271–272 (1979); *F.S. Royster Guano Co. v. Virginia*, 253 U.S. 412, 415 (1920). We have attempted to reconcile the principle with the reality by stating that, if a law neither burdens a fundamental right nor targets a suspect class, we will uphold the legislative classification so long as it bears a rational relation to some legitimate end. *See, e.g., Heller v. Doe*, 509 U.S. 312 (1993).

Amendment 2 fails, indeed defies, even this conventional inquiry. First, the amendment has the peculiar property of imposing a broad and undifferentiated disability on a single named group, an exceptional and, as we shall explain, invalid form of legislation. Second, its sheer breadth is so discontinuous with the reasons offered for it that the amendment seems inexplicable by anything but animus toward the class that it affects; it lacks a rational relationship to legitimate state interests.

AZ fails RBR

Taking the first point, even in the ordinary equal protection case calling for the most deferential of standards, we insist on knowing the relation between the classification adopted and the object to be attained. The search for the link between classification and objective gives substance to the Equal Protection Clause; it provides guidance and discipline for the legislature, which is entitled to know what sorts of laws it can pass; and it marks the limits of our own authority. In the ordinary case, a law will be sustained if it can be said to advance a legitimate government interest, even if the law seems unwise or works to the disadvantage of a particular group, or if the rationale for it seems tenuous. *See New Orleans v. Dukes*, 427 U.S. 297 (1976) (tourism benefits justified classification favoring pushcart vendors of certain longevity); *Williamson v. Lee Optical of Okla., Inc.*, 348 U.S. 483 (1955) (assumed health concerns justified law favoring optometrists over opticians); *Railway Express Agency, Inc. v. New York*, 336 U.S. 106 (1949) (potential traffic hazards justified exemption of vehicles advertising the owner's products from general advertising ban); *Kotch v. Board of River Port Pilot Comm'rs for Port of New Orleans*, 330 U.S. 552 (1947) (licensing scheme that disfavored persons unrelated to current river boat pilots justified by possible efficiency and safety benefits of a closely knit pilotage system). The laws challenged in the cases just cited were narrow enough in scope and grounded in a sufficient factual context for us to ascertain that there existed some relation between the classification and the purpose it served. By requiring that the classification bear a rational relationship to an independent and legitimate legislative end, we ensure that classifications are not drawn for the purpose of disadvantaging the group burdened by the law. *See United States Railroad Retirement Bd. v. Fritz*, 449 U.S. 166, 181 (1980) (STEVENS, J., concurring) ("If the adverse impact on the disfavored class is an apparent aim of the legislature, its impartiality would be suspect.").

① class/ objective

+ RBR

rational ∉ not adverse purpose

Amendment 2 confounds this normal process of judicial review. It is at once too narrow and too broad. It identifies persons by a single trait and then denies them protection across the board. The resulting disqualification of a class of persons from the right to seek specific protection from the law is unprecedented in our jurisprudence. The absence of precedent for Amendment 2 is itself instructive; "[d]iscriminations of an unusual character especially suggest careful

AZ ∉ too narrow + too broad

consideration to determine whether they are obnoxious to the constitutional provision." *Louisville Gas & Elec. Co. v. Coleman*, 277 U.S. 32, 37–38 (1928).

It is not within our constitutional tradition to enact laws of this sort. Central both to the idea of the rule of law and to our own Constitution's guarantee of equal protection is the principle that government and each of its parts remain open on impartial terms to all who seek its assistance. "'Equal protection of the laws is not achieved through indiscriminate imposition of inequalities.'" *Sweatt v. Painter*, 339 U.S. 629, 635 (1950) (quoting *Shelley v. Kraemer*, 334 U.S. 1, 22 (1948)). Respect for this principle explains why laws singling out a certain class of citizens for disfavored legal status or general hardships are rare. A law declaring that in general it shall be more difficult for one group of citizens than for all others to seek aid from the government is itself a denial of equal protection of the laws in the most literal sense. "The guaranty of 'equal protection of the laws is a pledge of the protection of equal laws.'" *Skinner v. Oklahoma ex rel. Williamson*, 316 U.S. 535, 541 (1942) (quoting *Yick Wo v. Hopkins*, 118 U.S. 356, 369 (1886)).

Davis v. Beason, 133 U.S. 333 (1890), not cited by the parties but relied upon by the dissent, is not evidence that Amendment 2 is within our constitutional tradition, and any reliance upon it as authority for sustaining the amendment is misplaced. In *Davis*, the Court approved an Idaho territorial statute denying Mormons, polygamists, and advocates of polygamy the right to vote and to hold office because, as the Court construed the statute, it "simply excludes from the privilege of voting, or of holding any office of honor, trust or profit, those who have been convicted of certain offences, and those who advocate a practical resistance to the laws of the Territory and justify and approve the commission of crimes forbidden by it." *Id.*, at 347. To the extent *Davis* held that persons advocating a certain practice may be denied the right to vote, it is no longer good law. *Brandenburg v. Ohio*, 395 U.S. 444 (1969) (per curiam). To the extent it held that the groups designated in the statute may be deprived of the right to vote because of their status, its ruling could not stand without surviving strict scrutiny, a most doubtful outcome. *Dunn v. Blumstein*, 405 U.S. 330, 337 (1972); *cf. United States v. Brown*, 381 U.S. 437 (1965); *United States v. Robel*, 389 U.S. 258 (1967). To the extent *Davis* held that a convicted felon may be denied the right to vote, its holding is not implicated by our decision and is unexceptionable. *See Richardson v. Ramirez*, 418 U.S. 24 (1974).

A second and related point is that laws of the kind now before us raise the inevitable inference that the disadvantage imposed is born of animosity toward the class of persons affected. "[I]f the constitutional conception of 'equal protection of the laws' means anything, it must at the very least mean that a bare . . . desire to harm a politically unpopular group cannot constitute a legitimate governmental interest." *Department of Agriculture v. Moreno*, 413 U.S. 528, 534 (1973). Even laws enacted for broad and ambitious purposes often can be explained by reference to legitimate public policies which justify the incidental disadvantages they impose on certain persons. Amendment 2, however, in making a general announcement that gays and lesbians shall not have any particular protections from the law, inflicts on them immediate, continuing, and real injuries that outrun and belie any legitimate justifications that may be claimed for it. We conclude that, in addition to the far-reaching deficiencies of Amendment 2 that we have noted, the principles it offends, in another sense, are conventional and venerable; a law must bear a rational relationship to a legitimate governmental purpose, *Kadrmas v. Dickinson Public Schools*, 487 U.S. 450, 462 (1988), and Amendment 2 does not.

The primary rationale the State offers for Amendment 2 is respect for other citizens' freedom of association, and in particular the liberties of landlords or employers who have personal or religious objections to homosexuality. Colorado also cites its interest in conserving resources to fight discrimination against other groups. The breadth of the Amendment is so far removed from these particular justifications that we find it impossible to credit them. We cannot say that Amendment 2 is directed to any identifiable legitimate purpose or discrete objective. It is a status-based enactment divorced from any factual context from which we could discern a relationship to legitimate state interests; it is a classification of persons undertaken for its own sake, something the Equal Protection Clause does not permit. "[C]lass legislation . . . [is] obnoxious to the prohibitions of the Fourteenth Amendment. . . ." *Civil Rights Cases*, 109 U.S., at 24.

We must conclude that Amendment 2 classifies homosexuals not to further a proper legislative end but to make them unequal to everyone else. This Colorado cannot do. A State cannot so deem a class of persons a stranger to its laws. Amendment 2 violates the Equal Protection Clause, and the judgment of the Supreme Court of Colorado is affirmed. It is so ordered.

JUSTICE SCALIA, with whom THE CHIEF JUSTICE and JUSTICE THOMAS join, dissenting.

The Court has mistaken a Kulturkampf for a fit of spite. The constitutional amendment before us here is not the manifestation of a "'bare . . . desire to harm'" homosexuals, but is rather a modest attempt by seemingly tolerant Coloradans to preserve traditional sexual mores against the efforts of a politically powerful minority to revise those mores through use of the laws. That objective, and the means chosen to achieve it, are not only unimpeachable under any constitutional doctrine hitherto pronounced (hence the opinion's heavy reliance upon principles of righteousness rather than judicial holdings); they have been specifically approved by the Congress of the United States and by this Court.

contradicts Bowers

In holding that homosexuality cannot be singled out for disfavorable treatment, the Court contradicts a decision, unchallenged here, pronounced only 10 years ago, *see Bowers v. Hardwick*, 478 U.S. 186 (1986), and places the prestige of this institution behind the proposition that opposition to homosexuality is as reprehensible as racial or religious bias. Whether it is or not is precisely the cultural debate that gave rise to the Colorado constitutional amendment (and to the preferential laws against which the amendment was directed). Since the Constitution of the United States says nothing about this subject, it is left to be resolved by normal democratic means, including the democratic adoption of provisions in state constitutions. This Court has no business imposing upon all Americans the resolution favored by the elite class from which the Members of this institution are selected, pronouncing that "animosity" toward homosexuality is evil. I vigorously dissent.

I

Let me first discuss Part II of the Court's opinion, its longest section, which is devoted to rejecting the State's arguments that Amendment 2 "puts gays and lesbians in the same position as all other persons," and "does no more than deny homosexuals special rights." The Court concludes that this reading of Amendment 2's language is "implausible" under the "authoritative construction" given Amendment 2 by the Supreme Court of Colorado.

"special rights" argument

In reaching this conclusion, the Court considers it unnecessary to decide the validity of the State's argument that Amendment 2 does not deprive homosexuals of the "protection [afforded by] general laws and policies that prohibit arbitrary discrimination in governmental and private settings." I agree that we need not resolve that dispute, because the Supreme Court of Colorado has resolved it for us. In *Evans v. Romer*, 882 P.2d 1335 (1994), the Colorado court stated:

> "It is significant to note that Colorado law currently proscribes discrimination against persons who are not suspect classes, including discrimination based on age; marital or family status; veterans' status; and for any legal, off-duty conduct such as smoking tobacco, § 24–34–402.5, 10A C.R.S. (1994 Supp.). *Of course Amendment 2 is not intended to have any effect on this legislation, but seeks only to prevent the adoption of anti-discrimination laws intended to protect gays, lesbians, and bisexuals.*" *Id.*, at 1346, n. 9 (emphasis added).

The Court utterly fails to distinguish this portion of the Colorado court's opinion. Colorado Rev. Stat. § 24–34–402.5 (Supp. 1995), which this passage authoritatively declares not to be affected by Amendment 2, was respondents' primary example of a generally applicable law whose protections would be unavailable to homosexuals under Amendment 2. The clear import of the Colorado court's conclusion that it is not affected is that "general laws and policies that prohibit arbitrary discrimination" would continue to prohibit discrimination on the basis of homosexual conduct as well. This analysis, which is fully in accord with (indeed, follows inescapably from) the text of the constitutional provision, lays to rest such horribles, raised in the course of oral argument, as the prospect that assaults upon homosexuals could not be prosecuted. The amendment prohibits *special treatment* of homosexuals, and nothing more. It would not affect, for example, a requirement of state law that pensions be paid to all retiring state employees with a certain length of service; homosexual employees, as well as others, would be entitled to that benefit. But it would prevent the State or any municipality from making death-benefit payments to the "life partner" of a homosexual when it does not make such payments to the long-time roommate of a nonhomosexual employee. Or again, it does not affect the requirement of the State's general insurance laws that customers be afforded coverage without discrimination unrelated to anticipated risk. Thus, homosexuals could not be denied coverage, or charged a greater premium, with respect to auto collision insurance; but neither the State nor any municipality could require that distinctive health insurance risks associated with homosexuality (if there are any) be ignored.

Despite all of its hand-wringing about the potential effect of Amendment 2 on general antidiscrimination laws, the Court's opinion ultimately does not dispute all this, but assumes it to be true. The only denial of equal treatment it contends homosexuals have suffered is this: They may not obtain *preferential* treatment without amending the state constitution. That is to say, the principle underlying the Court's opinion is that one who is accorded equal treatment under the laws, but cannot as readily as others obtain *preferential* treatment under the laws, has been denied equal protection of the laws. If merely stating this alleged "equal protection" violation does not suffice to refute it, our constitutional jurisprudence has achieved terminal silliness.

The central thesis of the Court's reasoning is that any group is denied equal protection when, to obtain advantage (or, presumably, to avoid disadvantage), it must have recourse to a more general and hence more difficult level of political decisionmaking than others. The world has never heard of such a principle, which is why the Court's opinion is so long on emotive utterance and so short on relevant legal citation. And it seems to me most unlikely that any multilevel democracy can function under such a principle. For *whenever* a disadvantage is imposed, or conferral of a benefit is prohibited, at one of the higher levels of democratic decisionmaking (*i.e.*, by the state legislature rather than local government, or by the people at large in the state constitution rather than the legislature), the affected group has (under this theory) been denied equal protection. To take the simplest of examples, consider a state law prohibiting the award of municipal contracts to relatives of mayors or city councilmen. Once such a law is passed, the group composed of such relatives must, in order to get the benefit of city contracts, persuade the state legislature—unlike all other citizens, who need only persuade the municipality. It is ridiculous to consider this a denial of equal protection, which is why the Court's theory is unheard-of.

The Court might reply that the example I have given is not a denial of equal protection only because the same "rational basis" (avoidance of corruption) which renders constitutional the *substantive discrimination* against relatives (i.e., the fact that they alone cannot obtain city contracts) also automatically suffices to sustain what might be called the *electoral-procedural* discrimination against them (*i.e.*, the fact that they must go to the state level to get this changed). This is of course a perfectly reasonable response, and would explain why "electoral-procedural discrimination" has not hitherto been heard of: a law that is valid in its substance is automatically valid in its level of enactment. But the Court cannot afford to make this argument, for as I shall discuss next, there is no doubt of a rational basis for the substance of the prohibition at issue here. The Court's entire novel theory rests upon the proposition that there is something *special*—something that cannot be justified by normal "rational basis" analysis—in making a disadvantaged group (or a nonpreferred group) resort to a higher decisionmaking level. That proposition finds no support in law or logic.

II

I turn next to whether there was a legitimate rational basis for the substance of the constitutional amendment—for the prohibition of special protection for homosexuals.[1] It is unsurprising that the Court avoids discussion of this question, since the answer is so obviously yes. The case most relevant to the issue before us today is not even mentioned in the Court's opinion: In *Bowers v. Hardwick*, 478 U.S. 186 (1986), we held that the Constitution does not prohibit what virtually all States had done from the founding of the Republic until very recent years—making homosexual conduct a crime. That holding is unassailable, except by those who think

---

[1]   The Court evidently agrees that "rational basis"—the normal test for compliance with the Equal Protection Clause—is the governing standard. The trial court rejected respondents' argument that homosexuals constitute a "suspect" or "quasi-suspect" class, and respondents elected not to appeal that ruling to the Supreme Court of Colorado. *See Evans v. Romer*, 882 P.2d 1335, 1341, n. 3 (Colo. 1994). And the Court implicitly rejects the Supreme Court of Colorado's holding, see *Evans v. Romer*, 854 P.2d 1270, 1282 (Colo. 1993), that Amendment 2 infringes upon a "fundamental right" of "independently identifiable classes" to "participate equally in the political process."

that the Constitution changes to suit current fashions. But in any event it is a given in the present case: Respondents' briefs did not urge overruling *Bowers,* and at oral argument respondents' counsel expressly disavowed any intent to seek such overruling. If it is constitutionally permissible for a State to make homosexual conduct criminal, surely it is constitutionally permissible for a State to enact other laws merely disfavoring homosexual conduct. (As the Court of Appeals for the District of Columbia Circuit has aptly put it: "If the Court [in *Bowers*] was unwilling to object to state laws that criminalize the behavior that defines the class, it is hardly open . . . to conclude that state sponsored discrimination against the class is invidious. After all, there can hardly be more palpable discrimination against the class than making the conduct that defines the class criminal." *Padula v. Webster,* 822 F.2d 97, 103 (1987).) And a fortiori it is constitutionally permissible for a State to adopt a provision not even disfavoring homosexual conduct, but merely prohibiting all levels of state government from bestowing special protections upon homosexual conduct. Respondents (who, unlike the Court, cannot afford the luxury of ignoring inconvenient precedent) counter *Bowers* with the argument that a greater-includes-the-lesser rationale cannot justify Amendment 2's application to individuals who do not engage in homosexual acts, but are merely of homosexual "orientation." Some courts of appeals have concluded that, with respect to laws of this sort at least, that is a distinction without a difference. *See Equality Foundation of Greater Cincinnati, Inc. v. Cincinnati,* 54 F.3d 261, 267 (6th Cir.1995) ("[F]or purposes of these proceedings, it is virtually impossible to distinguish or separate individuals of a particular *orientation* which predisposes them toward a particular sexual conduct from those who actually *engage* in that particular type of sexual conduct"); *Steffan v. Perry,* 41 F.3d 677, 689–690 (D.C. Cir. 1994). The Supreme Court of Colorado itself appears to be of this view. *See* 882 P.2d, at 1349–1350 ("Amendment 2 targets this class of persons based on four characteristics: sexual orientation; conduct; practices; and relationships. Each characteristic provides a potentially different way of identifying that class of persons who are gay, lesbian, or bisexual. These four characteristics are not truly severable from one another because each provides nothing more than a different way of identifying *the same class of persons*") (emphasis added).

But assuming that, in Amendment 2, a person of homosexual "orientation" is someone who does not engage in homosexual conduct but merely has a tendency or desire to do so, *Bowers* still suffices to establish a rational basis for the provision. If it is rational to criminalize the conduct, surely it is rational to deny special favor and protection to those with a self-avowed tendency or desire to engage in the conduct. Indeed, where criminal sanctions are not involved, homosexual "orientation" is an acceptable stand-in for homosexual conduct. A State "does not violate the Equal Protection Clause merely because the classifications made by its laws are imperfect," _Dandridge v. Williams_, 397 U.S. 471, 485 (1970). Just as a policy barring the hiring of methadone users as transit employees does not violate equal protection simply because some methadone users pose no threat to passenger safety, _see New York City Transit Authority v. Beazer_, 440 U.S. 568 (1979), and just as a mandatory retirement age of 50 for police officers does not violate equal protection even though it prematurely ends the careers of many policemen over 50 who still have the capacity to do the job, _see Massachusetts Bd. of Retirement v. Murgia_, 427 U.S. 307 (1976) (_per curiam_), Amendment 2 is not constitutionally invalid simply because it could have been drawn more precisely so as to withdraw special antidiscrimination protections only from those of homosexual "orientation" who actually engage in homosexual conduct. As JUSTICE KENNEDY wrote, when he was on the Court of Appeals, in a case involving discharge of homosexuals from the Navy: "Nearly any statute which classifies people may be irrational as applied in particular cases. Discharge of the particular plaintiffs before us would be rational, under minimal scrutiny, not because their particular cases present the dangers which justify Navy policy, but instead because the general policy of discharging all homosexuals is rational." _Beller v. Middendorf_, 632 F.2d 788, 808–809, n. 20 (9th Cir. 1980) (citation omitted). _See also Ben-Shalom v. Marsh_, 881 F.2d 454, 464 (7th Cir. 1989), cert. denied, 494 U.S. 1004 (1990).

Moreover, even if the provision regarding homosexual "orientation" were invalid, respondents' challenge to Amendment 2—which is a facial challenge—must fail. "A facial challenge to a legislative Act is, of course, the most difficult challenge to mount successfully, since the challenger must establish that no set of circumstances exists under which the Act would be valid." _United States v. Salerno_, 481 U.S. 739, 745 (1987). It would not be enough for respondents to establish (if they could) that Amendment 2 is unconstitutional as applied to those of homosexual "orientation"; since, under _Bowers_, Amendment 2 is unquestionably constitutional as applied to those who engage in homosexual conduct, the facial challenge cannot succeed. Some individuals of homosexual "orientation" who do not engage in homosexual acts might successfully bring an as-applied challenge to Amendment 2, but so far as the record indicates, none of the respondents is such a person. _See_ App. 4–5 (complaint describing each of the individual respondents as either "a gay man" or "a lesbian").[2]

---

[2] The Supreme Court of Colorado stated: "We hold that the portions of Amendment 2 that would remain if only the provision concerning sexual orientation were stricken are not autonomous and thus, not severable," 882 P.2d at 1349. That statement was premised, however, on the proposition that "[the] four characteristics [described in the Amendment—sexual orientation, conduct, practices, and relationships] are not truly severable from one another because each provides nothing more than a different way of identifying _the same class of persons_." _Id._, at 1349–1350 (emphasis added). As I have discussed above, if that premise is true—if the entire class affected by the Amendment takes part in homosexual conduct, practices

III

The foregoing suffices to establish what the Court's failure to cite any case remotely in point would lead one to suspect: No principle set forth in the Constitution, nor even any imagined by this Court in the past 200 years, prohibits what Colorado has done here. But the case for Colorado is much stronger than that. What it has done is not only unprohibited, but eminently reasonable, with close, congressionally approved precedent in earlier constitutional practice.

First, as to its eminent reasonableness. The Court's opinion contains grim, disapproving hints that Coloradans have been guilty of "animus" or "animosity" toward homosexuality, as though that has been established as un-American. Of course it is our moral heritage that one should not hate any human being or class of human beings. But I had thought that one could consider certain conduct reprehensible—murder, for example, or polygamy, or cruelty to animals—and could exhibit even "animus" toward such conduct. Surely that is the only sort of "animus" at issue here: moral disapproval of homosexual conduct, the same sort of moral disapproval that produced the centuries-old criminal laws that we held constitutional in *Bowers*. The Colorado amendment does not, to speak entirely precisely, prohibit giving favored status to people who are homosexuals; they can be favored for many reasons—for example, because they are senior citizens or members of racial minorities. But it prohibits giving them favored status *because of their homosexual conduct*—that is, it prohibits favored status *for homosexuality*.

But though Coloradans are, as I say, *entitled* to be hostile toward homosexual conduct, the fact is that the degree of hostility reflected by Amendment 2 is the smallest conceivable. The Court's portrayal of Coloradans as a society fallen victim to pointless, hate-filled "gay-bashing" is so false as to be comical. Colorado not only is one of the 25 States that have repealed their antisodomy laws, but was among the first to do so. *See* 1971 Colo. Sess. Laws, ch. 121, § 1. But the society that eliminates criminal punishment for homosexual acts does not necessarily abandon the view that homosexuality is morally wrong and socially harmful; often, abolition simply reflects the view that enforcement of such criminal laws involves unseemly intrusion into the intimate lives of citizens. *Cf.* Brief for Lambda Legal Defense and Education Fund, Inc., et al. as *Amici Curiae* in *Bowers v. Hardwick*, O.T.1985, No. 85–140, p. 25, n. 21 (antisodomy statutes are "unenforceable by any but the most offensive snooping and wasteful allocation of law enforcement resources"); Kadish, *The Crisis of Overcriminalization*, 374 The Annals of the American Academy of Political and Social Science 157, 161 (1967) ("To

---

and relationships—*Bowers* alone suffices to answer all constitutional objections. Separate consideration of persons of homosexual "orientation" is necessary only if one believes (as the Supreme Court of Colorado did not) that that is a distinct class.

obtain evidence [in sodomy cases], police are obliged to resort to behavior which tends to degrade and demean both themselves personally and law enforcement as an institution").

There is a problem, however, which arises when criminal sanction of homosexuality is eliminated but moral and social disapprobation of homosexuality is meant to be retained. The Court cannot be unaware of that problem; it is evident in many cities of the country, and occasionally bubbles to the surface of the news, in heated political disputes over such matters as the introduction into local schools of books teaching that homosexuality is an optional and fully acceptable "alternate life style." The problem (a problem, that is, for those who wish to retain social disapprobation of homosexuality) is that, because those who engage in homosexual conduct tend to reside in disproportionate numbers in certain communities, have high disposable income, and of course care about homosexual-rights issues much more ardently than the public at large, they possess political power much greater than their numbers, both locally and statewide. Quite understandably, they devote this political power to achieving not merely a grudging social toleration, but full social acceptance, of homosexuality. *See, e.g.,* Jacobs, *The Rhetorical Construction of Rights: The Case of the Gay Rights Movement, 1969–1991,* 72 Neb. L. Rev. 723, 724 (1993) ("The task of gay rights proponents is to move the center of public discourse along a continuum from the rhetoric of disapprobation, to rhetoric of tolerance, and finally to affirmation").

By the time Coloradans were asked to vote on Amendment 2, their exposure to homosexuals' quest for social endorsement was not limited to newspaper accounts of happenings in places such as New York, Los Angeles, San Francisco, and Key West. Three Colorado cities—Aspen, Boulder, and Denver—had enacted ordinances that listed "sexual orientation" as an impermissible ground for discrimination, equating the moral disapproval of homosexual conduct with racial and religious bigotry. *See* Aspen Municipal Code § 13–98 (1977); Boulder Rev. Municipal Code §§ 12–1–1 to 12–1–11 (1987); Denver Rev. Municipal Code, Art. IV §§ 28–91 to 28–116 (1991). The phenomenon had even appeared statewide: the Governor of Colorado had signed an executive order pronouncing that "in the State of Colorado we recognize the diversity in our pluralistic society and strive to bring an end to discrimination in any form," and directing state agencyheads to "ensure non-discrimination" in hiring and promotion based on, among other things, "sexual orientation." Executive Order No. D0035 (Dec. 10, 1990). I do not mean to be critical of these legislative successes; homosexuals are as entitled to use the legal system for reinforcement of their moral sentiments as are the rest of society. But they are subject to being countered by lawful, democratic countermeasures as well.

That is where Amendment 2 came in. It sought to counter both the geographic concentration and the disproportionate political power of homosexuals by (1) resolving the controversy at the statewide level, and (2) making the election a single-issue contest for both sides. It put directly, to all the citizens of the State, the question: Should homosexuality be given special protection? They answered no. The Court today asserts that this most democratic of procedures is unconstitutional. Lacking any cases to establish that facially absurd proposition, it simply asserts that it must be unconstitutional, because it has never happened before.

> "[Amendment 2] identifies persons by a single trait and then denies them protection across the board. The resulting disqualification of a class of persons from the right to seek specific protection from the law is unprecedented in our jurisprudence. The absence of precedent for Amendment 2 is itself instructive. . . .

> It is not within our constitutional tradition to enact laws of this sort. Central both to the idea of the rule of law and to our own Constitution's guarantee of equal protection is the principle that government and each of its parts remain open on impartial terms to all who seek its assistance."

As I have noted above, this is proved false every time a state law prohibiting or disfavoring certain conduct is passed, because such a law prevents the adversely affected group—whether drug addicts, or smokers, or gun owners, or motorcyclists—from changing the policy thus established in "each of [the] parts" of the State. What the Court says is even demonstrably false at the constitutional level. The Eighteenth Amendment to the Federal Constitution, for example, deprived those who drank alcohol not only of the power to alter the policy of prohibition locally or through state legislation, but even of the power to alter it through state constitutional amendment or federal legislation. The Establishment Clause of the First Amendment prevents theocrats from having their way by converting their fellow citizens at the local, state, or federal statutory level; as does the Republican Form of Government Clause prevent monarchists.

But there is a much closer analogy, one that involves precisely the effort by the majority of citizens to preserve its view of sexual morality statewide, against the efforts of a geographically concentrated and politically powerful minority to undermine it. The constitutions of the States of Arizona, Idaho, New Mexico, Oklahoma, and Utah to this day contain provisions stating that polygamy is "forever prohibited." Polygamists, and those who have a polygamous "orientation," have been "singled out" by these provisions for much more severe treatment than merely denial of favored status; and that treatment can only be changed by achieving amendment of the state constitutions. The Court's disposition today suggests that these provisions are unconstitutional, and that polygamy must be permitted in these States on a state-legislated, or perhaps even local-option, basis—unless, of course, polygamists for some reason have fewer constitutional rights than homosexuals.

The United States Congress, by the way, *required* the inclusion of these antipolygamy provisions in the constitutions of Arizona, New Mexico, Oklahoma, and Utah, as a condition of their admission to statehood. *See* Arizona Enabling Act, 36 Stat. 569; New Mexico Enabling Act, 36 Stat. 558; Oklahoma Enabling Act, 34 Stat. 269; Utah Enabling Act, 28 Stat. 108. (For Arizona, New Mexico, and Utah, moreover, the Enabling Acts required that the antipolygamy provisions be "irrevocable without the consent of the United States and the people of said State"—so that not only were "each of [the] parts" of these States not "open on impartial terms" to polygamists, but even the States as a whole were not; polygamists would have to persuade the whole country to their way of thinking.) Idaho adopted the constitutional provision on its own, but the 51st Congress, which admitted Idaho into the Union, found its constitution to be "republican in form and . . . in conformity with the Constitution of the United States." Act of Admission of Idaho, 26 Stat. 215 (emphasis added). Thus, this "singling out" of the sexual practices of a single group for statewide, democratic vote—so utterly alien to our constitutional system, the Court would have us believe—has not only happened, but has received the explicit approval of the United States Congress.

I cannot say that this Court has explicitly approved any of these state constitutional provisions; but it has approved a territorial statutory provision that went even further, depriving polygamists of the ability even to achieve a constitutional amendment, by depriving them of the power to vote. In *Davis v. Beason*, 133 U.S. 333 (1890), Justice Field wrote for a unanimous Court:

> "In our judgment, § 501 of the Revised Statutes of Idaho Territory, which provides that 'no person . . . who is a bigamist or polygamist or who teaches, advises, counsels, or encourages any person or persons to become bigamists or polygamists, or to commit any other crime defined by law, or to enter into what is known as plural or celestial marriage, or who is a member of any order, organization or association which teaches, advises, counsels, or encourages its members or devotees or any other persons to commit the crime of bigamy or polygamy, or any other crime defined by law . . . is permitted to vote at any election, or to hold any position or office of honor, trust, or profit within this

Territory,' *is not open to any constitutional or legal objection."*
Id., at 346–347 (emphasis added).

To the extent, if any, that this opinion permits the imposition of adverse consequences upon mere abstract advocacy of polygamy, it has of course been overruled by later cases. *See Brandenburg v. Ohio,* 395 U.S. 444 (1969) (per curiam). But the proposition that polygamy can be criminalized, and those engaging in that crime deprived of the vote, remains good law. *See Richardson v. Ramirez,* 418 U.S. 24, 53 (1974). *Beason* rejected the argument that "such discrimination is a denial of the equal protection of the laws." Brief for Appellant in *Davis v. Beason,* O.T. 1889, No. 1261, p. 41. Among the Justices joining in that rejection were the two whose views in other cases the Court today treats as equal-protection lodestars—Justice Harlan, who was to proclaim in *Plessy v. Ferguson,* 163 U.S. 537, 559 (1896) (dissenting opinion), that the Constitution "neither knows nor tolerates classes among citizens," quoted *ante,* at 1, and Justice Bradley, who had earlier declared that "class legislation . . . [is] obnoxious to the prohibitions of the Fourteenth Amendment," *Civil Rights Cases,* 109 U.S. 3, 24 (1883), quoted *ante,* at 14.[3]

This Court cited *Beason* with approval as recently as 1993, in an opinion authored by the same Justice who writes for the Court today. That opinion said: "Adverse impact will not always lead to a finding of impermissible targeting. For example, a social harm may have been a legitimate concern of government for reasons quite apart from discrimination. . . . *See, e.g.,* . . . *Davis v. Beason,* 133 U.S. 333 (1890)." *Church of Lukumi Babalu Aye, Inc. v. Hialeah,* 508 U.S. 520, 535 (1993). It remains to be explained how § 501 of the Idaho Revised Statutes was not an "impermissible targeting" of polygamists, but (the much more mild) Amendment 2 is an "impermissible targeting" of homosexuals. Has the Court concluded that the perceived social harm of polygamy is a

---

[3]   The Court labors mightily to get around *Beason,* but cannot escape the central fact that this Court found the statute at issue—which went much further than Amendment 2, denying polygamists not merely special treatment but the right *to vote*—"not open to any constitutional or legal objection," rejecting the appellant's argument (much like the argument of respondents today) that the statute impermissibly "singled him out," Brief for Appellant in *Davis v. Beason,* O.T.1889, No. 1261, p. 41. The Court adopts my conclusions that (a) insofar as *Beason* permits the imposition of adverse consequences based upon mere advocacy, it has been overruled by subsequent cases, and (b) insofar as *Beason* holds that convicted felons may be denied the right to vote, it remains good law. To these conclusions, it adds something new: the claim that "to the extent [*Beason*] held that the groups designated in the statute may be deprived of the right to vote because of their status, its ruling could not stand without surviving strict scrutiny, a most doubtful outcome." But if that is so, it is only because we have declared the right to *vote* to be a "fundamental political right," see, *e.g., Dunn v. Blumstein,* 405 U.S. 330, 336 (1972), deprivation of which triggers strict scrutiny. Amendment 2, of course, does not deny the fundamental right to vote, and the Court rejects the Colorado court's view that there exists a fundamental right to participate in the political process. Strict scrutiny is thus not in play here. Finally, the Court's suggestion that § 501 of the Revised Statutes of Idaho, and Amendment 2, deny rights on account of "status" (rather than conduct) opens up a broader debate involving the significance of *Bowers* to this case, a debate which the Court is otherwise unwilling to join.

"legitimate concern of government," and the perceived social harm of homosexuality is not?

IV

I strongly suspect that the answer to the last question is yes, which leads me to the last point I wish to make: The Court today, announcing that Amendment 2 "defies . . . conventional [constitutional] inquiry," and "confounds [the] normal process of judicial review," employs a constitutional theory heretofore unknown to frustrate Colorado's reasonable effort to preserve traditional American moral values. The Court's stern disapproval of "animosity" towards homosexuality might be compared with what an earlier Court (including the revered Justices Harlan and Bradley) said in *Murphy v. Ramsey,* 114 U.S. 15 (1885), rejecting a constitutional challenge to a United States statute that denied the franchise in federal territories to those who engaged in polygamous cohabitation:

> "[C]ertainly no legislation can be supposed more wholesome and necessary in the founding of a free, self-governing commonwealth, fit to take rank as one of the co-ordinate States of the Union, than that which seeks to establish it on the basis of the idea of the family, as consisting in and springing from the union for life of one man and one woman in the holy estate of matrimony; the sure foundation of all that is stable and noble in our civilization; the best guaranty of that reverent morality which is the source of all beneficent progress in social and political improvement." *Id.,* at 45.

I would not myself indulge in such official praise for heterosexual monogamy, because I think it no business of the courts (as opposed to the political branches) to take sides in this culture war.

But the Court today has done so, not only by inventing a novel and extravagant constitutional doctrine to take the victory away from traditional forces, but even by verbally disparaging as bigotry adherence to traditional attitudes. To suggest, for example, that this constitutional amendment springs from nothing more than " 'a bare . . . desire to harm a politically unpopular group,' " is nothing short of insulting. (It is also nothing short of preposterous to call "politically unpopular" a group which enjoys enormous influence in American media and politics, and which, as the trial court here noted, though composing no more than 4% of the population had the support of 46% of the voters on Amendment 2.)

When the Court takes sides in the culture wars, it tends to be with the knights rather than the villeins—and more specifically with the Templars, reflecting the views and values of the lawyer class from which the Court's Members are drawn. How that class feels about homosexuality will be evident to anyone who wishes to interview job applicants at virtually any of the Nation's law schools. The interviewer may refuse to offer a job because the applicant is a Republican; because he is an adulterer; because he went to the wrong prep school or belongs to the wrong country club; because he eats snails; because he is a womanizer; because she wears real-animal fur; or even because he hates the Chicago Cubs. But if the interviewer should wish not to be an associate or partner of an applicant because he disapproves of the applicant's homosexuality, *then* he will have violated the pledge which the Association of American Law Schools requires all its member-schools to exact from job interviewers: "assurance of the employer's willingness" to hire homosexuals. This law-school view of what "prejudices" must be stamped out may be contrasted with the more plebeian attitudes that apparently still prevail in the United States Congress, which has been unresponsive to repeated attempts to extend to homosexuals the protections of federal civil rights laws, *see, e.g.,* Employment Non-Discrimination Act of 1994, S. 2238, 103d Cong., 2d Sess. (1994); Civil Rights Amendments of 1975, H.R. 5452, 94th Cong., 1st Sess. (1975), and which took the pains to exclude them specifically from the Americans With Disabilities Act of 1990, see 42 U.S.C. § 12211(a) (1988 ed., Supp. V). * * *

Today's opinion has no foundation in American constitutional law, and barely pretends to. The people of Colorado have adopted an entirely reasonable provision which does not even disfavor homosexuals in any substantive sense, but merely denies them preferential treatment. Amendment 2 is designed to prevent piecemeal deterioration of the sexual morality favored by a majority of Coloradans, and is not only an appropriate means to that legitimate end, but a means that Americans have employed before. Striking it down is an act, not of judicial judgment, but of political will. I dissent.

NOTES

1.   For a sampling of scholarly commentary on *Romer*, see Akhil Reed Amar, *Attainder and Amendment 2:* Romer's *Rightness*, 95 MICH. L. REV. 203 (1996); Lynn Baker, *The Missing Pages of the Majority Opinion in* Romer v. Evans, 68 U. COLO. L. REV. 387 (1997); Dale Carpenter, *A Conservative Defense of* Romer v. Evans, 76 IND. L.J. 403 (2000); Richard Duncan, *The Narrow and Shallow Bite of* Romer *and the Eminent Rationality of Dual-Gender Marriage: A (Partial) Response to Professor Koppelman*, 6 WM. & MARY BILL RTS. J. 147 (1997); Daniel Farber & Suzanna Sherry, *The Pariah Principle*, 13 CONST. COMMENT. 257 (1996); Roderick M. Hills, Jr., *Is Amendment 2 Really a Bill of Attainder? Some Questions About Professor Amar's Analysis of* Romer, 95 MICH. L. REV. 236 (1996); Nan D. Hunter, *Proportional Equality: Readings of* Romer, 89 KY. L.J. 885 (2000); Louis Michael Seidman, Romer's *Radicalism: The Unexpected Revival of Warren Court Activism*, 1996 SUP. CT. REV. 67; Jane S. Schacter, Romer v. Evans *and*

Democracy's Domain, 50 VAND. L. REV. 361 (1997); Cass R. Sunstein, *The Supreme Court, 1995 Term—Foreword: Leaving Things Undecided*, 110 HARV. L. REV. 6, 53–71 (1996).

2.   From the time it was decided, *Romer* was greeted with uncertainty about its doctrinal basis. One reason is that the Colorado Supreme Court's decisions in the Amendment 2 case—like most of the legal and academic commentary—had focused on the applicability of the "political participation" theory in this context. In *Romer*, however, the U.S. Supreme Court ultimately declined to follow this path. As suggested by the opinion's reference to a "denial of equal protection of the laws in its most literal sense," the Court was apparently influenced by an amicus brief filed by a number of leading constitutional scholars. The brief, filed on behalf of Professors John Hart Ely, Gerald Gunther, Philip Kurland, Kathleen Sullivan, and Laurence Tribe, argued that Amendment 2 constituted an "inherent" violation of the equal protection clause:

> Colorado's Amendment 2 constitutes a *per se* violation of the Equal Protection Clause of the Fourteenth Amendment, which provides that "[n]o state shall . . . deny to any person within its jurisdiction the equal protection of the laws." That command is violated when a state's constitution renders some persons ineligible for "the . . . protection of the laws" from an entire category of mistreatment— here, the mistreatment of discrimination, however invidious and unwarranted. If Colorado had declared some people within its jurisdiction completely ineligible for the protection of its laws, existing or future, from some other form of mistreatment— unjustified physical assault, for example—no one would doubt that such state action would constitute a *per se* denial of the equal protection of the laws. Selectively decreeing some "person or class of persons," to use Amendment 2's language, ineligible for legal protection from mistreatment in which the wrong charged takes the form of *discrimination as such* is every bit as offensive on its face to the principle of equality before the law.
>
> States have no affirmative duty to enact or retain special laws for each individual or group who might be victimized by discriminatory treatment—that is, by injurious treatment that reflects prejudice and is neither privileged nor rationally justified by the context in which it occurs—just as they may well have no affirmative duty to enact or retain laws directed at other forms of wrongful treatment. But it is quite another matter for a state's constitution absolutely to preclude, for a selected set of persons, even the possibility of protection under any state or local law from a whole category of harmful conduct, including some that is undeniably wrongful. . . .
>
> To recognize that Amendment 2 works a *per se* violation of the Equal Protection Clause requires no benign or even neutral view of what Amendment 2 calls "homosexual . . . orientation, conduct,

practices or relationships." For literally *any* characteristic—even one on the basis of which a state may properly deny benefits or impose disabilities in a wide variety of circumstances—can sometimes become the basis for deprivations that are prejudiced rather than justified, and that are not privileged by the special context in which they occur. When Amendment 2 explicitly creates, for selected persons, a unique hole in the state's fabric of existing and potential legal protections against that admitted wrong, it provides a paradigm case of what it means for a state to structure its legal system so as to "deny" to "person[s] within its jurisdiction the equal protection of the laws."

Brief of Laurence H. Tribe et al. as Amici Curiae Supporting Respondents, *Romer v. Evans*, 517 U.S. 620, 116 S.Ct. 1620, 134 L.Ed.2d 855 (1996) (No. 94–1039), 1995 WL 17008432 at 1–2.

3.   Another reason for doctrinal uncertainty about *Romer* is that the rational basis standard applied by the Court is usually very forgiving to the government. Why didn't the government prevail in this case, given the relaxed standard applied? And, if the Court had, indeed, embraced the "per se" equal protection violation asserted in the scholars' amicus brief discussed above, why did the Court also apply rational basis? Wouldn't the very idea of a per se violation of the equal protection clause seem to obviate the need to apply any standard of review?

4.   It is notable that *Romer* simply applied rational basis without discussing the standard of review. Unlike the state court and federal appellate cases in the previous section probing heightened scrutiny for sexual orientation claims, you will find in the *Romer* opinion no analysis of whether heightened scrutiny for sexual orientation-based claims might be warranted. What might explain that conspicuous silence?

5.   A final reason that *Romer* has been regarded as enigmatic is its failure to mention—let alone distinguish—*Bowers v. Hardwick*, a case that was still good law when *Romer* was decided. That puzzling aspect of the opinion has receded in importance since the Court overruled *Hardwick* in *Lawrence*.

6.   To what extent, if any, is the *Romer* ruling traceable to the fact that Amendment 2 was passed through the initiative process? The Court did not focus on that issue in its opinion, but some research in political science suggests that direct democracy is particularly unfavorable terrain for minorities, including sexual minorities. For example, one leading study found that gay and lesbian citizens have faced measures putting their rights to a popular vote at an unusually high rate. Barbara Gamble, *Putting Civil Rights to a Popular Vote*, 41 AM. J. POL. SCI. 245–269 (1997). Gamble noted that nearly 60% of all state and local initiatives relating to civil rights in the period between 1959–1993 concerned the rights of gays and lesbians. Gamble's study also found that 88% of these gay-related initiatives proposed restricting lesbian and gay rights by repealing existing protective laws or

banning the enactment of protective laws in the future; and that voters approved some 79% of these restrictive measures. This study also reported a high rate of rights-restrictive measures affecting other minority groups. And, measures affecting minorities in general, and gays and lesbians in particular, both passed at a notably higher rate than the general pool of ballot measures, where voters have traditionally voted "no" in a high percentage of cases. *Id.* What might explain these patterns? What factors might make direct democracy inhospitable to sexual or other minorities?

7. North Carolina's H.B. 2, which focused on gender identity and bathrooms (see Section II.C., above), also repealed protections that had been enacted in the city of Charlotte to outlaw discrimination based on sexual orientation and gender identity. In addition, the bill provided that municipalities could not add any new antidiscrimination provisions that were not already protected by state law. Because sexual orientation and gender identity were not subject to statewide protection and thus could not be protected by localities, this law shares some characteristics of Colorado's Amendment 2. How strong do you think the argument is to invalidate the bill under *Romer*? Are there relevant differences?

In 2013, in *Windsor v. United States*, the Supreme Court invoked the equal protection clause (as well as considerations of federalism) to strike down a portion of DOMA, the Defense of Marriage Act. Two years later, the Supreme Court declared in *Obergefell v. Hodges* that same-sex couples have a fundamental right to marry. Most of the *Obergefell* opinion focused on the fundamental right to marry grounded in the Due Process Clause, but portions of it suggested—sometimes explicitly, sometimes implicitly—that the Equal Protection Clause is also relevant to understanding the decision. The two landmark opinions are covered in detail in Chapter 5 as part of that chapter's exploration of the marriage equality debate. Parts of the decisions relating to equality are excerpted here. As you read them, consider how—if at all—either one changes the approach the Court set out in *Romer*.

UNITED STATES V. WINDSOR

Supreme Court of the United States, 2013
133 S.Ct. 2675, 186 L.Ed.2d 808

[The Defense of Marriage Act was enacted by Congress in 1996. Section 3 of DOMA required that all federal agencies define marriage as "between one man and one woman as husband and wife." It was challenged by Edie Windsor, whose marriage to the late Thea Spyer was recognized in New York, but not by the Internal Revenue Service. The Obama Administration declined to defend the constitutionality of DOMA, so it was defended in court by a congressional group, the "Bipartisan Legal Advocacy Group" ("BLAG").]

* * * DOMA rejects the long-established precept that the incidents, benefits, and obligations of marriage are uniform for all married couples within each State, though they may vary, subject to constitutional guarantees, from one State to the next. * * * Here the State's decision to give this class of persons the right to marry conferred upon them a dignity and status of immense import. When the State used its historic and essential authority to define the marital relation in this way, its role and its power in making the decision enhanced the recognition, dignity, and protection of the class in their own community. DOMA, because of its reach and extent, departs from this history and tradition of reliance on state law to define marriage. " '[D]iscriminations of an unusual character especially suggest careful consideration to determine whether they are obnoxious to the constitutional provision.' " Romer v. Evans. * * *

DOMA seeks to injure the very class New York seeks to protect. By doing so it violates basic due process and equal protection principles applicable to the Federal Government. *See* U.S. Const., Amdt. 5; Bolling v. Sharpe, 347 U.S. 497, 74 S.Ct. 693, 98 L.Ed. 884 (1954). The Constitution's guarantee of equality "must at the very least mean that a bare congressional desire to harm a politically unpopular group cannot" justify disparate treatment of that group. Department of Agriculture v. Moreno. In determining whether a law is motived by an improper animus or purpose, " '[d]iscriminations of an unusual character' " especially require careful consideration. (quoting Romer). DOMA cannot survive under these principles. The responsibility of the States for the regulation of domestic relations is an important indicator of the substantial societal impact the State's classifications have in the daily lives and customs of its people. DOMA's unusual deviation from the usual tradition of recognizing and accepting state definitions of marriage here operates to deprive same-sex couples of the benefits and responsibilities that come with the federal recognition of their marriages. This is strong evidence of a law having the purpose and effect of disapproval of that class. The avowed purpose and practical effect of the law here in question are to impose a disadvantage, a separate status, and so a stigma upon all who enter into same-sex marriages made lawful by the unquestioned authority of the States.

The history of DOMA's enactment and its own text demonstrate that interference with the equal dignity of same-sex marriages, a dignity conferred by the States in the exercise of their sovereign power, was more than an incidental effect of the federal statute. It was its essence. The House Report announced its conclusion that "it is both appropriate and necessary for Congress to do what it can to defend the institution of traditional heterosexual marriage. . . . H.R. 3396 is appropriately entitled the 'Defense of Marriage Act.' The effort to redefine 'marriage' to extend to homosexual couples is a truly radical proposal that would fundamentally alter the institution of marriage." H.R.Rep. No. 104–664, pp. 12–13 (1996). The House concluded that DOMA expresses "both moral disapproval of homosexuality, and a moral conviction that heterosexuality better comports with traditional (especially Judeo-Christian) morality." *Id.*, at 16 (footnote deleted). The stated purpose of the law was to promote an "interest in protecting the traditional moral teachings reflected in heterosexual-only marriage laws." *Ibid.* Were there any doubt of this far-reaching purpose, the title of the Act confirms it: The Defense of Marriage. * * *

The Act's demonstrated purpose is to ensure that if any State decides to recognize same-sex marriages, those unions will be treated as second-class marriages for purposes of federal law. This raises a most serious question under the Constitution's Fifth Amendment.

DOMA's operation in practice confirms this purpose. When New York adopted a law to permit same-sex marriage, it sought to eliminate inequality; but DOMA frustrates that objective through a system-wide enactment with no identified connection to any particular area of federal law. DOMA writes inequality into the entire United States Code. The particular case at hand concerns the estate tax, but DOMA is more than a simple determination of what should or should not be allowed as an estate tax refund. Among the over 1,000 statutes and numerous federal regulations that DOMA controls are laws pertaining to Social Security, housing, taxes, criminal sanctions, copyright, and veterans' benefits. * * *

By creating two contradictory marriage regimes within the same State, DOMA forces same-sex couples to live as married for the purpose of state law but unmarried for the purpose of federal law, thus diminishing the stability and predictability of basic personal relations the State has found it proper to acknowledge and protect. By this dynamic DOMA undermines both the public and private significance of state-sanctioned same-sex marriages; for it tells those couples, and all the world, that their otherwise valid marriages are unworthy of federal recognition. This places same-sex couples in an unstable position of being in a second-tier marriage. The differentiation demeans the couple, whose moral and sexual choices the Constitution protects, see *Lawrence*, and whose relationship the State has sought to dignify. And it humiliates tens of thousands of children now being raised by same-sex couples. The law in question makes it even more difficult for the children to understand the integrity and closeness of their own family and its concord with other families in their community and in their daily lives. * * *

The liberty protected by the Fifth Amendment's Due Process Clause contains within it the prohibition against denying to any person the equal protection of the laws. While the Fifth Amendment itself withdraws from Government the power to degrade or demean in the way this law does, the equal protection guarantee of the Fourteenth Amendment makes that

Fifth Amendment right all the more specific and all the better understood and preserved. * * *

DOMA instructs all federal officials, and indeed all persons with whom same-sex couples interact, including their own children, that their marriage is less worthy than the marriages of others. The federal statute is invalid, for no legitimate purpose overcomes the purpose and effect to disparage and to injure those whom the State, by its marriage laws, sought to protect in personhood and dignity. By seeking to displace this protection and treating those persons as living in marriages less respected than others, the federal statute is in violation of the Fifth Amendment. This opinion and its holding are confined to those lawful marriages.

OBERGEFELL V. HODGES

Supreme Court of the United States 2015
___ U.S. ___, 135 S.Ct. 2584, 192 L.Ed.2d 609

[Two terms after it decided *Windsor*, the Court granted review in a case involving the laws of four states—Kentucky, Michigan, Ohio and Tennessee—that did not permit same-sex couples to marry.]

* * * [C]hanged understandings of marriage are characteristic of a Nation where new dimensions of freedom become apparent to new generations, often through perspectives that begin in pleas or protests and then are considered in the political sphere and the judicial process.

This dynamic can be seen in the Nation's experiences with the rights of gays and lesbians. Until the mid-20th century, same-sex intimacy long had been condemned as immoral by the state itself in most Western nations, a belief often embodied in the criminal law. For this reason, among others, many persons did not deem homosexuals to have dignity in their own distinct identity. A truthful declaration by same-sex couples of what was in their hearts had to remain unspoken. Even when a greater awareness of the humanity and integrity of homosexual persons came in the period after World War II, the argument that gays and lesbians had a just claim to dignity was in conflict with both law and widespread social conventions. Same-sex intimacy remained a crime in many States. Gays and lesbians were prohibited from most government employment, barred from military service, excluded under immigration laws, targeted by police, and burdened in their rights to associate. *See* Brief for Organization of American Historians as *Amicus Curiae* 5–28.

For much of the 20th century, moreover, homosexuality was treated as an illness. When the American Psychiatric Association published the first Diagnostic and Statistical Manual of Mental Disorders in 1952, homosexuality was classified as a mental disorder, a position adhered to until 1973. *See* Position Statement on Homosexuality and Civil Rights,

1973, in 131 Am. J. Psychiatry 497 (1974). Only in more recent years have psychiatrists and others recognized that sexual orientation is both a normal expression of human sexuality and immutable. *See* Brief for American Psychological Association et al. as *Amici Curiae* 7–17.

In the late 20th century, following substantial cultural and political developments, same-sex couples began to lead more open and public lives and to establish families. This development was followed by a quite extensive discussion of the issue in both governmental and private sectors and by a shift in public attitudes toward greater tolerance. As a result, questions about the rights of gays and lesbians soon reached the courts, where the issue could be discussed in the formal discourse of the law.

* * * The right of same-sex couples to marry that is part of the liberty promised by the Fourteenth Amendment is derived, too, from that Amendment's guarantee of the equal protection of the laws. The Due Process Clause and the Equal Protection Clause are connected in a profound way, though they set forth independent principles. Rights implicit in liberty and rights secured by equal protection may rest on different precepts and are not always co-extensive, yet in some instances each may be instructive as to the meaning and reach of the other. In any particular case one Clause may be thought to capture the essence of the right in a more accurate and comprehensive way, even as the two Clauses may converge in the identification and definition of the right. This interrelation of the two principles furthers our understanding of what freedom is and must become.

The Court's cases touching upon the right to marry reflect this dynamic. In *Loving* the Court invalidated a prohibition on interracial marriage under both the Equal Protection Clause and the Due Process Clause. The Court first declared the prohibition invalid because of its unequal treatment of interracial couples. It stated: "There can be no doubt that restricting the freedom to marry solely because of racial classifications violates the central meaning of the Equal Protection Clause." 388 U.S., at 12, 87 S.Ct. 1817. With this link to equal protection the Court proceeded to hold the prohibition offended central precepts of liberty: "To deny this fundamental freedom on so unsupportable a basis as the racial classifications embodied in these statutes, classifications so directly subversive of the principle of equality at the heart of the Fourteenth Amendment, is surely to deprive all the State's citizens of liberty without due process of law." The reasons why marriage is a fundamental right became more clear and compelling from a full awareness and understanding of the hurt that resulted from laws barring interracial unions.

The synergy between the two protections is illustrated further in *Zablocki*. There the Court invoked the Equal Protection Clause as its basis for invalidating the challenged law, which, as already noted, barred fathers who were behind on child-support payments from marrying without judicial approval. The equal protection analysis depended in central part on the Court's holding that the law burdened a right "of fundamental importance." It was the essential nature of the marriage right, discussed at length in *Zablocki*, see id., at 383–387, 98 S.Ct. 673, that made apparent the law's incompatibility with requirements of equality. Each concept—liberty and equal protection—leads to a stronger understanding of the other.

Indeed, in interpreting the Equal Protection Clause, the Court has recognized that new insights and societal understandings can reveal unjustified inequality within our most fundamental institutions that once passed unnoticed and unchallenged. To take but one period, this occurred with respect to marriage in the 1970's and 1980's. Notwithstanding the gradual erosion of the doctrine of coverture, invidious sex-based classifications in marriage remained common through the mid-20th century. *See* App. to Brief for Appellant in *Reed v. Reed,* O.T. 1971, No. 70–4, pp. 69–88 (an extensive reference to laws extant as of 1971 treating women as unequal to men in marriage). These classifications denied the equal dignity of men and women. One State's law, for example, provided in 1971 that "the husband is the head of the family and the wife is subject to him; her legal civil existence is merged in the husband, except so far as the law recognizes her separately, either for her own protection, or for her benefit." Ga. Code Ann. § 53–501 (1935). Responding to a new awareness, the Court invoked equal protection principles to invalidate laws imposing sex-based inequality on marriage. * * *

In *Lawrence* the Court acknowledged the interlocking nature of these constitutional safeguards in the context of the legal treatment of gays and lesbians. Although *Lawrence* elaborated its holding under the Due Process Clause, it acknowledged, and sought to remedy, the continuing inequality that resulted from laws making intimacy in the lives of gays and lesbians a crime against the State. *Lawrence* therefore drew upon principles of liberty and equality to define and protect the rights of gays and lesbians, holding the State "cannot demean their existence or control their destiny by making their private sexual conduct a crime."

This dynamic also applies to same-sex marriage. It is now clear that the challenged laws burden the liberty of same-sex couples, and it must be further acknowledged that they abridge central precepts of equality. Here the marriage laws enforced by the respondents are in essence unequal: same-sex couples are denied all the benefits afforded to opposite-sex couples and are barred from exercising a fundamental right. Especially against a long history of disapproval of their relationships, this denial to same-sex couples of the right to marry works a grave and continuing harm. The imposition of this disability on gays and lesbians serves to disrespect and subordinate them. And the Equal Protection Clause, like the Due Process Clause, prohibits this unjustified infringement of the fundamental right to marry.

NOTES

1.   How would you describe the current standard of review for sexual orientation-based discrimination under the equal protection clause? Notice that the Supreme Court has continued to avoid explicitly addressing that question. Why do you think the Court has steered clear of a question that equal protection doctrine traditionally considers so central?

2.   After *Romer*, many scholars identified "animus" as the key to that case, and linked it to other cases involving hostility toward a group. *See, e.g.,* Cass Sunstein *Foreword: Leaving Things Undecided*, 110 HARV. L. REV. 4, 53–64 (1996). Is it significant that *Windsor* mentions animus, but *Obergefell* does not? What might explain that? What role does animus now play in the analysis of sexual orientation-based discrimination under the equal protection clause? Note that if animus is a doctrinal driving force, it is crucial to define the term. For extended analyses of the concept of animus, see Dale Carpenter, *Windsor Products: Equal Protection from Animus*, 2013 S. Ct. Rev. 183; Susannah W. Pollvogt, *Unconstitutional Animus*, 81 FORDHAM L. REV. 887 (2012).

3.   While the *Obergefell* opinion does not assess the traditional criteria for heightened scrutiny, it does include in its discussion many of the issues that are relevant to that determination, such as the history of discrimination against LGBT persons, obstacles to effective political mobilization, the asserted immutability of sexual orientation, and what the Court considers the irrelevance of sexual orientation to the ability to participate in marriage and family life. What do you make of these ideas appearing in the opinion in the way that they do?

4.   For an argument that excluding transgender people from the protections of the Americans with Disabilities Act violates equal protection even under a rational basis test, see Barry, et al, *A Bare Desire to Harm: Transgender People and the Equal Protection Clause*, 57 B.C. L. REV. 507 (2016) (excerpted in Section II.E., above in connection with the question of heightened scrutiny). This argument draws heavily on *Windsor* and *Romer*, along with other cases emphasizing animus.

CHAPTER 4

WORKING

■ ■ ■

I. INTRODUCTION

A. BACKGROUND READINGS

Lesbians, gay men, bisexual, and transgender individuals confront significant discrimination, both explicit and subtle, in the workplace. Some employers fire or refuse to hire individuals solely on the basis of their articulated or perceived sexual orientation or gender identity. Those LGBT individuals who do have jobs often must hide their identity. Richard Mohr has argued that gay people (and the same is true of transgender individuals) begin to "underidentify with their jobs ... [feeling] no security ... [and consequently are prevented from] giving it a proper degree of commitment, a proper link to self...." Or LGBT employees become workaholics to "show themselves [they are] productive enough, worthy enough, good enough, [to] overcome the invisible stigma that lurks within them waiting to suppurate."[1] The following readings provide background information about the challenges facing LGBT individuals in the workplace.

PRIVATE EXPERIENCES IN THE PUBLIC DOMAIN: LESBIANS IN ORGANIZATIONS[*]
Marny Hall

THE LESBIAN CORPORATE EXPERIENCE

The danger of disclosure

Constantly occurring in the work setting were experiences that triggered the women's awareness of their lesbianism. Anti-gay jokes, or comments presuming heterosexuality, such as "Why don't you get married? ... [Y]ou're almost twenty-eight," stimulated an awareness of being different. Because the revelation of one's lesbianism could have serious consequences, these women were constantly preoccupied with concealing that aspect of their lives. Sometimes concealment occurred as automatically as retinal adjustment to light change. At other times, it

---

[1]   RICHARD D. MOHR, GAYS/JUSTICE: A STUDY OF ETHICS, SOCIETY, AND LAW 149 (1988).

[*]   Marny Hall, *Private Experiences in the Public Domain: Lesbians in Organizations, in* WOMEN'S STUDIES: ESSENTIAL READINGS 167–73 (Stevi Jackson et al. eds., 1993).

was deliberate and felt more stressful. Whether automatic or deliberate, the process of concealment called for constant attention to every nuance of social interaction. The background buzz of assumptions became centrally important for the lesbian because it signaled where vigilance was necessary or where she could relax and "be herself." The workplace reality for the lesbian, therefore, was one of heightened awareness and sensitivity toward the usually hidden matrices of behaviour, values and attitudes in self and others. * * *

Dangers of non-disclosure

Accompanying the need for protective secrecy was a "state-of-siege" mentality, a feeling of "us and them". Often the feeling associated with these states was anxiety or anger, or both, sometimes in the form of intellectual distance: "I don't fit in, and I don't necessarily want to"; "They're so ignorant"; "You just have to see where they're coming from."

Even if a subject's lesbianism continued to be a well-kept secret, it was perceived as a disadvantage that caused lesbians to receive "unfair treatment". No matter how long they had lived with their partners, lesbians couldn't tap corporate benefits, such as "family" health insurance or travel bonuses which included spouses. One woman, who had lived with her lover for seven years, had earned enough sales points for a company-sponsored trip to Hawaii; however, she had to go alone. There were no family allowances for lesbians who were relocated and whose partners chose to accompany them. Nor could lesbians play the management game, because they would never have the requisite opposite-sexed spouse and a country club membership in the suburbs.

Being secretive created inner conflicts: "I wanted to come out, but I just couldn't," as well as constant anxiety about discovery: "If my bosses knew, they'd find a way to get rid of me"; "In the case of my supervisees, sometimes it gets emotional, and they might hug me. What would go through their minds if they knew I was a lesbian?" Several women felt that their lesbianism, because it was invisible, was less of a hindrance than their gender, which they could not disguise. Being a woman was seen as a major disadvantage in the corporate world: "As a woman, I'm generally assumed to be incompetent whereas the men are assumed to be competent unless proven otherwise."

Their lesbianism reinforced separation between work and leisure. Some respondents contended that this was congruent with their needs: "I am a private person anyway. Even if I weren't gay, I wouldn't want to mix work with my life outside work." For the others the discontinuity was a source of frustration and anger: "These guys go home and their friends are the same people they see all day. For me, coming to work is bowing out of my world completely and going into theirs." * * *

Even though the non-disclosure of their homosexuality was crucial, several respondents felt the secret was not always within their control. For example, one woman was showing a friend from work the plans of the new house she and her lover had bought. Pointing-out the main bedroom, she accidentally said, "This is where we sleep." She was appalled to have revealed the intimate nature of her relationship. Other respondents felt they revealed their lesbianism through their physical appearance. A lesbian who wore jeans to a clerical job said, "The way I dress I was in a way forcing it down their throats." Another woman said, "At the time they started suspecting, I made a mistake and cut my hair short. That was the tip-off."

Many of the interviewees said their homosexuality had been revealed inadvertently. In one instance, a woman was featured in the business section of her home-town newspaper when she became the 300th member to join a local gay business organization. She had been assured, falsely, by the photographer who covered the event that the story would appear only in gay publications. Another woman said her co-workers found out about her when her lover, wearing jeans and short hair, stopped by her office one day to drop something off. These accidental disclosures generated embarrassment and fear and were perceived by respondents as an "Oh no!" experience. Even when these near-calamities did not trigger the expected dire consequences, the incidents themselves were remembered vividly. * * *

The neuterized/neutralized strategy

Femaleness is the discredited and visible side of one's lesbianism. Consequently if gender can be minimized, lesbianism is less likely to come into focus. Computer-related jobs were particularly popular. One can speculate that, because they combine the masculine aspects of technology with the female tradition of keyboard work, computers effectively de-gender their programmers. Consequently sexuality and sexual preference questions are neutralized. In a related strategy, women who are perceived as masculine can tap positive qualities attributed to males. In a corporation, the advantages occasioned by such perceptions may outweigh, or at least balance, the disadvantages of being seen as "unfeminine". * * *

Strategies that balance non-disclosure

All forms of non-disclosure, whether the occasional substitute of "he" for "she" when describing a weekend outing with a lover or the complete fabrication of a heterosexual life, leave a lesbian in a difficult moral position. Not only is she denying what she knows to be true, but she is also ignoring the strong exhortations of the lesbian community to come out. * * *

Denial and dissociation. Frequently respondents would insist they were not in the closet, and in response to further questioning would contradict themselves, for example, "No, I haven't actually told anyone I'm gay." They continued to deny, however, that they were being secretive. Others claimed they felt comfortable in the face of homophobic remarks. Though no respondent said it, I speculate that these respondents were using a dissociative strategy; it was not *they* who were being discussed contemptuously. One respondent distinguished between "dykey women", and gays who "handled their gayness discreetly". The dichotomization between good and bad gays is another dissociative strategy.

Avoidance. Several respondents simply avoided personal situations at work. Some regretted the absence of social interactions with co-workers. Others said they did not want to get close to co-workers because they had nothing in common with them.

Distraction. Respondents purposefully cultivated images that conveyed differentness—a feminist, a liberal—in order to distract from the more discreditable identification of lesbian. Unfavourable self-assessments about being duplicitous could thus be balanced by principled stand-taking.

Token disclosure. While concealing the true nature of their relationships, some respondents let it be known that they had done something with "a room-mate". This was a partial disclosure since their room-mates were also their lovers. Similarly, after Harvey Milk's assassination, one woman asked a homophobic job supervisor for time off to go to the funeral of a friend. She did not mention that the "friend" was Milk. In response to an anti-gay joke, one lesbian said, "You'd better get yourself some new material", revealing her irritation, but not her gay identity.

The most common partial-disclosure strategy was simply to disclose their homosexuality only to certain people they felt they could trust. Because this information could leak, such a partial disclosure often set off a new round of strategies to find out if one's secret had been more widely revealed.

All of these balancing strategies seemed to restore to some degree respondents' threatened sense of integrity.

Implications and conclusions

Rather like a horse that finds itself simultaneously reined in and spurred on, corporate lesbians are caught in a crossfire of conflicting cultural and subcultural imperatives. The strategies lesbians used to manoeuver their ways through this thicket of contradictions reveal that the old reductionist notion of "coming out" is not an act, but rather a never-ending and labyrinthine process of decision and indecision, of nuance and calculated presentations as well as impulsive and inadvertent revelations—a process, in short, as shifting as the contexts in which it occurs.

Is there, one might ask, a position beyond strategy, of simply acting naturally as one respondent claimed she did? Upon examination the "natural" stance is simply another ploy, an "as-if" strategy in which the respondent acted as if she were entitled to the same social prerogatives, could count on the same good will assumed by her heterosexual co-workers. According to Goffman, this sort of "open" strategy thrusts a new career upon the stigmatized person, "that of representing [her] category. [She] finds [herself] too eminent to avoid being presented by [her] own as an instance of them".[8] And, one might add, or tokenized by heterosexual co-workers.

And so the final irony for those who are thoroughly, consistently and extensively open at work is that they are effectively shorn of the authenticity and individuality they sought by this "naturalness". As Laing writes, "lonely and painful * * * to be misunderstood, but to be correctly understood is also to be in danger of being engulfed, when the 'understanding' occurs within a framework that one had hoped to break out of".[9] And Goffman notes, "There may be no 'authentic' solution at all".[10]

The rare lesbian who reveals her orientation, and who survives the consequences of violating the gendered expectations which structure the organization succumbs, then, to the organization in another way. Stylized out of existence, she forfeits her private mutinies, cannot mobilize the resistance necessary to shield her individuality from engulfment by the collective purpose of the organization. Homogenized, the token corporate lesbian becomes the consummate "organization (wo)man".

OUT AT WORK: A TRANS PERSPECTIVE*
Bay Windows

Andrea Dawn Verville is seated in the facility where she earns her living teaching adult education classes for unemployed and underemployed veterans. Clad in a woman's suit but without make-up, Verville says that until a legal name change comes through, she still identifies at her workplace by her male birth name.

---

8   E. Goffman, *Stigma*, Englewood Cliffs, NJ: Prentice Hall, 1964, p. 26.

9   R.D. Laing, *The Divided Self*, New York: Pantheon, 1970, p. 76.

10   Goffman, *Stigma*, p. 124.

*   Allen Richards, *Out at Work: A Trans Perspective*, BAY WINDOWS, June 27, 2003.

"Once the legal name change goes through, I will go full-time," Verville explains. Of her co-workers, she observes, "It's hard enough for people to take in a new person, but [it is particularly hard] to take in a new person and attach old names to her * * * . [My supervisor and I have agreed to] let things slide for now, until everything becomes legal in the courts of Massachusetts. Then it will be OK [for us] to say 'OK, these are the new rules we play by.' "

Verville identifies as a male-to-female (MTF) pre-operative transsexual. Still in the early stages of transition—she began undergoing hormone replacement therapy several months ago—Verville is nonetheless taking a bold step: Transitioning on a job she has held for the past several years. She admits to having had a high level of anxiety, she says, "because there is always the real threat of violence. Even here in Boston, there have been transgender people who have been killed in the past."

Ironically, Verville is confident that she could defend herself physically. Her self-described "hyper-masculine" past included stints in the Marines as a marksmanship instructor and aircraft mechanic, as well as receiving certification as a firefighter and working security jobs that on one occasion had her guarding former Vice President Al Gore.

But she is well aware of the disadvantages transgender individuals face in court and oftentimes in employment. In her case, however, Verville says, "I have the back-up of the administration." Verville's supervisor was supportive as she advised colleagues of her upcoming change. "It was the entire staff of the school, which was comprised of about twenty people," Verville recalls. "[At the end of a regular meeting], my boss said that I had an announcement to make. I basically laid everything out on the table and tried to allay some of their unspoken fears right off the bat. It was met with quiet acceptance and a 'Good for you' kind of thing."

"Afterward, that's when you start hearing people talking about you. Now, there's a slight level of humor, trying to break the ice and let them know that it's OK to come to me and talk about these things. It's not anything that most people have any sort of background with so part of who I am is an educator." * * *

* * * [W]hile transgender issues have moved farther into the mainstream in recent years, many trans people still have difficulty gaining acceptance in the mainstream workforce. According to Jennifer Levi, a staff attorney at Gay and Lesbian Advocates and Defenders (GLAD), transgendered individuals can face a host of workplace issues because of their gender identities. "It can be a difficult situation for trans people to transition during the course of employment, or it can be difficult if people have taken a job and then other co-workers learn that they are

transgender," says Levi. "The ultimate goal is for people to retain their jobs and to be able to work both in safety and just to be comfortable in the workplace."

Certainly, transgendered people have made gains toward better treatment in the workplace as well: Like Verville, others who spoke to Bay Windows for this story spoke positively of coming out or transitioning on the job.

Take Cole Thaler, a recent graduate of Northeastern University School of Law, who is now employed as a law clerk. Thaler, a female-to-male transgendered person (FTM) and co-founder of the Massachusetts transgender Political Coalition, said that his school records list him as female, which causes discrepancies when employers are checking references. "Generally I have had good experiences," he says. "I have been really lucky in that at all the jobs I have had since I identified as trans, all of my co-workers have been very willing to educate themselves and have been very respectful toward me."

Because he is not taking hormones and described himself as small of stature, Thaler explains, "I'm in a place where sometimes I pass and sometimes I don't, which has created any number of interesting situations in the workplace." For instance, Thaler once interviewed for a position for which one of his references referred to Thaler with male pronouns. Thaler explained to the interviewer that he identified as transgender; the interviewer then asked if that meant he would be using the men's restroom. Thaler said it was appropriate for him to do so if there was no single occupancy restroom. To this, the interviewer responded that he would send a memo out to other staff offering his support. "It set the pace so that when I came in people were expecting to see a guy and responded to me professionally," says Thaler.

"There is this sort of ethic of professionalism [in some high-level occupations] that has definitely worked to my advantage," Thaler admits. But there are still instances of highly paid white-collar workers being fired as well as the familiar stories of blue-collar individuals facing termination, he maintains. "I think it's just maybe less overt [in the white-collar world]."

Trans activist Holly Ryan credits the acceptance of her co-workers to her self-acceptance. Ryan, a purchasing director for a human service agency who also trains staff on dealing with trans individuals in rehabs, detoxes and educational facilities, transitioned on the job five years ago. She has been promoted three times since then. Ryan describes herself as expecting fair treatment and getting it. "I don't look at the ground. I don't whimper. I don't blame the world for anything. I just feel that, you know, it's going to be harder for me," she says. "But if I carry myself right, then it's not a problem. Not to say that there is not discrimination, but I think it's all in how you carry yourself."

The change did not require a huge leap of imagination for her co-workers, Ryan says. "I was pretty androgynous for years before that. I have long hair and I had electrolysis done even before I transitioned. I wore small hoop earrings. A lot of people thought that I was going to come out as gay," she explains. "I guess trans is the last thing on their minds. But when they thought about it for a day or two, they just said 'Oh, yeah, we get it now.' " Of her role in the company, Ryan says, "I'm not kept in the closet at my job. I'm out front."

Despite her own good fortune transitioning at work, Ryan personally knows of at least one person who hasn't fared as well: "I have a friend, who transitioned six months ago. Had a $75,000 a year job in manufacturing, came back, and three months later was fired for some other trumped up reason." * * *

While it appears that employers are becoming more open to gender diversity, climbing the ladder of success is still a challenge for many. Writer/activist Nancy Nangeroni, host of WMBR's Gender Talk, a radio program devoted to transgender issues, observes that many people start their own businesses rather than deal with the difficulties involved in attempting to be accepted as a trans person by potential employers.

Nangeroni, an MTF, is an MIT graduate who works as a design engineer. She transitioned on the job several years ago but within six months she knew staying at the company wasn't going to work for her. Nangeroni describes a feeling of undefined discomfort with her former co-workers, which she now acknowledges was at least partly on her end as well. A self-described former jock, Nangeroni had a falling out with a colleague with whom she had previously bonded over sports talk. "When I transitioned, he and I had a big blowout two or three months after I transitioned," Nangeroni recalls. "After that, he treated me with respect, I treated him with respect and it was much better. We agreed that we needed to be more professional and we were. So I respect him a lot for that."

After leaving that job, Nangeroni went on job interviews where she disclosed her trans status. "I think six or eight times I disclosed, and no offer. The first job that I didn't disclose, I got an offer," she notes. "So that pretty much was a lesson. Then later on, when the guy hired me, I asked him if he would have hired me if I had told him [I was trans]. He said no, because he would have wondered why I was telling him. He thought there would have been a problem."

"There's no point in my going for an interview if I'm going to tell them I'm trans," Nangeroni concludes. "It's just a waste of time.

"When I went to work at Lucent, they had previously had a person who transitioned there ten years before and it went badly. When I first arrived there, everyone loved me," Nangeroni recalled. "I started getting invited to all kinds of high level management meetings, including meetings in managers' homes. Until they found out I was a transsexual. Overnight everything changed. I never got another invitation."

But for Mike West, there are more pros than cons to coming out as trans. "I do plan on discussing my trans identity with potential employers and co-workers [when I return to work]," says West, a transitional male who is currently on long-term disability. "I have found that when I have been 100 percent honest with people that I get a very good response from them. I have actually had people approach me [to say] how impressed they are with my honesty and how much credit they give me for the whole thing. I think being honest also makes me relax more; there are no secrets. I'd be a liar if I said that someday I didn't hope that I have transitioned so well into my male role that I don't have to disclose the fact that I am transsexual. But at this moment in my life, I am still in the early stages of transition, so I feel it's best to just be up front and honest with everyone."

BIAS IN THE WORKPLACE: CONSISTENT EVIDENCE OF SEXUAL ORIENTATION AND GENDER IDENTITY DISCRIMINATION 1998–2008[*]

M.V. Lee Badgett et al.

Over the last ten years, many researchers have conducted studies to find out whether LGBT people face sexual orientation discrimination in the workplace. These studies include surveys of LGBT individuals' workplace experiences, wage comparisons between lesbian, gay, and bisexual (LGB) and heterosexual persons, analyses of discrimination complaints filed with administrative agencies, and testing studies and controlled experiments.

Studies conducted from the mid-1980s to mid-1990s revealed that 16% to 68% of LGB respondents reported experiencing employment discrimination at some point in their lives. Since the mid-1990s, an additional fifteen studies found that 15% to 43% of LGB respondents experienced discrimination in the workplace.

When asked more specific questions about the type of discrimination experienced, LGB respondents reported the following experiences that were related to their sexual orientation: 8% to 17% were fired or denied employment, 10% to 28% were denied a promotion or given negative

---

[*]   M.V. Lee Badgett, Brad Sears, Holning Lau, Deborah Ho, *Bias in the Workplace: Consistent Evidence of Sexual Orientation and Gender Identity Discrimination 1998–2008*, 84 CHI.-KENT L. REV. 559 (2009).

performance evaluations, 7% to 41% were verbally/physically abused or had their workplace vandalized, and 10% to 19% reported receiving unequal pay or benefits.

Although data on the transgender population are scarce, several studies have brought to light the presence of discrimination against this community. When transgender individuals were surveyed separately, they reported similar or higher levels of employment discrimination. In six studies conducted between 1996 and 2006, 20% to 57% of transgender respondents reported having experienced employment discrimination at some point in their life. More specifically, 13% to 56% were fired, 13% to 47% were denied employment, 22% to 31% were harassed, and 19% were denied a promotion based on their gender identity.

Beyond survey responses, collection and analysis of state-level discrimination complaint data allow another lens through which to measure sexual orientation discrimination. Individual complaints of discrimination filed with government agencies provide another measure of perceived discrimination. In 1997 the General Accounting Office (or GAO, now known as the Government Accountability Office) collected the number of complaints filed in states that outlaw sexual orientation discrimination and found that 1% of all discrimination complaints related to sexual orientation. However, comparisons of data from sixteen states and the District of Columbia show that the rate of sexual orientation discrimination complaints per LGB person is 5 per 10,000, which is roughly equivalent to gender-based discrimination complaints.

A wage or income gap between LGB people and heterosexual people with the same job and personal characteristics provides another indicator of sexual orientation discrimination. A growing number of studies using data from the National Health and Social Life Survey, the General Social Survey, the United States Census, and the National Health and Nutrition Examination Survey show that gay men earn 10% to 32% less than otherwise similar heterosexual men. The findings for lesbians, however, are less clear. In some studies they earn more than heterosexual women but less than heterosexual or gay men. [The fact that lesbians consistently earn less than men suggests that gender discrimination has a greater impact on lesbians' wages than sexual orientation discrimination.]

Controlled experiments reveal sexual orientation discrimination in workplace settings. In controlled experiments, researchers manufacture scenarios that allow comparisons of the treatment of LGB people with treatment of heterosexuals. Seven out of eight studies using controlled experiments related to employment and public accommodation find evidence of sexual orientation discrimination.

Despite the variations in methodology, context, and time period in the studies reviewed in this report, our review of the evidence demonstrates one disturbing and consistent pattern: sexual orientation-based and gender identity discrimination is a common occurrence in many workplaces across the country.

B. AMERICAN EMPLOYMENT LAW

In focusing on the working lives of LGBT individuals, this Chapter explores the landscape of employment discrimination law in the United States. Such an examination is an immense and complex task. Employment discrimination protections can be established by all three branches of the government—legislative (through statutes), executive (through rules, regulations, and executive orders), and judicial (through court decisions)—and by all levels of government—federal, state, and local. Moreover, employers, and therefore jobs themselves, are highly differentiated: military, civil service, public and private education, quasi-public utilities, government contractors, large and small corporations, partnerships, and other private employers. Employment discrimination law is also inconsistent, not only between jurisdictions and job types, but also on its own terms. The terrain is constantly shifting—particularly with the changing nature of the American judiciary and with the changing nature of American industry—and is thus difficult to capture in a study such as this.

This Chapter attempts to organize the vast subject of employment discrimination by dividing it into two parts—one explores the "private" workplace (corporate America and other non-governmental jobs), the other the "public" workplace (government employment). Employees in both are generally protected by antidiscrimination statutes such as Title VII. In addition, government employees are protected from discrimination by constitutional provisions, civil service rules, and executive orders.

II. PRIVATE EMPLOYMENT

The traditional concept governing relations between workers and employers in America has historically been "employment at will." "Employment at will" means that employment is solely within the discretion of, or "at the will of," the employer. An employee can be hired or fired for good reason, bad reason, or no reason at all.[2]

Throughout the last fifty years, the employment-at-will concept has been altered by expanding notions of rights for employees and restrictions on the unfettered discretion of employers. Some of these restrictions are statutory protections, created by Congress and state legislatures. The

---

[2]   *See generally* MICHAEL J. ZIMMER, CHARLES A. SULLIVAN & REBECCA HANNER WHITE, CASES AND MATERIALS ON EMPLOYMENT DISCRIMINATION 4–5 (6th ed. 2003).

*Title
VII*

most important of these laws is Title VII of the Civil Rights Act of 1964.[3]
Title VII makes it unlawful for an employer "to fail or refuse to hire or to
discharge any individual, or otherwise to discriminate against any
individual with respect to his compensation, terms, conditions, or
privileges of employment, because of such individual's race, color,
religion, sex, or national origin."[4] Congress has further extended
employment protections to bar discrimination on the basis of age, *see* Age
Discrimination in Employment Act,[5] disability, *see* Americans with
Disabilities Act,[6] and genetic information. *See* Genetic Information Non-
Discrimination Act.[7]

A. PROPOSED FEDERAL LAWS

ENDA

There have been several bills introduced in Congress during the last
four decades seeking to prohibit employment discrimination on the basis
of sexual orientation. Early efforts focused on simply amending Title VII
to include sexual orientation as a protected class. A later proposal, known
as the Employment Non-Discrimination Act (ENDA), called for the
enactment of a separate statute explicitly addressing the issue of sexual
orientation discrimination in employment.

When ENDA was first proposed in the mid-1990's, it did not include
a prohibition on discrimination on the basis of gender identity. Some of
the bill's supporters were opposed to including such a provision,
reasoning that the chances that Congress would enact the law would be
considerably diminished if gender identity was included as a protected
category. Not surprisingly, the transgender community was not pleased
with this decision and soon began working to add gender identity to the
bill. In 2004, the Human Rights Campaign, one of the leading LGBT

---

[3]　　　Pub. L. No. 88–352, § 701, 78 Stat. 241 (1964) (codified at 42 U.S.C.A.§§ 2000e to
2000e–17 (West 2007)).

[4]　　　42 U.S.C.A. § 2000e–2(a)(1).

[5]　　　Pub. L. No. 90–202, § 2, 81 Stat. 602 (1967) (codified at 29 U.S.C.A. §§ 621–634 (West
2007)).

[6]　　　Pub. L. No. 101–336, § 2, 104 Stat. 328 (1990) (codified at 42 U.S.C.A. §§ 12101–12213
(West 2007)). In enacting the Americans with Disabilities Act in 1990, Congress specifically
exempted these types of claims from the law's coverage:

　　(a)　　Homosexuality and Bisexuality. For purposes of the definition of "disability" in
　　section 3(2) [42 U.S.C. § 12102(2)], homosexuality and bisexuality are not impairments
　　and as such are not disabilities under this Act.

　　(b)　　Certain conditions. Under this Act, the term "disability" shall not include—

　　　　(1)　transvestism, transsexualism, pedophilia, exhibitionism, voyeurism, gender
　　　　identity disorders not resulting from physical impairments, or other sexual
　　　　behavior disorders; * * *

Id. at § 12211. The Supreme Court has held, however, that individuals who are HIV-positive,
even when they are asymptomatic, can be disabled within the meaning of the ADA. *See Bragdon
v. Abbott*, 524 U.S. 624, 118 S.Ct. 2196, 141 L.Ed.2d 540 (1998).

[7]　　　Pub. L. No. 110–233, 122 Stat. 881 (2008) (codified as amended in scattered sections of
2, 29, 42 U.S.C.).

rights organizations that lobby at the federal level, modified its position and came out in support of expanding ENDA to include gender identity.[8]

In 2007, a new ENDA bill, which included gender identity as a protected class for the first time, was introduced in the House of Representatives. But later that year, the bill was substituted with two different ones, one addressing sexual orientation and the other gender identity discrimination. The former was approved by the House of Representatives by a vote of 235 to 184. The Senate, however, did not take up the measure, and neither body voted on the gender identity version of ENDA.

In 2013, the Senate voted to pass an ENDA bill that included gender identity protection by a margin of 64 to 32. However, the House of Representatives did not vote on the measure.

ENDA completely exempted religious and religiously affiliated organizations from its scope. As the issue of religious exemptions from LGBT equality measures became more salient after large numbers of states began allowing same-sex couples to marry, growing numbers of LGBT rights supporters began to question ENDA's broad religious exemption. (We explore the issue of religious exemptions in Chapter 7.) In 2014, several leading LGBT rights organizations withdrew their support of ENDA because of its expansive religious exemption. A year later, many LGBT rights organizations rallied around a new bill introduced in Congress called the Equality Act. That bill would amend the Civil Rights Act of 1964, among other federal antidiscrimination laws, by adding sexual orientation and gender identity as protected categories. Unlike ENDA, the Equality Act's scope is not limited to employment discrimination, but also applies to, for example, discrimination by landlords and by places of public accommodation. The political climate that exists as this edition goes to press makes it unclear whether the Equality Act will become law in the near future.

Equality Act

B. TITLE VII

Title VII

The absence of a federal law explicitly prohibiting discrimination on the basis of either sexual orientation or gender identity means that the most important issue for LGBT rights under federal antidiscrimination law relates to Title VII's prohibition of discrimination on the basis of sex. Subsection 1, therefore, provides a brief primer on Title VII law as it applies to sex discrimination, with an emphasis on claims of sexual harassment and gender stereotyping. Some LGBT plaintiffs have succeeded in bringing Title VII sex employment discrimination cases under sexual harassment and/or gender stereotyping theories. And, more recently, some courts and the Equal Employment Opportunity

---

[8]   *See* Bob Roehr, *HRC Moves to Add Trans to ENDA*, WINDY CITY TIMES, Aug. 11, 2004.

Commission (EEOC) have adopted the view that sexual orientation and gender identity as such fall within the meaning of "sex" under Title VII. These issues are explored in Subsections 2 (sexual orientation) and 3 (gender identity).

1. Sex

The original version of the bill that eventually became Title VII did not include sex as a protected category. In fact, the amendment to prohibit sex discrimination was proposed by an *opponent* of Title VII on the floor of the House of Representatives. It was the legislator's hope that the amendment would prove to be so divisive that it would lead to the eventual defeat of the entire legislation. The amendment, however, was approved and so was, of course, Title VII.

The statute does not define "sex." Furthermore, because of the unusual way in which sex was added to the statute as a protected category, there is little legislative history to provide guidance on the meaning of the term. As a result, it has been largely up to the courts to define the term.

One of the earliest Supreme Court cases that addressed the meaning of "sex" under Title VII was *Phillips v. Martin Marrietta Corp.*[9] The employer in that case had a policy that excluded from its workplace women, but not men, with young children. The employer argued that it was not discriminating on the basis of sex because it was not refusing to hire all women, but only certain women, that is, women with young children. The Court rejected the notion that a "sex-plus" policy, namely, one that takes into account sex plus another factor (such as having children), is exempt from the scope of Title VII.

Perhaps surprisingly, given the reasoning of *Martin Marietta*, the Court several years later concluded that the exclusion of pregnancy from a disability insurance plan did not violate Title VII. The Court explained in *General Electric Co. v. Gilbert* that the insurance plan distinguished between pregnant women and nonpregnant persons (both men and women), and as such did not constitute sex discrimination.[10] Congress did not agree, and quickly amended Title VII by enacting the Pregnancy Discrimination Act of 1978, which explicitly prohibited discrimination on the basis of pregnancy.

The Court was more open to the idea that sexual harassment could constitute a form of sex discrimination under Title VII, concluding in *Meritor Savings Bank v. Vinson* that the statute is violated when the harassment is "sufficiently severe or pervasive 'to alter the conditions of [the victim's] employment and create an abusive working

---

[9]   400 U.S. 542, 91 S.Ct. 496, 27 L.Ed.2d 613 (1971).

[10]   429 U.S. 125, 97 S.Ct. 401, 50 L.Ed.2d 343 (1976).

environment.' "[11] The Court distinguished between two different categories of sexual harassment claims: "quid pro quo" cases and "hostile work environment" cases.[12] The former cases involve demands on employees to engage in sexual relationships in order to avoid being demoted or fired, or as a condition for promotion. The latter cases, which are more common, involve the creation of a workplace environment that is sufficiently hostile to the members of one sex so as to make it difficult for the subjects of the harassment to do their jobs.[13]

In "quid pro quo" cases, it is alleged that an employer or supervisor has taken a "tangible employment action" as a result of the employee's refusal to submit (or continue to submit) to sexual relations, which, if proven, by itself "constitutes a change in the terms and conditions of employment * * * actionable under Title VII."[14] On the other hand, in "hostile work environment" cases, the harassment usually takes place *before* a tangible employment decision is made regarding the employee. As a result, in order to establish that the harassment affects the terms and conditions of employment, the plaintiff must show that it is "severe or pervasive."[15] The Court has added that "in order to be actionable under the statute, a sexually objectionable environment must be both objectively and subjectively offensive, one that a reasonable person would find hostile or abusive, and one that the victim in fact did perceive to be so."[16]

In addition to recognizing sexual harassment, in its different manifestations, as a form of sex discrimination, the Court, in the following opinion, concluded that making employment decisions based on gender stereotypes also constitutes impermissible discrimination under Title VII.

PRICE WATERHOUSE V. HOPKINS

Supreme Court of the United States, 1989
490 U.S. 228, 109 S.Ct. 1775, 104 L.Ed.2d 268

JUSTICE BRENNAN.

Ann Hopkins was a senior manager in an office of Price Waterhouse when she was proposed for partnership in 1982. She was neither offered nor denied admission to the partnership; instead, her candidacy was held

---

[11]   477 U.S. 57, 67, 106 S.Ct. 2399, 2405, 91 L.Ed.2d 49, 60 (1986).

[12]   *Id.* at 65–66, 106 S. Ct. at 2404–05, L. Ed. 2d at 58–9.

[13]   For a further exploration of the two categories of sexual harassment cases, see HAROLD S. LEWIS, JR. & ELIZABETH J. NORMAN, EMPLOYMENT DISCRIMINATION LAW AND PRACTICE 98–120 (2nd ed. 2004).

[14]   *Burlington Indus., Inc. v. Ellerth,* 524 U.S. 742, 754, 118 S.Ct. 2257, 2265, 141 L.Ed.2d 633, 648 (1998).

[15]   *Id.* at 754, 118 S. Ct. at 2265, 141 L. Ed. 2d at 648.

[16]   *Faragher v. City of Boca Raton,* 524 U.S. 775, 787, 118 S.Ct. 2275, 2283, 141 L.Ed.2d 662, 676 (1998).

for reconsideration the following year. When the partners in her office later refused to repropose her for partnership, she sued Price Waterhouse under Title VII of the Civil Rights Act of 1964, charging that the firm had discriminated against her on the basis of sex in its decisions regarding partnership. * * *

Ann Hopkins had worked at Price Waterhouse's Office of Government Services in Washington, D.C., for five years when the partners in that office proposed her as a candidate for partnership. Of the 662 partners at the firm at that time, 7 were women. Of the 88 persons proposed for partnership that year, only 1—Hopkins—was a woman. Forty-seven of these candidates were admitted to the partnership, 21 were rejected, and 20—including Hopkins—were "held" for reconsideration the following year. Thirteen of the 32 partners who had submitted comments on Hopkins supported her bid for partnership. Three partners recommended that her candidacy be placed on hold, eight stated that they did not have an informed opinion about her, and eight recommended that she be denied partnership.

In a jointly prepared statement supporting her candidacy, the partners in Hopkins' office showcased her successful 2-year effort to secure a $25 million contract with the Department of State, labeling it "an outstanding performance" and one that Hopkins carried out "virtually at the partner level." * * *

The partners in Hopkins' office praised her character as well as her accomplishments, describing her in their joint statement as "an outstanding professional" who had a "deft touch," a "strong character, independence and integrity." Clients appear to have agreed with these assessments. At trial, one official from the State Department described her as "extremely competent, intelligent," "strong and forthright, very productive, energetic and creative." Another high-ranking official praised Hopkins' decisiveness, broadmindedness, and "intellectual clarity"; she was, in his words, "a stimulating conversationalist." Evaluations such as these led [the district court] Judge Gesell to conclude that Hopkins "had no difficulty dealing with clients and her clients appear to have been very pleased with her work" and that she "was generally viewed as a highly competent project leader who worked long hours, pushed vigorously to meet deadlines and demanded much from the multidisciplinary staffs with which she worked."

On too many occasions, however, Hopkins' aggressiveness apparently spilled over into abrasiveness. Staff members seem to have borne the brunt of Hopkins' brusqueness. Long before her bid for partnership, partners evaluating her work had counseled her to improve her relations with staff members. Although later evaluations indicate an improvement, Hopkins' perceived shortcomings in this important area eventually doomed her bid for partnership. Virtually all of the partners' negative remarks about Hopkins—even those of partners supporting her—had to do with her "interpersonal skills." Both "[s]upporters and opponents of her candidacy," stressed Judge Gesell, "indicated that she was sometimes overly aggressive, unduly harsh, difficult to work with and impatient with staff."

There were clear signs, though, that some of the partners reacted negatively to Hopkins' personality because she was a woman. One partner described her as "macho"; another suggested that she "overcompensated for being a woman"; a third advised her to take "a course at charm school". Several partners criticized her use of profanity; in response, one partner suggested that those partners objected to her swearing only "because it's a lady using foul language." Another supporter explained that Hopkins "ha[d] matured from a tough-talking somewhat masculine hard-nosed mgr to an authoritative, formidable, but much more appealing lady ptr candidate." But it was the man who, as Judge Gesell found, bore responsibility for explaining to Hopkins the reasons for the Policy Board's decision to place her candidacy on hold who delivered the *coup de grace*: in order to improve her chances for partnership, Thomas Beyer advised, Hopkins should "walk more femininely, talk more femininely, dress more femininely, wear make-up, have her hair styled, and wear jewelry."

Dr. Susan Fiske, a social psychologist and Associate Professor of Psychology at Carnegie-Mellon University, testified at trial that the partnership selection process at Price Waterhouse was likely influenced by sex stereotyping. Her testimony focused not only on the overtly sex-based comments of partners but also on gender-neutral remarks, made by partners who knew Hopkins only slightly, that were intensely critical of her. One partner, for example, baldly stated that Hopkins was "universally disliked" by staff, and another described her as "consistently annoying and irritating"; yet these were people who had had very little contact with Hopkins. According to Fiske, Hopkins' uniqueness (as the only woman in the pool of candidates) and the subjectivity of the evaluations made it likely that sharply critical remarks such as these were the product of sex stereotyping—although Fiske admitted that she could not say with certainty whether any particular comment was the result of stereotyping. Fiske based her opinion on a review of the submitted comments, explaining that it was commonly accepted practice for social psychologists to reach this kind of conclusion without having met any of the people involved in the decisionmaking process.

In previous years, other female candidates for partnership also had been evaluated in sex-based terms. As a general matter, Judge Gesell concluded, "[c]andidates were viewed favorably if partners believed they maintained their femin[in]ity while becoming effective professional managers"; in this environment, "[t]o be identified as a 'women's lib[b]er' was regarded as [a] negative comment." In fact, the judge found that in previous years "[o]ne partner repeatedly commented that he could not consider any woman seriously as a partnership candidate and believed that women were not even capable of functioning as senior managers— yet the firm took no action to discourage his comments and recorded his vote in the overall summary of the evaluations."

Judge Gesell found that Price Waterhouse legitimately emphasized interpersonal skills in its partnership decisions, and also found that the firm had not fabricated its complaints about Hopkins' interpersonal skills as a pretext for discrimination. Moreover, he concluded, the firm did not give decisive emphasis to such traits only because Hopkins was a woman; although there were male candidates who lacked these skills but who were admitted to partnership, the judge found that these candidates possessed other, positive traits that Hopkins lacked.

The judge went on to decide, however, that some of the partners' remarks about Hopkins stemmed from an impermissibly cabined view of the proper behavior of women, and that Price Waterhouse had done nothing to disavow reliance on such comments. He held that Price Waterhouse had unlawfully discriminated against Hopkins on the basis of sex by consciously giving credence and effect to partners' comments that resulted from sex stereotyping. * * *

In saying that gender played a motivating part in an employment decision, we mean that, if we asked the employer at the moment of the decision what its reasons were and if we received a truthful response, one of those reasons would be that the applicant or employee was a woman. In the specific context of sex stereotyping, an employer who acts on the basis of a belief that a woman cannot be aggressive, or that she must not be, has acted on the basis of gender.

Although the parties do not overtly dispute this last proposition, the placement by Price Waterhouse of "sex stereotyping" in quotation marks throughout its brief seems to us an insinuation either that such stereotyping was not present in this case or that it lacks legal relevance. We reject both possibilities. As to the existence of sex stereotyping in this case, we are not inclined to quarrel with the District Court's conclusion that a number of the partners' comments showed sex stereotyping at work. As for the legal relevance of sex stereotyping, we are beyond the day when an employer could evaluate employees by assuming or insisting that they matched the stereotype associated with their group, for " '[i]n forbidding employers to discriminate against individuals because of their sex, Congress intended to strike at the entire spectrum of disparate treatment of men and women resulting from sex stereotypes.' " *Los Angeles Dept. of Water and Power v. Manhart*, 435 U.S. 702, 707, n. 13, 98

S.Ct. 1370, 55 L.Ed.2d 657 (1978), quoting *Sprogis v. United Air Lines, Inc.*, 444 F.2d 1194, 1198 (7th Cir. 1971). An employer who objects to aggressiveness in women but whose positions require this trait places women in an intolerable and impermissible catch 22: out of a job if they behave aggressively and out of a job if they do not. Title VII lifts women out of this bind.

Remarks at work that are based on sex stereotypes do not inevitably prove that gender played a part in a particular employment decision. The plaintiff must show that the employer actually relied on her gender in making its decision. In making this showing, stereotyped remarks can certainly be *evidence* that gender played a part. In any event, the stereotyping in this case did not simply consist of stray remarks. On the contrary, Hopkins proved that Price Waterhouse invited partners to submit comments; that some of the comments stemmed from sex stereotypes; that an important part of the Policy Board's decision on Hopkins was an assessment of the submitted comments; and that Price Waterhouse in no way disclaimed reliance on the sex-linked evaluations. This is not, as Price Waterhouse suggests, "discrimination in the air"; rather, it is, as Hopkins puts it, "discrimination brought to ground and visited upon" an employee. By focusing on Hopkins' specific proof, however, we do not suggest a limitation on the possible ways of proving that stereotyping played a motivating role in an employment decision, and we refrain from deciding here which specific facts, "standing alone," would or would not establish a plaintiff's case, since such a decision is unnecessary in this case. * * *

In finding that some of the partners' comments reflected sex stereotyping, the District Court relied in part on Dr. Fiske's expert testimony. Without directly impugning Dr. Fiske's credentials or qualifications, Price Waterhouse insinuates that a social psychologist is unable to identify sex stereotyping in evaluations without investigating whether those evaluations have a basis in reality. This argument comes too late. At trial, counsel for Price Waterhouse twice assured the court that he did not question Dr. Fiske's expertise and failed to challenge the legitimacy of her discipline. Without contradiction from Price Waterhouse, Fiske testified that she discerned sex stereotyping in the partners' evaluations of Hopkins and she further explained that it was part of her business to identify stereotyping in written documents. We are not inclined to accept petitioner's belated and unsubstantiated characterization of Dr. Fiske's testimony as "gossamer evidence" based only on "intuitive hunches" and of her detection of sex stereotyping as "intuitively divined". Nor are we disposed to adopt the dissent's dismissive attitude toward Dr. Fiske's field of study and toward her own professional integrity.

Indeed, we are tempted to say that Dr. Fiske's expert testimony was merely icing on Hopkins' cake. It takes no special training to discern sex stereotyping in a description of an aggressive female employee as requiring "a course at charm school." Nor, turning to Thomas Beyer's memorable advice to Hopkins, does it require expertise in psychology to know that, if an employee's flawed "interpersonal skills" can be corrected by a soft-hued suit or a new shade of lipstick, perhaps it is the employee's sex and not her interpersonal skills that has drawn the criticism.

Price Waterhouse also charges that Hopkins produced no evidence that sex stereotyping played a role in the decision to place her candidacy on hold. As we have stressed, however, Hopkins showed that the partnership solicited evaluations from all of the firm's partners; that it generally relied very heavily on such evaluations in making its decision; that some of the partners' comments were the product of stereotyping; and that the firm in no way disclaimed reliance on those particular comments, either in Hopkins' case or in the past. Certainly a plausible— and, one might say, inevitable—conclusion to draw from this set of circumstances is that the Policy Board in making its decision did in fact take into account all of the partners' comments, including the comments that were motivated by stereotypical notions about women's proper deportment.

[Concurring opinions by JUSTICE WHITE and JUSTICE O'CONNOR, as well as a dissenting opinion by JUSTICE KENNEDY, are omitted.]

JESPERSEN V. HARRAH'S OPERATING COMPANY, INC.

United States Court of Appeals, Ninth Circuit, 2006 (en banc)
444 F.3d 1104

SCHROEDER, CHIEF JUDGE.

We took this sex discrimination case en banc in order to reaffirm our circuit law concerning appearance and grooming standards, and to clarify our evolving law of sex stereotyping claims. * * *

Plaintiff Darlene Jespersen worked successfully as a bartender at Harrah's for twenty years and compiled what by all accounts was an exemplary record. During Jespersen's entire tenure with Harrah's, the company maintained a policy encouraging female beverage servers to wear makeup. The parties agree, however, that the policy was not enforced until 2000. In February 2000, Harrah's implemented a "Beverage Department Image Transformation" program at twenty Harrah's locations, including its casino in Reno. Part of the program consisted of new grooming and appearance standards, called the "Personal Best" program. The program contained certain appearance standards that applied equally to both sexes, including a standard uniform of black pants, white shirt, black vest, and black bow tie.

Jespersen has never objected to any of these policies. The program also contained some sex-differentiated appearance requirements as to hair, nails, and makeup.

In April 2000, Harrah's amended that policy to require that women wear makeup. Jespersen's only objection here is to the makeup requirement. The amended policy provided in relevant part:

> All Beverage Service Personnel, in addition to being friendly, polite, courteous and responsive to our customer's needs, must possess the ability to physically perform the essential factors of the job as set forth in the standard job descriptions. They must be well groomed, appealing to the eye, be firm and body toned, and be comfortable with maintaining this look while wearing the specified uniform. Additional factors to be considered include, but are not limited to, hair styles, overall body contour, and degree of comfort the employee projects while wearing the uniform.

> * * *

> Beverage Bartenders and Barbacks will adhere to these additional guidelines:

> - Overall Guidelines (applied equally to male/ female):
>   - Appearance: Must maintain Personal Best image portrayed at time of hire.
>   - Jewelry, if issued, must be worn. Otherwise, tasteful and simple jewelry is permitted; no large chokers, chains or bracelets.
>   - No faddish hairstyles or unnatural colors are permitted.
> - Males:
>   - Hair must not extend below top of shirt collar. Ponytails are prohibited.
>   - Hands and fingernails must be clean and nails neatly trimmed at all times. No colored polish is permitted.
>   - Eye and facial makeup is not permitted.
>   - Shoes will be solid black leather or leather type with rubber (non skid) soles.
> - Females:
>   - Hair must be teased, curled, or styled every day you work. Hair must be worn down at all times, no exceptions.

- Stockings are to be of nude or natural color consistent with employee's skin tone. No runs.

- Nail polish can be clear, white, pink or red color only. No exotic nail art or length.

- Shoes will be solid black leather or leather type with rubber (non skid) soles.

- *Make up (face powder, blush and mascara) must be worn and applied neatly in complimentary colors. Lip color must be worn at all times.* (emphasis added).

Jespersen did not wear makeup on or off the job, and in her deposition stated that wearing it would conflict with her self-image. It is not disputed that she found the makeup requirement offensive, and felt so uncomfortable wearing makeup that she found it interfered with her ability to perform as a bartender. Unwilling to wear the makeup, and not qualifying for any open positions at the casino with a similar compensation scale, Jespersen left her employment with Harrah's.

After exhausting her administrative remedies with the Equal Employment Opportunity Commission and obtaining a right to sue notification, Jespersen filed this action in July 2001. In her complaint, Jespersen sought damages as well as declaratory and injunctive relief for discrimination and retaliation for opposition to discrimination, alleging that the "Personal Best" policy discriminated against women by "(1) subjecting them to terms and conditions of employment to which men are not similarly subjected, and (2) requiring that women conform to sex-based stereotypes as a term and condition of employment."

Harrah's moved for summary judgment, supporting its motion with documents giving the history and purpose of the appearance and grooming policies. Harrah's argued that the policy created similar standards for both men and women, and that where the standards differentiated on the basis of sex, as with the face and hair standards, any burdens imposed fell equally on both male and female bartenders.

In her deposition testimony, attached as a response to the motion for summary judgment, Jespersen described the personal indignity she felt as a result of attempting to comply with the makeup policy. Jespersen testified that when she wore the makeup she "felt very degraded and very demeaned." In addition, Jespersen testified that "it prohibited [her] from doing [her] job" because "[i]t affected [her] self-dignity * * * [and] took away [her] credibility as an individual and as a person." Jespersen made no cross-motion for summary judgment, taking the position that the case should go to the jury. Her response to Harrah's motion for summary judgment relied solely on her own deposition testimony regarding her subjective reaction to the makeup policy, and on favorable customer feedback and employer evaluation forms regarding her work.

The record therefore does not contain any affidavit or other evidence to establish that complying with the "Personal Best" standards caused burdens to fall unequally on men or women, and there is no evidence to suggest Harrah's motivation was to stereotype the women bartenders. Jespersen relied solely on evidence that she had been a good bartender, and that she had personal objections to complying with the policy, in order to support her argument that Harrah's " 'sells' and exploits its women employees." Jespersen contended that as a matter of law she had made a prima facie showing of gender discrimination, sufficient to survive summary judgment on both of her claims.

The district court granted Harrah's motion for summary judgment on all of Jespersen's claims. In this appeal, Jespersen maintains that the record before the district court was sufficient to create triable issues of material fact as to her unlawful discrimination claims of unequal burdens and sex stereotyping. We deal with each in turn.

UNEQUAL BURDENS

In order to assert a valid Title VII claim for sex discrimination, a plaintiff must make out a prima facie case establishing that the challenged employment action was either intentionally discriminatory or that it had a discriminatory effect on the basis of gender. *McDonnell Douglas Corp. v. Green,* 411 U.S. 792, 802, 93 S.Ct. 1817, 36 L.Ed.2d 668 (1973). Once a plaintiff establishes such a prima facie case, "[t]he burden then must shift to the employer to articulate some legitimate, nondiscriminatory reason for the employee's rejection." *McDonnell,* 411 U.S. at 802.

In this case, Jespersen argues that the makeup requirement itself establishes a prima facie case of discriminatory intent and must be justified by Harrah's as a bona fide occupational qualification. Our settled law in this circuit, however, does not support Jespersen's position that a sex-based difference in appearance standards alone, without any further showing of disparate effects, creates a prima facie case.

In *Gerdom v. Cont'l Airlines, Inc.,* 692 F.2d 602 (9th Cir.1982), we considered the Continental Airlines policy that imposed strict weight restrictions on female flight attendants, and held it constituted a violation of Title VII. We did so because the airline imposed no weight restriction whatsoever on a class of male employees who performed the same or similar functions as the flight attendants. Indeed, the policy was touted by the airline as intended to "create the public image of an airline which offered passengers service by thin, attractive women, whom executives referred to as Continental's 'girls.' " *Id.* at 604. In fact, Continental specifically argued that its policy was justified by its "desire to compete [with other airlines] by featuring attractive female cabin attendants[,]" a justification which this court recognized as "discriminatory on its face." *Id.* at 609. The weight restriction was part of an overall program to create a sexual image for the airline.

In contrast, this case involves an appearance policy that applied to both male and female bartenders, and was aimed at creating a professional and very similar look for all of them. All bartenders wore the same uniform. The policy only differentiated as to grooming standards. * * *

* * * [H]ere we deal with requirements that, on their face, are not more onerous for one gender than the other. Rather, Harrah's "Personal Best" policy contains sex-differentiated requirements regarding each employee's hair, hands, and face. While those individual requirements differ according to gender, none on its face places a greater burden on one gender than the other. Grooming standards that appropriately differentiate between the genders are not facially discriminatory.

We have long recognized that companies may differentiate between men and women in appearance and grooming policies, and so have other circuits. The material issue under our settled law is not whether the policies are different, but whether the policy imposed on the plaintiff creates an "unequal burden" for the plaintiff's gender * * * Under established equal burdens analysis, when an employer's grooming and appearance policy does not unreasonably burden one gender more than the other, that policy will not violate Title VII.

Jespersen asks us to take judicial notice of the fact that it costs more money and takes more time for a woman to comply with the makeup requirement than it takes for a man to comply with the requirement that he keep his hair short, but these are not matters appropriate for judicial notice. Judicial notice is reserved for matters "generally known within the territorial jurisdiction of the trial court" or "capable of accurate and ready determination by resort to sources whose accuracy cannot reasonably be questioned." Fed.R.Evid. 201. The time and cost of makeup and haircuts is in neither category. The facts that Jespersen would have this court judicially notice are not subject to the requisite "high degree of indisputability" generally required for such judicial notice. Fed.R.Evid. 201 advisory committee's note. * * *

SEX STEREOTYPING

* * * The stereotyping in *Price Waterhouse* interfered with Hopkins' ability to perform her work; the advice that she should take "a course at charm school" was intended to discourage her use of the forceful and aggressive techniques that made her successful in the first place. Impermissible sex stereotyping was clear because the very traits that she was asked to hide were the same traits considered praiseworthy in men.

Harrah's "Personal Best" policy is very different. The policy does not single out Jespersen. It applies to all of the bartenders, male and female. It requires all of the bartenders to wear exactly the same uniforms while interacting with the public in the context of the entertainment industry. It is for the most part unisex, from the black tie to the non-skid shoes. There is no evidence in this record to indicate that the policy was adopted to make women bartenders conform to a commonly-accepted stereotypical image of what women should wear. The record contains nothing to suggest the grooming standards would objectively inhibit a woman's ability to do the job. The only evidence in the record to support the stereotyping claim is Jespersen's own subjective reaction to the makeup requirement. * * *

We respect Jespersen's resolve to be true to herself and to the image that she wishes to project to the world. We cannot agree, however, that her objection to the makeup requirement, without more, can give rise to a claim of sex stereotyping under Title VII. If we were to do so, we would come perilously close to holding that every grooming, apparel, or appearance requirement that an individual finds personally offensive, or in conflict with his or her own self-image, can create a triable issue of sex discrimination.

This is not a case where the dress or appearance requirement is intended to be sexually provocative, and tending to stereotype women as sex objects * * * The "Personal Best" policy does not, on its face, indicate any discriminatory or sexually stereotypical intent on the part of Harrah's. * * *

Nor is there evidence in this record that Harrah's treated Jespersen any differently than it treated any other bartender, male or female, who did not comply with the written grooming standards applicable to all bartenders. Jespersen's claim here materially differs from Hopkins' claim in *Price Waterhouse* because Harrah's grooming standards do not require Jespersen to conform to a stereotypical image that would objectively impede her ability to perform her job requirements as a bartender. * * * AFFIRMED.

PREGERSON, CIRCUIT JUDGE, with whom JUDGES KOZINSKI, GRABER, and W. FLETCHER join, dissenting:

* * * The majority contends that it is bound to reject Jespersen's sex stereotyping claim because she presented too little evidence—only her "own subjective reaction to the makeup requirement." I disagree. Jespersen's evidence showed that Harrah's fired her because she did not comply with a grooming policy that imposed a facial uniform (full makeup) on only female bartenders. Harrah's stringent "Personal Best" policy required female beverage servers to wear foundation, blush, mascara, and lip color, and to ensure that lip color was on at all times.

Jespersen and her female colleagues were required to meet with professional image consultants who in turn created a facial template for each woman. Jespersen was required not simply to wear makeup; in addition, the consultants dictated where and how the makeup had to be applied.

Quite simply, her termination for failing to comply with a grooming policy that imposed a facial uniform on only female bartenders is discrimination "because of" sex. Such discrimination is clearly and unambiguously impermissible under Title VII, which requires that "gender must be *irrelevant* to employment decisions." *Price Waterhouse v. Hopkins*, 490 U.S. 228, 240, 109 S.Ct. 1775, 104 L.Ed.2d 268 (1989) (plurality opinion) (emphasis added).[2]

Notwithstanding Jespersen's failure to present additional evidence, little is required to make out a sex-stereotyping—as distinct from an undue burden—claim in this situation * * * *Price Waterhouse* recognizes that gender discrimination may manifest itself in stereotypical notions as to how women should dress and present themselves, not only as to how they should behave. * * *

* * * The fact that Harrah's required female bartenders to conform to a sex stereotype by wearing full makeup while working is not in dispute, and the policy is described at length in the majority opinion. This policy did not, as the majority suggests, impose a "grooming, apparel, or appearance requirement that an individual finds personally offensive," but rather one that treated Jespersen differently from male bartenders "because of" her sex. I believe that the fact that Harrah's designed and promoted a policy that required women to conform to a sex stereotype by wearing full makeup is sufficient "direct evidence" of discrimination.

The majority contends that Harrah's "Personal Best" appearance policy is very different from the policy at issue in *Price Waterhouse* in that it applies to both men and women. I disagree. As the majority concedes, "Harrah's 'Personal Best' policy contains sex-differentiated requirements regarding each employee's hair, hands, and face." The fact that a policy contains sex-differentiated requirements that affect people of both genders cannot excuse a particular requirement from scrutiny. By refusing to consider the makeup requirement separately, and instead stressing that the policy contained some gender-neutral requirements, such as color of clothing, as well as a variety of gender-differentiated requirements for "hair, hands, and face," the majority's approach would

---

[2]   Title VII identifies only one circumstance in which employers may take gender into account in making an employment decision-namely, "when gender is a 'bona fide occupational qualification [(BFOQ)] reasonably necessary to the normal operation of th[e] particular business or enterprise.' " *Price Waterhouse*, 490 U.S. at 242 (quoting 42 U.S.C. § 2000e–2(e)). Harrah's has not attempted to defend the "Personal Best" makeup requirement as a BFOQ. In fact, there is little doubt that the "Personal Best" policy is not a business necessity, as Harrah's quietly disposed of this policy after Jespersen filed this suit. . . .

permit otherwise impermissible gender stereotypes to be neutralized by the presence of a stereotype or burden that affects people of the opposite gender, or by some separate non-discriminatory requirement that applies to both men and women * * *

Because I believe that we should be careful not to insulate appearance requirements by viewing them in broad categories, such as "hair, hands, and face," I would consider the makeup requirement on its own terms. Viewed in isolation—or, at the very least, as part of a narrower category of requirements affecting employees' faces—the makeup or facial uniform requirement becomes closely analogous to the uniform policy held to constitute impermissible sex stereotyping in *Carroll v. Talman Federal Savings & Loan Ass'n of Chicago*, 604 F.2d 1028, 1029 (7th Cir.1979). In *Carroll*, the defendant bank required women to wear employer-issued uniforms, but permitted men to wear business attire of their own choosing. The Seventh Circuit found this rule discriminatory because it suggested to the public that the uniformed women held a "lesser professional status" and that women could not be trusted to choose appropriate business attire.

Just as the bank in *Carroll* deemed female employees incapable of achieving a professional appearance without assigned uniforms, Harrah's regarded women as unable to achieve a neat, attractive, and professional appearance without the facial uniform designed by a consultant and required by Harrah's. The inescapable message is that women's undoctored faces compare unfavorably to men's, not because of a physical difference between men's and women's faces, but because of a cultural assumption—and gender-based stereotype—that women's faces are incomplete, unattractive, or unprofessional without full makeup. We need not denounce all makeup as inherently offensive, just as there was no need to denounce all uniforms as inherently offensive in *Carroll*, to conclude that *requiring* female bartenders to wear full makeup is an impermissible sex stereotype and is evidence of discrimination because of sex. * * *

KOZINSKI, CIRCUIT JUDGE, with whom JUDGES GRABER and W. FLETCHER join, dissenting:

I agree with Judge Pregerson and join his dissent-subject to one caveat: I believe that Jespersen also presented a triable issue of fact on the question of disparate burden * * * I find it perfectly clear that Harrah's overall grooming policy is substantially more burdensome for women than for men. Every requirement that forces men to spend time or money on their appearance has a corresponding requirement that is as, or more, burdensome for women: short hair v. "teased, curled, or styled" hair; clean trimmed nails v. nail length and color requirements; black leather shoes v. black leather shoes. The requirement that women spend time and money applying full facial makeup has no corresponding requirement for men, making the "overall policy" more burdensome for the former than for the latter. The only question is how much.

It is true that Jespersen failed to present evidence about what it costs to buy makeup and how long it takes to apply it. But is there any doubt that putting on makeup costs money and takes time? Harrah's policy requires women to apply face powder, blush, mascara and lipstick. You don't need an expert witness to figure out that such items don't grow on trees.

Nor is there any rational doubt that application of makeup is an intricate and painstaking process that requires considerable time and care. Even those of us who don't wear makeup know how long it can take from the hundreds of hours we've spent over the years frantically tapping our toes and pointing to our wrists. It's hard to imagine that a woman could "put on her face," as they say, in the time it would take a man to shave—certainly not if she were to do the careful and thorough job Harrah's expects. Makeup, moreover, must be applied and removed every day; the policy burdens men with no such daily ritual. While a man could jog to the casino, slip into his uniform, and get right to work, a woman must travel to work so as to avoid smearing her makeup, or arrive early to put on her makeup there.

It might have been tidier if Jespersen had introduced evidence as to the time and cost associated with complying with the makeup requirement, but I can understand her failure to do so, as these hardly seem like questions reasonably subject to dispute. We could—and should—take judicial notice of these incontrovertible facts.

Alternatively, Jespersen did introduce evidence that she finds it burdensome to *wear* makeup because doing so is inconsistent with her self-image and interferes with her job performance. My colleagues dismiss this evidence, apparently on the ground that wearing makeup does not, as a matter of law, constitute a substantial burden. This presupposes that Jespersen is unreasonable or idiosyncratic in her discomfort. Why so? Whether to wear cosmetics—literally, the face one presents to the world—is an intensely personal choice. Makeup, moreover, touches delicate parts of the anatomy—the lips, the eyes, the cheeks—and can cause serious discomfort, sometimes even allergic reactions, for someone unaccustomed to wearing it. If you are used to wearing makeup—as most American women are—this may seem like no big deal. But those of us not used to wearing makeup would find a requirement that we do so highly intrusive. Imagine, for example, a rule that all judges wear face powder, blush, mascara and lipstick while on the bench. Like Jespersen, I would find such a regime burdensome and demeaning; it would interfere with my job performance. I suspect many of my colleagues would feel the same way.

Everyone accepts this as a reasonable reaction from a man, but why should it be different for a woman? It is not because of anatomical differences, such as a requirement that women wear bathing suits that cover their breasts. Women's faces, just like those of men, can be perfectly presentable without makeup; it is a cultural artifact that most women raised in the United States learn to put on—and presumably enjoy wearing—cosmetics. But cultural norms change; not so long ago a man wearing an earring was a gypsy, a pirate or an oddity. Today, a man wearing body piercing jewelry is hardly noticed. So, too, a large (and perhaps growing) number of women choose to present themselves to the world without makeup. I see no justification for forcing them to conform to Harrah's quaint notion of what a "real woman" looks like.

NOTES

1. As explored below in Subsections 2.A and 3, many of the gender stereotyping claims that have followed *Price Waterhouse* have been brought by LGBT employees. Such claims, of course, have also been raised in cases where neither issues of sexual orientation nor gender identity were present. In *Back v. Hastings on Hudson Union Free School District*, 365 F.3d 107 (2d Cir. 2004), for example, a female teacher who alleged she was denied tenure because the defendant did not believe she could be both a good worker and a good mother at the same time was allowed by the court to proceed with her gender-stereotyping lawsuit.

2. The *Jespersen* court has not been alone in upholding dress and grooming policies that are different for men and women. *See e.g., Harper v. Blockbuster Entm't Corp.*, 139 F.3d 1385 (11th Cir. 1998) (upholding employer's grooming policy, which prohibited men, but not women, from having long hair); *Tavora v. New York Mercantile Exch.*, 101 F.3d 907 (2d Cir. 1996) (same). *But see, e.g., Frank v. United Airlines, Inc.*, 216 F.3d 845 (9th Cir. 2000) (holding that airline's weight policy for flight attendants that based women's weight maximums on medium frame category, and men's maximums on large frame category, was discriminatory).

2. Sexual Orientation

In an important early case, the U.S. Court of Appeals for the Ninth Circuit held in 1979 that discrimination on the basis of sexual orientation is not "sex" discrimination within the meaning of Title VII.[17] In doing so, it quoted from an earlier ruling rejecting the view that Title VII protected transgender individuals from discrimination:

> The cases interpreting Title VII sex discrimination provisions agree that they were intended to place women on an equal footing with men. * * * Giving the statute its plain meaning, this court concludes that Congress had only the traditional notions of

---

[17]   *DeSantis v. Pacific Telephone & Telegraph*, 608 F.2d 327 (9th Cir. 1979).

"sex" in mind. Later legislative activity makes this narrow definition even more evident. Several bills have been introduced to amend the Civil Rights Act to prohibit discrimination against "sexual preference." None have [sic] been enacted into law. * * * Congress has not shown any intent other than to restrict the term "sex" to its traditional meaning. Therefore, this court will not expand Title VII's application in the absence of Congressional mandate.[18]

Many other courts have since agreed.[19] But there has been considerable less agreement among courts, as we will explore in this Subsection, on the extent to which the sexual orientation of plaintiffs impacts their ability to make out gender stereotyping and/or sexual harassment claims under Title VII.

a. Gender Stereotyping

DAWSON V. BUMBLE & BUMBLE

United States Court of Appeals, Second Circuit, 2005
398 F.3d 211

POOLER, CIRCUIT JUDGE:

This is an employment discrimination case. Plaintiff-Appellant Dawn Dawson, a self-described "lesbian female, who does not conform to gender norms in that she does not meet stereotyped expectations of femininity and may be perceived as more masculine than a stereotypical woman," claims that she suffered discrimination on the basis of sex, sex stereotyping, and/or sexual orientation in violation of federal, state, and municipal law. *See* Title VII of the Civil Rights Act of 1964 ("Title VII"), 42 U.S.C. § 2000e *et seq.;* New York State Human Rights Law, N.Y. Exec. Law § 290 *et seq.;* New York City Human Rights Law, N.Y.C. Admin. Code, Title 8. Dawson's former employer, Defendant-Appellee Bumble & Bumble, describes itself as "a prestigious, high-end hair salon in Manhattan, known for its innovative hair cutting techniques."

Dawson was hired by Bumble & Bumble in early 1999 as a "hair assistant." Dawson describes the duties of this position as including "assisting [hair] stylists in all aspects of their jobs, keeping their work

---

[18]   *Id.* at 329 (quoting *Holloway v. Arthur Andersen & Co.*, 566 F.2d 659, 662–63 (9th Cir. 1977)).

[19]   *See, e.g., Schroeder v. Hamilton Sch. Dist.*, 282 F.3d 946, 951 (7th Cir. 2002); *Bibby v. Philadelphia Coca-Cola Bottling Co.*, 260 F.3d 257, 265 (3d Cir. 2001); *Higgins v. New Balance Athletic Shoe, Inc.*, 194 F.3d 252, 259 (1st Cir. 1999); *Hopkins v. Baltimore Gas & Elec. Co.*, 77 F.3d 745, 751–52 & n. 3 (4th Cir. 1996); *Simonton v. Runyon*, 232 F.3d 33, 35–36 (2d Cir. 2000); *Williamson v. A.G. Edwards & Sons*, 876 F.2d 69, 70 (8th Cir. 1989). *See also Medina v. Income Support Div.*, 413 F.3d 1131, 1135 (10th Cir. 2005) (concluding that plaintiff, in effect, "alleg[ed] that she was discriminated against because she is a heterosexual" and holding that the "protections [of the statute] do not extend . . . to a person's sexuality.").

areas in the salon clean, escorting clients to different areas of the salon, shampooing clients' hair, and blow-drying clients' hair."

In addition to her duties as a hair assistant, Dawson was simultaneously enrolled in Bumble & Bumble's training program for hair stylists * * * Dawson alleges in her complaint that she "was confident that she would be able to graduate from the hair assistant training program to a stylist in an expedited fashion." We do not see, however, that Dawson disputes Bumble & Bumble's contention that "[o]nly about 10–15% of the total number of assistants at the Salon at any given time typically complete the educational program" and that it generally takes these successful candidates at least two and sometimes three years to complete the program.

The district court observed that the Bumble & Bumble salon is an unconventional workplace, a "heterogenous environment that strives for the avant garde and extols the unconventional." *Dawson v. Bumble & Bumble,* 246 F.Supp.2d 301, 311 (S.D.N.Y.2003). The district court also found that the salon's employees "embody many lifestyles and sexual preferences and reflect varying physical appearances, overall looks, and different manners of hair [,] dress and clothing." *Id.* at 310. Bumble & Bumble itself contends that "[i]f there is a 'norm' for Bumble employees, it is the norm of non-conformance." Thus, Bumble & Bumble asserts that the salon regularly employs "sexually 'non-stereotypical' individuals, including a female-to-male transsexual, [an] openly bisexual Education Coordinator, numerous other openly gay employees, and both male and female gay employees, including * * * lesbian employees with very androgynous looks." The district court found it to be particularly significant that Connie Voines, the manager of the salon and the individual who ultimately decided to terminate Dawson, is "a pre-surgery male-to-female transsexual who * * * at the time of the events in question, was transitioning from appearing male to appearing female." *Dawson,* 246 F.Supp.2d at 309.

Dawson does not seriously contest the depiction of the Bumble & Bumble salon as an environment in which conformance to gender norms was something less than a prerequisite for continued employment. When asked at her deposition if the salon employed "nonconformists" other than herself, Dawson replied: "It's like, you know, I don't think hairdressers are conformists anyway, so I would say the whole lot of them." Further, Dawson testified that she was not at all reticent about her lesbianism while working at the salon, but rather "discussed my life like anybody else would discuss their life and you know and I wasn't hidden about who I was." Dawson also stated that she was a willing participant in the sexually-charged banter that took place among the salon's employees, and that she would sometimes refer to herself as a "dyke." More generally, she stated that "lesbian jokes were brought up" and "you know, I like myself, I'm happy, so if this is light and funny, I'm with that."

The issue on which the parties disagree sharply is the quality of Dawson's performance as a hair assistant and as a participant in Bumble & Bumble's training program. Dawson alleges in her complaint that "her work was consistently praised by Connie Voines, * * * by other stylists, and clients" and that "several individuals who evaluated her work progress in the training program gave [her] positive feedback."

Dawson was terminated on July 15, 2000. According to Bumble & Bumble, Dawson's firing was the result of poor performance on the job and in the training program:

> Dawson's performance at the Salon was erratic: sometimes she performed well and with an enthusiastic attitude; other times, she did not. Over time, her performance on the Salon floor and in the educational program declined until it was unacceptable. For example, Dawson's performance in the basic cutting class was inadequate to advance to basic razor.

> Dawson also demonstrated significant performance deficiencies on the Salon floor. Several clients complained that she had been rude or abrupt with them or rough with their hair—more than with any other assistant. Similarly, several stylists complained that she was hostile or disrespectful. * * *

Appellee's Br. at 4–6 (internal citations omitted).

Dawson contends, however, that her failure to advance in Bumble & Bumble's training program and her termination are the result of discriminatory animus. As to the training program, Dawson alleges that it was repeatedly made clear to her that females rarely attained the position of hair stylist. Specifically, Dawson asserts that on one occasion when she asked Voines to place her in an editorial styling class, Voines stated, "How many women do you see doing editorial * * * They only want men with accents." Dawson also points to an affidavit from Amy Strober, another hair assistant, in which Strober states that when she asked to be assigned to a styling class, Voines said, "Do you know how many famous female editorial stylists there are? There is one."

With respect to her work on the salon floor as a hair assistant, Dawson alleges that she was subjected to a hostile work environment in that "[s]he was constantly harassed about her appearance, that she did not conform to the image of women, and that she should act in a manner less like a man and more like a woman." Dawson alleges that a range of invective was directed at her by fellow Bumble & Bumble employees: (1) two stylists, Howard McLaren and Raymond McLaren, repeatedly referred to her "in front of colleagues and clients, by the name 'Donald' ";

(2) a stylist named Ralph Formisano once stated that she was " 'wearing her sexuality like a costume,' implying that she did not conform to gender norms and appeared to be a lesbian"; and (3) a fellow hair assistant named Deniz Uzunoglu once "loudly proclaimed to [her], in extremely vulgar and threatening terms, that he thought she 'needed to have sex with a man.' "

In addition, Dawson asserts that the McLarens stated to educators in Bumble's education department that they wanted to fire her because of her " 'dyke' attitude." Finally, Dawson alleges that her termination took place as follows:

> On or about July 15, 2000, Voines informed Dawson that she was terminated because she "seemed unhappy" and because of the way she dressed and wore her hair. When Dawson asked for clarification, Voines stated that she could not send her to New Jersey or any place outside New York City. She added, "People won't understand you * * * you'll frighten them."

The United States District Court for the Southern District of New York granted Bumble & Bumble's motion for summary judgment with respect to all of Dawson's Title VII, NYSHRL, and NYCHRL claims. * * *

As already noted, Dawson defines herself in her complaint as "a lesbian female, who does not conform to gender norms in that she does not meet stereotyped expectations of femininity and may be perceived as more masculine than a stereotypical woman." In her brief on this appeal, Dawson further explains that she "is in three distinct, but somewhat interrelated protected classes * * * because (1) she is a woman [,] * * * (2) she does not conform to gender norms in that she appears more like a man than a woman, * * * [and] she is (3) gay." The district court, however, observed that "because the borders [between these classes] are so imprecise, it is not eviden[t] exactly what conduct by Bumble Dawson claims as the gravamen of the claims she asserts on sex or gender grounds, as opposed to what actions she bases on sexual orientation or sexual stereotyping." *Dawson,* 246 F.Supp.2d at 311. The district court further opined that

> Dawson's claims of sexual discrimination, as she articulates them in the Complaint and elaborates in her deposition, [possess a] somewhat protean quality, [such that it is] hard to grasp or pinpoint precisely what conduct she accuses of offending whatever behavioral norms she asserts govern the circumstances. At various times in her pleadings and testimony, she asserts that she was disparately treated because of the way she looked, because she was a woman, because she was not a man, because she was a lesbian, because she was a lesbian who did not conform to gender norms.

We find ourselves in full agreement with these assertions. Both in her complaint and in her briefing on this appeal, Dawson has significantly conflated her claims. As a result, it is often difficult to discern when Dawson is alleging that the various adverse employment actions allegedly visited upon her by Bumble & Bumble were motivated by animus toward her gender, her appearance, her sexual orientation, or some combination of these. The following excerpt from her deposition testimony, in which Dawson states the reasons why she believed she had been terminated, is indicative of the problem:

A.   Because of the way I look * * * [M]y visual presence was not acceptable. And the constant remarks about me being a lesbian * * * made it clear that they were none too happy with that.

Q.   * * * [I]s it fair to say that one of the things you're saying * * * is that you believe you were discriminated against because of your sexual orientation?

A.   Yes.

Q.   * * * Is it fair to state that another thing that you're complaining about in this action is that you were discriminated against because you're a lesbian who looks a certain way?

A.   Yes.

Such confusion as to the sources of the discriminatory animus allegedly visited upon Dawson complicates her claims under Title VII because "[t]he law is well-settled in this circuit and in all others to have reached the question that. * * * Title VII does not prohibit harassment or discrimination because of sexual orientation." *Simonton v. Runyon*, 232 F.3d 33, 35 (2d Cir.2000). Thus, to the extent that she is alleging discrimination based upon her lesbianism, Dawson cannot satisfy the first element of a prima facie case under Title VII because the statute does not recognize homosexuals as a protected class.

Realizing that discrimination based upon sexual orientation is not actionable under Title VII, Dawson avails herself of the "gender stereotyping" theory of Title VII liability according to which individuals who fail or refuse to comply with socially accepted gender roles are members of a protected class. * * *

When utilized by an avowedly homosexual plaintiff, however, gender stereotyping claims can easily present problems for an adjudicator. This is for the simple reason that "[s]tereotypical notions about how men and women should behave will often necessarily blur into ideas about heterosexuality and homosexuality." *Howell v. North Cent. Coll.*, 320 F.Supp.2d 717, 723 (N.D.Ill.2004). Like other courts, we have therefore recognized that a gender stereotyping claim should not be used to "bootstrap protection for sexual orientation into Title VII." *Simonton,* 232 F.3d at 38. * * *

Generally speaking, one can fail to conform to gender stereotypes in two ways: (1) through behavior or (2) through appearance. Dawson makes no assertion with respect to behavioral non-conformance. That is, unlike the plaintiff in *Price Waterhouse,* she was not told by anyone at Bumble & Bumble that her continued employment depended upon her acting and speaking in a more "feminine" manner. There is also no allegation that Dawson's work assignments were restricted in any way to those considered "appropriate" for a woman to perform.

Dawson's claim with respect to gender stereotyping thus rests upon the contention that her appearance was unacceptable in the eyes of Bumble & Bumble. Dawson states her position in this regard most comprehensively in an affidavit filed after she was deposed:

> My outward appearance does not conform to the traditional expectations of the way a woman would look. I do not conform to our society's gender norms because of the way I present myself, including my manner of dress, hair style, my lack of feminine jewelry, lack of feminine perfume, and lack of makeup. I also do not have a noticeable chest or wide hips, and my body type is more like a male than a female. In sum, my overall appearance is more like a male than a female. In fact, many people think that I look less like a female and more like a male.

Whatever the accuracy of this statement, the record in this case is simply devoid of any substantial evidence that Dawson was subjected to any adverse employment consequences as a result of her appearance. With respect to her "manner of dress," there is no evidence that the Bumble & Bumble salon even employed a formal dress code for its employees, let alone a dress code that reinforced gender stereotypes. On the contrary, Dawson has not contradicted the assertion of Connie Voines, the salon manager, to the effect that Dawson "generally wore leather pants and a jean jacket when working, none of which was objectionable from the Salon's point of view."

The only evidence presented by Dawson which tends to show that her style of dress was not acceptable comes in the form of alleged statements by co-workers. First, in her complaint Dawson alleges that she was "harassed by Ralph [Formisano], a stylist. He accused Dawson of 'wearing her sexuality like a costume,' implying that she did not conform to gender norms and appeared to be a lesbian." Only in her post-deposition affidavit does Dawson clearly state that this comment had anything to do with her "overall appearance" and was not simply concerned with her sexual orientation. Dawson's complaint also contains the allegation that "Howard and Raymond McLaren repeatedly referred to Dawson, in front of colleagues and clients, by the name 'Donald.'" Realizing that these comments also provide ambiguous support for a gender stereotyping claim, Dawson asserts in her brief on this appeal that she "believed the comments were related to her masculine appearance and/or her sexual orientation."

Bumble & Bumble *does* have a policy regarding hairstyles: employees must have their hair cut by Bumble & Bumble stylists as a means of advertising the salon's techniques. Dawson does not argue that this rule is discriminatory in itself, and any claim that it improperly enforces employees to conform to gender stereotypes is decisively belied by Connie Voines' uncontested assertion that for part of the time during which she was employed at the salon, Dawson was allowed to wear her hair "in a 'mohawk' style (in her case, extremely short in the back and on the sides, with a strip of longer hair down the center of her head)." Because this haircut was performed by a Bumble & Bumble stylist, the salon had no objection to it. Indeed, Voines states without contradiction that "many women [besides Dawson] who have worked at the Salon have had very short hair" and that one female employee had *all* of the hair on her head shaved down to only fuzz." * * *

In sum, in contrast to the plaintiff in *Price Waterhouse,* who proffered evidence that her promotion to partnership depended upon her changing her behavior to better conform to gender stereotypes, * * * Dawson has produced no substantial evidence from which we may plausibly infer that her alleged failure to conform her appearance to feminine stereotypes resulted in her suffering any adverse employment action at the hands of Bumble & Bumble. Thus, her Title VII claim based upon a gender stereotyping theory must fail. * * * AFFIRMED.

PROWEL V. WISE BUSINESS FORMS, INC.

United States Court of Appeals, Third Circuit, 2009
579 F.3d 285

HARDIMAN, CIRCUIT JUDGE.

Brian Prowel appeals the District Court's summary judgment in favor of his former employer, Wise Business Forms, Inc. Prowel sued under Title VII of the Civil Rights Act of 1964 and the Pennsylvania Human Relations Act, alleging that Wise harassed and retaliated against him because of sex * * * The principal issue on appeal is whether Prowel has marshaled sufficient facts for his claim of "gender stereotyping" discrimination to be submitted to a jury. * * *

Prowel began working for Wise in July 1991. A producer and distributor of business forms, Wise employed approximately 145 workers at its facility in Butler, Pennsylvania. From 1997 until his termination, Prowel operated a machine called a nale encoder, which encodes numbers and organizes business forms. On December 13, 2004, after 13 years with the company, Wise informed Prowel that it was laying him off for lack of work. * * *

Prowel identifies himself as an effeminate man and believes that his mannerisms caused him not to "fit in" with the other men at Wise. Prowel described the "genuine stereotypical male" at the plant as follows:

[B]lue jeans, t-shirt, blue collar worker, very rough around the edges. Most of the guys there hunted. Most of the guys there fished. If they drank, they drank beer, they didn't drink gin and tonic. Just you know, all into football, sports, all that kind of stuff, everything I wasn't.

In stark contrast to the other men at Wise, Prowel testified that he had a high voice and did not curse; was very well-groomed; wore what others would consider dressy clothes; was neat; filed his nails instead of ripping them off with a utility knife; crossed his legs and had a tendency to shake his foot "the way a woman would sit"; walked and carried himself in an effeminate manner; drove a clean car; had a rainbow decal on the trunk of his car; talked about things like art, music, interior design, and decor; and pushed the buttons on the nale encoder with "pizzazz."

Some of Prowel's co-workers reacted negatively to his demeanor and appearance. During the last two years of his employment at Wise, a female co-worker frequently called Prowel "Princess." In a similar vein, co-workers made comments such as: "Did you see what Rosebud was wearing?"; "Did you see Rosebud sitting there with his legs crossed, filing his nails?"; and "Look at the way he walks."

Prowel also testified that he is homosexual. At some point prior to November 1997, Prowel was "outed" at work when a newspaper clipping of a "man-seeking-man" ad was left at his workstation with a note that read: "Why don't you give him a call, big boy." Prowel reported the incident to two management-level personnel and asked that something be done. The culprit was never identified, however.

After Prowel was outed, some of his co-workers began causing problems for him, subjecting him to verbal and written attacks during the last seven years of his tenure at Wise. In addition to the nicknames "Princess" and "Rosebud," a female co-worker called him "fag" and said: "Listen, faggot, I don't have to put up with this from you." Prowel reported this to his shift supervisor but received no response.

At some point during the last two years of Prowel's employment, a pink, light-up, feather tiara with a package of lubricant jelly was left on his nale encoder. The items were removed after Prowel complained to Henry Nolan, the shift supervisor at that time. On March 24, 2004, as

Prowel entered the plant, he overheard a co-worker state: "I hate him. They should shoot all the fags." Prowel reported this remark to Nolan, who said he would look into it. Prowel also overheard conversations between co-workers, one of whom was a supervisor, who disapproved of how he lived his life. Finally, messages began to appear on the wall of the men's bathroom, claiming Prowel had AIDS and engaged in sexual relations with male co-workers. After Prowel complained, the company repainted the restroom. * * *

On December 13, 2004, Prowel was summoned to meet with his supervisors, who informed him that he was terminated effective immediately for lack of work. * * *

In evaluating Wise's motion for summary judgment, the District Court properly focused on our decision in *Bibby v. Philadelphia Coca Cola Bottling Co.,* 260 F.3d 257 (3d Cir.2001), wherein we stated: "Title VII does not prohibit discrimination based on sexual orientation. Congress has repeatedly rejected legislation that would have extended Title VII to cover sexual orientation." *Id.* at 261 (citations omitted). This does not mean, however, that a homosexual individual is barred from bringing a *sex discrimination* claim under Title VII, which plainly prohibits discrimination "because of sex."

Both Prowel and Wise rely heavily upon *Bibby.* Wise claims this appeal is indistinguishable from *Bibby* and therefore we should affirm its summary judgment for the same reason we affirmed summary judgment in *Bibby.* Prowel counters that reversal is required here because gender stereotyping was not at issue in *Bibby.* As we shall explain, *Bibby* does not dictate the result in this appeal. Because it guides our analysis, however, we shall review it in some detail.

John Bibby, a homosexual man, was a long-time employee of the Philadelphia Coca Cola Bottling Company. The company terminated Bibby after he sought sick leave, but ultimately reinstated him. After Bibby's reinstatement, he alleged that he was assaulted and harmed by co-workers and supervisors when he was subjected to crude remarks and derogatory sexual graffiti in the bathrooms.

Bibby filed a complaint with the Philadelphia Commission on Human Relations (PCHR), alleging sexual orientation discrimination. After the PCHR issued a right-to-sue letter, Bibby sued in federal court alleging, *inter alia,* sexual harassment in violation of Title VII. The district court granted summary judgment for the company because Bibby was harassed not "because of sex," but rather because of his sexual orientation, which is not cognizable under Title VII.

On appeal, this Court affirmed, holding that Bibby presented insufficient evidence to support a claim of same-sex harassment under Title VII. Despite acknowledging that harassment based on sexual orientation has no place in a just society, we explained that Congress chose not to include sexual orientation harassment in Title VII. Nevertheless, we stated that employees may—consistent with the Supreme Court's decision in *Price Waterhouse*—raise a Title VII *gender stereotyping* claim, provided they can demonstrate that "the[ir] harasser was acting to punish [their] noncompliance with gender stereotypes." *Id.* at 264. Because Bibby did not claim gender stereotyping, however, he could not prevail on that theory. We also concluded, in dicta, that even had we construed Bibby's claim to involve gender stereotyping, he did not marshal sufficient evidence to withstand summary judgment on that claim.

In light of the foregoing discussion, we disagree with both parties' arguments that *Bibby* dictates the outcome of this case. *Bibby* does not carry the day for Wise because in that case, the plaintiff failed to raise a gender stereotyping claim as Prowel has done here. Contrary to Prowel's argument, however, *Bibby* does not require that we reverse the District Court's summary judgment merely because we stated that a gender stereotyping claim is cognizable under Title VII; such has been the case since the Supreme Court's decision in *Price Waterhouse*. Instead, we must consider whether the record, when viewed in the light most favorable to Prowel, contains sufficient facts from which a reasonable jury could conclude that he was harassed and/or retaliated against "because of sex." * * *

As this appeal demonstrates, the line between sexual orientation discrimination and discrimination "because of sex" can be difficult to draw. In granting summary judgment for Wise, the District Court found that Prowel's claim fell clearly on one side of the line, holding that Prowel's sex discrimination claim was an artfully-pleaded claim of sexual orientation discrimination. However, our analysis—viewing the facts and inferences in favor of Prowel—leads us to conclude that the record is ambiguous on this dispositive question. Accordingly, Prowel's gender stereotyping claim must be submitted to a jury.

Wise claims it laid off Prowel because the company decided to reduce the number of nale encoder operators from three to two. This claim is not without support in the record. After Prowel was laid off, no one was hired to operate the nale encoder during his shift. Moreover, market conditions caused Wise to lay off 44 employees at its Pennsylvania facility between 2001 and September 2006, and the company's workforce shrank from 212 in 2001 to 145 in 2008. General Manager Straub testified that in determining which nale encoder operator to lay off, he considered various factors, including customer service, productivity, cooperativeness, willingness to perform other tasks (the frequency with which employees complained about working on other machines), future advancement opportunities, and cost. According to Wise, Prowel was laid off because:

comments on his daily production reports reflected an uncooperative and insubordinate attitude; he was the highest paid operator; he complained when asked to work on different machines; and he did not work to the best of his ability when operating the other machines.

Prowel asserts that these reasons were pretextual and he was terminated because of his complaints to management about harassment and his discussions with co-workers regarding a potential lawsuit against the company. In this respect, the record indicates that Prowel's work compared favorably to the other two nale encoder operators. Specifically, Prowel worked on other equipment fifty-four times during the last half of 2004 while a co-worker did so just once; Prowel also ran more jobs and impressions per hour than that same co-worker; and Prowel's attendance was significantly better than the third nale encoder operator. Finally, although Wise laid off forty-four workers between 2001 and 2006, it laid off no one in 2003, only Prowel in 2004, and just two in 2005. Although Prowel is unaware what role his sexual orientation played in his termination, he alleges that he was harassed and retaliated against not because of the quality of his work, but rather because he failed to conform to gender stereotypes.

The record demonstrates that Prowel has adduced evidence of harassment based on gender stereotypes. He acknowledged that he has a high voice and walks in an effeminate manner. In contrast with the typical male at Wise, Prowel testified that he: did not curse and was very well-groomed; filed his nails instead of ripping them off with a utility knife; crossed his legs and had a tendency to shake his foot "the way a woman would sit." Prowel also discussed things like art, music, interior design, and decor, and pushed the buttons on his nale encoder with "pizzazz." Prowel's effeminate traits did not go unnoticed by his co-workers, who commented: "Did you see what Rosebud was wearing?"; "Did you see Rosebud sitting there with his legs crossed, filing his nails?"; and "Look at the way he walks." Finally, a co-worker deposited a feathered, pink tiara at Prowel's workstation. When the aforementioned facts are considered in the light most favorable to Prowel, they constitute sufficient evidence of gender stereotyping harassment—namely, Prowel was harassed because he did not conform to Wise's vision of how a man should look, speak, and act-rather than harassment based solely on his sexual orientation.

To be sure, the District Court correctly noted that the record is replete with evidence of harassment motivated by Prowel's sexual orientation. Thus, it is possible that the harassment Prowel alleges was because of his sexual orientation, not his effeminacy. Nevertheless, this does not vitiate the possibility that Prowel was also harassed for his failure to conform to gender stereotypes. See 42 U.S.C. § 2000e–2(m) ("[A]n unlawful employment practice is established when the complaining party demonstrates that * * * sex * * * was a motivating factor for any employment practice, even though other factors also motivated the practice."). Because both scenarios are plausible, the case presents a question of fact for the jury and is not appropriate for summary judgment.

In support of the District Court's summary judgment, Wise argues persuasively that every case of sexual orientation discrimination cannot translate into a triable case of gender stereotyping discrimination, which would contradict Congress's decision not to make sexual orientation discrimination cognizable under Title VII. Nevertheless, Wise cannot persuasively argue that *because* Prowel is homosexual, he is precluded from bringing a gender stereotyping claim. There is no basis in the statutory or case law to support the notion that an effeminate *heterosexual* man can bring a gender stereotyping claim while an effeminate *homosexual* man may not. As long as the employee— regardless of his or her sexual orientation—marshals sufficient evidence such that a reasonable jury could conclude that harassment or discrimination occurred "because of sex," the case is not appropriate for summary judgment. For the reasons we have articulated, Prowel has adduced sufficient evidence to submit this claim to a jury.

NOTES

1.   Why the different outcomes in *Dawson* and *Prowel*? Were the plaintiff's facts in the latter case stronger than in the former? Did the nature of the workplace (a high-end hair salon vs. a printing plant) matter? Why did the *Dawson* court view the plaintiff's case as an improper effort to "bootstrap" a sexual orientation claim onto a gender stereotyping claim? Why was the *Prowel* court apparently not concerned about "bootstrapping"?

2.   Consider the following critique by Professor Zachary Kramer of judicial rulings (like *Dawson*) that have rejected, on "bootstrapping" grounds, Title VII sex discrimination claims brought by lesbian and gay plaintiffs:

> [T]here is a double standard at work in employment discrimination cases. For lesbian and gay employees, sexual orientation is a burden because courts are primed to reject otherwise actionable discrimination claims on the theory that such claims are an attempt to bootstrap protection for sexual orientation into Title VII. However, rather than being burdened by their sexual orientation in employment discrimination cases, heterosexual employees are not affected by theirs. Because heterosexuality is invisible in our culture, courts simply fail to recognize when an employee's discrimination claim implicates her heterosexuality. As a result, no court will ever conclude that a heterosexual employee is raising a sex discrimination claim as a means to bootstrap protection for

sexual orientation into Title VII. Put simply, heterosexuals and homosexuals are not similarly situated under Title VII.

Zachary A. Kramer, *Heterosexuality and Title VII*, 103 NW. U. L. REV. 205, 207–08 (2009). Kramer elaborates on the invisibility of heterosexuality by explaining that "in our culture, heterosexuals are typically thought of as not having a sexual orientation. Instead, heterosexuality is merely the normative baseline against which all other sexual orientations are tested. As such, heterosexuality tends to be missing altogether from discussions about sex and sexuality." *Id.* at 209. He adds that "the invisibility of heterosexuality has seeped into employment discrimination jurisprudence, creating a doctrinal privilege for heterosexual employees in the sense that they do not risk losing their discrimination claims because of their sexual orientation." *Id.* at 230.

    3.   Did Dawson lose in part because the employer seemed willing to hire and promote other LGBT individuals? Notice that Dawson claimed that she was discriminated against "because she was a lesbian who looks a certain way." Dawson's claim, therefore, might have been based on the idea that even an employer who is willing to promote gay men who are perceived to be effeminate, as well transgender employees who are gender nonconforming, might nonetheless be unwilling to promote lesbians who are perceived to be "too masculine." Is this claim analogous to one based on an employer's willingness to promote some racial minority groups and not others? An employer who refuses to promote African Americans while promoting Asians would clearly violate Title VII. Would not the same be true of an employer who refuses to promote "masculine" lesbians while promoting "feminine" gay men? Or is the problem that neither lesbians nor gay men, as such, are protected by the statute, while African Americans are protected?

b.   *Sexual Harassment*

ONCALE V. SUNDOWNER OFFSHORE SERVICES, INC.

Supreme Court of the United States, 1998
523 U.S. 75, 118 S.Ct. 998, 140 L.Ed.2d 201

JUSTICE SCALIA.

    This case presents the question whether workplace harassment can violate Title VII's prohibition against "discriminat[ion] * * * because of * * * sex," 42 U.S.C. § 2000e–2(a)(1), when the harasser and the harassed employee are of the same sex.

    The District Court having granted summary judgment for respondent, we must assume the facts to be as alleged by petitioner Joseph Oncale. The precise details are irrelevant to the legal point we must decide, and in the interest of both brevity and dignity we shall describe them only generally. In late October 1991, Oncale was working for respondent Sundowner Offshore Services on a Chevron U.S.A., Inc., oil platform in the Gulf of Mexico. He was employed as a roustabout on an eight-man crew which included respondents John Lyons, Danny Pippen, and Brandon Johnson. Lyons, the crane operator, and Pippen, the driller, had supervisory authority. On several occasions, Oncale was forcibly subjected to sex-related, humiliating actions against him by Lyons, Pippen and Johnson in the presence of the rest of the crew. Pippen and Lyons also physically assaulted Oncale in a sexual manner, and Lyons threatened him with rape.

Oncale's complaints to supervisory personnel produced no remedial action; in fact, the company's Safety Compliance Clerk, Valent Hohen, told Oncale that Lyons and Pippen "picked [on] him all the time too," and called him a name suggesting homosexuality. Oncale eventually quit—asking that his pink slip reflect that he "voluntarily left due to sexual harassment and verbal abuse." When asked at his deposition why he left Sundowner, Oncale stated "I felt that if I didn't leave my job, that I would be raped or forced to have sex."

Oncale filed a complaint against Sundowner in the United States District Court for the Eastern District of Louisiana, alleging that he was discriminated against in his employment because of his sex. Relying on the Fifth Circuit's decision in *Garcia v. Elf Atochem North America*, 28 F.3d 446, 451–452 (5th Cir. 1994), the district court held that "Mr. Oncale, a male, has no cause of action under Title VII for harassment by male co-workers." On appeal, a panel of the Fifth Circuit concluded that *Garcia* was binding Circuit precedent, and affirmed. 83 F.3d 118 (5th Cir. 1996). * * *

Title VII of the Civil Rights Act of 1964 provides, in relevant part, that "[i]t shall be an unlawful employment practice for an employer * * * to discriminate against any individual with respect to his compensation, terms, conditions, or privileges of employment, because of such individual's race, color, religion, sex, or national origin." 42 U.S.C. § 2000e–2(a)(1). We have held that this not only covers "terms" and "conditions" in the narrow contractual sense, but "evinces a congressional intent to strike at the entire spectrum of disparate treatment of men and women in employment." *Meritor Savings Bank, FSB v. Vinson*, 477 U.S. 57, 64, 106 S.Ct. 2399, 91 L.Ed.2d 49 (1986). "When the workplace is permeated with discriminatory intimidation, ridicule, and insult that is sufficiently severe or pervasive to alter the conditions of the victim's employment and create an abusive working environment, Title VII is violated." *Harris v. Forklift Systems, Inc.*, 510 U.S. 17, 21, 114 S.Ct. 367, 126 L.Ed.2d 295 (1993).

Title VII's prohibition of discrimination "because of * * * sex" protects men as well as women, *Newport News Shipbuilding & Dry Dock Co. v. EEOC*, 462 U.S. 669, 682, 103 S.Ct. 2622, 77 L.Ed.2d 89 (1983), and in the related context of racial discrimination in the workplace we have rejected any conclusive presumption that an employer will not discriminate against members of his own race. "Because of the many facets of human motivation, it would be unwise to presume as a matter of law that human beings of one definable group will not discriminate against other members of that group." *Castaneda v. Partida*, 430 U.S. 482, 499, 97 S.Ct. 1272, 51 L.Ed.2d 498 (1977). In *Johnson v. Transportation Agency, Santa Clara Cty.*, 480 U.S. 616, 107 S.Ct. 1442, 94 L.Ed.2d 615 (1987), a male employee claimed that his employer discriminated against him because of his sex when it preferred a female employee for promotion. Although we ultimately rejected the claim on other grounds, we did not consider it significant that the supervisor who made that decision was also a man. If our precedents leave any doubt on the question, we hold today that nothing in Title VII necessarily bars a claim of discrimination "because of * * * sex" merely because the plaintiff and the defendant (or the person charged with acting on behalf of the defendant) are of the same sex.

Courts have had little trouble with that principle in cases like *Johnson*, where an employee claims to have been passed over for a job or promotion. But when the issue arises in the context of a "hostile environment" sexual harassment claim, the state and federal courts have taken a bewildering variety of stances. Some, like the Fifth Circuit in this case, have held that same-sex sexual harassment claims are never cognizable under Title VII. Other decisions say that such claims are actionable only if the plaintiff can prove that the harasser is homosexual (and thus presumably motivated by sexual desire). *Compare McWilliams v. Fairfax County Board of Supervisors*, 72 F.3d 1191 (4th Cir. 1996), *with Wrightson v. Pizza Hut of America*, 99 F.3d 138 (4th Cir. 1996). Still others suggest that workplace harassment that is sexual in content is always actionable, regardless of the harasser's sex, sexual orientation, or motivations. *See Doe v. Belleville*, 119 F.3d 563 (7th Cir. 1997).

We see no justification in the statutory language or our precedents for a categorical rule excluding same-sex harassment claims from the coverage of Title VII. As some courts have observed, male-on-male sexual harassment in the workplace was assuredly not the principal evil Congress was concerned with when it enacted Title VII. But statutory prohibitions often go beyond the principal evil to cover reasonably comparable evils, and it is ultimately the provisions of our laws rather than the principal concerns of our legislators by which we are governed. Title VII prohibits "discriminat[ion] * * * because of * * * sex" in the "terms" or "conditions" of employment. Our holding that this includes sexual harassment must extend to sexual harassment of any kind that meets the statutory requirements.

Respondents and their amici contend that recognizing liability for same-sex harassment will transform Title VII into a general civility code for the American workplace. But that risk is no greater for same-sex than for opposite-sex harassment, and is adequately met by careful attention to the requirements of the statute. Title VII does not prohibit all verbal or physical harassment in the workplace; it is directed only at "discriminat[ion] * * * because of * * * sex." We have never held that workplace harassment, even harassment between men and women, is automatically discrimination because of sex merely because the words used have sexual content or connotations. "The critical issue, Title VII's text indicates, is whether members of one sex are exposed to disadvantageous terms or conditions of employment to which members of the other sex are not exposed." *Harris*, supra, at 25 (GINSBURG, J., concurring).

Courts and juries have found the inference of discrimination easy to draw in most male-female sexual harassment situations, because the challenged conduct typically involves explicit or implicit proposals of sexual activity; it is reasonable to assume those proposals would not have been made to someone of the same sex. The same chain of inference would be available to a plaintiff alleging same-sex harassment, if there were credible evidence that the harasser was homosexual. But harassing conduct need not be motivated by sexual desire to support an inference of discrimination on the basis of sex. A trier of fact might reasonably find such discrimination, for example, if a female victim is harassed in such sex-specific and derogatory terms by another woman as to make it clear that the harasser is motivated by general hostility to the presence of women in the workplace. A same-sex harassment plaintiff may also, of course, offer direct comparative evidence about how the alleged harasser treated members of both sexes in a mixed-sex workplace. Whatever evidentiary route the plaintiff chooses to follow, he or she must always prove that the conduct at issue was not merely tinged with offensive sexual connotations, but actually constituted "discrimina[tion] * * * because of * * * sex."

And there is another requirement that prevents Title VII from expanding into a general civility code: As we emphasized in *Meritor* and *Harris*, the statute does not reach genuine but innocuous differences in the ways men and women routinely interact with members of the same sex and of the opposite sex. The prohibition of harassment on the basis of sex requires neither asexuality nor androgyny in the workplace; it forbids only behavior so objectively offensive as to alter the "conditions" of the victim's employment. "Conduct that is not severe or pervasive enough to create an objectively hostile or abusive work environment—an environment that a reasonable person would find hostile or abusive—is beyond Title VII's purview." *Harris*, 510 U.S., at 21. We have always regarded that requirement as crucial, and as sufficient to ensure that courts and juries do not mistake ordinary socializing in the workplace—such as male-on-male horseplay or intersexual flirtation—for discriminatory "conditions of employment."

We have emphasized, moreover, that the objective severity of harassment should be judged from the perspective of a reasonable person in the plaintiff's position, considering "all the circumstances." *Harris*, 510 U.S., at 23. In same-sex (as in all) harassment cases, that inquiry requires careful consideration of the social context in which particular behavior occurs and is experienced by its target. A professional football player's working environment is not severely or pervasively abusive, for example, if the coach smacks him on the buttocks as he heads onto the field—even if the same behavior would reasonably be experienced as abusive by the coach's secretary (male or female) back at the office. The real social impact of workplace behavior often depends on a constellation of surrounding circumstances, expectations, and relationships which are not fully captured by a simple recitation of the words used or the physical acts performed. Common sense, and an appropriate sensitivity to social context, will enable courts and juries to distinguish between simple teasing or roughhousing among members of the same sex, and conduct which a reasonable person in the plaintiff's position would find severely hostile or abusive.

Because we conclude that sex discrimination consisting of same-sex sexual harassment is actionable under Title VII, the judgment of the Court of Appeals for the Fifth Circuit is reversed, and the case is remanded for further proceedings consistent with this opinion.

JUSTICE THOMAS, concurring.

I concur because the Court stresses that in every sexual harassment case, the plaintiff must plead and ultimately prove Title VII's statutory requirement that there be discrimination "because of * * * sex."

EQUAL EMPLOYMENT OPPORTUNITY COMMISSION V. BOH BROTHERS CONSTRUCTION COMPANY

United States Court of Appeals, Fifth Circuit, 2013 (en banc)
731 F.3d 444

JENNIFER WALKER ELROD, CIRCUIT JUDGE.

This Title VII case arises out of alleged sexual harassment by Chuck Wolfe, the superintendent of an all-male crew on a construction site operated by Boh Bros. Construction Company ("Boh Brothers"). During a three-day jury trial, the Equal Employment Opportunity Commission ("EEOC") presented evidence that Wolfe subjected Kerry Woods, an iron worker on Wolfe's crew, to almost-daily verbal and physical harassment because Woods did not conform to Wolfe's view of how a man should act. The jury found in favor of the EEOC on its hostile-environment claim, awarding compensatory and punitive damages. Boh Brothers appeals the district court's denial of its motion for judgment as a matter of law and motion for new trial. * * *

Woods is an iron worker and structural welder. Boh Brothers hired Woods on November 3, 2005, to work on crews repairing the Twin Spans bridges between New Orleans and Slidell after Hurricane Katrina. In January 2006, the company transferred Woods to a bridge-maintenance crew. Wolfe was the crew superintendent, with about five employees under his supervision.

The worksite was an undeniably vulgar place. Wolfe and the crew regularly used "very foul language" and "locker room talk." According to other crew members, Wolfe was a primary offender: he was "rough" and "mouthy" with his co-workers and often teased and "ribbed on" them.

By April 2006, Woods had become a specific and frequent target of Wolfe's abuse. Wolfe referred to Woods as "pu__y," "princess," and "fa__ot," often "two to three times a day." About two to three times per week—while Woods was bent over to perform a task—Wolfe approached him from behind and simulated anal intercourse with him. Woods felt "embarrassed and humiliated" by the name-calling and began to look over his shoulder before bending down. In addition, Wolfe exposed his penis to Woods about ten times while urinating, sometimes waving at Woods and smiling.

One time, Wolfe approached Woods while Woods was napping in his locked car during a break. According to Woods, Wolfe "looked like he was zipping his pants" and said, "[i]f your door wouldn't have been locked, my d_ck probably would have been in your mouth."

According to Wolfe, some of his teasing originated from Woods's use of Wet Ones instead of toilet paper, which Wolfe viewed as "kind of gay" and "feminine." In an interview with the EEOC, Wolfe explained:

> Mr. Woods sat at a table with a bunch of iron workers and told us that he brought, you know, feminine wipes—not feminine wipes—but Wet Ones or whatever to work with him because he didn't like it, didn't like to use toilet paper. It's [not] the kind of thing you'd want to say in front of a bunch [of] rough iron workers that they had there. They all picked on him about it. They said that's kind of feminine to bring these, that's for girls. To bring Wet Ones to work to wipe your ass, you damn sure don't sit in front of a bunch of iron workers and tell them about it. You keep that to yourself if in fact that's what you do.

Woods complained about Wolfe's treatment to his foreman, Tim Carpenter, "two or three times." Specifically, Woods said that he "didn't like how [Wolfe] spoke to" him and asked Carpenter to reprimand Wolfe for urinating on the bridge. According to Woods, he elected not to complain about all of Wolfe's behavior because he was afraid "to cause more of a conflict." * * *

* * * Woods [also met] with [Wayne] Duckworth, [the general superintendent for Boh Brothers' Heavy Highway Department]. * * * At the end of the conversation, Duckworth indicated that he would "look into" the alleged harassment. He sent Woods home without pay because, according to Duckworth, he feared "further problems" between Woods and Wolfe. Woods, believing that he had been fired, called Carpenter and asked him to intervene and "see if he could put [Woods] to work." Two days later, Carpenter called Woods and told him to report to work at the Almonaster yard.

Duckworth subsequently investigated Woods's complaint, although he did not document any aspect of his investigation. He spoke with both Wolfe and a crew foreman for about ten minutes each and determined that Wolfe's behavior, though unprofessional, did not constitute sexual harassment. Duckworth did not notify the company's general counsel about Woods's harassment allegations. * * *

Woods initially filed an EEOC charge questionnaire in November 2006, shortly after his removal from the Twin Spans maintenance crew, alleging he had been "fired" from that job and, three days later, hired to work at a different Boh Brothers location. In February 2007, Boh Brothers laid Woods off for lack of work. That March, Woods filed an EEOC charge of discrimination, alleging sexual harassment and, on the basis of his November 2006 removal from the maintenance crew, retaliation.

The EEOC brought this enforcement action on Woods's behalf in September 2009, claiming sexual harassment and retaliation under Title VII. Following a three-day trial, the jury returned a verdict in favor of Woods on the harassment claim and in favor of Boh Brothers on the retaliation claim. The jury awarded Woods $201,000 in compensatory damages and $250,000 in punitive damages. The district court reduced the compensatory damages award to $50,000 to comply with the $300,000 statutory damages cap. 42 U.S.C. § 1981a(b)(3)(D). Boh Brothers filed a renewed motion for judgment as a matter of law following entry of judgment and a motion for new trial, both of which the court denied. Boh Brothers timely appealed.

A panel of this court overturned the jury verdict. According to the panel, the evidence was insufficient as a matter of law to sustain the jury's finding that Wolfe discriminated against Woods "because of * * * sex" in violation of Title VII. *EEOC v. Boh Bros. Constr. Co., L.L.C.,* 689 F.3d 458, 459 (5th Cir.2012). The EEOC subsequently sought and obtained *en banc* review. * * *

[W]e must draw all reasonable inferences in the light most favorable to the verdict and cannot substitute other inferences that we might regard as more reasonable. * * *

[T]he most critical issues on appeal are whether the EEOC presented sufficient evidence that (1) Wolfe harassed Woods "because of * * * sex" as required by Title VII, and (2) Wolfe's harassment was severe or pervasive. We turn to the because-of-sex issue first.

At trial, the EEOC relied on gender-stereotyping evidence to prove that Woods suffered discrimination on the basis of sex. Specifically, the EEOC asserted that Wolfe harassed Woods because Woods was not a manly-enough man in Wolfe's eyes. On appeal, Boh Brothers argues that (1) the EEOC cannot, as a matter of law, rely on gender-stereotyping evidence to establish a same-sex harassment claim, and (2) even if it could, the evidence here was insufficient to sustain the jury verdict. As explained below, both of these arguments fail.

[Boh Brothers argued that the three evidentiary paths mentioned in *Oncale* "are the *exclusive* paths to success on a Title VII same-sex harassment claim." The court disagreed, noting that the *Oncale* Court "used 'for example' and '[w]hatever evidentiary route the plaintiff chooses to follow' in its discussion of those categories.'"] Boh Brothers further argues that, even if the EEOC's sex-stereotyping theory is cognizable in this context, the evidence is insufficient to support the jury's finding that Wolfe harassed Woods "because of * * * sex." We disagree.

In conducting this intent-based inquiry, we focus on the alleged harasser's subjective perception of the victim. Thus, even an employer's wrong or ill-informed assumptions about its employee may form the basis of a discrimination claim. *See, e.g., Black v. Pan Am. Labs., L.L.C.,* 646 F.3d 254, 260 (5th Cir.2011) (affirming a jury verdict in favor of a female sexual-harassment plaintiff who introduced evidence that decision-makers made sex-based comments—that "women [are] a detriment to the company," women "get hired on, get married, and/or get pregnant and they leave," and that the plaintiff did not need to worry about her sales quota because "it shouldn't matter to you, you're not the breadwinner anyway"—without requiring the plaintiff to show that her harasser's obviously sexist perceptions were true); *EEOC v. WC&M Enters., Inc.,* 496 F.3d 393, 401–02 (5th Cir.2007) (holding that a Muslim man's national-origin discrimination claim survived summary judgment even though his harassers did not know his country of origin). We do not require a plaintiff to prop up his employer's subjective discriminatory animus by proving that it was rooted in some objective truth; here, for example, that Woods was not, in fact, "manly." Rather, in considering the *motivation* behind a harasser's behavior, we look to evidence of the harasser's subjective view of the victim.

Applying these principles here, and drawing all reasonable inferences in the light most favorable to the verdict, there is enough evidence to support the jury's conclusion that Wolfe harassed Woods because of sex. Specifically, the EEOC offered evidence that Wolfe, the crew superintendent, thought that Woods was not a manly-enough man and taunted him tirelessly. Wolfe called Woods sex-based epithets like "fa—ot," "pu—y," and "princess," often "two to three times" per day. Wolfe himself admitted that these epithets were directed at Woods's masculinity:

Q. Now, when you said that Mr. Woods was kind of gay for using Wet Ones, you were saying that he was feminine; is that correct?

A. I didn't say he was gay. Said it * * * seemed kind of gay. * * *

Q. So you wouldn't say that he was gay, but you say his conduct was kind of gay?

A. Yes, sir[.]

Q. By saying that, you were saying he was feminine; correct?

A. Yes.

Q. You meant he was not being manly; is that correct?

A. Yes, sir.

Q. When you said that Mr. Woods'[s] conduct sounded like a homo, that again refers to Mr. Woods being feminine for using Wet Ones; is that correct?

A. Yes, sir * * *

Q. And * * * when you were talking with the EEOC investigator about the wet wipes or the Wet Ones, you initially called them feminine wipes; correct?

A. Yes, sir. I believe I did.

Q. And that's because you believed that Wet Ones [are] something that girls should use but men should not?

A. Or babies, yeah, that's correct.

Q. So you had stereotypes of how a man should act, and Mr. Woods didn't fit in to those stereotypes because he used Wet Ones and then talked about it in front of a bunch of hairy iron workers; correct?

A. I don't agree with that, no, no. He was an iron worker just like the rest of [t]hem. He performed and did his job just like everyone else. We was just playing. * * *

In addition to this name-calling, Wolfe mocked Woods with several other sexualized acts. For example, Woods testified that Wolfe would approach him from behind and "hump" him two to three times per week (which equates to more than 60 instances of simulated anal sex), that Wolfe exposed his genitals to Woods (sometimes while smiling and waving) about ten times, and that Wolfe suggested that he would put his penis in Woods's mouth.

Viewing the record as a whole, a jury could view Wolfe's behavior as an attempt to denigrate Woods because—at least in Wolfe's view—Woods fell outside of Wolfe's manly-man stereotype. Thus, we cannot say that no reasonable juror could have found that Woods suffered harassment because of his sex. Having reached this conclusion, we turn to the second critical question on appeal: whether the alleged abuse was sufficiently severe or pervasive to support Title VII liability.

Boh Brothers asserts that, even if Wolfe harassed Woods because of sex, the district court should have granted its Rule 50(b) motion because Wolfe's harassment was not severe or pervasive as a matter of law. * * * Woods specifically testified that he was a unique and constant target of Wolfe's abuse. For example, Woods testified on direct examination:

Q. In your experience, is it common on a construction site for this type of behavior you've described to take place?

A. No.

Q. Has any supervisor ever treated you like this at any other job you've held?

A. No.

Q. Has anybody ever treated you like this on any job you've held?

A. No.

Q. In your opinion, did Mr. Wolfe treat the other members of the maintenance crew the same way he treated you?

A. No.

Q. What was the difference?

A. He treated them—he treated them more like you're supposed to treat a grown man. He didn't pick—he didn't harass them like he harassed me all the time.

Q. Did you ever see Mr. Wolfe show somebody else his penis?

A.   No.

Q.   Did you ever hear Mr. Wolfe say anything about putting his penis in somebody's mouth to somebody else?

A.   No.

Wolfe himself conceded that he called *only* Woods "queer"; he did not recall whether he called anyone else "fa—ot," a name he used regarding Woods on a consistent basis. This, alongside all of the evidence discussed above * * * —the repeated humping, the reference to oral sex, etc.—is sufficient for a reasonable juror to conclude that Wolfe's harassment was sufficiently severe or pervasive to alter the conditions of Woods's employment. Wolfe hurled raw sex-based epithets uniquely at Woods two-to-three times a day, almost every day, for months on end. We have upheld a jury verdict on analogous facts. Accordingly, we conclude that there was sufficient evidence for a reasonable juror to conclude that Wolfe's harassment of Woods was severe or pervasive.

E. GRADY JOLLY, CIRCUIT JUDGE, dissenting,

Let me first acknowledge that the facts and language in this case, which occurred in an all-male workforce on an ironworker construction site, are not for tender ears. The vulgarities can cast turmoil in a strong stomach, but that does not mean that the laws of the United States have been violated, and it does not require Title VII and the EEOC to serve as federal enforcer of clean talk in a single sex workforce.

The majority notes that the EEOC "may rely on evidence that Wolfe viewed Woods as insufficiently masculine to prove its Title VII claim." That may be true, but the fatal vacuum in the majority's reasoning is that the EEOC, in fact, produced no evidence that Wolfe believed Woods was not a "manly man." This lack of regard for the very foundational requirement that some *reason* for alleged sexual discrimination be presented allows this alleged same-sex stereotyping case to untether Title VII from its current mooring in sexual discrimination. Its application now veers from the realm of valid action against actual *sexual* harassment to a new world, in which Title VII prevents not only sexual harassment, but also myriad other undesirable conduct—regardless of whether that conduct, in fact, even resembles *sexual discrimination*. Accordingly, I respectfully dissent.

While the Supreme Court has made clear that same-sex sexual harassment claims are cognizable under Title VII, it has further acknowledged that proving such claims is more demanding and cumbersome than proving traditional opposite-sex sexual harassment claims. *See Oncale v. Sundowner Offshore Servs., Inc.*, 523 U.S. 75, 80–81, 118 S.Ct. 998, 140 L.Ed.2d 201 (1998). Thus, in *Oncale* the Court recognized that there must be some identifiable basis for inferring that an alleged harasser is intending to discriminate against a victim on the basis of his or her sex in same-sex discrimination cases. For instance, the Court observed that same-sex harassment claims could be viable when there is credible evidence a harasser is homosexual, or when it has been made clear "the harasser is motivated by general hostility to the presence of [members of his or her same sex] in the workplace," or when there is "direct comparative evidence about how the alleged harasser treated members of both sexes in a mixed-sex workplace." *Id.* at 80. Each of these examples is a mechanism for ascertaining an intent to discriminate based upon sex. It is compelling, in the first instance, that none of these factors are present in this case.

But regardless of whether there are other methods for making this determination, the EEOC proffered no basis for inferring discriminatory intent based upon Woods's sex—subjective or objective. Rather, it moves quickly from asserting that other evidentiary paths are available to a conclusion that, because Wolfe targeted certain words and acts at Woods, Wolfe's mal intent to sexually discriminate against Woods was proved. This line of reasoning completely abdicates the burden prescribed to plaintiffs in same-sex sexual discrimination cases by the Supreme Court in *Oncale*—which is not simply to assert the basis for the inference of harassment based upon sex, but to further prove the truth of that assertion. The *Oncale* Court specifically held "[t]he same chain of inference" present in male-female sexual harassment claims—i.e., the assumption that certain "proposals would not have been made to someone of the same sex"—is available in same-sex sexual harassment cases only if an additional step is taken to illuminate the basis of the inference. *Id.* at 80, 118 S.Ct. 998. Unlike opposite sex Title VII claims, therefore, in same-sex suits a plaintiff must elucidate and prove the premise of his assertion that the harassment is *because of* sex—it is not assumed automatically.

In this case, the EEOC's proffered premise is that Wolfe subjectively believed Woods was somehow not "manly." But the only evidence the EEOC provided supporting this premise related to Woods's use of Wet Ones; Wolfe himself testified that, aside from this, he emphatically did not believe or consider Woods feminine, but, instead, Woods was "an iron worker just like the rest of [t]hem." And Woods himself offered no other explanation as to why he believed Wolfe was sexually harassing him, as opposed to simply taunting him as Wolfe did every other iron worker on the all-male job site. Indeed, Woods never stated that he felt Wolfe called him names and behaved crudely with him because Wolfe believed Woods did not conform to gender norms. Thus, even the plaintiff did not contend his alleged harasser harassed him because he did not act "manly."

Moreover, there is simply no evidence, garnered from Woods, Wolfe, or any of the other men who testified, that Woods failed objectively to conform to traditional "male gender norms." The majority notes that "[w]e do not require a plaintiff to prop up his employer's subjective discriminatory animus by proving that it was rooted in some objective truth." In other cases this assertion may be true. When, however, the subjective discriminatory animus of the employer is itself in question, objective evidence may be necessary to demonstrate the presence or absence of such an intent. *See, e.g., Medina v. Income Support Div., New Mexico,* 413 F.3d 1131, 1135 (10th Cir.2005) (finding no sexual harassment based upon gender stereotyping when "there [wa]s no evidence * * * that [the plaintiff] did not dress or behave like a stereotypical woman"). If a victim possesses no characteristics, exhibited or unexhibited, of nonconformance with gender stereotypes, then there would appear to be no basis for an alleged harasser to possess a subjective intent to discriminate against that victim because of nonconformance. And in cases such as this, where the alleged harasser does not consider the victim to be unmanly—and even the victim does not testify otherwise—and the alleged harasser further treats the victim with the same or similar disrespect with which he treats his other coworkers, we are left without anything tethering a claim of discrimination because of sex to the realities of the workplace. To reach any other conclusion is to say that when a supervisor persists in referring to an unquestionably manly man as a sissy, the laws of the United States have been broken, requiring the full force of the United States executive and judiciary to descend upon some small business and extract hundreds of thousands of dollars in fees and damages from its till. Such a result is simply at odds with Title VII, which is only violated in cases of discrimination based upon the victim's sex.

The majority * * * relies on the harassment, in and of itself, as a substitute for actual evidence reflecting a subjective intent of Wolfe to engage in *sex* discrimination against Woods—completely ignoring the all male iron worker environment where it occurred. The majority thus engages in a distraction from the proper legal analysis by treating this case as if it were sexual harassment between male and female when the inference of sex discrimination may be presumed by words and conduct. In same-sex sexual harassment cases, particularly in an all-male workforce where rowdy language is commonplace, the reason for harassment (i.e. whether it is because of *sex*) must be distilled and proved by the plaintiff, a showing which the majority has utterly failed in making. The majority should call it for what it is: immature and gutter behavior between and among male coworkers. And then drop it.

It is especially inappropriate in this case to assume that Wolfe's use of words like "pu—y" and "fa—ot" necessarily connoted a desire to sexually discriminate, because all of the evidence indicates Wolfe used these and similar words towards the other men on site on a daily basis. In fact, the record is replete with testimony that Wolfe was vulgar with everyone on site, aiming derogatory terms with sexual innuendoes at each of them, exposing himself to them, and pretending to "hump" several men on site. And while Wolfe was unquestionably the crudest ironworker on the site, the evidence indicates all the men were generally more vulgar here than they would have been in a mixed-sex society, and that such sexually-charged words were bandied about regularly. The EEOC has identified no basis for presuming that Wolfe directed these words and actions at Woods, particularly, or at any of the other ironworkers for that matter, out of a subjective intent to sexually discriminate against him or them. This failure should end the discussion and the case. * * *

Finally, the majority opinion takes no account of the overall social context in which this case occurred. It is important to the case, and to any conclusion of sexual harassment, that these actions occurred in an all-male environment and on the construction site. This setting is customarily vulgar and crude. And the Supreme Court has clearly and repeatedly held that "an appropriate sensitivity to social context," and a recognition that the same actions taken on "the field" versus in the office are importantly different, are considerations preventing Title VII from mutating into an all-encompassing code of civility. *Oncale,* 523 U.S. at 81. In fact, the Court explicitly found that "[t]he real social impact of workplace behavior depends on a constellation of surrounding circumstances, expectations, and relationships which are not fully captured by a simple recitation of the words used or the physical acts performed." *Id.* at 81–82. Despite this clear admonition, the majority quotes extensively from the record and recounts various actions in which Wolfe engaged without ever taking account of the environment surrounding these events, or explaining how behavior occurring on and characteristic of the construction site can constitute *sexual* harassment. * * *

EDITH H. JONES, CIRCUIT JUDGE, dissenting,

Bad facts often inspire bad law. And sex talk doesn't always mean that sex is involved. Supervisor Wolfe's conduct was, indeed, bad, boorish and juvenile. What elevated grossness in an all-male environment to a Title VII claim of employment discrimination "because of" Woods's "sex"? The EEOC had to offer an expert witness to explain its case. That should tell us something. In Title VII opposite-sex cases, we need no expert to explain the employment implications of sexual come-ons, put-downs, pat-downs, and stereotyping. Here, an all-male, heterosexual crew was performing a "macho" job. We know that men behave differently when women aren't around (as do women surrounded by women). No physical touching, threats, sexual *quid pro quo,* or employment retaliation was imposed on the plaintiff. Yet without such hard proof of sexually-motivated harassment, the majority affirms a substantial sexual harassment verdict for Kerry Woods. * * * [B]ased on this decision, every one of Woods's co-workers could have filed suit against Boh Brothers.

This decision, however, goes further than its application to single-sex workplaces. EEOC claimed to advocate that there is "no coarse workplace exclusion" from Title VII, especially for classically male locales like the oil patch. What it has persuaded the majority to adopt is the disturbing proposition that, to avoid exposure to Title VII liability, employers must purge every workplace of speech and gestures that might be viewed in any way as tokens of sex discrimination. Consider the attached memorandum, "Etiquette for Ironworkers," which suggests how prudent employers may respond to the majority decision. * * *

ETIQUETTE FOR IRONWORKERS

MEMO TO: Management

FROM: Legal Department of Apex Co.

DATE: September 2013

In keeping up with the newest developments in employment law, we have carefully reviewed and hired specialist outside counsel to give us a legal opinion concerning the implications of a recent Fifth Circuit en banc decision [in] *EEOC v. Boh Bros*. Like us, the employer in that case engaged in heavy construction and often operated in all-male crews. Like us, it had an unblemished record, years without a Title VII case. But the court ruled that common sexual epithets and vulgar gestures, when used too frequently by a male, heterosexual supervisor, can support a verdict against the company on behalf of another male, heterosexual plaintiff. Instead of looking on these actions as horseplay or, at worst, bullying, the court approved a jury verdict for "gender-stereotyping harassment." The EEOC intends to make this case an example for similar workplaces.

We need not advise you of the costs a company can incur in these cases. In addition to hundreds of thousands in outside legal fees, a judgment for damages may run into six figures. The EEOC requested, and got, a sweeping and intrusive injunction that will require significant expenditures in paperwork compliance costs and regular workplace sensitivity training for over one thousand employees.

To avert these consequences, we recommend that the company immediately issue the following rules for proper, non-gender-stereotyping workplace behavior. Employees should be informed that the rules apply across the board, to all-male, all-female, and mixed-sex offices and positions. The workplace must be cleansed of speech and actions that may be misperceived or twisted as reflecting gender stereotyping harassment.

NOTICE CONCERNING TITLE VII

To our Associates:

You are all aware of this company's unwavering policy to prevent discrimination of any kind based on sex, race, religion or national origin. Because of a new court decision, we must now focus on eliminating same-sex "gender stereotyping" of any kind as well. This means that men may expose this company to liability for their speech and behavior in the presence of other men, and women in the presence of other women. Although these rules will apply throughout the company, you IRONWORKERS have to take special notice. The rules apply throughout the workday, during breaks and lunch hours, and whenever two or more workers are gathered together.

1.   At the most general level, all employees must refrain from any communication—spoken, written, or gesticulated—that may create any suggestion of "sexual stereotyping" or "gender-based bullying." Please consider the broad implications of this prohibition, some of which follow. All employee interactions must be fully gender inclusive (or at least gender ambiguous). Careless phrases and jokes will not be tolerated if they may be interpreted to carry a stereotyping overtone.

2.   No more banter about bodily functions, sexual or otherwise, or human physical appearance. Those who do not enjoy references to sweat, toilet humor, tattoos, tight jeans, muscles, or large beards may feel singled out as not "man enough" for such speech.

3.   Do not discuss the appearance of women or any intimate sexual encounters, and do not refer to or use words that refer to sex in any way. This includes CUSS WORDS.

4.   Do not swivel your hips, make obscene gestures or mimic "twerking."

5.   Avoid discussing topics that may be viewed as "non-inclusive": bodybuilding, Boy Scouts, hunting, fishing, and riflery. Football and other "macho" sports may be an unwelcome subject to those who consider them boorishly aggressive.

6.   Do not engage in any competitive activity, like lifting heavy objects, on the worksite. This can create a sense of unmanly inferiority for non-participants.

7.   Do not use gender-stereotyped nicknames or name-calling. Supervisors may not encourage you to work harder by saying "put your backs into it," or "man up," and terms like "ladies" or "sissies" will be grounds for immediate discipline.

8.   Schoolyard humor, which is common at our jobsites to fill down-times and relieve boredom, raises sensitive issues. Some workers may be put off by jokes about personal grooming, scented deodorant, chest hair, or clothing as a form of gender hostility. Poking fun at a worker for drinking a diet soda, not being able to eat a raw jalapeno, using "Wet Ones" or "Purell" to clean himself, or calling someone a "wimp" or "wuss" or "geek" may get us sued and you in serious trouble.

9.   Asinine locker room behavior is forbidden. Examples of this would be comments about anatomy, crude gestures, actions like towel-swatting, simulated sexual acts, and any behavior that would make someone ill at ease with his personal expression of his gender. Relieving yourself in the presence of others is forbidden; the company is reconfiguring all restrooms to prevent any worker from observing another worker's bodily functions.

10. Avoid touching any coworker in any manner, except if asked to rescue the person from physical danger, and even then, avoid touching private areas.

PENALTIES: A first violation of these rules will result in a warning, a second violation in suspension without pay, and successive violations will result in termination. We will not call this a "three-strikes" policy, as that term might be interpreted to refer to the principally male sport of baseball. We need hardly explain that any worker terminated for same-sex gender stereotyping will have a hard time finding future employment.

The Company will conduct quarterly sensitivity sessions, where you can learn more about offensive gender stereotyping against fellow males and what you can do to prevent or correct it. As questions arise at any time, call our newly hired Sex Stereotype Counselor in the HR Department.

[Dissenting opinions by SMITH, J., and DEMOSS, J., are omitted].

NOTES

1.   The Court in *Oncale* concluded that it was appropriate to infer that different-sex sexual harassment constitutes sex discrimination "because the challenged conduct typically involves explicit or implicit proposals of sexual activity; it is reasonable to assume those proposals would not have been made to someone of the same sex." *Oncale v. Sundowner Offshore Services, Inc.*, 523 U.S. 75, 80, 118 S.Ct. 998, 140 L.Ed.2d 201 (1998). Why is it reasonable to so assume? Is it because most people are heterosexual?

2.   Plaintiffs in some post-*Oncale* same-sex sexual harassment cases have had a difficult time establishing that the harassment was "because of sex." Part of the problem seems to be that several courts have not been persuaded that the harassment was motivated by the plaintiffs' sex, as

opposed to by their sexual orientation. In *Simonton v. Runyon*, 232 F.3d 33, 35 (2d Cir. 2000), for example, the plaintiff (Simonton) alleged that

> his co-workers repeatedly assaulted him with such comments as "go fuck yourself, fag," "suck my dick," and "so you like it up the ass?" Notes were placed on the wall in the employees' bathroom with Simonton's name and the name of celebrities who had died of AIDS. Pornographic photographs were taped to his work area, male dolls were placed in his vehicle, and copies of Playgirl magazine were sent to his home. Pictures of an erect penis were posted in his work place, as were posters stating that Simonton suffered from mental illness as a result of "bung hole disorder." There were repeated statements that Simonton was a "fucking faggot."

Although the court noted that the alleged behavior was "morally reprehensible," it dismissed the Title VII claim, deeming it to be based on an allegation of sexual orientation, rather than sex, discrimination. Other courts have reached the same conclusion in similar cases. *See, e.g., Higgins v. New Balance Athletic Shoe, Inc.*, 194 F.3d 252 (1st Cir. 1999); *Bibby v. Philadelphia Coca-Cola Bottling Co.*, 260 F.3d 257 (3rd Cir. 2001).

3.   Christopher Vickers worked as a private police officer at an Ohio hospital. After some of his co-workers began suspecting that he might be gay, they started to harass him. They frequently called him a "fag," subjected him to vulgar gestures, and made lewd remarks suggesting that Vickers provide them with sexual favors. During a training on how to use handcuffs, one of the co-workers handcuffed Vickers and then simulated sex with him while another co-worker photographed the incident. "On other occasions, Vickers' co-workers repeatedly touched his crotch with a tape measure, grabbed Vickers' chest while making derogatory comments, tried to shove a sanitary napkin in Vickers' face, and simulated sex with a stuffed animal and then tried to push the stuffed animal into Vickers' crotch." *Vickers v. Fairfield Med. Ctr.*, 453 F.3d 757, 760 (6th Cir. 2006).

The Sixth Circuit Court of Appeals upheld the dismissal of Vickers's gender stereotyping claim by reasoning that "a gender stereotyping claim should not be used to bootstrap protection for sexual orientation into Title VII." *Id.* at 764. The court added that if Vickers succeeded with his claim, "any discrimination based on sexual orientation would be actionable under a sex stereotyping theory * * *, as all homosexuals, by definition, fail to conform to traditional gender norms in their sexual practices." *Id.* The court also rejected the sex harassment claim: "Nothing in Vickers' complaint indicates that his harassers acted out of sexual desire. Similarly, the complaint does not support an inference that there was general hostility toward men in the workplace. Finally, Vickers included no information regarding how women were treated in comparison to men at [the hospital]. In fact, defendants-appellees maintain that Vickers worked in an all-male workforce, an assertion that Vickers has apparently not disputed." *Id.* at 7654.

4. It is important that lawyers representing plaintiffs in same-sex sexual harassment cases under Title VII think carefully about how to handle evidence relating to harassment on the basis of sexual orientation. Focusing on such evidence, without linking it to discrimination "because of sex," might imperil the lawsuit. For example, the court in *Simonton, supra* Note 2, concluded that it was not possible "to infer from the [plaintiff's] complaint that the harassment [he] suffered was because of his sex and not, *as he urges throughout his complaint,* because of his sexual orientation." *Simonton,* 232 F.3d at 37 (emphasis added).

The fact, however, that there might have been discrimination on the basis of sexual orientation, alongside discrimination "because of sex," should not be held against plaintiffs in Title VII cases because "they do[ ] not need to allege that [they] suffered discrimination on the basis of [their] sex *alone* or that sexual orientation played no part in their treatment." *Centola v. Potter,* 183 F. Supp. 2d 403, 409 (D. Mass. 2002) (emphasis added). Part of the problem, of course, is that "the line between discrimination because of sexual orientation and discrimination because of sex is hardly clear." *Id.* at 408. While some judges may believe that they can neatly distinguish between both types of discrimination, it is not clear that the individuals who engage in the harassing conduct make such distinctions. Male supervisors and co-employees, for example, may dislike a male employee who is perceived to be gay and effeminate both because of his sexual orientation and because he does not "act like a man."

5. In *Rene v. MGM Grand Hotel,* 305 F.3d 1061 (9th Cir. 2002) (en banc), *cert. denied,* 538 U.S. 922, 123 S.Ct. 1573, 155 L.Ed.2d 313 (2003), the full U.S. Court of Appeals for the Ninth Circuit reversed the granting of a summary judgment motion filed by the employer in a same-sex sexual harassment case. The plaintiff in *Rene,* who worked as a butler for a Las Vegas hotel,

> provided extensive evidence that, over the course of a two-year period, his supervisor and several of his fellow butlers subjected him to a hostile work environment on almost a daily basis. The harassers' conduct included whistling and blowing kisses at Rene, calling him "sweetheart" and "muñeca" (Spanish for "doll"), telling crude jokes and giving sexually oriented "joke" gifts, and forcing Rene to look at pictures of naked men having sex. On "more times than [Rene said he] could possibly count," the harassment involved offensive physical conduct of a sexual nature. Rene gave deposition testimony that he was caressed and hugged and that his coworkers would "touch [his] body like they would to a woman." On numerous occasions, he said, they grabbed him in the crotch and poked their fingers in his anus through his clothing. When asked what he believed was the motivation behind this harassing behavior, Rene responded that the behavior occurred because he is gay.

Id. at 1064. The court, in a plurality opinion, concluded that the conduct in question was "of a sexual nature" and that it was therefore enough to establish a cause of action of sexual harassment under Title VII. *Id.* at 1068. The plurality noted that

> [i]n granting MGM Grand's motion for summary judgment, the district court did not deny that the sexual assaults alleged by Rene were so objectively offensive that they created a hostile working environment. Rather, it appears to have held that Rene's otherwise viable cause of action was defeated because he believed he was targeted because he is gay. This is not the law. We have surveyed the many cases finding a violation of Title VII based on the offensive touching of the genitalia, buttocks, or breasts of women. In none of those cases has a court denied relief because the victim was, or might have been, a lesbian. The sexual orientation of the victim was simply irrelevant. If sexual orientation is irrelevant for a female victim, we see no reason why it is not also irrelevant for a male victim.

Id. at 1066. A concurring opinion also sided with the plaintiff, but under the theory that he had made out a case of gender stereotyping harassment. *See id.* at 1064 (Pregerson, J., concurring). For its part, the dissent took issue with the notion that harassment of a "sexual nature" was enough to satisfy the statute's causation requirement in a same-sex sexual harassment case: "The alleged harassment in this case was not on account of the plaintiff's sex, i.e., this plaintiff was not treated differently from all the other male butlers because he was male. Rene contended [instead] that he was treated differently because he was homosexual." *Id.* at 1074 (Hug, J., dissenting). The dissenting opinion also concluded that the plaintiff did not claim "before the district court that the harassment [he] experienced was because he acted effeminately on the job, or for any reason other than his sexual orientation. The first line of the legal argument presented to the district court in opposition to the motion for summary judgment crystalizes this point in stating: 'The question raised by the motion is whether the conduct as alleged by Rene is prohibited by Title VII even though it was directed at Rene because of his sexual orientation.' " *Id.* at 1077.

6.   Courts have split on the question of whether Title VII polices the so-called "bisexual harasser" who sexually harasses subordinates regardless of their gender. Since an "equal opportunity" harasser arguably treats men and women in the same way, some courts have concluded that that harassment is not "because of sex." *See, e.g., EEOC v. Harbert-Yeargin, Inc.,* 266 F.3d 498, 520 (6th Cir. 2001) (noting that if the harasser "had been an equal opportunity gooser, there would be no cause of action here."); *Holman v. State of Indiana,* 211 F.3d 399, 403 (7th Cir. 2000) ("Title VII does not cover the 'equal opportunity' or 'bisexual' harasser * * * because such a person is not *discriminating* on the basis of sex."); *Barnes v. Costle,* 561 F.2d 983, 990 n. 55 (D.C. Cir. 1977) ("In case of the bisexual superior, the insistence upon sexual favors would not constitute gender discrimination because it would apply to

male and female employees alike."). Other courts have rejected this view. *See, e.g., Brown v. Henderson*, 257 F.3d 246, 254 (2d Cir. 2001) ("the inquiry into whether ill treatment was actually sex-based discrimination cannot be short-circuited by the mere fact that both men and women are involved"). *See also McDonnell v. Cisneros*, 84 F.3d 256, 260 (7th Cir. 1996) ("It would be exceedingly perverse if a male worker could buy his supervisors and his company immunity from Title VII liability by taking care to harass sexually an occasional male worker, though his preferred targets were female.").

7.   While the bisexuality of the harasser might undermine a sexual harassment claim, the homosexuality of the harasser might bolster it. Recall that in *Oncale*, the Supreme Court stated that

> [c]ourts and juries have found the inference of discrimination easy to draw in most male-female sexual harassment situations, because the challenged conduct typically involves explicit or implicit proposals of sexual activity; it is reasonable to assume those proposals would not have been made to someone of the same sex. *The same chain of inference would be available to a plaintiff alleging same-sex harassment, if there were credible evidence that the harasser was homosexual.*

Oncale, 523 U.S. at 80 (emphasis added). The emphasized sentence has given rise to cases in which plaintiffs have attempted to make out their harassment claims by trying to establish the same-sex sexual orientation of their harassers. *See, e.g., Love v. Motiva Enterprises*, 2009 WL 3334610, at *2–3 (Ct. App. 5th Cir. 2009); La Day v. Catalyst Technology, Inc., 302 F.3d 474, 480–81 (5th Cir. 2002); *Cooke v. Stefani Mgmt. Servs., Inc.*, 250 F.3d 564, 565–66 (7th Cir. 2001); *Shepherd v. Slater Steels Corp.*, 168 F.3d 998, 1009–1010 (7th Cir. 1999); *Merritt v. Delaware River Port Auth.*, 1999 WL 285900, at *3–4 (E.D. Pa. 1999). Although most of these courts spent time discussing the harassers' sexual orientation, it is not clear that *Oncale* requires that type of inquiry in cases where plaintiffs seek to use the existence of sexual desire to establish that the discrimination was "because of sex." As one federal Court of Appeals has put it,

> a plaintiff need not, in every first-evidentiary-route [i.e. sexual desire] case, establish that her harasser is homosexual in order to demonstrate that the harassing conduct was motivated by sexual desire. * * * [It is possible] that an alleged harasser may consider herself "heterosexual" but nonetheless propose or desire sexual activity with another woman in a harassing manner. In that scenario, evidence of homosexuality beyond that of her conduct itself may not be forthcoming, although the harasser still acted out of sexual desire. Indeed, aside from testimonial evidence or the fact of the harassing conduct, we find it would often be extremely difficult to obtain evidence tending to show a person's sexual orientation. Therefore, while the fact that the harasser is homosexual may support a finding that her conduct was motivated by sexual desire,

we do not read *Oncale* to require a plaintiff to demonstrate, in every first-evidentiary-route case, such a fact. We emphasize that *Oncale's* first evidentiary route turns on whether the harasser acted out of sexual desire. A plaintiff who makes this showing establishes that the harassment took place because of her sex, regardless whether she has also demonstrated that her harasser is homosexual.

Dick v. Phone Directories Company, Inc., 397 F.3d 1256, 1265 (10th Cir. 2005).

8. In addition to pursuing sexual harassment and/or gender stereotyping claims under Title VII, lesbians, gay men, and bisexuals in twenty-two states (CA, CO, CT, DE, HW, IA, IL, MA, MD, ME, MN, NH, NJ, NV, NM, NY, OR, RI, UT, VT, WI, WA) and the District of Columbia can sue under state statutes prohibiting employment discrimination on the basis of sexual orientation. For examples of such lawsuits, see *Wiedemeier v. AWS Convergence Technologies*, Inc. 2009 WL 3165746 (Cal.App. 2 Dist. 2009); *Dominguez v. Washington Mutual* Bank, 168 Cal.App.4th 714, 85 Cal.Rptr.3d 705 (2008); *Cookson v. Brewer Sch. Dep't*, 2009 ME 57, 974 A.2d 276 (2009); *Kwiatkowski v. Merrill Lynch*, 2008 WL 3875417 (N.J.Super.A.D. 2008); *Taylor v. N.Y.U Med. Ctr.*, 21 Misc.3d 23, 871 N.Y.S.2d 568 (App.Term 2008). There are also currently over 250 municipalities that have local ordinances prohibiting employment discrimination on the basis of sexual orientation.

c. *Sexual Orientation Discrimination as Per Se Sex Discrimination: The EEOC's Position*

BALDWIN V. FOXX

U.S. Equal Employment Opportunity Commission, 2015
2015 WL 4397641

At the time of events giving rise to this complaint, Complainant worked as a Supervisory Air Traffic Control Specialist at the Agency's Southern Region, Air Traffic Division, Air Traffic Control Tower/International Airport in Miami, Florida.

On August 28, 2012, Complainant contacted an EEO [Equal Employment Opportunity] Counselor and on December 21, 2012, filed a formal EEO complaint alleging that the Agency subjected him to discrimination on the bases of sex (male, sexual orientation) and reprisal for prior protected EEO activity when, on July 26, 2012, he learned that he was not selected for a permanent position as a Front Line Manager (FLM) at the Miami Tower TRACON facility (the Miami facility). * * * Complainant alleged that he was not selected because he is gay. He alleged that his supervisor, who was involved in the selection process for the permanent position, made several negative comments about Complainant's sexual orientation. For example, Complainant stated that in May 2011, when he mentioned that he and his partner had attended

Mardi Gras in New Orleans, the supervisor said, "We don't need to hear about that gay stuff." He also alleged that the supervisor told him on a number of occasions that he was "a distraction in the radar room" when his participation in conversations included mention of his male partner.

* * * Title VII's prohibition of sex discrimination means that employers may not "rel[y] upon sex-based considerations" or take gender into account when making employment decisions. This applies equally in claims brought by lesbian, gay, and bisexual individuals under Title VII.

When an employee raises a claim of sexual orientation discrimination as sex discrimination under Title VII, the question is not whether sexual orientation is explicitly listed in Title VII as a prohibited basis for employment actions. It is not. Rather, the question for purposes of Title VII coverage of a sexual orientation claim is the same as any other Title VII case involving allegations of sex discrimination—whether the agency has "relied on sex-based considerations" or "take[n] gender into account" when taking the challenged employment action.

In the case before us, we conclude that Complainant's claim of sexual orientation discrimination alleges that the Agency relied on sex-based considerations and took his sex into account in its employment decision regarding the permanent FLM position. Complainant, therefore, has stated a claim of sex discrimination. Indeed, we conclude that sexual orientation is inherently a "sex-based consideration," and an allegation of discrimination based on sexual orientation is necessarily an allegation of sex discrimination under Title VII. A complainant alleging that an agency took his or her sexual orientation into account in an employment action necessarily alleges that the agency took his or her sex into account.

Discrimination on the basis of sexual orientation is premised on sex-based preferences, assumptions, expectations, stereotypes, or norms. "Sexual orientation" as a concept cannot be defined or understood without reference to sex. A man is referred to as "gay" if he is physically and/or emotionally attracted to other men. A woman is referred to as "lesbian" if she is physically and/or emotionally attracted to other women. Someone is referred to as "heterosexual" or "straight" if he or she is physically and/or emotionally attracted to someone of the opposite-sex. It follows, then, that sexual orientation is inseparable from and inescapably linked to sex and, therefore, that allegations of sexual orientation discrimination involve sex-based considerations. One can describe this inescapable link between allegations of sexual orientation discrimination and sex discrimination in a number of ways.

Sexual orientation discrimination is sex discrimination because it necessarily entails treating an employee less favorably because of the employee's sex. For example, assume that an employer suspends a lesbian employee for displaying a photo of her female spouse on her desk, but does not suspend a male employee for displaying a photo of his female spouse on his desk. The lesbian employee in that example can allege that her employer took an adverse action against her that the employer would not have taken had she been male. That is a legitimate claim under Title VII that sex was unlawfully taken into account in the adverse employment action. The same result holds true if the person discriminated against is straight. Assume a woman is suspended because she has placed a picture of her husband on her desk but her gay colleague is not suspended after he places a picture of his husband on his desk. The straight female employee could bring a cognizable Title VII claim of disparate treatment because of sex.

The court in *Hall v. BNSF Ry. Co.*, No. 13–2160, 2014 WL 4719007 (W.D. Wash. 2014) adopted this analysis of Title VII. In that case, the court found that the plaintiff, a male who was married to another male, alleged sex discrimination under Title VII when he stated that he "experienced adverse employment action in the denial of the spousal health benefit, due to sex, where similarly situated females [married to males] were treated more favorably by getting the benefit." Id. at *2. The court recognized that the sexual orientation discrimination alleged by the plaintiff constituted an allegation that the employer was treating female employees with male partners more favorably than male employees with male partners simply because of the employee's sex.

Sexual orientation discrimination is also sex discrimination because it is associational discrimination on the basis of sex. That is, an employee alleging discrimination on the basis of sexual orientation is alleging that his or her employer took his or her sex into account by treating him or her differently for *associating* with a person of the same sex. For example, a gay man who alleges that his employer took an adverse employment action against him because he associated with or dated men states a claim of sex discrimination under Title VII; the fact that the employee is a man instead of a woman motivated the employer's discrimination against him. Similarly, a heterosexual man who alleges a gay supervisor denied him a promotion because he dates women instead of men states an actionable Title VII claim of discrimination because of his sex.

In applying Title VII's prohibition of race discrimination, courts and the Commission have consistently concluded that the statute prohibits discrimination based on an employee's association with a person of another race, such as an interracial marriage or friendship. This is because an employment action based on an employee's relationship with a person of another race necessarily involves considerations of the employee's race, and thus constitutes discrimination because of the employee's race.

This analysis is not limited to the context of race discrimination. Title VII "on its face treats each of the enumerated categories"—race, color, religion, sex, and national origin—"exactly the same." *Price Waterhouse*, 490 U.S. at 243 n.9 ("[O]ur specific references to gender throughout this opinion, and the principles we announce, apply with equal force to discrimination based on race, religion, or national origin.").

Therefore, Title VII similarly prohibits employers from treating an employee or applicant differently than other employees or applicants based on the fact that such individuals are in a same-sex marriage or because the employee has a personal association with someone of a particular sex. Adverse action on that basis is, "by definition," discrimination because of the employee or applicant's sex.

Sexual orientation discrimination also is sex discrimination because it necessarily involves discrimination based on gender stereotypes. In *Price Waterhouse*, the Court reaffirmed that Congress intended Title VII to "strike at the entire spectrum of disparate treatment of men and women resulting from sex stereotypes." 490 U.S. at 251. In the wake of *Price Waterhouse*, courts and the Commission have recognized that lesbian, gay, and bisexual individuals can bring claims of gender stereotyping under Title VII if such individuals demonstrate that they were treated adversely because they were viewed—based on their appearance, mannerisms, or conduct—as insufficiently "masculine" or "feminine." But as the Commission and a number of federal courts have concluded in cases dating from 2002 onwards, discrimination against people who are lesbian, gay, or bisexual on the basis of gender stereotypes often involves far more than assumptions about overt masculine or feminine behavior.

Sexual orientation discrimination and harassment "[are] often, if not always, motivated by a desire to enforce heterosexually defined gender norms." *Centola v. Potter*, 183 F. Supp. 2d 403, 410 (D. Mass. 2002). The *Centola* court continued:

> In fact, stereotypes about homosexuality are directly related to our stereotypes about the proper roles of men and women. While one paradigmatic form of stereotyping occurs when co-workers single out an effeminate man for scorn, in fact, the issue is far more complex. The harasser may discriminate against an openly gay co-worker, or a co-worker that he perceives to be gay, whether effeminate or not, because he thinks, "real" men should date women, and not other men.

Id. * * *

In the past, courts have often failed to view claims of discrimination by lesbian, gay, and bisexual employees in the straightforward manner described above. Indeed, many courts have gone to great lengths to distinguish adverse employment actions based on "sex" from adverse employment actions based on "sexual orientation." The stated justification for such intricate parsing of language has been the bare conclusion that "Title VII does not prohibit * * * discrimination because of sexual orientation." For that reason, courts have attempted to distinguish discrimination based on sexual orientation from discrimination based on sex, even while noting that the "borders [between the two classes] are * * * imprecise."

Some of these decisions reason that Congress in 1964 did not intend Title VII to apply to sexual orientation and, therefore, Title VII could not be interpreted to prohibit such discrimination. See, e.g., DeSantis v. Pacific Telephone & Telegraph Co., 608 F.2d 327, 329 (9th Cir. 1979) ("Congress had only the traditional notions of 'sex' in mind" when it passed Title VII and those "traditional notions" did not include sexual orientation or sexual preference), abrogated by Nichols v. Azteca Restaurant Enterprises, Inc., 256 F.3d 864, 875 (9th Cir. 2001).

Congress may not have envisioned the application of Title VII to these situations. But as a unanimous Court stated in *Oncale v. Sundowner Offshore Services, Inc.*, "statutory prohibitions often go beyond the principal evil [they were passed to combat] to cover reasonably comparable evils, and it is ultimately the provisions of our laws rather than the principal concerns of our legislators by which we are governed." 523 U.S. 75, 79, 7880 (1998) (holding that same-sex harassment is actionable under Title VII). Interpreting the sex discrimination prohibition of Title VII to exclude coverage of lesbian, gay or bisexual individuals who have experienced discrimination on the basis of sex inserts a limitation into the text that Congress has not included. Nothing in the text of Title VII "suggests that Congress intended to confine the benefits of [the] statute to heterosexual employees alone." Heller v. Columbia Edgewater Country Club, 195 F. Supp. 2d. 1212, 1222 (D. Or. 2002).

Some courts have also relied on the fact that Congress has debated but not yet passed legislation explicitly providing protections for sexual orientation. *See* Bibby v. Philadelphia Coca Cola Bottling Co., 260 F.3d 257, 261 (3d Cir. 2001) ("Congress has repeatedly rejected legislation that would extend Title VII to cover sexual orientation."). But the Supreme Court has ruled that "[c]ongressional inaction lacks persuasive significance because several equally tenable inferences may be drawn from such inaction, including the inference that the existing legislation already incorporated the offered change." Pension Benefit Guar. Corp. v. LTV Corp., 496 U.S. 633, 650 (1990).

The idea that congressional action is required (and inaction is therefore instructive in part) rests on the notion that protection against sexual orientation discrimination under Title VII would create a new class of covered persons. But analogous case law confirms this is not true. When courts held that Title VII protected persons who were discriminated against because of their relationships with persons of another race, the courts did not thereby create a new protected class of "people in interracial relationships." And when the Supreme Court decided that Title VII protected persons discriminated against because of gender stereotypes held by an employer, it did not thereby create a new protected class of "masculine women." Similarly, when ruling under Title VII that discrimination against an employee because he lacks religious beliefs is religious discrimination, the courts did not thereby create a new Title VII basis of "non-believers." These courts simply applied existing Title VII principles on race, sex, and religious discrimination to these situations. Further, the Supreme Court was not dissuaded by the absence of the word "mothers" in Title VII when it decided that the statute does not permit an employer to have one hiring policy for women with pre-school children and another for men with pre-school children. *See* Phillips v. Martin-Marietta, 400 U.S. 542, 543–44 (1971). The courts have gone where the principles of Title VII have directed.

Our task is the same. We apply the words of the statute Congress has charged us with enforcing. We therefore conclude that Complainant's allegations of discrimination on the basis of sexual orientation state a claim of discrimination on the basis of sex. We further conclude that allegations of discrimination on the basis of sexual orientation necessarily state a claim of discrimination on the basis of sex. An employee could show that the sexual orientation discrimination he or she experienced was sex discrimination because it involved treatment that would not have occurred but for the individual's sex; because it was based on the sex of the person(s) the individual associates with; and/or because it was premised on the fundamental sex stereotype, norm, or expectation that individuals should be attracted only to those of the opposite sex.[16] Agencies should treat claims of sexual orientation discrimination as complaints of sex discrimination under Title VII * * * .

NOTES

1.   How did the EEOC justify its interpretation of Title VII? Are you persuaded that, as a matter of statutory interpretation, the term "sex discrimination" is sufficiently expansive to include *any* claim of sexual orientation discrimination? Does this mean that there is nothing about sexual orientation discrimination that is distinct from sex discrimination?

2.   Some federal district courts have embraced the EEOC's position that discrimination on the basis of sexual orientation is "sex discrimination."

---

[16]   There may be other theories for establishing sexual orientation discrimination as sex discrimination, on which we express no opinion.

See, e.g., Isaacs v. Felder Sevcs., LLC, 143 F.Supp.3d 1190 (M.D. Ala.2015); *Videckis v. Pepperdine Univ.,* 150 F.Supp.3d 1151 (C.D. Ca.2015). Other district courts have held that the EEOC's guidance does not displace prior case law holding that Title VII does not prohibit sexual orientation discrimination. *See, e.g., Christiansen v. Omnicom Grp., Inc.,* 150 F.Supp.3d 1151 (S.D.N.Y.2016); *Hinton v. Virginia Union Univ.,* ___ F.Supp.3d ___, 2016 WL 2621967 (E.D.Va.2016); *Burrows v. Coll. of Cent. Florida,* 2015 WL 5257135 (M.D.Fla.2015.).

3. The U.S. Court of Appeals for the Seventh Circuit has agreed with the latter view, ruling that, despite the EEOC's position, it is bound by its prior decisions holding that Title VII does not prohibit sexual orientation discrimination. *Hively v. Ivy Tech Comm. Coll.,* ___ F.3d ___, 2016 WL 4039703 (7th Cir.2016) As the court saw it, the fact that Congress has not amended the statute in order to explicitly cover sexual orientation, despite all of the attention the issue has received in recent years, means that the understanding that "Congress intended a very narrow reading of the term 'sex' when it passed Title VII . . . appears to be correct." *Id.* at *3. At the same time, the court conceded that the narrow reading of Title VII "creates an uncomfortable result in which the more visibly and stereotypically gay or lesbian a plaintiff is in mannerisms, appearance, and behavior . . . the more likely a court is to recognize a claim of gender non-conformity which will be cognizable under Title VII as sex discrimination." *Id.* at *8. In contrast, "[p]laintiffs who do not look, act, or appear to be gender non-conforming but are merely known to be or perceived to be gay or lesbian do not fare as well in the federal courts." *Id.* Although the court opined that the different result in these cases was unsatisfying, it concluded that the problem could only be rectified by either a Supreme Court ruling or new legislation. *Id.*

4. The EEOC has also concluded that a "complaint of discrimination based on gender identity, change of sex, and/or transgender status is cognizable under Title VII" as "sex" discrimination. *Macy v. Holder,* EEOC Appeal No. 0120120821, 2012 WL 1435995. For a discussion of *Macy,* see *infra* Section II.B.3.

3. Gender Identity

ULANE V. EASTERN AIRLINES, INC.

United States Court of Appeals, Seventh Circuit, 1984
742 F.2d 1081, *cert. denied,* 471 U.S. 1017, 105 S.Ct. 2023, 85 L.Ed.2d 304 (1985)

HARLINGTON WOOD, JR., CIRCUIT JUDGE.

Plaintiff, as Kenneth Ulane, was hired in 1968 as a pilot for defendant, Eastern Air Lines, Inc., but was fired as Karen Frances Ulane in 1981. Ulane filed a timely charge of sex discrimination with the Equal Employment Opportunity Commission, which subsequently issued a right to sue letter. This suit followed. Counts I and II allege that Ulane's discharge violated Title VII of the Civil Rights Act of 1964: Count I alleges that Ulane was discriminated against as a female; Count II alleges that Ulane was discriminated against as a transsexual. The judge ruled in favor of Ulane on both counts after a bench trial. The court awarded her[2] reinstatement as a flying officer with full seniority and back pay, and attorneys' fees. This certified appeal followed pursuant to Federal Rule of Civil Procedure 54(b).

Counsel for Ulane opens their brief by explaining: "This is a Title VII case brought by a pilot who was fired by Eastern Airlines for no reason other than the fact that she ceased being a male and became a female." That explanation may give some cause to pause, but this briefly is the story.

Ulane became a licensed pilot in 1964, serving in the United States Army from that time until 1968 with a record of combat missions in Vietnam for which Ulane received the Air Medal with eight clusters. Upon discharge in 1968, Ulane began flying for Eastern. With Eastern, Ulane progressed from Second to First Officer, and also served as a flight instructor, logging over 8,000 flight hours.

Ulane was diagnosed a transsexual[3] in 1979. She explains that although embodied as a male, from early childhood she felt like a female. Ulane first sought psychiatric and medical assistance in 1968 while in the military. Later, Ulane began taking female hormones as part of her treatment, and eventually developed breasts from the hormones. In 1980, she underwent "sex reassignment surgery."[4] After the surgery, Illinois issued a revised birth certificate indicating Ulane was female, and the FAA certified her for flight status as a female. Ulane's own physician explained, however, that the operation would not create a biological female in the sense that Ulane would "have a uterus and ovaries and be able to bear babies." Ulane's chromosomes,[5] all concede, are unaffected by the hormones and surgery. Ulane, however, claims that the lack of change

---

[2]   Since Ulane considers herself to be female, and appears in public as female, we will use feminine pronouns in referring to her.

[3]   Transsexualism is a condition that exists when a physiologically normal person (*i.e.*, not a hermaphrodite—a person whose sex is not clearly defined due to a congenital condition) experiences discomfort or discontent about nature's choice of his or her particular sex and prefers to be the other sex. This discomfort is generally accompanied by a desire to utilize hormonal, surgical, and civil procedures to allow the individual to live in his or her preferred sex role. The diagnosis is appropriate only if the discomfort has been continuous for at least two years, and is not due to another mental disorder, such as schizophrenia. To be distinguished are homosexuals, who are sexually attracted to persons of the same sex, and transvestites, who are generally male heterosexuals who cross-dress, *i.e.*, dress as females, for sexual arousal rather than social comfort; both homosexuals and transvestites are content with the sex into which they were born.

[4]   Sex reassignment surgery for male-to-female transsexuals "involves the removal of the external male sexual organs and the construction of an artificial vagina by plastic surgery. It is supplemented by hormone treatments that facilitate the change in secondary sex characteristics," such as breast development.

[5]   The normal individual has 46 chromosomes, two of which designate sex. An XX configuration denotes female; XY denotes male. These chromosome patterns cannot be surgically altered.

in her chromosomes is irrelevant.[6] Eastern was not aware of Ulane's transsexuality, her hormone treatments, or her psychiatric counseling until she attempted to return to work after her reassignment surgery. Eastern knew Ulane only as one of its male pilots.

A. TITLE VII AND ULANE AS A TRANSSEXUAL.

The district judge first found under Count II that Eastern discharged Ulane because she was a transsexual, and that Title VII prohibits discrimination on this basis.[7] While we do not condone discrimination in any form, we are constrained to hold that Title VII does not protect transsexuals, and that the district court's order on this count therefore must be reversed for lack of jurisdiction.

[Title VII] provides in part that: "It shall be an unlawful employment practice for an employer to * * * discharge any individual * * * because of such individual's * * * sex * * * ." Other courts have held that the term "sex" as used in the statute is not synonymous with "sexual preference." *See, e.g., De Santis v. Pacific Telephone & Telegraph Co.*, 608 F.2d 327, 329–30 (9th Cir. 1979). The district court recognized this, and agreed that homosexuals and transvestites do not enjoy Title VII protection, but distinguished transsexuals as persons who, unlike homosexuals and transvestites, have sexual *identity* problems; the judge agreed that the term "sex" does not comprehend "sexual preference," but held that it does comprehend "sexual identity." The district judge based this holding on his finding that "sex is not a cut-and-dried matter of chromosomes," but is in part a psychological question—a question of self-perception; and in part a social matter—a question of how society perceives the individual. The district judge further supported his broad view of Title VII's coverage by recognizing Title VII as a remedial statute to be liberally construed. He concluded that it is reasonable to hold that the statutory word "sex" literally and scientifically applies to transsexuals even if it does not apply to homosexuals or transvestites.[10] We must disagree.

---

[6]   Biologically, sex is defined by chromosomes, internal and external genitalia, hormones, and gonads. Chromosomal sex cannot be changed, and a uterus and ovaries cannot be constructed. This leads some in the medical profession to conclude that hormone treatments and sex reassignment surgery can alter the evident makeup of an individual, but cannot change the individual's innate sex. Others disagree, arguing that one must look beyond chromosomes when determining an individual's sex and consider factors such as psychological sex or assumed sex role. These individuals conclude that post-operative male-to-female transsexuals do in fact qualify as females and are not merely "facsimiles."

[7]   Not all of the experts who testified agreed that Ulane is a transsexual. (Although doctors attempt to perform sex reassignment surgery only on transsexuals—as opposed, for example, on transvestites or schizophrenics, that an individual has undergone such surgery is not determinative of whether he or she is a true transsexual.) If Ulane is not a transsexual, then she is a transvestite. Even in the trial judge's view, transvestites are not covered by Title VII.

[10]   Judge Grady explained:

I have no problem with the idea that the statute was not intended and cannot reasonably be argued to have been intended to cover the matter of sexual preference, the preference of a sexual partner, or the matter of sexual gratification from wearing

Even though Title VII is a remedial statute, and even though some may define "sex" in such a way as to mean an individual's "sexual identity," our responsibility is to interpret this congressional legislation and determine what Congress intended when it decided to outlaw discrimination based on sex. The district judge did recognize that Congress manifested an intention to exclude homosexuals from Title VII coverage. Nonetheless, the judge defended his conclusion that Ulane's broad interpretation of the term "sex" was reasonable and could therefore be applied to the statute by noting that transsexuals are different than homosexuals, and that Congress never considered whether it should include or exclude transsexuals. While we recognize distinctions among homosexuals, transvestites, and transsexuals, we believe that the same reasons for holding that the first two groups do not enjoy Title VII coverage apply with equal force to deny protection for transsexuals.

It is a maxim of statutory construction that, unless otherwise defined, words should be given their ordinary, common meaning. The phrase in Title VII prohibiting discrimination based on sex, in its plain meaning, implies that it is unlawful to discriminate against women because they are women and against men because they are men. The words of Title VII do not outlaw discrimination against a person who has a sexual identity disorder, *i.e.*, a person born with a male body who believes himself to be female, or a person born with a female body who believes herself to be male; a prohibition against discrimination based on an individual's sex is not synonymous with a prohibition against discrimination based on an individual's sexual identity disorder or discontent with the sex into which they were born. The dearth of legislative history on section 2000e–2(a)(1) strongly reinforces the view that that section means nothing more than its plain language implies.

When Congress enacted the Civil Rights Act of 1964 it was primarily concerned with race discrimination. "Sex as a basis of discrimination was added as a floor amendment one day before the House approved Title VII, without prior hearing or debate." *Holloway v. Arthur Andersen & Co.*, 566 F.2d 659, 662 (9th Cir. 1977). This sex amendment was the gambit of a congressman seeking to scuttle adoption of the Civil Rights Act. The ploy failed and sex discrimination was abruptly added to the statute's prohibition against race discrimination.

The total lack of legislative history supporting the sex amendment coupled with the circumstances of the amendment's adoption clearly indicates that Congress never considered nor intended that this 1964 legislation apply to anything other than the traditional concept of sex. Had Congress intended more, surely the legislative history would have at least mentioned its intended broad coverage of homosexuals,

---

the clothes of the opposite sex. It seems to me an altogether different question as to whether the matter of sexual identity is comprehended by the word, "sex."

transvestites, or transsexuals, and would no doubt have sparked an interesting debate. There is not the slightest suggestion in the legislative record to support an all-encompassing interpretation.

Members of Congress have, moreover, on a number of occasions, attempted to amend Title VII to prohibit discrimination based upon "affectational or sexual orientation." Each of these attempts has failed. While the proposed amendments were directed toward homosexuals, their rejection strongly indicates that the phrase in the Civil Rights Act prohibiting discrimination on the basis of sex should be given a narrow, traditional interpretation, which would also exclude transsexuals. Furthermore, Congress has continued to reject these amendments even after courts have specifically held that Title VII does not protect transsexuals from discrimination.

Although the maxim that remedial statutes should be liberally construed is well recognized, that concept has reasonable bounds beyond which a court cannot go without transgressing the prerogatives of Congress. In our view, to include transsexuals within the reach of Title VII far exceeds mere statutory interpretation. Congress had a narrow view of sex in mind when it passed the Civil Rights Act, and it has rejected subsequent attempts to broaden the scope of its original interpretation. For us to now hold that Title VII protects transsexuals would take us out of the realm of interpreting and reviewing and into the realm of legislating. This we must not and will not do.

Congress has a right to deliberate on whether it wants such a broad sweeping of the untraditional and unusual within the term "sex" as used in Title VII. Only Congress can consider all the ramifications to society of such a broad view. We do not believe that the interpretation of the word "sex" as used in the statute is a mere matter of expert medical testimony or the credibility of witnesses produced in court. Congress may, at some future time, have some interest in testimony of that type, but it does not control our interpretation of Title VII based on the legislative history or lack thereof. If Congress believes that transsexuals should enjoy the protection of Title VII, it may so provide. Until that time, however, we decline in behalf of the Congress to judicially expand the definition of sex as used in Title VII beyond its common and traditional interpretation.

Our view of the application of Title VII to this type of case is not an original one. *Sommers v. Budget Marketing, Inc.*, 667 F.2d 748, 750 (8th Cir. 1982) (per curiam), and *Holloway v. Arthur Andersen & Co.*, 566 F.2d 659, 662–63 (9th Cir. 1977), the only two circuit court cases we found that have specifically addressed the issue, both held that discrimination against transsexuals does not fall within the ambit of Title VII. In *Sommers*, Budget Marketing fired an anatomical male who claimed to be female once Budget Marketing discovered that he had misrepresented himself as female when he applied for the job. In *Holloway*, Arthur Andersen, an accounting firm, dismissed the plaintiff after he informed his superior that he was undergoing treatment in preparation for sex change surgery. We agree with the Eighth and Ninth Circuits that if the term "sex" as it is used in Title VII is to mean more than biological male or biological female, the new definition must come from Congress.

B.   TITLE VII AND ULANE AS A FEMALE.

The trial judge originally found only that Eastern had discriminated against Ulane under Count II as a transsexual. The judge subsequently amended his findings to hold that Ulane is also female and has been discriminated against on this basis. Even if we accept the district judge's holding that Ulane is female, he made no factual findings necessary to support his conclusion that Eastern discriminated against her on this basis. All the district judge said was that his previous "findings and conclusions concerning sexual discrimination against the plaintiff by Eastern Airlines, Inc. apply with equal force whether plaintiff be regarded as a transsexual or a female." This is insufficient to support a finding that Ulane was discriminated against because she is *female* since the district judge's previous findings all centered around his conclusion that Eastern did not want "[a] *transsexual* in the cockpit" (emphasis added).

Ulane is entitled to any personal belief about her sexual identity she desires. After the surgery, hormones, appearance changes, and a new Illinois birth certificate and FAA pilot's certificate, it may be that society, as the trial judge found, considers Ulane to be female. But even if one believes that a woman can be so easily created from what remains of a man, that does not decide this case. If Eastern had considered Ulane to be female and had discriminated against her because she was female (*i.e.*, Eastern treated females less favorably than males), then the argument might be made that Title VII applied, but that is not this case. It is clear from the evidence that if Eastern did discriminate against Ulane, it was not because she is female, but because Ulane is a transsexual—a biological male who takes female hormones, cross-dresses, and has surgically altered parts of her body to make it appear to be female.

Since Ulane was not discriminated against as a female, and since Title VII is not so expansive in scope as to prohibit discrimination against transsexuals, we reverse the order of the trial court and remand for entry of judgment in favor of Eastern on Count I and dismissal of Count II. Reversed.

SMITH V. CITY OF SALEM

United States Court of Appeals, Sixth Circuit, 2004
378 F.3d 566

COLE, CIRCUIT JUDGE.

Plaintiff-Appellant Jimmie L. Smith appeals from a judgment of the United States District Court for the Northern District of Ohio dismissing his claims against his employer, Defendant-Appellant City of Salem, Ohio, and various City officials, and granting judgment on the pleadings to Defendants, pursuant to Federal Rule of Civil Procedure 12(c). Smith, who considers himself a transsexual and has been diagnosed with Gender Identity Disorder, alleged that Defendants discriminated against him in his employment on the basis of sex. He asserted claims pursuant to Title VII of the Civil Rights Act of 1964, 42 U.S.C. § 2000e *et seq.*, and 42 U.S.C. § 1983. The district court dismissed those claims pursuant to Rule 12(c). * * * For the following reasons, we reverse the judgment of the district court and remand the case for further proceedings consistent with this opinion. * * *

Smith is—and has been, at all times relevant to this action—employed by the city of Salem, Ohio, as a lieutenant in the Salem Fire Department (the "Fire Department"). Prior to the events surrounding this action, Smith worked for the Fire Department for seven years without any negative incidents. Smith—biologically and by birth a male—is a transsexual and has been diagnosed with Gender Identity Disorder ("GID"), which the American Psychiatric Association characterizes as a disjunction between an individual's sexual organs and sexual identity. American Psychiatric Association, Diagnostic and Statistical Manual of Mental Disorders 576–582 (4th ed. 2000). After being diagnosed with GID, Smith began "expressing a more feminine appearance on a full-time basis"—including at work—in accordance with international medical protocols for treating GID. Soon thereafter, Smith's co-workers began questioning him about his appearance and commenting that his appearance and mannerisms were not "masculine enough." As a result, Smith notified his immediate supervisor, Defendant Thomas Eastek, about his GID diagnosis and treatment. He also informed Eastek of the likelihood that his treatment would eventually include complete physical transformation from male to female. Smith had approached Eastek in order to answer any questions Eastek might have concerning his appearance and manner and so that Eastek could address Smith's co-workers' comments and inquiries. Smith specifically asked Eastek, and Eastek promised, not to divulge the substance of their conversation to any of his superiors, particularly to Defendant Walter Greenamyer, Chief of the Fire Department. In short order, however, Eastek told Greenamyer about Smith's behavior and his GID.

Greenamyer then met with Defendant C. Brooke Zellers, the Law Director for the City of Salem, with the intention of using Smith's transsexualism and its manifestations as a basis for terminating his employment. On April 18, 2001, Greenamyer and Zellers arranged a meeting of the City's executive body to discuss Smith and devise a plan for terminating his employment. The executive body included Defendants Larry D. DeJane, Salem's mayor; James A. Armeni, Salem's auditor; and Joseph S. Julian, Salem's service director. Also present was Salem Safety Director Henry L. Willard, now deceased, who was never a named defendant in this action. * * *

During the meeting, Greenamyer, DeJane, and Zellers agreed to arrange for the Salem Civil Service Commission to require Smith to undergo three separate psychological evaluations with physicians of the City's choosing. They hoped that Smith would either resign or refuse to comply. If he refused to comply, Defendants reasoned, they could terminate Smith's employment on the ground of insubordination. Willard, who remained silent during the meeting, telephoned Smith afterwards to inform him of the plan, calling Defendants' scheme a "witch hunt."

Two days after the meeting, on April 20, 2001, Smith's counsel telephoned DeJane to advise him of Smith's legal representation and the potential legal ramifications for the City if it followed through on the plan devised by Defendants during the April 18 meeting. On April 22, 2001, Smith received his "right to sue" letter from the U.S. Equal Employment Opportunity Commission ("EEOC"). Four days after that, on April 26, 2001, Greenamyer suspended Smith for one twenty-four hour shift, based on his alleged infraction of a City and/or Fire Department policy. * * *

Defendants do not challenge Smith's complaint with respect to any of the other elements necessary to establish discrimination and retaliation claims pursuant to Title VII. In any event, we affirmatively find that Smith has made out a *prima facie* case for both claims. To establish a *prima facie* case of employment discrimination pursuant to Title VII, Smith must show that: (1) he is a member of a protected class; (2) he suffered an adverse employment action; (3) he was qualified for the position in question; and (4) he was treated differently from similarly situated individuals outside of his protected class. His complaint asserts that he is a male with Gender Identity Disorder, and Title VII's prohibition of discrimination "because of * * * sex" protects men as well as women. The complaint also alleges both that Smith was qualified for the position in question—he had been a lieutenant in the Fire Department for seven years without any negative incidents—and that he would not have been treated differently, on account of his non-masculine behavior and GID, had he been a woman instead of a man. * * *

In his complaint, Smith asserts Title VII claims of retaliation and employment discrimination "because of * * * sex." The district court dismissed Smith's Title VII claims on the ground that he failed to state a claim for sex stereotyping pursuant to *Price Waterhouse v. Hopkins*, 490 U.S. 228, 109 S.Ct. 1775, 104 L.Ed.2d 268 (1989). The district court implied that Smith's claim was disingenuous, stating that he merely "invokes the term-of-art created by *Price Waterhouse*, that is, 'sex-stereotyping,'" as an end run around his "real" claim, which, the district court stated, was "based upon his transsexuality." The district court then held that "Title VII does not prohibit discrimination based on an individual's transsexualism."

Relying on *Price Waterhouse*—which held that Title VII's prohibition of discrimination "because of * * * sex" bars gender discrimination, including discrimination based on sex stereotypes—Smith contends on appeal that he was a victim of discrimination "because of * * * sex" both because of his gender non-conforming conduct and, more generally, because of his identification as a transsexual.

* * * As Judge Posner has pointed out, the term "gender" is one "borrowed from grammar to designate the sexes as viewed as social rather than biological classes." Richard A. Posner, Sex and Reason, 24–25 (1992). The Supreme Court made clear that in the context of Title VII, discrimination because of "sex" includes gender discrimination: "In the context of sex stereotyping, an employer who acts on the basis of a belief that a woman cannot be aggressive, or that she must not be, has acted on the basis of gender." *Price Waterhouse*, 490 U.S. at 250. The Court emphasized that "we are beyond the day when an employer could evaluate employees by assuming or insisting that they matched the stereotype associated with their group." *Id.* at 251.

Smith contends that the same theory of sex stereotyping applies here. His complaint sets forth the conduct and mannerisms which, he alleges, did not conform with his employers' and co-workers' sex stereotypes of how a man should look and behave. Smith's complaint states that, after being diagnosed with GID, he began to express a more feminine appearance and manner on a regular basis, including at work. The complaint states that his co-workers began commenting on his appearance and mannerisms as not being masculine enough; and that his supervisors at the Fire Department and other municipal agents knew about this allegedly unmasculine conduct and appearance. The complaint then describes a high-level meeting among Smith's supervisors and other municipal officials regarding his employment. Defendants allegedly schemed to compel Smith's resignation by forcing him to undergo multiple psychological evaluations of his gender non-conforming behavior. The complaint makes clear that these meetings took place soon after Smith assumed a more feminine appearance and manner and after his conversation about this with Eastek. In addition, the complaint alleges that Smith was suspended for twenty-four hours for allegedly violating an unenacted municipal policy, and that the suspension was ordered in retaliation for his pursuing legal remedies after he had been informed about Defendants' plan to intimidate him into resigning. In short, Smith claims that the discrimination he experienced was based on his failure to conform to sex stereotypes by expressing less masculine, and more feminine mannerisms and appearance.

Having alleged that his failure to conform to sex stereotypes concerning how a man should look and behave was the driving force behind Defendants' actions, Smith has sufficiently pleaded claims of sex stereotyping and gender discrimination.

In so holding, we find that the district court erred in relying on a series of pre-*Price Waterhouse* cases from other federal appellate courts holding that transsexuals, as a class, are not entitled to Title VII protection because "Congress had a narrow view of sex in mind" and "never considered nor intended that [Title VII] apply to anything other than the traditional concept of sex." *Ulane v. Eastern Airlines, Inc.*, 742 F.2d 1081, 1085, 1086 (7th Cir. 1984); *see also Holloway v. Arthur Andersen & Co.*, 566 F.2d 659, 661–63 (9th Cir. 1977) (refusing to extend protection of Title VII to transsexuals because discrimination against transsexuals is based on "gender" rather than "sex"). It is true that, in the past, federal appellate courts regarded Title VII as barring discrimination based only on "sex" (referring to an individual's anatomical and biological characteristics), but not on "gender" (referring to socially-constructed norms associated with a person's sex). In this earlier jurisprudence, male-to-female transsexuals * * *—as biological males whose outward behavior and emotional identity did not conform to socially-prescribed expectations of masculinity—were denied Title VII protection by courts because they were considered victims of "gender" rather than "sex" discrimination.

However, th[is] approach * * * has been eviscerated by *Price Waterhouse*. By holding that Title VII protected a woman who failed to conform to social expectations concerning how a woman should look and behave, the Supreme Court established that Title VII's reference to "sex" encompasses both the biological differences between men and women, and gender discrimination, that is, discrimination based on a failure to conform to stereotypical gender norms.

After *Price Waterhouse*, an employer who discriminates against women because, for instance, they do not wear dresses or makeup, is engaging in sex discrimination because the discrimination would not occur but for the victim's sex. It follows that employers who discriminate against men because they *do* wear dresses and makeup, or otherwise act femininely, are also engaging in sex discrimination, because the discrimination would not occur but for the victim's sex.

Yet some courts have held that this latter form of discrimination is of a different and somehow more permissible kind. For instance, the man who acts in ways typically associated with women is not described as engaging in the same activity as a woman who acts in ways typically associated with women, but is instead described as engaging in the different activity of being a transsexual (or in some instances, a homosexual or transvestite). Discrimination against the transsexual is then found not to be discrimination "because of * * * sex," but rather, discrimination against the plaintiff's unprotected status or mode of self-identification. In other words, these courts superimpose classifications such as "transsexual" on a plaintiff, and then legitimize discrimination based on the plaintiff's gender non-conformity by formalizing the non-conformity into an ostensibly unprotected classification. *See, e.g., Dillon v. Frank*, 952 F.2d 403, 1992 WL 5436 (6th Cir. 1992).

Such was the case here: despite the fact that Smith alleges that Defendants' discrimination was motivated by his appearance and mannerisms, which Defendants felt were inappropriate for his perceived sex, the district court expressly declined to discuss the applicability of *Price Waterhouse*. The district court therefore gave insufficient consideration to Smith's well-pleaded claims concerning his contra-gender behavior, but rather accounted for that behavior only insofar as it confirmed for the court Smith's status as a transsexual, which the district court held precluded Smith from Title VII protection.

Such analyses cannot be reconciled with *Price Waterhouse,* which does not make Title VII protection against sex stereotyping conditional or provide any reason to exclude Title VII coverage for non sex-stereotypical behavior simply because the person is a transsexual. As such, discrimination against a plaintiff who is a transsexual—and therefore fails to act and/or identify with his or her gender—is no different from the discrimination directed against Ann Hopkins in *Price Waterhouse*, who, in sex-stereotypical terms, did not act like a woman. Sex stereotyping based on a person's gender non-conforming behavior is impermissible discrimination, irrespective of the cause of that behavior; a label, such as "transsexual," is not fatal to a sex discrimination claim where the victim has suffered discrimination because of his or her gender non-conformity. Accordingly, we hold that Smith has stated a claim for relief pursuant to Title VII's prohibition of sex discrimination.

Finally, we note that, in its opinion, the district court repeatedly places the term "sex stereotyping" in quotation marks and refers to it as a "term of art" used by Smith to disingenuously plead discrimination because of transsexualism. Similarly, Defendants refer to sex

[handwritten margin note: but she identified as a woman]

stereotyping as "the *Price Waterhouse* loophole." These characterizations are almost identical to the treatment that Price Waterhouse itself gave sex stereotyping in its briefs to the U.S. Supreme Court. As we do now, the Supreme Court noted the practice with disfavor, stating:

> In the specific context of sex stereotyping, an employer who acts on the basis of a belief that a woman cannot be aggressive, or that she must not be, has acted on the basis of gender. Although the parties do not overtly dispute this last proposition, the placement by Price Waterhouse of "sex stereotyping" in quotation marks throughout its brief seems to us an insinuation either that such stereotyping was not present in this case or that it lacks legal relevance. We reject both possibilities.

Price Waterhouse, 490 U.S. at 250.

SCHROER V. BILLINGTON

U.S. District Court, District of Columbia, 2008
577 F. Supp. 2d 293

ROBERTSON, DISTRICT JUDGE.

Diane Schroer claims that she was denied employment by the Librarian of Congress because of sex, in violation of Title VII of the Civil Rights Act of 1964, 42 U.S.C. § 2000e–2(a)(1). Evidence was taken in a bench trial on August 19–22, 2008.

Diane Schroer is a male-to-female transsexual. Although born male, Schroer has a female gender identity—an internal, psychological sense of herself as a woman. In August 2004, before she changed her legal name or began presenting as a woman, Schroer applied for the position of Specialist in Terrorism and International Crime with the Congressional Research Service (CRS) at the Library of Congress. The terrorism specialist provides expert policy analysis to congressional committees, members of Congress and their staffs. The position requires a security clearance.

Schroer was well qualified for the job. She is a graduate of both the National War College and the Army Command and General Staff College, and she holds masters degrees in history and international relations. During Schroer's twenty-five years of service in the U.S. Armed Forces, she held important command and staff positions in the Armored Calvary, Airborne, Special Forces and Special Operations Units, and in combat operations in Haiti and Rwanda. Before her retirement from the military in January 2004, Schroer was a Colonel assigned to the U.S. Special Operations Command, serving as the director of a 120-person classified organization that tracked and targeted high-threat international terrorist organizations. In this position, Colonel Schroer analyzed sensitive intelligence reports, planned a range of classified and conventional operations, and regularly briefed senior military and government officials, including the Vice President, the Secretary of Defense, and the Chairman of the Joint Chiefs of Staff. At the time of her military retirement, Schroer held a Top Secret, Sensitive Compartmented Information security clearance, and had done so on a continuous basis since 1987. After her retirement, Schroer joined a private consulting firm, Benchmark International, where, when she applied for the CRS position, she was working as a program manager on an infrastructure security project for the National Guard.

When Schroer applied for the terrorism specialist position, she had been diagnosed with gender identity disorder and was working with a licensed clinical social worker * * * to develop a medically appropriate plan for transitioning from male to female. The transitioning process was guided by a set of treatment protocols formulated by the leading organization for the study and treatment of gender identity disorders, the Harry Benjamin International Gender Dysphoria Association. Because she had not yet begun presenting herself as a woman on a full-time basis, however, she applied for the position as "David J. Schroer," her legal name at the time. In October 2004, two months after submitting her application, Schroer was invited to interview with three members of the CRS staff * * * Charlotte Preece, the Assistant Director for Foreign Affairs, Defense and Trade, was the selecting official for the position. Schroer attended the interview dressed in traditionally masculine attire—a sport coat and slacks with a shirt and tie.

Schroer received the highest interview score of all eighteen candidates. In early December, Preece called Schroer, told her that she was on the shortlist of applicants still in the running, and asked for several writing samples and an updated list of references. After receiving these updated materials, the members of the selection committee unanimously recommended that Schroer be offered the job. In mid-December, Preece called Schroer [and] offered her the job * * * The next day, after Preece confirmed that the Library would be able to offer comparable pay, Schroer accepted the offer, and Preece began to fill out the paperwork necessary to finalize the hire.

Before Preece had completed and submitted these documents, Schroer asked her to lunch on December 20, 2004. Schroer's intention was to tell Preece about her transsexuality. She was about to begin the phase of her gender transition during which she would be dressing in traditionally feminine clothing and presenting as a woman on a full-time basis. She believed that starting work at CRS as a woman would be less disruptive than if she started as a man and later began presenting as a woman. * * * As they were sitting down to lunch, Preece stated that they were excited to have Schroer join CRS because she was "significantly better than the other candidates." Schroer asked why that was so, and Preece explained that her skills, her operational experience, her ability creatively to answer questions, and her contacts in the military and in defense industries made her application superior.

About a half hour into their lunch, Schroer told Preece that she needed to discuss a "personal matter." She began by asking Preece if she knew what "transgender" meant. Preece responded that she did, and Schroer went on to explain that she was transgender, that she would be transitioning from male to female, and that she would be starting work as "Diane." Preece's first reaction was to ask, "Why in the world would you want to do that?" Schroer explained that she did not see being transgender as a choice and that it was something she had lived with her entire life. Preece then asked her a series of questions, starting with whether she needed to change Schroer's name on the hiring documentation. Schroer responded that she did not because her legal name, at that point, was still David. Schroer went on to explain the Harry Benjamin Standards of Care and her own medical process for transitioning. She told Preece that she planned to have facial feminization surgery in early January and assured her that recovery from this surgery was quick and would pose no problem for a mid-January start date. In the context of explaining the Benjamin Standards of Care, Schroer explained that she would be living full-time as a woman for at least a year before having sex reassignment surgery. Such surgery, Schroer explained, could normally be accomplished during a two-week vacation period and would not interfere with the requirements of the job.

Preece then raised the issue of Schroer's security clearance, asking what name ought to appear on hiring documents. Schroer responded that she had several transgender friends who had retained their clearances while transitioning and said that she did not think it would be an issue in her case. Schroer also mentioned that her therapist would be available to answer any questions or provide additional background as needed. Because Schroer expected that there might be some concern about her appearance when presenting as a woman, she showed Preece three photographs of herself, wearing traditionally feminine professional attire. Although Preece did not say it to Schroer, her reaction on seeing these photos was that Schroer looked like "a man dressed in women's clothing." * * * Although Schroer initially thought that her conversation with Preece had gone well, she thought it "ominous" that Preece ended it by stating "Well, you've given me a lot to think about. I'll be in touch."

Preece did not finish Schroer's hiring memorandum when she returned to the Library after lunch. * * * Preece testified that at this point * * * she was leaning against hiring Schroer. She said that Schroer's transition raised five concerns for her. First, she was concerned about Schroer's ability to maintain her contacts within the military. * * *

Second, Preece was concerned with Schroer's credibility when testifying before Congress. * * * Third, Preece testified that she was concerned with Schroer's trustworthiness because she had not been up front about her transition from the beginning of the interview process. * * * Fourth, Preece thought that Schroer's transition might distract her from her job. * * * Finally, Preece was concerned with Schroer's ability to maintain her security clearance. In Preece's mind, "David Schroer" had a security clearance, but "Diane Schroer" did not * * * She had this concern, but she did not ask Schroer for any information on the people she knew who had undergone gender transitions while retaining their clearances. * * *

[The next day, after meeting with other Library officials, Preece decided that] she no longer wanted to recommend Schroer for the terrorism specialist position. Preece testified that the security clearance was the critical, deciding factor because of "how long it would take." She also testified, however, that she would have leaned against hiring Schroer even if she had no concerns regarding the security clearance, because her second candidate, John Rollins, presented "fewer complications"— because, unlike Schroer, he was not transitioning from male to female. * * *

Later that same afternoon, Preece called Schroer to rescind the job offer. She said, "Well, after a long and sleepless night, based on our conversation yesterday, I've determined that you are not a good fit, not what we want." Schroer replied that she was very disappointed. Preece ended the conversation by thanking Schroer for her honesty. Preece then called John Rollins, who had a lower total interview score than Schroer, and offered him the position. He accepted.

Since January 2005, Schroer has lived full-time as a woman. She has changed her legal name to Diane Schroer and obtained a Virginia driver's license and a United States Uniformed Services card reflecting her name change and gender transition.

* * * The Library argues that it had a number of non-discriminatory reasons for refusing to hire Schroer, including concerns about her ability to maintain or timely receive a security clearance, her trustworthiness, and the potential that her transition would distract her from her job. The Library also argues that a hiring decision based on transsexuality is not unlawful discrimination under Title VII.

[The court concluded that the three reasons for not hiring Schroer were pretextual. It then proceeded to address the legal issue of transsexuality and Title VII.]

Schroer contends that the Library's decision not to hire her is sex discrimination banned by Title VII, advancing two legal theories. The first is unlawful discrimination based on her failure to conform with sex stereotypes. The second is that discrimination on the basis of gender identity is literally discrimination "because of * * * sex."

A. *Sex Stereotyping*

Plaintiff's sex stereotyping theory is grounded in the Supreme Court's decision in *Price Waterhouse v. Hopkins,* 490 U.S. 228 (1989). * * * Schroer's case * * * rests on direct evidence, and compelling evidence, that the Library's hiring decision was infected by sex stereotypes. Charlotte Preece, the decisionmaker, admitted that when she viewed the photographs of Schroer in traditionally feminine attire, with a feminine hairstyle and makeup, she saw a man in women's clothing. In conversations Preece had with colleagues at the Library after her lunch with Schroer, she repeatedly mentioned these photographs. Preece testified that her difficulty comprehending Schroer's decision to undergo a gender transition was heightened because she viewed David Schroer not just as a man, but, in light of her Special Forces background, as a particularly masculine kind of man. Preece's perception of David Schroer as especially masculine made it all the more difficult for her to visualize Diane Schroer as anyone other than a man in a dress. Preece admitted that she believed that others at CRS, as well as Members of Congress and their staffs, would not take Diane Schroer seriously because they, too, would view her as a man in women's clothing.

What makes Schroer's sex stereotyping theory difficult is that, when the plaintiff is transsexual, direct evidence of discrimination based on sex stereotypes may look a great deal like discrimination based on transsexuality itself, a characteristic that, in and of itself, nearly all federal courts have said is unprotected by Title VII. *See Ulane v. Eastern Airlines,* 742 F.2d 1081, 1085 (7th Cir.1984). Take Preece's testimony regarding Schroer's credibility before Congress. As characterized by Schroer, the Library's credibility concern was that she "would not be deemed credible by Members of Congress and their staff because people would perceive her to be a woman, and would refuse to believe that she could possibly have the credentials that she had." Plaintiff argues that this is "quintessential sex stereotyping" because Diane Schroer is a woman and does have such a background. But Preece did not testify that she was concerned that Members of Congress would perceive Schroer simply to be a woman. Instead, she testified that "everyone would know that [Schroer] had transitioned from male to female because only a man could have her military experiences."

Ultimately, I do not think that it matters for purposes of Title VII liability whether the Library withdrew its offer of employment because it perceived Schroer to be an insufficiently masculine man, an insufficiently feminine woman, or an inherently gender-nonconforming transsexual. One or more of Preece's comments could be parsed in each of these three ways. While I would therefore conclude that Schroer is entitled to judgment based on a *Price Waterhouse*-type claim for sex stereotyping, I also conclude that she is entitled to judgment based on the language of the statute itself.

B. *Discrimination Because of Sex*

Schroer's second legal theory is that, because gender identity is a component of sex, discrimination on the basis of gender identity is sex discrimination. In support of this contention, Schroer adduced the testimony of Dr. Walter Bockting, a tenured associate professor at the University of Minnesota Medical School who specializes in gender identity disorders. Dr. Bockting testified that it has long been accepted in the relevant scientific community that there are nine factors that constitute a person's sex. One of these factors is gender identity, which Dr. Bockting defined as one's personal sense of being male or female.[7]

The Library adduced the testimony of Dr. Chester Schmidt, a professor of psychiatry at the Johns Hopkins University School of Medicine and also an expert in gender identity disorders. Dr. Schmidt disagreed with Dr. Bockting's view of the prevailing scientific consensus and testified that he and his colleagues regard gender identity as a component of "sexuality" rather than "sex." According to Dr. Schmidt, "sex" is made up of a number of facets, each of which has a determined biologic etiology. Dr. Schmidt does not believe that gender identity has a single, fixed etiology.

The testimony of both experts—on the science of gender identity and the relationship between intersex conditions and transsexuality—was impressive. Resolving the dispute between Dr. Schmidt and Dr. Bockting as to the proper scientific definition of sex, however, is not within this Court's competence. More importantly (because courts render opinions about scientific controversies with some regularity), deciding whether Dr. Bockting or Dr. Schmidt is right turns out to be unnecessary.

The evidence establishes that the Library was enthusiastic about hiring David Schroer—until she disclosed her transsexuality. The Library revoked the offer when it learned that a man named David intended to become, legally, culturally, and physically, a woman named Diane. This was discrimination "because of * * * sex." * * *

Imagine that an employee is fired because she converts from Christianity to Judaism. Imagine too that her employer testifies that he harbors no bias toward either Christians or Jews but only "converts." That would be a clear case of discrimination "because of religion." No court would take seriously the notion that "converts" are not covered by

---

[7]   The other eight factors, according to Dr. Bockting, are chromosomal sex, hypothalamic sex, fetal hormonal sex, pubertal hormonal sex, sex of assignment and rearing, internal morphological sex, external morphological sex, and gonads.

the statute. Discrimination "because of religion", easily encompasses discrimination because of a *change* of religion. But in cases where the plaintiff has changed her sex, and faces discrimination because of the decision to stop presenting as a man and to start appearing as a woman, courts have traditionally carved such persons out of the statute by concluding that "transsexuality" is unprotected by Title VII. In other words, courts have allowed their focus on the label "transsexual" to blind them to the statutory language itself.

In *Ulane v. Eastern Airlines,* the Seventh Circuit held that discrimination based on sex means only that "it is unlawful to discriminate against women because they are women and against men because they are men." The Court reasoned that the statute's legislative history "clearly indicates that Congress never considered nor intended that [Title VII] apply to anything other than the traditional concept of sex." 742 F.2d 1081, 1085 (7th Cir.1984). The Ninth Circuit took a similar approach, holding that Title VII did not extend protection to transsexuals because Congress's "manifest purpose" in enacting the statute was only "to ensure that men and women are treated equally." *Holloway v. Arthur Andersen & Co.,* 566 F.2d 659, 663 (9th Cir.1977). More recently, the Tenth Circuit has also held that because "sex" under Title VII means nothing more than "male and female," the statute only extends protection to transsexual employees "if they are discriminated against because they are male or because they are female." *Etsitty v. Utah Transit Authority,* 502 F.3d 1215, 1222 (10th Cir.2007).

The decisions holding that Title VII only prohibits discrimination against men because they are men, and discrimination against women because they are women, represent an elevation of "judge-supposed legislative intent over clear statutory text." *Zuni Pub. Sch. Dist. No. 89 v. Dep't of Educ.,* 550 U.S. 81, 127 S.Ct. 1534, 1551, 167 L.Ed.2d 449 (2007) (Scalia, J., dissenting).

For Diane Schroer to prevail on the facts of her case, however, it is not necessary to draw sweeping conclusions about the reach of Title VII. Even if the decisions that define the word "sex" in Title VII as referring only to anatomical or chromosomal sex are still good law—after that approach "has been eviscerated by *Price Waterhouse,*" *Smith* [*v. City of Salem*], 378 F.3d at 573—the Library's refusal to hire Schroer after being advised that she planned to change her anatomical sex by undergoing sex reassignment surgery was *literally* discrimination "because of * * * sex."

In 2007, a bill that would have banned employment discrimination on the basis of sexual orientation and gender identity was introduced in the House of Representatives. *See* H.R.2015, 110 Cong., 1st Sess. (2007). Two alternate bills were later introduced: one that banned discrimination only on the basis of sexual orientation, H.R. 3685, 110 Cong., 1st Sess.

(2007), and another that banned only gender identity discrimination, H.R. 3686, 110 Cong., 1st Sess. (2007). None of those bills was enacted.

The Library asserts that the introduction and non-passage of H.R.2015 and H.R. 3686 shows that transsexuals are not currently covered by Title VII and also that Congress is content with the status quo. However, as Schroer points out, another reasonable interpretation of that legislative non-history is that some Members of Congress believe that the *Ulane* court and others have interpreted "sex" in an unduly narrow manner, that Title VII means what it says, and that the statute requires, not amendment, but only correct interpretation.

In refusing to hire Diane Schroer because her appearance and background did not comport with the decisionmaker's sex stereotypes about how men and women should act and appear, and in response to Schroer's decision to transition, legally, culturally, and physically, from male to female, the Library of Congress violated Title VII's prohibition on sex discrimination.

NOTES

1.   The *Schroer* court's second holding, that discrimination on the basis of gender identity "was *literally* discrimination 'because of * * * sex,' " is noteworthy because most courts that have recognized Title VII claims in gender identity cases have instead adopted the gender stereotyping theory embraced by the U.S. Court of Appeals for the Sixth Circuit in *Smith. See, e.g., Barnes v. Cincinnati,* 401 F.3d 729 (6th Cir. 2005), *cert. denied,* 546 U.S. 1003, 126 S.Ct. 624, 163 L.Ed.2d 506 (2005); *Kastl v. Maricopa Co. Cmty. Coll. Dist.,* 325 Fed. Appx. 492, 493 (9th Cir. 2009); *Lopez v. River Oaks Imaging & Diagnostic Group, Inc.,* 542 F.Supp.2d 653, 667–68 (S.D.Tex. 2008). On the other hand, some courts continue to follow *Ulane* in holding that Title VII does not prohibit discrimination on the basis of gender identity. *See, e.g., Etsitty v. Utah Transit Authority,* 502 F.3d 1215, 1222 (10th Cir. 2007); *Oiler v. Winn-Dixie Louisiana, Inc.,* 2002 WL 31098541 (E.D. La. 2002).

2.   In 2012, the Equal Opportunity Employment Commission (EEOC), the agency charged with enforcing federal employment antidiscrimination law, reversed its earlier position by issuing a ruling explaining that a "complaint of discrimination based on gender identity, change of sex, and/or transgender status is cognizable under Title VII." *Macy v. Holder*, EEOC Appeal No. 0120120821, 2012 WL 1435995. In doing so, the EEOC explained that gender stereotyping was not a required element of the claim:

> Although most courts have found protection for transgender people under Title VII under a theory of gender stereotyping, evidence of gender stereotyping is simply one means of proving sex discrimination. Title VII prohibits discrimination based on sex whether motivated by hostility, by a desire to protect people of a

certain gender, by assumptions that disadvantage men [or women], by gender stereotypes, or by the desire to accommodate other people's prejudices or discomfort. While evidence that an employer has acted based on stereotypes about how men or women should act is certainly one means of demonstrating disparate treatment based on sex, "sex stereotyping" is not itself an independent cause of action. As the *Price Waterhouse* Court noted, while "stereotyped remarks can certainly be *evidence* that gender played a part" in an adverse employment action, the central question is always whether the "employer actually relied on [the employee's] gender in making its decision." [*Price Waterhouse v. Hopkins*, 490 U.S. 228, 251 (1989)].

Thus, a transgender person who has experienced discrimination based on his or her gender identity may establish a prima facie case of sex discrimination through any number of different formulations. * * * For example, Complainant could establish a case of sex discrimination under a theory of gender stereotyping by showing that she did not get the job * * * because the employer believed that biological men should consistently present as men and wear male clothing. Alternatively, if Complainant can prove that the reason that she did not get the job * * * is that the Director was willing to hire her when he thought she was a man, but was not willing to hire her once he found out that she was now a woman— she will have proven that the Director discriminated on the basis of sex. Under this theory, there would actually be no need, for purposes of establishing coverage under Title VII, for Complainant to compile any evidence that the Director was engaging in gender stereotyping.

In this respect, gender is no different from religion. Assume that an employee considers herself Christian and identifies as such. But assume that an employer finds out that the employee's parents are Muslim, believes that the employee should therefore be Muslim, and terminates the employee on that basis. No one would doubt that such an employer discriminated on the basis of religion. There would be no need for the employee who experienced the adverse employment action to demonstrate that the employer acted on the basis of some religious stereotype—although, clearly, discomfort with the choice made by the employee with regard to religion would presumably be at the root of the employer's actions. But for purposes of establishing a prima facie case that Title VII has been violated, the employee simply must demonstrate that the employer impermissibly used religion in making its employment decision.

3.   In addition to pursuing Title VII claims, transgender individuals in eighteen states (CA, CO, CT, DE, HW, IA, IL, MA, ME, MN, NJ, NM, NV, OR, RI, UT, VT, and WA) and the District of Columbia can sue under state statutes that prohibit employment discrimination on the basis of gender

identity. Furthermore, over one hundred municipalities have ordinances prohibiting that type of discrimination.

NOTE: BATHROOM ACCESS

The question of whether antidiscrimination laws require employers to allow their employees to use bathrooms that correspond to their gender identity has been the subject of some litigation. In *Goins v. West Group*, 635 N.W.2d 717 (Minn. 2001), the plaintiff, a female transgender employee, brought suit under Minnesota's sexual orientation discrimination law after her employer prohibited her from using bathrooms designated for women at work. The Minnesota law includes within the definition of "sexual orientation" the "having or being perceived as having a self-image or identity not traditionally associated with one's biological maleness or femaleness." The Minnesota Supreme Court ruled against the plaintiff, noting that

> Goins does not argue that an employer engages in impermissible discrimination by designating the use of restrooms according to gender. Rather, her claim is that the MHRA prohibits West's policy of designating restroom use according to biological gender, and requires instead that such designation be based on self-image of gender. Goins alleges that West engaged in impermissible discrimination by denying her access to a restroom consistent with her self-image of gender. We do not believe the MHRA can be read so broadly. As the district court observed, where financially feasible, the traditional and accepted practice in the employment setting is to provide restroom facilities that reflect the cultural preference for restroom designation based on biological gender. To conclude that the MHRA contemplates restrictions on an employer's ability to designate restroom facilities based on biological gender would likely restrain employer discretion in the gender designation of workplace shower and locker room facilities, a result not likely intended by the legislature. We believe, as does the Department of Human Rights, that the MHRA neither requires nor prohibits restroom designation according to self-image of gender or according to biological gender. While an employer may elect to offer education and training as proposed by Goins, it is not for us to condone or condemn the manner in which West enforced the disputed employment policy. Bearing in mind that the obligation of the judiciary in construing legislation is to give meaning to words accorded by common experience and understanding, to go beyond the parameters of a legislative enactment would amount to an intrusion upon the policy-making function of the legislature. Accordingly, absent more express guidance from the legislature, we conclude that an employer's designation of employee restroom use based on biological gender is not sexual orientation discrimination in violation of the MHRA.

Id. at 723.

For its part, the court in *Etsitty v. Utah Transit Authority*, 502 F.3d 1215 (10th Cir. 2007), held that an employer's concern about liability constituted a valid ground under Title VII to deny a female transgender employee the opportunity to use public bathrooms designated for women while wearing a work uniform. The court noted that "because an employer's requirement that employees use restrooms matching their biological sex does not expose biological males to disadvantageous terms and does not discriminate against employees who fail to conform to gender stereotypes, [the defendant's] proffered reason of concern over restroom usage is not discriminatory on the basis of sex." *Id*. at 1225.

Other courts have disagreed with the narrow understandings of antidiscrimination laws evident in rulings such as *Goins* and *Etsitty*. For example, the U.S. Court of Appeals for the Fourth Circuit sided with the Department of Education's position that Title IX of the Education Amendments of 1972, which prohibits sex discrimination by educational institutions that receive federal funds, requires covered schools to allow transgender students to use bathrooms that are congruent with their gender identity. *See G.G. v. Gloucester Cnty. Sch. Bd.*, 822 F.3d 709 (4th Cir. 2016), *stay granted by* 136 S.Ct. 2442 (2016). In doing so, the appellate court noted that the relevant Title IX "regulation is silent as to which restroom transgender individuals are to use when a school elects to provide sex-segregated restrooms, and the Department's interpretation, although perhaps not the intuitive one, is permitted by the varying physical, psychological, and social aspects—or, in the words of an older dictionary, 'the morphological, physiological, and behavioral peculiarities'—included in the term 'sex.'" *Id*. at 721.

For its part, the Maine Supreme Court has held that a school violated the state statute prohibiting discrimination on the basis of sexual orientation—as in Minnesota, gender identity under the Maine law falls within the statutory meaning of "sexual orientation"—when it excluded a transgender female student from girls' restrooms. *See Doe v. Regional School District 26*, 86 A.3d 600 (Me. 2014). In doing so, the court pointed out that the school had treated the plaintiff "differently from other students solely because of her status as a transgender girl." *Id*. at 606. *See also Mathis v. Fountain-Fort Carson School District*, Colorado Division of Civil Rights, Charge No. P20130034X, June 17, 2013.

In 2015, the Department of Labor's Occupational Safety and Health Administration (OSHA) issued a best practices guidance with the following "[c]ore [p]rinciple: All employees, including transgender employees, should have access to restrooms that correspond to their gender identity." *See* "A Guide to Restroom Access for Transgender Workers," Occupational Safety and Health Administration, 2015, p. 1, available at https://www.osha.gov/Publications/OSHA3795.pdf. The guidance notes that many companies have written policies ensuring that "*all* of their employees, including transgender employees, have prompt access to appropriate sanitary facilities." *Id*. at 2. The guidance adds that

[r]estricting employees to using only restrooms that are not consistent with their gender identity, or segregating them from other workers by requiring them to use gender-neutral or other specific restrooms, singles those employees out and may make them fear for their physical safety. Bathroom restrictions can result in employees avoiding using restrooms entirely while at work, which can lead to potentially serious physical injury or illness.

Id. at 1.

The issue of bathroom access has also received significant political and legislative attention. In 2015, voters in Houston repealed an ordinance enacted by the city council that prohibited discrimination on the basis of sexual orientation and gender identity. The main slogan used by the law's opponents was "No Men in Women's Bathrooms." *See* Manny Fernandez & Alan Blinder, "Opponents of Houston Rights Measure Focused on Bathrooms, and Won," N.Y. TIMES, Nov. 4, 2015, A17. In 2016, after the city of Charlotte enacted an ordinance prohibiting city contractors and places of public accommodation from discriminating on the basis of sexual orientation and gender identity, North Carolina enacted a law that *inter alia* prohibited schools and public agencies from permitting individuals to use bathrooms and changing facilities "designated . . . for a sex other than the [individuals'] biological sex." North Carolina House Bill 2 (2016). (The statute also prohibits municipalities from providing antidiscrimination protection to classes of individuals left unprotected by state law. For a discussion of this aspect of the statute, see *supra* Chapter 3, Section II.C.) This provision makes it illegal for covered entities to allow individuals to use bathrooms that correspond to their gender identity when it differs from their biological sex as stated in their birth certificates.

A few weeks later, the federal government sued the state in federal court contending that the new statute violated *inter alia* Title VII of the Civil Rights Act of 1964 and Title IX of the Education Amendments of 1972. In its complaint, the federal government asserted that:

Individuals are typically assigned a sex on their birth certificate solely on the basis of the appearance of the external genitalia at birth. Additional aspects of sex (for example, chromosomal makeup) typically are not assessed and considered at the time of birth, except in cases of infants born with ambiguous genitalia. An individual's "sex" consists of multiple factors, which may not always be in alignment. Among those factors are hormones, external genitalia, internal reproductive organs, chromosomes, and gender identity, which is an individual's internal sense of being male or female.

For individuals who have aspects of their sex that are not in alignment, the person's gender identity is the primary factor in terms of establishing that person's sex. External genitalia are, therefore, but one component of sex and not always determinative of a person's sex. Although there is not yet one definitive explanation for what determines gender identity, biological factors, most notably sexual differentiation in the brain, have a role in gender identity development. Transgender individuals are individuals who have a gender identity that does not match the sex they were assigned at birth. A transgender man's sex is male and a transgender woman's sex is female.

A transgender individual may begin to assert a gender identity inconsistent with their sex assigned at birth at any time from early childhood through adulthood. The decision by transgender individuals to assert their gender identity publicly is a deeply personal one that is made by the individual, often in consultation with family, medical and health care providers, and others.

Gender identity is innate and external efforts to change a person's gender identity can be harmful to a person's health and well-being. Gender identity and transgender status are inextricably linked to one's sex and are sex-related characteristics. Most states authorize changing the sex marker on one's birth certificate, but the requirements for doing so vary and are often onerous. Specifically, many states require surgical procedures. At least one state does not allow persons to change the sex marker on their birth certificates. Individuals born in North Carolina must have proof of certain surgeries, such as "sex reassignment surgery," in order to change the sex marker on their birth certificates. N.C. Gen. Stat. § 130A–118(b)(4). Surgery related to gender transitioning is generally unavailable to children under age 18. In addition, the great majority of transgender individuals do not have surgery as part of their gender transition. Determinations about such surgery are decisions about medical care made by physicians and patients on an individual basis. For some, health-related conditions or other medical criteria counsel against invasive surgery. For others, the high cost of surgical procedures, which are often excluded from health insurance coverage, present an insurmountable barrier.

Standards of medical care for surgery related to gender transitioning generally advise that transgender individuals present consistent with their gender identity on a day-to-day basis across all settings of life, including in bathrooms and changing facilities at school and at work, for a significant time period prior to undergoing surgery. * * *

H.B. 2 requires public agencies to follow a facially discriminatory policy of treating transgender individuals, whose gender identity may not match their birth certificates, differently from similarly situated non-transgender individuals. Because of Defendants' compliance with and implementation of H.B. 2, nontransgender employees of Defendants and of other public agencies in North Carolina may access bathrooms and changing facilities that are consistent with their gender identity in their places of work, while transgender employees may not access bathrooms and changing facilities that are consistent with their gender identity.

Defendants' compliance with and implementation of H.B. 2 stigmatizes and singles out transgender employees, results in their isolation and exclusion, and perpetuates a sense that they are not worthy of equal treatment and respect. Upon information and belief, transgender employees of Defendants and other public agencies in North Carolina have suffered and continue to suffer injury, including, without limitation, emotional harm, mental anguish, distress, humiliation, and indignity as a direct and proximate result of Defendants' compliance with and implementation of H.B. 2.[20]

United States of America v. North Carolina, U.S. District Court for the Middle District of North Carolina, No. 1:16-cv-425, May 10, 2016, pp. 7–11.

On the same day that the federal government filed its complaint against North Carolina, the state's governor filed suit against the federal government in federal court. (The leaders of the state Senate and House also filed a similar lawsuit.) In his complaint, the governor argued that

The Department [of Justice] contends that North Carolina's common sense privacy policy constitutes a pattern or practice of discriminating against transgender employees in the terms and conditions of their employment because it does not give employees an unfettered right to use the bathroom or changing facility of their choice based on gender identity. The Department's position is a baseless and blatant overreach. This is an attempt to unilaterally rewrite long-established federal civil rights laws in a manner that is wholly inconsistent with the intent of Congress and disregards decades of statutory interpretation by the Courts. The overwhelming weight of legal authority recognizes that transgender status is not a protected class under Title VII. If the United States desires a new protected class under Title VII, it must seek such action by the United States Congress.

McCrory v. United States of America, U.S. District Court for the Eastern District of North Carolina, No. 5:16-cv-238, May 10, 2016, p. 2. The governor's complaint added that

North Carolina does not treat transgender employees differently from non-transgender employees. All state employees are required to use the bathroom and changing facilities assigned to persons of their same biological sex, regardless of gender identity, or transgender status. * * *

Title VII does not prohibit employers, including state employers, from balancing the special circumstances posed by transgender

---

[20] *Editor's Note*: Some of the paragraphs in this excerpt have been combined.

employees with the right to bodily privacy held by non-transgender employees in the workplace. Title VII allows gender specific regulations in the workplace. *See Finnie v. Lee Cnty., Miss.*, 907 F. Supp. 2d 750, 772 (N.D. Miss. Jan. 17, 2012) (Title VII "was never intended to interfere in the promulgation and enforcement of personal appearance regulations by private employers."); *Jackson v. Houston Gen. Ins. Co.*, 122 F.3d 1066, 1066 (5th Cir. 1997) (an employer does not violate Title VII by imposing different grooming and dress standards for male and female employees); *Nichols v. Azteca Rest. Enterprises, Inc.*, 256 F.3d 864, 878 n.7 (9th Cir. 2001) ("We do not imply that all gender-based distinctions are actionable under Title VII. For example, our decision does not imply that there is any violation of Title VII occasioned by reasonable regulations that require male and female employees to conform to different dress and grooming standards"); *Jespersen v. Harrah's Operating Co., Inc.*, 444 F.3d 1104, 1109–10 (9th Cir.2006) (en banc) (holding that Harrah's grooming standards requiring women to wear makeup and styled hair and men to dress conservatively was not discriminatory because the policy did not impose unequal burdens on either sex); *Willingham v. Macon Tel. Pub. Co.*, 507 F.2d 1084, 1091–92 (5th Cir. 1975) (concluding that a grooming policy concerning hair length differences for males and females did not constitute sex discrimination and noting that such a policy relates "more closely to the employer's choice of how to run his business than to equality of employment opportunity").

Id. at 6, 8. The outcomes of these lawsuits are pending as this casebook goes to press.

III. PUBLIC EMPLOYMENT

The statutes that protect employees in the private sector from discrimination (like Title VII) usually also apply to public sector employees. What distinguishes public employment is that government employees, unlike their private sector counterparts, are protected not only by statutes, but also by constitutional law (as well as by civil service rules and executive orders).

The first Subsection that follows explores issues of gender identity and sexual orientation as they relate to general civilian jobs. The second Subsection addresses the military's "Don't Ask, Don't Tell" policy, which until it was repealed by Congress in 2010, was the last federal employment policy that made explicit distinctions on the basis of sexual orientation. The third Subsection discusses LGBT teachers.

A. CIVILIAN JOBS

GLENN V. BRUMBY

United States Court of Appeals, Eleventh Circuit, 2011
663 F.3d 1312

BARKETT, CIRCUIT JUDGE.

[For an excerpt setting forth the facts of the case, as well as the court's holding that "discriminating against someone on the basis of his or her gender non-conformity constitutes sex-based discrimination under the Equal Protection Clause," see Chapter 3, Section III.A.3]

We now turn to whether Glenn was fired on the basis of gender stereotyping. The first inquiry is whether Brumby acted on the basis of Glenn's gender-nonconformity. *See Vill. of Arlington Heights v. Metro. Hous. Dev. Corp.*, 429 U.S. 252, 266, 97 S.Ct. 555 (1977) (requiring proof of discriminatory intent). If so, we must then apply heightened scrutiny to decide whether that action was substantially related to a sufficiently important governmental interest.

A plaintiff can show discriminatory intent through direct or circumstantial evidence. In this case, Brumby testified at his deposition that he fired Glenn because he considered it "inappropriate" for her to appear at work dressed as a woman and that he found it "unsettling" and "unnatural" that Glenn would appear wearing women's clothing. Brumby testified that his decision to dismiss Glenn was based on his perception of Glenn as "a man dressed as a woman and made up as a woman," and Brumby admitted that his decision to fire Glenn was based on "the sheer fact of the transition." Brumby's testimony provides ample direct evidence to support the district court's conclusion that Brumby acted on the basis of Glenn's gender non-conformity.

If this were a Title VII case, the analysis would end here. *See Lewis v. Smith*, 731 F.2d 1535, 1537–38 (11th Cir.1984) ("If the evidence consists of direct testimony that the defendant acted with a discriminatory motive, and the trier of fact accepts this testimony, the ultimate issue of discrimination is proved."). However, because Glenn's claim is based on the Equal Protection Clause, we must, under heightened scrutiny, consider whether Brumby succeeded in showing an "exceedingly persuasive justification," *Virginia*, 518 U.S. at 546, 116 S.Ct. 2264, that is, that there was a "sufficiently important governmental interest" for his discriminatory conduct, *Cleburne*, 473 U.S. at 441, 105 S.Ct. 3249. This burden "is demanding and it rests entirely on the State." *Virginia*, 518 U.S. at 533, 116 S.Ct. 2264. The defendant's burden cannot be met by relying on a justification that is "hypothesized or invented post hoc in response to litigation." *Id.*

On appeal, Brumby advances only one putative justification for Glenn's firing: his purported concern that other women might object to Glenn's restroom use. However, Brumby presented insufficient evidence to show that he was actually motivated by concern over litigation regarding Glenn's restroom use. To support the justification that he now argues, Brumby points to a single statement in his deposition where he referred to a speculative concern about lawsuits arising if Glenn used the women's restroom. The district court recognized that this single reference, based on speculation, was overwhelmingly contradicted by specific evidence of Brumby's intent, and we agree. Indeed, Brumby testified that he viewed the possibility of a lawsuit by a co-worker if Glenn were retained as unlikely and the record indicates that the OLC, where Glenn worked, had only single-occupancy restrooms. Brumby advanced this argument before the district court only as a *conceivable* explanation for his decision to fire Glenn under rational basis review. *See Glenn*, 724 F.Supp.2d at 1302 ("Defendant based his entire defense on the argument that Plaintiff was not a member of a protected class and therefore his actions must only survive the rational relationship test."). The fact that such a hypothetical justification may have been sufficient to withstand rational-basis scrutiny, however, is wholly irrelevant to the heightened scrutiny analysis that is required here.

Brumby has advanced no other reason that could qualify as a governmental purpose, much less an "important" governmental purpose, and even less than that, a "sufficiently important governmental purpose" that was achieved by firing Glenn because of her gender non-conformity. *Cleburne*, 473 U.S. at 441, 105 S.Ct. 3249.

We therefore AFFIRM the judgment of the district court granting summary judgment in favor of Glenn on her sex-discrimination claim.

NOTES

1.   Since most federal circuits have held that sexual orientation does not constitute a suspect classification, most lesbian, gay, and bisexual plaintiffs in equal protection employment discrimination cases have failed to persuade courts to apply heightened scrutiny. Some plaintiffs, however, have succeeded in their claims by arguing that the discrimination in question did not pass muster under the type of rational-basis review called for by *Romer v. Evans*. Examples include the following cases:

- In *Quinn v. Nassau County Police Department*, 53 F. Supp. 2d 347 (E.D.N.Y. 1999), the plaintiff, who was a gay officer, endured years of harassment by his supervisors and fellow officers. "During a three-week jury trial, the plaintiff testified that approximately a year after he joined the police force in 1986, other officers learned he was gay and over a nine-year period, tormented him with pornographic cartoons and photographs, anti-gay remarks, and barbaric pranks." *Id.* at 350. After a trial on a Section 1983 claim, the jury awarded the plaintiff $380,000 in compensatory and punitive damages. In upholding the verdict, the court relied on *Romer* to hold "that a hostile work environment directed against homosexuals based on their sexual orientation constitute[s] an Equal Protection violation."

- In *Weaver v. Nebo School District*, 29 F. Supp. 2d 1279 (D. Utah 1998), a high school teacher was removed as the school's volleyball coach after she, in direct response to a student's question, stated that she was gay. The court concluded that the defendant, by its actions, violated both the First Amendment and the Equal Protection Clause. On the latter claim, the court noted that the only reason the plaintiff was removed was because of the "negative reaction" by the community to the plaintiff's sexual orientation, which amounted to an irrational justification for the decision under *Romer*. For other cases involving lesbian, gay, or bisexual teachers, see Section III.C, below.

- In *Miguel v. Guess*, 51 P.3d 89, 112 Wash.App. 536 (2002), a lesbian, who worked at a public hospital, alleged that she was dismissed because of her sexual orientation. The court relied on *Romer* to support its holding that "a state actor violates a homosexual employee's right of equal protection when it treats that person differently than it treats heterosexual employees, based solely upon the employee's sexual orientation."

2.   In 1998, President Bill Clinton issued an executive order prohibiting federal civilian agencies from discriminating on the basis of sexual orientation. *See* Exec. Order No. 13,087, 63 Fed. Reg. 30,097 (May 29, 1998). Sixteen years later, President Barack Obama signed an executive order adding gender identity to the list of prohibited bases for discrimination in the federal civilian workforce. The executive order also prohibits federal contractors from discriminating on the basis of sexual orientation or gender identity. *See* Exec. Order No. 13672, 79 Fed. Reg. 72,985 (Dec. 9, 2014).

SHAHAR V. BOWERS

United States Court of Appeals, Eleventh Circuit, 1997
114 F.3d 1097 (en banc), *cert. denied*, 522 U.S. 1049, 118 S.Ct. 693, 139 L.Ed.2d 638 (1998)

EDMONDSON, CIRCUIT JUDGE.

In this government-employment case, Plaintiff-Appellant contends that the Attorney General of the State of Georgia violated her federal constitutional rights by revoking an employment offer because of her purported "marriage"[1] to another woman. The district court concluded that Plaintiff's rights had not been violated. We affirm.

Given the culture and traditions of the Nation, considerable doubt exists that Plaintiff has a constitutionally protected federal right to be "married" to another woman: the question about the right of intimate association. Given especially that Plaintiff's religion requires a woman neither to "marry" another female—even in the case of lesbian couples—nor to marry at all, considerable doubt also exists that she has a constitutionally protected federal right to be "married" to another woman to engage in her religion: the question about the right of expressive association. * * *

Because even a favorable decision on these constitutional questions would entitle Plaintiff to no relief in this case, powerful considerations of judicial restraint call upon us not to decide these constitutional issues. * * * So, today we do stop short of making a final decision about such claimed rights. Instead, we assume (for the sake of argument only) that Plaintiff has these rights; but we conclude that the Attorney General's act—as an employer—was still lawful.

The facts are not much in dispute; but we accept Plaintiff's view when there is uncertainty. Plaintiff Robin Joy Shahar is a woman who has "married" another woman in a ceremony performed by a rabbi within the Reconstructionist Movement of Judaism. According to Shahar, though the State of Georgia does not recognize her "marriage" and she does not claim that the "marriage" has legal effect, she and her partner consider themselves to be "married."

Since August 1981, Defendant-Appellee Michael J. Bowers has been the Attorney General of the State of Georgia, a statewide elective office. He has been elected to the office four times. As the Attorney General, Bowers is the chief legal officer of the State of Georgia and head of the Georgia Department of Law (the "Department"). His responsibilities include enforcing the laws of the State by acting as a prosecutor in certain criminal actions; conducting investigations; representing Georgia, its agencies and officials in all civil litigation (including habeas corpus matters); and providing legal advice (including advice on the proper interpretation of Georgia law) to Georgia's executive branch.

While a law student, Shahar spent the summer of 1990 as a law clerk with the Department. In September 1990, the Attorney General offered Shahar the position of Staff Attorney when she graduated from law school. Shahar accepted the offer and was scheduled to begin work in September 1991.

---

[1]   For clarity's sake, we use the words "marriage" and "wedding" (in quotation marks) to refer to Shahar's relationship with her partner; we use the word marriage (absent quotation marks) to indicate legally recognized heterosexual marriage.

In the summer of 1990, Shahar began making plans for her "wedding." Her rabbi announced the expected "wedding" to the congregation at Shahar's synagogue in Atlanta. Shahar and her partner invited approximately 250 people, including two Department employees, to the "wedding." The written invitations characterized the ceremony as a "Jewish, lesbian-feminist, out-door wedding." The ceremony took place in a public park in South Carolina in June 1991.

In November 1990, Shahar filled out the required application for a Staff Attorney position. In response to the question on "marital status," Shahar indicated that she was "engaged." She altered "spouse's name" to read "future spouse's name" and filled in her partner's name: "Francine M. Greenfield." In response to the question "Do any of your relatives work for the State of Georgia?" she filled in the name of her partner as follows: "Francine Greenfield, future spouse."

Sometime in the spring of 1991, Shahar and her partner were working on their "wedding" invitations at an Atlanta restaurant. While there, they ran into Elizabeth Rowe and Susan Rutherford. Rowe was employed by the Department as a paralegal, Rutherford as an attorney. Rowe was invited to, and did attend, Shahar's ceremony. The four women had a brief conversation, which included some discussion of the "wedding" preparations.

In June 1991, Shahar told Deputy Attorney General Robert Coleman that she was getting married at the end of July, changing her last name, taking a trip to Greece and, accordingly, would not be starting work with the Department until mid-to-late September. At this point, Shahar did not say that she was "marrying" another woman. Senior Assistant Attorney General Jeffrey Milsteen, who had been co-chair of the summer clerk committee, was in Coleman's office at the time and heard Coleman congratulate Shahar. Milsteen later mentioned to Rutherford that Shahar was getting married. Rutherford then told Milsteen that Shahar was planning on "marrying" another woman. This revelation caused a stir.

Senior aides to the Attorney General became concerned about what they viewed as potential problems in the office resulting from the Department's employment of a Staff Attorney who purported to be part of a same-sex "marriage." As the Attorney General was out of the office that week, the five aides held several meetings among themselves to discuss the situation.

Upon the Attorney General's return to the office, he was informed of the situation. He held discussions with the senior aides, as well as a few other lawyers within the Department. After much discussion, the Attorney General decided, with the advice of his senior lawyers, to withdraw Shahar's job offer. In July 1991, he did so in writing. The pertinent letter stated that the withdrawal of Shahar's offer:

has become necessary in light of information which has only recently come to my attention relating to a purported marriage between you and another woman. As chief legal officer of this state, inaction on my part would constitute tacit approval of this purported marriage and jeopardize the proper functioning of this office. * * *

Shahar brought the present action against the Attorney General, individually and in his official capacity, seeking both damages and injunctive relief (including "reinstatement"). She said revoking her offer violated her free exercise and free association rights and her rights to equal protection. * * *

Bowers moved for summary judgment on all causes of action. On that same day, Shahar moved for partial summary judgment. The district court granted the Attorney General's motion for summary judgment and denied Shahar's.

Even when we assume, for argument's sake, that either the right to intimate association or the right to expressive association or both are present, we know they are not absolute. * * * Georgia and its elected Attorney General also have rights and duties which must be taken into account, especially where (as here) the State is acting as employer. * * * We also know that because the government's role as employer is different from its role as sovereign, we review its acts differently in the different contexts. * * * In reviewing Shahar's claim, we stress that this case is about the government acting as employer. * * *

We conclude that the appropriate test for evaluating the constitutional implications of the State of Georgia's decision—as an employer—to withdraw Shahar's job offer based on her "marriage" is the same test as the test for evaluating the constitutional implications of a government employer's decision based on an employee's exercise of her right to free speech, that is, the *Pickering* balancing test. [*Pickering v. Board of Education*, 391 U.S. 563, 88 S.Ct. 1731, 20 L.Ed.2d 811 (1968).] * * *

We have previously pointed out that government employees who have access to their employer's confidences or who act as spokespersons for their employers, as well as those employees with some policy-making role, are in a special class of employees and might seldom prevail under the First Amendment in keeping their jobs when they conflict with their employers.

Put differently, the government employer's interest in staffing its offices with persons the employer fully trusts is given great weight when the pertinent employee helps make policy, handles confidential information or must speak or act—for others to see—on the employer's behalf. Staff Attorneys inherently do (or must be ready to do) important things, which require the capacity to exercise good sense and discretion (as the Attorney General, using his considered judgment, defines those qualities): advise about policy; have access to confidential information (for example, litigation strategies); speak, write and act on behalf of the Attorney General and for the State.

In a case such as this one, the employee faces a difficult situation. In fact, we know of no federal appellate decision in which a subordinate prosecutor, state's attorney or like lawyer has prevailed in keeping his job over the chief lawyer's objection. * * * We conclude that the Attorney General—who is an elected official with great duties and with no job security except that which might come from his office's performing well—may properly limit the lawyers on his professional staff to persons in whom he has trust.

As both parties acknowledge, this case arises against the backdrop of an ongoing controversy in Georgia about homosexual sodomy, homosexual marriages, and other related issues, including a sodomy prosecution—in which the Attorney General's staff was engaged—resulting in the well-known Supreme Court decision in *Bowers v. Hardwick*, 478 U.S. 186, 190–92, 106 S.Ct. 2841, 92 L.Ed.2d 140 (1986) (criminal prosecution of homosexual sodomy does not violate substantive due process). When the Attorney General viewed Shahar's decision to "wed" openly—complete with changing her name—another woman (in a large "wedding") against this background of ongoing controversy, he saw her acts as having a realistic likelihood to affect her (and, therefore, the Department's) credibility, to interfere with the Department's ability to handle certain kinds of controversial matters (such as claims to same-sex marriage licenses, homosexual parental rights, employee benefits, insurance coverage of "domestic partners"), to interfere with the Department's efforts to enforce Georgia's laws against homosexual sodomy, and to create other difficulties within the Department which would be likely to harm the public perception of the Department.

In addition, because of Shahar's decision to participate in such a controversial same-sex "wedding" and "marriage" and the fact that she seemingly did not appreciate the importance of appearances and the need to avoid bringing "controversy" to the Department, the Attorney General lost confidence in her ability to make good judgments for the Department. Whatever our individual, personal estimates might be, we—as we observe throughout this opinion—cannot say that the Attorney General's worries and view of the circumstances that led him to take the adverse personnel action against Shahar are beyond the broad range of reasonable assessments of the facts.

We must decide whether Shahar's interests outweigh the disruption and other harm the Attorney General believes her employment could cause. *Pickering* balancing is never a precise mathematical process: it is a method of analysis by which a court compares the *relative* values of the things before it. A person often knows that "x" outweighs "y" even without first determining exactly what either "x" or "y" weighs. And it is this common experience that illustrates the workings of a *Pickering* balance.

To decide this case, we are willing to accord Shahar's claimed associational rights (which we have assumed to exist) substantial weight. But, we know that the weight due intimate associational rights, such as, those involved in even a state-authorized marriage, can be overcome by a government employer's interest in maintaining the effective functioning of his office.

In weighing her interest in her associational rights, Shahar asks us also to consider the "non-employment related context" of her "wedding" and "marriage" and that "[s]he took no action to transform her intimate association into a public or political statement." In addition, Shahar says that we should take into account that she has affirmatively disavowed a right to benefits from the Department based on her "marriage." To the extent that Shahar disclaims benefits bestowed by the State based on marriage, she is merely acknowledging what is undisputed, that Georgia law does not and has not recognized homosexual marriage. We fail to see how that technical acknowledgment counts for much in the balance.

If Shahar is arguing that she does not hold herself out as "married," the undisputed facts are to the contrary. Department employees, among many others, were invited to a "Jewish, lesbian-feminist, out-door wedding" which included exchanging wedding rings: the wearing of a wedding ring is an outward sign of having entered into marriage. Shahar listed her "marital status" on her employment application as "engaged" and indicated that her future spouse was a woman. She and her partner have both legally changed their family name to Shahar by filing a name change petition with the Fulton County Superior Court. They sought and received the married rate on their insurance. And, they, together, own the house in which they cohabit. These things were not done secretly, but openly.

Even if Shahar is not married to another woman, she, for appearance purposes, might as well be. We suppose that Shahar could have done more to "transform" her intimate relationship into a public statement. But after (as she says) "sanctifying" the relationship with a large "wedding" ceremony by which she became—and remains for all to see—"married," she has done enough to warrant the Attorney General's concern. He could conclude that her acts would give rise to a likelihood of confusion in the minds of members of the public: confusion about her marital status and about his attitude on same-sex marriage and related issues. * * *

As we have already written, the Attorney General's worry about his office being involved in litigation in which Shahar's special personal interest might appear to be in conflict with the State's position has been borne out in fact. This worry is not unreasonable. In addition, the Department, when the job offer was withdrawn, had already engaged in and won a recent battle about homosexual sodomy—highly visible litigation in which its lawyers worked to uphold the lawful prohibition of homosexual sodomy. This history makes it particularly reasonable for the Attorney General to worry about the internal consequences for his professional staff (for example, loss of morale, loss of cohesiveness and so forth) of allowing a lawyer, who openly—for instance, on her employment application and in statements to coworkers—represents herself to be "married" to a person of the same sex, to become part of his staff. Doubt and uncertainty of purpose can undo an office; he is not unreasonable to guard against that potentiality.

Shahar also argues that, at the Department, she would have handled mostly death penalty appeals and that the *Pickering* test requires evidence of potential interference with these particular duties. Even assuming Shahar is correct about her likely assignment within the Department, a particularized showing of interference with the provision of public services is not required. In addition, the Attorney General must be able to reassign his limited legal staff as the needs of his office require. * * *

In a similar way, it is not for this court to tie the Department's hands by telling it which Staff Attorneys may be assigned to which cases or duties or to force upon the Attorney General a Staff Attorney of limited utility. Such an interference by the federal judiciary into the internal organization of the executive branch of a state government is almost always unwarranted.

As we have already touched upon, the Attorney General, for balancing purposes, has pointed out, among other things, his concern about the public's reaction—the public that elected him and that he serves—to his having a Staff Attorney who is part of a same-sex "marriage." Shahar argues that he may not justify his decision by reference to perceived public hostility to her "marriage." We have held otherwise about the significance of public perception when law enforcement is involved. In *McMullen v. Carson*, 754 F.2d 936 (11th Cir. 1985), we held that a sheriff's clerical employee's First Amendment interest in an off-duty statement that he was employed by the sheriff's office and also was a recruiter for the Ku Klux Klan was outweighed by the sheriff's interest in esprit de corps and credibility in the community the sheriff policed. More important, we relied, in large part, on public perceptions of the employee's constitutionally protected act. *Id.* at 938–940.

In *McMullen*, both public perception and the anticipated effect that the employee's constitutionally protected activity would have on cohesion within the office were crucial in tipping the scales in the sheriff's favor. Nothing indicates that the employee had engaged in a criminal act or that he had joined an organization (he had joined the Invisible Empire) that had engaged in any criminal act. Given that it was additionally undisputed that neither the employee's statements nor his protected expressive association hindered his ability to perform his clerical duties and that the specific clerk "performed his duties in exemplary fashion," *id.* at 937, the two factors—public perception and anticipated effect— seemed to be the only ones weighing on the sheriff's side of the scale. But that was enough. * * *

Shahar says that by taking into account these concerns about public reaction, the Attorney General impermissibly discriminated against homosexuals; and she refers us to the Supreme Court's recent decision in *Romer v. Evans*, 517 U.S. 620, 116 S.Ct. 1620, 134 L.Ed.2d 855 (1996). * * *

Romer is about people's condition; this case is about a person's conduct. And, *Romer* is no employment case. Considering (in deciding to revoke a job offer) public reaction to a future Staff Attorney's conduct in taking part in a same-sex "wedding" and subsequent "marriage" is not the same kind of decision as an across-the-board denial of legal protection to a group because of their condition, that is, sexual orientation or preference. * * *

We do not decide today that the Attorney General did or did not do the right thing when he withdrew the pertinent employment offer. That decision is properly not ours to make. What we decide is much different and less: For the Law Department's professional staff, Georgia's Attorney General has made a personnel decision which none of the asserted federal constitutional provisions prohibited him from making. AFFIRMED.

[JUDGE TJOFLAT'S concurring opinion is omitted.]

GODBOLD, SENIOR CIRCUIT JUDGE, dissenting.

The Attorney General did not act reasonably. One must focus on what he knew and what he did. Post-event rationalizations of what he might have done, thought up afterwards in ivory towers, will not do. Two statements are central, the termination letter and the Attorney General's statement of position made to the panel of this court. The termination letter said in part:

> This action has become necessary in light of information which has only recently come to my attention relating to a purported marriage between you and another woman. As the chief legal officer of this state inaction on my part would constitute tacit

approval of this purported marriage and jeopardize the proper function of this office.

The Attorney General's position before the panel was expressed in a significant three-prong statement:

The Attorney General did not withdraw Shahar's offer of employment because of her association, religious or otherwise, with other homosexuals or her female partner, but rather because she invoked the civil and legal significance of being "married" to another woman. Shahar is still free to associate with her female partner, as well as other homosexuals, for religious and other purposes.

Examine the three prongs. They are: (1) Shahar's employment was not withdrawn for her association with her partner; (2) It was withdrawn because she invoked the civil and legal status of being married to another woman; (3) She is free to associate with her partner for religious reasons.

As to (1), the undisputed evidence is that in fact the Attorney General *did* terminate Shahar because of her religious-based association with her partner. As I explain below, he feared that he *might be* infringing on Shahar's religious beliefs, but he failed to make reasonable inquiry to determine if he was. As to (3), plainly Shahar was not free to associate with her partner for religious purposes. That is exactly what she had done, and it cost her employment agreement.

The prong that requires discussion is (2). The termination letter is plainly based on the Attorney General's conclusion that Shahar was falsely holding herself out as becoming married in the civil and legal sense, i.e., proposing to engage in a "purported marriage." In search of evidence of holding out by Shahar this court relies upon her use of the words "marriage" and "wedding." This implicates differing perceptions of what words mean. In a common law/statutory/traditional sense "marriage" describes a ceremony as a relationship or status between two persons as defined by common law or statute, involving two heterosexual persons, one male and one female. But, as this case tells us, that is not the only and ineluctable meaning. To a person of Shahar's faith as a Reconstructionist Jew "marriage" refers to the formal Jewish wedding ceremony recommended and carried out pursuant to the participants' Jewish faith by two persons (including two homosexuals) who have made a lifelong commitment to each other and are bound to each other by the ceremony in a relationship that can be terminated only within their faith and who, by engaging in the ceremony, made a commitment to the Jewish people as well. "Marriage" also refers to the status thereby conveyed upon them. In the eyes of Shahar and her partner they engaged in a Jewish marriage and they are accepted by their faith as married and accordingly they may use the term "marriage" to refer to the ceremonial event and to the status created by it.

This court, in its footnote 1, recognizes the duality of meaning that I have described for "wedding" and "marriage" [and "spouse"]. Throughout its opinion the court attempts to indicate (not always successfully) by quotation marks and limiting words which meaning it is referring to. But the decision of the en banc court is based upon, and approves, the Attorney General's attribution to these words of only a single meaning, the statutory/common-law/traditional meaning, and his perception that any other meaning is either false or non-existent, i.e., Shahar proposed to engage in a "purported marriage." The court simply adopts one perception and excludes the other as though it did not exist for Shahar and for others of her faith.

What the Attorney General knew was that Shahar had used the terms "marriage" and "spouse" and "marriage ceremony" in referring to the ceremony she planned and to the status to be created by it. She had used the terms "honeymoon" or "wedding trip" in describing her plans. Within the office there was information that she planned to send, or had sent, invitations to the ceremony and that some staff members were on the invitation list, and other information that, as the Attorney General described it, the planned ceremony would be "a big or church wedding, I don't remember which." Possessed of some, or all, of this knowledge, the Attorney General neither saw Shahar nor talked to her but built a Chinese wall around himself and concluded that she had falsely invoked the civil/statutory/common-law meaning that he attributed to the terms. We know that it occurred to him that assigning a single meaning to "marriage" and "wedding ceremony" might not be correct, for he talked with a female Jewish member of his staff, who told him that the wedding was to be performed by a rabbi from New York who performed homosexual marriages but that "she was not aware of homosexual marriages or gay and lesbian marriages being recognized in Judaism." At best the response was ambiguous—on the one hand the wedding was to be done by a rabbi, but on the other hand the staff member was not aware that it would be recognized in Judaism. As it turned out, she was correct about the rabbi but incorrect or uninformed about recognition of the marriage. * * *

The Attorney General and his staff acted in ignorance of the religious roots of the association that Shahar planned, the centrality of it to her faith, and the recognition of it by the religion to which she was committed. Staff members could recall no discussion of or inquiry into the religious aspects of the matter. The actions by the Attorney General do not meet the constitutional requirements of reasonableness.

BIRCH, CIRCUIT JUDGE, dissenting.

I might have found the majority's application of the *Pickering* balancing test more convincing were it not for the Supreme Court's recent decision in *Romer v. Evans*, 517 U.S. 620, 116 S.Ct. 1620, 134 L.Ed.2d 855 (1996). In my opinion, the Court's recognition in *Romer* that homosexuals, as a class, are entitled to some protection under the Equal Protection Clause bears on the validity—and therefore the weight in applying the *Pickering* balancing test—of Bowers' justifications for his action. With *Romer* in the balance, the scales tip decidedly in favor of Shahar because Bowers' asserted interests are not a legitimate basis for infringing Shahar's constitutionally-protected right of intimate association. For this reason, I dissent from the en banc court's affirmance of the district court's order granting summary judgment to Bowers. * * *

The *Pickering* balance in this case requires us to measure Shahar's right of intimate association against Bowers' asserted interests in infringing that right in the context of an employment relationship. The weight we accord to Bowers' asserted interests, however, hinges entirely on the reasonableness of his predictions as to how Shahar's homosexual relationship might affect or disrupt the Attorney General's office, significantly, it is undisputed that Bowers has made no showing of actual disruption to the office. When we closely examine these predictions, we discover that each one is based on a series of assumptions and unsupported inferences about Shahar *because of her status as a homosexual*. I cannot agree with the majority that these inferences and assumptions constitute a legitimate state interest to discriminate against Shahar in light of the Supreme Court's teaching just last term that mere "animosity toward the class" of homosexuals is not a rational basis for state action.

The first inference that Bowers drew from Shahar's status as a lesbian who married another woman is that the public might be hostile to her participation in a same-sex marriage and might view Shahar's employment by his Department as inconsistent with Georgia law. Bowers argued in his brief that "the public perception is that 'the natural consequence of a marriage is some sort of sexual conduct, * * * and if it's homosexual, it would have to be sodomy.'" As the Supreme Court made clear in *Palmore v. Sidoti*, 466 U.S. 429, 104 S.Ct. 1879, 80 L.Ed.2d 421 (1984), the government may not transform private biases into legitimate state interests by relying on the prejudices of the public. * * *

In applying the principle of *Palmore* to this case, the key question is not whether the government official reasonably could assume that the public might have a negative reaction to the employee's presence; it is whether the public's perception upon which the official relies is itself a legitimate basis for government action. If the public's perception is borne of no more than unsupported assumptions and stereotypes, it is irrational and cannot serve as the basis of legitimate government action. In this instance, the public's (alleged) blanket assumption that "if it's homosexual, it would have to be sodomy" is based not on anything set forth in the record but rather on public stereotyping and animosity toward homosexuals. Under the principles articulated in *Romer*, this does not provide the state with a legitimate, rational basis to discriminate against Shahar. Bowers' "concern" for the public's perception of homosexuals, therefore, is entitled to no weight in balancing Shahar's right of intimate association. * * *

Bowers' argument with respect to the alleged deleterious effect of Shahar's status and conduct on "morale" within the office is another attempt to legitimize his adverse action against Shahar on the basis of inferences that others—here, his employees—might derive from her status as a lesbian. The inferences from Shahar's acknowledged homosexuality that she is likely to violate Georgia's sodomy law, or would be unable or unwilling to enforce Georgia's sodomy or marriage laws, is no more justified on behalf of Bowers or his employees than it is on behalf of the public. Moreover, it is important to note that Bowers' speculation regarding Shahar's ability to handle certain types of cases is just that: speculation. Bowers has emphatically refused to meet with Shahar to discuss any of his concerns. Compounding this deficiency in Bowers' assertion that his prediction is "reasonable" is the fact that Bowers does not make the same assumption with respect to any of his other employees: He does not assume, for instance, that an unmarried employee who is openly dating an individual of the opposite sex has likely committed fornication, a criminal offense in Georgia, and thus may have a potential conflict in enforcing the fornication law. Nor, for that matter, does he apparently assume that married employees could well have committed sodomy—i.e., oral or anal sex, and could themselves have a potential conflict in enforcing Georgia's sodomy law.

In short, Bowers' asserted interests in taking adverse action against Shahar are based on inferences from her status as a homosexual which Bowers claims that he, the public, and department staff are entitled to make. In light of the Supreme Court's decision in *Romer*, these status-based inferences, unsupported by any facts in the record and explained only by animosity toward and stereotyping of homosexuals, do not constitute a legitimate interest that outweighs Shahar's First Amendment right of intimate association. Accordingly, I would reverse the district court's order granting summary judgment to Bowers.

[The dissenting opinions of JUDGES BARKETT and KRAVITCH are omitted.]

COVERING*
Kenji Yoshino

Assimilation is the magic in the American Dream. Just as in our actual dreams, magic permits us to transform into better, more beautiful creatures, so too in the American Dream, assimilation permits us to become not only Americans, but the kind of Americans we seek to be. Justice Scalia recently expressed this pro-assimilation sentiment when he joined a Supreme Court majority to strike down an affirmative action program. Calling for the end of race-consciousness by public actors, Scalia said: In the eyes of government, we are just one race here. It is American.[1] Packed into this statement is the idea that we should set aside the racial identifications that divide us—black, white, Asian, Latino—and embrace the Americanness that unites us all.

This vision of assimilation is profoundly seductive and is, at some level, not just American but human. Surrendering our individuality is what permits us to enter communities larger than the narrow stations of our individual lives. Especially when the traits that divide us are, like race, morally arbitrary, this surrender seems like something to be prized. Indeed, assimilation is not only often beneficial, but sometimes necessary. To speak a language, to wear clothes, to have manners—all are acts of assimilation.

This assimilationist dream has its grip on the law. The American legal antidiscrimination paradigm has been dominated by the cases of race, and, to a lesser extent, sex. The solicitude directed toward racial minorities and women has been justified in part by the fact that they are marked by immutable and visible characteristics—that is, that such groups cannot assimilate into mainstream society because they are marked as different. The law must step in because these groups are physiologically incapable of blending into the mainstream. In contrast, major strands of American antidiscrimination law direct much less concern toward groups that can assimilate. Such groups, after all, can engage in self-help by assimilating into mainstream society. In law, as in broader culture, assimilation is celebrated as the cure to many social ills. One would have to be antisocial to argue against it.

So it is with great trepidation but greater conviction that I come to do so. For the past few years, I have been working on issues relating to sexual minorities. That work has persuaded me that gays (by which I mean both lesbians and gay men) can proffer a new perspective on the relationship between assimilation and discrimination. I believe that the gay context demonstrates in a particularly trenchant manner that assimilation can be an effect of discrimination as well as an evasion of it.

---

*   Kenji Yoshino, *Covering*, 111 YALE L.J. 769 (2002).

[1]   Adarand Constructors v. Pena, 515 U.S. 200, 239 (1995) (Scalia, J., concurring).

My goal here is to develop this idea in the context of orientation, and then to demonstrate the applicability of this insight to the race-and sex-based contexts.

I believe gays may have theorized some dimensions of the relationship between assimilation and discrimination differently from either racial minorities or women. This is because gays are generally able to assimilate in more ways than either racial minorities or women. In fact or in the imagination of others, gays can assimilate in three ways: conversion, passing, and covering. Conversion means the underlying identity is altered. Conversion occurs when a lesbian changes her orientation to become straight. Passing means the underlying identity is not altered, but hidden. Passing occurs when a lesbian presents herself to the world as straight. Covering means the underlying identity is neither altered nor hidden, but is downplayed. Covering occurs when a lesbian both is, and says she is, a lesbian, but otherwise makes it easy for others to disattend her orientation.

Of these three forms of assimilation, covering will probably be least familiar. The term and concept come from sociologist Erving Goffman's groundbreaking work on stigma. Goffman observed that even persons who are ready to admit possession of a stigma * * * may nonetheless make a great effort to keep the stigma from looming large. Thus a lesbian might be comfortable being gay and saying she is gay, but might nonetheless modulate her identity to permit others to ignore her orientation. She might, for example, (1) not engage in public displays of same-sex affection; (2) not engage in gender-atypical activity that could code as gay; or (3) not engage in gay activism. * * *

[A]s the gay rights movement has become stronger, the assimilationist demands made on gays have become weaker, shifting in emphasis from conversion, to passing, to covering. A quick way of demonstrating that shift is to consider the gay-related issues that have figured in the mainstream press over the last decades. In the early 1970s, the press widely discussed the American Psychiatric Association's deletion of homosexuality from its taxonomy of mental disorders. The controversy over this deletion was a debate about conversion, that is, about whether gays were mentally diseased individuals who needed to change their orientations. In the early 1990s, the press debated the practice of outing—the revelation of an individual's homosexuality against her will—and the military's don't ask, don't tell policy. These topics pertained not to conversion, but to passing, that is, to whether a gay individual could or should self-identify as straight. Finally, at the turn of the millennium, the press has been devoting much of its gay-related coverage to same-sex marriage. The right of gays to marry is a question of covering, as it pertains not to the ability of gays to be gay or to self-identify as gay, but to their ability to signal that identity beyond the simple act of self-identification.

Again, the demand to cover may be the least intuitive. A recent example may clarify how gays are increasingly encountering covering demands. In 1990, a lesbian lawyer named Robin Shahar was fired from her job at the Georgia Attorney General's Office. Her employer emphasized that he had not fired Shahar for being a homosexual or for saying she was a homosexual, but for flaunting her homosexuality by engaging in a same-sex commitment ceremony. Thus Shahar was terminated not for failing to convert or to pass, but for failing to cover. As time progresses, I posit that more and more discrimination against gays will take the form of covering demands, rather than taking the historical forms of categorical exclusion or don't ask, don't tell. * * *

No historical moment has existed in which one demand has categorically supplanted another, as suggested by the coexistence of all three demands today. I thus am not arguing that we have definitively moved into a covering phase of anti-gay discrimination in which conversion and passing are no longer at issue. To the contrary, I believe that one of the challenging aspects of being gay today lies in the very multiplicity of the assimilationist demands that gays encounter. Moreover, the attenuation of assimilationist demands made on gays in the past few decades does not mean this shift is inexorable. The ascendance of the demand to convert in medical circles in the years after Freud's death is but one of many examples of how fragile progress in this area has been. * * *

Any real engagement with gay history * * * shows that in some instances, the shift from conversion to passing or covering can be experienced by gays as no shift at all. One such shift is the military's movement from its 1981 policy, which excluded gays on the basis of their homosexual status, to its 1993 don't ask, don't tell policy * * * which excludes gays on the basis of homosexual self-identification or homosexual conduct. The 1981 policy was a conversion policy, as it required gays to convert to heterosexuality to serve. The don't ask, don't tell policy is popularly understood as a passing policy (as its moniker would suggest) and is defended by the military as a covering policy. This shift thus appears to represent progress for gays—no longer will they be excluded for their status, but only for their self-identification or conduct. Yet this shift has not improved the material or dignitary conditions of gays in the military, as homosexual self-identification and homosexual conduct are sufficiently central to gay identity that burdening such acts is tantamount to burdening gay status. Indeed, exclusions under the new policy have skyrocketed, suggesting that the shift is the reverse of a progress narrative for gays. * * *

[It is generally thought] that gays can convert and pass, while racial minorities and women cannot. To a significant extent, the antidiscrimination jurisprudence arising under the equal protection guarantees of the Federal Constitution and Title VII of the Civil Rights Act of 1964 has accepted these distinctions, maintaining that racial minorities and women are more deserving of legal protection in part because they cannot convert or pass. Such jurisprudence embodies an assimilationist bias. It maintains that groups that can assimilate are less worthy of protection than groups that cannot. It further suggests that the only acceptable defense to a demand for assimilation is the inability to accede to it. In doing so, the jurisprudence reflects and reinforces a schism between gays on the one hand and racial minorities and women on the other.

* * * [E]ven if we accept these distinctions for the sake of argument, gays can still find common cause with racial minorities and women. Conversion and passing do not exhaust the forms of assimilation. There is also covering. And while racial minorities and women may be differently situated from gays along the axes of conversion and passing, all three groups are similarly situated along the axis of covering.

Like gays, racial minorities and women cover, and are asked to cover, all the time. The African-American woman who stops wearing cornrows to succeed at work may be covering. The native Hawaiian broadcaster who mutes his accent to retain his broadcasting job may be covering. The Latino venireperson who denies knowledge of Spanish to remain on a jury may be covering. Women also cover. The woman who seeks to downplay her status as a mother or her pregnancy for fear of being penalized as an inauthentic worker may be covering. The female scholar who eschews feminist topics may be covering. The woman who strives to be as aggressive or tearless as the stereotypical man may be covering. In all these instances, the individual is not attempting to change or hide her identity. Nonetheless, she is assimilating by making a disfavored trait easy for others to disattend.

Framing analogies among the covering strategies of these different groups merits some qualification. As an initial matter, these groups are obviously not distinct. When I state that women cover, I am focusing on how they cover as women—I do not foreclose the possibility that they will also cover along other dimensions. Understanding the intersectionality of identity is crucial to comprehending the difficulty of declaring that an individual is covering. For example, if a lesbian wears her hair long and down, is she covering her status as a gay person, refusing to cover as a woman, or exercising a grooming preference that has nothing to do with either axis of identity? If this question seems unanswerable, it is because—like most intersectional analysis—it honors the complexity of the underlying practice. * * *

* * * [T]he contemporary forms of discrimination to which racial minorities and women are most vulnerable often take the guise of enforced covering. A member of a racial minority cannot be sanctioned for failing to convert or to pass without having a Title VII employment discrimination claim. But he can be sanctioned for failing to cover—for wearing cornrows,[26] or lapsing into Spanish,[27] or for speaking with an accent.[28] Similarly, a woman generally cannot be burdened for failing to convert or to pass. Yet it is still true that for constitutional purposes, state actors can burden pregnancy without triggering a sex discrimination analysis.[29]

This commonality suggests that racial minorities and women have much to gain from a theory of discrimination that focuses on the harms of coerced assimilation. Members of these groups are not as impervious to the assimilationist bias in the current antidiscrimination paradigm as their inability to convert or to pass might suggest. If the only defense against an assimilationist demand is that one cannot accede to it, racial minorities and women are left completely unprotected against covering demands, as anyone is assumed to be able to cover. My model thus shows a ground on which racial minorities, women, and gays can make common cause. That common ground will become more evident as anti-gay claims shift in emphasis away from conversion and passing and toward covering.

———————

As the number of employers that welcome lesbian, gay, and bisexual employees grow, they may face resistance from other employees. The following case deals with some of the same legal issues as *Shahar*, except that it does so in the context of a heterosexual public employee who expressed anti-gay rights views that her employer claimed were inconsistent with its policies.

DIXON V. UNIVERSITY OF TOLEDO

United States Court of Appeals, Sixth Circuit, 2012
702 F.3d 269, *cert. denied*, 134 S.Ct. 119 (2013)

KAREN NELSON MOORE, CIRCUIT JUDGE.

In 2008, Plaintiff-Appellant Crystal Dixon, an African-American woman and then-interim Associate Vice President for Human Resources at the University of Toledo (the "University"), wrote an op-ed column in the *Toledo Free Press* rebuking comparisons drawn between the civil-

---

[26]   Rogers v. Am. Airlines, Inc., 527 F. Supp. 229 (S.D.N.Y. 1981).

[27]   Garcia v. Gloor, 618 F.2d 264 (5th Cir. 1980).

[28]   Kahakua v. Friday, No. 88–1668, 1989 WL 61762 (9th Cir. June 2, 1989).

[29]   Geduldig v. Aiello, 417 U.S. 484 (1974); see also Bray v. Alexandria Women's Health Clinic, 506 U.S. 263, 272 n.3 (1993) (noting the continuing vitality of *Geduldig*).

rights and gay-rights movements. Shortly thereafter, Dixon was fired. Claiming violations of her First and Fourteenth Amendment rights, Dixon subsequently filed a § 1983 suit against the University and Defendants-Appellees University President Lloyd Jacobs and University Vice President for Human Resources and Campus Safety William Logie (collectively, "the defendants"). The district court granted summary judgment to the defendants on all claims, and Dixon appeals.

The issues raised in this appeal turn primarily on the resolution of a narrow inquiry: whether the speech of a high-level Human Resources official who writes publicly against the very policies that her government employer charges her with creating, promoting, and enforcing is protected. We conclude that, given the nature of her position, Dixon did not engage in protected speech. We therefore affirm the judgment of the district court.

Dixon began her career at the University in January 2002. At this time, she was recruited by Logie to become the Administrative Director of Employee Relations at the Medical College of Ohio (the "College"). On July 1, 2006, the College merged with the University, and Dixon was promoted to Associate Vice President for Human Resources for the Health Sciences Campus. In July 2007, Dixon was promoted to interim Associate Vice President for Human Resources for both campuses, the position she held until she was terminated on May 8, 2008.

On April 4, 2008, Michael Miller, Editor-in-Chief of the *Toledo Free Press,* wrote an editorial titled "Gay rights and wrongs." In this piece, Miller implicitly compared the civil-rights movement with the gay-rights movement: "As a middle-aged, overweight white guy with graying facial hair, I am America's ruling demographic, so the gay rights struggle is something I experience secondhand, like my black friends' struggles and my wheelchair-bound friend's struggles." Miller then focused on a purported denial of healthcare benefits to same-sex couples at the University, explaining that "[w]hen [the College and the University] merged, [University] employees retained the domestic-partner benefits, but [College] employees were not offered them. So, people working for the same employer do not have access to the same benefits."

On April 18, 2008, Dixon responded to Miller with her op-ed column "Gay rights and wrongs: another perspective." Dixon addressed both points highlighted above, but did not identify her official position at the University. Dixon first rejected the comparison made by Miller between the gay-rights and civil-rights movements:

> As a Black woman who happens to be an alumnus of the University of Toledo's Graduate School, an employee and business owner, I take great umbrage at the notion that those choosing the homosexual lifestyle are "civil rights victims."

Here's why. I cannot wake up tomorrow and not be a Black woman. I am genetically and biologically a Black woman and very pleased to be so as my Creator intended. Daily, thousands of homosexuals make a life decision to leave the gay lifestyle evidenced by the growing population of PFOX (Parents and Friends of Ex Gays) and Exodus International just to name a few. * * *

Additionally, Dixon addressed Miller's discussion of the healthcare benefits system at the University:

The reference to the alleged benefits disparity at the University of Toledo was rather misleading. When the University of Toledo and former Medical University of Ohio merged, both entities had multiple contracts for different benefit plans at substantially different employee cost sharing levels. To suggest that homosexual employees on one campus are being denied benefits avoids the fact that ALL employees across the two campuses regardless of their sexual orientation, have different benefit plans. The university is working diligently to address this issue in a reasonable and cost-efficient manner, for all employees, not just one segment.

On April 21, 2008, as a result of her op-ed column, Dixon received a letter placing her on paid administrative leave. On May 4, 2008, Jacobs wrote a guest column in the *Toledo Free Press* responding to Dixon's op-ed column. Jacobs stated that "[a]lthough I recognize it is common knowledge that Crystal Dixon is associate vice president for Human Resources at the University of Toledo, her comments do not accord with the values of the University of Toledo." Jacobs then explained the various programs instituted at the University aimed at expanding and supporting diversity on campus.

A hearing was held on May 5, 2008, at which Dixon read a prepared statement reiterating the beliefs stated in her op-ed column, expressing her view that she had been speaking as a private citizen, and accusing the University of treating her differently than other employees. Dixon also asserted that her personal views did not affect her performance as Associate Vice President of Human Resources:

If the University is taking the Herculean leap to assume that my convictions affect my service to or decisions about those practicing homosexuality, please consider this: it is commonly believed/perceived that there are one, possibly two practicing homosexuals in the Human Resources Department. I hired both of them (one last year and one earlier this year)! I hired both of them with the perception that while they may be homosexual, more importantly they were competent, motivated and simply the best candidates for the jobs. One individual, I actually hired this year *after* observing a questionable exchange between he and his male roommate in the parking lot one day. * * *

On May 8, 2008, Dixon received a letter from Jacobs terminating her from the position of Associate Vice President for Human Resources for the following reasons:

> The public position you have taken in the Toledo Free Press is in direct contradiction to University policies and procedures as well as the Core Values of the Strategic Plan which is mission critical. Your position also calls into question your continued ability to lead a critical function within the Administration as personnel actions or decisions taken in your capacity as Associate Vice President for Human Resources could be challenged or placed at risk. The result is a loss of confidence in you as an administrator.

On December 1, 2008, Dixon filed suit in the U.S. District Court for the Northern District of Ohio against the University, Jacobs, and Logie. * * * On April 29, 2011, Dixon filed a motion for summary judgment, and the remaining defendants cross-moved for summary judgment in response. The district court granted the defendants' motion, and Dixon appealed. *Dixon v. University of Toledo,* 842 F.Supp.2d 1044 (N.D.Ohio 2012).

Dixon appeals the district court order granting summary judgment to the defendants on her First Amendment retaliation claim and her equal-protection claim. * * * Dixon argues that the district court erred in its First Amendment retaliation analysis, contending that the defendants "violated [her] right to freedom of speech by terminating her employment because she authored an opinion piece in a local newspaper in which she expressed her *personal* opinion and viewpoint on the issue of homosexuality and civil rights from the perspective of a Christian, African-American woman." Dixon further asserts that the district court misapprehended the equal-protection standard, arguing that "when government officials engage in discriminatory treatment based on the exercise of the fundamental right to freedom of speech they violate not only the First Amendment, but they also violate the equal protection guarantee of the Fourteenth Amendment."

First Amendment Retaliation

First Amendment retaliation claims are analyzed under a burden-shifting framework. A plaintiff must first make a prima facie case of retaliation, which comprises the following elements: "(1) he engaged in constitutionally protected speech or conduct; (2) an adverse action was taken against him that would deter a person of ordinary firmness from continuing to engage in that conduct; (3) there is a causal connection between elements one and two—that is, the adverse action was motivated at least in part by his protected conduct." *Scarbrough v. Morgan Cnty. Bd. of Educ.,* 470 F.3d 250, 255 (6th Cir.2006). If the employee establishes a prima facie case, the burden then shifts to the employer to demonstrate "by a preponderance of the evidence that the employment decision would have been the same absent the protected conduct." *Eckerman v. Tenn. Dep't of Safety,* 636 F.3d 202, 208 (6th Cir.2010).

Only the first element, whether the speech was protected, is at issue on appeal.[1] * * * In order to establish that her speech was protected, Dixon must first show that the speech touched on a matter of public concern. Dixon must then show that under the *Pickering* balancing test, her "free speech interests outweigh the efficiency interests of the government as employer." Finally, Dixon must demonstrate that the speech was not made pursuant to her official duties as Associate Vice President of Human Resources. * * *

Because the parties do not dispute that Dixon spoke on a matter of public concern, we turn to whether Dixon satisfies the *Pickering* requirement. The defendants argue that Dixon's speech falls into the presumption set forth in *Rose v. Stephens,* 291 F.3d 917 (6th Cir.2002). If this presumption applies, then Dixon's speech is not protected as a matter of law. Alternatively, the defendants argue that under the traditional *Pickering* balancing test, the balance of interests weighs in favor of the defendants rather than Dixon. The district court addressed both issues, concluding that the presumption applied to Dixon and that "the balance of [Dixon's] interest in making a comment of public concern is clearly outweighed by the University's interest as her employer in carrying out its own objectives." *Dixon,* 842 F.Supp.2d at 1051, 1053.

The *Rose* presumption dictates that "where a confidential or policymaking public employee is discharged on the basis of speech related to his political or policy views, the *Pickering* balance favors the government as a matter of law." *Rose,* 291 F.3d at 921. Therefore, in order for the presumption to apply, Dixon must (1) hold a confidential or policymaking position, and (2) have spoken on a matter related to political or policy views. An application of this presumption "renders the fact-intensive inquiry normally required by *Pickering* unnecessary because under these circumstances it is appropriate to presume that the government's interest in efficiency will predominate." *Rose,* 291 F.3d at 923.

Although there is no clear line drawn between policymaking and non-policymaking positions, we have previously outlined the following four

---

[1]   Termination is an adverse employment action, and it is clear that Dixon was terminated because of her speech.

categories of individuals to whom the *Rose* presumption will always apply:

> **Category One:** positions specifically named in relevant federal, state, county, or municipal law to which discretionary authority with respect to the enforcement of that law or the carrying out of some other policy of political concern is granted;

> **Category Two:** positions to which a significant portion of the total discretionary authority available to category one position-holders has been delegated; or positions not named in law, possessing by virtue of the jurisdiction's pattern or practice the same quantum or type of discretionary authority commonly held by category one positions in other jurisdictions;

> **Category Three:** confidential advisors who spend a significant portion of their time on the job advising category one or category two position-holders on how to exercise their statutory or delegated policymaking authority or other confidential employees who control the lines of communications to category one positions, category two positions or confidential advisors; and

> **Category Four:** positions that are part of a group of positions filled by balancing out political party representation, or that are filled by balancing out selections made by different governmental agents or bodies.

Latham v. Office of Attorney Gen. of Ohio, 395 F.3d 261, 267 (6th Cir.2005). "In determining whether an employee falls into one of these categories, we must examine the inherent duties of the position, rather than the actual tasks undertaken by the employee." *Id.* "While the inherent duties of the position are not necessarily those that appear in the written job description and authorizing statute, such descriptions can be instructive." *Id.*

The district court determined that as Associate Vice President for Human Resources, Dixon "was vested with a significant portion of the statutory authority available, placing her within category two." *Dixon,* 842 F.Supp.2d at 1051. The district court reasoned that her delegated appointing authority, including the authority to hire and fire, was significant and discretionary. Dixon contends on appeal that the district court erred in reaching this conclusion because "[a]lthough [Dixon] had authority to make some hiring decisions * * * she had *no* discretion to make policy regarding hiring practices nor was she delegated *any* such authority, let alone a 'significant portion' of it. Moreover, she had *no* authority, delegated or otherwise, to make any other policy of political concern." Appellant Br. at 26 (emphasis in original).

In Resolution No. 07–10–10, effective October 1, 2007, the Board of Trustees of the University delegated appointing authority to the Associate Vice President for Human Resources. Further, the official job description for Associate Vice President for Human Resources, which Dixon verified as accurate in her deposition, listed the most important job duty as "Policy Development and Application." Specifically, this duty requires that the Associate Vice President "[p]rovide leadership in recommending, implementing and overseeing human resource policies and procedures that support the university's strategic direction; reflect fair and equitable practices; and that are a model for innovative regulatory compliant and contemporary practice." The job description further notes that the Associate Vice President directs employee relations and "represent[s] the University in relevant employee relations actions brought before the * * * Ohio Civil Rights Commission, Equal Employment Opportunity Commission, * * * and other federal and state regulatory agencies."

Additionally, Dixon's own testimony regarding her job responsibilities reflects significant discretionary authority. Dixon testified that she was responsible for answering grievances, issuing disciplinary and corrective action, serving on various task forces, supervising approximately forty employees, overseeing benefits administration, setting compensation, and making presentations at town-hall meetings.

This evidence establishes that Dixon was delegated appointing authority and was responsible for recommending, implementing, and overseeing policy. The district court was thus correct in determining that these responsibilities constituted a policymaking position, i.e., that Dixon, as Associate Vice President for Human Resources, was a category-two policymaker.

In addition to holding a policymaking position, Dixon must have spoken on a political or policy issue in order to be subject to the *Rose* presumption. In *Rose*, we reasoned that "[t]he additional restriction that this presumption applies only to cases where the employee speaks on political or policy issues ensures that the content of the employee's speech directly implicates the loyalty requirements of the position and thus will adversely affect a central aspect of the working relationship in all cases." 291 F.3d at 923. Dixon argues that her op-ed column expressed a matter of personal concern and "was not speech that relates to either [her] political affiliation or substantive policy." Appellant Br. at 26–27.

Dixon's argument, however, ignores critical policies developed in and promoted by the Human Resources Department at the University. Dixon's public statement implying that LGBT individuals should not be compared with and afforded the same protections as African-Americans directly contradicts several such substantive policies instituted by the

University. For example, the University's Strategic Plan included pursuing a strategy that will "[r]ealize the strength and distinction to be derived from diversity in all its dimensions [and] recruit, retain, and celebrate a diverse university community." Additionally, the University enacted a Plan for Diversity that explicitly included sexual orientation. The University also included sexual orientation and gender identity and expression in its Equal Opportunity Policy and in its anti-harassment policy. Finally, as explained by Jacobs in his op-ed column, the University enacted the Spectrum Safe Places Program, which encourages "faculty, staff and graduate assistants and resident advisers to open their space as a Safe Place for Lesbian, Gay, Bisexual, Transgender, Queer, and Questioning * * * individuals."

Although Dixon correctly contends that she never explicitly stated that the University diversity policies should not extend to LGBT students and employees, by voicing her belief that members of the LGBT community do not possess an immutable characteristic in the way that she as an African-American woman does, the implication is clear: Dixon does not think LGBT students and employees of the University are entitled to civil-rights protections, even though the University, in part through the Human Resources Department, expressly provides them. In writing her op-ed column, Dixon not only spoke on policy issues, but also spoke on policy issues related directly to her position at the University.

In sum, the *Rose* presumption applies to Dixon because there is evidence establishing that she was a policymaker who engaged in speech on a policy issue related to her position. The government's interests thus outweigh Dixon's interests as a matter of law, and we affirm the district court's grant of summary judgment to the defendants on this basis. Because the *Rose* presumption is dispositive, it is unnecessary for us to consider the district court's *Pickering* [analysis]. * * *

Equal-Protection Claim

Dixon also alleges an equal-protection claim against the defendants, arguing on appeal that the defendants "punished Plaintiff because she expressed a 'less favored' viewpoint—one grounded in her strong Christian faith no less—in this very same forum in violation of the First Amendment (freedom of speech) *and* the Fourteenth Amendment (equal protection)." Appellant Br. at 34. The district court granted summary judgment to the defendants on this claim because Dixon "has not presented anyone who was 'similarly-situated' and engaged in similar conduct." *Dixon*, 842 F.Supp.2d at 1055.

"The Equal Protection Clause prohibits a state from denying to any person within its jurisdiction the equal protection of the laws." *Scarbrough*, 470 F.3d at 260. "The threshold element of an equal protection claim is disparate treatment; once disparate treatment is shown, the equal protection analysis to be applied is determined by the classification used by government decision-makers." *Id*. "Fundamentally, the Clause protects against invidious discrimination among similarly-situated individuals or implicating fundamental rights." *Id*. Although Dixon recites this standard in her argument, she has failed to produce sufficient evidence in support of her equal-protection claim. To begin, as discussed above, she has not shown that the defendants violated a fundamental right, as her speech was not protected. Moreover, Dixon has not shown that the individuals she argues were allowed to engage in public speech on the issue of LGBT rights and protections without penalty—Jacobs and Vice Provost Carol Bresnahan—are similarly situated.

Dixon's comparison with Jacobs is easily distinguishable. Jacobs, as President of the University, wrote an op-ed column detailing the University's stance on diversity, specifically as it relates to sexual orientation. Jacobs was speaking in his official capacity as the President of the University in order to explain the University's position on a policy matter. Dixon, on the other hand, wrote an op-ed column that was not commissioned by the University and that contradicted the very policies that she was charged with creating, promoting, and enforcing.

The comparison with Bresnahan, although intuitively more germane, fails because it is unsupported by sufficient evidence in the record. The evidence proffered by Dixon establishes that in December 2007, Bresnahan and her partner "became the first same-sex couple to file under the city's new domestic-partner registry." After she and her partner filed under the registry, Bresnahan was interviewed by the *Toledo Blade* and made the following statement regarding opposition of others to the registry: "It's their religious beliefs, and bigotry in the name of religion is still bigotry." Bresnahan was identified as Vice Provost of the University in the article, yet she was not terminated or disciplined as a result of this statement.

Importantly, however, the record is silent as to the responsibilities and authority of the vice-provost position at the University. "Inevitably, the degree to which others are viewed as similarly situated depends substantially on the facts and context of the case." *Loesel v. City of Frankenmuth,* 692 F.3d 452, 463 (6th Cir.2012). In this case, the critical inquiry centers on Dixon's role at the University. Therefore, in order to determine whether Bresnahan and Dixon are similarly situated, we must at the very least have before us a description of the duties inherent in Bresnahan's role at the University. Without such evidence, we cannot engage in an accurate comparison of the two individuals for the purposes of summary judgment in this case. Although Dixon has identified another administrator at the University who also spoke publicly on the issue of LGBT rights, Dixon has not shown that Bresnahan is similarly situated.

We thus affirm the district court's grant of summary judgment in favor of the defendants on the equal-protection claim.

NOTES

1.   Notice that the government employers prevailed in both *Shahar* and *Dixon*. Does this suggest that public employees in positions of responsibility would do well to make sure that their public actions and statements as they relate to LGBT rights issues are consistent with their employers' views? If it was constitutionally permissible for the University of Toledo to terminate Dixon for publicly expressing her views on LGBT rights issues, does that mean that the Georgia Attorney General could constitutionally terminate Shahar for publicizing and speaking about her commitment ceremony?

2.   Should it have mattered in *Dixon* that the plaintiff was apparently speaking as a private citizen and did not claim to be representing the views of the University? Should it have mattered that she did not directly criticize her employer or any of its policies?

B. THE MILITARY

Following President Clinton's election in November of 1992, a national debate on the subject erupted. Clinton had promised during his campaign that he would eliminate the ban on military service by gay people. At the outset of his term, in January of 1993, Clinton ordered his Administration to study the issue and propose a plan of action by July. Throughout the spring and early summer of 1993, Congress held hearings on the subject. In mid-July, the Department of Defense issued new military regulations, which are commonly referred to as the "Don't Ask, Don't Tell" (DADT) policy. The policy was codified by Congress in a law enacted in late 1993 and put into effect with new implementing Defense Department regulations in early 1994. The statute remained in place for seventeen years until Congress repealed it in 2010.

The first Subsection below provides a history of the military's approach to homosexuality, as well as excerpts from the DADT Act of 1993. The second Subsection traces the constitutional challenges to the military's personnel policies on sexual orientation from the 1950s until 2010. Finally, the third Subsection covers the end of DADT.

1.   Background Documents

U.S. MILITARY POLICY ON HOMOSEXUALITY
AND SODOMY—1916–1993[*]
RAND Corporation Report to the Secretary of Defense

U.S. MILITARY POLICY ON
HOMOSEXUALITY AND SODOMY

Since World War I, homosexuals have been restricted from serving in the Armed Forces of the United States through either personnel regulations or the application of the sodomy provisions of military law. Sodomy was defined as anal or oral sex between men or between a man and a woman. At the end of World War II, the legal definition was changed to include sexual relations between women as well.

Homosexuality and the Military, 1916 to 1940

Early attempts to regulate homosexual behaviors within the Armed Forces were sporadic and inchoate. The Articles of War of 1916 went into effect on 1 March 1917. As the first complete revision of military law in over 100 years, this new codification was the first legal document to address the incidence of sodomy within the military population. The first mention of sodomy in military law was in Article 93, which prohibited assault with the intent to commit sodomy.[2] In their 1920 revision, the Articles of War included sodomy as a separate offense. This statute did not change until 1951.

Between the two World Wars, the military attempted to screen and exclude homosexuals from service by utilizing contemporary biological theories about the causes and manifestations of homosexuality. In 1921, for example, the Army's "stigmata of degeneration" included men who appeared overly feminine, with sloping shoulders, broad hips, and an absence of secondary sex characteristics, including facial and body hair. Also among the exclusion criteria was the degenerative characteristic of "sexual psychopathy," which included sexual relations between men.

During the interwar period the military discharged homosexuals administratively more frequently than they formally court-martialed them, despite the official stance that sodomists had to be court-martialed under the Articles of War. Individuals suspected of homosexual acts were

---

[*]   SEXUAL ORIENTATION AND U.S. MILITARY PERSONNEL POLICY: OPTIONS AND ASSESSMENT 3–10 (RAND Corporation, National Defense Research Institute ed., 1993).

[2]   The Manuals for Court-Martial, 1917, defined sodomy as anal penetration of a man or woman by a man; both parties involved were equally guilty of the offense. In these regulations, penetration of the mouth did not constitute sodomy. In the regulations that accompanied the revision of the Articles of War in 1920, however, The Manuals for Courts-Martial redefined sodomy as anal or oral copulation between men or between a man and a woman (Jeffrey S. Davis, "Military Policy Toward Homosexuals: Scientific, Historical, and Legal Perspectives." *Military Law Review* 131, 1991, p. 73).

released under a "Section VIII" discharge for unsuitability. While in theory these could be honorable discharges, in cases of psychopathic behavior, the discharge was normally less-than-honorable, or "blue."

World War II: 1941 to 1946

In an attempt to rationalize policy concerning homosexuals in the months preceding America's entry into World War II, the Army Judge Advocate General tried to assess how existing policy was being applied in the field. In the absence of aggravating factors, the Army removed most sodomists from service through administrative proceedings. Court-martial was indicated, however, in those cases where force was employed, when minors were involved, or when the sexual partner was incapable of consent due to intoxication or other impairing condition.

During World War II, a lively debate took place among military authorities concerning the policies and practices regulating homosexual activity and the exclusion of homosexuals in the Armed Forces. Within the Army alone, for example, there were twenty-four separate revisions of regulations concerning homosexuality between 1941 and 1945, compared with eleven revisions before the war and seventeen between the end of the war and the passage of the Uniform Code of Military Justice in 1950. This debate had several causes. First, there was widespread variance in the treatment of individual cases within the military. Second, military authorities seemed increasingly willing to consult with and accept the recommendations of medical and psychiatric personnel with regard to homosexuals. The American Psychiatric Association's Military Mobilization Committee helped develop the procedures that would be used to evaluate the more than 18 million men who would be examined for induction during the course of the war. By the beginning of the war, Army and Navy Departments, along with Selective Service, had determined that overt homosexual behavior could be used to deny entry into the military.[5]

During World War II, the prewar practice of separating homosexuals from service through the use of the administrative discharge was continued and articulated as part of Army regulations. By the end of the war, military policy concerning homosexuality had undergone several important changes. First and most important, the "homosexual" had replaced the "sodomist" as the focal point of legal concern, although the criminal aspects of same-sex behaviors had been neither eliminated nor elucidated in any clear manner. People who engaged in same-sex behaviors could be separated from the service through their resignation or by administrative discharge. Even if no sexual activity had occurred, a growing body of policy supported the view that a homosexual personality

---

[5]   Alan Bérubé, *Coming Out Under Fire: The History of Gay Men and Women in World War Two*, New York: The Free Press, 1990, pp. 10–18.

could readily be identified, and that such persons were to be barred from military service at induction or separated from the service upon discovery.

The Cold War Era: 1946 to 1956

Immediately after the war, in 1946, the Army liberalized policies toward homosexual personnel by increasing the likelihood of their receiving an honorable discharge. Attitudes shifted soon afterward, however, and, in 1948, the provision for honorable discharge was deleted.[6] On October 11, 1949, the Department of Defense issued a memorandum that unified military policy toward homosexual behavior:

> Homosexual personnel, irrespective of sex, should not be permitted to serve in any branch of the Armed Services in any capacity, and prompt separation of known homosexuals from the Armed Forces be made mandatory.

The Eisenhower Administration, with the signing of Executive Order 10450 in 1953, codified "sexual perversion" as grounds for dismissal from federal jobs. By some estimates, dismissals from federal employment increased tenfold. In the military, the number of discharges for homosexuality remained about the same as it had been during World War II—roughly 2000 per year—but from the much smaller post-war force of 1.4 million. The rate of discharge in the military, therefore, was also approximately ten times greater than it had been during the war.

The Military and Homosexuality in the 1960s and 1970s

Within the military, the separation of homosexuals proceeded unchallenged throughout the late 1950s and early 1960s. DoD policy was revised in 1959, with the issuance of the first version of DoD Directive 1332.14 on the subject of Administrative Discharges. Section VII.I of that directive indicated that among the reasons for discharge for "unfitness" was "sexual perversion," including homosexual acts and sodomy. This remained the policy of the Department throughout the 1960s. * * *

The 1965 DoD directive revised the regulations surrounding the separation of homosexual personnel. Members facing a less-than-honorable discharge were allowed the chance to present their cases before administrative discharge boards and to be represented by counsel. By liberalizing the rights of service members, the 1965 separation directives marked a turning point in the legal history of homosexuals in the services. Before the 1965 directive, most service members accused of homosexuality cooperated without protest in order to protect others or to

---

[6] Those men and women with good service records, however, were to be separated from the service with a general, rather than a dishonorable, discharge.

avoid more severe punishment.[8] Inconsistency in the standards, in the documentation required, and in administrative procedures, however, led to a review during the Carter Administration of the policy and procedures for discharge.[9]

The results of the review were reflected in the new edition of DoD Directive 1332.14, issued on January 16, 1981. In a memorandum accompanying the new directive, outgoing Deputy Secretary of Defense Graham Claytor, noting that his revision "contains no change in policy," explained that the enclosure on homosexuality had been completely revised. The purpose of the new enclosure was to make it clear that, based on an investigative finding that a person "engaged in, has attempted to engage in, or has solicited another to engage in a homosexual act," discharge was mandatory.

The revised enclosure in 1981 also for the first time stated that "Homosexuality is incompatible with military service" and provided the following explanation for the exclusion of homosexuals:

> The presence of such members [homosexuals] adversely affects the ability of the armed forces to maintain discipline, good order, and morale; to foster mutual trust and confidence among servicemembers; to insure the integrity of the system of rank and command; to facilitate assignment and worldwide deployment of servicemembers who frequently must live and work under close conditions affording minimal privacy; to recruit and retain members of the armed forces; to maintain the public acceptability of military service; and to prevent breaches of security.

The revision also affected policy on discharges by making it clear that homosexuality alone did not require a *misconduct* discharge. In the absence of other actions (such as violence), the discharge could be under honorable conditions. As promulgated by Deputy Secretary Claytor, DoD Directive 1332.14 and its provisions concerning homosexuality remained the policy governing enlisted separations until January 1993.

---

[8]   Colin J. Williams and Martin S. Weinberg, *Homosexuals in the Military: A Study of Less Than Honorable Discharge*, New York: Harper and Row, 1971, p. 102. The procedures of interrogation are outlined on pp. 100–114.

[9]   The directive was issued in response to numerous court challenges, such as *Matlovich v. Secretary of the Air Force*, 591 F.2d 852, D.C. Cir. 1978, questioning why some open homosexuals were discharged while others were retained. The 1981 directive removed the military's discretion in deciding whether to retain an open homosexual, making such discharge mandatory.

1993 CONGRESSIONAL LAW
10 U.S.C.A. § 654 (2007)

§ 654.   Policy concerning homosexuality in the armed forces

(a)   Findings. Congress makes the following findings: * * *

(12) The worldwide deployment of United States military forces, the international responsibilities of the United States, and the potential for involvement of the armed forces in actual combat routinely make it necessary for members of the armed forces involuntarily to accept living conditions and working conditions that are often spartan, primitive, and characterized by forced intimacy with little or no privacy.

(13) The prohibition against homosexual conduct is a long-standing element of military law that continues to be necessary in the unique circumstances of military service.

(14) The armed forces must maintain personnel policies that exclude persons whose presence in the armed forces would create an unacceptable risk to the armed forces' high standards of morale, good order and discipline, and unit cohesion that are the essence of military capability.

(15) The presence in the armed forces of persons who demonstrate a propensity or intent to engage in homosexual acts would create an unacceptable risk to the high standards of morale, good order and discipline, and unit cohesion that are the essence of military capability.

(b)   Policy. A member of the armed forces shall be separated from the armed forces under regulations prescribed by the Secretary of Defense if one or more of the following findings is made and approved in accordance with procedures set forth in such regulations:

(1)   That the member has engaged in, attempted to engage in, or solicited another to engage in a homosexual act or acts unless there are further findings, made and approved in accordance with procedures set forth in such regulations, that the member has demonstrated that—

(A)   such conduct is a departure from the member's usual and customary behavior;

(B)   such conduct, under all the circumstances, is unlikely to recur;

(C)   such conduct was not accomplished by use of force, coercion, or intimidation;

(D) under the particular circumstances of the case, the member's continued presence in the armed forces is consistent with the interests of the armed forces in proper discipline, good order, and morale; and

(E) the member does not have a propensity or intent to engage in homosexual acts.

(2) That the member has stated that he or she is a homosexual or bisexual, or words to that effect, unless there is a further finding, made and approved in accordance with procedures set forth in the regulations, that the member has demonstrated that he or she is not a person who engages in, attempts to engage in, has a propensity to engage in, or intends to engage in homosexual acts.

(3) That the member has married or attempted to marry a person known to be of the same biological sex. * * *

(f) Definitions. In this section:

(1) The term "homosexual" means a person, regardless of sex, who engages in, attempts to engage in, has a propensity to engage in, or intends to engage in homosexual acts, and includes the terms "gay" and "lesbian".

(2) The term "bisexual" means a person who engages in, attempts to engage in, has a propensity to engage in, or intends to engage in homosexual and heterosexual acts.

(3) The term "homosexual act" means:

(A) any bodily contact, actively undertaken or passively permitted, between members of the same sex for the purpose of satisfying sexual desires; and

(B) any bodily contact which a reasonable person would understand to demonstrate a propensity or intent to engage in an act described in subparagraph (A).

2. Legal Challenges

Legal challenges to the military's sexual orientation personnel policy can be traced back to the 1950s and fall into several distinct historical periods. Early challenges were aimed at ensuring that discharges comported with basic notions of due process of law—such as notice and an opportunity to be heard—and generally did not question the constitutionality of the military's underlying approach.[21] In one of the earliest challenges to the constitutionality of the policy itself, the U.S.

---

[21]   See, e.g., Clackum v. United States, 148 Ct.Cl. 404, 296 F.2d 226 (Ct. Cl. 1960); Matlovich v. Secretary of the Air Force, 591 F.2d 852 (D.C. Cir. 1978).

Court of Appeals for the Ninth Circuit held in 1980 that it did not violate substantive due process principles.[22]

That ruling was followed by the election of Ronald Reagan and the adoption of regulations in 1981 that clarified and tightened the exclusionary policy. Several decisions in the early 1980s rejected the argument that those regulations impinged on a right to privacy,[23] thus foreshadowing the Supreme Court's decision in *Bowers v. Hardwick.*[24]

Bowers made it considerably more difficult for plaintiffs to argue that the right to privacy prohibited the government from making employment decisions based on sexual conduct. Accordingly, subsequent litigation challenging the military's policy focused on cases in which lesbians and gay men were discharged not for specific same-sex sexual conduct but solely on the basis of their sexual orientation. Such discharges were challenged under both the First Amendment and the Equal Protection Clause.

One of those cases was *Watkins v. United States Army*, in which a panel of the U.S. Court of Appeals for the Ninth Circuit first found the military regulations unconstitutional under the Equal Protection Clause, only to be vacated by the full circuit sitting en banc in a ruling that sided with Mr. Watkins, but only on estoppel grounds.[25] Several other post-*Bowers* federal appellate court rejected the argument that the military's 1981 policy violated the Constitution.[26]

Like the 1981 regulations, the 1993 DADT policy was repeatedly challenged in court. Most of those efforts were unsuccessful. The following case is representative of federal appellate court opinions rejecting constitutional challenges brought against the DADT policy.

---

[22]   *Beller v. Middendorf*, 632 F.2d 788 (9th Cir. 1980), *cert. denied*, 452 U.S. 905, 101 S.Ct. 3030, 69 L.Ed.2d 405 (1981).

[23]   *See, e.g., Rich v. Secretary of the Army*, 735 F.2d 1220 (10th Cir. 1984); *Dronenburg v. Zech*, 741 F.2d 1388 (D.C. Cir. 1984).

[24]   478 U.S. 186, 218–19 (1986).

[25]   Watkins v. United States Army, 837 F.2d. 1428, amended by 847 F.2d 1329 (9th Cir. 1988), different results reached on rehearing, 875 F.2d 699 (9th Cir. 1989) (en banc), cert. denied, 498 U.S. 957, 111 S.Ct. 384, 112 L.Ed.2d 395 (1990).

[26]   See, e.g., *Ben-Shalom v. Marsh*, 881 F.2d 454 (7th Cir. 1989), cert. denied, 494 U.S. 1004, 110 S.Ct. 1296, 108 L.Ed.2d 473 (1990); *Woodward v. United States*, 871 F.2d 1068 (Fed. Cir. 1989), cert. denied, 494 U.S. 1003, 110 S.Ct. 1295, 108 L.Ed.2d 473 (1990); *Steffan v. Perry*, 41 F.3d 677 (D.C. Cir. 1994) (en banc).

THOMASSON V. PERRY

United States Court of Appeals, Fourth Circuit, 1996

80 F.3d 915 (en banc), *cert. denied*, 519 U.S. 948, 117 S.Ct. 358, 136 L.Ed.2d 250 (1996)

WILKINSON, CHIEF JUDGE.

Paul G. Thomasson, the plaintiff in this case, rose to the rank of Lieutenant in his ten year Naval career. Thomasson's service record has been a commendable one. Thomasson consistently received the highest possible performance ratings, he was one of a few junior officers selected for a Joint Chiefs of Staff Internship, and his supervisors, including senior Naval officers, praised his work. Rear Admiral Lee F. Gunn, for example, stated in an evaluation that Thomasson was "a true 'front runner' who should be groomed for the most senior leadership in tomorrow's Navy."

In early March, 1994, soon after reading the Navy message implementing the DoD Directives, Thomasson wrote and presented a letter to four Admirals for whom he served. Noting in the letter that "the time has come when I can remain silent no longer," Thomasson stated "I am gay" and expressed strong disagreement with the military's policy. In accordance with that policy, the Navy initiated separation proceedings against him. In May, 1994, a three-member Board of Inquiry convened and conducted a two day hearing. At the hearing, the Navy conceded that Thomasson had an "enviable" service record * * * [but], it argued, Thomasson's letter gave rise to a presumption that he had a propensity or intent to engage in homosexual acts which, if unrebutted, warranted separation.

For his part, Thomasson presented a copy of his service record, live and written testimony from co-workers who expressed admiration for his capabilities and professionalism, a statement recounting his career and his decision to write the letter announcing that he was gay, and expert testimony on both homosexuality and the meaning of the military's policy. But Thomasson did not, as the district court observed, tender evidence to rebut the presumption that arose from his declaration of homosexuality; that is, he presented no specific evidence on whether he engaged in or had a propensity or intent to engage in homosexual acts. In fact, Thomasson's statement averred that he would "not go further in degrading myself by disproving a charge about sexual conduct that no one has made." The Navy argued that this defense fell short of rebutting the presumption that arose from Thomasson's declaration of his homosexuality, and therefore that he should be honorably discharged.

The Board unanimously found that Thomasson's announcement of his homosexuality gave rise to a presumption of a propensity or intent to engage in homosexual acts and that this presumption had not been rebutted. Because he thus violated Navy policy, Thomasson "failed to demonstrate acceptable qualities of leadership required of an officer in his grade" and the Board recommended that Thomasson be honorably discharged. A three-member Board of Review unanimously upheld this finding, and the Chief of Navy Personnel signed Thomasson's discharge orders. He was scheduled to be separated in February, 1995.

Thomasson brought this action in February, 1995, seeking declaratory and injunctive relief to prevent his discharge. The district court preliminarily enjoined Thomasson's discharge pending resolution of his claims. Ultimately, however, the court granted summary judgment for the government. * * * A panel of this court heard argument in September, 1995, and the full court subsequently voted to hear the case en banc.

II.

[The court begins with a lengthy review of the history of President Clinton's and Congress's action in enacting the military law at issue.]

Thomasson requests that we simply set aside these lengthy labors of the legislative process and supplant with our own judicial judgment the product of a serious and prolonged debate on a subject of paramount national importance. This would, however, be a step of substantial gravity. The courts were not created to award by judicial decree what was not achievable by political consensus. Our power to resolve particular controversies carries with it an obligation to respect general solutions. To overturn those solutions in the absence of a clear constitutional mandate would transform the judiciary into an instrument of disenfranchisement for all who use the political process to register the democratic will. * * *

III.

* * * None of this means, of course, that the statute before us may escape constitutional scrutiny. Rather, it is part of the process of constitutional scrutiny to recognize when the Constitution itself requires special deference. In the area of military affairs, the constitutional chartering of popular control is powerfully clear and purposefully redundant. Ultimately, "[t]he special status of the military has required, the Constitution has contemplated, Congress has created, and [the Supreme] Court has long recognized" that constitutional challenges to military personnel policies and decisions face heavy burdens. *Chappell v. Wallace*, 462 U.S. 296, 303–04, 103 S.Ct. 2362, 76 L.Ed.2d 586 (1983). It is with those burdens in mind that we address appellant's particular arguments.

IV.

We turn first to Thomasson's contention that the statute, on its face and as applied, contravenes the Fifth Amendment's guarantee of equal protection of the laws. * * *

A.

* * * The statutory classification here is not suspect, nor does it burden any fundamental right. Section 654(b) is aimed at service members who engage in or have a propensity to engage in homosexual acts. A class comprised of service members who engage in or have a propensity or intent to engage in such acts is not inherently suspect. *Steffan v. Perry*, 41 F.3d 677, 684 n. 3 (D.C. Cir. 1994) (en banc) (classification comprised of persons who engage in acts that the military can legitimately proscribe is not suspect). Similarly, there is no fundamental constitutional right on the part of a service member to engage in homosexual acts and there is a legitimate military interest in preventing the same. Heightened scrutiny of this statute would involve the judiciary in an inventive constitutional enterprise, and it would frustrate the elected branches of government in their efforts to deal with this question. Rational basis is accordingly the suitable standard of review.

B.

It is settled law that rational basis review "is not a license for courts to judge the wisdom, fairness, or logic of legislative choices." *F.C.C. v. Beach Communications, Inc.*, 508 U.S. 307, 313, 113 S.Ct. 2096, 124 L.Ed.2d 211 (1993). The question is simply whether the legislative classification is rationally related to a legitimate governmental interest. * * *

1.

Under these standards, the Act does not violate the equal protection guarantee. Instead, it reflects a legitimate legislative choice. Whether members of the judicial branch agree or disagree with that choice is irrelevant, for the Constitution envisions the rule of law, not the reign of judges. Congress, after months of discussion, concluded that those who engage in or have a propensity to engage in homosexual acts impair military readiness. The Act accordingly observes that the "long-standing" prohibition on homosexual conduct "continues to be necessary in the unique circumstances of military service," 10 U.S.C. § 654(a)(13), and that "[t]he presence in the armed forces of persons who demonstrate a propensity or intent to engage in homosexual acts would create an unacceptable risk to the high standards of morale, good order and discipline, and unit cohesion that are the essence of military capability," 10 U.S.C. § 654(a)(15).

These judgments reflect in turn Congress' view of military life, which can be, on a round-the-clock basis, "spartan, primitive, and characterized by forced intimacy with little or no privacy." 10 U.S.C. § 654(a)(12). Out of this forced intimacy are forged the bonds that create unit cohesion, which Congress found to be a "critical element[ ]" of combat readiness. 10 U.S.C.

§ 654(a)(7). In short, "to win wars, we create cohesive teams of warriors who will bond so tightly that they are prepared to go into battle and give their lives if necessary for the accomplishment of the mission and for the cohesion of the group. * * * We cannot allow anything to happen which would disrupt that feeling of cohesion within the force." Senate Hearings, at 708 (Statement of Chairman of the Joint Chiefs of Staff, General Colin L. Powell). Military leaders testified time and again how unit cohesion would be undermined: "[I]n my years of military service, I have experienced the fact that the introduction of an open homosexual into a small unit immediately polarizes that unit and destroys the very bonding that is so important for the unit's survival in time of war." S.Rep. No. 112, at 280 (Statement of General H. Norman Schwarzkopf).

It was legitimate, therefore, for Congress to conclude that sexual tensions and attractions could play havoc with a military unit's discipline and solidarity. It was appropriate for Congress to believe that a military force should be as free as possible of sexual attachments and pressures as it prepared to do battle. Any argument that Congress was misguided in this view is one of legislative policy, not constitutional law. Courts have held that military authorities may discharge those who engage in homosexual acts. Given that it is legitimate for Congress to proscribe homosexual acts, it is also legitimate for the government to seek to forestall these same dangers by trying to prevent the commission of such acts. The statements provision, by discharging those with a propensity or intent to engage in homosexual acts, operates in this preventive way. As the Senate Committee described the provision: "[i]t is appropriate for the armed forces to separate the individual from military service without waiting until the individual's propensity or intent * * * ripens into specific conduct prejudicial to good order and discipline." This goal is itself a valid one. No constitutional constraint prohibits the military from preventing acts that would threaten combat capability.

The conditions of military life, whether in barracks or aboard ship or in situations of collective peril, may throw service members into situations where sexual tensions are especially unwelcome. "Many soldiers experience a forced association 24 hours a day. They work together; they eat together; they share living space together; they train together; they shop for groceries together; they worship together. Same-gender sexual attraction in such a 'forced association' environment is something that civilians rarely experience and cannot fully understand." Senate Hearings, at 762 (Statement of General Gordon Sullivan). Section 654(b) thus accommodates the reasonable privacy concerns of heterosexual service members and reduces the sexual problems that may arise when some members of the unit have a propensity or intent to engage in homosexual acts and others do not. These same concerns for privacy and sexual tension explain the military's policy of providing service men and women with separate living quarters.

2.

* * * [T]he means chosen by Congress in the Act are rationally related to legitimate legislative ends. The presumption that declared homosexuals have a propensity or intent to engage in homosexual acts certainly has a rational factual basis. In fact, the presumption, which Thomasson was explicitly advised of, represents perhaps the most sensible inference raised by a declaration of one's sexual orientation. As the Senate Committee noted: "It would be irrational * * * to develop military personnel policies on the basis that all gays and lesbians will remain celibate. * * * "

Although Thomasson argues that some declared homosexuals have not engaged in or do not have a propensity or intent to engage in homosexual acts, "courts are compelled * * * to accept a legislature's generalizations even when there is an imperfect fit between means and ends." *Heller*, 113 S. Ct. at 2643. As a general matter, the legislature was certainly entitled to presume that a service member who declares that he is gay has a propensity to engage in homosexual acts. While some service members have rebutted that presumption before military boards of review, *see Richenberg v. Perry*, 909 F.Supp. 1303, 1313 (D. Neb. 1995); *Able v. United States*, 880 F.Supp. 968, 976 (D.N.Y. 1995), Thomasson did not demonstrate that he lacked a propensity to engage in homosexual acts. The general evidence offered at his discharge hearing had no bearing on this particular question.

Not only is the presumption rational, it is also permissible. Thomasson argues that it is illegitimate to separate him for a mere "propensity" to engage in acts. But in the civil context, the government can fashion general employment policies to prevent unsatisfactory conduct. In fact, the statements presumption is a reasonable means of allocating the burden of proof: It places the burden on the party with the most knowledge of the facts (here the military officer), and it frees the military from engaging in detective work. * * *

Finally, the statute is not, as Thomasson maintains, irrational due to any purported distinction between declared and undeclared homosexuals. The policy instead rationally initiates discharge proceedings when service members, by declaring their homosexuality, thereby provide affirmative evidence to military officials of their propensity or intent to engage in homosexual acts. Thomasson apparently argues that the failure of military authorities to inquire into all service members' propensity to engage in homosexual acts somehow renders the policy unconstitutionally imprecise. But the decision to stop questioning new recruits about their sexual orientation reflects an allocation of military resources and a balance of competing interests, one that does not undermine the basic constitutionality of the Act. Under rational basis review, a classification does not fail because it "is not made with mathematical nicety or because in practice it results in some inequality." *Dandridge v. Williams*, 397 U.S. 471, 485, 90 S.Ct. 1153, 25 L.Ed.2d 491 (1970). * * *

V.

Thomasson also argues that the statute, both on its face and as applied, violates the First Amendment. He was, he contends, separated from the service for doing nothing more than declaring he was gay. According to Thomasson, the statements provision of 10 U.S.C. § 654 thus operates to suppress speech on the basis of its content and viewpoint. It does so, he asserts, by making a specific category of speech—a statement declaring a service member's homosexuality—itself a basis for discharge. * * *

Thomasson, however, misinterprets the basic purpose of the policy. The statute does not target speech declaring homosexuality; rather, it targets homosexual acts and the propensity or intent to engage in homosexual acts, and permissibly uses the speech as evidence. The use of speech as evidence in this manner does not raise a constitutional issue— "the First Amendment does not prohibit the evidentiary use of speech to establish the elements of a crime," or, as is the case here, "to prove motive or intent." *Wisconsin v. Mitchell*, 508 U.S. 476, 489, 113 S.Ct. 2194, 124 L.Ed.2d 436 (1993). Discriminatory words often provide the basis for challenges to discriminatory acts under Title VII, for instance, *see Price Waterhouse v. Hopkins*, 490 U.S. 228, 251–52, 109 S.Ct. 1775, 104 L.Ed.2d 268 (1989) (plurality opinion), yet employers enjoy no First Amendment right to keep those words out of court. *See R.A.V. v. City of St. Paul*, 505 U.S. 377, 389, 112 S.Ct. 2538, 120 L.Ed.2d 305 (1992) (observing that "sexually derogatory 'fighting words,' among other words, may produce a violation of Title VII's general prohibition against sexual discrimination in employment practices").

There is no constitutional impediment, therefore, to the use of speech as relevant evidence of facts that may furnish a permissible basis for separation from military service. No First Amendment concern would arise, for instance, from the discharge of service members for declaring that they would refuse to follow orders, or that they were addicted to controlled substances. Such remarks provide evidence of activity that the military may validly proscribe. And, as we discussed above, the military may take measures to prevent the commission of sexual activity that it deems detrimental to its mission. * * *

Thomasson asserts, however, that this reasoning is not applicable to the new policy. He points to language in the DoD Directive stating that "sexual orientation is considered a personal and private matter" and "is not a bar to continued service." He infers from this language that speech disclosing one's homosexuality admits to nothing unlawful, and hence lacks any evidentiary value. According to Thomasson, the policy thus at bottom distinguishes declared homosexuals from undeclared homosexuals, penalizing only the former on the basis of their speech.

While imaginative, Thomasson's argument fails to alter our conclusion that the new policy is in fact directed at the propensity or intent of service members to engage in homosexual acts, and uses speech declaring homosexuality as evidence thereof. First, Thomasson's charge that such a declaration lacks any evidentiary value is patently erroneous. As we explained in rejecting Thomasson's equal protection challenge, a service member's statement that he is a homosexual has substantial evidentiary value regarding whether he has a propensity to engage in homosexual acts—"the military may reasonably assume that when a member states that he is a homosexual, that member means that he either engages or is likely to engage in homosexual conduct." *Steffan*, 41 F.3d at 686.

Second, the statutory provision does not at its core distinguish between declared and undeclared homosexuals, the central premise of Thomasson's First Amendment argument. Instead, it distinguishes service members who have a propensity or intent to engage in homosexual acts from other members, and uses a declaration of homosexuality as evidence. The statute's operation confirms as much. Service members who state that they are homosexual can avoid separation by rebutting the presumption that they have a propensity or intent to engage in homosexual acts. Although Thomasson chose not to come forward with evidence in this regard, other members subject to discharge under the statements provision have successfully demonstrated that they lack a propensity or intent to engage in homosexual acts. *See Richenberg*, 909 F.Supp. at 1313; *Able*, 880 F.Supp. at 976. Moreover, service members who have never spoken about their sexual orientation are still subject to separation if they are found to have engaged or attempted to engage in homosexual acts. In a similar vein, service members who have not publicly declared their homosexuality are nevertheless subject to discharge if they have made private statements to that effect, when those statements are brought to the attention of commanding officers and the evidence regarding any such private statement is credible. Again, the statute's essential concern is not with speech declaring homosexuality, as Thomasson alleges, but is instead with the propensity or intent to engage in acts which Congress has deemed detrimental to the military's mission.

Because the statute aims at this propensity, not at speech, it is not a viewpoint-based or content-based regulation. With respect to the former, the statute's treatment of a declaration of homosexuality is not based on a desire to suppress any viewpoint that the statement might convey. The declaration asserts a fact, one that the military uses as evidence of a propensity or intent to engage in homosexual acts. The military, however, allows service members to express views on issues that affect homosexuals. As the district court found, members are "free to affiliate with a group that opposes the policy, to make statements criticizing the policy, to attend demonstrations in favor of homosexual rights, to read homosexual newspapers, or engage in other such expressive activities."

The statute likewise does not discriminate on the basis of the content of speech. Whenever a provision prohibits certain acts, it necessarily chills speech that constitutes evidence of the acts. A regulation directed at acts thus inevitably restricts a certain type of speech; this policy is no exception. But effects of this variety do not establish a content-based restriction of speech. * * *

The military policy here is justified on a content-neutral, nonspeech basis: preventing the disruptions that homosexual activity among service members might have on military readiness. That the policy may hinge the commencement of administrative proceedings on a particular type of statement does not convert it into a content-based enactment. * * *

HALL, CIRCUIT JUDGE, dissenting (JUDGES ERVIN, MICHAEL and MOTZ join in this dissent):

I.

It is critical in this case to resist falling into discussion of generalities, as if each homosexual were a clone of some preening archetype. This case is about Lieutenant Paul Thomasson, and only him. The behavior of others is beside the point. Even without the challenged policy, some homosexuals would be unfit for military service, and some among them whose sexual misconduct were the root of their unfitness. The same, of course, can be said for heterosexuals. One need only to read the newspaper to know that the libidos of heterosexual American servicemen are not always restrained by military codes of conduct. But most are.

So, why was Lt. Paul Thomasson discharged?

It was not because of "conduct" in any ordinary sense of the word. To say his service record is "spotless" risks understatement; "sparkling" is a better choice. In his decade in the Navy, Lt. Thomasson rose through the ranks from ensign to full lieutenant. He has excelled in every task assigned him. In April 1991, he was chosen over numerous peers to be an intern to the Joint Chiefs of Staff at the Pentagon. He spent a year there, preparing briefs for Joint Chiefs Chairman Gen. Colin Powell and Secretary of Defense Richard Cheney, and he accompanied them to Congressional hearings on the military budget and force reductions. He was awarded the Joint Service Commendation Medal for "superlative performance" of that role, and, at the end of his internship, Gen. Powell thanked him in a personal letter for "contribut[ing] immeasurably" to the Joint Chiefs' success. Thomasson closed his career in the service of Rear Admiral Albert Konetzni, who, ironically, was in charge of implementing the policy on homosexuality at issue here; nevertheless, Admiral Konetzni recommended him for immediate promotion to Lieutenant Commander on the very day of his discharge.

The performance coin has no other side: the Navy does not complain that Thomasson ever rendered middling, let alone deficient, service. Moreover, the Navy has no proof that Thomasson has engaged in sodomy or broken any other conduct rule, high or petty. Conduct cannot be the cause of his discharge. Likewise, the discharge cannot be explained by Thomasson's homosexual status per se. Under the policy, homosexuals are expressly permitted to serve.

It is only because he has said that he is homosexual.

There is no difference between being and saying except that saying produces a reaction in others. The issue, then, is whether saying, and producing a reaction, is a ground for discharge that may constitutionally be applied to Lt. Thomasson. I believe that it is not.

II.

* * * There is a great deal of evidence that the statute was motivated by a desire to accommodate prejudice against homosexuals. In announcing the policy, the President stated that "those who oppose lifting the ban are clearly focused not on the conduct of individual gay service members, but on how nongay service members feel about gays in general and, in particular, those in the military service." Assistant Secretary of Defense Edwin Dorn testified that "much of the resistance to gays is grounded in fear and prejudice." Retired Admiral Thomas Moorer, former Chairman of the Joint Chiefs of Staff, served on an advisory committee during development of the new policy. He was quite blunt about his views: homosexuals engage in "a filthy, disease-ridden practice," are "inherently promiscuous," and have no place in the military. He stated that many other "military people" share his views. Finally, Lt. General John Otjen, who chaired the Military Working Group, stated that "there's a collective sense in the military * * * that homosexuality is wrong." Gen. Otjen believed that all members of the Military Working Group shared this "collective sense." Moreover, he conceded that, but for fear of and prejudice against homosexuals, the policy would be unnecessary. The evidence that prejudice against homosexuals is a purpose of "don't ask, don't tell" is therefore quite strong.

III.

A.

We are told, though, that tolerating this intolerance is essential to "unit cohesion." Even if accommodating the supposedly widespread disdain for gays were a permissible governmental purpose—and it is not—there is no evidence that the discharge of Lt. Thomasson will rationally further that purpose. Indeed, there is only speculation that the discharge of any homosexual would do so.

Dr. Lawrence J. Korb, Assistant Secretary of Defense under President Reagan, offered this critique of the "unit cohesion" rationale:

> There are at least three * * * major problems with the "unit cohesion" argument. First, it represents a severe and somewhat defeatist underestimation of the ability of today's servicemembers to keep their focus on professional military concerns; it also represents a uniquely curious (and, I believe, incorrect) admission that our soldiers and sailors could not effectively follow orders and do their jobs if we lifted the ban. Second, kowtowing to the prejudices of some by excluding others has never been an acceptable policy rationale, either in the military or in our society at large. And third, in the several units where acknowledged homosexuals are serving today (usually, by court order), there are no signs of unit disintegration or bad morale.

General Otjen, while a strong supporter of the "unit cohesion" hypothesis, admitted that it was based on the personal views of members of the Military Working Group rather than hard facts. The lack of real evidence is not for lack of investigating. In 1992, the General Accounting Office investigated similar organizations that permit open homosexuality in their ranks, and, the next year, the Secretary of Defense commissioned a study of analogous organizations and foreign militaries by the Defense Research Institute of the RAND Corporation. Both studies reported no serious problems resulting from the presence of open homosexuals.

In any event, we have in the record before us a real homosexual, a real unit, and hence a real test of the "unit cohesion" hypothesis. Lieutenant Thomasson served for over fifteen months after admitting his homosexuality. His stellar job performance continued. There were in fact persons in his unit who disapproved of homosexuality, but they continued to do their duty and had no difficulty working with Lt. Thomasson. In fact, some were forced to question their preconceptions in light of Lt. Thomasson's example. Not a single sailor testified that he had suffered even mildly diminished morale.

B.

The actual experience in Thomasson's unit should not surprise us. The ability of the American soldier to put duty before prejudice has been tested before. "Unit cohesion" is a facile way for the ins to put a patina of rationality on their efforts to exclude the outs. The concept has therefore been a favorite of those who, through the years, have resisted the irresistible erosion of white male domination of the armed forces. Though the prejudices underlying such resistance have doubtless outlived the erosion, they have not manifested themselves in a loss of "unit cohesion."

Race is the obvious example. "Don't ask, don't tell" was formulated when the chairman of the joint chiefs of staff was a black man, a black man whose presence in the otherwise all-white inner circle of our military caused no apparent friction or decay in its morale, performance, or cohesion. Likewise, I am enough of a realist to know that there are racists serving in our armed forces, racists to whom Gen. Powell's high rank must have been distasteful. They did their duty anyway. * * *

C.

Another incongruity of the "unit cohesion" hypothesis behind "don't tell" is that it encourages lying in the interest of building and maintaining "bonds of trust" among the troops. A relationship built on deception is anything but a "bond of trust."

* * * The sad corollary of this "policy of pretense" is that moral courage like that displayed by Lt. Thomasson is punished.

IV.

The policy also operates in an unconstitutional manner. Its bedrock is a presumption that everyone will fail to comply with rules of conduct— a declared homosexual is bound to misbehave, and the members of his unit will doubtless allow private prejudice to override discipline. A presumption of misconduct from a person's status, or even from his private prejudices, does not comport with due process.

An analogy offered by Lt. Thomasson at oral argument makes the point well. The Supreme Court has upheld the constitutionality of the military's uniform regulations, notwithstanding that they bar the wearing of yarmulkes. *Goldman v. Weinberger*, 475 U.S. 503, 106 S.Ct. 1310, 89 L.Ed.2d 478 (1986). Now suppose a serviceman writes a letter to his superior stating, "I am an Orthodox Jew." Has he broken the uniform regulations? Of course not. Should he be disciplined or discharged on account of his presumed "propensity" to wear a yarmulke? Of course not. Should he be discharged because his status and accompanying presumed propensity are presumed to stir up anti-Semitism among the majority gentiles? Of course not. In America, we presume that individuals obey the rules until they prove otherwise. If persons do not obey rules with which they disagree, or are presumed to act upon every urge or desire whatever the legal consequences, then rules are a vain exercise indeed. * * *

V.

The intolerability of a presumption of misconduct from a status renders irrelevant the majority's unremarkable holding that the First Amendment does not bar the evidentiary use of an "admission." Of course it does not. But Thomasson did not "admit" anything that could justify his discharge. He said, "I am gay." Let us take that as admitted. * * * Thomasson has not "admitted" any homosexual conduct.

The rejoinder, of course, is that the statute and policy define speech as "conduct." This definition fails to withstand constitutional scrutiny, for two reasons. First, as I have already discussed, it impermissibly presumes that homosexuals are unable to obey rules of conduct. Second, it creates a classification among homosexuals based solely on speech. Because there is no reason even to "rationally speculate" that declared homosexuals are more likely to break the rules than undeclared—the opposite speculation seems far more accurate—this rule must be targeted at suppressing the speech itself.

Here we meet up with the First Amendment, but on much different ground than the majority tackles it. Suppressing speech is "grave[ ] and most delicate" stuff. The military has a broader power to control speech than a civilian government, *Brown v. Glines*, 444 U.S. 348 (1980), but even there the power is exceedingly narrow: speech may be suppressed only if it is likely to interfere with vital prerequisites to military effectiveness. The "vital prerequisite" here is, I suppose, the accommodation of the prejudices of heterosexual servicemen. I very much doubt that such accommodation—never a legitimate legislative end—can ever be a "vital prerequisite" to the military's mission. In any event, Lt. Thomasson has proved beyond any doubt that his speech had no deleterious impact at all, let alone to some "vital prerequisite" to military effectiveness. If anything, the expulsion of a fine officer in retaliation for his speech will ultimately prove worse for the Navy * * *

In the final analysis, the expression of Lt. Thomasson's thoughts, without more, is the cause of his "honorable" banishment from the Navy. "I think we must let his mind alone." *American Communications Ass'n v. Douds*, 339 U.S. 382, 444, 70 S.Ct. 674, 94 L.Ed. 925 (1950) (Jackson, J., concurring and dissenting).

NOTES

1.   Several other federal appellate courts upheld the DADT policy in the years following *Thomasson. See, e.g., Cook v. Gates*, 528 F.3d 42 (1st Cir. 2008)*; Able v. United States*, 155 F.3d 628 (2d Cir. 1998); *Richenberg v. Perry*,

97 F.3d 256 (8th Cir. 1996), *cert. denied*, 522 U.S. 807, 118 S.Ct. 45, 139 L.Ed.2d 12 (1997).

2.   The number of annual discharges under the DADT policy were as follows:

1994	617
1995	772
1996	870
1997	1007
1998	1163
1999	1046
2000	1241
2001	1273
2002	906
2003	787
2004	668
2005	742
2006	612
2007	627
2008	619
2009	275

Log Cabin Republicans v. United States, 2010 WL 3526272 (C.D. Cal. 2010) at *28.

3.   The *Log Cabin* court was one of two federal district courts that struck down the DADT Act in 2010. (The other was *Witt v. Department of the Air Force*, 739 F.Supp.2d 1308 (W.D.Wash. 2010).) In striking down the statute, the *Log Cabin* court explained that the military's insistence that the ban promoted military effectiveness was significantly undermined by the fact that discharges under the policy had fallen by more than half since the start of the Afghanistan and Iraq wars. As the court put it, "if the presence of a homosexual soldier in the Armed Forces were a threat to military readiness or unit cohesion, it surely follows that in times of war it would be more urgent, not less, to discharge him or her, and to do so with dispatch." *Log Cabin Republicans*, 2010 WL 3526272 at *35.

The court also concluded that the plaintiff showed the following at trial:

- by impeding the efforts to recruit and retain an all-volunteer military force, the Act contributes to critical troop shortages and thus harms rather than furthers the Government's interest in military readiness;

- by causing the discharge of otherwise qualified servicemembers with critical skills such as Arabic, Chinese, Farsi, and Korean language fluency; military intelligence; counterterrorism; weapons development; and medical training, the Act harms rather than furthers the Government's interest in military readiness;

- by contributing to the necessity for the Armed Forces to permit enlistment through increased use of the "moral waiver" policy and lower educational and physical fitness standards, the Act harms rather than furthers the Government's interest in military readiness;

- Defendants' actions in delaying investigations regarding and enforcement of the Act until after a servicemember returns from combat deployment show that the Policy is not necessary to further the Government's interest in military readiness or unit cohesion;

- by causing the discharge of well-trained and competent servicemembers who are well-respected by their superiors and subordinates, the Act has harmed rather than furthered unit cohesion and morale;

- the Act is not necessary to protect the privacy of servicemembers because military housing quarters already provide sufficient protection for this interest.

Id. at 36. The court then held that

> [t]he Don't Ask, Don't Tell Act infringes the fundamental rights of United States servicemembers in many ways * * * [It] denies homosexuals serving in the Armed Forces the right to enjoy "intimate conduct" in their personal relationships. The Act denies them the right to speak about their loved ones while serving their country in uniform; * * * it discharges them for including information in a personal communication from which an unauthorized reader might discern their homosexuality. In order to justify the encroachment on these rights, Defendants [under *Witt v. Department of Air Force*, 527 F.3d 806 (9th Cir. 2008)] faced the burden at trial of showing the Don't Ask, Don't Tell Act was necessary to significantly further the Government's important interests in military readiness and unit cohesion. Defendants failed to meet that burden.

Id.

3. The End of "Don't Ask, Don't Tell"

The efforts to end the DADT policy were not limited to lawsuits. Many groups and individuals also tried for years to persuade Congress to repeal the DADT Act. Those efforts intensified after the 2008 elections, which not only resulted in the election of President Barack Obama (a strong critic of the military's exclusionary policy), but also handed both chambers of Congress to large Democratic majorities.

In the spring of 2010, the House of Representatives approved a Defense Authorization Act bill that included a repeal of DADT. Although the repeal's supporters believed that including the measure as part of the military's annual funding bill would make it more difficult for opponents to vote against it, Republican Senators during the fall of that year twice voted unanimously to block debate on the bill.

These defeats let repeal supporters in the House to change tactics by introducing a stand-alone bill calling for the end of DADT. That measure passed the House on December 15, 2010, by a vote of 250 to 175. Three days later, the Senate approved the bill by a vote of 65 to 31.

As Congress considered the ban's fate, senior military officials also expressed their views. Admiral Mike Mullen, the Chairman of the Joint Chiefs of Staff, told the Senate Armed Services Committee that "[n]o matter how I look at the issue, I cannot escape being troubled by the fact that we have in place a policy which forces young men and women to lie about who they are in order to defend their fellow citizens."[27] But General James Amos, commandant of the Marines Corps, expressed reservations about ending the policy, apparently reflecting the greater support for the ban in his branch of the Armed Services. Amos explained that "[t]here is nothing more intimate than young men and young women—and when you talk of infantry, we're talking [about] our young men—laying out, sleeping alongside of one another and sharing death, fear and loss of brothers. I don't know what the effect of [lifting the policy] will be on cohesion [and] combat effectiveness."[28]

Three weeks before Congress repealed the law, the Department of Defense issued a report on the findings of a working group named by the Secretary of Defense that spent nine months studying the implications of repealing the DADT policy. The working group solicited the views of hundreds of thousands of armed service members and conducted almost one hundred "information exchange meetings" with military personnel at dozens of military bases and installations around the world. The working group also received input from former and current lesbian and gay service members. The following is an excerpt from the report's executive summary.

---

[27]   Elisabeth Bumiller, *Top Defense Officials Seek to End "Don't Ask, Don't Tell,"* N.Y. TIMES, Feb. 2, 2010, at A1.

[28]   *Marines Commandant Says Ending Ban on Gays is Risky,* N.Y. TIMES, Nov. 7, 2010, at A15.

REPORT OF THE COMPREHENSIVE REVIEW OF THE ISSUES ASSOCIATED WITH A REPEAL OF "DON'T ASK, DON'T TELL"*

Department of Defense

The results of the Service member survey reveal a widespread attitude among a solid majority of Service members that repeal of Don't Ask, Don't Tell will not have a negative impact on their ability to conduct their military mission * * * The survey was one of the largest in the history of the military. We heard from over 115,000 Service members, or 28% of those solicited.

The results of the survey are best represented by the answers to three questions:

- When asked about how having a Service member in their immediate unit who said he or she is gay would affect the unit's ability to "work together to get the job done," 70% of Service members predicted it would have a positive, mixed, or no effect.

- When asked "in your career, have you ever worked in a unit with a co-worker that you believed to be homosexual," 69% of Service members reported that they had.

- When asked about the actual experience of serving in a unit with a co-worker who they believed was gay or lesbian, 92% stated that the unit's "ability to work together" was "very good," "good," or "neither good nor poor."

Consistently, the survey results revealed a large group of around 50–55% of Service members who thought that repeal of Don't Ask, Don't Tell would have mixed or no effect; another 15–20% who said repeal would have a positive effect; and about 30% who said it would have a negative effect. * * *

To be sure, these survey results reveal a significant minority—around 30% overall (and 40–60% in the Marine Corps and in various combat arms specialties)—who predicted in some form and to some degree negative views or concerns about the impact of a repeal of Don't Ask, Don't Tell. Any personnel policy change for which a group that size predicts negative consequences must be approached with caution. However, there are a number of other factors that still lead us to conclude that the risk of repeal to overall military effectiveness is low.

The reality is that there are gay men and lesbians already serving in today's U.S. military, and most Service members recognize this * * *

---

* U.S. Department of Defense, *Report of the Comprehensive Review of the Issues Associated with a Repeal of "Don't Ask, Don't Tell"* (2010).

[Sixty-nine percent] of the force recognizes that they have at some point served in a unit with a co-worker they believed to be gay or lesbian. Of those who have actually had this experience in their career, 92% stated that the unit's "ability to work together" was "very good," "good," or "neither good nor poor," while only 8% stated it was "poor" or "very poor." Anecdotally, we also heard a number of Service members tell us about a leader, co-worker, or fellow Service member they greatly liked, trusted, or admired, who they later learned was gay; and how once that person's sexual orientation was revealed to them, it made little or no difference to the relationship. Both the survey results and our own engagement of the force convinced us that when Service members had the actual experience of serving with someone they believe to be gay, in general unit performance was not affected negatively by this added dimension.

Yet, a frequent response among Service members at information exchange forums, when asked about the widespread recognition that gay men and lesbians are already in the military, were words to the effect of: "yes, but I don't know they are gay." Put another way, the concern with repeal among many is with "open" service.

In the course of our assessment, it became apparent to us that, aside from the moral and religious objections to homosexuality, much of the concern about "open" service is driven by misperceptions and stereotypes about what it would mean if gay Service members were allowed to be "open" about their sexual orientation. Repeatedly, we heard Service members express the view that "open" homosexuality would lead to widespread and overt displays of effeminacy among men, homosexual promiscuity, harassment and unwelcome advances within units, invasions of personal privacy, and an overall erosion of standards of conduct, unit cohesion, and morality. Based on our review, however, we conclude that these concerns about gay and lesbian Service members who are permitted to be "open" about their sexual orientation are exaggerated, and not consistent with the reported experiences of many Service members.

In today's civilian society, where there is no law that requires gay men and lesbians to conceal their sexual orientation in order to keep their job, most gay men and lesbians still tend to be discrete about their personal lives, and guarded about the people with whom they share information about their sexual orientation. We believe that, in the military environment, this would be true even more so. According to a survey conducted by RAND of a limited number of individuals who anonymously self-identified as gay and lesbian Service members, even if Don't Ask, Don't Tell were repealed, only 15% of gay and lesbian Service members would like to have their sexual orientation known to everyone in their unit. This conclusion is also consistent with what we heard from gay Service members in the course of this review. * * *

If gay and lesbian Service members in today's U.S. military were permitted to make reference to their sexual orientation, while subject to the same standards of conduct as all other Service members, we assess that most would continue to be private and discreet about their personal lives. This discretion would occur for reasons having nothing to do with law, but everything to do with a desire to fit in, co-exist, and succeed in the military environment. * * *

In communications with gay and lesbian current and former Service members, we repeatedly heard a patriotic desire to serve and defend the Nation, subject to the same rules as everyone else. In the words of one gay Service member, repeal would simply "take a knife out of my back. * * * You have no idea what it is like to have to serve in silence." Most said they did not desire special treatment, to use the military for social experimentation, or to advance a social agenda. Some of those separated under Don't Ask, Don't Tell would welcome the opportunity to rejoin the military if permitted. From them, we heard expressed many of the same values that we heard over and over again from Service members at large—love of country, honor, respect, integrity, and service over self. We simply cannot square the reality of these people with the perceptions about "open" service.

Given that we are in a time of war, the combat arms communities across all Services required special focus and analysis. Though the survey results demonstrate a solid majority of the overall U.S. military who predict mixed, positive or no effect in the event of repeal, these percentages are lower, and the percentage of those who predict negative effects are higher, in combat arms units. For example, * * * while the percentage of the overall U.S. military that predicts negative or very negative effects on their unit's ability to "work together to get the job done" is 30%, the percentage is 43% for the Marine Corps, 48% within Army combat arms units, and 58% within Marine combat arms units.

However, while a higher percentage of Service members in warfighting units predict negative effects of repeal, the percentage distinctions between warfighting units and the entire military are almost non-existent when asked about the actual experience of serving in a unit with someone believed to be gay. For example, when those in the overall military were asked about the experience of working with someone they believed to be gay or lesbian, 92% stated that their unit's "ability to work together," was "very good," "good" or "neither good nor poor." Meanwhile, in response to the same question, the percentage is 89% for those in Army combat arms units and 84% for those in Marine combat arms units—all very high percentages. * * *

Our assessment here is also informed by the lessons of history in this country. Though there are fundamental differences between matters of race, gender, and sexual orientation, we believe the U.S. military's prior experiences with racial and gender integration are relevant. In the late 1940s and early 1950s, our military took on the racial integration of its ranks, before the country at large had done so. Our military then was many times larger than it is today, had just returned from World War II, and was in the midst of Cold War tensions and the Korean War. By our assessment, the resistance to change at that time was far more intense: surveys of the military revealed opposition to racial integration of the Services at levels as high as 80–90%. Some of our best-known and most-revered military leaders from the World War II-era voiced opposition to the integration of blacks into the military, making strikingly similar predictions of the negative impact on unit cohesion. But by 1953, 95% of all African-American soldiers were serving in racially integrated units, while public buses in Montgomery, Alabama and other cities were still racially segregated.

Today, the U.S. military is probably the most racially diverse and integrated institution in the country—one in which an African American rose through the ranks to become the senior-most military officer in the country 20 years before Barack Obama was elected President.

The story is similar when it came to the integration of women into the military. In 1948, women were limited to 2% of active duty personnel in each Service, with significant limitations on the roles they could perform. Currently, women make up 14% of the force, and are permitted to serve in 92% of the occupational specialties. Along the way to gender integration, many of our Nation's military leaders predicted dire consequences for unit cohesion and military effectiveness if women were allowed to serve in large numbers. As with racial integration, this experience has not always been smooth. But, the consensus is the same: the introduction and integration of women into the force has made our military stronger.

The general lesson we take from these transformational experiences in history is that in matters of personnel change within the military, predictions and surveys tend to overestimate negative consequences, and underestimate the U.S. military's ability to adapt and incorporate within its ranks the diversity that is reflective of American society at large.

Our conclusions are also informed by the experiences of our foreign allies. To be sure, there is no perfect comparator to the U.S. military, and the cultures and attitudes toward homosexuality vary greatly among nations of the world. However, in recent times a number of other countries have transitioned to policies that permit open military service by gay men and lesbians. These include the United Kingdom, Canada, Australia, Germany, Italy, and Israel.

Significantly, prior to change, surveys of the militaries in Canada and the U.K. indicated much higher levels of resistance than our own survey results—as high as 65% for some areas—but the actual implementation of change in those countries went much more smoothly than expected, with little or no disruption. * * *

Our most significant recommendations are as follows:

Leadership, Training, and Education. Successful implementation of repeal of Don't Ask, Don't Tell will depend upon strong leadership, a clear message, and proactive education. * * *

Standards of Conduct. Throughout our engagement with the force, we heard many concerns expressed by Service members about possible inappropriate conduct that might take place in the event of repeal, including unprofessional relationships between Service members; public displays of affection; inappropriate dress and appearance; and acts of violence, harassment, and disrespect. Many of these concerns were about conduct that is already regulated in the military environment, regardless of the sexual orientation of the persons involved, or whether it involves persons of the same sex or the opposite sex. For instance, military standards of conduct—as reflected in the Uniform Code for Military Justice, Service regulations and policies, and unwritten Service customs and traditions—already prohibit fraternization and unprofessional relationships. They also address various forms of harassment and unprofessional behavior, prescribe appropriate dress and appearance, and provide guidelines on public displays of affection.

We believe that it is not necessary to establish an extensive set of new or revised standards of conduct in the event of repeal. Concerns for standards in the event of repeal can be adequately addressed through training and education about how already existing standards of conduct continue to apply to all Service members, regardless of sexual orientation, in a post-repeal environment. We do recommend, however, that the Department of Defense issue guidance that all standards of conduct apply uniformly, without regard to sexual orientation. We also recommend that the Department of Defense direct the Services to review their current standards to ensure that they are sexual-orientation neutral and that they provide adequate guidance to the extent each Service considers appropriate on unprofessional relationships, harassment, public displays of affection, and dress and appearance. Part of the education process should include a reminder to commanders about the tools they already have in hand to punish and remedy inappropriate conduct that may arise in a post-repeal environment. * * *

Moral and Religious Concerns. In the course of our review, we heard a large number of Service members raise religious and moral objections to homosexuality or to serving alongside someone who is gay.

Some feared repeal of Don't Ask, Don't Tell might limit their individual freedom of expression and free exercise of religion, or require them to change their personal beliefs about the morality of homosexuality. The views expressed to us in these terms cannot be downplayed or dismissed. Special attention should also be given to address the concerns of our community of 3,000 military chaplains. Some of the most intense and sharpest divergence of views about Don't Ask, Don't Tell exists among the chaplain corps. A large number of military chaplains (and their followers) believe that homosexuality is a sin and an abomination, and that they are required by God to condemn it as such.

However, the reality is that in today's U.S. military, people of sharply different moral values and religious convictions—including those who believe that abortion is murder and those who do not, and those who believe Jesus Christ is the Son of God and those who do not—and those who have no religious convictions at all, already co-exist, work, live, and fight together on a daily basis. The other reality is that policies regarding Service members' individual expression and free exercise of religion already exist, and we believe they are adequate. Service members will not be required to change their personal views and religious beliefs; they must, however, continue to respect and serve with others who hold different views and beliefs. * * *

Privacy and Cohabitation. In the course of our review we heard from a very large number of Service members about their discomfort with sharing bathroom facilities or living quarters with those they know to be gay or lesbian. Some went so far to suggest that a repeal of Don't Ask, Don't Tell may even require separate bathroom and shower facilities for gay men and lesbians. We disagree, and recommend against separate facilities. Though many regard the very discussion of this topic as offensive, given the number of Service members who raised it, we are obliged to address it. The creation of a third and possibly fourth category of bathroom facilities and living quarters, whether at bases or forward deployed areas, would be a logistical nightmare, expensive, and impossible to administer. And, even if it could be achieved and administered, separate facilities would, in our view, stigmatize gay and lesbian Service members in a manner reminiscent of "separate but equal" facilities for blacks prior to the 1960s. Accordingly, we recommend that the Department of Defense expressly prohibit berthing or billeting assignments or the designation of bathroom facilities based on sexual orientation. At the same time, commanders would retain the authority they currently have to alter berthing or billeting assignments or accommodate privacy concerns on an individualized, case-by-case basis, in the interests of morale, good order and discipline, and consistent with performance of mission. It should also be recognized that commanders already have the tools—from counseling, to non-judicial punishment, to

UCMJ prosecution—to deal with misbehavior in either living quarters or showers, whether the person who engages in the misconduct is gay or straight.

Most concerns we heard about showers and bathrooms were based on stereotype—that gay men and lesbians will behave as predators in these situations, or that permitting homosexual and heterosexual people of the same sex to shower together is tantamount to allowing men and women to shower together. However, common sense tells us that a situation in which people of different anatomy shower together is different from a situation in which people of the same anatomy but different sexual orientations shower together. The former is uncommon and unacceptable to almost everyone in this country; the latter is a situation most in the military have already experienced. Indeed, the survey results indicate 50% of Service members recognize they have already had the experience of sharing bathroom facilities with someone they believed to be gay. This is also a situation resembling what now exists in hundreds of thousands of college dorms, college and high school gyms, professional sports locker rooms, police and fire stations, and athletic clubs around the nation. And, as one gay former Service member told us, to fit in, co-exist, and conform to social norms, gay men have learned to avoid making heterosexuals feel uncomfortable or threatened in these situations. * * *

Benefits. As part of this review, we considered appropriate changes, in the event of repeal, to benefits to be accorded to same-sex partners and families of gay Service members. This issue is itself large and complex, and implicates the ongoing national political and legal debate regarding same-sex relationships. Members of the U.S. military are eligible for and receive a wide array of benefits and support resources, both for themselves and their families. A reality is that, given current law, particularly the Defense of Marriage Act, there are a number of those benefits that cannot legally be extended to gay and lesbian Service members and their same-sex partners, even if they are lawfully married in a state that permits same-sex marriage. An example of this is the Basic Allowance for Housing at the "with-dependent rate." The "with-dependent" rate is limited by statute to Service members with "dependents." The word "dependent" is also defined by statute and is limited to the Service member's "spouse" or dependent parents, unmarried children, or certain others under the age of 23 who are placed in the legal custody of the Service member. And, the Defense of Marriage Act limits the definition of the word "spouse" to mean "only a person of the opposite sex who is a husband or wife."

However, there are some benefits that are now, under current law and regulations, fully available to anyone of a Service member's choosing, including a same-sex partner, because they are "member-designated" benefits. Examples here are beneficiaries for Servicemembers' Group Life

Insurance and Thrift Savings Plan, missing member notification, and hospital visitation access. If Don't Ask, Don't Tell is repealed, Service members may designate a same-sex partner for these benefits without then having to conceal the nature of the relationship from the military * * *

Re-accession. In the event of repeal, we recommend that Service members who have been previously separated under Don't Ask, Don't Tell be permitted to apply for reentry into the military, pursuant to the same criteria as others who seek reentry. The fact that their separation was for homosexual conduct would not be considered as part of the Service member's application for re-accession.

UCMJ. We support the pre-existing proposals to repeal Article 125 of the Uniform Code of Military Justice and remove private consensual sodomy between adults as a criminal offense. This change in law is warranted irrespective of whether Don't Ask, Don't Tell is repealed, to resolve any constitutional concerns about the provision in light of *Lawrence v. Texas* and *United States v. Marcum.* We also support revising offenses involving sexual conduct or inappropriate relationships to ensure sexual orientation neutral application, consistent with the recommendations of this report. For example, the offense of adultery defined in the Manual for Courts-Martial should be revised to apply equally to heterosexual and homosexual sex that is engaged in by or with a married person.

NOTES

1. In 2012, the Palm Center, a research institute that focuses on issues of gender, sexuality, and the military, issued a report on the effects of the repeal of DADT on military effectiveness. Aaron Belkin et al., *One Year Out: An Assessment of DADT Reapeal's Impact on Military Readiness* (Palm Center, 2012), available at http://www.palmcenter.org/files/One%20Year%20 Out_0.pdf. The report found that the repeal had no impact on the cohesion of units that included openly gay, lesbian, or bisexual members. It also had no impact on recruiting, which remained robust. As for retention, the authors, after noting that some critics had predicted that the repeal would lead to mass resignations, found only two resignations (both involving chaplains) that were linked to the change in policy. Finally, the report found no evidence of an increase in the harassment of gay, lesbian, and bisexual members and no decline in morale among the troops.

2. In 1993, the same year that President Clinton announced the adoption of the DADT policy, the military "formally restricted women from artillery, armor, infantry, and other such ground-combat roles." Tanya L. Domi, *Women in Combat: Policy Catches up with Reality*, N. Y. TIMES, Feb. 8, 2013, A30. Two decades later, and only a year after the repeal of DADT, the military lifted its ban on women in combat. Elisabeth Bumiller and Thom

Shanker, *Military Chiefs' Personal Encounters Influenced Lifting Women's Combat Ban*, N.Y. TIMES, Jan. 24, 2013, A16.

3.   The DADT policy addressed issues of sexual orientation and not of gender identity. As a result, the repeal of DADT left in place medical regulations that prohibit transgender individuals from serving in the military. Under these regulations, the armed services had the authority to discharge, or refuse to admit, individuals on the basis of a "[h]istory of major abnormalities or defects of the genitalia such as change of sex [or] hermaphroditism." Instruction 6130.03, § 15(r), "Medical Standards for Appointment, Enlistment, or Induction in the Military Services," U.S. Department of Defense (2011). In addition, "[c]urrent or history of psychosexual conditions, including but not limited to transsexualism, exhibitionism, transvestism, voyeurism, and other paraphilias" constitute grounds for exclusion. *Id.* at § 29(r). *See also* "Standards of Medical Fitness," § 3–35, Army Regulation 40–501, U.S. Department of Defense (2011) ("A history of, or current manifestations of, personality disorders, disorders of impulse control not elsewhere classified, transvestism, voyeurism, other paraphilias, or factitious disorders, psychosexual conditions, transsexual, gender identity disorder to include major abnormalities or defects of the genitalia such as change of sex or a current attempt to change sex, hermaphroditism, pseudohermaphroditism, or pure gonadal dysgenesis or dysfunctional residuals from surgical correction of these conditions render an individual administratively unfit.").

4.   Legal challenges to the U.S. military's gender identity exclusionary regulations did not succeed. *See, e.g., Leyland v. Orr*, 828 F.2d 584, 586 (9th Cir. 1987); *DeGroat v. Townsend*, 495 F.Supp.2d 845, 850 (S.D. Ohio 2007); *Davis v. Alexander*, 510 F.Supp. 900, 904 (D. Minn. 1981). The military also successfully prosecuted biologically male service members for wearing female clothing under Article 134 of the Uniform Code of Military Justice, which prohibits "disorders and neglects to the prejudice of good order and discipline," as well as conduct that "bring[s] discredit upon the armed forces." 10 U.S.C. § 934 (2012). *See, e.g., United States v. Guerrero*, 33 M.J. 295 (Ct.Mil.App. 1991); *United States v. Davis*, 26 M.J. 445 (Ct.Mil.App. 1988).

5.   In 2015, the Secretary of Defense, after stating that the military's "current regulations regarding transgender service members are outdated and are causing uncertainty that distracts commanders from our core missions," appointed a working group to study "the policy and readiness implications of welcoming transgender persons to serve openly." Statement by Secretary of Defense Ash Carter on DOD Transgender Policy, Department of Defense, Press Release No. NR–272–15, July 13, 2015. A year later, the working group completed a report which concluded that allowing transgender individuals to serve openly in the military would not negatively impact its readiness. Agnes Gereben Schaefar et al., "Assessing Implications of Allowing Transgender Service Members to Serve Openly," RAND Corp., March, 2016. Shortly thereafter, the Secretary of Defense announced he was lifting the transgender ban effective immediately. Matthew Rosenberg, "Transgender

People will be Allowed to Serve Openly in the Military," N.Y. TIMES, June 30, 2016.

C. TEACHERS

The issue of lesbian, gay, and bisexual school teachers has given rise to a terrific amount of public concern, legislation, and litigation. These cases add an extra dimension to a standard government employee case— namely, the relationship of gay people to children. Two related issues arise in this context: first, the baseless concern that there is some connection between sexual orientation and child molestation; and second, a concern about whether gay people are good "role models" for children.

In 1977, the Washington Supreme Court upheld the firing of a gay school teacher. The court concluded that "the plaintiff's performance as a teacher was sufficiently impaired by his known homosexuality."[29] In particular, the court pointed to the fact that

> at least one student expressly objected to Gaylord teaching at the high school because of his homosexuality. Three fellow teachers testified against Gaylord remaining on the teaching staff, testifying it was objectionable to them both as teachers and parents. The vice-principal and the principal, as well as the retired superintendent of instruction, testified his presence on the faculty would create problems. * * * The testimony of the school teachers and administrative personnel constituted substantial evidence sufficient to support the findings as to the impairment of the teacher's efficiency.

> It is important to remember that Gaylord's homosexual conduct must be considered in the context of his position of teaching high school students. Such students could treat the retention of the high school teacher by the school board as indicating adult approval of his homosexuality. It would be unreasonable to assume as a matter of law a teacher's ability to perform as a teacher required to teach principles of morality is not impaired and creates no danger of encouraging expression of approval and of imitation. Likewise to say that school directors must wait for prior specific overt expression of homosexual conduct before they act to prevent harm from one who chooses to remain "erotically attracted to a notable degree towards persons of his own sex and is psychologically, if not actually disposed to engage in sexual activity prompted by this attraction" is to ask the school directors to take an unacceptable risk in discharging their

---

[29]   *Gaylord v. Tacoma Sch. Dist. No. 10*, 559 P.2d 1340, 1346, 88 Wash.2d 286, 297 (1977).

fiduciary responsibility of managing the affairs of the school district.[30]

A year later, California State Senator John Briggs proposed a statewide initiative calling for the firing of any school employee who engaged in "advocating, soliciting, imposing, encouraging or promoting of private or public homosexual activity directed at, or likely to come to the attention of schoolchildren and/or other employees."[31] The Briggs Initiative was defeated at the polls by California voters.

A law very similar to the Briggs Initiative was proposed in several states around the country and enacted in Oklahoma. The statute, provided as follows:

A.   As used in this section:

   1.   "Public homosexual activity" means the commission of an act defined in Section 886 of Title 21 of the Oklahoma Statutes, if such act is:

      a.   committed with a person of the same sex, and

      b.   indiscreet and not practiced in private;

   2.   "Public homosexual conduct" means advocating, soliciting, imposing, encouraging or promoting public or private homosexual activity in a manner that creates a substantial risk that such conduct will come to the attention of school children or school employees; * * *

B.   * * * [A] teacher, student teacher or a teachers' aide may be refused employment, or reemployment, dismissed, or suspended after a finding that the teacher or teachers' aide has:

   1.   Engaged in public homosexual conduct or activity; and

   2.   Has been rendered unfit, because of such conduct or activity, to hold a position as a teacher, student teacher or teachers' aide.

C.   The following factors shall be considered in making the determination whether the teacher, student teacher or teachers' aide has been rendered unfit for his position:

   1.   The likelihood that the activity or conduct may adversely affect students or school employees;

---

[30]   *Id.* at 1346–47, 88 Wash.2d at 298.

[31]   Karen M. Harbeck, *Gay and Lesbian Educators: Past History/Future Prospects, in* COMING OUT OF THE CLASSROOM CLOSET: GAY AND LESBIAN STUDENTS, TEACHERS, AND CURRICULA 121, 129 & n.25 (Karen M. Harbeck ed. 1992).

2.   The proximity in time or place the activity or conduct to
the teacher's, student teacher's or teachers' aide's official
duties;

3.   Any extenuating or aggravating circumstances; and

4.   Whether the conduct or activity is of a repeated or
continuing nature which tends to encourage or dispose
school children toward similar conduct or activity.[32]

The National Gay Task Force challenged the law in federal court.
The U.S. Court of Appeals for the Tenth Circuit Court rejected the due
process/privacy challenge to the statute because it "does not punish acts
performed in private between adults."[33] It also rejected the equal
protection challenge because "[s]urely a school may fire a teacher for
engaging in an indiscreet public act of oral or anal intercourse."[34] The
court, however, upheld the free speech challenge to the statute by noting
that

[t]he First Amendment protects "advocacy" even of illegal
conduct except when "advocacy" is "directed to inciting or
producing imminent lawless action and is likely to incite or
produce such action." *Brandenburg v. Ohio*, 395 U.S. 444, 447, 89
S.Ct. 1827, 23 L.Ed.2d 430 (1969). The First Amendment does
not permit someone to be punished for advocating illegal conduct
at some indefinite future time.

"Encouraging" and "promoting," like "advocating," do not
necessarily imply incitement to imminent action. A teacher who
went before the Oklahoma legislature or appeared on television
to urge the repeal of the Oklahoma anti-sodomy statute would be
"advocating," "promoting," and "encouraging" homosexual
sodomy and creating a substantial risk that his or her speech
would come to the attention of school children or school
employees if he or she said, "I think it is psychologically
damaging for people with homosexual desires to suppress those
desires. They should act on those desires and should be legally
free to do so." Such statements, which are aimed at legal and
social change, are at the core of First Amendment
protections. * * * Finally, the deterrent effect of § 6–103.15 is
both real and substantial. It applies to all teachers, substitute
teachers, and teachers aides in Oklahoma. To protect their jobs
they must restrict their expression. Thus, the § 6–103.15

---

[32]   OKLA.STAT. tit. 70, § 6–103.15 (1981).

[33]   *National Gay Task Force v. Board of Educ. of Oklahoma City*, 729 F.2d 1270, 1273
(10th Cir. 1984).

[34]   *Id.*

proscription of advocating, encouraging, or promoting homosexual activity is unconstitutionally overbroad.

We recognize that a state has interests in regulating the speech of teachers that differ from its interests in regulating the speech of the general citizenry. *Pickering v. Board of Education*, 391 U.S. 563, 568, 88 S.Ct. 1731, 20 L.Ed.2d 811 (1968). But a state's interests outweigh a teacher's interests only when the expression results in a material or substantial interference or disruption in the normal activities of the school. *See Tinker v. Des Moines Independent Community School District*, 393 U.S. 503, 89 S.Ct. 733, 21 L.Ed.2d 731 (1969). * * *

* * * An adverse effect on students or other employees is the only factor among those listed in § 6–103.15 that is even related to a material and substantial disruption. And although a material and substantial disruption is an adverse effect, many adverse effects are not material and substantial disruptions. The statute does not require that the teacher's public utterance occur in the classroom. Any public statement that would come to the attention of school children, their parents, or school employees that might lead someone to object to the teacher's social and political views would seem to justify a finding that the statement "may adversely affect" students or school employees.[35]

The U.S. Supreme Court granted certiorari and heard oral argument in the Oklahoma teachers case. However, Justice Powell fell ill, and the Court split 4–4 and thus, being evenly split, simply affirmed the Tenth Circuit's decision without an opinion of its own.[36]

SCHROEDER V. HAMILTON SCHOOL DISTRICT

United States Court of Appeals, Seventh Circuit, 2002
282 F.3d 946, *cert. denied*, 537 U.S. 974, 123 S.Ct. 435, 154 L.Ed.2d 330 (2002)

MANION, CIRCUIT JUDGE.

Tommy Schroeder, a school teacher, filed suit against his former employer, the Hamilton [Wisconsin] School District, the school district administrator, and several staff administrators (including school principals and human resource directors), pursuant to 42 U.S.C. § 1983, alleging that they violated his right to equal protection by failing to take reasonable measures to prevent students and parents, and occasionally fellow staff members, from harassing him about his homosexuality. The district court granted summary judgment for the defendants. Schroeder appeals, and we affirm.

---

[35]   *Id.* at 1274–75.

[36]   *Board of Educ. of Oklahoma City v. National Gay Task Force*, 470 U.S. 903, 105 S.Ct. 1858, 84 L.Ed.2d 776 (1984).

In 1990, after teaching for approximately 15 years in the Hamilton School District, Tommy Schroeder began teaching sixth grade at Templeton Middle School in Hamilton, Wisconsin. Shortly after arriving at Templeton, Schroeder disclosed his homosexuality to a few of his fellow staff members and, during his second or third year at the school, made the same disclosure at a public meeting. This information eventually spread throughout the Templeton community, and, beginning with the 1993–94 school year, Schroeder began receiving unpleasant inquiries and crude, occasionally cruel, taunts from students regarding his homosexuality.

While there were isolated incidents involving parents, as well as some of Schroeder's colleagues, the bulk of the harassment he endured at Templeton came from students. Some of the incidents were rather mild. For example, a fifth-grade girl asked Schroeder to verify a rumor that he was gay. Another student authored a note complaining that she had been disciplined by "the gay man." Finally, other students were found discussing Schroeder's homosexuality during homeroom. Many of the reported student comments and actions, however, were far worse—accusations that he had AIDS; a student calling him a faggot and remarking "How sad there are any gays in the world"; another student physically confronted Schroeder after shouting obscenities at him; catcalls in the hallways that he was a "queer" or a "faggot"; obscenities shouted at him during bus duty; harassing phone calls with students chanting "faggot, faggot, faggot" and other calls where he was asked whether he was a "faggot"; and bathroom graffiti identifying Schroeder as a "faggot," and describing, in the most explicit and vulgar terms, the type of sexual acts they presumed he engaged in with other men. He reported this harassment on several occasions, and the defendants "consequenced" (i.e., a term of art in education circles for student discipline) the students identified with the offensive behavior. Much of the harassment, however, was anonymous, and therefore went unpunished. As Patty Polczynski, the associate principal at Templeton, told Schroeder, "[i]t makes it difficult to consequence if you don't know who it is to consequence."

Because of the widespread, anonymous nature of the harassment, Schroeder demanded that the defendants conduct "sensitivity training" to condemn discrimination against homosexuals (presumably for the students at Templeton—the chief perpetrators of the harassment). Instead, Polczynski, after several meetings with Schroeder, circulated a memorandum to teachers and other staff noting that students were continuing to use "inappropriate and offensive racial and/or gender-related words or phrases," and that "[i]f you observe or overhear students using inappropriate language or gestures, please consequence them as you feel appropriate * * * ." Schroeder considered this memorandum to be a milquetoast response to the harassment he was receiving, especially in comparison to a previous Polczynski memorandum warning staff that "derogatory racial comments and symbols" were "totally unacceptable" and "contrary to [the school's] efforts to create a positive academic environment for all students." When the harassment continued, Schroeder expressed his frustration to Polczynski, and she responded by telling him that "you can't stop middle school kids from saying things. Guess you'll just have to ignore it."

Finally, after several requests for a transfer, Schroeder was moved to Lannon Elementary School in the fall of 1996, where he taught first-and second-grade classes. After a year's respite, the taunts resumed. This time, however, they came primarily from adults, presumably the parents of students at Lannon. At the beginning of his second year at Lannon, an anonymous memo was circulated by a parent proclaiming, "Mr. Schroeder openly admitted at a district meeting that he was homosexual. Is that a good role model for our 5-, 6- and 7-year-old children?" Schroeder also claims that he began hearing that certain staff members and parents were calling him a pedophile and accusing him of sexually abusing small boys. One parent removed his child from Schroeder's class because of Schroeder's homosexuality. Another parent's fear that Schroeder was a pedophile led defendant Richard Ladd, Lannon's principal, to raise the possibility of "proximity supervision" (i.e., meaning that Schroeder could not be alone with male students). The tires on Schroeder's car were slashed, and he began receiving anonymous, harassing phone calls at home (e.g. "Faggot, stay away from our kids" and "We just want you to know you * * * queer that when we pull out all our kids, you will have no job").

In February 1998, Schroeder, who has a protracted history of psychiatric problems, experienced a "mental breakdown." On February 11, 1998, Schroeder's last day at Lannon, Ladd approached him about complaints that he had received from some of his students' parents. Schroeder told Ladd that he did not want to talk about it, and that he was resigning. Later that day, Schroeder handed Ladd a letter of resignation. At this point, Ladd offered to arrange for a substitute teacher to take over Schroeder's class and requested that he take some time to think about whether he really wanted to resign. Schroeder declined the request, and never reported to work at Lannon again. Schroeder did, however, apply for medical leave and long-term disability insurance. Pursuant to terms of the collective bargaining agreement between the teacher's union and the Hamilton School District, the district terminated Schroeder's employment at the end of the 1998–99 school year.

Schroeder contends that the harassment he received from students, parents, and fellow teachers/staff members at Templeton and Lannon, coupled with the defendants' failure to properly address the problem, caused him to have a nervous breakdown that ultimately resulted in his termination. He therefore filed suit against the defendants, pursuant to 42 U.S.C. § 1983, alleging that they denied him equal protection of the law by failing to take effective steps to prevent him from being harassed on account of his sexual orientation. The parties filed cross motions for summary judgment, and the district court granted summary judgment in favor of the defendants. Schroeder appeals the decision. * * *

In order to establish an equal protection violation, Schroeder must show that the defendants: (1) treated him differently from others who were similarly situated, (2) intentionally treated him differently because of his membership in the class to which he belonged (i.e., homosexuals), and (3) because homosexuals do not enjoy any heightened protection under the Constitution, *see, e.g., Romer v. Evans*, 517 U.S. 620, 634–35, 116 S.Ct. 1620, 134 L.Ed.2d 855 (1996); *Bowers v. Hardwick*, 478 U.S. 186, 196, 106 S.Ct. 2841, 92 L.Ed.2d 140 (1986), that the discriminatory intent was not rationally related to a legitimate state interest. As we noted in *Nabozny v. Podlesny,*

> The gravamen of equal protection lies not in the fact of deprivation of a right but in the invidious classification of persons aggrieved by the state's action. A plaintiff must demonstrate intentional or purposeful discrimination to show an equal protection violation. Discriminatory purpose, however, implies more than intent as volition or intent as awareness of consequences. It implies that a decisionmaker singled out a particular group for disparate treatment and selected his course of action at least in part for the purpose of causing its adverse effects on the identifiable group.

[92 F.3d 446, 453–54 (7th Cir. 1996)].

* * * The district court's decision to grant the defendants' motion for summary judgment of this claim must be sustained if the defendants demonstrate that they did not deny Schroeder equal protection on account of his sexual orientation, or that they had a "rational basis" for doing so. * * *

Schroeder would have us *infer* differential treatment because: (1) a memorandum circulated by the associate principal at Templeton, Patty Polczynski, failed to address and condemn the widespread use by students of "heterosexist" and "anti-gay" comments in the same manner that a previous memorandum had done with respect to racist comments and symbols, and (2) while the Hamilton School District held several district-wide staff/teacher training sessions and conducted annual student orientation programs to implement its policies prohibiting race and sex discrimination, the district never held similar training sessions or student programs to address sexual orientation discrimination.

These events do not, however, demonstrate that Schroeder was treated differently from his non-homosexual colleagues, or that he was discriminated against on the basis of his homosexuality. First, as Schroeder acknowledges, the initial memorandum circulated by Polczynski was generated in response to the pervasive use of racist comments and symbols by students in the Hamilton School District. Polczynski explained her motivation for circulating the memorandum in the memorandum itself, noting that the derogatory racial comments being made by students were "contrary to [the school's] efforts to create a positive academic environment for all students." Additionally, the district-wide staff/teacher training sessions on race discrimination, referred to in Schroeder's appellate briefs, were conducted in the early 1990's when the Hamilton School District began busing black students into its schools from the Milwaukee County Schools. The training sessions and student orientation programs were conducted to ensure that incoming minority students were not subjected to racial discrimination, and to increase sensitivity to racial issues among school district personnel and students. By citing these examples, Schroeder attempts to set up a false dichotomy—i.e., disparity of treatment/protection given to blacks/women as compared with homosexuals. In reality, these examples merely demonstrate the school district's priorities for use of time and resources in favor of its students. And this is certainly understandable given the limited resources of today's public schools.

Furthermore, in a school setting, the well-being of students, not teachers, must be the primary concern of school administrators. Not only are schools primarily for the benefit of students, but it is also clear that children between the ages 6 to 14 are much more vulnerable to intimidation and mockery than teachers with advanced degrees and 20 years of experience. Likewise, with this vulnerability in mind, school administrators must be particularly steadfast in addressing and preventing any form of verbal or physical harassment/abuse directed at their students. They must also be cautious about using police tactics to deal with nonviolent harassment of a teacher by students, even if that harassment is offensive and cruel. * * *

* * * Schroeder [also] contends that the defendants discriminated against him because the Hamilton School District had policies against race and sex discrimination, but did not have one against sexual orientation discrimination. While this is most certainly true, the lack of such a policy is not evidence that the defendants were deliberately indifferent to his complaints of harassment. As previously noted, unlike blacks and women, homosexuals are not entitled to any heightened protection under the Constitution. Therefore, discrimination against homosexuals, or for that matter the elderly, overweight, undersized, or disfigured, will only constitute a violation of equal protection if it lacks a

rational basis. Here, there is no evidence that the defendants' decision not to implement a separate policy against sexual orientation discrimination was based on any animus toward Schroeder or homosexuals in general. Schroeder appears to suggest, however, that the only way the defendants could have prevented the harassment was by requiring all Hamilton School District personnel and students to attend mandatory training sessions on sexual orientation discrimination. There are several problems with this argument.

First of all, it is hardly reasonable to expect a school district to devote a substantial amount of resources to curb the harassment of one teacher, regardless of the basis for the harassment. In this case, other than Schroeder's situation, there is no evidence of any discrimination against homosexual teachers or students in the Hamilton School District. Instead, the evidence shows that one teacher, who happened to be a homosexual, was harassed because of his homosexuality. As emphasized in *Equal. Found. of Greater Cincinnati, Inc. v. City of Cincinnati*, 128 F.3d 289, 300–01 (6th Cir. 1997), another decision involving a claim of denial of equal protection on grounds of sexual orientation discrimination, it is not irrational to prioritize protective activities. It is in fact unavoidable, because of limitations of time and other resources. * * *

Schroeder's exhortation to adopt a specific policy requiring students to be sensitive to, or accepting of, homosexuals is especially problematic in an elementary or early middle school (i.e., sixth grade) setting. What would such a policy say? It is relatively simple to explain to a child that he or she should not criticize or offend someone because of the color of their skin, or because they are a boy or a girl. This is why blacks and women are described as "discrete and insular" groups. Unfortunately, there is no simple way of explaining to young students why it is wrong to mock homosexuals without discussing the underlying lifestyle or sexual behavior associated with such a designation.

Schools can, however, teach their students that it is wrong to mock anyone, for any reason. School administrators can, and should, insist that students behave in a courteous and respectful manner toward their teachers and other students. Such a policy would not require any discussion of homosexuality, or any other characteristic or behavior associated with it. If a student calls a teacher or another student a "faggot," he should be disciplined for violating the school's general civility code. If a student assaults a faculty member or another student because he is a homosexual, or because he is overweight, disfigured, undersized, or aged, he should be suspended or expelled for the assault. Students who are inconsiderate, disrespectful, mean, or even vicious, to others should be "consequenced" for what they do, not for the underlying motivation. Students must be taught—at school if not at home—that it is reprehensible to cruelly mock and malign staff members and other students—for any reason. In this case, the record is clear: When school administrators determined that a student harassed Schroeder by using derogatory terms like "faggot," the student was punished. By punishing these students, the defendants made it abundantly clear to the student population that such terms were totally unacceptable in polite society. This is all that was required of them.

That being said about disrespectful students, a short word about difficult parents. Schroeder asserts that he was also harassed by parents, and that the defendants did nothing about it because of his homosexuality. In support of his claim, Schroeder points to a memorandum, apparently circulated by a parent, which questions his qualifications to teach and criticizes the school's decision to blend first- and second-grade classes. The first paragraph alerted parents to the fact that Schroeder was an admitted homosexual, and presented the rhetorical question, "Is this a good role model for five-, six- and seven-year-old children?" Schroeder, like any well-qualified teacher, should be a good role model for his students, not because he is homosexual, but because he is an effective and enthusiastic teacher who wants them to learn. Regardless of the parental attitude displayed in the memorandum, however, school administrators have little or no power to "consequence" the parents of students. Obviously, if a child picks up foul language and prejudicial views from his parents at home, and then displays them at school, he should be disciplined. A student cannot, however, be disciplined for expressing a home-taught religious belief that homosexual acts are immoral. Administrators have to tiptoe on a narrow path when dealing with a child's unwarranted prejudices as opposed to his sincerely held religious beliefs. Beyond that, the Equal Protection Clause does not require a school district to do anything about parental unpleasantries unless they take place on school grounds. Schroeder could have reported the anonymous harassing phone calls he received, presumably from parents, to the telephone company, and any threats of physical violence to the police. School administrators have little authority to control parental activity. * * *

The question in this case is not whether the defendants did enough to engender a more positive attitude among its students and staff toward homosexuality. Rather, the only issue is whether the manner in which the defendants handled Schroeder's complaints of harassment denied him equal protection under the law. School administrators disciplined the identified students who misbehaved and degraded him, and made an effort to discover those not identified. There is no evidence that the defendants were deliberately indifferent to his situation, or that they did not make a sincere effort to deal with his complaints. On the contrary, the record shows that the school district was genuinely concerned about the treatment Schroeder experienced, and that it did what reasonably could be expected under the circumstances. The record is replete with memos, correspondence, and testimony indicating that various administrators and staff positively responded to his requests. In the absence of deliberate indifference, federal judges should not use rational basis review as a mechanism to impose their own social values on public school administrators who already have innumerable challenges to face.

Schroeder's breakdown and his current psychological condition are unfortunate. To the extent that student and parental harassment of him exacerbated his long history of personal and psychological problems, that is also unfortunate. There is, however, no evidence that the defendants denied him the equal protection of the law. * * * Affirmed.

[Concurring opinion by JUDGE POSNER is omitted.]

DIANE P. WOOD, CIRCUIT JUDGE, dissenting.

In this case, the majority holds that Tommy Schroeder, an openly homosexual teacher who was subjected to severe harassment on the job, cannot survive summary judgment on his claim under 42 U.S.C. § 1983 that defendant Hamilton School District and some of its administrators violated his rights under the Equal Protection Clause of the United States Constitution. In my view, this holding and the rationale both the majority and concurrence have used to reach it are inconsistent with the Supreme Court's recognition in *Romer v. Evans*, 517 U.S. 620, 116 S.Ct. 1620, 134 L.Ed.2d 855 (1996), that the Equal Protection Clause does protect homosexuals as a class and that this protection may not be denied simply because they may be an unpopular class in a given state or local community. I therefore respectfully dissent.

Because the majority has already furnished many of the relevant facts, I will simply highlight those that appear especially important to me. First, there is no dispute that Schroeder was a very good teacher; he taught successfully for the District for 22 years. Whatever psychiatric problems he may have had, it is clear that he had them under control until the unrelenting harassment to which he was subjected on the job caused him to have a full mental breakdown on February 11, 1998. He left the school that day a ruined man; when it became apparent that he could not return, the District terminated him. His vulnerability in no way excuses the District for the well-known reason that tortfeasors take their victims as they find them.

In addition, Schroeder complained repeatedly to the school officials about the vicious harassment the students and occasionally others directed toward him. His efforts to alert the District to the problem and to seek redress eliminate any possibility of the District's defeating this claim of intentional discrimination through a claim of lack of knowledge.

Despite the majority's efforts to find remedial efforts in the District's generalized responses, it is plain that the District never in any way took action specifically designed to inform the students that certain words or phrases that reflect negative views about homosexuals were out-of-bounds, nor in any other way did it tell them that harassment or discrimination based upon Schroeder's sexual orientation was impermissible. It would have been easy enough, as part of the philosophy of "courtesy to all" that the majority advocates, to prohibit certain words or actions without a detailed discussion of the sexual behavior of adults.

Finally, the District treated the class of homosexuals differently from the way it treated other classes, such as racial minorities or gender, as illustrated by the memorandum it circulated cautioning the community to avoid "offensive racial and/or gender related words or phrases." Even the majority concedes this when it admits that the District had no policy against discrimination based on sexual orientation and did have such policies against other forms of discrimination. Since even this court believes that discrimination based on sexual orientation is not "gender-related," *see, e.g., Spearman v. Ford Motor Co.*, 231 F.3d 1080, 1084 (7th Cir. 2000), there is every reason to think that the students of the Hamilton School District might have thought the same thing and concluded that the District's policy did not require them to avoid what is often referred to as gay-bashing.

The majority acknowledges that the core violation of the Equal Protection Clause is "precisely the selective withdrawal of police protection from a disfavored group * * * ." It also appears to admit that homosexuals might constitute one such group. Indeed so, as the Supreme Court's *Romer* decision makes clear. And, it is worth noting that *Romer* is the only decision from the Supreme Court in recent years to address an equal protection argument where the class of homosexuals were singled out for uniquely disfavored treatment. *Bowers v. Hardwick*, 478 U.S. 186, 106 S.Ct. 2841, 92 L.Ed.2d 140 (1986), looked only at the question whether the enforcement of the Georgia sodomy statute violated the fundamental rights (meaning substantive due process rights) of homosexuals in that state. The Court was careful to note that it was not addressing any equal protection argument. * * * The later case of *Boy Scouts of America v. Dale*, 530 U.S. 640, 120 S.Ct. 2446, 147 L.Ed.2d 554 (2000), dealt with the question whether the First Amendment associational rights of the Boy Scouts organization would be infringed if it was compelled to accept a scout leader it did not want. In that case, the reason the Boy Scouts did not want respondent Dale in its organization was Dale's sexual orientation. But the Equal Protection Clause naturally enough did not figure in the Court's opinion because the Boy Scouts is a private organization and thus not a "state actor" for purposes of the Fourteenth Amendment. That leaves us with *Romer* as the governing

Supreme Court decision on the applicability of the Equal Protection Clause to the class of homosexuals.

Nothing in *Romer* justifies a system under which a state or state actors like the District and its officials deliberately either omit altogether or give a diminished form of legal protection from verbal or physical assaults to individuals in certain disfavored classes. Yet both the majority opinion and the concurrence see no problem in the fact that the defendants intentionally responded less vigorously to the abuse that finally broke Schroeder than they themselves would have done for others. In fact, the majority seriously understates the case. *Never*, in the course of these events, did the administration ever attempt to dissuade either students, parents, or anyone else in the broader community of the school district, to refrain from discrimination or harassment based upon sexual orientation. Indeed, as I have already noted, school officials never even told the students that the words being used to describe Schroeder transgressed the general code of civility the majority is recommending to schools. Schroeder was just told to tough it out. The majority also makes the unwarranted factual finding that there was no evidence of hostility to Schroeder. Even a glance at the facts the majority itself has set out shows that this is, at a minimum, a disputed point of fact.

Last, the majority seems to believe that a lack of resources might have prevented the District from responding to Schroeder's complaints. This cannot be a serious point. Adding two words, "sexual orientation," to the memorandum that was circulated could hardly have added a second to the secretarial time involved, nor could it have added appreciably to the amount of toner consumed by the photocopying machine. This case is nothing like *Equality Foundation of Greater Cincinnati, Inc. v. City of Cincinnati*, 128 F.3d 289 (6th Cir. 1997). * * * *Equality Foundation* was a case in which the court upheld the city's refusal to include homosexuals in a specially protected class, whereas here the only thing Schroeder wants is the *same* treatment that everyone else is receiving—that is, the kind of treatment to which the Constitution entitles him, according to *Romer v. Evans*. The glaring absence of the words "sexual orientation" in the memorandum, coming on the heels of the offensive incidents and Schroeder's complaint about exactly that kind of harassment, implies official tolerance, if not endorsement, of the behavior in which the students and others had been engaging. As I believe the majority acknowledges, the mere fact that members of some religious groups think that homosexuality is immoral also in no way excuses a public school's tolerance of harassing *conduct* based on sexual preference. Some religions profess beliefs that are incompatible with the individual guarantees found in the Bill of Rights, as we have seen to our sorrow in the recent history of the Taliban group in Afghanistan, whose views about the role of women in society could never be adopted by a public body here. In this country, nondiscriminatory secular norms of conduct ordinarily prevail even if they conflict with particular religious beliefs or practices.

I do not disagree that each case of harassment or discrimination must be evaluated on its own facts. Nor do I quarrel with the proposition that proper allocation of investigative resources may require devoting less time and effort to some complaints than to others. That decision, however, must be made on a case-by-case basis. Systematically to put cases involving harassment based on homosexuality (or any other recognized classification) below the threshold for any action at all amounts to the kind of differential unfavorable treatment that the Equal Protection Clause reaches. I had thought that *Nabozny v. Podlesny*, 92 F.3d 446 (7th Cir. 1996), * * * settled the point that sexual orientation discrimination could not be treated in such a cavalier fashion.

Schroeder has shown that he suffered harassment so severe that he experienced a total mental breakdown; he has shown that a reasonable trier of fact could find that the school district officials acted intentionally when they failed to respond to his complaints; and he has shown that the trier of fact could also infer that his unfavorable treatment occurred because of his homosexuality. This is more than enough, in my view, to allow him to proceed to trial in his case against the District. I would Reverse the district court's judgment and Remand for that trial.

NOTES

1.   In *Rowland v. Mad River Local School District*, the school district did not renew plaintiff's contract to continue her work as a high school guidance counselor after she informed co-workers that she was bisexual. The plaintiff sued and a jury awarded her damages, finding a violation of her constitutional rights under the First Amendment and the Fourteenth Amendment's Equal Protection Clause. The U.S. Court of Appeals for the Sixth Circuit reversed, 730 F.2d 444 (6th Cir. 1984), rewriting the facts of the case to find that the plaintiff was actually dismissed for violating the confidentiality of her students. The court asserted that the breach of confidence rationale in no way related to plaintiff's sexual orientation and, thus, the equal protection and free speech issues were not addressed. Although certiorari was denied by the U.S. Supreme Court, Justice Brennan wrote a powerful dissenting opinion. 470 U.S. 1009–18, 105 S.Ct. 1373–79, 84 L.Ed.2d 392–98 (1985) (Brennan, J., dissenting from the denial of certiorari). His dissent is the first explication by a Supreme Court Justice of why classifications based on sexual orientation are suspect and should be carefully scrutinized by the courts.

2.   In *Collins v. Faith School District #46–2*, 574 N.W.2d 889, 1998 S.D. 17 (1998), a school board fired a teacher for discussing male homosexual sexual activities with his fourth grade class in the context of a sexual education program. The South Dakota Supreme Court overturned the board's

decision. The court held that the board's decision that the teacher was "incompetent" on the basis of this one class was irrational in light of his otherwise meritorious 29-year teaching record. *See also Glover v. Williamsburg Local Sch. Dist. Bd. of Educ.*, 20 F. Supp. 2d 1160 (S.D. Ohio 1998) (holding that non-renewal of teaching contract because of sexual orientation violates Equal Protection Clause).

3.   In *Lovell v. Comsewogue School District*, 214 F. Supp. 2d 319 (E.D.N.Y. 2002), a lesbian teacher alleged a violation of her constitutional rights to equal protection when the school refused to discipline students who were harassing her because of her sexual orientation. As in *Schroeder*, the teacher argued that the school took harassment on the basis of sexual orientation less seriously than harassment on other grounds, such as race. She alleged, for example "that when a black teacher had the word 'nigger' written on her blackboard, the school called in the Police Bias Unit and the School District held numerous faculty meetings concerning the incident. Similarly, when a student used the same racial epithet against another student, the offending student was suspended. On the other hand, when students harassed [her] due to her sexual orientation, including calling her a 'dyke,' no action was taken." *Id.* at 322. The court denied the defendant's motion to dismiss by concluding that "the use of disparaging remarks based on sexual orientation is sufficiently similar to the use of racial epithets [and] that [the plaintiff] was treated differently than other similarly situated teachers, which is sufficient to support a [*sic*] equal protection claim at this stage of the litigation." *Id.* at 322–23.

CHAPTER 5

COUPLING

▪ ▪ ▪

I. INTRODUCTION

Until relatively recently, no jurisdiction in the United States legally recognized same-sex relationships and, in the years leading up to *Lawrence*, some still criminalized same-sex sexual acts. The landscape shifted dramatically in the late 1990s and 2000s. Courts and legislatures began to extend relationship recognition, including eventually marriage, to same-sex couples. By 2012, voters were approving marriage equality in state referenda. In 2013, the Supreme Court weighed in by striking down Section 3 of the federal Defense of Marriage Act in *United States v. Windsor*. Then, in 2015, the campaign for marriage equality in the U.S. culminated in the Supreme Court's landmark decision in *Obergefell v. Hodges*. This Chapter explores the movement for marriage equality, including key judicial decisions. As it does, it considers the relationship between litigation and social change: How, if at all, did court decisions advance the cause of marriage equality? How, if at all, did litigation harm the cause? This Chapter also considers the relationship between marriage and family-based law and policy: Why did the LGBT movement coalesce around marriage? Is marriage the appropriate mechanism through which to extend rights and benefits to families? What comes after marriage equality in terms of relationship-based rights and recognition?

II. MARRIAGE AND THE CONSTITUTION

Marriage is fundamentally a matter for the states, but has long held a special place in federal constitutional law. As long ago as 1923, the U.S. Supreme Court stated that the liberty guaranteed by the due process clause includes the right to marry. *Meyer v. Nebraska*, 262 U.S. 390, 43 S.Ct. 625, 67 L.Ed. 1042 (1923). Decades later, the Court went on to elaborate the contours of that right. One of the most famous instances came in the following civil rights case.

LOVING V. VIRGINIA
Supreme Court of the United States, 1967
388 U.S. 1, 87 S.Ct. 1817, 18 L.Ed.2d 1010

MR. CHIEF JUSTICE WARREN.

This case presents a Constitutional question never addressed by this Court: whether a statutory scheme adopted by the State of Virginia to prevent marriages between persons solely on the basis of racial classifications violates the equal protection and due process clauses of the Fourteenth Amendment. For reasons which seem to us to reflect the central meaning of those Constitutional commands, we conclude that these statutes cannot stand consistently with the Fourteenth Amendment.

In June 1958, two residents of Virginia, Mildred Jeter, a Negro woman, and Richard Loving, a white man, were married in the District of Columbia pursuant to its laws. Shortly after their marriage, the Lovings returned to Virginia and established their marital abode in Caroline County. At the October Term, 1958, of the Circuit Court of Caroline County, a grand jury issued an indictment charging the Lovings with violating Virginia's ban on interracial marriages. On January 6, 1959, the Lovings pleaded guilty to the charge and were sentenced to one year in jail; however, the trial judge suspended the sentence for a period of 25 years on the condition that the Lovings leave the State and not return to Virginia together for 25 years. He stated in an opinion that:

> "Almighty God created the races white, black, yellow, malay and red, and He placed them on separate continents. And but for the interference with His arrangement there would be no cause for such marriages. The fact that He separated the races shows that He did not intend for the races to mix."

After their convictions, the Lovings took up residence in the District of Columbia. On November 6, 1963, they filed a motion in the state trial court to vacate the judgment and set aside the sentence on the ground that the statutes which they had violated were repugnant to the Fourteenth Amendment. * * * On January 22, 1965, the state trial judge denied the motion to vacate the sentences, and the Lovings perfected an appeal to the Supreme Court of Appeals of Virginia. . . .

The Supreme Court of Appeals upheld the constitutionality of the antimiscegenation statutes and, after modifying the sentence, affirmed the convictions.

The two statutes under which appellants were convicted and sentenced are part of a comprehensive statutory scheme aimed at prohibiting and punishing interracial marriages. The Lovings were convicted of violating § 20–58 of the Virginia Code:

"*Leaving State to evade law.* If any white person and colored person shall go out of this State, for the purpose of being married, and with the intention of returning, and be married out of it, and afterwards return to and reside in it, cohabiting as man and wife, they shall be punished as provided in § 20–59, and the marriage shall be governed by the same law as if it had been solemnized in this State. The fact of their cohabitation here as man and wife shall be evidence of their marriage."

Section 20–59, which defines the penalty for miscegenation, provides:

"*Punishment for marriage.* If any white person intermarry with a colored person, or any colored person intermarry with a white person, he shall be guilty of a felony and shall be punished by confinement in the penitentiary for not less than one nor more than five years."

Other central provisions in the Virginia statutory scheme are § 20–57, which automatically voids all marriages between "a white person and a colored person" without any judicial proceeding,[2] and §§ 20–54 and 1–14 which, respectively, define "white persons" and "colored persons and Indians" for purposes of the statutory prohibitions.[3] The Lovings have never disputed in the course of this litigation that Mrs. Loving is a "colored person" or that Mr. Loving is a "white person" within the meanings given those terms by the Virginia statutes.

---

[2]   Section 20–57 of the Virginia Code provides:

"*Marriages void without decree.* All marriages between a white person and a colored person shall be absolutely void without any decree of divorce or other legal process." *Va. Code Ann.*, § 20–57 (1960 Repl. Vol.).

[3]   Section 20–54 of the Virginia Code provides:

"*Intermarriage prohibited; meaning of term 'white persons.'* It shall hereafter be unlawful for any white person in this State to marry any save a white person, or a person with no other admixture of blood than white and American Indian. For the purpose of this chapter, the term 'white person' shall apply only to such person as has no trace whatever of any blood other than Caucasian; but persons who have one-sixteenth or less of the blood of the American Indian and have no other non-Caucasic blood shall be deemed to be white persons. All laws heretofore passed and now in effect regarding the intermarriage of white and colored persons shall apply to marriages prohibited by this chapter." *Va. Code Ann.*, § 20–54 (1960 Repl. Vol.).

The exception for persons with less than one-sixteenth "of the blood of the American Indian" is apparently accounted for, in the words of a tract issued by the Registrar of the State Bureau of Vital Statistics, by "the desire of all to recognize as an integral and honored part of the white race the descendants of John Rolfe and Pocahontas. . . ." Plecker, The New Family and Race Improvement, 17 Va.Health Bull., Extra No. 12, at 25–26 (New Family Series No. 5, 1925), cited in Wadlington, *The* Loving *Case: Virginia's Anti-Miscegenation Statute in Historical Perspective*, 52 VA. L. REV. 1189, 1202, n. 93 (1966).

Section 1–14 of the Virginia Code provides:

"*Colored persons and Indians defined.* Every person in whom there is ascertainable any Negro blood shall be deemed and taken to be a colored person, and every person not a colored person having one fourth or more of American Indian blood shall be deemed an American Indian; except that members of Indian tribes existing in this Commonwealth having one fourth or more of Indian blood and less than one sixteenth of Negro blood shall be deemed tribal Indians." *Va. Code Ann.* § 1–14 (1960 Repl. Vol.).

Virginia is now one of 16 States which prohibit and punish marriages on the basis of racial classifications.[4] Penalties for miscegenation arose as an incident to slavery and have been common in Virginia since the colonial period. The present statutory scheme dates from the adoption of the Racial Integrity Act of 1924, passed during the period of extreme nativism which followed the end of the First World War. The central features of this Act, and current Virginia law, are the absolute prohibition of a "white person" marrying other than another "white person," a prohibition against issuing marriage licenses until the issuing official is satisfied that the applicants' statements as to their race are correct, certificates of "racial composition" to be kept by both local and state registrars, and the carrying forward of earlier prohibitions against racial intermarriage.

I

In upholding the constitutionality of these provisions in the decision below, the Supreme Court of Appeals of Virginia referred to its 1955 decision in *Naim v. Naim*, 87 S.E.2d 749 (Va.1955), as stating the reasons supporting the validity of these laws. In *Naim*, the state court concluded that the State's legitimate purposes were "to preserve the racial integrity of its citizens," and to prevent "the corruption of blood," "a mongrel breed of citizens," and "the obliteration of racial pride," obviously an endorsement of the doctrine of White Supremacy. The court also reasoned that marriage has traditionally been subject to state regulation without federal intervention, and, consequently, the regulation of marriage should be left to exclusive state control by the Tenth Amendment.

While the state court is no doubt correct in asserting that marriage is a social relation subject to the State's police power, *Maynard v. Hill*, 125 U.S. 190 (1888), the State does not contend in its argument before this Court that its powers to regulate marriage are unlimited notwithstanding the commands of the Fourteenth Amendment. Nor could it do so in light of *Meyer v. Nebraska*, 262 U.S. 390 (1923), and *Skinner v. Oklahoma*, 316 U.S. 535 (1942). Instead, the State argues that the meaning of the Equal Protection Clause, as illuminated by the statements of the Framers, is only that state penal laws containing an interracial element as part of the definition of the offense must apply equally to whites and Negroes in the sense that members of each race are punished to the same degree. Thus,

---

4   After the initiation of this litigation, Maryland repealed its prohibitions against interracial marriage, *Md. Laws* 1967, c. 6, leaving Virginia and 15 other States [Alabama; Arkansas; Delaware; Florida; Georgia; Kentucky; Louisiana; Mississippi; Missouri; North Carolina; Oklahoma; South Carolina; Tennessee; Texas; West Virginia] with statutes outlawing interracial marriage. * * *

Over the past 15 years, 14 states have repealed laws outlawing interracial marriages: Arizona, California, Colorado, Idaho, Indiana, Maryland, Montana, Nebraska, Nevada, North Dakota, Oregon, South Dakota, Utah, and Wyoming. The first state court to recognize that miscegenation statutes violate the Equal Protection Clause was the Supreme Court of California. *Perez v. Sharp*, 198 P.2d 17 (Cal. 1948).

the State contends that, because its miscegenation statutes punish equally both the white and the Negro participants in an interracial marriage, these statutes, despite their reliance on racial classifications, do not constitute an invidious discrimination based upon race. The second argument advanced by the State assumes the validity of its equal application theory. The argument is that, if the Equal Protection Clause does not outlaw miscegenation statutes because of their reliance on racial classifications, the question of constitutionality would thus become whether there was any rational basis for a State to treat interracial marriages differently from other marriages. On this question, the State argues, the scientific evidence is substantially in doubt and, consequently, this Court should defer to the wisdom of the state legislature in adopting its policy of discouraging interracial marriages.

Because we reject the notion that the mere "equal application" of a statute containing racial classifications is enough to remove the classifications from the Fourteenth Amendment's proscription of all invidious racial discriminations, we do not accept the State's contention that these statutes should be upheld if there is any possible basis for concluding that they serve a rational purpose. The mere fact of equal application does not mean that our analysis of these statutes should follow the approach we have taken in cases involving no racial discrimination where the Equal Protection Clause has been arrayed against a statute discriminating between the kinds of advertising which may be displayed on trucks in New York City, *Railway Express Agency, Inc. v. New York*, 336 U.S. 106 (1949), or an exemption in Ohio's ad valorem tax for merchandise owned by a nonresident in a storage warehouse, *Allied Stores of Ohio, Inc. v. Bowers*, 358 U.S. 522 (1959). In these cases, involving distinctions not drawn according to race, the Court has merely asked whether there is any rational foundation for the discriminations, and has deferred to the wisdom of the state legislatures. In the case at bar, however, we deal with statutes containing racial classifications, and the fact of equal application does not immunize the statute from the very heavy burden of justification which the Fourteenth Amendment has traditionally required of state statutes drawn according to race.

The State argues that statements in the Thirty-ninth Congress about the time of the passage of the Fourteenth Amendment indicate that the Framers did not intend the Amendment to make unconstitutional state miscegenation laws. Many of the statements alluded to by the State concern the debates over the Freedmen's Bureau Bill, which President Johnson vetoed, and the Civil Rights Act of 1866, enacted over his veto. While these statements have some relevance to the intention of Congress in submitting the Fourteenth Amendment, it must be understood that they pertained to the passage of specific statutes and not to the broader, organic purpose of a constitutional amendment. As for the various statements directly concerning the Fourteenth Amendment, we have said in connection with a related problem, that although these historical sources "cast some light" they are not sufficient to resolve the problem; "[a]t best, they are inconclusive. The most avid proponents of the post-War Amendments undoubtedly intended them to remove all legal distinctions among 'all persons born or naturalized in the United States.' Their opponents, just as certainly, were antagonistic to both the letter and the spirit of the Amendments and wished them to have the most limited effect." *Brown v. Board of Education*, 347 U.S. 483, 489 (1954). *See also Strauder v. West Virginia*, 100 U.S. 303, 310 (1880). We have rejected the proposition that the debates in the Thirty-ninth Congress or in the state legislatures which ratified the Fourteenth Amendment supported the theory advanced by the State, that the requirement of equal protection of the laws is satisfied by penal laws defining offenses based on racial classifications so long as white and Negro participants in the offense were similarly punished. *McLaughlin v. Florida*, 379 U.S. 184 (1964).

The State finds support for its "equal application" theory in the decision of the Court in *Pace v. Alabama*, 106 U.S. 583 (1883). In that case, the Court upheld a conviction under an Alabama statute forbidding adultery or fornication between a white person and a Negro which imposed a greater penalty than that of a statute proscribing similar conduct by members of the same race. The Court reasoned that the statute could not be said to discriminate against Negroes because the punishment for each participant in the offense was the same. However, as recently as the 1964 Term, in rejecting the reasoning of that case, we stated "*Pace* represents a limited view of the Equal Protection Clause which has not withstood analysis in the subsequent decisions of this Court." *McLaughlin v. Florida*, 379 U.S. at 188. As we there demonstrated, the Equal Protection Clause requires the consideration of whether the classifications drawn by any statute constitute an arbitrary and invidious discrimination. The clear and central purpose of the Fourteenth Amendment was to eliminate all official state sources of invidious racial discrimination in the States. *Slaughter-House Cases*, 16 Wall. 36, 71 (1873); *Strauder v. West Virginia*, 100 U.S. 303, 307–308 (1880); *Ex parte Virginia*, 100 U.S. 339, 344–345 (1880); *Shelley v. Kraemer*, 334 U.S. 1 (1948); *Burton v. Wilmington Parking Authority*, 365 U.S. 715 (1961).

There can be no question but that Virginia's miscegenation statutes rest solely upon distinctions drawn according to race. The statutes proscribe generally accepted conduct if engaged in by members of different races. Over the years, this Court has consistently repudiated "[d]istinctions between citizens solely because of their ancestry" as being "odious to a free people whose institutions are founded upon the doctrine of equality." *Hirabayashi v. United States*, 320 U.S. 81, 100 (1943). At the very least, the Equal Protection Clause demands that racial classifications, especially suspect in criminal statutes, be subjected to the "most rigid scrutiny," *Korematsu v. United States*, 323 U.S. 214, 216 (1944), and, if they are ever to be upheld, they must be shown to be necessary to the accomplishment of some permissible state objective, independent of the racial discrimination which it was the object of the Fourteenth Amendment to eliminate. Indeed, two members of this Court have already stated that they "cannot conceive of a valid legislative purpose . . . which makes the color of a person's skin the test of whether his conduct is a criminal offense." *McLaughlin v. Florida*, 379 U.S. at 198 (Stewart, J., joined by Douglas, J., concurring).

There is patently no legitimate overriding purpose independent of invidious racial discrimination which justifies this classification. The fact that Virginia prohibits only interracial marriages involving white persons demonstrates that the racial classifications must stand on their own justification, as measures designed to maintain White Supremacy.[5] We have consistently denied the constitutionality of measures which restrict the rights of citizens on account of race. There can be no doubt that restricting the freedom to marry solely because of racial classifications violates the central meaning of the Equal Protection Clause.

II

These statutes also deprive the Lovings of liberty without due process of law in violation of the Due Process Clause of the Fourteenth Amendment. The freedom to marry has long been recognized as one of the vital personal rights essential to the orderly pursuit of happiness by free men.

Marriage is one of the "basic civil rights of man," fundamental to our very existence and survival. *Skinner v. Oklahoma*, 316 U.S. 535, 541 (1942). *See also Maynard v. Hill*, 125 U.S. 190 (1888). To deny this fundamental freedom on so unsupportable a basis as the racial classifications embodied in these statutes, classifications so directly subversive of the principle of equality at the heart of the Fourteenth Amendment, is surely to deprive all the State's citizens of liberty without due process of law. The Fourteenth Amendment requires that the

---

5   Appellants point out that the State's concern in these statutes, as expressed in the words of the 1924 Act's title, "An Act to Preserve Racial Integrity," extends only to the integrity of the white race. While Virginia prohibits whites from marrying any nonwhite (subject to the exception for the descendants of Pocahontas), Negroes, Orientals, and any other racial class may intermarry without statutory interference. Appellants contend that this distinction renders Virginia's miscegenation statutes arbitrary and unreasonable even assuming the constitutional validity of an official purpose to preserve "racial integrity." We need not reach this contention because we find the racial classifications in these statutes repugnant to the Fourteenth Amendment, even assuming an even-handed state purpose to protect the "integrity" of all races.

freedom of choice to marry not be restricted by invidious racial discriminations. Under our Constitution, the freedom to marry, or not marry, a person of another race resides with the individual and cannot be infringed by the State.

These convictions must be reversed. *It is so ordered.*

MR. JUSTICE STEWART, concurring.

I have previously expressed the belief that "it is simply not possible for a state law to be valid under our Constitution which makes the criminality of an act depend upon the race of the actor." *McLaughlin v. Florida,* 379 U.S. 184, 198 (concurring opinion). Because I adhere to that belief, I concur in the judgment of the Court.

NOTES

1. After *Loving,* the Supreme Court in *Zablocki v. Redhail* struck down a state statute that burdened the marriage rights of those who have outstanding child support obligations. 434 U.S. 374, 390–91, 98 S.Ct. 673, 683, 54 L.Ed.2d 618, 633 (1978). The Court described marriage as "the foundation of the family in our society" and explained that "the decision to marry has been placed on the same level of importance as decisions relating to procreation, childbirth, child rearing, and family relationships." *Id.* at 386. The Court also noted that because Wisconsin prohibited fornication, marriage constituted "the only relationship in which the State of Wisconsin allows sexual relations legally to take place." *Id.*

Then, in *Turner v. Safley,* the Court struck down a state regulation that burdened the marriage rights of prisoners. 482 U.S. 78, 100, 107 S.Ct. 2254, 2267, 96 L.Ed.2d 64, 86 (1987). The Court identified what it regarded as the central elements of marriage:

> It is settled that a prison inmate "retains those [constitutional] rights that are not inconsistent with his status as a prisoner or with the legitimate penological objectives of the corrections system." The right to marry, like many other rights, is subject to substantial restrictions as a result of incarceration. Many important attributes of marriage remain, however, after taking into account the limitations imposed by prison life. First, inmate marriages, like others, are expressions of emotional support and public commitment. These elements are an important and significant aspect of the marital relationship. In addition, many religions recognize marriage as having spiritual significance; for some inmates and their spouses, therefore, the commitment of marriage may be an exercise of religious faith as well as an expression of personal dedication. Third, most inmates eventually will be released by parole or commutation, and therefore most inmate marriages are formed in the expectation that they ultimately will be fully consummated. Finally, marital status often is a precondition to the

receipt of government benefits (e.g., Social Security benefits), property rights (e.g., tenancy by the entirety, inheritance rights), and other, less tangible benefits (e.g., legitimation of children born out of wedlock). These incidents of marriage, like the religious and personal aspects of the marriage commitment, are unaffected by the fact of confinement or the pursuit of legitimate corrections goals. . . . Taken together, we conclude that these remaining elements are sufficient to form a constitutionally protected marital relationship in the prison context.

482 U.S. at 95–96, 107 S.Ct. at 2265, 96 L.Ed. at 83. How does that description differ from the Court's earlier accounts of marriage?

2.   The right to marry established in *Loving* is closely related to the right of (marital) privacy established in *Griswold v. Connecticut*, 381 U.S. 479, 485–86, 85 S.Ct. 1678, 1682, 14 L.Ed.2d 510, 515–16 (1965) (striking down ban on contraceptive use by married couples), where the Court observed that marriage "is an association that promotes a way of life, not causes; a harmony in living, not political faiths; a bilateral loyalty, not commercial or social projects" and "for as noble a purpose as any involved in our prior decisions." 381 U.S. at 486.

3.   Although this Chapter is concerned primarily with same-sex relationships, it should be noted that lesbians and gay men sometimes find themselves in different-sex marriages. Moreover, different-sex marriages also include many bisexual women and men. *See generally* BRENDA MADDOX, MARRIED AND GAY: AN INTIMATE LOOK AT A DIFFERENT RELATIONSHIP (1982).

III. THE MOVEMENT FOR MARRIAGE EQUALITY

The following materials cover same-sex couples' quest for marriage. They are divided into six periods: (1) the 1970s, when same-sex couples first challenged their exclusion from marriage; (2) the late 1980s, when the LGBT movement seriously began to debate the desirability of marriage; (3) the 1990s, which saw the first state court decisions supporting same-sex couples' relationship rights, as well as the beginning of a forceful backlash against same-sex marriage; (4) the 2000s, which featured a string of state court decisions beginning with the first case to open marriage to same-sex couples and followed by mixed results in other states; (5) 2009 to 2013, during which federal litigation challenging state marriage bans and the federal Defense of Marriage Act moved forward and eventually culminated in the Supreme Court's decisions in *Hollingsworth v. Perry* and *United States v. Windsor*; and (6) 2013 to 2015, during which federal litigation challenging state marriage bans and the denial of interstate recognition of same-sex couples' marriages proliferated and ultimately concluded with the Supreme Court's 2015 decision in *Obergefell v. Hodges*.

Throughout these materials, we attend to the different arguments for and against marriage equality and consider claims sounding in both substantive due process (the fundamental right to marry) and equal protection (based on sex and sexual orientation). These doctrinal issues connect to standards and reasoning addressed in Chapters 2 and 3. We also introduce forms of nonmarital relationship recognition and contemplate the wisdom of such mechanisms. In addition, we use the movement for marriage equality to explore the relationship between litigation and social change, asking how court-based tactics influence the trajectories and outcomes of campaigns for social justice.

A. FIRST GENERATION CASES

While the LGBT movement focused on gay liberation in ways that might seem antithetical to the pursuit of marriage—a traditionally conservative and gender-hierarchical form of relationship—some lesbians, gay men, and bisexuals sought marriage rights. Of course, they did so at a time when lesbian and gay people enjoyed few legal protections; in fact, sodomy remained illegal in the vast majority of states. And marriage remained gender-differentiated as a legal matter; different rights and responsibilities were assigned to husbands and wives during marriage and at divorce. Same-sex couples entered court without an organized LGBT legal movement behind them; the public interest firms that would come to dominate the marriage equality cause had yet to form. At this early point, marriage cases emerged in Minnesota, Kentucky, and Washington State and represented signs of protest and resistance outside the major centers of LGBT life. *See* Michael Boucai, *Glorious Precedents: When Gay Marriage Was Radical*, 27 YALE J.L. & HUMAN. 1 (2015).

In response, courts routinely dismissed same-sex couples' claims. For example, in *Singer v. Hara*, the Washington Court of Appeals offered tautological reasoning in rejecting the plaintiffs' analogy to *Loving*: "The operative distinction lies in the relationship which is described by the term 'marriage' itself, and that relationship is the legal union of one man and one woman." 522 P.2d 1187, 1191 (Wash. App. 1974).

In addition to the *Singer* case, two other cases in the early 1970s upheld state marriage laws against constitutional challenges by same-sex couples—*Jones v. Hallahan*, 501 S.W.2d 588, 590 (Ky. Ct. App. 1973), and *Baker v. Nelson*, 191 N.W.2d 185, 187, 291 Minn. 310, 315 (1971). After the couple in *Baker* sought review by the U.S. Supreme Court, the Court dismissed their appeal for "want of a substantial federal question." 409 U.S. 810, 93 S.Ct. 37, 34 L.Ed.2d 65 (1972). The force of that precedent continued to influence marriage litigation until *Obergefell*. Courts also rejected same-sex marriage when it arose in different contexts. *See Anonymous v. Anonymous*, 325 N.Y.S.2d 499, 501, 67 Misc.2d 982, 982 (1971) (in case in which a man had married another man whom he thought was a woman, court relied on dictionary definitions of marriage in ruling that "[t]he marriage ceremony itself was a nullity").

Courts continued to reject same-sex marriage during the 1980s and into the 1990s. *See DeSanto v. Barnsley*, 476 A.2d 952, 328 Pa. Super. 181 (1984). In 1988, a circuit judge in Indiana denied two gay prisoners a license to marry and fined them $2,800 because "[t]heir claims about Indiana law and constitutional rights [were] wacky and sanctionably so." *See* Arthur Leonard, *Judge Denies Marriage License to Gay Male Prisoners*, 1988 LESBIAN/GAY L. NOTES 63. In October 1991, an Ohio probate judge denied a marriage license to a gay couple, asserting that state law prohibits same-sex marriage. *See* Arthur Leonard, *Gay Washingtonians Sue for Marriage License*, 1991 LESBIAN/GAY L. NOTES 3.

B. THE LGBT COMMUNITY'S DEBATE OVER MARRIAGE

Even as some same-sex couples sought the right to marry in court, the LGBT community had its own internal debate about whether marriage was a wise or desirable priority for the movement. While traces of this debate can be found in earlier LGBT organizing, the movement debate began in earnest in the late 1980s. The following exchange between Thomas Stoddard and Paula Ettelbrick, two leading LGBT advocates, inaugurated the debate in seminal essays that appeared under the heading *Gay Marriage: A Must or a Bust?* in OUT/LOOK magazine in 1989.

WHY GAY PEOPLE SHOULD SEEK THE RIGHT TO MARRY[*]
Thomas Stoddard

Even though, these days, few lesbians and gay men enter into marriages recognized by law, absolutely every gay person has an opinion on marriage as an "institution." (The word "institution" brings to mind, perhaps appropriately, museums.) After all, we all know quite a bit about the subject. Most of us grew up in marital households. Virtually all of us, regardless of race, creed, gender, and culture, have received lectures on the propriety, if not the sanctity, of marriage—which usually suggests that those who choose not to marry are both unhappy and unhealthy. We all have been witnesses, willing or not, to a lifelong parade of other people's marriages, from Uncle Harry and Aunt Bernice to the Prince and Princess of Wales. And at one point or another, some nosy relative has inevitably inquired of every gay person when he or she will finally "tie the knot" (an intriguing and probably apt cliché).

---

[*]   Thomas Stoddard, *Why Gay People Should Seek The Right To Marry*, OUT/LOOK, Fall 1989, at 9, 9–13.

I must confess at the outset that I am no fan of the "institution" of marriage as currently constructed and practiced. I may simply be unlucky, but I have seen preciously few marriages over the course of my forty years that invite admiration and emulation. All too often, marriage appears to petrify rather than satisfy and enrich, even for couples in their twenties and thirties who have had a chance to learn the lessons of feminism. Almost inevitably, the partners seem to fall into a "husband" role and a "wife" role, with such latter-day modifications as the wife who works in addition to raising the children and managing the household.

Let me be blunt: in its traditional form, marriage has been oppressive, especially (although not entirely) to women. Indeed, until the middle of the last century, marriage was, at its legal and social essence, an extension of the husband and his paternal family. Under the English common law, wives were among the husband's "chattel"—personal property—and could not, among other things, hold property in their own names. The common law crime of adultery demonstrates the unequal treatment accorded to husbands and wives: while a woman who slept with a man who wasn't her husband committed adultery, a man who slept with a woman not his wife committed fornication. A man was legally incapable of committing adultery, except as an accomplice to an errant wife. The underlying offense of adultery was not the sexual betrayal of one partner by the other, but the wife's engaging in conduct capable of tainting the husband's bloodlines. (I swear on my *Black's Law Dictionary* that I have not made this up!)

Nevertheless, despite the oppressive nature of marriage historically, and in spite of the general absence of edifying examples of modern heterosexual marriage, I believe very strongly that every lesbian and gay man should have the right to marry the same-sex partner of his or her choice, and that the gay rights movement should aggressively seek full legal recognition for same-sex marriages. To those who might not agree, I respectfully offer three explanations, one practical, one political and one philosophical.

THE PRACTICAL EXPLANATION

The legal status of marriage rewards the two individuals who travel to the altar (or its secular equivalent) with substantial economic and practical advantages. Married couples may reduce their tax liability by filing a joint return. They are entitled to special government benefits, such as those given surviving spouses and dependents through the Social Security program. They can inherit from one another even when there is no will. They are immune from subpoenas requiring testimony against the other spouse. And marriage to an American citizen gives a foreigner a right to residency in the United States.

Other advantages have arisen not by law but by custom. Most employers offer health insurance to their employees, and many will include an employee's spouse in the benefits package, usually at the employer's expense. Virtually no employer will include a partner who is not married to an employee, whether of the same sex or not. Indeed, very few insurance companies even offer the possibility of a group health plan covering "domestic partners" who are not married to one another. Two years ago, I tried to find such a policy for Lambda, and discovered that not one insurance company authorized to do business in New York—the second-largest state in the country with more than 17 million residents—would accommodate us. (Lambda has tried to make do by paying for individual insurance policies for the same-sex partners of its employees who otherwise would go uninsured but these individual policies are usually narrower in scope than group policies, often require applicants to furnish individual medical information not required under most group plans, and are typically much more expensive per person.)

In short, the law generally presumes in favor of every marital relationship, and acts to preserve and foster it, and to enhance the rights of the individuals who enter into it. It is usually possible, with enough money and the right advice, to replicate some of the benefits conferred by the legal status of marriage through the use of documents like wills and power of attorney forms, but that protection will inevitably, under current circumstances, be incomplete.

The law (as I suspect will come as no surprise to the readers of this journal) still looks upon lesbians and gay men with suspicion, and this suspicion casts a shadow over the documents they execute in recognition of a same-sex relationship. If a lesbian leaves property to her lover, her will may be invalidated on the grounds that it was executed under the "undue influence" of the would-be beneficiary. A property agreement may be denied validity because the underlying relationship is "meretricious"— akin to prostitution. (Astonishingly, until the mid-seventies, the law throughout the United States deemed "meretricious" virtually *any* formal economic arrangement between two people not married to one another, on the theory that an exchange of property between them was presumably payment for sexual services; the Supreme Court of California helped unravel this quaint legal fantasy in its 1976 ruling in the first famous "alimony" case, *Marvin v. Marvin.*) The law has progressed considerably beyond the uniformly oppressive state of affairs before 1969, but it is still far from enthusiastic about gay people and their relationships—to put it mildly.

Moreover, there are some barriers one simply cannot transcend outside of a formal marriage. When the Internal Revenue Code or the Immigration and Naturalization Act say "married," they mean "married" by definition of state statute. When the employer's group health plan says "spouse," it means "spouse" in the eyes of the law, not the eyes of the loving couple.

But there is another drawback. Couples seeking to protect their relationship through wills and other documents need knowledge, determination and—most importantly—money. No money, no lawyer. And no lawyer, no protection. Those who lack the sophistication or the wherewithal to retain a lawyer are simply stuck in most circumstances. Extending the right to marry to gay couples would assure that those at the bottom of the economic ladder have a chance to secure their relationship rights, too.

THE POLITICAL EXPLANATION

The claim that gay couples ought to be able to marry is not a new one. In the seventies, same-sex couples in three states—Minnesota, Kentucky and Washington—brought constitutional challenges to the marriage statutes, and in all three instances they failed. In each of the three, the court offered two basic justifications for limiting marriage to male-female couples: history and procreation. Witness this passage from the Supreme Court of Minnesota's 1971 opinion in *Baker v. Nelson*: "The institution of marriage as a union of man and woman, uniquely involving the procreating and rearing of children within a family, is as old as the book of Genesis. . . . This historic institution manifestly is more deeply founded than the asserted contemporary concept of marriage and societal interests for which petitioners contend."

Today no American jurisdiction recognizes the right of two women or two men to marry one another, although several nations in Northern Europe do. Even more telling, until earlier this year, there was little discussion within the gay rights movement about whether such a right should exist. As far as I can tell, no gay organization of any size, local or national, has yet declared the right to marry as one of its goals.

With all due respect to my colleagues and friends who take a different view, I believe it is time to renew the effort to overturn the existing marriage laws, and to do so in earnest, with a commitment of money and energy, through both the courts and the state legislatures. I am not naive about the likelihood of imminent victory. There is none. Nonetheless—and here I will not mince words—I would like to see the issue rise to the top of the agenda of every gay organization, including my own (although the judgment is hardly mine alone).

Why give it such prominence? Why devote resources to such a distant goal? Because marriage is, I believe, the political issue that most fully tests the dedication of people who are *not* gay to full equality for gay people, and also the issue most likely to lead ultimately to a world free from discrimination against lesbians and gay men.

Marriage is much more than a relationship sanctioned by law. It is the centerpiece of our entire social structure, the core of the traditional notion of "family." Even in its present tarnished state, the marital relationship inspires sentiments suggesting that it is something almost suprahuman. The Supreme Court, in striking down an anti-contraception statute in 1965, called marriage "noble" and "intimate to the degree of being sacred." The Roman Catholic Church and the Moral Majority would go—and have gone—considerably further.

Lesbians and gay men are now denied entry to this "noble" and "sacred" institution. The implicit message is this: two men or two women are incapable of achieving such an exalted domestic state. Gay relationships are somehow less significant, less valuable. Such relationships may, from time to time and from couple to couple, give the appearance of a marriage, but they can never be of the same quality or importance.

I resent—indeed, I loathe—that conception of same-sex relationships. And I am convinced that ultimately the only way to overturn it is to remove the barrier to marriage that now limits the freedom of every gay man and lesbian.

That is not to deny the value of "domestic partnership" ordinances, statutes that prohibit discrimination based on "marital status," and other legal advances that can enhance the rights (as well as the dignity) of gay couples. Without question, such advances move us further along the path to equality. But their value can only be partial. (The recently enacted San Francisco "domestic partnership" ordinance, for example, will have practical value only for gay people who happen to be employed by the City of San Francisco and want to include their non-marital spouses in part of the city's fringe benefit package; the vast majority of gay San Franciscans—those employed by someone other than the city—have only a symbolic victory to savor.) Measures of this kind can never assure full equality. Gay relationships will continue to be accorded a subsidiary status until the day that gay couples have *exactly* the same rights as their heterosexual counterparts. To my mind, that means either that the right to marry be extended to us, or that marriage be abolished in its present form for all gay couples, presumably to be replaced by some new legal entity—an unlikely alternative.

THE PHILOSOPHICAL EXPLANATION

I confessed at the outset that I personally found marriage in its present avatar rather, well, unattractive. Nonetheless, even from a philosophical perspective, I believe the right to marry should become a stated goal of the gay rights movement.

First, and most basically, the issue is not the desirability of marriage, but rather the desirability of the *right* to marry. That I think two lesbians or two gay men should be entitled to a marriage license does not mean that I think all gay people should find appropriate partners and exercise the right, should it eventually exist. I actually rather doubt that I, myself, would want to marry, even though I share a household with another man who is exceedingly dear to me. There are others who feel differently, for economic, symbolic, or romantic reasons. They should, to my mind, unquestionably have the opportunity to marry if they wish and otherwise meet the requirements of the state (like being old enough).

Furthermore, marriage may be unattractive and even oppressive as it is currently structured and practiced, but enlarging the concept to embrace same-sex couples would necessarily transform it into something new. If two women can marry, or two men, marriage—even for heterosexuals—need not be a union of a "husband" and a "wife." Extending the right to marry to gay people—that is, abolishing the traditional gender requirements of marriage—can be one of the means, perhaps the principal one, through which the institution divests itself of the sexist trappings of the past.

Some of my colleagues disagree with me. I welcome their thoughts and the debates and discussions our different perspectives will trigger. The movement for equality for lesbians and gay men can only be enriched through this collective exploration of the question of marriage. But I do believe many thousands of gay people want the right to marry. And I think, too, they will earn that right for themselves sooner than most of us imagine.

SINCE WHEN IS MARRIAGE A PATH TO LIBERATION?*
Paula Ettelbrick

"Marriage is a great institution, if you like living in institutions," according to a bit of T-shirt philosophy I saw recently. Certainly, marriage is an institution. It is one of the most venerable, impenetrable institutions in modern society. Marriage provides the ultimate form of acceptance for personal intimate relationships in our society, and gives those who marry an insider status of the most powerful kind.

Steeped in a patriarchal system that looks to ownership, property, and dominance of men over women as its basis, the institution of marriage long has been the focus of radical feminist revulsion. Marriage defines certain relationships as more valid than all others. Lesbian and gay relationships, being neither legally sanctioned or commingled by blood, are always at the bottom of the heap of social acceptance and importance.

---

* Paula Ettelbrick, *Since When Is Marriage a Path To Liberation?*, OUT/LOOK, Fall 1989, at 9, 14–17.

Given the imprimatur of social and personal approval which marriage provides, it is not surprising that some lesbians and gay men among us would look to legal marriage for self-affirmation. After all, those who marry can be instantaneously transformed from "outsiders" to "insiders," and we have a desperate need to become insiders.

It could make us feel OK about ourselves, perhaps even relieve some of the internalized homophobia that we all know so well. Society will then celebrate the birth of our children and mourn the death of our spouses. It would be easier to get health insurance for our spouses, family memberships to the local museum, and a right to inherit our spouse's cherished collection of lesbian mystery novels even if she failed to draft a will. Never again would she have to go to a family reunion and debate about the correct term for introducing our lover/partner/significant other to Aunt Flora. Everything would be quite easy and very nice.

So why does this unlikely event so deeply disturb me? For two major reasons. First, marriage will not liberate us as lesbians and gay men. In fact, it will constrain us, make us more invisible, force our assimilation into the mainstream, and undermine the goals of gay liberation. Second, attaining the right to marry will not transform our society from one that makes narrow, but dramatic, distinctions between those who are married and those who are not married to one that respects and encourages choice of relationships and family diversity. Marriage runs counter to two of the primary goals of the lesbian and gay movement: the affirmation of gay identity and culture; and the validation of many forms of relationships.

When analyzed from the standpoint of civil rights, certainly lesbians and gay men should have a right to marry. But obtaining a right does not always result in justice. White male firefighters in Birmingham, Alabama have been fighting for their "rights" to retain their jobs by overturning the city's affirmative action guidelines. If their "rights" prevail, the courts will have failed in rendering justice. The "right" fought for by the white male firefighters, as well as those who advocate strongly for the "rights" to legal marriage for gay people, will result, at best, in limited or narrowed "justice" for those closest to power at the expense of those who have been historically marginalized.

The fight for justice has as its goal the realignment of power imbalances among individuals and classes of people in society. A pure "rights" analysis often fails to incorporate a broader understanding of the underlying inequities that operate to deny justice to a fuller range of people and groups. In setting our priorities as a community, we must combine the concept of both rights and justice. At this point in time, making legal marriage for lesbian and gay couples a priority would set an agenda of gaining rights for a few, but would do nothing to correct the power imbalances between those who are married (whether gay or straight) and those who are not. Thus, justice would not be gained. Justice for gay men and lesbians will be achieved only when we are accepted and supported in this society *despite* our differences from the dominant culture and the choices we make regarding our relationships. Being queer is more than setting up house, sleeping with a person of the same gender, and seeking state approval for doing so. It is an identity, a culture with many variations. It is a way of dealing with the world by diminishing the constraints of gender roles which have for so long kept women and gay people oppressed and invisible. Being queer means pushing the parameters of sex, sexuality, and family, and in the process transforming the very fabric of society. Gay liberation is inexorably linked to women's liberation. Each is essential to the other.

The moment we argue, as some among us insist on doing, that we should be treated as equals because we are really just like married couples and hold the same values to be true, we undermine the very purpose of our movement and begin the dangerous process of silencing our different voices. As a lesbian, I am fundamentally different from non-lesbian women. That's the point. Marriage, as it exists today, is antithetical to my liberation as a lesbian and as a woman because it mainstreams my life and voice. I do not want to be known as "Mrs. Attached-To-Somebody-Else." Nor do I want to give the state the power to regulate my primary relationship.

Yet, the concept of equality in our legal system does not support differences, it only supports sameness. The very standard for equal protection is that people who are similarly situated must be treated equally. To make an argument for equal protection, we will be required to claim that gay and lesbian relationships are the same as straight relationships. To gain the right, we must compare ourselves to married couples. The law looks to the insiders as the norm, regardless of how flawed or unjust their institutions, and requires that those seeking the law's equal protection situate themselves in a similar posture to those who are already protected. In arguing for the right to legal marriage, lesbians and gay men would be forced to claim that we are just like heterosexual couples, have the same goals and purposes, and vow to structure our lives similarly. The law provides no room to argue that we are different, but are nonetheless entitled to equal protection.

The thought of emphasizing our sameness to married heterosexuals in order to obtain this "right" terrifies me. It rips away the very heart and soul of what I believe it is to be a lesbian in this world. It robs me of the opportunity to make a difference. We end up mimicking all that is bad about the institution of marriage in our effort to appear to be the same as straight couples.

By looking to our sameness and de-emphasizing our differences, we don't even place ourselves in a position of power that would allow us to transform marriage from an institution that emphasizes property and state regulation of relationships to an institution which recognizes one of many types of valid and respected relationships. Until the constitution is interpreted to respect and encourage differences, pursuing the legalization of same-sex marriage would be leading our movement into a trap; we would be demanding access to the very institution which, in its current form, would undermine *our* movement to recognize many different kinds of relationships. We would be perpetuating the elevation of married relationships and of "couples" in general, and further eclipsing other relationships of choice.

Ironically, gay marriage, instead of liberating gay sex and sexuality, would further outlaw all gay and lesbian sex which is not performed in a marital context. Just as sexually active non-married women face stigma and double standards around sex and sexual activity, so too would non-married gay people. The only legitimate gay sex would be that which is cloaked in and regulated by marriage. Its legitimacy would stem not from an acceptance of gay sexuality, but because the Supreme Court and society in general fiercely protect the privacy of marital relationships. Lesbians and gay men who did not seek the state's stamp of approval would clearly face increased sexual oppression.

Undoubtedly, whether we admit it or not, we all need to be accepted by the broader society. That motivation fuels our work to eliminate discrimination in the workplace and elsewhere, fight for custody of our children, create our own families, and so on. The growing discussion about the right to marry may be explained in part by this need for acceptance. Those closer to the norm or to power in this country are more likely to see marriage as a principle of freedom and equality. Those who are more acceptable to the mainstream because of race, gender, and economic status are more likely to want the right to marry. It is the final acceptance, the ultimate affirmation of identity.

On the other hand, more marginal members of the lesbian and gay community (women, people of color, working class and poor) are less likely to see marriage as having relevance to our struggles for survival. After all, what good is the affirmation of our relationships (that is, marital relationships) if we are rejected as women, black, or working class?

The path to acceptance is much more complicated for many of us. For instance, if we choose legal marriage, we may enjoy the right to add our spouse to our health insurance policy at work, since most employment policies are defined by one's marital status, not family relationship. However, that choice assumes that we have a job *and* that our employer provides us with health benefits. For women, particularly women of color who tend to occupy the low-paying jobs that do not provide healthcare benefits at all, it will not matter one bit if they are able to marry their women partners. The opportunity to marry will neither get them the health benefits nor transform them from outsider to insider.

Of course, a white man who marries another white man who has a full-time job with benefits will certainly be able to share in those benefits and overcome the only obstacle left to full societal assimilation—the goal of many in his class. In other words, gay marriage will not topple the system that allows only the privileged few to obtain decent health care. Nor will it close the privilege gap between those who are married and those who are not.

Marriage creates a two-tier system that allows the state to regulate relationships. It has become a facile mechanism for employers to dole out benefits, for businesses to provide special deals and incentives, and for the law to make distinctions in distributing meager public funds. None of these entities bothers to consider the relationship among people; the love, respect, and need to protect that exists among all kinds of family members. Rather, a simple certificate of the state, regardless of whether the spouses love, respect, or even see each other on a regular basis, dominates and is supported. None of this dynamic will change if gay men and lesbians are given the option of marriage.

Gay marriage will not help us address the systemic abuses inherent in a society that does not provide decent health care to all of its citizens, a right that should not depend on whether the individual (1) has sufficient resources to afford health care or health insurance, (2) is working and receives health insurance as part of compensation, or (3) is married to a partner who is working and has health coverage which is extended to spouses. It will not address the underlying unfairness that allows businesses to provide discounted services or goods to families and couples—who are defined to include straight, married people and their children, but not domestic partners.

Nor will it address the pain and anguish of an unmarried lesbian who receives word of her partner's accident, rushes to the hospital and is prohibited from entering the intensive ward or obtaining information about her condition solely because she is not a spouse or family member. Likewise, marriage will not help the gay victim of domestic violence who, because he chose not to marry, finds no protection under the law to keep his violent lover away.

If the laws change tomorrow and lesbians and gay men were allowed to marry, where would we find the incentive to continue the progressive movement we have started that is pushing for societal and legal recognition of all kinds of family relationships? To create other options and alternatives? To find a place in the law for the elderly couple who, for companionship and economic reasons, live together but do not marry? To recognize the right of a long-time, but unmarried, gay partner to stay in his rent-controlled apartment after the death of his lover, the only named tenant on the lease? To recognize the family relationship of the lesbian couple and the two gay men who are jointly sharing child-raising responsibilities? To get the law to acknowledge that we may have more than one relationship worthy of legal protection?

Marriage for lesbians and gay men still will not provide a real choice unless we continue the work our community has begun to spread the privilege around to other relationships. We must first break the tradition of piling benefits and privileges on to those who are married, while ignoring the real life needs of those who are not. Only when we de-institutionalize marriage and bridge the economic and privilege gap between the married and the unmarried will each of us have a true choice. Otherwise, our choice not to marry will continue to lack legal protection and societal respect.

The lesbian and gay community has laid the groundwork for revolutionizing society's views of family. The domestic partnership movement has been an important part of this progress insofar as it validates non-marital relationships. Because it is not limited to sexual or romantic relationships, domestic partnership provides an important opportunity for many who are not related by blood or marriage to claim certain minimal protections.

It is crucial, though, that we avoid the pitfall of framing the push for legal recognition of domestic partners (those who share a primary residence and financial responsibilities for each other) as a stepping stone to marriage. We must keep our eyes on the goals of providing true alternatives to marriage and of radically reordering society's views of family.

The goals of lesbian and gay liberation must simply be broader than the right to marry. Gay and lesbian marriages may minimally transform the institution of marriage by diluting its traditional patriarchal dynamic, but they will not transform society. They will not demolish the two-tier system of the "haves" and the "have-nots." We must not fool ourselves into believing that marriage will make it acceptable to be gay or lesbian. We will be liberated only when we are respected and accepted for our differences and the diversity we provide to this society. Marriage is not a path to that liberation.

NOTE

Professor Nan Hunter, another prominent LGBT advocate and scholar, suggested that Ettelbrick "essentialized" marriage and failed to appreciate the ways in which "[m]arriage between men or between women could . . . destabilize the cultural meaning of marriage," with positive implications for the institution. Nan D. Hunter, *Marriage, Law, and Gender: A Feminist Inquiry*, 1 L. & SEXUALITY 9, 17 (1991). Professor Hunter also pointed toward ways in which same-sex marriage could challenge gender-differentiated roles in the family.

C. SECOND GENERATION CASES

In 1993, as the intra-movement debate over marriage continued, Hawaii's Supreme Court reinstated a same-sex marriage challenge that had been dismissed by a trial court. *Baehr v. Lewin*, 852 P.2d 44, 68, 74 Haw. 530, 582 (1993). The court held that the denial of marriage licenses to same-sex couples constituted a claim of sex discrimination under the Hawaii state constitution, and it remanded the case for trial on the question of whether the state could satisfy strict scrutiny in defending its policy. The Hawaii Supreme Court's opinion on the sex discrimination claim is reprinted above, in Chapter 3, Section III.A.1. That opinion is widely seen to have opened the contemporary public debate over same-sex marriage. On remand, after a full trial on the merits, the trial court ruled that the state's ban on same-sex marriage was unconstitutional. *Baehr v. Miike*, 1996 WL 694235, at *22 (Haw. Cir. Ct. 1996). (The year before, a court in the District of Columbia had upheld that jurisdiction's marriage law. *Dean v. District of Columbia*, 653 A.2d 307 (D.C. 1995).) The Hawaii trial court decision was stayed pending the state's appeal to the Hawaii Supreme Court.

Blocking the trial court's decision and avoiding a decision on the merits by the state supreme court, Hawaii voters in November 1998 amended the state's constitution to permit the legislature to reserve marriage to different-sex couples—a reservation that the legislature, in fact, made. Legislative action associated with the ballot initiative on same-sex marriage also resulted in the enactment of the first statewide law providing rights and benefits to same-sex couples through a nonmarital designation. The "reciprocal beneficiaries" law included not only same-sex couples but also other pairings, such as blood relatives, excluded from marriage. The law included survivorship rights, health benefits, property rights, and legal standing regarding wrongful death and victims' rights. It went into effect on July 1, 1997. *See* HAW. REV. STAT. §§ 572C–1 to 572C–7 (2006).

In 1998, the Alaska electorate also amended its state constitution to block same-sex marriage. As in Hawaii, the amendment was a response to a court decision. In *Brause v. Bureau of Vital Statistics*, 1998 WL 88743, at *6 (Alaska Super. Ct. 1998), a trial court had affirmed the right to marry asserted by two gay men. In November 1998, the Alaska electorate amended the state constitution to read:

To be valid or recognized in this State, a marriage may exist only between one man and one woman.

ALASKA CONST. art. I, § 25 (amended 1998). The Alaska voters thereby ended the marriage litigation just as the Hawaii voters had ended the marriage challenge in their state.

Six years after the Hawaii Supreme Court's decision, the Vermont Supreme Court, in a landmark decision, ruled that same-sex couples must be provided the same benefits and protections as married couples. The court did not, however, require the state's legislature to open marriage to same-sex couples. In *Baker v. Vermont*, 744 A.2d 864, 170 Vt. 194 (1999), the court said:

> May the State of Vermont exclude same-sex couples from the benefits and protections that its laws provide to opposite-sex married couples? That is the fundamental question we address in this appeal, a question that the Court well knows arouses deeply-felt religious, moral, and political beliefs. Our constitutional responsibility to consider the legal merits of issues properly before us provides no exception for the controversial case. The issue before the Court, moreover, does not turn on the religious or moral debate over intimate same-sex relationships, but rather on the statutory and constitutional basis for the exclusion of same-sex couples from the secular benefits and protections offered married couples. We conclude that under the Common Benefits Clause of the Vermont Constitution, which, in pertinent part, reads, "That government is, or ought to be, instituted for the common benefit, protection, and security of the people, nation, or community, and not for the particular emolument or advantage of any single person, family, or set of persons, who are a part only of that community," Vt. Const., ch. I, art 7., plaintiffs may not be deprived of the statutory benefits and protections afforded persons of the opposite sex who choose to marry. We hold that the State is constitutionally required to extend to same-sex couples the common benefits and protections that flow from marriage under Vermont law. Whether this ultimately takes the form of inclusion within the marriage laws themselves or a parallel "domestic partnership" system or some equivalent statutory alternative, rests with the Legislature. Whatever system is chosen, however, must conform with the constitutional imperative to afford all Vermonters the common benefit, protection, and security of the law. . . .

[handwritten margin note: VT common benefit clause]

> While the laws relating to marriage have undergone many changes during the last century, largely toward the goal of equalizing the status of husbands and wives, the benefits of

marriage have not diminished in value. On the contrary, the benefits and protections incident to a marriage license under Vermont law have never been greater. They include, for example, the right to receive a portion of the estate of a spouse who dies intestate and protection against disinheritance through elective share provisions; preference in being appointed as the personal representative of a spouse who dies intestate; the right to bring a lawsuit for the wrongful death of a spouse; the right to bring an action for loss of consortium; the right to workers' compensation survivor benefits; the right to spousal benefits statutorily guaranteed to public employees, including health, life, disability, and accident insurance; the opportunity to be covered as a spouse under group life insurance policies issued to an employee; the opportunity to be covered as the insured's spouse under an individual health insurance policy; the right to claim an evidentiary privilege for marital communications; homestead rights and protections; the presumption of joint ownership of property and the concomitant right of survivorship; hospital visitation and other rights incident to the medical treatment of a family member; and the right to receive, and the obligation to provide, spousal support, maintenance, and property division in the event of separation or divorce. [statutory citations have been omitted]. . . .

It is important to state clearly the parameters of today's ruling. Although plaintiffs sought injunctive and declaratory relief designed to secure a marriage license, their claims and arguments here have focused primarily upon the consequences of official exclusion from the statutory benefits, protections, and security incident to marriage under Vermont law. While some future case may attempt to establish that—notwithstanding equal benefits and protections under Vermont law—the denial of a marriage license operates per se to deny constitutionally-protected rights, that is not the claim we address today. We hold only that plaintiffs are entitled under Chapter I, Article 7, of the Vermont Constitution to obtain the same benefits and protections afforded by Vermont law to married opposite-sex couples. We do not purport to infringe upon the prerogatives of the Legislature to craft an appropriate means of addressing this constitutional mandate, other than to note that the record here refers to a number of potentially constitutional statutory schemes from other jurisdictions. These include what are typically referred to as "domestic partnership" or "registered partnership" acts, which generally establish an alternative legal status to marriage for same-sex couples, impose similar formal requirements and limitations, create a parallel licensing or registration scheme, and extend all or most of the same rights and obligations provided by the law to married partners.

744 A.2d at 867, 883–86, 170 Vt. at 197–98, 221–25. In the wake of the state supreme court decision, the Vermont legislature complied with the court's mandate in 2000 by enacting a law recognizing "civil unions" for same-sex couples. VT. STAT. ANN. tit. 15, §§ 1201–1207 (2007).

After *Baker*, the U.S. Supreme Court decided *Lawrence* (2003). That case did not speak directly to marriage, but had powerful implications for the issue. Professor Carlos Ball explained *Lawrence*'s implications for the constitutional case for same-sex marriage:

> The Court in *Lawrence* understood that the Texas sodomy statute implicated liberty interests associated with personal relationships as much as liberty interests associated with sexual conduct. For the Court, in fact, it made no sense to discuss the freedom to engage in sexual conduct without bringing into the liberty analysis the ability of individuals to form and maintain the kinds of personal relationships that often accompany that conduct. The impact of the Texas sodomy statute on the freedom of individuals to form and maintain personal relationships, in other words, was for the Court as important as the statute's impact on the freedom of individuals to make decisions about their sexual conduct without fear of criminal repercussions. . . .

> The *Lawrence* Court recognized that the criminalization of particular kinds of sexual intimacy not only limits the autonomy of individuals to decide which kinds of sexual acts they want to engage in and with whom; it also, directly and necessarily, has an impact on the autonomy of individuals to build relationships that are based, in part, upon that sexual intimacy. Thus the Court, in one of the most important sentences in the opinion, noted that "[w]hen sexuality finds overt expression in intimate conduct with another person, the conduct can be but one element in a personal bond that is more enduring."

> The Court in *Lawrence* understood that relationships are central to the dignity and autonomy of all individuals, including those who are lesbian or gay. As the Court saw it, what was ultimately at issue in the case was the ability of individuals to "retain their dignity as free persons" in the face of regulations such as Texas's sodomy statute that "seek to control ... personal relationship[s]." The crucial point is this: The *Lawrence* Court understood that there is more to lesbian and gay individuals than their interest in having sex and that there is more to gay rights positions than simply the right to have sex.

[handwritten marginalia: connection]

Carlos A. Ball, *The Positive in the Fundamental Right to Marry: Same-Sex Marriage in the Aftermath of* Lawrence v. Texas, 88 MINN. L. REV. 1184, 1212–13 (2004).

Within six months of the *Lawrence* decision, the Massachusetts Supreme Judicial Court held that the denial of marriage licenses to same-sex couples violated its state's constitution. These developments—and reactions to them—are captured in the readings that follow.

D. MARRIAGE AND RELATIONSHIP RECOGNITION FOR SAME-SEX COUPLES

1. The Door Opens in Massachusetts

GOODRIDGE V. DEPARTMENT OF PUBLIC HEALTH

Supreme Judicial Court of Massachusetts, 2003
798 N.E.2d 941, 440 Mass. 309

MARSHALL, C.J.

The plaintiffs are fourteen individuals from five Massachusetts counties. * * *

In March and April, 2001, each of the plaintiff couples attempted to obtain a marriage license from a city or town clerk's office. * * *

In each case, the clerk either refused to accept the notice of intention to marry or denied a marriage license to the couple on the ground that Massachusetts does not recognize same-sex marriage. Because obtaining a marriage license is a necessary prerequisite to civil marriage in Massachusetts, denying marriage licenses to the plaintiffs was tantamount to denying them access to civil marriage itself, with its appurtenant social and legal protections, benefits, and obligations.[6]

On April 11, 2001, the plaintiffs filed suit in the Superior Court against the department and the commissioner seeking a judgment that "the exclusion of the [p]laintiff couples and other qualified same-sex couples from access to marriage licenses, and the legal and social status

---

[6] The complaint alleged various circumstances in which the absence of the full legal protections of civil marriage has harmed them and their children. For example, Hillary and Julie Goodridge alleged that, when Julie gave birth to their daughter (whom Hillary subsequently coadopted) during a delivery that required the infant's transfer to neonatal intensive care, Hillary "had difficulty gaining access to Julie and their newborn daughter at the hospital"; Gary Chalmers and Richard Linnell alleged that "Gary pays for a family health insurance policy at work which covers only him and their daughter because Massachusetts law does not consider Rich to be a 'dependent.' This means that their household must purchase a separate individual policy of health insurance for Rich at considerable expense. . . . Gary has a pension plan at work, but under state law, because he is a municipal employee, that plan does not allow him the same range of options in providing for his beneficiary that a married spouse has and thus he cannot provide the same security to his family that a married person could if he should predecease Rich."

of civil marriage, as well as the protections, benefits and obligations of marriage, violates Massachusetts law." * * *

A Superior Court judge ruled for the department. * * *

III

A

The larger question is whether, as the department claims, government action that bars same-sex couples from civil marriage constitutes a legitimate exercise of the State's authority to regulate conduct, or whether, as the plaintiffs claim, this categorical marriage exclusion violates the Massachusetts Constitution. * * *

For the reasons we explain below, we conclude that the marriage ban does not meet the rational basis test for either due process or equal protection. * * *

The department posits three legislative rationales for prohibiting same-sex couples from marrying: (1) providing a "favorable setting for procreation"; (2) ensuring the optimal setting for child rearing, which the department defines as "a two-parent family with one parent of each sex"; and (3) preserving scarce State and private financial resources. We consider each in turn.

The judge in the Superior Court endorsed the first rationale, holding that "the state's interest in regulating marriage is based on the traditional concept that marriage's primary purpose is procreation." This is incorrect. Fertility is not a condition of marriage, nor is it grounds for divorce. People who have never consummated their marriage, and never plan to, may be and stay married. People who cannot stir from their deathbed may marry. While it is certainly true that many, perhaps most, married couples have children together (assisted or unassisted), it is the exclusive and permanent commitment of the marriage partners to one another, not the begetting of children, that is the sine qua non of civil marriage.[23]

* * * The "marriage is procreation" argument singles out the one unbridgeable difference between same-sex and opposite-sex couples, and transforms that difference into the essence of legal marriage. Like Amendment 2 to the Constitution of Colorado, which effectively denied

---

[23]   It is hardly surprising that civil marriage developed historically as a means to regulate heterosexual conduct and to promote child rearing, because until very recently unassisted heterosexual relations were the only means short of adoption by which children could come into the world, and the absence of widely available and effective contraceptives made the link between heterosexual sex and procreation very strong indeed. Punitive notions of illegitimacy, and of homosexual identity, further cemented the common and legal understanding of marriage as an unquestionably heterosexual institution. But it is circular reasoning, not analysis, to maintain that marriage must remain a heterosexual institution because that is what it historically has been.

homosexual persons equality under the law and full access to the political process, the marriage restriction impermissibly "identifies persons by a single trait and then denies them protection across the board." *Romer v. Evans*, 517 U.S. 620, 633 (1996). In so doing, the State's action confers an official stamp of approval on the destructive stereotype that same-sex relationships are inherently unstable and inferior to opposite-sex relationships and are not worthy of respect.

The department's first stated rationale, equating marriage with unassisted heterosexual procreation, shades imperceptibly into its second: that confining marriage to opposite-sex couples ensures that children are raised in the "optimal" setting. Protecting the welfare of children is a paramount State policy. Restricting marriage to opposite-sex couples, however, cannot plausibly further this policy. "The demographic changes of the past century make it difficult to speak of an average American family. The composition of families varies greatly from household to household." *Troxel v. Granville*, 530 U.S. 57, 63 (2000). Massachusetts has responded supportively to the changing realities of the American family and has moved vigorously to strengthen the modern family in its many variations. Moreover, we have repudiated the common-law power of the State to provide varying levels of protection to children based on the circumstances of birth. The "best interests of the child" standard does not turn on a parent's sexual orientation or marital status.

The department has offered no evidence that forbidding marriage to people of the same sex will increase the number of couples choosing to enter into opposite-sex marriages in order to have and raise children. There is thus no rational relationship between the marriage statute and the Commonwealth's proffered goal of protecting the "optimal" child rearing unit. Moreover, the department readily concedes that people in same-sex couples may be "excellent" parents. These couples (including four of the plaintiff couples) have children for the reasons others do—to love them, to care for them, to nurture them. But the task of child rearing for same-sex couples is made infinitely harder by their status as outliers to the marriage laws. Given the wide range of public benefits reserved only for married couples, we do not credit the department's contention that the absence of access to civil marriage amounts to little more than an inconvenience to same-sex couples and their children. Excluding same-sex couples from civil marriage will not make children of opposite-sex marriages more secure, but it does prevent children of same-sex couples from enjoying the immeasurable advantages that flow from the assurance of a stable family structure in which children will be reared, educated, and socialized.[26]

---

[26] The [dissent's] claim that the constitutional rights to bear and raise a child are "not implicated or infringed" by the marriage ban does not stand up to scrutiny. The absolute foreclosure of the marriage option for the class of parents and would-be parents at issue here

(3)
conserving
resources

. . . The third rationale advanced by the department is that limiting marriage to opposite-sex couples furthers the Legislature's interest in conserving scarce State and private financial resources. The marriage restriction is rational, it argues, because the General Court logically could assume that same-sex couples are more financially independent than married couples and thus less needy of public marital benefits, such as tax advantages, or private marital benefits, such as employer-financed health plans that include spouses in their coverage.

4

An absolute statutory ban on same-sex marriage bears no rational relationship to the goal of economy. First, the department's conclusory generalization—that same-sex couples are less financially dependent on each other than opposite-sex couples—ignores that many same-sex couples, such as many of the plaintiffs in this case, have children and other dependents (here, aged parents) in their care. The department does not contend, nor could it, that these dependents are less needy or deserving than the dependents of married couples. Second, Massachusetts marriage laws do not condition receipt of public and private financial benefits to married individuals on a demonstration of financial dependence on each other; the benefits are available to married couples regardless of whether they mingle their finances or actually depend on each other for support. * * *

need for benefits

The department has had more than ample opportunity to articulate a constitutionally adequate justification for limiting civil marriage to opposite-sex unions. It has failed to do so.

The marriage ban works a deep and scarring hardship on a very real segment of the community for no rational reason. The absence of any reasonable relationship between, on the one hand, an absolute disqualification of same-sex couples who wish to enter into civil marriage and, on the other, protection of public health, safety, or general welfare, suggests that the marriage restriction is rooted in persistent prejudices against persons who are (or who are believed to be) homosexual. "The Constitution cannot control such prejudices but neither can it tolerate them. Private biases may be outside the reach of the law, but the law cannot, directly or indirectly, give them effect." *Palmore v. Sidoti*, 466 U.S. 429, 433 (1984). Limiting the protections, benefits, and obligations of civil marriage to opposite-sex couples violates the basic premises of individual liberty and equality under law protected by the Massachusetts Constitution.

IV

We consider next the plaintiffs' request for relief. * * *

---

imposes a heavy burden on their decision to have and raise children that is not suffered by any other class of parent.

In their complaint the plaintiffs request only a declaration that their exclusion and the exclusion of other qualified same-sex couples from access to civil marriage violates Massachusetts law. We declare that barring an individual from the protections, benefits, and obligations of civil marriage solely because that person would marry a person of the same sex violates the Massachusetts Constitution. We vacate the summary judgment for the department. We remand this case to the Superior Court for entry of judgment consistent with this opinion. Entry of judgment shall be stayed for 180 days to permit the Legislature to take such action as it may deem appropriate in light of this opinion.

GREANEY, J. (concurring).

I agree with the result reached by the court, the remedy ordered, and much of the reasoning in the court's opinion. In my view, however, the case is more directly resolved using traditional equal protection analysis. Analysis begins with the indisputable premise that the deprivation suffered by the plaintiffs is no mere legal inconvenience. The right to marry is not a privilege conferred by the State, but a fundamental right that is protected against unwarranted State interference. * * *

Because our marriage statutes intend, and state, the ordinary understanding that marriage under our law consists only of a union between a man and a woman, they create a statutory classification based on the sex of the two people who wish to marry. * * *

With these two propositions established (the infringement on a fundamental right and a sex-based classification), the enforcement of the marriage statutes as they are currently understood is forbidden by our Constitution unless the State can present a compelling purpose furthered by the statutes that can be accomplished in no other reasonable manner. This the State has not done. The justifications put forth by the State to sustain the statute's exclusion of the plaintiffs are insufficient for the reasons explained by the court. * * *

I do not doubt the sincerity of deeply held moral or religious beliefs that make inconceivable to some the notion that any change in the common-law definition of what constitutes a legal civil marriage is now, or ever would be, warranted. But, as matter of constitutional law, neither the mantra of tradition, nor individual conviction, can justify the perpetuation of a hierarchy in which couples of the same sex and their families are deemed less worthy of social and legal recognition than couples of the opposite sex and their families. *See Lawrence v. Texas.* * * *

SPINA, J. (dissenting, with whom SOSMAN and CORDY, JJ., join).

What is at stake in this case is not the unequal treatment of individuals or whether individual rights have been impermissibly burdened, but the power of the Legislature to effectuate social change without interference from the courts, pursuant to art. 30 of the Massachusetts Declaration of Rights. The power to regulate marriage lies with the Legislature, not with the judiciary. Today, the court has transformed its role as protector of individual rights into the role of creator of rights, and I respectfully dissent.

1. *Equal protection.* [The marriage law] creates no distinction between the sexes, but applies to men and women in precisely the same way. It does not create any disadvantage identified with gender, as both men and women are similarly limited to marrying a person of the opposite sex. Similarly, the marriage statutes do not discriminate on the basis of sexual orientation. The marriage statutes do not disqualify individuals on the basis of sexual orientation from entering into marriage. All individuals, with certain exceptions not relevant here, are free to marry. Whether an individual chooses not to marry because of sexual orientation or any other reason should be of no concern to the court. * * *

2. *Due process.* The marriage statutes do not impermissibly burden a right protected by our constitutional guarantee of due process implicit in art. 10 of our Declaration of Rights. There is no restriction on the right of any plaintiff to enter into marriage. Each is free to marry a willing person of the opposite sex. * * *

... Same-sex marriage, or the "right to marry the person of one's choice" as the court today defines that right, does not fall within the fundamental right to marry. Same-sex marriage is not "deeply rooted in this Nation's history," and the court does not suggest that it is. * * *

[JUSTICE SOSMAN's dissent, which JUSTICES SPINA and CORDY joined, is omitted.]

CORDY, J. (dissenting, with whom SPINA and SOSMAN, JJ., join).

The Massachusetts marriage statute does not impair the exercise of a recognized fundamental right, or discriminate on the basis of sex in violation of the equal rights amendment to the Massachusetts Constitution. Consequently, it is subject to review only to determine whether it satisfies the rational basis test. Because a conceivable rational basis exists upon which the Legislature could conclude that the marriage statute furthers the legitimate State purpose of ensuring, promoting, and supporting an optimal social structure for the bearing and raising of children, it is a valid exercise of the State's police power. * * *

* * * *State purpose.* The court's opinion concedes that the civil marriage statute serves legitimate State purposes, but further investigation and elaboration of those purposes is both helpful and necessary. Civil marriage is the institutional mechanism by which societies have sanctioned and recognized particular family structures, and the institution of marriage has existed as one of the fundamental

organizing principles of human society. Marriage has not been merely a contractual arrangement for legally defining the private relationship between two individuals (although that is certainly part of any marriage). Rather, on an institutional level, marriage is the "very basis of the whole fabric of civilized society," and it serves many important political, economic, social, educational, procreational, and personal functions.

Paramount among its many important functions, the institution of marriage has systematically provided for the regulation of heterosexual behavior, brought order to the resulting procreation, and ensured a stable family structure in which children will be reared, educated, and socialized. Admittedly, heterosexual intercourse, procreation, and child care are not necessarily conjoined (particularly in the modern age of widespread effective contraception and supportive social welfare programs), but an orderly society requires some mechanism for coping with the fact that sexual intercourse commonly results in pregnancy and childbirth. The institution of marriage is that mechanism.

The institution of marriage provides the important legal and normative link between heterosexual intercourse and procreation on the one hand and family responsibilities on the other. The partners in a marriage are expected to engage in exclusive sexual relations, with children the probable result and paternity presumed. Whereas the relationship between mother and child is demonstratively and predictably created and recognizable through the biological process of pregnancy and childbirth, there is no corresponding process for creating a relationship between father and child.... The alternative, a society without the institution of marriage, in which heterosexual intercourse, procreation, and child care are largely disconnected processes, would be chaotic.

The marital family is also the foremost setting for the education and socialization of children. Children learn about the world and their place in it primarily from those who raise them, and those children eventually grow up to exert some influence, great or small, positive or negative, on society. The institution of marriage encourages parents to remain committed to each other and to their children as they grow, thereby encouraging a stable venue for the education and socialization of children. * * *

It is undeniably true that dramatic historical shifts in our cultural, political, and economic landscape have altered some of our traditional notions about marriage, including the interpersonal dynamics within it, the range of responsibilities required of it as an institution, and the legal environment in which it exists. Nevertheless, the institution of marriage remains the principal weave of our social fabric. A family defined by heterosexual marriage continues to be the most prevalent social structure into which the vast majority of children are born, nurtured, and prepared for productive participation in civil society. It is difficult to imagine a State purpose more important and legitimate than ensuring, promoting, and supporting an optimal social structure within which to bear and raise children. At the very least, the marriage statute continues to serve this important State purpose. * * *

In considering whether such a rational basis exists, we defer to the decision-making process of the Legislature, and must make deferential assumptions about the information that it might consider and on which it may rely. We must assume that the Legislature (1) might conclude that the institution of civil marriage has successfully and continually provided this structure over several centuries; (2) might consider and credit studies that document negative consequences that too often follow children either born outside of marriage or raised in households lacking either a father or a mother figure, and scholarly commentary contending that children and families develop best when mothers and fathers are partners in their parenting; and (3) would be familiar with many recent studies that variously support the proposition that children raised in intact families headed by same-sex couples fare as well on many measures as children raised in similar families headed by opposite-sex couples; support the proposition that children of same-sex couples fare worse on some measures; or reveal notable differences between the two groups of children that warrant further study.

We must also assume that the Legislature would be aware of the critiques of the methodologies used in virtually all of the comparative studies of children raised in these different environments, cautioning that the sampling populations are not representative, that the observation periods are too limited in time, that the empirical data are unreliable, and that the hypotheses are too infused with political or agenda driven bias.

Taking all of this available information into account, the Legislature could rationally conclude that a family environment with married opposite-sex parents remains the optimal social structure in which to bear children, and that the raising of children by same-sex couples, who by definition cannot be the two sole biological parents of a child and cannot provide children with a parental authority figure of each gender,[29] presents an alternative structure for child rearing that has not yet proved

---

[29]   This family structure raises the prospect of children lacking any parent of their own gender. For example, a boy raised by two lesbians as his parents has no male parent. Contrary to the suggestion that concerns about such a family arrangement is [sic] based on "stereotypical" views about the differences between sexes, concern about such an arrangement remains rational. It is, for example, rational to posit that the child himself might invoke gender as a justification for the view that neither of his parents "understands" him, or that they "don't know what he is going through," particularly if his disagreement or dissatisfaction involves some issue pertaining to sex. Given that same-sex couples raising children are a very recent phenomenon, the ramifications of an adolescent child's having two parents but not one of his or her own gender have yet to be fully realized and cannot yet even be tested in significant numbers.

itself beyond reasonable scientific dispute to be as optimal as the biologically based marriage norm. Working from the assumption that a recognition of same-sex marriages will increase the number of children experiencing this alternative, the Legislature could conceivably conclude that declining to recognize same-sex marriages remains prudent until empirical questions about its impact on the upbringing of children are resolved.

* * * In addition, the Legislature could conclude that redefining the institution of marriage to permit same-sex couples to marry would impair the State's interest in promoting and supporting heterosexual marriage as the social institution that it has determined best normalizes, stabilizes, and links the acts of procreation and child rearing. While the plaintiffs argue that they only want to take part in the same stabilizing institution, the Legislature conceivably could conclude that permitting their participation would have the unintended effect of undermining to some degree marriage's ability to serve its social purpose.

* * * Given the critical importance of civil marriage as an organizing and stabilizing institution of society, it is eminently rational for the Legislature to postpone making fundamental changes to it until such time as there is unanimous scientific evidence, or popular consensus, or both, that such changes can safely be made.

There is no reason to believe that legislative processes are inadequate to effectuate legal changes in response to evolving evidence, social values, and views of fairness on the subject of same-sex relationships. Deliberate consideration of, and incremental responses to rapidly evolving scientific and social understanding is the norm of the political process—that it may seem painfully slow to those who are already persuaded by the arguments in favor of change is not a sufficient basis to conclude that the processes are constitutionally infirm. The Legislature is the appropriate branch, both constitutionally and practically, to consider and respond to it. It is not enough that we as Justices might be personally of the view that we have learned enough to decide what is best. So long as the question is at all debatable, it must be the Legislature that decides.

NOTES

1. Echoing the Vermont Supreme Court's resolution of the *Baker* case, the Massachusetts state legislature, after *Goodridge* was decided, asked the Supreme Judicial Court whether an equal benefits law short of full marriage recognition would satisfy the court's mandate. The Court replied that it would not. *Opinion of the Justices to the Senate*, 802 N.E.2d 565, 572, 440 Mass. 1201, 1210 (2004). On May 17, 2004, at the expiration of the Court's original 180-day mandate, same-sex couples began to marry in Massachusetts. *See* Yvonne Abraham & Rick Klein, *Free to Marry: Historic*

Date Arrives for Same-Sex Couples in Massachusetts, BOSTON GLOBE, May 17, 2004, at A1.

2.   Like the Hawaii decision before it, the *Goodridge* decision provoked a wave of backlash against same-sex marriage. The backlash is discussed below.

3.   Justice Cordy's dissent articulates the "responsible procreation" argument against same-sex marriage. This argument became particularly influential in litigation. You should consider its various iterations and responses by lawyers and courts in the remainder of this Chapter.

2.   Backlash and Countermobilization

Litigation seeking marriage equality met with intense countermobilization. Virtually as soon as the Hawaii Supreme Court signaled its apparent intention to announce a state constitutional right to marry, efforts to oppose that change in marriage law began. The passage of the federal Defense of Marriage Act (DOMA) and many state-law mini-DOMAs in the ensuing years evidenced substantial popular resistance to the legalization of same-sex marriage. After *Goodridge* was decided, that resistance reached a new level, when a federal constitutional amendment to ban same-sex marriage was endorsed by President George W. Bush. A leading version of the amendment proposed:

> Marriage in the United States shall consist only of the union of a man and a woman. Neither this Constitution, nor the constitution of any State, shall be construed to require that marriage or the legal incidents thereof be conferred upon any union other than the union of a man and a woman.

H.R.J. Res. 88, 109th Cong. (2006). Supporters of a federal amendment differed over whether to target only marriage, or also to prohibit nonmarital forms like civil unions.

In addition to promoting a federal constitutional amendment, opponents of same-sex marriage sought additional restrictions in the states. The early mini-DOMAs enacted after the *Baehr* decision in Hawaii generally focused on banning same-sex marriage on the state level and/or denying recognition to same-sex marriages performed in other states. Some were codified by statute, others by state constitutional amendment. After *Goodridge*, the trend was for states to pass constitutional amendments, not statutes. Indeed, some states that already had DOMA statutes on the books added new constitutional amendments. And many of the measures passed after *Goodridge* were so-called "super-DOMAs"— laws that reach beyond same-sex marriage to restrict civil unions and domestic partnerships, as well.

The backlash against same-sex marriage advocacy was widespread.[1] The following materials explore various dimensions of the backlash and ask whether (and how) litigation helps or hinders efforts for social change. We consider the competing perspectives of Professor Michael Klarman, a leading scholar on backlash against court decisions, and Mary Bonauto, the lawyer at Gay & Lesbian Advocates & Defenders (GLAD) who led the *Goodridge* litigation. We will return to the questions raised by these excerpts throughout the Chapter.

BROWN AND *LAWRENCE* (AND *GOODRIDGE*)[*]
Michael Klarman

Court rulings such as *Brown* and *Goodridge* produce political backlashes for three principal reasons: They raise the salience of an issue, they incite anger over "outside interference" or "judicial activism," and they alter the order in which social change would otherwise have occurred.

Brown was harder to ignore than earlier changes in southern racial practices. Most white southerners did not see black jurors or black police officers, who policed black neighborhoods only, and they would have been largely unaware of the dramatic increases in black voter registration that had occurred since World War II. Even some instances of integration—such as on city buses or golf courses—would have gone unnoticed by many white southerners. But they could not miss *Brown*, which received front-page coverage in virtually every newspaper in the country and was a constant topic of southern conversations. A northern white visitor found after *Brown* that segregation "is the foremost preoccupation of the Southern mind. . . . [It] intrudes into almost every conversation. It nags, it bothers and it will not be ignored." One white-supremacist leader credited the Court with "awakening us from a slumber of about 30 years," and an Alabama public official noted that white southerners owed the Justices "a debt of gratitude" for "causing us to become organized and unified."

Lawrence and, to an even greater extent, *Goodridge*, have dramatically raised the salience of gay-rights issues. Many other reforms on issues of sexual orientation—such as repeal of criminal prohibitions on sodomy, expansion of partnership benefits, and enactment of statutory protections against discrimination in employment and public

---

[1]   In 2010, the backlash took a new form when three Iowa supreme court justices who had ruled in favor of marriage equality lost their seats in a retention election. *See* John Gramlich, *Judges' Battles Signal a New Era for Retention Elections*, WASH. POST, Dec. 5, 2010, at A8. Normally, such elections return incumbent justices to the bench at a high rate. In the Iowa case, large sums were spent to defeat the justices.

[*]   Michael Klarman, Brown *and* Lawrence *(and* Goodridge*)*, 104 MICH. L. REV. 431, 473–85 (2005).

accommodations—have occurred without riveting public attention. Since *Goodridge*, though, same-sex marriage has constantly captured front-page newspaper headlines, and the issue received enormous attention during the 2004 presidential election campaign. Court rulings such as *Lawrence* and *Goodridge* forced people who previously had not paid much attention to gay-rights issues to notice what has been happening and to form an opinion on it. As one social conservative observed not long after the Massachusetts decision, "the more people focus on [gay marriage], the less they support it." Another critic of same-sex marriage noted that *Goodridge* "slapped American Christians in their face and woke them up." In the spring of 2004 in Oregon, the Christian Coalition sent out 75,000 voter guides opposing the reelection of Justice Rives Kistler of the state supreme court, denouncing him as "the only open homosexual supreme court judge in the nation"; it was the same-sex marriage issue that had given salience to the jurist's sexual orientation.

The second reason that rulings such as *Brown* and *Goodridge* produce political backlashes is that judicially mandated social reform may mobilize greater resistance than change accomplished through legislatures or with the acquiescence of other democratically operated institutions. *Brown* represented federal interference in southern race relations—something that white southerners, harboring deep historical resentments over military rule and "carpetbag" government during Reconstruction—could not easily tolerate. * * *

Goodridge, decided by the Massachusetts Supreme Court, cannot be seen as outside interference—at least with regard to ramifications for Massachusetts—in the same way that white southerners tended to regard the U.S. Supreme Court ruling in *Brown*. However, because it was a court decision, rather than a reform adopted by voters or popularly elected legislators, critics were able to deride it as the handiwork of arrogant "activist judges" defying the will of the people. * * * Karl Rove declared that President Bush believed that "5,000 years of human history should not be overthrown by the acts of a few liberal judges." The president himself stated during one of the presidential debates, "I'm deeply concerned that judges are making those decisions, and not the citizenry of the United States." Even a prominent gay-rights activist such as Andrew Sullivan, former editor of the New Republic, conceded that "court-imposed mandates rub people the wrong way, even those who support including gay couples within the family structure." The *Goodridge* ruling on same-sex marriage contrasts with other gay-rights reforms such as decriminalization of same-sex sodomy or the expansion of antidiscrimination laws to cover sexual orientation, where legislatures have been the driving force.

Moreover, because the Full Faith & Credit Clause of the federal constitution conceivably—though doubtfully—would place other states under some obligation to respect Massachusetts marriages, critics of *Goodridge* were able to rally support for a federal constitutional amendment, which was said to be necessary to protect the rest of the nation from the "activist judges" of Massachusetts. * * *

Third and perhaps most important, court decisions produce backlashes by commanding that social reform take place in a different order than might otherwise have occurred. On subjects such as race and sexual orientation, public attitudes often vary across a range of issues. Under Jim Crow, whites were generally more opposed to interracial marriage and the integration of grade schools than they were to desegregating transportation or permitting blacks to vote. Similarly, heterosexuals today tend to be far more committed to preventing same-sex marriage than to barring same-sex "civil unions" or to permitting employers to discriminate based on sexual orientation. Heterosexuals are least determined to retain criminal prohibitions on private, consensual, adult same-sex sodomy. * * *

By contrast, *Lawrence* dealt with an issue on which heterosexuals are most tolerant of change. Whatever most Americans today think of same-sex marriage or gays openly serving in the military, few favor punishing the private sexual conduct of gays and lesbians. As one leading social conservative put it after *Lawrence*, "even most Christians believe that what is done in the privacy of one's home is not the government's business." In 1961 all fifty states punished same-sex sodomy; in 1986 only twenty-five did so; and only thirteen states did so at the time of *Lawrence* (and only four of these had statutes that were explicitly addressed to same-sex sodomy). Even in those holdout states, virtually no prosecutions actually occurred. Thus, *Lawrence* was about as (politically) easy a constitutional case as the Court ever confronts: The Justices were asked to translate into constitutional law a social norm that commanded overwhelming popular support. Thus, they probably anticipated a relatively placid response to their ruling, unlike in *Brown*, where some of the Justices expected white southerners to respond with violence and school closures.

Goodridge produced a political backlash for the same reason that *Brown* did. By the early twenty-first century, most Americans were willing to accept decriminalization of same-sex sodomy, statutory bans on employment discrimination based on sexual orientation, and perhaps even civil unions for same-sex couples. Before *Lawrence* and, even more so, *Goodridge* gave same-sex marriage special prominence, many Democratic politicians—including most of those competing for the party's presidential nomination in 2004—supported civil unions, but not formal marriage, for gays and lesbians. This compromise position was an effort to appeal to homosexual voters, who disproportionately support the Democratic party, without alienating those heterosexuals who are willing to countenance progressive change on issues involving sexual orientation but not same-sex marriage.

After *Goodridge*, that compromise position became untenable. With gay and lesbian couples demanding marriage licenses across the country, it became harder to divert public attention from same-sex marriage to civil unions. * * *

Inspired by the ruling of the Massachusetts court, thousands of same-sex couples applied for and received marriage licenses in San Francisco and in Multnomah County, Oregon, and smaller numbers did so in several other cities across the nation. Office-holders in local communities where public opinion supported same-sex marriage had obvious incentives to grant such licenses; their defiance of higher authority converted them into local heroes (much as southern governors such as Orval Faubus and George Wallace became virtually unbeatable politically by defying federal-court integration orders after *Brown*). For example, Mayor Newsom, who had won a narrow victory in the San Francisco mayoral election in December 2003, saw his approval ratings rise to a staggering eighty-five percent after he ordered local officials to begin issuing marriage licenses in February 2004. As the threat that same-sex marriage would expand beyond the boundaries of Massachusetts became real, opponents mobilized behind state and federal constitutional amendments to limit marriage to unions between men and women.

After the 2004 election, many prominent Democrats blamed Mayor Newsom of San Francisco for providing conservatives with an issue to rally around. Senator Dianne Feinstein of California observed that the thousands of same-sex weddings in San Francisco "energized a very conservative vote" and that the "whole issue has been too much, too fast, too soon. And people aren't ready for it." Representative Barney Frank of Massachusetts, one of the few openly gay representatives in the U.S. Congress, said that Newsom had "helped to galvanize Mr. Bush's conservative supporters in those states by playing into people's fears of same-sex weddings." * * *

Thus, the most significant short-term consequence of *Goodridge*, as with *Brown*, may have been the political backlash that it inspired. By outpacing public opinion on issues of social reform, such rulings mobilize opponents, undercut moderates, and retard the cause they purport to advance. And while the violent southern backlash produced by *Brown* generated a counterbacklash in northern opinion, in the wake of *Goodridge* gays and lesbians have not faced the sort of pervasive public violence that outrages moderates and turns the tide of public opinion once and for all. * * *

The future may be even easier to predict with regard to gay rights. Although the election results in 2004 confirm that most Americans are not yet ready for same-sex marriage, on other gay-rights issues the trend is plainly in the direction of expanded rights. In 2004, voters in Cincinnati overturned a city ordinance adopted ten years earlier that had barred the city council from passing any laws giving "minority or protected status" to gays and lesbians. In both North Carolina and Idaho, states not normally considered strong bastions of gay rights, voters elected their first openly gay state legislators, and voters in Dallas County, Texas elected as sheriff an openly lesbian Democrat—the first woman ever to hold the post and the first Democrat to do so in nearly three decades. On January 1, 2005, the nation's most far-reaching domestic partnership law went into effect in California, granting nearly all the rights of married couples to thousands of same-sex partners. Moreover, despite election results revealing powerful public opposition to same-sex marriage, lower courts—even in socially conservative states— have continued to expand gay rights in other contexts. In December 2004, a state court in Arkansas invalidated a regulation banning gays and lesbians from serving as foster parents, and the Montana Supreme Court ruled that public universities in the state were constitutionally obliged to provide gay employees with insurance coverage for domestic partners. * * *

The demographics of public opinion on issues of sexual orientation virtually ensure that one day in the not-too-distant future a substantial majority of Americans will support same-sex marriage: young people are much more likely to support gay rights than are their elders. Indeed, a poll taken in June 2003 showed that sixty-one percent of respondents aged eighteen to twenty-nine already supported the legalization of same-sex marriage, while among those aged 65 and over just twenty-two percent did so. There is little reason to believe that as people get older, their attitudes on such issues become more conservative (unlike attitudes toward wealth redistribution, which do become more conservative as people age and acquire more property). As an older generation holding more traditional views about sexual orientation fades from the scene and today's youth become tomorrow's policymakers, same-sex marriage will become increasingly accepted.

GOODRIDGE IN CONTEXT[*]
Mary L. Bonauto

At GLAD [Gay & Lesbian Advocates & Defenders], we had assumed that some day we would have to litigate the denial of marriage. My own

---

[*]   Mary L. Bonauto, Goodridge *in Context*, 40 HARV. C.R.-C.L. L. REV. 1, 21–69 (2005). Bonauto was the lead lawyer in the *Goodridge* litigation.

experience with GLAD's intake calls demonstrated over and over again that many of the people who called us with legal problems could trace their problems to nonrecognition of their relationships. I had turned down requests for representation in such cases several times. The real question was when would LGBT people denied marriage rights get a fair hearing in court, in the legislature, and in public opinion in Massachusetts. . . . [W]ith each passing year, the increase in support for ending discrimination against LGBT people by non-LGBT people became phenomenal. This increase was essential because, as Rev. Dr. Martin Luther King, Jr. explained, no minority can succeed without the assistance of the majority. For this and other reasons, some of which are discussed below, we thought the answer was, "In 2001." * * *

GLAD did not litigate the marriage issue in Massachusetts precipitously. Short of constitutional litigation, we had made concerted efforts to secure rights and protections for LGBT families through other means, but knew those tools could not address the enormous architecture of protections provided by marriage. For example . . . GLAD used statutory construction principles to include LGBT families within the meanings of words like "person" in the adoption context. We worked within the equitable powers of the courts to address the needs of LGBT families when the legislature had not spoken, as in the de facto parenting case. We tried to secure a rule of even-handedness—that LGBT people should be able to contract regarding their affairs under ordinary rules of contract. We were unable to persuade the court that the term "dependent" could include same-sex domestic partners, a failure that effectively nullified governmental domestic partner programs for health insurance. * * *

[F]rom our perspective on the ground, we thought the conventional wisdom that a civil union "compromise" would be more palatable than marriage was overstated. Much of the public debate in Vermont in the early months of 2000 had to do with the fundamental humanity and equal citizenship of LGBT people, i.e., the same issues involved in seeking marriage. Thus, any alleged advantage of civil unions seemed de minimis and certainly outweighed by the enormous legal disadvantages of civil unions vis-a-vis marriage for couples. Although this is too crude a formulation, we expected that those who opposed any rights for LGBT people would reject both marriage and civil unions and that those who accepted civil unions could come to see marriage as the fairer and simpler alternative over time. Those who protested most vociferously opposed marriage, civil unions, and any legal protections whatsoever. In short, we considered and rejected the idea of litigating for civil unions as opposed to marriage.

Second, we believed that the public education accompanying the case as well as the Vermont court ruling enormously advanced the standing of

LGBT families and people in Vermont. We hoped that a case in Massachusetts, along with public education and legislative involvement, would make relationship recognition and access to legal protections an increasingly urgent priority in all branches of government.

Third, we anticipated political fallout in both states and expected (with enormous work) we could weather it. We saw that significant numbers of non-LGBT people came to the fore when the courts finally rejected discrimination in Vermont and anticipated that would be true in Massachusetts as well. Despite some legislators being turned out of office for their civil union votes, there was no undoing of the court decision in Vermont: the legislature refused to advance for electoral consideration any amendment to the state constitution that would have either reversed the *Baker* [*v. Vermont*] decision or amended the constitution to add a restriction on marriage. * * *

Another factor sped the timing of the decision to litigate: we knew we would soon be on the defense in a constitutional amendment campaign. The Massachusetts Citizens Alliance, later known as Massachusetts Citizens for Marriage, was planning to come straight at the marriage issue with a citizen initiative to place an anti-LGBT marriage amendment on the ballot by November 2004. In order for the measure to advance, it needed the support of 50 of 200 legislators in a joint session. At GLAD, we knew no ballot campaign on marriage had yet been won and we assumed the issues would be framed in a way favorable to our opponents, putting LGBT people and families on the defense. In short, we calculated that the signature gathering process would succeed, that 50 or more legislators would support it, and that we would likely be facing a ballot measure in 2004.

Knowing that the legislature and public would be embroiled in the marriage and amendment discussions in any event, and aware of the generally favorable momentum toward relationship recognition, we viewed an affirmative marriage case as an opportunity to frame the issues positively and in the voices of LGBT people. We also thought the best defense was the same thing that had moved us forward so far: shining a light (this time through a lawsuit) on the lives of the real people affected and the bedrock American principles of fairness and equality. We knew we had a window of opportunity: a constitutional amendment must be approved by two legislatures before it can be put out to the voters for ratification at a general election.

If the case were resolved successfully, then Massachusetts voters would have the chance to see for themselves that relationship recognition and marriage rights for LGBT people were fair before they voted on the question of taking away those rights. If we lost the case, there would be less impetus to vote in favor of an amendment. Even more importantly, many more people in the electorate would understand the harms to our communities from being denied relationship recognition and marriage rights, thus increasing pressure on the Massachusetts legislature to take steps to ameliorate the discrimination. * * *

[Bonauto then discusses anti-same-sex-marriage initiatives around the country after *Goodridge*.]

Is all of this legislative activity a "backlash" to *Goodridge*, or to San Francisco Mayor Gavin Newsom's move to issue marriage licenses starting in February? On balance, it is more "lash" than "backlash." Without a doubt, these developments have agitated some and spurred others to take more drastic steps to preempt the otherwise natural course of events. Thirty-seven states enacted laws or constitutional amendments denying marriage to LGBT people before *Goodridge* was even decided. The proposed federal amendment was drafted in 2000–2001, and Congress passed the Defense of Marriage Act in 1996, both long before any state ended the exclusion of same-sex couples from marriage. The new marriage restrictions and amendments are not spontaneous developments, but the result of a premeditated campaign. George Chauncey's overview shows how marriage has been an obsession of the radical right, and Evan Wolfson notes, on the eve of the 1996 Presidential Caucuses in Iowa, leading "family values" groups—the same ones active in Massachusetts and around the country today—forced the candidates to take a position on a so-called Marriage Protection Pledge, the sole purpose of which was to deny marriage rights to LGBT people without "protecting" marriage in any other way. * * *

Beyond accelerating the conversation about fairness, staying the course means allowing legal systems and private entities to take measure of these new legal developments. In Massachusetts, some employers and trusts initially withheld employment benefits but then changed course to explicitly include same-sex married couples within their benefit plans.

* * * The public policy discussions are advancing as well and will continue. Already, some states have begun ameliorating the harsh consequences of the total exclusion of LGBT people from marriage. While the steps taken toward statewide domestic partnership registries in Maine and New Jersey are modest, they are particularly notable because Maine's follows a legislative enactment of a state anti-LGBT marriage law, and New Jersey's accompanies pending marriage litigation. California's newest law, effective January 1, 2005, provides registered domestic partners with almost every state-conferred right and responsibility of married persons and may soon be superceded by marriage. * * *

Many in the LGBT community feel lifted up by the *Goodridge* decision, just as the *Brown* decision had a "powerfully inspirational effect" on politically minded African Americans. We need this spirit, just as we need urgency because the harms to families and their children demand it. We must not be self-abnegating, but we also need the tempering influence of a longer term perspective: the nearly sixty years it took to dismantle the "separate but equal" doctrine, and the even longer fight for women to win the right to vote—plus the fact that it took a constitutional amendment to do so. While the path of LGBT people will be different from those in other justice movements, I draw solace from California's *Perez* case where that state's high court, in a four-to-three decision with a bitter dissent, ended race discrimination in marriage in that state. It was the first state supreme court to do so, and the existing legal precedents around the country were contrary, and the cultural landscape was inauspicious. Yet, many of us are now grateful that the court saw the issue as one of human equality and dignity and broke what had been a logjam of discrimination. A large number of states repealed their bans on interracial marriage by the time the U.S. Supreme Court decided *Loving v. Virginia* nineteen years later. While Dr. King was correct that progress is anything but inevitable, it is certainly a better bet that with determined time and effort, LGBT people will be part of constitutional history in this country, a story of the "extension of constitutional rights and protections to people once formerly ignored or excluded."

NOTES

1. The reality of same-sex marriage, achieved first through litigation, likely affects public perception. As Professor Carlos Ball explains, "Although implacable opponents of same-sex marriage are unlikely to allow facts such as these to weaken their resolve, more open-minded citizens are likely to be persuaded of the moral legitimacy behind claims for gay equality by simply observing and getting to know lesbian and gay couples as married couples." Carlos A. Ball, *The Backlash Thesis and Same-Sex Marriage: Learning from* Brown v. Board of Education *and its Aftermath*, 14 WM. & MARY BILL RTS. J. 1493, 1527 (2006).

2. The ferocity and scope of the backlash against same-sex marriage rulings raise the question of why the earliest state court constitutional ruling in favor of interracial marriage—by the California Supreme Court in 1948— did not trigger comparable backlash. Opinion polls suggest that interracial marriage was subject to very high rates of disapproval when the California Supreme Court struck down that state's ban on interracial unions in *Perez v. Sharp*, 32 Cal. 2d 711, 198 P.2d 17 (1948). Under Professor Klarman's analysis, above, one might have expected a backlash. The disparity in the aftermaths is likely traceable to a range of legal, political, and cultural differences between the historical episodes that suggest that broad generalizations about backlash against court decisions should be avoided in favor of a fact-intensive, contextualized inquiry. *See* Jane S. Schacter, *Courts*

and the Politics of Backlash: Marriage Equality Litigation, Then and Now, 82 S. CAL. L. REV. 1153 (2009).

3. Marriage Litigation in State Courts After Goodridge

After *Goodridge* made same-sex marriage a reality for the first time in the United States, several important questions came to the fore. One was whether other state supreme courts would follow *Goodridge*'s lead. Another was whether courts would use the doctrinal apparatus of fundamental rights, grounded in substantive due process, or would instead employ equality analysis. Note that *Goodridge* blended the two frameworks. A third question was whether courts would apply some form of rational basis review (as the court did in *Goodridge*) or would deem heightened scrutiny appropriate. After *Goodridge,* state supreme courts varied on each of these points.

In *Hernandez v. Robles,* the highest court in New York held that excluding same-sex couples from marriage did not violate the state constitution. 855 N.E.2d 1 (N.Y. 2006). The court found that because the exclusion implicated neither a fundamental right nor a suspect or quasi-suspect classification, only rational basis review applied. *Id.* at 10–11. The court then accepted the "responsible procreation" argument—which Justice Cordy articulated in *Goodridge*—as a justification for the exclusion of same-sex couples from marriage:

> [T]he Legislature could rationally decide that, for the welfare of children, it is more important to promote stability, and to avoid instability, in opposite-sex than in same-sex relationships. Heterosexual intercourse has a natural tendency to lead to the birth of children; homosexual intercourse does not. Despite the advances of science, it remains true that the vast majority of children are born as a result of a sexual relationship between a man and a woman, and the Legislature could find that this will continue to be true. The Legislature could also find that such relationships are all too often casual or temporary. It could find that an important function of marriage is to create more stability and permanence in the relationships that cause children to be born. It thus could choose to offer an inducement—in the form of marriage and its attendant benefits—to opposite-sex couples who make a solemn, long-term commitment to each other.

Id. at 7. The court also accepted the related interest in dual-gender parenting:

> The Legislature could rationally believe that it is better, other things being equal, for children to grow up with both a mother and a father. Intuition and experience suggest that a child

benefits from having before his or her eyes, every day, living models of what both a man and a woman are like.

Id.

Courts in other states also rejected same-sex couples' marriage claims under a rational basis standard. *See Conaway v. Deane*, 932 A.2d 571 (Md. 2007); *Andersen v. King Cty.*, 138 P.3d 963 (Wash. 2006). In contrast to *Goodridge*, the rational basis review applied in *Hernandez* and these other state court decisions was more deferential to the government. This difference raises questions first addressed in Chapter 3.

Eventually, courts in other states held marriage bans unconstititonal and did so by applying heightened scrutiny based on the existence of a fundamental right and/or a suspect or quasi-suspect classification. In 2008, the California Supreme Court applied strict scrutiny to the state's statutory marriage ban because it found a violation of same-sex couples' fundamental right to marry and ruled that gays and lesbians constituted a suspect class. *In re Marriage Cases*, 183 P.3d 384 (Cal. 2008). Importantly, both holdings were based on state, rather than federal, constitutional law. Soon after, the Connecticut and Iowa Supreme Courts ruled the exclusion of same-sex couples from marriage unconstitutional after finding that classifications based on sexual orientation were quasi-suspect and thus merited heightened scrutiny for state equal protection purposes. *Kerrigan v. Comm'n of Pub. Health*, 957 A.2d 407 (Conn. 2008); *Varnum v. Brien*, 763 N.W.2d 862 (Iowa 2009).

While the earliest victories for the marriage equality movement came through litigation, eventually legislatures began to pass marriage equality bills. In 2009, Vermont became the first state to enact marriage equality legislation.

Same-sex marriage advocates had suffered a string of defeats in public initiative battles dating back to the 1990s, but that too eventually changed. In November 2012, voters in Maine, Maryland, and Washington approved marriage equality at the ballot box; in addition, voters in Minnesota rejected a constitutional amendment banning same-sex marriage, and lawmakers in the state subsequently passed marriage equality legislation.

4. Alternatives to Marriage: Civil Unions, Domestic Partnerships, and Other Forms of Relationship Recognition

As Vermont's *Baker* litigation demonstrated, same-sex couples' demands for marriage were at times met with the rights and benefits of marriage without the label of "marriage." In Vermont, this was termed "civil union." Even before Vermont, many municipalities had enacted domestic partnership ordinances, and many public and private employers had offered domestic partner benefits to employees' unmarried partners. The following materials consider these alternative sources of relationship recognition. We begin by examining how courts approached the constitutional status of state-law regimes that provided the rights and benefits of marriage under a different title. We then examine a variety of recognition mechanisms, including those that furnish some but not all of the rights available through marriage.

LEWIS V. HARRIS

Supreme Court of New Jersey, 2006
908 A.2d 196, 188 N.J. 415

Raised here is the perplexing question—"what's in a name?"—and is a name itself of constitutional magnitude after the State is required to provide full statutory rights and benefits to same-sex couples? We are mindful that in the cultural clash over same-sex marriage, the word marriage itself—independent of the rights and benefits of marriage—has an evocative and important meaning to both parties. Under our equal protection jurisprudence, however, plaintiffs' claimed right to the name of marriage is surely not the same now that equal rights and benefits must be conferred on committed same-sex couples. * * *

[I]t is not our role to suggest whether the Legislature should either amend the marriage statutes to include same-sex couples or enact a civil union scheme. Our role here is limited to constitutional adjudication, and therefore we must steer clear of the swift and treacherous currents of social policy when we have no constitutional compass with which to navigate. * * *

Our decision today significantly advances the civil rights of gays and lesbians. We have decided that our State Constitution guarantees that every statutory right and benefit conferred to heterosexual couples through civil marriage must be made available to committed same-sex couples. Now the Legislature must determine whether to alter the long accepted definition of marriage. The great engine for social change in this country has always been the democratic process. Although courts can ensure equal treatment, they cannot guarantee social acceptance, which must come through the evolving ethos of a maturing society. Plaintiffs' quest does not end here. Their next appeal must be to their fellow citizens whose voices are heard through their popularly elected representatives. * * *

NOTE

After *Lewis*, the New Jersey legislature voted to allow civil unions for same-sex couples. The bill took effect in February 2007. *See* N.J. STAT. ANN. §§ 37:1–1 to 37:1–36 (2007). Couples in civil unions had the same legal rights and responsibilities as married couples under New Jersey law. LGBT rights advocates continued to push for marriage legislatively while also challenging civil unions in state court as constitutionally inadequate. After the U.S. Supreme Court struck down Section 3 of the Defense of Marriage Act (DOMA) and federal agencies began providing federal rights and benefits to married same-sex couples, the New Jersey courts determined that civil unions failed to satisfy the equality mandate announced in *Lewis*. *See Garden State Equality v. Dow*, 79 A.3d 1036, 216 N.J. 314 (N.J. 2013). Accordingly, same-sex couples obtained the right to marry in New Jersey.

In other cases, same-sex couples challenged the constitutional adequacy of separate nonmarital regimes after the state legislature provided comprehensive state-law protections through civil unions or domestic partnerships. The Connecticut Supreme Court reasoned that, because "of the exalted status of marriage in our society, it is hardly surprising that civil unions are perceived to be inferior to marriage." *Kerrigan v. Comm'n of Pub. Health*, 957 A.2d 407, 418 (Conn. 2008). Accordingly, as explained above, the court held that excluding same-sex couples from marriage violated the state constitution. Similarly, in its landmark decision, the California Supreme Court held:

> [B]y drawing a distinction between the name assigned to the family relationship available to opposite-sex couples and the name assigned to the family relationship available to same-sex couples, and by reserving the historic and highly respected designation of marriage exclusively to opposite-sex couples while offering same-sex couples only the new and unfamiliar designation of domestic partnership . . . [the state denies] same-sex couples the equal dignity and respect that is a core element of the constitutional right to marry.

In re Marriage Cases, 183 P.3d 384, 434–35 (Cal. 2008). Interestingly, the court questioned "[w]hether or not the name 'marriage,' in the abstract, is considered a core element of the state constitutional right to marry," but nonetheless held that "one of the core elements of this fundamental right is the right of same-sex couples to have their official family relationship accorded the same dignity, respect, and stature as that accorded to all other officially recognized family relationships." *Id.* at 434. In other words, so long as the state licensed marriage, it could not withhold that designation from same-sex couples.

———————

While the cases discussed above addressed the constitutional adequacy of nonmarital recognition when same-sex couples are excluded from marriage, there are other important questions about the desirability of nonmarital recognition more generally. That is, putting aside the question of same-sex couples' rights, consider whether laws furnishing rights to—and imposing obligations on—unmarried couples and other nonmarital families are wise from a public policy perspective. If so, what rights should such laws include? What relationships should they cover?

The term "civil union" was commonly used to describe a form of recognition that granted to same-sex couples (and in some cases unmarried different-sex couples) all the rights of marriage that a state itself could bestow. Some laws denominated "domestic partnership" laws were equally broad. For instance, California's law, which as noted above the California Supreme Court rejected as a substitute for marriage, provided domestic partners with the state-law rights and benefits of marriage. It is currently open to same-sex couples, as well as to different-sex couples in which one member is over 62. Other domestic partnership regimes, however, have included only limited benefits. These may be state laws, local ordinances, or employer programs. Aside from civil unions and domestic partnerships, some states have offered statuses such as "designated beneficiary" or "reciprocal beneficiary." These regimes provide fewer rights and often include relationships other than intimate couples, such as blood relatives and close friends.[2] Compare the following "domestic partnership" law from California with the "designated beneficiary" law from Colorado:

CALIFORNIA DOMESTIC PARTNERSHIP STATUTE

§ 297.   Domestic partners defined; Requirements for establishing domestic partnership

(a) Domestic partners are two adults who have chosen to share one another's lives in an intimate and committed relationship of mutual caring.

(b) A domestic partnership shall be established in California when both persons file a Declaration of Domestic Partnership with the Secretary of State pursuant to this division, and, at the time of filing, all of the following requirements are met:

   (1) Both persons have a common residence.

   (2) Neither person is married to someone else or is a member of another domestic partnership with someone else that has not been terminated, dissolved, or adjudged a nullity.

   (3) The two persons are not related by blood in a way that would prevent them from being married to each other in this state.

   (4) Both persons are at least 18 years of age.

   (5) Either of the following:

---

[2]   Vermont's reciprocal beneficiary law includes only blood relatives excluded from marriage. 15 VT. STAT. ANN. § 1301.

(A) Both persons are members of the same sex.

(B) One or both of the persons meet the eligibility criteria under Title II of the Social Security Act as defined in 42 U.S.C. Section 402(a) for old-age insurance benefits or Title XVI of the Social Security Act as defined in 42 U.S.C. Section 1381 for aged individuals. Notwithstanding any other provision of this section, persons of opposite sexes may not constitute a domestic partnership unless one or both of the persons are over the age of 62.

(6) Both persons are capable of consenting to the domestic partnership.

§ 297.5. Rights, protections, benefits and responsibilities of present, former, and surviving registered domestic partners; Federal provisions; Long-term care plans; Constitutional provisions and provisions adopted by initiative

(a) Registered domestic partners shall have the same rights, protections, and benefits, and shall be subject to the same responsibilities, obligations, and duties under law, whether they derive from statutes, administrative regulations, court rules, government policies, common law, or any other provisions or sources of law, as are granted to and imposed upon spouses.

(b) Former registered domestic partners shall have the same rights, protections, and benefits, and shall be subject to the same responsibilities, obligations, and duties under law, whether they derive from statutes, administrative regulations, court rules, government policies, common law, or any other provisions or sources of law, as are granted to and imposed upon former spouses.

(c) A surviving registered domestic partner, following the death of the other partner, shall have the same rights, protections, and benefits, and shall be subject to the same responsibilities, obligations, and duties under law, whether they derive from statutes, administrative regulations, court rules, government policies, common law, or any other provisions or sources of law, as are granted to and imposed upon a widow or a widower.

(d) The rights and obligations of registered domestic partners with respect to a child of either of them shall be the same as those of spouses. The rights and obligations of former or surviving registered domestic partners with respect to a child of either of them shall be the same as those of former or surviving spouses.

CAL. FAM. CODE §§ 297, 297.5 (2005).

Colorado Designated Beneficiary Statute

15–22–104. Requirements for a valid designated beneficiary agreement.

(1) A designated beneficiary agreement shall be legally recognized if:

    (a)   The parties to the designated beneficiary agreement satisfy all of the following criteria:

        (I)   Both are at least eighteen years of age;

        (II)   Both are competent to enter into a contract;

        (III) Neither party is married to another person;

        (IV) Neither party is a party to another designated beneficiary agreement; and

        (V)   Both parties enter into the designated beneficiary agreement without force, fraud, or duress[.]

COLO. REV. STAT. § 15–22–106

[Unlike California's domestic partnership law, which assigns a predetermined package of rights and responsibilities to the partners, the Colorado law allows the beneficiaries to choose rights and responsibilities from a menu. The menu offers only a limited set of rights. These include the right to act as a proxy decision-maker or surrogate decision-maker for medical care; the right to inherit real or personal property through intestate succession; the right to sue for wrongful death; and the right to direct the disposition of the beneficiary's remains. COLO. REV. STAT. § 15–22–105.]

NOTES

1. Government bodies and private employers offering nonmarital rights and benefits often had to decide whether to limit these forms of recognition to same-sex couples only, or to extend them to different-sex couples who do not marry. As a matter of policy, how would you approach that question? How, if at all, would your position have changed when same-sex couples gained access to marriage?

2. Nonmarital rights are more robust in many other countries, but often these rights are granted to cohabiting couples without the need for the couple to register their partnership. Formal partnership regimes also exist in other countries. Denmark first provided nonmarital recognition to same-sex couples in 1989. Many other countries eventually followed suit through civil partnership laws. Some regimes were limited to same-sex couples, while others included different-sex couples as well.

———

In the absence of marriage or statutory schemes offering nonmarital rights, same-sex couples sought to create or receive some of the rights and benefits automatically enjoyed by married couples. These included: rights to spousal shares of marital property upon death of one partner; tax benefits (including joint income tax returns, dependency deductions, gift tax exemptions, and exemptions for alimony and property settlements); rights in tort law (including emotional distress, wrongful death actions, and loss of consortium); rights in criminal law (including immunity from compelled testimony, and the marital communication privilege); non-exclusion under zoning laws; visitation privileges in hospitals and other institutions; authority to make decisions for an ill spouse; employee benefits for spouses (including health insurance, medical leave, and bereavement leave); government benefits (including Social Security and veterans payments to spouses, workers compensation for those whose spouses move for job-related reasons); and lower fees for married couples (including automobile and life insurance, family travel rates, and family memberships).

Same-sex couples used a variety of legal instruments as a means of asserting their rights. These include the simple (wills, powers of attorney) to the complicated (adoption). *See, e.g., Whorton v. Dillingham*, 248 Cal. Rptr. 405, 202 Cal. App. 3d 447 (1988); *Jones v. Daly*, 176 Cal. Rptr. 130, 122 Cal. App. 3d 500 (1981). Of course, contractual arrangements can only go so far.

Another strategy was to seek recognition for purposes of specific benefits and programs. In 1989, LGBT rights lawyers achieved a landmark victory in *Braschi v. Stahl Associates Co.*, 543 N.E.2d 49, 74 N.Y.2d 201, 544 N.Y.S.2d 784 (1989). Braschi, a gay man, sought to remain in his rent-controlled New York City apartment after the death of his partner, Blanchard. The rent-control law allowed a "surviving spouse of the deceased tenant or some other member of the deceased tenant's *family* who has been living with the tenant" to remain in the apartment. In the following passage, the court adopted a functional, rather than formal, definition of family:

> [W]e conclude that the term family, as used in 9 NYCRR 2204.6(d), should not be rigidly restricted to those people who have formalized their relationship by obtaining, for instance, a marriage certificate or an adoption order. The intended protection against sudden eviction should not rest on fictitious legal distinctions or genetic history, but instead should find its foundation in the reality of family life. In the context of eviction, a more realistic, and certainly equally valid, view of a family includes two adult lifetime partners whose relationship is long term and characterized by an emotional and financial commitment and interdependence. This view comports both with

our society's traditional concept of "family" and with the expectations of individuals who live in such nuclear units. In fact, Webster's Dictionary defines "family" *first* as "a group of people united by certain convictions or common affiliation" (WEBSTER'S NINTH NEW COLLEGIATE DICTIONARY 448 (1984). . . . Hence, it is reasonable to conclude that, in using the term "family," the Legislature intended to extend protection to those who reside in households having all of the normal familial characteristics. Appellant Braschi should therefore be afforded the opportunity to prove that he and Blanchard had such a household.

This definition of "family" is consistent with both of the competing purposes of the rent-control laws: the protection of individuals from sudden dislocation and the gradual transition to a free market system. Family members, whether or not related by blood, or law who have always treated the apartment as their family home will be protected against the hardship of eviction following the death of the named tenant, thereby furthering the Legislature's goals of preventing dislocation and preserving family units which might otherwise be broken apart upon eviction. . . .

Appellant and Blanchard lived together as permanent life partners for more than 10 years. They regarded one another, and were regarded by friends and family, as spouses. * * * In addition to their interwoven social lives, appellant clearly considered the apartment his home. He lists the apartment as his address on his driver's license and passport, and receives all his mail at the apartment address. . . . Financially, the two men shared all obligations including a household budget. . . . Additionally, Blanchard executed a power of attorney in appellant's favor so that appellant could make necessary decisions—financial, medical and personal—for him during his illness. Finally, appellant was the named beneficiary of Blanchard's life insurance policy, as well as the primary legatee and coexecutor of Blanchard's estate. Hence, a court examining these facts could reasonably conclude that these men were much more than mere roommates.

NOTES

1.   Even as the *Braschi* court adopted a functional definition of family, it seems to have hewed to a model of family shaped by marriage. The court may have treated the couple as a family because they functioned like a married couple, despite the fact that they were in a same-sex relationship.

See, e.g., Ariela R. Dubler, *Wifely Behavior: A Legal History of Acting Married,* 100 COLUM. L. REV. 957, 1020 (2000).

2. The question of guardianship rights for a same-sex partner was litigated in an early Minnesota case that became a powerful symbol of the need for the law to recognize same-sex couples. In *In re Guardianship of Kowalski,* 478 N.W.2d 790, 797 (Minn. Ct. App. 1991), the Court of Appeals of Minnesota granted the petition for guardianship of Sharon Kowalski that had been filed by Sharon's partner, Karen Thompson. Sharon had suffered severe brain damage in a car accident. The guardianship petition was challenged by Sharon's family. The family had not been aware of Sharon's sexual orientation before the accident, and they disapproved of the lesbian relationship. They sought guardianship in a third-party, a family friend. Karen remained active in Sharon's care, visiting her at least three times a week, re-outfitting their home to be accessible, and taking Sharon for weekend visits, despite a previous four-year period in which she was refused visitation rights by the family. The trial court awarded guardianship to the family friend "despite the uncontradicted medical testimony" that Sharon expressed a preference to be cared for by Karen, that Karen had a strong interest in Sharon's care and an "exceptional" understanding of Sharon's needs, and that Karen was "strongly equipped" to provide care for Sharon outside of an institutional setting. *Id.* at 793–94. The Court of Appeals reversed and held that, in light of the overwhelming evidence, Karen's petition for guardianship should be granted. *See id.* at 797.

As alternative sources of recognition proliferated, LGBT activists and scholars continued to debate the desirability of pursuing marriage as *the* relationship recognition form. That is, the debate that began in earnest in the late 1980s, with the seminal essays by Stoddard and Ettelbrick, continued. Yet the debate adapted to the changing legal landscape, focusing less on whether to seek marriage and more on whether (and how) to seek marriage while at the same time pursuing pluralistic family law reform. In 2006, a coalition of LGBT activists and authors, along with allies, issued the following statement.

BEYOND SAME-SEX MARRIAGE: A NEW STRATEGIC VISION FOR ALL OUR FAMILIES AND RELATIONSHIPS*
Various Signatories

The time has come to reframe the narrow terms of the marriage debate in the United States. Conservatives are seeking to enshrine discrimination in the U.S. Constitution through the Federal Marriage

---

* This is the executive summary of a document entitled *Beyond Same-Sex Marriage: A New Strategic Vision For All Our Families and Relationships,* which is available at http://www.beyondmarriage.org.

Amendment. But their opposition to same-sex marriage is only one part of a broader pro-marriage, "family values" agenda that includes abstinence-only sex education, stringent divorce laws, coercive marriage promotion policies directed toward women on welfare, and attacks on reproductive freedom. Moreover, a thirty-year political assault on the social safety net has left households with more burdens and constraints and fewer resources.

Meanwhile, the LGBT movement has recently focused on marriage equality as a stand-alone issue. While this strategy may secure rights and benefits for some LGBT families, it has left us isolated and vulnerable to a virulent backlash. We must respond to the full scope of the conservative marriage agenda by building alliances across issues and constituencies. Our strategies must be visionary, creative, and practical to counter the right's powerful and effective use of marriage as a "wedge" issue that pits one group against another. The struggle for marriage rights should be part of a larger effort to strengthen the stability and security of diverse households and families. To that end, we advocate:

- Legal recognition for a wide range of relationships, households and families—regardless of kinship or conjugal status.

- Access for all, regardless of marital or citizenship status, to vital government support programs including but not limited to health care, housing, Social Security and pension plans, disaster recovery assistance, unemployment insurance and welfare assistance.

- Separation of church and state in all matters, including regulation and recognition of relationships, households and families.

- Freedom from state regulation of our sexual lives and gender choices, identities and expression.

Marriage is not the only worthy form of family or relationship, and it should not be legally and economically privileged above all others. A majority of people—whatever their sexual and gender identities—do not live in traditional nuclear families. They stand to gain from alternative forms of household recognition beyond one-size-fits-all marriage. For example:

- Single parent households
- Senior citizens living together and serving as each other's caregivers (think *Golden Girls*)
- Blended and extended families

- Children being raised in multiple households or by unmarried parents

- Adult children living with and caring for their parents

- Senior citizens who are the primary caregivers to their grandchildren or other relatives

- Close friends or siblings living in non-conjugal relationships and serving as each other's primary support and caregivers

- Households in which there is more than one conjugal partner

- Care-giving relationships that provide support to those living with extended illness such as HIV/AIDS.

The current debate over marriage, same-sex and otherwise, ignores the needs and desires of so many in a nation where household diversity is the demographic norm. We seek to reframe this debate. Our call speaks to the widespread hunger for authentic and just community in ways that are both pragmatic and visionary. It follows in the best tradition of the progressive LGBT movement, which invented alternative legal statuses such as domestic partnership and reciprocal beneficiary. We seek to build on these historic accomplishments by continuing to diversify and democratize partnership and household recognition. We advocate the expansion of existing legal statuses, social services and benefits to support the needs of all our households.

We call on colleagues working in various social justice movements and campaigns * * * to join us in our call for government support of *all* our households.

NOTES

1. Other activists and scholars lamented that the focus on marriage equality eclipsed other important goals. Professor Angela Harris, for example, argued that the LGBT community had historically worked:

> to queer "the family," to bring its contradictions and its inadequacies to the surface, to make it visible as a set of economic and political entitlements, a tentacular institution with roots in the state and the market and not simply a private relation of intimacy.

Angela Harris, *From Stonewall to the Suburbs?: Toward a Political Economy of Sexuality*, 14 WM. & MARY BILL RTS. J. 1539, 1568 (2006). The focus on marriage, Harris argued, would diminish and potentially undermine the work of expanding the meaning of family.

2. The Stoddard-Ettelbrick debate was revisited, modernized, and reconfigured to some extent in *Updating the LGBT Intra-Community Debate on Same-Sex Marriage*, 61 RUTGERS L. REV. 493 (2009). Professor Nancy

Polikoff, one of the most prominent critics of the LGBT movement's focus on marriage, updated and defended Ettelbrick's view in *Equality and Justice for Lesbian and Gay Families and Relationships*:

> I advocate law reform that values all families and relationships. This does not mean that the law should treat all relationships in the same way. It means that we should identify the purpose of any law and include within that law the relationships that will further its purpose. Marriage should never be the dividing line between who is in and who is out.

> I do not start with marriage, or with the package of rights that marriage gives different-sex couples, and work down from there, strategizing about how many of those rights politicians are willing to grant same-sex couples who sign up with the state in a status called civil union or domestic partnership. Instead, I start by identifying the needs of all LGBT people and work up from there to craft legislative proposals to meet those needs.

> Laws that value all families are not primarily about legitimating gay relationships that mirror marriage. They are about ensuring that every relationship and every family has the legal framework for economic and emotional security. Laws that value all families value same-sex couples but not only same-sex couples. Lesbian, gay, bisexual, and transgender people live in varied households and families. A valuing-all-families approach strives to meet the needs of all of them, making real the vision in the Beyond Same-Sex Marriage statement that "marriage is not the only worthy form of family or relationship, and it should not be legally and economically privileged above all others."

61 RUTGERS L. REV. 529, 558–60. In 2008, Professor Polikoff published BEYOND (STRAIGHT AND GAY) MARRIAGE, a book that examined in depth the ways that marriage as an institution leaves unmet the important material needs of many individuals—LGBT and straight.

In his symposium essay, *A Little Older, a Little Wiser, and Still Committed*, Professor Mark Strasser defended Stoddard's view:

> Two issues should not be conflated: (1) whether married individuals are more willing to sacrifice for the sake of the family, thereby making all members of the family better off in the long run, and (2) whether women in different-sex marriages are often asked to bear disproportionate burdens. Both (1) and (2) may be true. The point here is merely that the recognition of same-sex marriage would likely result in LGBT couples investing more in their families, redounding to the benefit of all. It is simply unclear whether the recognition of same-sex marriage would promote egalitarian sharing of burdens in different-sex relationships.

61 RUTGERS L. REV. 507, 519.

In the same issue, Professor Edward Stein charted a middle path between the two views:

> My look backward from today to 1989 indicates that both Stoddard and Ettelbrick were right. The aggressive push for marriage equality has made a surprising amount of progress: not only has it produced substantial legal reform in a few states, but it has also contributed to a significant change in attitudes toward LGBT people and their families. The pluralist, reformed-minded approach has also borne fruit. Various alternatives to marriage have been developed, functional accounts of family have been embraced, and the institution of marriage and its legal significance have changed. The different strategies that Stoddard and Ettelbrick proposed have both worked and, rather than being in opposition to each other, have worked well together. When, for example, attempts to achieve marriage equality have failed, alternative forms of relationship recognition have been created instead of same-sex marriage. This has happened, for example, in Maryland, where domestic partnership laws were passed after the state's supreme court rejected a legal challenge to prohibitions on same-sex marriages. Sometimes, the relationship-recognition form that results is effectively a consolation prize from the perspective of the marriage-equality approach, but these alternative forms, under the influence of Ettelbrick's approach, may blossom into relationship pluralism, especially if the new form of relationship recognition develops in a sedimentary fashion. The two approaches also work synergistically in that, as functional and alternative family forms are implemented and people get used to them, resistance to same-sex marriage often weakens. By giving domestic partner benefits to employees in same-sex relationships, employers and some municipalities helped people get used to same-sex relationships and gave them recognition. This process helped facilitate support for and acceptance of same-sex marriages, civil unions, and more robust domestic partnerships. Similarly, people living in states that have had civil union or domestic partner laws for some years tend to be more supportive of same-sex relationships. The Vermont legislature, which in 1999 struggled to respond to their state supreme court's order to give same-sex relationships the same rights and benefits that different-sex couples received through marriage, just recently, and by an overwhelming majority, enacted legislation giving full marriage equality to same-sex couples. This demonstrates how recognition of nonmarital same-sex relationships can pave the way to full marriage equality for same-sex couples.

Marriage or Liberation?: Reflections on Two Strategies in the Struggle for Lesbian and Gay Rights and Relationship Recognition, 61 RUTGERS L. REV. 567, 591.

Consider where you would situate yourself among the positions articulated by Professors Polikoff, Strasser, and Stein.

E. FEDERAL LITIGATION FOR MARRIAGE EQUALITY

1. Federal Challenges to State Restrictions on Marriage: The Case Against California's Proposition 8

The marriage litigation discussed up to this point was pursued in state court and decided on state constitutional grounds. LGBT advocates carefully avoided federal court for fear of creating damaging precedent and prematurely presenting the issue to the U.S. Supreme Court. After all, the Court rarely invalidates the laws of a majority of states. Accordingly, LGBT advocates hoped to achieve marriage equality in additional states before pressing federal constitutional claims in federal court. But advocates from the established movement organizations could only exert so much control. Other lawyers and couples were eager to press the issue in federal court. The first sustained, organized, and well-funded case in federal court emerged from California. It provides a window through which to revisit questions about the relationship between litigation and social change raised in the materials after *Goodridge*.

First, we explain the state-law developments that led up to federal litigation in California. The same-sex marriage debate was highly visible and sharply contested in the state. In March 2000, the voters passed a statute, Proposition 22, that defined marriage as limited to a man and a woman. In 2004, San Francisco Mayor Gavin Newsom made national headlines by directing that marriage licenses be issued to same-sex couples in the city, Prop 22 notwithstanding. Mayor Newsom's argument was that he was authorized to act because Prop 22 violated the California Constitution.

Unlike in Massachusetts, LGBT rights advocates in California deliberately avoided litigation challenging the state's marriage law. They were not merely concerned about the uncertainty of litigation but were also worried that a favorable decision could easily be reversed through the state initiative system. Yet Mayor Newsom's actions pushed the issue in California and invited litigation by opponents of same-sex marriage seeking to halt the marriages.

The marriages permitted by Newsom's action were eventually voided by the California Supreme Court in *Lockyer v. City & County of San Francisco*, 33 Cal. 4th 1055, 17 Cal. Rptr. 3d 225, 95 P.3d 459 (2004). The opinion in *Lockyer*, however, expressly turned on the finding that, in the absence of a judicial determination that Prop 22 was unconstitutional, city officials lacked authority to act based on their own views of the measure's constitutional defects. The court's opinion reserved for another day the question of whether Prop 22 violated the state constitution.

Soon after the *Lockyer* decision, several lawsuits were brought to challenge the constitutionality of Prop 22. With the issue now in the courts, LGBT rights advocates affirmatively litigated for marriage equality in the state. In California, events outside the control of LGBT rights lawyers forced them into litigation involving the constitutionality of the state's marriage ban. This feature is noteworthy, given that backlash critics often blame advocates for the choice to litigate prematurely. *See* Scott L. Cummings & Douglas NeJaime, *Lawyering for Marriage Equality*, 57 UCLA L. REV. 1235, 1240–41 (2010) (explaining how the situation in California calls into question a central assumption of the backlash thesis).

In May 2008, the California Supreme Court overturned Prop 22 under the California Constitution in *In re Marriage Cases*, 43 Cal. 4th 757, 76 Cal. Rptr. 3d 683, 183 P.3d 384 (2008), discussed earlier in this Chapter. With its ruling, the California Supreme Court became the first state supreme court in the country to follow *Goodridge*. Same-sex couples began to marry in June 2008, but did not enjoy that freedom for long. Even before the *Marriage Cases* decision, efforts were underway to replace Prop 22—a statute—with a state constitutional amendment limiting marriage to a man and a woman. Opponents of same-sex marriage completed their efforts in time to qualify Prop 8 for the November 2008 ballot. Prop 8 went on to pass at the polls with 52% of the vote. The level of support was down substantially from the 61% approval Prop 22 had secured in 2000, but was enough to bring same-sex marriage to a halt in the nation's most populous state. After its passage, Prop 8 came to represent the face of the same-sex marriage debate in the United States. In the following materials, we explore the campaign that led to passage of the measure, the litigation it spawned, and its ultimate demise after it made its way all the way to the U.S. Supreme Court.

a. Proposition 8

Full Text of Proposition 8

This initiative measure is submitted to the people in accordance with the provisions of Article II, Section 8, of the California Constitution.

This initiative measure expressly amends the California Constitution by adding a section thereto; therefore, new provisions proposed to be added are printed in italic type to indicate that they are new.

SECTION 1. Title This measure shall be known and may be cited as the "California Marriage Protection Act."

SECTION 2. Section 7.5 is added to Article I of the California Constitution, to read:

SEC. 7.5. Only marriage between a man and a woman is valid or recognized in California.

The Official Ballot Pamphlet from Proposition

Arguments for Proposition 8

Proposition 8 is simple and straightforward. It contains the same 14 words that were previously approved in 2000 by over 61% of California voters: "Only marriage between a man and a woman is valid or recognized in California."

Because four activist judges in San Francisco wrongly overturned the people's vote, we need to pass this measure as a constitutional amendment to RESTORE THE DEFINITION OF MARRIAGE as a man and a woman.

Proposition 8 is about preserving marriage; *it's not an attack on the gay lifestyle.* Proposition 8 doesn't take away any rights or benefits of gay or lesbian domestic partnerships. Under California law, "domestic partners shall have the same rights, protections, and benefits" as married spouses. (Family Code § 297.5.) There are NO exceptions. Proposition 8 WILL NOT change this.

YES on Proposition 8 does three simple things:

— *It restores the definition of marriage* to what the vast majority of California voters already approved and human history has understood marriage to be.

— *It overturns the outrageous decision of four activist Supreme Court judges who ignored the will of the people.*

— *It protects our children from being taught in public schools that "same-sex marriage" is the same as traditional marriage.*

Proposition 8 protects marriage as an essential institution of society. While death, divorce, or other circumstances may prevent the ideal, the best situation for a child is to be raised by a married mother and father.

The narrow decision of the California Supreme Court isn't just about "live and let live." State law may require teachers to instruct children as young as kindergarteners about marriage. (Education Code § 51890.) If the gay marriage ruling is not overturned, TEACHERS COULD BE REQUIRED to teach young children there is *no difference* between gay marriage and traditional marriage.

We should not accept a court decision that may result in public schools teaching our kids that gay marriage is okay. That is an issue for parents to discuss with their children according to their own values and beliefs. *It shouldn't be forced on us against our will.*

Some will try to tell you that Proposition 8 takes away legal rights of gay domestic partnerships. That is false. Proposition 8 DOES NOT take away any of those rights and does not interfere with gays living the lifestyle they choose.

However, while gays have the right to their private lives, *they do not have the right to redefine marriage for everyone else.*

CALIFORNIANS HAVE NEVER VOTED FOR SAME-SEX MARRIAGE. If gay activists want to legalize gay marriage, they should put it on the ballot. Instead, they have gone behind the backs of voters and convinced four activist judges in San Francisco to redefine marriage for the rest of society. That is the wrong approach.

Voting YES on Proposition 8 RESTORES the definition of marriage that was approved by over 61% of voters. Voting YES overturns the decision of four activist judges. Voting YES *protects our children.*

Please vote YES on Proposition 8 to RESTORE the meaning of marriage.

RON PRENTICE, President

California Family Council

ROSEMARIE "ROSIE" AVILA, Governing Board Member

Santa Ana Unified School District

BISHOP GEORGE McKINNEY, Director

Coalition of African American Pastors

———

Arguments Against Proposition 8

OUR CALIFORNIA CONSTITUTION—the law of our land— SHOULD GUARANTEE THE SAME FREEDOMS AND RIGHTS TO EVERYONE—NO ONE group SHOULD be singled out to BE TREATED DIFFERENTLY.

In fact, our nation was founded on the principle that all people should be treated equally. EQUAL PROTECTION UNDER THE LAW IS THE FOUNDATION OF AMERICAN SOCIETY.

That's what this election is about—equality, freedom, and fairness, for all.

Marriage is the institution that conveys dignity and respect to the lifetime commitment of any couple. PROPOSITION 8 WOULD DENY LESBIAN AND GAY COUPLES that same DIGNITY AND RESPECT.

That's why Proposition 8 is wrong for California.

Regardless of how you feel about this issue, the freedom to marry is fundamental to our society, just like the freedoms of religion and speech.

PROPOSITION 8 MANDATES ONE SET OF RULES FOR GAY AND LESBIAN COUPLES AND ANOTHER SET FOR EVERYONE ELSE. That's just not fair. OUR LAWS SHOULD TREAT EVERYONE EQUALLY.

In fact, the government has no business telling people who can and cannot get married. Just like government has no business telling us what to read, watch on TV, or do in our private lives. We don't need Prop. 8; WE DON'T NEED MORE GOVERNMENT IN OUR LIVES.

REGARDLESS OF HOW ANYONE FEELS ABOUT MARRIAGE FOR GAY AND LESBIAN COUPLES, PEOPLE SHOULD NOT BE SINGLED OUT FOR UNFAIR TREATMENT UNDER THE LAWS OF OUR STATE. Those committed and loving couples who want to accept the responsibility that comes with marriage should be treated like everyone else.

DOMESTIC PARTNERSHIPS ARE NOT MARRIAGE.

When you're married and your spouse is sick or hurt, there is no confusion: you get into the ambulance or hospital room with no questions asked. IN EVERYDAY LIFE, AND ESPECIALLY IN EMERGENCY SITUATIONS, DOMESTIC PARTNERSHIPS ARE SIMPLY NOT ENOUGH. Only marriage provides the certainty and the security that people know they can count on in their times of greatest need.

EQUALITY UNDER THE LAW IS A FUNDAMENTAL CONSTITUTIONAL GUARANTEE. Prop. 8 separates one group of Californians from another and excludes them from enjoying the same rights as other loving couples.

Forty-six years ago I married my college sweetheart, Julia. We raised three children—two boys and one girl. The boys are married, with children of their own. Our daughter, Liz, a lesbian, can now also be married—if she so chooses.

All we have ever wanted for our daughter is that she be treated with the same dignity and respect as her brothers—with the same freedoms and responsibilities as every other Californian.

My wife and I never treated our children differently, we never loved them any differently, and now the law doesn't treat them differently, either.

Each of our children now has the same rights as the others, to choose the person to love, commit to, and to marry.

Don't take away the equality, freedom, and fairness that everyone in California—straight, gay, or lesbian—deserves.

Please join us in voting NO on Prop. 8.

SAMUEL THORON, Former President

Parents, Families and Friends of Lesbians and Gays

JULIA MILLER THORON, Parent

NOTES

1. How would you assess the competing arguments in the ballot pamphlet? Are each side's arguments the most effective available for its position?

2. More money was spent by both sides in the Prop 8 campaign than had ever been spent on any initiative involving a social issue. Expenses exceeded $80 million, with donations coming from individuals in all fifty states and from around the world. The vast sums of funding in the campaigns largely went to the television ads, some of which echoed the themes in the ballot arguments. For an in-depth analysis of several of the major ads used in the campaign, see Melissa Murray, *Marriage Rights and Parental Rights: Parents, the State, and Proposition 8*, 5 STAN. J. C.R. & C.L. 357 (2009).

3. One of the more controversial aspects of the funding of Prop 8 was the substantial role played by the Mormon Church. *See* Jesse McKinley & Kirk Johnson, *Mormons Tipped Scale in Ban on Gay Marriage*, N.Y. Times, Nov. 15, 2008, at A1. Proceedings before the California Fair Political Practices Commission resulted in the Church's agreement to pay a $5,500 fine for failing to report $37,000 worth of assistance to the pro-Prop 8 campaign shortly before the 2008 election. Bob Egelko, *Judge Poses Tough Questions for Each Side of Prop 8 Debate*, S.F. CHRONICLE, June 9, 2010, at C5.

b. State Court Challenge

Shortly following its passage, Prop 8 was challenged in state court. The central claim was that Prop 8 was procedurally invalid because it constituted a "revision" to—and not a mere "amendment" of—the state constitution, and therefore could not, under the terms of the state constitution, be enacted through a ballot initiative alone. Then-Attorney General Jerry Brown contested the claim that Prop 8 was a "revision," but nevertheless asserted that it violated the state constitution because it denied same-sex couples a fundamental right made inalienable under that document. Because of Brown's stance, ProtectMarriage.com was permitted to intervene.

In *Strauss v. Horton*, 46 Cal. 4th 364, 93 Cal. Rptr. 3d 591, 207 P.3d 48 (2009), the state supreme court rejected the challenge to Prop 8. Chief Justice George, who authored the opinion in the *Marriage Cases*, wrote for the majority:

> [A]s originally adopted, the constitutional amendment/revision dichotomy in California—which mirrored the framework set forth in many other state constitutions of the same vintage— indicates that the category of *constitutional revision* referred to the kind of wholesale or fundamental alteration of the constitutional structure that appropriately could be undertaken only by a constitutional convention, in contrast to the category of *constitutional amendment,* which included any and all of the more discrete changes to the Constitution that thereafter might be proposed. . . .

> [A]mong the various constitutional protections recognized in the *Marriage Cases* as available to same-sex couples, it is only the designation of marriage—albeit significant—that has been removed by this initiative measure.

> Taking into consideration the actual limited effect of Proposition 8 upon the preexisting state constitutional right of privacy and due process and upon the guarantee of equal protection of the laws, and after comparing this initiative measure to the many other constitutional changes that have been reviewed and evaluated in numerous prior decisions of this court, we conclude Proposition 8 constitutes a constitutional amendment rather than a constitutional revision. As a quantitative matter, petitioners concede that Proposition 8—which adds but a single, simple section to the Constitution—does not constitute a revision. As a qualitative matter, the act of limiting access to the designation of marriage to opposite-sex couples does not have a substantial or, indeed, even a minimal effect on *the governmental plan or framework of California* that existed prior to the

amendment. Contrary to petitioners' claim in this regard, the measure does not transform or undermine the judicial function; this court will continue to exercise its traditional responsibility to faithfully enforce *all* of the provisions of the California Constitution, which now include the new section added through the voters' approval of Proposition 8. Furthermore, the judiciary's authority in applying the state Constitution always has been limited by the content of the provisions set forth in our Constitution, and that limitation remains unchanged.

The court also upheld the validity of the approximately 18,000 same-sex marriages that had occurred between the *Marriage Cases* decision and Prop 8's passage.

c. Moving to the Federal Courts

Strauss was immediately followed by the announcement of a federal lawsuit challenging the constitutionality of Prop 8. As the next reading explains, the decision to go to federal court marked a new—and controversial—chapter in same-sex marriage advocacy.

GAY ON TRIAL: WHY MORE THAN MARRIAGE IS AT STAKE IN THE FEDERAL LEGAL CHALLENGE TO PROP 8[*]

Gabriel Arana

On Nov. 4, 2008, when the polls closed on the West Coast and media outlets reported that California voters had passed Proposition 8, gay-rights supporters across the country were stunned. How could the purported gay haven of *California*—home to Hollywood, Harvey Milk, and the Castro—have rejected same-sex marriage?

After months of scapegoating, soul-searching, and regrouping, gay-rights leaders settled on a two-part strategy: Fight the measure in state court and work on overturning it at the ballot box in 2010 or 2012. The state Supreme Court challenge to Prop 8, which argued that the measure was not an "amendment" to the California Constitution but a "revision" requiring legislative approval, was widely considered a long shot. Few were surprised when the court upheld Prop 8.

What did come as a surprise was the news, that same day, that two relative strangers to civil-rights litigation, David Boies and Ted Olson, had filed a suit against the amendment in federal court. It was a decision so rash that it could only have come from outsiders. Olson, a prominent figure in the conservative legal movement, had represented George W. Bush in *Bush v. Gore*, a case in which he faced off against Boies, a high-

---

[*] Gabriel Arana, *Gay on Trial: Why More than Marriage is at Stake in the Federal Legal Challenge to Prop. 8*, THE AMERICAN PROSPECT, November 23, 2009.

profile lawyer who made his name defending Wall Street, not civil rights. They intend to take their challenge to Prop 8 all the way. * * *

For decades, groups like the ACLU and Lambda have taken an incremental approach to fighting for gay rights in court, concentrating on establishing legal precedents and popular support in states before going federal. In California, Connecticut, New York, and Iowa, gay-rights attorneys have pursued many big-ticket cases, with mixed results. But in federal courts, their aims have been more modest; it was only in 2003 that Lambda succeeded in decriminalizing sodomy nationwide.

To some, both within the movement and outside it, this tentative approach has been frustrating. As Olson said, "People should not have to beg to be treated equally or wait for decades for popular approval to be treated equally." But even among those of us who believe LGBT Americans deserve equal rights *now*, the fear is that jumping the gun will lead to harmful court precedents and social backlash [as followed the Hawaii Supreme Court's 1993 ruling]. * * *

"The debate is never about whether equality means equality for gay people, too. There have been debates about timing as long as there have been queer people to have a conversation," says Jennifer Pizer, the Lambda attorney who argued the state-level challenge to Prop 8. "The question always is a matter of how much development of the doctrine and how much social and political change should be achieved before asking the ultimate question." * * *

The fact that two straight, white-shoe lawyers have taken on the case shows the broad support gay rights have gained. But there is also the sense that Boies and Olson stand to lose nothing. The possible reward, on the other hand, is clear: For two attorneys who have pursued high-profile cases throughout their careers, this could be the defining win that puts them in history books. *Perry v. Schwarzenegger* is one of the rare cases that redraws battle lines and upsets traditional alliances. Like *Brown v. Board of Education* or *Roe v. Wade*, it has the potential to change American life. * * *

The stakes are high. If *Perry v. Schwarzenegger* reaches the Supreme Court and Boies and Olson are successful, gays and lesbians nationwide would not only have the right to marry, they stand to gain many of the legal rights they have sought for decades. In the eyes of the law, gay people would be equal to straight people, and any legislation that discriminated against them could be challenged and easily struck down against this precedent. However, defeat could legitimize such discrimination against LGBT Americans, making it far more difficult to sue for parental or housing rights. The door to any federal litigation on marriage equality would be shut for decades.

This is risky because Boies and Olson are entering a legal no-man's land. The coalition of lawyers who fought to overturn Prop 8 at the state level decided not to mount a federal challenge "because federal litigation puts in play the federal doctrines that as yet are underdeveloped," Pizer says. Marriage and family law tend to be state law, she explains, and the federal framework is sketchy.

Legal experts say getting judges to recognize gays as a suspect class will be a tough sell; the Supreme Court has long refused to make age or disability a protected category. And even those who think the legal arguments are compelling say that swaying a conservative Supreme Court is the real challenge. "If you just look at the criteria, they'll be able to make a very powerful case," says William Eskridge, a professor at Yale Law School who was involved in gay-marriage litigation in the early 1990s. "[But] if the case comes to the Supreme Court in the next three years, given its membership, the conventional wisdom is that they don't have five votes." * * *

The quandary for the court in January is, in effect, how to name a reality that we do not all share. The real fight is not over marriage itself. *Perry v. Schwarzenegger* is only about gay marriage in the sense that *Roe v. Wade* was about privacy, or *Brown v. Board of Education* was about school choice. The case is really about the place of gay people in society. * * *

As Eskridge points out, the best turn the Prop 8 case could take is that it would be rendered moot by California voters. * * * But even if Boies and Olson lose the case, it would not be the disaster that some gay-rights supporters fear. A Supreme Court loss could galvanize a movement that, at least in California, was dumbstruck that gay rights didn't just come as a matter of course. Indeed, * * * the promise of equality seems to lie increasingly in local, grass-roots efforts. Decades of fervent activism are what made the legislative victories in Vermont and New Hampshire possible, and they are an indication of public support that no court can grant. It is better not to be the victim of discrimination in the first place than to have the law on your side when you are.

NOTES

1. The decision by Olson and Boies to file in federal court starkly raises the question of who should decide matters of crucial strategy in law reform litigation. For a scholarly perspective, see William B. Rubenstein, *Divided We Litigate: Addressing Disputes Among Group Members and Lawyers in Civil Rights Campaigns*, 106 YALE L.J. 1623 (1997). Do you think it was wise to file in federal court? Why or why not? What role do you think the consensus of major LGBT rights organizations should play in determining the path forged in such cases?

2. How does the involvement of Ted Olson—most famous for representing George W. Bush in *Bush v. Gore*—affect the cause? Is there a "conservative" case for same-sex marriage that is different from a "progressive" case? If so, how?

3. As you assess the wisdom of the federal litigation, consider the character of the marriage backlash. As we have seen, after 1993, same-sex marriage produced a sweeping *policy* backlash around the country, reflected in a rash of anti-marriage measures at both the state and federal levels. Prop 22 and Prop 8 were parts of this response. Yet, over the same time period, there was no *public opinion* backlash. Quite the contrary, polls showed that public attitudes toward same-sex marriage warmed considerably, with Gallup showing majority support by 2013. *See, e.g.*, Lydia Saad, *In U.S., 52% Back Law to Legalize Gay Marriage in 50 States*, GALLUP, INC., July 29, 2013, *available at* http://www.gallup.com/poll/163730/back-law-legalize-gay-marri age-states.aspx (last accessed Dec. 11, 2013) ("Gallup used two separate approaches to measure public support for gay marriage this month, and they produced similar results: 52% would vote for a federal law legalizing same-sex marriages in all 50 states, and 54% think gay marriages should be recognized as valid, with the same rights as marriages between men and women."). When Gallup first asked about the legality of same-sex marriage in 1996, it found that 68% of Americans were opposed while only 27% were in favor. Jeffrey M. Jones, *American's Opposition to Gay Marriage Eases Slightly*, GALLUP, INC., May 4, 2010, *available at* http://www.gallup.com/poll/ 128291/americans-opposition-gay-marriage-eases-slightly.aspx (last accessed Dec. 11, 2013). Does rising public support of this kind suggest that court decisions in favor of marriage equality may have speeded public acceptance, even as they also helped to generate measures like Prop 8?

Judge Vaughn Walker of the Northern District of California was assigned the *Perry* case. Contrary to prior practice in the state court litigation on marriage equality, he decided to hold a full trial on the merits. The trial ultimately lasted thirteen days and produced a transcript of 3115 pages.[3] Both sides offered expert testimony on questions relevant to Prop 8's constitutionality, though many more experts testified in favor of marriage equality. This included historian George Chauncey, whose testimony is excerpted in Chapter 1. In August 2010, Judge Walker issued the following opinion.

---

[3] The trial transcripts are available at http://www.afer.org/our-work/hearing-transcripts/.

PERRY V. SCHWARZENEGGER

District Court of Northern California, 2010
704 F.Supp.2d 921

WALKER, J.

[Plaintiffs, same-sex couples wishing to marry in California, claimed that Prop 8 deprived them of due process and equal protection of the laws contrary to the Fourteenth Amendment. The Governor and Attorney General appeared in court, but declined to defend the measure. The initiative's sponsors, known as ProtectMarriage.com-Yes on 8, a Project of California Renewal ("Protect Marriage"), were permitted to intervene in the district court proceedings.]

* * * A state's interest in an enactment must of course be secular in nature. The state does not have an interest in enforcing private moral or religious beliefs without an accompanying secular purpose. *See Lawrence v. Texas,* 539 U.S. 558, 571 (2003).

Perhaps recognizing that Proposition 8 must advance a secular purpose to be constitutional, proponents abandoned previous arguments from the campaign that had asserted the moral superiority of opposite-sex couples. Instead, in this litigation, proponents asserted that Proposition 8:

1.   Maintains California's definition of marriage as excluding same-sex couples;

2.   Affirms the will of California citizens to exclude same-sex couples from marriage;

3.   Promotes stability in relationships between a man and a woman because they naturally (and at times unintentionally) produce children; and

4.   Promotes "statistically optimal" child-rearing households; that is, households in which children are raised by a man and a woman married to each other.

While proponents vigorously defended the constitutionality of Proposition 8, they did so based on legal conclusions and cross-examinations of some of plaintiffs' witnesses, eschewing all but a rather limited factual presentation. * * *

At oral argument on proponents' motion for summary judgment, the court posed to proponents' counsel the assumption that "the state's interest in marriage is procreative" and inquired how permitting same-sex marriage impairs or adversely affects that interest. Counsel replied that the inquiry was "not the legally relevant question," but when pressed for an answer, counsel replied: "Your honor, my answer is: I don't know. I don't know."

Despite this response, proponents in their trial brief promised to "demonstrate that redefining marriage to encompass same-sex relationships" would effect some twenty-three specific harmful consequences. At trial, however, proponents presented only one witness, David Blankenhorn, to address the government interest in marriage. Blankenhorn's testimony is addressed at length hereafter; suffice it to say that he provided no credible evidence to support any of the claimed adverse effects proponents promised to demonstrate. During closing arguments, proponents again focused on the contention that "responsible procreation is really at the heart of society's interest in regulating marriage." When asked to identify the evidence at trial that supported this contention, proponents' counsel replied, "you don't have to have evidence of this point."

Proponents' procreation argument, distilled to its essence, is as follows: the state has an interest in encouraging sexual activity between people of the opposite sex to occur in stable marriages because such sexual activity may lead to pregnancy and children, and the state has an interest in encouraging parents to raise children in stable households. The state therefore, the argument goes, has an interest in encouraging all opposite-sex sexual activity, whether responsible or irresponsible, procreative or otherwise, to occur within a stable marriage, as this encourages the development of a social norm that opposite-sex sexual activity should occur within marriage. Entrenchment of this norm increases the probability that procreation will occur within a marital union. Because same-sex couples' sexual activity does not lead to procreation, according to proponents the state has no interest in encouraging their sexual activity to occur within a stable marriage. Thus, according to proponents, the state's only interest is in opposite-sex sexual activity. * * *

[JUDGE WALKER then discusses the evidence presented at trial by the various expert witnesses and then presents an extensive set of findings of fact.]

CONCLUSIONS OF LAW

* * * The freedom to marry is recognized as a fundamental right protected by the Due Process Clause.

* * * The parties do not dispute that the right to marry is fundamental. The question presented here is whether plaintiffs seek to exercise the fundamental right to marry; or, because they are couples of the same sex, whether they seek recognition of a new right.

To determine whether a right is fundamental under the Due Process Clause, the court inquires into whether the right is rooted "in our Nation's history, legal traditions, and practices." *Glucksberg,* 521 U.S. at 710. Here, because the right to marry is fundamental, the court looks to the evidence presented at trial to determine: (1) the history, tradition and practice of marriage in the United States; and (2) whether plaintiffs seek to exercise their right to marry or seek to exercise some other right. * * *

The marital bargain in California (along with other states) traditionally required that a woman's legal and economic identity be subsumed by her husband's upon marriage under the doctrine of coverture; this once-unquestioned aspect of marriage now is regarded as antithetical to the notion of marriage as a union of equals. As states moved to recognize the equality of the sexes, they eliminated laws and practices like coverture that had made gender a proxy for a spouse's role within a marriage. Marriage was thus transformed from a male-dominated institution into an institution recognizing men and women as equals. Yet, individuals retained the right to marry; that right did not become different simply because the institution of marriage became compatible with gender equality.

The evidence at trial shows that marriage in the United States traditionally has not been open to same-sex couples. The evidence suggests many reasons for this tradition of exclusion, including gender roles mandated through coverture, social disapproval of same-sex relationships, and the reality that the vast majority of people are heterosexual and have had no reason to challenge the restriction. The evidence shows that the movement of marriage away from a gendered institution and toward an institution free from state-mandated gender roles reflects an evolution in the understanding of gender rather than a change in marriage. The evidence did not show any historical purpose for excluding same-sex couples from marriage, as states have never required spouses to have an ability or willingness to procreate in order to marry. Rather, the exclusion exists as an artifact of a time when the genders were seen as having distinct roles in society and in marriage. That time has passed.

The right to marry has been historically and remains the right to choose a spouse and, with mutual consent, join together and form a household. Race and gender restrictions shaped marriage during eras of race and gender inequality, but such restrictions were never part of the historical core of the institution of marriage. Today, gender is not relevant to the state in determining spouses' obligations to each other and to their dependents. Relative gender composition aside, same-sex couples are situated identically to opposite-sex couples in terms of their ability to perform the rights and obligations of marriage under California law. Gender no longer forms an essential part of marriage; marriage under law is a union of equals. * * *

Plaintiffs do not seek recognition of a new right. To characterize plaintiffs' objective as "the right to same-sex marriage" would suggest that plaintiffs seek something different from what opposite-sex couples across the state enjoy—namely, marriage. Rather, plaintiffs ask California to recognize their relationships for what they are: marriages. * * *

Because plaintiffs seek to exercise their fundamental right to marry, their claim is subject to strict scrutiny. *Zablocki,* 434 U.S. at 388. That the majority of California voters supported Proposition 8 is irrelevant, as "fundamental rights may not be submitted to [a] vote; they depend on the outcome of no elections." Under strict scrutiny, the state bears the burden of producing evidence to show that Proposition 8 is narrowly tailored to a compelling government interest. Because the government defendants declined to advance such arguments, proponents seized the role of asserting the existence of a compelling California interest in Proposition 8.

As explained in detail in the equal protection analysis, Proposition 8 cannot withstand rational basis review. Still less can Proposition 8 survive the strict scrutiny required by plaintiffs' due process claim. The minimal evidentiary presentation made by proponents does not meet the heavy burden of production necessary to show that Proposition 8 is narrowly tailored to a compelling government interest. Proposition 8 cannot, therefore, withstand strict scrutiny. Moreover, proponents do not assert that the availability of domestic partnerships satisfies plaintiffs' fundamental right to marry; proponents stipulated that "[t]here is a significant symbolic disparity between domestic partnership and marriage." Accordingly, Proposition 8 violates the Due Process Clause of the Fourteenth Amendment.

EQUAL PROTECTION

* * * The guarantee of equal protection coexists, of course, with the reality that most legislation must classify for some purpose or another. *See Romer v. Evans,* 517 U.S. 620, 631 (1996). When a law creates a classification but neither targets a suspect class nor burdens a fundamental right, the court presumes the law is valid and will uphold it as long as it is rationally related to some legitimate government interest. * * *

The court defers to legislative (or in this case, popular) judgment if there is at least a debatable question whether the underlying basis for the classification is rational. Even under the most deferential standard of review, however, the court must "insist on knowing the relation between the classification adopted and the object to be attained." *Romer,* 517 U.S. at 632; *Heller,* 509 U.S. at 321 (basis for a classification must "find some footing in the realities of the subject addressed by the legislation"). The court may look to evidence to determine whether the basis for the underlying debate is rational. *Plyler v. Doe,* 457 U.S. 202, 228 (1982) (finding an asserted interest in preserving state resources by prohibiting undocumented children from attending public school to be irrational because "the available evidence suggests that illegal aliens underutilize public services, while contributing their labor to the local economy and tax money to the state fisc"). * * *

Yet, to survive rational basis review, a law must do more than disadvantage or otherwise harm a particular group. *United States Department of Agriculture v. Moreno*, 413 U.S. 528 (1973).

SEXUAL ORIENTATION OR SEX DISCRIMINATION

Plaintiffs challenge Proposition 8 as violating the Equal Protection Clause because Proposition 8 discriminates both on the basis of sex and on the basis of sexual orientation. Sexual orientation discrimination can take the form of sex discrimination. Thus, Proposition 8 operates to restrict Perry's choice of marital partner because of her sex. But Proposition 8 also operates to restrict Perry's choice of marital partner because of her sexual orientation; her desire to marry another woman arises only because she is a lesbian. * * *

STANDARD OF REVIEW

* * * The trial record shows that strict scrutiny is the appropriate standard of review to apply to legislative classifications based on sexual orientation. All classifications based on sexual orientation appear suspect, as the evidence shows that California would rarely, if ever, have a reason to categorize individuals based on their sexual orientation. Here, however, strict scrutiny is unnecessary. Proposition 8 fails to survive even rational basis review.

PROPOSITION 8 DOES NOT SURVIVE RATIONAL BASIS

Proposition 8 cannot withstand any level of scrutiny under the Equal Protection Clause, as excluding same-sex couples from marriage is simply not rationally related to a legitimate state interest. One example of a legitimate state interest in not issuing marriage licenses to a particular group might be a scarcity of marriage licenses or county officials to issue them. But marriage licenses in California are not a limited commodity, and the existence of 18,000 same-sex married couples in California shows that the state has the resources to allow both same-sex and opposite-sex couples to wed. * * *

PURPORTED INTEREST #1: RESERVING MARRIAGE AS A UNION BETWEEN A MAN AND A WOMAN AND EXCLUDING ANY OTHER RELATIONSHIP

Proponents first argue that Proposition 8 is rational because it preserves: (1) "the traditional institution of marriage as the union of a man and a woman"; (2) "the traditional social and legal purposes, functions, and structure of marriage"; and (3) "the traditional meaning of marriage as it has always been defined in the English language." * * *

Tradition alone, however, cannot form a rational basis for a law.

* * * [T]he evidence shows that the tradition of gender restrictions arose when spouses were legally required to adhere to specific gender roles. California has eliminated all legally mandated gender roles except the requirement that a marriage consist of one man and one woman. Proposition 8 thus enshrines in the California Constitution a gender restriction that the evidence shows to be nothing more than an artifact of a foregone notion that men and women fulfill different roles in civic life.

The tradition of restricting marriage to opposite-sex couples does not further any state interest. Rather, the evidence shows that Proposition 8 harms the state's interest in equality, because it mandates that men and women be treated differently based only on antiquated and discredited notions of gender. * * *

PURPORTED INTEREST #2: PROCEEDING WITH CAUTION WHEN IMPLEMENTING SOCIAL CHANGES

Proponents next argue that Proposition 8 is related to state interests in: (1) "[a]cting incrementally and with caution when considering a radical transformation to the fundamental nature of a bedrock social institution"; (2) "[d]ecreasing the probability of weakening the institution of marriage"; (3) "[d]ecreasing the probability of adverse consequences that could result from weakening the institution of marriage"; and (4) "[d]ecreasing the probability of the potential adverse consequences of same-sex marriage." * * *

[P]roponents presented no reliable evidence that allowing same-sex couples to marry will have any negative effects on society or on the institution of marriage. The process of allowing same-sex couples to marry is straightforward, and no evidence suggests that the state needs any significant lead time to integrate same-sex couples into marriage. The evidence shows that allowing same-sex couples to marry will be simple for California to implement because it has already done so; no change need be phased in. California need not restructure any institution to allow same-sex couples to marry. * * *

PURPORTED INTEREST #3: PROMOTING OPPOSITE-SEX PARENTING OVER SAME-SEX PARENTING

* * * Proponents argue Proposition 8: (1) promotes "stability and responsibility in naturally procreative relationships"; (2) promotes "enduring and stable family structures for the responsible raising and care of children by their biological parents"; (3) increases "the probability that natural procreation will occur within stable, enduring, and supporting family structures"; (4) promotes "the natural and mutually

beneficial bond between parents and their biological children"; (5) increases "the probability that each child will be raised by both of his or her biological parents"; (6) increases "the probability that each child will be raised by both a father and a mother"; and (7) increases "the probability that each child will have a legally recognized father and mother."

The evidence supports two points which together show Proposition 8 does not advance any of the identified interests: (1) same-sex parents and opposite-sex parents are of equal quality, and (2) Proposition 8 does not make it more likely that opposite-sex couples will marry and raise offspring biologically related to both parents. * * *

Proponents argue Proposition 8 advances a state interest in encouraging the formation of stable households. Instead, the evidence shows that Proposition 8 undermines that state interest, because same-sex households have become less stable by the passage of Proposition 8. * * *

PURPORTED INTEREST #4: PROTECTING THE FREEDOM OF THOSE WHO OPPOSE MARRIAGE FOR SAME-SEX COUPLES

Proponents next argue that Proposition 8 protects the First Amendment freedom of those who disagree with allowing marriage for couples of the same sex. Proponents argue that Proposition 8: (1) preserves "the prerogative and responsibility of parents to provide for the ethical and moral development and education of their own children"; and (2) accommodates "the First Amendment rights of individuals and institutions that oppose same-sex marriage on religious or moral grounds."

These purported interests fail as a matter of law. Proposition 8 does not affect any First Amendment right or responsibility of parents to educate their children. Californians are prevented from distinguishing between same-sex partners and opposite-sex spouses in public accommodations, as California antidiscrimination law requires identical treatment for same-sex unions and opposite-sex marriages. . . .

To the extent proponents argue that one of the rights of those morally opposed to same-sex unions is the right to prevent same-sex couples from marrying, as explained presently those individuals' moral views are an insufficient basis upon which to enact a legislative classification.

PURPORTED INTEREST #5: TREATING SAME-SEX COUPLES DIFFERENTLY FROM OPPOSITE-SEX COUPLES

Proponents argue that Proposition 8 advances a state interest in treating same-sex couples differently from opposite-sex couples by: (1)

"[u]sing different names for different things"; (2) "[m]aintaining the flexibility to separately address the needs of different types of relationships"; (3) "[e]nsuring that California marriages are recognized in other jurisdictions"; and (4) "[c]onforming California's definition of marriage to federal law."

Here, proponents assume a premise that the evidence thoroughly rebutted: rather than being different, same-sex and opposite-sex unions are, for all purposes relevant to California law, exactly the same. The evidence shows conclusively that moral and religious views form the only basis for a belief that same-sex couples are different from opposite-sex couples. The evidence fatally undermines any purported state interest in treating couples differently; thus, these interests do not provide a rational basis supporting Proposition 8.

In addition, proponents appear to claim that Proposition 8 advances a state interest in easing administrative burdens associated with issuing and recognizing marriage licenses. . . . Even assuming the state were to have an interest in administrative convenience, Proposition 8 actually creates an administrative burden on California because California must maintain a parallel institution for same-sex couples to provide the equivalent rights and benefits afforded to married couples. * * *

PURPORTED INTEREST #6: THE CATCHALL INTEREST

Finally, proponents assert that Proposition 8 advances "[a]ny other conceivable legitimate interests identified by the parties, amici, or the court at any stage of the proceedings." * * *

Many of the purported interests identified by proponents are nothing more than a fear or unarticulated dislike of same-sex couples. . . . The evidence shows that, by every available metric, opposite-sex couples are not better than their same-sex counterparts; instead, as partners, parents and citizens, opposite-sex couples and same-sex couples are equal. Proposition 8 violates the Equal Protection Clause because it does not treat them equally.

A PRIVATE MORAL VIEW THAT SAME-SEX COUPLES ARE INFERIOR TO OPPOSITE-SEX COUPLES IS NOT A PROPER BASIS FOR LEGISLATION

In the absence of a rational basis, what remains of proponents' case is an inference, amply supported by evidence in the record, that Proposition 8 was premised on the belief that same-sex couples simply are not as good as opposite-sex couples. Whether that belief is based on moral disapproval of homosexuality, animus towards gays and lesbians or simply a belief that a relationship between a man and a woman is inherently better than a relationship between two men or two women, this belief is not a proper basis on which to legislate. * * *

The arguments surrounding Proposition 8 raise a question similar to that addressed in *Lawrence*, when the Court asked whether a majority of citizens could use the power of the state to enforce "profound and deep convictions accepted as ethical and moral principles" through the criminal code. 539 U.S. at 571. The question here is whether California voters can enforce those same principles through regulation of marriage licenses. They cannot. California's obligation is to treat its citizens equally, not to "mandate [its] own moral code." *Id.* (citing *Planned Parenthood of Southeastern Pa. v. Casey,* 505 U.S. 833 (1992)). "[M]oral disapproval, without any other asserted state interest," has never been a rational basis for legislation. *Lawrence,* 539 U.S. at 582 (O'Connor, J, concurring). Tradition alone cannot support legislation. *See Williams,* 399 U.S. at 239; *Romer,* 517 U.S. at 635; *Lawrence,* 539 U.S. at 579. * * *

The evidence at trial regarding the campaign to pass Proposition 8 uncloaks the most likely explanation for its passage: a desire to advance the belief that opposite-sex couples are morally superior to same-sex couples. The campaign relied heavily on negative stereotypes about gays and lesbians and focused on protecting children from inchoate threats vaguely associated with gays and lesbians. * * *

Because Proposition 8 disadvantages gays and lesbians without any rational justification, Proposition 8 violates the Equal Protection Clause of the Fourteenth Amendment.

NOTE

The proponents of Prop 8, who had intervened at the district court, appealed Judge Walker's ruling to the Ninth Circuit Court of Appeals. None of the state defendants appealed the judgment, and the question was raised whether intervenors had Article III standing to appeal a judgment when state officials chose not to appeal. The Ninth Circuit asked the California Supreme Court for its opinion on whether state law authorized ballot sponsors to appeal in the unusual circumstances presented in *Perry,* and the state court answered affirmatively. *See Perry v. Brown,* 52 Cal. 4th 1116, 134 Cal. Rptr. 3d 499, 265 P.3d 1002 (2011). Thereafter, the Ninth Circuit found that the initiative proponents had federal Article III standing and ruled that Prop 8 was unconstitutional. In doing so, the court adopted a narrower line of reasoning than the district court and limited its ruling to the unique situation in California, where voters had eliminated same-sex couples' existing right to marry while maintaining a comprehensive domestic partnership scheme. The Ninth Circuit explained:

> All that Proposition 8 accomplished was to take away from same-sex couples the right to be granted marriage licenses and thus legally to use the designation of 'marriage,' which symbolizes state legitimization and societal recognition of their committed relationships. Proposition 8 serves no purpose, and has no effect,

other than to lessen the status and human dignity of gays and lesbians in California, and to officially reclassify their relationships and families as inferior to those of opposite-sex couples. The Constitution simply does not allow for "laws of this sort."

Perry v. Brown, 671 F.3d 1052, 1063–64 (9th Cir. 2012). The court relied extensively on *Romer v. Evans*, 517 U.S. 620 (1996).

d.   Prop 8 at the U.S. Supreme Court

After the Ninth Circuit's ruling, the proponents of Prop 8 sought certiorari from the U.S. Supreme Court. At the same time that the Court accepted a case challenging Section 3 of the federal Defense of Marriage Act (discussed below), the Court accepted the Prop 8 case, now captioned *Hollingsworth v. Perry*. In addition to briefing the merits, the Court specifically asked the parties to address whether the Prop 8 proponents had standing to appeal the district court's adverse ruling.

Ultimately, the Court did not address the merits of Prop 8 and instead, in a 5–4 decision, held that the proponents lacked standing to appeal. Writing for the Court, Chief Justice Roberts explained:

> Federal courts have authority under the Constitution to answer such questions only if necessary to do so in the course of deciding an actual "case" or "controversy." As used in the Constitution, those words do not include every sort of dispute, but only those "historically viewed as capable of resolution through the judicial process." This is an essential limit on our power: It ensures that we act *as judges,* and do not engage in policymaking properly left to elected representatives.

> For there to be such a case or controversy, it is not enough that the party invoking the power of the court have a keen interest in the issue. That party must also have "standing," which requires, among other things, that it have suffered a concrete and particularized injury. Because we find that petitioners do not have standing, we have no authority to decide this case on the merits, and neither did the Ninth Circuit.

Hollingsworth v. Perry, 570 U.S. ___, 133 S.Ct. 2652, 2659, 186 L.Ed.2d 768 (2013) (citations omitted). Accordingly, the Court vacated the Ninth Circuit's ruling, thus leaving Judge Walker's district court decision as the decisive ruling in the case.

The Justices themselves may have been concerned about the political reaction to a broad substantive ruling and therefore may have wished to avoid the merits for institutional reasons. Indeed, Justice Kennedy, writing for the dissenting Justices, raised the tension that confronted the Court:

Of course, the Court must be cautious before entering a realm of controversy where the legal community and society at large are still formulating ideas and approaches to a most difficult subject. But it is shortsighted to misconstrue principles of justiciability to avoid that subject.

Id. at 2674 (Kennedy, J., dissenting). Ultimately, Justice Kennedy would have reached the merits in order to preserve the integrity of the state initiative system.

In reaching its decision, the Court was likely influenced by considerations regarding its own role in ongoing social change efforts. Consider this assessment:

[W]e must understand the Court's resolution against the backdrop of some of the justices' reluctance to reach the merits. From the beginning of the litigation, the Olson-Boies team had, against the advice of the country's leading LGBT rights lawyers, sought a Supreme Court decision holding that a state cannot exclude same-sex couples from marriage. . . . Olson and Boies consistently argued that Proposition 8 deprived same-sex couples of their fundamental right to marry and that sexual orientation-based classifications should be subjected to heightened scrutiny for equal protection purposes. A victory based on either theory likely would have yielded a "fifty-state solution," leading the Court to strike down, in one fell swoop, the restrictive marriage laws of thirty-eight states.

Some of the justices were clearly reluctant to produce such a sweeping result. Concerned with their own institutional legitimacy and the backlash a broad decision could produce, justices both supportive of and hostile to constitutional claims to marriage equality may have wanted to sidestep the ongoing political and cultural battle.

Douglas NeJaime, *The View From Below: Public Interest Lawyering, Social Change, and Adjudication*, 61 UCLA L. REV. DISC. 182, 195–96 (2013).

Nonetheless, the decision constituted a significant victory for the LGBT rights movement. After the Court's ruling, same-sex couples once again had access to marriage in California, the most populous state in the country. And the ruling aided the marriage equality campaign's momentum. Yet, given that the case did not produce the sweeping victory that the lawyers sought, consider "whether the *Perry* lawyers, and Olson and Boies in particular, had been too optimistic. Had they asked the justices to do too much too soon? Had the LGBT movement lawyers been right to discourage a federal lawsuit until more states had moved into the marriage equality column?" *Id.* at 197.

The federal litigation challenging Prop 8 ultimately produced its demise but in unexpected ways—without a U.S. Supreme Court decision on the merits and without a direct impact on marriage bans in other states. Even as the Court avoided the substantive question in the Prop 8 case, it addressed the issue of same-sex marriage in *Windsor*, the case challenging Section 3 of the federal Defense of Marriage Act. It is to that case we now turn.

2. Federal Recognition of Same-Sex Couples' Marriages: The Case Against DOMA

a. The Federal Defense of Marriage Act

Soon after the Hawaii Supreme Court issued its 1993 decision in *Baehr*, opponents of same-sex marriage argued that, absent legislation, Hawaii would set off a national chain reaction in which the federal government and other states would be compelled to recognize same-sex marriage. Accordingly, in 1996, Congress passed, and President Bill Clinton signed, the Defense of Marriage Act ("DOMA"):

DEFENSE OF MARRIAGE ACT
Pub. L. No. 104–199, 110 Stat. 2419 (1996)

An Act to define and protect the institution of marriage.

SECTION 2. POWERS RESERVED TO THE STATES.

(a) IN GENERAL. Chapter 115 of title 28, United States Code, is amended by adding after section 1738B the following:

§ 1738C. Certain acts, records, and proceedings and the effect thereof

No State, territory, or possession of the United States, or Indian tribe, shall be required to give effect to any public act, record, or judicial proceeding of any other State, territory, possession, or tribe respecting a relationship between persons of the same sex that is treated as a marriage under the laws of such other State, territory, possession, or tribe, or a right or claim arising from such relationship. [28 U.S.C.A. § 1738C (2007).]

SECTION 3. DEFINITION OF MARRIAGE.

(a) IN GENERAL. Chapter 1 of title 1, United States Code, is amended by adding at the end the following:

Sec. 7.   Definition of "marriage" and "spouse"

In determining the meaning of any Act of Congress, or of any ruling, regulation, or interpretation of the various administrative bureaus and agencies of the United States, the word "marriage" means only a legal union between one man and

one woman as husband and wife, and the word "spouse" refers
only to a person of the opposite sex who is a husband or a wife. [1
U.S.C.A. § 7 (2007).]

Note that DOMA has two different sections. One states that federal
law does not require any state to recognize a same-sex marriage duly
entered into in another state. The other provides that, for purposes of any
federal law, the definition of marriage is limited to one man and one
woman.

b.   DOMA Litigation and the Executive Branch's Position

DOMA's definition of marriage applied to an enormous array of
federal programs and, in one fell swoop, severely limited the benefits and
protections available to same-sex couples across many areas of law. For
many years, the organized LGBT rights movement steered clear of
challenging DOMA in federal court, for many of the same reasons that
federal lawsuits against state mini-DOMAs were avoided before the *Perry*
litigation was brought to challenge Prop 8. A lawsuit filed in
Massachusetts in 2009 changed that. Lawyers at GLAD brought suit on
behalf of married same-sex couples disadvantaged in relation to
particular federal programs. In a parallel suit, lawyers for the state of
Massachusetts challenged DOMA as applied to the state, which
authorized marriage for same-sex couples. These lawsuits challenged only
Section 3 of DOMA, regarding the federal definition of marriage, and did
not raise claims against Section 2, regarding interstate recognition. In
June 2010, just a few weeks before Judge Walker issued his *Perry*
decision, a federal district judge in Massachusetts struck down Section 3
of DOMA as unconstitutional.

After this favorable result, LGBT advocates filed additional
challenges to Section 3 of DOMA in other federal district courts. Two such
cases, *Windsor v. United States*, 833 F. Supp. 2d 394 (S.D.N.Y. 2012), and
Pedersen v. Office of Personnel Management, 881 F. Supp. 2d 294 (D.
Conn. 2012), were filed in federal district courts in the Second Circuit.
Unlike the First Circuit, where the Massachusetts district court sat, the
Second Circuit lacked precedent on the question of whether sexual
orientation-based classifications merit heightened scrutiny for federal
equal protection purposes.

In response, Attorney General Eric Holder, who had been defending
Section 3 of DOMA on behalf of the United States, announced that
President Obama's position on DOMA had shifted in light of resolution of
this new issue. On February 23, 2011, the Attorney General sent the
letter excerpted below to the Speaker of the House, Republican John
Boehner. As you review the letter, consider whether you think it is
appropriate for the President unilaterally to decline to defend a statute in
the circumstances presented here. Does it pose any systemic risks?

The Honorable John A. Boehner

Speaker

U.S. House of Representatives

Washington, DC 20515

Re: Defense of Marriage Act

Dear Mr. Speaker:

After careful consideration, including review of a recommendation from me, the President of the United States has made the determination that Section 3 of the Defense of Marriage Act ("DOMA"), 1 U.S.C. § 7, as applied to same-sex couples who are legally married under state law, violates the equal protection component of the Fifth Amendment. Pursuant to 28 U.S.C. § 530D, I am writing to advise you of the Executive Branch's determination and to inform you of the steps the Department will take in two pending DOMA cases to implement that determination.

Section 3 violates EP

While the Department has previously defended DOMA against legal challenges involving legally married same-sex couples, recent lawsuits that challenge the constitutionality of DOMA Section 3 have caused the President and the Department to conduct a new examination of the defense of this provision. In particular, in November 2011, plaintiffs filed two new lawsuits challenging the constitutionality of Section 3 of DOMA in jurisdictions without precedent on whether sexual-orientation classifications are subject to rational basis review or whether they must satisfy some form of heightened scrutiny. . . . Previously, the Administration has defended Section 3 in jurisdictions where circuit courts have already held that classifications based on sexual orientation are subject to rational basis review, and it has advanced arguments to defend DOMA Section 3 under the binding standard that has applied in those cases.

These new lawsuits, by contrast, will require the Department to take an affirmative position on the level of scrutiny that should be applied to DOMA Section 3 in a circuit without binding precedent on the issue. As described more fully below, the President and I have concluded that classifications based on sexual orientation warrant heightened scrutiny and that, as applied to same-sex couples legally married under state law, Section 3 of DOMA is unconstitutional.

Standard of Review

The Supreme Court has yet to rule on the appropriate level of scrutiny for classifications based on sexual orientation. It has, however, rendered a number of decisions that set forth the criteria that should inform this and any other judgment as to whether heightened scrutiny applies. [The criteria cited here are discussed in Chapter 3, Section 2, above.] * * *

Each of these factors counsels in favor of being suspicious of classifications based on sexual orientation. First and most importantly, there is, regrettably, a significant history of purposeful discrimination against gay and lesbian people, by governmental as well as private entities, based on prejudice and stereotypes that continue to have ramifications today. Indeed, until very recently, states have "demean[ed] the[ ] existence" of gays and lesbians "by making their private sexual conduct a crime." *Lawrence v. Texas*, 539 U.S. 558, 578 (2003).

Second, while sexual orientation carries no visible badge, a growing scientific consensus accepts that sexual orientation is a characteristic that is immutable, *see* Richard A. Posner, Sex and Reason 101 (1992); it is undoubtedly unfair to require sexual orientation to be hidden from view to avoid discrimination, *see* Don't Ask, Don't Tell Repeal Act of 2010. . . .

Third, the adoption of laws like those at issue in *Romer v. Evans*, 517 U.S. 620 (1996), and *Lawrence*, the longstanding ban on gays and lesbians in the military, and the absence of federal protection for employment discrimination on the basis of sexual orientation show the group to have limited political power and "ability to attract the [favorable] attention of the lawmakers." *Cleburne*, 473 U.S. at 445. And while the enactment of the Matthew Shepard Act and pending repeal of Don't Ask, Don't Tell indicate that the political process is not closed *entirely* to gay and lesbian people, that is not the standard by which the Court has judged "political powerlessness." Indeed, when the Court ruled that gender-based classifications were subject to heightened scrutiny, women already had won major political victories such as the Nineteenth Amendment (right to vote) and protection under Title VII (employment discrimination).

Finally, there is a growing acknowledgment that sexual orientation "bears no relation to ability to perform or contribute to society. . . ." *Frontiero v. Richardson*, 411 U.S. 677, 686 (1973) (plurality). Recent evolutions in legislation (including the pending repeal of Don't Ask, Don't Tell), in community practices and attitudes, in case law (including the Supreme Court's holdings in *Lawrence* and *Romer*), and in social science regarding sexual orientation all make clear that sexual orientation is not a characteristic that generally bears on legitimate policy objectives. *See, e.g.,* Statement by the President on the Don't Ask, Don't Tell Repeal Act of 2010 ("It is time to recognize that sacrifice, valor and integrity are no more defined by sexual orientation than they are by race or gender, religion or creed.")

To be sure, there is substantial circuit court authority applying rational basis review to sexual-orientation classifications. We have carefully examined each of those decisions. Many of them reason only that if consensual same-sex sodomy may be criminalized under *Bowers v. Hardwick*, then it follows that no heightened review is appropriate—a line of reasoning that does not survive the overruling of *Bowers* in *Lawrence v. Texas*, 539 U.S. 558 (2003). Others rely on claims regarding "procreational responsibility" that the Department has disavowed already in litigation as unreasonable, or claims regarding the immutability of sexual orientation that we do not believe can be reconciled with more recent social science understandings. And none engages in an examination of all the factors that the Supreme Court has identified as relevant to a decision about the appropriate level of scrutiny. Finally, many of the more recent decisions have relied on the fact that the Supreme Court has not recognized that gays and lesbians constitute a suspect class or the fact that the Court has applied rational basis review in its most recent decisions addressing classifications based on sexual orientation, *Lawrence* and *Romer*. But neither of those decisions reached, let alone resolved, the level of scrutiny issue because in both the Court concluded that the laws could not even survive the more deferential rational basis standard.

Application to Section 3 of DOMA

* * * [U]nder heightened scrutiny, the United States cannot defend Section 3 by advancing hypothetical rationales, independent of the legislative record, as it has done in circuits where precedent mandates application of rational basis review. Instead, the United States can defend Section 3 only by invoking Congress' actual justifications for the law.

Moreover, the legislative record underlying DOMA's passage contains discussion and debate that undermines any defense under heightened scrutiny. The record contains numerous expressions reflecting moral disapproval of gays and lesbians and their intimate and family relationships—precisely the kind of stereotype-based thinking and animus the Equal Protection Clause is designed to guard against. * * *

Application to Second Circuit Cases

After careful consideration, including a review of my recommendation, the President has concluded that given a number of factors, including a documented history of discrimination, classifications based on sexual orientation should be subject to a heightened standard of scrutiny. The President has also concluded that Section 3 of DOMA, as applied to legally married same-sex couples, fails to meet that standard and is therefore unconstitutional. * * *

Notwithstanding this determination, the President has informed me that Section 3 will continue to be enforced by the Executive Branch. To that end, the President has instructed Executive agencies to continue to comply with Section 3 of DOMA, consistent with the Executive's obligation to take care that the laws be faithfully executed, unless and until Congress repeals Section 3 or the judicial branch renders a definitive verdict against the law's constitutionality. This course of action respects the actions of the prior Congress that enacted DOMA, and it recognizes the judiciary as the final arbiter of the constitutional claims raised.

continue to comply

As you know, the Department has a longstanding practice of defending the constitutionality of duly-enacted statutes if reasonable arguments can be made in their defense, a practice that accords the respect appropriately due to a coequal branch of government. However, the Department in the past has declined to defend statutes despite the availability of professionally responsible arguments, in part because the Department does not consider every plausible argument to be a "reasonable" one. "[D]ifferent cases can raise very different issues with respect to statutes of doubtful constitutional validity," and thus there are "a variety of factors that bear on whether the Department will defend the constitutionality of a statute." Letter to Hon. Orrin G. Hatch from Assistant Attorney General Andrew Fois at 7 (Mar. 22, 1996). This is the rare case where the proper course is to forgo the defense of this statute. Moreover, the Department has declined to defend a statute "in cases in which it is manifest that the President has concluded that the statute is unconstitutional," as is the case here. Seth P. Waxman, *Defending Congress*, 79 N.C. L. Rev. 1073, 1083 (2001).

In light of the foregoing, I will instruct the Department's lawyers to immediately inform the district courts in *Windsor* and

Pedersen of the Executive Branch's view that heightened scrutiny is the appropriate standard of review and that, consistent with that standard, Section 3 of DOMA may not be constitutionally applied to same-sex couples whose marriages are legally recognized under state law. If asked by the district courts in the Second Circuit for the position of the United States in the event those courts determine that the applicable standard is rational basis, the Department will state that, consistent with the position it has taken in prior cases, a reasonable argument for Section 3's constitutionality may be proffered under that permissive standard. Our attorneys will also notify the courts of our interest in providing Congress a full and fair opportunity to participate in the litigation in those cases. We will remain parties to the case and continue to represent the interests of the United States throughout the litigation. * * *

Sincerely yours,

Eric H. Holder, Jr.

Attorney General

———————

Ultimately, the Second Circuit Court of Appeals in *Windsor* agreed with the Justice Department and held that intermediate scrutiny should apply to classifications based on sexual orientation:

> Analysis of these four factors supports our conclusion that homosexuals compose a class that is subject to heightened scrutiny. We further conclude that the class is quasi-suspect (rather than suspect) based on the weight of the factors and on analogy to the classifications recognized as suspect and quasi-suspect. While homosexuals have been the target of significant and long-standing discrimination in public and private spheres, this mistreatment "is not sufficient to require 'our most exacting scrutiny.' "

Windsor v. United States, 699 F.3d 169, 185 (2d Cir. 2012). Applying intermediate scrutiny, the court found Section 3 of DOMA unconstitutional. *See id.* at 185–88. Meanwhile, the First Circuit also found Section 3 unconstitutional, but did so without applying intermediate scrutiny. *See Gill v. Office of Pers. Mgmt.*, 682 F.3d 1 (1st Cir. 2012).

c.   *DOMA at the U.S. Supreme Court*

As the number of federal court decisions invalidating Section 3 of DOMA grew, the U.S. Supreme Court granted certiorari in *Windsor*. As in

[handwritten margin note: Windsor – heightened scrutiny]

Hollingsworth v. Perry, the Court confronted significant questions of justiciability. Given that the federal executive branch refused to defend DOMA, the Bipartisan Legal Advisory Group (BLAG), composed of five Congressional leaders, intervened to defend the law. BLAG's decision divided along party lines, with the three Republican members voting to defend DOMA. In *Windsor*, the Court considered whether, given the President's agreement with the plaintiff and the Second Circuit, a case or controversy existed, and whether BLAG had standing. While some Justices would have found these issues dispositive such that they would not have reached the merits, a majority reached the merits and ultimately struck down Section 3 of DOMA.

UNITED STATES V. WINDSOR

Supreme Court of the United States, 2013
570 U.S. ___, 133 S.Ct. 2675, 186 L.Ed.2d 808

JUSTICE KENNEDY delivered the opinion of the Court.

Two women then resident in New York were married in a lawful ceremony in Ontario, Canada, in 2007. Edith Windsor and Thea Spyer returned to their home in New York City. When Spyer died in 2009, she left her entire estate to Windsor. Windsor sought to claim the estate tax exemption for surviving spouses. She was barred from doing so, however, by a federal law, the Defense of Marriage Act, which excludes a same-sex partner from the definition of "spouse" as that term is used in federal statutes. Windsor paid the taxes but filed suit to challenge the constitutionality of this provision. The United States District Court and the Court of Appeals ruled that this portion of the statute is unconstitutional and ordered the United States to pay Windsor a refund. This Court granted certiorari and now affirms the judgment in Windsor's favor.

I

In 1996, as some States were beginning to consider the concept of same-sex marriage, see, *e.g., Baehr v. Lewin*, 74 Haw. 530, 852 P. 2d 44 (1993), and before any State had acted to permit it, Congress enacted the Defense of Marriage Act (DOMA), 110 Stat. 2419. DOMA contains two operative sections: Section 2, which has not been challenged here, allows States to refuse to recognize same-sex marriages performed under the laws of other States. *See* 28 U.S.C. § 1738C.

Section 3 is at issue here. It amends the Dictionary Act in Title 1, § 7, of the United States Code to provide a federal definition of "marriage" and "spouse." Section 3 of DOMA provides as follows:

"In determining the meaning of any Act of Congress, or of any ruling, regulation, or interpretation of the various administrative bureaus and agencies of the United States, the word 'marriage' means only a legal union between one man and one woman as husband and wife, and the word 'spouse' refers only to a person of the opposite sex who is a husband or a wife." 1 U.S.C. § 7.

The definitional provision does not by its terms forbid States from enacting laws permitting same-sex marriages or civil unions or providing state benefits to residents in that status. The enactment's comprehensive definition of marriage for purposes of all federal statutes and other regulations or directives covered by its terms, however, does control over 1,000 federal laws in which marital or spousal status is addressed as a matter of federal law.

Edith Windsor and Thea Spyer met in New York City in 1963 and began a long-term relationship. Windsor and Spyer registered as domestic partners when New York City gave that right to same-sex couples in 1993. Concerned about Spyer's health, the couple made the 2007 trip to Canada for their marriage, but they continued to reside in New York City. The State of New York deems their Ontario marriage to be a valid one.

Spyer died in February 2009, and left her entire estate to Windsor. Because DOMA denies federal recognition to same-sex spouses, Windsor did not qualify for the marital exemption from the federal estate tax, which excludes from taxation "any interest in property which passes or has passed from the decedent to his surviving spouse." Windsor paid $363,053 in estate taxes and sought a refund. The Internal Revenue Service denied the refund, concluding that, under DOMA, Windsor was not a "surviving spouse." Windsor commenced this refund suit in the United States District Court for the Southern District of New York. She contended that DOMA violates the guarantee of equal protection, as applied to the Federal Government through the Fifth Amendment.

While the tax refund suit was pending, the Attorney General of the United States notified the Speaker of the House of Representatives, pursuant to 28 U.S.C. § 530D, that the Department of Justice would no longer defend the constitutionality of DOMA's § 3. * * *

Although "the President * * * instructed the Department not to defend the statute in *Windsor*," he also decided "that Section 3 will continue to be enforced by the Executive Branch" and that the United States had an "interest in providing Congress a full and fair opportunity to participate in the litigation of those cases." The stated rationale for this dual-track procedure (determination of unconstitutionality coupled with ongoing enforcement) was to "recogniz[e] the judiciary as the final arbiter of the constitutional claims raised."

In response to the notice from the Attorney General, the Bipartisan Legal Advisory Group (BLAG) of the House of Representatives voted to intervene in the litigation to defend the constitutionality of § 3 of DOMA. * * *

On the merits of the tax refund suit, the District Court ruled against the United States. It held that § 3 of DOMA is unconstitutional and ordered the Treasury to refund the tax with interest. * * * [T]he Court of Appeals for the Second Circuit affirmed the District Court's judgment. It applied heightened scrutiny to classifications based on sexual orientation, as both the Department and Windsor had urged. The United States has not complied with the judgment. Windsor has not received her refund, and the Executive Branch continues to enforce § 3 of DOMA. * * *

[In Part II, the Court found that "prudential and Article III requirements are met" such that it did not need to determine BLAG's standing and could proceed directly to the merits.]

III

* * * It seems fair to conclude that, until recent years, many citizens had not even considered the possibility that two persons of the same sex might aspire to occupy the same status and dignity as that of a man and woman in lawful marriage. For marriage between a man and a woman no doubt had been thought of by most people as essential to the very definition of that term and to its role and function throughout the history of civilization. That belief, for many who long have held it, became even more urgent, more cherished when challenged. For others, however, came the beginnings of a new perspective, a new insight. Accordingly some States concluded that same-sex marriage ought to be given recognition and validity in the law for those same-sex couples who wish to define themselves by their commitment to each other. The limitation of lawful marriage to heterosexual couples, which for centuries had been deemed both necessary and fundamental, came to be seen in New York and certain other States as an unjust exclusion.

Slowly at first and then in rapid course, the laws of New York came to acknowledge the urgency of this issue for same-sex couples who wanted to affirm their commitment to one another before their children, their family, their friends, and their community. And so New York recognized same-sex marriages performed elsewhere; and then it later amended its own marriage laws to permit same-sex marriage. New York, in common with, as of this writing, 11 other States and the District of Columbia, decided that same-sex couples should have the right to marry and so live with pride in themselves and their union and in a status of equality with all other married persons. After a statewide deliberative process that enabled its citizens to discuss and weigh arguments for and against same-sex marriage, New York acted to enlarge the definition of marriage to correct what its citizens and elected representatives perceived to be an injustice that they had not earlier known or understood.

Against this background of lawful same-sex marriage in some States, the design, purpose, and effect of DOMA should be considered as the beginning point in deciding whether it is valid under the Constitution. By history and tradition the definition and regulation of marriage, as will be discussed in more detail, has been treated as being within the authority and realm of the separate States. Yet it is further established that Congress, in enacting discrete statutes, can make determinations that bear on marital rights and privileges. * * * Congress has the power both to ensure efficiency in the administration of its programs and to choose what larger goals and policies to pursue. * * *

Though * * * discrete examples establish the constitutionality of limited federal laws that regulate the meaning of marriage in order to further federal policy, DOMA has a far greater reach; for it enacts a directive applicable to over 1,000 federal statutes and the whole realm of federal regulations. And its operation is directed to a class of persons that the laws of New York, and of 11 other States, have sought to protect.

In order to assess the validity of that intervention it is necessary to discuss the extent of the state power and authority over marriage as a matter of history and tradition. State laws defining and regulating marriage, of course, must respect the constitutional rights of persons, see, e.g., *Loving v. Virginia*, 388 U.S. 1 (1967); but, subject to those guarantees, "regulation of domestic relations" is "an area that has long been regarded as a virtually exclusive province of the States." [citation omitted]

The recognition of civil marriages is central to state domestic relations law applicable to its residents and citizens. The definition of marriage is the foundation of the State's broader authority to regulate the subject of domestic relations with respect to the "[p]rotection of offspring, property interests, and the enforcement of marital responsibilities." "[T]he states, at the time of the adoption of the Constitution, possessed full power over the subject of marriage and divorce ... [and] the Constitution delegated no authority to the Government of the United States on the subject of marriage and divorce." [citations omitted]

* * * The significance of state responsibilities for the definition and regulation of marriage dates to the Nation's beginning; for "when the Constitution was adopted the common understanding was that the domestic relations of husband and wife and parent and child were matters reserved to the States." [citation omitted] Marriage laws vary in some respects from State to State. For example, the required minimum age is 16 in Vermont, but only 13 in New Hampshire. Likewise the permissible degree of consanguinity can vary (most States permit first

cousins to marry, but a handful—such as Iowa and Washington, prohibit the practice). But these rules are in every event consistent within each State.

Against this background DOMA rejects the long-established precept that the incidents, benefits, and obligations of marriage are uniform for all married couples within each State, though they may vary, subject to constitutional guarantees, from one State to the next. Despite these considerations, it is unnecessary to decide whether this federal intrusion on state power is a violation of the Constitution because it disrupts the federal balance. The State's power in defining the marital relation is of central relevance in this case quite apart from principles of federalism. Here the State's decision to give this class of persons the right to marry conferred upon them a dignity and status of immense import. When the State used its historic and essential authority to define the marital relation in this way, its role and its power in making the decision enhanced the recognition, dignity, and protection of the class in their own community. DOMA, because of its reach and extent, departs from this history and tradition of reliance on state law to define marriage. "'[D]iscriminations of an unusual character especially suggest careful consideration to determine whether they are obnoxious to the constitutional provision.'" *Romer v. Evans*, 517 U.S. 620, 633 (1996).

The Federal Government uses this state-defined class for the opposite purpose—to impose restrictions and disabilities. That result requires this Court now to address whether the resulting injury and indignity is a deprivation of an essential part of the liberty protected by the Fifth Amendment. What the State of New York treats as alike the federal law deems unlike by a law designed to injure the same class the State seeks to protect.

In acting first to recognize and then to allow same-sex marriages, New York was responding "to the initiative of those who [sought] a voice in shaping the destiny of their own times." These actions were without doubt a proper exercise of its sovereign authority within our federal system, all in the way that the Framers of the Constitution intended. The dynamics of state government in the federal system are to allow the formation of consensus respecting the way the members of a discrete community treat each other in their daily contact and constant interaction with each other.

The States' interest in defining and regulating the marital relation, subject to constitutional guarantees, stems from the understanding that marriage is more than a routine classification for purposes of certain statutory benefits. Private, consensual sexual intimacy between two adult persons of the same sex may not be punished by the State, and it can form "but one element in a personal bond that is more enduring."

Lawrence v. Texas, 539 U.S. 558, 567 (2003). By its recognition of the validity of same-sex marriages performed in other jurisdictions and then by authorizing same-sex unions and same-sex marriages, New York sought to give further protection and dignity to that bond. For same-sex couples who wished to be married, the State acted to give their lawful conduct a lawful status. This status is a far-reaching legal acknowledgment of the intimate relationship between two people, a relationship deemed by the State worthy of dignity in the community equal with all other marriages. It reflects both the community's considered perspective on the historical roots of the institution of marriage and its evolving understanding of the meaning of equality.

IV

DOMA seeks to injure the very class New York seeks to protect. By doing so it violates basic due process and equal protection principles applicable to the Federal Government. *See* U.S. Const., Amdt. 5; *Bolling v. Sharpe*, 347 U.S. 497 (1954). The Constitution's guarantee of equality "must at the very least mean that a bare congressional desire to harm a politically unpopular group cannot" justify disparate treatment of that group. *Department of Agriculture v. Moreno*, 413 U.S. 528, 534–535 (1973). In determining whether a law is motived by an improper animus or purpose, " '[d]iscriminations of an unusual character' " especially require careful consideration. *Supra*, at 19 (quoting *Romer*, *supra*, at 633). DOMA cannot survive under these principles. The responsibility of the States for the regulation of domestic relations is an important indicator of the substantial societal impact the State's classifications have in the daily lives and customs of its people. DOMA's unusual deviation from the usual tradition of recognizing and accepting state definitions of marriage here operates to deprive same-sex couples of the benefits and responsibilities that come with the federal recognition of their marriages. This is strong evidence of a law having the purpose and effect of disapproval of that class. The avowed purpose and practical effect of the law here in question are to impose a disadvantage, a separate status, and so a stigma upon all who enter into same-sex marriages made lawful by the unquestioned authority of the States.

The history of DOMA's enactment and its own text demonstrate that interference with the equal dignity of same-sex marriages, a dignity conferred by the States in the exercise of their sovereign power, was more than an incidental effect of the federal statute. It was its essence. The House Report announced its conclusion that "it is both appropriate and necessary for Congress to do what it can to defend the institution of traditional heterosexual marriage. . . . H. R. 3396 is appropriately entitled the 'Defense of Marriage Act.' The effort to redefine 'marriage' to extend to homosexual couples is a truly radical proposal that would fundamentally alter the institution of marriage." The House concluded that DOMA expresses "both moral disapproval of homosexuality, and a moral conviction that heterosexuality better comports with traditional (especially Judeo-Christian) morality." The stated purpose of the law was to promote an "interest in protecting the traditional moral teachings reflected in heterosexual-only marriage laws." Were there any doubt of this far-reaching purpose, the title of the Act confirms it: The Defense of Marriage.

The arguments put forward by BLAG are just as candid about the congressional purpose to influence or interfere with state sovereign choices about who may be married. As the title and dynamics of the bill indicate, its purpose is to discourage enactment of state same-sex marriage laws and to restrict the freedom and choice of couples married under those laws if they are enacted. The congressional goal was "to put a thumb on the scales and influence a state's decision as to how to shape its own marriage laws." The Act's demonstrated purpose is to ensure that if any State decides to recognize same-sex marriages, those unions will be treated as second-class marriages for purposes of federal law. This raises a most serious question under the Constitution's Fifth Amendment.

DOMA's operation in practice confirms this purpose. When New York adopted a law to permit same-sex marriage, it sought to eliminate inequality; but DOMA frustrates that objective through a system-wide enactment with no identified connection to any particular area of federal law. DOMA writes inequality into the entire United States Code. The particular case at hand concerns the estate tax, but DOMA is more than a simple determination of what should or should not be allowed as an estate tax refund. Among the over 1,000 statutes and numerous federal regulations that DOMA controls are laws pertaining to Social Security, housing, taxes, criminal sanctions, copyright, and veterans' benefits.

DOMA's principal effect is to identify a subset of state-sanctioned marriages and make them unequal. The principal purpose is to impose inequality, not for other reasons like governmental efficiency. Responsibilities, as well as rights, enhance the dignity and integrity of the person. And DOMA contrives to deprive some couples married under the laws of their State, but not other couples, of both rights and responsibilities. By creating two contradictory marriage regimes within the same State, DOMA forces same-sex couples to live as married for the purpose of state law but unmarried for the purpose of federal law, thus diminishing the stability and predictability of basic personal relations the State has found it proper to acknowledge and protect. By this dynamic DOMA undermines both the public and private significance of state-sanctioned same-sex marriages; for it tells those couples, and all the world, that their otherwise valid marriages are unworthy of federal recognition. This places same-sex couples in an unstable position of being in a second-tier marriage. The differentiation demeans the couple, whose moral and sexual choices the Constitution protects, see *Lawrence*, 539 U.S. 558, and whose relationship the State has sought to dignify. And it humiliates tens of thousands of children now being raised by same-sex couples. The law in question makes it even more difficult for the children to understand the integrity and closeness of their own family and its concord with other families in their community and in their daily lives.

Under DOMA, same-sex married couples have their lives burdened, by reason of government decree, in visible and public ways. By its great reach, DOMA touches many aspects of married and family life, from the mundane to the profound. It prevents same-sex married couples from obtaining government healthcare benefits they would otherwise receive. It deprives them of the Bankruptcy Code's special protections for domestic-support obligations. It forces them to follow a complicated procedure to file their state and federal taxes jointly. It prohibits them from being buried together in veterans' cemeteries.

* * * DOMA also brings financial harm to children of same-sex couples. It raises the cost of health care for families by taxing health benefits provided by employers to their workers' same-sex spouses. And it denies or reduces benefits allowed to families upon the loss of a spouse and parent, benefits that are an integral part of family security.

DOMA divests married same-sex couples of the duties and responsibilities that are an essential part of married life and that they in most cases would be honored to accept were DOMA not in force. * * *

* * *

The power the Constitution grants it also restrains. And though Congress has great authority to design laws to fit its own conception of sound national policy, it cannot deny the liberty protected by the Due Process Clause of the Fifth Amendment.

What has been explained to this point should more than suffice to establish that the principal purpose and the necessary effect of this law are to demean those persons who are in a lawful same-sex marriage. This requires the Court to hold, as it now does, that DOMA is unconstitutional as a deprivation of the liberty of the person protected by the Fifth Amendment of the Constitution.

The liberty protected by the Fifth Amendment's Due Process Clause contains within it the prohibition against denying to any person the equal protection of the laws. *See Bolling*, 347 U. S., at 499–500; *Adarand Constructors, Inc. v. Peña*, 515 U.S. 200, 217–218 (1995). While the Fifth Amendment itself withdraws from Government the power to degrade or demean in the way this law does, the equal protection guarantee of the Fourteenth Amendment makes that Fifth Amendment right all the more specific and all the better understood and preserved.

The class to which DOMA directs its restrictions and restraints are those persons who are joined in same-sex marriages made lawful by the State. DOMA singles out a class of persons deemed by a State entitled to recognition and protection to enhance their own liberty. It imposes a disability on the class by refusing to acknowledge a status the State finds to be dignified and proper. DOMA instructs all federal officials, and indeed all persons with whom same-sex couples interact, including their own children, that their marriage is less worthy than the marriages of others. The federal statute is invalid, for no legitimate purpose overcomes the purpose and effect to disparage and to injure those whom the State, by its marriage laws, sought to protect in personhood and dignity. By seeking to displace this protection and treating those persons as living in marriages less respected than others, the federal statute is in violation of the Fifth Amendment. This opinion and its holding are confined to those lawful marriages.

The judgment of the Court of Appeals for the Second Circuit is affirmed.

It is so ordered.

CHIEF JUSTICE ROBERTS, dissenting.

* * * [W]hile I disagree with the result to which the majority's analysis leads it in this case, I think it more important to point out that its analysis leads no further. The Court does not have before it, and the logic of its opinion does not decide, the distinct question whether the States, in the exercise of their "historic and essential authority to define the marital relation," may continue to utilize the traditional definition of marriage.

The majority goes out of its way to make this explicit in the penultimate sentence of its opinion. It states that "[t]his opinion and its holding are confined to those lawful marriages,"—referring to same-sex marriages that a State has already recognized as a result of the local "community's considered perspective on the historical roots of the institution of marriage and its evolving understanding of the meaning of equality." Justice SCALIA believes this is a " 'bald, unreasoned disclaime[r].' " In my view, though, the disclaimer is a logical and necessary consequence of the argument the majority has chosen to adopt. The dominant theme of the majority opinion is that the Federal Government's intrusion into an area "central to state domestic relations law applicable to its residents and citizens" is sufficiently "unusual" to set off alarm bells. I think the majority goes off course, as I have said, but it is undeniable that its judgment is based on federalism.

* * * We may in the future have to resolve challenges to state marriage definitions affecting same-sex couples. That issue, however, is not before us in this case. * * * I write only to highlight the limits of the

majority's holding and reasoning today, lest its opinion be taken to resolve not only a question that I believe is not properly before us—DOMA's constitutionality—but also a question that all agree, and the Court explicitly acknowledges, is not at issue.

JUSTICE SCALIA, with whom JUSTICE THOMAS joins, and with whom THE CHIEF JUSTICE joins as to Part I, dissenting.[4]

This case is about power in several respects. It is about the power of our people to govern themselves, and the power of this Court to pronounce the law. Today's opinion aggrandizes the latter, with the predictable consequence of diminishing the former. We have no power to decide this case. And even if we did, we have no power under the Constitution to invalidate this democratically adopted legislation. The Court's errors on both points spring forth from the same diseased root: an exalted conception of the role of this institution in America. * * *

II.

* * * I think that this Court has, and the Court of Appeals had, no power to decide this suit. We should vacate the decision below and remand to the Court of Appeals for the Second Circuit, with instructions to dismiss the appeal. Given that the majority has volunteered its view of the merits, however, I proceed to discuss that as well.

A

There are many remarkable things about the majority's merits holding. The first is how rootless and shifting its justifications are. For example, the opinion starts with seven full pages about the traditional power of States to define domestic relations—initially fooling many readers, I am sure, into thinking that this is a federalism opinion. But we are eventually told that "it is unnecessary to decide whether this federal intrusion on state power is a violation of the Constitution," and that "[t]he State's power in defining the marital relation is of central relevance in this case quite apart from principles of federalism" because "the State's decision to give this class of persons the right to marry conferred upon them a dignity and status of immense import." *Ante*, at 18. But no one questions the power of the States to define marriage (with the concomitant conferral of dignity and status), so what is the point of devoting seven pages to describing how long and well established that power is? Even after the opinion has formally disclaimed reliance upon principles of federalism, mentions of "the usual tradition of recognizing and accepting state definitions of marriage" continue. See, *e.g.*, *ante*, at 20. What to make of this? The opinion never explains. My guess is that the majority, while reluctant to suggest that defining the meaning of

---

"marriage" in federal statutes is unsupported by any of the Federal Government's enumerated powers, nonetheless needs some rhetorical basis to support its pretense that today's prohibition of laws excluding same-sex marriage is confined to the Federal Government (leaving the second, state-law shoe to be dropped later, maybe next Term). But I am only guessing.

Equally perplexing are the opinion's references to "the Constitution's guarantee of equality." *Ibid.* Near the end of the opinion, we are told that although the "equal protection guarantee of the Fourteenth Amendment makes [the] Fifth Amendment [due process] right all the more specific and all the better understood and preserved"—what can *that* mean?—"the Fifth Amendment itself withdraws from Government the power to degrade or demean in the way this law does." *Ante*, at 25. The only possible interpretation of this statement is that the Equal Protection Clause, even the Equal Protection Clause as incorporated in the Due Process Clause, is not the basis for today's holding. But the portion of the majority opinion that explains why DOMA is unconstitutional (Part IV) begins by citing *Bolling v. Sharpe*, 347 U.S. 497 (1954), *Department of Agriculture v. Moreno*, 413 U.S. 528 (1973), and *Romer v. Evans*, 517 U.S. 620 (1996)—all of which are equal-protection cases. And those three cases are the only authorities that the Court cites in Part IV about the Constitution's meaning, except for its citation of *Lawrence v. Texas*, 539 U.S. 558 (2003) (not an equal-protection case) to support its passing assertion that the Constitution protects the "moral and sexual choices" of same-sex couples.

Moreover, if this is meant to be an equal-protection opinion, it is a confusing one. The opinion does not resolve and indeed does not even mention what had been the central question in this litigation: whether, under the Equal Protection Clause, laws restricting marriage to a man and a woman are reviewed for more than mere rationality. That is the issue that divided the parties and the court below. In accord with my previously expressed skepticism about the Court's "tiers of scrutiny" approach, I would review this classification only for its rationality. *See United States v. Virginia*, 518 U.S. 515, 567–570 (1996) (SCALIA, J., dissenting). As nearly as I can tell, the Court agrees with that; its opinion does not apply strict scrutiny, and its central propositions are taken from rational-basis cases like *Moreno*. But the Court certainly does not apply anything that resembles that deferential framework.

The majority opinion need not get into the strict-vs.-rational-basis scrutiny question, and need not justify its holding under either, because it says that DOMA is unconstitutional as "a deprivation of the liberty of the person protected by the Fifth Amendment of the Constitution"; that it violates "basic due process" principles; and that it inflicts an "injury and indignity" of a kind that denies "an essential part of the liberty protected by the Fifth Amendment". The majority never utters the dread words "substantive due process," perhaps sensing the disrepute into which that doctrine has fallen, but that is what those statements mean. Yet the opinion does not argue that same-sex marriage is "deeply rooted in this Nation's history and tradition," a claim that would of course be quite absurd. So would the further suggestion (also necessary, under our substantive-due-process precedents) that a world in which DOMA exists is one bereft of " 'ordered liberty.' " [citations omitted]

Some might conclude that this loaf could have used a while longer in the oven. But that would be wrong; it is already overcooked. The most expert care in preparation cannot redeem a bad recipe. The sum of all the Court's nonspecific hand-waving is that this law is invalid (maybe on equal-protection grounds, maybe on substantive-due-process grounds, and perhaps with some amorphous federalism component playing a role) because it is motivated by a " 'bare . . . desire to harm' " couples in same-sex marriages. It is this proposition with which I will therefore engage.

B

As I have observed before, the Constitution does not forbid the government to enforce traditional moral and sexual norms. *See Lawrence v. Texas*, 539 U.S. 558, 599 (2003) (SCALIA, J., dissenting). I will not swell the U.S. Reports with restatements of that point. It is enough to say that the Constitution neither requires nor forbids our society to approve of same-sex marriage, much as it neither requires nor forbids us to approve of no-fault divorce, polygamy, or the consumption of alcohol.

However, even setting aside traditional moral disapproval of same-sex marriage (or indeed same-sex sex), there are many perfectly valid—indeed, downright boring—justifying rationales for this legislation. Their existence ought to be the end of this case. For they give the lie to the Court's conclusion that only those with hateful hearts could have voted "aye" on this Act. And more importantly, they serve to make the contents of the legislators' hearts quite irrelevant: "It is a familiar principle of constitutional law that this Court will not strike down an otherwise constitutional statute on the basis of an alleged illicit legislative motive." *United States v. O'Brien*, 391 U.S. 367, 383 (1968). Or at least it was a familiar principle. By holding to the contrary, the majority has declared open season on any law that (in the opinion of the law's opponents and any panel of like-minded federal judges) can be characterized as mean-spirited.

The majority concludes that the only motive for this Act was the "bare . . . desire to harm a politically unpopular group." Bear in mind that the object of this condemnation is not the legislature of some once-Confederate Southern state (familiar objects of the Court's scorn, see, *e.g., Edwards v. Aguillard*, 482 U.S. 578 (1987)), but our respected coordinate branches, the Congress and Presidency of the United States. Laying such a charge against them should require the most extraordinary evidence, and I would have thought that every attempt would be made to indulge a more anodyne explanation for the statute. The majority does the opposite—affirmatively concealing from the reader the arguments that exist in justification. It makes only a passing mention of the "arguments put forward" by the Act's defenders, and does not even trouble to paraphrase or describe them. *See ante*, at 21. I imagine that this is because it is harder to maintain the illusion of the Act's supporters as unhinged members of a wild-eyed lynch mob when one first describes their views as they see them.

To choose just one of these defenders' arguments, DOMA avoids difficult choice-of-law issues that will now arise absent a uniform federal definition of marriage. *See, e.g.*, Baude, Beyond DOMA: Choice of State Law in Federal Statutes, 64 Stan. L. Rev. 1371 (2012). Imagine a pair of women who marry in Albany and then move to Alabama, which does not "recognize as valid any marriage of parties of the same sex." When the couple files their next federal tax return, may it be a joint one? Which State's law controls, for federal-law purposes: their State of celebration (which recognizes the marriage) or their State of domicile (which does not)? (Does the answer depend on whether they were just visiting in Albany?) Are these questions to be answered as a matter of federal common law, or perhaps by borrowing a State's choice-of-law rules? If so, *which* State's? And what about States where the status of an out-of-state same-sex marriage is an unsettled question under local law? DOMA avoided all of this uncertainty by specifying which marriages would be recognized for federal purposes. That is a classic purpose for a definitional provision. [citations omitted]

Further, DOMA preserves the intended effects of prior legislation against then-unforeseen changes in circumstance. When Congress provided (for example) that a special estate-tax exemption would exist for spouses, this exemption reached only *opposite-sex* spouses—those being the only sort that were recognized in any State at the time of DOMA's passage. When it became clear that changes in state law might one day alter that balance, DOMA's definitional section was enacted to ensure that state-level experimentation did not automatically alter the basic operation of federal law, unless and until Congress made the further judgment to do so on its own. That is not animus—just stabilizing prudence. Congress has hardly demonstrated itself unwilling to make such further, revising judgments upon due deliberation. [citations omitted]

The Court mentions none of this. Instead, it accuses the Congress that enacted this law and the President who signed it of something much worse than, for example, having acted in excess of enumerated federal powers—or even having drawn distinctions that prove to be irrational. Those legal errors may be made in good faith, errors though they are. But the majority says that the supporters of this Act acted with malice—with the "purpose" "to disparage and to injure" same-sex couples. It says that the motivation for DOMA was to "demean," to "impose inequality," to "impose . . . a stigma," to deny people "equal dignity," to brand gay people as "unworthy," and to "humiliat[e]" their children.

I am sure these accusations are quite untrue. To be sure (as the majority points out), the legislation is called the Defense of Marriage Act. But to defend traditional marriage is not to condemn, demean, or humiliate those who would prefer other arrangements, any more than to defend the Constitution of the United States is to condemn, demean, or humiliate other constitutions. To hurl such accusations so casually demeans *this institution*. In the majority's judgment, any resistance to its holding is beyond the pale of reasoned disagreement. To question its high-handed invalidation of a presumptively valid statute is to act (the majority is sure) with *the purpose* to "disparage," "injure," "degrade," "demean," and "humiliate" our fellow human beings, our fellow citizens, who are homosexual. All that, simply for supporting an Act that did no more than codify an aspect of marriage that had been unquestioned in our society for most of its existence—indeed, had been unquestioned in virtually all societies for virtually all of human history. It is one thing for a society to elect change; it is another for a court of law to impose change by adjudging those who oppose it hostes humani generis, enemies of the human race.

* * *

The penultimate sentence of the majority's opinion is a naked declaration that "[t]his opinion and its holding are confined" to those couples "joined in same-sex marriages made lawful by the State." I have heard such "bald, unreasoned disclaimer[s]" before. *Lawrence*, 539 U. S., at 604. When the Court declared a constitutional right to homosexual sodomy, we were assured that the case had nothing, nothing at all to do with "whether the government must give formal recognition to any relationship that homosexual persons seek to enter." *Id.*, at 578. Now we are told that DOMA is invalid because it "demeans the couple, whose moral and sexual choices the Constitution protects," *ante*, at 23—with an accompanying citation of *Lawrence*. It takes real cheek for today's majority to assure us, as it is going out the door, that a constitutional requirement to give formal recognition to same-sex marriage is not at issue here—when what has preceded that assurance is a lecture on how superior the majority's moral judgment in favor of same-sex marriage is to the Congress's hateful moral judgment against it. I promise you this: The only thing that will "confine" the Court's holding is its sense of what it can get away with.

I do not mean to suggest disagreement with THE CHIEF JUSTICE's view that lower federal courts and state courts can distinguish today's case when the issue before them is state denial of marital status to same-sex couples—or even that this Court could theoretically do so. Lord, an opinion with such scatter-shot rationales as this one (federalism noises among them) can be distinguished in many ways. And deserves to be. State and lower federal courts should take the Court at its word and distinguish away.

In my opinion, however, the view that this Court will take of state prohibition of same-sex marriage is indicated beyond mistaking by today's opinion. As I have said, the real rationale of today's opinion, whatever disappearing trail of its legalistic argle-bargle one chooses to follow, is that DOMA is motivated by " 'bare . . . desire to harm' " couples in same-sex marriages. How easy it is, indeed how inevitable, to reach the same conclusion with regard to state laws denying same-sex couples marital status. Consider how easy (inevitable) it is to make the following substitutions in a passage from today's opinion:

> "~~DOMA's~~ *This state law's* principal effect is to identify a subset of ~~state-sanctioned marriages~~ *constitutionally protected sexual relationships*, see *Lawrence*, and make them unequal. The principal purpose is to impose inequality, not for other reasons like governmental efficiency. Responsibilities, as well as rights, enhance the dignity and integrity of the person. And ~~DOMA~~ *this state law* contrives to deprive some couples ~~married under the laws of their State~~ *enjoying constitutionally protected sexual relationships,* but not other couples, of both rights and responsibilities."

Or try this passage:

> "~~[DOMA]~~ *This state law* tells those couples, and all the world, that their otherwise valid ~~marriages~~ *relationships* are unworthy of ~~federal~~ *state* recognition. This places same-sex couples in an unstable position of being in a second-tier ~~marriage~~ *relationship*. The differentiation demeans the couple, whose moral and sexual choices the Constitution protects, see *Lawrence*. . . ."

Or this—which does not even require alteration, except as to the invented number:

> "And it humiliates ~~tens of~~ thousands of children now being raised by same-sex couples. The law in question makes it even more difficult for the children to understand the integrity and closeness of their own family and its concord with other families in their community and in their daily lives."

Similarly transposable passages—deliberately transposable, I think—abound. In sum, that Court which finds it so horrific that Congress irrationally and hatefully robbed same-sex couples of the "personhood and dignity" which state legislatures conferred upon them, will of a certitude be similarly appalled by state legislatures' irrational and hateful failure to acknowledge that "personhood and dignity" in the first place. As far as this Court is concerned, no one should be fooled; it is just a matter of listening and waiting for the other shoe.

By formally declaring anyone opposed to same-sex marriage an enemy of human decency, the majority arms well every challenger to a state law restricting marriage to its traditional definition. Henceforth those challengers will lead with this Court's declaration that there is "no legitimate purpose" served by such a law, and will claim that the traditional definition has "the purpose and effect to disparage and to injure" the "personhood and dignity" of same-sex couples. The majority's limiting assurance will be meaningless in the face of language like that, as the majority well knows. That is why the language is there. The result will be a judicial distortion of our society's debate over marriage—a debate that can seem in need of our clumsy "help" only to a member of this institution.

As to that debate: Few public controversies touch an institution so central to the lives of so many, and few inspire such attendant passion by good people on all sides. Few public controversies will ever demonstrate so vividly the beauty of what our Framers gave us, a gift the Court pawns today to buy its stolen moment in the spotlight: a system of government that permits us to rule ourselves. Since DOMA's passage, citizens on all sides of the question have seen victories and they have seen defeats. There have been plebiscites, legislation, persuasion, and loud voices—in other words, democracy. Victories in one place for some are offset by victories in other places for others. [citations omitted] Even in a single State, the question has come out differently on different occasions. Compare Maine Question 1 (permitting "the State of Maine to issue marriage licenses to same-sex couples") (approved by a popular vote, 53% to 47%, on November 6, 2012) with Maine Question 1 (rejecting "the new law that lets same-sex couples marry") (approved by a popular vote, 53% to 47%, on November 3, 2009).

In the majority's telling, this story is black-and-white: Hate your neighbor or come along with us. The truth is more complicated. It is hard to admit that one's political opponents are not monsters, especially in a struggle like this one, and the challenge in the end proves more than today's Court can handle. Too bad. A reminder that disagreement over something so fundamental as marriage can still be politically legitimate would have been a fit task for what in earlier times was called the judicial temperament. We might have covered ourselves with honor today, by promising all sides of this debate that it was theirs to settle and that we would respect their resolution. We might have let the People decide.

But that the majority will not do. Some will rejoice in today's decision, and some will despair at it; that is the nature of a controversy that matters so much to so many. But the Court has cheated both sides, robbing the winners of an honest victory, and the losers of the peace that comes from a fair defeat. We owed both of them better. I dissent.

JUSTICE ALITO, with whom JUSTICE THOMAS joins as to Parts II and III, dissenting.[5]

Our Nation is engaged in a heated debate about same-sex marriage. That debate is, at bottom, about the nature of the institution of marriage. Respondent Edith Windsor, supported by the United States, asks this Court to intervene in that debate, and although she couches her argument in different terms, what she seeks is a holding that enshrines in the Constitution a particular understanding of marriage under which the sex of the partners makes no difference. The Constitution, however, does not dictate that choice. It leaves the choice to the people, acting through their elected representatives at both the federal and state levels. I would therefore hold that Congress did not violate Windsor's constitutional rights by enacting § 3 of [DOMA]. * * *

II

* * * Same-sex marriage presents a highly emotional and important question of public policy—but not a difficult question of constitutional law. The Constitution does not guarantee the right to enter into a same-sex marriage. Indeed, no provision of the Constitution speaks to the issue.

The Court has sometimes found the Due Process Clauses to have a substantive component that guarantees liberties beyond the absence of physical restraint. And the Court's holding that "DOMA is unconstitutional as a deprivation of the liberty of the person protected by the Fifth Amendment of the Constitution," suggests that substantive due process may partially underlie the Court's decision today. But it is well established that any "substantive" component to the Due Process Clause protects only "those fundamental rights and liberties which are, objectively, 'deeply rooted in this Nation's history and tradition,'" as well as "'implicit in the concept of ordered liberty,' such that 'neither liberty nor justice would exist if they were sacrificed.'" [citations omitted]

It is beyond dispute that the right to same-sex marriage is not deeply rooted in this Nation's history and tradition. In this country, no State permitted same-sex marriage until the Massachusetts Supreme Judicial

---

5 *Editor's Note*: In Part I, Justice Alito explained his view that BLAG had Article III standing in the case such that the Court should reach the merits.

Court held in 2003 that limiting marriage to opposite-sex couples violated the State Constitution. * * *

What Windsor and the United States seek, therefore, is not the protection of a deeply rooted right but the recognition of a very new right, and they seek this innovation not from a legislative body elected by the people, but from unelected judges. Faced with such a request, judges have cause for both caution and humility.

The family is an ancient and universal human institution. Family structure reflects the characteristics of a civilization, and changes in family structure and in the popular understanding of marriage and the family can have profound effects. Past changes in the understanding of marriage—for example, the gradual ascendance of the idea that romantic love is a prerequisite to marriage—have had far-reaching consequences. But the process by which such consequences come about is complex, involving the interaction of numerous factors, and tends to occur over an extended period of time.

We can expect something similar to take place if same-sex marriage becomes widely accepted. The long-term consequences of this change are not now known and are unlikely to be ascertainable for some time to come. There are those who think that allowing same-sex marriage will seriously undermine the institution of marriage. Others think that recognition of same-sex marriage will fortify a now-shaky institution.

At present, no one—including social scientists, philosophers, and historians—can predict with any certainty what the long-term ramifications of widespread acceptance of same-sex marriage will be. And judges are certainly not equipped to make such an assessment. The Members of this Court have the authority and the responsibility to interpret and apply the Constitution. Thus, if the Constitution contained a provision guaranteeing the right to marry a person of the same sex, it would be our duty to enforce that right. But the Constitution simply does not speak to the issue of same-sex marriage. In our system of government, ultimate sovereignty rests with the people, and the people have the right to control their own destiny. Any change on a question so fundamental should be made by the people through their elected officials.

III

Perhaps because they cannot show that same-sex marriage is a fundamental right under our Constitution, Windsor and the United States couch their arguments in equal protection terms. They argue that § 3 of DOMA discriminates on the basis of sexual orientation, that classifications based on sexual orientation should trigger a form of "heightened" scrutiny, and that § 3 cannot survive such scrutiny. They further maintain that the governmental interests that § 3 purports to serve are not sufficiently important and that it has not been adequately shown that § 3 serves those interests very well. The Court's holding, too, seems to rest on "the equal protection guarantee of the Fourteenth Amendment"—although the Court is careful not to adopt most of Windsor's and the United States' argument.

In my view, the approach that Windsor and the United States advocate is misguided. Our equal protection framework, upon which Windsor and the United States rely, is a judicial construct that provides a useful mechanism for analyzing a certain universe of equal protection cases. But that framework is ill suited for use in evaluating the constitutionality of laws based on the traditional understanding of marriage, which fundamentally turn on what marriage is. * * *

By asking the Court to strike down DOMA as not satisfying some form of heightened scrutiny, Windsor and the United States are really seeking to have the Court resolve a debate between two competing views of marriage.

The first and older view, which I will call the "traditional" or "conjugal" view, sees marriage as an intrinsically opposite-sex institution. BLAG notes that virtually every culture, including many not influenced by the Abrahamic religions, has limited marriage to people of the opposite sex. And BLAG attempts to explain this phenomenon by arguing that the institution of marriage was created for the purpose of channeling heterosexual intercourse into a structure that supports child rearing. * * * While modern cultural changes have weakened the link between marriage and procreation in the popular mind, there is no doubt that, throughout human history and across many cultures, marriage has been viewed as an exclusively opposite-sex institution and as one inextricably linked to procreation and biological kinship.

The other, newer view is what I will call the "consent-based" vision of marriage, a vision that primarily defines marriage as the solemnization of mutual commitment—marked by strong emotional attachment and sexual attraction—between two persons. At least as it applies to heterosexual couples, this view of marriage now plays a very prominent role in the popular understanding of the institution. Indeed, our popular culture is infused with this understanding of marriage. Proponents of same-sex marriage argue that because gender differentiation is not relevant to this vision, the exclusion of same-sex couples from the institution of marriage is rank discrimination.

The Constitution does not codify either of these views of marriage (although I suspect it would have been hard at the time of the adoption of the Constitution or the Fifth Amendment to find Americans who did not take the traditional view for granted). The silence of the Constitution on this question should be enough to end the matter as far as the judiciary is concerned. Yet, Windsor and the United States implicitly ask us to endorse the consent-based view of marriage and to reject the traditional view, thereby arrogating to ourselves the power to decide a question that philosophers, historians, social scientists, and theologians are better qualified to explore.[7] Because our constitutional order assigns the resolution of questions of this nature to the people, I would not presume to enshrine either vision of marriage in our constitutional jurisprudence.

Legislatures, however, have little choice but to decide between the two views. We have long made clear that neither the political branches of the Federal Government nor state governments are required to be neutral between competing visions of the good, provided that the vision of the good that they adopt is not countermanded by the Constitution. Accordingly, both Congress and the States are entitled to enact laws recognizing either of the two understandings of marriage. * * *

* * *

For these reasons, I would hold that § 3 of DOMA does not violate the Fifth Amendment. I respectfully dissent.

NOTES

1.   Justice Kennedy's majority opinion includes elements of equality, liberty, and federalism. What role did each doctrinal area play? On what doctrinal principle does the decision ultimately rest? What role does dignity play in Justice Kennedy's reasoning?

2.   What level of scrutiny does Justice Kennedy apply? Why did he not explicitly engage the issue of heightened scrutiny addressed by the Second Circuit?

In a significant decision involving peremptory challenges based on sexual orientation, the Ninth Circuit Court of Appeals held that *Windsor* requires the application of heightened scrutiny to sexual orientation classifications. *SmithKline Beecham Corp. v. Abbott Labs.*, 740 F.3d 471 (9th Cir. 2014). The court reasoned that while *Windsor* "did not expressly announce the level of scrutiny it applied to the equal protection claim . . . an express declaration is not necessary." *Id.* at 480. The court then explained:

---

[7]   The degree to which this question is intractable to typical judicial processes of decisionmaking was highlighted by the trial in *Hollingsworth v. Perry*. In that case, the trial judge, after receiving testimony from some expert witnesses, purported to make "findings of fact" on such questions as why marriage came to be, what marriage is, and the effect legalizing same-sex marriage would have on opposite-sex marriage.

At times, the trial reached the heights of parody, as when the trial judge questioned his ability to take into account the views of great thinkers of the past because they were unavailable to testify in person in his courtroom.

And, if this spectacle were not enough, some professors of constitutional law have argued that we are bound to accept the trial judge's findings—including those on major philosophical questions and predictions about the future—unless they are "clearly erroneous." Only an arrogant legal culture that has lost all appreciation of its own limitations could take such a suggestion seriously.

"Unlike in rational basis review, hypothetical reasons for DOMA's enactment were not a basis of the Court's inquiry." *Id.* at 481. It continued:

> Rational basis is ordinarily unconcerned with the inequality that results from the challenged state action. Due to this distinctive feature of rational basis review, words like *harm* or *injury* rarely appear in the Court's decisions applying rational basis review. *Windsor*, however, uses these words repeatedly.

Id. at 482 (citation omitted). Finally, the court noted that "[a]bsent from *Windsor*'s review of DOMA are the 'strong presumption' in favor of constitutionality of laws and the 'extremely deferential' posture toward government action that are the marks of rational basis review." *Id.* at 483. What do you think of the Ninth Circuit's reasoning? Do you agree?

3.   How does Justice Kennedy analyze the governmental interests put forward to support DOMA? Why are those interests not valid justifications for the law?

4.   In his dissent, Chief Justice Roberts emphasizes the federalism dimensions of the majority opinion to distinguish the constitutional question regarding state marriage prohibitions. For his part, Justice Scalia suggests a closer relationship between the Court's decision and the constitutionality of state marriage bans. To what extent did principles of federalism guide the Court's decision? What does the equal protection reasoning in *Windsor* reveal about the constitutionality of state laws excluding same-sex couples from marriage?

5.   Even though *Windsor* did not involve a claim to the fundamental right to marry, Justices Scalia and Alito both engage this issue. Does excluding same-sex couples from marriage infringe on the fundamental right to marry? Is there anything in Justice Kennedy's opinion that reveals his outlook on this question? For analysis of *Windsor*'s right-to-marry dimensions, see Douglas NeJaime, Windsor's *Right to Marry*, 123 YALE L.J. ONLINE 219 (2013).

6.   In his dissent, Justice Alito explains how the debate over same-sex marriage implicates a broader debate over the meaning and purpose of marriage. What is the distinction between the "conjugal" and "consent-based" understandings of marriage? How do same-sex couples relate to each? What does Justice Kennedy's opinion suggest are the central features of marriage? How do these features relate to the view of marriage espoused by the Court in *Loving* and *Turner*, excerpted at the beginning of this Chapter?

7.   Justice Kennedy concludes that DOMA "humiliates tens of thousands of children now being raised by same-sex couples." How does this argument relate to the claims of same-sex marriage opponents regarding procreation and childrearing? What is the relationship between marriage and parenting? What *should* it be?

8.   Justice Scalia argues in his dissent that avoiding "difficult choice-of-law issues that will now arise absent a uniform federal definition of marriage" provides a rational basis for the law. After *Windsor*, federal agencies confronted these choice-of-law issues as they considered how marital status would be determined for purposes of various federal statutes. A place-of-residence (or place-of-domicile) rule was adopted in the few instances that statutes dictated such a result. *See* U.S. Dep't of Labor, Wage and Hour Div., *Fact Sheet #28F: Qualifying Reasons for Leave under the Family and Medical Leave Act* (Aug. 2013) ("Spouse means a husband or wife as defined or recognized under state law for purposes of marriage in the state where the employee resides, including 'common law' marriage and same-sex marriage."). But most federal agencies adopted a place-of-celebration rule. This meant that if couples married in a state that recognized same-sex couples' marriage, they would be eligible for the particular federal benefits even if the state where they resided refused to recognize their marriage. In one of the most significant announcements, the Internal Revenue Service explained its reasoning:

> [I]ndividuals of the same sex will be considered to be lawfully married under the [Internal Revenue] Code as long as they were married in a state whose laws authorize the marriage of two individuals of the same sex, even if they are domiciled in a state that does not recognize the validity of same-sex marriages. For over half a century, for Federal income tax purposes, the Service has recognized marriages based on the laws of the state in which they were entered into, without regard to subsequent changes in domicile, to achieve uniformity, stability, and efficiency in the application and administration of the Code. Given our increasingly mobile society, it is important to have a uniform rule of recognition that can be applied with certainty by the Service and taxpayers alike for all Federal tax purposes. Those overriding tax administration policy goals generally apply with equal force in the context of same-sex marriages. * * *
>
> A rule of recognition based on the state of a taxpayer's current domicile would also raise significant challenges for employers that operate in more than one state, or that have employees (or former employees) who live in more than one state, or move between states with different marriage recognition rules. Substantial financial and administrative burdens would be placed on those employers, as well as the administrators of employee benefit plans.

Rev. Rul. 2013–17, 2013–38 I.R.B. 201, at § 3.

9.   After *Windsor*, the federal government extended federal rights and benefits to married same-sex couples but did not extend such rights and benefits to same-sex couples in civil unions or domestic partnerships. This development furnished additional support after *Windsor* to same-sex couples' claims that state-level nonmarital recognition failed to satisfy equal

protection requirements. By providing same-sex couples the state-law rights of marriage through a nonmarital status but withholding marriage itself, states effectively precluded same-sex couples from receiving the full panoply of federal rights attached to marriage. The New Jersey Supreme Court, in considering the adequacy of civil unions after *Windsor*, explained that because *Windsor* "paved the way to extending federal benefits to married same-sex couples" and "because a number of federal agencies responded and now provide various benefits to married same-sex couples," "same-sex couples in New Jersey [were] being deprived of the full rights and benefits the State Constitution guarantees." *Garden State Equality v. Dow*, 79 A.3d 1036, 1042, 216 N.J. 314, 325 (N.J. 2013). Accordingly, same-sex couples in New Jersey gained access to marriage after *Windsor*.

10. After *Windsor*, county clerks in New Mexico began to issue marriage licenses to same-sex couples. The state supreme court ultimately resolved the issue. The court held that sexual orientation merited intermediate scrutiny for state equal protection purposes, and under that standard the court invalidated same-sex couples' exclusion from marriage. *Griego v. Oliver*, 316 P.3d 865, 880–89 (N.M. 2013).

11. *Windsor* did not involve Section 2 of DOMA, which related to interstate recognition of same-sex marriage. When DOMA was passed in 1996, supporters of the law pointed to the Full Faith and Credit Clause in Article IV of the federal Constitution to argue that states would have to recognize same-sex marriages from other states. That Clause provides that:

> Full faith and credit shall be given in each State to the public Acts, Records, and judicial Proceedings of every other State. And the Congress may by general Laws prescribe the manner in which such Acts, Records, and Proceedings shall be proved, and the effect thereof.

U.S. CONST. art. IV, § 1. However, the idea that the Full Faith and Credit Clause would, in fact, compel interstate recognition of same-sex marriage was hardly the inevitability that opponents claimed. Nevertheless, the claim proved politically potent. And many states passed their own laws defining marriage as an exclusively different-sex union and expressly declining to recognize same-sex marriages performed in other states. While many of the earlier decisions on interstate recognition were decided on the basis of comity principles, the issue, as *Obergefell v. Hodges* demonstrates in the next section, ultimately became part of the same constitutional debate as the permissibility of states' refusal to license marriage for same-sex couples.

3. Nationwide Marriage Equality

Hollingworth v. Perry, discussed earlier in this Chapter, presented the Supreme Court with the question of whether state bans on same-sex marriage were constitutional. Yet, because the Court did not reach the merits in that case, the reasoning in *Windsor* became more significant to ongoing advocacy for marriage equality. As one commentator explained, the Court's "approach, as public interest lawyers had hoped when they filed federal lawsuits challenging DOMA, significantly moved forward the marriage equality cause. But it did not decisively settle the question. In this sense, *Windsor*, like *Perry*, is a point along the way to marriage equality—it fuels, rather than ends, social movement activity and public interest lawyering." NeJaime, *The View From Below, supra*, at 204.

In *Windsor*'s wake, same-sex couples around the country filed a number of lawsuits in federal and state courts challenging state marriage bans. In addition to federal constitutional claims based on the fundamental right to marry, the plaintiffs in these suits asserted federal equal protection claims that relied on the Court's reasoning in *Windsor*. At the same time, federal lawsuits initiated before the Court's *Windsor* decision moved forward with new energy.

Of the 66 federal and state rulings after *Windsor*, 61 favored same-sex couples. As federal courts held that the federal Constitution required marriage equality, many states and other defenders of same-sex marriage bans sought review by the U.S. Supreme Court. The Court denied petitions for certiorari in cases from the Fourth, Seventh, Ninth, and Tenth Circuits, thus allowing court decisions striking down same-sex marriage bans in many states to take effect.

Suddenly, litigation was bringing marriage equality to more and more states, including those that had long resisted same-sex marriage and where LGBT rights lawyers had avoided pressing the issue. Professor Jane Schacter details this shift, beginning with the pre-*Windsor* landcape:

> For almost all of the first two decades of the contemporary marriage equality movement, LGBT rights litigators chose favorable states for litigation, and made only claims grounded in the state constitution. Litigating on this basis prevented a feared loss in the Supreme Court. . . . It did not take long after *Windsor* was decided to see where the litigation road would be going. Federal lawsuits were newly filed, or were rejuvenated, in states all over the country. One of the first federal district court opinions to be issued after *Windsor* was in the unlikely state of Utah—the very state that had been the first to pass a state mini-DOMA after the 1993 Hawaii bombshell in *Baehr v. Lewin*. The 2013 Utah ruling was followed by district court judgments in Oklahoma, Kentucky, Idaho, and Tennessee, among others, where public support for marriage equality would not be expected to be high.

Federal litigation in states hostile to same-sex marriage reflected change in one interesting respect. In most of the states that legalized same-sex marriage before *Windsor*, there is polling evidence that a majority or plurality (or something close to it) supported same-sex marriage at the time of legalization.... [T]his pattern held whether it was judicial or legislative action that led to legalizing same-sex marriage. Based on available polling evidence close to the time same-sex marriage was legalized, two exceptions to this pattern were Iowa (where polls reflected low support) and California (where two 2008 polls pointed in different directions).

Jane S. Schacter, *What Marriage Equality Can Tell Us About Popular Constitutionalism (and Vice-Versa)*, 52 HOUS. L. REV. 1147, 1171–72 (2015). Asking "[w]hat happened after *Windsor*?", Professor Schacter then considers polling data in the 23 states that legalized same-sex marriage between the *Windsor* ruling and the end of 2014.

Here, the picture is more variable. The two states that proceeded by legislation (Illinois and Hawaii) show majority or plurality support in the polls. Those that proceeded through post-*Windsor* state court rulings that became final (New Jersey and New Mexico) show majority or (very narrow) plurality support. States that legalized by way of federal court ruling—nineteen of the twenty-three—are a mixed bag. Nine show significant evidence of majority or plurality popular support (Arizona, California, Colorado, Indiana, Nevada, Oregon, Pennsylvania, Virginia, and Wisconsin); seven show significant evidence of opposition (Idaho, North Carolina, Oklahoma, South Carolina, Utah, West Virginia, and Wyoming); and three are inconclusive with multiple polls pointing in different directions (Alaska, Montana, and Kansas).

It is not surprising that the polling would change as the debate moves into what LGBT activists call "low equality" states like some of these, along with others, like Alabama, Louisiana, and Mississippi. Many of these states were among the holdout states on other issues of cultural constitutional policy, such as interracial marriage (the subject of *Loving v. Virginia*), and the criminalization of sodomy (the subject of *Lawrence v. Texas*).

Id. at 1172–73.

While federal appellate courts across the country had ruled in favor of same-sex couples, eventually the federal Court of Appeals for the Sixth Circuit ruled against same-sex couples in a case that consolidated appeals from Kentucky, Michigan, Ohio, and Tennessee. *DeBoer v. Snyder*, 772

F.3d 388 (6th Cir. 2014). The Supreme Court granted certiorari in that case, which was captioned *Obergefell v. Hodges*.

OBERGEFELL V. HODGES

Supreme Court of the United States, 2015
576 U.S__, 135 S.Ct. 2584, 192 L.Ed.2d 609

JUSTICE KENNEDY delivered the opinion of the Court.

The Constitution promises liberty to all within its reach, a liberty that includes certain specific rights that allow persons, within a lawful realm, to define and express their identity. The petitioners in these cases seek to find that liberty by marrying someone of the same sex and having their marriages deemed lawful on the same terms and conditions as marriages between persons of the opposite sex.

I

These cases come from Michigan, Kentucky, Ohio, and Tennessee, States that define marriage as a union between one man and one woman. The petitioners are 14 same-sex couples and two men whose same-sex partners are deceased. The respondents are state officials responsible for enforcing the laws in question. The petitioners claim the respondents violate the Fourteenth Amendment by denying them the right to marry or to have their marriages, lawfully performed in another State, given full recognition.

Petitioners filed these suits in United States District Courts in their home States. Each District Court ruled in their favor. The respondents appealed the decisions against them to the United States Court of Appeals for the Sixth Circuit. It consolidated the cases and reversed the judgments of the District Courts. *DeBoer v. Snyder*, 772 F.3d 388 (2014). The Court of Appeals held that a State has no constitutional obligation to license same-sex marriages or to recognize same-sex marriages performed out of State.

The petitioners sought certiorari. This Court granted review. * * *

II

Before addressing the principles and precedents that govern these cases, it is appropriate to note the history of the subject now before the Court.

A

From their beginning to their most recent page, the annals of human history reveal the transcendent importance of marriage. The lifelong union of a man and a woman always has promised nobility and dignity to all persons, without regard to their station in life. Marriage is sacred to those who live by their religions and offers unique fulfillment to those who find meaning in the secular realm. Its dynamic allows two people to find a life that could not be found alone, for a marriage becomes greater than just the two persons. Rising from the most basic human needs, marriage is essential to our most profound hopes and aspirations.

The centrality of marriage to the human condition makes it unsurprising that the institution has existed for millennia and across civilizations. Since the dawn of history, marriage has transformed strangers into relatives, binding families and societies together. * * * There are untold references to the beauty of marriage in religious and philosophical texts spanning time, cultures, and faiths, as well as in art and literature in all their forms. It is fair and necessary to say these references were based on the understanding that marriage is a union between two persons of the opposite sex.

That history is the beginning of these cases. The respondents say it should be the end as well. To them, it would demean a timeless institution if the concept and lawful status of marriage were extended to two persons of the same sex. Marriage, in their view, is by its nature a gender-differentiated union of man and woman. This view long has been held—and continues to be held—in good faith by reasonable and sincere people here and throughout the world.

The petitioners acknowledge this history but contend that these cases cannot end there. Were their intent to demean the revered idea and reality of marriage, the petitioners' claims would be of a different order. But that is neither their purpose nor their submission. To the contrary, it is the enduring importance of marriage that underlies the petitioners' contentions. This, they say, is their whole point. Far from seeking to devalue marriage, the petitioners seek it for themselves because of their respect—and need—for its privileges and responsibilities. And their immutable nature dictates that same-sex marriage is their only real path to this profound commitment.

* * * Petitioner James Obergefell, a plaintiff in the Ohio case, met John Arthur over two decades ago. They fell in love and started a life together, establishing a lasting, committed relation. In 2011, however, Arthur was diagnosed with amyotrophic lateral sclerosis, or ALS. This debilitating disease is progressive, with no known cure. Two years ago, Obergefell and Arthur decided to commit to one another, resolving to marry before Arthur died. To fulfill their mutual promise, they traveled from Ohio to Maryland, where same-sex marriage was legal. It was difficult for Arthur to move, and so the couple were wed inside a medical transport plane as it remained on the tarmac in Baltimore. Three months later, Arthur died. Ohio law does not permit Obergefell to be listed as the surviving spouse on Arthur's death certificate. By statute, they must remain strangers even in death, a state-imposed separation Obergefell

deems "hurtful for the rest of time." He brought suit to be shown as the surviving spouse on Arthur's death certificate.

April DeBoer and Jayne Rowse are co-plaintiffs in the case from Michigan. They celebrated a commitment ceremony to honor their permanent relation in 2007. They both work as nurses, DeBoer in a neonatal unit and Rowse in an emergency unit. In 2009, DeBoer and Rowse fostered and then adopted a baby boy. Later that same year, they welcomed another son into their family. The new baby, born prematurely and abandoned by his biological mother, required around-the-clock care. The next year, a baby girl with special needs joined their family. Michigan, however, permits only opposite-sex married couples or single individuals to adopt, so each child can have only one woman as his or her legal parent. If an emergency were to arise, schools and hospitals may treat the three children as if they had only one parent. And, were tragedy to befall either DeBoer or Rowse, the other would have no legal rights over the children she had not been permitted to adopt. This couple seeks relief from the continuing uncertainty their unmarried status creates in their lives. * * *

The cases now before the Court involve other petitioners as well, each with their own experiences. Their stories reveal that they seek not to denigrate marriage but rather to live their lives, or honor their spouses' memory, joined by its bond.

B

The ancient origins of marriage confirm its centrality, but it has not stood in isolation from developments in law and society. The history of marriage is one of both continuity and change. That institution—even as confined to opposite-sex relations—has evolved over time.

For example, marriage was once viewed as an arrangement by the couple's parents based on political, religious, and financial concerns; but by the time of the Nation's founding it was understood to be a voluntary contract between a man and a woman. *See* N. Cott, Public Vows: A History of Marriage and the Nation 9–17 (2000); S. Coontz, Marriage, A History 15–16 (2005). As the role and status of women changed, the institution further evolved. Under the centuries-old doctrine of coverture, a married man and woman were treated by the State as a single, male-dominated legal entity. *See* 1 W. Blackstone, Commentaries on the Laws of England 430 (1765). As women gained legal, political, and property rights, and as society began to understand that women have their own equal dignity, the law of coverture was abandoned. *See* Brief for Historians of Marriage et al. as Amici Curiae 16–19. These and other developments in the institution of marriage over the past centuries were not mere superficial changes. Rather, they worked deep transformations in its structure, affecting aspects of marriage long viewed by many as essential. *See generally* N. Cott, Public Vows; S. Coontz, Marriage; H. Hartog, Man & Wife in America: A History (2000).

These new insights have strengthened, not weakened, the institution of marriage. Indeed, changed understandings of marriage are characteristic of a Nation where new dimensions of freedom become apparent to new generations, often through perspectives that begin in pleas or protests and then are considered in the political sphere and the judicial process.

This dynamic can be seen in the Nation's experiences with the rights of gays and lesbians. Until the mid-20th century, same-sex intimacy long had been condemned as immoral by the state itself in most Western nations, a belief often embodied in the criminal law. For this reason, among others, many persons did not deem homosexuals to have dignity in their own distinct identity. A truthful declaration by same-sex couples of what was in their hearts had to remain unspoken. Even when a greater awareness of the humanity and integrity of homosexual persons came in the period after World War II, the argument that gays and lesbians had a just claim to dignity was in conflict with both law and widespread social conventions. Same-sex intimacy remained a crime in many States. Gays and lesbians were prohibited from most government employment, barred from military service, excluded under immigration laws, targeted by police, and burdened in their rights to associate. *See* Brief for Organization of American Historians as *Amicus Curiae* 5–28.

For much of the 20th century, moreover, homosexuality was treated as an illness. When the American Psychiatric Association published the first Diagnostic and Statistical Manual of Mental Disorders in 1952, homosexuality was classified as a mental disorder, a position adhered to until 1973. *See* Position Statement on Homosexuality and Civil Rights, 1973, in 131 Am. J. Psychiatry 497 (1974). Only in more recent years have psychiatrists and others recognized that sexual orientation is both a normal expression of human sexuality and immutable. *See* Brief for American Psychological Association et al. as *Amici Curiae* 7–17.

In the late 20th century, following substantial cultural and political developments, same-sex couples began to lead more open and public lives and to establish families. This development was followed by a quite extensive discussion of the issue in both governmental and private sectors and by a shift in public attitudes toward greater tolerance. As a result, questions about the rights of gays and lesbians soon reached the courts, where the issue could be discussed in the formal discourse of the law.

This Court first gave detailed consideration to the legal status of homosexuals in *Bowers v. Hardwick*, 478 U.S. 186 (1986). There it upheld the constitutionality of a Georgia law deemed to criminalize certain homosexual acts. Ten years later, in *Romer v. Evans*, 517 U.S. 620 (1996), the Court invalidated an amendment to Colorado's Constitution that sought to foreclose any branch or political subdivision of the State from protecting persons against discrimination based on sexual orientation. Then, in 2003, the Court overruled Bowers, holding that laws making same-sex intimacy a crime "demea[n] the lives of homosexual persons." *Lawrence v. Texas*, 539 U.S. 558, 575.

Against this background, the legal question of same-sex marriage arose. In 1993, the Hawaii Supreme Court held Hawaii's law restricting marriage to opposite-sex couples constituted a classification on the basis of sex and was therefore subject to strict scrutiny under the Hawaii Constitution. *Baehr v. Lewin*, 74 Haw. 530, 852 P. 2d 44. Although this decision did not mandate that same-sex marriage be allowed, some States were concerned by its implications and reaffirmed in their laws that marriage is defined as a union between opposite-sex partners. So too in 1996, Congress passed the Defense of Marriage Act (DOMA), 110 Stat. 2419, defining marriage for all federal-law purposes as "only a legal union between one man and one woman as husband and wife." 1 U.S.C. § 7.

The new and widespread discussion of the subject led other States to a different conclusion. In 2003, the Supreme Judicial Court of Massachusetts held the State's Constitution guaranteed same-sex couples the right to marry. *See Goodridge v. Department of Public Health*, 798 N. E. 2d 941 (2003). After that ruling, some additional States granted marriage rights to same-sex couples, either through judicial or legislative processes. Two Terms ago, in *United States v. Windsor*, 570 U.S. (2013), this Court invalidated DOMA to the extent it barred the Federal Government from treating same-sex marriages as valid even when they were lawful in the State where they were licensed. DOMA, the Court held, impermissibly disparaged those same-sex couples "who wanted to affirm their commitment to one another before their children, their family, their friends, and their community."

Numerous cases about same-sex marriage have reached the United States Courts of Appeals in recent years. In accordance with the judicial duty to base their decisions on principled reasons and neutral discussions, without scornful or disparaging commentary, courts have written a substantial body of law considering all sides of these issues. That case law helps to explain and formulate the underlying principles this Court now must consider. With the exception of the opinion here under review and one other, see *Citizens for Equal Protection v. Bruning*, 455 F. 3d 859, 864–868 (CA8 2006), the Courts of Appeals have held that excluding same-sex couples from marriage violates the Constitution. There also have been many thoughtful District Court decisions addressing same-sex marriage—and most of them, too, have concluded same-sex couples must be allowed to marry. In addition the highest courts of many States have contributed to this ongoing dialogue in decisions interpreting their own State Constitutions.

After years of litigation, legislation, referenda, and the discussions that attended these public acts, the States are now divided on the issue of same-sex marriage.

III

Under the Due Process Clause of the Fourteenth Amendment, no State shall "deprive any person of life, liberty, or property, without due process of law." The fundamental liberties protected by this Clause include most of the rights enumerated in the Bill of Rights. *See Duncan v. Louisiana*, 391 U.S. 145, 147–149 (1968). In addition these liberties extend to certain personal choices central to individual dignity and autonomy, including intimate choices that define personal identity and beliefs. *See, e.g., Eisenstadt v. Baird*, 405 U.S. 438, 453 (1972); *Griswold v. Connecticut*, 381 U.S. 479, 484–486 (1965).

The identification and protection of fundamental rights is an enduring part of the judicial duty to interpret the Constitution. That responsibility, however, "has not been reduced to any formula." *Poe v. Ullman*, 367 U.S. 497, 542 (1961) (Harlan, J., dissenting). Rather, it requires courts to exercise reasoned judgment in identifying interests of the person so fundamental that the State must accord them its respect. That process is guided by many of the same considerations relevant to analysis of other constitutional provisions that set forth broad principles rather than specific requirements. History and tradition guide and discipline this inquiry but do not set its outer boundaries. *See Lawrence, supra*, at 572. That method respects our history and learns from it without allowing the past alone to rule the present.

The nature of injustice is that we may not always see it in our own times. The generations that wrote and ratified the Bill of Rights and the Fourteenth Amendment did not presume to know the extent of freedom in all of its dimensions, and so they entrusted to future generations a charter protecting the right of all persons to enjoy liberty as we learn its meaning. When new insight reveals discord between the Constitution's central protections and a received legal stricture, a claim to liberty must be addressed. Applying these established tenets, the Court has long held the right to marry is protected by the Constitution. In *Loving v. Virginia*, 388 U.S. 1, 12 (1967), which invalidated bans on interracial unions, a unanimous Court held marriage is "one of the vital personal rights essential to the orderly pursuit of happiness by free men." The Court reaffirmed that holding in *Zablocki v. Redhail*, 434 U.S. 374, 384 (1978), which held the right to marry was burdened by a law prohibiting fathers who were behind on child support from marrying. The Court again applied this principle in *Turner v. Safley*, 482 U.S. 78, 95 (1987), which held the right to marry was abridged by regulations limiting the privilege of prison inmates to marry. Over time and in other contexts, the Court has reiterated that the right to marry is fundamental under the Due Process Clause. * * *

It cannot be denied that this Court's cases describing the right to marry presumed a relationship involving opposite-sex partners. The Court, like many institutions, has made assumptions defined by the world and time of which it is a part. This was evident in *Baker v. Nelson*, 409 U.S. 810, a one-line summary decision issued in 1972, holding the exclusion of same-sex couples from marriage did not present a substantial federal question.

Still, there are other, more instructive precedents. This Court's cases have expressed constitutional principles of broader reach. In defining the right to marry these cases have identified essential attributes of that right based in history, tradition, and other constitutional liberties inherent in this intimate bond. *See, e.g., Lawrence*, 539 U. S., at 574; *Turner, supra*, at 95; *Zablocki, supra*, at 384; *Loving, supra*, at 12; *Griswold, supra*, at 486. And in assessing whether the force and rationale of its cases apply to same-sex couples, the Court must respect the basic reasons why the right to marry has been long protected. *See, e.g., Eisenstadt, supra*, at 453–454; *Poe, supra*, at 542–553 (HARLAN, J., dissenting).

This analysis compels the conclusion that same-sex couples may exercise the right to marry. The four principles and traditions to be discussed demonstrate that the reasons marriage is fundamental under the Constitution apply with equal force to same-sex couples.

A first premise of the Court's relevant precedents is that the right to personal choice regarding marriage is inherent in the concept of individual autonomy. This abiding connection between marriage and liberty is why *Loving* invalidated interracial marriage bans under the Due Process Clause. *See* 388 U. S., at 12; *see also Zablocki, supra*, at 384 (observing *Loving* held "the right to marry is of fundamental importance for all individuals"). Like choices concerning contraception, family relationships, procreation, and childrearing, all of which are protected by the Constitution, decisions concerning marriage are among the most intimate that an individual can make. *See Lawrence, supra*, at 574. Indeed, the Court has noted it would be contradictory "to recognize a right of privacy with respect to other matters of family life and not with respect to the decision to enter the relationship that is the foundation of the family in our society." *Zablocki, supra*, at 386.

Choices about marriage shape an individual's destiny. As the Supreme Judicial Court of Massachusetts has explained, because "it fulfils yearnings for security, safe haven, and connection that express our common humanity, civil marriage is an esteemed institution, and the decision whether and whom to marry is among life's momentous acts of self-definition." *Goodridge*, 798 N.E.2d, at 955.

The nature of marriage is that, through its enduring bond, two persons together can find other freedoms, such as expression, intimacy, and spirituality. This is true for all persons, whatever their sexual orientation. *See Windsor*, 570 U.S., at ___. There is dignity in the bond between two men or two women who seek to marry and in their autonomy to make such profound choices. *Cf. Loving, supra,* at 12 ("[T]he freedom to marry, or not marry, a person of another race resides with the individual and cannot be infringed by the State").

A second principle in this Court's jurisprudence is that the right to marry is fundamental because it supports a two-person union unlike any other in its importance to the committed individuals. This point was central to *Griswold v. Connecticut*, which held the Constitution protects the right of married couples to use contraception. Suggesting that marriage is a right "older than the Bill of Rights," *Griswold* described marriage this way:

> "Marriage is a coming together for better or for worse, hopefully enduring, and intimate to the degree of being sacred. It is an association that promotes a way of life, not causes; a harmony in living, not political faiths; a bilateral loyalty, not commercial or social projects. Yet it is an association for as noble a purpose as any involved in our prior decisions."

And in *Turner*, the Court again acknowledged the intimate association protected by this right, holding prisoners could not be denied the right to marry because their committed relationships satisfied the basic reasons why marriage is a fundamental right. The right to marry thus dignifies couples who "wish to define themselves by their commitment to each other." *Windsor, supra,* at ___. Marriage responds to the universal fear that a lonely person might call out only to find no one there. It offers the hope of companionship and understanding and assurance that while both still live there will be someone to care for the other.

As this Court held in *Lawrence*, same-sex couples have the same right as opposite-sex couples to enjoy intimate association. *Lawrence* invalidated laws that made same-sex intimacy a *criminal* act. And it acknowledged that "[w]hen sexuality finds overt expression in intimate conduct with another person, the conduct can be but one element in a personal bond that is more enduring." 539 U.S., at 567. But while *Lawrence* confirmed a dimension of freedom that allows individuals to engage in intimate association without criminal liability, it does not follow that freedom stops there. Outlaw to outcast may be a step forward, but it does not achieve the full promise of liberty.

A third basis for protecting the right to marry is that it safeguards children and families and thus draws meaning from related rights of childrearing, procreation, and education. *See Pierce v. Society of Sisters*, 268 U.S. 510 (1925); *Meyer*, 262 U. S., at 399. The Court has recognized these connections by describing the varied rights as a unified whole: "[T]he right to 'marry, establish a home and bring up children' is a central part of the liberty protected by the Due Process Clause." *Zablocki*, 434 U.S., at 384. Under the laws of the several States, some of marriage's protections for children and families are material. But marriage also confers more profound benefits. By giving recognition and legal structure to their parents' relationship, marriage allows children "to understand the integrity and closeness of their own family and its concord with other families in their community and in their daily lives." *Windsor, supra*, at ___. Marriage also affords the permanency and stability important to children's best interests. *See* Brief for Scholars of the Constitutional Rights of Children as *Amici Curiae* 22–27.

As all parties agree, many same-sex couples provide loving and nurturing homes to their children, whether biological or adopted. And hundreds of thousands of children are presently being raised by such couples. *See* Brief for Gary J. Gates as *Amicus Curiae* 4. Most States have allowed gays and lesbians to adopt, either as individuals or as couples, and many adopted and foster children have same-sex parents, see *id.,* at 5. This provides powerful confirmation from the law itself that gays and lesbians can create loving, supportive families.

Excluding same-sex couples from marriage thus conflicts with a central premise of the right to marry. Without the recognition, stability, and predictability marriage offers, their children suffer the stigma of knowing their families are somehow lesser. They also suffer the significant material costs of being raised by unmarried parents, relegated through no fault of their own to a more difficult and uncertain family life. The marriage laws at issue here thus harm and humiliate the children of same-sex couples. *See Windsor, supra*, at ___.

That is not to say the right to marry is less meaningful for those who do not or cannot have children. An ability, desire, or promise to procreate is not and has not been a prerequisite for a valid marriage in any State. In light of precedent protecting the right of a married couple not to procreate, it cannot be said the Court or the States have conditioned the right to marry on the capacity or commitment to procreate. The constitutional marriage right has many aspects, of which childbearing is only one.

Fourth and finally, this Court's cases and the Nation's traditions make clear that marriage is a keystone of our social order. Alexis de Tocqueville recognized this truth on his travels through the United States almost two centuries ago:

> "There is certainly no country in the world where the tie of marriage is so much respected as in America. . . . [W]hen the American retires from the turmoil of public life to the bosom of his family, he finds in it the image of order and of peace. . . . [H]e afterwards carries [that image] with him into public affairs." 1 Democracy in America 309 (H. Reeve transl., rev. ed. 1990).

In *Maynard v. Hill*, 125 U.S. 190, 211 (1888), the Court echoed de Tocqueville, explaining that marriage is "the foundation of the family and of society, without which there would be neither civilization nor progress." Marriage, the *Maynard* Court said, has long been "'a great public institution, giving character to our whole civil polity.'" Id., at 213. This idea has been reiterated even as the institution has evolved in substantial ways over time, superseding rules related to parental consent, gender, and race once thought by many to be essential. *See generally* N. Cott, Public Vows. Marriage remains a building block of our national community.

For that reason, just as a couple vows to support each other, so does society pledge to support the couple, offering symbolic recognition and material benefits to protect and nourish the union. Indeed, while the States are in general free to vary the benefits they confer on all married couples, they have throughout our history made marriage the basis for an expanding list of governmental rights, benefits, and responsibilities. These aspects of marital status include: taxation; inheritance and property rights; rules of intestate succession; spousal privilege in the law of evidence; hospital access; medical decisionmaking authority; adoption rights; the rights and benefits of survivors; birth and death certificates; professional ethics rules; campaign finance restrictions; workers' compensation benefits; health insurance; and child custody, support, and visitation rules. *See* Brief for United States as Amicus Curiae 6–9; Brief for American Bar Association as Amicus Curiae 8–29. Valid marriage under state law is also a significant status for over a thousand provisions of federal law. *See Windsor*, 570 U. S., at ___. The States have contributed to the fundamental character of the marriage right by placing that institution at the center of so many facets of the legal and social order.

There is no difference between same- and opposite-sex couples with respect to this principle. Yet by virtue of their exclusion from that institution, same-sex couples are denied the constellation of benefits that the States have linked to marriage. This harm results in more than just material burdens. Same-sex couples are consigned to an instability many opposite-sex couples would deem intolerable in their own lives. As the State itself makes marriage all the more precious by the significance it attaches to it, exclusion from that status has the effect of teaching that gays and lesbians are unequal in important respects. It demeans gays and lesbians for the State to lock them out of a central institution of the Nation's society. Same-sex couples, too, may aspire to the transcendent purposes of marriage and seek fulfillment in its highest meaning.

The limitation of marriage to opposite-sex couples may long have seemed natural and just, but its inconsistency with the central meaning of the fundamental right to marry is now manifest. With that knowledge must come the recognition that laws excluding same-sex couples from the marriage right impose stigma and injury of the kind prohibited by our basic charter.

Objecting that this does not reflect an appropriate framing of the issue, the respondents refer to *Washington v. Glucksberg*, 521 U.S. 702, 721 (1997), which called for a " 'careful description' " of fundamental rights. They assert the petitioners do not seek to exercise the right to marry but rather a new and nonexistent "right to same-sex marriage." Brief for Respondent in No. 14–556, p. 8. *Glucksberg* did insist that liberty under the Due Process Clause must be defined in a most circumscribed manner, with central reference to specific historical practices. Yet while that approach may have been appropriate for the asserted right there involved (physician-assisted suicide), it is inconsistent with the approach this Court has used in discussing other fundamental rights, including marriage and intimacy. *Loving* did not ask about a "right to interracial marriage"; *Turner* did not ask about a "right of inmates to marry"; and *Zablocki* did not ask about a "right of fathers with unpaid child support duties to marry." Rather, each case inquired about the right to marry in its comprehensive sense, asking if there was a sufficient justification for excluding the relevant class from the right.

That principle applies here. If rights were defined by who exercised them in the past, then received practices could serve as their own continued justification and new groups could not invoke rights once denied. This Court has rejected that approach, both with respect to the right to marry and the rights of gays and lesbians. *See Loving,* 388 U.S., at 12; *Lawrence,* 539 U.S., at 566–567.

The right to marry is fundamental as a matter of history and tradition, but rights come not from ancient sources alone. They rise, too, from a better informed understanding of how constitutional imperatives define a liberty that remains urgent in our own era. Many who deem same-sex marriage to be wrong reach that conclusion based on decent and honorable religious or philosophical premises, and neither they nor their beliefs are disparaged here. But when that sincere, personal opposition becomes enacted law and public policy, the necessary consequence is to put the imprimatur of the State itself on an exclusion that soon demeans or stigmatizes those whose own liberty is then denied. Under the Constitution, same-sex couples seek in marriage the same legal treatment as opposite-sex couples, and it would disparage their choices and diminish their personhood to deny them this right.

The right of same-sex couples to marry that is part of the liberty promised by the Fourteenth Amendment is derived, too, from that Amendment's guarantee of the equal protection of the laws. The Due Process Clause and the Equal Protection Clause are connected in a profound way, though they set forth independent principles. Rights implicit in liberty and rights secured by equal protection may rest on different precepts and are not always co-extensive, yet in some instances each may be instructive as to the meaning and reach of the other. In any particular case one Clause may be thought to capture the essence of the right in a more accurate and comprehensive way, even as the two Clauses may converge in the identification and definition of the right. This interrelation of the two principles furthers our understanding of what freedom is and must become.

The Court's cases touching upon the right to marry reflect this dynamic. In *Loving* the Court invalidated a prohibition on interracial marriage under both the Equal Protection Clause and the Due Process Clause. The Court first declared the prohibition invalid because of its unequal treatment of interracial couples. It stated: "There can be no doubt that restricting the freedom to marry solely because of racial classifications violates the central meaning of the Equal Protection Clause." 388 U. S., at 12. With this link to equal protection the Court proceeded to hold the prohibition offended central precepts of liberty: "To deny this fundamental freedom on so unsupportable a basis as the racial classifications embodied in these statutes, classifications so directly subversive of the principle of equality at the heart of the Fourteenth Amendment, is surely to deprive all the State's citizens of liberty without due process of law." Ibid. The reasons why marriage is a fundamental right became more clear and compelling from a full awareness and understanding of the hurt that resulted from laws barring interracial unions. * * *

In *Lawrence* the Court acknowledged the interlocking nature of these constitutional safeguards in the context of the legal treatment of gays and lesbians. Although *Lawrence* elaborated its holding under the Due Process Clause, it acknowledged, and sought to remedy, the continuing inequality that resulted from laws making intimacy in the lives of gays and lesbians a crime against the State. *Lawrence* therefore drew upon principles of liberty and equality to define and protect the rights of gays and lesbians, holding the State "cannot demean their existence or control their destiny by making their private sexual conduct a crime."

This dynamic also applies to same-sex marriage. It is now clear that the challenged laws burden the liberty of same-sex couples, and it must be further acknowledged that they abridge central precepts of equality. Here the marriage laws enforced by the respondents are in essence unequal: same-sex couples are denied all the benefits afforded to opposite-sex couples and are barred from exercising a fundamental right. Especially against a long history of disapproval of their relationships, this denial to same-sex couples of the right to marry works a grave and continuing harm. The imposition of this disability on gays and lesbians serves to disrespect and subordinate them. And the Equal Protection Clause, like the Due Process Clause, prohibits this unjustified infringement of the fundamental right to marry. See, *e.g., Zablocki, supra,* at 383–388; *Skinner,* 316 U. S., at 541.

These considerations lead to the conclusion that the right to marry is a fundamental right inherent in the liberty of the person, and under the Due Process and Equal Protection Clauses of the Fourteenth Amendment couples of the same-sex may not be deprived of that right and that liberty. The Court now holds that same-sex couples may exercise the fundamental right to marry. No longer may this liberty be denied to them. *Baker* v. *Nelson* must be and now is overruled, and the State laws challenged by Petitioners in these cases are now held invalid to the extent they exclude same-sex couples from civil marriage on the same terms and conditions as opposite-sex couples.

IV

There may be an initial inclination in these cases to proceed with caution—to await further legislation, litigation, and debate. The respondents warn there has been insufficient democratic discourse before deciding an issue so basic as the definition of marriage. * * *

Yet there has been far more deliberation than this argument acknowledges. There have been referenda, legislative debates, and grassroots campaigns, as well as countless studies, papers, books, and other popular and scholarly writings. There has been extensive litigation in state and federal courts. Judicial opinions addressing the issue have been informed by the contentions of parties and counsel, which, in turn, reflect the more general, societal discussion of same-sex marriage and its meaning that has occurred over the past decades. As more than 100 *amici* make clear in their filings, many of the central institutions in American life—state and local governments, the military, large and small businesses, labor unions, religious organizations, law enforcement, civic groups, professional organizations, and universities—have devoted substantial attention to the question. This has led to an enhanced understanding of the issue—an understanding reflected in the arguments now presented for resolution as a matter of constitutional law.

Of course, the Constitution contemplates that democracy is the appropriate process for change, so long as that process does not abridge fundamental rights. * * *

The dynamic of our constitutional system is that individuals need not await legislative action before asserting a fundamental right. The Nation's courts are open to injured individuals who come to them to vindicate their own direct, personal stake in our basic charter. An individual can invoke a right to constitutional protection when he or she is harmed, even if the broader public disagrees and even if the legislature refuses to act. The idea of the Constitution "was to withdraw certain subjects from the vicissitudes of political controversy, to place them beyond the reach of majorities and officials and to establish them as legal principles to be applied by the courts." *West Virginia Bd. of Ed.* v. *Barnette*, 319 U.S. 624, 638 (1943). This is why "fundamental rights may not be submitted to a vote; they depend on the outcome of no elections." *Ibid.* It is of no moment whether advocates of same-sex marriage now enjoy or lack momentum in the democratic process. The issue before the Court here is the legal question whether the Constitution protects the right of same-sex couples to marry.

This is not the first time the Court has been asked to adopt a cautious approach to recognizing and protecting fundamental rights. In *Bowers*, a bare majority upheld a law criminalizing same-sex intimacy. That approach might have been viewed as a cautious endorsement of the democratic process, which had only just begun to consider the rights of gays and lesbians. Yet, in effect, *Bowers* upheld state action that denied gays and lesbians a fundamental right and caused them pain and humiliation. As evidenced by the dissents in that case, the facts and principles necessary to a correct holding were known to the *Bowers* Court. That is why *Lawrence* held *Bowers* was "not correct when it was decided." 539 U. S., at 578. Although *Bowers* was eventually repudiated in *Lawrence*, men and women were harmed in the interim, and the substantial effects of these injuries no doubt lingered long after *Bowers* was overruled. Dignitary wounds cannot always be healed with the stroke of a pen. * * *

The respondents also argue allowing same-sex couples to wed will harm marriage as an institution by leading to fewer opposite-sex marriages. This may occur, the respondents contend, because licensing same-sex marriage severs the connection between natural procreation and marriage. That argument, however, rests on a counterintuitive view of opposite-sex couple's decisionmaking processes regarding marriage and parenthood. Decisions about whether to marry and raise children are based on many personal, romantic, and practical considerations; and it is unrealistic to conclude that an opposite-sex couple would choose not to marry simply because same-sex couples may do so. *See Kitchen* v. *Herbert*, 755 F. 3d 1193, 1223 (CA10 2014) ("[I]t is wholly illogical to believe that state recognition of the love and commitment between same-sex couples will alter the most intimate and personal decisions of opposite-sex couples"). The respondents have not shown a foundation for the conclusion that allowing same-sex marriage will cause the harmful outcomes they describe. Indeed, with respect to this asserted basis for excluding same-sex couples from the right to marry, it is appropriate to observe these cases involve only the rights of two consenting adults whose marriages would pose no risk of harm to themselves or third parties.

Finally, it must be emphasized that religions, and those who adhere to religious doctrines, may continue to advocate with utmost, sincere conviction that, by divine precepts, same-sex marriage should not be condoned. The First Amendment ensures that religious organizations and persons are given proper protection as they seek to teach the principles that are so fulfilling and so central to their lives and faiths, and to their own deep aspirations to continue the family structure they have long revered. The same is true of those who oppose same-sex marriage for other reasons. In turn, those who believe allowing same-sex marriage is proper or indeed essential, whether as a matter of religious conviction or secular belief, may engage those who disagree with their view in an open and searching debate. The Constitution, however, does not permit the State to bar same-sex couples from marriage on the same terms as accorded to couples of the opposite sex.

V

These cases also present the question whether the Constitution requires States to recognize same-sex marriages validly performed out of State. * * *

The Court, in this decision, holds same-sex couples may exercise the fundamental right to marry in all States. It follows that the Court also must hold—and it now does hold—that there is no lawful basis for a State to refuse to recognize a lawful same-sex marriage performed in another State on the ground of its same-sex character.

* * *

No union is more profound than marriage, for it embodies the highest ideals of love, fidelity, devotion, sacrifice, and family. In forming a marital union, two people become something greater than once they were. As some of the petitioners in these cases demonstrate, marriage embodies a love that may endure even past death. It would misunderstand these men and women to say they disrespect the idea of marriage. Their plea is that they do respect it, respect it so deeply that they seek to find its fulfillment for themselves. Their hope is not to be condemned to live in loneliness, excluded from one of civilization's oldest institutions. They ask for equal dignity in the eyes of the law. The Constitution grants them that right.

The judgment of the Court of Appeals for the Sixth Circuit is reversed.

It is so ordered.

CHIEF JUSTICE ROBERTS, with whom JUSTICE SCALIA and JUSTICE THOMAS join, dissenting.

Petitioners make strong arguments rooted in social policy and considerations of fairness. They contend that same-sex couples should be allowed to affirm their love and commitment through marriage, just like opposite-sex couples. That position has undeniable appeal; over the past six years, voters and legislators in eleven States and the District of Columbia have revised their laws to allow marriage between two people of the same sex.

But this Court is not a legislature. Whether same-sex marriage is a good idea should be of no concern to us. Under the Constitution, judges have power to say what the law is, not what it should be. The people who ratified the Constitution authorized courts to exercise "neither force nor will but merely judgment." The Federalist No. 78, p. 465 (C. Rossiter ed. 1961) (A. Hamilton).

Although the policy arguments for extending marriage to same-sex couples may be compelling, the legal arguments for requiring such an extension are not. The fundamental right to marry does not include a right to make a State change its definition of marriage. And a State's decision to maintain the meaning of marriage that has persisted in every culture throughout human history can hardly be called irrational. In short, our Constitution does not enact any one theory of marriage. The people of a State are free to expand marriage to include same-sex couples, or to retain the historic definition.

Today, however, the Court takes the extraordinary step of ordering every State to license and recognize same-sex marriage. Many people will rejoice at this decision, and I begrudge none their celebration. But for those who believe in a government of laws, not of men, the majority's approach is deeply disheartening. Supporters of same-sex marriage have achieved considerable success persuading their fellow citizens—through the democratic process—to adopt their view. That ends today. Five lawyers have closed the debate and enacted their own vision of marriage as a matter of constitutional law. Stealing this issue from the people will for many cast a cloud over same-sex marriage, making a dramatic social change that much more difficult to accept.

The majority's decision is an act of will, not legal judgment. The right it announces has no basis in the Constitution or this Court's precedent. The majority expressly disclaims judicial "caution" and omits even a pretense of humility, openly relying on its desire to remake society according to its own "new insight" into the "nature of injustice." As a result, the Court invalidates the marriage laws of more than half the States and orders the transformation of a social institution that has formed the basis of human society for millennia, for the Kalahari Bushmen and the Han Chinese, the Carthaginians and the Aztecs. Just who do we think we are?

It can be tempting for judges to confuse our own preferences with the requirements of the law. But as this Court has been reminded throughout our history, the Constitution "is made for people of fundamentally differing views." *Lochner* v. *New York*, 198 U.S. 45, 76 (1905) (Holmes, J., dissenting). Accordingly, "courts are not concerned with the wisdom or policy of legislation." *Id.*, at 69 (Harlan, J., dissenting). The majority today neglects that restrained conception of the judicial role. It seizes for itself a question the Constitution leaves to the people, at a time when the people are engaged in a vibrant debate on that question. And it answers that question based not on neutral principles of constitutional law, but on its own "understanding of what freedom is and must become." I have no choice but to dissent.

Understand well what this dissent is about: It is not about whether, in my judgment, the institution of marriage should be changed to include same-sex couples. It is instead about whether, in our democratic republic, that decision should rest with the people acting through their elected representatives, or with five lawyers who happen to hold commissions authorizing them to resolve legal disputes according to law. The Constitution leaves no doubt about the answer.

I

Petitioners and their *amici* base their arguments on the "right to marry" and the imperative of "marriage equality." There is no serious dispute that, under our precedents, the Constitution protects a right to marry and requires States to apply their marriage laws equally. The real question in these cases is what constitutes "marriage," or—more precisely—*who decides* what constitutes "marriage"?

The majority largely ignores these questions, relegating ages of human experience with marriage to a paragraph or two. Even if history and precedent are not "the end" of these cases, *ante*, at 4, I would not "sweep away what has so long been settled" without showing greater respect for all that preceded us. *Town of Greece* v. *Galloway*, 572 U.S. ___ (2014). * * *

As the majority acknowledges, marriage "has existed for millennia and across civilizations." For all those millennia, across all those civilizations, "marriage" referred to only one relationship: the union of a man and a woman. *See* Tr. of Oral Arg. on Question 1, p. 12 (petitioners conceding that they are not aware of any society that permitted same-sex marriage before 2001). As the Court explained two Terms ago, "until recent years, . . . marriage between a man and a woman no doubt had been thought of by most people as essential to the very definition of that term and to its role and function throughout the history of civilization." *United States* v. *Windsor*, 570 U.S. (2013).

This universal definition of marriage as the union of a man and a woman is no historical coincidence. Marriage did not come about as a result of a political movement, discovery, disease, war, religious doctrine, or any other moving force of world history—and certainly not as a result of a prehistoric decision to exclude gays and lesbians. It arose in the nature of things to meet a vital need: ensuring that children are conceived by a mother and father committed to raising them in the stable conditions of a lifelong relationship.

The premises supporting this concept of marriage are so fundamental that they rarely require articulation. The human race must procreate to survive. Procreation occurs through sexual relations between a man and a woman. When sexual relations result in the conception of a child, that child's prospects are generally better if the mother and father stay together rather than going their separate ways. Therefore, for the good of children and society, sexual relations that can lead to procreation should occur only between a man and a woman committed to a lasting bond.

Society has recognized that bond as marriage. And by bestowing a respected status and material benefits on married couples, society encourages men and women to conduct sexual relations within marriage rather than without. As one prominent scholar put it, "Marriage is a socially arranged solution for the problem of getting people to stay together and care for children that the mere desire for children, and the sex that makes children possible, does not solve." J. Q. Wilson, The Marriage Problem 41 (2002). * * *

The Constitution itself says nothing about marriage, and the Framers thereby entrusted the States with "[t]he whole subject of the domestic relations of husband and wife." *Windsor*, 570 U. S., at ___. There is no dispute that every State at the founding—and every State throughout our history until a dozen years ago—defined marriage in the traditional, biologically rooted way. * * *

As the majority notes, some aspects of marriage have changed over time. Arranged marriages have largely given way to pairings based on romantic love. States have replaced coverture, the doctrine by which a married man and woman became a single legal entity, with laws that respect each participant's separate status. Racial restrictions on marriage, which "arose as an incident to slavery" to promote "White Supremacy," were repealed by many States and ultimately struck down by this Court. *Loving*, 388 U. S., at 6–7.

The majority observes that these developments "were not mere superficial changes" in marriage, but rather "worked deep transformations in its structure." They did not, however, work any transformation in the core structure of marriage as the union between a man and a woman. If you had asked a person on the street how marriage was defined, no one would ever have said, "Marriage is the union of a man and a woman, where the woman is subject to coverture." The majority may be right that the "history of marriage is one of both continuity and change," but the core meaning of marriage has endured. * * *

II

* * * The majority purports to identify four "principles and traditions" in this Court's due process precedents that support a fundamental right for same-sex couples to marry. *Ante*, at 12. In reality, however, the majority's approach has no basis in principle or tradition, except for the unprincipled tradition of judicial policymaking that characterized discredited decisions such as *Lochner* v. *New York*, 198 U.S. 45. Stripped of its shiny rhetorical gloss, the majority's argument is that the Due Process Clause gives same-sex couples a fundamental right to marry because it will be good for them and for society. If I were a legislator, I would certainly consider that view as a matter of social policy. But as a judge, I find the majority's position indefensible as a matter of constitutional law. * * *

Petitioners' "fundamental right" claim falls into the most sensitive category of constitutional adjudication. Petitioners do not contend that their States' marriage laws violate an *enumerated* constitutional right, such as the freedom of speech protected by the First Amendment. There is, after all, no "Companionship and Understanding" or "Nobility and Dignity" Clause in the Constitution. They argue instead that the laws violate a right *implied* by the Fourteenth Amendment's requirement that "liberty" may not be deprived without "due process of law."

This Court has interpreted the Due Process Clause to include a "substantive" component that protects certain liberty interests against state deprivation "no matter what process is provided." *Reno* v. *Flores*, 507 U.S. 292, 302 (1993). * * *

Allowing unelected federal judges to select which unenumerated rights rank as "fundamental"—and to strike down state laws on the basis of that determination—raises obvious concerns about the judicial role.

Our precedents have accordingly insisted that judges "exercise the utmost care" in identifying implied fundamental rights, "lest the liberty protected by the Due Process Clause be subtly transformed into the policy preferences of the Members of this Court." *Washington* v. *Glucksberg*, 521 U.S. 702, 720 (1997). * * *

Rejecting *Lochner* does not require disavowing the doctrine of implied fundamental rights, and this Court has not done so. But to avoid repeating *Lochner*'s error of converting personal preferences into constitutional mandates, our modern substantive due process cases have stressed the need for "judicial self-restraint." *Collins* v. *Harker Heights*, 503 U.S. 115, 125 (1992). Our precedents have required that implied fundamental rights be "objectively, deeply rooted in this Nation's history and tradition," and "implicit in the concept of ordered liberty, such that neither liberty nor justice would exist if they were sacrificed." *Glucksberg*, 521 U. S., at 720–721.

Although the Court articulated the importance of history and tradition to the fundamental rights inquiry most precisely in *Glucksberg*, many other cases both before and after have adopted the same approach. * * *

Neither *Lawrence* nor any other precedent in the privacy line of cases supports the right that petitioners assert here. Unlike criminal laws banning contraceptives and sodomy, the marriage laws at issue here involve no government intrusion. They create no crime and impose no punishment. Same-sex couples remain free to live together, to engage in intimate conduct, and to raise their families as they see fit. No one is "condemned to live in loneliness" by the laws challenged in these cases— no one. At the same time, the laws in no way interfere with the "right to be let alone."

* * * [T]he privacy cases provide no support for the majority's position, because petitioners do not seek privacy. Quite the opposite, they seek public recognition of their relationships, along with corresponding government benefits. Our cases have consistently refused to allow litigants to convert the shield provided by constitutional liberties into a sword to demand positive entitlements from the State. Thus, although the right to privacy recognized by our precedents certainly plays a role in protecting the intimate conduct of same-sex couples, it provides no affirmative right to redefine marriage and no basis for striking down the laws at issue here. * * *

Perhaps recognizing how little support it can derive from precedent, the majority goes out of its way to jettison the "careful" approach to implied fundamental rights taken by this Court in *Glucksberg*. It is revealing that the majority's position requires it to effectively overrule *Glucksberg*, the leading modern case setting the bounds of substantive due process. At least this part of the majority opinion has the virtue of candor. Nobody could rightly accuse the majority of taking a careful approach.

Ultimately, only one precedent offers any support for the majority's methodology: *Lochner* v. *New York*, 198 U.S. 45. The majority opens its opinion by announcing petitioners' right to "define and express their identity." The majority later explains that "the right to personal choice regarding marriage is inherent in the concept of individual autonomy." This freewheeling notion of individual autonomy echoes nothing so much as "the general right of an individual to be *free in his person* and in his power to contract in relation to his own labor." *Lochner*, 198 U. S., at 58 (emphasis added). * * *

One immediate question invited by the majority's position is whether States may retain the definition of marriage as a union of two people. Cf. *Brown* v. *Buhman*, 947 F. Supp. 2d 1170 (Utah 2013), appeal pending, No. 14–4117 (CA10). Although the majority randomly inserts the adjective "two" in various places, it offers no reason at all why the two-person element of the core definition of marriage may be preserved while the man-woman element may not. Indeed, from the standpoint of history and tradition, a leap from opposite-sex marriage to same-sex marriage is much greater than one from a two-person union to plural unions, which have deep roots in some cultures around the world. If the majority is willing to take the big leap, it is hard to see how it can say no to the shorter one.

It is striking how much of the majority's reasoning would apply with equal force to the claim of a fundamental right to plural marriage. If "[t]here is dignity in the bond between two men or two women who seek to marry and in their autonomy to make such profound choices," why would there be any less dignity in the bond between three people who, in exercising their autonomy, seek to make the profound choice to marry? If a same-sex couple has the constitutional right to marry because their children would otherwise "suffer the stigma of knowing their families are somehow lesser," why wouldn't the same reasoning apply to a family of three or more persons raising children? If not having the opportunity to marry "serves to disrespect and subordinate" gay and lesbian couples, why wouldn't the same "imposition of this disability," serve to disrespect and subordinate people who find fulfillment in polyamorous relationships? *See* Bennett, Polyamory: The Next Sexual Revolution? Newsweek, July 28, 2009 (estimating 500,000 polyamorous families in the United States); Li, Married Lesbian "Throuple" Expecting First Child, N.Y. Post, Apr. 23, 2014; Otter, Three May Not Be a Crowd: The Case for a Constitutional Right to Plural Marriage, 64 Emory L. J. 1977 (2015).

I do not mean to equate marriage between same-sex couples with plural marriages in all respects. There may well be relevant differences that compel different legal analysis. But if there are, petitioners have not pointed to any. When asked about a plural marital union at oral argument, petitioners asserted that a State "doesn't have such an institution." But that is exactly the point: the States at issue here do not have an institution of same-sex marriage, either. * * *

III

In addition to their due process argument, petitioners contend that the Equal Protection Clause requires their States to license and recognize same-sex marriages. The majority does not seriously engage with this claim. Its discussion is, quite frankly, difficult to follow. The central point seems to be that there is a "synergy between" the Equal Protection Clause and the Due Process Clause, and that some precedents relying on one Clause have also relied on the other. *Ante*, at 20. Absent from this portion of the opinion, however, is anything resembling our usual framework for deciding equal protection cases. It is casebook doctrine that the "modern Supreme Court's treatment of equal protection claims has used a means-ends methodology in which judges ask whether the classification the government is using is sufficiently related to the goals it is pursuing." G. Stone, L. Seidman, C. Sunstein, M. Tushnet, & P. Karlan, Constitutional Law 453 (7th ed. 2013). The majority's approach today is different[.] * * *

The majority goes on to assert in conclusory fashion that the Equal Protection Clause provides an alternative basis for its holding. Yet the majority fails to provide even a single sentence explaining how the Equal Protection Clause supplies independent weight for its position, nor does it attempt to justify its gratuitous violation of the canon against unnecessarily resolving constitutional questions. In any event, the marriage laws at issue here do not violate the Equal Protection Clause, because distinguishing between opposite-sex and same-sex couples is rationally related to the States' "legitimate state interest" in "preserving the traditional institution of marriage." *Lawrence*, 539 U.S., at 585 (O'Connor, J., concurring in judgment).

It is important to note with precision which laws petitioners have challenged. Although they discuss some of the ancillary legal benefits that accompany marriage, such as hospital visitation rights and recognition of spousal status on official documents, petitioners' lawsuits target the laws defining marriage generally rather than those allocating benefits specifically. The equal protection analysis might be different, in my view, if we were confronted with a more focused challenge to the denial of certain tangible benefits. Of course, those more selective claims will not arise now that the Court has taken the drastic step of requiring every State to license and recognize marriages between same-sex couples.

IV

* * * Those who founded our country would not recognize the majority's conception of the judicial role. They after all risked their lives and fortunes for the precious right to govern themselves. They would never have imagined yielding that right on a question of social policy to unaccountable and unelected judges. And they certainly would not have been satisfied by a system empowering judges to override policy judgments so long as they do so after "a quite extensive discussion." *Ante*, at 8. In our democracy, debate about the content of the law is not an exhaustion requirement to be checked off before courts can impose their will. * * *

When decisions are reached through democratic means, some people will inevitably be disappointed with the results. But those whose views do not prevail at least know that they have had their say, and accordingly are—in the tradition of our political culture—reconciled to the result of a fair and honest debate. In addition, they can gear up to raise the issue later, hoping to persuade enough on the winning side to think again. "That is exactly how our system of government is supposed to work." *Post*, at 2–3 (Scalia, J., dissenting).

But today the Court puts a stop to all that. By deciding this question under the Constitution, the Court removes it from the realm of democratic decision. There will be consequences to shutting down the political process on an issue of such profound public significance. Closing debate tends to close minds. People denied a voice are less likely to accept the ruling of a court on an issue that does not seem to be the sort of thing courts usually decide. As a thoughtful commentator observed about another issue, "The political process was moving . . . , not swiftly enough for advocates of quick, complete change, but majoritarian institutions were listening and acting. Heavy-handed judicial intervention was difficult to justify and appears to have provoked, not resolved, conflict." Ginsburg, Some Thoughts on Autonomy and Equality in Relation to *Roe v. Wade*, 63 N. C. L. Rev. 375, 385–386 (1985). Indeed, however heartened the proponents of same-sex marriage might be on this day, it is worth acknowledging what they have lost, and lost forever: the opportunity to win the true acceptance that comes from persuading their fellow citizens of the justice of their cause. And they lose this just when the winds of change were freshening at their backs.

Federal courts are blunt instruments when it comes to creating rights. They have constitutional power only to resolve concrete cases or controversies; they do not have the flexibility of legislatures to address concerns of parties not before the court or to anticipate problems that may arise from the exercise of a new right. Today's decision, for example, creates serious questions about religious liberty. Many good and decent people oppose same-sex marriage as a tenet of faith, and their freedom to exercise religion is—unlike the right imagined by the majority—actually spelled out in the Constitution. Amdt. 1.

Respect for sincere religious conviction has led voters and legislators in every State that has adopted same-sex marriage democratically to include accommodations for religious practice. The majority's decision imposing same-sex marriage cannot, of course, create any such accommodations. The majority graciously suggests that religious believers may continue to "advocate" and "teach" their views of marriage. The First Amendment guarantees, however, the freedom to *exercise* religion. Ominously, that is not a word the majority uses.

Hard questions arise when people of faith exercise religion in ways that may be seen to conflict with the new right to same-sex marriage— when, for example, a religious college provides married student housing only to opposite-sex married couples, or a religious adoption agency declines to place children with same-sex married couples. Indeed, the Solicitor General candidly acknowledged that the tax exemptions of some religious institutions would be in question if they opposed same-sex marriage. There is little doubt that these and similar questions will soon be before this Court. Unfortunately, people of faith can take no comfort in the treatment they receive from the majority today.

Perhaps the most discouraging aspect of today's decision is the extent to which the majority feels compelled to sully those on the other side of the debate. The majority offers a cursory assurance that it does not intend to disparage people who, as a matter of conscience, cannot accept same-sex marriage. That disclaimer is hard to square with the very next sentence, in which the majority explains that "the necessary consequence" of laws codifying the traditional definition of marriage is to "demea[n] or stigmatiz[e]" same-sex couples. The majority reiterates such characterizations over and over. By the majority's account, Americans who did nothing more than follow the understanding of marriage that has existed for our entire history—in particular, the tens of millions of people who voted to reaffirm their States' enduring definition of marriage—have acted to "lock . . . out," "disparage," "disrespect and subordinate," and inflict "[d]ignitary wounds" upon their gay and lesbian neighbors. These apparent assaults on the character of fairminded people will have an effect, in society and in court. *See post*, at 6–7 (Alito, J., dissenting). Moreover, they are entirely gratuitous. It is one thing for the majority to conclude that the Constitution protects a right to same-sex marriage; it is something else to portray everyone who does not share the majority's "better informed understanding" as bigoted.

In the face of all this, a much different view of the Court's role is possible. That view is more modest and restrained. It is more skeptical that the legal abilities of judges also reflect insight into moral and philosophical issues. It is more sensitive to the fact that judges are unelected and unaccountable, and that the legitimacy of their power depends on confining it to the exercise of legal judgment. It is more attuned to the lessons of history, and what it has meant for the country and Court when Justices have exceeded their proper bounds. And it is less pretentious than to suppose that while people around the world have viewed an institution in a particular way for thousands of years, the present generation and the present Court are the ones chosen to burst the bonds of that history and tradition.

* * *

If you are among the many Americans—of whatever sexual orientation—who favor expanding same-sex marriage, by all means celebrate today's decision. Celebrate the achievement of a desired goal. Celebrate the opportunity for a new expression of commitment to a partner. Celebrate the availability of new benefits. But do not celebrate the Constitution. It had nothing to do with it.

I respectfully dissent.

JUSTICE SCALIA, with whom JUSTICE THOMAS joins, dissenting.

Scalia Dissent

* * * The substance of today's decree is not of immense personal importance to me. The law can recognize as marriage whatever sexual attachments and living arrangements it wishes, and can accord them favorable civil consequences, from tax treatment to rights of inheritance. Those civil consequences—and the public approval that conferring the name of marriage evidences—can perhaps have adverse social effects, but no more adverse than the effects of many other controversial laws. So it is not of special importance to me what the law says about marriage. It is of overwhelming importance, however, who it is that rules me. Today's decree says that my Ruler, and the Ruler of 320 million Americans coast-to-coast, is a majority of the nine lawyers on the Supreme Court. The opinion in these cases is the furthest extension in fact—and the furthest extension one can even imagine—of the Court's claimed power to create "liberties" that the Constitution and its Amendments neglect to mention. This practice of constitutional revision by an unelected committee of nine, always accompanied (as it is today) by extravagant praise of liberty, robs the People of the most important liberty they asserted in the Declaration of Independence and won in the Revolution of 1776: the freedom to govern themselves.

I

Until the courts put a stop to it, public debate over same-sex marriage displayed American democracy at its best. Individuals on both sides of the issue passionately, but respectfully, attempted to persuade

democratic system

their fellow citizens to accept their views. Americans considered the arguments and put the question to a vote. The electorates of 11 States, either directly or through their representatives, chose to expand the traditional definition of marriage. Many more decided not to. Win or lose, advocates for both sides continued pressing their cases, secure in the knowledge that an electoral loss can be negated by a later electoral win. That is exactly how our system of government is supposed to work.

The Constitution places some constraints on self-rule—constraints adopted *by the People themselves* when they ratified the Constitution and its Amendments. Forbidden are laws "impairing the Obligation of Contracts," denying "Full Faith and Credit" to the "public Acts" of other States, prohibiting the free exercise of religion, abridging the freedom of speech, infringing the right to keep and bear arms, authorizing unreasonable searches and seizures, and so forth. Aside from these limitations, those powers "reserved to the States respectively, or to the people" can be exercised as the States or the People desire. These cases ask us to decide whether the Fourteenth Amendment contains a limitation that requires the States to license and recognize marriages between two people of the same sex. Does it remove *that* issue from the political process?

Of course not. It would be surprising to find a prescription regarding marriage in the Federal Constitution since, as the author of today's opinion reminded us only two years ago (in an opinion joined by the same Justices who join him today):

> "[R]egulation of domestic relations is an area that has long been regarded as a virtually exclusive province of the States."

> "[T]he Federal Government, through our history, has deferred to state-law policy decisions with respect to domestic relations."

But we need not speculate. When the Fourteenth Amendment was ratified in 1868, every State limited marriage to one man and one woman, and no one doubted the constitutionality of doing so. That resolves these cases. When it comes to determining the meaning of a vague constitutional provision—such as "due process of law" or "equal protection of the laws"—it is unquestionable that the People who ratified that provision did not understand it to prohibit a practice that remained both universal and uncontroversial in the years after ratification. We have no basis for striking down a practice that is not expressly prohibited by the Fourteenth Amendment's text, and that bears the endorsement of a long tradition of open, widespread, and unchallenged use dating back to the Amendment's ratification. Since there is no doubt whatever that the People never decided to prohibit the limitation of marriage to opposite-sex couples, the public debate over same-sex marriage must be allowed to continue.

But the Court ends this debate, in an opinion lacking even a thin veneer of law. Buried beneath the mummeries and straining-to-be-memorable passages of the opinion is a candid and startling assertion: No matter *what* it was the People ratified, the Fourteenth Amendment protects those rights that the Judiciary, in its "reasoned judgment," thinks the Fourteenth Amendment ought to protect. That is so because "[t]he generations that wrote and ratified the Bill of Rights and the Fourteenth Amendment did not presume to know the extent of freedom in all of its dimensions. . . ." One would think that sentence would continue: " . . . and therefore they provided for a means by which the People could amend the Constitution," or perhaps " . . . and therefore they left the creation of additional liberties, such as the freedom to marry someone of the same sex, to the People, through the never-ending process of legislation." But no. What logically follows, in the majority's judge-empowering estimation, is: "and so they entrusted to future generations a charter protecting the right of all persons to enjoy liberty as we learn its meaning." The "we," needless to say, is the nine of us. "History and tradition guide and discipline [our] inquiry but do not set its outer boundaries." Thus, rather than focusing on *the People's* understanding of "liberty"—at the time of ratification or even today—the majority focuses on four "principles and traditions" that, *in the majority's view*, prohibit States from defining marriage as an institution consisting of one man and one woman.

This is a naked judicial claim to legislative—indeed, *super-legislative*—power; a claim fundamentally at odds with our system of government. Except as limited by a constitutional prohibition agreed to by the People, the States are free to adopt whatever laws they like, even those that offend the esteemed Justices' "reasoned judgment." A system of government that makes the People subordinate to a committee of nine unelected lawyers does not deserve to be called a democracy.

Judges are selected precisely for their skill as lawyers; whether they reflect the policy views of a particular constituency is not (or should not be) relevant. Not surprisingly then, the Federal Judiciary is hardly a cross-section of America. Take, for example, this Court, which consists of only nine men and women, all of them successful lawyers who studied at Harvard or Yale Law School. Four of the nine are natives of New York City. Eight of them grew up in east- and west-coast States. Only one hails from the vast expanse in-between. Not a single Southwesterner or even, to tell the truth, a genuine Westerner (California does not count). Not a single evangelical Christian (a group that comprises about one quarter of Americans), or even a Protestant of any denomination. The strikingly unrepresentative character of the body voting on today's social upheaval would be irrelevant if they were functioning as *judges*, answering the legal question whether the American people had ever ratified a constitutional provision that was understood to proscribe the traditional definition of marriage. But of course the Justices in today's majority are not voting on that basis; *they say they are not*. And to allow the policy question of same-sex marriage to be considered and resolved by a select, patrician, highly unrepresentative panel of nine is to violate a principle even more fundamental than no taxation without representation: no social transformation without representation.

II

But what really astounds is the hubris reflected in today's judicial Putsch. The five Justices who compose today's majority are entirely comfortable concluding that every State violated the Constitution for all of the 135 years between the Fourteenth Amendment's ratification and Massachusetts' permitting of same-sex marriages in 2003. They have discovered in the Fourteenth Amendment a "fundamental right" overlooked by every person alive at the time of ratification, and almost everyone else in the time since. They see what lesser legal minds—minds like Thomas Cooley, John Marshall Harlan, Oliver Wendell Holmes, Jr., Learned Hand, Louis Brandeis, William Howard Taft, Benjamin Cardozo, Hugo Black, Felix Frankfurter, Robert Jackson, and Henry Friendly—could not. They are certain that the People ratified the Fourteenth Amendment to bestow on them the power to remove questions from the democratic process when that is called for by their "reasoned judgment." These Justices know that limiting marriage to one man and one woman is contrary to reason; they know that an institution as old as government itself, and accepted by every nation in history until 15 years ago, cannot possibly be supported by anything other than ignorance or bigotry. And they are willing to say that any citizen who does not agree with that, who adheres to what was, until 15 years ago, the unanimous judgment of all generations and all societies, stands against the Constitution.

The opinion is couched in a style that is as pretentious as its content is egotistic. It is one thing for separate concurring or dissenting opinions to contain extravagances, even silly extravagances, of thought and expression; it is something else for the official opinion of the Court to do so.[22] Of course the opinion's showy profundities are often profoundly incoherent. "The nature of marriage is that, through its enduring bond, two persons together can find other freedoms, such as expression, intimacy, and spirituality." (Really? Who ever thought that intimacy and spirituality [whatever that means] were freedoms? And if intimacy is, one would think Freedom of Intimacy is abridged rather than expanded by

---

[22]   If, even as the price to be paid for a fifth vote, I ever joined an opinion for the Court that began: "The Constitution promises liberty to all within its reach, a liberty that includes certain specific rights that allow persons, within a lawful realm, to define and express their identity," I would hide my head in a bag. The Supreme Court of the United States has descended from the disciplined legal reasoning of John Marshall and Joseph Story to the mystical aphorisms of the fortune cookie.

marriage. Ask the nearest hippie. Expression, sure enough, *is* a freedom, but anyone in a long-lasting marriage will attest that that happy state constricts, rather than expands, what one can prudently say.) Rights, we are told, can "rise ... from a better informed understanding of how constitutional imperatives define a liberty that remains urgent in our own era." (Huh? How can a better informed understanding of how constitutional imperatives [whatever that means] define [whatever that means] an urgent liberty [never mind], give birth to a right?) And we are told that, "[i]n any particular case," either the Equal Protection or Due Process Clause "may be thought to capture the essence of [a] right in a more accurate and comprehensive way," than the other, "even as the two Clauses may converge in the identification and definition of the right." (What say? What possible "essence" does substantive due process "capture" in an "accurate and comprehensive way"? It stands for nothing whatever, except those freedoms and entitlements that this Court *really* likes. And the Equal Protection Clause, as employed today, identifies nothing except a difference in treatment that this Court *really* dislikes. Hardly a distillation of essence. If the opinion is correct that the two clauses "converge in the identification and definition of [a] right," that is only because the majority's likes and dislikes are predictably compatible.) I could go on. The world does not expect logic and precision in poetry or inspirational pop-philosophy; it demands them in the law. The stuff contained in today's opinion has to diminish this Court's reputation for clear thinking and sober analysis.

* * *

Hubris is sometimes defined as o'erweening pride; and pride, we know, goeth before a fall. The Judiciary is the "least dangerous" of the federal branches because it has "neither Force nor Will, but merely judgment; and must ultimately depend upon the aid of the executive arm" and the States, "even for the efficacy of its judgments." With each decision of ours that takes from the People a question properly left to them—with each decision that is unabashedly based not on law, but on the "reasoned judgment" of a bare majority of this Court—we move one step closer to being reminded of our impotence.

JUSTICE THOMAS, with whom JUSTICE SCALIA joins, dissenting.

The Court's decision today is at odds not only with the Constitution, but with the principles upon which our Nation was built. Since well before 1787, liberty has been understood as freedom from government action, not entitlement to government benefits. The Framers created our Constitution to preserve that understanding of liberty. Yet the majority invokes our Constitution in the name of a "liberty" that the Framers would not have recognized, to the detriment of the liberty they sought to protect. Along the way, it rejects the idea—captured in our Declaration of

Independence—that human dignity is innate and suggests instead that it comes from the Government. This distortion of our Constitution not only ignores the text, it inverts the relationship between the individual and the state in our Republic. I cannot agree with it.

* * * Even if the doctrine of substantive due process were somehow defensible—it is not—petitioners still would not have a claim. To invoke the protection of the Due Process Clause at all—whether under a theory of "substantive" or "procedural" due process—a party must first identify a deprivation of "life, liberty, or property." The majority claims these state laws deprive petitioners of "liberty," but the concept of "liberty" it conjures up bears no resemblance to any plausible meaning of that word as it is used in the Due Process Clauses.

* * * As used in the Due Process Clauses, "liberty" most likely refers to "the power of loco-motion, of changing situation, or removing one's person to whatsoever place one's own inclination may direct; without imprisonment or restraint, unless by due course of law." 1 W. Blackstone, Commentaries on the Laws of England 130 (1769) (Blackstone). That definition is drawn from the historical roots of the Clauses and is consistent with our Constitution's text and structure. * * *

Even assuming that the "liberty" in those Clauses encompasses something more than freedom from physical restraint, it would not include the types of rights claimed by the majority. In the American legal tradition, liberty has long been understood as individual freedom *from* governmental action, not as a right *to* a particular governmental entitlement. * * *

Whether we define "liberty" as locomotion or freedom from governmental action more broadly, petitioners have in no way been deprived of it.

Petitioners cannot claim, under the most plausible definition of "liberty," that they have been imprisoned or physically restrained by the States for participating in same-sex relationships. To the contrary, they have been able to cohabitate and raise their children in peace. They have been able to hold civil marriage ceremonies in States that recognize same-sex marriages and private religious ceremonies in all States. They have been able to travel freely around the country, making their homes where they please. Far from being incarcerated or physically restrained, petitioners have been left alone to order their lives as they see fit.

Nor, under the broader definition, can they claim that the States have restricted their ability to go about their daily lives as they would be able to absent governmental restrictions. Petitioners do not ask this Court to order the States to stop restricting their ability to enter same-sex relationships, to engage in intimate behavior, to make vows to their partners in public ceremonies, to engage in religious wedding ceremonies, to hold themselves out as married, or to raise children. The States have imposed no such restrictions. Nor have the States prevented petitioners from approximating a number of incidents of marriage through private legal means, such as wills, trusts, and powers of attorney. * * *

Petitioners' misconception of liberty carries over into their discussion of our precedents identifying a right to marry, not one of which has expanded the concept of "liberty" beyond the concept of negative liberty. Those precedents all involved absolute prohibitions on private actions associated with marriage. *Loving*, for example, involved a couple who was criminally prosecuted for marrying in the District of Columbia and cohabiting in Virginia. They were each sentenced to a year of imprisonment, suspended for a term of 25 years on the condition that they not reenter the Commonwealth together during that time. In a similar vein, *Zablocki* involved a man who was prohibited, on pain of criminal penalty, from "marry[ing] in Wisconsin or elsewhere" because of his outstanding child-support obligations. And *Turner* involved state inmates who were prohibited from entering marriages without the permission of the superintendent of the prison, permission that could not be granted absent compelling reasons. In *none* of those cases were individuals denied solely governmental recognition and benefits associated with marriage.

* * * Numerous *amici*—even some not supporting the States—have cautioned the Court that its decision here will "have unavoidable and wide-ranging implications for religious liberty." Brief for General Conference of Seventh-Day Adventists et al. as *Amici Curiae* 5. In our society, marriage is not simply a governmental institution; it is a religious institution as well. Today's decision might change the former, but it cannot change the latter. It appears all but inevitable that the two will come into conflict, particularly as individuals and churches are confronted with demands to participate in and endorse civil marriages between same-sex couples.

The majority appears unmoved by that inevitability. It makes only a weak gesture toward religious liberty in a single paragraph. And even that gesture indicates a misunderstanding of religious liberty in our Nation's tradition. Religious liberty is about more than just the protection for "religious organizations and persons . . . as they seek to teach the principles that are so fulfilling and so central to their lives and faiths." Religious liberty is about freedom of action in matters of religion generally, and the scope of that liberty is directly correlated to the civil restraints placed upon religious practice.

Although our Constitution provides some protection against such governmental restrictions on religious practices, the People have long elected to afford broader protections than this Court's constitutional precedents mandate. Had the majority allowed the definition of marriage to be left to the political process—as the Constitution requires—the People could have considered the religious liberty implications of deviating from the traditional definition as part of their deliberative process. Instead, the majority's decision short-circuits that process, with potentially ruinous consequences for religious liberty. * * *

JUSTICE ALITO, with whom JUSTICE SCALIA and JUSTICE THOMAS join, dissenting.

Until the federal courts intervened, the American people were engaged in a debate about whether their States should recognize same-sex marriage. The question in these cases, however, is not what States *should* do about same-sex marriage but whether the Constitution answers that question for them. It does not. The Constitution leaves that question to be decided by the people of each State.

I

The Constitution says nothing about a right to same-sex marriage, but the Court holds that the term "liberty" in the Due Process Clause of the Fourteenth Amendment encompasses this right. * * *

To prevent five unelected Justices from imposing their personal vision of liberty upon the American people, the Court has held that "liberty" under the Due Process Clause should be understood to protect only those rights that are " 'deeply rooted in this Nation's history and tradition.' " *Washington* v. *Glucksberg*, 521 U.S. 701, 720–721 (1997). And it is beyond dispute that the right to same-sex marriage is not among those rights. *See United States* v. *Windsor*, 570 U.S. (2013) (Alito, J., dissenting). * * *

For today's majority, it does not matter that the right to same-sex marriage lacks deep roots or even that it is contrary to long-established tradition. The Justices in the majority claim the authority to confer constitutional protection upon that right simply because they believe that it is fundamental.

II

Attempting to circumvent the problem presented by the newness of the right found in these cases, the majority claims that the issue is the right to equal treatment. Noting that marriage is a fundamental right, the majority argues that a State has no valid reason for denying that right to same-sex couples. This reasoning is dependent upon a particular understanding of the purpose of civil marriage. Although the Court expresses the point in loftier terms, its argument is that the fundamental purpose of marriage is to promote the well-being of those who choose to marry. Marriage provides emotional fulfillment and the promise of support in times of need. And by benefiting persons who choose to wed, marriage indirectly benefits society because persons who live in stable, fulfilling, and supportive relationships make better citizens. It is for these reasons, the argument goes, that States encourage and formalize marriage, confer special benefits on married persons, and also impose some special obligations. This understanding of the States' reasons for recognizing marriage enables the majority to argue that same-sex marriage serves the States' objectives in the same way as opposite-sex marriage.

This understanding of marriage, which focuses almost entirely on the happiness of persons who choose to marry, is shared by many people today, but it is not the traditional one. For millennia, marriage was inextricably linked to the one thing that only an opposite-sex couple can do: procreate.

Adherents to different schools of philosophy use different terms to explain why society should formalize marriage and attach special benefits and obligations to persons who marry. Here, the States defending their adherence to the traditional understanding of marriage have explained their position using the pragmatic vocabulary that characterizes most American political discourse. Their basic argument is that States formalize and promote marriage, unlike other fulfilling human relationships, in order to encourage potentially procreative conduct to take place within a lasting unit that has long been thought to provide the best atmosphere for raising children. They thus argue that there are reasonable secular grounds for restricting marriage to opposite-sex couples.

If this traditional understanding of the purpose of marriage does not ring true to all ears today, that is probably because the tie between marriage and procreation has frayed. Today, for instance, more than 40% of all children in this country are born to unmarried women. This development undoubtedly is both a cause and a result of changes in our society's understanding of marriage.

While, for many, the attributes of marriage in 21st-century America have changed, those States that do not want to recognize same-sex marriage have not yet given up on the traditional understanding. They worry that by officially abandoning the older understanding, they may contribute to marriage's further decay. It is far beyond the outer reaches of this Court's authority to say that a State may not adhere to the understanding of marriage that has long prevailed, not just in this country and others with similar cultural roots, but also in a great variety of countries and cultures all around the globe. * * *

III

Today's decision usurps the constitutional right of the people to decide whether to keep or alter the traditional understanding of marriage. The decision will also have other important consequences.

It will be used to vilify Americans who are unwilling to assent to the new orthodoxy. In the course of its opinion, the majority compares traditional marriage laws to laws that denied equal treatment for African-Americans and women. The implications of this analogy will be exploited by those who are determined to stamp out every vestige of dissent.

Perhaps recognizing how its reasoning may be used, the majority attempts, toward the end of its opinion, to reassure those who oppose same-sex marriage that their rights of conscience will be protected. We will soon see whether this proves to be true. I assume that those who cling to old beliefs will be able to whisper their thoughts in the recesses of their homes, but if they repeat those views in public, they will risk being labeled as bigots and treated as such by governments, employers, and schools. * * *

NOTES

1. As you have already seen, the claim to marriage equality has been based on theories of both substantive due process and equal protection. Justice Kennedy focuses most centrally on substantive due process, finding that same-sex couples have a fundamental right to marry. Why do you think Justice Kennedy focuses on substantive due process, instead of basing his ruling primarily on equal protection, as he did in *Romer* and *Windsor*?

2. In explaining why the fundamental right to marry applies to same-sex couples, how does Justice Kennedy conceptualize marriage? What view of marriage does Justice Alito take in dissent? Does Justice Alito accurately characterize the majority's view of marriage?

3. Both Chief Justice Roberts and Justice Thomas point out that the petitioners were not complaining of improper governmental intrusion into their lives. They also argue that the Court's relevant due process precedents have been generally limited to the right to privacy and "to be left alone." Does Justice Kennedy respond to this line of reasoning? Does the fundamental right to marry recognized in *Loving, Zablocki*, and *Turner* impose a duty on the government to act affirmatively (rather than simply "leaving individuals alone")? How does Justice Thomas distinguish those three cases?

4. Even as substantive due process is central in the Court's decision, Justice Kennedy also relies on equal protection. How does his reasoning about equality compare to his approach in *Windsor*? Why is animus not a significant concept in the equal protection analysis in *Obergefell*? Does

Justice Kennedy focus more on discriminatory intent or discriminatory effect? Why does it matter?

5.   What level of scrutiny does the Court apply to the state marriage bans? The Court holds that same-sex couples have a fundamental right to marry. Does it then apply strict scrutiny? Does it analyze the governmental interests put forward in defense of the laws? The Court also holds that the marriage laws violate equal protection. Does it apply heightened scrutiny to laws that discriminate based on sexual orientation? After *Obergefell*, what level of scrutiny should lower federal courts apply to classifications based on sexual orientation?

6.   As he did in earlier decisions, Justice Kennedy invokes the dignity of LGBT people. What doctrinal and conceptual role does dignity play in the opinion? In dissent, Justice Thomas notes that "the Constitution contains no 'dignity' Clause." Why does that matter?

7.   The majority and dissents have very different views about constitutional interpretation. How would you describe the model to which Justice Kennedy subscribes? What about the dissenting justices? Why does Chief Justice Roberts invoke *Lochner* in this debate? What differences do you observe among the dissenting justices? Whose views do you find most appealing?

8.   The views of constitutional interpretation taken by the Justices relate to their views about the Court's role. How does the majority think about the Court as an institution, the role of judicial review, and the relationship between social change and constitutional meaning? What is the critique of the Court lodged by the dissenters? How should we think of the role of the Court—and courts generally—in a constitutional democracy, particularly when contentious issues are involved? Consider these questions in light of the materials introduced throughout this Chapter that analyzed whether, as a descriptive matter, litigation accelerates social change, and whether, as a normative matter, courts should push forward social change?

9.   Chief Justice Roberts raises the possibility of plural marriage in his dissent. Indeed, he cites an article about a lesbian "throuple," in which three women in a relationship intend to co-parent. Is Chief Justice Roberts correct to raise the prospect of plural marriage? Does Justice Kennedy do anything to respond? Could he have avoided this issue by using a different doctrinal basis for the decision? After *Obergefell*, how might those desiring multiple-partner marriage make a constitutional claim? How would the government defend the two-person restriction in marriage laws? Who would win? Who *should* win?

10. Same-sex parenting figures prominently in Justice Kennedy's analysis. He recognizes that same-sex couples are raising children, and he appears to validate same-sex-couple-headed families. How might *Obergefell* affect state laws that discriminate against same-sex couples in family formation? May a state limit adoption to different-sex couples after *Obergefell*? Same-sex couples often use assisted reproductive technologies

(ART) to have children, with lesbians commonly relying on donor insemination and gay men increasingly turning to surrogacy. After *Obergefell*, may a state withhold parental status from a nonbiological mother when her spouse gives birth to a child conceived through donor insemination? May a state prohibit surrogacy or refuse to enforce surrogacy agreements? Does *Obergefell* speak to these issues, or is it "only" a case about the right to marry?

11. Both the majority and the dissents raise the issue of religious objections to same-sex marriage. Should the Court have addressed the specific contours of religious liberty in its decision? What conflicts do the dissenters see as likely to arise in the wake of *Obergefell*? How should these conflicts be resolved? Chapter 7 considers the debate over religious liberty and same-sex marriage.

IV. WHAT'S NEXT AFTER MARRIAGE?

Obergefell made marriage equality a nationwide reality. But that does not mean that work around marriage for same-sex couples has ended. In the U.S., issues percolating before *Obergefell* have gained widespread attention. Religious objections to laws protecting same-sex couples have proliferated; individuals and institutions seek religious exemptions, both through legislative efforts and through litigation under constitutional and statutory provisions protecting religious liberty. We explore these issues in Chapter 7. The onset of marriage equality in states without antidiscrimination law explicitly covering sexual orientation has also exposed the vulnerability of LGB people. Individuals who have married their same-sex partner—an act that can essentially out them—have been fired by their employers. Antidiscrimination law is covered in Chapter 4.

While the marriage equality question has been settled by the Supreme Court in the U.S.—though some conservative advocates seek to nullify or overturn the decision—efforts to achieve marriage equality move forward in other countries, particularly in Europe, Latin America, and Australia. As of late 2016, more than twenty countries, including the U.S., have opened marriage to same-sex couples nationwide. The Netherlands first allowed same-sex couples to marry in 2001. These countries eventually did the same: Belgium (2003), Spain (2005), Canada (2005), South Africa (2006), Norway (2009), Sweden (2009), Portugal (2010), Iceland (2010), Argentina (2010), Denmark (2012), Brazil (2013), France (2013), Uruguay (2013), New Zealand (2013), Great Britain (England and Wales, 2013; Scotland, 2014), Luxembourg (2014), Ireland (2015), Colombia (2016), and Finland (signed 2015, effective 2017). Same-sex couples can marry in parts of Mexico. Efforts to bring marriage equality to more countries continue through both legislative work and litigation.

Yet, rather than focus on continuing efforts aimed at marriage, this last section focuses on the demographics of marriage in the U.S. and the status of families living outside marriage. Justice Kennedy's opinion is in many ways an ode to marriage. Is that good or bad? Were marriage critics right to worry about the implications of making marriage a priority of the LGBT movement? Justice Kennedy described marriage as "a keystone of our social order," and he claimed that same-sex couples' children "suffer the significant material costs of being raised by unmarried parents." Consider the perspectives of those who warned against making marriage an LGBT movement priority and who worried that the focus on marriage would crowd out other strategies. What might they say today?

In the wake of *Obergefell*, Professor Melissa Murray criticized the Court's marriage-promoting rhetoric:

> *Obergefell* builds the case for equal access to marriage on the premise that marriage is the most profound, dignified, and fundamental institution into which individuals may enter. Alternatives to marriage . . . are by comparison, undignified, less profound, and less valuable. On this account, the rationale for marriage equality rests—perhaps ironically—on the fundamental *inequality* of other relationships and kinship forms.

Melissa Murray, Obergefell v. Hodges *and Nonmarriage Inequality*, 104 CALIF. L. REV. (forthcoming 2016).

Supporting Professor Murray's concerns, in August 2016, the Illinois Supreme Court refused to allow a woman who had been in a long-term nonmarital relationship with her same-sex partner to bring a claim to enforce mutual property rights arising out of the relationship. *Blumenthal v. Brewer*, 2016 IL 118781 (Ill. Aug. 18, 2016). The court relied on *Obergefell*, which it viewed as consistent with judicial and legislative trends "uphold[ing] the institution of marriage." *Id.* at *26.

In contrast, also in August 2016, New York's highest court overturned a decades-old precedent preventing nonbiological unmarried parents from seeking custody of the children they raised with the biological mother. *In re Brooke S.B.*, ___ N.E.3d ___, 2016 WL 4507780 (N.Y. Aug 30, 2016). The court reasoned that the earlier precedent's "foundational premise of heterosexual parenting and nonrecognition of same-sex couples is unsustainable, particularly in light of . . . [*Obergefell*]." *Id.* at *20. This decision is discussed in Chapter 6.

What does *Obergefell* mean for unmarried couples? What does it mean for nonmarital parents and children? Should LGBT advocates continue to fight for rights and benefits for nonmarital families? If so, how? The materials below consider these questions.

A. THE DEMOGRAPHICS OF MARRIAGE
AND NONMARRIAGE

The concerns raised by Professor Murray are especially significant because of the shifting demographics of marriage. As marriage became an LGBT movement priority, marriage rates in the heterosexual population were declining. Married families make up only about half of U.S. households.

Importantly, the marriage decline has not fallen evenly across society. Instead, marriage has become a status correlated with privilege. Whites are more likely to marry than their African-American and Latino counterparts. College-educated individuals are more likely to marry than those with only a high school diploma. Those with higher incomes are more likely to marry than those with lower incomes. And now highly educated men and highly educated women are more likely than in past decades to marry one another; economists believe this phenomenon they call "assortative mating" produces and perpetuates inequality across society by consolidating privilege and reducing marriage's role as a driver of social mobility.

As rates of marriage have declined, rates of nonmarital and single parenthood have risen. More than half of births to women under 30 occur outside marriage. Rates of nonmarital birth to cohabiting couples has increased, now accounting for more than half of nonmarital births. Yet marriage continues to be the family form through which the government distributes important rights and benefits.

If same-sex couples simply replicate the dynamics seen among heterosexuals, marriage may reflect ongoing inequalities among LGBT people. Data from the Census Bureau's 2013 American Community Survey, which of course do not include the most recent—and biggest— wave of same-sex marriages, provide preliminary indications of similarities and differences between different-sex and same-sex couples.

While marriage clearly skews white in the different-sex couple population, at this point the same feature is not observable in same-sex couples. For different-sex couples, the married population is 74% white and 26% non-white, while the unmarried couple population is 64% white and 36% non-white. For same-sex couples, both the married and unmarried couple populations are 77% white and 23% non-white. Married same-sex couples are as racially diverse as the general same-sex couple population.

Yet the story of economic privilege is similar—with significant disparities between married and unmarried couples in both the same-sex and different-sex populations. Still, there are two important features to note: First, the economic differences between married and unmarried couples are not as stark among same-sex couples. Married same-sex couples' median income exceeds their unmarried counterparts by 27%. The margin between married and unmarried different-sex couples is much wider at 46%. Second, married same-sex couples have a higher median household income—more than $100,000—than any of the other three groups—not only unmarried same-sex and different-sex couples but also married different-sex couples.

Rates of childrearing do not differ significantly between married and unmarried different-sex couples. But among same-sex couples, married couples are more likely to be raising children than their unmarried counterparts. And the racial diversity observed in marriage exists in parenting as well. Among same-sex couples raising children, 32% of those married and 35% of those unmarried are non-white. For different-sex couples, there is greater disparity—34% and 49%, respectively.

As with different-sex couples, married same-sex couples with children have more resources than their unmarried counterparts. Again, they have a higher median household income than even married different-sex couples with children—$100,000, compared to $83,550. Also, unmarried same-sex couples raising children have a median household income of $67,900, higher than unmarried different-sex couples' $46,000.

Parenting cuts differently based on gender. More than three-quarters of same-sex couples raising a child under 18 are female. Among married same-sex couples, 36% of female couples are raising children, compared to 17% of male couples. Yet male couples are raising children with more resources. In fact, married male couples raising adopted or foster children have a median household income over $200,000. For more extensive treatment of these data, see Gary J. Gates, *Demographics of Married and Unmarried Same-Sex Couples: Analyses of the 2013 American Community Survey* (Williams Institute 2015).

Family formation for same-sex couples often takes more cumbersome—and costly—steps than for different-sex couples. Married same-sex couples, for instance, are five times more likely than their different-sex counterparts to be raising adopted or foster children. Marriage, therefore, may constitute merely another deliberate step toward family formation for same-sex couples. Furthermore, because marriage offers routes to legal parentage without a biological connection—something often not at issue for heterosexuals—same-sex couples forming families with children through assisted reproductive technologies or adoption may view marriage as critical to familial recognition.

Yet even if marriage and parenting are more connected for same-sex couples than for different-sex couples, there will remain substantial numbers of LGBT people raising children outside marriage, often with less resources. And inequality between married and unmarried same-sex couples will persist. What should the LGBT movement do about that? What other movements might work in coalition with LGBT advocates on these issues?

B. NONMARITAL RECOGNITION BEFORE AND AFTER MARRIAGE EQUALITY

While the materials in this Chapter revealed a lively internal LGBT community debate about marriage in the late 1980s and 1990s, that debate became more muted as the marriage equality campaign gained steam. Why? One likely explanation is the widespread backlash against same-sex marriage advocacy by opponents of LGBT rights. Consider Professor Jane Schacter's view:

> For all the fiery rhetoric and deep disagreements dividing opponents and proponents of same-sex marriage, . . . there are some surprising points of confluence between the two sides in how they frame the debate. First, both supporters and opponents of same-sex marriage characterize the institution of marriage as a centrally important and positive force in communal life. Such a characterization is, of course, utterly predictable for those opposing same-sex marriage. . . . Yet it is hardly obvious that prominent supporters of LGBT rights would also have such high praise for marriage. . . . A second point of confluence is that both sides frame the marriage debate as something of an epochal showdown on LGBT equality. Both, in other words, seem to see the stakes as high, the outcome as a proxy statement about LGBT equality, and the struggle as a cultural moment of truth. . . . The fact that the public debate about same-sex marriage has been framed as the true test of LGBT equality undoubtedly has been a prime force in quieting any internal resistance to same-sex marriage. The internal critics have always had political commitments that place them in deep and passionate opposition to the "external" critics of same-sex marriage—the cultural and religious traditionalists who oppose LGBT equality in all its forms. Indeed, the internal and external resistance to same-sex marriage are strikingly converse to one another. The internal resistance to marriage advocacy came from those strongly committed to gay equality, but doubtful about the institution of marriage. The external resistance comes from those strongly opposed to gay equality, but reverent about the traditional institution of marriage.

Jane S. Schacter, *The Other Same-Sex Marriage Debate*, 84 CHICAGO-KENT L. REV. 379, 381–83 (2009). In this article, Professor Schacter asks, in counterfactual fashion, whether it is possible to imagine the history unfolding differently. Might LGBT advocates have affirmatively sought an institution separate from marriage—one that might have allowed more flexibility than marriage, and thus met a wider range of needs? Might LGBT advocates, alternatively, have sought to eliminate civil marriage, leaving marriage to religious institutions, while the state offered a secular partnership to all couples? Would either of these courses, or another one you might imagine, have been preferable to concentrating heavily on securing access to marriage per se? Why or why not?

Professor Douglas NeJaime analyzes the viability of these alternative paths in a world where same-sex couples did not have access to marriage. Through a case study of domestic partnership work in California in the 1980s and 1990s, he shows how marriage anchored nonmarital recognition, even before the movement made explicit claims to marriage. In this excerpt, Professor NeJaime summarizes some of the case study's implications:

> Even for activists resisting marriage, marriage functioned like a riptide. Advocates were swimming with *and* against marriage, often at the same time. That is, they challenged marriage's role even as they submitted to its pull. LGBT advocates' claims [to nonmarital recognition] did not simply succeed or fail on their own, but were met with reactions from a range of relevant actors who shaped the content and influenced the viability of those claims. Government actors, including judges and lawmakers, privileged marriage in law and policy. Countermovement activists, who influenced officials and mobilized voters, sought to both restore the centrality of marriage and cut back on LGBT rights. And private institutions, including employers and insurers sympathetic to sexual orientation equality, acted on financial incentives to limit the types of nonmarital relationships that would qualify for benefits. Overall, then, marriage constituted a deeply entrenched legal norm, a powerful but controversial cultural priority, and a well-understood limiting principle. Both supportive and hostile responses filtered LGBT claims through the lens of marriage, and such responses often redirected advocates' energy and constrained potentially more transformative visions.

> . . . Marriage rendered intimate couples the appropriate targets of reform. Those who mapped onto a particular notion of the marital family gained support by distinguishing themselves from other relationships that failed to fit the marital mold. Furthermore, marriage distinguished same-sex couples from their different-sex, unmarried counterparts. This produced an emphasis on marriage access over marriage choice in ways that gradually propped up marriage as an LGBT movement goal. Indeed, supportive allies frequently cast domestic partnership as a compromise solution that avoided the more radical possibility of same-sex marriage.

Accordingly, the power of marriage as a legal and cultural norm structured claims, debates, and outcomes regarding family reform such that advocates did not—and could not—simply reject marriage. Even if advocates hoped otherwise, domestic partnership in many ways solidified, rather than resisted, the power of marriage.

Douglas NeJaime, *Before Marriage: The Unexplored History of Nonmarital Recognition and Its Relationship to Marriage*, 102 CALIF. L. REV. 87, 161 (2014).

Professor NeJaime's analysis suggests that so long as same-sex couples were excluded from marriage, their efforts for relationship recognition would be framed in relation to marriage and would be seen as a deliberately unstable compromise measure. It should not be surprising, then, that once same-sex couples began to access marriage, some nonmarital recognition mechanisms were rolled back. Once Connecticut offered marriage to same-sex couples, it converted civil unions, which had been available only to same-sex couples, into marriages by statute: "Two persons who are parties to a civil union . . . that has not been dissolved or annulled by the parties or merged into a marriage . . . as of October 1, 2010, shall be deemed to be married . . . and such civil union shall be merged into such marriage by operation of law on said date." CT. STAT. ANN. § 46b–38rr (2009). Some public and private employers also ceased offering domestic partner benefits once same-sex couples gained access to marriage. *See* Nancy D. Polikoff, *What Marriage Equality Arguments Portend for Domestic Partner Employee Benefits*, 37 N.Y.U. REV. L. & SOC. CHANGE 49 (2012).

Should states and employers do away with forms of nonmarital recognition after marriage equality? Why or why not? Which forms of nonmarital recognition do you think are most likely to remain? Washington, D.C., which offered domestic partnerships to same-sex and different-sex couples, maintained its nonmarital status after it opened marriage to same-sex couples. *See* D.C. Code § 32–701 (2012). Perhaps the inclusion of different-sex couples, who already had access to marriage, is key to a nonmarital recognition regime's survival. Statutory regimes like the designated beneficiary system in Colorado have also remained. Perhaps statuses that include fewer rights and benefits than marriage and include relationships other than intimate couples are most likely to remain.

C. THE FUTURE OF MARRIAGE AND NONMARRIAGE

The post-marriage-equality moment seems to present a critical point. The achievement of marriage equality may open space for other family law efforts that help nonmarital families. Who should lead these efforts? And what should be the specific goals of these efforts?

Since the primary advocacy for nonmarital relationship rights came from LGBT advocates, the onset of marriage equality may reduce incentives for those advocates—and their constituents—to mobilize around nonmarital rights. Even domestic partnership policies at private employers were frequently the product of work by LGBT employee groups. If LGBT individuals and advocates are no longer as motivated to seek nonmarital rights—precisely because they have achieved access to marriage—then who is likely to push for such reforms? Different-sex couples have taken advantage of domestic partnership policies, but they were rarely driving efforts to achieve such policies. What kinds of new coalitions might emerge between LGBT groups and other groups? How might LGBT organizing relate to increased attention to economic inequality, some of which certainly relates to family law and policy?

For those committed to supporting nonmarital families, what are the best approaches in law and policy? Much of LGBT advocacy aimed at nonmarital couples focused on formal recognition, like civil unions and domestic partnerships. But historically, systems that require couples to affirmatively register their relationships have been taken up at greater rates by those with more education and more income. If the demographics of nonmarital recognition regimes look similar to the demographics of marriage, perhaps the solution to supporting nonmarital families should be found elsewhere. What could be done to support unmarried couples and nonmarital childrearing? Is the piecemeal extension of rights and obligations, as we saw in *Braschi* and *Kowalski* earlier in this Chapter, a better path? What are the downsides of this approach?

What about reducing marriage's role as a gateway to rights and obligations, and instead attaching such rights and obligations to families that feature the kinds of dependency relationships the state seeks to support? For instance, the American Law Institute in 2002 proposed recognition of same-sex and different-sex couples who are "not married to one another, [but] who for a significant period of time share a primary residence and a life together as a couple." AMERICAN LAW INSTITUTE, PRINCIPLES OF THE LAW OF FAMILY DISSOLUTION: ANALYSIS AND RECOMMENDATIONS, § 6.03 (2002). The time of cohabitation would be less if the couple had a child together. These couples would then automatically have rights and obligations similar to spouses regarding property, support, and parental rights. Of course, this regime technically only kicks in at dissolution.

Professor Nancy Polikoff's approach, which she terms "valuing all families," would look to the purpose of a particular law and then seek to have the law capture those who fulfill the law's purpose. For instance, she argues, "Any law that permits ... caregiving leave [like the federal Family and Medical Leave Act] but limits who may take such leave to spouses or a narrow group of family members defeats the important purpose of such a law—facilitating caregiving by those who are willing to provide such care to those with whom they have close personal relationships." Nancy D. Polikoff, *Ending Marriage as We Know It*, 32 HOFSTRA L. REV. 201, 231 (2003). Consider the following excerpt from Professor Polikoff:

VALUING ALL FAMILIES*
Nancy D. Polikoff

Today we take for granted that marriage is not the right dividing line for the rights or obligations of parents. The political forces behind [the conservative campaign for] "marriage promotion" today rarely admit they want to return children born outside marriage to second-class status, but they are ever willing to extol a special legal status for marriage at the expense of many—even most—American families.

For example, when the American Law Institute (ALI) proposed treating separating domestic partners identically to divorcing married couples, "marriage movement" ideologues called it a "war on the traditional family." One spokesperson said, "Anyone who cares about the state of marriage, which is weak enough already, if you want it to become weaker still, knock away legal protections marriage enjoys." But the ALI was not knocking any protections away from marriage; it was extending them to unmarried couples who also needed them. Since the 5.5 million cohabiting couples no longer break any laws or violate social taboos, it's inexcusable that their dissolution might leave one partner economically devastated solely for the lack of a marriage license.

And if we care about the well-being of all children, we need to change the laws that now privilege marriage at the expense of children. Without a valid prenuptial agreement, in almost every state a husband cannot disinherit his wife (and vice-versa). But every state except Massachusetts and Louisiana allows a parent to disinherit minor children. When a man had no obligation to support children born to anyone except his wife, and when the rarity of divorce made it unlikely that a man's children would be living with anyone other than his current wife, the guaranteed inheritance for a wife might have, to some extent, protected the economic well-being of children. This is no longer the case.

When Pfc. Hannah McKinney deployed for Iraq, she left behind a man she had just married and a two-year-old son from an earlier relationship whom she entrusted to her parents. Hannah died in Iraq, and the military paid a $100,000 death benefit to her husband, not to her parents, who will raise her son.

This federal benefit—originally a much smaller dollar figure—was created in 1908. Divorce was rare and a man had no obligation to support his children unless his wife gave birth to them. Congress might have reasonably assumed that if a service member was married and had children, then those children would be with his surviving spouse.

---

*   Nancy D. Polikoff, Valuing All Families, 48 SANTA CLARA L. REV. 741, 744–47 (2008).

Congress might have thought that by paying the spouse, the government was providing for the children. As Hannah's example demonstrates, that assumption no longer holds true.

These are just a few examples of laws that need rethinking given the composition of today's families. Husbands and wives receive many "special rights"—spousal employment benefits, Social Security and workers compensation survivors benefits, and the ability to request ongoing support when a relationship dissolves, to give just a few examples—simply because they are married. A woman married to a retired worker for nine months is entitled to social security benefits based on his life-long earnings when he dies; a woman who lived with an unmarried partner for twenty-nine years, even if she raised children with him, is not eligible. The benefits look like part of the package of rewards for marrying, and are justified as proper incentives to marry. * * *

The composition of today's families and households differs from that of earlier times. When Congress enacted social security benefits for wives and widows in 1939 (husbands and widowers were not equally entitled until the 1970s), only 15% of married women worked outside the home. Some workers compensation death benefit schemes—which also treated widowers less favorably than widows—were passed when only 7% of married women worked outside the home. Now, in 60% of married couples, both spouses work outside the home; 63.5% of women with children under the age of 6 and 75.0% of women with children in school [are] in the work force.

Today, less than 50% of all households contain a married couple, down from 78% in 1950. Since 1950, the divorce rate has increased about 40%. During that same period, the percentage of births to unmarried women has gone from 4% to almost 37%. We've got to revise our laws to protect the economic security and emotional peace of mind of the full variety of today's families and relationships. * * *

CHAPTER 6

PARENTING

■ ■ ■

There are large numbers of families in the United States headed by LGBT individuals. It is estimated that "as many as 6 million American children and adults have an LGBT parent."[1] It is also estimated that "nearly half of LGBT women (48%)" and "a fifth of LGBT men (20%)" are raising a child under 18.[2]

This Chapter explores how LGBT individuals become legal parents. The Chapter is divided into two Sections. The first explores how LGBT people can become legal parents based on biological links with their children. The second discusses how LGBT individuals can become legal parents in the absence of biological links with their children. As we will see throughout the Chapter, although biology can play an important role in establishing parental rights, a biological connection is neither a necessary nor (in some instances) a sufficient factor for establishing the existence of legal parentage.

I. PARENTHOOD BASED ON BIOLOGY

A. DISPUTES BETWEEN LGBT PARENTS AND OTHER PARENTS

Some cases involving parenting by lesbians, gay men, and bisexuals concern the dissolution of different-sex marriages. Sexual orientation is sometimes put at issue in these cases when heterosexual parents attempt to use the sexuality of gay, lesbian, and bisexual parents as grounds for limiting the latter's custodial or visitation rights.

---

[1] Gary J. Gates, *LGBT Parenting in the United States* (Williams Institute, 2013), p.1, available at http://williamsinstitute.law.ucla.edu/wp-content/uploads/LGBT-Parenting.pdf.

[2] *Id.* "An estimated 39% of individuals in same-sex couples who have children under age 18 in the home are people of color, compared to 36% of different-sex couples who are non-White." *Id.* In addition, "[a]mong children under age 18 living with same-sex couples, half (50%) are non-White compared to 41% of children living with different-sex couples." *Id.* There is also evidence that same-sex couples raising children face economic disadvantages. The median annual household income of same-sex couples with children under 18 is lower ($63,000) than that of different-sex couples with children ($74,000). In addition, single LGBT adults raising children are three times as likely to report income near the poverty threshold than single non-LGBT parents. *Id.* As for married or partnered LGBT couples with children, they are two times as likely as non-LGBT couples with children to report household income near the poverty line. *Id.*

There is a thread in the older case law that supported the concept that a same-sex sexual orientation alone was a per se reason for denying custody or visitation rights.[3] The vast majority of courts today eschew such language in favor of a nexus test: parents' sexuality and sexual relationships may be taken into account only when they may have adverse effects on their children.[4] While an improvement on a per se test, the nexus test by no means produces determinant results in favor of lesbian, gay, or bisexual parents; perhaps not surprisingly, courts have articulated a nexus test in cases that both protect and discriminate against these parents.[5] Accordingly, in reviewing the materials that follow, you should consider in what circumstances courts find that the

---

[3]   *E.g.,* *S v. S,* 608 S.W.2d 64, 65, 66 (Ky. Ct. App. 1980) (while "wife denies any overt lesbian relationship in the presence of the child and there is no proof to the contrary," court denies her custody based both on testimony that " 'there is social stigma attached to homosexuality' " and speculation from data on parental modeling on children); *S.E.G. v. R.A.G.,* 735 S.W.2d 164, 166 (Mo. Ct. App. 1987) ("Such conduct [i.e., lesbian mother showing affection toward and sleeping with her partner] can never be kept private enough to be a neutral factor in the development of a child's values and character."); *M.J.P. v. J.G.P.,* 640 P.2d 966, 967, 1982 OK 13 (1982) ("The question before us is whether this acknowledged, open homosexual relationship involving the custodial parent was shown by the facts to be sufficient change of condition to warrant modification of a child custody order? We answer in the affirmative."); *Dailey v. Dailey,* 635 S.W.2d 391, 396 (Tenn. Ct. App. 1981) ("To permit this small child to be subjected to the type of sexually related behavior that has been carried on in his presence in the past under the proof in this record could provide nothing but harmful effects on his life in the future."); *Roe v. Roe,* 324 S.E.2d 691, 694, 228 Va. 722, 728 (1985) ("[W]e have no hesitancy in saying that the conditions under which this child must live daily are not only unlawful but also impose an intolerable burden upon her by reason of the social condemnation attached to them.").

[4]   *E.g.,* *S.N.E. v. R.L.B.,* 699 P.2d 875 (Alaska 1985) (finding that social stigma, real or imagined, associated with parent's homosexuality does not affect child's best interests); *Jacoby v. Jacoby,* 763 So.2d 410, 413 (Fla. Dist. Ct. App. 2000) (holding that "[f]or a court to properly consider conduct such as [the mother's] sexual orientation on the issue of custody, the conduct must have a direct effect or impact upon the children"); *Hassenstab v. Hassenstab,* 570 N.W.2d 368, 372–73, 6 Neb.App. 13, 18–19 (Ct. App. 1997) (affirming refusal to modify custody based on mother's lesbian relationship in absence of evidence child was directly exposed to sexual activity or harmed by mother's relationship); *Inscoe v. Inscoe,* 700 N.E.2d 70, 82, 121 Ohio App.3d 396, 415 (Ct. App. 1997) (ruling that trial court "may consider a parent's sexual orientation only if the sexual orientation has a direct adverse impact" on the child); *Fox v. Fox,* 904 P.2d 66, 69, 1995 OK 87 (1995) (holding that lesbian mother's "sexual proclivities" are not grounds for changing custody absent evidence of "significant change of circumstances which directly and adversely affects the children"); *Van Driel v. Van Driel,* 525 N.W.2d 37, 39 (S.D. 1994) (explicitly rejecting *per se* test and holding that lesbian mother's "conduct must be shown to have had some harmful effect on the children"). *See also In re Marriage of Birdsall,* 243 Cal.Rptr. 287, 291, 197 Cal.App.3d 1024, 1031 (1988) (holding that a parent is not unfit, as a matter of law, merely because he or she is homosexual); *McGriff v. McGriff,* 99 P.3d 111, 117, 140 Idaho 642, 648 (2004) (holding that "[s]exual orientation, in and of itself cannot be the basis for awarding or removing custody"); *Teegarden v. Teegarden,* 642 N.E.2d 1007, 1010 (Ind. Ct. App. 1994) (holding that lesbian mother's custody could not be conditioned on her behavior absent evidence that such behavior would adversely affect children); *Paul C. v. Tracy C.,* 622 N.Y.S.2d 159, 160, 209 A.D.2d 955, 956 (App. Div. 1994) (holding that mother's alleged lesbian relationship did not preclude her from custody absent evidence that such relationship had negative affect on children).

[5]   *Compare, e.g., In re Marriage of Martins,* 269 Ill.App.3d 380, 390, 206 Ill.Dec. 562, 645 N.E.2d 567, 574 (Ct. App. 1995) (granting custody to father after finding lesbian mother's "lifestyle had adversely affected the children") *with Large v. Large,* 1993 WL 498127, at *5 (Ohio Ct. App. 1993) (affirming grant of custody to lesbian mother after finding no evidence indicating that her sexual orientation negatively effected children).

relevant nexus does exist and consider upon whom the burden of proof, vis-à-vis this nexus, is placed.

It should be noted that custody and/or visitation cases involving transgender parents are fewer in number than those involving gay, lesbian, or bisexual parents. Nonetheless, there are some similarities between the two groups of cases as courts struggle to determine what role, if any, gender identity should play in the assignation of parental rights and responsibilities.[6] The second case below, *Magnuson v. Magnuson*, involves a custody dispute between a transgender parent and her former wife.[7]

EX PARTE J.M.F.

Supreme Court of Alabama, 1998
730 So.2d 1190

LYONS, JUSTICE.

I.

The parties were divorced in January 1993, after a six-year marriage, and the trial court awarded custody of the parties' minor daughter to the mother. Shortly thereafter, the mother began a homosexual relationship with G.S., and in April 1992 she and her daughter moved into an apartment with G.S. Although the apartment had three bedrooms, the mother began sharing a bedroom with G.S. The father was aware of the relationship but, according to him, his conversations with the mother led him to believe that the mother and G.S. would maintain a discreet relationship, that they would not share a bedroom, and that they would represent themselves to the child and others as being merely roommates.

The father subsequently remarried, and the child regularly visited him and his new wife in their home. During the course of these visits, the father learned that his former wife and G.S. were sharing a bedroom, that the child occasionally slept with them in their bed, and that they kissed in the presence of the child. The father also noticed one instance where the child, while playing a game with her stepmother, grabbed the stepmother's breast in a way that appeared to him to be inappropriate. During visitation, the child remarked to the father that "girls could marry girls and boys could marry boys."

After the father learned that the mother and G.S. were not conducting a discreet relationship but were, in fact, openly displaying

---

[6]   *See* Helen Y. Chang, *My Father is a Woman, Oh No!: The Failure of the Courts to Uphold Individual Substantive Due Process Rights for Transgender Parents Under the Guise of the Best Interest of the Child*, 43 SANTA CLARA L. REV. 649, 685–98 (2003) (arguing that courts in cases involving transgender parents should apply the same nexus test that many courts apply in cases involving gay, lesbian, or bisexual parents).

[7]   170 P.3d 65, 141 Wash. App. 347 (2007),

their affair to the child, and after observing the effect that this was having upon the child, he moved to modify the divorce judgment in order to obtain custody of the daughter. The child underwent expert psychological evaluation and was represented in the modification proceedings by a guardian ad litem.

The evidence presented during the * * * proceeding shows that since the divorce, the mother and G.S. have not conducted their relationship with discretion and have not concealed the nature of their union from the child. The mother and G.S. have exchanged rings and have a committed relationship as "life partners" that includes ongoing sexual activity. The mother and G.S. share a bed and the child has at times slept in the bed with them. They kiss and show romantic affection for each other in the child's presence.[1]

The mother has explained to the daughter that she and G.S. love each other the way that the child's father and stepmother love each other. The mother and G.S. testified that G.S. shares in the child's upbringing in the way of a devoted stepmother and that the child accepts and loves her as a parental figure. G.S. regularly attends school functions and meetings with the mother, accompanies the child on school field trips, and eats lunch with the child at school twice a month.

The record contains evidence indicating that the child has remarked several times that girls may marry girls and that boys may marry boys. The mother and G.S. have homosexual couples as guests in their home, and they have taken the daughter with them on an overnight trip to visit a male homosexual couple; during this visit, the child slept with the mother and G.S. in one room, while their hosts shared a bedroom.

During her testimony, the mother repeatedly denied that her lifestyle had resulted in, or would result in, problems for the child. She denied that other children would shun the child based upon the obvious relationship between her mother and G.S., which they regularly display to those at the child's school. The mother stated in deposition testimony that if others showed "prejudice" against the child it would be "up to the child" to decide how to deal with it because "kids have to deal with peer pressure in their own ways anyway." The mother pointed out that children reject other children for a variety of reasons and that her daughter was "going to have to learn about prejudice in her daily life anyway." The mother was confident that the child could decide for herself what to tell her friends and that whatever the child was comfortable with would be fine.

---

[1]   The record contains no evidence indicating that the mother and G.S. have displayed any sexual activity in the presence of the child, other than hand-holding and kissing that is not prolonged.

The other evidence adduced during the trial showed, without dispute, that the child has a loving relationship with her father and her stepmother and that she accepts the stepmother as a parental figure. It is undisputed that she enjoys visiting them in their home and that the father and stepmother share in the care of the child when she is with them. The stepmother testified as to her love for the child and her commitment to sharing the responsibility of her upbringing. The father and the stepmother are both employed and can make satisfactory arrangements for the care of the child while they are working; the father, in particular, has a flexible work schedule in his job as an electrician that allows him to be available to care for the child.

There was also expert testimony at trial from the psychologists who examined the child. Dr. Sharon Gotlieb, who was the child's primary therapist, opined that the child's relationship with her mother is excellent, that the two are well bonded, and that the child exhibited no pathology or mental illness. She also stated that the child had a good relationship with G.S. and that the relationship is beneficial to the child. Dr. Gotlieb expressed concern that a change in custody would have a substantial detrimental effect on the child, perhaps causing her to have immediate and/or long-term behavior problems, school problems, or depression. Dr. Gotlieb did testify that a child is best served by having both a male and a female role model in the house, rather than two male, or two female, role models; however, she qualified this statement by opining that the gender of a new adult introduced into the home of a custodial parent after the biological parents divorced would make no difference to the child because the principal role models in her life would remain her parents.

Dr. Daniel McKeever, a pastoral counselor, testified that the father brought the child to him to be evaluated after observing her touching herself "excessively" in the genital area. He testified that, utilizing play therapy, he detected that the child might have issues of anger and sexuality, based upon his perceptions of the child's play with anatomically correct dolls. He also expressed a suspicion that the child might have experienced sexual abuse; however, he also stated that he had only two appointments with the child and that the father's suspicion of sexual abuse stemmed from the fact of the mother's lesbianism. Dr. McKeever did not interview the mother, G.S., or the child's stepmother.

Dr. Karen Turnbow, the court-appointed psychologist, stated in her report to the court that her evaluation of the child revealed no indication of sexual abuse or exposure to sexual acts. She reported that she spent time with both parents, with G.S., and with the child's stepmother, and concluded that the child has a good relationship with each of them and is resilient. Dr. Turnbow stated that, based upon her review of available literature on the subject of a child being reared by an openly homosexual parent, she did not think the homosexuality of a parent should be the sole consideration in a custody situation; rather, she said, the literature suggested that custody should be determined on the basis of individual character and parenting skills.

Dr. James B. Collier testified on behalf of the mother concerning scientific studies as to the effect growing up in a homosexual household had on children. He testified that he had reviewed at least 50 articles, all from journals that are subject to peer review, and that these studies consistently found no adverse consequences for children growing up in such a household.

In addition to the foregoing evidence, the trial court also had before it the report of Terry M. Cromer, the child's appointed guardian ad litem; the report summarized the evidence and scientific studies submitted to the court and presented Cromer's own observations. Cromer confirmed the unanimous opinion of all the psychologists that the child was pretty, well-groomed, intelligent, energetic, healthy, and generally happy. He also confirmed that the child is bonded with both parents and enjoys a loving relationship with both. He recognized that, as Dr. Collier and Dr. Gotlieb had stated, there were studies that had determined that there is generally no significant difference in various factors between a child who has been reared by a heterosexual couple and one who has been reared by a homosexual couple. He also pointed out that there are studies that come to the opposite conclusion and that the child's therapist, Dr. Gotlieb, appeared reluctant to consider studies which suggest that a child reared by homosexual parents could suffer exclusion, isolation, a drop in school grades, and other problems. After summarizing the evidence, Cromer recommended to the trial court that it grant the father's motion to change custody.

After considering all the evidence, the trial court entered an order changing custody to the father, finding that the change would materially promote the child's best interests and setting forth the mother's visitation rights. The trial court initially restricted the mother's visits by ordering that she not "exercise her right of visitation with the minor child of the parties in the presence of a person to whom she is not related by blood or marriage." However, upon motion of the mother, the trial court modified the order to provide that the restriction "shall not apply and be considered as being applicable to the general public, casual, professional, platonic or business relationships."

In reviewing the trial court's judgment, the Court of Civil Appeals pointed out that, in Alabama, evidence of a parent's heterosexual misconduct cannot, in itself, support a change of custody unless the trial court finds that the misconduct has a detrimental effect upon the child. The Court of Civil Appeals emphasized that this standard has been applied in other jurisdictions to cases involving homosexual conduct on the part of a custodial parent, and it adopted this standard for use in such cases in Alabama. In applying this standard, the Court of Civil Appeals determined that the record contained no evidence indicating that the mother's relationship with G.S. has a detrimental effect upon the child, and it thus concluded that the trial court had improperly changed custody based solely upon the mother's homosexuality.

II.

It is, of course, well established that a noncustodial parent seeking a change of custody must show not only that he or she is fit to have custody, but that the change would materially promote the child's best interests. This requires a showing that the positive good brought about by the modification would more than offset the inherently disruptive effect caused by uprooting the child. Where a parent seeks a change of custody based solely upon the heterosexual misconduct of the custodial parent, our law requires that there be an additional showing that the misconduct has a detrimental effect upon the child.

In this case, however, the father has not sought to change the custody of the child based upon the fact that the mother is engaged in a homosexual affair; indeed, the father was aware of the mother's feelings for G.S. at the time of the divorce and was aware that they cohabitated thereafter, but he did not immediately seek a change of custody. The father sought custody of the child only after he had remarried and had discovered that the mother and G.S. were not conducting a discreet affair in the guise of "roommates" but were, instead, presenting themselves openly to the child as affectionate "life partners" with a relationship similar to that of the father and the stepmother. This is, therefore, not a custody case based solely upon the mother's sexual conduct, where the "substantial detrimental effect" element might be applicable. Rather, it is a custody case based upon two distinct changes in the circumstances of the parties: (1) the change in the father's life, from single parenthood to marriage and the creation of a two-parent, heterosexual home environment, and (2) the change in the mother's homosexual relationship, from a discreet affair to the creation of an openly homosexual home environment. The father was not, as the Court of Civil Appeals erroneously held, required to show that the mother's relationship with the child was having a "substantial detrimental effect" upon the child. Rather, he was required to establish that, based upon the changes in the circumstances of the parties, a change in custody would materially promote the child's best interests and that the positive good brought by this change would more than offset the inherently disruptive effect of uprooting the child.

III.

* * * The trial court was presented with evidence of two important changes in the circumstances of the parties that had occurred since their divorce; we will address both of those changes. There is evidence that the mother had expressed feelings for G.S. just before the divorce and that the father was aware of this. There is evidence that, when the mother subsequently moved into a three-bedroom apartment with G.S. and the child, she represented to the father that she and G.S. would not share a room and would represent themselves to be roommates. However, the mother and G.S. subsequently established an open lesbian relationship, which they explained to the child and which they demonstrate with affection in the presence of the child on a regular basis.

The mother has testified that she has not had any significant concern about the adverse effect her transformation from a married heterosexual to a committed homosexual could have on the child. The mother has repeatedly denied that the child will suffer any ill effects from the mother's choice of lifestyle; however, the mother has also testified that it will be up to the child to cope with any ridicule or prejudice that the child might suffer as she gets older, because, she said, "all children have to cope with prejudice anyway."

The mother and G.S. have homosexual couples as guests in their home, and the evidence suggests that the child believes that "girls can marry girls." Both the mother and G.S. have testified that they would not discourage the child from adopting a homosexual lifestyle. In short, the mother and G.S. have established a two-parent home environment where their homosexual relationship is openly practiced and presented to the child as the social and moral equivalent of a heterosexual marriage.[3]

The trial court also heard evidence indicating that the father is no longer a single parent, but has now established a happy marriage with a woman who loves the child, assists in her care, and has demonstrated a commitment to sharing the responsibility of rearing the child should the father gain custody of her. The child has consistently expressed love for the stepmother and acceptance of her as a parental figure. The father and the stepmother have a house with ample room for the child, and they are able to provide for her material needs, as well as her emotional and physical needs. In short, the father and the stepmother have established a two-parent home environment where heterosexual marriage is presented as the moral and societal norm.

---

[3] Act 98–500, Ala. Acts 1998, approved by the Governor on May 1, 1998, forbids the issuance of a marriage license "in the State of Alabama to parties of the same sex" and provides that the State of Alabama "shall not recognize as valid any marriage of parties of the same sex that occurred or was alleged to have occurred" anywhere else.

The trial court had before it a number of scientific studies as to the effect of child-rearing by homosexual couples, and much of the information presented by those studies suggests that a homosexual couple with good parenting skills is just as likely to successfully rear a child as is a heterosexual couple. The trial court was also presented with studies indicating that a child reared by a homosexual couple is more likely to experience isolation, behavioral problems, and depression and that the optimum environment for rearing a child is one where both a male and a female role model are present, living together in a marriage relationship. There was evidence that the child displayed conduct that gave her father cause for concern.

After carefully considering all of the evidence, we simply cannot hold that the trial court abused its discretion in determining that the positive good brought about by placing the child in the custody of her father would more than offset the inherent disruption brought about by uprooting the child from her mother's custody. While the evidence shows that the mother loves the child and has provided her with good care, it also shows that she has chosen to expose the child continuously to a lifestyle that is "neither legal in this state, nor moral in the eyes of most of its citizens." *Ex parte D.W.W.*, 717 So.2d 793, 796 (Ala.1998).[4] The record contains evidence from which the trial court could have concluded that "[a] child raised by two women or two men is deprived of extremely valuable developmental experience and the opportunity for optimal individual growth and interpersonal development" and that "the degree of harm to children from the homosexual conduct of a parent is uncertain * * * and the range of potential harm is enormous." Lynn D. Wardle, *The Potential Impact of Homosexual Parenting on Children*, 1997 U. Ill. L. Rev. 833, 895 (1997).

While much study, and even more controversy, continue to center upon the effects of homosexual parenting, the inestimable developmental benefit of a loving home environment that is anchored by a successful marriage is undisputed. The father's circumstances have changed, and he is now able to provide this benefit to the child. The mother's circumstances have also changed, in that she is unable, while choosing to conduct an open cohabitation with her lesbian life partner, to provide this benefit. The trial court's change of custody based upon the changed

---

[4]   Under Ala. Code 1975, § 13A–6–65, it is a Class A misdemeanor to engage in consensual "deviate sexual intercourse with another person"; this statute was specifically altered by the legislature from the original draft of the "Alabama Criminal Code" proposed to the legislature, so as "to make all homosexual conduct criminal." *See* Commentary to § 13A–6–65 and § 13A–1–1.

In addition, Alabama has established that "[c]ourse materials and instruction" in the public schools "that relate to [sex] education" shall emphasize, "in a factual manner and from a public health perspective, that homosexuality is not a lifestyle acceptable to the general public and that homosexual conduct is a criminal offense under the laws of the state." Ala. Code 1975, § 16–40A–2(c)(8).

circumstances of the parties was not an abuse of discretion; thus, the Court of Civil Appeals erred in reversing the trial court's judgment. * * *

The judgment of the Court of Civil Appeals is reversed and the cause is remanded for that court to enter a judgment affirming the trial court's order insofar as it changes custody and to consider the issue regarding the restrictions placed upon the mother's visitation rights.

MAGNUSON V. MAGNUSON

Court of Appeals of Washington, 2007
170 P.3d 65, 141 Wash.App. 347

BROWN, J.

In this parenting plan dispute, Robert S. Magnuson contends the trial court erred by improperly considering transgender status when it granted primary residential placement of the parties' children to Dr. Tracy A. Magnuson. But the court properly focused on the children's needs in making the residential placement decision, not transgender status, conforming to principles established in sexual preference cases. We agree with this extension of principle. Accordingly, we affirm.

In 1985, "Robbie"[1] Magnuson and Tracy A. Magnuson (now Berg) were married. They had two children, Brian (born October 4, 1991) and Meridith (born December 29, 1998). Tracy is a surgeon and Robbie is an attorney. Robbie eventually "announced that [s]he needed to, and would be transitioning from male to female." She took a leave of absence from work and ultimately resigned. Robbie and Tracy separated in October 2004, and Tracy filed to dissolve their marriage.

After an eight-day trial, the court entered numerous findings, including: "Both parents are good and loving parents. * * * The children's relationship with each parent is approximately equal. Each has performed equal but very different roles with the children. * * * Historically, the parties were a dual professional family, relying on the assistance of nannies[,] and [i]t is somewhat disingenuous for either parent to claim the historical role of primary parent in this case."

The court found both parents acted in ways adversely affecting the children's stability. For example, Tracy denigrated Robbie in front of the children; Robbie's conduct had an "unimaginable impact on Meridith" when she showed up at Meridith's school, pushed Meridith's maternal grandmother out of the way, and "grabbed Meridith, such that observers actually thought a kidnapping was going on." Further, "[Robbie] has indicated she will be undergoing sexual reassignment surgery sometime

---

[1] Each party is referred to by first name to avoid confusion without disrespect to individual or professional status. Similarly, Robbie is referred to by pronoun in the female gender consistent with the preference shown in Robbie's briefing and to conform to and avoid confusion with the trial court's quoted findings of fact.

in the very near future * * * [Robbie's] surgery may be everything [she] has hoped for, or it may be disastrous. No one knows what is ahead[,] and [t]he impact of gender reassignment surgery on the children is unknown."

The court found while Robbie left her job, Tracy "maintained her professional career, has provided for the children in the 'former' family home, and provides an oasis of stability in all of this ongoing change." A previous shared co-equal residential placement did not work, and "[t]hese children, in particular, need environmental and parental stability." Finally, "[w]hile the margin is somewhat slim in this particular case, [Tracy] is in a more stable and predictable place in her life right now to act as the children's primary care giver." Robbie appealed.

The issue is whether the trial court abused its discretion by impermissibly considering Robbie's transgender status in granting residential placement of the parties' two minor children to Tracy. Robbie contends the court erred in rejecting the guardian ad litem's (GAL) recommendation, in finding "[t]he impact of gender reassignment surgery on the children is unknown" [Factual Finding 2.21 X], in failing to properly address the factors in RCW 26.09.187(3)(a), and in restricting Robbie's parental rights.

We review a trial court's child placement decision for abuse of discretion. Trial courts have broad discretion and are not bound by GAL recommendations. * * * Certain factors must be considered when establishing the residential provisions in a permanent parenting plan. RCW 26.09.187(3)(a). These include: the parent/child relationship, the parents' responsibilities in performing parenting functions, parent agreements, "[e]ach parent's past and potential for future performance of parenting functions," the child's "emotional needs and developmental level," the child's relationships and activities, including schooling, the parent's wishes, the wishes of a mature child, and the parents' employment schedules. RCW 26.09.187(3)(a)(iii)(iv).

First, the trial court carefully considered each child's relationship with each parent before [ruling]. The court did not interview the children, but relied upon specific evidence given by the parties and the GAL when finding the impact of Robbie's surgery on the children was unknown. The court acted within its fact-finding discretion when drawing inferences from the given evidence of the children's present uncomfortable and nervous behavior to make the future impact finding. While Robbie points to evidence of the children's adjustment, we are in no position to find facts, reweigh the evidence, or decide witness credibility.

Second, the court was not bound by the GAL's recommendation. The court's oral ruling and its extensive findings of fact show the factors in RCW 26.09.187(3)(a) that were considered; the court is not required to enter written findings on each factor. The record does not support

Robbie's assertion that by rejecting the GAL's recommendation, the court impermissibly based its placement decision on transgender status.

Indeed, the court found Robbie was "undergoing an authentic gender transformation," and "has a right to be happy in her chosen life ahead." And, Robbie received substantial residential time with the children without limitation or restriction. *See In re Marriage of Cabalquinto*, 100 Wash.2d 325, 329, 669 P.2d 886 (1983) ("Visitation rights must be determined with reference to the needs of the child rather than the sexual preferences of the parent."). The *Cabalquinto* court's reasoning in a sexual preference visitation context is equally applicable in this transgender residential placement context.

In sum, the need of each child, not Robbie's transgender status, was the court's focus in determining residential placement. The court focused on the children's need for "environmental and parental stability" in granting the majority of residential time to Tracy, a permissible statutory factor addressing the children's emotional needs. RCW 26.09.187(3)(a). * * * Affirmed.

KULIK, J. (dissenting).

I agree with the majority's conclusion that the Supreme Court's reasoning in *In re Marriage of Cabalquinto*, 100 Wash.2d 325, 669 P.2d 886 (1983) is equally applicable to transgender persons. *Cabalquinto* held that a trial court cannot restrict a parent's rights based on sexual orientation, and the majority here extends that holding to transgender persons. However, the trial court erred by doing exactly what the majority here prohibits—the court awarded primary residential placement to Tracy based on Robbie's transgender status. This is a manifest abuse of discretion and, therefore, I respectfully dissent. * * *

The trial court's Findings of Fact (FF) 2.21 X provides: "The impact of gender reassignment surgery on the children is unknown." But the trial court's other findings refute the assertion that substantial evidence supports FF 2.21 X. Contrary to the unrebutted expert opinion of Dr. Walter Bockting, the court found that the impact of the gender reassignment surgery on the children was unknown. Dr. Bockting is a national expert in transgender parenting. He presented uncontradicted testimony that transgender status does not ultimately have an impact on the parent's ability to parent.

The court found that the children had approximately equal relationships with each parent. Significantly, the court made no finding that Robbie's transgender status endangered the physical, mental, or emotional health of the children. And, the trial court found that Robbie was the more nurturing parent.

The guardian ad litem (GAL) conducted an exhaustive investigation. He interviewed 23 lay witnesses and 15 professional and expert witnesses, and prepared a 214-page report. The court found that the GAL had done a thorough job and had performed his role in an exemplary way.

The GAL testified that Robbie was the primary parent based on sabbaticals and involvement with the children on a day-to-day basis. The GAL concluded that Robbie was the more nurturing and engaged parent, and he recommended that the court designate Robbie as the primary residential parent. The GAL also concluded that Tracy had always been the secondary parent. Another expert, Dr. Paul Wert, the court-appointed psychologist, stated that psychologically and emotionally, Robbie was capable of continuing to extensively parent.

The trial court also erroneously based its decision to place the children with Tracy on a misreading of RCW 26.09.187(3)(a)(I). Under this statute, the greatest weight shall be given to the "relative strength, nature, and stability of the child's relationship with each parent." RCW 26.09.187(3)(a)(I). Here, the trial court found a lack of stability based on Robbie's transgender status. "The respondent has indicated she will be undergoing sexual reassignment surgery sometime in the very near future. Said surgery may be everything respondent has hoped for, or it may be disastrous. No one knows what is ahead."

However, the statute requires a review of the stability of the child's relationship with the parent—not a review of whether the parent may have a surgery that impacts the parent. The trial court's conclusion that Robbie's life was not stable because of her planned surgery was directly and impermissibly related to Robbie's transgender status. And again, there was no evidence and no finding that Robbie's transgender status would cause any harm or detriment to the children.

Moreover, the proper test of parental fitness is the present condition of the parent. The court's speculation about the future is not an appropriate basis for awarding custody.

Finally, the trial court itself recognized that Robbie's transgender status caused no harm to the children when it placed no restrictions on Robbie's visitation with the children. The court agreed that the children's relationships with each parent were approximately equal. Apparently, the only difference between the parents was that Robbie, the primary parent, planned to have gender reassignment surgery.

"A trial court abuses its discretion when its decision is manifestly unreasonable or based on untenable grounds." *In re Parentage of J.H.*, 112 Wash.App. 486, 492, 49 P.3d 154 (2002). One parent's transgender status is not a tenable ground upon which to decide residential placement. Accordingly, I respectfully dissent.

MOIX v. MOIX

Supreme Court of Arkansas, 2013
430 S.W.3d 680, 2013 Ark. 478

CLIFF HOOFMAN, JUSTICE.

Appellant John Moix appeals from the circuit court's visitation order, which contained a provision prohibiting his long-term, domestic partner from being present during any overnight visitation with appellant's minor child. On appeal, appellant argues that the circuit court's order violated his state and federal constitutional rights to privacy and equal protection, and that the circuit court erred by finding that such a non-cohabitation restriction was required in the absence of any finding of harm to the child. * * * We reverse and remand.

John and Libby Moix were divorced in 2004. The divorce decree incorporated the parties' settlement agreement, which provided that the parties would share joint custody of their three sons, with appellee serving as the primary custodian and appellant receiving reasonable visitation. The settlement agreement also stated that neither party was to have overnight guests of the opposite sex.

In May 2005, appellee filed a petition to modify visitation, alleging that since the entry of the divorce decree, appellant had been having a romantic relationship with a live-in male companion and that the children had been exposed to that relationship on multiple occasions. Appellee asserted that appellant and his partner had recently separated after they were involved in a physical altercation in which appellant was seriously injured, although they had since resumed their relationship and were again residing together. Appellee requested that, due to this change in circumstances, the circuit court grant her sole custody of the children and limit appellant's visitation in such a way as to limit the children's exposure to the illicit relationship and to the danger caused by the volatility of his companion. Appellant agreed to the entry of an order of modification, filed on July 18, 2005, which provided that the existing custody arrangement would continue with the two older twin boys, but that appellee would receive full custody of R.M., who was five years old at the time. The order also restricted appellant to visitation with R.M. on every other weekend and every Wednesday, with no overnight visitation.

Despite the agreed order modifying visitation, it is undisputed by the parties that the order was not followed and that appellant had liberal overnight visitation with R.M. until late 2009 or early 2010, when he became addicted to prescription drugs and sought inpatient treatment after being involved in a hit-and-run accident. After he completed his treatment, appellant was limited to daytime visitation at the discretion of appellee. In May 2012, appellant filed a motion for modification of visitation and child support, in which he alleged that appellee had remarried in 2010 and that she had informed him that R.M. had a new father and no longer needed him. Appellant asserted that the severe reduction in his visitation coincided with appellee's remarriage and that his son had expressed the desire to spend more time with him. Because there had been a material change in circumstances based on appellee's remarriage, her new husband usurping his role as father of R.M., and the fact that R.M. was now twelve years old and wished to spend more time with his father, appellant requested that the circuit court modify visitation to allow overnight visits, as well as holiday and extended summer visitation.

In her response, appellee denied that there had been a material change in circumstances or that it was in R.M.'s best interest to have increased visitation. She asserted that any change in appellant's circumstances had been detrimental, pointing to his arrest for driving while under the influence of prescription drugs and the fact that he had lost his pharmacist license. She further alleged that appellant's relationship with his boyfriend had been volatile and that it was not in R.M.'s best interest to have overnight visitation in such an environment.

At the hearing held on October 9, 2012, appellant testified that he had been a pharmacist for twenty-three years and that he had had previous problems with a prescription-drug addiction in 1993, although he had completed treatment and remained sober until his recent relapse subsequent to his divorce. He testified that he gradually relapsed from 2004 until February 2010, when he was arrested for a DWI after being involved in a hit-and-run accident. Appellant completed several months of inpatient treatment and testified that he had completely abstained from alcohol and prescription drugs since February 2010. He further testified that he was now under a ten-year contract with the pharmacy board, pursuant to which he had been able to regain his pharmacist license, and that he has to call every morning to see if he must undergo a drug screen. So far, appellant stated that he had undergone fifty-nine random drug screens, all of which had been negative. He testified that he has also been regularly attending AA and NA meetings as required under the contract.

With regard to his relationship with his partner, Chad Cornelius, appellant testified that they had been in a committed, monogamous relationship for at least seven years and that they had applied for a marriage license in Iowa. Appellant stated that he had enjoyed overnight visitation with R.M. for five years before appellee forbade it and that even though Chad had been present, R.M. had never been exposed to any type of romantic behavior between them. Appellant testified that he and Chad had never slept in the same bed during any of R.M.'s previous visits and that if overnight visitation were again allowed, he would continue to abstain from bed sharing or other romantic behavior in the presence of his son. Appellant stated that Chad has a son from his previous marriage who often stays overnight at their home and that R.M. and Chad's son have a close relationship that would be greatly hindered if Chad were not allowed to be present during any overnight visits. According to appellant, he and Chad had not had any altercations since the one in 2005, which did not occur in the presence of R.M., and he stated that Chad is a positive role model for his son. Appellant also noted that his two older sons had lived with him during their senior year in high school, that they continued to spend weekends at his home during college, and that one of his sons is moving back home. He testified that all of his children are happy and emotionally, mentally, and physically stable.

Chad also testified and stated that he was a registered nurse at a hospital focusing on children and adolescents with behavioral-health issues. Chad testified that he has had to pass multiple state and federal background checks as a condition of his employment. He agreed that he and appellant had been in a committed relationship since 2005 and that they would like to get married. Chad also confirmed that he always slept in another room when R.M. visited. He testified that his sixteen-year-old son has a great relationship with R.M. Chad confirmed that appellant had been completely abstinent from drugs and alcohol since February 2010, and Chad stated that he personally does not drink alcohol in their home.

[Three other witnesses testified on behalf of the appellant, telling the court that both he and Chad were good and responsible parents.] The final witness to testify was appellee. She testified that she had obtained the 2005 modification order after she became concerned about appellant's and Chad's relationship and how it would affect R.M. She stated that appellant's relationship was not the sole reason why she was contesting his attempt to increase visitation. According to appellee, appellant had complained to her about Chad acting in a threatening and controlling manner, and she indicated that their relationship was unstable and unhealthy. She also indicated that she had found needles and vials of steroids in a guest bedroom of appellant's home while cleaning it in 2009 and that appellant had told her that Chad had a past history of steroid use. She testified that she would like to see appellant exhibit a longer period of being drug and alcohol free before allowing expanded visitation. Appellee further stated that appellant had shared information about the court proceedings with R.M., which she did not feel was appropriate. She admitted that R.M. had a loving relationship with his father and that it was important that they spend time together, but testified that it was not in R.M.'s best interest to have overnight or extended visitation at the present time due to his recent drug issues and his relationship with Chad.

In rebuttal testimony, appellant responded to appellee's allegation about finding needles and steroids in his home. He testified that he was not aware of these items, that he had never used intravenous drugs at any point, and that he was not aware that Chad had ever used them.

The circuit court entered an order on November 14, 2012, granting appellant's motion for modification of visitation. The court found that there had been a material change in circumstances and that it was in R.M.'s best interest to have more time with his father. Appellant was awarded visitation on every other weekend, as well as one evening during the week, in addition to extended summer and holiday visitation. However, the court found that it was required by the public policy of this state to impose a non-cohabitation restriction preventing Chad from being present during any overnight visits. The court noted that appellant and Chad were in a long-term committed relationship, that they had resided together since at least 2007, and that Chad posed "no threat to the health, safety, or welfare" of R.M. Other than the prohibition on unmarried cohabitation with a romantic partner in the presence of a minor child, the circuit court found no other factors present to militate against overnight visitation in this case. The court further found that the non-cohabitation policy, and the mandatory application of that policy, survive both federal and state constitutional scrutiny. Appellant filed a timely notice of appeal from the circuit court's order.

In domestic relations cases, we review the evidence de novo and will not reverse the circuit court's findings unless they are clearly erroneous. We also give special deference to the circuit court's superior position in evaluating the witnesses, their testimony, and the child's best interest. Because a circuit court maintains continuing jurisdiction over visitation, it may modify or vacate a prior visitation order when it becomes aware of a material change in circumstances since the previous order. The party seeking modification has the burden of demonstrating such a material change in circumstances. With regard to visitation, the primary consideration is the best interest of the child. Important factors for the court to consider in determining reasonable visitation are the wishes of the child, the capacity of the party desiring visitation to supervise and care for the child, problems of transportation and prior conduct in abusing visitation, the work schedule or stability of the parties, and relationship with siblings and other relatives. We have held that fixing visitation rights is a matter that lies within the sound discretion of the circuit court.

In his first two points on appeal, appellant argues that the non-cohabitation agreement imposed by the circuit court violates his federal and state constitutional rights to privacy and equal protection. However, because we find merit in appellant's final argument, there is no need to address these constitutional arguments. * * *

In his third and final point on appeal, appellant argues that, contrary to the circuit court's belief, our prior cases do not require the imposition of non-cohabitation provisions in the absence of any finding of evidence of harm to the minor child. * * *

As the circuit court in this case recognized, under the long-standing public policy of the courts in this state, a parent's extramarital cohabitation with a romantic partner in the presence of children, or a parent's promiscuous conduct or lifestyle, has never been condoned. *See, e.g., Alphin v. Alphin,* 364 Ark. 332, 219 S.W.3d 160 (2005); *Taylor v. Taylor,* 353 Ark. 69, 110 S.W.3d 731 (2003); *Campbell v. Campbell,* 336 Ark. 379, 985 S.W.2d 724 (1999). In *Campbell, supra,* this court made it clear that the purpose of non-cohabitation provisions are to promote a stable environment for the children and not merely to monitor a parent's sexual conduct.

We have also repeatedly held, however, that the primary consideration in domestic relations cases is the welfare and best interest of the children and that all other considerations are secondary. Therefore, we have emphasized in more recent cases that the policy against romantic cohabitation in the presence of children must be considered under the circumstances of each particular case and in light of the best interest of the children. For example, in *Taylor, supra,* we reversed the trial court's modification of custody where the finding of a material change in circumstances was based on the trial court's concern about protecting the children from future harm based on public misperception. In that case, the evidence showed that the custodial parent resided with a lesbian woman and that the two sometimes shared a bed, although they denied a romantic or sexual relationship. We cited cases from other states in support of the proposition that there must be concrete proof of likely harm to the children from the parent's living arrangement before a change in custody can be made. We held that "evidence-based factors must govern," rather than stereotypical presumptions of future harm.

We further discussed the issue of non-cohabitation agreements in *Arkansas Department of Human Services v. Cole,* 2011 Ark. 145, 380 S.W.3d 429. In *Cole,* we held that the Arkansas Adoption and Foster Care Act of 2008 (Act 1), which prohibited an individual from adopting or serving as a foster parent if that individual was cohabiting with a sexual partner outside of marriage, was unconstitutional because it violated the fundamental right to privacy implicit in the Arkansas Constitution. In response to the appellants' argument in that case that our holding would render non-cohabitation agreements in custody or dependency-neglect cases unenforceable, we stated the following:

We strongly disagree with the State and [the Family Council Action Committee's] conclusion that if this court finds that the categorical ban on adoption and fostering for sexual cohabitors put in place by Act 1 violates an individual's fundamental right to sexual privacy in one's home, state courts and DHS will be prohibited henceforth from considering and enforcing non-cohabitation agreements and orders in deciding child-custody and visitation cases as well as dependency-neglect cases. That simply is not the case. The overriding concern in all of these situations is the best interest of the child. *To arrive at what is in the child's best interest, the circuit courts and state agencies look at all the factors, including a non-cohabitation order if one exists, and make the best-interest determination on a case-by-case basis.* Act 1's blanket ban provides for no such individualized consideration or case-by-case analysis in adoption or foster-care cases and makes the bald assumption that in all cases where adoption or foster care is the issue it is always against the best interest of the child to be placed in a home where an individual is cohabiting with a sexual partner outside of marriage.

But in addition to case-by-case analysis, there is another difference between cohabitation in the child-custody or dependency-neglect context and cohabiting sexual partners who wish to adopt or become foster parents. Third-party strangers who cohabit with a divorced parent are unknown in many cases to the circuit court and have not undergone the rigorous screening associated with foster care or adoption. By everyone's account, applicants for foster care must comply with a raft of DHS regulations that include criminal background checks, home studies, family histories, support systems, and the like. Adoption, under the auspices of the trial court, requires similar screening. Unsuitable and undesirable adoptive and foster parents are thereby weeded out in the screening process. The same does not pertain to a third-party stranger who cohabits with a divorced or single parent.

Id. at 16–17, 380 S.W.3d 429, 380 S.W.3d 438 (emphasis added). Thus, we agree with appellant that the public policy against romantic cohabitation is not a "blanket ban," as it may not override the primary consideration for the circuit court in such cases, which is determining what is in the best interest of the children involved.

In the present case, the circuit court found from the evidence presented that appellant and his partner are in a long-term, committed romantic relationship and that "Mr. Cornelius poses no threat to the health, safety, or welfare of the minor child." The court further found that, "[o]ther than the prohibition of unmarried cohabitation with a romantic partner in the presence of the minor child, there are no other factors that would militate against overnight visitation." However, because the circuit court also stated that the mandatory application of our public policy against unmarried cohabitation required it to include a non-cohabitation provision, it made no finding on whether such a provision was in the best interest of R.M. Therefore, we reverse and remand for the circuit court to make this determination.

HUDSON GOODSON, JUSTICE, dissenting.

The majority in this case finds error in the circuit court's conclusion that the restriction on overnight visitation was in the best interest of the child. I must dissent.

Arkansas's appellate courts have steadfastly upheld chancery court orders that prohibit parents from allowing romantic partners to stay or reside in the home when the children are present. This court has gone so far as to say that "a parent's unmarried cohabitation with a romantic partner, or a parent's promiscuous conduct or lifestyle, *in the presence of a child* cannot be abided." *Taylor v. Taylor,* 353 Ark. 69, 80, 110 S.W.3d 731, 737 (2003) (emphasis supplied). This rule has been applied regardless of whether the parent is heterosexual or homosexual. *See Taylor,* 345 Ark. 300, 47 S.W.3d 222 (2001). The laudable purpose of the prohibition is to promote a stable environment for children; it is not imposed merely to monitor a parent's sexual conduct.

In our 2001 decision in *Taylor,* this court affirmed the circuit court's requirement that the mother's female sexual companion move out of the home as a condition of retaining custody of her children. There was no showing of harm occasioned by the companion's presence, as the circuit court expressed the willingness to allow the companion to babysit when the mother was at work. Nonetheless, we held that the circuit court acted within its authority and was not clearly erroneous in determining that it was not in the children's best interests for the mother to continue cohabitating with another adult with whom she was romantically involved. This court said,

> As emphasized by our court's earlier decisions, the trial court's use of the non-cohabitation restriction is a material factor to consider when determining custody issues. Such a restriction or prohibition aids in structuring the home place so as to reduce the possibilities (or opportunities) where children may be present and subjected to a single parent's sexual encounters, whether they be heterosexual or homosexual.

Taylor, 345 Ark. at 304–305, 47 S.W.3d at 225.

We have not completely abandoned the restriction in subsequent caselaw. In *Arkansas Department of Human Services v. Cole,* 2011 Ark. 145, 380 S.W.3d 429, this court determined that Act 1's categorical ban prohibiting sexual cohabitors from adopting or fostering children was unconstitutional as a violation of the fundamental right of privacy found in the Arkansas Constitution. However, we did not disavow the restriction on overnight romantic guests, as we expressly rejected the argument that striking down the categorical ban would prevent our courts from considering and enforcing non-cohabitation orders and agreements in domestic-relations cases.

The primary consideration regarding visitation is the best interest of the child. In its oral ruling from the bench, the circuit court recognized this guiding principle. The court also recognized the settled law permitting the imposition of a restriction on overnight visitation in the presence of sexual partners. Contrary to the majority's assertion, the circuit court did not neglect to make a determination that the restriction was in the best interest of the child. The court quite plainly stated that "the best interest dictates that that be the continued policy of the Court" to not permit overnight visitation in the presence of the child. I would affirm the circuit court's decision in keeping with our time-tested law. The court acted well within in its authority to conclude that the restriction promoted the best interest of this child.

[Dissenting opinion by BAKER, J., is omitted].

NOTES

1. *Openness of Relationship.* It appears that the lesbian mother lost in *Ex parte J.M.F.* because she was not sufficiently "discreet" in her relationship with her partner to satisfy the Alabama Supreme Court. Notice how the court did not require the petitioning father to establish that the mother's relationship with another woman adversely affected the child. Instead, the openness of the relationship, both inside and outside of the home, seems to have been enough to justify taking custody away from the lesbian mother and awarding it to the remarried father.

The North Carolina Supreme Court reached a similar conclusion in *Pulliam v. Smith*, 348 N.C. 616, 501 S.E.2d 898 (1998). After Carol and Frederick were divorced in 1991, they entered into a consent decree by which they would have joint legal custody and Frederick would have physical custody of their two children, ages three and six. The mother remarried and subsequently brought a motion to modify the custody judgment based on the fact that Frederick's gay partner had moved in with him and the children. The trial court granted the custody modification petition, but the intermediate appellate court, as in *Ex parte J.M.F.*, reversed concluding that there was insufficient evidence that the father's living arrangement adversely affected the children. The North Carolina Supreme Court reversed, noting that

> uncontroverted evidence was presented that defendant-father and Mr. Tipton engaged in oral sex approximately once a week in the home with the children present [in the home]. Defendant-father and

Mr. Tipton intended to continue such homosexual activity in the home. Defendant-father saw nothing wrong with such conduct and would not counsel the two minor children that such conduct was improper.

Evidence was also presented tending to show that the children had seen the two men demonstrate physical affection, including kissing each other on the lips. This activity took place in the home in front of the children as the "provider" of this couple prepared to leave for work. The minor child Joey had observed his father and Mr. Tipton in bed together.

The evidence further tended to show that the door of the bedroom occupied by defendant-father and Mr. Tipton was directly across the hall and approximately three feet from the door to the children's bedroom. Defendant-father and Mr. Tipton testified that both their bedroom door and the children's bedroom door were open at all times, except when the two men engaged in sexual activity. Further, testimony tended to show that the children went in and out of the two men's bedroom at will, often during the night when the two men were in bed together.

Defendant testified that he had told the children that society was not accepting of such a homosexual relationship. There was also evidence that Mr. Tipton kept photographs of "drag queens" in the home, despite his admission that the children should not be exposed to such material. Further, evidence was presented that Mr. Tipton had, on at least one occasion, taken the children away from the home without defendant's knowledge of their whereabouts.

* * * We conclude that activities such as the regular commission of sexual acts in the home by unmarried people, failing and refusing to counsel the children against such conduct while acknowledging this conduct to them, allowing the children to see unmarried persons known by the children to be sexual partners in bed together, keeping admittedly improper sexual material in the home, and Mr. Tipton's taking the children out of the home without their father's knowledge of their whereabouts support the trial court's findings of "improper influences" which are "detrimental to the best interest and welfare of the two minor children."

We do not agree with the conclusion of Justice Webb's dissent that the only basis upon which the trial court changed custody was that the defendant is a "practicing homosexual." Instead, we conclude that the trial court could and did order a change in custody *based in part* on proper findings of fact to the effect that defendant-father was regularly engaging in sexual acts with Mr. Tipton in the home while the children were present and upon other improper conduct by these two men. The trial court did not rely on the mere fact that defendant is a homosexual or a "practicing homosexual." Nor does this Court hold that the mere homosexual status of a parent is sufficient, taken alone, to support denying such parent custody of his or her child or children. That question is not presented by the facts of this case. * * *

* * * [E]vidence was [also] presented that when Joey was told that defendant-father was involved in a homosexual relationship, Joey was emotionally distraught, covering his face with his hands and running into the bathroom. Later, Joey cried, grasped onto his mother, and asked his mother to get him out of defendant's home. Evidence was also presented that sometime thereafter, Joey told his stepfather, William Pulliam, that he wanted his mother to come and get him and take him to Wichita where she lived. Further, evidence was presented that Joey expressed confusion over defendant's homosexual relationship with Mr. Tipton by asking Mr. Tipton if he was Joey's stepfather.

The trial court could reasonably find from this substantial evidence, as well as the other evidence discussed above, that "[t]he activity of the Defendant will likely create emotional difficulties for the two minor children."

Id. at 900–04.

2. *The Nexus Test.* The court in *Pulliam*, unlike in *J.M.F.*, attempted to base its ruling on ostensible evidence of harm caused by the gay father's relationship with another man. In doing so, the court seemed to be applying the nexus test, which requires the introduction of proof of harm to the children before courts can take into account the sexual orientation and relationships of parent litigants. Many courts have applied the nexus test to reject the claims by heterosexual parents that the same-sex sexual orientation and relationships of their former spouses justify limiting the latter's custodial and visitation rights. For example, the Florida Court of Appeals in *Jacoby v. Jacoby*, 763 So.2d 410 (Fla. Ct. App. 2000), reasoned as follows:

For a court to properly consider conduct such as Mrs. Jacoby's [same-sex] sexual orientation on the issue of custody, the conduct must have a direct effect or impact upon the children. *See Maradie v. Maradie*, 680 So.2d 538 (Fla. 1st DCA 1996). "[T]he mere possibility of negative impact on the child is not enough." *Id.* at 543. The connection between the conduct and the harm to the children must have an evidentiary basis; it cannot be assumed. We have reviewed the [trial] court's comments concerning the negative impact of the mother's sexual orientation on the children, and have found them to be conclusory or unsupported by the evidence.

For example, the final judgment stated that "[t]here is no doubt that the husband feels the current living arrangement of the wife is immoral and an inappropriate place in which to rear their children. . . . Obviously, this opinion is shared by others in the community." But the latter is not obvious to us from this record. In fact, there was no evidence addressing "the community's" beliefs about the morality of homosexuals or their child rearing abilities. * * *

But even if the court's comments about the community's beliefs and possible reactions were correct and supported by the evidence in this record, the law cannot give effect to private biases. *See Palmore v. Sidoti*, 466 U.S. 429, 433 (1984). Moreover, even if the law were to permit consideration of the biases of others, and even if we were to accept the assumption that such would necessarily harm the children, the bias and ensuing harm would flow not from the fact that the children were *living* with a homosexual mother, but from the fact that she *is* a homosexual. The circuit court's reliance on perceived biases was an improper basis for a residential custody determination.

Id. at 413. For similar rulings, *see. e.g., S.N.E. v. R.L.B.*, 699 P.2d 875 (Alaska 1985); *McGriff v. McGriff*, 99 P.3d 111 (Idaho 2004); *In re Marriage of R.S.*, 677 N.E.2d 1297 (Ill. Ct. App. 1996); *D.H. v. J.H.*, 418 N.E.2d 286 (Ind. Ct. App. 1981); *Hassenstab v. Hassenstab*, 570 N.W.2d 368 (Neb. Ct. App. 1997); *Damron v. Damron*, 670 N.W.2d 871, 873 (N.D. 2003); *Inscoe v. Inscoe*, 700 N.E.2d 70 (Ohio Ct. App. 1997); *Fox v. Fox*, 904 P.2d 66 (Okla. 1995); *Stroman v. Williams*, 353 S.E.2d 704 (S.C. Ct. App. 1987); *Van Driel v. Van Driel*, 525 N.W.2d 37 (S.D. 1994); *Matter of Marriage of Cabalquinto*, 669 P.2d 886 (Wash. 1983); *Black v. Black*, 2016 WL 917786 (Wash. Ct. App.). For a historical review of LGBT parenting cases, see CARLOS A. BALL, THE RIGHT TO BE PARENTS: LGBT FAMILIES AND THE TRANSFORMATION OF PARENTHOOD (2012).

3. *Social Science Data.* A recurring issue in cases between LGBT parents and their former heterosexual spouses is whether sexuality affects parenting ability. Social scientists have studied this question for decades, generally concluding that there are no meaningful differences in the children of lesbians and gay men when compared to children of heterosexual parents—in other words, that a parent's sexual orientation and gender has no discernable impact on the child's well-being or upbringing.

In a 1997 law review article, Professor Lynn Wardle argued that this social science research was methodologically flawed because it relied *inter alia* on small, non-random samples that seldom used married heterosexual families as the control groups. *See* Lynn D. Wardle, *The Potential Impact of Homosexual Parenting on Children*, 1997 U. ILL. L. REV. 833. Despite the literarure's purported flaws, Wardle used the data to argue that the studies suggested that children raised by lesbians and gay men are at risk of the following potential harms: a greater incidence of same-sex sexual activity, which then allegedly leads to a greater incidence of HIV, drug abuse, and suicide; negative effects on gender roles, gender identity, and self-esteem; and a greater likelihood of being sexually molested. Wardle's article touched off a lively debate in the scholarly literature; for a response, see, e.g., Carlos A. Ball & Janice Farrell Pea, *Warring with Wardle: Morality, Social Science, and Gay and Lesbian Parents*, 1998 U. ILL. L. REV. 253.

Most of the responses to Wardle continued to insist that children raised by gay parents were no different than those raised by heterosexuals. But in 2001, the sociologists Judith Stacey and Timothy Biblarz published an article in the *American Sociological Review* that received significant attention because it contended that there might be an association between the gender and sexual orientation of lesbian mothers, on the one hand, and the gender attitudes/interests and openness to same-sex sexual attraction and relationships of their children on the other. Judith Stacey & Timothy J. Biblarz, *(How) Does the Sexual Orientation of Parents Matter?*, 66 AM. SOC. REV. 159, 167–71, 176–79 (2001). Stacey and Biblarz reported on evidence suggesting that "lesbian parenting may free daughters and sons from a broad but uneven range of traditional gender prescriptions." *Id.* at 167. They also reported that while "the young adults reared by lesbian mothers were * * * significantly more likely to report having thought they might experience homoerotic attraction or relationship, * * * they were not statistically more likely to self-identify as bisexual, lesbian, or gay." *Id.* at 177.

In an article reviewing the social science studies on the children of lesbians and gay men, including several conducted after the publication of the Stacey and Biblarz article, Professor Carlos Ball divides the literature into three distinct subject areas of investigation. *See* Carlos A. Ball, *Social Science Studies and the Children of Lesbians and Gay Men: The Rational Basis Perspective*, 21 WILL. & MARY BILL RIGHTS J. 691 (2013). The first area addresses the children's psychological adjustment and social functioning, "including matters such as behavioral adjustment, emotional well-being, self-esteem, school performance, and peer relations. The second area consists of the gender attitudes and interests of the children of lesbians and gay men. Finally, the third area relates to the sexual orientation of those children." *Id.* at 697. In terms of the first area of study, Ball concludes that "the social science evidence showing a lack of an association between parental sexual orientation and the psychological and social functioning of children is so conclusive and so uniform, that efforts to impose marriage and parenting restrictions on lesbians and gay men based on concerns about such functioning are irrational (and therefore unconstitutional) because they lack a defensible factual foundation." *Id.* at 698.

But Ball found that the social science literature is somewhat less consistent on the questions of gender role development and sexual orientation, with a minority of studies suggesting possible associations with parental sexual orientation. "Specifically, * * * a minority of studies suggest that the daughters of lesbian mothers evince attitudes and engage in play and school activities that are less consistent with traditional gender expectations when compared to the daughters of heterosexual parents.

Similarly, * * * a minority of studies suggest that the daughters of lesbian mothers express a greater interest in participating in same-sex relationships than do the daughters of heterosexual parents." *Id.* at 699. Ball then proceeded to argue that even if these indicia of possible differences can be shown to exist conclusively, they cannot constitutionally be used to justify the differential treatment of lesbians and gay men in matters associated with parenting because the state does not have a legitimate interest "in encouraging individuals to behave in certain ways (or to pursue certain preferences) based on their gender" or "in attempting to influence the sexual orientation of individuals, or in discouraging individuals (including adolescents) from engaging in same-sex as opposed to different-sex sexual conduct." *Id.* at 701. Do you agree? If so, does that mean that much of the social science literature on the children of lesbians and gay men is constitutionally *irrelevant*?

4.   *Transgender Parents.* The Nevada Supreme Court in *Daly v. Daly*, 102 Nev. 66, 715 P.2d 56 (1986), *overruled on other grounds by In re Termination of Parental Rights as to N.J.*, 116 Nev. 790, 8 P.3d 126 (2000), upheld the termination of the parental rights of a male-to-female transgender parent. The child in the case was born more than a dozen years before her father underwent sex-reassignment surgery. When the mother learned of the impending surgery, she petitioned to have the father's parental rights terminated. The court found the termination to be in the child's best interest because of "the substantial risk of emotional or mental injury were she forced to visit with her father." *Id.* at 59. Similarly, the court in *M.B. v. D.W.*, 236 S.W.3d 31 (Ky.Ct.App. 2007), terminated the parental rights of a male-to-female transsexual parent so that her former wife's new husband could adopt the child.

In contrast, the court in *Christian v. Randall*, 516 P.2d 132, 33 Colo.App. 129 (Ct. App. 1973), refused to transfer custody from a female-to-male transgender parent who had custody of the children for many years after the divorce and before he underwent sex-change surgery. The court noted that the sex change did not "adversely affect respondent's relationship with the children nor impair their emotional development." 516 P.2d at 134, 33 Colo.App. at 133. *Cf. In re Marriage of D.F.D & D.G.D.*, 862 P.2d 368, 376, 261 Mont. 186, 200 (1993) (concluding that trial court erred in denying joint custody to father who had in the past dressed in women's clothes in private).

5.   *Visitation.* As *Moix* illustrates, many lesbian, gay, and bisexual parents, following the dissolution of different-sex relationships, have had to contend with court-imposed visitation restrictions. Some courts have sought to prohibit children from staying overnight with their lesbian, gay, or bisexual parents. *See, e.g., North v. North*, 648 A.2d 1025, 1033, 102 Md.App. 1, 16 (Ct. Spec. App. 1994) (holding that lower court abused its discretion by denying father overnight visitation based on fear that he would display or discuss his "homosexual lifestyle" with children). Other courts have allowed

overnight visits as long as particular others are not present. In one case, for example, an appellate court upheld a visitation restriction on a gay dad that prohibited the overnight presence of any non-blood related person. *Marlow v. Marlow*, 702 N.E.2d 733, 738 (Ind. Ct. App. 1998). In another case, a court vacated a visitation restriction prohibiting overnight visitation in the presence of a lesbian mother's female partner. *Eldridge v. Eldridge*, 42 S.W.3d 82, 90 (Tenn. 2001). *See also A.O.V. v. J.R.V.*, 2007 WL 581871, at *6 (Va. Ct. App. 2007) (holding that trial judge did not "abuse his discretion by prohibiting the father from allowing his [male] companion to occupy the home overnight or engaging in displays of affection while the children visit."). Other courts have imposed restrictions on the presence of certain individuals (usually the parent's same-sex partner) regardless of the time of day. *See, e.g., Ex parte D.W.W.*, 717 So.2d 793, 796–97 (Ala. 1998) (upholding visitation restriction that prohibited mother's lesbian partner from being present during visit); *Weigand v. Houghton*, 730 So.2d 581 (Miss. 1999) (same). In addition, some courts have expressed concerns about parents who are actively involved in the LGBT community. One court, for example, upheld an order requiring that a gay father "not include in the children's activities during periods of visitation, any social, religious or educational functions sponsored by or which otherwise promote the homosexual lifestyle." *Marlow, supra,* 702 N.E.2d at 735. Another court, in upholding a restriction prohibiting the presence of a lesbian mother's partner during visitation, noted with concern that "[b]oth women are active in the homosexual community [and that] [t]hey frequent gay bars and have discussed taking the children to a homosexual church." *See Ex parte D.W.W.,* supra 717 So.2d at 796. Finally, at least one court has upheld similar visitation restrictions imposed on a transgender parent. *See J.L.S. v. D.K.S.*, 943 S.W.2d 766, 772 (Mo. Ct. App. 1997) (upholding visitation restriction imposed on female transgender parent that she not "cohabit with other transsexuals or sleep with another female" during visits).

Other courts, like the Arkansas Supreme Court in *Moix*, have rejected visitation restrictions in cases involving lesbian, gay, and bisexual parents in the absence of a showing that such restrictions are necessary to avoid the risk of harm to children. In *Mongerson v. Mongerson*, 678 S.E.2d 891 (Ga. 2009), for example, the Georgia Supreme Court unanimously overturned a trial judge's ruling that granted visitation to a gay father on the condition that he not "expos[e] the children to his homosexual partners and friends." *Id.* at 894. The court explained that "the prohibition * * * assumes, without evidentiary support, that the children will suffer harm from any such contact. Such an arbitrary classification based on sexual orientation flies in the face of our public policy that encourages divorced parents to participate in the raising of their children." *Id.* at 895. *See also In re Marriage of Dorworth*, 33 P.3d 1260, 1262 (Colo. Ct. App. 2001) (vacating visitation restriction that prohibited presence of any other person at night at home of bisexual father); *Gould v. Dickens*, 143 S.W.3d 639, 644 (Mo. Ct. App. 2004) (vacating visitation restriction prohibiting overnight visitation when lesbian mother shared a bed with her female partner).

B. SPERM DONORS

THOMAS S. v. ROBIN Y.

Supreme Court of New York, Appellate Division, 1994
618 N.Y.S.2d 356, 209 A.D.2d 298

MEMORANDUM DECISION.

This appeal presents the narrow issue of whether a sperm donor who is known to his child as her father and who, despite residing in California, has had considerable contact with her at the instance of her mother, is entitled to an order of filiation, as mandated by Family Court Act § 542. We hold that he is. The broader issue of visitation, while argued extensively in the briefs, has not been adequately explored, and we therefore remand this issue for a hearing.

The child, Ry R.-Y., now 12 years old, lives with her mother, respondent Robin Y., the mother's lifetime companion, Sandra R., and Sandra's child, Cade, now 14, who was also conceived through artificial insemination by a donor known to her mother. Petitioner, who is also gay, was sought out by Robin Y. as a known donor and, after several attempts in both New York and California, Robin Y. successfully inseminated herself with petitioner's semen in February 1981 at the home of a mutual friend.

Ry was born on November 16, 1981 in San Francisco, where the household temporarily relocated in connection with Sandra R.'s employment. Like Cade, Ry was given the last names of R. and Y. Petitioner is not listed on Ry's birth certificate, and R. and Y. paid all expenses associated with the pregnancy and delivery. Petitioner was, however, informed of the birth and brought congratulatory flowers to R. and Y.'s home. Later that year, the household moved back to New York where they currently occupy an apartment located in a building owned by Sandra R.

For the first three years of her life, petitioner saw Ry only once or twice while in New York on business. In accordance with an oral agreement with R. and Y., he did not call, support or give presents to her during this period. When Cade, at the age of approximately five years, started asking questions about her father, R. and Y., as they had agreed between themselves, made arrangements for Ry and Cade to meet their biological fathers.

Petitioner testified that there were approximately 26 visits with the R. and Y. family over the following six-year period, ranging in duration from a few days to two weeks. Robin Y. estimates that appellant spent a total of sixty days with the R.-Y. family over the course of those six years, and petitioner estimates 148 days. Whatever the figure, it appears that all parties concerned developed a comfortable relationship with one another. Photographs included in the exhibits depict a warm and amicable relationship between petitioner and Ry, and there are numerous cards and letters from Ry to petitioner in which she expressed her love for him.

In July 1990, petitioner asked Robin Y. for permission to take Ry and Cade to see his parents and stay at a beach house with some of his siblings and their children. It seems that petitioner felt awkward about introducing R. and Y. to his parents. R. and Y., however, were not willing to allow petitioner to take the girls unless the mothers accompanied them.

It was apparently during the course of these negotiations that petitioner revealed his desire to establish a paternal relationship with Ry. Y. and R. regarded this as a breach of their oral agreement, insisting that visitation continue on the same terms as over the past six years, *viz.*, with their supervision. They also rejected petitioner's suggestion to consult a family counselor or mediator. Unable to resolve his differences with R. and Y. and unable to see his daughter for a period of several months, petitioner moved, by order to show cause, for an order of filiation and for visitation.

During the course of the proceedings, Family Court ordered blood tests and a psychiatric evaluation of Ry. * * * The tests indicated a 99.9% probability of petitioner's paternity. Psychiatric evaluation revealed a belief on Ry's part that any relationship with petitioner would necessarily disrupt her relationship with Robin Y. and Sandra R. and might therefore undermine the legitimacy of her perception of the family unit. It also revealed that, since these proceedings were instituted, Ry has expressed a desire to end all contact with petitioner.

Family Court found by clear and convincing evidence, based upon the blood tests, that petitioner is the biological father of Ry. Nevertheless, citing the doctrine of equitable estoppel, the court refused to enter an order of filiation and dismissed the proceeding. The court characterized petitioner as an "outsider attacking her [Ry's] family and refusing to give it respect", concluding that "a declaration of paternity would be a statement that her family is other than what she knows it to be and needs it to be" and, therefore, "would not be in her best interests." The court added, "Even were there an adjudication of paternity, I would deny [petitioner's] application for visitation."

It is appropriate to begin with the observation that the effect of Family Court's order is to cut off the parental rights of a man who is conceded by all concerned—the child, her mother and the court—to be the biological father. The legal question that confronts us is not, as Family Court framed it, whether an established family unit is to be broken up. Custody of the child is not now, and is unlikely ever to be, an issue between the parties. Rather the question is whether the rights of a biological parent are to be terminated. Absent strict adherence to statutory provisions, termination of those rights is in violation of well established standards of due process and cannot stand.

The asserted sanctity of the family unit is an uncompelling ground for the drastic step of depriving petitioner of procedural due process. Whatever concerns and misgivings Family Court and the dissenters may entertain about visitation, custody and the child's best interests, it is clear that they are appropriately reserved for a later stage of the proceedings. * * *

The emphasis placed on custody, both by respondent and the dissent, is out of all proportion to its relevance to this proceeding. First, Thomas S. has never asserted a desire to gain custody of Ry. Second, as noted, custody and visitation are matters for subsequent hearings. Finally, the extent of petitioner's involvement in Ry's life is at once characterized by the dissent as both inadequate and overly intrusive. He is vilified for failing to sufficiently undertake his parental responsibility to provide ongoing support for the child and her education, without any consideration for whether support was necessary, solicited or even deemed desirable by her mother and Sandra R. He is criticized for having only a limited experience with the day-to-day events in his child's life, without regard for the three-thousand-mile distance between residences or the degree to which access to the child was limited by respondent and Sandra R. At the same time, petitioner's desire to communicate and visit with his daughter is portrayed as a threat to the stability and legitimacy of the family unit constituted by Ry, respondent and Sandra R. It is distressing that petitioner, who seems to have exhibited sensitivity and respect for the relationship between respondent and her domestic partner, is proposed to be compensated for his understanding by judicial extinguishment of his rights as a father. Such a result is offensive to the Court's sense of equity. Moreover, such an injustice hardly serves to promote tolerance and restraint among persons who may confront similar circumstances. It discourages resolution of disputes involving novel and complex familial relationships without resort to litigation which, ideally, should only be pursued as a last resort. * * *

Family Court's disposition is no more compelled by the equities of this matter than by the law. The notion that a lesbian mother should enjoy a parental relationship with her daughter but a gay father should not is so innately discriminatory as to be unworthy of comment. Merely because petitioner does not have custody of his daughter does not compel the conclusion, embraced by the dissent, that he may not assert any right to maintain a parental relationship with her. While much is made by Family Court of the alleged oral understanding between the parties that petitioner would not assume a parental role towards Ry, any such agreement is unenforceable for failure to comply with explicit statutory requirements for surrender of parental rights as the dissent concedes. * * *

Family Court presumed to apply the doctrine of equitable estoppel to foreclose any attempt by petitioner to obtain judicial consideration of his rights as a parent. However, the doctrine is more appropriately applied against the mother than against petitioner. If respondent now finds petitioner's involvement in his daughter's life to be inconvenient, she cannot deny that her predicament is the result of her own action. Not content with the knowledge of the identity of the biological father that her chosen method of conception afforded, Robin Y. initiated and fostered a relationship between petitioner and Ry. However strenuously this relationship may be gainsaid by respondent, its nature, duration and constancy during the six years prior to the commencement of this proceeding amply demonstrate petitioner's interest and concern for his child so as to preclude summary termination of his parental rights. Nor, given that Ry has known petitioner to be her father since the age of three, is there any credibility to the suggestion that mere acknowledgment of petitioner's legal status will result in a shock to the child's sensibilities. According to the testimony of the court-appointed psychiatrist, Ry's recently expressed desire to sever contact with petitioner, coinciding as it does with the onset of the instant dispute, is based on concerns communicated to her by Robin Y. and Sandra R. These fears are based on the misapprehension that visitation by petitioner necessarily poses an immediate threat to the stability of the household. In any event, Family Court's precipitous pronouncement notwithstanding, visitation is a matter yet to be determined, and the value of therapy in reestablishing the relationship between Ry and her father is an appropriate consideration in that context. Finally, entry of an order of filiation has the advantage of supplying a further source of support, should the necessity arise, together with the potential for substantial inheritance.

We reject the dissent's view that the alleged agreement between the parties constitutes evidence of a lack of commitment to his child on the part of petitioner. As the dissenters concede, legal impediments and public policy considerations bar enforcement of the oral agreement, and it can therefore be accorded no force or effect. It is the longstanding rule of equity, now extended to law, that the facts be viewed in their fullest. The Court cannot simply ignore the significant events that have transpired since Ry's third birthday. In any event, we regard the determination of this matter in any manner that departs from the express procedures delineated in article 5 of the Family Court Act as a violation of petitioner's statutory and Constitutional rights.

Having initiated and encouraged, over a substantial period of time, the relationship between petitioner and his daughter, respondent is estopped to deny his right to legal recognition of that relationship. The provisions of Family Ct. Act § 542(a) are clear and unambiguous and, therefore, there is no room for judicial interpretation. Having found that petitioner is the father of Ry R.-Y., Family Court was commanded by statutory direction to enter an order of filiation.

ELLERIN, JUSTICE (dissenting).

The question before us on this appeal is whether petitioner must be granted an order of filiation, pursuant to Family Court Act § 542, establishing his paternity of the child borne by respondent in November, 1981 as a result of having been artificially inseminated with petitioner's sperm or whether the doctrine of equitable estoppel may be applied to preclude the issuance of such order. * * *

The facts as found by the trial court are as follows. The child Ry was conceived by respondent Robin Y using sperm donated by appellant Thomas S., a gay man, while Robin was living in a stable life partnership relationship with another lesbian mother, Sandra R., and Sandra's then infant child Cade. At the time of appellant's providing his sperm, it was agreed, albeit not in writing, that he would have no parental rights or obligations and that the child would be brought up with Cade in a 2 parent household with 2 mothers. Appellant further agreed that he would make himself known to the child if the child wished to know the identity of her biological progenitor.

Notwithstanding the agreement, it is the manner in which the parties acted during the period from the child's birth up to the time of the commencement of this proceeding that is of critical significance. For the first 3 years of Ry's life there was virtually no contact with appellant. He was neither present at, nor involved with any arrangements for or costs of, her birth. His name was not on her birth certificate, he was not in any way involved in her care or support nor did he indicate the slightest desire to learn of her progress or condition even though for the first 8 months of her life Ry and her family resided in San Francisco where appellant lived.

It was only in 1985 when Cade, then almost 5 years old, began to ask about her biological origins, that contact was made with both Cade's sperm donor and with appellant, both of whom lived in California. At that time Ry was almost 3 and a half years old. In the ensuing 6 years there were periodic contacts between appellant, and both children, usually with both mothers present and always at the complete discretion of the mothers.

The record clearly establishes that for Ry's first 9 and half years of life the appellant at no time sought to establish a true parental relationship with her either by way of seeking to legally establish his paternity and assuming the responsibilities and obligations which that status entailed or by any involvement in her upbringing or schooling or by attempting to provide any support for her. He was not there when she cut her baby teeth, started to walk, was sick or in need of parental comfort or guidance, nor did he seek to involve himself in the every day decisions which are peculiarly the domain of parents—decisions as to what schools she should attend, what camps, what doctors should be consulted, the extent of her after school and social activities, the need for tutors and the like. Perhaps Ry herself best stated it when she said that to her a parent is a person who a child depends on to care for her needs.

The net of petitioner's relationship with Ry during the 6 years that he occasionally saw her until she was almost 10 years old was that of a close family friend or fond surrogate uncle who, while acknowledging that he was her biological sperm donor, fully recognized that her family unit consisted of her two mothers and her sister Cade and that he was not a family member of that unit. Throughout this period he fully acquiesced in the mothers' arrangement for meetings—i.e., to include all 4 members of the Ry family and with Cade to be treated by him in precisely the same way as Ry. While respondent Robin Y. was always agreeable to continuing periodic meetings and contacts with appellant on the same basis, it was appellant who summarily sought to alter this *modus operandi* of the preceding 6 years. He asked that the children visit him by themselves, without the other members of those whom he had always recognized as her family, so that he could introduce Ry to his own biological family, including his parents and siblings. He made clear that he would not feel comfortable introducing the mothers to his family. After respondent refused to accede to this attempt to markedly alter the prior course of the relationship between appellant and Ry's family, fueled by respondent's apprehension of future legal proceedings seeking to undermine that family relationship, appellant filed the instant petition for filiation.

The trial court, sensitive to the issues involved, appointed a law guardian for the child and obtained the agreement of all parties to submit the child to a psychiatric evaluation. Both the law guardian and the psychiatrist strongly recommended against the declaration of paternity and further recommended that there be no court-ordered visitation. * * *

At the outset, it must be emphasized that this proceeding was brought for the purpose of establishing, in the first instance, petitioner's parental status. While, concededly, petitioner provided the sperm for the artificial insemination that resulted in Ry's birth, petitioner at no time, for the almost 10 years prior to the commencement of this proceeding, established any paternal rights either by way of a legal proceeding or by way of fulfilling any of the duties and responsibilities incidental to parenthood. In that setting, the majority's characterization of the denial of the petition as akin to the "termination of [petitioner's] parental rights" is both puzzling and inaccurate. Until it can be established that petitioner has some parental rights, the very relief sought in this proceeding, the question of any "termination" of petitioner's rights never arises and the majority's recourse to Social Services Law § 384–b, governing termination of parental rights, is misplaced.

Nor, it should be made clear, is this case in any way a referendum on the comparative parenting abilities of lesbian mothers versus gay fathers, a gratuitous rhetorical inquiry posed by the majority. That petitioner is a gay man is wholly irrelevant to the question of whether his conduct for a period of almost 10 years during which he acquiesced in, and indeed fostered, Ry's belief that her family unit consisted of her 2 mothers and her sister Cade and that he did not occupy, nor seek to exercise, any parental or family role, should preclude his present attempt to establish parental status. It is the import of appellant's conduct and not his sexual orientation that is controlling. An identical standard would apply if any or all of the parties involved in this case were heterosexual.

The threshold issue that must first be determined is what rights, if any, arise from the fact that petitioner was the sperm donor and paternal biological progenitor of the child Ry. The Court of Appeals has made clear that absent "a full commitment to the responsibilities of parenthood" the mere existence of a biological link does not merit constitutional protection. Thus, an unwed biological father does not automatically have parental rights which must be recognized by the state independent of the child's best interests, since such rights come into existence only if the father has sufficiently grasped the opportunity to "promptly manifest[ed] his willingness to take on parental responsibilities" and it is only when "the opportunity, of limited duration, to manifest a willingness to be a parent" is grasped that an interest arises worthy of protection as a matter of due process.

While providing support for the child, and the child's education, would appear to be a minimal requirement for the manifestation of parenthood, the criteria which are particularly relevant in determining whether an unwed biological father has sufficiently undertaken his parental responsibilities to give him a protected parental interest may be garnered by reference to Domestic Relations Law § 111 which governs adoptions and delineates the various criteria which must be met before an unwed father has any protected right vis-a-vis the child. That statute provides that when the child is more than six months old, the father has a protected parental right to the extent of requiring his consent to the child's adoption, *only if* he has, maintained substantial and continuous or repeated contact with the child as manifested by: (i) the payment by the father toward the support of the child of a fair and reasonable sum, according to the father's means, and either (ii) the father's visiting the child at least monthly when physically and financially able to do so and not prevented from doing so by the person or authorized agency having lawful custody of the child, or (iii) the father's regular communication with the child or with the person or agency having the care or custody of the child, when physically and financially unable to visit the child or prevented from doing so by the person or authorized agency having lawful custody of the child.

In this case there is no question that petitioner has never sought to contribute to the ongoing support of the child, or to see to her educational or other needs despite the fact that he is a professional of substantial means. On the contrary, all of the child's economic and educational needs have been provided for through her mothers and she has enjoyed a comfortable standard of living. Nor, after not seeing the child at all for the first 3 years of her life, has petitioner ever sought to visit the child on anything close to a monthly basis. His failure to do so cannot be attributed to respondent since, until very recently, the pattern of occasional visits was one with which he was in full agreement. Whether viewed within the framework of the statutory criteria or the common understanding of what parenthood entails vis-a-vis the multiple daily facets of a child's life, petitioner's conduct until the commencement of this proceeding fell far short of manifesting the willingness to take on the parental responsibilities necessary to invest him with any constitutionally recognized parental "rights" which could be terminated subject to the provisions of Social Services Law § 384–b.

Petitioner argues that, *de hors* any constitutional considerations, Family Court Act § 542 requires that an order of filiation be granted because he is unquestionably the child's biological progenitor. Irrespective of the seemingly mandatory language of Family Court Act § 542, biological fatherhood does not create an absolute right to an order of filiation, and, indeed, the courts of this state have frequently applied the doctrine of equitable estoppel to forestall the entry of such an order regardless of biological relation.

An equitable estoppel will be applied in the interest of fairness where the misleading words or conduct of a party induces justifiable reliance by another to his or her substantial detriment, and may include a situation where the failure of a party to promptly assert a right creates circumstances making it inequitable to permit the right to be exercised after considerable time has elapsed.

Appropriate circumstances for application of an estoppel in a paternity proceeding have been found in a wide variety of situations. For example, in *Matter of Ettore I. v. Angela D.*, 513 N.Y.S.2d 733 (App. Div. 1987), the petitioner was estopped from asserting paternity where he had taken no action for three years and both the child and the mother's husband had regarded the child as the husband's own and had formed a parent-child relationship.

In *Terrence M. v. Gale C.*, 597 N.Y.S.2d 333 (App. Div. 1993), petitioner was estopped from attempting to establish his paternity where he had failed to support or attempt to establish any relationship with the child for almost the entire period of the child's minority. In that case, the person whom the child had previously thought of as her father had never been married to her mother and was, at the time of the proceeding, deceased. * * *

This leads to the issue of whether an estoppel should be applied under the facts of this case. While frequently paternity cases which have involved the application of equitable estoppel have concerned the preservation of the legitimacy of the child in its legal definition, no authority is cited to support the majority's conclusion that the preservation of legitimacy in its legal sense is a *sine qua non* for the imposition of equitable estoppel. On the contrary, the paramount purpose of the equitable estoppel doctrine is to promote fairness and justice, and in considering whether it should be applied in a paternity case the overriding consideration is whether imposition of the estoppel will serve the best interests of the child. * * *

* * * While the child has always known that petitioner is her biological progenitor, it had consistently been demonstrated by petitioner himself that this factor did not confer upon him any authority or power over her life, that it did not mean that Sandra R. was less her mother than Robin Y., and that it did not mean that her sister was not her full sister. To now grant him the standing to claim the very considerable authority and power held by a parent, against her wishes, would change her life in drastic ways. For this reason, I believe that the elements of misrepresentation, reliance and detriment have clearly been established and that the evidence demonstrates that an order of filiation is not in this child's best interests. Under these circumstances, the doctrine should be applied. * * *

Finally, it should be noted that, contrary to respondent's arguments, the fact that the child was conceived by artificial insemination is wholly irrelevant on the question of whether or not petitioner has acquired any parental rights. In this state, the only differentiation drawn between the familial status of a child conceived as a result of artificial insemination, as opposed to intercourse occurs when the child is born to a woman who makes a mutual decision with her husband to conceive a child in this fashion, which is memorialized in a written, signed statement and where the insemination is performed by a licensed physician who certifies that he has performed the procedure. In such a case, Domestic Relations Law § 73 automatically bestows the parental rights of the biological father upon the mother's husband, who is deemed the legal father for all purposes. That statute, of course, has no application to this case and the conclusion that petitioner has no protected parental rights is predicated upon his failure for almost 10 years to manifest his willingness to assume the responsibilities of parenthood or to be a parent irrespective of the manner of the child's conception.

NOTES

1. *Use of an Unknown Sperm Donor*. Using an unknown sperm donor is often considered the best way to guarantee that he will not assert parental rights at a later time. The anonymity of the woman and the donor may be maintained through the use of a sperm bank. Sperm banks often screen donors for health problems. They also keep records on the physical characteristics of donors. Thus, although the mother does not know the donor's identity, she may still screen for certain physical traits and can more safely assume that her own health will not be jeopardized by the insemination.

Some sperm banks have adopted policies that allow the children, usually when they reach the age of eighteen, to learn the identity of the anonymous donors as long as they, at the time of donation, consented to have their identity revealed. These sperm banks inform prospective mothers whether donors have agreed to have their identity revealed in the future so that they can take this information into account when choosing a donor.

2. *Use of a Known Sperm Donor*. Some prospective mothers choose known donors because they want to have the option of revealing their identities to the children. Many of these mothers also choose to have the donors play a role in their children's lives. One study of lesbian couples who chose known donors found that they

> struggled with how to maintain themselves as lesbian-headed two-parent families in the face of normative cognitive prescriptions about the two-parent family. Although some solved this problem by simply eliminating the biological father from the picture altogether, replacing him with male role models who had no legal or social claim to father status, others attempted a compromise in which the biological father remained present but was redefined from father to sperm donor and, in some cases, to uncle or close family friend. Men who agreed to play this role often relinquished both their social and legal claim to co-parent status, making it possible for the nonbiological mother to fill that role.

Susan E. Dalton & Denise D. Bielby, *"That's Our Kind of Constellation":* *Lesbian Mothers Negotiate Institutionalized Understandings of Gender*

Within the Family, 14 GENDER & SOCIETY 36, 49 (2000). Dalton and Bielby report that, as *Thomas S.* illustrates, it is difficult for some lesbian coparents to manage a sperm donor's involvement with their family while at the same time making it clear that the donor is not a parent. As one of the lesbian mothers put it, "We were not looking for another parent, we were looking for somebody the kids could know, and that's a hard thing to ask somebody. * * * I think to ask somebody to be an anonymous donor is fairly easy [as is] to ask them to be an involved parent, but [the] * * * in-between, we want you to be a known person but not involved is [not so easy]. * * * [It] takes a fairly special person to be able to have that sort of a role." *Id.* For an extensive study of thirty-four families headed by lesbian mothers whose children were conceived through donor insemination, see MAUREEN SULLIVAN, THE FAMILY OF WOMAN: LESBIAN MOTHERS, THEIR CHILDREN, AND THE UNDOING OF GENDER (2004). *See also* NANCY J. MEZEY, NEW CHOICES, NEW FAMILIES: HOW LESBIANS DECIDE ABOUT MOTHERHOOD (2008).

What advice would you give prospective mothers when choosing between anonymous and known donors? What are the advantages and disadvantages of each option? If a lesbian couple chooses to use sperm provided by a known donor, what advice would you give them regarding the possible legal implications of that choice? How can they best protect themselves against a possible future parental claim by the known donor?

3.   *Use of a Known Sperm Donor and Parentage Statutes.* The Uniform Parentage Act (UPA) of 1973 deemed a known sperm donor not to be the father of a child conceived by a *married* woman as long as the sperm was provided to a licensed physician. Uniform Parentage Act § (5)(b) (1973). Several states adopted the UPA as written, but others (like California) did not distinguish between married and unmarried women. *See* 1975 Cal. Stat. 3197–98 (codified as amended at Cal. Fam. Code § 7613 (West 2016)). For an application of the California statute, see *Jhordan C. v. Mary K.*, 224 Cal.Rptr. 530, 534, 179 Cal.App.3d 386, 392 (1986).

A more recent version of the UPA also does not differentiate among women based on their marital status (or on the sperm being provided to a licensed physician). *See* Uniform Parentage Act § 703 (2002). Although some state statutes continue to distinguish between married and unmarried women for purposes of terminating the parental rights of known donors, *see, e.g.*, MINN. STAT. ANN. § 257.56(2) (West 2007); MO. ANN. STAT. § 210.824(2) (West 2004); MONT. CODE ANN. § 40–6–106(2) (2007), most statutes do not. The laws that do not take marital status into account can be divided into two groups. Under the first set of statutes, the donor is not a parent and there is "no statutory mechanism for producing a different result even if the parties intend a different outcome." Nancy Polikoff, *A Mother Should Not Have to Adopt Her Own Child: Parentage Laws for Children of Lesbian Couples in the Twenty-First Century*, 5 STAN. J. CIV. RTS. & LIBERTIES 201, 241 (2009) (footnote omitted). In the second group, "the donor is not a parent unless the donor and recipient agree in writing to the contrary." *Id.* at 242 (footnote omitted). For example, the relevant California statute states that "[t]he donor of semen provided to a licensed physician and surgeon or to a licensed sperm bank for use in assisted reproduction by a woman other than the donor's spouse is treated in law as if he were not the natural parent of a child thereby conceived, unless otherwise agreed to in a writing signed by the donor and the woman prior to the conception of the child." Cal. Fam. Code § 7613(b)(1) (West 2016).

4. *Contract—Use of an Alternative Insemination Donor's Agreement.* In *In re R.C.*, 775 P.2d 27, 35 (Colo. 1989) (en banc), the court held that a statute, which would have otherwise extinguished the rights of a known donor, was inapplicable in a case where there was an agreement between the parties that the donor would have parental rights. In *Matter of Marriage of Leckie & Voorhies*, 875 P.2d 521, 521–22, 128 Or.App. 289, 291–93 (Ct. App. 1994), a donor's agreement that he would not "demand, request, or compel any guardianship or custody," and that he would "have no parental rights whatsoever with said child," was held to control his later claim to filiation, particularly in the absence of "any conduct legally sufficient to vitiate his waiver."

5. *Function—Ongoing Contact with Child.* As *Thomas S.* makes clear, ongoing contact between donor and child may also preclude the extinguishment of the donor's rights. *See* Fred A. Bernstein, *This Child Does Have Two Mothers * * * and a Sperm Donor with Visitation*, 22 N.Y.U. REV. L. & SOC. CHANGE 1, 22–27 (1996); *see also Tripp v. Hinckley*, 736 N.Y.S.2d 506, 508, 290 A.D.2d 767, 768 (App. Div. 2002) (upholding extended visitation rights of donor who was involved in the children's lives after they were born).

C. CO-MATERNITY/OVA SHARING

D.M.T. v. T.M.H.
Supreme Court of Florida, 2013
129 So.3d 320

PARIENTE, J.

The child at the center of this dispute was born on January 4, 2004. Her birth mother, D.M.T., and her biological mother, T.M.H., were in a long-term committed relationship at the time of the child's birth, and the child began her life by living with both parents. The Fifth District set forth the undisputed facts of this case as follows:

> [T.M.H.] and [D.M.T.] were involved in a committed relationship from 1995 until 2006. They lived together and owned real property as joint tenants, evidenced by a deed in the record. Additionally, both women deposited their income into a joint bank account and used those funds to pay their bills.

> The couple decided to have a baby that they would raise together as equal parental partners. They sought reproductive medical

assistance, where they learned [D.M.T.] was infertile. [T.M.H.] and [D.M.T.], using funds from their joint bank account, paid a reproductive doctor to withdraw ova from [T.M.H.], have them fertilized, and implant the fertilized ova into [D.M.T.]. The two women told the reproductive doctor that they intended to raise the child as a couple, and they went for counseling with a mental health professional to prepare themselves for parenthood. The in vitro fertilization procedure that was utilized proved successful, and a child was conceived.

The child was born in Brevard County on January 4, 2004. The couple gave the child a hyphenation of their last names. Although the birth certificate lists only [D.M.T.] as the mother and does not indicate a father, a maternity test revealed that there is a 99.99% certainty that [T.M.H.] is the biological mother of the child. [T.M.H.] and [D.M.T.] sent out birth announcements with both of their names declaring, "We Proudly Announce the Birth of Our Beautiful Daughter." Both women participated at their child's baptism, and they both took an active role in the child's early education.

The women separated in May 2006, and the child lived with [D.M.T.]. Initially, [T.M.H.] made regular child support payments, which [D.M.T.] accepted. [T.M.H.] ended the support payments when she and [D.M.T.] agreed to divide the child's time evenly between them. They continued to divide the costs of education.

T.M.H., 79 So.3d at 788–89.

Eventually, the couple's relationship severely deteriorated, and, as is all too commonly seen in child custody proceedings, one parent, D.M.T., unfortunately severed the other parent's, T.M.H.'s, contact with the daughter the couple had jointly planned for, conceived, and raised as a family. Until that time, the child "did not distinguish between one [woman] being the biological or the birth parent." *Id.* at 789. Each party was simply a parent to this child up until and including the point at which D.M.T., the birth mother, absconded to an undisclosed location with the child after the parties' relationship soured.

After finally locating the birth mother in Australia, T.M.H., the biological mother, served the birth mother with a petition to establish parental rights to the couple's child and for declaratory relief, including an adjudication of parentage pursuant to chapter 742, Florida Statutes (2008), and a declaration of statutory invalidity with respect to section 742.14, the assisted reproductive technology statute. In response to the biological mother's action, the birth mother filed a motion for summary judgment, alleging that the biological mother lacked parental rights as a matter of law regardless of the couple's original intent with respect to raising the child. The trial court held a hearing and granted the birth mother's summary judgment motion, explaining that it felt constrained by the current state of the law and expressing hope that an appellate court would reverse its ruling. * * * The biological mother appealed the trial court's ruling to the Fifth District Court of Appeal, [which reversed]. * * *

I. SECTIONS 742.13 AND 742.14

* * * Section 742.14, which is Florida's assisted reproductive technology statute, is entitled "Donation of eggs, sperm, or preembryos" and has provided as follows since 1993:

> The donor of any egg, sperm, or preembryo, *other than the commissioning couple* or a father who has executed *a preplanned adoption* agreement under § 63.212, *shall relinquish all maternal or paternal rights and obligations* with respect to the donation or the resulting children. Only reasonable compensation directly related to the donation of eggs, sperm, and preembryos shall be permitted.

§ 742.14, Fla. Stat. (emphasis added). The term "commissioning couple," as used in section 742.14, is defined in section 742.13(2) as "the *intended mother and father* of a child who will be conceived by means of assisted reproductive technology using the eggs or sperm of at least one of the intended parents." § 742.13(2), Fla. Stat. (emphasis added).

The Fifth District concluded that the assisted reproductive technology statute did not apply to T.M.H. since she always intended to parent the child conceived through her provision of biological material to her partner. Therefore, according to the Fifth District, T.M.H. is not considered a "donor" as that term is used in the statute.

We reject the Fifth District's construction of the assisted reproductive technology statute. The plain language of section 742.14 does not provide for the subjective intentions of someone in T.M.H.'s position to be taken into consideration in determining whether he or she is a "donor" under the terms of the statute. Rather, the statute identifies only two categories of individuals who do not relinquish parental rights as to their provision of biological material during the course of assisted reproductive technology—(1) members of a "commissioning couple"; and (2) fathers who have executed a preplanned adoption agreement. Indeed, the structure of section 742.14 designates these groups as fitting within the term "donor," and then provides that they are specifically exempted from the statutory relinquishment of parental rights. If the statute did not apply to these groups, then they would not need to be exempted from its requirements.

In providing for these two exceptions, the Legislature expressed its intent not to allow the subjective intentions of all other individuals who provide eggs, sperm, or preembryos during the course of assisted reproductive technology to become an issue in need of litigation. Instead, the Legislature articulated a policy of treating all individuals who provide eggs, sperm, or preembryos as part of assisted reproductive technology as "donor[s]" bound by the terms of the statute, and then exempting two specific groups in accordance with the purpose behind the statutory enactment.

To hold that section 742.14 does not apply to T.M.H. in this case because of her subjective intention not to give her egg away would essentially create a third exception in the statute. This Court, however, is "not at liberty to add words to the statute that were not placed there by the Legislature." *Lawnwood Med. Ctr., Inc. v. Seeger,* 990 So.2d 503, 512 (Fla.2008). * * *

II. The Constitutionality of the Statutes

1. Constitutional Right of Parenting

It is a basic tenet of our society and our law that individuals have the fundamental constitutionally protected rights to procreate and to be a parent to their children. * * *

Moreover, "we recognize the sanctity of the biological connection" between parents and children, and thus, "we look carefully at anything that would sever the biological parent-child link." *Baby E.A.W.,* 658 So.2d at 967. With respect to the link between a biological father and his child, we have previously explained that constitutional protection of the individual's right to be a parent applies "when an unwed [biological] father demonstrates a full commitment to the responsibilities of parenthood by coming forward to participate in raising his child." *Id.* at 966–67. The approach this Court has taken regarding the rights of biological but unwed fathers echoes the United States Supreme Court's recognition that a biological father's constitutional rights are inchoate and develop into a fundamental right to be a parent "[w]hen an unwed father demonstrates a full commitment to the responsibilities of parenthood by 'com[ing] forward to participate in the rearing of his child,' * * * [because] his interest in personal contact with his child acquires *substantial protection under the due process clause."* *Lehr,* 463 U.S. at 261, 103 S.Ct. 2985. * * *

In this case, the biological mother asserts that she has a protected constitutional interest to be a parent to her child, which is a fundamental right unquestionably protected by the Florida and federal Due Process Clauses and specifically by Florida's state constitutional privacy provision. While acknowledging that a mere biological link between parent and child is insufficient to merit substantial constitutional protection, the biological mother argues that we should analogize the nature of her interest to the interest possessed by unwed biological fathers, whose parental rights are inchoate but develop into a fundamental right to be a parent when the biological father demonstrates "a full commitment to the responsibilities of parenthood." *T.M.H.*, 79 So.3d at 797. We agree.

This Court has previously stated that the biological relationship between parent and child provides "the opportunity to assume parental responsibilities." *Doe,* 543 So.2d at 748. In other words, although an unmarried man who impregnates an unmarried woman does not automatically have a fundamental right to be a parent to the child, his right to be a parent develops substantial constitutional protection as a fundamental right if he assumes responsibility for the care and raising of that child. * * *

In this case, the biological connection between mother and daughter is not in dispute. Additionally, T.M.H. and her former partner D.M.T. demonstrated an intent to jointly raise the child through their actions before and after the child's birth, and T.M.H. actively participated as a parent for the first several years of the child's life. Importantly for constitutional purposes, T.M.H. also assumed full parental responsibilities until her contact with her child was suddenly cut off. In this way, this case is wholly unlike cases such as *Lamaritata v. Lucas,* 823 So.2d 316, 319 (Fla. 2d DCA 2002), relied on by the dissent, where the parties seeking the assistance of reproductive technology "joined forces solely for the purpose of artificially inseminating Ms. Lamaritata" and specifically agreed that the individual providing genetic material would not have any rights or obligations with respect to the child.

This case is also completely different from cases involving *nonparents* seeking to establish legal rights to a child, such as *Beagle,* 678 So.2d 1271, which involved grandparents' rights, and *Troxel,* which is relied on by the dissent. *Troxel* concerned a state nonparental visitation statute described as "breathtakingly broad," permitting "*[a]ny person* " to petition the court for visitation rights "*at any time,*" and the court to grant such visitation rights whenever "visitation may serve *the best interest of the child.*" *Troxel,* 530 U.S. at 61, 67, 120 S.Ct. 2054.

Contrary to *Troxel,* which involved a nonparent, there is no doubt that the common law would grant constitutional due process and privacy protection, in the form of a fundamental right to be a parent, to an unwed biological father in this situation who had the proverbial one night stand with a mother but then assumed parental responsibilities for the first several years of the child's life. Of course, the common law was developed before the scientific advancements in reproductive technology that allow individuals to exercise their basic right and desire to have children in ways that were not contemplated by society centuries or even decades ago.

As explained by the Fifth District in this case, it is difficult to understand how rigid legal rules "established during a time so far removed in history when the science of in vitro fertilization was a remote thought in the minds of the scientists of the times [have] much currency today." *T.M.H.*, 79 So.3d at 796. Although the right to procreate has long been described as "one of the basic civil rights" individuals hold, *Skinner*, 316 U.S. at 541, 62 S.Ct. 1110, advances in science and technology now provide innumerable ways for traditional and non-traditional couples alike to conceive a child and, we conclude, in so doing to exercise their "inalienable rights * * * to enjoy and defend life and liberty, [and] to pursue happiness." Art. I, § 2, Fla. Const. * * *

It would indeed be anomalous if, under Florida law, an unwed biological father would have more constitutionally protected rights to parent a child after a one night stand than an unwed biological mother who, with a committed partner and as part of a loving relationship, planned for the birth of a child and remains committed to supporting and raising her own daughter. As the Fifth District stated, "it would pose a substantial equal protection problem to deny an unwed genetic mother the ability to assert parental rights after she established a parental relationship with her child while allowing an unwed genetic father to do so." *T.M.H.*, 79 So.3d at 797 n. 8.

Although the biological mother in this case is seeking vindication of her right to be a parent to her child, this right comes with critical legal and financial responsibilities, including possible child support payments. *See* § 61.29, Fla. Stat. (2012). Unquestionably, these responsibilities are part and parcel of the fundamental right to be a parent. T.M.H., the biological mother, demonstrated her commitment to accepting these responsibilities until her contact with the child was cut off. Because T.M.H. accepted responsibility for raising her child from the beginning and did in fact parent and support the child until D.M.T. prevented her from doing so, we hold that T.M.H.'s inchoate interest has developed into a protected fundamental right to be a parent to her child.

2. Abridgment of Fundamental Right

We subject statutes that interfere with an individual's fundamental rights to strict scrutiny analysis, which requires the State to prove that the legislation furthers a compelling governmental interest through the least intrusive means. * * * Therefore, the burden falls on the birth mother to demonstrate that application of the assisted reproductive technology statute to deprive the biological mother of her fundamental right to be a parent furthers a compelling governmental interest through the least intrusive means. This showing has not been made.

We recognize the important role section 742.14 plays in protecting couples seeking to use assisted reproductive technology to conceive a child from parental rights claims brought by typical third-party providers of the genetic material used in assisted reproductive technology, as well as the State's corresponding interest in furthering that objective. This case, however, does not implicate those concerns. Quite simply, based on the factual situation before us, we do not discern even a legitimate State interest in applying section 742.14 to deny T.M.H. her right to be a parent to her daughter.

This is significant to our as-applied constitutional analysis of the statutory scheme, which is intended to provide statutory protection to a "commissioning couple" from a parental rights claim by a third-party provider of biological material used in assisted reproductive technology. We therefore reject the dissent's assertion that our analysis has no "logical end point" or "obvious stopping point," as our conclusion is based on the specific facts presented in this case, as set forth in the Fifth District's certified question, which establish that T.M.H. was an intended parent and assumed full parental responsibilities until her contact with the child was cut off. * * *

[3.] Classification Based on Sexual Orientation

We next address the equal protection challenge to the statute, as confronted by the Fifth District, under both the Florida and United States Constitutions. Specifically * * * we address whether the statute is unconstitutional as applied under the Florida and federal Equal Protection Clauses by exempting heterosexual couples, but not same-sex couples, from the automatic relinquishment of parental rights when seeking the assistance of reproductive technology to conceive a child with the intent to become the child's parents. Put another way, as Judge Monaco succinctly explained in his concurring opinion below, "[b]ut for the fact that [the biological mother] and [the birth mother] are of the same sex, we would probably consider them to be a 'commissioning couple' under the statute, and the outcome of this case would be easy." *T.M.H.*, 79 So.3d at 804 (Monaco, J., concurring). * * *

Sexual orientation has not been determined to constitute a protected class and therefore sexual orientation does not provide an independent basis for using heightened scrutiny to review State action that results in unequal treatment to homosexuals. *See Romer*, 517 U.S. at 630–32, 116 S.Ct. 1620. Further, even though our state constitution recognizes gender as a specific class, *see* art. I, § 2, Fla. Const., it does not separately recognize sexual orientation as a protected class, and thus we do not rely on our state's Equal Protection Clause to apply a heightened scrutiny examination to statutes discriminating on the basis of sexual orientation. *See Fla. Dep't of Children & Families v. Adoption of X.X.G.*, 45 So.3d 79,

81, 83 (Fla. 3d DCA 2010) (applying rational basis review to a statute prohibiting homosexuals from adopting).

Accordingly, we apply a rational basis analysis to our review of this claim. The specific question we confront is whether the classification between heterosexual and same-sex couples drawn by the assisted reproductive technology statute bears some rational relationship to a legitimate state purpose.

D.M.T. argues that defining the term "commissioning couple" in section 742.13(2), as applied in section 742.14, to include only one male and one female is related to the State's legitimate interest in not extending rights to same-sex couples. Specifically, she cites to Florida law that declines to recognize same-sex marriages and prohibits homosexuals from adopting children. We reject this argument as unavailing for several reasons.

First, section 742.14 does not operate to *grant* parental rights to biological parents, but only to provide for the *relinquishment* of those rights in the case of the typical egg or sperm donor. In other words, section 742.14 allows a member of a "commissioning couple" to preserve his or her interest in the child conceived through assisted reproductive technology; however, that individual becomes a parent only if he or she has some legal basis to be recognized as a parent. This could be due to a biological connection plus the assumption of parental responsibilities, as we have demonstrated applies in this case, or through application of another statute. *See, e.g.,* § 63.032(12), Fla. Stat. (2008) (defining the term "parent" to mean "a woman who gives birth to a child or a man whose consent to the adoption of the child would be required"). That is, sections 742.13 and 742.14 do not create a statutory basis for an individual who would not otherwise have parental rights to claim those rights. Therefore, because section 742.14 does not operate to grant rights, but only to eliminate rights that are already held or that may develop, any State interest that could potentially exist in not extending rights to same-sex couples is not implicated.

Second, there is no indication that the exception provided in section 742.14 for a "commissioning couple" extends only to married couples, so the state constitutional provision against same-sex marriage is also not implicated. By contrast, in the next statutory provisions, sections 742.15–16, Florida Statutes, which relate to gestational surrogacy, the Legislature has specifically provided that the "commissioning couple" must be "legally married" in order to claim protection under the statutes. *See* § 742.15(1), Fla. Stat. (2008). * * *

Third, we reject D.M.T.'s contention that recognizing T.M.H.'s parental rights in this case would undermine the State interest in providing certainty to couples using assisted reproductive technology to become parents because it would increase litigation regarding the intentions of individuals providing genetic material for use in assisted reproductive technology. No one disputes that the State has an interest in ensuring that the parental rights of children conceived through the use of assisted reproductive technology are defined by law, in making sure children have parents to care for them, and in preventing litigation that disrupts families.

In reality, however, the issue of an unmarried mother and father's intent under the statute, including whether they qualify as a "commissioning couple," has been the subject of prior litigation in the courts of this state. Since intent, pursuant to the definition of "commissioning couple" found in section 742.13(2) and used in section 742.14, is the determinative element regarding whether two individuals seeking the assistance of reproductive technology to conceive qualify as a "commissioning couple," it is of course relevant to the inquiry. We conclude, though, that the State does not have a legitimate interest in precluding same-sex couples from being given the same opportunity as heterosexual couples to demonstrate that intent. Consistent with equal protection, a same-sex couple must be afforded the equivalent chance as a heterosexual couple to establish their intentions in using assisted reproductive technology to conceive a child. * * *

III. Waiver of Rights

Lastly, we address the birth mother's contention that, regardless of the application of section 742.14 in this case, the biological mother waived any parental rights to this child by signing a standard informed consent form during the couple's process of seeking medical assistance to conceive. * * *

While it is uncontroverted that the biological mother signed a standard "Informed Consent Oocyte Recipient" form for the Fertility and Reproductive Medicine Center for Women with the birth mother listed as the recipient, the biological mother signed this form as the birth mother's partner and *not* as the individual providing the egg for the couple. Clearly, then, this informed consent does not on its face apply to waive the biological mother's rights to the child, even though this is the document that the birth mother relied on in her initial motion to dismiss and motion for judgment on the pleadings. * * *

[C]ourts that have considered similar standard informed consents used in reproductive technology have held that waiver provisions like the one [in this case] are inapplicable in circumstances like those in this case. This is because it is uncontested that the biological mother was not an anonymous donor, but rather, that the parties were in a committed relationship where reproductive technology was used—with one woman providing her egg and the other partner bearing the child—so that both women became the child's parents.

We reject the dissent's reliance on *Lamaritata* to argue that the biological mother waived her parental rights. *Lamaritata* is completely distinguishable from this case. As the dissent acknowledges, the parties in *Lamaritata* specifically entered into a contract whereby they agreed that the donor would have no parental rights and obligations associated with any child conceived from the use of assisted reproductive technology. * * * As the Second District explained, there were "no facts to show that [the parties] ha[d] any type of relationship that would fall under the rubric of 'couple.' Further, they did not commission or contract to jointly raise the children as mother and father." *Lamaritata,* 823 So.2d at 319. * * *

Despite the dissent's view to the contrary, the facts of this case clearly demonstrate that exactly the opposite of the facts in *Lamaritata* are true here. Not only did the biological mother assume parental obligations, but the couple's actions before and after the child's birth— including their use of funds from their joint bank account, their statements to the reproductive doctor that they intended to raise the child as a couple, the counseling they underwent to prepare themselves for parenthood, the use of a hyphenated last name for the child, and the joint birth announcement—reveal that the couple's agreement in actuality was to both parent the child they intended to conceive. * * *

We also reject the dissent's reliance on *Wakeman v. Dixon,* 921 So.2d 669 (Fla. 1st DCA 2006). Like the Fifth District, we conclude that *Wakeman* "is clearly distinguishable from the instant case because there, one lesbian partner was the birth mother and the partner claiming parental rights was not the biological mother." *T.M.H.,* 79 So.3d at 794 n. 6. As the Fifth District correctly observed, the First District in *Wakeman* held that the individual seeking parental rights was neither a "biological" nor a "natural" parent, whereas in this case, T.M.H. "would fall into both categories under the *Wakeman* rationale." *T.M.H.,* 79 So.3d at 794 n. 6. * * *

POLSTON, C.J., dissenting.

Unlike the majority, I do not believe that sections 742.14 and 742.13(2), Florida Statutes, violate T.M.H.'s constitutional rights to due process, privacy, and equal protection. Instead, contract law, common law, Florida statutory law, and the United States and Florida Constitutions all provide that T.M.H. does not have parental rights with respect to the child born to D.M.T. Therefore, I respectfully dissent.

I refer to the parties in this case using the birth mother's initials, D.M.T., and the egg donor's initials, T.M.H. The majority refers to T.M.H. as the biological mother, but the term might appear to answer the very question addressed by this Court, namely whether T.M.H. is a legal parent. Furthermore, the terms the majority uses to distinguish the parties (birth mother and biological mother) are confusing because "both the genetic and gestational roles in bringing this child into the world are 'biological' processes." *T.M.H. v. D.M.T.*, 79 So.3d 787, 807 (Fla. 5th DCA 2011) (Lawson, J., dissenting). * * *

* * * T.M.H. signed at the time of her egg donation two waivers of all claims and rights she might have regarding any resulting child. Specifically, the informed consent donor form that T.M.H. signed at the time she donated her eggs includes the following language:

> I, the undersigned, [T.M.H.,] forever hereafter relinquish any claims to jurisdiction over the offspring that might result from this donation and waive any and all rights to future consent, notice, or consultation regarding the donation. I agree that the recipient may regard the donated eggs as her own and any offspring resulted there from as her own children.

In addition to this informed consent donor form, T.M.H. also signed an "Informed Consent Oocyte Recipient" form on the line reserved for the recipient's partner. And, very similar to the donor form, the recipient form provides as follows:

> I/We understand that the egg donor has relinquished any claim to, or jurisdiction over the offspring that might result from this donation and waive any and all rights to future consent, notice, or consultation regarding such donation. The donor understands that the recipient may regard the donated eggs as her own and any offspring resulting there from as her own children.

Therefore, T.M.H. signed two contracts that expressly waived any rights she might have with respect to any child resulting from her egg donation.

A person may waive fully vested, fundamental parental rights by completing a form. *See, e.g.,* § 39.806(1)(a), Fla. Stat. (providing that grounds for the termination of parental rights may be established "[w]hen the parent or parents have voluntarily executed a written surrender of the child and consented to the entry of an order giving custody of the child to the department for subsequent adoption"). * * * Further, * * * individuals may waive various constitutional rights, including the right to counsel, the right to remain silent, and the right to a jury.

If one can waive fully vested parental rights and various constitutional rights by signing a written form, an egg donor can certainly waive any potential interest in a possible future child by completing a form. Consequently, I would give effect to the plain language of the two forms that T.M.H. signed and conclude that T.M.H. contractually waived any claim of parental rights.

* * * Notably, the Second District Court of Appeal's decision in *Lamaritata*, 823 So.2d 316, is very persuasively on point. In *Lamaritata*, a donor and recipient "entered into a contract whereby the donor would provide sperm to [the] recipient with the expectation that she would become pregnant through artificial insemination and deliver offspring." 823 So.2d at 318. Further, their "agreement provided that if childbirth resulted, the donor would have no parental rights and obligations." *Id.* The Second District held that "[b]oth the contract between the parties and the Florida statute controlling these arrangements provide that there are no parental rights or responsibilities resulting to the donor of sperm." *Id.* at 319 (citing § 742.14, Fla. Stat.). As a result, "the sperm donor is a nonparent, a statutory stranger to the children." *Id.* The donor's status as a nonparent continued to be true, even though the donor and recipient "entered into subsequent stipulations, purportedly to give visitation rights to this [donor.]" *Id.* The Second District explained that the subsequent visitation rights agreement between the parties was not enforceable because "[t]here are numerous Florida cases holding that nonparents are not entitled to visitation rights." *Id.*

In this case, like the donor in *Lamaritata*, T.M.H. signed a contract at the time of donation waiving any claims or rights to any potential child. And similar to the parties in *Lamaritata*, T.M.H. and D.M.T. agreed at some point to co-parent the child as evidenced by T.M.H. participating in parenting decisions for a period of time after the child's birth, although the parenting agreement in this case appears to have been oral and not formally executed. However, just as the Second District concluded in *Lamaritata*, I would hold that the donor in this case is a nonparent by operation of the waivers of rights she signed (as well as by operation of section 742.14). Because T.M.H. is not a legal parent, any agreement, oral or otherwise, that may have existed between the parties for T.M.H. to co-parent is unenforceable under Florida law. * * *

[Furthermore,] [p]roviding T.M.H. access to visitation and other incidents of a parental relationship over D.M.T.'s objection would violate D.M.T.'s due process and privacy rights as the child's legal parent. *See Wakeman*, 921 So.2d at 671 (holding that co-parenting agreement between same-sex couple was unenforceable and explaining that a non-legal parent "cannot be granted by statute the right to visitation with minor children, because, absent evidence of a demonstrable harm to the child, such a grant unconstitutionally interferes with a natural parent's privacy right to rear his or her child").

The majority skips any analysis of D.M.T.'s constitutional rights as the legal parent. Instead, the majority concludes as a matter of substantive due process and privacy that, because T.M.H. at some point established a relationship with the child, the promotion of stability and certainty in families employing assisted reproductive technology is an insufficient state interest to support the termination of that relationship. The majority's conclusion is based upon its argument that T.M.H. has a fundamental interest in her relationship with the child that is protected by the due process clauses of the United States and Florida Constitutions and the privacy clause of the Florida Constitution.

But contrary to the majority's description of the asserted interest as the elimination of an already established parental relationship, section 742.14 operates *at the time of donation* to eliminate any interests or obligations a sperm donor or egg donor may have with regard to a future, potential child. At the time of the donation of biological material, any interest in a potential parental relationship would have to be deemed an inchoate interest and not even possibly a fundamental interest protected by the due process and privacy clauses as there is indisputably no child or parental relationship with a child at that point.

Moreover, the majority's analysis ignores a vital aspect of substantive due process jurisprudence. The United States Supreme Court has recognized the temptation for members of a court to improperly constitutionalize their own preferences and thereby impose them upon the rest of the citizenry in perpetuity and, therefore, has "insisted not merely that the interest denominated as a 'liberty' be 'fundamental' (a concept that, in isolation, is hard to objectify), but also that it be an interest traditionally protected by our society." *Michael H. v. Gerald D.,* 491 U.S. 110, 122, 109 S.Ct. 2333, 105 L.Ed.2d 91 (1989). In other words, due process only affords protections to rights "so rooted in the traditions and conscience of our people as to be ranked as fundamental." *Snyder v. Massachusetts,* 291 U.S. 97, 105, 54 S.Ct. 330, 78 L.Ed. 674 (1934). * * *

Therefore, * * * the substantive due process issue in the present case really comes down to whether relationships like the one between T.M.H. and the child born to D.M.T. "ha[ve] been treated as a protected family unit under the historic practices of our society, or whether on any other basis [they have] been accorded special protection." [*Michael H.,* 491 U.S]. at 124, 109 S.Ct. 2333. Of course, it is impossible to conclude that such relationships have been treated in this manner. In fact, our history indicates that quite the opposite is true as our society has historically protected the legal rights of birth mothers and the traditional family.

* * * But not only does the majority's analysis skip the vital question of whether the alleged right is "so rooted in the traditions and conscience of our people as to be ranked as fundamental," it also suffers from the problem of having no seeming or logical end point. Does the majority's analysis now mean that section 742.14 is unconstitutional as applied to

all sperm and egg donors since they are also denied the opportunity to develop parental relationships with children resulting from their biological material? Or perhaps the majority would limit its holding to those sperm and egg donors who may later develop relationships with resulting children despite the operation of the statute? However, does this mean that a child could have a constitutional right to two mothers and a father (or two fathers), perhaps where a married, heterosexual couple agrees to and then subsequently raises a child with the egg donor, an egg donor who is in a committed relationship with a man other than the genetic father? Or perhaps this new constitutional right to employ assisted reproductive technology without the relinquishment of any donor rights and obligations only applies to those in same-sex relationships? Additionally, does this newly created constitutional right now override all waivers of parental rights, including voluntary waivers leading to adoption?

* * * The majority also concludes that sections 742.14 and 742.13(2) violate the equal protection clauses of the United States and Florida Constitutions. * * * However, the Legislature had a legitimate state purpose in enacting these statutes. * * *

The rationale underlying sections 742.14 and 742.13(2) is the promotion of stability, certainty, and permanence in families employing assisted reproductive technology. And the State has a legitimate interest in regulating assisted reproductive technology and its social and economic effects. The statutes are rationally related to this legitimate interest since allowing claims of parentage by egg and sperm donors could disrupt the certainty, stability, and permanence that generally proves beneficial to families employing assisted reproductive technology, including the constitutionally protected parental rights of legal birth mothers "to make decisions concerning the care, custody, and control of their children." *Troxel,* 530 U.S. at 66, 120 S.Ct. 2054. Accordingly, because it pursues a legitimate purpose by rational means, Florida's decision to treat T.M.H. differently from a commissioning couple cannot be deemed a denial of equal protection.

Furthermore, as Judge Lawson aptly noted,

the statute in question here is not directed just at men or women, heterosexuals or homosexuals, or any other narrow class. It places broad limits on the right of all citizens to make a parentage claim after donating genetic material to another. And * * * the statute does not bar [T.M.H.] (or any women, irrespective of sexual preference) from using assisted reproductive technology to conceive, bear and give birth to a child of her own, using her own body. This appears, at least on its face, to be a rational way to address this difficult social policy issue, irrespective of whether it reflects a policy choice that the majority or I would prefer.

T.M.H., 79 So.3d at 823 (Lawson, J., dissenting). Simply put, T.M.H. did not have to choose this way. The statute does not prohibit T.M.H. from engaging in any sexual activity, using assisted reproductive technology to pass along her genes to a child gestated by another, or parenting a child that she personally gave birth to or legally adopted. The statute does not stand in the way of T.M.H. having children.

ST. MARY V. DAMON
Supreme Court of Nevada, 2013
309 P.3d 1027

SAITTA, J.:

This appeal concerns the establishment of custodial rights over a minor child born to former female partners, appellant Sha'Kayla St. Mary and respondent Veronica Lynn Damon. The couple became romantically involved and decided to have a child. They drafted a co-parenting agreement, and eventually, St. Mary gave birth to a child through in vitro fertilization, using Damon's egg and an anonymous donor's sperm. Thereafter, their relationship ended, leading to the underlying dispute concerning the parties' custodial rights over the child. * * *

Approximately one year after entering into a romantic relationship with each other, St. Mary and Damon moved in together. They planned to have a child, deciding that Damon would have her egg fertilized by a sperm donor, and St. Mary would carry the fertilized egg and give birth to the child. In October 2007, Damon's eggs were implanted into St. Mary. Around the same time, Damon drafted a co-parenting agreement, which she and St. Mary signed. The agreement indicated that Damon and St. Mary sought to "jointly and equally share parental responsibility, with both of [them] providing support and guidance." In it, they stated that they would "make every effort to jointly share the responsibilities of raising [their] child," including paying for expenses and making major child-related decisions. The agreement provided that if their relationship ended, they would each work to ensure that the other maintained a close relationship with the child, share the duties of raising the child, and make a "good-faith effort to jointly make all major decisions affecting" the child.

St. Mary gave birth to a child in June 2008. The hospital birth confirmation report and certificate of live birth listed only St. Mary as the child's mother. The child was given both parties' last names, however, in the hyphenated form of St. Mary-Damon.

For several months, St. Mary primarily stayed home caring for the child during the day while Damon worked. But, nearly one year after the child's birth, their romantic relationship ended, St. Mary moved out of the home, and St. Mary and Damon disagreed about how to share their time with the child. St. Mary signed an affidavit declaring that Damon was the biological mother of the child, and in 2009, Damon filed an ex parte petition with the district court to establish maternity, seeking to have the child's birth certificate amended to add Damon as a mother. The district court issued an order stating that St. Mary gave birth to the child and that Damon "is the biological and legal mother of said child." The 2009 order also directed that the birth certificate be amended to add Damon's name as a mother.

Thereafter, St. Mary instituted the underlying case by filing a complaint and motion, in a separate district court case, to establish custody, visitation, and child support. In response, Damon contended that, due to her biological connection, she was entitled to sole custody of the child. Damon attached the 2009 order to her opposition.

During a hearing on St. Mary's complaint, the district court orally advised St. Mary that she had the burden of establishing her visitation rights as a surrogate, and the court scheduled an evidentiary hearing regarding her visitation. In a subsequent hearing, the district court ruled that the issues surrounding the parties' co-parenting agreement would be addressed at the evidentiary hearing.

Damon filed a motion to limit the scope of the evidentiary hearing to the issue of third-party visitation, excluding any parentage and custody issues. She asserted that the district court had already determined that St. Mary must establish her visitation rights as a surrogate and, as a result, there was no need to provide evidence to determine parentage. St. Mary opposed the motion, arguing that she was entitled to a full evidentiary hearing because limiting the hearing's scope to third-party visitation would, in effect, deny her parental rights without any opportunity to be heard on the matter.

The district court held the evidentiary hearing. Before taking evidence, the district court considered Damon's motion to limit the hearing's scope. Apparently looking to the 2009 birth certificate order and believing that Damon's status as the sole legal and biological mother had already been determined, the court decided that it would only consider the issue of third-party visitation. The limitation of the hearing's scope was significant. The district court barred consideration of St. Mary's assertion of custody rights, which concern a parent's legal basis to direct the upbringing of his or her child, and limited the hearing to a lesser right of third-party visitation.

The hearing moved forward with the parties focusing on the visitation issue. St. Mary and Damon gave conflicting testimonies regarding their relationship, the co-parenting agreement's purpose, and their intentions in using in vitro fertilization to produce the child. St. Mary testified that she and Damon intended to create the child together, wanted the child to be their child, and fertilized and implanted Damon's eggs into St. Mary so that both women would be "related" to the child. But Damon testified that she and St. Mary orally agreed that St. Mary would be a mere surrogate. St. Mary further testified that she and Damon created the co-parenting agreement together, believing that it would be required by the fertility clinic as a prerequisite for the performance of the reproductive procedure. St. Mary indicated that despite the fertility clinic not asking for the agreement before the procedure, she and Damon completed the agreement after the procedure. Damon asserted that she and St. Mary did not intend to create an enforceable co-parenting agreement but created the agreement to satisfy the fertility clinic's requirements and to seek insurance coverage for the pregnancy.

Following the hearing, in March 2011, the district court issued an order providing that St. Mary was entitled to third-party visitation but not custody. The court reiterated that the scope of the evidentiary hearing had been limited to the issue of third-party visitation and noted that St. Mary could not be awarded custody of the child because previous orders determined that she "has no biological or legal rights whatsoever under Nevada law." Relying on NRS 126.045, which was repealed by the 2013 Legislature, the court also concluded that the co-parenting agreement was null and void because under that statute "a surrogate agreement is only for married couples, which only include one man and one woman." *See* Nev. Stat., ch. 213, § 36, at 813 (repealing NRS 126.045). The 2011 order further provided that although St. Mary gave birth to the child, she "was simply a carrier for [the child]," and that she must "realize that [Damon] is the mother." As a result, St. Mary was granted third-party visitation rights and denied any rights as a legal mother. This appeal from the 2011 order followed.

St. Mary argues that the district court erred in determining that, legally, she was a surrogate and not the child's legal mother and in deeming the co-parenting agreement unenforceable as a matter of law. As a result of our de novo review of these legal questions, we agree.

St. Mary may be the child's legal mother

To determine parentage in Nevada, courts must look to the Nevada Parentage Act, which is modeled after the Uniform Parentage Act (UPA). As the Legislature's adoption of the UPA recognizes, the relationship between a parent and a child is of fundamental societal and constitutional dimension. In Nevada, all of the "rights, privileges, duties and obligations" accompanying parenthood are conferred on those persons who are deemed to have a parent-child relationship with the child, regardless of the parents' marital status. Surrogates who bear a child conceived through assisted conception for another, on the other hand, are often not entitled to claim parental rights. *See* NRS 126.045 (2009) (defining "[s]urrogate" as "an adult woman who enters into an agreement to bear a child conceived through assisted conception for the intended parents," who are treated as the natural parents); 2013 Nev. Stat., ch. 213, §§ 10, 23, 27 at 807–08, 810–11 (replacing the term "surrogate" with "[g]estational carrier" and defining such as a woman "who is not an intended parent and who enters into a gestational agreement," wherein she gives up "legal and physical custody" of the child to the intended parent or parents and may "relinquish all rights and duties as the parent[ ] of a child conceived through assisted reproduction"). Accordingly, whether St. Mary is treated as someone other than a legal mother, such as a surrogate, is of the upmost significance.

The multiple ways to prove maternity

Given the medical advances and changing family dynamics of the age, determining a child's parents today can be more complicated than it was in the past. To this end, although perhaps not encompassing every possibility, the Nevada Parentage Act provides several ways to determine a child's legal mother: a mother with a parent-child relationship with the child "incident to which the law confers or imposes rights, privileges, duties, and obligations." NRS 126.021(3). Under the pre-2013 and current versions of NRS 126.041(1), a woman's status as a legal mother can be established by "proof of her having given birth to the child." *See* NRS 126.041 (2009). In maternity actions under NRS Chapter 126, the statutes under which paternity may be determined apply "[i]nsofar as practicable." NRS 126.231. Paternity may be established in a variety of ways, including through presumptions based on marriage and cohabitation, NRS 126.051(1)(a)-(c), presumptions based on receiving the child into the home and openly holding oneself out as a parent, NRS 126.051(1)(d), genetic testing, NRS 126.051(2), and voluntary acknowledgment, NRS 126.053. Hence, a determination of parentage rests upon a wide array of considerations rather than genetics alone.

This case presents a situation where two women proffered evidence that could establish or generate a conclusive presumption of maternity to either woman. St. Mary testified that she gave birth to the child, thereby offering proof to establish that she is the child's legal mother. Damon showed that her egg was used to produce the child, demonstrating a genetic relationship to the child that may be a basis for concluding that she is the child's legal mother. By dividing the reproductive roles of conceiving a child, St. Mary and Damon each assumed functions traditionally used to evidence a legal maternal relationship. Hence, this matter raises the issue of whether the Nevada Parentage Act and its policies preclude a child from having two legal mothers where two women split the genetic and physical functions of creating a child.

The law does not preclude a child from having two legal mothers

When the district court apparently referenced the 2009 birth certificate order to conclude that Damon's status as the exclusive legal and biological mother was determined and that, as a result, it would not consider St. Mary's assertions of maternity or custody at the evidentiary hearing, it impliedly operated on the premise that a child, created by artificial insemination through an anonymous sperm donor, may not have two mothers under the law. However, contrary to this premise, the Nevada Parentage Act and its policies do not preclude such a child from having two legal mothers.

Although NRS 126.051(3) contains procedures for rebutting paternity presumptions by clear and convincing evidence or "a court decree establishing *paternity* * * * by another *man*," (emphases added), and while NRS 126.051(3) arguably applies in maternity cases, we decline to read this provision of the statute as conveying clear legislative intent to deprive a child conceived by artificial insemination of the emotional, financial, and physical support of an intended mother who "actively assisted in the decision and process of bringing [the child] into this world." *In re T.P.S.*, 365 Ill.Dec. 567, 978 N.E.2d 1070, 1077 (Ill.App.Ct.2012). In Nevada, as in other states, the best interest of the child is the paramount concern in determining the custody and care of children. Both the Legislature and this court have acknowledged that, generally, a child's best interest is served by maintaining two actively involved parents. Certainly, the Legislature has not instructed that children born to unregistered domestic partners bear any less rights to the best-interest considerations set forth in these statutes than children born to registered domestic partners, married persons, and unmarried persons. Ultimately, "the preservation and strengthening of family life is a part of the public policy of this State." NRS 128.005(1). * * *

Nonetheless, the district court determined that St. Mary was not the child's legal mother. The court appears to have grounded this conclusion on the 2009 order, which provided that Damon was the child's legal mother and required Damon's name to be added to the child's birth certificate. But while that order stated that Damon was "the biological and legal mother" of the child, it in no way purported to undo or deny St. Mary's parent-child relationship with the child. The order did not require the removal of St. Mary's name from the birth certificate or provide that St. Mary was not the child's legal mother. Rather, it acknowledged Damon's relationship with the child without denying the same of St. Mary. Moreover, whether St. Mary had rights to the child was not an issue that Damon's 2009 petition sought to resolve because it requested that "maternity be established" and "[t]hat the birth certificate be amended to add the biological mother's name of * * * D[amon]."

Further, the district court's finding that St. Mary was a mere surrogate went beyond the limited scope of the hearing, which the district court prefaced by confirming that it would not consider parentage. Because this argument was not resolved by the 2009 order or any other prior determination, and since the Nevada Parentage Act did not bar a consideration of the evidence regarding St. Mary's claims for maternity and custody rights, the district court erred in refusing to consider the parentage issue and limiting the scope of the evidentiary hearing based on its conclusion that St. Mary was a surrogate—which was a conclusion that was made without an evidentiary hearing on that issue.

* * * Although St. Mary's parentage can be established by virtue of her having given birth to the child, the parties dispute whether they intended for St. Mary to be the child's parent or simply a surrogate or gestational carrier who lacked a legal parent-child relationship to the child. Therefore, upon remand, the district court must hold an evidentiary hearing to determine whether St. Mary is the child's legal mother or if she is someone without a legal relationship to the child, during which the court may consider any relevant evidence for establishing maternity under the Nevada Parentage Act.

The co-parenting agreement was not a surrogacy agreement and was consistent with Nevada's public policy

St. Mary asserts that the co-parenting agreement demonstrates the parties' intent regarding parentage and custody of the child and that the district court erred in determining that the co-parenting agreement was an unenforceable surrogacy agreement under NRS 126.045. Damon responds that, because the agreement was between an unmarried intended parent and a surrogate and purported to resolve issues of parentage and child custody, the district court correctly deemed that the co-parenting agreement was prohibited by NRS 126.045 (2009).

At the time of the district court's determinations, NRS 126.045 (2009) governed contracts between two married persons and a gestational carrier, or surrogate, for assisted reproduction. It required such contracts to specify the parties' rights, including the "[p]arentage of the child," the "[c]ustody of the child in the event of a change of circumstances," and the "respective responsibilities and liabilities of the contracting parties." NRS 126.045(1)(a)–(c) (2009). Additionally, the statute defined a "[s]urrogate" as "an adult woman who enters into an agreement to bear a child conceived through assisted conception for the intended parents," and "[i]ntended parents" were defined as "a man and woman, married to each other," who agree to "be the parents of a child born to a surrogate through assisted conception." NRS 126.045(4)(b), (c) (2009). Here, St. Mary and Damon's co-parenting agreement was not within the scope of NRS 126.045. The agreement lacked any language intimating that St. Mary acted as a surrogate, such as language indicating that she surrendered custody of the child or relinquished her rights as a mother to the child. Rather, the agreement expressed that St. Mary would share the parental duties of raising the child and would jointly make major parenting decisions with Damon.

Nevertheless, Damon insists that, because the agreement covered issues of parentage and child custody, it necessarily addressed issues contemplated by NRS 126.045 and, as a result, is void for failing to meet the statute's other terms. In other words, Damon argues that outside of NRS 126.045, agreements (at least those with a non-parent) concerning parentage, custody, and responsibilities over a child are void. But, as explained above, parentage is governed by NRS Chapter 126. In the event that both parties are determined to be the child's parents, nothing in Nevada law prevents two parents from entering into agreements that demonstrate their intent concerning child custody.

"Parties are free to contract, and the courts will enforce their contracts if they are not unconscionable, illegal, or in violation of public policy." *Rivero v. Rivero,* 125 Nev. 410, 429, 216 P.3d 213, 226 (2009). It is presumed that fit parents act in the best interest of their children. *Troxel v. Granville,* 530 U.S. 57, 68, 120 S.Ct. 2054, 147 L.Ed.2d 49 (2000). Thus, public policy favors fit parents entering agreements to resolve issues pertaining to their minor child's custody, care, and visitation.

When a child has the opportunity to be supported by two loving and fit parents pursuant to a co-parenting agreement, this opportunity is to be given due consideration and must not be foreclosed on account of the parents being of the same sex. * * * To bar the enforceability of a co-parenting agreement on the basis of the parents' genders conflicts with the Nevada Parentage Act's policies of promoting the child's best interest with the support of two parents.

St. Mary and Damon's co-parenting agreement was aligned with Nevada's policy of allowing parents to agree on how to best provide for their child. Within their co-parenting agreement, St. Mary and Damon sought to provide for their child's best interest by agreeing to share the responsibilities of raising the child, even if the relationship between St. Mary and Damon ended. The agreement's language provides the indicia of an effort by St. Mary and Damon to make the child's best interest their priority. Thus, in the event that St. Mary is found to be a legal mother, the district court must consider the parties' co-parenting agreement in making its child custody determination. * * *

[W]e reverse the 2011 order. We remand this matter to the district court for further proceedings to determine the child's parentage, custody, and visitation.

NOTES

1. Notice that in *D.M.T. v. T.M.H.*, it was the woman who carried the child to term who contended that her former partner (who provided the egg) was not the child's legal parent. In contrast, in *St. Mary v. Damon*, it was the woman who contributed the egg who claimed that her former partner (who carried the child to term) was not the child's legal parent. As a general matter, should the law in these cases prioritize the genetic contribution over the gestational one (or vice-versa) or should the law treat women in both categories as similarly situated for purposes of determining parenthood? Are there reasons to believe that the partner who carried the child to term in *St. Mary* was more of a "surrogate" than the partner who did so in *T.M.H.*? We return to surrogacy issues at the end of the Chapter.

2. As in *T.M.H.*, the petitioner in *K.M. v. E.G.*, 37 Cal.4th 130, 33 Cal.Rptr.3d 61, 117 P.3d 673 (2005), both provided her eggs so that her female partner could become pregnant and signed an informed consent form seemingly waiving all parental rights. After the children were born, the two women raised them together. When the couple's relationship later dissolved, the gestational mother tried to end all contact between her former partner and the children. The California Supreme Court, in siding with the former partner, rejected the analogy, accepted by the lower courts, between women in her situation and known sperm donors whose parental rights are legally terminated when they provide their sperm to licensed physicians. Sperm donors, the court noted, are not usually in relationships with the recipients and they rarely plan on living with them in the same home where the children will be raised. *See id*. 117 P.3d at 680–81. The genetic relationship between the female former partner and the children, when coupled with the inapplicability of the known sperm donor nonpaternity statute, meant that the children had two mothers. *Id*. The court also held that the signing of the informed consent form did not waive the genetic mother's rights because a "woman who supplies ova to be used to impregnate her lesbian partner, with the understanding that the resulting child will be raised in their joint home, cannot waive her responsibility to support that child. Nor can such a purported waiver effectively cause that woman to relinquish her parental rights." *Id*. at 682.

II. PARENTHOOD BASED ON FACTORS OTHER THAN BIOLOGY

Adoption has traditionally constituted the primary way in which individuals who are not biologically related to children establish their parental status. As this Section explores, many LGBT individuals, when allowed by law, have pursued the adoption option. But, as this Section also shows, many states have opened non-adoptive routes to legal parentage for nonbiological LGBT parents. Several developments influenced this shift, including the increasing numbers of post-dissolution parenting claims by unmarried nonbiological LGBT parents; the increasing legal recognition of family formation, primarily by different-sex couples, through assisted reproduction; and marriage equality. This Section covers both the traditional adoption route and non-adoptive statutory and equitable routes to parentage.

A. ADOPTION

Many lesbian, gay, and bisexual individuals become parents through adoption. Some adopt children who are part of the foster care system, others pursue private adoptions, while yet others seek to adopt their partners' legal children through second-parent adoptions. In the absence of biological links with children, adoption generally offers the most legally secure (albeit oftentimes expensive) mechanism for establishing legal parenthood. This section explores the question of adoption, with a particular emphasis on second-parent adoptions.

Distinct from the traditional form of adoption, which extinguishes the parental rights and obligations of legal parents, second parent-adoption leaves the parental rights of one legally recognized parent intact and creates another legally recognized parent for the child. All jurisdictions allow individuals to adopt their spouses' children without the latter having to terminate their parental rights. Before marriage equality, same-sex couples could not avail themselves of the "spousal adoption" option. As a result, the question of whether the same-sex partners of legal parents could adopt the latter's children without first terminating the parents' legal rights was litigated in many jurisdictions. Answering this question required courts to interpret a particular state's adoption statute. The first judicial decision below is representative of rulings that have allowed unmarried partners of parents to petition for adoption; the second opinion is representative of rulings that have concluded differently.

With nationwide marriage equality, same-sex couples who choose to marry can now, regardless of where they live, avail themselves of the "spousal adoption" option. (Even before marriage equality, many domestic parternship and civil union statutes opened stepparent adoption to registered same-sex couples.) But the issue of second-parent adoption remains a highly salient one for unmarried couples, regardless of their gender or sexual orientation. In jurisdictions that do not allow second-parent adoptions, the unmarried partners of legal parents are not able to adopt the latter's children without first seeking to terminate their partners' parental rights. As a practical matter, this means that unmarried individuals in those jurisdictions are not able to adopt the children in question regardless of the extent to which they have functioned as parents and of the extent to which doing so is in the children's best interests.

IN RE ADOPTION OF TAMMY

Supreme Judicial Court of Massachusetts, 1993
619 N.E.2d 315, 416 Mass. 205

GREANEY, JUSTICE.

We summarize the relevant facts as found by the judge. Helen and Susan have lived together in a committed relationship, which they consider to be permanent, for more than ten years. In June, 1983, they jointly purchased a house in Cambridge. Both women are physicians specializing in surgery. At the time the petition was filed, Helen maintained a private practice in general surgery at Mount Auburn Hospital and Susan, a nationally recognized expert in the field of breast cancer, was director of the Faulkner Breast Center and a surgical oncologist at the Dana Farber Cancer Institute. Both women also held positions on the faculty of Harvard Medical School.

For several years prior to the birth of Tammy, Helen and Susan planned to have a child, biologically related to both of them, whom they would jointly parent. Helen first attempted to conceive a child through artificial insemination by Susan's brother. When those efforts failed, Susan successfully conceived a child through artificial insemination by Helen's biological cousin, Francis. The women attended childbirth classes together and Helen was present when Susan gave birth to Tammy on April 30, 1988. Although Tammy's birth certificate reflects Francis as her biological father, she was given a hyphenated surname using Susan and Helen's last names.

Since her birth, Tammy has lived with, and been raised and supported by, Helen and Susan. Tammy views both women as her parents, calling Helen "mama" and Susan "mommy." Tammy has strong emotional and psychological bonds with both Helen and Susan. Together, Helen and Susan have provided Tammy with a comfortable home, and have created a warm and stable environment which is supportive of Tammy's growth and over-all well being. Both women jointly and equally participate in parenting Tammy, and both have a strong financial commitment to her. During the work week, Helen usually has lunch at home with Tammy, and on weekends both women spend time together with Tammy at special events or running errands. When Helen and Susan are working, Tammy is cared for by a nanny. The three vacation together at least ten days every three to four months, frequently spending time with Helen's and Susan's respective extended families in California and Mexico. Francis does not participate in parenting Tammy and does not support her. His intention was to assist Helen and Susan in having a child, and he does not intend to be involved with Tammy, except as a distant relative. Francis signed an adoption surrender and supports the joint adoption by both women.

Helen and Susan, recognizing that the laws of the Commonwealth do not permit them to enter into a legally cognizable marriage, believe that the best interests of Tammy require legal recognition of her identical emotional relationship to both women. Susan expressed her understanding that it may not be in her own long-term interest to permit Helen to adopt Tammy because, in the event that Helen and Susan separate, Helen would have equal rights to primary custody. Susan indicated, however, that she has no reservation about allowing Helen to adopt. Apart from the emotional security and current practical ramifications which legal recognition of the reality of her parental relationships will provide Tammy, Susan indicated that the adoption is important for Tammy in terms of potential inheritance from Helen. Helen and her living issue are the beneficiaries of three irrevocable family trusts. Unless Tammy is adopted, Helen's share of the trusts may pass to others. Although Susan and Helen have established a substantial trust fund for Tammy, it is comparatively small in relation to Tammy's potential inheritance under Helen's family trusts.

Over a dozen witnesses, including mental health professionals, teachers, colleagues, neighbors, blood relatives and a priest and nun, testified to the fact that Helen and Susan participate equally in raising Tammy, that Tammy relates to both women as her parents, and that the three form a healthy, happy, and stable family unit. Educators familiar with Tammy testified that she is an extremely well-adjusted, bright, creative, cheerful child who interacts well with other children and adults. A priest and nun from the parties' church testified that Helen and Susan are active parishioners, that they routinely take Tammy to church and church-related activities, and that they attend to the spiritual and moral development of Tammy in an exemplary fashion. Teachers from Tammy's school testified that Helen and Susan both actively participate as volunteers in the school community and communicate frequently with school officials. Neighbors testified that they would have no hesitation in leaving their own children in the care of Helen or Susan. Susan's father, brother, and maternal aunt, and Helen's cousin testified in favor of the joint adoption. Members of both women's extended families attested to the fact that they consider Helen and Susan to be equal parents of Tammy. Both families unreservedly endorsed the adoption petition.

The Department of Social Services (department) conducted a home study in connection with the adoption petition which recommended the adoption, concluding that "the petitioners and their home are suitable for the proper rearing of this child." Tammy's pediatrician reported to the department that Tammy receives regular pediatric care and that she "could not have more excellent parents than Helen and Susan." A court-appointed guardian ad litem, Dr. Steven Nickman, assistant clinical professor of psychiatry at Harvard Medical School, conducted a clinical assessment of Tammy and her family with a view toward determining whether or not it would be in Tammy's best interests to be adopted by Helen and Susan. Dr. Nickman considered the ramifications of the fact that Tammy will be brought up in a "non-standard" family. As part of his report, he reviewed and referenced literature on child psychiatry and child psychology which supports the conclusion that children raised by lesbian parents develop normally. In sum, he stated that "the fact that this parent-child constellation came into being as a result of thoughtful planning and a strong desire on the part of these women to be parents to a child and to give that child the love, the wisdom and the knowledge that they possess * * * [needs to be taken into account]. * * * The maturity of these women, their status in the community, and their seriousness of purpose stands in contrast to the caretaking environments of a vast number of children who are born to heterosexual parents but who are variously abused, neglected and otherwise deprived of security and happiness." Dr. Nickman concluded that "there is every reason for [Helen] to become a legal parent to Tammy just as [Susan] is," and he recommended that the court so order. An attorney appointed to represent Tammy's interests also strongly recommended that the joint petition be granted.

Despite the overwhelming support for the joint adoption and the judge's conclusion that joint adoption is clearly in Tammy's best interests, the question remains whether there is anything in the law of the Commonwealth that would prevent this adoption. The law of adoption is purely statutory, and the governing statute, is to be strictly followed in all its essential particulars. To the extent that any ambiguity or vagueness exists in the statute, judicial construction should enhance, rather than defeat, its purpose. The primary purpose of the adoption statute, particularly with regard to children under the age of fourteen, is undoubtedly the advancement of the best interests of the subject child. With these considerations in mind, we examine the statute to determine whether adoption in the circumstances of this case is permitted.

1. The initial question is whether the Probate Court judge had jurisdiction to enter a judgment on a joint petition for adoption brought by two unmarried cohabitants in the petitioners' circumstances. We answer this question in the affirmative.

There is nothing on the face of the statute which precludes the joint adoption of a child by two unmarried cohabitants such as the petitioners. [The law] provides that "[a] person of full age may petition the probate court in the county where he resides for leave to adopt as his child another person younger than himself, unless such other person is his or her wife or husband, or brother, sister, uncle or aunt, of the whole or half blood." Other than requiring that a spouse join in the petition, if the petitioner is married and the spouse is competent to join therein, the statute does not expressly prohibit or require joinder by any person. Although the singular "a person" is used, it is a legislatively mandated rule of statutory construction that "[w]ords importing the singular number may extend and be applied to several persons" unless the resulting construction is "inconsistent with the manifest intent of the law-making body or repugnant to the context of the same statute." In the context of adoption, where the legislative intent to promote the best interests of the child is evidenced throughout the governing statute, and the adoption of a child by two unmarried individuals accomplishes that goal, construing the term "person" as "persons" clearly enhances, rather than defeats, the purpose of the statute. Furthermore, it is apparent from the first sentence of [the law] that the Legislature considered and defined those combinations of persons which would lead to adoptions in violation of public policy. Clearly absent is any prohibition of adoption by two unmarried individuals like the petitioners.

While the Legislature may not have envisioned adoption by same-sex partners, there is no indication that it attempted to define all possible categories of persons leading to adoptions in the best interests of children. Rather than limit the potential categories of persons entitled to adopt * * * the Legislature used general language to define who may adopt and who may be adopted. The Probate Court has thus been granted jurisdiction to consider a variety of adoption petitions. The limitations on adoption that do exist derive from the written consent requirements contained in § 2, from specific conditions set forth in § 2A, which must be satisfied prior to the adoption of a child under the age of fourteen, and from several statutory and judicial directives which essentially restrict adoptions to those which have been found by a judge to be in the best interests of the subject child.

In this case all requirements in §§ 2 and 2A are met, and there is no question that the judge's findings demonstrate that the directives set forth in §§ 5B and 6, and in case law, have been satisfied. Adoption will not result in any tangible change in Tammy's daily life; it will, however, serve to provide her with a significant legal relationship which may be important in her future. At the most practical level, adoption will entitle Tammy to inherit from Helen's family trusts and from Helen and her family under the law of intestate succession to receive support from Helen, who will be legally obligated to provide such support to be eligible for coverage under Helen's health insurance policies, and to be eligible for social security benefits in the event of Helen's disability or death.

Of equal, if not greater significance, adoption will enable Tammy to preserve her unique filial ties to Helen in the event that Helen and Susan separate, or Susan predeceases Helen. As the case law and commentary on the subject illustrate, when the functional parents of children born in circumstances similar to Tammy separate or one dies, the children often remain in legal limbo for years while their future is disputed in the courts. In some cases, children have been denied the affection of a functional parent who has been with them since birth, even when it is apparent that this outcome is contrary to the children's best interests. Adoption serves to establish legal rights and responsibilities so that, in the event that problems arise in the future, issues of custody and visitation may be promptly resolved by reference to the best interests of the child within the recognized framework of the law. There is no jurisdictional bar in the statute to the judge's consideration of this joint petition. The conclusion that the adoption is in the best interests of Tammy is also well warranted.

2. The judge also posed the question whether Susan's legal relationship to Tammy must be terminated if Tammy is adopted. Section 6 provides that, on entry of an adoption decree, "all rights, duties and other legal consequences of the natural relation of child and parent shall * * * terminate between the child so adopted and his natural parents and kindred." Although [the law] clearly permits a child's natural parent to be an adoptive parent, § 6 does not contain any express exceptions to its termination provision. The Legislature obviously did not intend that a natural parent's legal relationship to its child be terminated when the natural parent is a party to the adoption petition.

Section 6 clearly is directed to the more usual circumstances of adoption, where the child is adopted by persons who are not the child's natural parents (either because the natural parents have elected to relinquish the child for adoption or their parental rights have been involuntarily terminated). The purpose of the termination provision is to protect the security of the child's newly-created family unit by eliminating involvement with the child's natural parents. Although it is not uncommon for a natural parent to join in the adoption petition of a spouse who is not the child's natural parent, the statute has never been construed to require the termination of the natural parent's legal relationship to the child in these circumstances. Nor has § 6 been construed to apply when the natural mother petitions alone to adopt her child born out of wedlock. Reading the adoption statute as a whole, we conclude that the termination provision contained in § 6 was intended to apply only when the natural parents (or parent) are not parties to the adoption petition.

3. We conclude that the Probate Court has jurisdiction to enter a decree on a joint adoption petition brought by the two petitioners when

the judge has found that joint adoption is in the subject child's best interests. We further conclude that, when a natural parent is a party to a joint adoption petition, that parent's legal relationship to the child does not terminate on entry of the adoption decree.

[Dissenting opinions by JUSTICE NOLAN and JUSTICE LYNCH are omitted.]

IN RE ADOPTION OF LUKE

Supreme Court of Nebraska, 2002
640 N.W.2d 374, 263 Neb. 365

PER CURIAM.

B.P. is the biological mother of Luke, a minor child born on December 20, 1997. Luke was conceived by artificial insemination using semen from an anonymous donor from the University of Nebraska Medical Center's genetic semen bank. Accordingly, Luke's biological father is unknown and is not a party to this action. For purposes of the Nebraska adoption statutes, Luke was born "out of wedlock."

On October 2, 2000, appellants jointly filed a verified petition in which A.E. sought to adopt Luke. B.P. indicated her "consent" in the petition and in other supporting documents. B.P. did not file a relinquishment of her parental rights to Luke. To the contrary, she indicated on an affidavit attached to the petition that she did not intend to relinquish Luke. The only relief sought in this proceeding was the adoption of Luke by A.E.

A home study of appellants' household was conducted by an adoption specialist. The specialist recommended A.E.'s adoption of Luke be approved by the court.

In an order filed December 1, 2000, the county court denied the petition for adoption. * * *

For an adoption to be valid under Nebraska's adoption statutes, the record must show the following factors: (1) the existence of an adult person or persons entitled to adopt, (2) the existence of a child eligible for adoption, (3) compliance with statutory procedures providing for adoption, and (4) evidence that the proposed adoption is in the child's best interests. Neb. Rev. Stat. § 43–101 et seq. The absence of any one of the necessary factors will preclude the adoption. In this case, Luke was not eligible for adoption, the county court determined that his adoption by A.E. was precluded on this basis, and we affirm on this basis.

The county court stated that "the statu[t]es permit a single adult person to adopt a child after all necessary consents and relinquishments have been filed." On this record, B.P. did not relinquish her parental rights to Luke, and therefore, he was not eligible for adoption by A.E. The county court's denial of the petition due to an absence of a relinquishment was correct. The county court also stated that Nebraska's adoption statutes do not provide for "two non-married persons to adopt a minor child, no matter how qualified they are." Because A.E. alone sought to adopt Luke, the issue of whether two nonmarried persons are entitled to adopt was not presented to the county court in this case. Thus, that issue is not before this court on appeal, and we do not consider it.

Appellants argue that the county court erred in concluding that it could not grant the adoption of Luke by A.E. as an additional parent without a relinquishment of the parental rights of B.P. Appellants contend that "consent is an alternative to a relinquishment," and that where B.P. intended to preserve her parental rights upon the adoption of Luke by A.E., only B.P.'s consent, which was given, was required. * * *

The State responds that the Nebraska adoption statutory scheme does not provide for adoption without relinquishment except in the case of a stepparent where "an adult husband or wife" seeks to "adopt a child of the other spouse." § 43–101(1).[2] The State contends that stepparent adoption is the only explicit adoption scenario outlined in the Nebraska adoption statutes and that it is implicit in this statutorily permitted scenario that the existing parent intends to continue parenting and, therefore, need not relinquish his or her parental rights to the child in question. * * *

With respect to * * * Luke, who is the subject of this case, § 43–101 provides that "any minor child may be adopted." Elsewhere in chapter 43, however, numerous statutory substantive and procedural provisions are set forth which must be read together with § 43–101 and met before "any minor child," § 43–101, is in fact eligible for adoption and a decree of adoption may be properly entered. The statutes which provide for the consequences of adoption also bear on the issue of Luke's eligibility. Reading the various provisions of chapter 43 in pari materia, we conclude that with the exception of the stepparent adoption, the parent or parents possessing existing parental rights must relinquish the child before "any minor child may be adopted by any adult person or persons." Under Nebraska's statutory adoption scheme, the minor child, Luke, was not eligible for adoption by A.E. because B.P. had not relinquished him and the county court's reading of the statute was correct.

---

[2]   Section 43–101 is entitled "Children eligible for adoption." Section 43–101(1) provides as follows:

Except as otherwise provided in the Nebraska Indian Child Welfare Act, any minor child may be adopted by any adult person or persons and any adult child may be adopted by the spouse of such child's parent in the cases and subject to sections 43–101 to 43–115, except that no person having a husband or wife may adopt a minor child unless the husband or wife joins in the petition therefor. If the husband or wife so joins in the petition therefor, the adoption shall be by them jointly, except that an adult husband or wife may adopt a child of the other spouse whether born in or out of wedlock.

In *In re Adoption of Kassandra B. & Nicholas B.*, 540 N.W.2d 554, 558 (Neb. 1995), we observed that as to the biological parent, "termination of his or her parental rights is the foundation of our adoption statutes." This pronouncement is reflected in the adoption statutes, which require relinquishment or termination prior to adoption, except when a stepparent adopts, and is further reflected in case law interpreting the adoption statutes.

Appellants argue that B.P.'s consent was the equivalent of relinquishment for purposes of the present case. We do not agree. Section § 43–104 provides that "no adoption shall be decreed unless written consents thereto are filed in the court of the county in which the person or persons desiring to adopt reside." * * *

A consent to the proceedings by a parent or parents under § 43–104 is not required when a relinquishment has been executed. § 43–104(3)(a). A relinquishment would preclude the necessity of a consent. B.P. did not sign a relinquishment in this case, and her "consent" is not the equivalent of relinquishment.

We have stated that the consent granted by a court under § 43–104 does nothing more than permit the trial court to entertain the adoption proceedings. *Klein v. Klein*, 230 Neb. 385, 431 N.W.2d 646 (1988). We read "consent" in § 43–104 to mean that the person, persons, or entity authorized to consent to the proceedings has agreed that the proposed adoption should be entertained by the trial court. In the instant case, B.P. "consented" to the proceedings and Luke is not ineligible for adoption due to a lack of such consent; however, B.P.'s consent to the proceedings was not tantamount to a relinquishment of parental rights.

The importance of "relinquishment" in the adoption statutes is apparent in § 43–109, which provides in relevant part:

> If, upon the hearing, the court finds that such adoption is for the best interests of such minor child or such adult child, a decree of adoption shall be entered. No decree of adoption shall be entered unless * * * (c) the court record includes an affidavit or affidavits signed by the *relinquishing biological parent*, or parents if both are available, in which it is affirmed that, pursuant to section 43–106.02, prior to the relinquishment of the child for adoption, the *relinquishing parent* was, or parents if both are available were, (i) presented a copy or copies of the nonconsent form provided for in section 43–146.06 and (ii) given an explanation of the effects of filing or not filing the nonconsent form.

(Emphasis supplied.) The affidavit noted in § 43–109(c) refers to the form completed by the relinquishing parent or parents which indicates whether the parent or parents agree to the release of information about the relinquishing parent or parents to the adopted child. * * *

We have held that in a private adoption case where the prospective adoptive parent was not a spouse of the biological parent, there must be a relinquishment by the biological parent and the relinquishment must be valid in order for the child to become eligible for adoption. *See Gray v. Maxwell*, 293 N.W.2d 90 (Neb. 1993) (stating that where biological mother was paid sum of money in excess of legitimate expenses of confinement and birth in consideration for executing relinquishment, such relinquishment was against public policy and was invalid). In the instant case, B.P. swore in the affidavit required under § 43–109 that "I do not intend to relinquish [Luke] for the ultimate purpose of adoption." Having refused to relinquish Luke, B.P. is not a "relinquishing biological parent." The affidavit B.P. signed did not meet the requirements of § 43–109. Therefore, Luke was not eligible for adoption and "[n]o decree of adoption shall be entered."

The provisions contained in the adoption statutes found at §§ 43–110 and 43–111, pertaining to the consequences of adoption, further buttress our conclusion that "termination" of existing parental rights is the foundation of our adoption statutes. Section 43–110, entitled "Decree; effect as between parties," provides as follows:

> After a decree of adoption is entered, the usual relation of parent and child and all the rights, duties and other legal consequences of the natural relation of child and parent shall thereafter exist between such adopted child and the person or persons adopting such child and his, her or their kindred.

We have stated that the "purpose of § 43–110 is to terminate any relationship which existed between the natural parent and the child and to create a new relationship between the adoptive parent and the child." *In re Estate of Luckey; Bailey v. Luckey*, 291 N.W.2d 235, 237–38 (Neb. 1980).

Section 43–111, entitled "Decree; effect as to natural parents," provides:

> Except as provided in section 43–106.01 and the Nebraska Indian Child Welfare Act, after a decree of adoption has been entered, the natural parents of the adopted child shall be relieved of all parental duties toward and all responsibilities for such child and have no rights over such adopted child or to his or her property by descent and distribution.

We have read this section as requiring a relinquishment prior to a private placement adoption. *Gray v. Maxwell, supra.*

Thus, under Nebraska's adoption statutes, the legal consequence of an adoption is that "the natural relation of child and parent shall thereafter exist between such adopted child and the person or persons adopting such child," § 43–110, and the adoption serves to relieve the natural parents of "all parental duties toward and all responsibilities for such child and have no rights over such adopted child," § 43–111. The pleadings in this case indicate that only A.E. sought to adopt Luke. Had the county court permitted the adoption of Luke by A.E., a new relationship between A.E. and Luke would have been created pursuant to § 43–110, and, as an unintended consequence, B.P. would have been relieved of her natural rights to Luke pursuant to § 43–111. In the instant case, B.P. manifestly did not want the consequences ordained by § 43–111 to attach had the county court granted the petition for adoption of Luke by A.E. * * *

Appellants urge this court to ignore the language of § 43–111 and to interpret the adoption statutes as permitting the adoption of Luke by A.E. as a parent in addition to the existing parent, B.P., without consequence to the parental rights of B.P. Appellants acknowledge that the exception providing for a stepparent adoption under § 43–101 permits the addition of a stepparent without relieving the natural parent of rights which would otherwise result under § 43–111. Appellants urge this court to read into the adoption statutes an additional exception for second-parent adoptions and to disregard the fact that the adoption statutes explicitly provide for stepparent adoptions and do not explicitly provide for second-parent adoptions.

The adoption statutes permit only the paradigms which are explicit. With the exception of the statutory stepparent adoption scenario outlined in § 43–101, the adoption statutes neither provide for nor expressly designate who may adopt. When construing a statute, appellate courts are guided by the presumption that the Legislature intended a sensible, rather than an absurd, result in enacting a statute. Because the Nebraska adoption statutes explicitly provide for a stepparent adoption following which the existing parent will inherently continue raising the child, we conclude it would be an absurd result under the statutes as written to require relinquishment by the existing parent in the explicit statutorily permitted case of a stepparent adoption. As compared to a stepparent adoption, however, it is not inherent in § 43–101 that the "person or persons" seeking to adopt will necessarily be in addition to the existing parent who will continue to raise the child. Reading the adoption statutes in their entirety, it is clear that aside from the stepparent adoption scenario, the parents' parental rights must be terminated or the child must be relinquished in order for the child to be eligible for adoption by "any adult person or persons" under § 43–101. * * * AFFIRMED.

[Dissenting opinion by JUSTICE WRIGHT is omitted.]

NOTES

1. In addition to Massachusetts, second-parent adoptions have been approved by the highest courts in California, Idaho, New York, Pennsylvania, and Vermont. *See Sharon S. v. Superior Court*, 73 P.3d 554, 574, 31 Cal.4th 417, 446, 2 Cal.Rptr.3d 699, 729 (2003); *Matter of Jacob*, 660 N.E.2d 397, 405, 86 N.Y.2d 651, 669, 636 N.Y.S.2d 716, 724 (1995); *In re Adoption of Doe*, 326 P.3d 347, 156 Idaho 345 (2014); *Adoption of R.B.F. & R.C.F.*, 803 A.2d 1195, 1203, 569 Pa. 269, 283 (2002); *In re Adoption of B.L.V.B.*, 628 A.2d 1271, 1276, 160 Vt. 368, 377 (1993).

2. Some states have allowed second-parent adoptions through statutory amendments. *See, e.g.*, CONN. GEN. STAT. ANN. § 45a–724(a)(3) (2016) (providing that "any parent of a minor child may agree in writing with one other person who shares parental responsibility for the child with such parent that the other person shall adopt or join in the adoption of the child"). In 2010, New York amended its adoption statute to permit "two unmarried adult intimate partners" to adopt together. N.Y. DOM. REL. L. § 210 (2016). A few years later, a New York court held that a close friend (a gay man) of an adoptive parent (a straight woman) could seek to become the child's second parent under the provision. *See In re the Adoption of G.*, 978 N.Y.S.2d 622, 42 Misc.3d 812 (Surr. Ct. 2013). The court explained that "[t]he legislative history of the ... amendment ... supports the interpretation of the phrase 'intimate partners' to include a relationship such as the one we have here: very close, loving friends, who have an intimate connection, which includes planning for and raising a child together. Indeed, the experience of jointly and intentionally parenting a child is itself of the most intimate nature." *Id.* at 821.

3. In addition to Nebraska, appellate courts in North Carolina, Ohio, and Wisconsin have denied second-parent adoption petitions. *See Boseman v. Jarrell*, 704 S.E.2d 494, 501, 364 N.C. 537, 547 (2010); *In re Adoption of Doe*, 719 N.E.2d 1071, 1073, 130 Ohio App.3d 288, 292 (1998); *In Interest of Angel Lace M.*, 516 N.W.2d 678, 687, 184 Wis.2d 492, 519 (1994). Interestingly, the North Carolina Supreme Court in *Boseman*, after concluding that the state adoption statute did not allow second-parent adoptions, proceeded to affirm the granting of joint custody following the dissolution of a lesbian relationship because the biological mother had invited her partner to form a family unit and to raise the child together. *Boseman*, 704 S.E.2d at 504, 364 N.C. at 552.

4. Although it would seem that second-parent adoptions make clear that both individuals in question are to be deemed legal parents, difficulties sometimes arise. Here is a case in point: E.L. was the biological mother of three children conceived through donor insemination. In order to secure the parental rights of V.L., her partner and intended co-parent, the two women pursued a second-parent adoption in their home-state of Georgia. E.L. consented to V.L. adopting the children, and a court ruled in favor of the adoption. The trouble started when the women broke up years later and E.L.

tried to cut off V.L.'s parental rights. At this point, the women were living in Alabama. Once having agreed to the adoption, E.L. now argued that the Georgia court had no authority to issue the adoption decree. The Alabama Supreme Court agreed and ruled that Alabama courts could ignore the Georgia adoption decree and thereby deny V.L. any chance to seek visitation or custody of her adopted children. *See Ex parte E.L.*, 2015 WL 5511249 (Ala.2015).

The Supreme Court reversed the Alabama court in summary fashion. *See V.L. v. E.L.*, ___ U.S. ___, 136 S.Ct. 1017, 194 L.Ed.2d 92 (2016). The Court ordered no briefing and heard no oral argument. Rather, in a *per curiam* opinion with no dissents, the justices relied on the Full Faith and Credit Clause, which straightforwardly requires one state to respect the judgments of another state's courts. Alabama's highest court had tried to get around this settled rule by invoking an exception to full faith and credit for judgments that are entered by an out-of-state court that lacked jurisdiction. The Supreme Court held that the exception did not apply because the Georgia court that ordered the adoption unquestionably was the court with jurisdiction to hear adoption matters. What the Alabama Supreme Court was really doing, the Court explained, was taking issue with the Georgia court's conclusion that Georgia law allowed an adoption in these circumstances. That argument, said the justices, is not about jurisdiction but about the merits of the case. *Id.*

5.   In 1977, Florida enacted a law prohibiting lesbians and gay men from adopting. 1977 FLA. LAWS, CH. 77–140, § 1, FLA. STAT. § 63.042(3) (2002). The statute provided that "[n]o person eligible to adopt under the statute may adopt if that person is a homosexual." *Id.* In 2004, the U.S. Court of Appeals for the Eleventh Circuit upheld the statute's constitutionality. *Lofton v. Secretary of Dep't of Children & Family Servs.*, 358 F.3d 804 (11th Cir. 2004), *cert. denied*, 543 U.S. 1081, 125 S.Ct. 869, 160 L.Ed.2d 825 (2005). Several years later, a Florida appellate court struck down the law because it violated the state constitution's guarantee of equal protection. *Florida Department of Children and Families v. In re Matter of Adoption of X.X.G. and N.R.G.*, 45 So.3d 79 (Fla.Ct.App. 2010). Florida argued that there was "a rational basis for the prohibition on homosexual adoption because children will have better role models, and face less discrimination, if they are placed in non-homosexual households, preferably with a husband and wife as the parents." *Id.* at 85. But the court, after noting that one-third of Florida's adoptions were by single individuals and that the state allowed lesbians and gay men to serve as foster parents and as legal guardians, concluded that there was no rational basis for categorically prohibiting gay people from adopting. *Id.* at 87. In doing so, the court reviewed the social science literature on parenting by lesbians and gay men, noting that "[t]hese reports and studies find that there are no differences in the parenting of homosexuals or the adjustment of their children. . . . [B]ased on the robust nature of the evidence available in the field, this Court is satisfied that the issue is so far beyond dispute that it would be irrational to hold otherwise; the best

interests of children are not preserved by prohibiting homosexual adoption."
Id.

6. Utah law gives a preference to married couples over single adults in adoption placements. UTAH CODE ANN. §§ 78A–6–307(19), 78B–6–117(4) (2016). *See also* ARIZ. REV. STAT. § 8–103 (2016) (granting preferences to married couples over single adults in adoption). Utah law also prohibits a child from being adopted "by a person who is cohabiting in a relationship that is not a legally valid and binding marriage under the laws of this state. For purposes of this Subsection[,] 'cohabiting' means residing with another person and being involved in a sexual relationship with that person." UTAH CODE ANN. § 78–30–1–3(b) (2016). Before same-sex couples could marry in Utah, this provision made it impossible for lesbians and gay men who lived with their partners to adopt. Note, however, that unlike the former Florida ban, the Utah statute is facially neutral as to sexual orientation.

While some states, like Utah, prohibit unmarried couples from adopting jointly, they allow married same-sex couples to adopt. Mississippi, in contrast, has a statute prohibiting "adoptions by couples of the same gender." MISS. CODE ANN. § 93–17–3(5) (2006). In 2016, after a federal district court issued a preliminary injunction prohibiting enforcement of the law on the ground that it is likely inconsistent with *Obergefell, see Campaign for Southern Equality v. Mississippi Department of Human Services,* ___ F.Supp.3d ___, 2016 WL 1306202 (Miss. Dist. Ct. 2016), the state announced it would not appeal. *See* "Mississippi's Gay Adoption Ban is Dead," CLARION-LEDGER, May 3, 2016.

7. As discussed in *Moix v. Moix, supra* Section 1.A., Arkansas voters in 2008 approved a measure prohibiting cohabiting couples from serving as adoptive or foster care parents. The Arkansas Supreme Court later held that the measure violated the fundamental right to privacy under the state constitution because it penalized individuals for their sexual intimacy choices. *See Arkansas Dep't Human Services v. Cole,* 380 S.W.3d 429, 2011 Ark. 145 (2011). An earlier Arkansas regulation prohibiting the placement of foster children with lesbians and gay men was struck down by the Arkansas Supreme Court in 2006. *See Department of Human Services v. Howard,* 367 Ark. 55, 238 S.W.3d 1 (2006).

8. Is there is a relevant difference between categorically prohibiting lesbians and gay men to adopt (or to serve as foster care parents) and allowing decision makers to take the sexual orientation of prospective parents into account when making particular placement decisions? Professor Michael Wald, in an article that forcefully argues against categorical restrictions based on sexual orientation, suggests that in making case-by-case adoption and foster care placement decisions, judges and agencies should be permitted to take sexual orientation into account as long as it is one of several factors that are considered. *See* Michael S. Wald, *Adults' Sexual Orientation and State Determinations Regarding Placement of Children,* 40 FAM. L. Q. 381, 417–422 (2006). Wald explains that "[c]aseworkers or courts

could consider the difficulties or advantages a particular child is likely to face in living with a gay family as one of the factors in determining the best placement. Even if the difficulties are related to the fact of stigma, as a general rule, children should not be made to bear the costs of remedying biases that are deemed undesirable by policymakers." *Id.* at 417–18.

Professor Wald adds that the case for allowing decision-makers to take sexual orientation into account is stronger in foster care placements than in adoption placements because "children tend to enter foster care at older ages and face very difficult adjustments. Asking these youth to adjust to a home where the caretakers are of a different sexual orientation may be unwise in some situations. The youth may bring biases that will undermine the chances of a successful placement. Getting foster youth to develop the emotional commitment and sense of trust needed for successful placements is challenging under the best of circumstances. It is likely to be impossible if the youth is resistant." *Id.* at 421. What is your position on this? Do you agree with Professor Wald or do you think that a prospective parent's sexual orientation (and gender identity) should *never* be a factor in the placement of children?

9.   Professor Wald seems to have had in mind heterosexual adolescents who may object to being placed in the homes of LGBT individuals. What about LGBT youth? Should officials attempt to place LGBT adolescents with LGBT foster or adoptive parents before considering placements with heterosexual parents? For arguments against this type of "sexual orientation matching" policy, see Joseph Evall, *Sexual Orientation and Adoptive Matching*, 25 FAM. L.Q. 347 (1991).

B. DE FACTO PARENTHOOD AND STATUTORY "HOLDING OUT" PROVISIONS

In some jurisdictions, individuals who do not have a biological or adoptive relationship with children they have helped raise alongside legally recognized parents may be able to establish a parent-child relationship without having to adopt the child. Courts in some states have granted these individuals standing to sue for custody and/or visitation under the equitable doctrine of *de facto* parenthood (sometimes referred to as *in loco parentis*, functional parenthood, or psychological parenthood). In addition, some jurisdictions have statutory provisions that recognize as parents individuals who have "held out" children as their own despite the absence of biological or adoptive links with those children. As the two cases that follow show, these ways of attaining parentage status can be of assistance to the former same-sex partners of legal parents. These two ways of establishing parenthood status are particularly important for LGBT individuals who have not married their children's legal parents or who have not adopted the children.[8]

V.C. v. M.J.B.

Supreme Court of New Jersey, 2000

748 A.2d 539, 163 N.J. 200

LONG, J.

The following facts were established at trial. V.C. and M.J.B., who are lesbians, met in 1992 and began dating on July 4, 1993. On July 9, 1993, M.J.B. went to see a fertility specialist to begin artificial insemination procedures. She prepared for that appointment by recording her body temperature for eight to nine months prior for purposes of tracking her ovulation schedule. She had been planning to be artificially inseminated since late 1980. According to M.J.B., she made the final decision to become pregnant independently and before beginning her relationship with V.C. Two individuals who knew M.J.B. before she began dating V.C., confirmed that M.J.B. had been planning to become pregnant through artificial insemination for years prior to the beginning of the parties' relationship.

According to V.C., early in their relationship, the two discussed having children. However, V.C. did not become aware of M.J.B.'s visits with the specialist and her decision to have a baby by artificial insemination until September 1993. In fact, the doctor's records of M.J.B.'s first appointment indicate that M.J.B. was single and that she "desires children."

Nonetheless, V.C. claimed that the parties jointly decided to have children and that she and M.J.B. jointly researched and decided which sperm donor they should use. M.J.B. acknowledged that she consulted V.C. on the issue but maintained that she individually made the final choice about which sperm donor to use.

Between November 1993 and February 1994, M.J.B. underwent several insemination procedures. V.C. attended at least two of those sessions. In December 1993, V.C. moved into M.J.B.'s apartment. Two months later, on February 7, 1994, the doctor informed M.J.B. that she

---

[8] There are different reasons why individuals may not seek to adopt children whom they are helping to raise. First, as noted in the previous section, some jurisdictions do not allow the unmarried partners of legal parents to adopt without first terminating the latter's parental rights. Second, adoption is oftentimes expensive, making it unaffordable for some couples and individuals. Third, most individuals who are functioning as parents consider themselves the children's parent, leading them to believe it is not necessary to adopt their own children, especially while the relationships with the legal parents remain happy ones. *See* CARLOS A. BALL, THE RIGHT TO BE PARENTS: LGBT FAMILIES AND THE TRANSFORMATION OF PARENTHOOD 104 (2012).

was pregnant. M.J.B. called V.C. at work to tell her the good news. Eventually, M.J.B. was informed that she was having twins.

During M.J.B.'s pregnancy, both M.J.B. and V.C. prepared for the birth of the twins by attending pre-natal and Lamaze classes. In April 1994, the parties moved to a larger apartment to accommodate the pending births. V.C. contended that during that time they jointly decided on the children's names. M.J.B. admitted consulting V.C., but maintained that she made the final decision regarding names.

The children were born on September 29, 1994. V.C. took M.J.B. to the hospital and she was present in the delivery room at the birth of the children. At the hospital, the nurses and staff treated V.C. as if she were a mother. Immediately following the birth, the nurses gave one child to M.J.B. to hold and the other to V.C., and took pictures of the four of them together. After the children were born, M.J.B. took a three-month maternity leave and V.C. took a three-week vacation.

The parties opened joint bank accounts for their household expenses, and prepared wills, powers of attorney, and named each other as the beneficiary for their respective life insurance policies. At some point, the parties also opened savings accounts for the children, and named V.C. as custodian for one account and M.J.B. as custodian for the other.

The parties also decided to have the children call M.J.B. "Mommy" and V.C. "Meema." M.J.B. conceded that she referred to V.C. as a "mother" of the children. In addition, M.J.B. supported the notion, both publicly and privately, that during the twenty-three months after the children were born, the parties and the children functioned as a family unit. M.J.B. sent cards and letters to V.C. that referred to V.C. as the children's mother, and indicated that the four of them were a family. The children also gave cards to V.C. that indicated that V.C. was their mother. M.J.B. encouraged a relationship between V.C. and the children and sought to create a "happy, cohesive environment for the children." M.J.B. admitted that, when the parties' relationship was intact, she sometimes thought of the four of them as a family. However, although M.J.B. sometimes considered the children "theirs," other times she considered them "hers".

M.J.B. agreed that both parties cared for the children but insisted that she made substantive decisions regarding their lives. For instance, M.J.B. maintained that she independently researched and made the final decisions regarding the children's pediatrician and day care center. V.C. countered that she was equally involved in all decision-making regarding the children. Specifically, V.C. claimed that she participated in choosing a day care center for the children, and it is clear that M.J.B. brought V.C. to visit the center she selected prior to making a final decision.

M.J.B. acknowledged that V.C. assumed substantial responsibility for the children, but maintained that V.C. was a mere helper and not a co-parent. However, according to V.C., she acted as a co-parent to the children and had equal parenting responsibility. Indeed, M.J.B. listed V.C. as the "other mother" on the children's pediatrician and day care registration forms. M.J.B. also gave V.C. medical power of attorney over the children. * * *

Together the parties purchased a home in February 1995. Later that year, V.C. asked M.J.B. to marry her, and M.J.B. accepted. In July 1995, the parties held a commitment ceremony where they were "married." At the ceremony, V.C., M.J.B. and the twins were blessed as a "family." * * *

* * * [I]n August 1996, M.J.B. ended the relationship. The parties then took turns living in the house with the children until November 1996. In December 1996, V.C. moved out. M.J.B. permitted V.C. to visit with the children until May 1997. During that time, V.C. spent approximately every other weekend with the children, and contributed money toward the household expenses.

In May 1997, M.J.B. went away on business and left the children with V.C. for two weeks. However, later that month, M.J.B. refused to continue V.C.'s visitation with the children, and at some point, M.J.B. stopped accepting V.C.'s money. M.J.B. asserted that she did not want to continue the children's contact with V.C. because she believed that V.C. was not properly caring for the children, and that the children were suffering distress from continued contact with V.C. Both parties became involved with new partners after the dissolution of their relationship. Eventually, V.C. filed this complaint for joint legal custody.

At trial, expert witnesses appeared for both parties. Dr. Allwyn J. Levine testified on behalf of V.C., and Dr. David Brodzinsky testified on behalf of M.J.B. Both experts arrived at similar conclusions after having examined the women individually and with the children, and after examining the children separately.

Dr. Levine concluded that both children view V.C. as a maternal figure and that V.C. regards herself as one of the children's mothers. "[B]ecause the children were basically parented from birth" by V.C. and M.J.B. "until they physically separated," Dr. Levine concluded that the children view the parties "as inter-changeable maternal mothering objects" and "have established a maternal bond with both of the women."

Dr. Levine likened the parties' relationship to a heterosexual marriage. Consequently, the children would be affected by the loss of V.C. just as if they had been denied contact with their father after a divorce. Dr. Levine explained that the children would benefit from continued contact with V.C. because they had a bonded relationship with her. Dr. Levine further noted that if the children felt abandoned by V.C., they might also feel unnecessary guilt and assume that they made V.C. angry or somehow caused the parties' separation. * * *

Likewise, Dr. Brodzinsky concluded that V.C. and the children enjoyed a bonded relationship that benefitted both children. Dr. Brodzinsky determined that the children regarded V.C. as a member of their family. * * * In contrast to Dr. Levine's opinion, Dr. Brodzinsky believed that the loss of V.C. was not akin to the loss of a parent in a heterosexual divorce. The doctor explained that societal views foster the expectation that a child and a parent will continue their relationship after a divorce, but that no similar expectation would exist for the children's relationship with V.C. * * *

The trial court denied V.C.'s applications for joint legal custody and visitation because it concluded that she failed to establish that the bonded relationship she enjoyed with the children had risen to the level of psychological or *de facto* parenthood. In so doing, the court gave significant weight to the fact that the decision to have children was M.J.B.'s, and not a joint decision between M.J.B. and V.C.

Finding that V.C. did not qualify as a psychological parent to the children, the trial court opined that it would "only be able to consider [V.C.'s] petition for custody if [she] was able [to] prove [M.J.B.] to be an unfit parent." Because V.C. did not allege that M.J.B. was an unfit parent, the trial court held that V.C. lacked standing to petition for joint legal custody. The court also denied V.C.'s application for visitation, determining that even a step-parent would not be granted such visitation except for equitable reasons, not present here. Further, it resolved that visitation was not in the children's best interests because M.J.B. harbored animosity toward V.C. that would "inevitably pass[ ] along to the children." According to the trial court, the case might have been different had V.C. "enjoyed a longer and more irreplaceable relationship with the children. * * * " Upon the entry of judgment, V.C. appealed. [The Appellate Division reversed the trial court's judgment.] * * *

There are no statutes explicitly addressing whether a former unmarried domestic partner has standing to seek custody and visitation with her former partner's biological children. That is not to say, however, that the current statutory scheme dealing with issues of custody and visitation does not provide some guiding principles. N.J.S.A. 9:2–3 prescribes:

> When the parents of a minor child live separately, or are about to do so, the Superior Court, in an action brought by either parent, shall have the same power to make judgments or orders concerning care, custody, education and maintenance as concerning a child whose parents are divorced. * * *

Further, N.J.S.A. 9:2–4 provides, in part, that

[t]he Legislature finds and declares that it is in the public policy of this State to assure minor children of frequent and continuing contact with both parents after the parents have separated or dissolved their marriage and that it is in the public interest to encourage parents to share the rights and responsibilities of child rearing in order to effect this policy. In any proceeding involving the custody of a minor child, the rights of both parents shall be equal. * * *

By that scheme, the Legislature has expressed the view that children should not generally be denied continuing contact with parents after the relationship between the parties ends.

N.J.S.A. 9:2–13(f) provides that "[t]he word 'parent,' when not otherwise described by the context, means a natural parent or parent by previous adoption." M.J.B. argues that because V.C. is not a natural or adoptive parent, we lack jurisdiction to consider her claims. That is an incomplete interpretation of the Act. Although the statutory definition of parent focuses on natural and adoptive parents, it also includes the phrase, "when not otherwise described by the context." That language evinces a legislative intent to leave open the possibility that individuals other than natural or adoptive parents may qualify as "parents," depending on the circumstances.

By including the words "when not otherwise described by the context" in the statute, the Legislature obviously envisioned a case where the specific relationship between a child and a person not specifically denominated by the statute would qualify as "parental" under the scheme of Title 9. Although the Legislature may not have considered the precise case before us, it is hard to imagine what it could have had in mind in adding the "context" language other than a situation such as this, in which a person not related to a child by blood or adoption has stood in a parental role vis-a-vis the child. It is that contention by V.C. that brings this case before the court and affords us jurisdiction over V.C.'s complaint.

Separate and apart from the statute, M.J.B. contends that there is no legal precedent for this action by V.C. She asserts, correctly, that a legal parent has a fundamental right to the care, custody and nurturance of his or her child. Various constitutional provisions have been cited as the source of that right, which is deeply imbedded in our collective consciousness and traditions. In general, however, the right of a legal parent to the care and custody of his or her child derives from the notion of privacy. According to M.J.B., that right entitles her to absolute preference over V.C. in connection with custody and visitation of the twins. She argues that V.C., a stranger, has no standing to bring this action. We disagree.

The right of parents to the care and custody of their children is not absolute. For example, a legal parent's fundamental right to custody and control of a child may be infringed upon by the state if the parent endangers the health or safety of the child. Likewise, if there is a showing of unfitness, abandonment or gross misconduct, a parent's right to custody of her child may be usurped.

According to M.J.B., because there is no allegation by V.C. of unfitness, abandonment or gross misconduct, there is no reason advanced to interfere with any of her constitutional prerogatives. What she elides from consideration, however, is the "exceptional circumstances" category (occasionally denominated as extraordinary circumstances) that has been recognized as an alternative basis for a third party to seek custody and visitation of another person's child. The "exceptional circumstances" category contemplates the intervention of the Court in the exercise of its *parens patriae* power to protect a child.

Subsumed within that category is the subset known as the psychological parent cases in which a third party has stepped in to assume the role of the legal parent who has been unable or unwilling to undertake the obligations of parenthood. * * *

At the heart of the psychological parent cases is a recognition that children have a strong interest in maintaining the ties that connect them to adults who love and provide for them. That interest, for constitutional as well as social purposes, lies in the emotional bonds that develop between family members as a result of shared daily life. That point was emphasized in *Lehr v. Robertson*, 463 U.S. 248, 261 (1983), where the Supreme Court held that a stepfather's *actual* relationship with a child was the determining factor when considering the degree of protection that the parent-child link must be afforded. The Court stressed that "the importance of the familial relationship, to the individuals involved and to the society, stems from the emotional attachments that derive from the intimacy of daily association, and from the role it plays in 'promot[ing] a way of life' through the instruction of children as well as from the fact of blood relationship."

To be sure, prior cases in New Jersey have arisen in the context of a third party taking over the role of an unwilling, absent or incapacitated parent. The question presented here is different; V.C. did not step into M.J.B.'s shoes, but labored alongside her in their family. However, because we view this issue as falling broadly within the contours we have previously described, and because V.C. invokes the "exceptional circumstances" doctrine based on her claim to be a psychological parent to the twins, she has standing to maintain this action separate and apart from the statute.

The next issue we confront is how a party may establish that he or she has, in fact, become a psychological parent to the child of a fit and involved legal parent. That is a question which many of our sister states have attempted to answer. Some have enacted statutes to address the subject by deconstructing psychological parenthood to its fundamental elements, including: the substantial nature of the relationship between the third party and the child, *see, e.g.,* Ariz. Rev. Stat. Ann. § 25–415(G)(1) (West 2000); whether or not the third party and the child actually lived together, *see, e.g.,* Minn. Stat. Ann. § 257.022(2b) (West 1999); Tex. Fam. Code Ann. § 102.003(a)(9) (West 1999); and whether the unrelated third party had previously provided financial support for the child, *see, e.g.,* 1999 Nev. Stat. 125A.330(3)(I). * * *

The most thoughtful and inclusive definition of *de facto* parenthood is the test enunciated in *Custody of H.S.H.-K.,* 533 N.W.2d 419, 421 (Wisc. 1995), and adopted by the Appellate Division majority here. It addresses the main fears and concerns both legislatures and courts have advanced when addressing the notion of psychological parenthood. Under that test,

> [t]o demonstrate the existence of the petitioner's parent-like relationship with the child, the petitioner must prove four elements: (1) that the biological or adoptive parent consented to, and fostered, the petitioner's formation and establishment of a parent-like relationship with the child; (2) that the petitioner and the child lived together in the same household; (3) that the petitioner assumed the obligations of parenthood by taking significant responsibility for the child's care, education and development, including contributing towards the child's support, without expectation of financial compensation [a petitioner's contribution to a child's support need not be monetary]; and (4) that the petitioner has been in a parental role for a length of time sufficient to have established with the child a bonded, dependent relationship parental in nature. * * *

Prong one is critical because it makes the biological or adoptive parent a participant in the creation of the psychological parent's relationship with the child. Without such a requirement, a paid nanny or babysitter could theoretically qualify for parental status. To avoid that result, in order for a third party to be deemed a psychological parent, the legal parent must have fostered the formation of the parental relationship between the third party and the child. By fostered is meant that the legal parent ceded over to the third party a measure of parental authority and autonomy and granted to that third party rights and duties vis-a-vis the child that the third party's status would not otherwise warrant. Ordinarily, a relationship based on payment by the legal parent to the third party will not qualify.

The requirement of cooperation by the legal parent is critical because it places control within his or her hands. That parent has the absolute ability to maintain a zone of autonomous privacy for herself and her child. However, if she wishes to maintain that zone of privacy she cannot invite a third party to function as a parent to her child and cannot cede over to that third party parental authority the exercise of which may create a profound bond with the child.

Two further points concerning the consent requirement need to be clarified. First, a psychological parent-child relationship that is voluntarily created by the legally recognized parent may not be unilaterally terminated after the relationship between the adults ends. Although the intent of the legally recognized parent is critical to the psychological parent analysis, the focus is on that party's intent during the formation and pendency of the parent-child relationship. The reason is that the ending of the relationship between the legal parent and the third party does not end the bond that the legal parent fostered and that actually developed between the child and the psychological parent. Thus, the right of the legal parent "[does] not extend to erasing a relationship between her partner and her child which she voluntarily created and actively fostered simply because after the party's separation she regretted having done so." *J.A.L. v. E.P.H.*, 682 A.2d 1314, 1322 (Pa. Super. Ct. 1996).

In practice, that may mean protecting those relationships despite the later, contrary wishes of the legal parent in order to advance the interests of the child. As long as the legal parent consents to the continuation of the relationship between another adult who is a psychological parent and the child after the termination of the adult parties' relationship, the courts need not be involved. Only when that consent is withdrawn are courts called on to protect the child's relationship with the psychological parent.

The second issue that needs to be clarified is that participation in the decision to have a child is not a prerequisite to a finding that one has become a psychological parent to the child. We make that point because the trial court appeared to view the fact that M.J.B. alone made the decision to have the twins as pivotal to the question of the existence of a psychological parent relationship between V.C. and the children. Although joint participation in the family's decision to have a child is probative evidence of the legally recognized parent's intentions, not having participated in the decision does not preclude a finding of the third party's psychological parenthood. Such circumstances parallel the situation in which a woman, already pregnant or a mother, becomes involved with or marries a man who is not the biological or adoptive father of the child, but thereafter fully functions in every respect as a father. There is nothing about that scenario that would justify precluding the possibility of denominating that person as a psychological parent. It goes without saying that adoption proceedings in these circumstances would eliminate the need for a psychological parent inquiry altogether and would be preferable to court intervention. However, the failure of the parties to pursue that option is not preclusive of a finding of psychological parenthood where all the other indicia of that status are present.

Concerning the remaining prongs of the *H.S.H.-K.* test, we accept Wisconsin's formulation with these additional comments. The third prong, a finding that a third party assumed the obligations of parenthood, is not contingent on financial contributions made by the third party. Financial contribution may be considered but should not be given inordinate weight when determining whether a third party has assumed the obligations of parenthood. Obviously, as we have indicated, the assumption of a parental role is much more complex than mere financial support. It is determined by the nature, quality, and extent of the functions undertaken by the third party and the response of the child to that nurturance.

Indeed, we can conceive of a case in which the third party is the stay-at-home mother or father who undertakes all of the daily domestic and child care activities in a household with preschool children while the legal parent is the breadwinner engaged in her occupation or profession. Although it is always possible to put a price on the contributions of the stay-at-home parent, *see* Martha M. Ertman, *Commercializing Marriage: A Proposal for Valuing Women's Work Through Premarital Security Agreements*, 77 Tex. L. Rev. 17, 43 (1998) (outlining different economic models for placing value on homemaker's contribution), our point is that such an analysis is not necessary because it is the nature of what is done that will determine whether a parent-child bond has developed, not how much it is worth in dollars.

It bears repeating that the fourth prong is most important because it requires the existence of a parent-child bond. A necessary corollary is that the third party must have functioned as a parent for a long enough time that such a bond has developed. What is crucial here is not the amount of time but the nature of the relationship. How much time is necessary will turn on the facts of each case including an assessment of exactly what functions the putative parent performed, as well as at what period and stage of the child's life and development such actions were taken. Most importantly, a determination will have to be made about the actuality and strength of the parent-child bond. Generally, that will require expert testimony.

The standards to which we have referred will govern all cases in which a third party asserts psychological parent status as a basis for a custody or visitation action regarding the child of a legal parent, with whom the third party has lived in a familial setting.

This opinion should not be viewed as an incursion on the general right of a fit legal parent to raise his or her child without outside interference. What we have addressed here is a specific set of circumstances involving the volitional choice of a legal parent to cede a measure of parental authority to a third party; to allow that party to function as a parent in the day-to-day life of the child; and to foster the forging of a parental bond between the third party and the child. In such circumstances, the legal parent has created a family with the third party and the child, and has invited the third party into the otherwise inviolable realm of family privacy. By virtue of her own actions, the legal parent's expectation of autonomous privacy in her relationship with her child is necessarily reduced from that which would have been the case had she never invited the third party into their lives. Most important, where that invitation and its consequences have altered her child's life by essentially giving him or her another parent, the legal parent's options are constrained. It is the child's best interest that is preeminent as it would be if two legal parents were in a conflict over custody and visitation.

Once a third party has been determined to be a psychological parent to a child, under the previously described standards, he or she stands in parity with the legal parent. Custody and visitation issues between them are to be determined on a best interests standard giving weight to the factors set forth in N.J.S.A. 9:2–4. * * *

That is not to suggest that a person's status as a legal parent does not play a part in custody or visitation proceedings in those circumstances. Indeed, as the Appellate Division stated in *Todd v. Sheridan*, 633 A.2d 1009 (App. Div. 1993):

> No fair reading of [*Zack v. Fiebert*, 563 A.2d 58, 235 N.J.Super. 424 (App.Div.1989)] prohibits a judge from considering any aspect of either party's character or status in assessing the best interests of the child. N.J.S.A. 9:2–4. Obviously, as the trial judge recognized, he was not free to give an absolute preference to [the natural parent] because that would have undermined the salutary aims *Zack* was meant to accomplish. However, he was free to consider [the natural parent's] status as [the child's] biological father as one weight in the best interests balance.

We agree. The legal parent's status is a significant weight in the best interests balance because eventually, in the search for self-knowledge, the child's interest in his or her roots will emerge. Thus, under ordinary circumstances when the evidence concerning the child's best interests (as between a legal parent and psychological parent) is in equipoise, custody will be awarded to the legal parent.

Visitation, however, will be the presumptive rule, subject to the considerations set forth in N.J.S.A. 9:2–4, as would be the case if two natural parents were in conflict. As we said in *Beck v. Beck*, 86 N.J. 480, 495, 432 A.2d 63 (1981), visitation rights are almost "invariably" granted to the non-custodial parent. Indeed, "[t]he denial of visitation rights is such an extraordinary proscription that it should be invoked only in those exceptional cases where it clearly and convincingly appears that the granting of visitation will cause physical or emotional harm to the children or where it is demonstrated that the parent is unfit." *Barron v. Barron*, 184 N.J.Super. 297, 303, 445 A.2d 1182 (Ch. Div. 1982). Once the parent-child bond is forged, the rights and duties of the parties should be crafted to reflect that reality.

Ordinarily, when we announce a new standard, we remand the case to the trial court for reconsideration. That is not necessary here. This full record informs us that M.J.B. fostered and cultivated, in every way, the development of a parent-child bond between V.C. and the twins; that they all lived together in the same household as a family; that despite M.J.B.'s after-the-fact characterizations of V.C. as a "stranger" and a "nanny," V.C. assumed many of the day-to-day obligations of parenthood toward the twins, including financial support; and that a bonded relationship developed between V.C. and the twins that is parental in nature. In short, we agree with the Appellate Division that V.C. is a psychological parent to the twins.

That said, the issue is whether V.C. should be granted joint legal custody and visitation. As we have stated, the best interests standard applies and the factors set forth in N.J.S.A. 9:2–4 come into play. Under that statute V.C. and M.J.B. are essentially equal. Each appears to be a fully capable, loving parent committed to the safety and welfare of the twins. Although there is animosity between V.C. and M.J.B., that is not a determinant of whether V.C. can continue in the children's lives.

We note that V.C. is not seeking joint physical custody, but joint legal custody for decision making. However, due to the pendency of this case, V.C. has not been involved in the decision-making for the twins for nearly four years. To interject her into the decisional realm at this point would be unnecessarily disruptive for all involved. We will not, therefore, order joint legal custody in this case.

Visitation, however, is another matter. V.C. and the twins have been visiting during nearly all of the four years since V.C. parted company from M.J.B. Continued visitation in those circumstances is presumed. Nothing suggests that V.C. should be precluded from continuing to see the children on a regular basis. Indeed, it is clear that continued regular visitation is in the twins' best interests because V.C. is their psychological parent. We thus affirm the judgment of the Appellate Division.

[Concurring opinion by JUSTICE O'HERN is omitted.]

CHATTERJEE V. KING
Supreme Court of New Mexico, 2012
280 P.3d 283

CHÁVEZ, JUSTICE.

Bani Chatterjee (Chatterjee) and Taya King (King) are two women who were in a committed, long-term domestic relationship when they agreed to bring a child into their relationship. Chatterjee pleaded in the district court that during the course of their relationship, and with Chatterjee's active participation, King adopted a child (Child) from Russia. Chatterjee supported King and Child financially, lived in the family home, and co-parented Child for a number of years before their commitment to each other foundered and they dissolved their relationship. Chatterjee never adopted Child. After they ended their relationship, King moved to Colorado and sought to prevent Chatterjee from having any contact with Child.

Chatterjee filed a petition in the district court to establish parentage and determine custody and timesharing (Petition). Chatterjee alleged that she was a presumed natural parent under the * * * New Mexico Uniform Parentage Act. She further claimed to be the equitable or de facto parent of Child, and as such, was entitled to relief.[2] In response to Chatterjee's Petition, King filed a motion to dismiss * * * argu[ing] that Chatterjee was a third party who was seeking custody and visitation of Child and that * * * third part[ies] are prohibited from receiving custody rights absent a showing of unfitness of the natural or adoptive parent. The district court dismissed the Petition for failure to state a claim upon which relief could be granted.

Chatterjee then appealed to the Court of Appeals, which * * * held that Chatterjee did not have standing to seek joint custody absent a showing of King's unfitness because she is neither the biological nor the adoptive mother of Child. The Court further held that presumptions establishing a father and child relationship cannot be applied to women, and a mother and child relationship can only be established through biology or adoption. * * * The Court of Appeals reversed the district court's dismissal concerning the opportunity for Chatterjee to seek standing for visitation and remanded to the district court, instructing the district court to determine whether visitation with Chatterjee would be in Child's best interests. On remand, the district court appointed a guardian ad litem for Child and accepted the guardian ad litem's recommendation

---

[2]   Because we find that a plain reading of the Uniform Parentage Act gives Chatterjee standing to seek custody, we do not reach her arguments on extraordinary circumstances or constitutionality.

that contact and visitation with Chatterjee would be in Child's best interests.

The question in this case is whether Chatterjee has pleaded sufficient facts in her Petition to give her standing to pursue joint custody of Child under the Dissolution of Marriage Act. Whether Chatterjee has standing to pursue joint custody depends on whether Chatterjee has pleaded facts sufficient to establish that she is an interested party under Section 40–11–21 of the New Mexico Uniform Parentage Act (UPA). Her pleading sets forth facts, which, if true, establish that she has a personal, financial, and custodial relationship with Child and has openly held Child out as her daughter, although she is neither Child's biological nor adoptive mother. * * *

Chatterjee argues that the Court of Appeals erred in holding that none of the UPA provisions relating to the father and child relationship may be applied to women. She claims that this holding directly contradicts the plain language of Section 40–11–21. King responds that the UPA provisions establishing paternity should not be applied to women because the UPA expressly provides the ways in which maternity can be established. We agree with Chatterjee. We find support for Chatterjee's argument not only in the plain language of the statute itself, but also in the purpose of the UPA, the application of paternity provisions to women in jurisdictions with similar UPA provisions, and in public policy that encourages the love and support of children from able and willing parents. * * *

We begin our analysis with Section 40–11–2 of the UPA, which states that a " 'parent and child relationship' means the legal relationship existing between a child and his natural or adoptive parents incident to which the law confers or imposes rights, privileges, duties and obligations. It includes the mother and child relationship and the father and child relationship." For a mother, Section 40–11–4(A) provides that "the natural mother may be established by proof of her having given birth to the child, *or as provided by Section* [40–11–21 NMSA 1978]." (Emphasis added.) Section 40–11–21 states that "[a]ny interested party may bring an action to determine the existence or nonexistence of a mother and child relationship. Insofar as practicable, the provisions of the Uniform Parentage Act applicable to the father and child relationship apply."

The Court of Appeals held that reading Section 40–11–21 to allow Chatterjee to establish parentage through Section 40–11–5(A)(4) was impracticable. The Court also held that reading Section 40–11–5 to apply to women would render Section 40–11–4(A), which provides for how a woman may establish natural motherhood, " 'surplusage or meaningless.' " It reasoned that the Legislature, in enacting Section 40–

11–4(A), created separate sections for how a woman as opposed to a man can prove natural parenthood, implying that it intended each sex to have different means available for proving parenthood. The Court therefore concluded that applying the means for proving paternity to proving maternity would contravene the Legislature's intent. We disagree.

It is practicable to apply Section 40–11–5 to determine maternity in certain circumstances. "Practicable" is defined as "reasonably capable of being accomplished; feasible." *Black's Law Dictionary* 1291 (9th ed. 2009). Section 40–11–5(A)(4), which establishes a parental presumption, is reasonably capable of being accomplished by either a man or a woman. Section 40–11–5(A)(4) provides, in relevant part, that "[a] man is presumed to be the natural father of a child if * * * while the child is under the age of majority, he openly holds out the child as his natural child and has established a personal, financial or custodial relationship with the child." Because the presumption is based on a person's conduct, not a biological connection, a woman is capable of holding out a child as her natural child and establishing a personal, financial, or custodial relationship with that child. This is particularly true when, as is alleged in this case, the relationship between the child and both the presumptive and the adoptive parent occurred simultaneously.

In addition, by limiting proof of natural motherhood to biology under Section 40–11–4(A), the Court of Appeals renders meaningless the clear instruction in Section 40–11–4(A) that a "natural mother may [also] be established * * * as provided by Section 21 [40–11–21 NMSA 1978]." A straightforward reading of Section 40–11–4(A) is that motherhood may be established by giving birth, by adoption, and in any other way in which a father and child relationship may be established when it is practicable to do so. Because it is practicable for a woman to hold a child out as her own, the plain language instructs us to recognize that Section 40–11–5(A)(4) relating to the father and child relationship also applies to the mother and child relationship. * * *

Moreover, we seek to avoid an interpretation of a statute that would raise constitutional concerns. In *New Mexico Right to Choose/NARAL v. Johnson,* 126 N.M. 788, 975 P.2d 841, we held that classifications based on gender are presumptively unconstitutional. In this case, the Court of Appeals' reading would yield different results for a man than for a woman in precisely the same situation. If this Court interpreted Section 40–11–5(A)(4) as applying only to males, then a man in a same-sex relationship claiming to be a natural parent because he held out a child as his own would have standing simply by virtue of his gender, while a woman in the same position would not. In other words, if two men were in Chatterjee's and King's exact situation, Chatterjee's male counterpart would have standing under Section 40–11–5(A)(4) of the UPA to establish parentage, while Chatterjee would not. We avoid this disparate treatment, giving effect to the Legislature's intent, with a plain and simple application of Section 40–11–5(A)(4) to both men and women under Section 40–11–21. * * *

The Oregon Court of Appeals has also applied statutes establishing parentage presumptions based on marital status to women. *Shineovich & Kemp,* 229 Or.App. 670, 214 P.3d 29, 39–40 (2009). Although this case dealt with a parentage presumption arising from artificial insemination, it presented essentially the same issue facing this Court: whether a statute creating a presumption of parentage written in terms of paternity should be applied to similarly situated women.

In *Shineovich,* the Oregon Court of Appeals held that a statute recognizing a husband's parentage based on his consent to assisted reproduction was unconstitutional unless it was equally applied to women in same-sex relationships who consent to their partners' inseminations. * * * The court held that the statute was unconstitutional because it did not require that there be at least the possibility of a biological relationship with the child. In other words, all it required was conduct that indicated an intent to parent. The statute simply creates a presumption that the consenting husband of an artificially inseminated woman is the child's legal parent, regardless of biological connection. The court held that the Oregon statute that provided standing was unconstitutional as applied because there was no compelling justification to deny same-sex couples the right to enjoy that presumption. Therefore, the court extended the presumption to similarly situated women. * * *

* * * [T]he state has a strong interest in ensuring that a child will be cared for, financially and otherwise, by two parents. If that care is lacking, the state will ultimately assume the responsibility of caring for the child. This is one of the primary reasons that the original UPA was created, and it makes little sense to read the statute without keeping this overarching legislative goal in mind.

The original UPA was also written to address the interest that children have in their own support. The rationale underlying the original UPA is that every child should be treated equally, regardless of the marital status of the child's parents. In deciding illegitimacy cases, the United States Supreme Court recognized that it is "illogical and unjust" for a state to deny a child's essential right to be supported by two parents simply because the child's parents are not married. *Gomez v. Perez,* 409 U.S. 535, 538, 93 S.Ct. 872, 35 L.Ed.2d 56 (1973). The Court also noted, regarding irresponsible parenthood, that "no child is responsible for his [or her] birth and penalizing the illegitimate child is an ineffectual * * * way of deterring the parent." *Weber v. Aetna Cas. & Sur. Co.,* 406 U.S. 164, 175, 92 S.Ct. 1400, 31 L.Ed.2d 768 (1972). With this in mind, we see no reason for children to be penalized because of the decisions that their parents make, legal or otherwise.

Consistent with the underlying policy-based rationale of the New Mexico UPA that equality in child welfare requires laws that achieve equality in parentage, Child's need for love and support is no less critical simply because her second parent also happens to be a woman. Experts in child psychology recognize that sometimes the law is too limiting when it comes to actually addressing what is in the child's best interests. The attachment bonds that form between a child and a parent are formed regardless of a biological or legal connection. The law needs to address traditional expectations in light of current realities to keep up with the changing demographic of American families and to protect the children born into them. * * *

It is inappropriate to deny Chatterjee the opportunity to establish parentage, when denying Chatterjee this opportunity would only serve to harm both Child and the state. In our view, it is against public policy to deny parental rights and responsibilities based solely on the sex of either or both of the parents. The better view is to recognize that the child's best interests are served when intending parents physically, emotionally, and financially support the child from the time the child comes into their lives. This is especially true when both parents are able and willing to care for the child. Therefore, we hold that the Legislature intended that Section 40–11–5(A)(4) be applied to a woman who is seeking to establish a natural parent and child relationship with a child whom she has held out as her natural child from the moment the child came into the lives of both the adoptive mother and the presumptive mother. * * *

The fact that Chatterjee did not adopt Child does not impact our decision. Section 40–11–5 of the New Mexico UPA delineates the ways in which parentage can be presumed. Thus, our Legislature has recognized that there will be many situations in which someone is caring for a child but has not taken any steps to legalize that relationship. While taking legal action is the best way to ensure that both the alleged parent and the child have rights arising from that relationship, both our Legislature and this Court have indicated a willingness to confer rights to relationships that have not been legally established. This is so because parental rights are not automatically conferred when there is a biological relationship, but rather when an alleged parent has taken the responsibility of caring for a child. Considering the specific facts of this case, we hold that Chatterjee has alleged sufficient facts to attempt to establish that she is an interested party, and therefore she has standing to establish parentage under Section 40–11–21 of the New Mexico UPA.

BOSSON, JUSTICE (specially concurring).

I agree with the outcome reached by the majority, but on narrower grounds. I write out of concern that this Opinion might be interpreted to expand the population of presumed parents in a manner that would shake settled expectations of custody rights and child support responsibilities. If interpreted narrowly, the majority Opinion applies existing law to evolving, contemporary fact patterns, which is a good thing. If interpreted broadly, however, the majority Opinion could be read to impose seismic changes in custody and child support relationships that neither the New Mexico Uniform Parentage Act (UPA), nor sound policy authorizes, at least not in my judgment.

The majority Opinion holds that Chatterjee has standing to pursue shared custody of Child because the presumptions of paternity listed in Section 40–11–5 of the applicable UPA apply equally to women as presumptions of maternity when practicable. In order to reach this conclusion, I believe we need to address other questions that do not hinge upon Chatterjee's gender. *First, when is a nonadoptive, nonbiological individual a presumed parent under the holding-out provision of the UPA? Then, when does biology (the lack of a biological relationship) rebut such a presumption of parentage?*

Without answering these questions, the majority Opinion concludes that Chatterjee has standing to pursue custody because "[h]er pleading sets forth facts, which, if true, establish that she has a personal, financial, and custodial relationship with Child and has openly held Child out as her daughter, although she is neither Child's biological nor adoptive mother." But is concluding that Chatterjee has openly held out Child as her daughter the end of the inquiry? Not in my opinion.

Let me explain my concerns through a hypothetical. Suppose a hypothetical Mother has two children with men who are no longer involved in their lives for whatever reason, including death. Eventually, Mother begins a serious relationship with a hypothetical Man who moves in and lives happily with Mother and her two young children. Man assists in financial aspects of the household, which almost automatically includes expenses that support the children. At times he refers to himself as the children's father, for example in conversations with neighbors, perhaps on school documents and so forth, either for convenience purposes or perhaps because he truly does wish to become the children's father. Mother may or may not know that Man refers to himself in this way, but we will assume she does. Mother actively considers the possibility of marriage and that some day Man might adopt her two children.

After a few years, however, the relationship sours, and Mother asks Man to leave. It is over. But Man decides he does not want it to end entirely; he wants to share legal custody over the two children. Perhaps his motives are pure; perhaps he is just vindictive and extortionate.

Whatever the motive, he alleges standing as a presumed father who has held out the children as his "own" and has established a financial, personal, and custodial relationship with them. He files in court and, as a presumed father, demands a full-blown custody hearing to prove his merits. The best interests of the children, he argues, require his presence in their lives, and Mother, whether out of spite or sincerity, is not acting in a manner consistent with those best interests. Mother finds herself in a custody battle to retain control over her own children.

A claim of presumed parenthood can be equally abused in the other direction. Perhaps Man chooses to end the relationship, never really interested in custody over the children. But it is the Mother who demands permanent child support from him, alleging that Man has become, however reluctantly, a presumed father by virtue of his holding out.

Neither of these scenarios strikes me as desirable from a policy point of view. They appear to run counter to conventional expectations among both professionals and the public at large. After all, the Mother in my hypothetical, completely fit as a parent, has never agreed to surrender her custodial rights to anyone. Should my hypothetical Man even have standing to pursue his claim? According to my reading of the UPA, such claims veer far outside the essential intent and structure of the statute. Yet we need to be careful, lest the majority Opinion be read to lay a legal basis for such claims.

The majority Opinion is not clear what facts Chatterjee has alleged sufficient to establish that she openly held out Child as her own. Therefore, it is also not clear whether hypothetical Man, like Chatterjee, would have standing to pursue custody as a "presumed parent" under the holding-out provision. I believe Chatterjee's situation is distinct, and I write to explain why. Without this clarification and resulting narrowing of the Opinion, I fear the consequences of my hypothetical. As explained earlier, I fear that Man could force Mother to defend her sole custody rights in court, leaving the ultimate determination to a best-interests analysis by a judge, and only after prolonged, highly expensive, and totally unnecessary litigation. And, to make matters worse, if Man has deeper pockets than Mother, he might well win.

The majority states that "New Mexico courts have long recognized that children may form parent-child bonds with persons other than their legal parents." While I do not disagree, the point seems irrelevant, unless everything boils down to a "best interests" determination. For most of this Court's history, "the primary purpose of paternity suits [was] to insure the putative father meets his obligation to help support the child." *Aldridge ex rel. Aldridge v. Mims,* 118 N.M. 661, 665, 884 P.2d 817, 821 (Ct.App.1994). * * * In fact, there is only one prior New Mexico case in which a litigant cited the UPA as the basis for establishing parentage and thus, for standing to gain custody rights *for* a presumed father as opposed to child support *from* one. *See Lane v. Lane,* 121 N.M. 414, 912 P.2d 290. All other New Mexico cases apply the UPA to establish paternity in the child support context or in the context of paternal grandparents seeking visitation rights. And * * * the putative father in *Lane* was not successful under the holding-out provisions of the UPA. Given this limited history, this case poses questions of first impression regarding the UPA for which we truly do not have precedent. While it is self-evident that Chatterjee should have the same rights as a similarly-situated male, the more basic question asks whether and under what circumstances should such a male have standing to be considered a presumed natural parent under the Act.

We have certain traditional legal avenues for asserting parental rights over nonbiological children, primarily through adoption. Adoption can be complicated but, at the very least, it has a set legal protocol. It alerts everyone concerned, just like executing a will, of the solemnity of the occasion and its permanent consequences. * * *

We should be wary of interpreting statutes in a way that would dilute the need for such formality, relying instead upon the more ambiguous standard of "best interests." * * * The holding out provision under Section 40–11–5(A)(4) requires that "[a man] openly holds out the child as his natural child and has established a personal, financial or custodial relationship with the child." Although, "natural" in the context of "natural child," again, likely means biological in most cases, the provision does not require an assertion of, or an actual, biological relationship. It just requires that a presumed parent *hold a child out* as a natural child, meaning treating the child in the same way that a person would treat his or her biological child. Whether Chatterjee can allege that she has established a personal, financial, or custodial relationship with Child is not yet at issue. Whether Chatterjee "openly held out [Child] as [her] natural child," and exactly what that means, definitely is at issue. So too, is what my hypothetical Man should be required to allege by way of holding out before he could gain "presumed natural parent" status under the UPA and force hypothetical Mother to defend her sole custody status in court.

Cases from our own Court of Appeals as well as from California jurisprudence illustrate at least three common themes that define holding out a child as one's natural child. In each, the presumed parent (1) acted as a parent from the time the child was born or adopted; (2) assumed ongoing responsibilities to the child through legal and financial declarations; and (3) was recognized by the child's family, including another parent or the child, as the child's parent. This strikes me as a narrower class of presumed parents and significantly so, one that might just deter hypothetical Man from pursuit of custody. * * *

Under this high standard for "hold[ing] out," my hypothetical Man rightfully would have a difficult case to allege, much less prove, that he was a "presumed natural parent." In the hypothetical, Man was not involved in bringing Mother's children into the household, unlike Chatterjee who helped create the essential familial relationship. The children would not use or have Man's name. Man may or may not have listed the children formally on any legal documents as his own or as dependents in any formalized manner. It is not clear what role the children or the children's Mother would have considered hypothetical Man to have. To even come close to presumed parent status, Man must not just prove, but he must initially allege such facts. Hypothetical Man would have to make clear whether the children or Mother represented Man to others as the children's father, and in what context, or whether anyone else in the children's family would have believed Man to be the children's father. There would have to be evidence and allegations that hypothetical Man had assumed ongoing financial or legal obligations for the children.

Absent most of the foregoing, I do not believe that hypothetical Man could even allege that he has held himself out as a presumed natural parent. Thus, unlike Chatterjee, he would not have standing under the UPA, thereby avoiding the seismic shift in settled legal expectations that I outlined at the beginning of this discussion. Similarly, hypothetical Mother could not seek child support from hypothetical Man under the holding-out provision. All this follows, and justly so, as long as we take a disciplined view of what it really takes to become a presumed natural parent.

NOTES

1.   Courts are divided on the question of whether the equitable doctrine of *de facto* parenthood (as already noted, also sometimes referred to as *in loco parentis*, functional parenthood, or psychological parenthood) allows unmarried partners of legal parents to exercise rights over the children after the relationships between the adults end. Some courts, like the New Jersey court in *V.C. v. M.J.B.*, have ruled that it does. For other cases in which courts have ruled similarly in the context of dissolving same-sex relationships, *see, e.g., In re E.L.M.C.*, 100 P.3d 546, 555 (Colo. Ct. App. 2004); *King v. S.B.*, 837 N.E.2d 965, 967 (Ind. 2005); *Conover v. Conover*, 141 A.3d 31 (Md. Ct. App. 2016) *C.E.W. v. D.E.W.*, 845 A.2d 1146, 1152, 2004 Me. 43 (2004); *E.N.O. v. L.M.M.*, 711 N.E.2d 886, 893, 429 Mass. 824, 832 (1999); *Latham v. Schwerdtfeger*, 802 N.W.2d 66, 74, 282 Neb. 121, 132 (2011); *Mason v. Dwinnell*, 660 S.E.2d 58, 65, 190 N.C.App. 209, 220 (2008); *Ramey v. Sutton*, 362 P.3d 217 (Ok. 2015); *T.B. v. L.R.M.*, 753 A.2d 873, 888, 2000 PA Super 168 (2000), *aff'd*, 786 A.2d 913, 567 Pa. 222 (2001); *Rubano v. Dicenzo*, 759 A.2d 959, 967 (R.I. 2000); *In re Parentage of L.B.*, 122 P.3d 161, 177, 155 Wash.2d 679, 708 (2005) (en banc); *Custody of H.S.H.-K*, 533 N.W.2d

419, 437, 193 Wis.2d 649, 699 (1995). It is important to remember that nonbiological parents in dissolving different-sex relationships can also benefit from the *de facto* parenthood doctrine.

2.   Other courts have rejected the equitable doctrine of *de facto* parenthood in cases involving same-sex partners. *See, e.g., Smith v. Gordon,* 968 A.2d 1, 2 (Del. 2009) (abrogated by DEL. CODE. ANN. TIT. 13, § 8–201(a)(4), (b)(6) (2009)); *Matter of Visitation with C.B.L.,* 309 Ill.App.3d 888, 895, 243 Ill.Dec. 284, 723 N.E.2d 316, 321 (1999); *Wakeman v. Dixon,* 921 So.2d 669, 671 (Fla. Dist. Ct. App. 2006) (en banc)*; B.F. v. T.D.,* 194 S.W.3d 310, 312 (Ky. 2006); *White v. White,* 293 S.W.3d 1, 15–16 (Mo.Ct.App. 2009); *In re Thompson,* 11 S.W.3d 913, 919 (Tenn.Ct.App. 1999); *Jones v. Barlow,* 154 P.3d 808, 815, 2007 UT 20 (2007); *Stadter v. Spirko,* 52 Va.App. 81, 91, 661 S.E.2d 494, 498–99 (2008). *See also Lake v. Putnam,* ___ N.W.2d ___, 2016 WL 3606081 (Mich. Ct. App. 2016) (limiting application of equitable parenthood doctrine to cases involving married couples). Several of these decisions were issued after the prestigious American Law Institute ("ALI") urged states to adopt equitable parenthood doctrines as part of their relationship dissolution laws. *See* PRINCIPLES OF THE LAW OF FAMILY DISSOLUTION: ANALYSIS AND RECOMMENDATIONS § 2.03 (American Law Institute ed., 2002).

3.   The Uniform Parentage Act, which was promulgated in 1973 and amended in 2002, has been adopted, often in modified form, by nineteen states. Note that the court in *Chatterjee* relied on the state's UPA, rather than on the equitable doctrine of *de facto* parenthood, to grant standing to the lesbian co-parent in the case. In particular, the court relied on the UPA's "holding out" provision, concluding that it applied to putative mothers, not just fathers. How would you characterize the concurring Justice's concerns about the potential application of the majority opinion? Do you think it was crucial for the outcome of the case that the petitioner in *Chatterjee* was involved in the decision to bring the child into the home from the very beginning? Is that the main difference between the facts in the case and the concurring Justice's hypothetical involving Mother and Man? Should parentage presumptions based on "holding out" apply to individuals who were not involved in the decision to bring the child into the home—that is, to individuals who became involved with the legal parent only after that parent had a child? In *In re Nicholas H.,* 46 P.3d 932 (Cal. 2002), the California Supreme Court applied its state's "holding out" presumption to a nonbiological father who became involved with the mother after she became pregnant. For its part, the New York Court of Appeals has ruled that nonbiological and nonadoptive petitioners have standing in custody and visitation cases as long as they can establish, by clear and convincing evidence, that they had entered into "into a pre-conception agreement to conceive and raise a child as co-parents." *Matter of Brooke S.B. v. Elizabeth A. C.C.,* ___ N.E.3d ___, 2016 WL 4507780 (N.Y. 2016). The court left for another day cases in which "a biological or adoptive parent consented to the creation of a parent-like relationship between his or her partner and child

after conception." *Id.* (emphasis added). The court in *Brooke S.B.* overruled a decades-old precedent categorically refusing to grant standing as a parent to individuals who lacked a biological or adoptive relationship to the child. *See Alison D. v. Virginia M.*, 77 N.Y.2d 651, 656, 569 N.Y.S.2d 586, 572 N.E.2d 27, 29 (1991).

4. The Kansas Supreme Court, in *Frazier v. Goudschaal*, 296 Kan. 730, 751, 295 P.3d 542, 556 (2013), held that a parenting agreement entered into by a lesbian couple was enforceable, and that, as a result, the biological parent's former partner was entitled to a determination of whether granting her custody was in the child's best interests. In rejecting the biological mother's argument that the enforcement of the agreement violated her constitutional rights, the court explained that she

> overlooks * * * the fact that she exercised her due process right to decide upon the care, custody, and control of her children and asserted her preference as a parent when she entered into the coparenting agreement with Frazier. If a parent has a constitutional right to make the decisions regarding the care, custody, and control of his or her children, free of government interference, then that parent should have the right to enter into a coparenting agreement to share custody with another without having the government interfere by nullifying that agreement, so long as it is in the best interests of the children. Further, * * * parental preference can be waived and * * * the courts should not be required to assign to a mother any more rights than that mother has claimed for herself.

Id. at 557. Although some courts have held that parenting agreements are relevant to determining how custody should be arranged *after* there has been a determination that the party seeking to enforce the contract is a legal parent, see, e.g., *St. Mary v. Damon*, 309 P.3d 1027 (Nev. 2013), discussed in *supra* Section I.C., the *Frazier* court concluded that the agreement was strong evidence that the lesbian partner who was not biologically related to the child was, in fact, a legal parent.

5. What role should the lack of a biological connection between a functional or *de facto* parent and the child play in determining whether the former can seek custody (rather than just visitation)? Notice that the New Jersey Supreme Court in *V.C. v. M.J.B.* ruled that a parent's biological connection should be given "*a significant weight* in the best interests balance because eventually, in the search for self-knowledge, the child's interest in his or her roots will emerge." 163 N.J. 200, 228, 748 A.2d 539, 554 (2000) (emphasis added). Do you agree with this type of presumption in favor of granting custody to the biological parent over the nonbiological one?

In *Jones v. Jones*, 884 A.2d 915, 919, 2005 PA Super 337 (2005), a Pennsylvania appellate court upheld the granting of custody to the nonbiological mother rather than to the biological mother. The court, after reviewing Pennsylvania cases, concluded that the best interests analysis is weighted in favor of the biological parent over someone who is *in loco parentis* ("in the place of a parent") with the children. The court added that "[t]he burden of proof is not evenly balanced, as [biological] parents have a *prima facie* right to custody, which will be forfeited only if convincing reasons appear that the child's best interest will be served by an award to the third party." *Id.* It is not necessary, however, for a person who is *in loco parentis* with the children "to establish that the biological parent is unfit." *Id.* at 917. In reviewing the evidence presented below, the appellate court concluded that the trial judge did not err: "While the scale was tipped in favor of Boring [the biological mother], Jones [the nonbiological mother] produced clear and convincing reasons to even the scale and then tip it on her side. Jones did not establish that Boring was unfit, and was not required to do so, but Jones did clearly and convincingly establish that the children would be better off with her as the primary custodian and that the children's relationship with *both* parties would be better fostered if custody were awarded to Jones." 884 A.2d at 918.

6.   De facto parenthood doctrines and "holding out" presumptions may be relevant not only when nonbiological parents *assert parental rights*, but also when biological or adoptive parents, or the government, seek *to impose child support obligations* on nonbiological parents. *See L.S.K. v. H.A.N.*, 813 A.2d 872 (Pa. Super.Ct. 2002). *See also Elisa B. v. Superior Court*, 117 P.3d 660, 37 Cal.4th 108, 33 Cal.Rptr.3d 46 (2005) (holding that, under California Uniform Parentage Act, the former lesbian partner of biological mother who consented and participated in alternative insemination, with the understanding that she would help raise child, was liable for child support); *Karin T. v. Michael T.*, 484 N.Y.S.2d 780, 127 Misc.2d 14 (Fam. Ct. 1985) (male transgender individual who agreed to be child's co-parent is responsible for child support). For rulings in which courts have concluded that the LGBT individuals' degree of involvement in the child's life did not justify the imposition of child support obligations, see *T.F. v. B.L.*, 813 N.E.2d 1244, 1253, 442 Mass. 522, 533 (2004); *State ex rel. D.R.M.*, 34 P.3d 887, 898, 109 Wash.App. 182, 203 (Ct.App. 2001).

C. ALTERNATIVE INSEMINATION STATUTES AND THE MARITAL PRESUMPTION

As we saw in *Thomas S.* earlier in this Chapter, lesbian couples often have children through donor insemination. Statutes in many states provide that sperm donors do not have parental rights or obligations. However, the applicability of some of those statutes depends on the *marital status* of the woman being inseminated. These statutes provide that the donor of semen used to inseminate a *married* woman (other than the donor's wife) is treated as if he were not the child's parent. Other statutes, though, simply provide that the donor of semen used to inseminate a woman other than the donor's wife is treated as if he were not the child's parent, regardless of the woman's marital status.

Even if donor-insemination statutes do not recognize the sperm donor as a legal father when the woman giving birth is unmarried, they generally do not recognize the woman's unmarried partner, if she has one, as a legal parent—even if that unmarried partner is the child's intended parent. Instead, most donor-insemination statutes provide for the recognition of the woman's partner—the second parent—only when the woman is married. These statutes provide that when a married woman is inseminated with donor sperm, her husband, provided he consented to the insemination, is the legal father. Before marriage equality, the second parent in same-sex relationships was not treated as a legal parent under these donor-insemination provisions. Nonetheless, recognizing the barrier erected for same-sex couples excluded from marriage, some states applied donor-insemination statutes to recognize the nonbiological co-parent as a legal parent.[9]

Now, in the age of marriage equality, if the woman giving birth is married to another woman, that woman should ordinarily be deemed the child's second parent. Courts in some states have ordered state authorities to apply these donor-insemination statutes to married lesbian couples. This has been the case even if the statute in question includes terms like "husband" and "father.[10] As a federal district court reasoned after *Obergefell*, the state cannot "extend the benefits of the assisted-reproduction statutes to male spouses in opposite-sex couples but not [to] female spouses in same-sex couples."[11]

Rather than leave the issue to judicial interpretation, some states have made their donor-insemination statutes explicitly gender neutral. However, many donor-insemination provisions continue to differentiate based on *marital status*. In order to qualify for protection, the same-sex couple must be married.[12]

Many states do not have statutes specifically regulating donor insemination. And even in states with donor-insemination statutes, the intended parents may fail to comply with the statutory requirements. For instance, some statutes require the involvement of a licensed physician, thus excluding couples who engage in at-home insemination. If a donor-insemination statute does not exist or does not apply, the marital

---

9   *See, e.g., Shineovich and Kemp*, 214 P.3d 29 (Or. App. 2009) (holding that failure to apply donor insemination statute in cases involving lesbian co-parents violated equal protection guarantees).

10   *See, e.g., Della Corte v. Ramirez*, 961 N.E.2d 601, 603 (Mass. App. Ct. 2012) ("We do not read 'husband' to exclude same-sex married couples, but determine that same-sex married partners are similarly situated to heterosexual couples in these circumstances.").

11   *Roe v. Patton*, 2015 WL 4476734, at *3 (D. Utah July 22, 2015).

12   For an exception, in which the statute is both gender-neutral and marital-status-neutral, see Cal. Fam. Code § 7613(a) (2016) ("If a woman conceives through assisted reproduction with semen or ova or both donated by a donor not her spouse, with the consent of another intended parent, that intended parent is treated in law as if he or she were the natural parent of a child thereby conceived.").

presumption—also called the presumption of legitimacy—would govern *married* couples. Under the marital presumption, when a woman gives birth to a child, her husband is presumed to be the legal parent. The marital presumption can be rebutted in some circumstances—for instance, in light of evidence showing that the husband is not the biological father. With marriage equality, the question has arisen as to whether the marital presumption applies to female same-sex couples who have children through donor insemination. Some of the conflicts, as the next case shows, involve birth certificates, which constitute evidence of parentage.

GARTNER V. IOWA DEPARTMENT OF PUBLIC HEALTH

Supreme Court of Iowa, 2013
830 N.W.2d 335

WIGGINS, JUSTICE.

In this appeal, we must decide whether Iowa Code section 144.13(2) (2011) requires the Iowa Department of Public Health to list as a parent on a child's birth certificate the nonbirthing spouse in a lesbian marriage when the child was born to one of the spouses during the couple's marriage. * * *

[We] find section 144.13(2) as applied to married lesbian couples violates the equal protection clauses found in article I, sections 1 and 6 of the Iowa Constitution. Accordingly, the Department must presumptively list on a child's birth certificate the nonbirthing spouse in a lesbian marriage when the child was born to one of the spouses during their marriage. * * *

Background Facts and Proceedings

Melissa and Heather Gartner are a lesbian couple. They have been in a loving, committed relationship since December 2003. * * *

Heather conceived their first child by anonymous donor insemination. Melissa participated in every step of Heather's pregnancy, which included choosing the anonymous sperm donor. Melissa was present for the birth of the couple's first child.

Because Melissa and Heather were not legally married at the time of the first child's birth, the couple went through formal adoption procedures to ensure Melissa's name was on the child's birth certificate. The Gartners successfully navigated the adoption process after both Melissa and Heather underwent background checks for criminal misconduct and sexual abuse. Heather characterized the adoption process as expensive, intrusive, and laborious. Once the couple finalized the adoption, the Department issued the child's birth certificate, which named both Heather and Melissa as parents.

Two years later, in April 2009, we decided *Varnum v. Brien*, 763 N.W.2d 862 (Iowa 2009), which held Iowa's Defense of Marriage Act unconstitutional. Thereafter, the state began solemnizing same-sex marriages. Melissa and Heather Gartner subsequently married in Des Moines on June 13. Heather was approximately six months pregnant with the couple's second child, Mackenzie Jean Gartner, at the time of their marriage.

Three months later, on September 19, Heather gave birth to Mackenzie. Heather conceived Mackenzie using the same anonymous donor as for their first child.

The day after Mackenzie's birth, Heather and Melissa completed a form at the hospital to obtain Mackenzie's birth certificate. The Department provided the form. On the form, the Gartners indicated that both Heather and Melissa are Mackenzie's parents and that they are legally married.

The Department issued Mackenzie's birth certificate on approximately November 19. The certificate only listed Heather as Mackenzie's parent. The space for the second parent's name was blank.

After receiving Mackenzie's birth certificate naming only Heather, the Gartners sent a letter to the Department requesting a birth certificate recognizing both Heather and Melissa as Mackenzie's parents. The Department denied the request. The Department refused to place the name of the nonbirthing spouse in a lesbian marriage on the birth certificate without the spouse first adopting the child, pursuant to Iowa Code section 144.23(1). The Department indicated: "The system for registration of births in Iowa currently recognizes the biological and 'gendered' roles of 'mother' and 'father,' grounded in the biological fact that a child has one biological mother and one biological father. . . ." * * *

We must decide if we can interpret Iowa Code section 144.13(2), otherwise known as Iowa's presumption of parentage statute, to require the Department to list as a parent on a child's birth certificate the nonbirthing lesbian spouse, when the other spouse conceived the child during the marriage using an anonymous sperm donor. If we cannot adopt such an interpretation of the statute, we then must determine whether the Department's refusal to list the nonbirthing lesbian spouse on the child's birth certificate violates the equal protection clauses in article I, sections 1 and 6 of the Iowa Constitution.

Iowa's Presumption of Parentage Statute

Iowa's Vital Statistics Code requires filing a certificate of birth with the Department within seven days of a live birth occurring in the state. Iowa Code § 144.13(1)(a). The state uses the birth certificate to establish the fact a birth occurred, as well as to identify the child for immunization purposes. Id. § 144.13(1)(a), (d).

For purposes of preparing a birth certificate, the Code includes a presumption of parentage. *See id.* § 144.13(2). The legislature articulated the following procedure for preparing a child's birth certificate, based upon the presumption of parentage:

> If the mother was married at the time of conception, birth, or at any time during the period between conception and birth, the name of the husband shall be entered on the certificate as the father of the child unless paternity has been determined otherwise by a court of competent jurisdiction, in which case the name of the father as determined by the court shall be entered by the department.

Id. The statute is rebuttable under the preponderance standard "by clear, strong and satisfactory evidence." The challenging party must also demonstrate a parental relationship with the child. Here, rebutting the presumption is a nonissue, because Heather conceived Mackenzie using an anonymous sperm donor. * * *

Legislatures across the nation have adopted statutes codifying a presumption of parentage in order to address several key social policies. Specifically, "the presumption protected the legitimacy of children, which in turn entitled them to the financial support, inheritance rights, and filiation obligations of their parents." Diane S. Kaplan, *Why Truth Is Not a Defense in Paternity Actions,* 10 Tex. J. Women & L. 69, 70 (2000). It thwarted the possibility that children would become wards of the state and promoted familial stability by preventing "a third-party putative father from insinuating himself onto an intact family by claiming to have sired one of the family's children." *Id.* at 70–71. Moreover, at a time when "genetic origins were more a matter of suspicion than science," the presumption served judicial efficiency by curtailing debates between parents as to the biological nature of their parent-child relationship. *Id.* at 71. * * *

Specific to Iowa, our court long ago articulated the principal bases for presuming a child born in wedlock is the legitimate issue of the marital spouses:

> This rule is founded on decency, morality, and public policy. By that rule, the child is protected in his inheritance and safeguarded against future humiliation and shame. Likewise, under the rule, the family relationship is kept sacred and the peace and harmony thereof preserved. No one, by incompetent evidence, can malign the virtue of the mother, and no one, by such evidence, can interrupt the harmony of the family relationship and undermine the sanctity of the home."

Heath v. Heath, 222 Iowa 660, 661, 269 N.W. 761, 761 (Iowa 1936). Taking these policies individually, we recognize the strong stigma accompanying illegitimacy. The presumption counteracts the stigma by protecting the integrity of the marital family, even when a biological connection is not present. The presumption in Iowa even protects the child if the parents' marriage later terminates. * * * Finally, the presumption in Iowa functions to ensure a child's right to financial support against a spouse's claim of not being a biological parent. * * *

Statutory Interpretation of Iowa Code Section 144.13(2)

* * * A specific rule of construction found in Iowa Code section 4.1 applies to statutes containing gendered terms and assists us in ascertaining the legislature's intent. Section 4.1 provides: "Words of one gender include the other genders." Iowa Code § 4.1(17). This is not, however, a blanket rule applicable to all types of statutes. Instead, courts construing statutes can only utilize this rule when the statute uses a specific type of gendered language.

When the statute refers to only *one* gender and the gender referenced is *masculine,* section 4.1(17) extends the statute to include females. * * * Thus, when a statute employs a masculine term, we will construe the scope of the statute to include the corresponding feminine term.

However, when the statute refers to only *one* gender and the gender referenced is *feminine,* section 4.1(17) does not extend the scope of the statute to include males. *Young v. O'Keefe,* 246 Iowa 1182, 1188, 69 N.W.2d 534, 537 (1955). There, the court found that a husband could not recover under a pension statute, because the court could not enlarge the term "widow," as it referred to the surviving spouse who was eligible for survivor benefits, to include "widowers." *Id.* at 1186–89, 69 N.W.2d at 537–38 ("Nowhere . . . do we find any statute or authority permitting substitution of the *masculine* for the *feminine.*").

Finally, when the statute employs *both* masculine and feminine words, section 4.1(17) does not apply. *Cf. State ex rel. Mitchell v. McChesney,* 190 Iowa 731, 733–34, 180 N.W. 857, 858 (1921). Reading such a statute in a gender-neutral manner "would destroy or change" the plain and unambiguous language, and would "nullif[y] the intent of the Legislature." *Id.* at 734, 180 N.W. at 858.

Iowa's presumption of parentage statute expressly uses *both* masculine and feminine words by referring to a mother, father, and husband. *See* Iowa Code § 144.13(2). Accordingly, section 4.1(17) does not apply. If we applied the rule and imposed a gender-neutral interpretation of the presumption, we would destroy the legislature's intent to *unambiguously* differentiate between the roles assigned to the two sexes. Only a male can be a husband or father. Only a female can be a wife or mother. The legislature used plain and unambiguous language to convey its intent. Thus, we cannot nullify the intent of the legislature by finding otherwise through statutory construction.

* * * [W]e cannot use the rules of statutory construction to extend, enlarge, or otherwise change the plain meaning of section 144.13(2)

Accordingly, we proceed to the second step of our analysis and determine whether the constitutional guarantees of equal protection and due process require applying the presumption of parentage to lesbian married couples.

Constitutional Analysis

* * * [W]ith respect to the government's purpose of identifying a child as part of their family and providing a basis for verifying the birth of a child, married lesbian couples are similarly situated to spouses and parents in an opposite-sex marriage. * * *

The Gartners argue the refusal of the Department to list both of the spouses in a lesbian marriage on the birth certificate of a child born during marriage classifies a person based on sex and sexual orientation under the Iowa Constitution. The Department contends the refusal only classifies individuals based on sex. Nonetheless, the Department concedes that even if we classify the refusal on sex, an intermediate level of scrutiny applies.

In *Varnum*, we rejected the argument that the [Iowa] Defense of Marriage Act classified individuals based on sex and analyzed the classification based on sexual orientation. The legislature's purposeful use of "husband" in section 144.13(2) does not allow married lesbian couples to have the nonbirthing spouse's name on the birth certificate when one of the spouses in that relationship gives birth to the child. Therefore, as in *Varnum*, the refusal to list the nonbirthing lesbian spouse on the child's birth certificate "differentiates implicitly on the basis of sexual orientation." * * *

Under *Varnum*, a sexual-orientation-based classification is subject to a heightened level of scrutiny under the Iowa Constitution. Neither the Gartners nor the Department asks us to overturn *Varnum*, which requires the state to allow same-sex couples to marry. Therefore, it would be inappropriate for this court to revisit the *Varnum* decision. Instead, our task is to measure the Department's classification against the heightened-level-of-scrutiny standard.

Heightened scrutiny requires the State to show the statutory classification is substantially related to an important governmental objective. Accordingly, we must evaluate whether the governmental objectives proffered by the State are important and whether the statutory classification substantially relates to those objectives.

Our construction of the statute is the same as the Department's. The plain language of the statute requires the Department to put a husband's name on the birth certificate if a married opposite-sex couple has a child born during the marriage and if the couple used an anonymous sperm donor to conceive the child. Thus, the statute treats married lesbian couples who conceive through artificial insemination using an anonymous sperm donor differently than married opposite-sex couples who conceive a child in the same manner. We must analyze this differential treatment to determine if it is substantially related to an important governmental objective.

In the Department's response to the Gartners' request for admissions, the State admitted Iowa Code section 144.13(2) requires the Department to put a male's name on a child's birth certificate if a married opposite-sex couple has a child born during the marriage and if the couple utilized an anonymous sperm donor to conceive the child. However, this is not true if paternity has been determined otherwise by a court of competent jurisdiction.

The Department enumerates three objectives supporting section 144.13(2)'s differing treatment of married, lesbian and opposite-sex couples. Specifically, the Department argues the government has an interest in the accuracy of birth certificates, the efficiency and effectiveness of government administration, and the determination of paternity.

First, we understand that ensuring the accuracy of birth records for identification of biological parents is a laudable goal. However, the present system does not always accurately identify the biological father. When a married opposite-sex couple conceives a child using an anonymous sperm donor, the child's birth certificate reflects the male spouse as the father, not the biological father who donated the sperm. In that situation, the Department is not aware the couple conceived the child by an anonymous sperm donor.

Furthermore, the Department claims that the only way a married lesbian couple, who uses an anonymous sperm donor to conceive the child, can list the nonbirthing spouse as the parent on the birth certificate is to go through an adoption proceeding. This will not make the birth certificate any more accurate than applying the presumption of parentage for married lesbian couples, because the birth certificate still will not identify the biological father. The birth records of this state do not contain a statistical database listing the children conceived using anonymous sperm donors. Thus, the classification is not substantially related to the asserted governmental purpose of accuracy.

The Department next asserts the refusal to apply the presumption of parentage to nonbirthing spouses in lesbian marriages serves administrative efficiency and effectiveness. The Department argues that it takes valuable resources to reissue a birth certificate when a challenger successfully rebuts the presumption of parentage. However, when couples use an anonymous sperm donor, there will be no rebuttal of paternity. * * *

It is *more* efficient for the Department to list, presumptively, the nonbirthing spouse as the parent on the birth certificate when the child is born, rather than to require the Department to issue a birth certificate with only one spouse's name on the certificate and then later, after an adoption is complete, reissue the certificate. These realities demonstrate that the disparate treatment of married lesbian couples is less effective and efficient, and that some other unarticulated reason, such as stereotype or prejudice, may explain the real objective of the State.

The third proffered reason for the Department's action is the government's interest in establishing paternity to ensure financial support of the child and the fundamental legal rights of the father. When a lesbian couple is married, it is just as important to establish who is financially responsible for the child and the legal rights of the nonbirthing spouse. As we said in *Varnum*

> [Same-sex couples] are in committed and loving relationships, many raising families, just like heterosexual couples. Moreover, official recognition of their status provides an institutional basis for defining their fundamental relational rights and responsibilities, just as it does for heterosexual couples. Society benefits, for example, from providing same-sex couples a stable framework within which to raise their children. * * *

It is important for our laws to recognize that married lesbian couples who have children enjoy the same benefits and burdens as married opposite-sex couples who have children. By naming the nonbirthing spouse on the birth certificate of a married lesbian couple's child, the child is ensured support from that parent and the parent establishes fundamental legal rights at the moment of birth. Therefore, the only explanation for not listing the nonbirthing lesbian spouse on the birth certificate is stereotype or prejudice. The exclusion of the nonbirthing spouse on the birth certificate of a child born to a married lesbian couple is not substantially related to the objective of establishing parentage.

Thus, section 144.13(2) fails to comport with the guarantees of equal protection under article I, sections 1 and 6 of the Iowa Constitution. The Department has been unable to identify a constitutionally adequate justification for refusing to list on a child's birth certificate the nonbirthing spouse in a lesbian marriage, when the child was conceived using an anonymous sperm donor and was born to the other spouse during the marriage. Thus, the language in section 144.13(2) limiting the requirement to "the name of the husband" on the birth certificate is unconstitutional as applied to married lesbian couples who have a child born to them during marriage.

We find the presumption of parentage statute violates equal protection under the Iowa Constitution as applied to married lesbian couples. However, we are not required to strike down the statute because our obligation is to preserve as much of a statute as possible, within constitutional restraints. Accordingly, instead of striking section 144.13(2) from the Code, we will preserve it as to married opposite-sex couples and require the Department to apply the statute to married lesbian couples. Therefore, we affirm the district court and order the Department to issue a birth certificate naming Melissa Gartner as the parent of the child, Mackenzie Jean Gartner. * * *

Consider the following excerpt, which places the *Gartner* conflict in the broader context of the relationship between marriage equality and parentage.

MARRIAGE EQUALITY AND THE NEW PARENTHOOD*
Douglas NeJaime

While the marital presumption always had the capacity to embody functional parenthood, it often did so by masking, rather than owning, biological reality. Even when the mother's husband was not the biological father, the law could act on the fiction that he was. But with same-sex couples, where there can be no mistake about biological fact, the marital presumption is detached from notions of biology on a wholesale basis. With same-sex marriage, the presumption makes sense only because it provides an indication of intent and "holding out"—the very concepts elaborated on behalf of unmarried same-sex parents in earlier advocacy. * * *

In the wake of *Obergefell*, disputes over the marital presumption have proliferated. * * *

[T]he conceptual underpinnings of donor-insemination regulation, which premises marital parentage on intent and conduct, may become generalizable through marriage equality. Previously, donor insemination constituted an exception to the normal operation of presumptions. Many states, including California, maintain a separate provision setting out intent-based rules for married couples using donor insemination. The assumption, of course, is that donor insemination makes the biological

---

* Douglas NeJaime, *Marriage Equality and the New Parenthood*, 129 HARV. L. REV. 1185, 1242–49 (2016).

reality explicit in ways that complicate application of the marital presumption and point toward a competing claim by the sperm donor. For those states that nonetheless route donor insemination through the general marital presumption, the biological reality for most different-sex couples can remain hidden. With same-sex marriage, however, the logic of alternative insemination informs the logic of the marital presumption more generally, such that the presumption effectively becomes a de facto donor-insemination statute.

In states that remain hostile to LGBT equality, resistance to application of the marital presumption to same-sex couples surely represents further enactment of anti-LGBT sentiment. Yet the refusal to apply the marital presumption to same-sex couples can be understood not merely as continuing resistance to LGBT equality, but also as an attempt to recenter biology as a dominant marker of parentage and to maintain the primacy of gendered notions of parenting. * * *

Application of the marital presumption to nonbiological mothers in same-sex marriages would ratify developments in parentage law, which witnessed the extensive recognition of married, nonbiological parents. It would also give meaning to marriage equality, which validated same-sex couples' intentional and functional parent-child relationships. * * *

Applying the marital presumption to same-sex couples is important not only from a sexual-orientation-equality perspective, but also from a more general family law perspective. The push and pull between biology and function continues to play out in disputes involving different-sex parents. In fact, in some states, biology has gained prominence in the context of married different-sex couples in which the husband seeks to disestablish paternity. Even when a man has served as a father for a substantial period of time, some courts have allowed the introduction of genetic evidence to terminate his parental obligations. These types of disputes arise at divorce, when, at a particularly unsettling time for children, courts may terminate an established parent-child relationship.

Paternity disestablishment is troubling from the perspective of a model of parenthood that values functional relationships and children's best interests, and it should be seen as connected to conflicts over the application of the marital presumption to same-sex couples. If the marital presumption applies to lesbian mothers in a way that is relatively insulated from rebuttal by genetic evidence, then it may similarly apply to husbands who have been serving as (nonbiological) fathers. Of course, competing claims by biological fathers present an additional consideration. Still, it is important to see that part of what is at stake in paternity disestablishment is a model of parenthood that values parent-child relationships regardless of biology. * * *

NOTES

1.   The *Gartner* court did not rule that the parentage statute's marital presumption automatically applied to female same-sex couples. Instead, it found that the statute by its terms applied only to different-sex couples—because of the use of the term "husband"—but that application of the statute to female same-sex couples was unconstitutional. Could the court have avoided the constitutional question? Could it have interpreted the statute in a gender-neutral way?

2.   *Gartner* predates *Obergefell*. As Professor NeJaime notes, after *Obergefell*, many states have had to address whether, and in what circumstances, the marital presumption should apply to female same-sex couples. As a general matter, because *Obergefell* requires that same-sex couples have access to the rights and obligations of marriage on equal terms with different-sex couples, over the objection of many states, the marital presumption is increasingly being read to reach the woman married to the birth mother. Nonetheless, litigation over this question continues.

3.   Under what circumstances, if any, should an individual be able to challenge the marital presumption? Who should be able to rebut the presumption? What evidence should be required to rebut the presumption? States generally allow the marital presumption to be challenged in three situations: (1) the mother challenges her husband's paternity; (2) the husband seeks to disestablish his paternity; and (3) the biological father (who is not the mother's husband) seeks to establish his paternity. Biological evidence is introduced to challenge the presumption. States differ over when these challenges can be brought, and when a court can refuse to even allow the introduction of biological evidence to rebut the presumption. For instance, many states require that a challenge be brought within the first two years of the child's life, and some states allow a judge to exclude biological evidence if doing so is in the best interest of the child. For an exploration of state variation regarding the circumstances under which the marital presumption can be challenged, see Theresa Glennon, *Somebody's Child: Evaluating the Erosion of the Marital Presumption of Paternity*, 102 W. VA. L. REV. 547 (2000). If biological evidence can rebut the presumption, what does that mean for lesbian couples? Should different rules apply to same-sex and different-sex couples?

4.   Just as with donor-insemination statutes, some states have made their marital presumptions explicitly gender neutral. For instance, Maine law provides that "[a] person is presumed to be the parent of a child if . . . [t]he person and the woman giving birth to the child are married to each other and the child is born during the marriage." ME. STAT., T. 19A § 1881(1) (2016). *See also* CAL. FAM. CODE § 7611(a) (2014); 750 ILL. COMP. STAT. ANN. 46/204 (2015); N.H. REV. STAT. § 168–B:2 (2014).

5.   After *Obergefell*, the Uniform Law Commission created a committee to revise and amend the Uniform Parentage Act (UPA). The committee's proposal features parentage presumptions, including the marital

presumption, the "holding out" presumption, and donor-insemination provisions, that apply in gender-neutral ways so as to reach female same-sex couples. For updates on the revision process, which is expected to conclude at some point in 2017, and to review the documents produced by the committee, see Uniform Law Commission, Amendments to the Uniform Parentage Act (2002), http://uniformlaws.org/Committee.aspx?title=Amend ments%20to%20Uniform%20Parentage%20Act%20%282002%29.

6. Given that marriage equality is thought to provide family-based equality for married same-sex couples, one might expect parentage for men in same-sex couples to operate similarly to parentage for women in same-sex couples. Yet because the marital presumption springs from a husband's (or spouse's) relationship to a *birth mother*, the presumption does not usually apply to male same-sex couples. Among states that have made their marital presumptions gender neutral, only Washington state expressly applies its presumption to male same-sex couples. *See* WASH. REV. CODE ANN. § 26.26.116 (2011) ("In the context of a marriage or a domestic partnership, a person is presumed to be the parent of a child if: The person and the mother or father of the child are married to each other or in a domestic partnership with each other and the child is born during the marriage or domestic partnership.").

D. SURROGACY

While female same-sex couples commonly use donor insemination to have children, male same-sex couples have increasingly turned to surrogacy to have children. Because the marital presumption does not generally apply to male same-sex couples, gay male couples must rely on parentage rules specifically governing surrogacy or, in the absence of such rules, resort to the adoption process. That is, in the absence of parentage rules recognizing a *nonbiological* intended father, that father would have to adopt the child after the surrogate relinquishes her parental rights. The following materials address surrogacy specifically for male same-sex couples, but you should keep in mind that different-sex couples also engage in surrogacy and thus would be subject to the relevant rules and regulations.

THE RIGHT TO BE PARENTS: LGBT FAMILIES AND THE TRANSFORMATION OF PARENTHOOD*

Carlos A. Ball

It is not only lesbian women who have used alternative insemination and other forms of reproductive assistance to have children; so have gay men. But for the latter, of course, the process is complicated by the fact that they must rely not only on donated gametes (in their case eggs or

---

* Carlos A. Ball, THE RIGHT TO BE PARENTS: LGBT FAMILIES AND THE TRANSFORMATION OF PARENTHOOD (2012).

ova), but also on the assistance of a surrogate to carry the fertilized embryo to term.

There are two different types of surrogacy. The first, known as "traditional surrogacy," involves the use of sperm—from either the intended father or a donor—to inseminate the surrogate mother. In these types of cases, the birth mother is linked to the child both genetically and through gestation.

The second type of surrogacy, known as "gestational surrogacy," involves the retrieval of ova from either the intended mother or a donor. The ova is then fertilized in vitro (that is, outside of the womb) with the sperm of the intended father or of a donor, after which the embryo is placed in the surrogate's womb. In these situations, the birth mother is linked to the child through gestation but not through genetics.

When surrogacy pregnancies first began taking place in the United States with some frequency—around the mid-1980s—in vitro technology was not very advanced and was quite expensive, making traditional surrogacy the only realistic option for many individuals interested in pursuing surrogacy as a way of becoming parents. In 1986, the country became riveted by the story of Mary Beth Whitehead, a married woman who agreed to serve as a traditional surrogate by being inseminated with the sperm of a married man so that he and his wife could raise the resulting child. But the day after the baby was born, Whitehead changed her mind, and a protracted and highly visible lawsuit—known as the *Baby M.* case—ensued over who was the child's mother. Eventually, the New Jersey Supreme Court held that the surrogacy agreement entered into by Whitehead and the child's biological father violated public policy because it effectively called for the sale of a child. As a result, the court held that Whitehead—and not the father's wife—was the child's mother.[25]

Shortly after the *Baby M.* case, several states enacted laws prohibiting surrogacy agreements. With time, however, the political opposition to surrogacy diminished, in part because advances in reproductive technology made gestational surrogacy easier (and less costly) to achieve. The fact that gestational surrogates are not genetically related to the children has meant that they have generally not been viewed as either victims or as baby sellers. In fact, the media now routinely portray surrogate mothers in a positive light, highlighting their generosity in wanting to help prospective parents—both infertile heterosexuals and gay men—have children.

In addition, legislators these days seem less interested in discouraging surrogacy than they are, as one commentator has put it, in "providing certainty about parental status and protecting all participants,

---

[25]   *Matter of Baby M.*, 537 A.2d 1227 (N.J. 1988).

especially children." An example of this shift is a statute unanimously passed by the Illinois legislature in 2004 which creates a presumption that, in cases of gestational surrogacy, it is the intended parents and not the surrogate mothers who are the children's legal parents.[28] In other states, however, surrogacy of any kind remains strictly prohibited.

Although it is difficult to determine precise numbers, it appears that thousands of gay men have in recent years pursued the opportunity to have children with the assistance of surrogate mothers. While the majority of these surrogacy arrangements seem to have gone as planned with the mother relinquishing parental rights after birth, some have ended up in litigation.

Several of the surrogacy cases in which gay men are litigants have involved relatively rare instances of traditional surrogacy where the issue is usually not whether the surrogate mother should be deemed a parent (she usually is), but is instead who should have custody of the child. In one case, a New York trial court concluded that the biological gay father should have sole custody despite the objection of the surrogate mother, a former friend who had volunteered to help him have the child.[29] In another case, an Ohio appellate court ruled that a woman who was inseminated with the sperm of an anonymous donor did not have to share custody with her gay brother (and his male partner) even though there was evidence that she had agreed, prior to conception, that the brother could raise the child.[30]

There have also been some legal disputes between gay men and gestational surrogates. In 2009, a New Jersey trial court held that the *Baby M.* precedent also applied to gestational surrogacy. As a result, the court ruled that a gestational surrogate who had agreed to help a gay couple—one of whom was her brother—have children was a legal parent of the resulting twin girls.[31] But two years earlier, a Minnesota appellate court upheld the gestational surrogacy agreement between a gay man and his niece, holding that the former, and not the latter, was the child's legal parent.[32]

---

[28]   750 ILLINOIS COMP. ST. § 47/1–75 (2010).

[29]   *C. on Behalf of T. v. G. & E.*, Supreme Court of New York, New York County, *New York Law Journal*, Jan. 12, 2001, 29.

[30]   *Decker v. Decker*, 2001 WL 1167475 (Ohio Ct.App. Sept. 28, 2001).

[31]   *A.G.R. v. D.R.H. & S.H.*, Superior Court of New Jersey, Hudson County, No. FD-09-001838-07, December 23, 2009.

[32]   *In re Paternity and Custody of Baby Boy A.*, 2007 WL 4304448 (Minn.Ct.App. Dec. 11, 2007).

RAFTOPOL V. RAMEY

Connecticut Supreme Court, 2011
12 A.3d 783, 299 Conn. 681

McLACHLAN, J.

This appeal raises the question of whether Connecticut law permits an intended parent who is neither the biological nor the adoptive parent of a child to become a legal parent of that child by means of a valid gestational agreement. The use of technology to accomplish reproduction by means other than sexual intercourse no longer may be considered "new" science, and, indeed, the legislature has recognized the validity of such agreements. Moreover, no one can deny that assisted reproductive technology implicates an essential matter of public policy—it is a basic expectation that our legal system should enable each of us to identify our legal parents with reasonable promptness and certainty. Despite the facts that assisted reproductive technology has been available for some time, and that the technology implicates the important issue of the determination of legal parentage, our laws, and the laws of most other states, have struggled unsuccessfully to keep pace with the complex legal issues that continue to arise as a result of the technology. It is our view that our laws should provide an answer to the following two basic questions: (1) who are the legal parents of children born as a result of such technology; and (2) what steps must such persons take to clarify their status as legal parents of such children? Our answers to these questions are limited by the scope of the question presented on appeal, and, even more importantly, by the fact that the broad public policy issues raised by modern reproductive technology and implicated by this appeal more appropriately would be addressed by the legislature. When, as in the present case, however, a statutory scheme is susceptible to an interpretation whereby a child born as a result of a gestational agreement could be deemed to have no legal parent, which rationally could not have been the legislature's intent, the court is bound to interpret the scheme in a manner that confers legal parentage on the intended parents pursuant to the legally valid gestational agreement.

The defendant department of public health (department) appeals from the judgment of the trial court in favor of the plaintiff Shawn Hargon, an intended parent under the gestational agreement. On appeal, the department argues that the trial court lacked subject matter jurisdiction both to terminate the putative parental rights of the gestational carrier, the defendant Karma A. Ramey, and to declare Hargon a legal parent of the children to whom Ramey gave birth, and, consequently, to order the department to issue a replacement birth certificate pursuant to General Statutes § 7–48a, naming Hargon and the named plaintiff, Anthony Raftopol, the children's biological father, as the children's parents. The department also argues that the trial court improperly concluded that § 7–48a conferred parental status on Hargon solely on the ground that he was an intended parent and party to a valid gestational agreement. We conclude that the trial court had jurisdiction to issue the declaratory judgment. Moreover, we conclude that the trial court's judgment declaring Hargon to be the parent of the children and ordering the department to place his name on the replacement birth certificate is supported by the applicable statutes. Accordingly, we affirm the judgment of the trial court.

The record reflects the following facts, either as found by the trial court or undisputed. The plaintiffs, who were domestic partners living in Bucharest, Romania, entered into a written agreement (gestational agreement), dated July 29, 2007, with Ramey, in which she agreed to act as a gestational carrier for the plaintiffs. Pursuant to the gestational agreement, eggs were recovered from a third party egg donor and fertilized with sperm contributed by Raftopol. Three of the resulting frozen embryos were subsequently implanted in Ramey's uterus. As a result of the procedures, Ramey gave birth to two children on April 19, 2008. DNA testing confirmed that Raftopol was the biological father of the children. Pursuant to the gestational agreement, Ramey had agreed to terminate her parental rights to any children resulting from the procedures, and to sign any forms necessary for the issuance of a replacement birth certificate naming the plaintiffs as the parents of such children. Ramey also had agreed to consent to the adoption of any such children by Hargon and to cooperate fully to obtain this goal.

Prior to the expected delivery date, the plaintiffs brought this action, seeking a declaratory judgment that the gestational agreement was valid, that the plaintiffs were the legal parents of the children and requesting that the court order the department to issue a replacement birth certificate reflecting that they, and not Ramey, were parents of the children. The department responded that the court lacked jurisdiction over the matter because Hargon did not allege that he had conceived the children and because the court lacked jurisdiction to terminate the parental rights of the gestational carrier, the egg donor, and any husbands either may have, which the department argued would be a necessary prerequisite to the declaration that Hargon is a parent of the children. Finally, the department contended that the allegations of the complaint did not sufficiently establish the paternity of the children. Following a hearing, the trial court issued a ruling declaring that: (1) the gestational agreement is valid; (2) Raftopol is the genetic and legal father of the children; (3) Hargon is the legal father of the children; and (4) Ramey is not the genetic or legal mother of the children. The court therefore ordered the department to issue a replacement birth certificate pursuant to § 7–48a. This appeal followed.

I

We first turn to the issue of whether the trial court lacked subject matter jurisdiction to declare Hargon a legal parent of the children because Hargon was not biologically related to the children and did not adopt them. Included within this issue is the question of whether the court was required, as a prerequisite to making any determination regarding Hargon's parental status, to terminate Ramey's parental rights, and, if so, whether the court had jurisdiction to terminate those rights. We conclude that * * * because Ramey did not have any parental rights with respect to the children, the termination of those nonexistent rights was not a necessary prerequisite to a determination of Hargon's parental status with respect to the children. * * *

Our statutes and case law establish that a gestational carrier who bears no biological relationship to the child she has carried does not have parental rights with respect to that child. We have long recognized that there are three ways by which a person may become a parent: conception, adoption or pursuant to the artificial insemination statutes. The definitional section of chapter 803 of the General Statutes, which deals with termination of parental rights and adoption, defines " '[p]arent' " as "a biological or adoptive parent." * * * In 1975, the legislature provided the third means by which a person may gain parental status. Public Acts 1975, No. 75–233, now codified at General Statutes § 45a–774. Section 45a–774 provides: "Any child or children born as a result of A.I.D. shall be deemed to acquire, in all respects, the status of a naturally conceived legitimate child of the husband and wife who consented to and requested the use of A.I.D." "A.I.D." is defined as "artificial insemination with the use of donated sperm or eggs from an identified or anonymous donor." General Statutes § 45a–771a (2). "Artificial insemination" is specifically defined to include both "intrauterine insemination and in vitro fertilization. . . ." General Statutes § 45a–771a (1). Accordingly, a child born to a married woman and conceived through artificial insemination by an egg or sperm donor is the child of the wife and husband who requested and consented to the use of A.I.D.

* * * Under any of the three specified ways of acquiring parental status, as set forth both in our statutes and interpretive case law, Ramey is not a parent of the children in the present case. It is undisputed that she is neither the biological nor the adoptive mother to the children. Nor does she fall within the parameters of the artificial insemination statutes. Accordingly, Ramey did not have parental rights that required termination before Hargon could acquire parental status with respect to the children. * * *

II

* * * [W]e turn to the merits of the department's claim that the trial court improperly concluded that § 7–48a conferred parental status on Hargon by virtue of the gestational agreement. The plaintiffs contend that § 7–48a evidences a legislative recognition of the validity of intended parentage. Accordingly, they claim that, pursuant to § 7–48a, a court of competent jurisdiction may declare Hargon to be the parent of the children, and, consistent with that declaratory ruling, may order the department to issue a replacement birth certificate reflecting his parental status. The department claims that the legislature intended that § 7–48a would allow only intended parents who are also the genetic parents of the children to gain legal parental status without first adopting the children. We conclude that § 7–48a allows an intended parent who is a party to a *valid* gestational agreement to become a parent without first adopting the children, without respect to that intended parent's genetic relationship to the children. Consistent with that conclusion, we conclude that the trial court properly ordered the department to issue a replacement birth certificate listing Hargon as parent of the children. We emphasize that the court's order to the department to place Hargon's name on the replacement birth certificate *follows from* its declaratory judgment concluding that Hargon is a parent to the children. No one should misunderstand this opinion to state that the department, by placing Hargon's name on the replacement birth certificate, or by refusing to do so, confers or declines to confer parental status on Hargon. In this particular case, that relationship was created by the valid gestational agreement, and that relationship is accurately reflected by naming Hargon as a parent to the children on the replacement birth certificate. A birth certificate is a vital record that must accurately reflect legal relationships between parents and children—it does not create those relationships.

Preliminarily, we must note that because in the present case the department has not challenged the trial court's finding that the gestational agreement at issue is valid, that issue has not been presented to us. Accordingly, our analysis is predicated on this important starting point: we assume without deciding that the gestational agreement at issue is valid. The question of whether § 7–48a allows a nonbiological intended parent to acquire parental status through a valid gestational agreement without first adopting the children presents a question of statutory interpretation, over which we exercise plenary review.

* * * [W]e begin with the text of the statute. Section 7–48a provides in relevant part: "On and after January 1, 2002, each birth certificate shall be filed with the name of the birth mother recorded. *If the birth is subject to a gestational agreement,* the Department of Public Health shall create a replacement certificate in accordance with an order from a court of competent jurisdiction not later than forty-five days after receipt of such order or forty-five days after the birth of the child, whichever is later. Such replacement certificate shall include all information required to be included in a certificate of birth of this state as of the date of the birth * * * " (Emphasis added.) What is clear from the text of the statute is that if the birth is subject to a "gestational agreement" and if a court of competent jurisdiction orders the department to do so, the department is both authorized and required to issue a replacement birth certificate in accordance with that order. It follows that, because some gestational agreements would justify a court order to the department to issue a replacement birth certificate, at least some gestational agreements are valid under Connecticut law. Beyond that, however, the statutory text gives rise to numerous ambiguities. For example, although § 7–48a initially provides that the name of the birth mother shall be placed on the birth certificate, it does not define the term "birth mother." Nor, more significantly, does § 7–48a define the key phrase, "gestational agreement."

Section 7–48a says nothing about the nature and scope of the court order. It is, therefore, not clear whether § 7–48a sets forth merely procedural guidelines or effects a substantive change in the law. In other words, it is possible that the "court order" contemplated by the statute is merely a ministerial order for the issuance of a replacement birth certificate. It is also possible that § 7–48a effects a substantive change in the law, creating a new means by which a person may become a parent, thus justifying an order declaring parentage. That is, does § 7–48a contemplate, as happened in the present case, a court issuing a declaratory judgment that the intended parents are, by virtue of the gestational agreement, legal parents, and an order consistent with that judgment directing the department to issue the replacement birth certificate? Additionally, § 7–48a does not set forth any guidelines as to who may qualify, and by what means, to be named as a parent on a replacement birth certificate. In other words, it is unclear from the text of § 7–48a: (1) which types of gestational agreements are intended to be included within the statutory phrase "gestational agreement"; (2) whether a court may order the department to issue a replacement birth certificate naming an intended parent as the parent, despite the fact that the intended parent is the parent neither by conception nor adoption; and (3) whether the statute creates a new means by which persons may become legal parents.

* * * [W]e conclude that the plain language of § 7–48a does not unambiguously indicate whether the legislature intended § 7–48a to authorize the Superior Court to declare an intended parent who bears no biological relationship to a child to be a legal parent of that child absent adoption proceedings.

Moreover, the department's contention that the *only* reasonable interpretation of the plain language of § 7–48a is that only biological intended parents may gain legal parental status solely by virtue of being parties to a valid gestational agreement, runs afoul of a basic principle of statutory construction. We often have stated that "it is axiomatic that those who promulgate statutes . . . do not intend to promulgate statutes . . . that lead to absurd consequences or bizarre results." Accordingly, "[w]e construe a statute in a manner that will not . . . lead to absurd results." The department's contention that the legislature expressed an intent, via the plain language of § 7–48a, that only a biological intended parent may gain parental status absent adoption proceedings, when examined in relation to the artificial insemination statutes, leads to the not very remote possibility of a child who comes into the world with no parents—a parentless child. Specifically, General Statutes § 45a–775 provides: "An identified or anonymous donor of sperm or eggs used in A.I.D., or any person claiming by or through such donor, shall not have any right or interest in any child born as a result of A.I.D." As we previously have noted, the definitional section defines " 'A.I.D.,' " or " '[a]rtificial insemination with donor sperm or eggs' " to include in vitro fertilization. General Statutes § 45a–771a. Thus, neither an egg or sperm donor, nor their spouses, if any, gain parental status by virtue of the contribution of gametes for use in in vitro fertilization. Furthermore, as we already [explained], a gestational carrier who is a party to a valid gestational agreement does not have any parental rights. A corollary to this conclusion is that any spouse of the gestational carrier similarly would not acquire parental status by virtue of a valid gestational agreement. Following this process of elimination, it takes little imagination to visualize the absurd consequence. Suppose an infertile couple who desire to have children but cannot supply the womb, the eggs, or the sperm—a scenario far more likely than the hypothetical imaginary horrible. These intended parents would need to rely on third party egg and sperm donors to produce embryos that are implanted in a gestational carrier pursuant to a gestational agreement. If § 7–48a confers parental status only on biological intended parents, the intended parents are not the parents of any resulting child, nor are the gestational carrier, any spouse she may have, the gamete donors, or any spouses each may have. Every possible parent to the child would be eliminated as a matter of law, yielding the result of a child who is born parentless, not due to the death of the parents, but simply due to elimination by operation of law. The legislature cannot be presumed to have intended this consequence, which is so absurd as to be Kafkaesque. Thus, our examination of the language of the statute * * * yields only ambiguity and the department's interpretation of the language of the statute leads to an absurd result. The mere fact, however, that the department's proposed interpretation of § 7–48a leads to an absurd result does not necessarily lead to the conclusion, based on the language of the statute, that § 7–48a confers parental status on Hargon by virtue of the gestational agreement. As we have explained, there are many ambiguities in § 7–48a—the nature and scope of "an order from a court of competent jurisdiction," the types of gestational agreements that would give rise to such an order, whatever it may be, who may be an intended parent, just to name a few. In light of the many remaining ambiguities, we turn to extratextual sources in order to discern the intent of the legislature.

Section 7–48a initially was enacted by No. 01–163, § 28, of the 2001 Public Acts (P.A. 01–163), and, at the time of passage, provided merely: "On and after January 1, 2002, each birth certificate shall contain the name of the birth mother, *except by the order of a court of competent jurisdiction.*" (Emphasis added.) The raised bill that preceded P.A. 01–163 had been much more detailed, and provided in relevant part: "(a) On receipt of a certified copy of an order of a court of competent jurisdiction approving a gestational agreement, the department shall prepare a new birth certificate for the child born of the agreement. The new birth certificate shall include all the information required to be set forth in a certificate of birth of this state as of the date of birth, *except that the intended parent or parents under this agreement shall be named as the parent or parents. . . .*" (Emphasis added.) Raised Bill No. 6569, January 2001 Sess., § 27. Thus, although the original language specifically had provided that an intended parent's name should be placed on the replacement birth certificate, that language was omitted from the final language in P.A. 01–163 that was codified at § 7–48a. During discussion of the amendment during house proceedings, Representative Mary U. Eberle remarked on the omission of the original language, observing: "This amendment makes a number of technical corrections and changes . . . *and* it removes the language on gestational agreements and simply substitutes the requirement that the mother on the birth certificate shall be the birth mother unless—except by order of a court of competent jurisdiction." (Emphasis added.) 44 H.R. Proc., Pt. 11, 2001 Sess., p. 3719. Representative Eberle's remarks indicate that the amendment, in addition to and separate from certain technical changes, deleted the language that had referred to gestational agreements and had provided that intended parents be named as parents on replacement certificates. The omission of this language in the raised bill suggests one of two possibilities: (1) the legislature considered, then rejected, the notion of parenthood created solely by intent; or (2) the legislature left it to the courts to decide what additional information the department could be ordered to place on birth certificates.

Section 7–48a was amended in 2004 to add language requiring the department to issue a replacement birth certificate in accordance with an order from a court of competent jurisdiction. Public Acts 2004, No. 04–

255, § 28. Representative Donald B. Sherer offered some background on the amendment during the floor discussion of the bill, observing: "A number of years ago ... this legislature changed the birth certificate registration law to permit a court of [competent jurisdiction] being the Superior Court to find parentage *in accordance with the biological relationship to a child* rather than the birth mother if she wasn't the biological mother." (Emphasis added.) 47 H.R. Proc., Pt. 14, 2004 Sess., pp. 4456–57. Although Representative Sherer did not directly state that the finding of parentage contemplated by § 7–48a could be confined to those intended parents who share a biological relationship with the children, but are not the birth parents, his remark does provide some support for that interpretation.

A subsequent exchange could be read more broadly. At one point during the discussion of the amendment, Representative Lenny T. Winkler remarked: "[F]rom what I understand it's been difficult for some individuals to adopt and they've been required to go to [P]robate [Court] and this would avoid that and make it easier, could you explain that all?" *Id.*, at p. 4459. Representative Sherer responded: "That's correct. There's been the difficult situation where due to the birth being, the parents not being the birth parents the only way to obtain a new birth certificate would be to go to [P]robate [C]ourt and basically adopt their own child, which no one really thinks is the right thing to do." *Id.* This exchange indicates that the legislature was focused on allowing nonbirth parents, which could include the intended parents under a gestational agreement, to circumvent Probate Court. The exchange leaves open the possibility that the legislature intended that nonbiological intended parents would benefit from the rule. Both exchanges also clarify one ambiguity in § 7–48a. Sherer stated that the "court of [competent jurisdiction]," referred to in the statute, is the Superior Court, and that the intent of the statute is to circumvent proceedings in the Probate Court because of the difficulty some parties to gestational agreements had encountered in adopting. This legislative history clarifies that § 7–48a does not merely provide for a ministerial order by a court, but rather, has effected a substantive change in the law and has created a new way by which persons may become legal parents.

With respect to whether this substantive change in the law was intended to include nonbiological intended parents, we recognize that the legislative history is inconclusive, but we already have rejected, on the basis of our plain language analysis, the department's contention that only biological intended parents may acquire legal parentage solely by virtue of a valid gestational agreement. On the basis of our analysis of both the text of the statute, as well as its legislative history, we conclude that the legislature intended § 7–48a to confer parental status on an intended parent who is a party to a valid gestational agreement irrespective of that intended parent's genetic relationship to the children. Such intended parents need not adopt the children in order to become legal parents. They acquire that status by operation of law, upon an order by a court of competent jurisdiction pursuant to § 7–48a.

Consistent with our conclusion that § 7–48a confers parental status on a nongenetic, intended parent who is a party to a valid gestational agreement, we also conclude that the trial court properly ordered the department to issue a replacement birth certificate listing Hargon as a parent of the children. * * *

The department also contends that courts in other jurisdictions have concluded that the legislature is the appropriate body to devise new rules for the regulation of gestational agreements. See, e.g., *In re C.K.G.*, 173 S.W.3d 714, 730 (Tenn.2005) (deciding maternity question presented by artificial insemination with donated egg narrowly in recognition that, due to "far-reaching, profoundly complex, and competing public policy considerations implicated by" use of assisted reproductive technology, legislature is appropriate body to craft "general rule to adjudicate all controversies" that arise from its use).

We agree that the legislature is the appropriate body to craft specific rules and procedures governing gestational agreements. That precept does not conflict with our decision today, which interprets § 7–48a in accordance with well established rules of statutory construction. Our decision is grounded on and guided by the intent of the legislature. Moreover, because we agree with the department that the legislature is the appropriate body to establish specific standards, rules and procedures governing gestational agreements, and because our starting point in this decision is an unchallenged ruling that the instant gestational agreement is valid, we have confined the scope of our holding to valid gestational agreements.

Indeed, this appeal highlights the fact that our existing statutes addressing parentage do not address the public policy concerns raised by modern assisted reproductive technology. * * * [T]his area of law needs to be clarified so that families are not left in a state of confusion. Our existing statutory scheme only partially addresses these issues. Parentage, however, is not an issue that should be addressed in a "piecemeal" fashion. As we already have observed in this opinion, our existing statutes provide few answers and raise many questions. It is decidedly not the role of this court to make the public policy determinations necessary to establish the specific rules and procedures governing the validity of gestational agreements or set the standards for valid gestational agreements. The legislature will be required to grapple with numerous questions implicating significant public policy issues— that body, with the ability to hold public hearings and seek out expert assistance, is the appropriate one to make such public policy determinations.

We highlight some of the issues that remain unresolved in our current statutory scheme by looking to the laws of other jurisdictions that have grappled with these public policy issues. In jurisdictions that have addressed the issues raised by the use of assisted reproductive technology,[35] it appears that there are three general approaches to the determination of legal parentage. Those three approaches define parentage based on: (1) the intent of the parties; see, e.g., *Johnson v. Calvert,* 5 Cal.4th 84, 93, 851 P.2d 776, 19 Cal.Rptr.2d 494, cert. denied, 510 U.S. 874, 114 S.Ct. 206, 126 L.Ed.2d 163 (1993); Nev.Rev.Stat. § 126.045(2) (2009); (2) the genetic relatedness of the parties; see, e.g., *Culliton v. Beth Israel Deaconess Medical Center,* 435 Mass. at 286–87, 756 N.E.2d 1133; *Belsito v. Clark,* 67 Ohio Misc.2d 54, 64–66, 644 N.E.2d 760 (1994); or (3) giving birth. See, e.g., *McDonald v. McDonald,* 196 App.Div.2d 7, 9, 608 N.Y.S.2d 477 (1994).[36]

How a state defines parentage is merely the starting point. Additional issues that some states have addressed, for example, include whether to recognize compensated gestational agreements,[37] whether to limit the availability to married couples,[38] infertile intended parents,[39]

---

[35] Connecticut is not alone in failing to enact laws addressing the issues implicated by assisted reproductive technology. An astonishing twenty states have not weighed in at all on the validity of gestational agreements, including Alaska, Colorado, Delaware, Georgia, Hawaii, Idaho, Maine, Maryland, Minnesota, Mississippi, Missouri, Montana, North Carolina, Oklahoma, Oregon, Rhode Island, South Carolina, South Dakota, Vermont and Wyoming.

[36] Some states have barred gestational agreements altogether, including Arizona, Indiana, Michigan, New York, North Dakota and the District of Columbia. *See* Ariz. Rev. Stat. § 25–218(A) (2007); Ind. Code §§ 31–20–1–1 and 31–20–1–2 (LexisNexis 2009); Mich. Comp. Laws § 722.855 (2005); N.Y. Dom. Rel. Law §§ 122 and 123 (McKinney 2010); N.D. Cent. Code § 14–18–05 (2009); D.C.Code Ann. § 16–402 (LexisNexis 2008). Two states, Alabama and Iowa, have only gone so far as to *decriminalize* surrogacy. *See* Ala. Code §§ 26–10A–33 and 26–10A–34 (2009); Iowa Code Ann. § 710.11 (West 2003).

[37] Ten states prohibit compensated gestational agreements, including Florida, Kansas, Kentucky, Louisiana, Nebraska, Nevada, New Hampshire, New Mexico, Virginia and Washington. *See* Fla. Stat. Ann. § 742.15(4) (West 2010); Opinions, Kan. Atty. Gen. No. 96–73 (September 11, 1996) (compensation for gestational agreement does not fall within statutory exception permitting fee for professional service rendered in connection with adoption); Ky. Rev. Stat. Ann. § 199.590(4) (LexisNexis 2007); La. Rev. Stat. Ann. § 9:2713 (2005); Neb. Rev.Stat. § 25–21,200 (1995); Nev. Rev. Stat. § 126.045(3) (2009); N.H.Rev.Stat. Ann. §§ 168–B:16 (IV) and 168–B:25 (V) (2002); N.M. Stat. Ann. § 32A–5–34 (F) (West 2006); Va. Code Ann. § 20–160(B)(4) (2008); Wn. Rev. Code Ann. § 26.26.240 (West 2005). Illinois, Texas and West Virginia, on the other hand, appear to authorize compensated gestational agreements. *See* 750 Ill. Comp. Stat. Ann. 47/25 (d)(3) (West 2009); Tex. Fam. Code Ann. §§ 160.751 through 160.753 (Vernon 2008); W. Va.Code § 48–22–803(e)(3) (LexisNexis 2009).

[38] Some states require that intended parents be married. See, e.g., Fla. Stat. Ann. § 742.15(1) (West 2010); Nev. Rev. Stat. § 126.045(4)(b) (2009); Tex. Fam. Code Ann. § 160.754(b) (Vernon 2008). * * *

[39] Some states require that one or both of the intended parents must have a "medical need" for the use of a gestational carrier. See, e.g., Fla. Stat. Ann. § 742.15(2) (West 2010); 750 Ill. Comp. Stat. Ann. 47/20(b)(2) (West 2009); N.H. Rev. Stat. Ann. § 168–B:17(II) (2002); Va. Code Ann. § 20–160(B)(8) (2008).

age limitations,[40] what protections to put in place to safeguard the gestational carrier's right to make decisions regarding healthcare and termination of the pregnancy until the child has been delivered,[41] whether to require that the spouse of the gestational carrier either consent or be made a party to the contract,[42] what measures to put in place to safeguard the legal rights of the parties,[43] who should be required to obtain health insurance coverage,[44] whether to require that at least one intended parent contribute genetic material,[45] and whether to require mental and physical health evaluations and home studies.[46] * * *

---

[40]   For example, Florida requires that both the gestational carrier and the intended parents be eighteen years or older. Fla. Stat. Ann. § 742.15(1) (West 2010). Illinois requires that the gestational carrier must be at least twenty-one years of age. 750 Ill. Comp. Stat. Ann. 47/20 (a)(1) (West 2009). New Hampshire requires that all parties to the contract must be at least twenty-one years of age. N.H. Rev. Stat. Ann. § 168–B:17(I) (2002).

[41]   See, e.g., Fla. Stat. Ann. § 742.15(3)(a) (West 2010).

[42]   See, e.g., 750 Ill. Comp. Stat. Ann. 47/25(b)(2)(i) (West 2009); Va. Code Ann. § 20–160(B)(10) (2008).

[43]   Illinois, New Hampshire and Virginia, each of which has enacted a comprehensive statutory scheme addressing issues that arise from the use of assisted reproductive technology, each incorporate numerous provisions safeguarding the legal rights of the parties to gestational agreements. For example, among the many legal protections incorporated into Illinois' statutory scheme are the requirements that gestational agreements be in writing, and that the gestational carrier and intended parents must be represented by separate counsel. 750 Ill. Comp. Stat. Ann. 47/25(b)(1) and (3) (West 2009). Additionally, the parties must sign acknowledgments that they have received information regarding the "legal, financial, and contractual rights, expectations, penalties and obligations of the surrogacy agreement. . . ." 750 Ill. Comp. Stat. Ann. 47/25(b)(3.5) (West 2009). The gestational agreement also must be witnessed by two competent adults. 750 Ill. Comp. Stat. Ann. 47/25(b)(5) (West 2009). A gestational carrier and the intended parents each must have consulted with counsel regarding the potential legal consequences of the gestational agreement. 750 Ill. Comp. Stat. Ann. 47/20(a)(5) and (b)(4) (West 2009).

New Hampshire requires judicial preauthorization of a gestational agreement, prior to the medical procedure to impregnate the gestational carrier. N.H. Rev. Stat. Ann. § 168–B:16 (I)(b) (2002). At the hearing, the court must make findings that all parties to the gestational agreement have given their informed consent and that the agreement contains no unconscionable terms. N.H. Rev. Stat. Ann. § 168–B:23(III)(a) and (b) (2002). The contract must be signed by the gestational carrier and her spouse if she is married. N.H. Rev. Stat. Ann. § 168–B:25(2002). In addition, New Hampshire requires that a gestational agreement provide that the gestational carrier has the right to keep the child if, within seventy-two hours after the birth of the child, the carrier executes a signed statement of her intent to keep the child and delivers the writing to the intended parents and the attending physician or the hospital medical director or designee. N.H. Rev. Stat. Ann. § 168–B:25(IV) (2002).

Similar to New Hampshire, Virginia requires that a petition for court approval of a surrogacy contract be filed prior to the performance of assisted conception. One of the required findings by the court is that the parties have voluntarily entered into the gestational agreement and understand its terms. Va.Code Ann. § 20–160(B)(4) (2008).

[44]   Illinois requires that the gestational carrier be covered by health insurance and provides that either the gestational carrier or the intended parents may obtain coverage. 750 Ill. Comp. Stat. 47/20(a)(6) (West 2009).

[45]   See, e.g., 750 Ill. Comp. Stat. Ann. 47/20(b)(1) (West 2009); N.H. Rev. Stat. Ann. § 168–B:17 (III) (2002); Va. Code Ann. § 20–160(B)(9) (2008).

In addition to requiring that at least one intended parent must contribute a gamete, New Hampshire bars the use of a third party egg donor—the egg must either come from the intended mother or the gestational carrier. N.H. Rev. Stat. Ann. § 168–B:17(III) and (IV) (2002).

Texas does not appear to require that one of the intended parents contribute genetic material, and allows a donor egg to be used, but prohibits the use of the gestational carrier's eggs in the assisted reproduction procedure. Tex. Fam. Code Ann. § 160.754(c) (Vernon 2008).

We emphasize that the legislature is the appropriate body to make the public policy determinations implicated by these issues. Because of the uncertainties created by the existing statutory scheme, we respectfully would suggest that the legislature consider doing so. Particularly important will be a determination of which types of gestational agreements are valid, as that determination will decide who may benefit from the streamlined process to parentage created by § 7–48a. As we have stated previously in this opinion, in the language of § 7–48a, the legislature already implicitly has recognized that at least some gestational agreements are valid. That general recognition of validity has little practical use, however, until the legislature clarifies specifically what requirements must be met in order for a gestational agreement to be valid. For today, we answer only the narrow question presented in this appeal: Upon a court order pursuant to § 7–48a, intended parents who are parties to a valid gestational agreement acquire parental status and are entitled to be named as parents on the replacement birth certificate, without respect to their biological relationship to the children.

The judgment is affirmed.

[Concurring opinion by ZARELLA, J., is omitted.]

NOTES

1.   Pay particular attention to the types of surrogacy restrictions, noted by the court in *Raftapol*, which some states have codified into law. Which of those restrictions, if any, do you think are appropriate? Is it good policy, for example, to allow so-called altruistic surrogacy (i.e., the surrogate can only be reimbursed for expenses) but not so-called compensated surrogacy (i.e., the surrogate can be compensated for more than expenses)? What about limiting intended parenthood through surrogacy to instances in which the couples are married? In which there is a medical necessity for the surrogacy? How about the requirement that at least one of the intended parents contribute genetic material?

2.   The surrogate in *Raftapol* did not seek to exercise parental rights. But that was precisely what the surrogate attempted to do in *In re Paternity and Custody of Baby Boy A*, 2007 WL 4304448 (Minn. Ct. App.). The gestational surrogate in *Baby Boy A.* was the niece of the child's father, a gay

---

Nevada requires that both intended parents must contribute the gametes used in the assisted reproduction procedure. Nev. Rev. Stat. § 126.045(4)(a) (2009).

[46]   See, e.g., 750 Ill. Comp. Stat. Ann. 47/20(a)(3) and (4), and (b)(3) (West 2009) (gestational carrier must have mental and physical health evaluation; intended parents must have mental health evaluation); N.H. Rev. Stat. Ann. § 168–B:18(II) and (III) (2002) (all parties must undergo "nonmedical evaluation" and home study to determine ability to parent and to adjust to and assume risks of contract and ability to provide child with food, clothing, shelter, medical care and necessities); N.H. Rev. Stat. Ann. § 168–B:19 (I) (2002) (participants in medical procedures must be medically evaluated); Va. Code Ann. § 20–160(B)(2) and (6) (2008) (court shall order home study of all parties to contract; all parties have submitted to physical and psychological evaluations).

man who provided his genetic material for the creation of the embryo (with a donated egg) that doctors in Illinois implanted in the surrogate's uterus. Before the medical procedure took place, the parties signed a gestational surrogacy agreement (GSA). The agreement stated that it was the surrogate's intent not to exercise parental rights over the child and that the uncle was "the genetic and intended parent [who] shall exclusively have . . . custody and all parental rights, duties, and obligations." *Id.* at *2. After the child was born in Minnesota, the surrogate argued *inter alia* that the GSA was unenforceable under Minnesota law because the state lacked a statute allowing the assignation of parental rights "pursuant to a private contract." *Id.* at *6. However, the court noted that no provision of state law *prohibited* parties from entering into a GSA. (The Minnesota legislature is one of many state legislatures that has not weighed in on the validity of gestational surrogacy agreements. *See Raftapol, supra*, note 15.) The court added that

> [b]ecause there is no Minnesota legislative or judicial pronouncement that prohibits such agreements, we conclude that GSAs do not violate any articulated public policy of this state. By this opinion, however, we neither condemn nor condone gestational surrogacy. That is not our function. But a child has been born in this state as the result of the procedure, and the judiciary has been asked to determine the child's parentage and custody. That is our function.

Id. at *7. The court then proceeded to hold that Illinois law, which was the law that the parties had agreed in the GSA should be applied, recognized the father as the child's sole parent. *Id.* at *8.

3.   Some different sex-couples have escaped restrictive regulation of surrogacy by using their gametes. In those situations, the law often recognizes the intended parents as the legal parents based on their biological connections. *See, e.g., Johnson v. Calvert*, 851 P.2d 776 (Cal. 1993). For male same-sex couples, as well as different-sex couples using a gestational surrogate and an egg donor, at least one of the intended parents cannot rely on a biological connection to establish parentage. That parent would need to turn to statutory provisions like those in Connecticut that provide for the parentage of the nonbiological intended parent. Even in states without such legislation, some trial courts have granted judgments of parentage to nonbiological intended parents; these courts usually find statutory authority to adjudicate parentage, just as they would in circumstances involving contested paternity. In the absence of a statutory framework regulating gestational surrogacy or a trial court willing to grant parentage judgments, the nonbiological intended parent would need to adopt the child.

4.   Given that gay men have increasingly engaged in surrogacy to have children, surrogacy has increasingly been framed as related to sexual orientation equality. As Professor NeJaime explains: "Family-based LGBT equality may be particularly significant to the status of assisted reproduction, which is central to same-sex family formation. Marriage equality may further

normalize various forms of [assisted reproduction technology] for all families. Surrogacy, for instance, continues to be heavily restricted as a legal matter. But as states embrace same-sex family formation, they may increasingly accommodate the mechanisms commonly used by same-sex couples to have children." NeJaime, *supra*, at 1253. Is that a good thing? Should states loosen their restrictions on surrogacy? Should surrogacy be seen as connected to sexual orientation equality? As a political matter? As a constitutional matter?

5.   For an article surveying the surrogacy laws of all fifty states (many of which are silent on the enforceability of surrogacy agreements), see Darra L. Hofman, *"Mama's Baby, Daddy's Maybe:" A State-By-State Survey of Surrogacy Laws and Their Disparate Gender Impact*, 35 WM. MITCHELL L. REV. 449 (2009).

CHAPTER 7

SEXUALITY, GENDER, & THE FIRST AMENDMENT

■ ■ ■

I. INTRODUCTION

Sexual orientation and gender identity have vital expressive dimensions. Key milestones of an open life—coming out, meeting other LGBT people, finding a partner, participating in social and political activity—depend to some extent on self-identification. Free expression enables LGBT persons to create their own groups, communities, and cultures. Absent self-identification, LGBT people would never be able to meet with one another to form meaningful friendships; intimate relationships; support, lobbying, or educational groups; or, for example, legal-aid organizations.

This Chapter explores the role of First Amendment freedoms in the lives of LGBT individuals and in the LGBT community. Section II of this Chapter focuses on the lives of high school and college students and on issues associated with asserting sexual and gender identity at school. (In Chapter 4, we have already seen issues that arise as LGBT persons are open about their identities at work). Section II considers a broader set of issues that have come to the fore over the last few decades, as private, non-governmental organizations (like the Boy Scouts and religiously-affiliated entities) have sought to deny equal access to LGBT people and asserted their own expressive liberties as a justification for doing so. Section III then considers the debate over religious liberty that is, in some sense, the outgrowth of earlier debates like the one about the Boy Scouts' exclusionary policy. Although the Boy Scouts has since largely abandoned that policy, the broad questions it posed are very much alive in debates over religious liberty. While some of the conflicts over religious liberty arise under the First Amendment's Free Exercise Clause, most of the issues arise under statutory frameworks that protect religious liberty or provide religious exemptions. These debates have become especially salient with the rise of marriage equality.

The organizing legal principle of this Chapter is the First Amendment, along with statutory frameworks that purport to protect First Amendment values of religious freedom. We will see expressive liberties asserted as both a "sword" in favor of LGBT presence and inclusion and as a "shield" against it—that is, as a source of constitutional protection claimed by those seeking to exclude LGBT persons from areas of social life. The historical trajectory of First Amendment claims in the realm of LGBT issues has been toward such "shield" claims that pit values of equality against values of liberty.

II. FREE SPEECH AND SCHOOLS

A. ASSERTING LGBT IDENTITY

FRICKE V. LYNCH

United States District Court, District of Rhode Island, 1980
491 F. Supp. 381

PETTINE, CHIEF JUDGE.

Most of the time, a young man's choice of a date for the senior prom is of no great interest to anyone other than the student, his companion, and, perhaps, a few of their classmates. But in Aaron Fricke's case, the school authorities actively disapprove of his choice, the other students are upset, the community is abuzz, and out-of-state newspapers consider the matter newsworthy. All this fuss arises because Aaron Fricke's intended escort is another young man. Claiming that the school's refusal to allow him to bring a male escort violates his First and Fourteenth Amendment rights, Fricke seeks a preliminary injunction ordering the school officials to allow him to attend with a male escort.

Two days of testimony have revealed the following facts. The senior reception at Cumberland High School is a formal dinner-dance sponsored and run by the senior class. It is held shortly before graduation but is not a part of the graduation ceremonies. This year the students have decided to hold the dance at the Pleasant Valley Country Club in Sutton, Massachusetts on Friday, May 30. All seniors except those on suspension are eligible to attend the dance; no one is required to go. All students who attend must bring an escort, although their dates need not be seniors or even Cumberland High School students. Each student is asked the name of his date at the time he buys the tickets.

The principal testified that school dances are chaperoned by him, two assistant principals, and one or two class advisers. They are sometimes joined by other teachers who volunteer to help chaperone; such teachers are not paid. Often these teachers will drop in for part of the dance. Additionally, police officers are on duty at the dance. Usually two officers attend; last year three plainclothes officers were at the junior prom.

The seeds of the present conflict were planted a year ago when Paul Guilbert, then a junior at Cumberland High School, sought permission to bring a male escort to the junior prom. The principal, Richard Lynch (the defendant here), denied the request, fearing that student reaction could lead to a disruption at the dance and possibly to physical harm to Guilbert. The request and its denial were widely publicized and led to widespread community and student reaction adverse to Paul. Some students taunted and spit at him, and once someone slapped him; in response, principal Lynch arranged an escort system, in which Lynch or an assistant principal accompanied Paul as he went from one class to the next. No other incidents or violence occurred. Paul did not attend the prom. At that time Aaron Fricke (plaintiff here) was a friend of Paul's and supported his position regarding the dance.

This year, during or after an assembly in April in which senior class events were discussed, Aaron Fricke, a senior at Cumberland High School, decided that he wanted to attend the senior reception with a male companion. Aaron considers himself a homosexual, and has never dated girls, although he does socialize with female friends. He has never taken a girl to a school dance. Until this April, he had not "come out of the closet" by publicly acknowledging his sexual orientation.

Aaron asked principal Lynch for permission to bring a male escort, which Lynch denied. A week later (during vacation), Aaron asked Paul Guilbert—who now lives in New York—to be his escort (if allowed), and Paul accepted. Aaron met again with Lynch, at which time they discussed Aaron's commitment to homosexuality; Aaron indicated that although it was possible he might someday be bisexual, at the present he is exclusively homosexual and could not conscientiously date girls. Lynch gave Aaron written reasons for his action;[2] his prime concern was the fear that a disruption would occur and Aaron or, especially, Paul would be hurt. He indicated in court that he would allow Aaron to bring a male escort if there were no threat of violence.

After Aaron filed suit in this Court, an event reported by the Rhode Island and Boston papers, a student shoved and, the next day, punched

---

[2]   Principal Lynch sent the following letter to Aaron's home and handed it to him in person:

I am denying your request for the following reasons:

   1. The real and present threat of physical harm to you, your male escort and to others;

   2. The adverse effect among your classmates, other students, the school and the town of Cumberland, which is certain to follow approval of such a request for overt homosexual interaction (male or female) at a class function;

   3. Since the dance is being held out of state and this is a function of the students of Cumberland High School, the school department is powerless to insure protection in Sutton, Massachusetts. That protection would be required of property as well as persons and would expose all concerned to liability for harm which might occur;

   4. It is long-standing school policy that no unescorted student, male or female, is permitted to attend. To enforce this rule, a student must identify his or her escort before the committee will sell the ticket. I suspect that other objections will be raised by your fellow students, the Cumberland School Department, parents and other citizens, which will heighten the potential for harm.

Aaron. The unprovoked, surprise assault necessitated five stitches under Aaron's right eye. The assailant was suspended for nine days. After this, Aaron was given a special parking space closer to the school doors and has been provided with an escort (principal or assistant principal) between classes. No further incidents have occurred. * * *

Aaron contends that the school's action violates his First Amendment right of association, his First Amendment right to free speech, and his Fourteenth Amendment right to equal protection of the laws. (The equal protection claim is a "hybrid" one—that he has been treated differently than others because of the content of his communication.)[3]

The starting point in my analysis of Aaron's First Amendment free speech claim must be, of course, to determine whether the action he proposes to take has a "communicative content sufficient to bring it within the ambit of the First Amendment." *Gay Students Organization v. Bonner*, 509 F.2d 652 (1st Cir. 1974) (hereinafter *Bonner*). . . . [T]he "speech pure" / "speech plus" demarcation is problematic, both in logic and in practice. This normally difficult task is made somewhat easier here, however, by the precedent set in *Bonner, supra.* In that case, the University of New Hampshire prohibited the Gay Students' Organization (GSO) from holding dances and other social events. The First Circuit explicitly rejected the idea that traditional First Amendment rights of expression were not involved. The Court found that not only did discussion and exchange of ideas take place at informal social functions, but also that:

> beyond the specific communications at such events is the basic "message" GSO seeks to convey—that homosexuals exist, that they feel repressed by existing laws and attitudes, that they wish to emerge from their isolation, and that public understanding of their attitudes and problems is desirable for society.

Here too the proposed activity has significant expressive content. Aaron testified that he wants to go because he feels he has a right to attend and participate just like all the other students and that it would be dishonest to his own sexual identity to take a girl to the dance. He went on to acknowledge that he feels his attendance would have a certain political element and would be a statement for equal rights and human rights. Admittedly, his explanation of his "message" was hesitant and not nearly as articulate as Judge Coffin's restatement of the GSO's message, cited above. Nevertheless, I believe Aaron's testimony that he is sincerely—

---

[3]   The plaintiff has not advanced the plausible arguments that homosexuals constitute a suspect class, *see* L. Tribe, *American Constitutional Law* (1978) at 944–45 n. 17, or that one has a constitutional right to be a homosexual, *see, e.g., Acanfora v. Board of Education,* 359 F. Supp. 843 (D. Md. 1973), *aff'd on other grounds,* 491 F.2d 498 (4th Cir. 1974). The first amendment aspect of the case makes it unnecessary for me to reach these issues, although they may very well be applicable to this kind of case.

although perhaps not irrevocably—committed to a homosexual orientation and that attending the dance with another young man would be a political statement. While mere communicative intent may not always transform conduct into speech, *United States v. O'Brien*, 391 U.S. 367, 376 (1968), *Bonner* makes clear that this exact type of conduct as a vehicle for transmitting this very message can be considered protected speech.

Accordingly, the school's action must be judged by the standards articulated in *United States v. O'Brien*, 391 U.S. 367 (1968), and applied in *Bonner*: (1) was the regulation within the constitutional power of the government; (2) did it further an important or substantial governmental interest; (3) was the governmental interest unrelated to the suppression of free expression; and (4) was the incidental restriction on alleged first amendment freedoms no greater than essential to the furtherance of that interest?

I need not dwell on the first two *O'Brien* requirements: the school unquestionably has an important interest in student safety and has the power to regulate students' conduct to ensure safety. As to the suppression of free expression, Lynch's testimony indicated that his personal views on homosexuality did not affect his decision, and that but for the threat of violence he would let the two young men go together. Thus the government's interest here is not in squelching a particular message because it objects to its content as such. On the other hand, the school's interest is in suppressing certain speech activity because of the reaction its message may engender. Surely this is still suppression of free expression.

It is also clear that the school's action fails to meet the last criterion set out in *O'Brien*, the requirement that the government employ the "least restrictive alternative" before curtailing speech. The plaintiff argues, and I agree, that the school can take appropriate security measures to control the risk of harm. Lynch testified that he did not know if adequate security could be provided, and that he would still need to sit down and make the necessary arrangements. In fact he has not made any effort to determine the need for and logistics of additional security. Although Lynch did not say that any additional security measures would be adequate, from the testimony I find that significant measures could be taken and would—in all probability—critically reduce the likelihood of any disturbance. As Lynch's own testimony indicates, police officers and teachers will be present at the dance, and have been quite successful in the past in controlling whatever problems arise, including unauthorized drinking. Despite the ever-present possibility of violence at sports events, adequate discipline has been maintained. From Lynch's testimony, I have every reason to believe that additional school or law enforcement personnel could be used to "shore up security" and would be effective. It should also be noted that Lynch testified that if he considered it impossible to provide adequate security he would move to cancel the dance. The Court appreciates that controlling high school students is no easy task. It is, of course, impossible to guarantee that no harm will occur, no matter what measures are taken. But only one student so far has attempted to harm Aaron, and no evidence was introduced of other threats. The measures taken already, especially the escort system, have been highly effective in preventing any further problems at school. Appropriate security measures coupled with a firm, clearly communicated attitude by the administration that any disturbance will not be tolerated appear to be a realistic, and less restrictive, alternative to prohibiting Aaron from attending the dance with the date of his choice.

The analysis so far has been along traditional First Amendment lines, making no real allowance for the fact that this case arises in a high school setting. The most difficult problem this controversy presents is how this setting should affect the result. *Tinker v. Des Moines Independent Community School District*, 393 U.S. 503 (1969), makes clear that high school students do not "shed their constitutional rights to freedom of speech or expression at the schoolhouse gate." * * *

Tinker did, however, indicate that there are limits on first amendment rights within the school:

A student's rights, therefore, do not embrace merely the classroom hours. When he is in the cafeteria, or on the playing field, or on the campus during the authorized hours, he may express his opinions, even on controversial subjects like the conflict in Vietnam, if he does so without "materially and substantially interfer[ing] with the requirements of appropriate discipline in the operation of the school" and without colliding with the rights of others. *But conduct by the student, in class or out of it, which for any reason—whether it stems from time, place or type of behavior—materially disrupts classwork or involves substantial disorder or invasion of the rights of others is, of course, not immunized by the constitutional guarantee of freedom of speech.*

It seems to me that here, not unlike in *Tinker*, the school administrators were acting on "an undifferentiated fear or apprehension of disturbance." True, Aaron was punched and then security measures were taken, but since that incident he has not been threatened with violence nor has he been attacked. There has been no disruption at the school; classes have not been cancelled, suspended, or interrupted. In short, while the defendants have perhaps shown more of a basis for fear of harm than in *Tinker*, they have failed to make a "showing" that Aaron's conduct would "materially and substantially interfere" with school discipline. However, even if the Court assumes that there is justifiable fear and that Aaron's peaceful speech leads, or may lead, to a violent reaction from others, the question remains: may the school prohibit the speech, or must it protect the speaker?

It is certainly clear that outside of the classroom the fear—however justified—of a violent reaction is not sufficient reason to restrain such speech in advance, and an actual hostile reaction is rarely an adequate basis for curtailing free speech. Thus, the question here is whether the interest in school discipline and order, recognized in *Tinker*, requires a different approach.

After considerable thought and research, I have concluded that even a legitimate interest in school discipline does not outweigh a student's right to peacefully express his views in an appropriate time, place, and manner.[5] To rule otherwise would completely subvert free speech in the schools by granting other students a "heckler's veto," allowing them to decide—through prohibited and violent methods—what speech will be heard. The First Amendment does not tolerate mob rule by unruly school children. This conclusion is bolstered by the fact that any disturbance here, however great, would not interfere with the main business of school—education. No classes or school work would be affected; at the very worst an optional social event, conducted by the students for their own enjoyment, would be marred. In such a context, the school does have an obligation to take reasonable measures to protect and foster free speech, not to stand helpless before unauthorized student violence. * * *

The present case is so difficult because the court is keenly sensitive to the testimony regarding the concerns of a possible disturbance, and of

---

[5]   The second reason relied upon by the *Bonner* court in finding the GSO social events to be speech-related was the interpretation placed upon those events by the community. There the university prohibited the gay social events because the community considered them "shocking and offensive," "a spectacle, an abomination," an "affront" to townspeople, "grandstanding," inflammatory, "undermin[ing] the university within the state," and distasteful. The first circuit concluded that "[we] do not see how these statements can be interpreted to avoid the conclusion that the regulation imposed was based in large measure, if not exclusively, on the content of the GSO's expression." *Bonner* at 661. I quite agree that these statements of community outrage indicate that the *content*, i.e. the homosexual-ness, of the GSO's activities led to the strong reaction and the prohibition, not the fact that they were dances. With all due respect, however, I am puzzled by how this reaction proves the *expressive* nature of these activities. Community outrage per se does not transform conduct into speech, or even indicate that it is speech; communities have reacted with outrage similar to that of the citizens of New Hampshire to such non-expressive activities as Hester Prynne's adultery, the dumping of chemicals into Love Canal, and the Son of Sam murders. It is hard in *Bonner* to separate the community's opposition to the GSO's acts from its opposition to its message (if the acts had a message); surely they opposed both. Same-sex dancing may have an expressive element, but it is also action, and potentially objectionable as such.

Insofar as *Bonner* directs me to consider community reaction in assessing expressive content, I conclude that the community disapproves of the content of Aaron's message and that the vehemence of their opposition to his intended escort is based in part on this disapproval of what he is trying to communicate. The school here professes to be unconcerned with the content of the plaintiff's message, but their concern with townspeople's reaction is, indirectly, content-related.

physical harm to Aaron or Paul. However, I am convinced that meaningful security measures are possible, and the First Amendment requires that such steps be taken to protect—rather than to stifle—free expression. Some may feel that Aaron's attendance at the reception and the message he will thereby convey is trivial compared to other social debates, but to engage in this kind of a weighing in process is to make the content-based evaluation forbidden by the First Amendment.

As to the other concern raised by *Tinker*, some people might say that Aaron Fricke's conduct would infringe the rights of the other students, and is thus unprotected by *Tinker*. This view is misguided, however. Aaron's conduct is quiet and peaceful; it demands no response from others and—in a crowd of some five hundred people—can be easily ignored. Any disturbance that might interfere with the rights of others would be caused by those students who resort to violence, not by Aaron and his companion, who do not want a fight.

Because the free speech claim is dispositive, I find it unnecessary to reach the plaintiff's right of association argument or to deal at length with his equal protection claim.[6] I find that the plaintiff has established a probability of success on the merits and has shown irreparable harm; accordingly his request for a preliminary injunction is hereby granted.

As a final note, I would add that the social problems presented by homosexuality are emotionally charged; community norms are in flux, and the psychiatric profession itself is divided in its attitude toward homosexuality. This Court's role, of course, is not to mandate social norms or impose its own view of acceptable behavior. It is instead, to interpret and apply the Constitution as best it can. The Constitution is not self-explanatory, and answers to knotty problems are inevitably inexact. All that an individual judge can do is to apply the legal precedents as accurately and as honestly as he can, uninfluenced by personal predilections or the fear of community reaction, hoping each time to disprove the legal maxim that "hard cases make bad law."

---

[6]   This case can also be profitably analyzed under the Equal Protection Clause of the fourteenth amendment. In preventing Aaron Fricke from attending the senior reception, the school has afforded disparate treatment to a certain class of students—those wishing to attend the reception with companions of the same sex. Ordinarily, a government classification need only bear a rational relationship to a legitimate public purpose; ... [however] [w]here, as here, government classification impinges on a first amendment right, the government is held to a higher level of scrutiny. *Chicago Police Department v. Mosley*, 408 U.S. 92 (1972). I find that principal Lynch's reason for prohibiting Aaron's attendance at the reception—the potential for disruption—is not sufficiently compelling to justify a classification that would abridge first amendment rights.

MCMILLEN V. ITAWAMBA COUNTY SCHOOL DISTRICT

United States District Court, Northern District of Mississippi, 2010

702 F. Supp. 2d 699

DAVIDSON, DISTRICT JUDGE.

Plaintiff, Constance McMillen ("Constance"), is a senior at Itawamba Agricultural High School ("IAHS") in Fulton, Mississippi. Constance has been openly identified as a lesbian at school since the eighth grade. Last semester, Constance asked her girlfriend, who is a fellow student at IAHS, to be her date to the IAHS Junior and Senior prom ("prom") and her girlfriend accepted her invitation.

According to a Memorandum to IAHS Juniors and Seniors issued on February 5, 2010, the prom was scheduled to be held in the IAHS Commons on April 2, 2010. . . . Constance approached the assistant principal, Rick Mitchell, to ask permission to bring her girlfriend as her date to the prom. Constance was informed that they could attend with two guys as their dates but could not attend together as a couple.

Constance then met with Principal Trae Wiygul ("Wiygul") and Superintendent Teresa McNeese ("McNeese") to ask for permission to bring her girlfriend as her date to the prom and was told the two could attend separately but not together as a couple. In addition, Constance was informed that she and her girlfriend would not be allowed to slow dance together because it could "push people's buttons." Constance testified that Superintendent McNeese also informed her that if she and her girlfriend made anyone uncomfortable while at the prom, they would be "kicked out." Constance also inquired as to whether she would be allowed to wear a tuxedo to the prom. Both Wiygul and McNeese informed Constance that only boys were allowed to wear tuxedos. Further, after checking with the Itawamba County Board of Education, Superintendent McNeese informed Constance that girls were not allowed to even wear slacks and a nice top but must wear a dress. Disappointed by Defendants' answers, Constance contacted the ACLU. The ACLU then sent Defendants a letter demanding it change its policies which prevent Constance from attending the prom with a same-sex date and from wearing a tuxedo. * * *

On March 10, 2010, after [a] special meeting was held, the Itawamba County Board of Education, issued a statement to the press, announcing its intent to cancel the prom. The School Board stated in its announcement, in part:

> Due to the distractions to the educational process caused by recent events, the Itawamba School District has decided to not host a prom at Itawamba Agricultural High School this year. It is our hope that private citizens will organize an event for the juniors and seniors. However, at this time, we feel that it is in

the best interest of the Itawamba County School District, after
taking into consideration the education, safety, and well being of
our students, that the Itawamba County School District not host
a junior/senior prom at [IAHS].

* * * Constance testified that she considered it important to attend prom
because it is a "part of high school that everyone remembers" and that she
wanted to share that with her girlfriend who is special to her. Constance
wants to attend the prom with her girlfriend because she does not want to
hide her sexual orientation. Constance further testified that she feels that
the school is attempting to force her to pretend that she is someone she is
not by going with a male date. Constance testified that she believes gay
students have the same right as straight students to not only attend the
prom with the person they are dating but also to dance with that person.
According to Constance, "if [she] cannot share the prom experience with
[her] girlfriend then there is not any point in going." Constance also
believes that students should not be forced to wear clothes that conform
to traditional gender norms and testified that she wants to wear a tuxedo
to the prom so that she can express to her school community that "it's
perfectly okay for a woman to wear a tuxedo, and that the school
shouldn't be allowed to make girls wear a dress if that's not what they are
comfortable in." Constance does not want to attend the prom if IAHS does
not allow female students to wear tuxedos. * * *

In order for the court to grant a preliminary injunction, Constance
must establish the following elements:

(1) a substantial likelihood of success on the merits;

(2) a substantial threat that the plaintiff will suffer irreparable
injury if the injunction is denied;

(3) that the threatened injury to the plaintiff outweighs any
damage that an injunction might cause the defendant; and

(4) that granting the injunction will not disserve the public
interest.

a.   Substantial Likelihood of Success on the Merits

The First Amendment of the Constitution states that "Congress shall
make no law . . . abridging the freedom of speech." U.S. Const. amend. I.
"[I]f the constitutional conception of 'equal protection of the laws' means
anything, it must at the very least mean that a bare desire to harm a
politically unpopular group cannot constitute a legitimate governmental
interest." *Romer v. Evans*, 517 U.S. 620, 634–35, 116 S. Ct. 1620, 1628
134 L. Ed. 2d 855 (1996). The United States Supreme Court has
"recognized that the 'vigilant protection of constitutional freedoms is
nowhere more vital than in the community of American schools.'" The
Fifth Circuit has established that the "expression of one's identity and

affiliation to unique social groups" may constitute "speech" as envisioned by the First Amendment. *See Canady v. Bossier Parish Sch. Bd.*, 240 F.3d 437, 441 (5th Cir. 2001). The United States Supreme Court has also held that "states and their agencies, such as the Defendant, cannot set-out homosexuals for special treatment, neither inclusive or [sic] exclusive." *Collins v. Scottsboro City Bd. of Educ.*, CV-2008-90 (38th Judicial District March 28, 2008) (*citing Romer v. Evans*, 517 U.S. 620, 116 S. Ct. 1620, 134 L. Ed. 2d 855 (1996)). * * *

In *Fricke v. Lynch*, 491 F. Supp. 381, 385 (D.R.I. 1980), a factually similar case, the United States District Court of Rhode Island held that a male high school student's desire to take a same-sex date to his prom had significant expressive content which brought it within the ambit of the First Amendment. *See Fricke v. Lynch*, 491 F. Supp. at 385. The Rhode Island district court found that Fricke's belief that he had "a right to attend and participate just like all other students and that it would be dishonest to his own sexual identity to take a girl to the dance" coupled with the fact he felt "his attendance would have a certain political element and would be a statement for equal rights and human rights" is "the exact type of conduct" that "can be considered protected speech." *Id.* at 385.

In *Gay Students Organization of New Hampshire v. Bonner*, 509 F.2d 652, 659 (1st Cir. 1974), the First Circuit opined that "GSO social functions do not constitute 'pure speech', but conduct may have a communicative content sufficient to bring it within the ambit of the First Amendment." * * * The First Circuit held that the University's policy banning the GSO from holding social functions was content related and "the curtailing of expression which [the University] find[s] abhorrent or offensive cannot provide the important governmental interest upon which impairment of First Amendment freedoms must be predicated." *Gay Students Org.*, 509 F.2d at 662 (citations omitted).

According to the clearly established case law, Defendants have violated her First Amendment rights by denying Constance's request to bring her girlfriend as her date to the prom.

Constance further believes that females should be allowed to dress in non-gender-conforming attire, and that, in particular, she should be permitted to wear a tuxedo to the prom. In *Canady,* the Fifth Circuit recognized that "[c]lothing may also symbolize ethnic heritage religious beliefs, and political and social views." *Canady,* 240 F.3d at 440. The Fifth Circuit stated that "the choice to wear clothing as a symbol of an opinion or cause is undoubtedly protected under the First Amendment if the message is likely to be understood by those intended to view it." *Id.* at 441 (*citing Texas v. Johnson*, 491 U.S. 397, 404, 109 S. Ct. 2533, 105 L. Ed. 2d 342 (1989)).

The United States Supreme Court has held that "[i]n deciding whether particular conduct possesses sufficient communicative elements to bring the First Amendment into play, we have asked whether '[a]n intent to convey a particularized message was present, and [whether] the likelihood was great that the message would be understood by those who viewed it.' " * * *

In *Tinker*, students were suspended from school for wearing black armbands in protest of the Vietnam War. *See Tinker*, 393 U.S. at 508–14, 89 S. Ct. 733. The United States Supreme Court held that students may wear color patterns or styles with the intent to express a particular matter unless school officials can demonstrate the expression would "substantially interfere with the work of the school or impinge upon the rights of the other students." *Id.* at 509, 89 S. Ct. 733 (citations omitted).

In *ACT-UP v. Walp*, 755 F. Supp. 1281 (M.D. Pa. 1991), the District Court of the Middle District of Pennsylvania found that the Pennsylvania House of Representatives violated the Plaintiffs' First Amendment rights when it closed the gallery during the governor's speech to prevent members of ACT-UP from expressing their views in an attempt to raise public awareness of acquired immune deficiency syndrome (AIDS). * * *

In the case *sub judice*, Constance requested permission to wear a tuxedo, or even pants and a nice shirt, to her prom with the intent of communicating to the school community her social and political views that women should not be constrained to wear clothing that has traditionally been deemed "female" attire. * * *

The record shows Constance has been openly gay since eighth grade and she intended to communicate a message by wearing a tuxedo and to express her identity through attending prom with a same-sex date. The Court finds this expression and communication of her viewpoint is the type of speech that falls squarely within the purview of the First Amendment. * * * The Court finds that Constance's First Amendment rights have been violated and therefore, she has established * * * a substantial likelihood of success on the merits with respect to her First Amendment claim.

[The court went on to find that Constance had demonstrated both a substantial threat of imminent injury and that the threat of injury to her outweighed any injury that granting an injunction might cause.] * * *

d.   Public Interest

"[I]t is in the public's interest to protect rights guaranteed under the Constitution of the United States." The United States Supreme Court has stated, "[t]he right to speak freely and to promote diversity of ideas and programs is therefore one of the chief distinctions that sets us apart from totalitarian regimes." * * *

However, the Court is of the opinion that its failure to grant an injunction in this instance does not disserve the public interest. Defendants testified that a parent sponsored prom which is open to *all* IAHS students has been planned and is scheduled for April 2, 2010. Though the details of the "private" prom are unknown to the Court, Defendants have made representations, upon which this Court relies, that *all* IAHS students, including the Plaintiff, are welcome and encouraged to attend. The Court finds that requiring Defendants to step-back into a sponsorship role at this late date would only confuse and confound the community on the issue. Parents have taken the initiative to plan and pay for a "private" prom for the Juniors and Seniors of IAHS and to now require Defendants to host one as it had originally planned would defeat the purpose and efforts of those individuals.

In addition, the power and interests of an Article III Court has its limits and under the circumstances, the Court cannot go into the business of planning and overseeing a prom hosted by Defendants, especially in light of the fact that the parents of IAHS students have already undertaken such tasks. Therefore, the Court finds that issuing an injunction would be disruptive to the efforts of the community and would not be in the public's interest. * * *

[T]he Court finds that Plaintiff's motion for preliminary injunction should be denied. This case remains active and Plaintiff, is she so desires, will be permitted to amend her Complaint to seek compensatory damages and any other appropriate relief.

DOE V. YUNITS

Superior Court of Massachusetts, 2000
2000 WL 33162199

GILES, JUDGE.

Plaintiff Pat Doe ("plaintiff"), a fifteen-year-old student, has brought this action by her next friend, Jane Doe, requesting that this court prohibit defendants from excluding the plaintiff from South Junior High School ("South Junior High"), Brockton, Massachusetts, on the basis of the plaintiff's sex, disability, or gender identity and expression. Plaintiff has been diagnosed with gender identity disorder, which means that, although plaintiff was born biologically male, she has a female gender identity. Plaintiff seeks to attend school wearing clothes and fashion accouterments that are consistent with her gender identity. Defendants have informed plaintiff that she could not enroll in school this academic year if she wore girls' clothes or accessories. . . .

Plaintiff began attending South Junior High, a Brockton public school, in September 1998, as a 7th grader. In early 1999, plaintiff first began to express her female gender identity by wearing girls' make-up, shirts, and fashion accessories to school. South Junior High has a dress code which prohibits, among other things, "clothing which could be disruptive or distractive to the educational process or which could affect the safety of students." In early 1999, the principal, Kenneth Cardone ("Cardone"), would often send the plaintiff home to change if she arrived at school wearing girls' apparel. On some occasions, plaintiff would change and return to school; other times, she would remain home, too upset to return. In June 1999, after being referred to a therapist by the South Junior High, plaintiff was diagnosed with gender identity disorder. Plaintiff's treating therapist, Judith Havens ("Havens"), determined that it was medically and clinically necessary for plaintiff to wear clothing consistent with the female gender and that failure to do so could cause harm to plaintiff's mental health.

Plaintiff returned to school in September 1999, as an 8th grader, and was instructed by Cardone to come to his office every day so that he could approve the plaintiff's appearance. Some days the plaintiff would be sent home to change, sometimes returning to school dressed differently and sometimes remaining home. During the 1999–2000 school year, plaintiff stopped attending school, citing the hostile environment created by Cardone. Because of plaintiff's many absences during the 1999–2000 school year, plaintiff was required to repeat the 8th grade this year.

Over the course of the 1998–1999 and 1999–2000 school years, plaintiff sometimes arrived at school wearing such items as skirts and dresses, wigs, high-heeled shoes, and padded bras with tight shirts. The school faculty and administration became concerned because the plaintiff was experiencing trouble with some of her classmates. Defendants cite one occasion when the school adjustment counselor had to restrain a male student because he was threatening to punch the plaintiff for allegedly spreading rumors that the two had engaged in oral sex. Defendants also point to an instance when a school official had to break up a confrontation between the plaintiff and a male student to whom plaintiff persistently blew kisses. At another time, plaintiff grabbed the buttock of a male student in the school cafeteria. Plaintiff also has been known to primp, pose, apply make-up, and flirt with other students in class. Defendants also advance that the plaintiff sometimes called attention to herself by yelling and dancing in the halls. Plaintiff has been suspended at least three times for using the ladies' restroom after being warned not to.

On Friday, September 1, 2000, Cardone and Dr. Kenneth Sennett ("Sennett"), Senior Director for Pupil Personnel Services, met with the plaintiff relative to repeating the 8th grade. At that meeting, Cardone and Sennett informed the plaintiff that she would not be allowed to attend South Junior High if she were to wear any outfits disruptive to the educational process, specifically padded bras, skirts or dresses, or wigs. On September 21, 2000, plaintiff's grandmother tried to enroll plaintiff in school and was told by Cardone and Sennett that plaintiff would not be permitted to enroll if she wore any girls' clothing or accessories. Defendants allege that they have not barred the plaintiff from school but have merely provided limits on the type of dress the plaintiff may wear. Defendants claim it is the plaintiff's own choice not to attend school because of the guidelines they have placed on her attire. Plaintiff is not currently attending school, but the school has provided a home tutor for her to allow her to keep pace with her classmates. * * *

The Massachusetts Declaration of Rights, Article XVI (as amended by Article 77) provides, "the right of free speech shall not be abridged". . . . The analysis of this article is guided by federal free speech analysis. According to federal analysis, this court must first determine whether the plaintiff's symbolic acts constitute expressive speech which is protected, in this case, by Article VXI of the Massachusetts Declaration of Rights. *See Texas v. Johnson, supra,* [491 U.S. 397, 109 S. Ct. 2533, 105 L. Ed. 2d 342 (1989)] citing *Spence v. Washington, supra,* [418 U.S. 405, 94 S. Ct. 2727, 41 L. Ed. 2d 842 (1974)]. If the speech is expressive, the court must next determine if the defendants' conduct was impermissible because it was meant to suppress that speech. *See Texas v. Johnson,* 491 U.S. 397, 403, 105 L. Ed. 2d 342, 109 S. Ct. 2533 (1989), citing *United States v. O'Brien,* 391 U.S. 367, 377, 20 L. Ed. 2d 672, 88 S. Ct. 1673 (1968); see also *Spence v. Washington,* 418 U.S. 405, 414 n. 8, 41 L. Ed. 2d 842, 94 S. Ct. 2727 (1974). If the defendants' conduct is not related to the suppression of speech, furthers an important or substantial governmental interest, and is within the constitutional powers of the government, and if the incidental restriction on speech is no greater than necessary, the government's conduct is permissible. *See United States v. O'Brien, supra.* In addition, because this case involves public school students, suppression of speech that "materially and substantially interferes with the work of the school" is permissible. *See Tinker v. Des Moines Community School District,* 393 U.S. 503, 21 L. Ed. 2d 731, 738, 89 S. Ct. 733 (1969). * * *

Symbolic acts constitute expression if the actor's intent to convey a particularized message is likely to be understood by those perceiving the message. . . .

Plaintiff in this case is likely to establish that, by dressing in clothing and accessories traditionally associated with the female gender, she is expressing her identification with that gender. In addition, plaintiff's ability to express herself and her gender identity through dress is important to her health and well-being, as attested to by her treating therapist. Therefore, plaintiff's expression is not merely a personal preference but a necessary symbol of her very identity. . . .

This court must next determine if the plaintiff's message was understood by those perceiving it, i.e., the school faculty and plaintiff's fellow students. In the case at bar, defendants contend that junior high school students are too young to understand plaintiff's expression of her female gender identity through dress and that "not every defiant act by a high school student is constitutionally protected speech." *Id.* at 558. However . . . here there is strong evidence that plaintiff's message is well understood by faculty and students. The school's vehement response and some students' hostile reactions are proof of the fact that the plaintiff's message clearly has been received. Moreover, plaintiff is likely to establish, through testimony, that her fellow students are well aware of the fact that she is a biological male more comfortable wearing traditionally "female"-type clothing because of her identification with that gender. * * *

Plaintiff also will probably prevail on the merits of the second prong of the *Texas v. Johnson* test, that is, the defendants' conduct was meant to suppress plaintiff's speech. Defendants in this case have prohibited the plaintiff from wearing items of clothing that are traditionally labeled girls' clothing, such as dresses and skirts, padded bras, and wigs. This constitutes direct suppression of speech because biological females who wear items such as tight skirts to school are unlikely to be disciplined by school officials, as admitted by defendants' counsel at oral argument. . . . Therefore, the test set out in *United States v. O'Brien*, which permits restrictions on speech where the government motivation is not directly related to the content of the speech, cannot apply here. Further, defendants' argument that the school's policy is a content-neutral regulation of speech is without merit because, as has been discussed, the school is prohibiting the plaintiff from wearing clothes a biological female would be allowed to wear. Therefore, the plaintiff has a likelihood of fulfilling the *Texas v. Johnson* test that her speech conveyed a particularized message understood by others and that the defendants' conduct was meant to suppress that speech. * * *

This court also must consider if the plaintiff's speech "materially and substantially interferes with the work of the school." . . . Defendants argue that they are merely preventing disruptive conduct on the part of the plaintiff by restricting her attire at school. Their argument is unpersuasive. Given the state of the record thus far, the plaintiff has demonstrated a likelihood of proving that defendants, rather than attempting to restrict plaintiff's wearing of distracting items of clothing, are seeking to ban her from donning apparel that can be labeled "girls' clothes" and to encourage more conventional, male-oriented attire. Defendants argue that any other student who came to school dressed in distracting clothing would be disciplined as the plaintiff was. However, defendants overlook the fact that, if a female student came to school in a frilly dress or blouse, make-up, or padded bra, she would go, and presumably has gone, unnoticed by school officials. Defendants do not find plaintiff's clothing distracting *per se*, but, essentially, distracting simply because plaintiff is a biological male.

In addition to the expression of her female gender identity through dress, however, plaintiff has engaged in behavior in class and towards other students that can be seen as detrimental to the learning process. This deportment, however, is separate from plaintiff's dress. Defendants vaguely cite instances when the principal became aware of threats by students to beat up the "boy who dressed like a girl" to support the notion that plaintiff's dress alone is disruptive. To rule in defendants' favor in this regard, however, would grant those contentious students a "heckler's veto." *See Fricke v. Lynch*, 491 F. Supp. 381, 387 (D.R.I. 1980). The majority of defendants' evidence of plaintiff's disruption is based on plaintiff's actions as distinct from her mode of dress. Some of these acts may be a further expression of gender identity, such as applying make-up in class; but many are instances of misconduct for which any student would be punished. Regardless of plaintiff's gender identity, any student should be punished for engaging in harassing behavior towards classmates. Plaintiff is not immune from such punishment but, by the same token, should not be punished on the basis of dress alone.

Plaintiff has framed this issue narrowly as a question of whether or not it is appropriate for defendants to restrict the manner in which she can dress. Defendants, on the other hand, appear unable to distinguish between instances of conduct connected to plaintiff's expression of her female gender identity, such as the wearing of a wig or padded bra, and separate from it, such as grabbing a male student's buttocks or blowing kisses to a male student. The line between expression and flagrant behavior can blur, thereby rendering this case difficult for the court. It seems, however, that expression of gender identity through dress can be divorced from conduct in school that warrants punishment, regardless of the gender or gender identity of the offender. Therefore, a school should not be allowed to bar or discipline a student because of gender-identified dress but should be permitted to ban clothing that would be inappropriate if worn by any student, such as a theatrical costume, and to punish conduct that would be deemed offensive if committed by any student, such as harassing, threatening, or obscene behavior. *See Bethel v. Fraser*, 478 U.S. 675, 92 L. Ed. 2d 549, 106 S. Ct. 3159 (1986).

NOTES

1.   *Proms.* Aaron Fricke told his story of going to the prom in detail in Aaron Fricke, *One Life, One Prom, in* THE CHRISTOPHER STREET READER 21 (Michael Denneny et al. eds., 1983). There are reasons to believe that things may have changed since Fricke's struggle, at least in some parts of the country. Commentator Andrew Sullivan observes:

I grew up in a world where I literally never heard the word "homosexual" until I went to college. It is not uncommon to meet gay men in their early 20s who took a boy as their date to the high school prom. . . . [T]he psychological impact [of this cultural shift] on the younger generation cannot be overstated.

Andrew Sullivan, *The End of Gay Culture and the Future of Gay Life*, CHI. SUN-TIMES, Nov. 27, 2005, at B1. *See also* Julie Hubbard, *Bleckley School Officials Allowing Gay Prom Date*, MACON TELEGRAPH, Mar. 23, 2010 (story of gay teen receiving permission to bring his male prom date). In some schools, openly gay and lesbian students have been elected as homecoming king or queen. *Lesbian Becomes College Homecoming King*, ASSOCIATED PRESS, Mar. 2, 2006; Sarah Kershaw et al., *Gay Students Force New Look at Homecoming Traditions*, N.Y. TIMES, Nov. 27, 2004, at A12. In a twist, a lesbian couple fought for the right to run together for prom court. Their high school initially turned them down, insisting that there be both a male and female elected, but relented after the ACLU supported the couple. The couple did not win the election, but succeeded in getting the rules changed. Alayna Schulman, *Updated: Two Girls Fight for Chance to Be Foothill's 'Queen and Queen,'* http://www.redding.com/news/local/two-girls-fight-for-chance-to-be-foothills-prom-queen-and-queen-316cd1da-8083-5a5e-e053-0100007f30fe-377350321.html. In other high schools, gay students have staged their own prom. *See, e.g.*, Cheryl Winkelman, *Tracy's Inaugural Gay Prom Goes Smoothly Despite Threats*, ALAMEDA TIMES-STAR, Apr. 14, 2006.

Transgender students have also made their presence more visible at school dances. In 2013, Cassidy Lynn Campbell of Huntington Beach, California became the first transgender student to be elected homecoming queen at a public high school. Treye Green, *Who Is Cassidy Lynn Campbell? Meet Transgender Teen Crowned High School's Homecoming Queen*, INT'L BUS. TIMES (Sept. 21, 2013, 5:52 PM), http://www.ibtimes.com/who-cassidy-lynn-campbell-meet-transgender-teen-crowned-high-schools-homecoming-queen-1409254. Other transgender high school students have also been elected prom queen or king. *See, e.g.*, Ross Forman, *Lesbian Wins Prom King at Lane Tech*, WINDY CITY TIMES (June 23, 2013), http://www.windycitymedia group.com/lgbt/Lesbian-wins-prom-king-at-Lane-Tech/43366.html; *Transgender Teen Elected Prom Queen*, THE ADVOCATE (May 31, 2011, 5:40 PM), http://www.advocate.com/news/daily-news/2011/05/31/transgender-teen-elected-prom-queen.

However, as the events surrounding Constance McMillen's 2010 lawsuit reflect, problems still arise. Eventually, two private proms were held in Constance's community, both organized by parents. One, which a majority of the students attended, was not mentioned to McMillen. The second, which McMillen attended, had only five other student attendees and was deemed by media accounts to be a "fake prom." Subsequently, McMillen became a poster-child for the LGBT movement, including appearances on numerous TV shows and serving as a Grand Marshall of the 2010 New York City Pride Parade. *School Wrong, but Prom Won't Go On*, THE ADVOCATE, March 23,

2010, *available* at http://www.advocate.com/News/Daily_News/2010/03/23/ McMillens_School_Wrong_But_Prom_Wont_Have_to_Go_On/. In addition, she won a $35,000 settlement from the school district for the violation of her rights, found by the district judge who had previously denied injunctive relief. *See* Chris Joyner, *Mississippi School District Pays Lesbian Teen Over Prom*, USA TODAY, July 21, 2010, at 3A.

2.   *Gender Identity and Dress*. Compare the *Fricke*, *McMillen* and *Doe* cases. How are they similar and how are they different? The two issues intersect in a concrete way when a transgender student seeks to attend a prom in gender-variant clothing. *See* Meg Kissinger & Meg Jones, *Crossing the Line?; Lake Geneva Student Who Wore Dress to Prom Is Suspended, Fined $249*, MILWAUKEE J. SENTINEL, May 11, 2005, at B1; Shamus Toomey, *No Prom but Lots of Support for Man Who Wore Gown: School Officials Say He Violated Dress Code*, CHI. SUN-TIMES, May 26, 2006, at 4.

3.   *Gender Identity and School Bathrooms*. Among the most pressing issues for transgender youth in schools is access to bathrooms that correspond with gender identity. In a major ruling in 2016, the Fourth Circuit held that Gloucester High School must allow Gavin Grimm, a transgender boy, to use the bathroom consistent with his gender identity. *G.G. v. Gloucester County School Board*, 822 F. 3d 709 (4th Cir. 2016). Grimm had used the boys' room without incident for two months before some complaints from the community led the school district to require that students use the bathroom that corresponds to the sex they were assigned at birth or be furnished a private bathroom. Grimm relied on Title IX, a federal statute that bans sex discrimination in federally-funded schools. As this edition of the casebook goes to the press, the Supreme Court has stayed the preliminary injunction that had granted relief to Grimm while it decides whether to grant certiorari in the case. *Gloucester County School Board v. G.G.*, 136 S.Ct. 2442 (Aug. 3, 2016). Recall that we have seen similar issues about whether discrimination based on gender identity is a form of sex discrimination in Chapter 3, Section II.C and Chapter 4, Section II.B.3. Although Grimm was not litigated as a First Amendment case, several articles have argued that both dress and restroom access at school have significant expressive dimensions for transgender students. Laurel Grbach, Note and Comment, *Transgender Students Dress: Free Speech and Protected Expression in Public Schools*, 22 TEMP. POL. & CIV. RTS. L. REV. 526 (2013); Jeffrey Kosbie, *(No) State Interests in Regulating Gender: How Suppression of Gender Nonconformity Violates Freedom of Speech*, 19 WM. & MARY J. WOMEN & L. 187 (2013); Danielle Weatherby, *From Jack to Jill: Gender Expression as Protected Speech in the Modern Schoolhouse*, 39 N.Y.U. REV. L. & SOC. CHANGE 89 (2015).

4.   In general, the social and psychological obstacles for LGBT students can be intense. Rates of harassment directed against LGBT teenagers are high. *See* Rebecca Bethard, *Chalk Talk: New York's Harvey Milk School: A Viable Alternative*, 33 J.L. & Educ. 417, 417–18 (2004) (reporting a 1999 study indicating that 41.7% of LGBT students did not feel safe in school and

that 69% had experienced harassment). A 1989 report on youth suicide issued by the U.S. Department of Health and Human Services (HHS) reported that gay and lesbian youth were more likely to suffer chronic depression and alcoholism and were "2 to 3 times more likely to attempt suicide than other young people." Paul Gibson, *Gay Male and Lesbian Youth Suicide*, *in* U.S. Dep't of Health & Human Servs., 3 Report of the Secretary's Task Force on Youth Suicide 110 (Marcia R. Feinleib ed., 1989). The report also found that such youth were more often forced to leave their homes as "push-aways" or "throw-aways" rather than running away on their own. *Id.* at 112. Gibson's stated assumptions that homosexuality was natural and that homosexuals should not be subject to discrimination proved quite controversial and drew public disapproval of the report from then-HHS Secretary Louis W. Sullivan.

In 2011, the U.S. Centers for Disease Control and Prevention (CDC) released the results of a new study on lesbian, gay, and bisexual youth. Dana Rudolph, *Gay, Lesbian, Bisexual Youth More at Risk, Federal Study Finds*, Keen News Serv. (June 8, 2011), http://www.keennewsservice.com/2011/06/08/gay-lesbian-bisexual-youth-more-at-risk-federal-study-finds/. The CDC found that gay and lesbian students had higher risks than heterosexual students in seven of ten major health risk categories: behaviors related to violence, attempted suicide, tobacco use, alcohol use, other drug use, sexual behaviors, and weight management. *Id.* Bisexual students were at even higher risk. *Id.*

Recent state-level reports also suggest that LGBT youths continue to have higher incidence of suicide attempts. *See, e.g.*, Cal. Safe Sch. Coal. & 4-H Ctr. for Youth Dev., Univ. Cal., Davis, Safe Place to Learn: Consequence of Harassment Based on Actual or Perceived Sexual Orientation and Gender Non-Conformity and Steps for Making Schools Safer 8 (2004), *available at* http://casafeschools.org/SafePlacetoLearnLow.pdf (finding that 45% of "students harassed based on actual or perceived sexual orientation . . . seriously consider[ed] suicide" and 35% "made a plan for suicide," compared to 14% and 9% for other students); Mass. Dep't of Educ., 2003 Youth Risk Behavior Survey Results 49 (2004) (finding that 32% of "sexual minority youth" attempt suicide, as compared to 7% of other students). Such suicides received increased news coverage in 2010, when a spate of a half-dozen teenagers killed themselves after anti-gay bullying. *See* Jeremy Hubbard, *Fifth Gay Teen Suicide in Three Weeks Sparks Debate*, ABC News (Oct. 3, 2010), http://abcnews.go.com/US/gay-teen-suicide-sparks-debate/story?id=11788128. The suicides led to the "It Gets Better" campaign, organized by columnist Dan Savage, in which individuals posted videos to YouTube indicating support for gay youth, including such visible supporters as President Obama. *See* Brian Stelter, *Campaign Offers Help to Gay Youths*, N.Y. Times, Oct. 19, 2010, at A16.

5.   Many states have enacted laws providing protection to gay students against discrimination and/or bullying based on their sexual orientation and/or gender identity. For a state-by-state review of these laws, http://www.glsen.org/article/state-maps (maintained by the Gay, Lesbian and Straight

Education Network ("GLSEN"). But laws against bullying and harassment have resulted in some pushback, as evidenced by the eight states with "no promo homo" laws that bar teachers from speaking in a positive light (or at all, in some states) about LGBT issues. *See id.*

6. In recent years, gay-straight alliances have proliferated in high schools across the country. In part, this growth has been spurred by the federal Equal Access Act, enacted in 1984, which prohibits public secondary schools in certain circumstances from discriminating against students desiring to hold meetings on the basis of political, religious, philosophical, or other content of the speech. The EAA has increasingly become part of the litigation landscape. In an example of a successful case, the American Civil Liberties Union pressured a public high school in Corpus Christi, Texas into recognizing a gay-straight alliance by threatening to sue under the EAA. *Flour Bluff High School Acknowledges Gay-Straight Alliance Club Has the Right to Meet*, AMERICAN CIVIL LIBERTIES UNION (Mar. 9, 2011), https://www.aclu.org/lgbt-rights/flour-bluff-high-school-acknowledges-gay-straight-alliance-club-has-right-meet. For a general overview, see Todd A. DeMitchell & Richard Fossey, *Student Speech: School Boards, Gay/Straight Alliances, and the Equal Access Act*, 2008 B.Y.U. EDUC. & L.J. 89 (2008); Eric W. Schulze, *Gay-Related Student Groups and the Equal Access Act*, 196 ED. L. REP. 369 (2005). In 2011, the U.S. Department of Education issued guidelines about the Act intended "to provide schools with the information and resources they need to help ensure that all students, including LGBT and gender non-conforming students, have a safe place to learn, meet, share experiences, and discuss matters that are important to them." *Key Policy Letters from the Education Secretary and Deputy Secretary*, U.S. DEP'T OF EDUC. (June 14, 2011), http://www2.ed.gov/policy/elsec/guid/secletter/110607. html.

7. In light of the obstacles confronted by openly gay students in some high schools, consider the idea that school districts ought to offer students the option of attending a separate LGBT school, like the Harvey Milk High School in New York. That school aims to protect LGBT youth from physical violence and emotional harm. For more about Harvey Milk High, see *The Harvey Milk High School*, Hetrick-Martin Inst., http://www.hmi.org/page. aspx?pid=230). The Harvey Milk program has inspired some others around the country. *See* Jessica Caefati, *Gay High Schools Offer Haven From Bullies," http://www.usnews.com/education/articles/2008/12/31/gay-high-schools-offer-a-haven-from-bullies* (discussing Alliance High School in Milwaukee); *Charter High School*, http://www.lalgbtcenter.org/charter_high_school (describing the independent school for LGBT students and straight allies operated by the Los Angeles LGBT Center).

8. Anti-gay bullying and harassment cases are not restricted to incidents at K–12 schools. One particularly controversial case involved college roommates at Rutgers University. In 2010, Dharun Ravi and another classmate, Molly Wei, used a webcam to spy on Ravi's roommate, Tyler Clementi, having sex with a man. Lisa W. Foderaro, *Private Moment Made*

Public, Then a Fatal Jump, N.Y. Times, Sept. 30, 2010, at A1. Ravi and Wei streamed Clementi's sexual encounter on the Internet and encouraged their friends to watch. *Id.* Only three days later, Clementi committed suicide. In 2012, Wei made a deal with the prosecution, but Ravi was convicted on fifteen charges and sentenced to thirty days in jail. Kate Zernike, *Judge Defends Penalty in Rutgers Spying Case, Saying It Fits Crime*, N.Y. Times, May 31, 2012, at A22. Ravi's trial raised questions as to whether his actions should be considered a hate crime. *See, e.g.*, Lila Shapiro, *Dharun Ravi Appeals Highlight the Continued Hate-Crime Law Debate*, Huffington Post (June 13, 2012, 4:51 PM), http://www.huffingtonpost.com/2012/06/13/dharun-ravi-appeals-hate-crime_n_1594320.html. The case brought tremendous attention to the anti-LGBT bullying issue. For a review of the case that urges a nuanced understanding of students like Tyler Clementi, see Andrew Gilden, *Cyberbullying and the Innocence Narrative*, 48 Harv. C.R.-C.L. L. Rev. 357 (2013) (arguing that the media oversimplified Clementi's narrative by painting him as only a victim).

9. In the 1970s and 1980s, the major litigation battles on college campuses involved securing recognition, funding, and equal facility access for LGBT student groups on campus. Many state universities fought student groups on this score, and the groups compiled an impressive record of litigation victories. *See, e.g., Gay & Lesbian Students Ass'n v. Gohn*, 850 F.2d 361 (8th Cir. 1988); *Gay Student Servs. v. Tex. A & M Univ.*, 737 F.2d 1317 (5th Cir. 1984), *cert. denied*, 471 U.S. 1001, 105 S.Ct. 1860, 85 L.Ed.2d 155 (1985); *Gay Lib v. Univ. of Mo.*, 558 F.2d 848 (8th Cir. 1977), *cert. denied sub nom. Ratchford v. Gay Lib*, 434 U.S. 1080, 98 S. Ct. 1276, 55 L. ed. 2d 789 (1978); *Gay Alliance of Students v. Matthews*, 544 F.2d 162 (4th Cir. 1976); *Gay Students Org. of Univ. of N.H. v. Bonner*, 509 F.2d 652 (1st Cir. 1974); *Student Coalition for Gay Rights v. Austin Peay State Univ.*, 477 F. Supp. 1267 (M.D. Tenn. 1979); *Wood v. Davison*, 351 F. Supp. 543 (N.D. Ga. 1972). *See also* Jane S. Schacter, *Sexual Orientation, Social Change, and the Courts*, 54 Drake L. Rev. 861, 873 (2006) ("By interpreting the First Amendment to require that universities recognize and provide space to gay student groups, courts helped to establish a visible gay presence on college campuses. Student activism was the driving force in establishing this presence, but the substantial string of litigation victories was necessary to counter the recalcitrance of several universities. This was no small accomplishment. Coerced gay invisibility has historically been a central part of gay inequality. And, these cases facilitated not only visibility, but subsequent student and university activism in support of a broader range of non-discrimination policies.").

10. Compared to students at public universities, LGBT students wishing to organize on private college campuses have confronted additional obstacles. In 1987 in the District of Columbia, gay students at a private Catholic school, Georgetown University, filed suit under the local human rights act, which prohibits discrimination in public and private educational institutions on the basis of sexual orientation. Georgetown interposed a First

Amendment defense, arguing that forced recognition of the gay student group would violate its rights of free exercise of religion. The District of Columbia's highest court, the D.C. Court of Appeals, reached a compromise that neither party contemplated in their pleadings. It chose not to interpret the local human rights law as requiring Georgetown to "endorse" the student group, agreeing that this would violate the school's First Amendment rights. It did interpret the law, however, to require Georgetown to grant equal benefits to the group. "Although a compelling state interest may justify regulation of religiously motivated conduct," the court reasoned, "nothing can penetrate the constitutional shield protecting against official coercion to renounce a religious belief or to endorse a principle opposed to that belief." *Gay Rights Coalition of Georgetown Univ. Law Ctr. v. Georgetown Univ.*, 536 A.2d 1, 25 (D.C. 1987). With regard to the use of University resources, the court held that the District's compelling interest in eradicating discrimination on the basis of sexual orientation outweighed the University's First Amendment religious rights. Over time, Georgetown became more hospitable to LGBT students. In 2008, the school opened an LGBTQ resource center in response to student protests about the school's response to anti-gay incidents. Kyle Spencer, *A Rainbow over Catholic Colleges*, N.Y. Times, July 30, 2013, at ED22. In 2013, Georgetown elected its first openly gay student body president. *Id.*

11. LGBT students can face particular difficulties at religiously affiliated colleges and universities. Some Christian schools prohibit "homosexual behavior," raising questions for gay and lesbian students about whether they could lose scholarships or be expelled for holding hands with a partner or posting a picture on a gay website. Erik Eckholm, *Even on Religious Campuses, Students Fight for Gay Identity*, N.Y. Times, Apr. 19, 2011, at A1. For an overview of recent developments at several schools, see David R. Wheeler, *The LGBT Politics of Christian Colleges*, THE ATLANTIC, March 14, 2016, http://www.theatlantic.com/education/archive/2016/03/the-lgbt-politics-of-christian-colleges/473373/.

12. Transgender students face additional challenges when they attend, or wish to attend, single-sex colleges and universities. Smith College rejected a transgender woman's application in 2013 because government documents listed the applicant as male. Zach Howard, *Elite Women's College Rejects Transgender Student, Prompts Outcry*, Reuters (Mar. 28, 2013, 4:51 PM), http://www.reuters.com/article/2013/03/28/us-usa-college-transgender-idUSB RE92R0YT20130328. In response, activists pressured Smith to form a committee to address transgender applications. Glennisha Morgan, *Smith College Plans Committee to Address Transgender Student Applicants*, Huffington Post (May 5, 2013, 8:38 PM), http://www.huffingtonpost.com/2013/05/03/smith-college-transgender-committee-_n_3209606.html.   Ultimately, Smith changed its policy. *See Transgender Students at Women's Colleges*, N.Y. TIMES, May 5, 2015, http://www.nytimes.com/2015/05/05/opinion/transgender-students-at-womens-colleges.html?_r=0 (editorial noting with approval that Smith joined some other women's colleges in deciding to admit

transgender women and permitting current students admitted as females, but transitioning to male, to remain at Smith).

B. COUNTERING ASSERTIONS OF LGBT IDENTITY

HARPER V. POWAY UNIFIED SCHOOL DISTRICT

United States Court of Appeals, Ninth Circuit, 2006
445 F.3d 1166, *vacated* 127 S. Ct. 1484 (2007) (mem.)

REINHARDT, CIRCUIT JUDGE.

May a public high school prohibit students from wearing T-shirts with messages that condemn and denigrate other students on the basis of their sexual orientation? Appellant in this action is a sophomore at Poway High School who was ordered not to wear a T-shirt to school that read, "BE ASHAMED, OUR SCHOOL EMBRACED WHAT GOD HAS CONDEMNED" handwritten on the front, and "HOMOSEXUALITY IS SHAMEFUL" handwritten on the back. He appeals the district court's order denying his motion for a preliminary injunction. Because he is not likely to succeed on the merits, we affirm the district court's order. Poway High School ("the School") has had a history of conflict among its students over issues of sexual orientation. In 2003, the School permitted a student group called the Gay-Straight Alliance to hold a "Day of Silence" at the School which, in the words of an Assistant Principal, is intended to "teach tolerance of others, particularly those of a different sexual orientation." During the days surrounding the 2003 "Day of Silence," a series of incidents and altercations occurred on the school campus as a result of anti-homosexual comments that were made by students. One such confrontation required the Principal to separate students physically. According to David LeMaster, a teacher at Poway, several students were suspended as a result of these conflicts. Moreover, a week or so after the "Day of Silence," a group of heterosexual students informally organized a "Straight-Pride Day," during which they wore T-shirts which displayed derogatory remarks about homosexuals. According to Assistant Principal Lynell Antrim, some students were asked to remove the shirts and did so, while others "had an altercation and were suspended for their actions."

Because of these conflicts in 2003, when the Gay-Straight Alliance sought to hold another "Day of Silence" in 2004, the School required the organization to consult with the Principal to "problem solve" and find ways to reduce tensions and potential altercations. On April 21, 2004, the date of the 2004 "Day of Silence," appellant Tyler Chase Harper wore a T-shirt to school on which "I WILL NOT ACCEPT WHAT GOD HAS CONDEMNED," was handwritten on the front and "HOMOSEXUALITY IS SHAMEFUL 'Romans 1:27' " was handwritten on the back. There is no evidence in the record that any school staff saw Harper's T-shirt on that day. The next day, April 22, 2004, Harper wore the same T-shirt to school, except that the front of the shirt read "BE ASHAMED, OUR SCHOOL EMBRACED WHAT GOD HAS CONDEMNED," while the back retained the same message as before, "HOMOSEXUALITY IS SHAMEFUL 'Romans 1:27.'" LeMaster, Harper's second period teacher, noticed Harper's shirt and observed "several students off-task talking about" the shirt. LeMaster, recalling the altercations that erupted as a result of "anti-homosexual speech" during the previous year's "Day of Silence," explained to Harper that he believed that the shirt was "inflammatory," that it violated the School's dress code, and that it "created a negative and hostile working environment for others." When Harper refused to remove his shirt and asked to speak to an administrator, LeMaster gave him a dress code violation card to take to the front office.

When Harper arrived at the front office, he met Assistant Principal Antrim. She told Harper that the "Day of Silence" was "not about the school promoting homosexuality but rather it was a student activity trying to raise other students' awareness regarding tolerance in their judgement [sic] of others." Antrim believed that Harper's shirt "was inflammatory under the circumstances and could cause disruption in the educational setting." Like LeMaster, she also recalled the altercations that had arisen as a result of anti-homosexual speech one year prior. According to her affidavit, she "discussed [with Harper] ways that he and students of his faith could bring a positive light onto this issue without the condemnation that he displayed on his shirt." Harper was informed that if he removed the shirt he could return to class. When Harper again refused to remove his shirt, the Principal, Scott Fisher, spoke with him, explaining his concern that the shirt was "inflammatory" and that it was the School's "intent to avoid physical conflict on campus." Fisher also explained to Harper that it was not healthy for students to be addressed in such a derogatory manner. According to Fisher, Harper informed him that he had already been "confronted by a group of students on campus" and was "involved in a tense verbal conversation" earlier that morning. The Principal eventually decided that Harper could not wear his shirt on campus, a decision that, he asserts, was influenced by "the fact that during the previous year, there was tension on campus surrounding the Day of Silence between certain gay and straight students." Fisher proposed some alternatives to wearing the shirt, all of which Harper turned down. Harper asked two times to be suspended. Fisher "told him that [he] did not want him suspended from school, nor did [he] want him to have something in his disciplinary record because of a stance he felt strongly about." Instead, Fisher told Harper that he would be required to remain in the front office for the remainder of the school day. * * *

Harper remained in the office for the last period of the day, after which he was instructed to proceed directly off campus. Harper was not suspended, no disciplinary record was placed in his file, and he received full attendance credit for the day.

[Harper filed a lawsuit raising several constitutional claims, including one based on his right to free speech. The district c-ourt denied Harper's motion for a preliminary injunction. Harper then filed an interlocutory appeal.]

The district court concluded that Harper failed to demonstrate a likelihood of success on the merits of his claim that the School violated his First Amendment right to free speech because, under *Tinker v. Des Moines Independent Community School District*, the evidence in the record was sufficient to permit the school officials to "reasonably . . . forecast substantial disruption of or material interference with school activities." 393 U.S. 503, 514 (1969). . . . We affirm the district court's denial of the requested preliminary injunction. Although we, like the district court, rely on *Tinker*, we rely on a different provision—that schools may prohibit speech that "intrudes upon . . . the rights of other students." *Tinker*, 393 U.S. at 508.

Public schools are places where impressionable young persons spend much of their time while growing up. They do so in order to receive what society hopes will be a fair and full education—an education without which they will almost certainly fail in later life, likely sooner rather than later. *See Brown v. Bd. of Educ.*, 347 U.S. 483, 493 (1954) ("[I]t is doubtful that any child may reasonably be expected to succeed in life if he is denied the opportunity of an education."). The public school, with its free education, is the key to our democracy. Almost all young Americans attend public schools. During the time they do—from first grade through twelfth—students are discovering what and who they are. Often, they are insecure. Generally, they are vulnerable to cruel, inhuman, and prejudiced treatment by others.

The courts have construed the First Amendment as applied to public schools in a manner that attempts to strike a balance between the free speech rights of students and the special need to maintain a safe, secure and effective learning environment. . . . In *Tinker*, the Supreme Court confirmed a student's right to free speech in public schools. In balancing that right against the state interest in maintaining an ordered and effective public education system, however, the Court declared that a student's speech rights could be curtailed under two circumstances. First, a school may regulate student speech that would "impinge upon the rights of other students." Second, a school may prohibit student speech that would result in "substantial disruption of or material interference with school activities." Because, as we explain below, the School's prohibition of the wearing of the demeaning T-shirt is constitutionally permissible under the first of the *Tinker* prongs, we conclude that the district court did not abuse its discretion in finding that Harper failed to demonstrate a likelihood of success on the merits of his free speech claim.

* * * Harper argues that *Tinker*'s reference to the "rights of other students" should be construed narrowly to involve only circumstances in which a student's right to be free from direct physical confrontation is infringed. * * *

We conclude that Harper's wearing of his T-shirt "colli[des] with the rights of other students" in the most fundamental way. Public school students who may be injured by verbal assaults on the basis of a core identifying characteristic such as race, religion, or sexual orientation, have a right to be free from such attacks while on school campuses. As *Tinker* clearly states, students have the right to "be secure and to be let alone." *Id.* Being secure involves not only freedom from physical assaults but from psychological attacks that cause young people to question their self-worth and their rightful place in society. The "right to be let alone" has been recognized by the Supreme Court, of course, as " 'the most comprehensive of rights and the right most valued by civilized men.' " Indeed, the "recognizable privacy interest in avoiding unwanted communication" is perhaps most important "when persons are 'powerless to avoid' it." Because minors are subject to mandatory attendance requirements, the Court has emphasized "the obvious concern on the part of parents, and school authorities acting in loco parentis, to protect children—especially in a captive audience. . . ." Although name-calling is ordinarily protected outside the school context, "[s]tudents cannot hide behind the First Amendment to protect their 'right' to abuse and intimidate other students at school."

Speech that attacks high school students who are members of minority groups that have historically been oppressed, subjected to verbal and physical abuse, and made to feel inferior, serves to injure and intimidate them, as well as to damage their sense of security and interfere with their opportunity to learn. The demeaning of young gay and lesbian students in a school environment is detrimental not only to their psychological health and well-being, but also to their educational development. Indeed, studies demonstrate that "academic underachievement, truancy, and dropout are prevalent among homosexual youth and are the probable consequences of violence and verbal and physical abuse at school." Susanne M. Stronski Huwiler and Gary Remafedi, *Adolescent Homosexuality*, 33 REV. JUR. U.I.P.R. REV. JUR. U.I.P.R. 151, 164 (1999); see also Thomas A. Mayes, *Confronting Same-Sex, Student-to-Student Sexual Harassment: Recommendations for Educators and Policy Makers*, 29 FORDHAM URB. L.J. 641, 655 (2001) (describing how gay students are at a greater risk of school failure and dropping out, most likely as a result of "social pressure and isolation"); Amy Lovell, *"Other Students Always Used to Say, 'Look At The Dykes' "*:

Protecting Students From Peer Sexual Orientation Harassment, 86 CAL. L. REV. 617, 625–28 (1998) (summarizing the negative effects on gay students of peer sexual orientation harassment). One study has found that among teenage victims of anti-gay discrimination, 75% experienced a decline in academic performance, 39% had truancy problems and 28% dropped out of school. *See* Courtney Weiner, Note, *Sex Education: Recognizing Anti-Gay Harassment as Sex Discrimination Under Title VII and Title IX*, 37 COLUM. HUM. RTS. L. REV. 189, 225 (2005). Another study confirmed that gay students had difficulty concentrating in school and feared for their safety as a result of peer harassment, and that verbal abuse led some gay students to skip school and others to drop out altogether. HUMAN RIGHTS WATCH, HATRED IN THE HALLWAYS (1999), http://hrw.org/reports/2001/uslgbt/Final-05.htm#P609_91364. Indeed, gay teens suffer a school dropout rate over three times the national average. NAT'L MENTAL HEALTH ASS'N, BULLYING IN SCHOOLS: HARASSMENT PUTS GAY YOUTH AT RISK, http://www.nmha.org/pbedu/backtoschool/bullying GayYouth.pdf; see also Maurice R. Dyson, *Safe Rules or Gays' Schools? The Dilemma of Sexual Orientation Segregation in Public Education*, 7 U. PA. J. CONST. L. 183, 187 (2004) (gay teens face greater risks of "dropping out [and] performing poorly in school"); Kelli Armstrong, *The Silent Minority Within a Minority: Focusing on the Needs of Gay Youth in Our Public Schools*, 24 GOLDEN GATE U. L. REV. 67, 76–77 (1994) (describing how abuse by peers causes gay youth to experience social isolation and drop out of school). In short, it is well established that attacks on students on the basis of their sexual orientation are harmful not only to the students' health and welfare, but also to their educational performance and their ultimate potential for success in life.

Those who administer our public educational institutions need not tolerate verbal assaults that may destroy the self-esteem of our most vulnerable teenagers and interfere with their educational development. * * *

The dissent claims that we should not take notice of the fact that gay students are harmed by derogatory messages such as Harper's because there is no "evidence" that they are in fact injured by being shamed or humiliated by their peers. It is simply not a novel concept, however, that such attacks on young minority students can be harmful to their self-esteem and to their ability to learn. As long ago as in *Brown v. Board of Education*, the Supreme Court recognized that "[a] sense of inferiority affects the motivation of a child to learn." 347 U.S. at 494, 74 S.Ct. 686 (internal quotation marks omitted). If a school permitted its students to wear shirts reading, "Negroes: Go Back To Africa," no one would doubt that the message would be harmful to young black students. So, too, in the case of gay students, with regard to messages such as those written on Harper's T-shirt. As our dissenting colleague recently concluded, "[y]ou don't need an expert witness to figure out" the self-evident effect of certain policies or messages. *Jespersen v. Harrah's Operating Co., Inc.*, 444 F.3d 1104, 1117, at *13 (9th Cir. 2006) (Kozinski, Circuit Judge, dissenting). * * *

The dissent takes comfort in the fact that there is a political disagreement regarding homosexuality in this country. We do not deny that there is, just as there was a longstanding political disagreement about racial equality that reached its peak in the 1950's and about whether religious minorities should hold high office that lasted at least until after the 1960 presidential election, or whether blacks or Jews should be permitted to attend private universities and prep schools, work in various industries such as banks, brokerage houses, and Wall Street law firms, or stay at prominent resorts or hotels. Such disagreements may justify social or political debate, but they do not justify students in high schools or elementary schools assaulting their fellow students with demeaning statements: by calling gay students shameful, by labeling black students inferior or by wearing T-shirts saying that Jews are doomed to Hell. Perhaps our dissenting colleague believes that one can condemn homosexuality without condemning homosexuals. If so, he is wrong. To say that homosexuality is shameful is to say, necessarily, that gays and lesbians are shameful. There are numerous locations and opportunities available to those who wish to advance such an argument. It is not necessary to do so by directly condemning, to their faces, young students trying to obtain a fair and full education in our public schools. * * *

In his declaration in the district court, the school principal justified his actions on the basis that "any shirt which is worn on campus which speaks in a derogatory manner towards an individual or group of individuals is not healthy for young people. . . ." If, by this, the principal meant that all such shirts may be banned under *Tinker*, we do not agree. T-shirts proclaiming, "Young Republicans Suck," or "Young Democrats Suck," for example, may not be very civil but they would certainly not be sufficiently damaging to the individual or the educational process to warrant a limitation on the wearer's First Amendment rights. Similarly, T-shirts that denigrate the President, his administration, or his policies, or otherwise invite political disagreement or debate, including debates over the war in Iraq, would not fall within the "rights of others" *Tinker* prong.

Although we hold that the School's restriction of Harper's right to carry messages on his T-shirt was permissible under *Tinker*, we reaffirm the importance of preserving student speech about controversial issues generally and protecting the bedrock principle that students "may not be confined to the expression of those sentiments that are officially approved." *Tinker*. It is essential that students have the opportunity to

SEXUALITY, GENDER, & THE FIRST AMENDMENT

engage in full and open political expression, both in and out of the school environment. Engaging in controversial political speech, even when it is offensive to others, is an important right of all Americans and learning the value of such freedoms is an essential part of a public school education. Indeed, the inculcation of "the fundamental values necessary to the maintenance of a democratic political system" is "truly the 'work of the schools.'" Limitations on student speech must be narrow, and applied with sensitivity and for reasons that are consistent with the fundamental First Amendment mandate. Accordingly, we limit our holding to instances of derogatory and injurious remarks directed at students' minority status such as race, religion, and sexual orientation. Moreover, our decision is based not only on the type and degree of injury the speech involved causes to impressionable young people, but on the locale in which it takes place. *See Tinker* (student rights must be construed "in light of the special characteristics of the school environment"). Thus, it is limited to conduct that occurs in public high schools (and in elementary schools). As young students acquire more strength and maturity, and specifically as they reach college age, they become adequately equipped emotionally and intellectually to deal with the type of verbal assaults that may be prohibited during their earlier years. Accordingly, we do not condone the use in public colleges or other public institutions of higher learning of restrictions similar to those permitted here.

Finally, we emphasize that the School's actions here were no more than necessary to prevent the intrusion on the rights of other students. Aside from prohibiting the wearing of the shirt, the School did not take the additional step of punishing the speaker: Harper was not suspended from school nor was the incident made a part of his disciplinary record. * * *

The dissent claims that although the School may have been justified in banning discussion of the subject of sexual orientation altogether, it cannot "gag[ ] only those who oppose the Day of Silence." As we have explained, however, although *Tinker* does not allow schools to restrict the non-invasive, non-disruptive expression of political viewpoints, it does permit school authorities to restrict "one particular opinion" if the expression would "impinge upon the rights of other students" or substantially disrupt school activities. *Tinker.* Accordingly, a school may permit students to discuss a particular subject without being required to allow them to launch injurious verbal assaults that intrude upon the rights of other students.

"A school need not tolerate student speech that is inconsistent with its basic educational mission, [ ] even though the government could not censor similar speech outside the school." Part of a school's "basic educational mission" is the inculcation of "fundamental values of habits and manners of civility essential to a democratic society." For this reason, public schools may permit, and even encourage, discussions of tolerance, equality, and democracy without being required to provide equal time for student or other speech espousing intolerance, bigotry, or hatred. As we have explained, because a school sponsors a "Day of Religious Tolerance," it need not permit its students to wear T-shirts reading, "Jews Are Christ-Killers" or "All Muslims Are Evil Doers." Such expressions would be "wholly inconsistent with the 'fundamental values' of public school education." Similarly, a school that permits a "Day of Racial Tolerance," may restrict a student from displaying a swastika or a Confederate Flag. * * *

We again emphasize that we do not suggest that all debate as to issues relating to tolerance or equality may be prohibited. As we have stated repeatedly, we consider here only the question of T-shirts, banners, and other similar items bearing slogans that injure students with respect to their core characteristics. Other issues must await another day. * * *

KOZINSKI, CIRCUIT JUDGE, dissenting:

While I find this a difficult and troubling case, I can agree with neither the majority's rationale nor its conclusion. On the record to date, the school authorities have offered no lawful justification for banning Harper's t-shirt and the district court should therefore have enjoined them from doing so pending the outcome of this case. * * *

School authorities may ban student speech based on the existence of "any facts which might reasonably [lead] school authorities to forecast substantial disruption." *Tinker*. The school authorities here have shown precious little to support an inference that Harper's t-shirt would "materially disrupt[ ] classwork." [Although the majority opinion ruled only on the "rights of others" prong of *Tinker*, the dissent offered a lengthy challenge to the factual basis for a finding of "substantial disruption" under the other *Tinker* prong. Much of this part of the dissent is omitted].

But there is a more fundamental issue here. The record reveals quite clearly that Harper's t-shirt was not an out-of-the-blue affront to fellow students who were minding their own business. Rather, Harper wore his t-shirt in response to the Day of Silence, a political activity that was sponsored or at the very least tolerated by school authorities. The Day of Silence is a protest sponsored by the Gay, Lesbian and Straight Education Network (GLSEN). According to a GLSEN press release, the Day of Silence is "an annual, national student-led effort in which participants take a vow of silence to peacefully protest the discrimination and harassment faced by lesbian, gay, bisexual and transgender (LGBT) youth in schools." Press Release, GLSEN, A New Record for the Day of Silence (Apr. 14, 2004), available at http://www.glsen.org/cgi-bin/iowa/all/news/record/1655.html. The point of this protest, as I understand it, is to promote tolerance toward all students, regardless of their sexual orientation.

Tolerance is a civic virtue, but not one practiced by all members of our society toward all others. This may be unfortunate, but it is a reality we must accept in a pluralistic society. Specifically, tolerance toward homosexuality and homosexual conduct is anathema to those who believe that intimate relations among people of the same sex are immoral or sinful. So long as the subject is kept out of the school environment, these differences of opinion need not clash. But a visible and highly publicized political action by those on one side of the issue will provoke those on the other side to express a different point of view, if only to avoid the implication that they agree. *See* Robert Bolt, A Man for All Seasons act 2, at 88 (1962) ("The maxim of the law is 'Silence gives consent.' ").

Given the history of violent confrontation between those who support the Day of Silence and those who oppose it, the school authorities may have been justified in banning the subject altogether by denying both sides permission to express their views during the school day. I find it far more problematic—and more than a little ironic—to try to solve the problem of violent confrontations by gagging only those who oppose the Day of Silence and the point of view it represents. * * *

I cannot imagine that my colleagues would approve this in other situations. Say, for example, one school group—perhaps the Young Republicans—were to organize a day of support for the war in Iraq by encouraging students to wear a yellow armband. And suppose that other students responded by wearing t-shirts with messages such as "Marines are Murderers" and "U.S. Bombs Kill Babies." If a student whose brother was killed in Iraq assaulted a student wearing one of the anti-war t-shirts, would we approve a school's response that banned the t-shirts but continued to permit the yellow armbands? Not to worry, says the majority, because students can still sport t-shirts that criticize "the President, his administration, or his policies, or otherwise invite political disagreement or debate." But acceptance of homosexuality is a political disagreement and debate. It's not at all clear to me how one can criticize public officers and their policies without also addressing the controversial policies they adopt. For example, in 2004, San Francisco mayor Gavin Newsom issued marriage licenses to nearly 4,000 gay and lesbian couples. While some people view this as a courageous and principled action, others consider it an abomination. It's not at all clear to me how those in the latter camp could go about expressing their vehement disagreement with Mayor Newsom's policy without also expressing disdain for those who turned out at City Hall to take advantage of the policy.

[The dissent then moved on to the "rights of others" analysis]. Tinker does contain an additional ground for banning student speech, namely where it is an "invasion of the rights of others." The school authorities suggest that Harper's t-shirt violates California Education Code § 201(a), which provides that "[a]ll pupils have the right to participate fully in the educational process, free from discrimination and harassment." Defendants cite no California case holding that the passive display by one student of a message another student finds offensive violates this provision, and I am reluctant to so conclude on my own. The interaction between harassment law and the First Amendment is a difficult and unsettled one because much of what harassment law seeks to prohibit, the First Amendment seems to protect. Certainly, state law cannot trump the First Amendment by defining "harassment" as any conduct that another person finds offensive; far too much core First Amendment speech could thus be squelched.

* * * The "rights of others" language in *Tinker* can only refer to traditional rights, such as those against assault, defamation, invasion of privacy, extortion and blackmail, whose interplay with the First Amendment is well established. Surely, this language is not meant to give state legislatures the power to define the First Amendment rights of students out of existence by giving others the right not to hear that speech. Otherwise, a state legislature could effectively overrule *Tinker* by granting students an affirmative right not to be offended. To the extent that state law purports to prohibit such language in the school context, it is patently unconstitutional. * * *

Nor can I join my colleagues in concluding that Harper's t-shirt violated the rights of other students by disparaging their homosexual status. As I understand the opinion, my colleagues are saying that messages such as Harper's are so offensive and demeaning that they interfere with the ability of homosexual students to partake of the educational environment. * * *

[This argument] raises many problems, the first of which is that it finds no support in the record. What my colleagues say could be true, but the only support they provide are a few law review articles, a couple of press releases by advocacy groups and some pop psychology. Aside from the fact that published articles are hardly an adequate substitute for record evidence, the cited materials are just not specific enough to be particularly helpful. None would seem to meet the standard of *Daubert v. Merrell Dow Pharmaceuticals, Inc.*, 509 U.S. 579, 592–94 (1993).

The first article, written by physicians but apparently not peer-reviewed, makes a general statement to the effect that academic under-achievement and other problems of homosexual youths "are the probable consequence of violence and verbal and physical abuse at school." Susanne M. Stronski Huwiler & Gary Remafedi, *Adolescent Homosexuality*, 33 REV. JUR. U.I.P.R. 151, 164 (1999). The article does not explain what the authors mean by "verbal . . . abuse," so it's not clear that Harper's t-shirt is even covered by the article's findings. Nor does the article explain the degree to which statements, as opposed to physical abuse, are responsible for the ill effects it discusses. The second article, written by a lawyer, not a health-care professional, merely points to general problems suffered by gay and lesbian youths during their school years—problems that are reinforced by a variety of school practices and policies. *See* Thomas A. Mayes, *Confronting Same-Sex, Student-to-Student Sexual Harassment: Recommendations for Educators and Policy Makers*, 29 FORDHAM URB. L.J. 641, 655–58 (2001). The other articles the majority cites also focus on physical abuse or threats, which the school can and should stamp out in a viewpoint neutral way. The majority finally resorts to press releases from advocacy groups—hardly a source "whose accuracy cannot reasonably be questioned." Fed.R.Evid. 201(b). What the materials the majority cites do establish is that the success of gay and lesbian teens in school is a complicated phenomenon, influenced by many factors. Even taking the sources on their own terms, none provides support for the notion that disparaging statements by other students, in the context of a political debate, materially interfere with the ability of homosexual students to profit from the school environment.

Nor do I find the proposition at the heart of the majority's opinion—that homosexual students are severely harmed by any and all statements casting aspersions on their sexual orientation—so self-evident as to require no evidentiary support. We take judicial notice of facts that aren't reasonably subject to dispute—gravity, the temperature at which ice melts, that commercial goods cost money, that time flows forward but not backward. But the fact that we can take judicial notice of certain indisputable facts does not mean that all facts are indisputable. Predicting the effect of certain kinds of statements on the learning ability of high school students is simply not the kind of "fact" that is judicially noticeable under any fair reading of Federal Rule of Evidence 201. Even the articles that the majority cites admit that the research on these effects is not unanimous. We have no business assuming without proof that the educational progress of homosexual students would be stunted by Harper's statement.

I find it significant, moreover, that Harper did not thrust his view of homosexuality into the school environment as part of a campaign to demean or embarrass other students. Rather, he was responding to public statements made by others with whom he disagreed. Whatever one might think are the psychological effects of unprovoked demeaning statements by one student against another, the effects may be quite different when they are part of a political give-and-take. By participating in the Day of Silence activities, homosexual students perforce acknowledge that their status is not universally admired or accepted; the whole point of the Day of Silence, as I understand it, is to dispute views like those characterized by Harper's t-shirt. Supporters of the Day of Silence may prefer to see views such as Harper's channeled into public discourse rather than officially suppressed but whispered behind backs or scribbled on bathroom walls. Confronting—and refuting—such views in a public forum may well empower homosexual students, contributing to their sense of self-esteem.

Beyond the question of evidentiary support, I have considerable difficulty understanding the source and sweep of the novel doctrine the majority announces today. Not all statements that demean other students can be banned by schools; the majority is very clear about this. The new doctrine applies only to statements that demean students based on their "minority status such as race, religion, and sexual orientation." Is this a right created by state law? By federal law? By common law? And if interference with the learning process is the keystone to the new right, how come it's limited to those characteristics that are associated with minority status? Students may well have their self-esteem bruised by being demeaned for being white or Christian, or having bad acne or weight problems, or being poor or stupid or any one of the infinite number of characteristics that will not qualify them for minority status. Under the rule the majority announces today, schools would be able to ban t-shirts with pictures of Mohammed wearing a bomb turban but not those with pictures of a Crucifix dipped in urine—yet Muslim and Christian children, respectively, may have their learning equally disrupted.

Even the concept of minority status is not free from doubt. In defining what is a minority—and hence protected—do we look to the national community, the state, the locality or the school? In a school that has 60 percent black students and 40 percent white students, will the school be able to ban t-shirts with anti-black racist messages but not those with anti-white racist messages, or vice versa? Must a Salt Lake City high school prohibit or permit Big Love t-shirts?

And at what level of generality do we define a minority group? If the Pope speaks out against gay marriage, can gay students wear to school t-shirts saying "Catholics Are Bigots," or will they be demeaning the core characteristic of a religious minority? And, are Catholics part of a monolithic Christian majority, or a minority sect that has endured centuries of discrimination in America? * * *

The fundamental problem with the majority's approach is that it has no anchor anywhere in the record or in the law. It is entirely a judicial creation, hatched to deal with the situation before us, but likely to cause innumerable problems in the future. Respectfully, I cannot go along. * * *

I also have sympathy for defendants' position that students in school are a captive audience and should not be forced to endure speech that they find offensive and demeaning. There is surely something to the notion that a Jewish student might not be able to devote his full attention to school activities if the fellow in the seat next to him is wearing a t-shirt with the message "Hitler Had the Right Idea" in front and "Let's Finish the Job!" on the back. This t-shirt may well interfere with the educational experience even if the two students never come to blows or even have words about it.

Perhaps school authorities should have greater latitude to control student speech than allowed them by [*Tinker*]. Perhaps the narrow exceptions of *Tinker* should be broadened and multiplied. Perhaps *Tinker* should be overruled. But that is a job for the Supreme Court, not for us. While I sympathize with my colleagues' effort to tinker with the law in this area, I am not convinced we have the authority to do so, which is why I must respectfully dissent.

Exhibit A

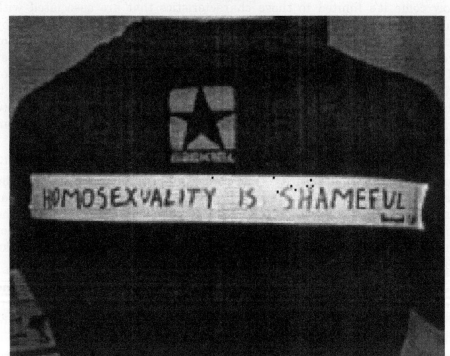

NOTES

1.   After the Ninth Circuit's decision, the Supreme Court granted certiorari, vacated the judgment, and remanded the case with instructions to the Ninth Circuit to dismiss it as moot. *Harper ex rel. Harper v. Poway Unified Sch. Dist.*, 127 S. Ct. 1484 (2007) (mem.). By the time the Court acted, Tyler Harper had graduated. In its decision, the Court also denied the

motion to intervene filed on behalf of Tyler Harper's younger sister, who had sought to continue the case.

2.   The *Harper* case is hardly an isolated incident. There have been a number of recent flashpoints of controversy involving LGBT students and schools. For other cases involving students wearing t-shirts expressing a view on LGBT issues, see *Nuxoll v. Indian Prairie School District #204*, 523 F.3d 668 (7th Cir. 2008); *Okwedy v. Molinari*, 333 F.3d 339 (2d Cir. 2003). For scholarly perspectives, see Michael Kent Curtis, *Be Careful What You Wish for: Dueling High School T-Shirts, and the Perils of Suppression*, 44 WAKE FOREST L. REV. 431 (2009); Shannon Gilreath, *"Tell Your Faggot Friend He Owes Me $500 for My Broken Hand": Thoughts on a Substantive Equality Theory of Free* Speech, 44 WAKE FOREST L. REV. 557 (2009); John E. Taylor, Tinker *and Viewpoint Discrimination*, 77 U.M.K.C. L. REV. 569 (2009). There have also been curricular controversies. One high profile case involved parental protests in Massachusetts about grade school children reading books featuring gay families. *See Parker v. Hurley*, 514 F.3d 87 (1st Cir. 2008), *cert. denied*, 129 S.Ct. 56, 172 L.Ed.2d 24 (2008). That controversy made its way to the Proposition 8 campaign in 2008, and provided the basis for claims about how schoolchildren would be affected by legalizing marriage in California. For more on the Proposition 8 campaign, see Chapter 5.

III. FREE (ANTI-GAY) SPEECH

In this Section and the next one, we move beyond the focus on schools and look more broadly at the legal issues that arise when *private, non-governmental* organizations deny equal access and opportunities to LGBT people. In such cases, those who are excluded or whose identities are suppressed cannot rely on constitutional protections applicable to state actors, but must seek legal recourse—if any—in the application of non-discrimination statutes and principles to the private actors. Conversely, the private actors often raise the First Amendment as a defense, alleging that the application of a law prohibiting them from discriminating against LGBT people violates their First Amendment rights. The structures of some of these cases recall disputes about the entry of racial minorities and women into the nation's public life. The unit accordingly begins with the *Roberts* case, in which the U.S. Supreme Court considered the constitutionality of the Jaycees' ban on women members. The cases and notes that follow consider the exclusion of openly gay persons from parades and groups like the Boy Scouts. In the next Section, we move from objections to LGBT inclusion grounded in free speech to those grounded in religious liberty. As you review materials in both Sections, consider the overarching question of how courts should resolve conflicts between LGBT equality on the one hand, and expressive or religious liberty on the other.

ROBERTS V. UNITED STATES JAYCEES

Supreme Court of the United States, 1984
468 U.S. 609, 104 S.Ct. 3244, 82 L.Ed.2d 462

JUSTICE BRENNAN delivered the opinion of the Court.

This case requires us to address a conflict between a State's efforts to eliminate gender-based discrimination against its citizens and the constitutional freedom of association asserted by members of a private organization. In the decision under review, the Court of Appeals for the Eighth Circuit concluded that, by requiring the United States Jaycees to admit women as full voting members, the Minnesota Human Rights Act violates the First and Fourteenth Amendment rights [of association] of the organization's members. We . . . reverse. * * *

Our decisions have referred to constitutionally protected "freedom of association" in two distinct senses. In one line of decisions, the Court has concluded that choices to enter into and maintain certain intimate human relationships must be secured against undue intrusion by the State because of the role of such relationships in safeguarding the individual freedom that is central to our constitutional scheme. In this respect, freedom of association receives protection as a fundamental element of personal liberty. In another set of decisions, the Court has recognized a right to associate for the purpose of engaging in those activities protected by the First Amendment—speech, assembly, petition for the redress of grievances, and the exercise of religion. The Constitution guarantees freedom of association of this kind as an indispensable means of preserving other individual liberties.

The intrinsic and instrumental features of constitutionally protected association may, of course, coincide. In particular, when the State interferes with individuals' selection of those with whom they wish to join in a common endeavor, freedom of association in both of its forms may be implicated. The Jaycees contend that this is such a case. Still, the nature and degree of constitutional protection afforded freedom of association may vary depending on the extent to which one or the other aspect of the constitutionally protected liberty is at stake in a given case. We therefore find it useful to consider separately the effect of applying the Minnesota statute to the Jaycees on what could be called its members' freedom of intimate association and their freedom of expressive association.

A

The Court has long recognized that, because the Bill of Rights is designed to secure individual liberty, it must afford the formation and preservation of certain kinds of highly personal relationships a substantial measure of sanctuary from unjustified interference by the State. *E.g., Pierce v. Society of Sisters*, 268 U.S. 510, 534–535 (1925); *Meyer v. Nebraska*, 262 U.S. 390, 399 (1923). Without precisely identifying every consideration that may underlie this type of constitutional protection, we have noted that certain kinds of personal bonds have played a critical role in the culture and traditions of the Nation by cultivating and transmitting shared ideals and beliefs; they thereby foster diversity and act as critical buffers between the individual and the power of the State. *See, e.g., Zablocki v. Redhail*, 434 U.S. 374, 383–386 (1978); *Moore v. East Cleveland*, 431 U.S. 494, 503–504 (1977) (plurality opinion); *Wisconsin v. Yoder*, 406 U.S. 205, 232 (1972); *Griswold v. Connecticut*, 381 U.S. 479, 482–485 (1965). Moreover, the constitutional shelter afforded such relationships reflects the realization that individuals draw much of their emotional enrichment from close ties with others. Protecting these relationships from unwarranted state interference therefore safeguards the ability independently to define one's identity that is central to any concept of liberty. *See, e.g., Quilloin v. Walcott*, 434 U.S. 246, 255 (1978); *Smith v. Organization of Foster Families*, 431 U.S. 816, 844 (1977); *Cleveland Board of Education v. LaFleur*, 414 U.S. 632, 639–640 (1974); *Stanley v. Illinois*, 405 U.S. 645, 651–652 (1972); *Stanley v. Georgia*, 394 U.S. 557, 564 (1969); *Olmstead v. United States*, 277 U.S. 438, 478 (1928) (Brandeis, J., dissenting).

The personal affiliations that exemplify these considerations, and that therefore suggest some relevant limitations on the relationships that might be entitled to this sort of constitutional protection, are those that attend the creation and sustenance of a family—marriage, *e.g., Zablocki v. Redhail*; childbirth, *e.g., Carey v. Population Services International*; the raising and education of children, *e.g., Smith v. Organization of Foster Families*; and cohabitation with one's relatives, *e.g., Moore v. East Cleveland*. Family relationships, by their nature, involve deep attachments and commitments to the necessarily few other individuals with whom one shares not only a special community of thoughts, experiences, and beliefs but also distinctively personal aspects of one's life. Among other things, therefore, they are distinguished by such attributes as relative smallness, a high degree of selectivity in decisions to begin and maintain the affiliation, and seclusion from others in critical aspects of the relationship. As a general matter, only relationships with these sorts of qualities are likely to reflect the considerations that have led to an understanding of freedom of association as an intrinsic element of personal liberty. Conversely, an association lacking these qualities— such as a large business enterprise—seems remote from the concerns giving rise to this constitutional protection. Accordingly, the Constitution undoubtedly imposes constraints on the State's power to control the selection of one's spouse that would not apply to regulations affecting the choice of one's fellow employees. *Compare Loving v. Virginia*, 388 U.S. 1, 12 (1967), *with Railway Mail Assn. v. Corsi*, 326 U.S. 88, 93–94 (1945).

Between these poles, of course, lies a broad range of human relationships that may make greater or lesser claims to constitutional protection from particular incursions by the State. Determining the limits of state authority over an individual's freedom to enter into a particular association therefore unavoidably entails a careful assessment of where that relationship's objective characteristics locate it on a spectrum from the most intimate to the most attenuated of personal attachments. We need not mark the potentially significant points on this terrain with any precision. We note only that factors that may be relevant include size, purpose, policies, selectivity, congeniality, and other characteristics that in a particular case may be pertinent. In this case, however, several features of the Jaycees clearly place the organization outside of the category of relationships worthy of this kind of constitutional protection.

The undisputed facts reveal that the local chapters of the Jaycees are large and basically unselective groups. At the time of the state administrative hearing, the Minneapolis chapter had approximately 430 members, while the St. Paul chapter had about 400. Apart from age and sex, neither the national organization nor the local chapters employ any criteria for judging applicants for membership, and new members are routinely recruited and admitted with no inquiry into their backgrounds. In fact, a local officer testified that he could recall no instance in which an applicant had been denied membership on any basis other than age or sex. Furthermore, despite their inability to vote, hold office, or receive certain awards, women affiliated with the Jaycees attend various meetings, participate in selected projects, and engage in many of the organization's social functions. Indeed, numerous non-members of both genders regularly participate in a substantial portion of activities central to the decision of many members to associate with one another, including many of the organization's various community programs, awards ceremonies, and recruitment meetings.

In short, the local chapters of the Jaycees are neither small nor selective. Moreover, much of the activity central to the formation and maintenance of the association involves the participation of strangers to that relationship. Accordingly, we conclude that the Jaycees chapters lack the distinctive characteristics that might afford constitutional protection to the decision of its members to exclude women. We turn therefore to consider the extent to which application of the Minnesota statute to compel the Jaycees to accept women infringes the group's freedom of expressive association.

B

An individual's freedom to speak, to worship, and to petition the government for the redress of grievances could not be vigorously protected from interference by the State unless a correlative freedom to engage in group effort toward those ends were not also guaranteed. *See, e.g., Citizens Against Rent Control/Coalition for Fair Housing v. Berkeley*, 454 U.S. 290, 294 (1981). According protection to collective effort on behalf of shared goals is especially important in preserving political and cultural diversity and in shielding dissident expression from suppression by the majority. *See, e.g., Gilmore v. City of Montgomery*, 417 U.S., at 575; *Griswold v. Connecticut*, 381 U.S., at 482–485; *NAACP v. Button*, 371 U.S. 415, 431 (1963); *NAACP v. Alabama ex rel. Patterson*, 357 U.S., at 462. Consequently, we have long understood as implicit in the right to engage in activities protected by the First Amendment a corresponding right to associate with others in pursuit of a wide variety of political, social, economic, educational, religious, and cultural ends. *See, e.g., NAACP v. Claiborne Hardware Co.*, 458 U.S. 886, 907–909, 932–933; *Larson v. Valente*, 456 U.S. 228, 244–246 (1982); *In re Primus*, 436 U.S. 412, 426 (1978); *Abood v. Detroit Board of Education*, 431 U.S. 209, 231 (1977). In view of the various protected activities in which the Jaycees engage (*see infra*) that right is plainly implicated in this case.

Government actions that may unconstitutionally infringe upon this freedom can take a number of forms. Among other things, government may seek to impose penalties or withhold benefits from individuals because of their membership in a disfavored group, *e.g., Healy v. James*, 408 U.S. 169, 180–184 (1972); it may attempt to require disclosure of the fact of membership in a group seeking anonymity, *e.g., Brown v. Socialist Workers '74 Campaign Committee*, 459 U.S. 87, 91–92 (1982); and it may try to interfere with the internal organization or affairs of the group, *e.g., Cousins v. Wigoda*, 419 U.S. 477, 487–488 (1975). By requiring the Jaycees to admit women as full voting members, the Minnesota Act works an infringement of the last type. There can be no clearer example of an intrusion into the internal structure or affairs of an association than a regulation that forces the group to accept members it does not desire. Such a regulation may impair the ability of the original members to express only those views that brought them together. Freedom of association therefore plainly presupposes a freedom not to associate. *See Abood v. Detroit Board of Education*, 431 U.S., at 234–235.

The right to associate for expressive purposes is not, however, absolute. Infringements on that right may be justified by regulations adopted to serve compelling state interests, unrelated to the suppression of ideas, that cannot be achieved through means significantly less restrictive of associational freedoms. We are persuaded that Minnesota's compelling interest in eradicating discrimination against its female citizens justifies the impact that application of the statute to the Jaycees may have on the male members' associational freedoms.

On its face, the Minnesota Act does not aim at the suppression of speech, does not distinguish between prohibited and permitted activity on the basis of viewpoint, and does not license enforcement authorities to administer the statute on the basis of such constitutionally impermissible criteria. Nor does the Jaycees contend that the Act has been applied in this case for the purpose of hampering the organization's ability to express its views. Instead, as the Minnesota Supreme Court explained, the Act reflects the State's strong historical commitment to eliminating discrimination and assuring its citizens equal access to publicly available goods and services. That goal, which is unrelated to the suppression of expression, plainly serves compelling state interests of the highest order. * * *

By prohibiting gender discrimination in places of public accommodation, the Minnesota Act protects the State's citizenry from a number of serious social and personal harms. In the context of reviewing state actions under the Equal Protection Clause, this Court has frequently noted that discrimination based on archaic and overbroad assumptions about the relative needs and capacities of the sexes forces individuals to labor under stereotypical notions that often bear no relationship to their actual abilities. It thereby both deprives persons of their individual dignity and denies society the benefits of wide participation in political, economic, and cultural life. These concerns are strongly implicated with respect to gender discrimination in the allocation of publicly available goods and services. Thus, in upholding Title II of the Civil Rights Act of 1964, which forbids race discrimination in public accommodations, we emphasized that its "fundamental object . . . was to vindicate 'the deprivation of personal dignity that surely accompanies denials of equal access to public establishments.' " *Heart of Atlanta Motel, Inc. v. United States*, 379 U.S. 241, 250 (1964). That stigmatizing injury, and the denial of equal opportunities that accompanies it, is surely felt as strongly by persons suffering discrimination on the basis of their sex as by those treated differently because of their race.

Nor is the state interest in assuring equal access limited to the provision of purely tangible goods and services. A State enjoys broad authority to create rights of public access on behalf of its citizens. *PruneYard Shopping Center v. Robins*, 447 U.S. 74, 81–88 (1980). Like many States and municipalities, Minnesota has adopted a functional definition of public accommodations that reaches various forms of public, quasi-commercial conduct. This expansive definition reflects a recognition of the changing nature of the American economy and of the importance, both to the individual and to society, of removing the barriers to economic advancement and political and social integration that have historically plagued certain disadvantaged groups, including women. Thus, in explaining its conclusion that the Jaycees local chapters are "place[s] of public accommodations" within the meaning of the Act, the Minnesota court noted the various commercial programs and benefits offered to members and stated that "[l]eadership skills are 'goods,' [and] business contacts and employment promotions are 'privileges' and 'advantages'. . . ." Assuring women equal access to such goods, privileges, and advantages clearly furthers compelling state interests.

In applying the Act to the Jaycees, the State has advanced those interests through the least restrictive means of achieving its ends. Indeed, the Jaycees has failed to demonstrate that the Act imposes any serious burdens on the male members' freedom of expressive association. To be sure, as the Court of Appeals noted, a "not insubstantial part" of the Jaycees' activities constitutes protected expression on political, economic, cultural, and social affairs. Over the years, the national and local levels of the organization have taken public positions on a number of diverse issues, and members of the Jaycees regularly engage in a variety of civic, charitable, lobbying, fundraising, and other activities worthy of constitutional protection under the First Amendment. There is, however, no basis in the record for concluding that admission of women as full voting members will impede the organization's ability to engage in these protected activities or to disseminate its preferred views. The Act requires no change in the Jaycees' creed of promoting the interests of young men, and it imposes no restrictions on the organization's ability to exclude individuals with ideologies or philosophies different from those of its existing members. Moreover, the Jaycees already invites women to share the group's views and philosophy and to participate in much of its training and community activities. Accordingly, any claim that admission of women as full voting members will impair a symbolic message conveyed by the very fact that women are not permitted to vote is attenuated at best.

While acknowledging that "the specific content of most of the resolutions adopted over the years by the Jaycees has nothing to do with sex," the Court of Appeals nonetheless entertained the hypothesis that women members might have a different view or agenda with respect to these matters so that, if they are allowed to vote, "some change in the Jaycees' philosophical cast can reasonably be expected." It is similarly arguable that, insofar as the Jaycees is organized to promote the views of young men whatever those views happen to be, admission of women as voting members will change the message communicated by the group's speech because of the gender-based assumptions of the audience. Neither supposition, however, is supported by the record. In claiming that women might have a different attitude about such issues as the federal budget, school prayer, voting rights, and foreign relations, or that the organization's public positions would have a different effect if the group were not "a purely young men's association," the Jaycees relies solely on unsupported generalizations about the relative interests and perspectives of men and women. Although such generalizations may or may not have a statistical basis in fact with respect to particular positions adopted by the Jaycees, we have repeatedly condemned legal decisionmaking that relies uncritically on such assumptions. *See, e.g., Palmore v. Sidoti*, 466 U.S. 429, 433–434 (1984). In the absence of a showing far more substantial than that attempted by the Jaycees, we decline to indulge in the sexual stereotyping that underlies appellee's contention that, by allowing women to vote, application of the Minnesota Act will change the content or impact of the organization's speech.

In any event, even if enforcement of the Act causes some incidental abridgment of the Jaycees' protected speech, that effect is no greater than is necessary to accomplish the State's legitimate purposes. As we have explained, acts of invidious discrimination in the distribution of publicly available goods, services, and other advantages cause unique evils that government has a compelling interest to prevent—wholly apart from the point of view such conduct may transmit. Accordingly, like violence or other types of potentially expressive activities that produce special harms distinct from their communicative impact, such practices are entitled to no constitutional protection. In prohibiting such practices, the Minnesota Act therefore "responds precisely to the substantive problem which legitimately concerns" the State and abridges no more speech or associational freedom than is necessary to accomplish that purpose.

HURLEY V. IRISH-AMERICAN GAY, LESBIAN & BISEXUAL GROUP OF BOSTON

Supreme Court of the United States, 1995
515 U.S. 557, 115 S.Ct. 2338, 132 L.Ed.2d 487

JUSTICE SOUTER delivered the opinion of the Court.

The issue in this case is whether Massachusetts may require private citizens who organize a parade to include among the marchers a group imparting a message the organizers do not wish to convey. We hold that such a mandate violates the First Amendment.

I

March 17 is set aside for two celebrations in South Boston. As early as 1737, some people in Boston observed the feast of the apostle to Ireland, and since 1776 the day has marked the evacuation of royal troops and Loyalists from the city, prompted by the guns captured at Ticonderoga and set up on Dorchester Heights under General Washington's command. Washington himself reportedly drew on the earlier tradition in choosing "St. Patrick" as the response to "Boston," the password used in the colonial lines on evacuation day. Although the General Court of Massachusetts did not officially designate March 17 as Evacuation Day until 1938, the City Council of Boston had previously sponsored public celebrations of Evacuation Day, including notable commemorations on the centennial in 1876, and on the 125th anniversary in 1901, with its parade, salute, concert, and fireworks display.

The tradition of formal sponsorship by the city came to an end in 1947, however, when Mayor James Michael Curley himself granted authority to organize and conduct the St. Patrick's Day-Evacuation Day Parade to the petitioner South Boston Allied War Veterans Council, an unincorporated association of individuals elected from various South Boston veterans groups. Every year since that time, the Council has applied for and received a permit for the parade, which at times has included as many as 20,000 marchers and drawn up to 1 million watchers. No other applicant has ever applied for that permit. Through 1992, the city allowed the Council to use the city's official seal, and provided printing services as well as direct funding.

1992 was the year that a number of gay, lesbian, and bisexual descendants of the Irish immigrants joined together with other supporters to form the respondent organization, GLIB, to march in the parade as a way to express pride in their Irish heritage as openly gay, lesbian, and bisexual individuals, to demonstrate that there are such men and women among those so descended, and to express their solidarity with like individuals who sought to march in New York's St. Patrick's Day Parade. Although the Council denied GLIB's application to take part in the 1992 parade, GLIB obtained a state-court order to include its contingent, which marched "uneventfully" among that year's 10,000 participants and 750,000 spectators.

In 1993, after the Council had again refused to admit GLIB to the upcoming parade, the organization and some of its members filed this suit against the Council, the individual petitioner John J. "Wacko" Hurley, and the City of Boston, alleging violations of the State and Federal Constitutions and of the state public accommodations law, which prohibits "any distinction, discrimination or restriction on account of . . . sexual orientation . . . relative to the admission of any person to, or treatment in any place of public accommodation, resort or amusement." After finding that "[f]or at least the past 47 years, the Parade has traveled the same basic route along the public streets of South Boston, providing entertainment, amusement, and recreation to participants and spectators alike," the state trial court ruled that the parade fell within the statutory definition of a public accommodation. The court found that the Council had no written criteria and employed no particular procedures for admission, voted on new applications in batches, had occasionally admitted groups who simply showed up at the parade without having submitted an application, and did "not generally inquire into the specific messages or views of each applicant." The court consequently rejected the Council's contention that the parade was "private" (in the sense of being exclusive), holding instead that "the lack of genuine selectivity in choosing participants and sponsors demonstrates that the Parade is a public event." It found the parade to be "eclectic," containing a wide variety of "patriotic, commercial, political, moral, artistic, religious, athletic, public service, trade union, and eleemosynary themes," as well as conflicting messages. While noting that the Council had indeed excluded the Ku Klux Klan and ROAR (an antibusing group), it attributed little significance to these facts, concluding ultimately that "[t]he only common theme among the participants and sponsors is their public involvement in the Parade."

The court rejected the Council's assertion that the exclusion of "groups with sexual themes merely formalized [the fact] that the Parade expresses traditional religious and social values," and found the Council's "final position [to be] that GLIB would be excluded because of its values and its message, *i.e.*, its members' sexual orientation." This position, in the court's view, was not only violative of the public accommodations law but "paradoxical" as well, since "a proper celebration of St. Patrick's and Evacuation Day requires diversity and inclusiveness." The court rejected the notion that GLIB's admission would trample on the Council's First Amendment rights since the court understood that constitutional protection of any interest in expressive association would "requir[e] focus on a specific message, theme, or group" absent from the parade. "Given the [Council's] lack of selectivity in choosing participants and failure to circumscribe the marchers' message," the court found it "impossible to discern any specific expressive purpose entitling the Parade to protection under the First Amendment." It concluded that the parade is "not an exercise of [the Council's] constitutionally protected right of expressive association," but instead "an open recreational event that is subject to the public accommodations law."

The court held that because the statute did not mandate inclusion of GLIB but only prohibited discrimination based on sexual orientation, any infringement on the Council's right to expressive association was only "incidental" and "no greater than necessary to accomplish the statute's legitimate purpose" of eradicating discrimination (citing *Roberts v. United States Jaycees*, 468 U.S. 609, 628–629 (1984)). Accordingly, it ruled that "GLIB is entitled to participate in the Parade on the same terms and conditions as other participants."

The Supreme Judicial Court of Massachusetts affirmed, seeing nothing clearly erroneous in the trial judge's findings that GLIB was excluded from the parade based on the sexual orientation of its members, that it was impossible to detect an expressive purpose in the parade, that there was no state action, and that the parade was a public accommodation within the meaning of [the Massachusetts statute]. * * *

We granted certiorari to determine whether the requirement to admit a parade contingent expressing a message not of the private organizers' own choosing violates the First Amendment. We hold that it does and reverse.

II

Given the scope of the issues as originally joined in this case, it is worth noting some that have fallen aside in the course of the litigation, before reaching us. Although the Council presents us with a First Amendment claim, respondents do not. Neither do they press a claim that the Council's action has denied them equal protection of the laws in violation of the Fourteenth Amendment. While the guarantees of free speech and equal protection guard only against encroachment by the government and "erec[t] no shield against merely private conduct," *Shelley v. Kraemer*, 334 U.S. 1 (1948), respondents originally argued that the Council's conduct was not purely private, but had the character of state action. The trial court's review of the city's involvement led it to find otherwise, however, and although the Supreme Judicial Court did not squarely address the issue, it appears to have affirmed the trial court's decision on that point as well as the others. In any event, respondents have not brought that question up either in a cross-petition for certiorari or in their briefs filed in this Court. When asked at oral argument whether they challenged the conclusion by the Massachusetts' courts that no state action is involved in the parade, respondents' counsel answered that they "do not press that issue here." In this Court, then, their claim for inclusion in the parade rests solely on the Massachusetts public accommodations law.

There is no corresponding concession from the other side, however, and certainly not to the state courts' characterization of the parade as lacking the element of expression for purposes of the First Amendment. Accordingly, our review of petitioners' claim that their activity is indeed in the nature of protected speech carries with it a constitutional duty to conduct an independent examination of the record as a whole, without deference to the trial court. *See Bose Corp. v. Consumers Union of United States, Inc.*, 466 U.S. 485, 499 (1984). The "requirement of independent appellate review . . . is a rule of federal constitutional law," *id.*, at 510, which does not limit our deference to a trial court on matters of witness credibility, *Harte-Hanks Communications, Inc. v. Connaughton*, 491 U.S. 657, 688 (1989), but which generally requires us to "review the finding of facts by a State court . . . where a conclusion of law as to a Federal right and a finding of fact are so intermingled as to make it necessary, in order to pass upon the Federal question, to analyze the facts," *Fiske v. Kansas*, 274 U.S. 380, 385–386 (1927). This obligation rests upon us simply because the reaches of the First Amendment are ultimately defined by the facts it is held to embrace, and we must thus decide for ourselves whether a given course of conduct falls on the near or far side of the line of constitutional protection. Even where a speech case has originally been tried in a federal court, subject to the provision of Federal Rule of Civil Procedure 52(a) that "[f]indings of fact . . . shall not be set aside unless clearly erroneous," we are obliged to make a fresh examination of crucial facts. Hence, in this case, though we are confronted with the state courts' conclusion that the factual characteristics of petitioners' activity place it within the vast realm of non-expressive conduct, our obligation is to "'make an independent examination of the whole record,' . . . so as to assure ourselves that th[is] judgment does not constitute a forbidden intrusion on the field of free expression." *New York Times Co. v. Sullivan*, 376 U.S. 254, 285 (1964) (footnote omitted), quoting *Edwards v. South Carolina*, 372 U.S. 229, 235 (1963).

III

A

If there were no reason for a group of people to march from here to there except to reach a destination, they could make the trip without expressing any message beyond the fact of the march itself. Some people might call such a procession a parade, but it would not be much of one. Real "[p]arades are public dramas of social relations, and in them performers define who can be a social actor and what subjects and ideas are available for communication and consideration." S. Davis, Parades and Power: Street Theatre in Nineteenth-Century Philadelphia 6 (1986). Hence, we use the word "parade" to indicate marchers who are making some sort of collective point, not just to each other but to bystanders along the way. Indeed a parade's dependence on watchers is so extreme that nowadays, as with Bishop Berkeley's celebrated tree, "if a parade or demonstration receives no media coverage, it may as well not have happened." *Id.*, at 171. Parades are thus a form of expression, not just motion, and the inherent expressiveness of marching to make a point explains our cases involving protest marches. * * *

The protected expression that inheres in a parade is not limited to its banners and songs, however, for the Constitution looks beyond written or spoken words as mediums of expression. Noting that "[s]ymbolism is a primitive but effective way of communicating ideas," *West Virginia Bd. of Ed. v. Barnette*, 319 U.S. 624, 632 (1943), our cases have recognized that the First Amendment shields such acts as saluting a flag (and refusing to do so), *id.*, at 632, 642, wearing an arm band to protest a war, *Tinker v. Des Moines Independent Community School Dist.*, 393 U.S. 503, 505–506 (1969), displaying a red flag, *Stromberg v. California*, 283 U.S. 359, 369 (1931), and even "[m]arching, walking or parading" in uniforms displaying the swastika, *National Socialist Party of America v. Skokie*, 432 U.S. 43 (1977). As some of these examples show, a narrow, succinctly articulable message is not a condition of constitutional protection, which if confined to expressions conveying a "particularized message," *cf. Spence v. Washington*, 418 U.S. 405, 411 (1974) (*per curiam*), would never reach the unquestionably shielded painting of Jackson Pollock, music of Arnold Schonberg, or Jabberwocky verse of Lewis Carroll.

Not many marches, then, are beyond the realm of expressive parades, and the South Boston celebration is not one of them. Spectators line the streets; people march in costumes and uniforms, carrying flags and banners with all sorts of messages (*e.g.*, "England get out of Ireland," "Say no to drugs"); marching bands and pipers play, floats are pulled along, and the whole show is broadcast over Boston television. To be sure, we agree with the state courts that in spite of excluding some applicants, the Council is rather lenient in admitting participants. But a private speaker does not forfeit constitutional protection simply by combining multifarious voices, or by failing to edit their themes to isolate an exact message as the exclusive subject matter of the speech. Nor, under our precedent, does First Amendment protection require a speaker to generate, as an original matter, each item featured in the communication. Cable operators, for example, are engaged in protected speech activities even when they only select programming originally produced by others. *Turner Broadcasting System, Inc. v. FCC*, 512 U.S. 622, 636, 114 S.Ct. 2445, 129 L.Ed.2d 497 (1994). For that matter, the presentation of an edited compilation of speech generated by other persons is a staple of most newspapers' opinion pages, which, of course, fall squarely within the core of First Amendment security, *Miami Herald Publishing Co. v. Tornillo*, 418 U.S. 241 (1974), as does even the simple selection of a paid noncommercial advertisement for inclusion in a daily paper, see *New York Times*, 376 U.S., at 265–266. The selection of contingents to make a parade is entitled to similar protection.

Respondents' participation as a unit in the parade was equally expressive. GLIB was formed for the very purpose of marching in it, as the trial court found, in order to celebrate its members' identity as openly gay, lesbian, and bisexual descendants of the Irish immigrants, to show that there are such individuals in the community, and to support the like men and women who sought to march in the New York parade. The organization distributed a fact sheet describing the members' intentions, and the record otherwise corroborates the expressive nature of GLIB's participation. In 1993, members of GLIB marched behind a shamrock-strewn banner with the simple inscription "Irish American Gay, Lesbian and Bisexual Group of Boston." GLIB understandably seeks to communicate its ideas as part of the existing parade, rather than staging one of its own.

B

The Massachusetts public accommodations law under which respondents brought suit has a venerable history. . . .

As with many public accommodations statutes across the Nation, the legislature continued to broaden the scope of legislation, to the point that the law today prohibits discrimination on the basis of "race, color, religious creed, national origin, sex, sexual orientation . . . deafness, blindness or any physical or mental disability or ancestry" in "the admission of any person to, or treatment in any place of public accommodation, resort or amusement." Provisions like these are well within the State's usual power to enact when a legislature has reason to believe that a given group is the target of discrimination, and they do not, as a general matter, violate the First or Fourteenth Amendments. Nor is this statute unusual in any obvious way, since it does not, on its face, target speech or discriminate on the basis of its content, the focal point of its prohibition being rather on the act of discriminating against individuals in the provision of publicly available goods, privileges, and services on the proscribed grounds.

C

In the case before us, however, the Massachusetts law has been applied in a peculiar way. Its enforcement does not address any dispute about the participation of openly gay, lesbian, or bisexual individuals in various units admitted to the parade. The petitioners disclaim any intent to exclude homosexuals as such, and no individual member of GLIB claims to have been excluded from parading as a member of any group that the Council has approved to march. Instead, the disagreement goes to the admission of GLIB as its own parade unit carrying its own banner. Since every participating unit affects the message conveyed by the private organizers, the state courts' application of the statute produced an order essentially requiring petitioners to alter the expressive content of their parade. Although the state courts spoke of the parade as a place of public accommodation, once the expressive character of both the parade and the marching GLIB contingent is understood, it becomes apparent that the state courts' application of the statute had the effect of declaring the sponsors' speech itself to be the public accommodation. Under this approach any contingent of protected individuals with a message would have the right to participate in petitioners' speech, so that the communication produced by the private organizers would be shaped by all those protected by the law who wished to join in with some expressive demonstration of their own. But this use of the State's power violates the fundamental rule of protection under the First Amendment, that a speaker has the autonomy to choose the content of his own message.

"Since *all* speech inherently involves choices of what to say and what to leave unsaid," *Pacific Gas & Electric Co. v. Public Utilities Comm'n of Cal.*, 475 U.S. 1, 11 (1986) (plurality opinion) (emphasis in original), one important manifestation of the principle of free speech is that one who chooses to speak may also decide "what not to say," *id.*, at 16. Although the State may at times "prescribe what shall be orthodox in commercial advertising" by requiring the dissemination of "purely factual and uncontroversial information," *Zauderer v. Office of Disciplinary Counsel of Supreme Court of Ohio*, 471 U.S. 626, 651 (1985), outside that context it may not compel affirmance of a belief with which the speaker disagrees, see *Barnette*, 319 U.S., at 642. Indeed this general rule, that the speaker has the right to tailor the speech, applies not only to expressions of value, opinion, or endorsement, but equally to statements of fact the speaker would rather avoid, subject, perhaps, to the permissive law of defamation. Nor is the rule's benefit restricted to the press, being enjoyed by business corporations generally and by ordinary people engaged in unsophisticated expression as well as by professional publishers. Its point is simply the point of all speech protection, which is to shield just those choices of content that in someone's eyes are misguided, or even hurtful.

Petitioners' claim to the benefit of this principle of autonomy to control one's own speech is as sound as the South Boston parade is expressive. Rather like a composer, the Council selects the expressive units of the parade from potential participants, and though the score may not produce a particularized message, each contingent's expression in the Council's eyes comports with what merits celebration on that day. Even if this view gives the Council credit for a more considered judgment than it actively made, the Council clearly decided to exclude a message it did not like from the communication it chose to make, and that is enough to invoke its right as a private speaker to shape its expression by speaking on one subject while remaining silent on another. The message it disfavored is not difficult to identify. Although GLIB's point (like the Council's) is not wholly articulate, a contingent marching behind the organization's banner would at least bear witness to the fact that some Irish are gay, lesbian, or bisexual, and the presence of the organized marchers would suggest their view that people of their sexual orientations have as much claim to unqualified social acceptance as heterosexuals and indeed as members of parade units organized around other identifying characteristics. The parade's organizers may not believe these facts about Irish sexuality to be so, or they may object to unqualified social acceptance of gays and lesbians or have some other reason for wishing to keep GLIB's message out of the parade. But whatever the reason, it boils down to the choice of a speaker not to propound a particular point of view, and that choice is presumed to lie beyond the government's power to control.

Respondents argue that any tension between this rule and the Massachusetts law falls short of unconstitutionality, citing the most recent of our cases on the general subject of compelled access for expressive purposes, *Turner Broadcasting System Inc. v. FCC,*, 512 U.S. 622, 114 S.Ct. 2445, 129 L.Ed.2d 497 (1994). There we reviewed regulations requiring cable operators to set aside channels for designated broadcast signals, and applied only intermediate scrutiny. Respondents contend on this authority that admission of GLIB to the parade would not threaten the core principle of speaker's autonomy because the Council, like a cable operator, is merely "a conduit" for the speech of participants in the parade "rather than itself a speaker." But this metaphor is not apt here, because GLIB's participation would likely be perceived as having resulted from the Council's customary determination about a unit admitted to the parade, that its message was worthy of presentation and quite possibly of support as well. A newspaper, similarly, "is more than a passive receptacle or conduit for news, comment, and advertising," and we have held that "[t]he choice of material . . . and the decisions made as to limitations on the size and content . . . and treatment of public issues . . . —whether fair or unfair—constitute the exercise of editorial control and judgment" upon which the State can not intrude. *Tornillo*, 418 U.S., at 258. Indeed, in *Pacific Gas & Electric*, we invalidated coerced access to the envelope of a private utility's bill and newsletter because the utility "may be forced either to appear to agree with [the intruding leaflet] or to respond." 475 U.S., at 15 (plurality) (citation omitted). The plurality made the further point that if "the government [were] freely able to compel . . . speakers to propound political messages with which they disagree, . . . protection [of a speaker's freedom] would be empty, for the government could require speakers to affirm in one breath that which they deny in the next." *Id.*, at 16. Thus, when dissemination of a view contrary to one's own is forced upon a speaker intimately connected with the communication advanced, the speaker's right to autonomy over the message is compromised.

In *Turner Broadcasting*, we found this problem absent in the cable context, because "[g]iven cable's long history of serving as a conduit for broadcast signals, there appears little risk that cable viewers would assume that the broadcast stations carried on a cable system convey ideas or messages endorsed by the cable operator." We stressed that the viewer is frequently apprised of the identity of the broadcaster whose signal is being received via cable and that it is "common practice for broadcasters to disclaim any identity of viewpoint between the management and the speakers who use the broadcast facility."

Parades and demonstrations, in contrast, are not understood to be so neutrally presented or selectively viewed. Unlike the programming offered on various channels by a cable network, the parade does not consist of individual, unrelated segments that happen to be transmitted together for individual selection by members of the audience. Although each parade unit generally identifies itself, each is understood to contribute something to a common theme, and accordingly there is no customary practice whereby private sponsors disavow "any identity of viewpoint" between themselves and the selected participants. Practice follows practicability here, for such disclaimers would be quite curious in a moving parade. Without deciding on the precise significance of the likelihood of misattribution, it nonetheless becomes clear that in the context of an expressive parade, as with a protest march, the parade's overall message is distilled from the individual presentations along the way, and each unit's expression is perceived by spectators as part of the whole.

An additional distinction between *Turner Broadcasting* and this case points to the fundamental weakness of any attempt to justify the state court order's limitation on the Council's autonomy as a speaker. A cable is not only a conduit for speech produced by others and selected by cable operators for transmission, but a franchised channel giving monopolistic opportunity to shut out some speakers. This power gives rise to the government's interest in limiting monopolistic autonomy in order to allow for the survival of broadcasters who might otherwise be silenced and consequently destroyed. The government's interest in *Turner Broadcasting* was not the alteration of speech, but the survival of speakers. In thus identifying an interest going beyond abridgment of speech itself, the defenders of the law at issue in *Turner Broadcasting* addressed the threshold requirement of any review under the Speech Clause, whatever the ultimate level of scrutiny, that a challenged restriction on speech serve a compelling, or at least important, governmental object.

In this case, of course, there is no assertion comparable to the *Turner Broadcasting* claim that some speakers will be destroyed in the absence of the challenged law. True, the size and success of petitioners' parade makes it an enviable vehicle for the dissemination of GLIB's views, but that fact, without more, would fall far short of supporting a claim that petitioners enjoy an abiding monopoly of access to spectators. Considering that GLIB presumably would have had a fair shot (under neutral criteria developed by the city) at obtaining a parade permit of its own, respondents have not shown that petitioners enjoy the capacity to "silence the voice of competing speakers," as cable operators do with respect to program providers who wish to reach subscribers. Nor has any other legitimate interest been identified in support of applying the Massachusetts statute in this way to expressive activity like the parade.

The statute is a piece of protective legislation that announces no purpose beyond the object both expressed and apparent in its provisions, which is to prevent any denial of access to (or discriminatory treatment in) public accommodations on proscribed grounds, including sexual orientation. On its face, the object of the law is to ensure by statute for gays and lesbians desiring to make use of public accommodations what the old common law promised to any member of the public wanting a meal at the inn, that accepting the usual terms of service, they will not be turned away merely on the proprietor's exercise of personal preference. When the law is applied to expressive activity in the way it was done here, its apparent object is simply to require speakers to modify the content of their expression to whatever extent beneficiaries of the law choose to alter it with messages of their own. But in the absence of some further, legitimate end, this object is merely to allow exactly what the general rule of speaker's autonomy forbids.

It might, of course, have been argued that a broader objective is apparent: that the ultimate point of forbidding acts of discrimination toward certain classes is to produce a society free of the corresponding biases. Requiring access to a speaker's message would thus be not an end in itself, but a means to produce speakers free of the biases, whose expressive conduct would be at least neutral toward the particular classes, obviating any future need for correction. But if this indeed is the point of applying the state law to expressive conduct, it is a decidedly fatal objective. Having availed itself of the public thoroughfares "for purposes of assembly [and] communicating thoughts between citizens," the Council is engaged in a use of the streets that has "from ancient times, been a part of the privileges, immunities, rights, and liberties of citizens." *Hague v. Committee for Industrial Organization*, 307 U.S. 496, 515 (1939) (opinion of Roberts, J.). Our tradition of free speech commands that a speaker who takes to the street corner to express his views in this way should be free from interference by the State based on the content of what he says. The very idea that a noncommercial speech restriction be used to produce thoughts and statements acceptable to some groups or, indeed, all people, grates on the First Amendment, for it amounts to nothing less than a proposal to limit speech in the service of orthodox expression. The Speech Clause has no more certain antithesis. While the law is free to promote all sorts of conduct in place of harmful behavior, it is not free to interfere with speech for no better reason than promoting an approved message or discouraging a disfavored one, however enlightened either purpose may strike the government. * * *

New York State Club Association is also instructive by the contrast it provides. There, we turned back a facial challenge to a state antidiscrimination statute on the assumption that the expressive associational character of a dining club with over 400 members could be sufficiently attenuated to permit application of the law even to such a private organization, but we also recognized that the State did not prohibit exclusion of those whose views were at odds with positions espoused by the general club memberships. *See also Roberts*, 468 U.S., at 627. In other words, although the association provided public benefits to which a State could ensure equal access, it was also engaged in expressive activity; compelled access to the benefit, which was upheld, did not trespass on the organization's message itself. If we were to analyze this case strictly along those lines, GLIB would lose. Assuming the parade to be large enough and a source of benefits (apart from its expression) that would generally justify a mandated access provision, GLIB could nonetheless be refused admission as an expressive contingent with its own message just as readily as a private club could exclude an applicant whose manifest views were at odds with a position taken by the club's existing members.

IV

Our holding today rests not on any particular view about the Council's message but on the Nation's commitment to protect freedom of speech. Disapproval of a private speaker's statement does not legitimize use of the Commonwealth's power to compel the speaker to alter the message by including one more acceptable to others. Accordingly, the judgment of the Supreme Judicial Court is reversed and the case remanded for proceedings not inconsistent with this opinion. *It is so ordered.*

NOTES

1. *Roberts*. Chief Justice Burger and Justice Blackmun, both former members of Twin Cities chapters of the Jaycees, recused themselves from *Roberts*. Justice O'Connor filed a concurrence in which she criticized the majority's opinion for overlooking the commercial nature of the opportunities afforded to men by membership in the Jaycees. "An association must choose its market. Once it enters the marketplace of commerce in any substantial degree it loses the complete control over its membership that it would otherwise enjoy if it confined its affairs to the marketplace of ideas." *Roberts*, 468 U.S. at 636, 104 S. Ct. at 3259 (O'Connor, J., concurring in part and in judgment).

2. *Hurley*. After years of controversy, the organizers of the St. Patrick's Day Parade in Boston dropped the ban on gay marchers in March, 2015. *See* Katharine Q. Seelye and Jess Bidgood, *Boston Celebrates End of Ban as Gays March in St. Patrick's Parade*, N.Y. Times, March 16, 2015, http://www.ny times.com/2015/03/16/us/boston-celebrates-end-of-ban-as-gays-march-in-st-patricks-parade.html?_r=0. New York's parade had likewise been enmeshed in years of controversy. It permitted gay marchers before Boston's parade did, but banned gay advocacy groups from participating. In March 2016, it changed policy and permitted LGBT groups to march. *See* Marc Santora and William Neuman, *With Mayor Bill de Blasio Marching, St. Patrick's Day*

Parade Walks Peaceful Path, N.Y. Tɪᴍᴇs, March 17, 2016, http://www.nytimes.com/2016/03/18/nyregion/with-mayor-bill-de-blasio-marching-st-patricks-day-parade-walks-peaceful-path.html. After the changes in each city, mayors who had previously boycotted the parades marched.

Bᴏʏ Sᴄᴏᴜᴛs ᴏғ Aᴍᴇʀɪᴄᴀ ᴠ. Dᴀʟᴇ

Supreme Court of the United States, 2000
530 U.S. 640, 120 S.Ct. 2446, 147 L.Ed.2d 554

Cʜɪᴇғ Jᴜsᴛɪᴄᴇ Rᴇʜɴǫᴜɪsᴛ delivered the opinion of the Court.

James Dale entered scouting in 1978 at the age of eight by joining Monmouth Council's Cub Scout Pack 142. Dale became a Boy Scout in 1981 and remained a Scout until he turned 18. By all accounts, Dale was an exemplary Scout. In 1988, he achieved the rank of Eagle Scout, one of Scouting's highest honors. Dale applied for adult membership in the Boy Scouts in 1989. The Boy Scouts approved his application for the position of assistant scoutmaster of Troop 73. Around the same time, Dale left home to attend Rutgers University. After arriving at Rutgers, Dale first acknowledged to himself and others that he is gay. He quickly became involved with, and eventually became the copresident of, the Rutgers University Lesbian/Gay Alliance. In 1990, Dale attended a seminar addressing the psychological and health needs of lesbian and gay teenagers. A newspaper covering the event interviewed Dale about his advocacy of homosexual teenagers' need for gay role models. In early July 1990, the newspaper published the interview and Dale's photograph over a caption identifying him as the copresident of the Lesbian/Gay Alliance.

Later that month, Dale received a letter from Monmouth Council Executive James Kay revoking his adult membership. Dale wrote to Kay requesting the reason for Monmouth Council's decision. Kay responded by letter that the Boy Scouts "specifically forbid membership to homosexuals." In 1992, Dale filed a complaint against the Boy Scouts in the New Jersey Superior Court [alleging violations of a New Jersey statute that prohibits discrimination on the basis of sexual orientation by places of public accommodation. The New Jersey Supreme Court ruled in Dale's favor.]

In *Roberts v. United States Jaycees*, 468 U.S. 609 (1984), we observed that "implicit in the right to engage in activities protected by the First Amendment" is "a corresponding right to associate with others in pursuit of a wide variety of political, social, economic, educational, religious, and cultural ends." This right is crucial in preventing the majority from imposing its views on groups that would rather express other, perhaps unpopular, ideas. Government actions that may unconstitutionally burden this freedom may take many forms, one of which is "intrusion into the internal structure or affairs of an association" like a "regulation that forces the group to accept members it does not desire." *Id.* at 623. Forcing a group to accept certain members may impair the ability of the group to express those views, and only those views, that it intends to express. Thus, "[f]reedom of association . . . plainly presupposes a freedom not to associate." *Id.*

The forced inclusion of an unwanted person in a group infringes the group's freedom of expressive association if the presence of that person affects in a significant way the group's ability to advocate public or private viewpoints. But the freedom of expressive association, like many freedoms, is not absolute. [It can] be overridden "by regulations adopted to serve compelling state interests, unrelated to the suppression of ideas, that cannot be achieved through means significantly less restrictive of associational freedoms." *Id.* at 623.

To determine whether a group is protected by the First Amendment's expressive associational right, we must determine whether the group engages in "expressive association." The First Amendment's protection of expressive association is not reserved for advocacy groups. But to come within its ambit, a group must engage in some form of expression, whether it be public or private. * * *

The Boy Scouts is a private, nonprofit organization. According to its mission statement:

It is the mission of the Boy Scouts of America to serve others by helping to instill values in young people and, in other ways, to prepare them to make ethical choices over their lifetime in achieving their full potential. The values we strive to instill are based on those found in the Scout Oath and Law:

<u>Scout Oath</u> On my honor I will do my best:

To do my duty to God and my country and to obey the Scout Law;

To help other people at all times;

To keep myself physically strong, mentally awake, and morally straight.

<u>Scout Law</u> A Scout is:

Trustworthy	Obedient
Loyal	Cheerful
Helpful	Thrifty
Friendly	Brave
Courteous	Clean
Kind	Reverent.

Thus, the general mission of the Boy Scouts is clear: "[T]o instill values in young people." The Boy Scouts seeks to instill these values by having its adult leaders spend time with the youth members, instructing and engaging them in activities like camping, archery, and fishing. During the time spent with the youth members, the scoutmasters and assistant scoutmasters inculcate them with the Boy Scouts' values—both expressly and by example. It seems indisputable that an association that seeks to transmit such a system of values engages in expressive activity.

Given that the Boy Scouts engages in expressive activity, we must determine whether the forced inclusion of Dale as an assistant scoutmaster would significantly affect the Boy Scouts' ability to advocate public or private viewpoints. This inquiry necessarily requires us first to explore, to a limited extent, the nature of the Boy Scouts' view of homosexuality.

The values the Boy Scouts seeks to instill are "based on" those listed in the Scout Oath and Law. The Boy Scouts explains that the Scout Oath and Law provide "a positive moral code for living; they are a list of 'do's' rather than 'don'ts.'" The Boy Scouts asserts that homosexual conduct is inconsistent with the values embodied in the Scout Oath and Law, particularly with the values represented by the terms "morally straight" and "clean."

Obviously, the Scout Oath and Law do not expressly mention sexuality or sexual orientation. And the terms "morally straight" and "clean" are by no means self-defining. Different people would attribute to those terms very different meanings. For example, some people may believe that engaging in homosexual conduct is not at odds with being "morally straight" and "clean." And others may believe that engaging in homosexual conduct is contrary to being "morally straight" and "clean." The Boy Scouts says it falls within the latter category. * * *

The Boy Scouts asserts that it "teach[es] that homosexual conduct is not morally straight," and that it does "not want to promote homosexual conduct as a legitimate form of behavior." We accept the Boy Scouts' assertion. We need not inquire further to determine the nature of the Boy Scouts' expression with respect to homosexuality. . . . We cannot doubt that the Boy Scouts sincerely holds this view.

We must then determine whether Dale's presence as an assistant scoutmaster would significantly burden the Boy Scouts' desire to not "promote homosexual conduct as a legitimate form of behavior." As we give deference to an association's assertions regarding the nature of its expression, we must also give deference to an association's view of what would impair its expression. That is not to say that an expressive association can erect a shield against antidiscrimination laws simply by asserting that mere acceptance of a member from a particular group would impair its message. But here Dale, by his own admission, is one of a group of gay Scouts who have "become leaders in their community and are open and honest about their sexual orientation." Dale was the copresident of a gay and lesbian organization at college and remains a gay rights activist. Dale's presence in the Boy Scouts would, at the very least, force the organization to send a message, both to the youth members and the world, that the Boy Scouts accepts homosexual conduct as a legitimate form of behavior.

Hurley [*v. Irish-American Gay, Lesbian and Bisexual Group of Boston, Inc.*, 515 U.S. 557 (1995)], is illustrative on this point. . . . As the presence of GLIB in Boston's St. Patrick's Day parade would have interfered with the parade organizers' choice not to propound a particular point of view, the presence of Dale as an assistant scoutmaster would just as surely interfere with the Boy Scout's choice not to propound a point of view contrary to its beliefs.

The New Jersey Supreme Court determined that the Boy Scouts' ability to disseminate its message was not significantly affected by the forced inclusion of Dale as an assistant scoutmaster because of the following findings:

> Boy Scout members do not associate for the purpose of disseminating the belief that homosexuality is immoral; Boy Scouts discourages its leaders from disseminating any views on sexual issues; and Boy Scouts includes sponsors and members who subscribe to different views in respect of homosexuality.

Boy Scouts of America v. Dale, 734 A.2d 1196, 1223 (N.J. 1999). We disagree with the New Jersey Supreme Court's conclusion drawn from these findings.

First, associations do not have to associate for the "purpose" of disseminating a certain message in order to be entitled to the protections of the First Amendment. An association must merely engage in expressive activity that could be impaired in order to be entitled to protection. For example, the purpose of the St. Patrick's Day parade in *Hurley* was not to espouse any views about sexual orientation, but we held that the parade organizers had a right to exclude certain participants nonetheless.

Second, even if the Boy Scouts discourages Scout leaders from disseminating views on sexual issues—a fact that the Boy Scouts disputes with contrary evidence—the First Amendment protects the Boy Scouts' method of expression. If the Boy Scouts wishes Scout leaders to avoid questions of sexuality and teach only by example, this fact does not negate the sincerity of its belief discussed above.

Third, the First Amendment simply does not require that every member of a group agree on every issue in order for the group's policy to be "expressive association." The Boy Scouts takes an official position with respect to homosexual conduct, and that is sufficient for First Amendment purposes. In this same vein, Dale makes much of the claim that the Boy Scouts does not revoke the membership of heterosexual Scout leaders that openly disagree with the Boy Scouts' policy on sexual orientation. But if this is true, it is irrelevant.[1] The presence of an avowed homosexual and gay rights activist in an assistant scoutmaster's uniform sends a distinctly different message from the presence of a heterosexual assistant scoutmaster who is on record as disagreeing with Boy Scouts policy. The Boy Scouts has a First Amendment right to choose to send one message but not the other. The fact that the organization does not trumpet its views from the housetops, or that it tolerates dissent within its ranks, does not mean that its views receive no First Amendment protection.

Having determined that the Boy Scouts is an expressive association and that the forced inclusion of Dale would significantly affect its expression, we inquire whether the application of New Jersey's public accommodations law to require that the Boy Scouts accept Dale as an assistant scoutmaster runs afoul of the Scouts' freedom of expressive association. We conclude that it does. * * *

[A] state requirement that the Boy Scouts retain Dale as an assistant scoutmaster would significantly burden the organization's right to oppose or disfavor homosexual conduct. The state interests embodied in New Jersey's public accommodations law do not justify such a severe intrusion on the Boy Scouts' rights to freedom of expressive association. That being the case, we hold that the First Amendment prohibits the State from imposing such a requirement through the application of its public accommodations law.

JUSTICE STEVENS' dissent makes much of its observation that the public perception of homosexuality in this country has changed. Indeed, it appears that homosexuality has gained greater societal acceptance. But this is scarcely an argument for denying First Amendment protection to those who refuse to accept these views. The First Amendment protects expression, be it of the popular variety or not. And the fact that an idea may be embraced and advocated by increasing numbers of people is all the more reason to protect the First Amendment rights of those who wish to voice a different view.

---

[1]   The record evidence sheds doubt on Dale's assertion. For example, the National Director of the Boy Scouts certified that "any persons who advocate to Scouting youth that homosexual conduct is" consistent with Scouting values will not be registered as adult leaders. And the Monmouth Council Scout Executive testified that the advocacy of the morality of homosexuality to youth members by any adult member is grounds for revocation of the adult's membership.

JUSTICE STEVENS, with whom JUSTICE SOUTER, JUSTICE GINSBURG and JUSTICE BREYER join, dissenting.

[Justice Stevens's dissent begins with a lengthy review of the factual record, aimed at demonstrating that the Boy Scouts, as an organization, did not maintain an explicit anti-gay policy or propound a consistent or coherent anti-gay message.]

[O]ther than [in] a single sentence, BSA fails to show that it ever taught Scouts that homosexuality is not "morally straight" or "clean," [phrases used in the Scout oath] or that such a view was part of the group's collective efforts to foster a belief. Furthermore, BSA's policy statements fail to establish any clear, consistent, and unequivocal position on homosexuality. * * *

[BSA] was clearly on notice by 1990 that it might well be subjected to state public accommodation antidiscrimination laws, and that a court might one day reject its claimed right to associate. Yet it took no steps prior to Dale's expulsion to clarify how its exclusivity was connected to its expression. It speaks volumes about the credibility of BSA's claim to a shared goal that homosexuality is incompatible with Scouting that since at least 1984 it had been aware of this issue . . . yet it did nothing in the intervening six years (or even in the years after Dale's expulsion) to explain clearly and openly why the presence of homosexuals would affect its expressive activities, or to make the view of "morally straight" and "clean" taken in its 1991 and 1992 policies a part of the values actually instilled in Scouts through the Handbook, lessons, or otherwise.

* * * The relevant question is whether the mere inclusion of the person at issue would "impose any serious burden," "affect in any significant way," or be "a substantial restraint upon" the organization's "shared goals," "basic goals," or "collective effort to foster beliefs." Accordingly, it is necessary to examine what, exactly, are BSA's shared goals and the degree to which its expressive activities would be burdened, affected, or restrained by including homosexuals.

The evidence before this Court makes it exceptionally clear that BSA has, at most, simply adopted an exclusionary membership policy and has no shared goal of disapproving of homosexuality. BSA's mission statement and federal charter say nothing on the matter; its official membership policy is silent; its Scout Oath and Law—and accompanying definitions—are devoid of any view on the topic; its guidance for Scouts and Scoutmasters on sexuality declare that such matters are "not construed to be Scouting's proper area," but are the province of a Scout's parents and pastor; and BSA's posture respecting religion tolerates a wide variety of views on the issue of homosexuality. Moreover, there is simply no evidence that BSA otherwise teaches anything in this area, or that it instructs Scouts on matters involving homosexuality in ways not conveyed in the Boy Scout or Scoutmaster Handbooks. In short, Boy Scouts of America is simply silent on homosexuality. There is no shared goal or collective effort to foster a belief about homosexuality at all—let alone one that is significantly burdened by admitting homosexuals.

* * * The majority pretermits this entire analysis. It finds that BSA in fact " 'teach[es] that homosexual conduct is not morally straight.' " This conclusion, remarkably, rests entirely on statements in BSA's briefs. Moreover, the majority insists that we must "give deference to an association's assertions regarding the nature of its expression" and "we must also give deference to an association's view of what would impair its expression." So long as the record "contains written evidence" to support a group's bare assertion, "[w]e need not inquire further." Once the organization "asserts" that it engages in particular expression, "[w]e cannot doubt" the truth of that assertion.

This is an astounding view of the law. I am unaware of any previous instance in which our analysis of the scope of a constitutional right was determined by looking at what a litigant asserts in his or her brief and inquiring no further. It is even more astonishing in the First Amendment area, because, as the majority itself acknowledges, "we are obligated to independently review the factual record." It is an odd form of independent review that consists of deferring entirely to whatever a litigant claims. But the majority insists that our inquiry must be "limited," because "it is not the role of the courts to reject a group's expressed values because they disagree with those values or find them internally inconsistent."

But nothing in our cases calls for this Court to do any such thing. An organization can adopt the message of its choice, and it is not this Court's place to disagree with it. But we must inquire whether the group is, in fact, expressing a message (whatever it may be) and whether that message (if one is expressed) is significantly affected by a State's antidiscrimination law. More critically, that inquiry requires our independent analysis, rather than deference to a group's litigating posture. Reflection on the subject dictates that such an inquiry is required.

Surely there are instances in which an organization that truly aims to foster a belief at odds with the purposes of a State's antidiscrimination laws will have a First Amendment right to association that precludes forced compliance with those laws. But that right is not a freedom to discriminate at will, nor is it a right to maintain an exclusionary membership policy simply out of fear of what the public reaction would be if the group's membership were opened up. It is an implicit right designed to protect the enumerated rights of the First Amendment, not a license to act on any discriminatory impulse. To prevail in asserting a right of expressive association as a defense to a charge of violating an antidiscrimination law, the organization must at least show it has adopted and advocated an unequivocal position inconsistent with a position advocated or epitomized by the person whom the organization seeks to exclude. If this Court were to defer to whatever position an organization is prepared to assert in its briefs, there would be no way to mark the proper boundary between genuine exercises of the right to associate, on the one hand, and sham claims that are simply attempts to insulate nonexpressive private discrimination, on the other hand. Shielding a litigant's claim from judicial scrutiny would, in turn, render civil rights legislation a nullity, and turn this important constitutional right into a farce. Accordingly, the Court's prescription of total deference will not do. . . .

Even if BSA's right to associate argument fails, it nonetheless might have a First Amendment right to refrain from including debate and dialogue about homosexuality as part of its mission to instill values in Scouts. . . . Dale's right to advocate certain beliefs in a public forum or in a private debate does not include a right to advocate these ideas when he is working as a Scoutmaster. And BSA cannot be compelled to include a message about homosexuality among the values it actually chooses to teach its Scouts, if it would prefer to remain silent on that subject. * * *

In its briefs, BSA implies, even if it does not directly argue, that Dale would use his Scoutmaster position as a "bully pulpit" to convey immoral messages to his troop, and therefore his inclusion in the group would compel BSA to include a message it does not want to impart. Even though the majority does not endorse that argument, I think it is important to explain why it lacks merit, before considering the argument the majority does accept. BSA has not contended, nor does the record support, that Dale had ever advocated a view on homosexuality to his troop before his membership was revoked. Accordingly, BSA's revocation could only have been based on an assumption that he would do so in the future. But the only information BSA had at the time it revoked Dale's membership was a newspaper article describing a seminar at Rutgers University on the topic of homosexual teenagers that Dale attended. The relevant passage reads:

> James Dale, 19, co-president of the Rutgers University Lesbian Gay Alliance with Sharice Richardson, also 19, said he lived a double life while in high school, pretending to be straight while attending a military academy. He remembers dating girls and even laughing at homophobic jokes while at school, only admitting his homosexuality during his second year at Rutgers. " 'I was looking for a role model, someone who was gay and accepting of me,' Dale said, adding he wasn't just seeking sexual experiences, but a community that would take him in and provide him with a support network and friends."

Nothing in that article, however, even remotely suggests that Dale would advocate any views on homosexuality to his troop. . . . [T]here is no basis for BSA to presume that a homosexual will be unable to comply with BSA's policy not to discuss sexual matters any more than it would presume that politically or religiously active members could not resist the urge to proselytize or politicize during troop meetings.[19] As BSA itself puts it, its rights are "not implicated *unless* a prospective leader *presents himself* as a role model inconsistent with Boy Scouting's understanding of the Scout Oath and Law."

The majority, though, does not rest its conclusion on the claim that Dale will use his position as a bully pulpit. Rather, it contends that Dale's mere presence among the Boy Scouts will itself force the group to convey a message about homosexuality—even if Dale has no intention of doing so. The majority holds that "[t]he presence of an avowed homosexual and gay rights activist in an assistant scoutmaster's uniform sends a distinc[t] . . . message," and, accordingly, BSA is entitled to exclude that message. In particular, "Dale's presence in the Boy Scouts would, at the very least, force the organization to send a message, both to the youth members and the world, that the Boy Scouts accepts homosexual conduct as a legitimate form of behavior."

The majority's argument relies exclusively on *Hurley*. Dale's inclusion in the Boy Scouts is nothing like the case in *Hurley*. . . . His participation sends no cognizable message to the Scouts or to the world. Unlike GLIB, Dale did not carry a banner or a sign; he did not distribute any fact sheet; and he expressed no intent to send any message. If there is any kind of message being sent, then, it is by the mere act of joining the Boy Scouts. Such an act does not constitute an instance of symbolic speech under the First Amendment. * * *

The only apparent explanation for the majority's holding, then, is that homosexuals are simply so different from the rest of society that their presence alone—unlike any other individual's—should be singled out for special First Amendment treatment. Under the majority's reasoning, an openly gay male is irreversibly affixed with the label "homosexual." That label, even though unseen, communicates a message that permits his exclusion wherever he goes. His openness is the sole and sufficient justification for his ostracism. Though unintended, reliance on such a justification is tantamount to a constitutionally prescribed symbol of inferiority. As counsel for the Boy Scouts remarked, Dale "put a banner

---

[19]   Consider, in this regard, that a heterosexual, as well as a homosexual, could advocate to the Scouts the view that homosexuality is not immoral. BSA acknowledges as much by stating that a heterosexual who advocates that view to Scouts would be expelled as well. But BSA does not expel heterosexual members who take that view outside of their participation in Scouting, as long as they do not advocate that position to the Scouts. And if there is no reason to presume that such a heterosexual will openly violate BSA's desire to express no view on the subject, what reason—other than blatant stereotyping—could justify a contrary presumption for homosexuals?

around his neck when he . . . got himself into the newspaper. . . . He created a reputation. . . . He can't take that banner off. He put it on himself and, indeed, he has continued to put it on himself." * * *

Furthermore, it is not likely that BSA would be understood to send any message, either to Scouts or to the world, simply by admitting someone as a member. Over the years, BSA has generously welcomed over 87 million young Americans into its ranks. In 1992 over one million adults were active BSA members. The notion that an organization of that size and enormous prestige implicitly endorses the views that each of those adults may express in a non-Scouting context is simply mind boggling. Indeed, in this case there is no evidence that the young Scouts in Dale's troop, or members of their families, were even aware of his sexual orientation, either before or after his public statements at Rutgers University. It is equally farfetched to assert that Dale's open declaration of his homosexuality, reported in a local newspaper, will effectively force BSA to send a message to anyone simply because it allows Dale to be an Assistant Scoutmaster. For an Olympic gold medal winner or a Wimbledon tennis champion, being "openly gay" perhaps communicates a message—for example, that openness about one's sexual orientation is more virtuous than concealment; that a homosexual person can be a capable and virtuous person who should be judged like anyone else; and that homosexuality is not immoral—but it certainly does not follow that they necessarily send a message on behalf of the organizations that sponsor the activities in which they excel. The fact that such persons participate in these organizations is not usually construed to convey a message on behalf of those organizations any more than does the inclusion of women, African-Americans, religious minorities, or any other discrete group. Surely the organizations are not forced by antidiscrimination laws to take any position on the legitimacy of any individual's private beliefs or private conduct.

The State of New Jersey has decided that people who are open and frank about their sexual orientation are entitled to equal access to employment as school teachers, police officers, librarians, athletic coaches, and a host of other jobs filled by citizens who serve as role models for children and adults alike. Dozens of Scout units throughout the State are sponsored by public agencies, such as schools and fire departments, that employ such role models. BSA's affiliation with numerous public agencies that comply with New Jersey's law against discrimination cannot be understood to convey any particular message endorsing or condoning the activities of all these people.

NOTES

1.   Over a series of years, the Boy Scouts of America largely abandoned the policy they defended in *Dale*. In May 2013, the leadership voted to allow

openly gay youths to participate in the organization. Erik Eckholm, *Boy Scouts End Longtime Ban on Openly Gay Youths*, N.Y. Times, May 23, 2013, at A1. But the group still barred openly gay adults and leaders from participating. This first major policy change followed a vocal campaign by members of the scouting community, including a campaign in which many Eagle Scouts renounced their status or returned their badges in protest of the Boy Scouts' exclusionary policies. Gabriel Rodriguez, *This Brave Eagle Scout Won't Tolerate the Boy Scouts' Anti-Gay Policy*, PolicyMic (April 7, 2013), http://www.policymic.com/articles/33409/this-brave-eagle-scout-won-t-tolerate-the-boy-scouts-anti-gay-policy. In July 2015, the Boy Scouts dropped their ban on gay scout leaders, though left discretion for church-sponsored units to choose leaders consistent with their views. Erik Eckholm, *Boy Scouts End Ban on Gay Leaders, Over Protests by Mormon Church*, N. Y. Times, July 27, 2015.

2.   Not all youth organizations similar to the Boy Scouts pursued policies of exclusion. The Girl Scouts of the United States of America explicitly address homosexuality in its membership policy:

> As a private organization, Girl Scouts of the U.S.A. respects the values and beliefs of its members and does not intrude into personal matters. Therefore, there are no membership policies on sexual preference. However, Girl Scouts of the U.S.A. has firm standards relating to the appropriate conduct of adult volunteers and staff. The Girl Scout organization does not condone or permit sexual displays of any sort by its members during Girl Scout activities, nor does it permit the advocacy or promotion of a personal lifestyle or sexual preference. These are private matters for girls and their families to address.

Girl Scouts of the United States of America, Statements on GSUSA Membership Policies (Oct. 1991). Indeed, in October 2011, a Girl Scout troop in Colorado admitted a transgender member, Bobby Montoya. Katia Hetter, *Girl Scouts Accepts Transgender Kid, Provokes Cookie Boycott*, CNN (Jan. 13, 2012, 7:23 PM), http://www.cnn.com/2012/01/13/living/girl-scout-boycott/. The Girl Scouts of Colorado said, "If a child identifies as a girl and the child's family presents her as a girl, Girl Scouts of Colorado welcomes her as a Girl Scout." *Id.*

3.   Not all supporters of gay equality necessarily regarded the *Dale* decision as wrongly decided. Professor Dale Carpenter, for example, argued that:

> The First Amendment created gay America. For advocates of gay legal and social equality there has been no more reliable and important constitutional text. The freedoms it guarantees have protected gay cultural and political institutions from state regulation designed to impose a contrary vision of the good life. Gay organizations, clubs, bars, politicians, journals, newspapers, radio

programs, television shows—all these would be swept away in the absence of a strong First Amendment.

The First Amendment, evenhanded and detached from passions to an unusual degree for a jurisprudence, sheltered gays even when most of the country thought they were not just immoral, but also sick and dangerous. . . .

By contrast, the Due Process Clause (in its substantive dimension) has been faithless. The Equal Protection Clause has been impotent. The Ninth Amendment has been missing in action. . . . And the Fourteenth Amendment's Privileges and Immunities Clause has not been seen since it was banished at the age of five.

Dale Carpenter, *Expressive Association and Anti-Discrimination Law After Dale*, 85 MINN. L. REV. 1515, 1525–27 (2001).

4.   For scholarly commentary on *Dale* from different perspectives, see Yaacov Ben-Shemesh, *Multiculturalism and the Anti-Discrimination Principle: Law and Intercultural Conflicts*, 1 LAW & ETHICS HUM. RTS. 271 (2007); Erwin Chemerinsky & Catherine Fisk, *The Expressive Interest of Associations*, 9 WM. & MARY BILL RTS. J. 595 (2001); Richard A. Epstein, *The Constitutional Perils of Moderation: The Case of the Boy Scouts*, 74 S. CAL. L. REV. 119 (2000); Nancy J. Knauer, *"Simply So Different": The Uniquely Expressive Character of the Openly Gay Individual After* Boy Scouts of America v. Dale, 89 KY. L.J. 997 (2001); Andrew Koppelman, *Sign of the Times:* Dale v. Boy Scouts of America *and the Changing Meaning of Nondiscrimination*, 23 CARDOZO L. REV. 1819 (2002); Jed Rubenfeld, *The First Amendment's Purpose*, 53 STAN. L. REV. 767 (2001); Seana Valentine Shiffrin, *What Is Really Wrong with Compelled Association*, 99 NW. U. L. REV. 839 (2005); Laurence H. Tribe, *Disentangling Symmetries: Speech, Association, Parenthood*, 28 PEPP. L. REV. 641 (2001); Neal Troum, *Expressive Association and the Right to Exclude: Reading Between the Lines in* Boy Scouts of America v. Dale, 35 CREIGHTON L. REV. 641 (2002).

5.   Six years after *Dale*, the Supreme Court decided *Rumsfeld v. Forum for Academic and Institutional Rights, Inc.*, 547 U.S. 47, 126 S.Ct. 1297, 164 L.Ed.2d 156 (2006). In *FAIR*, a group of law schools challenged the Solomon Amendment, a federal law that denied federal funding to universities if the university's law school (or any other unit) did not give military employers the same access to on-campus recruiting as it gave other employers. The Solomon Amendment was enacted when the military still barred openly lesbian and gay service members under the "Don't Ask, Don' Tell" policy. Many law schools sought to deny the military full access to on-campus recruiting because of antidiscrimination policies that did not allow any employer to discriminate based on a student's sexual orientation. FAIR argued that the Solomon Amendment violated law schools' speech and associational rights because it forced schools to express approval or acceptance of the military's discriminatory policy when, in fact, they objected to the policy. In *FAIR*, the Court rejected these First Amendment claims, holding that the law schools

were expressing no message of approval by permitting full access to military recruiters. Notice the contrast with *Dale*, where the Court deferred to the Boy Scouts' understanding of the message they would send by allowing openly gay scoutmasters. The FAIR court refused to defer to the law schools' view of what allowing access to military recruiters would express, and said the law schools remained free to say whatever they wished about the government's military policy as long as equal access was provided to recruiters. Can *Dale* and *FAIR* be reconciled?

IV. THE CONFLICT BETWEEN LGBT EQUALITY AND RELIGIOUS LIBERTY

A. RELIGIOUS PERSPECTIVES ON LGBT EQUALITY AND SAME-SEX RELATIONSHIPS

This section turns its focus to objections to LGBT equality that are grounded in religious liberty. This conflict intensified with the advent of same-sex marriage, but the debate is broader and reaches a range of LGBT equality measures, including antidiscrimination laws. Nor are the positions of all religious entities the same. Religious bodies have taken a variety of perspectives on homosexuality, LGBT rights, and marriage for same-sex couples. While some religious groups have opposed advances on LGBT issues, others have promoted the interests of LGBT individuals and their families. In this Chapter, however, we focus on religiously-grounded objections to LGBT equality measures and the legal frameworks used to address these objections.

To better understand the religious basis for opposition, we begin with the position of the U.S. Conference of Catholic Bishops, which links marriage to both procreative sex and gender differentiation.

BETWEEN MAN AND WOMAN: QUESTIONS AND ANSWERS ABOUT MARRIAGE AND SAME-SEX UNIONS*

We, the Catholic bishops of the United States, offer here some basic truths to assist people in understanding Catholic teaching about marriage and to enable them to promote marriage and its sacredness.

1. What is marriage?

Marriage, as instituted by God, is a faithful, exclusive, lifelong union of a man and a woman joined in an intimate community of life and love. They commit themselves completely to each other and to the wondrous

---

*   *Between Man and Woman: Questions and Answers About Marriage and Same-Sex Unions* was developed by the Committee on Marriage and Family Life of the U.S. Conference of Catholic Bishops and was approved for publication by the full body of bishops in November 2003.

responsibility of bringing children into the world and caring for them. The call to marriage is woven deeply into the human spirit. Man and woman are equal. However, as created, they are different from but made for each other. This complementarity, including sexual difference, draws them together in a mutually loving union that should be always open to the procreation of children (see *Catechism of the Catholic Church* [CCC], nos. 1602–1605). These truths about marriage are present in the order of nature and can be perceived by the light of human reason. They have been confirmed by divine Revelation in Sacred Scripture. * * *

3.   Why can marriage exist only between a man and a woman?

The natural structure of human sexuality makes man and woman complementary partners for the transmission of human life. Only a union of male and female can express the sexual complementarity willed by God for marriage. The permanent and exclusive commitment of marriage is the necessary context for the expression of sexual love intended by God both to serve the transmission of human life and to build up the bond between husband and wife (see CCC, nos. 1639–1640).

In marriage, husband and wife give themselves totally to each other in their masculinity and femininity (see CCC, no. 1643). They are equal as human beings but different as man and woman, fulfilling each other through this natural difference. This unique complementarity makes possible the conjugal bond that is the core of marriage.

4.   Why is a same-sex union not equivalent to a marriage?

For several reasons a same-sex union contradicts the nature of marriage: It is not based on the natural complementarity of male and female; it cannot cooperate with God to create new life; and the natural purpose of sexual union cannot be achieved by a same-sex union. Persons in same-sex unions cannot enter into a true conjugal union. Therefore, it is wrong to equate their relationship to a marriage. * * *

6.   Does denying marriage to homosexual persons demonstrate unjust discrimination and a lack of respect for them as persons?

It is not unjust to deny legal status to same-sex unions because marriage and same-sex unions are essentially different realities. In fact, justice requires society to do so. To uphold God's intent for marriage, in which sexual relations have their proper and exclusive place, is not to offend the dignity of homosexual persons. Christians must give witness to the whole moral truth and oppose as immoral both homosexual acts and unjust discrimination against homosexual persons. The *Catechism of the Catholic Church* urges that homosexual persons "be accepted with respect, compassion, and sensitivity" (no. 2358). It also encourages chaste friendships. "Chastity is expressed notably in *friendship with one's* *neighbor.* Whether it develops between persons of the same or opposite sex, friendship represents a great good for all" (no. 2347). * * *

NOTE

Of course, the Catholic Church is not the only major religious institution opposed to same-sex marriage and LGBT equality. Many evangelical Protestant churches, which cover a range of denominations, have expressed opposition to LGBT advances. The Church of Jesus Christ of Latter-day Saints (the Mormon Church) also opposes marriage for same-sex couples. And some Islamic and Orthodox Jewish institutions oppose LGBT equality. For an example of a cross-denominational statement opposing LGBT equality, see *Manhattan Declaration: A Call to Christian Conscience*, Manhattan Declaration (Nov. 2009). Nonetheless, faith communities continue to engage in their own internal debates over the role of LGBT people, and some have recently moved toward acceptance of marriage for same-sex couples. *See, e.g.,* Laurie Goodstein, *Largest Presbyterian Denomination Gives Final Approval for Same-Sex Marriage*, N.Y. TIMES (Mar. 17, 2015).

B. LITIGATING FOR EXEMPTIONS FROM ANTI-DISCRIMINATION LAWS

The next two cases bring squarely into focus the legal tension between some religious beliefs and antidiscrimination laws. Both pit First Amendment rights against LGBT equality claims. The first case involves speech and association claims arising under the First Amendment. The second case involves speech and free exercise claims arising principally under the First Amendment. As you consider these cases, think about if and how the religious nature of the claims changes the issue from what we have seen thus far. Notice, as well, that the second case involves a *commercial* actor who resists application of a non-discrimination norm. How should that fact weigh in the analysis?

CHRISTIAN LEGAL SOCIETY V. MARTINEZ

Supreme Court of the United States, 2010
561 U.S. 661, 130 S.Ct. 2971, 177 L.Ed.2d 838

JUSTICE GINSBURG delivered the opinion of the Court.

In a series of decisions, this Court has emphasized that the First Amendment generally precludes public universities from denying student organizations access to school-sponsored forums because of the groups' viewpoints. *See Rosenberger* v. *Rector and Visitors of Univ. of Va.*, 515 U.S. 819 (1995); *Widmar* v. *Vincent*, 454 U.S. 263 (1981); *Healy* v. *James*, 408 U.S. 169 (1972). This case concerns a novel question regarding student activities at public universities: May a public law school condition its official recognition of a student group—and the attendant use of school funds and facilities—on the organization's agreement to open eligibility for membership and leadership to all students?

In the view of petitioner Christian Legal Society (CLS), an accept-all-comers policy impairs its First Amendment rights to free speech, expressive association, and free exercise of religion by prompting it, on pain of relinquishing the advantages of recognition, to accept members who do not share the organization's core beliefs about religion and sexual orientation. From the perspective of respondent Hastings College of the Law (Hastings or the Law School), CLS seeks special dispensation from an across-the-board open-access requirement designed to further the reasonable educational purposes underpinning the school's student-organization program. * * *

Founded in 1878, Hastings was the first law school in the University of California public-school system. Like many institutions of higher education, Hastings encourages students to form extracurricular associations that "contribute to the Hastings community and experience." These groups offer students "opportunities to pursue academic and social interests outside of the classroom [to] further their education" and to help them "develo[p] leadership skills."

Through its "Registered Student Organization" (RSO) program, Hastings extends official recognition to student groups. Several benefits attend this school-approved status. RSOs are eligible to seek financial assistance from the Law School, which subsidizes their events using funds from a mandatory student-activity fee imposed on all students. RSOs may also use Law-School channels to communicate with students: They may place announcements in a weekly Office-of-Student-Services newsletter, advertise events on designated bulletin boards, send e-mails using a Hastings-organization address, and participate in an annual Student Organizations Fair designed to advance recruitment efforts. In addition, RSOs may apply for permission to use the Law School's facilities for meetings and office space. Finally, Hastings allows officially recognized groups to use its name and logo.

In exchange for these benefits, RSOs must abide by certain conditions. Only a "non-commercial organization whose membership is limited to Hastings students may become [an RSO]." A prospective RSO must submit its bylaws to Hastings for approval, and if it intends to use the Law School's name or logo, it must sign a license agreement. Critical here, all RSOs must undertake to comply with Hastings' "Policies and Regulations Applying to College Activities, Organizations and Students."

The Law School's Policy on Nondiscrimination (Nondiscrimination Policy), which binds RSOs, states:

"[Hastings] is committed to a policy against legally impermissible, arbitrary or unreasonable discriminatory practices. All groups, including administration, faculty, student governments, [Hastings]-owned student residence facilities and programs sponsored by [Hastings], are governed by this policy of nondiscrimination. [Hasting's] policy on nondiscrimination is to comply fully with applicable law.

"[Hastings] shall not discriminate unlawfully on the basis of race, color, religion, national origin, ancestry, disability, age, sex or sexual orientation. This nondiscrimination policy covers admission, access and treatment in Hastings-sponsored programs and activities."

Hastings interprets the Nondiscrimination Policy, as it relates to the RSO program, to mandate acceptance of all comers: School-approved groups must "allow any student to participate, become a member, or seek leadership positions in the organization, regardless of [her] status or beliefs." Other law schools have adopted similar all-comers policies. See, *e.g.,* Georgetown University Law Center, Office of Student Life: Student Organizations, available at http://www.law.georgetown.edu/StudentLife/ StudentOrgs/NewGroup.htm (All Internet materials as visited June 24, 2010, and included in Clerk of Court's case file) (Membership in registered groups must be "open to all students."); Hofstra Law School Student Handbook 2009–2010, p.49, available at http://law.hofstra.edu/ pdf/StudentLife/StudentAffairs/Handbook/stuhb_handbook.pdf ("[Student] organizations are open to all students."). From Hastings' adoption of its Nondiscrimination Policy in 1990 until the events stirring this litigation, "no student organization at Hastings . . . ever sought an exemption from the Policy."

In 2004, CLS became the first student group to do so. At the beginning of the academic year, the leaders of a predecessor Christian organization—which had been an RSO at Hastings for a decade—formed CLS by affiliating with the national Christian Legal Society (CLS-National). CLS-National, an association of Christian lawyers and law students, charters student chapters at law schools throughout the country. CLS chapters must adopt bylaws that, *inter alia,* require members and officers to sign a "Statement of Faith" and to conduct their lives in accord with prescribed principles.[1] Among those tenets is the

---

[1]   The Statement of Faith provides: "Trusting in Jesus Christ as my Savior, I believe in:

- One God, eternally existent in three persons, Father, Son and Holy Spirit.
- God the Father Almighty, Maker of heaven and earth.
- The Deity of our Lord, Jesus Christ, God's only Son conceived of the Holy Spirit, born of the Virgin Mary; His vicarious death for our sins through which we receive eternal life; His bodily resurrection and personal return.
- The presence and power of the Holy Spirit in the work of regeneration.
- The Bible as the inspired Word of God." App. 226.

belief that sexual activity should not occur outside of marriage between a man and a woman; CLS thus interprets its bylaws to exclude from affiliation anyone who engages in "unrepentant homosexual conduct." CLS also excludes students who hold religious convictions different from those in the Statement of Faith.

On September 17, 2004, CLS submitted to Hastings an application for RSO status, accompanied by all required documents, including the set of bylaws mandated by CLS-National. Several days later, the Law School rejected the application; CLS's bylaws, Hastings explained, did not comply with the Nondiscrimination Policy because CLS barred students based on religion and sexual orientation.

CLS formally requested an exemption from the Nondiscrimination Policy, but Hastings declined to grant one. "[T]o be one of our student-recognized organizations," Hastings reiterated, "CLS must open its membership to all students irrespective of their religious beliefs or sexual orientation." If CLS instead chose to operate outside the RSO program, Hastings stated, the school "would be pleased to provide [CLS] the use of Hastings facilities for its meetings and activities." CLS would also have access to chalkboards and generally available campus bulletin boards to announce its events. In other words, Hastings would do nothing to suppress CLS's endeavors, but neither would it lend RSO-level support for them.

Refusing to alter its bylaws, CLS did not obtain RSO status. It did, however, operate independently during the 2004–2005 academic year. . . .

On October 22, 2004, CLS filed suit against various Hastings officers and administrators . . . alleg[ing] that Hastings' refusal to grant the organization RSO status violated CLS's First and Fourteenth Amendment rights to free speech, expressive association, and free exercise of religion.

On cross-motions for summary judgment, the U.S. District Court for the Northern District of California ruled in favor of Hastings. The Law School's all-comers condition on access to a limited public forum, the court held, was both reasonable and viewpoint neutral, and therefore did not violate CLS's right to free speech.

Nor, in the District Court's view, did the Law School impermissibly impair CLS's right to expressive association. * * *

The court also rejected CLS's Free Exercise Clause argument. "[T]he Nondiscrimination Policy does not target or single out religious beliefs," the court noted; rather, the policy "is neutral and of general applicability." * * *

On appeal, the Ninth Circuit affirmed in an opinion that stated, in full:

> "The parties stipulate that Hastings imposes an open membership rule on all student groups—all groups must accept all comers as voting members even if those individuals disagree with the mission of the group. The conditions on recognition are therefore viewpoint neutral and reasonable. *Truth v. Kent Sch. Dist.*, 542 F. 3d 634, 649–50 (9th Cir. 2008)." *Christian Legal Soc. Chapter of Univ. of Cal.* v. *Kane*, 319 Fed. Appx. 645, 645–646 (CA9 2009).

[We] now affirm the Ninth Circuit's judgment.

Before considering the merits of CLS's constitutional arguments, we must resolve a preliminary issue: CLS urges us to review the Nondiscrimination Policy as written—prohibiting discrimination on several enumerated bases, including religion and sexual orientation—and not as a requirement that all RSOs accept all comers. The written terms of the Nondiscrimination Policy, CLS contends, "targe[t] solely those groups whose beliefs are based on religion or that disapprove of a particular kind of sexual behavior," and leave other associations free to limit membership and leadership to individuals committed to the group's ideology. Brief for Petitioner 19 (internal quotation marks omitted). For example, "[a] political ... group can insist that its leaders support its purposes and beliefs," CLS alleges, but "a religious group cannot."

CLS's assertion runs headlong into the stipulation of facts it jointly submitted with Hastings at the summary-judgment stage. In that filing, the parties specified:

> "Hastings requires that registered student organizations allow *any* student to participate, become a member, or seek leadership positions in the organization, regardless of [her] status or beliefs. Thus, for example, the Hastings Democratic Caucus cannot bar students holding Republican political beliefs from becoming members or seeking leadership positions in the organization." * * *

In support of the argument that Hastings' all-comers policy treads on its First Amendment rights to free speech and expressive association, CLS draws on two lines of decisions. First, in a progression of cases, this Court has employed forum analysis to determine when a governmental entity, in regulating property in its charge, may place limitations on speech. Recognizing a State's right "to preserve the property under its control for the use to which it is lawfully dedicated," *Cornelius* v. *NAACP Legal Defense & Ed. Fund, Inc.*, 473 U.S. 788, 800 (1985) (internal quotation marks omitted), the Court has permitted restrictions on access to a limited public forum, like the RSO program here, with this key caveat: Any access barrier must be reasonable and viewpoint neutral. * * *

Second, as evidenced by another set of decisions, this Court has rigorously reviewed laws and regulations that constrain associational freedom. In the context of public accommodations, we have subjected restrictions on that freedom to close scrutiny; such restrictions are permitted only if they serve "compelling state interests" that are "unrelated to the suppression of ideas"—interests that cannot be advanced "through . . . significantly less restrictive [means]." *Roberts* v. *United States Jaycees*, 468 U.S. 609, 623 (1984). *See also, e.g., Boy Scouts of America* v. *Dale*, 530 U.S. 640, 648 (2000). "Freedom of association," we have recognized, "plainly presupposes a freedom not to associate." *Roberts*, 468 U.S., at 623. Insisting that an organization embrace unwelcome members, we have therefore concluded, "directly and immediately affects associational rights." *Dale*, 530 U.S., at 659.

CLS would have us engage each line of cases independently, but its expressive-association and free-speech arguments merge: *Who* speaks on its behalf, CLS reasons, colors *what* concept is conveyed. It therefore makes little sense to treat CLS's speech and association claims as discrete. Instead, three observations lead us to conclude that our limited-public-forum precedents supply the appropriate framework for assessing both CLS's speech and association rights.

First, the same considerations that have led us to apply a less restrictive level of scrutiny to speech in limited public forums as compared to other environments apply with equal force to expressive association occurring in limited public forums. . . .

Second, and closely related, the strict scrutiny we have applied in some settings to laws that burden expressive association would, in practical effect, invalidate a defining characteristic of limited public forums—the State may "reserv[e] [them] for certain groups." *Rosenberger*, 515 U.S., at 829. . . .

Third, this case fits comfortably within the limited-public-forum category, for CLS, in seeking what is effectively a state subsidy, faces only indirect pressure to modify its membership policies; CLS may exclude any person for any reason if it forgoes the benefits of official recognition. The expressive-association precedents on which CLS relies, in contrast, involved regulations that *compelled* a group to include unwanted members, with no choice to opt out. See, *e.g., Dale*, 530 U.S., at 648 (regulation "forc[ed] [the Boy Scouts] to accept members it [did] not desire" (internal quotation marks omitted)); *Roberts*, 468 U. S., at 623 ("There can be no clearer example of an intrusion into the internal structure or affairs of an association than" forced inclusion of unwelcome participants.).

In diverse contexts, our decisions have distinguished between policies that require action and those that withhold benefits. Application of the less-restrictive limited-public-forum analysis better accounts for the fact that Hastings, through its RSO program, is dangling the carrot of subsidy, not wielding the stick of prohibition.

In sum, we are persuaded that our limited-public-forum precedents adequately respect both CLS's speech and expressive-association rights, and fairly balance those rights against Hastings' interests as property owner and educational institution. We turn to the merits of the instant dispute, therefore, with the limited-public-forum decisions as our guide. * * *

"Once it has opened a limited [public] forum," we emphasized, "the State must respect the lawful boundaries it has itself set." The constitutional constraints on the boundaries the State may set bear repetition here: "The State may not exclude speech where its distinction is not reasonable in light of the purpose served by the forum, . . . nor may it discriminate against speech on the basis of . . . viewpoint." *Rosenberger*, 515 U.S., at 829.

Our inquiry is shaped by the educational context in which it arises: "First Amendment rights," we have observed, "must be analyzed in light of the special characteristics of the school environment." *Widmar*, 454 U.S., at 268, n. 5 (internal quotation marks omitted). * * *

A college's commission—and its concomitant license to choose among pedagogical approaches—is not confined to the classroom, for extracurricular programs are, today, essential parts of the educational process. Schools, we have emphasized, enjoy "a significant measure of authority over the type of officially recognized activities in which their students participate."

With appropriate regard for school administrators' judgment, we review the justifications Hastings offers in defense of its all-comers requirement. First, the open-access policy "ensures that the leadership, educational, and social opportunities afforded by [RSOs] are available to all students." Just as "Hastings does not allow its professors to host classes open only to those students with a certain status or belief," so the Law School may decide, reasonably in our view, "that the . . . educational experience is best promoted when all participants in the forum must provide equal access to all students." RSOs, we count it significant, are eligible for financial assistance drawn from mandatory student-activity fees; the all-comers policy ensures that no Hastings student is forced to fund a group that would reject her as a member.

Second, the all-comers requirement helps Hastings police the written terms of its Nondiscrimination Policy without inquiring into an RSO's motivation for membership restrictions. To bring the RSO program within CLS's view of the Constitution's limits, CLS proposes that Hastings permit exclusion because of *belief* but forbid discrimination due to *status*. But that proposal would impose on Hastings a daunting labor. How should the Law School go about determining whether a student organization cloaked prohibited status exclusion in belief-based garb? If a hypothetical Male-Superiority Club barred a female student from running for its presidency, for example, how could the Law School tell whether the group rejected her bid because of her sex or because, by seeking to lead the club, she manifested a lack of belief in its fundamental philosophy?

This case itself is instructive in this regard. CLS contends that it does not exclude individuals because of sexual orientation, but rather "on the basis of a conjunction of conduct and the belief that the conduct is not wrong." Our decisions have declined to distinguish between status and conduct in this context. *See Lawrence* v. *Texas*, 539 U.S. 558, 575 (2003) ("When homosexual *conduct* is made criminal by the law of the State, that declaration in and of itself is an invitation to subject homosexual *persons* to discrimination." (emphasis added)); *id.,* at 583 (O'Connor, J., concurring in judgment) ("While it is true that the law applies only to conduct, the conduct targeted by this law is conduct that is closely correlated with being homosexual. Under such circumstances, [the] law is targeted at more than conduct. It is instead directed toward gay persons as a class.").

Third, the Law School reasonably adheres to the view that an all-comers policy, to the extent it brings together individuals with diverse backgrounds and beliefs, "encourages tolerance, cooperation, and learning among students." And if the policy sometimes produces discord, Hastings can rationally rank among RSO-program goals development of conflict-resolution skills, toleration, and readiness to find common ground.

Fourth, Hastings' policy, which incorporates—in fact, subsumes—state-law proscriptions on discrimination, conveys the Law School's decision "to decline to subsidize with public monies and benefits conduct of which the people of California disapprove." State law, of course, may not *command* that public universities take action impermissible under the First Amendment.

In sum, the several justifications Hastings asserts in support of its all-comers requirement are surely reasonable in light of the RSO forum's purposes.

The Law School's policy is all the more creditworthy in view of the "substantial alternative channels that remain open for [CLS-student] communication to take place." If restrictions on access to a limited public forum are viewpoint discriminatory, the ability of a group to exist outside the forum would not cure the constitutional shortcoming. But when access barriers are viewpoint neutral, our decisions have counted it

significant that other available avenues for the group to exercise its First
Amendment rights lessen the burden created by those barriers.

In this case, Hastings offered CLS access to school facilities to
conduct meetings and the use of chalkboards and generally available
bulletin boards to advertise events. Although CLS could not take
advantage of RSO-specific methods of communication, the advent of
electronic media and social-networking sites reduces the importance of
those channels.

Private groups, from fraternities and sororities to social clubs and
secret societies, commonly maintain a presence at universities without
official school affiliation. Based on the record before us, CLS was
similarly situated: It hosted a variety of activities the year after Hastings
denied it recognition, and the number of students attending those
meetings and events doubled.

CLS nevertheless deems Hastings' all-comers policy "frankly absurd."
"There can be no diversity of viewpoints in a forum," it asserts, "if groups
are not permitted to form around viewpoints." *Id.*, at 50; accord *post*, at 25
(Alito, J., dissenting). This catchphrase confuses CLS's preferred policy
with constitutional limitation—the *advisability* of Hastings' policy does
not control its *permissibility*.

CLS also assails the reasonableness of the all-comers policy in light
of the RSO forum's function by forecasting that the policy will facilitate
hostile takeovers; if organizations must open their arms to all, CLS
contends, saboteurs will infiltrate groups to subvert their mission and
message. This supposition strikes us as more hypothetical than real. CLS
points to no history or prospect of RSO-hijackings at Hastings. Students
tend to self-sort and presumably will not endeavor en masse to join—let
alone seek leadership positions in—groups pursuing missions wholly at
odds with their personal beliefs. And if a rogue student intent on
sabotaging an organization's objectives nevertheless attempted a
takeover, the members of that group would not likely elect her as an
officer.

RSOs, moreover, in harmony with the all-comers policy, may
condition eligibility for membership and leadership on attendance, the
payment of dues, or other neutral requirements designed to ensure that
students join because of their commitment to a group's vitality, not its
demise. Several RSOs at Hastings limit their membership rolls and
officer slates in just this way.

Hastings, furthermore, could reasonably expect more from its law
students than the disruptive behavior CLS hypothesizes—and to build
this expectation into its educational approach. A reasonable policy need
not anticipate and preemptively close off every opportunity for avoidance
or manipulation. If students begin to exploit an all-comers policy by

hijacking organizations to distort or destroy their missions, Hastings presumably would revisit and revise its policy. *See* Tr. of Oral Arg. 41 (counsel for Hastings); Brief for Hastings 38.

Finally, CLS asserts (and the dissent repeats, *post*, at 29) that the Law School lacks any legitimate interest—let alone one reasonably related to the RSO forum's purposes—in urging "religious groups not to favor co-religionists for purposes of their religious activities." CLS's analytical error lies in focusing on the benefits it must forgo while ignoring the interests of those it seeks to fence out: Exclusion, after all, has two sides. Hastings, caught in the crossfire between a group's desire to exclude and students' demand for equal access, may reasonably draw a line in the sand permitting *all* organizations to express what they wish but *no* group to discriminate in membership.

D.

We next consider whether Hastings' all-comers policy is viewpoint neutral.

Although this aspect of limited-public-forum analysis has been the constitutional sticking point in our prior decisions . . . we need not dwell on it here. It is, after all, hard to imagine a more viewpoint-neutral policy than one requiring *all* student groups to accept *all* comers. In contrast to *Healy*, *Widmar*, and *Rosenberger*, in which universities singled out organizations for disfavored treatment because of their points of view, Hastings' all-comers requirement draws no distinction between groups based on their message or perspective. An all-comers condition on access to RSO status, in short, is textbook viewpoint neutral. . . .

Hastings' requirement that student groups accept all comers, we are satisfied, "is justified without reference to the content [or viewpoint] of the regulated speech." The Law School's policy aims at the *act* of rejecting would-be group members without reference to the reasons motivating that behavior: Hastings' "desire to redress th[e] perceived harms" of exclusionary membership policies "provides an adequate explanation for its [all-comers condition] over and above mere disagreement with [any student group's] beliefs or biases." CLS's conduct—not its Christian perspective—is, from Hastings' vantage point, what stands between the group and RSO status. "In the end," as Hastings observes, "CLS is simply confusing its *own* viewpoint-based objections to . . . nondiscrimination laws (which it is entitled to have and [to] voice) with viewpoint *discrimination*." * * *

JUSTICE ALITO, with whom THE CHIEF JUSTICE, JUSTICE SCALIA, and JUSTICE THOMAS join, dissenting.

The proudest boast of our free speech jurisprudence is that we protect the freedom to express "the thought that we hate." Today's decision rests on a very different principle: no freedom for expression that offends prevailing standards of political correctness in our country's institutions of higher learning. * * *

The Court's treatment of this case is deeply disappointing. The Court does not address the constitutionality of the very different policy that Hastings invoked when it denied CLS's application for registration. Nor does the Court address the constitutionality of the policy that Hastings now purports to follow. And the Court ignores strong evidence that the accept-all-comers policy is not viewpoint neutral because it was announced as a pretext to justify viewpoint discrimination. Brushing aside inconvenient precedent, the Court arms public educational institutions with a handy weapon for suppressing the speech of unpopular groups—groups to which, as Hastings candidly puts it, these institutions "do not wish to . . . lend their name[s]." * * *

The Court bases all of its analysis on the proposition that the relevant Hastings' policy is the so-called accept-all-comers policy. This frees the Court from the difficult task of defending the constitutionality of either the policy that Hastings actually—and repeatedly—invoked when it denied registration, *i.e.*, the school's written Nondiscrimination Policy, or the policy that Hastings belatedly unveiled when it filed its brief in this Court. Overwhelming evidence, however, shows that Hastings denied CLS's application pursuant to the Nondiscrimination Policy and that the accept-all-comers policy was nowhere to be found until it was mentioned by a former dean in a deposition taken well after this case began. [The dissent then supplies its view of the facts and its reading of the joint stipulation]. * * *

I must comment on the majority's emphasis on funding. According to the majority, CLS is "seeking what is effectively a state subsidy," and the question presented in this case centers on the "use of school funds." In fact, funding plays a very small role in this case. Most of what CLS sought and was denied—such as permission to set up a table on the law school patio—would have been virtually cost free. If every such activity is regarded as a matter of funding, the First Amendment rights of students at public universities will be at the mercy of the administration. As CLS notes, "[t]o university students, the campus is their world. The right to meet on campus and use campus channels of communication is at least as important to university students as the right to gather on the town square and use local communication forums is to the citizen." * * *

The Court pays little attention to *Healy* and instead focuses solely on the question whether Hastings' registration policy represents a permissible regulation in a limited public forum. While I think that *Healy* is largely controlling, I am content to address the constitutionality of

Hastings' actions under our limited public forum cases, which lead to exactly the same conclusion.

In this case, the forum consists of the RSO program. Once a public university opens a limited public forum, it "must respect the lawful boundaries it has itself set." The university "may not exclude speech where its distinction is not 'reasonable in light of the purpose served by the forum.'" And the university must maintain strict viewpoint neutrality.

This requirement of viewpoint neutrality extends to the expression of religious viewpoints. In an unbroken line of decisions analyzing private religious speech in limited public forums, we have made it perfectly clear that "[r]eligion is [a] viewpoint from which ideas are conveyed." * * *

Analyzed under this framework, Hastings' refusal to register CLS pursuant to its Nondiscrimination Policy plainly fails. As previously noted, when Hastings refused to register CLS, it claimed that the CLS bylaws impermissibly discriminated on the basis of religion and sexual orientation. As interpreted by Hastings and applied to CLS, both of these grounds constituted viewpoint discrimination. * * *

Here, the Nondiscrimination Policy permitted membership requirements that expressed a secular viewpoint. *See* App. 93. (For example, the Hastings Democratic Caucus and the Hastings Republicans were allowed to exclude members who disagreed with their parties' platforms.) But religious groups were not permitted to express a religious viewpoint by limiting membership to students who shared their religious viewpoints. Under established precedent, this was viewpoint discrimination.

It bears emphasis that permitting religious groups to limit membership to those who share the groups' beliefs would not have the effect of allowing other groups to discriminate on the basis of religion. It would not mean, for example, that fraternities or sororities could exclude students on that basis. As our cases have recognized, the right of expressive association permits a group to exclude an applicant for membership only if the admission of that person would "affec[t] in a significant way the group's ability to advocate public or private viewpoints." *Dale*, 530 U.S., at 648. Groups that do not engage in expressive association have no such right. Similarly, groups that are dedicated to expressing a viewpoint on a secular topic (for example, a political or ideological viewpoint) would have no basis for limiting membership based on religion because the presence of members with diverse religious beliefs would have no effect on the group's ability to express its views. But for religious groups, the situation is very different. This point was put well by a coalition of Muslim, Christian, Jewish, and Sikh groups: "Of course there is a strong interest in prohibiting religious discrimination where religion is irrelevant. But it is fundamentally confused to apply a rule against religious discrimination to a religious association."

The Hastings Nondiscrimination Policy, as interpreted by the law school, also discriminated on the basis of viewpoint regarding sexual morality. CLS has a particular viewpoint on this subject, namely, that sexual conduct outside marriage between a man and a woman is wrongful. Hastings would not allow CLS to express this viewpoint by limiting membership to persons willing to express a sincere agreement with CLS's views. By contrast, nothing in the Nondiscrimination Policy prohibited a group from expressing a contrary viewpoint by limiting membership to persons willing to endorse that group's beliefs. A Free Love Club could require members to affirm that they reject the traditional view of sexual morality to which CLS adheres. It is hard to see how this can be viewed as anything other than viewpoint discrimination. * * *

I come now to the version of Hastings' policy that the Court has chosen to address. This is not the policy that Hastings invoked when CLS was denied registration. Nor is it the policy that Hastings now proclaims—and presumably implements. It is a policy that, as far as the record establishes, was in force only from the time when it was first disclosed by the former dean in July 2005 until Hastings filed its brief in this Court in March 2010. Why we should train our attention on this particular policy and not the other two is a puzzle. But in any event, it is clear that the accept-all-comers policy is not reasonable in light of the purpose of the RSO forum, and it is impossible to say on the present record that it is viewpoint neutral.

Once a state university opens a limited forum, it "must respect the lawful boundaries it has itself set." *Rosenberger*, 515 U.S., at 829. Hastings' regulations on the registration of student groups impose only two substantive limitations: A group seeking registration must have student members and must be non-commercial. Access to the forum is not limited to groups devoted to particular purposes. The regulations provide that a group applying for registration must submit an official document including "a statement of *its purpose*," *id.* but the regulations make no attempt to define the limits of acceptable purposes. The regulations do not require a group seeking registration to show that it has a certain number of members or that its program is of interest to any particular number of Hastings students. Nor do the regulations require that a group serve a need not met by existing groups. * * *

Taken as a whole, the regulations plainly contemplate the creation of a forum within which Hastings students are free to form and obtain registration of essentially the same broad range of private groups that nonstudents may form off campus. That is precisely what the parties in this case stipulated: The RSO forum "seeks to promote a diversity of viewpoints *among* registered student organizations, including viewpoints on religion and human sexuality."

The way in which the RSO forum actually developed corroborates this design. As noted, Hastings had more than 60 RSOs in 2004–2005, each with its own independently devised purpose. Some addressed serious social issues; others—for example, the wine appreciation and ultimate Frisbee clubs—were simply recreational. Some organizations focused on a subject but did not claim to promote a particular viewpoint on that subject (for example, the Association of Communications, Sports & Entertainment Law); others were defined, not by subject, but by viewpoint. The forum did not have a single Party Politics Club; rather, it featured both the Hastings Democratic Caucus and the Hastings Republicans. There was no Reproductive Issues Club; the forum included separate pro-choice and pro-life organizations. Students did not see fit to create a Monotheistic Religions Club, but they have formed the Hastings Jewish Law Students Association and the Hastings Association of Muslim Law Students. In short, the RSO forum, true to its design, has allowed Hastings students to replicate on campus a broad array of private, independent, noncommercial organizations that is very similar to those that nonstudents have formed in the outside world.

The accept-all-comers policy is antithetical to the design of the RSO forum for the same reason that a state-imposed accept-all-comers policy would violate the First Amendment rights of private groups if applied off campus. As explained above, a group's First Amendment right of expressive association is burdened by the "forced inclusion" of members whose presence would "affec[t] in a significant way the group's ability to advocate public or private viewpoints." *Dale*, 530 U.S., at 648. The Court has therefore held that the government may not compel a group that engages in "expressive association" to admit such a member unless the government has a compelling interest, " 'unrelated to the suppression of ideas, that cannot be achieved through means significantly less restrictive of associational freedoms.' " * * *

In sum, Hastings' accept-all-comers policy is not reasonable in light of the stipulated purpose of the RSO forum: to promote a diversity of viewpoints   *"among"*—not   within—"registered   student organizations." * * *

One final aspect of the Court's decision warrants comment. In response to the argument that the accept-all-comers-policy would permit a small and unpopular group to be taken over by students who wish to silence its message, the Court states that the policy would permit a registered group to impose membership requirements "designed to ensure that students join because of their commitment to a group's vitality, not its demise." *Ante*, at 27. With this concession, the Court tacitly recognizes that Hastings does not really have an accept-all-comers policy—it has an accept-some-dissident-comers policy—and the line between members who merely seek to change a group's message (who apparently must be admitted) and those who seek a group's "demise" (who may be kept out) is hopelessly vague.

Here is an example. Not all Christian denominations agree with CLS's views on sexual morality and other matters. During a recent year, CLS had seven members. Suppose that 10 students who are members of denominations that disagree with CLS decided that CLS was misrepresenting true Christian doctrine. Suppose that these students joined CLS, elected officers who shared their views, ended the group's affiliation with the national organization, and changed the group's message. The new leadership would likely proclaim that the group was "vital" but rectified, while CLS, I assume, would take the view that the old group had suffered its "demise." Whether a change represents reform or transformation may depend very much on the eye of the beholder.

Justice Kennedy takes a similarly mistaken tack. He contends that CLS "would have a substantial case on the merits if it were shown that the all-comers policy was . . . used to infiltrate the group or challenge its leadership in order to stifle its views," *ante*, at 4 (concurring opinion), but he does not explain on what ground such a claim could succeed. The Court holds that the accept-all-comers policy is viewpoint neutral and reasonable in light of the purposes of the RSO forum. How could those characteristics be altered by a change in the membership of one of the forum's registered groups? No explanation is apparent.

In the end, the Court refuses to acknowledge the consequences of its holding. A true accept-all-comers policy permits small unpopular groups to be taken over by students who wish to change the views that the group expresses. Rules requiring that members attend meetings, pay dues, and behave politely, see *ante*, at 27, would not eliminate this threat.

The possibility of such takeovers, however, is by no means the most important effect of the Court's holding. There are religious groups that cannot in good conscience agree in their bylaws that they will admit persons who do not share their faith, and for these groups, the consequence of an accept-all-comers policy is marginalization. *See* Brief for Evangelical Scholars (Officers and 24 Former Presidents of the Evangelical Theological Society) et al. as *Amici Curiae* 19 (affirmance in this case "will allow every public college and university in the United States to exclude all evangelical Christian organizations"); Brief for Agudath Israel of America as *Amicus Curiae* 3, 8 (affirmance would "point a judicial dagger at the heart of the Orthodox Jewish community in the

United States" and permit that community to be relegated to the status of "a second-class group"); Brief for Union of Orthodox Jewish Congregations of America as *Amicus Curiae* 3 (affirmance "could significantly affect the ability of [affiliated] student clubs and youth movements . . . to prescribe requirements for their membership and leaders based on religious beliefs and commitments"). This is where the Court's decision leads.

I do not think it is an exaggeration to say that today's decision is a serious setback for freedom of expression in this country. Our First Amendment reflects a "profound national commitment to the principle that debate on public issues should be uninhibited, robust, and wide-open." *New York Times Co.* v. *Sullivan*, 376 U.S. 254, 270 (1964). Even if the United States is the only Nation that shares this commitment to the same extent, I would not change our law to conform to the international norm. I fear that the Court's decision marks a turn in that direction. Even those who find CLS's views objectionable should be concerned about the way the group has been treated—by Hastings, the Court of Appeals, and now this Court. I can only hope that this decision will turn out to be an aberration.

ELANE PHOTOGRAPHY, LLC v. WILLOCK

Supreme Court of New Mexico, 2013
309 P. 3d 53

CHAVEZ, JUDGE.

[Vanessa Willock and Misti Collingsworth were planning a commitment ceremony. Willock e-mailed a local business, Elane Photography, to inquire about its services. The lead photographer and co-owner of the business, Elaine Huguenin, replied that she would not photograph a same-sex ceremony because she considered it to violate her religious beliefs, and that she photographed only "traditional weddings." The couple filed a complaint alleging discrimination in violation of the New Mexico Human Rights Act's provisions prohibiting discrimination based on sexual orientation by businesses that meet the definition of a public accommodation. On appeal from a judgment against it, Elane Photography did not contest that it was a public accommodation, but argued that applying the statute to it violated its rights under the Free Speech and Free Exercise Clause of the First Amendment. The New Mexico Supreme Court first rejected Elane's argument that the refusal to serve the same-sex couple was not based on their sexual orientation. On this point, the court invoked the analysis of status and conduct in *CLS v. Martinez*, among other things. The court then turned to the First Amendment issues].

* * * Elane Photography observes that photography is an expressive art form and that photographs can fall within the constitutional protections of free speech. *See Hurley v. Irish-Am. Gay, Lesbian & Bisexual Grp. of Boston*, 515 U.S. 557, 569, 115 S. Ct. 2338, 132 L. Ed. 2d 487 (1995) (observing that abstract art and instrumental music are "unquestionably shielded" by the First Amendment). Elane Photography also states that in the course of its business, it creates and edits photographs for its clients so as to tell a positive story about each wedding it photographs, and the company and its owners would prefer not to send a positive message about same-sex weddings or same-sex marriage. Elane Photography concludes that by requiring it to photograph same-sex weddings on the same basis that it photographs opposite-sex weddings, the NMHRA unconstitutionally compels it to "create and engage in expression" that sends a positive message about same-sex marriage not shared by its owner.

The compelled-speech doctrine on which Elane Photography relies is comprised of two lines of cases. The first line of cases establishes the proposition that the government may not require an individual to "speak the government's message." *Rumsfeld v. Forum for Academic & Institutional Rights, Inc.*, 547 U.S. 47, 63, 126 S. Ct. 1297, 164 L. Ed. 2d 156 (2006). The second line of cases prohibits the government from requiring a private actor "to host or accommodate another speaker's message." *Id.*

The right to refrain from speaking was established in *West Virginia State Board of Education v. Barnette*, in which the United States Supreme Court held that the State of West Virginia could not constitutionally require students to salute the American flag and recite the Pledge of Allegiance. The Court held that a state could not require "affirmation of a belief and an attitude of mind," and that the state had impermissibly "invade[d] the sphere of intellect and spirit which it is the purpose of the First Amendment to our Constitution to reserve from all official control."

Similarly, in *Wooley v. Maynard,* the United States Supreme Court held that the State of New Hampshire could not constitutionally punish a man for covering the state motto on the license plate of his car. The *Wooley* plaintiffs considered "Live Free or Die," the state motto, "repugnant to their moral, religious, and political beliefs," and they raised a First Amendment challenge to the state's law forbidding residents to hide or alter the motto. * * *

However, [*Barnette* and *Wooley*] . . . involve situations in which the speakers were compelled to publicly "speak the government's message." *Rumsfeld.* * * * Both cases stand for the proposition that the First Amendment does not permit the government to "prescribe what shall be orthodox in politics, nationalism, religion, or other matters of opinion or force citizens to confess by word or act their faith therein." However, unlike the laws at issue in *Wooley* and *Barnette,* the NMHRA does not require Elane Photography to recite or display any message. It does not even require Elane Photography to take photographs. The NMHRA only mandates that if Elane Photography operates a business as a public accommodation, it cannot discriminate against potential clients based on their sexual orientation.

Furthermore, the laws at issue in *Wooley* and *Barnette* had little purpose other than to promote the government-sanctioned message. * * * Antidiscrimination laws have important purposes that go beyond expressing government values: they ensure that services are freely available in the market, and they protect individuals from humiliation and dignitary harm. * * *

Elane Photography's argument here is more analogous to the claims raised by the law schools in *Rumsfeld.* In that case, a federal law made universities' federal funding contingent on the universities allowing military recruiters access to university facilities and services on the same basis as other, non-military recruiters. A group of law schools that objected to the ban on gays in the military challenged the law on a number of constitutional grounds, including that the law in question compelled them to speak the government's message. In order to assist the military recruiters, schools had to provide services that involved speech, "such as sending e-mails and distributing flyers."

The United States Supreme Court held that this requirement did not constitute compelled speech. The Court observed that the federal law "neither limits what law schools may say nor requires them to say anything." Schools were compelled only to provide the type of speech-related services to military recruiters that they provided to non-military recruiters. "There [was] nothing ... approaching a Government-mandated pledge or motto that the school [had to] endorse."

The same situation is true in the instant case. Like the law in *Rumsfeld,* the NMHRA does not require any affirmation of belief by regulated public accommodations; instead, it requires businesses that offer services to the public at large to provide those services without regard for race, sex, sexual orientation, or other protected classifications. The fact that these services may involve speech or other expressive services does not render the NMHRA unconstitutional. *See Rumsfeld* ("The compelled speech to which the law schools point is plainly incidental to the [law's] regulation of conduct, and it has never been deemed an abridgment of freedom of speech or press to make a course of conduct illegal merely because the conduct was in part initiated, evidenced, or carried out by means of language, either spoken, written, or printed." (internal quotation marks and citation omitted)). Elane Photography is compelled to take photographs of same-sex weddings only to the extent that it would provide the same services to a heterosexual couple. *See id.* (speech assisting military recruiters was "only 'compelled' if, and to the extent, the school provide[d] such speech for other recruiters").

The second line of compelled-speech cases deals with situations in which a government entity has required a speaker to "host or accommodate another speaker's message." *Id.* at 63, 126 S.Ct. 1297. Elane Photography argues that a same-sex wedding or commitment ceremony is an expressive event, and that by requiring it to accept a client who is having a same-sex wedding, the NMHRA compels it to facilitate the messages inherent in that event. Elane Photography argues that there are two messages conveyed by a same-sex wedding or commitment ceremony: first, that such ceremonies exist, and second, that these occasions deserve celebration and approval. Elane Photography does not wish to convey either of these messages.

The United States Supreme Court has never found a compelled-speech violation arising from the application of antidiscrimination laws to a for-profit public accommodation.... [The Court] has found constitutional problems with some applications of state public accommodation laws, but those problems have arisen when states have applied their public accommodation laws to free-speech events such as privately organized parades, and private membership organizations. Elane Photography, however, is an ordinary public accommodation, a "clearly commercial entit[y]," that sells goods and services to the public.

* * * If Elane Photography took photographs on its own time and sold them at a gallery, or if it was hired by certain clients but did not offer its services to the general public, the [public accommodations] law would not apply to Elane Photography's choice of whom to photograph or not. The difference in the present case is that the photographs that are allegedly compelled by the NMHRA are photographs that Elane Photography produces for hire in the ordinary course of its business as a public accommodation. This determination has no relation to the artistic merit of photographs produced by Elane Photography. If Annie Leibovitz or Peter Lindbergh worked as public accommodations in New Mexico, they would be subject to the provisions of the NMHRA. Unlike the defendants in *Hurley* or the other cases in which the United States Supreme Court has found compelled-speech violations, Elane Photography sells its expressive services to the public. It may be that Elane Photography expresses its clients' messages in its photographs, but only because it is hired to do so.

* * * *Hurley* is different from the instant case in two significant ways. First, the Massachusetts courts appear to have erroneously classified the privately organized parade as a public accommodation. *See id.* ("[T]he state courts' application of the statute had the effect of declaring the sponsors' speech itself to be the public accommodation."). Second, parades by their nature express a message to the public. By requiring the parade organizers to include GLIB, the Massachusetts courts directly altered the expressive content of the parade. The presence of a group in a parade carries expressive weight, and Hurley implicated associational rights as well as free-speech rights. Elane Photography argues that photographs are also inherently expressive, so *Hurley* must apply to this case as well. However, the NMHRA applies not to Elane Photography's photographs but to its business operation, and in particular, its business decision not to offer its services to protected classes of people. While photography may be expressive, the operation of a photography business is not. By way of analogy, the NMHRA could not dictate which groups a parade organizer had to include. However, if a business sold parade-planning services, and that business operated as a public accommodation, the NMHRA would prohibit that business from refusing to offer parade-planning services to persons because of their sexual orientation. Thus, Elane Photography's reliance on *Hurley* is misplaced.

* * * Elane Photography also argues that if it is compelled to photograph same-sex weddings, observers will believe that it and its owners approve of same-sex marriage. * * * The *Hurley* Court observed that admitting GLIB or any other organization into a parade would likely be perceived as a message from the parade organizers "that [GLIB's] message was worthy of presentation and quite possibly of support as well."

* * * The *Rumsfeld* Court held that students "can appreciate the difference between speech a school sponsors and speech the school permits because legally required to do so," and that the law schools were free to express their disagreement with the military's policy.

* * * Elane Photography makes an argument very similar to one rejected by the *Rumsfeld* Court: by treating customers alike, regardless of whether they are having same-sex or opposite-sex weddings, Elane Photography is concerned that it will send the message that it sees nothing wrong with same-sex marriage. Reasonable observers are unlikely to interpret Elane Photography's photographs as an endorsement of the photographed events. It is well known to the public that wedding photographers are hired by paying customers and that a photographer may not share the happy couple's views on issues ranging from the minor (the color scheme, the hors d'oeuvres) to the decidedly major (the religious service, the choice of bride or groom). As in *Rumsfeld* . . . Elane Photography is free to disavow, implicitly or explicitly, any

messages that it believes the photographs convey. We note that after *Rumsfeld,* many law schools published open letters expressing their continued opposition to military policies and military recruitment on campus.

* * * [The Court then turned to the First Amendment free exercise claim]. It is an open question whether Elane Photography, which is a limited liability company rather than a natural person, has First Amendment free exercise rights. Several federal courts have recently addressed this question with differing outcomes. However, it is not necessary for this Court to address whether Elane Photography has a constitutionally protected right to exercise its religion. Assuming that Elane Photography has such rights, they are not offended by enforcement of the NMHRA.

Under established law, "the right of free exercise does not relieve an individual of the obligation to comply with a valid and neutral law of general applicability on the ground that the law proscribes (or prescribes) conduct that his religion prescribes (or proscribes)." *Emp't Div., Dep't of Human Res. of Or. v. Smith,* 494 U.S. 872, 879 (1990). In order to state a valid First Amendment free exercise claim, a party must show [among others] that the law in question is not a "neutral law of general applicability," *id.* * * *

The United States Supreme Court elaborated on the rule concerning "law that is neutral and of general applicability" in *Church of the Lukumi Babalu Aye, Inc. v. City of Hialeah,* 508 U.S. 520, 531, 546 (1993). A law is not neutral "if [its] object . . . is to infringe upon or restrict practices because of their religious motivation." It is not generally applicable if it "impose[s] burdens only on conduct motivated by religious belief" while permitting exceptions for secular conduct or for favored religions. *Id.* These inquiries are related; the Court observed that improper intent could be inferred if the law was a " 'religious gerrymander' " that burdened religion but exempted similar secular activity. If a law is neither neutral nor generally applicable, it "must be justified by a compelling governmental interest and must be narrowly tailored to advance that interest."

* * * In *Lukumi Babalu Aye,* the city of Hialeah had passed several ordinances that prohibited religious sacrifice of animals but exempted secular slaughterhouses, kosher slaughterhouses, hunting, fishing, euthanasia of unwanted animals, and extermination of pests. The Court held that this was a "religious gerrymander," the result of which was "that few if any killings of animals [were] prohibited other than Santeria sacrifice." The Court concluded that "[t]he ordinances had as their object the suppression of religion" and were therefore nonneutral. The Court then examined whether the ordinances were generally applicable and

whether the government was selectively burdening only religiously motivated conduct. The Court did not precisely define the standard for assessing general applicability, but it did observe that the Hialeah ordinances were grossly under-inclusive with respect to the laws' stated goals, and it concluded that the laws burdened "only . . . conduct motivated by religious belief." The Court applied strict scrutiny to the ordinances and found them unconstitutional.

* * * Elane Photography argues that the NMHRA is not generally applicable and that this Court therefore should apply strict scrutiny to the application of the NMHRA to Elane Photography. Elane Photography identifies several exemptions from the antidiscrimination provisions of the NMHRA and argues that these exemptions make it not generally applicable. Specifically, Elane Photography points to Section 28–1–9(A)(1), which exempts sales or rentals of single-family homes if the owner does not own more than three houses, and Section 28–1–9(D), which exempts owners who live in small multi-family dwellings and rent out the other units. Elane Photography argues that these exemptions . . . "impermissibly prefer the secular to the religious."

This is a misreading of Section 28–1–9. Unlike the exemptions in *Lukumi Babalu Aye,* the exemptions in Section 28–1–9(A) and (D) apply equally to religious and secular conduct. Neither subsection discusses motivation; homeowners who meet the criteria of Section 28–1–9(A) and (D) are permitted to discriminate regardless of whether they do so on religious or nonreligious grounds. Therefore, the NMHRA does not target only religiously motivated discrimination, and these exemptions do not prevent the NMHRA from being generally applicable. These exemptions also do not indicate any animus toward religion by the Legislature that might render the law nonneutral; similar exemptions commonly appear in housing discrimination laws, including the federal Fair Housing Act. . . .

Elane Photography also argues that the exemptions to the NMHRA for religious organizations undercut the purpose of the statute. In particular, Elane Photography highlights Section 28–1–9(B) and (C), which in its reading permits religious organizations to "decline same-sex couples as customers."

Once again, Elane Photography's interpretation rests on a distorted reading of the statute. Section 28–1–9(B) allows religious organizations to "limit[ ] admission to or giv[e] preference to persons of the same religion or denomination or [to make] selections of buyers, lessees or tenants" that promote the organization's religious principles. In the context of "buyers, lessees or tenants," "buyers" clearly refers to purchasers of real estate rather than retail customers. *Id.* Subsection (C) exempts religious organizations from provisions of the NMHRA governing sexual orientation and gender identity, but only regarding "employment or renting." If a religious organization sold goods or services to the general public, neither subsection would allow the organization to turn away same-sex couples while catering to opposite-sex couples of all faiths. Subsection (B) permits religious organizations to serve only or primarily people of their own faith, as well as to discriminate in certain limited real estate transactions; Subsection (C) applies only to employment and, again, to real estate.

In other words, neither of the religious exemptions in Section 28–1–9 would permit a religious organization to take the actions that Elane Photography did in this case. Furthermore, these exemptions do not prevent the NMHRA from being generally applicable. Exemptions for religious organizations are common in a wide variety of laws, and they reflect the attempts of the Legislature to respect free exercise rights by reducing legal burdens on religion. Such exemptions are generally permissible, and in some situations they may be constitutionally mandated, *see Hosanna-Tabor Evangelical Lutheran Church & Sch. v. EEOC*, ___ U.S. ___, ___, 132 S.Ct. 694, 705–06 (2012) (holding that the First Amendment precludes the application of employment discrimination laws to disputes between religious organizations and their ministers).

The exemptions in the NMHRA are ordinary exemptions for religious organizations and for certain limited employment and real-estate transactions. The exemptions do not prefer secular conduct over religious conduct or evince any hostility toward religion. We hold that the NMHRA is a neutral law of general applicability, and as such it does not offend the Free Exercise Clause of the First Amendment. * * *

NOTES

1. For academic analysis of the CLS case, see Richard A. Epstein, *Church and State at the Crossroads*: Christian Legal Society v. Martinez, 2010 CATO SUP. CT. REV. 105 (2010); William N. Eskridge, Jr., *Noah's Curse: How Religion Often Conflates Status, Belief, and Conduct to Distort Antidiscrimination Norms*, 45 GA. L. REV. 657 (2011); John D. Inazu, *The Unsettling "Well-Settled" Law of Freedom of Association*, 43 CONN. L. REV. 149 (2010) (positing that Freedom of Association has been misunderstood since *Roberts v. Jaycees* and that *CLS* continues in this tradition of incorrectly decided Supreme Court cases); Kathleen M. Sullivan, *Two Concepts of the Freedom of Speech*, 124 HARV. L. REV. 143 (2010); *Symposium, Christian Legal Society v. Martinez*, 38 HASTINGS CON. L.Q. (2011).

2. There is a burgeoning academic literature on the kinds of issues posed in *Elane Photography* and the larger conflict implicated by the case. For a variety of perspectives, see Thomas C. Berg, *What Same-Sex Marriage and Religious-Liberty Claims Have in Common*, 5 NW. J.L. & SOC. POL'Y 206 (2010); Jennifer Gerarda Brown, *Peacemaking in the Culture War Between Gay Rights and Religious Liberty*, 95 IOWA L. REV. 747 (2010); Chai R.

Feldblum, *Moral Conflict and Liberty: Gay Rights and Religion*, 72 BROOK. L. REV. 61 (2006); James Gottry, Note, *Just Shoot Me: Antidiscrimination Laws Take Aim at First Amendment Freedoms*, 64 VAND. L. REV. 961 (2011); Laura K. Klein, *Rights Clash: How Conflicts Between Gay Rights and Religious Freedom Challenge the Legal System*, 98 GEO. L.J. 505 (2010); Douglas Laycock & Thomas C. Berg, *Protecting Same-Sex Marriage and Religious Liberty*, 99 VA. L. REV. IN BRIEF 1 (2013); Douglas NeJaime, *Inclusion, Accommodation and Recognition: Accounting for Differences Based on Religion and Sexual Orientation*, 32 HARV. J. L. & GENDER 303 (2009); Douglas NeJaime, *Marriage Inequality: Same-Sex Relationships, Religious Exemptions, and the Production of Sexual Orientation Discrimination*, 100 CALIF. L. REV. 1169 (2012); *Symposium, Religious Liberty and Non-Discrimination Law*, 5 NW. J. L. & SOC. POL. 206 (2010); Laura S. Underkuffler, *Odious Discrimination and the Religious Exemption Question*, 32 CARDOZO L. REV. 2069 (2011); Robin Fretwell Wilson, *The Calculus of Accommodation: Contraception, Abortion, Same-Sex Marriage, and Other Clashes Between Religion and the State*, 53 B.C. L. REV. 1417 (2012).

C. THE PURSUIT OF LEGISLATIVE EXEMPTIONS FROM SAME-SEX MARRIAGE AND ANTIDISCRIMINATION LAWS

Cases like *CLS* and *Elane Photography* illustrate litigation that aims to secure religiously-based exemptions from equality laws. As the outcome of these cases suggests, and *Elane Photography* in particular reflects, constitutional claims may not succeed. Indeed, there are particular obstacles that proponents of constitutional religious liberty claims grounded in the First Amendment face. Although the First Amendment includes a free exercise clause, which restricts lawmakers from "prohibiting the free exercise of religion," under current First Amendment doctrine this constitutional protection does not lead to obligations to accommodate religious objections to neutral and generally applicable laws, like antidiscrimination laws or laws regulating marriage. For this reason, attempts to win religious accommodations in the LGBT context have focused heavily on legislation. In the end, it is statutory, rather than constitutional, reasoning that most frequently shapes the question of religious liberty in the LGBT context. This section explores developments in the pursuit of robust statutory exemptions to LGBT equality mandates.

Debates over religious liberty intensified with the Supreme Court's decision in *Obergefell v. Hodges* recognizing same-sex couples' constitutional right to marry. Indeed, the dissenting justices devoted significant attention to conflicts between same-sex marriage and religious freedom. Before *Obergefell* and the string of federal court decisions in 2014 and 2015 that led up to it, much of the religious liberty focus was on legislative proposals in states that were relatively friendly to same-sex marriage and had antidiscrimination laws covering sexual orientation. In fact, in some of these states, limited religious exemptions constituted a key part of the effort to pass marriage legislatively. But for most of the states that ushered in marriage equality in 2014 and 2015, same-sex couples did not enjoy state-level protections against discrimination based on sexual orientation. (And federal antidiscrimination law does not expressly include sexual orientation.) In these states, same-sex couples may face discrimination and have no recourse under antidiscrimination law, regardless of whether religious exemptions exist. That is, private individuals and organizations may engage in discrimination, for religious or non-religious reasons, because sexual orientation discrimination is not expressly prohibited. Nonetheless, in many of these states, lawmakers and social conservative advocates turned to religious exemption campaigns both to preempt any future antidiscrimination obligations that may exist at the state and federal levels and to override local nondiscrimination ordinances that included sexual orientation. These religious exemption efforts can be broken down into two main strategies: legislation specifically related to marriage and/or LGBT nondiscrimination, and legislation that broadly protects religious liberty as a civil right and leaves to courts the adjudication of specific disputes.

1. Targeted Exemptions

The first strategy aims at targeted, specific legislative exemptions. While numerous bills have been introduced across the country, only a handful have passed up to this point. For example, North Carolina enacted a law that allows public officials to decline to officiate same-sex weddings: "Every magistrate has the right to recuse from performing all lawful marriages . . . based upon any sincerely held religious objection. . . . Every assistant register of deeds and deputy register of deeds has the right to recuse from issuing all lawful marriage licenses . . . based upon any sincerely held religious objection." N.C. GEN. STAT. § 51–5.5 (2015).

Indeed, the religious objections of public officials have received significant attention in *Obergefell*'s wake. In the most high-profile case, Kim Davis, the clerk for Rowan County, Kentucky, claimed that her religious beliefs prevented her from issuing marriage licenses to same-sex couples or from allowing others in her office to do so (since the license would include her name). *See* Appellant Kim Davis's Emergency Motion for Immediate Consideration and Motion for Injunction Pending Appeal at 7–8, *Miller v. Davis*, Case No. 15–5961 (6th Cir. Sept. 7, 2015). When the courts ordered her to perform her duties and the U.S. Supreme Court denied her relief, she was jailed for refusing to comply. She was eventually released as deputy clerks in her office began to issue marriage licenses to same-sex couples. When Kentucky's newly elected Republican governor took office, he issued an executive order removing county clerks' names from marriage licenses in a move that sought to satisfy Davis and her supporters.

Other exemption statutes have focused on private actors. Michigan enacted a statute allowing private adoption agencies to refuse to work with same-sex couples based on religious objections. It provides that "a child placing agency shall not be required to provide adoption services if those adoption services conflict with . . . the child placing agency's sincerely held religious beliefs. . . ." MICH. COMP. LAWS § 710.23g (2015).

In 2016, Mississippi enacted the most far-reaching religious exemptions statute aimed at LGBT people. Mississippi's law covers both public and private actors and targets both same-sex couples and transgender individuals.

Mississippi House Bill No. 1523 (2016)

Section 2. The sincerely held religious beliefs or moral convictions protected by this act are the belief or conviction that:

(a) Marriage is or should be recognized as the union of one man and one woman;

(b) Sexual relations are properly reserved to such a marriage; and

(c) Male (man) or female (woman) refer to an individual's immutable biological sex as objectively determined by anatomy and genetics at time of birth.

Section 3. (1) The state government shall not take any discriminatory action against a religious organization wholly or partially on the basis that such organization:

(a) Solemnizes or declines to solemnize any marriage, or provides or declines to provide services, accommodations, facilities, goods or privileges for a purpose related to the solemnization, formation, celebration or recognition of any marriage, based upon or in a manner consistent with a sincerely held religious belief or moral conviction described in Section 2 of this act;

(b) Makes any employment-related decision including, but not limited to, the decision whether or not to hire, terminate or discipline an individual whose conduct or religious beliefs are inconsistent with those of the religious organization, based upon or in a manner consistent with a sincerely held religious belief or moral conviction described in Section 2 of this act; or

(c) Makes any decision concerning the sale, rental, occupancy of, or terms and conditions of occupying a dwelling or other housing under its control, based upon or in a manner consistent with a sincerely held religious belief or moral conviction described in Section 2 of this act.

(2) The state government shall not take any discriminatory action against a religious organization that advertises, provides or facilitates adoption or foster care, wholly or partially on the basis that such organization has provided or declined to provide any adoption or foster care service, or related service, based upon or in a manner consistent with a sincerely held religious belief or moral conviction described in Section 2 of this act.

(3) The state government shall not take any discriminatory action against a person who the state grants custody of a foster or adoptive child, or who seeks from the state custody of a foster or adoptive child, wholly or partially on the basis that the person guides, instructs, or raises a child, or intends to guide, instruct, or raise a child based upon or in a manner consistent with a sincerely held religious belief or moral conviction described in Section 2 of this act.

(4) The state government shall not take any discriminatory action against a person wholly or partially on the basis that the person declines to participate in the provision of treatments, counseling, or surgeries related to sex reassignment or gender identity transitioning or declines to participate in the provision of psychological, counseling, or fertility services based upon a sincerely held religious belief or moral conviction described in Section 2 of this act.

This subsection (4) shall not be construed to allow any person to deny visitation, recognition of a designated representative for health care decision-making, or emergency medical treatment necessary to cure an illness or injury as required by law.

(5) The state government shall not take any discriminatory action against a person wholly or partially on the basis that the person has provided or declined to provide the following services, accommodations, facilities, goods, or privileges for a purpose related to the solemnization, formation, celebration, or recognition of any marriage, based upon or in a manner consistent with a sincerely held religious belief or moral conviction described in Section 2 of this act:

(a) Photography, poetry, videography, disc-jockey services, wedding planning, printing, publishing or similar marriage-related goods or services; or

(b) Floral arrangements, dress making, cake or pastry artistry, assembly-hall or other wedding-venue rentals, limousine or other car-service rentals, jewelry sales and services, or similar marriage-related services, accommodations, facilities or goods.

(6) The state government shall not take any discriminatory action against a person wholly or partially on the basis that the person establishes sex-specific standards or policies concerning employee or student dress or grooming, or concerning access to restrooms, spas, baths, showers, dressing rooms, locker rooms, or other intimate facilities or settings, based upon or in a manner consistent with a sincerely held religious belief or moral conviction described in Section 2 of this act. * * *

(8)(a) Any person employed or acting on behalf of the state government who has authority to authorize or license marriages, including, but not limited to, clerks, registers of deeds or their deputies, may seek recusal from authorizing or licensing lawful marriages based upon or in a manner consistent with a sincerely held religious belief or moral conviction described in Section 2 of this act. Any person making such recusal shall provide prior written notice to the State Registrar of Vital Records who shall keep a record of such recusal, and the state government shall not take any discriminatory action against that person wholly or partially on the basis of such recusal. The person who is recusing himself or herself shall take all necessary steps to ensure that the authorization and licensing of any legally valid marriage is not impeded or delayed as a result of any recusal.

(b) Any person employed or acting on behalf of the state government who has authority to perform or solemnize marriages, including, but not limited to, judges, magistrates, justices of the peace or their deputies, may seek recusal from performing or solemnizing lawful marriages based upon or in a manner consistent with a sincerely held religious belief or moral conviction described in Section 2 of this act. Any person making such recusal shall provide prior written notice to the Administrative Office of Courts, and the state government shall not take any discriminatory action against that person wholly or partially on the basis of such recusal. The Administrative Office of Courts shall take all necessary steps to ensure that the performance or solemnization of any legally valid marriage is not impeded or delayed as a result of any recusal. * * *

NOTES

1.   On what grounds might Mississippi's religious exemptions law be challenged? Does it present First Amendment problems? Equal protection problems? Due process issues? In June 2016, a federal district court preliminarily enjoined enforcement of HB 1523 under both the Fourteenth Amendment's Equal Protection Clause and the First Amendment's Establishment Clause. Focusing on how the law authorizes refusals that produce material and dignitary harms, the Court reasoned that the law gives individuals "an absolute right to refuse service to LGBT citizens without regard for the impact on their employer, coworkers, or those being denied

service." Memorandum Opinion and Order at *56, *Barber v. Bryant*, Case No. 3:16-cv-00417, 2016 WL 3562647 (S.D. Miss. June 30, 2016).

The Establishment Clause is not a principal focus of this chapter, but the *Barber* decision suggests it may become a part of the legal landscape in this area. The Supreme Court has interpreted the Establishment Clause to prevent religious accommodations that impose "significant burdens" on third parties. *See Estate of Thornton v. Caldor, Inc.*, 472 U.S. 703, 710 (1985). Exemptions from laws protecting LGBT equality or reproductive healthcare have the capacity to inflict such third-party harms on specific individuals. Note that such third-party concerns are not unique to the Establishment Clause. Courts have also raised such concerns in considering the proper scope of constitutional free exercise protections as well as statutory religious liberty laws.

2. Regardless of HB 1523, under constitutional free exercise protections, religious institutions would not be compelled to solemnize any same-sex couple's marriage. But the Mississippi law would allow businesses to refuse to provide "accommodations, facilities, goods, or privileges for a purpose related to the solemnization, formation, celebration, or recognition of any marriage." What does it mean to "recognize" a marriage in this context? Does such "recognition" move beyond the wedding itself? Could a restaurant refuse to host a same-sex couple's anniversary dinner? Could an inn refuse to lodge a married same-sex couple? On the far-reaching nature of terms like "recognition" in religious exemption statutes, see Douglas NeJaime, *Marriage Inequality: Same-Sex Relationships, Religious Exemptions, and the Production of Sexual Orientation Discrimination*, 100 CALIF. L. REV. 1169, 1230–32 (2012).

3. The Mississippi law would also allow healthcare providers to refuse to "participate" in gender-identity-related healthcare services. Many states have healthcare refusal laws that allow healthcare providers to refuse to perform abortions or sterilizations. As Professors Douglas NeJaime and Reva Siegel explain, in the late 1990s and 2000s, healthcare refusal laws were "self-consciously expanded to reach an ever-widening number of persons who might count themselves as complicit [in the objected-to act]. Fueled by complicity-based objections, refusal laws expanded to cover acts and actors only remotely connected to the challenged healthcare service." Douglas NeJaime & Reva B. Siegel, *Conscience Wars: Complicity-Based Conscience Claims in Religion and Politics*, 124 YALE L.J. 2516, 2541 (2015). The laws came to cover not only abortion and sterilization but also contraception; they protected not only doctors and nurses but other healthcare employees, including pharmacists; and they included not only direct performance of the procedure but also referrals, counseling, and (in the case of contraception) sale and distribution.

In 2004, well before it passed the 2016 measure, Mississippi enacted the most expansive healthcare refusal law in the country. It defines "health care service" to include "any phase of patient medical care, treatment or procedure, including, but not limited to, the following: patient referral, counseling, therapy, testing, diagnosis or prognosis, research, instruction, prescribing, dispensing or administering any device, drug, or medication, surgery, or any other care or treatment rendered by health care providers or health care institutions." MISS. CODE ANN. § 41–107–3(a). And it defines "health care provider" to include "any individual who may be asked to participate in any way in a health care service, including, but not limited to: a physician, physician's assistant, nurse, nurses' aide, medical assistant, hospital employee, clinic employee, nursing home employee, pharmacist, pharmacy employee, researcher, medical or nursing school faculty, student or employee, counselor, social worker or any professional, paraprofessional, or any other person who furnishes, or assists in the furnishing of, a health care procedure." *Id.* at § 41–107–3(b).

Does the inclusion of gender-identity-related healthcare services in Mississippi's 2016 religious exemption statute add anything, given the 2004 healthcare refusal law? What other healthcare services might be denied to LGBT people under the healthcare refusal law? What about assisted reproductive technologies like donor insemination and *in vitro* fertilization?

4. Notice that Mississippi's religious exemption law, like its healthcare refusal law, includes not only "religious beliefs" but also "moral convictions." Why might lawmakers have included this language? Should exemption statutes privilege religious beliefs or instead cover conscience generally? Are there special risks to including both religious and secular conscientious objection in domains like LGBT equality and reproductive healthcare?

5. Given that Mississippi does not have a state antidiscrimination law that includes sexual orientation and gender identity, why would it pass a religious exemptions statute specifically relating to LGBT people?

6. Where unable to pass a legislative exemption scheme, some governors have issued executive orders that provide religious exemptions. For instance, in Kansas, the governor extended a far-reaching exemption to religiously affiliated organizations. It includes the following provision:

> The State Government shall not take any discriminatory action against a religious organization, including those providing social services, wholly or partially on the basis that such organization declines or will decline to solemnize any marriage or to provide services, accommodations, facilities, goods, or privileges for a purpose related to the solemnization, formation, celebration or recognition of any marriage, based upon or consistent with a sincerely held religious belief or moral conviction. . . .

Kan. Exec. Order No. 15–05, 34 Kan. Reg. 835 (July 16, 2015).

7. Most of the activity relating to religious exemptions in the LGBT context has occurred at the state level. But federal efforts have also been made. Congress considered, but did not pass, a bill titled the First Amendment Defense Act, which provided that the federal government "shall

not take any discriminatory action against a person . . . on the basis that such person believes or acts in accordance with a religious belief or moral conviction that marriage is or should be recognized as the union of one man and one woman, or that sexual relations are properly reserved to such a marriage." H.R. 3133, 113th Cong. (2013).

2.   Religious Freedom Restoration Acts

Mississippi passed its broad religious exemptions statute aimed specifically at LGBT people in 2016. But in 2014, Mississippi enacted a general religious liberty statute that mirrors the federal Religious Freedom Restoration Act (RFRA). This illustrates the second strategy to secure religious exemptions: enact, strengthen, and litigate under state RFRAs.

The Supreme Court in *Employment Division v. Smith*, 494 U.S. 872 (1990), held that under the First Amendment's free exercise clause, claims to exemption from neutral and generally applicable laws are subject to only a rational basis form of review. In response, Congress enacted RFRA with bipartisan support. RFRA provides:

> Government may substantially burden a person's exercise of religion only if it demonstrates that application of the burden to the person—(1) is in furtherance of a compelling governmental interest; and (2) is the least restrictive means of furthering that compelling governmental interest.

42 U.S.C. § 2000bb–1(b).

When the Court in *City of Boerne v. Flores*, 521 U.S. 507 (1997), struck down the federal RFRA as applied to the states (based on the conclusion that Congress had exceeded its authority), many states responded by enacting their own RFRAs. But for many years, even though the state RFRA tests sound like the language of strict scrutiny, claims to religious exemptions under RFRAs largely failed. *See* Christopher C. Lund, *Religious Liberty After* Gonzales: *A Look at State RFRAs*, 55 S.D. L. REV. 466 (2010) (explaining how in the relatively few state RFRA cases, courts required a strong showing of "substantial burden" and gave the government latitude in assessing the "compelling governmental interest" and "least restrictive means").

Two developments coincided to shift the salience and power of RFRAs. First, opponents of the Affordable Care Act (ACA), the comprehensive healthcare law passed under President Obama, used RFRA to challenge the law's contraceptive coverage requirements. The law required that employer-provided health insurance include coverage for certain contraceptives. After failing to secure an exemption from this requirement in Congress, some for-profit corporations sought a religious exemption from the law's requirement under RFRA. Second, opponents of same-sex marriage and LGBT equality turned to religious liberty claims, including claims under state RFRAs and efforts to pass additional RFRAs, as they dealt with the onset of marriage equality and anticipated the eventual decision in *Obergefell*.

Efforts focused on RFRAs received an important boost when the Supreme Court ruled in favor of the for-profit corporations invoking the federal RFRA to challenge the ACA's contraceptive coverage requirements.

BURWELL V. HOBBY LOBBY STORES, INC.

United States Supreme Court, 2014
573 U.S. ___, 134 S.Ct. 2751, 189 L.Ed.2d 675

JUSTICE ALITO delivered the opinion of the Court.

We must decide in these cases whether the Religious Freedom Restoration Act of 1993 (RFRA), 107 Stat. 1488, 42 U.S.C. §§ 2000bb *et seq.*, permits the United States Department of Health and Human Services (HHS) to demand that three closely held corporations provide health-insurance coverage for methods of contraception that violate the sincerely held religious beliefs of the companies' owners. We hold that the regulations that impose this obligation violate RFRA, which prohibits the Federal Government from taking any action that substantially burdens the exercise of religion unless that action constitutes the least restrictive means of serving a compelling government interest.

* * * Since RFRA applies in these cases, we must decide whether the challenged HHS regulations substantially burden the exercise of religion, and we hold that they do. The owners of the businesses have religious objections to abortion, and according to their religious beliefs the four contraceptive methods at issue are abortifacients. If the owners comply with the HHS mandate, they believe they will be facilitating abortions, and if they do not comply, they will pay a very heavy price—as much as $1.3 million per day, or about $475 million per year, in the case of one of the companies. If these consequences do not amount to a substantial burden, it is hard to see what would.

Under RFRA, a Government action that imposes a substantial burden on religious exercise must serve a compelling government interest, and we assume that the HHS regulations satisfy this requirement. But in order for the HHS mandate to be sustained, it must also constitute the least restrictive means of serving that interest, and the mandate plainly fails that test. There are other ways in which Congress or HHS could equally ensure that every woman has cost-free access to the particular contraceptives at issue here and, indeed, to all FDA-approved contraceptives.

In fact, HHS has already devised and implemented a system that seeks to respect the religious liberty of religious nonprofit corporations while ensuring that the employees of these entities have precisely the same access to all FDA-approved contraceptives as employees of companies whose owners have no religious objections to providing such coverage. The employees of these religious nonprofit corporations still have access to insurance coverage without cost sharing for all FDA-approved contraceptives[.] * * * Although HHS has made this system available to religious nonprofits that have religious objections to the contraceptive mandate, HHS has provided no reason why the same system cannot be made available when the owners of for-profit corporations [such as Hobby Lobby] have similar religious objections. * * *

As this description of our reasoning shows, our holding is very specific. We do not hold, as the principal dissent alleges, that for-profit corporations and other commercial enterprises can "opt out of any law (saving only tax laws) they judge incompatible with their sincerely held religious beliefs." Nor do we hold * * * that such corporations have free rein to take steps that impose "disadvantages . . . on others" or that require "the general public [to] pick up the tab." And we certainly do not hold or suggest that "RFRA demands accommodation of a for-profit corporation's religious beliefs no matter the impact that accommodation may have on . . . thousands of women employed by Hobby Lobby." The effect of the HHS-created accommodation on the women employed by Hobby Lobby and the other companies involved in these cases would be precisely zero. Under that accommodation, these women would still be entitled to all FDA-approved contraceptives without cost sharing.

[The Court then proceeds to work through the specifics of the RFRA analysis it just summarized in opening its opinion.] * * * In opposing the requirement to provide coverage for the contraceptives to which they object, the [claimants] argued that "it is immoral and sinful for [them] to intentionally participate in, pay for, facilitate, or otherwise support these drugs."

* * * [They] have a sincere religious belief that life begins at conception. They therefore object on religious grounds to providing health insurance that covers methods of birth control that * * * may result in the destruction of an embryo.

* * * [The claimants] and their companies sincerely believe that providing the insurance coverage demanded by the HHS regulations lies on the forbidden side of the line, and it is not for us to say that their religious beliefs are mistaken or insubstantial. Instead, our "narrow function . . . in this context is to determine" whether the line drawn reflects "an honest conviction," and there is no dispute that it does.

Since the HHS contraceptive mandate imposes a substantial burden on the exercise of religion, we must move on and decide whether HHS has shown that the mandate both "(1) is in furtherance of a compelling governmental interest; and (2) is the least restrictive means of furthering that compelling governmental interest."

HHS asserts that the contraceptive mandate serves a variety of important interests, but many of these are couched in very broad terms, such as promoting "public health" and "gender equality." * * *

The objecting parties contend that HHS has not shown that the mandate serves a compelling government interest, and it is arguable that there are features of ACA that support that view. * * *

We find it unnecessary to adjudicate this issue. We will assume that the interest in guaranteeing cost-free access to the four challenged contraceptive methods is compelling within the meaning of RFRA[.]

* * * HHS has not shown that it lacks other means of achieving its desired goal without imposing a substantial burden on the exercise of religion by the objecting parties in these cases.

The most straightforward way of doing this would be for the Government to assume the cost of providing the four contraceptives at issue to any women who are unable to obtain them under their health-insurance policies due to their employers' religious objections. * * *

In the end, however, we need not rely on the option of a new, government-funded program in order to conclude that the HHS regulations fail the least-restrictive-means test. HHS itself has demonstrated that it has at its disposal an approach that is less restrictive than requiring employers to fund contraceptive methods that violate their religious beliefs. As we explained above, HHS has already established an accommodation for nonprofit organizations with religious objections. * * *

The principal dissent identifies no reason why this accommodation would fail to protect the asserted needs of women as effectively as the contraceptive mandate, and there is none. Under the accommodation, the plaintiffs' female employees would continue to receive contraceptive coverage without cost sharing for all FDA-approved contraceptives, and they would continue to "face minimal logistical and administrative obstacles," because their employers' insurers would be responsible for providing information and coverage.

* * * Our decision should not be understood to hold that an insurance-coverage mandate must necessarily fall if it conflicts with an employer's religious beliefs. Other coverage requirements, such as immunizations, may be supported by different interests (for example, the need to combat the spread of infectious diseases). * * *

The principal dissent raises the possibility that discrimination in hiring, for example on the basis of race, might be cloaked as religious practice to escape legal sanction. Our decision today provides no such shield. The Government has a compelling interest in providing an equal opportunity to participate in the workforce without regard to race, and prohibitions on racial discrimination are precisely tailored to achieve that critical goal.

* * * The contraceptive mandate, as applied to closely held corporations, violates RFRA.

JUSTICE KENNEDY, concurring.

* * * The Government must demonstrate that the application of a substantial burden to a person's exercise of religion "(1) is in furtherance of a compelling governmental interest; and (2) is the least restrictive means of furthering that compelling governmental interest."

As to RFRA's first requirement, the Department of Health and Human Services (HHS) makes the case that the mandate serves the Government's compelling interest in providing insurance coverage that is necessary to protect the health of female employees, coverage that is significantly more costly than for a male employee. * * * It is important to confirm that a premise of the Court's opinion is its assumption that the HHS regulation here at issue furthers a legitimate and compelling interest in the health of female employees.

But the Government has not made the second showing required by RFRA, that the means it uses to regulate is the least restrictive way to further its interest. As the Court's opinion explains, the record in these cases shows that there is an existing, recognized, workable, and already-implemented framework to provide coverage.

* * * Among the reasons the United States is so open, so tolerant, and so free is that no person may be restricted or demeaned by government in exercising his or her religion. Yet neither may that same exercise unduly restrict other persons, such as employees, in protecting their own interests, interests the law deems compelling. In these cases the means to reconcile those two priorities are at hand in the existing accommodation the Government has designed, identified, and used for circumstances closely parallel to those presented here.

JUSTICE GINSBURG, with whom JUSTICES BREYER, KAGAN, and SOTOMAYOR join, dissenting.[1]

* * * No doubt the [owners of Hobby Lobby] and all who share their beliefs may decline to acquire for themselves the contraceptives in

---

[1] *Editor's Note*: Justices Breyer and Kagan joined all of the dissent with the exception of a section of the dissent not excerpted here that rejected the majority's conclusion that for-profit corporations qualify as "person[s]" entitled to religious exemptions under RFRA.

question. But that choice may not be imposed on employees who hold other beliefs. Working for Hobby Lobby * * * should not deprive employees of the preventive care available to workers at the shop next door, at least in the absence of directions from the Legislature or Administration to do so.

Why should decisions of this order be made by Congress or the regulatory authority, and not this Court? [The claimants] do not stand alone as commercial enterprises seeking exemptions from generally applicable laws on the basis of their religious beliefs. See, e.g., Newman v. Piggie Park Enterprises, Inc., (D.S.C.1966) (owner of restaurant chain refused to serve black patrons based on his religious beliefs opposing racial integration); In re Minnesota ex rel. McClure (Minn. 1985) (born-again Christians who owned closely held, for-profit health clubs believed that the Bible proscribed hiring or retaining an "individua[l] living with but not married to a person of the opposite sex," "a young, single woman working without her father's consent or a married woman working without her husband's consent," and any person "antagonistic to the Bible," including "fornicators and homosexuals"); Elane Photography, LLC v. Willock, (N.M. 2013) (for-profit photography business owned by a husband and wife refused to photograph a lesbian couple's commitment ceremony based on the religious beliefs of the company's owners). Would RFRA require exemptions in cases of this ilk? And if not, how does the Court divine which religious beliefs are worthy of accommodation, and which are not? Isn't the Court disarmed from making such a judgment given its recognition that "courts must not presume to determine . . . the plausibility of a religious claim"?

Would the exemption the Court holds RFRA demands for employers with religiously grounded objections to the use of certain contraceptives extend to employers with religiously grounded objections to blood transfusions (Jehovah's Witnesses); antidepressants (Scientologists); medications derived from pigs, including anesthesia, intravenous fluids, and pills coated with gelatin (certain Muslims, Jews, and Hindus); and vaccinations (Christian Scientists, among others)?

* * * There is an overriding interest, I believe, in keeping the courts "out of the business of evaluating the relative merits of differing religious claims," or the sincerity with which an asserted religious belief is held. Indeed, approving some religious claims while deeming others unworthy of accommodation could be "perceived as favoring one religion over another," the very "risk the Establishment Clause was designed to preclude." The Court, I fear, has ventured into a minefield, by its immoderate reading of RFRA. * * *

NOTES

1. One of the major disputes in *Hobby Lobby*, which the excerpt above omits, involved whether closely-held for-profit corporations are protected under RFRA. The Court ruled that they are. For commentary on the relationship between religious liberty and corporations, see THE RISE OF CORPORATE RELIGIOUS LIBERTY (Micah Schwartzman, Chad Flanders, & Zöe Robinson eds., Oxford University Press, 2016).

2. In order to state a claim under RFRA, the claimant must show that the challenged law creates a "substantial burden" on the claimant's exercise of religion. How does Justice Alito reason about the "substantial burden" inquiry? How is analysis of the claimant's religious sincerity different than analysis of the claimant's burden? What role should the Court play in assessing whether the claimant's religious exercise is substantially burdened? The RFRA standard requires that the claimant satisfy the "substantial burden" prong before the burden shifts to the government to show a compelling governmental interest and narrow tailoring. If the Court does not independently assess whether the claimant is substantially burdened, how is the RFRA standard altered? What might be the effect of such an alteration?

3. What does the Court hold with regard to the government's compelling interest? After *Hobby Lobby*, is there any basis to question whether the contraceptive coverage requirement is supported by a compelling governmental interest? What is Justice Kennedy's view of the compelling governmental interest? How might his view have mattered to the way in which the case was decided by the Court?

4. The Court decides the case based on the "least restrictive means" analysis. Why is the contraceptive coverage requirement not the least restrictive means of furthering the government's compelling ends? The Court suggests that one alternative is for the government to take on the cost of contraceptive coverage itself. Should this constitute an alternative for purposes of the "least restrict means" inquiry? Does the alternative need to be practical? Does it need to be politically possible? What external factors, if any, should discipline the consideration of alternative means?

5. The Court also suggests that the accommodation offered to religiously affiliated nonprofit organizations constitutes a less restrictive alternative for closely-held for-profit corporations with religious objections. Religiously affiliated nonprofits with objections to providing contraceptive coverage as part of employee insurance benefits were required to submit a form to the federal government registering their objection so that the government could arrange for contraceptive coverage for the organizations' employees through alternative routes. But Justice Alito expressly left open the question of whether successful RFRA challenges might be leveled against this accommodation. Indeed, mere days after the Court issued its decision in *Hobby Lobby*, the Court provisionally granted an accommodation to a religiously affiliated college challenging the nonprofit accommodation.

Wheaton College v. Burwell, ___ U.S. ___, 134 S.Ct. 2806, 189 L.Ed.2d 856 (2014). After that, the federal government allowed objecting nonprofits simply to notify the government of their objection. Religiously affiliated nonprofits also challenged this accommodation. Cases challenging the accommodation mechanism offered to religious affiliated nonprofits proliferated in *Hobby Lobby*'s wake and eventually made their way to the Supreme Court. As the Catholic organization Little Sisters of the Poor argued in its petition to the Court:

> [T]hese organizations do not merely object to paying for or being the direct provider of contraceptive coverage; they object to facilitating, or being complicit in, access to contraceptives; to paving the way for contraceptives to be provided under their plans; and to directly transferring their own obligations onto others. Being forced to "comply" with the mandate via the regulatory "accommodation" is no more compatible with their religious beliefs than being forced to comply with that mandate directly.

Petition for Writ of Certiorari at 10, Little Sisters of the Poor Home for the Aged v. Burwell, No. 15–105 (U.S. July 23, 2015). Do the accommodation mechanisms substantially burden the religiously affiliated nonprofits' exercise of religion? Is the accommodation the least restrictive means of furthering the government's compelling interest? In May of 2016, the U.S. Supreme Court (per curium) remanded a set of four of these cases to the lower courts to afford "an opportunity to arrive at an approach going forward that accommodates petitioners' religious exercise while at the same time ensuring that women covered by petitioners' health plans 'receive full and equal health coverage, including contraceptive coverage.' " *Zubik v. Burwell,* 136 S.Ct. 1557, 1560 (2016).

6.   Justice Alito states that the closely-held for-profit corporations in *Hobby Lobby* could be accommodated with "precisely zero" effect on the corporations' employees. What leads him to make this statement? Throughout constitutional and statutory law on religious liberty, we see a concern with third-party harm that reflects an intuition that third parties should not be forced to bear the costs of another's religious exercise. What is Justice Kennedy's view on the issue of third-party harm? What about Justice Ginsburg? Does she believe the effect would be "zero"?

7.   The majority and dissent disagree over the reach of the Court's decision. Justice Alito suggests that the decision "is concerned solely with the contraceptive mandate." But Justice Ginsburg warns that there is no limiting principle that would prevent application of the Court's ruling to other exemption claims in the health insurance context, as well as exemption claims in the antidiscrimination context. How does Justice Alito respond to these concerns? Does his response mitigate the concerns raised by Justice Ginsburg?

D. SCHOLARLY PERSPECTIVES ON THE RELIGIOUS LIBERTY DEBATE

The *Hobby Lobby* decision both reflected and fueled significant conflict over the meaning and contours of religious liberty. As the debate between the majority and dissent about the reach of the decision suggests, many understood the case as related to ongoing disputes over religious liberty in the LGBT context. In the excerpt below, Professor Douglas Laycock, one of the country's leading religious liberty scholars, situates religious liberty disputes over abortion and contraception, such as the one that arose in *Hobby Lobby*, within the same so-called "culture war" conflicts as religious liberty disputes over same-sex marriage and LGBT rights. He proposes generous religious accommodations; in fact, he supported the claimants in *Hobby Lobby*. Professor Laycock advocates broad religious exemptions as a principled matter, but also sees such exemptions as a way to settle ongoing conflicts over contentious issues.

RELIGIOUS LIBERTY AND THE CULTURE WARS[*]
Douglas Laycock

[T]he biggest problem for religious liberty in our time is deep disagreements over sexual morality.

* * * The Sexual Revolution that began in earnest in the 1960s continues to make important gains, most dramatically with respect to same-sex relationships. And conservative churches in this country have persistently been on the losing side of this Revolution. They have opposed not just the Sexual Revolution's excesses; they have opposed its core. Each of the remaining sexual issues—abortion, same-sex marriage, contraception, sterilization, emergency contraception—has the same fundamental structure: what one side views as a grave evil, the other side views as a fundamental human right. For tens of millions of Americans, conservative churches have made themselves the enemy of liberty.

In the view of the pro-life and traditional marriage movements, abortion and same-sex marriage are so evil that they must be prohibited for everybody. And that means, in the view of pro-choice women, same-sex couples, and many who support their causes, that religious conservatives are attempting to interfere with the most intimate and personal of human decisions, and to impose their controversial views of morality on the entire population.

* * * The stakes are high. Many disputes over the free exercise of religion involve unusual practices of small religions, unusual laws of little importance, or both. But these disputes over same-sex marriage,

---

[*]   Douglas Laycock, *Religious Liberty and the Culture Wars*, 2014 U. ILL. L. REV. 839, 846, 866, 869, 871–73, 876, 877–78.

contraception, emergency contraception, and abortion involve core teachings of large and mainstream religious organizations on one side, and important government programs backed by powerful interest groups on the other. They present claims of fundamental right on both sides—the right to exercise one's religion and not to violate God's will as one understands it, and the right to control one's own sex life, one's own body, and one's own health care. Both religion and sex are intensely personal. Both religion and sex are spheres that we normally try to protect from government interference.

* * * In the winter and spring of 2014, Religious Freedom Restoration Acts became politically toxic. Resentment of the federal RFRA because of the contraception litigation, an overreaching bill in Kansas that was not a RFRA at all, and proposed amendments to clarify that the Arizona RFRA applies to business people, combined with anti-gay statements from the Arizona bill's sponsor, enabled opponents to create an overwhelming public reaction that took down the Kansas and Arizona bills and proposed state RFRAs in Georgia and Ohio. These various bills were very different, but the avalanche of publicity generally failed to distinguish among them, and thus inevitably mischaracterized them.

For many people, this hostility to religious liberty is a growing intuitive reaction. They are tired of hearing from the Catholic bishops and the evangelical preachers—tired of hearing about their religion, tired of hearing their claims to religious liberty, tired of them trying to restrict other people's sex lives. "Increasingly, people identify and link organized religion with anti-gay attitudes, sexual conservatism, a whole range of those kind of social cultural values."

For others, it is a more thought out position. The academic arguments against religious liberty grow more elaborated in the law reviews, more hostile in the list serves. Arguments created to win a particular battle about contraception or marriage are rarely limited to those issues. These arguments have obvious implications for other religious liberty claims, and if accepted by courts, the precedents apply to all religious liberty claims.

I cannot offer a full analysis of the legal issues in these cases. But I do want to highlight the sweep of the arguments that are being made against claims to religious liberty. The interest groups now arrayed against religious liberty tend to assume that any interest they care about is compelling, and to state those interests at the grandest level of generality. There is a compelling interest in women's health, or even more broadly, in public health; there is a compelling interest in nondiscrimination. Such sweeping claims avoid the proper inquiry, which is whether enforcement of the government's interest as applied to the particular religious claimant—and to all others whose similar claims cannot be fairly distinguished—is necessary to serve a compelling government interest.

Not that that matters, because the opponents of religious liberty also insist that every individual application of their interests is compelling. They say there is a compelling interest in avoiding any inconvenience or affront; no potential customer should ever be referred elsewhere. They say that they are entitled to have personal services available even when the services are entirely unwanted. No same-sex couple in its right mind would want to be counseled by a counselor who believes that the couple's relationship is fundamentally wrong. But supporters of gay rights insist that every counselor be available to same-sex couples. The purpose of such arguments is not to obtain counseling, but to drive conservative believers out of the profession.

The same logic is applied to every other occupation or profession in any way connected to one of these disputes. If you don't want to do abortions, do not work in obstetrics and gynecology. You should not be permitted to deliver babies unless you are also willing to kill babies on request. If you don't want to do same-sex weddings, don't be a wedding planner or a caterer or the owner of a bridal shop, however small. And even: if religious nonprofits don't want to provide contraception, they don't have to run "a hospital, school, or charity." Never mind that churches for centuries have treated education, and care of the sick and the destitute, as part of their missions.

* * * These arguments are made with a completely one-sided sense of each side's turf. If we are to preserve liberty for both sides in the culture wars, then we have to preserve some space where each side can live its own values and where its rules control.

* * * Even on the hot-button culture-war issues, religious liberty provides a model for resolving or ameliorating social conflict. We could still create a society in which both sides can live their own values, if we care enough about liberty to protect it for both sides.

One of the ironies of the culture wars is that religious minorities and gays and lesbians make essentially parallel demands on the larger society. I cannot fundamentally change who I am, they each say. You cannot interfere with those things constitutive of my identity; on the most fundamental things, you must let me live my life according to my own values. We can honor both sides' version of that claim if we will try.

And in all but a tiny fraction of these cases, the issue is not whether any other individual can obtain contraception, or whether a same-sex couple can have a wedding with the full panoply of catering, clothes, photographs, flowers, and all the rest. All those things are readily available in the market place in most of the country. The issue is whether the religious conscientious objector must be the one who provides these things. * * *

[L]ive-and-let-live solutions would be quite possible if either side would accept them. * * *

_____

In contrast to Professor Laycock's position, other scholars have questioned religious exemptions from laws protecting rights to abortion, contraception, same-sex marriage, and LGBT nondiscrimination. Consider the essay below, which opposes expansive exemptions on principled grounds while also questioning the notion that such exemptions would resolve conflict. While many supporters of reproductive rights and LGBT equality have offered powerful critiques of *Hobby Lobby*, in what follows Professors Douglas NeJaime and Reva Siegel provide a constructive reading of the case as part of a legal response to the religious exemption claims being asserted. They first provide a political diagnosis of why the claims are appearing. As you read, remember the position of the U.S. Conference of Catholic Bishops with which we began this section.

CONSCIENCE AND THE CULTURE WARS*
Douglas NeJaime and Reva B. Siegel

These days, conservatives seem to own "conscience." Consider the current objection to marriage equality. "Some citizens may conclude that they cannot in good conscience participate in a same-sex ceremony, from priests and pastors to bakers and florists," argues the Heritage Foundation's Ryan Anderson. "The government should not force them to choose between their religious beliefs and their livelihood." Serving same-sex couples, business owners assert, would make them complicit in relationships they deem sinful, and so they claim religious exemptions from state and local antidiscrimination laws.

Conscience is also the rallying cry of conservatives opposed to the Affordable Care Act. In *Burwell v. Hobby Lobby Stores*, decided by the Supreme Court in June 2014, employers challenged the ACA's required coverage of contraception on the grounds that it would make them complicit in their employees' use of drugs that the employers believe cause abortion. The Court ruled 5–4 in favor of the employers' conscience objections.

Religious liberty challenges to the ACA arise under a law known as the Religious Freedom Restoration Act (RFRA), which allows people to claim exemptions from federal laws that "substantially burden" their

_____

    * Douglas NeJaime & Reva B. Siegel, *Conscience and the Culture Wars*, AMERICAN PROSPECT (Summer 2015).

religious practice. Opponents of same-sex marriage are moving to enact or to strengthen state laws mirroring the federal RFRA, as high-profile conflicts in Arizona, Indiana, and Arkansas have illustrated.

Partisan divides over religious conscience claims are not surprising in light of today's culture wars. But from a historical perspective, the partisan divide is remarkable. Liberals have long respected conscientious objection to military service and advocated that the government accommodate the beliefs and practices of religious minorities.

The new conservative campaign for religious exemptions follows a well-established pattern. When advocates suffer defeat and their arguments lose legitimacy, they look for new ways to frame their views, often borrowing from their opponents. * * *

In the debate over same-sex marriage, the opponents at first defended traditional marriage by appealing to moral disapproval of homosexuality. When these arguments began to lose credibility, opponents emphasized the importance of preserving sex-differentiated procreation and parenting. Today many have reframed the defense of traditional marriage as necessary to preserve religious liberty, to promote pluralism, and to avoid discrimination against religious conservatives. Again, conservatives are speaking in the language of civil rights. As Jeb Bush has put it, "People that act on their conscience shouldn't be discriminated against, for sure."

This is how RFRA has been drawn into the culture wars. After failing to prohibit abortion and same-sex marriage, conservatives have sought to create religious exemptions from laws that protect the right to abortion or same-sex marriage. Without change in numbers or belief, religious conservatives have shifted from *speaking as a majority* seeking to enforce traditional morality to *speaking as a minority* seeking exemptions from laws that depart from traditional morality. If unable to protect traditional sexual morality through laws of general application, conservatives can protect traditional values through liberal frames—by asserting claims to religious exemption and by appealing to secular commitments to pluralism and nondiscrimination.

* * * The new claims being made by conservatives today are fundamentally different from the claims of religious liberty that led to the passage of RFRA. These differences are crucial to judging whether and how to accommodate the demands for religious exemption.

The Roots of RFRA

RFRA has not always provoked partisan conflict. More than two decades ago, Congress enacted the law with near unanimous bipartisan support. The immediate stimulus was a Supreme Court decision in a case involving Native Americans who were denied unemployment benefits after being fired for their use of peyote during religious rituals. Many people across the ideological spectrum thought that the Constitution protected claims of this kind under the First Amendment's guarantee of the right to "free exercise" of religion. After all, in the famous case of *Sherbert v. Verner*, the Warren Court had provided free-exercise protection to a Seventh-day Adventist who had been denied unemployment compensation when she refused to accept a job because of her Sabbath observance. But in the case involving the use of peyote in Native American religious ceremonies, the Court interpreted guarantees of free exercise more narrowly, as prohibiting only state action singling out the faithful for discriminatory treatment. Justice Antonin Scalia, a recent Reagan appointee, wrote the Court's opinion.

As Scalia's position indicated, conservatives have not always supported expansive judicial protections for the free exercise of religion. Some conservatives in the Reagan administration favored limiting judicial enforcement of free-exercise rights as part of their general effort to contain the role of the courts in matters of religion. Nevertheless, the Court's decision denying claims for religious exemption in the peyote case alienated Republicans and Democrats alike, and in 1993, Congress rallied to restore protection for religious liberty through RFRA. Signed into law by President Bill Clinton, the statute commands that the government may not "substantially burden a person's exercise of religion" unless doing so is "the least restrictive means of furthering [a] compelling governmental interest."

But in enacting RFRA, Congress did not contemplate religious liberty cases of the kind we are now seeing. The statute itself names three free-exercise cases, all of them involving members of minority religions who sought exemptions based on unconventional beliefs generally not considered by lawmakers when they adopted the challenged laws. Few imagined that opponents of abortion would assert claims under RFRA. In fact, Catholics wanted to make RFRA abortion-neutral, fearful that advocates for choice might assert conscience-based claims for exemptions from abortion bans if the Court overturned *Roe v. Wade*.

Conscience Claims in Health Care

Conscience-based claims against abortion developed from a different body of law—not RFRA, but laws that allow medical personnel to refuse to provide health care services on religious grounds. In the wake of *Roe*, newly enacted federal and state laws authorized doctors with religious or moral objections to refuse to perform abortions or sterilizations. After the Court narrowed but upheld *Roe* in 1992, abortion opponents invoked religious liberty to expand health care refusal laws, authorizing many more individuals and institutions to deny health care services they deemed sinful—abortion prominently, but also increasingly contraception.

The latest wave of health care refusal legislation uses concepts of complicity to authorize conscience objections in broadly defined circumstances. Mississippi, for example, allows health care providers to assert conscience objections to providing "any phase of patient medical care, treatment or procedure, including, but not limited to, the following: patient referral, counseling, therapy, testing, diagnosis or prognosis, research, instruction, prescribing, dispensing or administering any device, drug, or medication, surgery, or any other care or treatment rendered by health care providers or health care institutions." The Mississippi law also defines "health care provider" as expansively as possible. Like laws adopted in some other states, the one in Mississippi is based on a model statute promulgated by the anti-abortion group Americans United for Life.

Laws authorizing health care providers to refuse patient care illustrate how conservatives are now using the ideas of conscience and religious liberty. States like Mississippi could accommodate the conscience objections of health care providers while ensuring alternative care for patients. But health care refusal laws rarely require institutions to provide alternative care; many even authorize providers to refuse to inform patients that they are being denied services that they may want. Expansive health care refusal laws of the kind Mississippi has enacted thereby serve to restrict access to abortion.

For decades, constrained by constitutional rulings, conservatives have used claims on conscience to restrict access to abortion. Now, as laws recognizing same-sex marriage spread, religious conservatives have begun to look to health care refusals as an inspiration and a model for restraining another development they could not entirely block. As Ryan Anderson writes in the *National Review*, "Whatever the Court does will cause less damage if we . . . highlight the importance of religious liberty. Even if the Court were to one day redefine marriage, governmental recognition of same-sex relationships as marriage need not and should not require third parties to recognize a same-sex relationship as a marriage." * * *

Conscience is now a rallying cry for a cross-denominational coalition opposing abortion and same-sex marriage and supporting religious liberty. For example, the "Manhattan Declaration"—a 2009 manifesto of conservative Christian principles endorsed by Catholic and evangelical Protestant leaders as well as conservative political activists—is subtitled "A Call of Christian Conscience." The declaration asks Christians to unite across denominational lines in support of three central principles: "the sanctity of human life, the dignity of marriage as a union of husband and wife, and the freedom of religion." Alongside planks opposing abortion and same-sex marriage, the statement offers support for claims of conscientious refusal to be complicit in either one. * * *

[T]he cross-denominational coalition asserting conscience claims in health care and marriage has the backing of the Republican Party, which invokes conscience to decry a so-called "war on religion." The 2012 Republican Party platform declared, "The most offensive instance of this war on religion has been the current Administration's attempt to compel faith-related institutions, as well as believing individuals, to contravene their deeply held religious, moral, or ethical beliefs regarding health services, traditional marriage, or abortion." * * *

Why Complicity Claims Are Different

* * * [O]ne can challenge the Court's decision in *Hobby Lobby* and reject the conscience claims of bakers and florists without abandoning support for all religious exemptions.

Today's conflicts over marriage and health care feature a special kind of conscience claim—claims about *complicity*. The employers in *Hobby Lobby* objected that the ACA forced them to provide "insurance coverage for items that risk killing an embryo [and thereby] makes them complicit in abortion." Similarly, businesses in the wedding industry object to "facilitating" same-sex weddings. These complicity claims concern the conduct of third parties, other citizens who do not share the objector's beliefs, and so differ in fundamental ways from many other religious-liberty claims. For instance, in the recently decided *Holt v. Hobbs* case, a prisoner sought a religious exemption from the prison's general prohibition on beards; he was not seeking to avoid complicity in what he believed were someone else's sinful acts.

To be sure, complicity claims are bona fide faith claims. For example, Catholic principles of "cooperation" and "scandal" warn the faithful against complicity in the sins of others. Further, there should be no doubt that RFRA's broad language covers complicity claims. But unlike the claims that concerned Congress when it enacted RFRA, the accommodation of complicity claims is more likely to result in harm to third parties, such as women seeking access to contraception and abortion or same-sex couples going about their everyday lives.

In the free-exercise cases that Congress invoked in passing RFRA, religious minorities sought exemptions based on unconventional beliefs or practices generally not considered by lawmakers when they adopted the challenged laws. The costs of accommodating their claims were minimal and widely shared. For instance, granting exemptions from the drug laws to Native Americans who use peyote in ritual ceremonies only modestly detracts from the public interest in health and safety.

Complicity-based conscience claims differ from these other claims. Because complicity claims single out other citizens as sinners, their accommodation can inflict targeted harm. Complicity claims are increasingly entangled in culture-war politics as a means of mobilizing the faithful against the practices of people who depart from traditional morality. For these reasons, accommodation of the claims is fraught with significance not only for the claimants but also for those whose conduct the claimants condemn. These third-party effects need to be taken into account in weighing whether and how the government should accommodate complicity-based claims of conscience.

Why *Hobby Lobby* May Help

Supreme Court decisions have often limited the accommodation of religious liberty out of a concern about third-party harm. In the initial outcry over the Court's expansive interpretation of RFRA in *Hobby Lobby*, few paused to notice the language of limitation in the decision. The dissenting opinion by Justice Ruth Bader Ginsburg wasn't the only one to invoke third-party harm as a limiting principle on accommodating claims of conscience. The majority opinion by Justice Samuel Alito and the concurring opinion by Justice Anthony Kennedy also did so.

In fact, concern about third-party harm structured the majority's decision. The Court did not hold that religious liberty trumped the government's interest in women's health. Instead, it recognized the claim for accommodation on the narrower ground that the government could promote women's access to contraception by means that did not burden the plaintiffs' religious liberty. In fact, the majority opinion emphasized that the government could accommodate the plaintiffs' religious beliefs with "precisely zero" effect on their female employees because the government could in theory provide contraception without involving the employer.

The Court's reasoning in *Hobby Lobby* shows that the courts must take third-party harm into account in applying RFRA. Under the law, whenever the government "substantially burdens" a person's exercise of religion, it must demonstrate two things: the burden furthers a "compelling governmental interest" and is the "least restrictive means" of doing so.

These considerations are directly relevant to third-party harm. For example, if granting a religious accommodation would inflict harm on people protected by an antidiscrimination law or undermine societal values and goals the law promotes, unencumbered enforcement of the law is the least restrictive means of achieving the government's compelling ends. If, however, the government can accommodate the religious claimant in ways that do not impair pursuit of the compelling interests in banning discrimination, RFRA requires the accommodation.

This interpretation of the law does not dictate the outcome of a specific case, but it suggests that any accommodation of religious exercise must minimize, to the extent feasible, adverse effects on third parties. * * *

NOTES

1.   How is the conflict over abortion and contraception related to the conflict over same-sex marriage and LGBT equality as a matter of religion? As a matter of politics?

2.   What do you think of Professor Laycock's argument that "religious liberty provides a model for resolving or ameliorating social conflict"? Is each side too unwilling to compromise? Is a live-and-let-live solution possible? What should such a solution look like?

3.   What do you think of the approach advanced by Professors NeJaime and Siegel? Are they sufficiently protective of conscience? Are they too protective? Should the law take account of both the material and dignitary harms of discrimination? If so, how do we know when material harms are present? And how do we know when dignitary harms exist?

4.   Look back at the Mississippi religious exemptions law, House Bill 1523, covered earlier in this section. Does the law take account of third-party harm? Is there any provision that seeks to protect the same-sex couple refused goods or services? If so, is the focus on material harms only, or does it also consider dignitary harms?

5.   Does the NeJaime/Siegel approach take adequate account of the harm suffered by religious objectors? What exactly is the harm experienced when a religious objector is obligated to serve a same-sex couple? Under *Hobby Lobby*, would being forced to comply with a law that prohibits sexual orientation discrimination impose, in RFRA's language, a "substantial burden" on religious exercise?

6.   Interestingly, while more than 20 states currently have RFRAs, they tend to be states that do not currently have antidiscrimination laws that include sexual orientation and gender identity. Accordingly, most of the conflicts between religious liberty and LGBT equality have not posed questions about RFRA's coverage. And in the cases to date, religious objectors who have refused service to same-sex couples in states that do have inclusive antidiscrimination laws have failed to prevail under constitutional religious liberty protections. These cases include bakeries refusing to provide wedding cakes, florists refusing to provide floral arrangements, event spaces refusing to rent to same-sex couples, and inns refusing to lodge same-sex couples. *See, e.g., Craig v. Masterpiece Cakeshop, Inc.*, 370 P.3d 272 (Colo. App. 2015) (holding that the bakery owner's refusal to provide a cake for a same-sex couple's wedding violated the state's antidiscrimination law and that the owner was not entitled to a religious exemption); *Melissa Elaine Klein* and *Aaron Wayne Klein*, Nos. 44–14 and 44–15, 2015 WL 4503460 (Or. Comm'r of the Bureau of Labor and Indus. July 2, 2015) (same); *State of Washington v. Arlene's Flowers*, No. 13–2–00871–5 (Wa. Super. Ct. February 18, 2015) (holding that a florist who refused to sell flowers to a same-sex couple for their wedding violated the state's antidiscrimination law and is not entitled to a religious exemption); *Gifford v. McCarthy*, No. 520410, 2016 WL 155543

(N.Y. App. Div. Jan. 14, 2016) (upholding an administrative judge's decision that the owners' refusal to rent space to a lesbian couple for their wedding violated the state's public accommodation statute and that the owners were not entitled to a religious exemption); *Cervelli v. Aloha Bed & Breakfast*, No. 11–1–3103–12 (Haw. Cir. Ct. Apr. 15, 2013) (holding that a bed-and-breakfast owner's refusal to rent a room to a lesbian couple violated the state's public accommodation statute and that the owner was not entitled to a religious exemption).

The *Elane Photography* case excerpted above arose in New Mexico, one of the only states with both sexual orientation antidiscrimination law and a RFRA. In that case, the state supreme court rejected the religious exemption claim of a photography company that refused to photograph a same-sex couple's commitment ceremony. *Elane Photography, LLC v. Willock*, 309 P.3d 53 (N.M. Ct. App. 2013), *cert. denied*, 134 S.Ct. 1787 (2014). The court interpreted New Mexico's RFRA not to apply to an action in which the government is not a party. This case is excerpted above because the court also rejected the business's First Amendment claims.

Attempts continue to pass additional RFRAs or to amend existing RFRAs to provide greater coverage for businesses and individuals with religious objections to LGBT equality. It appears that conflicts over religious liberty will continue to frame fights over LGBT equality.

INDEX

References are to Pages